LABOUR LAW:
CASES AND MATERIALS

AUSTRALIA AND NEW ZEALAND
The Law Book Company Ltd.
Sydney : Melbourne : Perth

CANADA AND U.S.A.
The Carswell Company Ltd.
Agincourt, Ontario

INDIA
N.M. Tripathi Private Ltd.
Bombay
and
Eastern Law House Private Ltd.
Calcutta and Delhi
M.P.P. House
Bangalore

ISRAEL
Steimatzky's Agency Ltd.
Jerusalem : Tel-Aviv : Haifa

MALAYSIA : SINGAPORE : BRUNEI
Malayan Law Journal (Pte.) Ltd.
Singapore and Kuala Lumpur

PAKISTAN
Pakistan Law House
Karachi

LABOUR LAW: CASES AND MATERIALS

ROGER BENEDICTUS
M.A. (Oxon.), LL.M. (Lond.)
Senior Lecturer in Law at the University of Leicester

and

BRIAN BERCUSSON
LL.M. (McGill), Ph.D. (Cantab.)
Senior Lecturer, Queen Mary College, University of London
Associate Professor of Law at the
European University Institute Florence

LONDON
SWEET & MAXWELL
1987

Published in 1987 by
Sweet & Maxwell Limited
of 11 New Fetter Lane, London.
Computerset by Promenade Graphics Limited, Cheltenham.
Printed in Great Britain by
Adlard & Son Limited, The Garden City Press,
Letchworth, Herts.

British Library Cataloguing in Publication Data

Benedictus, Roger
Labour law: cases and materials.
1. Labour laws and legislation—Great
Britain—Cases
I. Title II. Bercusson, Brian
344.104'1125'0264 KD3006.3

ISBN 0–421–27870–6

To Tanya and Catherine

PREFACE

What is the justification for this book of cases and materials on British labour law? Two other collections of cases and materials are currently available: P. Davies and M. Freedland's *Labour Law: Text and Materials* was first published in 1979, with a second edition in 1983, while P. Elias, B. Napier and P. Wallington's *Labour Law* was published in 1980. The standards of scholarship displayed by these works are incontrovertible. Davies and Freedland, as their title indicates, have written at least half a textbook, and their commentary is constantly thoughtful and illuminating. Elias, Napier and Wallington included more and longer extracts, and have written lengthy and penetrating notes referring extensively to the labour law literature. However, to a large extent, the two books share a common viewpoint as to subject-matter, identification of problems, and selection of materials, albeit the order in which they are arranged differs.

In compiling this book, as we explain more fully in our introduction, we have sought to express an alternative approach to labour law: to define a different subject-matter; to identify problems, only some of which have hitherto been treated in the literature; to use, more extensively, industrial relations materials such as collective agreements; and to analyse cases, statutes and other materials more consistently from a policy viewpoint. It is our hope that the value of our book will be found in this new approach so that it contributes to the current debates on labour law, and does not merely replicate the excellent work of others.

Now, our regrets. During its lengthy gestation the book developed in a way which eventually proved unacceptable to Professor Roger Rideout of University College, London. He had been deeply involved in all the earlier stages of the book's preparation but to our great disappointment, he finally insisted on withdrawing from the project before the final draft was submitted to the publishers. We do want to put on record here the fact that Roger Rideout provided an enormous critical stimulus to the preparation of the manuscript, both through the initial drafts of some chapters and analysis of others, for which we are both very grateful.

We have exercised as much self-restraint as possible with regard to text. We have also not sought to provide a compendium of references to the extensive literature on labour law and industrial relations. No doubt such text and references would enhance the value of the materials collected, but they would have lengthened both the book and the time of preparation beyond the present endurance of the authors and publisher.

The patience of the latter is worthy of a memoir at least as long as this book. Equal gratitude is due to our long-suffering spouses to whom the book is dedicated, while grateful acknowledgements must also be given to the practical assistance of Colin Bourn, Jit Singh and Janet Feather, and to Barbara Goodman and her ever cheerful and helpful assistants in the Law Faculty office at Leicester.

April 1987

Brian Bercusson
Roger Benedictus
Florence and Leicester

ACKNOWLEDGEMENTS

We wish to express our appreciation to the following for their permission to reprint items from the material listed below. ACAS: *The ACAS Role in Conciliation, Arbitration and Mediation* (1979), *Annual Report* 1981, Appendix B, ACAS evidence to the Megaw Committee of Inquiry into Civil Service Pay; George Allen & Unwin (Publishers) Ltd.: B. C. Roberts, *National Wages Policy in War and Peace* (1958); Anglo-German Foundation for the Study of Industrial Society: Trade Union Research Unit, Ruskin College, Oxford, *Working Time in Britain: The Effects of Changes in Pattern and Duration in Selected Industries* (1981); Barry Rose/Kluwer Law Publishers: B. Bercusson, "Labour Law" in A. Martin and P. Archer, *More Law Reform Now* (1983); Basil Blackwell: R. Hyman and I. Brough, *Social Values and Industrial Relations* (1975), B. Weekes *et al*, *Industrial Relations and the Limits of the Law* (1975); British Institute of International and Comparative Law: G. England, "Loss of jobs in strikes: the position in England and Canada compared" (1976) I.C.L.Q. 583; British Journal of Industrial Relations: W. Brown, "A consideration of custom and practice" (1972) 10 B.J.I.R. 42, R. H. Fryer, A. J. Fairclough and T. B. Manson, "Facilities for female shop stewards: the EPA and collective agreements" (1978) 16 B.J.I.R. 160, S. Hill, "Norms, groups and power: the sociology of workplace industrial relations" (1974) 12 B.J.I.R. 213, R. Hyman, "Inequality, ideology and industrial relations" (1974) 14 B.J.I.R. 50, G. Latta and R. Lewis, "Trade union legal services" (1974) 12 B.J.I.R. 56, P. Lewis, "An analysis of why legislation has failed to provide employment protection for unfairly dismissed employees" (1981) 19 B.J.I.R. 316, W. Streeck, "Qualitative demands and the neo-corporatist manageability of industrial relations" (1981) 19 B.J.I.R. 149, M. Terry, "The inevitable growth of informality" (1977) 15 B.J.I.R. 76; Butterworths & Company (Publishers) Ltd.: *All England Law Reports*, P. S. Atiyah, *Vicarious Liability in the Law of Torts* (1980); Cambridge University Press: C. Craig, J. Rubery, R. Tarling, F. Wilkinson, *Labour Market Structure, Industrial Organisation and Low Pay* (1982); Camden NALGO: Camden NALGO Equal Rights Working Party Report, Summary of Recommendations, August 1976; Faber and Faber Ltd.: A. Fox, *Beyond Contract: Work, Power and Trust Relations* (1974); Gower Publishing Group: S. Brittain and P. Lilley, *The Delusion of Incomes Policy* (1977), W. W. Daniel and N. Millward, *Workplace Industrial Relations in Britain* (1983); W. A. Brown, "The structure of pay bargaining in Britain" in F. T. Blackaby, *The Future of Pay Bargaining* (1980); Harvard Law Review:

H. Shulman, "Reason, contract and law in labor relations" (1955) 68 H.L.R. 999; Heinemann Educational Books Ltd.: H. Clegg, *How to Run an Incomes Policy* (1971); Her Majesty's Stationery Office: ACAS Industrial Relations Handbook 1980, Central Arbitration Committee, *Annual Reports* 1980, 1981, 1982, *CAC Awards,* Nos. 80/73, 79/74, 79/451, *Official Reports,* Cmnd. 3623, Cmnd. 8128, *Department of Employment Gazette* March 1982, June 1982, October 1982, April 1983, May 1983, *Department of Employment Manpower Papers* No. 14 (1975), No. 15 (1978), *Department of Employment Research Papers* No. 23 June 1981, No. 35 January 1982, No. 38 September 1982, No. 53 July 1985, *Industrial Tribunal Reports,* Ministry of Labour, *Industrial Relations Handbook* (1961), Research Paper No. 1 for the Royal Commission on Trade Unions and Employers' Associations 1967, "Selection Procedure for Civil Service Appointments", The Civil Service, Vol. 4, Memorandum No. 9 October 1966; R. Hyman: *Disputes Procedure in Action* (1972); The Incorporated Council of Law Reporting for England and Wales: *The Law Reports;* Industrial Law Journal: C. Bourn, "Statutory exemptions for collective agreements" (1979) 8 I.L.J. 85, B. Bercusson, "The future of fair wages policy" (1982) 11 I.L.J. 271, H. Collins, "Capitalist discipline and corporatist law" (1982) 11 I.L.J. 78, B. A. Hepple and B. W. Napier, "Temporary workers and the law" (1978) 7 I.L.J. 84, O. Kahn-Freund, book review of "Fair Wages Resolutions" (1978) by B. Bercusson, (1979) 8 I.L.J. 188, M. Mellish and N. Collis-Squires, "Legal and social norms in discipline and dismissal" (1976) 5 I.L.J. 164, R. Upex and A. Morris, "Maternity rights—illusion or reality?" (1981) 10 I.L.J. 218; Industrial Relations Services: *Industrial Relations Law Reports, Industrial Relations Review and Report*; The Institute of Advanced Legal Studies: C. Crouch, "Changing perceptions of a public interest" in Lord Wedderburn of Charlton and W. T. Murphy, *Labour Law and the Community* (1982), B. A. Hepple, "Labour law and public employees in Britain" in Lord Wedderburn of Charlton and W. T. Murphy, *Labour Law and the Community* (1982), R. W. Rideout, "Arbitration and the public interest: regulated arbitration" in Lord Wedderburn of Charlton and W. T. Murphy, *Labour Law and the Community* (1982), Kluwer Law Publishers: H. Barbagelata, "Different categories of workers" in R. Blanpain, *Comparative Labour Law and Industrial Relations* (1980); Labour Research Department: *Bargaining Report Wages, Rates, Hours and Holidays* (1982); The London School of Economics and Political Science: Sidney and Beatrice Webb, *Industrial Democracy*; Longman Group UK Ltd., K. W. Wedderburn in Aaron and Wedderburn *Industrial Conflict: a Comparative Legal Survey* (1972); Macmillan Press Ltd.: L. Lustgarten, *Legal Control of Racial Discrimination* (1980), J. Gennard, *Financing Strikers* (1977); MCB Publications: *Knights Industrial Reports;* The Modern Law Review: B. Bercusson, "One hundred years of conspiracy and protection of property: time for a change" (1977) M.L.R. 268, O. Kahn-Freund, "A note on status and contract in British labour law" (1967) 30 M.L.R. 635, P. Lewis, "Interpretation of 'practicable' and 'just' in relation to 're-employment' in unfair dismissal cases" (1982) 45 M.L.R. 382; Organisation for Economic Co-operation and

Development: Employment and Manpower Policy Measures, in *Ministers of Labour and the Problem of Employment* (1976) Vol. 1; Open University Press: R. Hyman, "Trade unions, control and resistance" in G. Esland and G. Salaman, *The Politics of Work and Occupations* (1980); Oxford University Press: P. S. Atiyah, *The Rise and Fall of Freedom of Contract,* (1979), J. Clark and Lord Wedderburn of Charlton, "Modern labour law: problems, functions and policies" in R. Lewis, J. Clark and Lord Wedderburn, *Labour Law and Industrial Relations* (1982) P. Willman, *Fairness, Collective Bargaining and Incomes Policy* (1982); Penguin Books Ltd.: K. W. Wedderburn, *The Worker and the Law* (1965) (2nd ed. 1971); Policy Studies Institute: W. W. Daniel and N. McIntosh, *Incomes Policy and Collective Bargaining at the Workplace: a study of the productivity criterion cases.* PEP Broadsheet 541 May 1973, W. W. Daniel and N. Millward, *Incomes Policy and Collective Bargaining at the Workplace: a study of the productivity criterion cases,* PEP Broadsheet 541 May 1973, Metcalfe, *Alternatives to Unemployment: Special Employment Measures in Britain* (1982); Stevens & Sons Ltd.: M. R. Freedland, "The obligation to work and to pay for work" (1977) *Current Legal Problems* 181, G. S. Goodwin-Gill, "Judicial reasoning and the 'right' to picket" (1975) 91 L.Q.R. 173, L. Lustgarten, "The new meaning of discrimination" (1978) Public Law 178; Sweet & Maxwell Ltd.: B. Bercusson, Annotation to EPCA, s.57(3), in B. A. Hepple and P. O'Higgins, *The Encyclopedia of Labour Relations Law,* B. Bercusson, Introduction, and annotation to s.12 of EPCA, in C. D. Drake and B. Bercusson, *The Employment Acts 1974–1980* (1981), P. Davies and M. Freedland, *Kahn-Freund's Labour and the Law* (3rd ed. 1983), R. Rideout, *Principles of Labour Law* (3rd ed. 1971), Tavistock Publications Ltd.: F. F. Piven and R. A. Cloward, *Regulating the Poor* (1972), Times Newspapers Ltd.: *National Union of Mineworkers* v. *Gormley, The Times,* October 21, 1977; Brian Towers: B. Towers, *British Incomes Policy;* The University of California Press: K. W. Wedderburn and P. L. Davies, *Employment Grievances and Disputes Procedures in Great Britain* (1969); The Yale Law Journal Company and Fred B. Rothman & Company: J. Getman, "Labor arbitration and the dispute resolution" (1979) 88 Yale Law Journal 916.

Due to constraints on space, footnotes have had to be omitted from extracts.

CONTENTS

TABLE OF CASES

(Page references in **bold** indicate the page upon which the section is set out.)

TABLE OF STATUTES

(Page references in **bold** indicate the page upon which the section is set out.)

LIST OF ABBREVIATIONS

Legislation

EA 1980	Employment Act 1980
EA 1982	Employment Act 1982
EPA	Employment Protection Act 1975
EPCA	Employment Protection (Consolidation) Act 1978
IRA	Industrial Relations Act 1971
TUA	Trade Union Act 1984
TULRA	Trade Union and Labour Relations Act 1974 (as amended by the Trade Union and Labour Relations (Amendment) Act 1976 (TULR(A)A))

Institutions

ACAS	Advisory, Conciliation and Arbitration Service
CAC	Central Arbitration Committee
CBI	Confederation of British Industry
CRE	Commission for Racial Equality
EAT	Employment Appeal Tribunal
EOC	Equal Opportunities Commission
ILO	International Labour Organisation
IRC	Independent Review Committee
IT	Industrial Tribunal
MSC	Manpower Services Commission
NIRC	National Industrial Relation Court (1972–1974)
TUC	Trades Union Congress

Trade Unions

AEU	Amalgamated Engineering Union (formerly AUEW)
APCCS	Association of Professional, Executive, Clerical and Computer Staff
APEX	see APCCS
ASTMS	Association of Scientific, Technical and Managerial Staffs
AUEW	Amalgamated Union of Engineering Workers
AUEW-TASS	Amalgamated Union of Engineering Workers—Technical, Administrative and Supervisory Section

EETPU	Electrical, Electronic, Telecommunication and Plumbing Union
GMBATU	General, Municipal, Boilermakers' and Allied Trade Union (formerly GMWU)
GMWU	General and Municipal Workers' Union
IPCS	Institution of Professional Civil Servants
NASD	National Amalgamated Stevedores and Dockers Society
NATSOPA	National Society of Operative Printers, Graphical and Media Personnel
NGA	National Graphical Association
NUGSAT	National Union of Gold, Silver and Allied Trades
NUJ	National Union of Journalists
NUM	National Union of Mineworkers
NUPE	National Union of Public Employees
OPAS	Operative Printers' Assistants' Society
SOGAT	Society of Graphical and Allied Trades
TASS	previously AUEW-TASS
USDAW	Union of Shop, Distributive and Allied Workers

Specialist Journals and Law Reports

B.J.I.R.	British Journal of Industrial Relations
B.J.L.S.	British Journal of Law and Society
I.C.R.	Industrial Court Reports (1972–4), subsequently Industrial Cases Reports
I.L.J.	Industrial Law Journal
I.R.L.R.	Industrial Relations Law Reports
I.R.R.R.	Industrial Relations Review and Report
I.T.R.	Industrial Tribunal Reports (1966–1978)
K.I.R.	Knights Industrial Reports

INTRODUCTION

In a review of "Labour Law Today" ((1981) 44 M.L.R. 589) Lord Wedderburn of Charlton presented a broad survey of the "story of labour law in Britain." He traced the development of the subject from the position in 1946 when in Kahn-Freund's words "labour law was the contract of employment and a bit about protective legislation. By 1950," he stated, "there was still no satisfactory book dealing with the law about individual employment relationships; collective labour relations; statutory regulation; collective agreements; trade unions; and industrial conflict" ((1979) 8 I.L.J. 199). It was Kahn-Freund who made the breakthrough, providing "both an analytical and historical framework for thinking about *all* aspects of British labour law."

The essence of the break-through was to abandon the hitherto exclusive reliance on legal categories of contract, tort and legislation as the basis for the organisation of the subject. Rather, using those legal concepts as tools, Kahn-Freund in *Labour and the Law* (1972) presented his brilliant analysis of collective bargaining with chapters on trade unions and trade disputes. The decisive shift was to a new organisational framework: "collective" labour law came into its own.

Thereafter a new orthodoxy developed which prescribed a division between individual employment law and collective labour law. Once this major extension of the boundaries of the subject had been made, however, it remained relatively static. Concepts and categories were taken from the discipline of industrial relations and injected into labour law. Textbooks now preceded their treatment of collective labour law with descriptions of the industrial relations system in Britain, with particular emphasis on the development of collective bargaining. Having thus set the scene, however, the remaining discussion of collective labour law followed the traditional paths dictated by legal concepts, case-law or the incidence of legislation: legal enforceability of collective agreements; statutory provisions on collective bargaining; the case-law on industrial action.

In this book we have selected extracts from cases and materials in accordance with a principle which suggests a different structure of labour law from that normally encountered in the literature.

Currently, British labour law starts from the assumption that the legal concepts and institutional forms which govern the organisation of work and workers are the subject-matter of labour law. The alternative starting point for readers proposed here is that the subject-matter of labour law is work and workers. Work is the application of human labour to the production of goods or the provision of services. Workers are the human beings carrying out this activity. Our premise is that the current focus of attention in British labour law on the legal concepts and institutional forms which govern work and workers has serious weaknesses.

Defining the subject-matter in terms of concepts and institutions means that it is the difficulties with these concepts and institutions which become the concerns of labour lawyers. So if a problem of work or workers is not catered for by a legal concept or industrial relations institution, it is not dealt with. Our re-definition of the subject-matter of labour law acknowledges that important problems exist affecting work and workers, some of which do not happen to have involved a distinct legal concept or industrial relations institution (see, for example, the treatment of changes at the workplace (Chapter 3, section 2), discipline at work (Chapter 7), systems of pay determination (Chapter 5, section 4) and Custom and Practice (Chapter 12, section 4)).

These problems are recognisable through the experience of work and workers, which is inevitably complex and subject to constant change. Labour lawyers' own experience and perceptions of work and workers must vary, so that different problems may be identified by those seeing the same reality from different points of view. The contents of this book, therefore, must necessarily be to some extent a subjective selection of problems derived from our experience of and perspective on the problems of work and workers. While we think that our selection covers most of the conventional "topics" of labour law, what matters in the final resort is not readers' acceptance of our selection but their appreciation that labour law must address the day-to-day problems of work and workers rather than lawyers' concerns with legal concepts and institutions. Hence our inclusion of materials on less familiar themes, such as access to work or work and the family, which are scarcely catered for in the current labour law literature or have their nature distorted by the emphasis on the legal concept or industrial relations institution rather than on the problem itself.

The way in which problems are analysed is different once the focus is shifted from concepts and institutions to problems of work and workers. Many rules dealing with the problems of work and workers derive from collective agreements and industrial relations custom and practice. These latter phenomena are worthy of attention not simply because they may have a particular legal status or have assumed an institutional form, but because they contribute a multitude of rules governing work and workers.

We have here suggested a framework not dictated by conventional legal patterns (*eg* common law development, statutory interpretation); rather, our proposed emphasis on the problems of work and workers means that the reader's attention is focussed on policy issues: how is a problem dealt with by rules derived from different sources? What are the policies underlying such rules? To what extent has a policy been successfully implemented? And what alternative policies and methods of implementation might be adopted?

Policy analysis of this sort is a real challenge: British tribunals and courts are less than forthcoming as to their policy preferences in reaching decisions, and are reticent in their recognition of the policy consequences of such decisions. The extracts presented in this book have been selected primarily not for their technical analysis of the common law or of statutory language, but rather for the light they shed on judicial and legislative policy preferences and the political consequences of judicial and legislative decisions.

These elements: a different subject-matter, the different problems thrown up as a consequence of this alternative focus, and the different methods and materials used to illuminate the ways in which these problems are resolved, contribute, we submit, to what we hope will develop into a new approach to labour law. It can be summarised as a perception of labour law as being concerned with the problems of workers and of work and the policy solutions adopted to deal with them.

The problems on which we have selected material are evident from the tables of contents. We begin with material on workers and their relations with the State, with employers and with other workers. Next there is material on the problem of access to work, focussing on legal control of the employer's discretion in hiring employees, followed by material on problems of the definition and changing nature of the work obligation undertaken by workers. In Chapter 4 on the Quantity of Work, the reader is exposed to the often overlapping issues of hours of work, overtime obligations and redundancy, and the sequence of problems arising in redundancy situations: from preventing redundancy, to consultation, selection, notice, and finally redundancy payments. The following chapters have material on some of the major incidents of work: pay and benefits, discipline, and discrimination and inequality; on external factors with a major impact on work: sickness and injury, and family life; and a selection of material allowing the reader to explore the policies underlying the substantive and procedural rules which affect termination of work. The last four chapters are devoted to materials on trade unions, collective bargaining, industrial conflict and the internal affairs of trade unions, the traditional concerns of labour law, but once again with the emphasis on problems and policy. So, in Chapter 12 on Collective Bargaining, the reader can investigate the implications of complex bargaining structures and of collective agreements on a variety of subjects for workers' contractual terms of employment. Chapter 13 on Industrial Conflict concludes with a selection of materials on some key issues of law and policy. Chapter 14 on the Internal Affairs of Trade Unions provides scope for discussion of legal controls of union policy-making and executive action, drawing on the litigation arising from the miners' strike of 1984–85.

We think that this collection of cases and materials has a number of advantages. Problems of great practical importance are highlighted which do not normally receive adequate attention. For example, hitherto there has rarely been available to students of labour law in conventional works opportunity for comprehensive analysis of discipline at work, it usually having been treated as a mere by-product of the contract of employment, the Truck Acts or the Code of Practice in unfair dismissal cases. Again, the materials on "access to work" challenge the reader by exposing the policy issues underlying the legal rules.

The approach adopted in this book also seeks to narrow the present gap between practitioners (whether they be lawyers, union officials and members, employers and personnel officers, or policymakers) and academic labour lawyers. Our focus on practical problems enables students of labour law at all levels to apply to them their theoretical perspectives and their legal and other skills. Some of the difficulties which beset labour law are attributable to this gap between theory and practice. For example, the debate over the "floor of rights" can be seen to be based on a premise which tends to isolate statutes from the problems of industrial relations practice. It may be true that statutes provide a number of legal entitlements—but so what? There are practical problems of coverage: at what point do the gaps in the floor affecting, for example, part-timers, temporary workers, unorganised workers, or civil servants, become so wide that whether a floor exists or not is more appropriate for philosophical than legal debate? There are difficulties of enforcement: is there machinery to combat widespread evasion, or is it used? There are conflicts over standards: are the statutory standards effectively superseded by collective practice? Problems such as these render questionable the value of a notion of a floor of rights. To promote it may be to assume that the establishment of statutory rights is a solution to practical problems.

The closer approximation of labour law studies to labour problems would give the lie to the assertion that law is in some sense singularly irrelevant to or a mere secondary force in British labour relations. Study of the relation of insurance to tort law, or of police practice to criminal law, or of business and consumer affairs policy to contract law, or of corporate practice to company law, show no less subservient a relationship of law to practice. British lawyers should strive constructively to encourage the closer alignment of law and practice. The closer legal analysis is brought to bear on practical problems, the more lawyers can contribute to the solution of those problems.

CHAPTER 1

WORKERS

1. IDEOLOGY AND SUBORDINATION

The modern legal concept of work and workers is shaped by the ideology of classical liberalism, as described in the following extract.

A. Fox, BEYOND CONTRACT: WORK, POWER AND TRUST RELATIONS (1974), pp. 164–167

. . . Hobbes argues that men in society are driven into an endless struggle for power over others; not necessarily because they themselves seek ever more power and gratification but because if they are to defend what they have against the power-hungry predators they cannot opt out of the contest. . . . Since no society could permit this to take place through physical violence, Hobbes must be assuming one which provides peaceful, non-violent ways by which every man can constantly seek power over others without destroying the social fabric. This Macpherson terms 'the possessive market society'—a society in which, by contrast with one based on custom and status, there is no authoritative allocation of work or rewards and in which, by contrast with a society of independent producers who exchange only their products in the market, there is a market in labour as well as in products. If a single criterion of the possessive market society is sought it would be that man's labour is a commodity, ie that a man's energy and skill are his own, yet are regarded not as integral parts of his personality but as alienable possessions, the use and disposal of which he is free to hand over to others for a price. Such a concept also includes the characteristic that where labour has become a commodity, market relations so shape or permeate all social relations that we may refer not simply to a market *economy* but to a market *society*. . . .

Hobbes's perspective was amended by Locke in ways which need not concern us here, but the essential picture of possessive market society remained. The normality and justice of the market in labour was as much a commonplace of seventeenth century thinking as the normality and justice of the markets in commodities and capital. To Locke a man's labour was so unquestionably his own property that he might freely sell it for wages, with the labour thus sold becoming the property of the buyer who was then entitled to appropriate the produce of that labour. And the implications went further. To insist that a man's labour is his own is not only to say that it is his to alienate in a wage contract; it is also to say that his labour and its productivity is something for which he owes no debt to civil society—a further perspective on the separation of economics and ethics. The traditional view that property and labour were social functions with social obligations was thereby undermined.

The failure to appreciate the social function of labour (*eg* housewives' domestic labour, see O. Clarke and A. Ogus, "What is a wife worth?" (1978) 5 B.J.L.S.1) and the focus solely on its quality as a market commodity have implications for relations at work.

R. Hyman, "Trade unions, control and resistance" in THE POLITICS OF WORK AND OCCUPATIONS (G. Esland and G. Salaman ed., 1980) pp. 303–307

For the great majority of the "occupied population" (in Britain, over 90 per cent), work equals wage-labour. Labour relations are thus, at the outset, market relations. The prospective worker must find an employer willing to pay a wage or salary in return for the disposal of his/her skill, knowledge or physical capacities; and can expect such employment to last only so long as this willingness continues. Labour thus has the status of a commodity; and as with all market relationships, the interests of buyers and sellers are antagonistic. The wages and conditions sought by the employee as the means to a decent life, both within and outside work, are a *cost* cutting into the employer's profits. . . .

If labour within capitalism is in one sense a commodity like any other, in another sense it is quite unlike all other types of commodity. For while the employment contract may well specify precisely what the worker receives from the employer, what he/she provides in return is rarely defined specifically. . . .

. . . Rather than agreeing to expend a given amount of effort, the employee surrenders his/her *capacity to work*; and it is the function of management, through its hierarchy of control, to transform this capacity into actual productive activity. Hence Marx's vital distinction between labour and labour power: the wage or salary is not the price of labour as such but of labour power, the ability to work; but the realization of this potential is by no means a simple economic exchange, it is a process which occurs 'outside the limits of the market'. The cobbler who sells a pair of boots is separated from the commodity after the moment of sale, and is engaged in no necessary and continuing relationship with the customer; but the worker's labour power cannot be detached from his/her physical presence, and this necessitates an ongoing social relationship with the employer (or the employer's agents) throughout the labour process itself. Issues of control inevitably pervade this relationship: the conflictual character of job control and the commodity status of labour are reciprocally dependent aspects of social relations of production within capitalism.

Different legal formulations of the concept of the worker are possible. Labour law starts with the relationship of employment—the contract of service. The supremacy of ideology in this concept is apparent, as the following extract illustrates.

H. Barbagelata, "Different categories of workers" in COMPARATIVE LABOUR LAW AND INDUSTRIAL RELATIONS (R. Blanpain ed. 1980), p. 320

1. The expression "worker" like its corresponding word in all languages does not have a single universal meaning in social and labour law. In a broad sense a worker is one who performs personal services for an employer in return for a promise of economic compensation. But individual employment law and sometimes the law of collective labour relations narrows down this definition of "worker". In most countries regardless of the economic legal and political system, labour law and industrial relations apply only to those workers who are in a subordinate employment relationship with an employer, so-called *employees,* as distinct from independent workers, the so-called self-employed.

2. In most systems the chief source of the individual employment relationship is the *contract of employment*. But this concept does not explain much. Personal services can also be rendered under other contracts, such as those by an independent contractor, an agent or with a partner. For this reason individual contracts of employment have to be carefully differentiated from other forms of contract and this is of great practical importance as well as a source of considerable difficulty.

3. In truth the definition of the "employee" and the "contract of employment", as distinct from other voluntary relationships where personal services are rendered in return for money, is not determined by a single criterion. There is, however, a convergence in modern legal doctrine towards the recognition of submission of the employee to the employer's command or control as to the time, place and manner in which the work is to be done as a necessary criterion. This criterion of subordination or dependency is of Continental European origin and was originally distinct from the Common Law test of control derived from the old law of master and servant. But the conception of a power of control in the Common Law countries has been influenced by the Continental doctrines of subordination and integration, especially as a result of the work of the late Sir Otto Kahn-Freund. This implies a functional dependency inherent in the employment relationship.

This emphasis on subordination in labour law may be contrasted with different approaches in other legal contexts. The worker as such may be an object of taxation, a subject of social security, protected by legislation on health and safety, a member of a trade union—as well as being related to the employer through a contract of service. The legal concept of the worker may vary in different contexts according to the policy pursued by the legal rules affecting the workers. For example, the use of an alternative concept of the worker in the law of vicarious liability was considered by Atiyah (P. S. Atiyah, *Vicarious Liability in the Law of Torts* (1967) pp. 31–33):

> ". . . the classification of a particular factual situation must always be considered in the light of the purpose for which the classification is being made. Thus in a case of vicarious liability the enquiry is always whether one person is legally responsible for the acts of another. The relationship between the parties may therefore be classified as a master-servant relationship *for this purpose* even though the relationship might not be so classified for other purposes. . . .
> [This] approach has the merit of emphasising that legal concepts are tools to be used intelligently for the purpose in hand and not to be applied blindly to a variety of uses. . . ."

The problems of relying on the contract of employment have been debated, *eg* in the law on unemployment benefit where *income* is a more important criterion than subordination (see A. I. Ogus and E. Barendt, *The Law of Social Security* (1978), pp. 82–83). The point was made by Rideout in *Principles of Labour Law* (3rd ed., 1979), p. 11:

> "It may be that the next stage should be to say that certain elements pointing to or from service should be weighted according to the purpose for which the distinction is required. So, if vicarious liability is the issue, control should be of primary importance, whilst if qualification to receive industrial injury benefits is to be decided the main consideration should be the worker's lack of capital and his economic dependence on the payment he receives from a regular employer for his work."

Laws affecting workers, despite the very different contexts in which they function and the diverse policies pursued, frequently adopt the contract of service and subordination as the criteria defining the objects of their attention. Increasingly, however, the incongruence of the contract of service with the objectives of the law requires amendment, qualification or elaboration of the ideological element of subordination.

2. LEGAL RELATIONSHIPS

The worker has three principal relationships which are affected by law: (a) with the State; (b) with the employer; and (c) with other workers.

(A) Relations with the State

This relationship embraces a number of areas: taxation (via the compulsory PAYE system), social security (via the compulsory National Insurance system), regulatory legislation providing rights (the "floor of rights") and imposing obligations at work. There may be special obligations *vis-à-vis* the State where the worker is in the public sector (*e.g.* restrictions on the disclosure of information under the Official Secrets Acts 1911 and 1920), or the State may enforce professional monopolies (*e.g.* pharmaceutical chemists' exclusive rights to sell by retail medicinal products under the Medicines Act, 1968, s. 10), or impose qualifications for engaging in certain work (*e.g.* the need for drivers of heavy goods vehicles to be licensed to drive vehicles of that class: see the Road Traffic Act 1972, s. 112(1)). In national emergencies, such as in war-time, the State may have the power of "direction of labour," or conversely, certain parts of the State machinery may be expressly precluded from directing labour (as are the courts under TULRA, s. 16).

The scope and complexity of the worker's relations with the State raise the fundamental issue of whether labour law's focus on the employment relationship and reliance on the contract of employment is adequate. Concepts based on the employment relationship and the contract of employment are of little help in analysing the position of important occupations such as the professions, yet law is central to understanding these categories of workers.

Labour law needs analytical tools to examine the role of the State. In 1954 Kahn-Freund declared that the contract of employment was "the corner-stone of the edifice" of labour law (A. Flanders and H. A. Clegg (1954), "Legal Framework" in *The System of Industrial Relations in Great Britain*, p. 47). Over a decade later, Rideout opined that he had "examined this corner-stone and found it to have a core of rubble" ("The Contract of Employment" in (1966) *Current Legal Problems* 111 at 122). Rideout went on to question whether legal theory permitted employment to be explained in terms of contract, and contrasted the rival claims of "a contract or a status of employment." These rival claims were the subject of an illuminating essay by Kahn-Freund, from which the following extract is taken.

O. Kahn-Freund, "*A note on status and contract in British labour law*" (1967) 30 M.L.R. 635 at 635, 640–642

THE labour law of Great Britain shares with that of the other nations in our orbit of civilisation two essential jurisprudential features: it is based on the contractual foundation of the obligation to work and of the obligation to pay wages, and it is at the same time permeated by a tendency to formulate and to enforce an evergrowing number of imperative norms for the protection of the worker, norms which the parties to the contract cannot validly set aside to the detriment of the economically weaker party. This dual insistence on agreement as the legal basis of at least some of the essential rights and obligations and on mandatory regulation as the source of the content of the relationship has given rise to a jurisprudential dilemma which has so far not been clearly faced in the literature on the subject.

The dilemma arises from the ambiguity of the term "status". . . . [not that concept as used by Sir Henry Maine in his celebrated dictum that "Western society is moving from 'contract' to 'status'," but rather in a sense analysed by Kahn-Freund as "something radically different from what Maine had referred to in his observation". . . .]

. . . the law operates upon an existing contractual relation, but it moulds this relation through mandatory norms which can not be contracted out to the detriment of the weaker party (employee, passenger, customer in general). It is this phenomenon which is characteristic of the legal developments of our time, nowhere more so than in the field of labour law.

How can we explain the conceptual confusion between two legal phenomena as different as the imposition of rights and duties irrespective of the volition of the person concerned, and the shaping of a contractual relation into which he has freely entered?. . . .

. . . The reason appears to be that the positive regulation of the substance of contractual relations has only within fairly recent times become one of the recognised functions of the legislature. The law of contract was developed by the courts, and the principal conceptual instruments which they handled were the intention of the parties . . . and public policy which, in a few extreme cases, may destroy a contract, but which cannot mould it. Thus the idea of the positive regulation by law of the content of contractual relations is, as English legal history goes, fairly new. . . .

. . . . Hence the tendency to think of anything that is imperative or compulsory as imposed in the way status is imposed. We have the extensive phenomenon of a body of affirmative rules regulating the substance of contracts of employment, of hire-purchase, etc. But this is incompletely absorbed into the conceptual structure of the law.

(*B*) *Relations with the Employer*

(i) The development of the concept of the contract of employment

On the one hand, there is a consensus that: "The contract of employment is, both historically and currently, the central legal institution of our labour laws" (P. Davies and M. Freedland, *Labour Law: Text and Materials* (1979), p. 2); or "It is contract, in one form or another, which dominates the law of individual employment" (P. Elias, B. Napier, P. Wallington, *Cases and Materials on Labour Law* (1981), p. 372). On the other hand, there is the criticism that "historically the law of contract has never come to terms with the reality of industrial life" (Mr. Justice P. Pain, in [1981] 10 I.L.J. 137 at 143). The following extract illuminates the development of the concept of the contract of employment. It does so by reviewing the historical development of the employment relationship from pre-industrial labour to industrial employment.

A. Fox, BEYOND CONTRACT: WORK, POWER AND TRUST RELATIONS (1974), pp. 188–190

One of the master symbols of the emergent social order has been seen to be contract. Voluntary agreement forged through bargaining over specific terms, the essence of economic exchange, was seen as the mechanism which articulated atomistic, self-regarding individuals into the collaborative aggregates and linked processes necessary for civil society. How did the employment relation fit into this contractual society and into the ideologies prevalent within it? Can the contract of employment be seen as simply another manifestation of this increasingly pervasive form of exchange?. . . .

From the fourteenth century the law of employment, such as it was, had relied on the legal imagery of "master and servant." The law of master and servant "was rooted in a society in which everyone was presumed to belong somewhere, and the great parameters of belonging were kinship, locality, religion, occupation, and social class. In all spheres of life, including spiritual communion, *subordination to legitimate authority* was thought to be a natural, inevitable, and even welcome accompaniment of moral grace and practical virtue" (Selznick: his italics).

Master and servant law looked to the household as a model and saw in it the foundations of orderly society. Hill, noting that the government of a family was likened "to that of a ship, a corporate town, or a state," quotes a seventeenth century writer to the effect that "In a family, the master or *pater-familias*, who is a kind of petty monarch there, hath authority to prescribe to his children and servants. . . . " Servants included wage earners; all those who worked for an employer for a wage. The reason for this usage was that the household model was appropriate not only to the—overwhelmingly predominant—agricultural family unit in which hired labour supplemented the work of family members, but also to the pattern of work and training among skilled artisans. Within this setting, the relation of master and servant was diffuse and paternalistic. Work was carried out in the master's house or in a small shop near by, with the workman living as a member of the household. The positions of the master and servant were conceived in status terms. This was perfectly compatible with the notion that some terms of their association, such as its duration and the wages to be paid, could be contractual and therefore subject to bargaining and mutual assent. But beyond this it was never contemplated that the parties would design their own relationship. By far the greater part of the framework of mutual rights and obligations within which they connected themselves was to be taken as given. Its sources were custom, ideology, and the law, which between them defined the expectations and obligations accepted by all who entered into the master-servant relation. The servant was seen as contributing personal service, conceived not as specific labour duties but as a general contribution to the needs of the enterprise, be it household, farm, or workshop. "In some vague but important sense, it was assumed that the whole person was committed to the relation" (Selznick). . . .

So long as the family farm and the small family business predominated, this patriarchal paternalistic concept corresponded to economic realities in the sense that the division of labour and the social setting of work provided a context in which the participants could readily act out the concept if they chose to. And provided reality could be shown to approximate for at least part of the time to a genuinely reciprocal exchange, the concept could offer a legitimizing service by appearing to provide something of a justification for class domination.

Given the growth of industrialism, however, with its increasing division of labour, impersonal markets, and the segmental and specific relations thereby created, the old traditional diffuse relationship was not only structurally undermined in the practical sense that changing forms made it increasingly difficult to operate, it was also challenged in principle . . . (by) . . . the doctrinal assertion of contract as economic exchange, purged of all traditional particularistic bonds and ties which might obscure economic calculation and impede the mobility of resources (including labour) in their ever vigilant search for the highest return. Many employers were ready to embrace a doctrine which divested their authority of any diffuse sense of duty, obligation, and responsibility towards those they employed. From this point of view the old master-servant law needed streamlining down towards the concept of contract. To define the employment relation as contract was to emphasize: (a) the limited nature of the commitment made by the parties to each other and (b) the high value placed on the freedom of individuals, whatever their station, to enter contractual relations and define for themselves the terms of the bargain (Selznick).

The first of these propositions was acceptable enough to employers with respect to many of the work roles they had in mind, though . . . its appeal was to lose some of its bloom. The second, however, as we have noted, could only be seen as explosive if ever it were to be applied in its full literalness to the employment contract. The pure milk of the contract gospel had to be diluted if the entrepreneur was to enjoy practical and moral support in his unfettered command over labour resources. The law did not, therefore, treat the conditions of employment as the outcome of free bargaining and mutual assent. The concept of contract had to be adapted to maintain, in Selznick's phrase, "the organizational strength of the business enterprise". This was done by marrying contractualism to the traditional master-servant notions. Although contract theory ostensibly gave full discretion to the parties in defining the nature and scope of authority, in fact the law imported into the employment contract a set of implied terms reserving full authority of direction and control to the employer.

Thus once the contract was defined as an employment contract the master-servant model was brought into play—though of course not all the original aspects of it. The notion of the employer's diffuse obligations was distinctly in decline. What was most important for the propertied classes was that element which legitimized the employer's prerogative.

(ii) The legal definition of the employment relationship

The case law ranges over a variety of *tests* for determining whether the relationship in question is one of employment. Some of these tests relate to the *work* (its place: at home or in a factory or peripatetic; or duration: temporary, permanent, or irregular); some to the *worker* (his or her discretion or skills or equipment used); or the *employer's* role (in supervision or control, hiring and dismissal, or form of payment). None of these has proved adequate by itself, and in combination many give conflicting indications.

One consequence has been that considerable confusion exists over the question of whether a particular relationship is one of a contract of service (an employee) or of a contract for services (a self-employed person). Specifically, is the question one of law (on which an appeal can be made to higher tribunals) or one of fact for the Industrial Tribunal alone to decide?

O'Kelly v. Trusthouse Forte plc
[1983] I.R.L.R. 369
Court of Appeal

The E.A.T. interpreted a passage in a judgment of Stephenson L.J. in *Young & Woods Ltd.* v *West* [1980] I.R.L.R. 210 as authority for the proposition that the question of whether a worker is employed under a contract of employment is one of pure law upon which an appellate tribunal can reach its own view. The Court of Appeal disagreed with this interpretation of Stephenson L.J.'s view.

Sir John Donaldson M.R.: There is no doubt that there are pure questions of law which throw a court back to questions of fact . . . facts whose nature, quality and degrees are known with complete precision will no doubt always produce the same answer. But this is not real life. In reality every Tribunal of fact will find and assess the factual circumstances in ways which differ to a greater or lesser extent and so can give rise to different conclusions, each of which is unassailable on appeal. In this sense, but in this sense alone, their conclusions are conclusions of fact. More accurately they are conclusions of law which are wholly dependent upon conclusions of fact.

The test to be applied in identifying whether a contract is one of employment or for services is a pure question of law and so is its application to the facts. But it is for the tribunal of fact not only to find those facts but to assess them qualitatively and within limits, which are indefinable in the abstract, those findings and that assessment will dictate the correct legal answer. In the familiar phrase "it is all a question of fact and degree."

It is only if the weight given to a particular factor shows a self-misdirection in law that an appellate court with a limited jurisdiction can interfere. It is difficult to demonstrate such a misdirection and, to the extent that it is not done, the issue is one of fact. . . .

In the instant appeal the Industrial Tribunal directed itself to "consider all aspects of the relationship, no single factor being in itself decisive and each of which may vary in weight and direction, and having given such balance to the factors as seems appropriate, to determine whether the person was carrying on business on his own account." This is wholly correct as a matter of law and it is not for this court or for the EAT to re-weigh the facts.

Ackner L.J.: It was objected by Mr Irvine [counsel for the employer] that if the Employment Appeal Tribunal and the Court of Appeal were entitled to intervene where in their opinion the Industrial Tribunal had reached the wrong, although an arguable, decision this would lead to a multiplicity of litigation. In my judgment the contrary would be the case. Without the Employment Appeal Tribunal being entitled to intervene where in its view the Industrial Tribunal has wrongly evaluated the weight of a relevant consideration(s) then it will be open to Industrial Tribunals to reach differing conclusions, so long as they are reasonably maintainable, on essentially the same facts. This is clearly highly undesirable, particularly where a substantial number of statutory provisions impose duties on an employer in relation to his employees, or confer benefits on employees, where they work under a contract of service, but not under a contract for services. . . . To permit conflicting decisions on the basis that a broad band exists where a tribunal or a court might be said reasonably entitled to decide the issue either way would seem most unsatisfactory.

In practice, the problem of whether a worker is employed under a contract of service has given rise to a phenomenon widely suspected and recently confirmed by research in North London. This concerns the choice by employers of whether they took on their own employees, or preferred "self-employed" contractors.

P. Leighton, "*Employment contracts: a choice of relationships*", DEPARTMENT OF EMPLOYMENT GAZETTE, (October 1982), p. 433 at 438

A factor which was highly influential was the impact of tax, social security and insurance legislation. Employers in mini-cabbing, some in insurance and most engaged in the repair of domestic appliances generally accepted the so-called advantages of self-employed status. Sometimes it was euphemistically referred to as "having freedom to regulate your income more effectively" or, more usually, "having the opportunity to fiddle". It was in the less structured occupations that this view was most prevalent. From the employer's viewpoint there are many administrative and financial savings to be derived from the use of self-employed staff. These are not limited to social security but involve liability insurance and employment benefits such as sick pay and paid holidays. It should be said that the law does not require many such benefits to be provided even for direct employees and several employers in the survey (in employment agencies and domestic appliances) did not do so for their direct labour. There is, though, a frequent misconception that using direct labour increases these costs and responsibilities *per se*, and so the use of self-employed staff has much to commend it. If this attitude is coupled with enthusiasm for the "philosophy" of self-employment more generally it will make the choice of employment relationship almost inevitable.

The policy issue is whether the courts will permit parties to label their relationship unilaterally, whatever the consequences for legal regulation of the employment relationship.

(a) A policy approach to defining the employment relationship

The cases in which it is difficult to determine the legal nature of the employment relationship may be better assessed, as Rideout has said: "according to the purpose for which the distinction is required." To that end, in some cases, the judges do have express regard to policy when holding the contract to be one of service or not. The following are illustrations.

1. Employment status and taxation. In the following case, the court considered the legal definition of the employment relationship in the context of taxation policy.

Massey v. Crown Life Insurance Co.
[1978] I.R.L.R. 31; [1978] 2 All E.R. 576
Court of Appeal

On the advice of his accountant, Mr Massey, the manager of a branch of an insurance company, changed his agreement with his employer in 1973 so as to become self-employed and began paying income tax under Schedule D accordingly. When his employment was terminated subsequently, he claimed compensation for unfair dismissal, for which only "employees" are eligible.

Lord Denning M.R. : The law, as I see it, is this: if the true relationship of the parties is that of master and servant under a contract of service, the parties cannot alter the truth of that relationship by putting a different label upon it. If they should put a different label upon it and use it as a dishonest device to deceive the Revenue, I should have thought it was illegal and could not be enforced by either party and they could not get any advantage out of it—at any rate not in any case where they had to rely upon it as the basis of a claim: see *Alexander* v *Rayson* [1936] 1 KB 169. An arrangement between two parties to put forward a dishonest description of their relationship so as to deceive the Revenue would clearly be illegal and unenforceable. On the other hand, if their relationship is ambiguous and is capable of being one or the other, then the parties can remove that ambiguity, by the very agreement itself which they make with one another. The agreement itself then becomes the best material from which to gather the true legal relationship between them. This is clearly seen by referring back to the case of *The Commissioners of Inland Revenue* v *His Grace the Duke of Westminster* [1936] A.C. 1. The duke had a gardener and paid him for his work a weekly sum. But, in order to avoid tax, his solicitors drew up a deed in which it said that his earnings were not really wages, but were an annual payment payable by weekly instalments. The House of Lords held that, to find out what the true relationship was and what the true nature of these payments were, you had to look at the deed. Lord Tomlin said (at p. 19) that "every man is entitled, if he can, to order his affairs so that the tax attaching under the appropriate Acts is less than it otherwise would be." The gardener did the same work as before but the legal relationship was changed by the deed drawn up by the solicitors. . . .

It seems to me on the authorities that, when it is a situation which is in doubt or which is ambiguous, so that it can be brought under one relationship or the other, it is open to the parties by agreement to stipulate what the legal situation between them shall be. That was said in the *Ready Mixed Concrete* case [1968] 2 Q.B. 497 by MacKenna J. He said (at p. 513) that "if it were doubtful what rights and duties the parties wished to provide for, a declaration of this kind might help in resolving the doubt and fixing them in the sense required to give effect to that intention".

So the way in which they draw up their agreement and express it may be a very important factor in defining what the true relation was between them. If they declare that he is self-employed, that may be decisive.

Coming back to this case, for myself I have considerable doubt whether Mr Massey was really a servant from 1971 to 1973. It looks to me much more as if he was even in that time a commission agent. He could take on other work. He did in fact work for another insurance broker. He was paid on commission. He received a minimum sum but over and above that he was paid on commission as many commission agents are. So I think it is very doubtful whether he was under a contract of service from 1971 to 1973. But I am perfectly clear that afterwards in 1973, when this agreement was drawn up and re-cast, although the same work was done under it, the relation was no longer a master and servant relationship. It was an employer and independent contractor relationship. The change to "John I. Massey & Associates" was an unnecessary complication. It is significant that the Tribunal found that both sides agreed that the agreement was, and was intended to be, a genuine transaction and not something which was done solely for the purpose of deceiving the Inspector of Taxes. They said, "Had we thought otherwise, we would have held the agreement to be tainted with illegality with the consequence that it would have been void."

It seems to me that those findings of the Industrial Tribunal were well-justified in the circumstances of this case. Mr Massey was not an employee. He was not employed under a contract of service so as to be able to avail himself of the unfair dismissal provisions. . . .

In most of these cases, I expect that it will be found that the parties do deliberately agree for the man to be "self-employed" or "on the lump." It is done especially so as to obtain the tax benefits. When such an agreement is made, it affords strong evidence that that is the real relationship. If it is so found, the man must accept it. He cannot afterwards assert that he was only a servant.

In the present case there is a perfectly genuine agreement entered into at the instance of Mr Massey on the footing that he is "self-employed." He gets the benefit of it by avoiding tax deductions and getting his pension contributions returned. I do not see that he can come along afterwards and say it is something else in order to claim that he has been unfairly dismissed. Having made his bed as being "self-employed," he must lie on it. He is not under a contract of service.

2. Employment status and health and safety. In the following case, the policy of protecting the health and safety of workers was considered as a factor in determining employment status.

M. J. Ferguson v. John Dawson & Partners (Contractors) Ltd.
[1976] I.R.L.R. 346
Court of Appeal

Mr Ferguson claimed damages for injuries suffered at work. The employer claimed that he was not an employee, but a labour-only subcontractor working under a contract for services ("on the lump"), and hence not protected by statutory health and safety provisions governing employees.

MEGAW L.J.: My own view would have been that a declaration by the parties, even if it be incorporated in the contract, that the workman is to be, or is to be deemed to be, self-employed, an independent contractor, ought to be wholly disregarded—not merely treated as not being conclusive—if the remainder of the contractual terms, governing the realities of the relationship, show the relationship of employer and employee. The Roman soldier would not have been a self-employed labour-only sub-contractor because of any verbal exchange between him and the centurion when he enlisted. I find difficulty in accepting that the parties, by a mere expression of intention as to what the legal relationship should be, can in any way influence the conclusion of law as to what the relationship is. I think that it would be contrary to the public interest if that were so: for it would mean that the parties, by their own whim, by the use of a verbal formula, unrelated to the reality of the relationship, could influence the decision on whom the responsibility for the safety of workmen, as imposed by statutory regulations, should rest . . . .

. . . . The parties cannot transfer a statute-imposed duty of care for safety of workmen from an employer to the workman himself merely because the parties agree, in effect, that the workman shall be deemed to be self-employed, where the true essence of the contract is, otherwise, a contract of service.

LAWTON L.J. (dissenting): I appreciate that there are powerful arguments for thinking that 'working on the lump' is socially undesirable and that many men who do so work do not appreciate that they may be depriving themselves of safeguards which statutory regulations enact must be provided for employed men; but these considerations are not sufficiently strong to make labour bargains of this kind void as being against public policy. If in a particular case the evidence leaves the court in doubt as to what the parties had agreed, there would, no doubt, be a finding which was more in accordance with public policy than against it. That is not this case. In my judgment there is no doubt what the parties intended and it was that the plaintiff should not be a servant of the defendants. Anyway public policy is an awkward horse for a judge to ride, particularly when it wants to go in more than one direction. Maybe the law should try to save workmen from their folly; but it should not encourage them to change a status which they have freely chosen when it suits them to do so. In my judgment it would be contrary to public policy to allow a man to say he was self-employed for the purpose of avoiding the incidence of taxation but a servant for the purpose of claiming compensation. For these reasons I would allow the appeal.

3. Employment status and statutory rights. In the following case, the policy of upholding employment rights was considered mainly relevant to determining the legal status of the worker.

Young & Woods Ltd. v. West
[1980] I.R.L.R. 201
Court of Appeal

When Mr West began employment as a skilled sheet metal worker in a factory, he was offered the choice of being paid as an employee, or as a self-employed worker. He chose the latter. However, when he was sacked, he claimed unfair dismissal under legislation applicable only to employees.

STEPHENSON L.J.: Mr Clifford [counsel for the employer] has submitted that, though a party cannot alter the true relationship, if the parties genuinely and expressly intend to establish a person (on the employer's books) to do a job as a self-employed person, then he cannot make a claim as an employee for the purpose of getting compensation for unfair dismissal. Either, he says, the parties cannot resile from the position which they have deliberately and openly taken up in any circumstances or, if that is putting the matter too high, the presumption created by their deliberately and openly chosen relationship is rebuttable, but not easily rebuttable.

I am satisfied that the parties can resile from the position which they have deliberately and openly chosen to take up and that to reach any other conclusion would be, in effect, to permit the parties to contract out of the [Employment Protection Consolidation] Act [1978] and to deprive, in particular, a person who works as an employee within the definition of the Act under a contract of service of the benefits which this statute confers upon him. If I consider the policy of the Act I can see the dangers, pointed out by Lord Justice Ackner in the course of the argument, of employers anxious to escape from their statutory liabilities under this legislation or the Factories Acts offering this choice to persons whom they intend to employ, as Mr West was employed, as employees within the definition of the Act and pressing them to take that employment—it may be even insisting upon their taking that employment—on the terms that it shall not be called that employment at all, but shall be called a contract for services with a self-employed person I, therefore, reject Mr Clifford's submission in its extreme form.

4. Business and profit or employment and pay. In the following two cases, the courts seemed to be weighing up the values of individual business enterprise in determining the employment status of the worker concerned.

Market Investigations Ltd. v. Minister of Social Security
[1969] 2 W.L.R. 2; [1968] 3 All E.R. 732
Queen's Bench Division

COOKE J.: . . . the fundamental test to be applied is this: "Is the person who has engaged himself to perform these services performing them as a person in business on his own account?". If the answer to that question is "yes", then the contract is a contract for services. If the answer is "no" then the contract is a contract of service. No exhaustive list has been compiled and *perhaps* no exhaustive list can be compiled of considerations which are relevant in determining that question, nor can strict rules be laid down as to the relative weight which the various considerations should carry in particular cases. The most than can be said is that control will no doubt always have to be considered, although it can no longer be regarded as the sole determining factor; and that factors, which may be of importance, are such matters as whether the man performing the services provides his own equipment, whether he hires his own helpers, what degree of financial risk he takes, what degree of responsibility for investment and management he has, and whether and how far he has an opportunity of profiting from sound management in the performance of his task. The application of the general test may be easier in a case where the person who engages himself to perform the services does so in the course of an already established business of his own; but this factor is not decisive, and a person who engages himself to perform services for another may well be an independent contractor even though he has not entered into the contract in the course of an existing business carried on by him.

Hitchcock v. Post Office
[1980] I.C.R. 100
Employment Appeal Tribunal

The case concerned the employment status of a sub-postmaster who ran a post office as part of some other retail business.

SLYNN J.: We accept, as Mr Carr [counsel for the Post Office] quite rightly has accepted, that there is here a substantial measure of control which relates to the conduct of the Post Office's business. It might be, if there were no other factors present, that that control would be sufficient to make the contract one of service rather than for services. But there are other factors present. The question in this case, it seems to us, is really whether the control which does exist is such that it prevents the contract from being one for services rather than of service. Accordingly we must look at the matter as a whole. We consider here that great importance has to be attached to the fact that the applicant provided the premises and a certain amount of the equipment at his own expense. The sub-post office came into what was his general store. It was a part of his own business . . . . Moreover it seems to us that even though there may be less chance of making profit, or risk of loss than in many businesses, there was still here the chance of profit and the risk of loss . . . . It is true that, here, part of the payment made to him was for the use of the premises and part was for his own services . . . . In our view, the essential position was that the applicant, although under control as to the way in which much of the work was done, was carrying on business on his own account. The economic reality of it was that this was his shop, his premises, and it was he who was conducting this sub-post office business even if on behalf of the Post Office. We do not consider that it can be said that he, although doing work for them, was so integrated into their business that he became a servant. The position of a head postmaster who is a full-time employee of the Post Office, and who provides no premises, no employees of his own, seems to us to be entirely different. The very fact here that the applicant was carrying on this business with employees of his own seems to us to indicate very strongly that he was not employed under a contract of service. We do not consider that the element of control here—which, as the industrial tribunal found, is not so much of a managerial nature but is connected with the protection of the Post Office's own property and public interest—is such as to prevent this being a contract for services in the generally understood sense.

(b) A non-policy or "factual" approach to defining the employment relationship

The cases above illustrate that policy considerations are often a factor in the decisions judges make as to whether a contract of service exists. It is difficult, however, to gauge the significance of policy considerations when these are weighed in the judgments against other "factual" tests. The sterility of purely "factual" tests is evident in *O'Kelly* v. *Trusthouse Forte plc* [1983] I.R.L.R. 369 (C.A.), which concerned an application for interim relief under the Employment Protection Consolidation Act 1978, s.77 on a complaint of dismissal for trade union reasons. The three judges of the Court of Appeal did not even advert to the policy of protecting employees against anti-union employers. They were concerned only that the applicants might not be "employees," *ie* the court might unwittingly protect them from the alleged anti-union defendant. In the following case, in contrast, the court was obviously influenced by what it saw as a deliberate legislative policy to broaden the application of statutory obligations.

Mirror Group Newspapers Ltd. v. Gunning
[1985] I.R.L.R. 60
Employment Appeal Tribunal

The appellants refused to transfer a newspaper distribution agency to Mrs Gunning, who claimed this was based on discrimination because of her sex. The industrial tribunal held the distribution agency came within the definition of "employment" under the Sex Discrimination Act 1975, s.82(1): "a contract personally to execute any work or labour."

WAITE J.: The expression "employment under . . . a contract personally to execute any work or labour" has in our view to be read as a whole. The legislative purpose in applying the word "any" to the expression "work or labour" was, we believe, to indicate that the formula was meant to be a wide and flexible one. It would be a matter for the Tribunal upon the terms of each particular agreement, properly construed according to its context, firstly to determine whether any (and if so which) of the duties requiring execution by the contracting party constituted work or labour, secondly to assess the extent to which he was required to undertake responsibility for their execution in his own person, and thirdly to look at the agreement as a whole, asking itself whether, having regard to those findings, the contract is properly to be regarded in essence as a contract for the execution of work or labour or as a bargain of some other kind. . . . [The judge then quoted from the last paragraph given above of the judgment of Sir John Donaldson M.R. in *O'Kelly*'s case (above p. 20), and adapted that direction to the Sex Discrimination Act 1975. He continued:]

The argument that if Tribunals in other cases were permitted to adopt the criteria applied in the present case, and to characterise as "employment" for the purposes of the anti-discrimination Acts transactions containing so slight an element of personal involvement as the agency here concerned, bizarre or absurd consequences would result, did not impress the majority of us. We do not share those fears, and we do not think that Parliament did either. We would expect the view of the legislature to have been that any anti-discrimination legislation would need, in order to be effective at all, to define the potential range of the mischief broadly and boldly. The anti-discrimination Acts include sections which enable behaviour *prima facie* of a discriminatory character to be justified in particular circumstances, and we would regard it as probable that it was Parliament's intention to leave it to the practical good sense of the Tribunals to interpret the Acts as a whole in a way which would ensure the enforcement of their letter only to the extent required by their spirit.

In most cases, however, the courts will abjure overt policy as a consideration in determining employment status. The "usual strategy of legal analysis" was demonstrated in the following extract from a research project attempting to classify employment status in six industries: employment agencies, computing, insurance, mini-cabbing, the direct selling of goods and the repair of domestic appliances.

P. Leighton, "*Employment and self-employment: some problems of law and practice*" (in 1976) DEPARTMENT OF EMPLOYMENT GAZETTE (May 1983), at pp. 199–200

First, directly appropriate case law was located, that is, cases which dealt with the specific trades. Generally, this was not very productive. Though there have been decisions on insurance (*Massey* above p. 15) direct selling (*Hamerton* [1978] I.C.R. 166) and driving (*BSM* and *Dick Evans "U" Drive* [1978] I.C.R. 894) inspection revealed that they often turned on an unusual or narrow legal point. Secondly other relevant cases were considered including those on people working at home (*Cope* [1978] I.C.R. 1210) those who spent little time at their headquarters (*the Market Investigations* case p. 18 above), and those who exercised considerable professional judgment and independence (*Wallis, Addison, Midland Sinfonia* [1979] I.R.L.R. 136, [1981] I.C.R. 281, [1981] I.C.R. 454). Again these revealed little that could be applied to the specific circumstances of the 25 firms under study. Nonetheless with this material in hand together with earlier broader case law a "check list" was drawn up in the hope of reckoning the "balance" of the various items. Occasionally, as we shall see, virtually all the items pointed in one direction and so the conclusion was straightforward. In most situations, however it became necessary to pose a broader question. With the possible exception of workers in employment businesses all the selected industries had the characteristic of allowing the "entrepreneurial spirit" to thrive. It was felt that the "business on your own account" test of *Market Investigations* was generally appropriate. At the same time it was thought that the elusively broad, but relevant concept of "control" must be given considerable weight. The factors included in the check list are set out below.

The "check list"

(1) The "label" given by the parties—this was for information only and could be disregarded for current purposes.

(2) Pay—how described (for example "fee" or "wage"); how computed (basic salary or commission or percentage); and whether PAYE deducted.
(3) Hours of work—whether full-time, regular, flexible.
(4) Other employment benefits such as sick pay, pensions and fringe benefits.
(5) Supervision and discipline—presence of a rule book, sanctions, code of discipline.
(6) The dominance of the employment relationship—is there more than one employer being worked for?
(7) The provision of capital, tools, transport and equipment.

It should be noted that each item had its own complexities and problems. For example, working part-time or short-time does not necessarily increase the likelihood of self-employed status (*Market Investigations, Cope*), but if coupled with other factors such as flexibility of working procedures or the payment of remuneration on a fee or lump sum basis, self-employment may well be the correct legal status (*WHPT Housing Association* and *Midland Sinfonia*). Similarly, it appears that the provision of employment benefits increases the likelihood of direct employment, but its absence does not necessarily lead to a conclusion of self-employment (*Market Investigations*).

Job location was considered a neutral factor which had to be set alongside other factors, for case law suggests that working off the business premises does not necessarily increase the tendency to self-employment (*Hamerton*). Working off-premises frequently heightens the need for adequate supervision and discipline, which would therefore tend to suggest direct employment.

Before considering the application of this approach to the case studies a cautionary note ought to be sounded. Any application of the tests of employment status necessarily involves not only consideration of what might be termed the static aspects of the relationship—employment benefits, hours, basis of calculation of pay, for example—but also a monitoring of the day to day execution of the contract. Only then can the vital issues of supervision, flexibility, dependence, and the like be properly examined.

As put in a recent Court of Appeal decision denying a Methodist minister status as an employee ("In the spiritual sense, the minister sets out to serve God as his master . . . ." *The President of the Methodist Conference* v. *Parfitt* [1984] I.R.L.R. 141 (C.A.), *per* May J. at p. 146):

> "The tasks which people carry out and the contexts in which they do so daily become so much more numerous, more diverse and more sophisticated that no one test or set of tests is apt to separate contracts of service and contracts for services in all cases."

The uncertain results derived from applying the "check-list" approach are demonstrated in the following case.

Withers v. Flackwell Heath Football Supporters' Club
[1981] I.R.L.R. 307
Employment Appeal Tribunal

The question arose whether Mr Withers, who worked as a bar steward, was an employee or was self-employed.

BRISTOW J.: It is clear from the authorities that when you have to decide whether you have to deal with a contract of employment or a contract for services by an independent contractor (a problem which the cases show has given the lawyers considerable trouble in recent years, and which has become of increasing importance in view of the employment protection legislation of the last 10 years) there is no rule of thumb for reaching the right conclusion. The degree of control exercised by the person for whom the work is being done, the terminology the parties use, whether the man doing the work uses his own gear, all are to be taken into account. "Is he on his own business rather than the business of the party for whom the work is being done?" is the ultimate question. As the Tribunal found, and as we ourselves have found, formulating the question in that way—as it was formulated by Cooke J. in *Market Investigations Ltd* v *Minister of Social Security* [1968] 3 All E.R. 372, a formulation subsequently approved by the Court of Appeal—does not of itself make it easy to answer in this particular fact situation. That both parties put the self-contradictory label "self-employed" on their relationship is far from conclusive and is to be disregarded when the reality is that the label, and the fiscal consequences which flow from its use, are adopted simply for fiscal reasons. In each case it is clear that you must look at all the circumstances and judge what is the reality of the situation.

Here the fact situation is unusual and, not surprisingly, quite unlike the fact situations in the authorities which were cited to us. Taking into account the considerations canvassed in those cases we found that there were pointers in each direction, and at first we found it difficult to agree upon what the right answer is. But, like the Industrial Tribunals, we have the advantage of a membership which includes those who are more closely involved in the industrial scene in which these problems are thrown up than lawyers alone can be; and the question which we in the end posed ourselves, and the answer to which first produced agreement between the three members of the court, was couched in industrial rather than legal terminology: "If you had asked Mr Withers while he was running the club bar. 'Are you your own boss?' could he have honestly given any other answer than 'No'? In our judgment, clearly not.

We like to think that if a similar question had been asked in any of the cases cited to us, the answer would have produced the correct conclusion as readily as it produced what we, in the end, agree was plainly the correct conclusion here. If that is right, we think that our elementary lay approach may be helpful to the members of Industrial Tribunals in fact situations which are not easy to fit into the alternative legal concepts.

The cases which emphasise policy, and the multiplicity of differences between employments in terms of place, hours, payment systems, methods of work, degrees of supervision and so on raise the question of whether confining employment relationships to two categories only, employee or self-employed, is adequate. The different qualities of various types of employment might be better dealt with by rules specifically devised to cater for these difference. Such a solution was envisaged in a study of "temporary workers."

B. A. Hepple and B. W. Napier, "*Temporary workers and the law,*" (1978) 7 I.L.J. 84 at 99

The "temporary worker" needs to be separately identified as a category within British labour law. At present rights are haphazardly allocated to short-term workers—and many of these workers are denied legal protection—simply on grounds of various ill-assorted and inexplicable lengths of service. What needs to be identified are the valid reasons why temporary work is required, for example: (1) to meet seasonal changes in demand, particularly for catering work and retail distribution: (2) to fill gaps caused by illness, pregnancy and confinement, medical suspension and holidays of permanent staff; (3) to provide training including working holidays for young persons from abroad; and (4) to perform specific tasks, such as a short-term research project funded from a source outside the undertaking. A Temporary Work Act could make special provision for groups such as these, including the "contracting out" of certain statutory provisions, while preventing the illegitimate use of short-term workers in order to evade statutory duties.

Similar arguments could be made to support legal definitions of and the attribution of specific rights and duties to other groups of workers. The boundary between status and contract becomes blurred, the more the law determines that the relationship of the parties carries with it certain automatic rights and obligations.

(C) *Relations with Other Workers*

The legal relations of workers with each other take place within a number of different frameworks. One framework is within an *organisation of workers* (a trade union or professional association). By virtue of the contract of membership, closed shop arrangements, demarcation agreements and statutory provisions, a worker's relation to other workers is subject to extensive regulation.

Within the *enterprise*, rules governing the relationships between workers are derived from, *eg* collective agreements governing redundancy selection, statutory provisions on equal pay requiring parity of terms and conditions, participation in pension fund schemes, and, occasionally, under schemes providing for self-management in a co-operative arrangement. There is nothing, however, to parallel the complexity of rules and structures in company law governing the relations between shareholders who own, and directors who manage, the enterprise.

Outside the enterprise or organisation of workers, legal regulation of workers' relations with each other is even more diffuse: laws prohibiting discrimination, statutes which (in the past) allowed for claims for parity of terms and conditions between workers in the same industry (Fair Wages Resolution 1946 (revoked in September 1983); Schedule 11 to the Employment Protection Act 1975 (repealed by the Employment Act 1980)); the activities of the TUC and the Labour Party—these demonstrate the heterogeneity of relationships which exist, but which have not been reduced to a systematic legal formulation of workers' relations with each other. (For an illustration of how relations between workers *outside* the enterprise, and *apart* from the trade union could be significant, see the issues surrounding sympathetic or secondary industrial action, where ties of class, industry, skill or geography among workers may be important (see Chapter 13 on *Industrial Conflict*, p. 596)).

3. THE IMPLICATIONS FOR LABOUR LAW OF THE CHANGING RELATIONSHIPS OF WORKERS

The extracts above illustrate the tension in labour law between the focus on the worker's relationships with the employer, and his or her wider net of relationships with the State and with other workers. This may be reflected in movement between notions of status and contract in labour law, by emphasis on policy in determining the substance or even the existence of a contract of employment, or by a recognition that the employment relationship is often subject to the worker's relations with trade unions, and/or with other workers in the same enterprise or outside it.

This tension emerges particularly sharply in the debate over "industrial democracy." This concept involves both the worker's relation to the enterprise and his or her relation to the State. In either case, albeit indirectly, the relationship with other workers is of vital importance.

To shift the emphasis in labour law to the relationship between workers and the State has profound implications for labour law. Even merely to shift the emphasis in labour law to the relationship between workers and the enterprises in which they work involves overlaps with the law governing others interested in the enterprise: shareholders, creditors, consumers and so on. Thus the overlap with shareholders was a major concern of the proposal to put worker directors on the boards of companies (*cf* the Bullock Report on Industrial Democracy (Cmnd. 6706 1977)). The position *vis-à-vis* creditors is particularly acute in the event of insolvency, when wages owed are given preferential status in the distribution of the assets of the enterprise (*c.f.* the Insolvency Act 1986, Sched. 6, paras. 9–15). The position *vis-à-vis* consumers is particularly sensitive in the case of disputes in essential services.

In sum, labour law is concerned with workers and their problems, but the subject-matter can change depending on whether the principal relationship is with the employer, or with others.

CHAPTER 2

ACCESS TO WORK

Access to work means establishing the link between the workers and work. Employers, as owners of the means of production in factories, offices and shops, control access to work, though there are large numbers of self-employed workers, farmers, professionals and others. This chapter examines the extent to which law plays a role in regulating employers' control over work opportunities, and in particular their discretion in selecting among job applicants. We begin by isolating four factors in the sphere of access to work which might encourage legal intervention.

1. FACTORS ENCOURAGING LEGAL INTERVENTION

(A) *The Nature of the Work*

Some work requires skills and qualifications. Other work may be done by almost anybody. Employers accused of discriminating, *eg* on grounds of sex, may defend themselves by referring to the nature of the work. Legislation may control the exercise of their discretion in this regard.

Noble v. David Gold & Son (Holdings) Ltd.
[1980] I.R.L.R. 252; [1980] I.C.R. 543
Court of Appeal

LAWTON L.J.: An Act of Parliament such as the Sex Discrimination Act 1975 may try to change our attitudes towards one another, but it cannot make a woman behave like a man or deprive people of their commonsense. The Act to which I refer provided, subject to a few exceptions, that employers when offering jobs must not assume that women are less capable of doing them than men, and vice versa. This does not mean, however, that a particular applicant for a job, whether male or female, can do it. Much will depend upon the applicant's personal attributes. If the job is one which requires the lifting of heavy loads, a woman of slight build may not be capable of doing that kind of work but one with the physique of an international discus thrower may be. Whether a woman applicant for a job can physically do it must be a matter of judgement for the employer, and he should base his judgement on his own assessment of the candidate, based upon her physique and his experience of what other women doing that kind of job have been able to do. What he must not do is to assume that all women are incapable of doing a particular job.

The law may also prevent access to work unless certain qualifications are met. This is commonly found in the professions: see the Solicitors Act 1974, ss. 19–23; Medical Act 1969; Pharmacy and Poisons Act 1954, s.18; concerning solicitors: see *Reynolds* v. *Hoyle* [1976] 1 W.L.R. 207 (Q.B.D.); doctors: *Tarnesby* v. *Kensington, Chelsea and Westminster Area Health Authority* (*Teaching*) [1981] I.R.L.R. 369 (H.L.); and for barristers: *Engineers' and Managers' Association* v. *ACAS* [1979] I.C.R. 637 (C.A.), at pp. 640–642. The monopoly enjoyed by members of professions over certain types of work by virtue of the statutory exclusion of others is one instance of how law is used to control access to work.

(*B*) *The Nature of the Employer*

An administrative system of regulating access to work may exist, as it does with regard to the civil service where work is distributed in accordance with prescribed standards.

Evidence submitted to the Committee under the Chairmanship of Lord Fulton on The Civil Service (1966–1968), Vol. 4, Memorandum No. 9 submitted by The Civil Service Commission (October 1966) *"Selection Procedure for Civil Service Appointments,"* p. 297

Selection for established posts in the Civil Service is by written examination, by interview before a Selection Board, by objective or aptitude tests, or by extended tests and interviews (commonly if inaccurately termed "Group Selection tests") lasting some two days, or by a combination of these methods. Whatever method is employed the aim is the same: to assess each candidate's intellectual ability, personality, potentiality and, where relevant, his professional or technical skill in relation to the requirements of the post to be filled, and to recommend for appointment those considered suitable.

Could legally prescribed procedures and standards controlling access to work be made mandatory on private sector employers? Lustgarten drew the following conclusions about industrial practice.

L. Lustgarten, *"The new meaning of discrimination"* [1978] PUBLIC LAW 178 at 184–185

How commonly [testing of job applicants] occurs is an empirical question of paramount importance . . . there appears to be only one study that casts any light on the answer. This document is based on a survey of members of the Institute of Personnel Management conducted in 1968 and, as its authors readily acknowledge, it falls far short of a comprehensive study and the sample can certainly not be taken as representative of British industry. Its conclusions may be briefly summarised:

1. Compared with an earlier survey of selection procedures in British industry conducted in the early 1960s, the use of testing is increasing; roughly 45 per cent. of the firms responding used them for some jobs.
2. Larger firms are substantially more likely to operate employment tests than smaller ones. No particular industry seems markedly more or less prone to do so than the average.
3. Tests are most frequently used for clerical staff; least frequently for managers/supervisors and "operatives."
4. General ability/intelligence tests are by far the most common type of test used.
5. Of those firms using tests, less than one in five conducted any form of evaluation of their effectiveness, and virtually none of these did so in a manner that would meet the most elementary scientific standard of accuracy.

One can draw only the most hesitant conclusions from this research but it appears that use of tests, though of growing importance, is nowhere near the norm in British industry, particularly for shop floor workers. Other formal requirements, notably scholastic credentials, are also used to an unknown extent. It seems likely that they would mostly be required for certain white collar and trainee positions. Thus one may hypothesise that few unskilled or semi-skilled jobs are subject to any articulated "requirement or condition."

At present, those who control work opportunities—employers—enjoy, in the private sector, a discretion largely unfettered by law or by any other procedure or standard as to whom they will grant access to work.

(C) *The Organisation of the Workforce*

The organisation of the workforce can determine access to work opportunities. One common illustration is the pre-entry closed shop, where access to jobs requires union membership. An organisation of workers which effectively controls the supply of labour may, by its internal rules, control access to work. Such control of work opportunities through autonomous regulation is one of the hall-marks of a professional organisation: for examples see *Carter* v. *The Law Society* [1973] I.C.R. 113 (N.I.R.C.); *Pratt* v. *British Medical Association* [1919] 1 K.B. 244.

Unlike such organisations which benefit from statutory protection, trade unions, to be effective, need to be able to take industrial action to enforce their control over access to work. The Employment Act 1982, ss. 12–14 removed their statutory immunity in tort and thus exposed them to common law liability in tort for industrial action when attempting in some circumstances to control access to work.

The following case illustrates the employer-union conflict over access to work.

Messenger Newspapers Group Ltd. v. National Graphical Association (1982)
[1984] I.R.L.R. 397
Queen's Bench Division

The plaintiff group of companies, owned 51 per cent. by Mr Shah, had established a subsidiary typesetting company in 1979 in Stockport, Fineward Ltd., which had a formal recognition agreement, including provision for a closed shop, with the NGA. In 1981, the group expanded by setting up another typesetting company in Bury (CAPS Ltd.,) and in 1983, another in Warrington (Messenger Printing Ltd.,). No agreements with the NGA were reached with respect to these two subsidiaries. This led to an official dispute with the NGA, assisted by SOGAT and the NUJ.

CAULFIELD J.: Enshrined in the rules of the defendant union, and faithfully obeyed by its members, except Shah and two or three others, is the closed shop. From the evidence I have heard, the closed shop is to the members of the defendant union an article of faith . . . .

The issues in this case arise because the plaintiff company, led by its chairman, Shah, has sought to assert the rights recently confirmed by Parliament in the statutes to which I will refer in more detail later, an assertion the plaintiff could not have made but for the legislation.

The closed shop principle and practice is not peculiar to the defendant union. Other unions whose activities are not without relevance to the issues raised in this action and who are associated with the newspaper industry themselves practise and jealously preserve so far as they can the same principle and practice. Two of those unions are SOGAT and the NUJ, with which the plaintiff asserts the defendant conspired . . . .

[Disputes followed with Shah over his refusal to accept, with respect to the companies in Bury and Warrington, what was described by the judge as]:

. . . the usual undertaking given by companies who apply for recognition by the NGA. If Shah had accepted it he would have agreed to observe the national agreements, rules and regulations of the defendant as they then existed or as they were subsequently amended; he would agree to employ members of the NGA in all operations which are deemed to fall under their jurisdiction; and as regards vacancies in the company, he would have agreed to notify any future vacancies in the firm to the local branch of the NGA, who would where possible supply suitable labour for the vacant positions.

[The position was summarised by the judge as follows:]

. . . There was a recognition agreement at Fineward; there was no recognition agreement elsewhere. If Shah had enlarged his business at Fineward at the expense of Warrington or Bury, then he would have been subject to the NGA agreement, and he was virtually telling the union "We are going to expand, but we are going to expand without recognition by the NGA". He was at that stage telling the union "I will not accept the closed shop in respect of any place where I expand".

From that letter the closed shop at Fineward was threatened, and it is plain on the evidence that the group—that is the plaintiff—would not expand at Fineward which was subject to the closed shop but would expand without the closed shop at Bury and eventually Warrington through its subsidiaries.

Expansion on Shah's evidence, which I accept, did take place. A press was bought for use at Warrington at very great cost. There was expenditure, too, at Bury. These purchases came to the knowledge of the union in Manchester, and brought a letter from the Manchester branch of the NGA on 20.7.82. . . . which disclosed that the defendant knew what was happening:

> "Dear Mr Shah,
>
> It has been brought to my attention that your company has purchased a Web Offset machine from the Co-operative Press, Chester Road, and according to information I have received it is to be installed in an office in Warrington New Town.
>
> The purpose of this letter is firstly to introduce myself as secretary of the Manchester branch and to express the hope that the venture you are about to undertake will be a successful one.
>
> I take it as read that when your machine is installed you will contact me in order that suitable arrangements can be made to have your office placed on the list of recognised offices and also to discuss the question of NGA recognition and the engagement of suitable labour. . . ."

So, long before the assertion of a trade dispute at Stockport was made by the defendant, it is plain that the plaintiff and the defendant were preparing for war. . . .

[As to the union's industrial action, including picketing, which followed, the judge concluded:]

. . . there was an open conspiracy between the defendant, SOGAT and the NUJ to effect two unlawful ends, one being the disruption of the plaintiff's business, and the other being the enforcement of the defendant's closed shop by a variety of unlawful means, including unlawful interference with the plaintiff's business, inducing or attempting to induce breaches of contract and intimidation.

[He further found two other torts:]

. . . The two torts which I think have been established, and established conclusively, are, firstly, unlawful interference with the plaintiff's business; and secondly, intimidation. As to the first, I have made my findings of fact. The Norwest Co-operative Society plainly withdrew their advertising for a period at the instigation of the defendant. . . . Secondly, there is overwhelming evidence which I have accepted that the plaintiff has established the tort of intimidation. Save for a brief period at Stockport at the outset, there has been unlawful picketing throughout. I am confident there is no tort created by the recent legislation. Unlawful picketing is not in itself a tort. I am wholly satisfied that the purpose of the defendant's activities was, as I have said more than once in this judgment, to compel the plaintiff to accept the closed shop, which in itself is unlawful because of the combined effect of s.12 and s.14 of the 1982 Act.

This last statement is suspect since sections 12–14 outlaw pressures to impose union membership requirements, but do not themselves make the closed shop unlawful (see below, p. 595). Without the means to enforce it, however, union control of access to work is very vulnerable. This vulnerability is enhanced by the Employment Act 1980, s.4, which, in the circumstances of a closed shop, allows a complaint by a person not to be unreasonably refused membership in a trade union. A remedy is thus provided where a union unreasonably denies access to work, whereas no remedy exists if an employer denies an employee access—even on trade union grounds: see *City of Birmingham District Council* v. *Beyer* [1977] I.R.L.R. 211, below p. 34.

(D) *The Role of the State*

Government can affect access to work, not only through control of public expenditure and the creation thereby of jobs in the private and public sectors, but through mechanisms aimed specifically at the labour market. Three examples will illustrate this.

First, national emergencies can lead to the State taking extensive powers in the sphere of access to work. The following extract describes the Government's approach during the second world war, and in the reconstruction period after the war.

B.C. Roberts, NATIONAL WAGES POLICY IN WAR AND PEACE (1958), pp. 35–36, 55–56, 63

The Minister of Labour had power, under the Emergency Powers Act of 1940, to direct any person to perform any task that might be required, at any place and under specified terms and conditions of employment. No Minister in modern British history had ever been given such drastic powers over the lives of persons and immense care had to be taken to see that these powers were exercised fairly. It seems that the Minister was, if anything, over cautious in the use of his powers to direct and coerce. He succeeded, however, in mobilizing both for the services and for essential work the manpower of the country to a degree unreached in any other nation. . . .

The Government, stimulated by the convertability crisis of 1947, eventually screwed up its courage to go beyond exhortation and, with the support of the unions, introduced a Control of Engagements Order which took effect in October 1947. Workers covered by the Order were compelled to use the Labour Exchanges when changing employment and could be directed to essential jobs . . . .

. . . Though it had been possible in wartime to conscript and direct labour to wherever it was required, in peacetime direction, even when accepted in preference to a national wage policy, proved to be abortive. It was a failure because the Ministry of Labour dared not use the powers at its command. The net result was that the much vaunted manpower planning of the Labour Government was reduced to a farce; the targets were missed by such huge margins that their continued publication became an acute source of embarrassment and they were discontinued.

A second example of State intervention may exist where the State provides services in connection with the labour market.

"*Employment and Manpower Policy Measures*" (Appendix to the Recommendations of the Council on a General Employment and Manpower Policy) in *Ministers of Labour and the Problems of Employment* (1976) O.E.C.D., Vol. 1, pp. 85–88

(c) Facilitating manpower adaptation, better labour market functioning and work environment improvements

— development of the public employment service, including:
   (i) improvement of information about vacancies and job seekers,

comprehensive statistics, fuller notification of vacancies, establishment of "job banks" by computer techniques;
(ii) advance notice concerning employment variations;
(iii) manpower forecasting, vocational guidance and testing facilities;
(iv) co-operation with employers and trade unions to develop manpower planning in enterprises;

— promotion of occupational mobility by recurrent education and training;
— transitional arrangements for young people moving from school to work (sandwich courses, work-related instruction, etc.);
— facilitating geographical mobility (financial assistance for distant job search, moving allowances, and help with resettlement and social adjustment in a new environment);
— co-operation between authorities responsible for manpower policy, public transportation and residential construction to provide travel facilities and housing in appropriate areas;
— child-care facilities for mothers and other persons with family responsibilities desiring employment;
— training and orientation facilities for persons wishing to return to employment;
— special incentives to alleviate patterns of male-female occupational segregation;
— reception services in cities receiving large numbers of migrants from rural areas;
— rehabilitation, training, new work experience opportunities, and guidance and adjustment assistance for socially and medically handicapped;
— better access to suitable training opportunities for older workers;
— adjustment of work organisation and work places, to overcome individual handicaps;
— transferable pension rights;
— elimination of age limits for hiring in private and public employment.

The Employment and Training Act 1973 created the Manpower Services Commission (MSC). The Commission comprises a chairman, together with three members each from employers and trade unions, two from local authorities and one from the educational world. The manpower services of the Department of Employment were transferred to the MSC. It is empowered "to make such arrangements as it considers appropriate for the purpose of assisting persons to select, train for, obtain and retain employment suitable for their ages and capacities and to obtain suitable employees" (section 2). The Secretary of State for Employment retains overall control and responsibility, approving the MSC's plans and budget, issuing directions and being accountable to Parliament for its activities.

The MSC's pursuit of an active manpower policy by way of services to the unemployed, training and re-training workers and assistance to special groups has been overtaken by concern with extremely high unemployment levels. The shift from "manpower adjustment" functions to those of job creation was evident in the MSC's Draft Corporate Plan 1983–87. This included the provision of 130,000 places on the Community Programme in 1983/84, offering full-time or part-time jobs for up to 12 months for long-term unemployed people, at a cost of £382 million in 1983/84 rising to £631 million in 1985/86, and the placing of 460,000 young people on the Youth Training Scheme in 1983/84, at a cost of £873 million in 1983/84 rising to £1085 million in 1985/86. Total Government expenditure by the Commission was due to be £1906 million in 1983/84, rising to £2382 million in 1985/86 (see summary in 293 *Industrial Relations Review and Report* 14).

The third example of State regulation of access to work is that of immigration controls. The Aliens Restriction (Amendment) Act 1919 and the Aliens Order 1920 introduced a system of work permits. Entry was prohibited unless the immigrant had "a permit in writing for his engagement issued to that employer by the Ministry of Labour." Similar arrangements are still used to regulate immigration.

2. LEGAL PERSPECTIVES ON ACCESS TO WORK

If access to work is not controlled by law, what does control it? The answer seems to be the imperfect workings of the *labour market*. Work as a commodity in a capitalist economy is exchanged for wages in a labour market. The nature of the market is one where those who control the means of production meet and engage those who possess labour power. The operation of the market varies from industry to industry and place to place, from those industries and places where a few large employers and trade unions may dominate the job or labour supply, to others where hundreds of small employers and unorganised workers meet to establish employment relationships. The decision of employers to engage, or of workers to accept, employment is effectively the exercise of a discretion or freedom. Lawyers are familiar with the degrees to which the exercise of discretion or freedom can be controlled. The extent to which, and the way in which, this freedom is regulated depends, in part at least, on how it is perceived.

(A) *Access to Work as a Matter of Private Contract*

At common law, access to work is perceived as a matter of private contract in a free market. The assumption is that of freedom of contract: both parties are free to enter into, or refuse to enter into a contract of employment. As put by Lord Davey in *Allen* v. *Flood* [1898] A.C. 1 (H.L.) at p. 172:

> "[An employer] may refuse to employ [a workman] from the most mistaken, capricious, malicious, or morally reprehensible motives that can be conceived, but the workman has no right of action against him."

The Webbs described the operation of the doctrine of freedom of contract in a chapter entitled "The Higgling of the Market."

S. and B. Webb, INDUSTRIAL DEMOCRACY 1897 (1920, reprinted New York 1965), pp. 655–657

We begin with the bargain between the workman and the capitalist employer. We assume that there is only a single situation vacant and only one candidate for it. When the workman applies for the post to the employer's foreman, the two parties to the bargain differ considerably in strategic strength. There is first the difference of alternative. If the foreman, and the capitalist employer for whom he acts, fail to come to terms with the workman, they may be put to some inconvenience in arranging the work of the establishment. They may have to persuade the other workmen to work harder or to work overtime; they may even be compelled to leave a machine vacant, and thus run the risk of some delay in the completion of an order. Even if the workman remains obdurate, the worst that the capitalist suffers is a fractional decrease of the year's profit. Meanwhile, he and his foreman, with their wives and families, find their housekeeping quite unaffected; they go on eating and drinking, working and enjoying themselves, whether the bargain with the indivdual workman has been made or not. Very different is the case with the wage-earner. If he refuses the foreman's terms even for a day, he irrevocably loses his whole day's subsistence. If he has absolutely no other resources than his labor, hunger brings him to his knees the very next morning. Even if he has a little hoard, or a couple of rooms full of furniture, he and his family can only exist by the immediate sacrifice of their cherished provision against calamity, or the stripping of their home. Sooner or later he must come to terms, on pain of starvation or the workhouse. And since success in the higgling of the market is largely determined by the relative eagerness of the parties to come to terms—especially if this eagerness cannot be hid—it is now agreed, even if on this ground alone, "that manual labourers as a class are at a disadvantage in bargaining."

The Webbs did note the effect of the doctrine when the labour market tables were turned, and the workers' superior bargaining power gave them the upper hand (see pp. 215–217).

To perceive access to work as a matter of freedom of private contract has the result described by the Webbs in the final chapter of their book (p. 847):

> "What particular individuals, sections, or classes usually mean by 'freedom of contract' . . . is freedom of opportunity to use the power that they happen to possess; that is to say, to compel other less powerful people to accept their terms. This sort of personal freedom in a community composed of unequal units is not distinguishable from compulsion."

This is still the perspective retained by the common law today.

City of Birmingham District Council v. Beyer
[1977] I.R.L.R. 211; [1978] 1 All E.R. 910
Employment Appeal Tribunal

Mr Beyer, a noted trade unionist, was convinced that no large employer who recognised him would give him a job because of his record of union activism. Using a false name and bogus references, he was engaged on October 4, 1975 by the defendant. He was recognised an hour later and dismissed. On September 10, 1976 he managed, unrecognised, to get a job again with the defendant. He was again dismissed within hours when he was discovered, on the grounds of his previous year's deception. Mr Beyer's successful claim of unfair dismissal before an Industrial Tribunal was reversed on appeal.

KILNER BROWN J.: . . . the reasoning of the Industrial Tribunal in this case is tantamount to saying that an employer must not refuse to employ Mr Beyer and that he is entitled to compel the Birmingham Corporation to give him a job. As far as we are aware, on secondhand information, there is no place on earth where it is correct to say that a man has a right to a job. A government may have a duty to provide and pay for as many jobs as possible but until there is work available for all, obviously the employer must have a vested right to pick and choose. There is nothing in the legislation which we have to administer which lays down that an employer may not refuse to employ a man unless he has reasonable grounds for refusing. That may come about one day, but it is not the law at present.

(B) *Access to Work as a Matter of Public Policy*

The general common law view is that access to work is a matter of private contract. Nonetheless, there have been legal interventions in the labour market as a matter of public policy: anti-discrimination laws, statutes regulating professions or employment in the Civil Service, regulation of the closed shop, direction of labour in national emergencies, manpower services and immigration controls. However, only exceptional circumstances are said to warrant intervention. To illustrate how the legal process might be brought to bear on the problem of access to work, we focus on the selection process.

Recent legislation shows how legal controls could be imposed on the exercise of the employer's discretion in selecting an employee. The law prohibiting discrimination on grounds of sex or race (and see also the Rehabilitation of Offenders Act 1974, s.4(3)(*b*)) enables an unsuccessful applicant for a job to complain that the employer has exercised his discretion in an unlawful manner. In the case law under these statutes we can see the beginnings of a legal requirement that the employer *justify* his decision not to employ the complainant.

Humphreys v. Board of Managers of St. George's Church of England (Aided) Primary School
[1978] I.C.R. 546
Employment Appeal Tribunal

A woman teacher applicant for a vacant teaching post complained of sex discrimination when a considerably less well qualified male applicant was appointed.

PHILLIPS J.: The complainant's case, put quite simply, was that this was a situation where the less well qualified, and markedly the less well qualified, person was appointed and where the person with markedly the less teaching experience was appointed. She says, but says no more than, that at least indicates a case which needs looking into and which demands an explanation. . . .

It is a question about which we have already said something in *Oxford* v *Department of Health and Social Security* [1977] I.C.R. 884. All we need do for present purposes is to repeat what was said then by a different division of the Appeal Tribunal. We pointed out that the burden of proof, formally at least, was upon the applicant; that it is a burden which may move very easily to the respondent as a result of the evidence by the applicant. In that case . . . the judgment of the Appeal Tribunal continued, at p. 887:

> " . . . It further seems to us that, while the burden of proof lies upon the applicant, it would only be in exceptional or frivolous cases that it would be right for the Industrial Tribunal to find at the end of the applicant's case that there was no case to answer and that it was not necessary to hear what the respondents had to say about it."

We repeat and endorse these observations. In truth an application of this kind, and the nature of the hearing before an Industrial Tribunal, if justice is to be done, must partake of something at all events of the nature of an inquiry into what has gone on . . . Here was a lady against whom nothing had been said, who was far and away the better qualified educationally, and who had by far and away the longer relevant service. In those circumstances we think that the Industrial Tribunal would have been wiser, and it could have been expected that they would have thought it better, to hear what the employers or the representatives present had to say about it.

At present the law is strictly limited to allowing tribunals to scrutinise employers' hiring decisions only for the taint of racial or sexist bias. Contrast might fruitfully be made with controls on the discretion of workers to refuse job offers, with the sanction of disqualification from unemployment benefit. One of the grounds upon which a worker may be disqualified by the insurance officer is set out in the Social Security Act 1975, s.20(1)(*b*):

> "(Where) after a situation in any suitable employment has been properly notified to him as vacant or about to become vacant, he has without good cause refused or failed to apply for that situation or refused to accept that situation when offered to him."

The burden is on the claimant to prove either that the employment was not suitable or that he had good cause for refusing it or failing to apply for it. Guidance as to what is suitable employment is supplied by section 20(4) of the 1975 Act.

The problems of subjecting the employer's discretion in hiring to public policy enforceable through legal regulation are manifold. They include the development of policy principles applicable to the decision to engage. Parallels could perhaps be drawn with existing legal controls over the employer's discretion in dismissals. There does seem to be an imbalance in a system which strictly controls the "fairness" of dismissal while leaving that of hiring virtually unrestrained by law. The overlap in public policy is illustrated in those cases where an employee on a fixed-term contract is not rehired. The law treats this refusal to rehire as a dismissal, and requires the employer to demonstrate the fairness of the decision (for an illustration, see *Terry* v. *East Sussex County Council* [1976] I.R.L.R. 332 (E.A.T.), below, Chapter 10 on *Termination of Work*, p. 303).

(C) *Access to Work as a Matter of Legal Entitlement: A "Right to Work"*

The concept of access to work as a matter of legal entitlement—a "right to work"—exists in law in a very peculiar way. The most obvious repository of a corresponding duty would seem to be the employer—he who controls the work opportunity access to which is sought. But the common law does not impose any obligation on the employer to provide work. Rather, the "right to work" is found in the context of the common law's policy against "restraints of trade." The courts have used this latter doctrine not against employers who refuse access to work or close down establishments throwing people out of work—but against *others* who interfere with access to work. Trade unions were initially held to be unlawful conspiracies in restraint of trade (*Hornby* v. *Close* (1867) 8 B.&S. 175 (Q.B.D.)), a doctrine only avoided by statutory reversal (see now TULRA, s.2(5)). In contrast, professional organisations have been permitted to justify such restraint on work opportunities because, as one judge put it: "They are not only necessary in the interests of the profession but of the public, who trust to the peculiarly high standing and integrity of a profession to serve it well" (*Pharmaceutical Society of Great Britain* v. *Dickson* [1970] A.C. 403 at 436 (H.L.), *per* Lord Upjohn). The social power possessed by some organisations controlling access to work has occasionally led some judges to consider a substantive "right to work" (see *Nagle* v. *Feilden* [1966] 2 Q.B. 633 (C.A.), below, p. 626 and cases on admission to trade unions in Chapter 14. It was the implications of such a right on employers in a labour market which led the House of Lords to reject the notion in the following case.

Allen v. Flood
[1898] A.C. 1
House of Lords

Ironworkers informed their employers that unless certain shipwrights were discharged, all the ironworkers would stop work. The employers therefore discharged the shipwrights and refused to employ them again. The shipwrights brought an action against the ironworkers. If the shipwrights had a "right to work," then interference with this right might be unlawful. The trial judge responded affirmatively to this idea; the Court of Appeal, by a 6–2 majority agreed; but the House of Lords, by a 6–3 majority, held that there was no such 'right to work' susceptible to interference.

Lord Herschell: I do not doubt that everyone has a right to pursue his trade or employment without "molestation" or "obstruction" if those terms are used to imply some act in itself wrongful. This is only a branch of a much wider proposition, namely, that everyone has a right to do any lawful act he pleases without molestation or obstruction. If it be intended to assert that an act not otherwise wrongful always becomes so if it interferes with another's trade or employment, and needs to be excused or justified, I say that such a proposition in my opinion has no solid foundation in reason to rest upon. . . .

. . . In my opinion a man cannot be called upon to justify either act or word merely because it interferes with another's trade or calling, any more than he is bound to justify or excuse his act or word under any other circumstances, unless it be shewn to be in its nature wrongful, and thus to require justification.

LORD DAVEY: It was, however, argued that the act of the appellant in the present case was a violation of the right which every man has to pursue a lawful trade and calling, and that the violation of this right is actionable. . . . The right which a man has to pursue his trade or calling is qualified by the equal right of others to do the same and compete with him, though to his damage. And it is obvious that a general abstract right of this character stands on a different footing from such a private particular rights as the right to performance of a contract into which one has entered. A man has no right to be employed by any particular employer, and has no right to any particular employment if it depends on the will of another.

Could the law require the employer to provide work which is available? To start with, the "right to work" needs to be distinguished from the mere right to challenge an employer's discretion in refusing work (on which see (B) *Access to Work as a Matter of Public Policy*, p. 35 *et seq.*). The latter is more a right to equal opportunity to work, a right not to be discriminated against. Provided the employer could justify giving the job to another applicant for an approved reason, there would be no infringement of right.

A "right to work" would appear more substantial. The issue is not the employer's choice, but the applicant's entitlement. The job becomes something, entitlement to which is not controlled by the employer at all. It is thus questionable whether such a "right" is consistent with private ownership or control by employers of the means of production which provide opportunities for work.

A less radical alternative would be for access to work opportunities to be governed by legal principles which would vary considerably in the roles given to the employer and the applicant. Rules as to the allocation of work opportunities are already in existence in a multiplicity of disparate cases. Present law covers numerous situations where a worker out of a job may claim access to work as of right, and if the employer refuses, he may be penalised. Examples include:

(a) reinstatement/re-engagement after unfair dismissal (EPCA, ss.68, *et seq.* see below, Chapter 10 *Termination of Work*, pp. 394 *et seq.*);
(b) the right to return to work after maternity absence (EPCA, ss.45 *et seq.* see below, Chapter 8 *Work and Family*, pp. 272 *et seq.*);
(c) the right to a suitable available vacancy where a pregnant employee is incapable of doing her own job (EPCA, s.60);
(d) the right to a vacancy in the event of redundancy (*Vokes* v. *Bear* [1973] I.R.L.R. 363 (N.I.R.C.); see below, Chapter 4 *Quantity of Work*, p. 121).

In addition, there is an enormous reservoir of custom and practice governing the allocation of work opportunities in various industries, and numerous cases involving judicial consideration of the fairness of promotions, transfers and redeployments.

The principles developed in these different sources are not as yet harmonised. But they constitute a breach in the common law's refusal to contemplate a "right to work" *vis-à-vis* the employer. The starting point is an entitlement of the applicant, as opposed to the common law's starting point of the employer's right to hire whom he wishes.

(D) *Access to Work as a Matter of Social Security*

The extent to which work is necessary for an individual to sustain him or herself and for society to produce the sustenance for itself makes access to work very much a matter of social policy. The link between labour law and social welfare law was evident from a very early date.

P. S. Atiyah, THE RISE AND FALL OF FREEDOM OF CONTRACT (1979), pp. 67–68

The labour force was, in many ways, the subject of the greatest degree of regulation. The Statute of Artificers (usually called the Statute of Apprentices) was passed in 1563 and remained on the Statute book until 1819; the Poor Law Act of 1601—which provided for much else besides poor relief—remained largely operative until the twentieth century. Between them, these Acts attempted "to banish idleness, to advance husbandry and to yield to the hired person, both in times of scarcity and in times of plenty, a convenient proportion of wages." They controlled entry into the class of skilled workmen by providing for a compulsory seven years' apprenticeship; they reserved the superior trades for the sons of the better off; they assumed a universal duty to work on all the able-bodied; and empowered justices to require unemployed artificers to work in husbandry; they required permission for a workman to transfer from one employer to another; they severely restricted the freedom of movement of the poor by enabling a person without means to be removed by order of the justices to his original parish or last place of settlement; and they empowered justices to fix wage rates for virtually all classes of workmen. On the other hand, there was a *quid pro quo* for all this: the Poor Law recognized the right of the indigent to poor relief, to be provided at the charge of the parish, and there were also other provisions for the benefit of labourers and artisans such as attempts to ensure that they were employed under contracts of a year's duration.

The relation between the social security system and the sphere of work regulation is analysed in the following extract.

F.F. Piven and R.A. Cloward, REGULATING THE POOR (1972), pp. 3–4

. . . . Since the early sixteenth century, many Western governments have come to make provision for the care of the destitute, often known as poor relief. . . .

Relief arrangements are ancillary to economic arrangements. Their chief function is to regulate labor, and they do that in two general ways. First, when mass unemployment leads to outbreaks of turmoil, relief programs are ordinarily initiated or expanded to absorb and control enough of the unemployed to restore order; then, as turbulence subsides, the relief system contracts, expelling those who are needed to populate the labor market. Relief also performs a labor-regulating function in this shrunken state, however. Some of the aged, the disabled, the insane, and others who are of no use as workers are left on the relief rolls, and their treatment is so degrading and punitive as to instill in the laboring masses a fear of the fate that awaits them should they relax into beggary and pauperism. To demean and punish those who do not work is to exalt by contrast even the meanest labor at the meanest wages.

For a critique of this analysis, see the book review by J. Higgins, (1978) 7 Journal of Social Policy 189.

CHAPTER 3

THE WORK OBLIGATION

One of the most important problems currently facing the parties to the employment relationship, and especially workers, is that of changes at work as a result of new technology, reorganisation of production, re-training and new methods of work. So what is the employee's work obligation: how is it defined in law, and to what extent does the law require the worker to be flexible? And when change *is* introduced, how does law regulate the process of change? Two other problems we examine are closely connected to the work obligation: quality control of work, and safety.

1. DEFINITION AND FLEXIBILITY

Here we examine the role of the law of contract in defining the work obligation, the techniques used by judges to control the content of the work obligation and the contribution of statute to achieving flexibility.

(A) Contractual Definition

The common law purports to look solely at the contractual obligation. The job is defined by the contract of employment. But the enormous variety of jobs can present the courts with problems of defining the work obligation in a contract. Contrast:

(a) where the job in question consists of performing limited physical tasks to a specified speed and standard (*eg* manual workers on an assembly line, or clerical workers);
(b) where the job consists of a number of differing activities each requiring different skills and each to be undertaken at different times or for varying amounts of time—at the discretion of the employer (*eg* skilled maintenance workers, various white-collar jobs);
(c) where the job consists of an unforeseeable mix of activities involving changes in skills and work performed, supervision and responsibility, etc. (*eg* social workers, higher management).

The law, perhaps through contract, has to try to define each of these different work obligations. Contrast the following cases.

Peter Carnie & Son Ltd. v. Paton
[1979] I.R.L.R. 260
Employment Appeal Tribunal

LORD McDONALD: The respondent was first employed by a previous owner of the garage on 15.5.72. No written particulars of his employment were ever provided but a record kept by that previous owner was produced which indicated that the respondent was employed in "general garage duties/stores."

The respondent performed a variety of duties in this connection and the Tribunal have found that when his employment began he was a general handyman. The appellants expanded their car hire business and as time went on the respondent became increasingly involved in this. In 1975 he began dealing with car hire reception. He had however many other duties in connection with the hiring of cars. He also continued to perform numerous handyman functions. These are fully set out in the reasons given by the Industrial Tribunal. They conclude that, speaking very roughly, the respondent devoted about 75% of his time to car hire work. 25% of his time related to the reception side of car hire work.

The respondent liked reception work, but the appellants were not entirely satisfied with him performing these duties. They had some difficulty in making other arrangements but eventually shortly before the respondent went on holiday on 12.8.78 they were able to tell him that when he returned from holiday he would no longer be required to work at the reception side of the car hire business. He was informed that he would be expected to concentrate more on other aspects of the car hire business and that he would continue to do general duties as he was already doing. He was not therefore being instructed to do different work from what he had been doing already. It was simply a matter of removing one aspect of his work in order that he might concentrate more on the remaining aspects. As the Industrial Tribunal tersely say: "The applicant was not pleased." . . . .

The majority of the Tribunal took the view that the proposed change involved that the respondent would lose the most pleasant part of his duties. They also took the view that by being withdrawn from the work of a receptionist he would lose status. Thereafter they went so far as to say;

> "By removing that part of his job which he enjoyed most, and by diminishing his status to some extent, the respondents were in significant breach of contract entitling the applicant to terminate his employment without notice."

In our opinion the majority have clearly applied the reasonableness test in this connection and not the proper test, namely, the contract test. There is no finding that the respondent was employed as a car hire receptionist. Reception duties were merely part of his general duties and this is implicit in the findings in fact of the entire Tribunal. It is unreasonable, if not indeed absurd, to suggest that an employee who is engaged on general duties can insist upon doing only those duties which he likes most. Moreover while there may be cases where a change in duties involving diminution in status could amount to breach of contract, we do not see how any reasonable Tribunal, in the circumstances of the present case, could conclude that that applied here.

We agree entirely with the reasoning of the chairman who dissented. On the facts as found by the Tribunal it is clear that the appellants were not contractually bound to retain the respondent on reception duties. Again on the facts as found by the whole Tribunal the respondent's employment included a variety of unskilled duties of a general nature. That inevitably involved that these duties might be altered from time to time in order to meet the varying needs of the business. To suggest that a variation of this nature amounts either to a material breach going to the root of the contract of employment or indicates that the employers no longer intend to be bound by an essential term of the contract will simply not do . . . .

McNeill v. Charles Crimin (Electrical Contractors) Ltd.

[1984] I.R.L.R. 179
Employment Appeal Tribunal

Mr McNeill, a foreman electrician, was transferred from a site on which he was foreman to another where he was to carry out electrical work under the supervision of another electrician. A majority of the Industrial Tribunal hearing his complaint held this was not a material breach of his contract of employment.

LORD McDONALD: In our opinion in the present case the majority have overstated the position by concluding that a breach sufficiently material to go to the root of a contract involved a substantial alteration in the terms and conditions of employment on a permanent basis. We are not concerned in this field of the law with the question of reasonableness. We are concerned with the interpretation of the terms and conditions of employment. If these require an employee to work in a certain place and in a certain capacity, it is in our view a breach of these conditions for the employer to seek to insist that he should work elsewhere and in a different capacity albeit on a temporary basis . . . .

. . . In so far as elements of fact arise in connection with this matter the lay members of this Appeal Tribunal are strongly of the view that to require a foreman to work under and take instructions from an ordinary operative is such that they would in practice regard [it] as total abandonment of the foreman's contract of employment on the part of the employer.

The courts in theory see the contract as needing to define precisely the work purchased by the employer. The employer, however, is more interested in flexibility and mobility so as to maximise production in the light of changing requirements. In the following cases, the courts found little difficulty in reconciling legal doctrine with employers' prerogatives.

Glitz v. Watford Electric Co. Ltd.

[1979] I.R.L.R. 89
Employment Appeal Tribunal

ARNOLD J.: The main point which is put forward on behalf of Miss Glitz is this: that in November 1975 she was in a contractual relationship with this company which did not extend to include an obligation on her part to work on the duplicator if the company asked her to do so . . . . This brings into the forefront of the matter the question of what her job was. As we have already indicated, in our view it was part of a contractual arrangement between Miss Glitz and the company that they should employ her and she should work as a copy typist/general clerical duties clerk. That was the contractual term which had been introduced on the occasion of her joining the company at the beginning of November 1974 and that had continued as the contractual ambit of the respective obligations right through the piece until, at least, November 1977.

Now the question whether operating the duplicator was part of her contractual obligation falls, as we think, to be answered by reference to the question whether the operation of the duplicator falls, in the context of the case, within the ambit of general clerical duties and that it is not a determinant factor either that at the time that she was engaged it was contemplated, as it undoubtedly was, that the duplicator would be operated by somebody other than herself or that, in fact, she did not operate the duplicator all through the piece from November 1974 to November 1977. We answer that question of construction in the way that the Tribunal did by concluding that, in the context of this case, with a small clerical staff in a small office, the ambit of general clerical duties is wide enough to include the operation of a duplicator.

This points up a matter which we think lies very near to the heart of this case and that is this: it is very easy for people to think that the ambit of their contractual obligations is the same as the ambit of the duties which they in fact perform. As was pointed out to us by the trade union official who has very ably represented Miss Glitz before us, in a big company or at any rate in a company with a big clerical department that particular problem would never arise because the job description embodied in the contractual documents would tend to be a specialised description precisely because, in a big unit, the employment of specialists as such can be readily afforded. That, in our view, makes it all the more necessary, where one is dealing with a small unit, such as the small unit which one is dealing with here, where the job description tends to be wide precisely because to run a small unit one has to have flexibility, that it should be pointed out to employees, if it is not apparent that they understand this, either specifically or by means of some general hand-out or otherwise, that the ambit of the obligation in the contract of employment may very well be wider than the particular duties upon which the person concerned is normally engaged. But that circumstance can make no difference to our conclusion that the operation of the duplicator did lie within the ambit of the contractual sphere of operations of Miss Glitz.

Cresswell v. Board of Inland Revenue
[1984] I.R.L.R. 190
Chancery Division

Employees, including tax officers, refused to cooperate with a changeover from a traditional manual method of operation to computerisation of PAYE ("COP"), and complained that the employers were acting in breach of contract in requiring them to operate the computerised system.

WALTON J.: The description of the job of a Tax Officer is like the description of the job of any other grade, namely "the general duties appropriate to the grade concerned." Bearing this in mind, it will be convenient, as a form of shorthand, to refer to the jobs as those of Clerical Assistant [C.A.], [Tax Officer] TO or [Tax Officer Higher Grade] TOHG as the case may be.

Granted that down to the present the work of each of these three grades has been done manually, with pen, paper and pocket calculator, if the employer changes this so as largely to remove the necessity to use pen and paper but requires the person concerned to use a computer instead, or in some cases in addition, is the nature of the job thereby fundamentally changed? I do not think that the drawing of parallels with other situations really assists because, at the end of the day, it is the precise impact which is made by the computerisation programme on the day-to-day work of these three grades which is in question. . . .

. . . there can really be no doubt as to the fact that an employee is expected to adapt himself to new methods and techniques introduced in the course of his employment (*cf. North Riding Garages Ltd.* v *Butterwick* [1967] 2 Q.B. 56; see p. 79 below). Of course, in a proper case the employer must provide any necessary training or re-training . . . it will, in all cases, be a question of pure fact as to whether the re-training involved the acquisition of such esoteric skills that it would not be reasonable to expect the employee to acquire them. In an age when the computer has forced its way into the school room and where electronic games are played by schoolchildren in their own homes as a matter of everyday occurrence, it can hardly be considered that to ask an employee to acquire basic skills as to retrieving information from a computer or feeding such information into a computer is something in the slightest esoteric or, even nowadays, unusual . . . .

Of course the changes in working methods and practices which COP brings in its train are great—although I think that the evidence has tended to exaggerate them. But that, as it seems to me, is not the point. COP merely introduces up to date modern methods for dealing with bulk problems: it leaves the jobs done by those who operate the new methodology precisely the same as before, although the content of some of the jobs, most notably that of the grade CA, will have been considerably altered, but in no case altered anything like sufficiently to fall outside the original description of the proper functions of the grade concerned.

Moreover, the contrary conclusion would fly in the face of common sense. Although doubtless, all of us, being conservative (with a small "c") by nature desire nothing better than to be left to deepen out accustomed ruts, and hate change, a TO has no right to remain in perpetuity doing one defined type of work in one particular way.

(B) *Judicial Control of the Work Obligation*

The common law principle of contractual definition of the work obligation would seem to allow the parties to the contract of employment, or trade unions and employers' associations, their bargaining agents, to control the content of the work obligation. In practice, most contracts do have some definition of the job. Indeed, under EPCA, s. 1(1)(*g*) the employer is obliged to provide a "job title," and many contracts of employment spell out the work obligation explicitly in job descriptions. However, the informality of the employment relationship, the vagueness of contractual language and the variety of sources, written and oral, from which the contractual terms may be drawn—enable the courts in disputed cases to determine the content of the work obligation.

On the face of it, it is for the parties to the employment relationship to define the scope of an employee's duty. The courts may infer that the employee warrants to display a certain skill, but the scope of that commitment is a matter for agreement. There is no presumption of total service. The remainder of this section is concerned with the degree to which contractual definition of the work obligation is in the hands of the parties, and the degree to which, by various devices, the courts have given themselves power to construct the contract. Three techniques of judicial control of the work obligation will be highlighted.

(i) Choosing among a variety of sources of terms of employment

Contractual obligations may be constructed from a variety of sources, *e.g.* job advertisements, works rules, collective agreements, written statements of particulars (issued under EPCA, s. 1), and so on. The following cases illustrate the degree of choice open to the court in establishing the exact nature of the work obligation using such sources.

Pedersen v. Camden London Borough Council
[1981] I.C.R. 674; [1981] I.R.L.R. 173
Court of Appeal

LAWTON L.J.: The employee first entered the employment of Camden London Borough Council on June 28, 1971. He started work as a catering assistant, but after a few weeks most of his work took place at the assembly rooms of the old St. Pancras Town Hall. There he worked as a barman and ran buffets and supplied refreshments as required. In 1973, the employers were minded to make an appointment as "bar steward/catering assistant." They advertised the job fairly extensively in a number of newspapers circulating in the London area and in the catering trade, and in addition, they posted a copy of the advertisement on the staff notice board. The advertisement was in these terms:

> "Required in the catering service of a large London borough to be responsible for the efficient running and trading performance at the council's assembly rooms bar and such other temporary bars as are set up from time to time. Duties will include general cleaning, washing up and control of bar stocks and other catering duties as assigned when not on bar duty. Evening work as required. 35-hour, seven-day week; additional hours may be worked at overtime rates. Must be experienced with knowledge of stock control preparatory work . . . ."

The salary offered in the advertisement was higher than that which the employee was getting as a catering assistant. He saw either the notice on the notice board, or one of the advertisements, because he applied for the job. His application was accepted, and by a letter dated August 23, 1973, the employers wrote to him as follows:

> "Dear Mr Pedersen,
> With reference to your application for the post of bar steward and catering assistant in the Buildings, Works and Services Division of my department, I am pleased to inform you that you have been appointed to such post, with effect from July 19, 1973. Your grading takes into account the fact that you will be required to work a 35-hour week, which will be primarily related to the preparation and operation of the bar(s) and which will include evenings, weekends and bank holidays. You will be granted time off in lieu for any hours worked on a bank holiday. Your actual hours will be arranged, in advance whenever possible, by the catering officer or his representative. When you are not required for bar duty, the catering officer will assign to you other additional catering duties. Your other conditions of service are as set out on the attached document."

The only relevant part of the "attached document" which was given to the employee pursuant to section 4 of the Contracts of Employment Act 1963 [now EPCA, s.1] was that his job was described as "bar steward and catering assistant." The reference in the letter of August 23, 1973, to "grading" had this consequence for the employee: he was up-graded. As a result of his getting the new job, he was in higher standing in the employers' hierarchy than he had been as a mere catering assistant.

From 1973 until April 1977 the employee worked mostly as a barman in charge of the bar at the assembly rooms at the old St. Pancras Town Hall and from time to time at such other places where bars were set up. His employment between those years was not all that smooth, from the point of view of industrial relations. He was not an easy employee to have on the staff; but he did continue and he was still concerned mostly with doing work as a bar steward up to April 1, 1977.

[The employee was then transferred to do mainly catering duties; he refused and left.]

I take the view that the terms of the contract are set out in the letter of August 23, 1973, but in construing that letter, the court is entitled to look at the surrounding circumstances and, in particular, at what had led to the employee applying for the job which was on offer. What had led to his applying for the job was the advertisement. The advertisement, in my opinion, had stressed very clearly indeed that the primary function of any applicant would be to perform the duties of a bar steward. The advertisement is not part of the contract; it is merely a document leading up to the making of the contract, so the terms of the contract have got to be found in the letter. But there is a link, in my opinion, between the written terms of contract and the advertisement, and it comes in the opening sentence of the letter, which is in the terms: "With reference to your application for the post of bar steward and catering assistant in the Buildings, Works and Services Division of my department . . . " By looking at the time factor it is clear that that application was made pursuant to the advertisements which had appeared for that particular job.

Then I come to look at the body of the letter, and the opening words of the main paragraph start by a reference to the grading, and, as I have already commented, there was an up-grading so far as the employee was concerned. He was to be given a better status in the employers' hierarchy. Then come the words: " . . . you will be required to work a 35-hour week, which will be primarily related to the preparation and operation of the bar(s) and will include evenings, weekends and bank holidays."

A great deal turns upon the meaning to be put upon the word "primarily" in that context. Mr Winberg [counsel for the employers] submitted that it related solely to the division of hours and had no relation to functions. I do not agree. In the context of this letter, looked at against the circumstances to which I have already referred, in my judgment what the letter was saying was that the primary function and duty of the employee was to be a bar steward; and that the subsequent reference to his duty to do additional catering work was something which was secondary to the main function which he was to perform, namely, that of bar steward.

On that construction of the contract, in my judgment it follows that if his conditions of work became such that his primary function was not to be a bar steward but to be a catering assistant, or alternatively if his function as a bar steward was substantially reduced, then there was a change in his conditions of work which could be a breach of his contract.

The Court of Appeal restored the decision of the Industrial Tribunal, reversing that of the E.A.T., which had reached the opposite conclusion ([1979] I.R.L.R. 377). In the next case, the judge could choose among a signed contract of employment form, an oral promise, a written statement of particulars, custom and practice and a collective agreement.

Hawker Siddeley Power Engineering Ltd. v. Rump
[1979] I.R.L.R. 425
Employment Appeal Tribunal

Soon after the respondent began his employment in 1973, he was asked to sign a contract of employment form which indicated that he would be liable to travel all over the country. The respondent explained to one of the company's managers, a Mr Davidson, that he was not prepared to travel beyond the south of England because his wife suffered from a nervous condition. According to the respondent, Mr Davidson told him there was enough work in southern England and promised him "sign that contract and I'll get in touch with the office and you'll only work in southern England."

During his employment, the respondent was not required to travel outside southern England. In 1976, he was issued with a further document pursuant to section 4 of the Contracts of Employment Act (now EPCA, s.4) which expressly stated that: "You may be required to transfer from one workplace to another on the instruction of the Employer in accordance with the provisions of the appropriate Working Rule Agreement."

On March 16, 1978, the respondent was orally instructed to go to Scotland; he refused.

TALBOT J.: The first submission with which we will deal is that, when one examines what took place between Mr Davidson and Mr Rump, there should not be implied or added to his contract of employment the oral term that he would not be required to work outside the southern part of England . . . .

We are, therefore, invited to find that what took place here was no more than a *de facto* arrangement and there should not be implied from that *de facto* arrangement any term as suggested of this contract. But when we refer back to the nature of the agreement—we will repeat the important words, Mr Davidson saying: "Sign that contract and I will get in touch with the office and you will only work in Southern England,"—we are driven to the conclusion that there was a direct promise which must have become part of the contract of employment because it was following upon that that Mr Rump signed the contract, and there was, therefore, this term in the contract.

Having found thus far, the submission of Mr Reynolds (for the appellants) went on in this way:

> "The agreement of July 1976, signed by Mr Rump, was a variation of the 1973 agreement. It did not contain any oral term nor was there any evidence to indicate that it became part of the 1976 agreement and therefore the binding agreement which has to be considered is not that which was reached in 1973, together with the oral term, but the 1976 agreement without the oral term."

Mr Reynolds submitted, therefore, that being a binding agreement, Mr Rump is bound by its terms. We need not refer to the terms in detail because it is without doubt that they required him to travel for his work wherever they required him to go within the British Isles and, being thus bound, his refusal to travel to Scotland was a breach of his agreement and thereby resulted in the termination of his employment. . . .

It is quite clear that when Mr Rump was required to sign (and did sign) particulars of his contract in 1976 there is no evidence to suggest that it was brought to his attention that there would be no oral term which would limit his mobility to the south of England. We find it very difficult to believe that on the facts of this case the mere putting in front of Mr Rump of this 1976 document and inviting him to sign it could be a variation by agreement so as to exclude that very important oral term which he had secured in 1973 . . .

In our view this was, in effect, a unilateral variation—if it was a variation at all—which would not be binding upon Mr Rump.

(ii) Implication and interpretation of terms of employment: "reasonableness" and "business efficacy"

The ability of the judge to control the work obligation is even more obvious in cases where the worker begins employment with nothing in writing and little stated orally—as in the following case of a one-sentence "hiring."

Ferguson v. John Dawson & Partners (Contractors) Ltd.
[1976] I.R.L.R. 346; [1976] 1 W.L.R. 1213
Court of Appeal

MEGAW L.J.: The evidence was simply this: the plaintiff came with four other Irishmen, already working for the defendants, and he asked, or perhaps one of his friends asked, if he could "come along." Mr Murray's evidence is: "I said he could start on Monday and that was it. But I did inform him there were no cards: we were purely working as a lump labour force". . . .

The defendants, as I have said, contend that the contract which governed the legal relationship between the plaintiff and the defendants for the three months up to the time of the accident was a single-term contract. The single term, derived from Mr Murray's words "I did inform him that there were no cards, we were purely working as a lump labour force," was that the plaintiff's status vis-à-vis the defendants was to be, or was to be deemed to be, "self-employed labour-only sub-contractor."

I shall assume for present purposes, though counsel for the plaintiff was not disposed to accept the assumption, that this is a correct interpretation of the intended, and understood, meaning of the Delphic words which were spoken by Mr Murray and tacitly accepted by the plaintiff.

I am not, however, prepared to accept the defendants' further contention that there were no other terms of the contract. Indeed, if there were no other terms, the only conclusion in law, I think, would be the absurd conclusion that there was no contract at all during the three months in which the plaintiff was working for the defendants. Counsel for the defendants, when this was put to him, was disposed to accept that there must have been a contractual term as to remuneration. There must, as I think, have been many other contractual terms, also, necessarily to be implied, even though they were not mentioned in the brief conversation when Mr Murray and the plaintiff agreed that the plaintiff should start work on the following Monday. This is so, whether the contract was a contract of service or for services. For example, what sort of work could the defendants require the plaintiff to do? Was he to work in his own time or during stated hours and, if so, what hours? Where could he be required to work? What notice, if any, was required by either side for the termination of the contract? What control could the defendants through Mr Murray exercise over the order in which the plaintiff did such work as he might be required to do, or the manner of doing it?

In my opinion, the law is not so divorced from reality as to assume that the same considerations as to the ascertainment of the relevant contractual terms, if a legal analysis of the terms has to be made for any purpose, applies to a contract of the nature with which we are here concerned, the taking on of a labourer on casual application to a site agent on a building site, as applies to commercial contracts between business men, whether made orally after discussion of terms or made in writing with elaborate provisions. The terms—even the essential terms—of a contract of the present nature would often not be spoken or written at the time when the workman is taken on. They would be understood by reference to the known circumstances and the existing practices and conventions of a particular trade or a particular contractor or a particular site. Moreover, if and in so far as they were not implied, by common knowledge of what the practice was, at the time when the labourer was first taken on—the date when the legal analysis would regard the contractor (*sic*) as being made—terms could well be added thereafter, as particular questions of the rights and obligations of the parties arose during the progress of the work. Again, to apply legal analysis, such terms would be treated as having been added, or the contract as being varied.

The power of judges to imply terms in the absence of express provision can be exercised to further various policy objectives as regards flexibility and mobility. For example, the "business efficacy" test of implied terms was advanced to justify a quite different effect in the following two cases.

G.K.N. Ltd. v. Lloyd

[1972] I.C.R. 214
National Industrial Relations Court

The employee was the senior camshaft straightener in the employer's foundry. He became redundant in that job and, in accordance with a negotiated shop agreement, he was required to work in a different foundry as a labourer doing unskilled work at a substantially reduced wage. The employer claimed that the contract of employment contained an implied term that the employee could be required to undertake other skilled or unskilled work at reduced rates of pay on a day or shift basis.

Sir John Donaldson: Mr Turiff [for the employers] put forward the implied term arising by custom or by necessary implication of law in order to give business efficacy to the contract of service. Whether or not such a term was to be implied as a matter of custom is a mixed question of fact and law. So far as the factual content is concerned, there was evidence on either side, and the Industrial Tribunal, which was the tribunal of fact, considered that

> "The implications for the employee were clearly drastic, and we should require considerably more evidence than we have in this case before we could find it proved."

The implications are indeed drastic and we are not surprised that the Tribunal was not satisfied. Had it been satisfied, an issue would have arisen as to whether such a custom was sufficiently reasonable to be effective in law. Similarly, we are quite unable to hold that any such term is necessary in order to give business efficacy to the contract. No doubt, transfers between jobs were from time to time necessary to keep the foundry in production, but business efficacy does not require that this should be at the expense of the employees. Transfers which involve depriving a skilled man of the pleasure of exercising his skills and impose upon him the hardships of shift work, as opposed to day work, might be thought to merit more, rather than less, pay.

Express Lift Co. Ltd. v. Bowles
[1977] I.R.L.R. 99; [1977] I.C.R. 474
Employment Appeal Tribunal

A collective agreement existed which on the face of it incorporated into the individual contract of employment an obligation to work anywhere in the U.K. The respondent argued that that term should be qualified by an implied limitation to work at such places as should be reasonable. An Industrial Tribunal held that he had been unfairly dismissed.

KILNER BROWN J.: We start with the basic fact that the implied term, which was observed by both sides, was that men could be sent anywhere in the United Kingdom. There was no evidence that exceptions had been made. In the absence of evidence we would conclude that any exception would have to be by agreement. In other words it would be a variation by mutual consent.

A number of authorities, some 100 years old, have been cited to establish what we would have thought was clear enough in 1976. One cannot have a unilateral variation of an implied term. Nor can a court read into a term something which is not there . . . .

These various propositions were brought together by Lord Wright when he used the following words in *Luxor (Eastbourne) Ltd* v *Cooper* [1971] A.C. at p.137:

> " 'It is well recognised however that there may be cases where obviously some term must be implied if the intention of the parties is not to be defeated, some term of which it can be predicated that "it goes without saying," some term not expressed but necessary to give to the transaction such business efficacy as the parties must have intended. This does not mean that the court can embark on a reconstruction of the agreement on equitable principles or on a view of what the parties should in the opinion of the court reasonably have contemplated.' "

There are two questions in the analysis involved in this instant case. First, was there an implied term recognised by both parties? There was. It was to work wherever required in the United Kingdom. Second, was there a further implied term that it contemplated exceptions in special circumstances? If it was not necessary to make the contract work there is no room for such a further implied term. Certainly the Court cannot introduce it because it appears reasonable or equitable so to do.

Regrettably that is precisely what this Tribunal purported to do.

The law is not so harsh nor so devoid of common sense as we were at one time disposed to feel it must be if we followed the guidance of the quoted observations. We unanimously recognise that in a contract of employment between master and servant the overriding consideration is that both parties require certainty and must know what the contract involves. The only way in which this applicant could have escaped the obligation to go where his employer required him was to have agreed a variation of the implied term. Unfortunately this man did not do so.

The policy implications of other tests for implied terms are both more obvious and more vague, *eg* "reasonableness" was adverted to in *G.K.N. Ltd.* v. *Lloyd* and also in the following case.

Jones v. Associated Tunnelling Co. Ltd.
[1981] I.R.L.R. 477
Employment Appeal Tribunal

Mr Jones was first employed in December 1964 to work at Chatterley Whitfield Colliery some two miles from his home. The only reference to his place of employment was the word "Chatterley." In 1969 Mr Jones ceased working at Chatterley and started to work at Hem Heath Colliery, some 12 to 13 miles from his home. He worked there until 1980 when he was offered work at another place equally accessible to his home. He refused this work, and claimed a redundancy payment. (In 1973 and again in 1976 he was given written statements of particulars (Doc. A4) which are, however, irrelevant for the purposes of our extract.)

BROWNE-WILKINSON J.: We prefer to approach the case by considering first whether, as a matter of law, during the period from 12.12.64 down to the date of the issue of A4 on 8.10.73 there was any and, if so what, term to be implied in the contract giving the employers the power to alter Mr Jones's place of work from one colliery to another. Apart from the point we will consider in a moment, we have no doubt that it is right to imply into the contract a term to the effect suggested by the Industrial Tribunal, *ie* a right to transfer to any site within daily commuting reach of Mr Jones's home.

The starting point must be that a contract of employment cannot simply be silent on the place of work: if there is no express term, there must be either some rule of law that in all contracts of employment the employer is (or alternatively is not) entitled to transfer the employee from his original place of work or some term regulating the matter must be implied into each contract. We know of no rule of law laying down the position in relation to all contracts of employment, nor do we think it either desirable or possible to lay down a single rule. It is impossible to conceive of any fixed rule which will be equally appropriate to the case of, say, an employee of a touring repertory theatre and the librarian of the British Museum. Therefore, the position must be regulated by the express or implied agreement of the parties in each case. In order to give the contract business efficacy, it is necessary to imply *some* term into each contract of employment.

The term to be implied must depend on the circumstances of each case. The authorities show that it may be relevant to consider the nature of the employer's business, whether or not the employee has in fact been moved during the employment, what the employee was told when he was employed, and whether there is any provision made to cover the employee's expenses when working away from daily reach of his home. These are only examples; all the circumstances of each case have to be considered: see *O'Brien* v *Associated Fire Alarms* [1969] 1 All ER 93; *Stevenson* v *Teesside Bridge and Engineering Ltd* [1971] 1 All ER 296; *Times Newspapers* v *Bartlett* (1976) 11 ITR 106.

Looking at the circumstances of this case, what would the parties have said had an officious bystander asked them "At what sites can Mr Jones be asked to work?" The employers might have replied "Anywhere in the United Kingdom." But the Industrial Tribunal's findings indicate that Mr Jones, as one would expect, would have objected to being transferred anywhere outside daily reach of his home. The employers were in business as contractors working at different sites; so the parties must have envisaged a degree of mobility. In 1969, Mr Jones himself was moved from his original place of work to Hem Heath Colliery without objection. All the statements of terms and conditions subsequently issued contain mobility clauses, albeit in varying terms. From these factors we think that the plain inference is that the employers were to have *some* power to move Mr Jones's place of work and that the reasonable term to imply (as the lowest common denominator of what the parties would have agreed if asked) is a power to direct Mr Jones to work at any place within reasonable daily reach of Mr Jones's home. Such a term would permit Mr Jones to be required to work at Florence Colliery.

This approach, however, is challenged by Mr Hughes on behalf of Mr Jones. He submits that in order to imply a term, it is not enough to say that some term has to be implied and for the court then to imply a reasonable term. He submits that before any term can be implied it is necessary to show precisely what term the parties (if asked) would have said was obvious. In this case, as in all contracts of employment, it is impossible to state with certainty what the term as to mobility would have been. It might have been the term that the Industrial Tribunal suggested, but it might also have been mobility within a defined area or within a given radius of Mr Jones's home. Therefore, says Mr Hughes, it is not possible to imply any term since one cannot be certain what that term should be.

The foundation for this submission is the decision of the House of Lords in *Trollope and Colls Ltd* v *North Western Metropolitan Regional Hospital Board* [1973] 2 All ER 260. . . .

In our judgement, that decision is distinguishable from the present case. In that case, there was no need to imply any term: the express terms of the contract were unambiguous and covered the event which had happened, albeit in a way which was surprising in its result. Therefore any term which was to be implied would be varying the unambiguous express terms of the contract. In the case of contracts of employment containing no mobility clause, the position is quite different. As we have sought to show, it is essential to imply *some* term into the contract in order to give the contract business efficacy: there must be some term laying down the place of work. In such a case, it seems to us that there is no alternative but for the Tribunal or court to imply a term which the parties, if reasonable, would probably have agreed if they had directed their minds to the problem. Such a term will not vary the express contractual terms. This view is supported by the very many cases in which the courts have decided what terms as to mobility ought to be included in a contract of employment: see for example the cases cited above. If Mr Hughes's submission were correct, all those cases would have been wrongly decided since it is never possible to state with certainty exactly what the parties would have agreed as to mobility if they had directed their minds to the question.

We therefore reach the conclusion that we are entitled to hold, and do hold, that the right term to imply into Mr Jones's contract from the outset was that he could be required to work at any place within reasonable daily commuting distance from his home.

In this case, therefore, the courts first discovered that there was no agreement as to the intention of either party and then implied a term which represented what the court saw as an acceptable compromise. One of the qualities of the use of a "reasonableness" test is that "reasonable" implied terms of a contract may vary from time to time according to changes in policy objectives, in our case, with respect to the work obligation.

Wetherall (Bond St. W.1) Ltd. v. Lynn
[1977] I.R.L.R. 333; [1978] 1 W.L.R. 200
Employment Appeal Tribunal

The employee had been promoted in 1976 to the position of retail stock controller, but received a written warning three months later from the retail director. He also alleged that the retail director had made allegations about his efficiency in front of junior members of staff.

BRISTOW J.: For example, you are employed as a machine minder. It will usually be at any rate an implied term of your contract that you keep your machine clean. But except in dire emergency if your employer orders you to clean the lavatories that would be likely to be a repudiation of the contract. You could also describe the order as unreasonable, inequitable, unfair. For example, to treat Mr Lynn as Mrs Black did in this case, undermining his authority by blackguarding him in the presence of his subordinates, is a repudiation because it shows that she did not intend to perform the obligation implicit in his contract of service that she would not undermine the authority with which his contract invested him. You could also describe her conduct as unreasonable, inequitable, unfair.

What is conduct on the part of the employer showing an intention not to be bound by the contract will depend on the circumstances of each case, and upon the terms of the contract, express or to be implied, in each case; these terms will reflect the changes in the relationship between employer and employee as social standards change.

(iii) The work obligation as service: the duty to obey orders

As a technique of controlling the employee's work obligation, judges are sometimes tempted to imply a duty to obey orders in almost absolute terms (see *Turner* v. *Mason* (1845) 14 M. & W. 112). Although formally it is only an *implied* term, they tend to express the *nature* of the contractual work obligation in terms of service and obedience. In the following case, the Court of Appeal held the work obligation required the employee to assist the proper functioning of the undertaking whatever the formal terms of the contract of employment.

Secretary of State for Employment v. Amalgamated Society of Locomotive Engineers and Firemen (No. 2)
[1972] 2 Q.B. 455; [1972] 2 All E.R. 949
Court of Appeal

The respondent trade unions had called upon their members employed by British Railways to work-to-rule. The Secretary of

State was empowered by the Industrial Relations Act 1971 (now repealed) to make certain orders if conduct constituting industrial action also involved a breach of contract. His action in making such an order was challenged on several grounds, one of which was that the work-to-rule did not involve a breach of contract.

LORD DENNING M.R.: For this purpose, of course, we must consider what their contracts of employment are and see whether this conduct is in breach of those contracts. So we have been referred to the contracts of employment. They are contained in a series of collective agreements made by the Railways Board with the trade unions. The terms are set out in some books which have been put before us. They contain detailed provisions on all sorts of matters, such as hours of duty, meal times, rates of pay, rest days and so forth.

The Rule Book is entirely different. It has 280 pages and 239 rules with many sub-rules. Each man signs a form saying that he will abide by the rules. But these rules are in no way terms of the contract of employment. They are only instructions to a man as to how he is to do his work. . . .

. . . . Rule 126(i), which was specially emphasised in the instructions to the men, provides:

> "The Driver and Fireman MUST . . . satisfy themselves that the engine is in proper order."

Rule 176 is a compendious rule which is worth noting:

> "Inspectors, Shunters, Guards, Drivers, Signalmen and all others concerned, must make every effort to facilitate the working of trains and prevent any avoidable delay."

Those rules are to be construed reasonably. They must be fitted in sensibly the one with the other. They must be construed according to the usual course of dealing and to the way they have been applied in practice. When the rules are so construed the railway system, as we all know, works efficiently and safely. But if some of those rules are construed unreasonably, as, for instance, the driver takes too long examining his engine or seeing that all is in order, the system may be in danger of being disrupted. It is only when they are construed unreasonably that the railway system grinds to a halt. It is, I should think, clearly a breach of contract first to construe the rules unreasonably, and then to put that unreasonable construction into practice . . . .

Now I quite agree that a man is not bound positively to do more for his employer than his contract requires. He can withdraw his goodwill if he pleases. But what he must not do is wilfully to obstruct the employer as he goes about his business . . . .

BUCKLEY L.J.: . . . It does not mean that the employer could require a man to do anything which lay outside his obligations under the contract, such as to work excess hours of work or to work an unsafe system of work or anything of that kind, but it does mean that within the terms of the contract the employee must serve the employer faithfully with a view to promoting those commercial interests for which he is employed. The contrary view is, in my opinion, one which proceeds upon much too narrow and formalistic an approach to the legal relations of employer and employee . . . .

ROSKILL L.J.: Mr Wedderburn this morning, in a happy phrase, said that the implication which the Crown and the Railways Board sought was designed not to make the contract work, but to make the workers work. If I thought that that aphorism accurately stated the position I would not hesitate to refuse to imply such a term. The courts will only imply a term when it is so clear that the only reason why it has not been expressly included is because the parties thought the need for the provision was self-evident. . . . Accordingly, I have no hesitation in implying a term into the contract of service that each employee will not, in obeying his lawful instructions, seek to obey them in a wholly unreasonable way which has the effect of disrupting the system, the efficient running of which he is employed to ensure. I prefer to rest my decision that work-to-rule is a breach of contract on this ground rather than on the alternative ground, clearly equally tenable, advanced by the Solicitor-General, that work-to-rule involves a breach of the positive obligation of faithful service owed by employee to his master.

Contrast the following case, where "reasonableness" allowed for some consideration of the employee's interests.

London Borough of Redbridge v. Fishman
[1978] I.R.L.R. 69; [1978] I.C.R. 569
Employment Appeal Tribunal

In July 1973 Mrs Fishman was appointed as "a full time permanent teacher in charge of the Resources Centre" at Wanstead High School. She was informed that when the Resources Centre was built, she would be required to apply herself almost full-time to its work, engaging in classroom teaching only to an extent sufficient to keep her in touch with practical requirements. In the autumn of 1975, a new head teacher was appointed who did not believe so strongly in the idea of Resources Centres. In January 1976, Mrs Fishman agreed to teach twelve periods of English per week. But when, later in the year, she was asked to teach 18 periods of English per week, which was three-quarters of the normal classroom teaching requirement, she refused. After a period of suspension, she was dismissed for refusal to obey that instruction.

Phillips J.: The view of the Industrial Tribunal was that there was no justification for the London Borough of Redbridge to have dismissed Mrs Fishman for misconduct. They took the view that Mrs Fishman was being required to do work which was different from that which she had been employed to do, and that while there is "flexibility" in the contract of employment of a teacher, and teachers can be required to help out and to do teaching other than that for which they are particularly engaged, the post which Mrs Fishman had been offered and accepted was a unique post which expressly excluded general classroom teaching. They found that Mrs Fishman was well within her rights and behaved reasonably in refusing to accept the Headmistress's instruction to teach 18 periods of English. . . .

Mr Scrivener, on behalf of the London Borough of Redbridge, has attacked the decision of the Industrial Tribunal on the ground that they misunderstood the contractual position. In a school, he says, there are only three categories of employees: the headmaster, the assistant masters and the non-teaching staff. He submits that all assistant masters are appointed without any job description and that any master can be required to teach any subject. While accepting that appointments of a particular kind may be advertised, offered and accepted—for example "to teach German in the sixth form, with subsidiary history in the lower forms"—he claims that as a matter of contract the master appointed may be required to teach any subject at any time, even to the total exclusion of teaching German. He does not shrink from the proposition put to him in the course of argument that if this submission is right the teacher engaged to teach the violin to the upper school may be drafted to teaching woodwork to the junior school, and vice-versa. We have found this a startling proposition, and one which we would have expected to be more acceptable in Dotheboys Hall or Llanabba Castle than in the more progressive London Borough of Redbridge. . . .

In accordance with the Articles of Government for County Secondary Schools, under Clause 4 it is the duty of the Headmaster (1) to control the internal organisation, management and discipline of the school; (2) to exercise supervision over the teaching and non-teaching staff. These are the provisions relied upon in support of the proposition that a teacher is a professional man appointed as a teacher, and as such capable of undertaking any teaching, and liable whatever the precise terms of the appointment to be drafted under the direction of the Headmaster to undertake any teaching as occasion may demand. We do not accept this proposition. No doubt there is need for flexibility, and for teachers normally engaged in one type of teaching at a particular level to be ready to undertake other teaching at different levels, but we think that Mr Scrivener's submission goes too far; in our judgment the Headmaster is entitled to require teachers to do work other than that for which they have been engaged, provided that the request is reasonable. In fact this seems to have been the approach of the London Borough of Redbridge, and when she was finally dismissed it was on the ground that she had refused to accept the *reasonable* instructions of the Headmistress. In our judgment this is the correct approach. What is reasonable will depend on the circumstances, and no doubt will differ from time to time, and from place to place; amongst other things, bearing in mind the particular duties which the teacher was engaged to undertake. And it would be relevant to take account of the custom and practice of the profession.

Accordingly, it becomes relevant to enquire what it was that Mrs Fishman was engaged to do . . . .

. . . we think that Mrs Fishman was being employed as an assistant teacher who was going to be the Director of the Resources Centre, and whose main activities were going to be devoted to that end, her teaching commitment being ancillary to it. We do not mean by this that she could not under any circumstances be required by the Headmistress to undertake what may be described as ordinary teaching duties, at least to some extent. Indeed, when she was asked to take 12 periods of English she was ready to do so, albeit reluctantly, and did so. She only objected, and ultimately refused to accept the instruction of the Headmistress, when she was instructed to take 18 periods of English. The point of her objection was that a commitment of this kind would make it impossible for her to carry out her duties as Director of the Resources Centre in the way in which that post had been originally planned.

2. CHANGES IN THE WORK OBLIGATION

The concept of a fixed definition of tasks to be performed by the worker is at odds with the employer's need for flexibility to meet the changing requirements of production. Trade unions have accepted very broad flexibility clauses in many industries, but have sought compensation for this concession in terms of job security or income.

Unfortunately, there is no legal concept or category which corresponds to the problem of changes at work. The law is to be found in doctrines of variations in the contract of employment, rules on dismissal for refusal to accept changes, and redundancy claims. Little account is taken of the role played by collective agreements on changes at work. Yet detailed rules and procedures already exist in practice governing changes: status quo clauses, trial periods, training and re-training provisions, procedures for resolving disputes arising from changes and many other sophisticated mechanisms.

Changes may be proposed by either side, though more often legal disputes arise as a result of changes initiated by the employer. If everybody concerned consents, there will be no dispute, and hence no need for legal intervention. But if there is a dispute, then the law may be invoked. Such disputes present themselves in a number of ways.

(A) Unilateral Changes By the Employer

(i) Changes and contracts

(a) The problem of consent

In practice, changes are often unilaterally imposed by an employer. In law, the obligations in the contract of employment, including the work obligation, can only be changed by mutual consent. Even so, the changes initiated by the employer may be implemented in practice for a period of time before any legal challenge is made (*eg* through proceedings for unfair dismissal or redundancy payments following dismissal). If it is found by a tribunal or court that the employee did not consent, the unilateral change in the work obligation:

(i) will be a breach of contract;
(ii) may constitute a constructive dismissal which is unfair (see below, pp. 307 *et seq.*);
(iii) may amount to a dismissal for redundancy (see below, pp. 137 *et seq.*).

If it is found that the employee did consent, he will be bound by the changed obligation. An initial question is, therefore, when does implementation of unilateral changes *imply* that the employee has consented. For example, in the following case, the employee protested.

Marriott v. Oxford and District Co-operative Society Ltd. (No. 2)
[1970] 1 Q.B. 186; [1969] 3 All E.R. 1126
Court of Appeal

The appellant was employed by the respondents as a foreman. After some years of such employment, the respondents concluded that there was insufficient work for a foreman and offered the appellant the position of supervisor at a reduced wage. He protested and attempted to find work elsewhere. Later he was notified that his wages would be reduced by £1 per week. Again he protested but did not leave the respondent's employment at once. Three or four weeks after the reduction of his wages had taken effect, he left to take another job.

Cross L.J.: So, as I see it, the only question for us to determine is whether the letter of 24th January [giving notice of reduction of wages] was a termination of the contract by the employer . . . . The letter says, in effect, "You will have to leave our employment at the end of the month unless you accept the reduction of £1 a week." So it can be argued that it would only have operated as a termination by the employer if Mr Marriott had not accepted the terms. But in all the circumstances of this case, including the fact that Mr Marriott continued to protest about the reduction even after he received the letter, I think that it would be wrong to treat the fact that he went on working and put up with the reduction for a few weeks as showing that agreement was reached without a previous termination of the contract by the employer. If one looks at the realities of the case, the contract was terminated by the employer by that letter.

In contrast, it was the wording, and not the realities of the matter which led the court to construe a letter from the employer as not a termination in *Burdett-Coutts* v. *Hertfordshire County Council* [1984] I.R.L.R. 91 (Q.B.D.). The letter announced wage reductions, together with the hope that the employees would continue in service. The letter was interpreted by the court as an attempt unilaterally to change terms of employment, not a termination. Hence the employees were able to obtain a declaration that the employers had acted unlawfully.

In the following case, an employee's protest was recognised to be "unrealistic" in the ordinary circumstances of employers' unilaterally imposing changes.

Jones v. Associated Tunnelling Co. Ltd.
[1981] I.R.L.R. 477
Employment Appeal Tribunal

After working some four years at Hem Heath Colliery, Mr Jones was given a written statement of particulars in 1973 and again in 1976, both of which stated that he could be required to work elsewhere. He continued at Hem Heath until 1980, when he was ordered to move, and refused.

Browne-Wilkinson J.: If, as in the present case, there is no evidence of any oral discussion varying the original terms, the fact that a statement of terms and conditions containing different terms has been issued cannot be compelling evidence of an express oral variation. The most that can be said is that by continuing to work without objection after receiving such further statement, the employee may have impliedly agreed to the variation recorded in the second statement or is estopped from denying it.

In our view, to imply an agreement to vary or to raise an estoppel against the employee on the grounds that he has not objected to a false record by the employers of the terms actually agreed is a course which should be adopted with great caution. If the variation relates to a matter which has immediate practical application (*eg*, the rate of pay) and the employee continues to work without objection after effect has been given to the variation (*eg*, his pay packet has been reduced) then obviously he may well be taken to have impliedly agreed. But where, as in the present case, the variation has no immediate practical effect the position is not the same. It is the view of both members of this Tribunal with experience in industrial relations (with which the Chairman, without such experience, agrees) that it is asking too much of the ordinary employee to require him either to object to an erroneous statement of his terms of employment having no immediate practical impact on him or be taken to have assented to the variation. So to hold would involve an unrealistic view of the inclination and ability of the ordinary employee to read and fully understand such statements.

Even if he does read the statement and can understand it, it would be unrealistic of the law to require him to risk a confrontation with his employer on a matter which has no immediate practical impact on the employee. For those reasons, as at present advised, we would not be inclined to imply any assent to a variation from mere failure by the employee to object to the unilateral alteration by the employer of the terms of employment contained in a statutory statement.

Contrast the view of the same judge in a case where an employee was taken on by the Civil Service in 1948 on the understanding that his age of retirement would be 65, a fact confirmed in 1952, 1969, and orally in January 1981. A document was sent to him in November 1981 telling him the practice had changed: as from April 1982 he would be retired at age 61. Browne-Wilkinson J. held (*DHSS* v. *Coy* [1983] I.R.L.R. 474, at 477):

> "If there has been a clear change of policy communicated to the employees, then as from that moment onwards the only possible conclusion which a Tribunal could reach on the matter would be that the only reasonable expectation of employees would be that the new policy would thereafter be implemented."

While finding that the E.A.T. was not justified in its application of this approach in the case before them, a majority of the Court of Appeal did not appear to dissent from it ([1984] I.R.L.R. 360). In his minority dissenting judgment, Sir John Donaldson M.R. espoused an attitude very supportive of it. The House of Lords reversed the Court of Appeal and reinforced the view expressed by Browne-Wilkinson J. ([1985] I.R.L.R. 263, *per* Lord Diplock, at p. 267):

> "Administrative policies may change with changing circumstances, including changes in the political complexion of governments. The liberty to make such changes is something that is inherent in our constitutional form of government. When a change in administrative policy takes place and is communicated in a departmental circular to, among others, those employees in the category whose age at which they would be compulsorily retired was stated in a previous circular to be a higher age than 60 years, any reasonable expectations that may have been aroused in them by any previous circular are destroyed and are replaced by such other reasonable expectations as to the earliest date at which they can be compelled to retire if the administrative policy announced in the new circular is applied to them."

The issue of consent is particularly problematic where the change in the work obligation is informally implemented on the shop floor and only challenged much later. The following case illustrates management's attempt to deny consent to such a change.

Simmonds v. Dowty Seals Ltd.
[1978] I.R.L.R. 425
Employment Appeal Tribunal

When Mr Simmonds started work in April 1969, his written particulars gave his hours of work as 7.30 am to 4.30 pm. In April 1972, however, following an informal agreement with the tool room foreman and the works manager, Mr Simmonds went on to the night shift, initially for a trial period, and then, as he thought, permanently. The written particulars of his terms of employment were never altered to take account of the change in his hours of work and no record of the agreement as to his working night shifts was made. Subsequently, there were changes in the management so that the people now in charge were unaware of this agreement. In August 1976, he worked for two weeks on day shift, but wrote to the company making it clear that he would do so only if he received his normal night shift premium. In September 1976, the deputy personnel manager sent him a memorandum which refuted his claim that he was a permanent night shift worker, and pointed out that if he was requested to work day shifts, the company was not obliged to pay him any night shift premium.

Mr Simmonds terminated his employment in April 1977 after he had been ordered to go on to day work. An Industrial Tribunal initially dismissed his claim for constructive dismissal, holding that his contract had never been varied from one for day work and, furthermore, that by working days in August 1976 without making an issue of it, he had accepted the company's view of his contractual obligations. Mr Simmonds appealed against this decision.

Bristow J.: The question comes down to this. As from the successful conclusion of Mr Simmonds's trial period on nights in 1972, what was his contract?

Was it, as Mr Barnes on his behalf contends, a contract under which his obligation was to work nights instead of days? Was it, as Mr Belcourt for the company contends, a contract under which his obligation was to work days, and nights if required? That is to say, was he then in the same position as he would have been if he had not written "No" to "Are you prepared to work night shift if necessary?" on the application form dated 19.4.69?

This question has to be decided on the evidence. The company's witnesses were in the difficult position that they could only speak of the company's policy as they knew it after they joined [in 1973–74]. It is not surprising that in the absence of any documentation of change in Mr Simmonds's terms of employment, and in view of the fact that if his obligation was simply to work nights instead of days he would as a tool maker have been in a wholly exceptional situation. Mr Martindale [the personnel manager] found it genuinely impossible to accept the proposition that he had a verbal agreement in 1972 to do just that. If Mr Martindale [the personnel manager] had been in the saddle in 1972 and the matter had come to his attention, he would not have allowed such an alteration in Mr Simmonds's terms of employment to be agreed. It may well be that if Mr Martindale's predecessor had been involved in what went on between Mr Simmonds, Mr Hitchman and Mr Hennequin in 1972, he too would not have allowed such an alteration to be made. But he was not.

The evidence is that on the management side it was only Mr Hitchman, the tool room foreman who knew nothing about the company's shift work policy, and Mr Hennequin, the works manager, who were involved. We must conclude that the matter never got to the personnel department. If it had, the appropriate officer should have made a note that Mr Simmonds's obligation was no longer to work days only. Had the note been made, it would have answered the question: was the new obligation to work nights only, or nights or days as required? . . .

That the personnel department would not have agreed any arrangements made between Mr Simmonds and Mr Hitchman that Mr Simmonds should be obliged to work nights only, as against company policy and the normal company arrangements, is neither here nor there because there is no evidence that the personnel department knew anything about it, and the absence of any alteration in Mr Simmonds's documents, something to which Mr Martindale attached importance, suggests strongly that it did not. The picture is that Mr Hitchman, who told Mr Hennequin of the requirement for a tool maker on nights, was the man who was left to make the arrangements. Mr Simmonds was not ready to turn his domestic life upside down without consideration with his family and a three months' trial. We see nothing inconsistent with the good sense of the situation as it could well have appeared to Mr Hitchman, and to Mr Hennequin if Mr Hitchman kept him fully in the picture, that if Mr Simmonds wanted his obligation to be nights only because although he was prepared to turn his domestic life upside down for the good extra money he was not prepared to do it on an "as required" basis, Mr Hitchman, Mr Hennequin and Mr Simmonds should have come to such an agreement.

Such an agreement would be binding on the company and would not require to be in writing in order to have legal effect. That there was such an agreement would be entirely consistent with everything that happened afterwards. Mr Hitchman's evidence is to the effect that that was the agreement he supposed himself to be making. Mr Simmonds's evidence and the whole of his subsequent behaviour is consistent with such an agreement having been made. The company's 1976 standpoint, because based as it had to be not on knowledge of what had been agreed in 1972, but on the basis of no documentation and of company policy, is in no way inconsistent with such an agreement having been made.

We bear in mind that it is for Mr Simmonds to prove that there was an agreement in 1972 that his obligation thereafter was to work nights only instead of days only. In our judgment the evidence in this case leads to the conclusion that there was such an agreement. If there was, it is conceded that what the company did in April 1977 was a repudiation of that agreement, so that although it was Mr Simmonds who gave notice it was the company that was responsible in law for bringing the contract of employment to an end.

Accordingly we allow the appeal. Since Mr Simmonds's employment was determined because the company required him to do something which turns out to have been outside the terms of his contract under threat of disciplinary action if he would not, he was unfairly dismissed.

(*b*) *Trial periods at common law and under statute*

At common law, significant change which is unilaterally imposed on an employee may amount to a repudiation by the employer of the contract of employment. The right of the employee to accept the employer's repudiation and terminate the contract, however may be waived—and a waiver might be implied by delay in "accepting" the repudiation, *ie* terminating the contract.

Shields Furniture Ltd. v. Goff
[1973] I.C.R. 187
National Industrial Relations Court

BRIGHTMAN J.: In the case before us the employees were never asked if they were willing to work at Fulham. They were simply told on Monday that on Tuesday their work was being moved two-and-a-half miles away. What is an employee expected to do in these circumstances? He does not want to be out of a job. Nor, if he is a conscientious workman, does he want to let his employer down if this can be avoided. In most cases, therefore, he goes to the new job. He goes with an open mind. There is a period when he is uncommitted. During that period he makes up his mind whether he will accept the new employment in which case he is not entitled to a redundancy payment, or whether he will leave, or, in legal language, accept the employer's repudiation. So what we have to decide is whether on the primary facts the proper inference is that the employee accepted the new employment.

In our view the proper inference is that the employees did not commit themselves to working at Fulham instead of Markham Street, but accepted the employer's repudiation of the Markham Street contract. We do not think that the three weeks that the employees worked at Fulham and the (subsequent) two weeks' holiday was so long an elapsed period of time that one ought to assume an agreed variation or replacement of their previous contract. The employers never asked them to consider whether they wished to be discharged at Markham Street or to take on new work at Fulham. They were given no period of time in which to assess the position. The employers directed them to Fulham which they had no contractual right to do. The employees reacted to that direction in the way that most employees would react: they went. They did not protest, but went to work and waited to see to what extent conditions would be improved. In those circumstances the time they allowed to go by was not so long as to imply the agreed substitution of a different contract.

In the following case, *Goff* was used explicitly to create a "common law trial period."

Air Canada v. Lee
[1978] I.R.L.R. 392
Employment Appeal Tribunal

Mrs Lee was employed at premises in Dover Street on the third floor in a room with plenty of light and air. Under her contract of employment, she was not "mobile." After their lease expired, the employers moved to an office in Regent Street, where Mrs Lee would have to work in the basement of the new premises. She was not happy with the proposed site and agreed to move to the new location on a trial basis and was never served with a notice of dismissal. She was employed at the new site for some two months and then gave notice of resignation.

PHILLIPS J.: [The judge quoted from *Goff* (above) and continued:] It is here entirely obvious that Mrs Lee never did accept [employment at the new premises]. The trial period, which had never been precisely fixed, expired and she then did what she could have done at the date of the removal to Regent Street: she said "No, I won't work in the basement. I want my redundancy payment . . . ."

We would add this word of caution: in that case, as in this case, the duration of the trial period was unspecified. That of course does not mean that it can last forever, but only for what is a reasonable period in all the circumstances. Amongst the circumstances will be included the steps the employers take, during a trial period the length of which is unspecified, to enquire how things are coming along and what the employee is going to do. If they make no such enquiries, and if it is only a comparatively short period, or a reasonable period, then it carries on until either the employee announces his decision, or a period of time has expired which is long enough for it to be said that it would be unreasonable to consider the trial period as still subsisting.

Under EPCA, if there is a dismissal for redundancy (*i.e.* loss of the previous job but the employee is offered a different but suitable job), there is an automatic *statutory* four week trial period (section 84(3)-(7)). There is then no repudiation. This situation may be difficult to distinguish from the case where the employee is told he must take a new job, on pain of dismissal (a repudiatory act)—in which case a "common law trial period" comes into effect.

Turvey v. Cheyney & Son Ltd.
[1979] I.C.R. 341; [1979] I.R.L.R. 105
Employment Appeal Tribunal

Four polishers were offered jobs in different departments when work in the polishing department diminished. They indicated that they would undertake the new work for a trial period. After more than four weeks, they all left of their own accord because the new work did not suit them.

BRISTOW J.: It is clear law that where one party to a contract acts in such a way as to show he no longer intends to be bound, the other party can decide at his option whether or not to treat the contract as at an end. Moreover he does not necessarily have to make up his mind at once but is entitled to a reasonable time in which to do so.

The application of this common law principle to contracts of employment is illustrated in *Shields Furniture Ltd* v *Goff* [1973] ICR 187 [above p. 64], where Brightman J said that the mere fact that an employee started to work under the terms of a new contract offered him by the employer did not constitute an acceptance of the new contract so that he must be regarded as having made up his mind not to rely on the repudiation of the old contract. You have to see whether the employee is accepting the new contract by his conduct, or whether he is giving it a try to see whether he will accept it or not.

If, as in this case with the three employees, the employee says that he is giving it a trial, clearly he has not accepted the new contract simply by doing that. If having started by expressly giving it a trial he goes on working under the new terms without any more being said about it, the time will come when a reasonable time for making up his mind has expired, and he will be taken to have made a new contract or renewed the old one with variations. Each case will depend on its own facts, and it will be for the Industrial Tribunal to say whether or not, on the facts which it finds, a new contract has been made or the old contract has been renewed with variations. Since the answer must vary with the circumstances we will call the period which at common law the employee has to make up his mind period X.

So, in the case of a dismissal [for redundancy plus the offer of alternative employment under what is now EPCA, s.84] the employee, who has no common law protection producing period X in which he can make up his mind if he likes the new job, because no repudiation of the contract is involved, is given the [statutory] trial period [EPCA, s.84(4)]. By [EPCA, s.84(6)] if he terminates his new or renewed contract, or gives notice to do so during the trial period and acts on the notice, or if the employer, for a reason connected with the change, does the same, the employee is treated as dismissed when the old contract came to an end or would have done had he not accepted the new job.

This is an improvement in the position of the employee who is dismissed under [EPCA, s.83(2)(*a*) and (*b*)] circumstances. It is also an improvement in the protection of the employee under [s.83(2)(*c*)] circumstances. He has a period X in which to make up his mind. If his decision is not to take the new job, he is treated as dismissed at the moment he brings period X to an end by leaving the new job. If his decision is to take the new job and he brings period X to an end by making a new contract or renewing the old one with variations he then has the further trial period created by EPCA, s.84(4) in which to make up his mind, before losing his right to say, "You dismissed me by repudiating the old contract." He is then in the [EPCA, s.84(3)] situation. So he has his common law period X protection plus his statutory trial period protection.

It will be seen that our view of how [EPCA, s.84] as amended takes effect differs in some respects from its construction by this Court as expressed by Phillips J in the *Air Canada* case [[1978] IRLR 394, above p. 64] in his extempore judgment. But the basis of the decision in the *Air Canada* case was that the employee was in a [EPCA, s.83(2)(*c*)] situation, and that what we have called her period X had not come to an end before she herself gave notice. In those circumstances applying the opening words of [EPCA, s.84(3)], no question of the statutory trial period arose because neither was her contract of employment renewed nor was she re-engaged under a new contract.

It follows that in the case before us the Industrial Tribunal went wrong in law, and it is clear from their reasons that the approach they made to a factual situation which looks simple enough and must occur in practice very often caused them to fail to consider and resolve the fundamental questions which have now to be decided so that you can apply [EPCA, s.84] correctly. They are these:

1. Has the employee been dismissed, so that [EPCA, s.83(2)(*a*)] applies? Or does [EPCA, s.83(2)(*b*)] apply (this we think will be rare in redundancy cases)? Or has the employee been told, without being dismissed within the meaning of [EPCA s.83(2)(*a*) or (*b*)], that his work is coming to an end and he is being offered another job but that if he will not take it he will be dismissed? This is a repudiation of his contract putting him in the [EPCA, s.83(2)(*c*)] situation with period X, within which to make up his mind.

2. If he is in the [EPCA, s.83(2)(*a*)] or [EPCA, s.83(2)(*b*)] situation, the Tribunal will go straight on to deal with [EPCA, s.84(3)] and the subsequent sub-sections creating the trial period. If he is in the [EPCA, s.83(2)(*c*)] situation and starts working in the new job, making it clear, expressly or by implication, that he does so on trial without committing himself to a new contract or a renewed contract with variations, then, when he leaves the job, is period X still in existence, or has it elapsed because his conduct shows that he has by then committed himself to the new contract or contract with vari-

ations? In answering this question the considerations examined by Phillips J in the *Air Canada* case at p.394 paragraphs 9 and 11 should be taken into account together with any other circumstances which a Tribunal may think throw light on what can be a difficult question.

If, but only if, the answer is that there is a new contract or a contract renewed with variations and so period X has expired before the employee walks out, the Tribunal then goes on to deal with [EPCA, s.84(3)] and the subsequent sub-sections creating the trial period.

The force of the *statutory* trial period in cases of changes at work is evident from a case where it was held to override and thus invalidate a redeployment agreement whereby, as part of his contract of employment, the employee agreed to allow changes in his work obligation in the event of redundancy (*Tocher* v. *General Motors Scotland Ltd.* [1981] I.R.L.R. 55). Further, even where the employee appears to acquiesce in changes unilaterally imposed, it appears possible to rely on these "repudiatory" acts in claiming constructive dismissal based on a later subsequent breach—this later breach being the "last straw" (see *Lewis* v. *Motorworld Garages Ltd.* [1985] I.R.L.R. 465, see Chap. 10, p. 307).

(ii) Changes and dismissal

Employees risk dismissal if they resist change. Should this occur the question will arise whether a dismissal for refusal to accept change is fair and also whether the employee is entitled to statutory redundancy compensation. The policy issue is between the right of management unilaterally to change the work obligation and the right of the worker to adhere to the obligation he has accepted. The protection of the employee depends on the court insisting that an employer demanding work changes compensate the employee who does not wish to accept them and, so, loses his employment.

(a) Unfair dismissal on "economic" grounds

The questions raised in the cases are, first, whether refusing to change is a fair reason for dismissing an employee (EPCA, s.57(1)); and secondly, whether the employer has acted reasonably in dismissing the employee for that reason (EPCA, s.57(3)).

Hollister v. National Farmers Union
[1979] I.C.R. 542; [1979] I.R.L.R. 238
Court of Appeal

In 1976 the London Headquarters of the NFU decided that insurance business for the county of Cornwall would be transferred from the Cornish Mutual Association to the NFU Mutual. This involved different terms and conditions of employment and methods of working for the Cornish group secretaries who had previously handled the business and who had substantially been remunerated by commission upon it. Mr Hollister was one of the secretaries. He protested, but was eventually told either to accept the change or be dismissed. He refused to agree the new terms and was dismissed.

LORD DENNING M.R.: The question which is being discussed in this case is whether the reorganisation of the business, which the National Farmers'

Union felt they had to undertake in 1976, coupled with Mr Hollister's refusal to accept the new agreement, was a substantial reason of such a kind as to justify the dismissal of the employee. Upon that there have only been one or two cases. One we were particularly referred to was the case of *Ellis* v *Brighton Co-operative Society Ltd* [1976] I.R.L.R. 419, where it was recognised by the Court that reorganisation of business may on occasion be a sufficient reason justifying the dismissal of an employee. They went on to say: "Where there has been a properly consulted-upon reorganisation which, if it is not done, is going to bring the whole business to a standstill, a failure to go along with the new arrangements may well—it is not bound to but it may well—constitute 'some other substantial reason'." Certainly, I think, everyone would agree with that. But in the present case Mr Justice Arnold expanded it a little so as not to limit it to where it came absolutely to a standstill but to where there was some sound, good business reason for the reorganisation. I must say I see no reason to differ from Mr Justice Arnold's view on that. It must depend in all the circumstances whether the reorganisation was such that the only sensible thing to do was to terminate the employee's contract unless he would agree to a new arrangement. It seems to me that that paragraph may well be satisfied, and indeed was satisfied, in this case, having regard to the commercial necessity of rearrangements being made and the termination of the relationship with the Cornish Mutual, and the setting up of a new relationship via the National Farmers' Union Mutual Insurance Limited. On that rearrangement being made, it was absolutely essential for new contracts to be made with the existing group secretaries: and the only way to deal with it was to terminate the agreements and offer them reasonable new ones. It seems to me that that would be, and was, a substantial reason of a kind sufficient to justify this kind of dismissal.

See also *Bowater Containers Ltd.* v. *McCormack* [1980] I.R.L.R. 50 (E.A.T.), where Talbot J., quoting *Hollister*, held dismissal to be fair for a substantial reason where an employee refused "to undertake his part in the new reorganisation which was beneficial to the efficient running of the company."

To justify changes in terms of "sound, good business reasons" or "commercial necessity" carries the risk of overlooking the employees' interests. An attempt to include these interests was made in the following case.

Evans v. Elementa Holdings Ltd.
[1982] I.R.L.R. 143
Employment Appeal Tribunal

Mr Evans, alone of all the employees concerned, refused to accept a new contract offered by his employer, because of what he regarded as an excessive new obligation to work overtime. He was dismissed.

Browne-Wilkinson J.: The question under EPCA s.57(3) is whether the employers' conduct in dismissing [the appellant] was reasonable. But, as the Industrial Tribunal recognised, that question necessarily required the Industrial Tribunal to find whether it was reasonable for Mr Evans to decline the new terms of the contract. If it was reasonable for him to decline those terms, then obviously it would have been unreasonable for the employers to dismiss him for such refusal. It was therefore a necessary part of the Industrial Tribunal's decision on this point that the terms of the contract were not objectionable or oppressive. So far as we can see, at no stage do they analyse what is, or would have been, the effect of this alteration in the contractual position. In our view, it is simply not a possible view to have reached, after analysis, to say that Mr Evans was unreasonable in refusing to accept a contract which imposed upon him an unlimited obligation to work overtime, he being a man who under his existing contract did not have to work on Saturdays or do any overtime. That is particularly so in the light of certain evidence which was given which might suggest that the employers were envisaging that for the future he would, like his colleagues, be expected to work overtime three Saturdays out of four. If it had been shown in this case that there was some immediate need for the employers to increase the overtime worked or to require mandatory overtime as opposed to voluntary overtime, that might have fundamentally altered the position. But there was no evidence of any kind directed towards a need to change the provisions as to overtime for the current working needs of the company. On the contrary, there was evidence that the workload had not increased and there was evidence that the number of setters-out had fallen from three to one. That is inconsistent with a view that overall there was a need for more work to be done though flexibility might have been required . . . .

This case turns on the imposition of a new contract of employment, not new working practices. If he had accepted the new contract, he would have bound himself for the future to perform the contract in its revised form. Managements change and if, in the future, a new management were to require substantial overtime, he would have had no answer.

This passage was disagreed with by another division of the E.A.T. in *Chubb Fire Security Ltd.* v. *Harper* [1983] I.R.L.R. 311 (E.A.T.), (para. 9). The approach proposed by Balcombe J. in that case was instead to ask (para. 8):

> " . . . was [the employer] acting reasonably in deciding that the advantages to them of implementing the proposed re-organisation outweighed any disadvantage which they should have contemplated [the employee] might suffer."

Even this did not go far enough for another division of the E.A.T. in the following case.

Richmond Precision Engineering Ltd. v. Pearce

[1985] I.R.L.R. 179
Employment Appeal Tribunal

After a take-over occurred of the business employing Mr Pearce, employees were notified of certain modifications to be made to terms and conditions of employment. For Mr Pearce, these changes involved a reduction in his hourly rate by 10p; an increase in his basic weekly hours of work from 39 to 40; a reduction in his annual holiday entitlement from five weeks to four weeks; loss of a £25 a month contribution towards petrol costs; and loss of the benefit of an occupational pension scheme. Mr Pearce refused to accept these new terms and was eventually dismissed in consequence.

An Industrial Tribunal, relying on *Chubb's* case, balanced the advantages to the employer against the disadvantages to the employee, and upheld the complaint of unfair dismissal.

Beldam J.: In the present case, the employers were faced with a situation in which they had to try to integrate the workforce at Hudsons with their own workforce. No possible criticism could be levelled, nor has any been sought to be levelled, at the way in which they went about discussing this matter and negotiating with the employees. They negotiated with this respondent. They went as far as they felt that they could. In the finding which the Tribunal made that the offer was pitched just that little bit too low, it seems to us that the Tribunal were falling into the trap of substituting what they would have regarded as a reasonable offer for what a reasonable employer might be expected to offer in these circumstances. And the circumstances in this case clearly included the terms and conditions and rates of pay of their existing workforce. They did not therefore consider, or apparently consider, the range of offers which might be open to the reasonable employer in these circumstances. It would be quite impossible, in the judgment of this Tribunal, to say that the offer which the appellants made to this respondent was not within the range of offers which were, in all the circumstances, reasonable.

The task of weighing the advantages to the employer against the disadvantages to the employee is merely one factor which the Tribunal have to take into account when determining the question in accordance with the equity and substantial merits of the case. Merely because there are disadvantages to the employee, it does not, by any manner of means follow, that the employer has acted unreasonably in treating his failure to accept the terms which they have offered as a reason to dismiss . . . .

That led them to place far too much emphasis, in our judgment, on the disadvantages which they thought that the respondent would suffer. In finding that the offer was pitched just that little bit too low, the Tribunal regarded merely one of the factors which they had to take into account; it should have directed itself that what it had to consider was whether it was an offer, from the employer's point of view, which a reasonable employer could make, in the circumstances which faced that employer.

Pearce was decided on December 13, 1984, and did not refer to the following case decided six weeks earlier, in which the Court of Appeal prescribed in very narrow terms the grounds on which the E.A.T. should overturn industrial tribunal decisions (see below, Chapter 10 on *Termination of Work*, pp. 324 *et seq.*—a prescription which goes some way towards explaining their decision).

Kent County Council v. Gilham
[1985] I.R.L.R. 18
Court of Appeal

To achieve savings, the employer proposed to reduce pay and holiday entitlement fixed by national collective agreements. When the unions refused to re-negotiate terms, the employer effected the cuts unilaterally, terminating the employees' contracts and offering new ones at the reduced rates. The employees refused to accept the new contracts and claimed unfair dismissal. An Industrial Tribunal upheld the complaints, finding that the employer had no substantial reason and, even if he did, he had acted unreasonably. The E.A.T. and the Court of Appeal reversed the finding that the employer had no substantial reason, but refused to disturb the Tribunal's finding that the employer had acted unreasonably.

GRIFFITHS L.J.: The "substantial reason" put forward by the Council was the need "to achieve economies forced upon the employer by a national policy to reduce spending in the public sector and by offering new contracts on reduced terms to avoid a closure of all or a major part of the school meals service."

It is quite impossible to argue that such a reason could not be a substantial reason for dismissing a dinner lady. The hurdle over which the employer has to jump at this stage of an enquiry into an unfair dismissal complaint is designed to deter employers from dismissing employees for some trivial or unworthy reason. If he does so, the dismissal is deemed unfair without the need to look further into its merits. But if on the face of it the reason *could* justify the dismissal, then it passes as a substantial reason, and the enquiry moves on to [EPCA] s.57(3), and the question of reasonableness. . . .

[The judge then referred] to the decisions of two other Industrial Tribunals in both of which, on a very similar issue, the decision had gone in favour of the local authority . . . .

[The judge nonetheless refused to overturn the Tribunal's assessment of the reasonableness of the employer's action:]

The [appellant] Council put no evidence before the Tribunal of any efforts on their part to instil some sense of urgency into the national negotiations, and it was in my view legitimate for the Tribunal to ask itself whether in the circumstances a reasonable employer would defer a decision to breach a national agreement until there had been time for the matter to be considered at national level. This would not of itself necessarily be a decisive matter, but it was one of the factors to be weighed in the balance and to which the Tribunal was entitled to give such weight as they thought fit.

The next submission was that the Industrial Tribunal erred in law in that it held that the Council's departure from a collective agreement was in itself necessarily unfair regardless of any other interest the Council had to consider, or duties it had to fulfil. There is no doubt that the Tribunal did consider that the breach of a national agreement was a very serious matter, as indeed did the two other Industrial Tribunals who have considered a similar problem. But, reading the decision as a whole, it is clear that the Tribunal balanced this factor against the difficulties that the Council faced and the need to make cuts in their educational budget. . . .

DILLON L.J.: It is of obvious importance, in the fields of employment law and of industrial relations, that national agreements negotiated between employers and trade unions as to wages and conditions of employment should not be breached unilaterally by an employer. It could not therefore be said that no reasonable Tribunal could have regarded the Council's decision, to breach the national agreement and dismiss the dinner ladies unless they were prepared to accept a reduction of pay, as unreasonable. . . .

It is said that the Industrial Tribunal erred in that they regarded the sanctity of national agreements as paramount, and of such importance as inexorably to override all other considerations. I do not, however, so read their decision; in particular they clearly had very much in mind the difficult position in which the Council had been placed by the Government's direction, and they weighed the various factors against each other. . . .

The reported decisions contain, as it seems to me, a good deal of what I would venture to call over-sophistication as to the approach to be adopted by Industrial Tribunals to the question of reasonableness. In my judgment it is sufficient for the Tribunal to answer directly the simple question posed by subsection (3) [of EPCA, s.57]; "In all the circumstances, did the employer act reasonably or unreasonably in treating the reason in the particular case as a sufficient reason for dismissing the employee?" That is a question of fact, and it is to be treated as a question of fact and not a sophistication of law. A

Tribunal may in a particular case react to the facts by saying, "What the employer did is not what we ourselves would have done, but we cannot say that it was unreasonable." That again, however, is an answer on the facts to a question of fact, and not a guideline of law to be applied by all other Tribunals in all other cases. Because the question is one of fact, and there are many different Industrial Tribunals, it is quite likely that different Tribunals will reach different conclusions on the question of reasonableness on very similar facts. That is inherent in the system which Parliament has set up, and is no indication that any Tribunal had misdirected itself or erred in law.

The pyramid comprising Industrial Tribunal review of employer decisions at the base (*Pearce*), and E.A.T. review of Industrial Tribunal decisions in the middle (*Gilham*), was crowned by pronouncements on judicial review of administrative action. In the following case the possibility was canvassed that, in the case of public authorities, judicial review could invoke the same considerations of "reasonableness".

R. v. Hertfordshire County Council *ex p.* National Union of Public Employees

[1985] I.R.L.R. 258

Court of Appeal

Two councils, to make economies, gave notice to school meals service employees terminating their contracts of employment and offering re-employment on terms less favourable than those negotiated nationally. The applicants sought judicial review of these decisions.

DILLON L.J.: The obvious question that arises is whether it was reasonable for the councils to solve their difficulties by, in effect, imposing cuts in pay on the dinner ladies, when the dinner ladies, or many of them, are among the lowest paid of the councils' employees, and their previous terms of pay and employment, which were in effect being unilaterally abrogated by the councils, had been the subject of a nationally negotiated wages agreement. That is not, however, the question which the court is asked to decide in these proceedings.

The proper Tribunals to decide whether the councils acted reasonably are the Industrial Tribunals, which, with their lay members, have a special expertise in this field. It is plain however, from the judgments of this court in *Gilham* v *Kent County Council* [above p. 70], decided on 1.11.84, that the question is one on which different Industrial Tribunals could reasonably come to opposite conclusions.

The question raised in these proceedings is a more sophisticated and, from the point of view of the appellants, much more difficult question. The appellants say, invoking the judgments in the *Wednesbury* case [1948] 1 KB 223, that in reaching their decision to dismiss the dinner ladies and only offer them re-employment on less favourable terms, the councils have come to a conclusion so unreasonable that no reasonable authorities could ever have come to it. They say accordingly that the decision, as a decision of a public authority, is *ultra vires* and void. Such a contention is , however, as it seems to me, untenable in the light of *Gilham's* case; there this court held the decisions of the various Industrial Tribunals each way on the dismissal of dinner ladies in very similar circumstances to be all valid, whereas if the appellants' contention in the present case is correct the court ought to have overruled the decisions of the Tribunals in the cases of *Gregory* v *Devon County Council* (IT 36077/83) and *Golledge* v *Somerset County Council* (IT 15211/83) as unreasonable and perverse. [These were the two decisions cited in *Gilham* in which the actions of the local authority were upheld as reasonable.]

I am not called on to say whether or not the dismissals, in the present case, of the dinner ladies by the Hertfordshire and East Sussex County Councils were reasonable or fair. I have no doubt however that the contention that the decisions were so unreasonable that no reasonable authorities could have made them goes too far and must fail.

These cases represent a remarkable conjunction of principles. It must be a matter of concern that issues as different as controlling employers' changes to terms and conditions of work, the review of the decisions of Industrial Tribunals as "industrial juries" by the E.A.T., and the supervision of administrative authorities by the courts should all be resolved by a principle of "reasonableness." This is a conjunction of either sublime simplicity or stark poverty.

The policy behind the substantive principle that unilateral changes in contractual terms are "some other substantial reason of a kind such as to justify the dismissal" within EPCA, s.57(1)(*b*) is highlighted by cases on transfers of undertakings between employers under the Transfer of Undertakings (Protection of Employment) Regulations 1981 (S.I. 1981 No.1794). Regulation 8(2) provides that:

> "Where an economic, technical or organisational reason entailing changes in the workforce of either the transferor or the transferee before or after a relevant transfer is the reason or principal reason for dismissing an employee . . . [the dismissal shall] be regarded as having been for a substantial reason of a kind as to justify the dismissal . . . ."

The interpretation of this provision by the E.A.T. contrasts with that adopted by the same body with respect to "economic" dismissals under unfair dismissal legislation, for policy reasons made explicit in the following case.

Berriman v. Delabole Slate Ltd.
[1984] I.R.L.R. 394
Employment Appeal Tribunal

Following the transfer of the undertaking in which Mr Berriman was employed, the transferee employer wrote informing him that they proposed to alter his pay, entailing a substantial reduction in his guaranteed weekly wage.

NOLAN J.: [The E.A.T. held that there were no "changes in the workforce" so as to bring the dismissal within the scope of Regulation 8(2), and continued:] Mr Tabachnik, counsel for the employer, reminded us firstly in this connection of cases such as *Hollister* [above p. 67], in which it has been recognised that ordinary, prudent, commercial requirements may necessitate the reduction of the work force and changes in the terms of employment of workers. He says it cannot be supposed that Regulation 8 should have been designed to make new rules applicable in the case where there has been a transfer of an undertaking different from those which apply, as a matter of well settled law, to undertakings which have not been transferred.

The difficulty we find with that argument is that, as it seems to us, the provisions of para. 8 clearly are designed to make new provision, not previously in the legislation, dealing with the transfer of undertakings.

Mr Tabachnik said that if employers, such as the respondent employers in the present case, were subject to the requirements of keeping the employees taken over from the previous employer on a range of pay which they have previously enjoyed and, as a necessary practical consequence, were required to bring up the rates of pay of their own previous employees to those of the new employees, that would be an impossibly onerous requirement and one which would reduce the likelihood of amalgamations and transfers which would be of general benefit to the business community and to employees.

We see the force of that argument but the converse appears to us to be equally important, namely, as we understand the argument for the respondent company, that the consequence would be that employers were indeed entitled, when taking over another business, to require a reduction in the pay of the employees taken over without thereby infringing the provisions of the employment legislation.

The Court of Appeal rejected the employer's appeal ([1985] I.R.L.R. 305, *per* Browne-Wilkinson L.J. at p. 308):

> " . . . it is far from clear that it was the intention of the legislature (or of the EEC Directive 77/187 which required the regulations to be made) that immediately following a transfer the employees of the transferred undertaking could be made to accept new terms of service. The purpose of the directive was 'the safeguarding of employees' rights in the event of transfers' and the regulations themselves include in their name the words 'Protection of Employment.' Amongst the most crucial rights of employees are their existing terms of service. We are not satisfied that there is a clear statutory intention to ensure that, following a transfer, the transferee company can insist on equating the terms and conditions of the 'transferred' employees to those of his existing employees notwithstanding the fact that such alteration may constitute a detriment to the transferred employees."

The policy justification put forward for finding dismissals unfair in *Berriman* would seem to apply with equal force to changes in terms *not* connected with transfers of undertakings.

The substantive issue of fairness in the general law of unfair dismissal has thus been decided by the judges in the interests of the employer desiring change. The main restrictions so far placed by the courts are procedural ones. The employer should adopt certain procedures in introducing the change—otherwise the dismissal will be for a "fair" reason (EPCA, s.57(1)), but may be unreasonably implemented (s.57(3))—and hence unfair. So, for example, the employer:

(a) must have and produce evidence that he adequately considered the case for and against the reorganisation or changes leading to the dismissal;

(b) needs to indicate that he considered alternatives to dismissing the employee; and
(c) should have discussed or consulted with the employee about the changes affecting him or her.

The following cases illustrate this common law development of procedural restrictions on employer-initiated changes at work.

Banerjee v. City & East London Area Health Authority
[1979] I.R.L.R. 147
Employment Appeal Tribunal

When one of two part-time consultant surgeons (the other being the appellant) decided to give up the job, the respondent Authority decided to appoint a single consultant. This course of action was suggested by two advisory bodies, the surgical division committee and the district management team. It was claimed to be in accordance with the Authority's policy of rationalisation and the custom and practice of amalgamating part-time posts. In view of this decision, the appellant was dismissed. An Industrial Tribunal held that his dismissal was either on grounds of redundancy or for "some other substantial reason" and that it was fair.

ARNOLD J.: If an employer comes along and says "We have evolved such-and-such a policy" and either "we regard it as a matter of importance" or "the advantages which are to be discerned from this policy are so-and-so," subject to there being any effective cross-examination, it seems to us that it must inevitably follow that the evaluation by the employer of the policy as a matter of importance, a matter in which substantial advantage is discerned, if it is properly the subject matter of another reason, can be seen to be the subject of a substantial other reason. But in this case what is the state of the evidence? One knows that there was the policy, because Miss Keogh [the respondent's medical staffing officer] said so—a policy of rationalising and appointing one person to fill separate part-time employments. We know that it was logical to do this from a consultant's point of view, because Mr Woodward [a member of the surgical division committee] said so. We know that it was the custom and practice to amalgamate part-time posts. And that is all we know. We have not the least idea, and the Tribunal had not the least idea, what advantages this policy was supposed, or thought likely, or hoped, to bring. We have no idea, and the Tribunal had no idea, what importance was attached to this policy by the Health Authority.

Our conclusion upon the matter is that no Tribunal, on that evidence, was entitled to conclude that it was a substantial other reason. Therefore, holding as we do that there was no material upon which redundancy could be determined, and no material upon which substantiality could be afforded as an appropriate description of the other reason (which undoubtedly as a reason there was), we do not think that the Health Authority has brought the matter within the ambit of what is now EPCA, s. 57(1)(*b*). . . .

When a question of unfair dismissal comes up, the officer of the employing company who has taken the decision to dismiss, or one of those who have been party to the decision to dismiss, comes along and says, "The reason we dismissed was" this or that. "We have considered keeping him on. We considered the advantages of each course, and we decided" so-and-so. It may very well be that if that course had been taken by this Authority the onus would have been discharged. We do not believe that it is enough to say, "This is our policy, this is the recommendation which we received from a body appointed to advise us, and that is that." We do not take the view that any Tribunal, on the material which was available to this Tribunal, could legitimately have concluded that the onus lying on the Authority under [what is now EPCA, s. 57(3)] was discharged in this case.

The first part of the extract from the decision in the following case goes further to suggest not only a need for adequate consideration but some degree of objectivity in listing the sufficiency of the economic reason.

Ladbroke Courage Holidays Ltd. v. Asten
[1981] I.R.L.R. 59
Employment Appeal Tribunal

Mr Asten was dismissed on the grounds, *inter alia*, that the company's Regional Controller had been instructed to reduce the wages bill. The Industrial Tribunal held this was "some other substantial reason," but went on to hold that dismissal for this reason was nonetheless unfair: firstly, because the company failed to produce any evidence that there was a real need to reduce the wages bill; secondly, because there was no consultation or discussion with Mr Asten prior to the dismissal. If there had been, said the Tribunal, the company probably would not have reached the decision to dismiss him.

WATERHOUSE J.: The way that the Industrial Tribunal dealt with the matter in their statement of reasons was, first of all, to criticise the sufficiency of the reasons in the light of the general circumstances; and then, after criticising the quality of evidence produced by the appellants, they continued.

"In our view, if an employer seeks to rely on business re-organisation or economic necessity as a reason for a dismissal, it is incumbent on them to produce some evidence to show that there was a re-organisation or that there was some economic need for economy. In deciding whether a dismissal was fair or unfair, we consider it very material to know whether the employer was making profits or losses. We do not consider that an employer can satisfy a Tribunal that it was fair to dismiss an employee merely by proving that a Regional Controller had instructions to reduce his wages bill, without any evidence as to the reason why the instructions were given."

We cannot detect any error of law in that statement. It is clear from the wording of EPCA, s.57(3) that, whether the reason for dismissal is redundancy or some other substantial reason, the employer must satisfy the Tribunal that in the circumstances, having regard to equity and the substantial merits of the case, he acted reasonably in treating it as a sufficient reason for dismissing the employee [the burden on the employer was removed by the Employment Act 1980.] In our view, the basis of the appellants' decision to reduce the wages bill was a circumstance which the Industrial Tribunal were entitled to investigate before reaching a conclusion on the employer's case under s.57(3).

There are more substantial hurdles for the appellants to surmount, however, because, in paragraph 9 of the statement of reasons, the Tribunal went on to say that there were even stronger reasons for holding that the dismissal in the instant case was unfair. They said that there was no discussion or consultation with the respondent prior to the decision to dismiss him . . . .

Thus, there are two parts of the Tribunal's conclusions that are relevant. Firstly, they say that there should have been consultation with the respondent. If that consultation had taken place, the fact that the actual economies were very limited would have been made apparent to the appellants and the position could have been solved in a number of different ways. Secondly, the result of the discussion, in the view of the Industrial Tribunal, would have been that the appellants would have appreciated that their decision was not justified in the circumstances.

. . . we cannot accept that there was any error by the Industrial Tribunal in their finding as to the relevance of the failure of consultation in this case. In our judgment, it was plainly open to the Industrial Tribunal to consider, as they did, that any reasonable employer would have consulted the respondent in this case before dismissing him. Indeed, the evidence before the Industrial Tribunal, to which we have been referred briefly, indicates that he was a very reasonable man with whom fruitful discussion could take place. In the light of the economic factors discussed quite accurately by the Industrial Tribunal in paragraph 9 of their reasons, there was obviously much to be discussed and several different possibilities to be considered. One of the considerations was that the respondent was already going to take March off without pay because his wife was expecting a baby in April. Another consideration was that there would be a need for a seasonal bars manager or a seasonal head barman from April 1980 onwards. Yet another factor was that the intention of the appellants was that, if they dismissed the respondent, they would pay him a month's pay and make an *ex gratia* payment of two weeks' salary in addition.

In all these circumstances, it was open to the Tribunal to reach the conclusion that consultation should have taken place and that consultation was likely to have been fruitful, bearing in mind the personal position and attitude of the respondent. They were entitled to hold that the appellants had failed to establish their case under s.57(3) and, accordingly, the finding of unfair dismissal must be upheld.

The view that, despite these apparent safeguards, the employer is entitled to take his own economic decisions is well illustrated in the following decision.

Orr v. Vaughan
[1981] I.R.L.R. 63
Employment Appeal Tribunal

The appellant had two beauty salons. At the end of 1979 her bookkeeper told her that there was not enough money to pay all the bills and the wages and that something had to be done. According to the bookkeeper, the loss was coming from the Silvermere salon and she advised the appellant to take on more of the work there herself and cut down on the staff costs.

The appellant decided to take over the work principally of Miss Vaughan, and Miss Vaughan was given notice of dismissal.

SLYNN J.: The Industrial Tribunal formed a view about the way this matter had been conducted. They were not satisfied that there really had been any kind of proper investigation into whether the Silvermere salon was losing money. The books, which were produced, did not show it. The Tribunal thought that Mrs Sutton had never attempted to get out, from the record which she kept, the precise income and expenditure attributable to the Silvermere salon. Moreover, having heard the evidence, they were not satisfied that the books did show that the business at Silvermere was losing money. They came to the conclusion that Mrs Orr had not taken reasonable steps and had not behaved like a responsible employer in investigating the financial position before coming to the conclusion that it was Silvermere which was losing money . . . .

. . . . They thought that there was no more than an intuition that the Silvermere business was not flourishing; that what was said by Mrs Orr to be facts in relation to the business had not been shown to be facts at all. They said, "You really cannot regard it as another substantial reason when you have not really gone into the state of the business before doing your so-called reorganisation."

Mrs Orr has appealed against that decision. Mr Supperstone, who has appeared on her behalf, has drawn our attention to a number of authorities. He has stressed that it is sufficient if there is a reorganisation of a business for a sound good business reason. It does not have to be shown now, as was at one time thought, that the alternative to a re-organisation is that the business will come to an end. As the Court of Appeal stated in *Hollister* v *National Farmers Union* [1979] IRLR 238 at p. 240 [above p. 67], it is sufficient to establish that there has been a substantial reason of a kind such as to justify the dismissal, if there is a good commercial reason for it.

It is said here that Mrs Orr was entitled to come to the view, on the information which was before her, given to her by her book-keeper, that she should dispense with the services of one of her employees in order to cut down costs because the business was not working profitably . . . . that it is not for this Industrial Tribunal to substitute its own view of what it would have done . . . .

We fully appreciate the submissions which Mr Supperstone, ably and concisely, has put before us. At the end of the day, it is largely for the employer to decide, on the material which is available to the employer, what is to be done by way of re-organisation of the business; and it is for the employer to decide whether the requirements of the business for employees to carry out the particular work have ceased or diminished. If an employer acts on reasonable information reasonably acquired, then that is the test and no more.

We have to consider whether this Tribunal has applied a different test and has imposed upon the employer a higher burden than is required . . . . What is clear here is that this Tribunal did take all the factors into account. They felt that this decision had not been arrived at in a reasonable way. It is not just a case where the employer had information to show that there had to be a re-organisation. It is one where, having gone into it carefully in their reasons, the Tribunal concluded that reasonable inquiries had not been made and that really, on the information, Mrs Orr could not be satisfied that it was the Silvermere business, which she wished to keep separate, which was losing money . . . .

In the result, although, as we say, we appreciate the criticism which can be made of some of the individual points, and although a different Tribunal might have come to a different view on the assessment of the evidence as a whole, we find if quite impossible to say that this Tribunal has in any way misdirected itself in law. Nor has it imposed on the employer a higher burden than the statute requires. It does not seem to us possible to say that this decision is, on the findings of fact, a decision to which no reasonable Tribunal, properly directing itself in law, could possibly have come.

(*b*) *Redundancy and changed work obligations*

Statutory protection of employees in redundancy situations depends on the definition of redundancy in EPCA s.81(2)(*b*): "the fact that the requirements of that business for employees to carry out work of a particular kind have ceased or diminished." There is some division of opinion in the courts as to whether this redundancy protection applies to dismissals resulting from changes in the work obligation or wholesale reorganisations of the business. From a technical viewpoint, the question is whether it is requirements of the business for *employees* or for *work* which is emphasised. The former allows for protection of employees dismissed; the latter protects the business. From a policy viewpoint, the question is whether the employer's interest in the business or the employees' interests in employment or compensation are paramount. An early case demonstrated a tendency to favour employers' interests where changes are made.

North Riding Garages Ltd. v. Butterwick
[1967] I.T.R. 229
Queen's Bench Division

> The workshop manager at a garage was asked by the new owners, following a take-over of the business, to undertake new duties, including the giving of estimates of repair costs to customers. When he was unable to undertake this task adequately, he was dismissed. At an Industrial Tribunal his claim for a redundancy payment succeeded on the grounds that the employer's requirements for a workshop manager, the duties previously undertaken by the employee, had ceased when they reorganised the garage.

WIDGERY J.: It is, we think, important to observe that a claim under [what has been re-enacted as EPCA, s.81(2)(*b*)] is conditional upon a change in the requirements of the business. If the requirement of the business for employees to carry out work of a particular kind increases or remains constant no redundancy payment can be claimed by an employee, in work of that kind, whose dismissal is attributable to personal deficiencies which prevent him from satisfying his employer. The very fact of dismissal shows that the employee's services are no longer required by his employer and that he may, in a popular sense, be said to have become redundant. But if the dismissal was attributable to age, physical disability or inability to meet his employer's standards he was not dismissed on account of redundancy within the meaning of the Act. For the purpose of this Act an employee who remains in the same kind of work is expected to adapt himself to new methods and techniques and cannot complain if his employer insists on higher standards of efficiency than those previously required; but if new methods alter the nature of the work required to be done it may follow that no requirement remains for employees to do work of the particular kind which has been superseded and that they are truly redundant. Thus if a motor manufacturer decides to use plastics instead of wood in the bodywork of his cars and dismisses his woodworkers, they may well be entitled to redundancy payments on the footing that their dismissal is attributable to a cessation of the requirement of the business for employees to carry out work of a particular kind, namely woodworking.

If one looks at the primary facts disclosed by the evidence in this case, it is difficult to see what is the particular kind of work in which a requirement for employees has ceased or diminished. The vehicle workshop remained, as did the requirement for a workshop manager, and we do not understand the Tribunal to have found that the volume of repair work had diminished to such an extent as to make the respondent's dismissal wholly or mainly attributable to that fact. The only possible conclusion which appears to us to have been open to the Tribunal on the evidence was that the respondent was dismissed because he could not do his job in accordance with the new methods and new standards required by the appellants.

Cf. Murphy v. *Epsom College*, p. 85 below.

The same considerations are apparent in the following case, where policy was emphasised in terms similar to those in the cases on unfair dismissal: reorganisations for "efficiency" are not redundancies either.

Johnson v. Nottinghamshire Combined Police Authority

[1974] I.R.L.R. 20
Court of Appeal

The appellants were female clerks at a police station working from 9.30 a.m. to 5.30 or 6.00 p.m. Monday to Friday. The police proposed that they should work separate shifts: one from 8.00 a.m. to 3.00 p.m. and the other from 1.00 p.m. to 8.00 p.m. six days a week, exchanging rotas each week. This involved the same number of hours as they had worked before and there would be no change in the actual work. The women refused to accept the change because it could not be fitted in with their home duties. They were dismissed, and two other ladies were appointed who were ready to undertake the new hours. An Industrial Tribunal and the N.I.R.C. rejected their claim for redundancy payments.

Lord Denning M.R.: . . . an employer is entitled to reorganise his business so as to improve its efficiency and, in so doing, to propose to his staff a change in the terms and conditions of their employment: and to dispense with their services if they do not agree. Such a change does not automatically give the staff a right to redundancy payments. It only does so if the change in the terms and conditions is due to a redundancy situation. The question in every case is: was the change due to a redundancy situation, or not? If the change is due to a redundancy situation, he is entitled to a redundancy payment. If it is not due to it, he is not.

Typical of redundancy situations are these: there may be a recession in trade so that not so many men are needed. There may be a change in the kind of work done, as from wood to fibre glass, so that woodworkers are no longer needed (see *Hindle* v. *Percival Boats* [1969] 1 WLR 174). The business may be no longer profitable so that the employer has to cut down somewhere. Or, he may be overstaffed. The employer may meet such a situation by dispensing with the services of some of the men or alternatively he may lower the wages or put men on part time. If he does it by making a change in the terms and conditions of employment, it is due to a redundancy situation. Those who lose or leave their work in consequence are entitled to redundancy payments.

It is often difficult to know whether the employer's proposals are due to a redundancy situation or not. But at this point the statute comes in to help the employee by providing that he is presumed to be dismissed by reason of redundancy: see [now EPCA, s.91(2)]. So in all the cases where there is a change in the terms and conditions of employment, it is for the employer to prove that it was done for efficiency, and not so as to meet a redundancy situation.

It remains to apply these principles to a change in hours of work. It is a change in the terms and conditions of employment. It does not automatically give rise to a right to redundancy payments. If the employer proves that it was due to a reorganisation so as to achieve more efficient working, the man is not entitled to redundancy payments . . . .

. . . . If the employer requires the same number of employees as before—for the same tasks as before—but requires them at different hours, there is no redundancy situation. If the change in hours is unfair to a particular employee, in the situation in which she finds herself, it might give rise to a claim for unfair dismissal . . . : but it does not give rise to a redundancy payment. [See Lord Denning M.R. in *Hollister*, above, p. 67.]

In the present case the police authorities proved that the change in the hours of work was not due to a redundancy situation, but to a reorganisation in the interests of efficiency. The same work was done by the ladies afterwards as it was before. But they did it at different hours. I think that the Industrial Tribunal and the [N.I.R.C.] were quite right. I would dismiss the appeal.

Stephenson L.J.: I will assume that an alteration of method or hour or of the type of person employed or of status or responsibility—or even of remuneration—may alter the work done to such an extent that it would in common sense be regarded as a different task or job so that the change required by the employer and rejected by the employee would be a change in kind. No longer would an employee be said to do the same job or the employer to require the same task to be performed. But that is not the case. If these appellants were asked, "Why did you leave your job?" they might answer, "Because it isn't the job it was." But if asked, "Who is doing your job now?", I doubt if either of them would reply, "Nobody. It has gone, or been done away with." It has not. It is the same job done to a different time schedule.

The next case was a determined effort to avoid the strict consequences of the *Johnson* case.

Kykot v. Smith Hartley Ltd.
[1975] I.R.L.R. 372
Queen's Bench Division

Mr Kykot's employers reorganised his working hours so that, instead of working on the night shift, as he had done since 1967, he was to work a rotating day shift. The reorganisation was occasioned by the desire of another night worker to change to day work. Mr

Kykot refused to accept the change and left. Subsequently, the night shift ceased. A Leeds Industrial Tribunal, relying on the *Johnson* case (above p. 80), held that the reason for the dismissal was not redundancy.

PHILLIPS J.: I think the Tribunal is saying that the case before them was on all-fours with *Johnson's* case, and that *Johnson's* case laid down propositions of law to be applied in all cases where what is in issue is a change in the hours to be worked. But, the facts in *Johnson's* case . . . are different from those in the present case . . . . It is quite plain that in the present case there was a reduction in the total number of persons employed. Indeed, the whole of the night shift was being closed down and not all those thereby released were being absorbed in the day shift . . . .

There is a second difference in circumstances between *Johnson's* case . . . and this case; that is, there was a good deal of evidence (about which I express no view) that, . . . there was a falling-off in trade. There was a recession . . . . All *Johnson's* case is saying is that, if there is a reorganisation with the aim of improving efficiency, and persons have to be moved from one shift to another (a change which they may not be required to accept, because the conditions of their contracts of employment do not require it), it cannot be said automatically that in those circumstances there is what Lord Denning has called "a redundancy situation" . . . .

In truth, all these cases of redundancy claims ultimately raise questions of fact and the decided cases are only of value in enunciating the principles. For that purpose, and by way of illustration as to what happens in particular circumstances, they are, of course, extremely valuable. I am not saying for a moment that *Johnson's* case is irrelevant to the situation in this case, but it has to be remembered that there were important points of distinction, which I repeat for clarity: firstly, the reorganisation, as I read it, did result in fewer people being employed; secondly, there was a background of recession at the time . . . .

. . . in an ordinary case, as I understand it, if there is a situation which could be described as a redundancy situation and which requires two fewer persons to be employed in the business than heretofore, the fact that work is offered to the applicant in a part of the business to which he cannot, in accordance with his contract, be required to transfer does not necessarily prevent him from having a claim on the grounds of the dismissal which arises, because he refuses to take up that work, being by reason of redundancy . . . .

There is one other point which was argued, about which I should say a word. The Tribunal decided, as I have explained already, that the applicant was employed as a "weaver full stop" and not as a "weaver on the night shift." That is, of course, eminently a question of fact for the Tribunal, but there is room for the belief (and I say no more) that its members reached the conclusion which they did by treating it almost, if not entirely, as a question of law out of deference to the decision in *Johnson's* case. It is not a question of law, nor does *Johnson's* case say that it is. *Johnson's* case merely indicates some of the relevant considerations.

Phillips J.'s attempted distinction was subsequently reduced in impact by the Court of Appeal's reiteration of the *Johnson* principle, again emphasising the policy issue. In the following case, the benefit to employers and detriment to workers were explicit.

Lesney Products & Co. Ltd. v. Nolan
[1977] I.R.L.R. 77
Court of Appeal

Because of falling sales, the employer eliminated the nightshift and reorganised the single day shift with overtime into two day shifts. All those who had been working the existing day shift were offered employment on the new double day shift. Those who refused, including Mrs Nolan, were dismissed.

LORD DENNING M.R.: Now the matter comes before this Court. I must say that it is a difficult case. The relevant principles were stated by this Court in *Johnson* v *Nottinghamshire Combined Police Authority* [1974] I.R.L.R 20 . . . [see above p. 80].

In applying that principle, it is important that nothing should be done to impair the ability of employers to reorganise their work force and their terms and conditions of work so as to improve efficiency. They may re-organise it so as to reduce overtime and thus to save themselves money, but that does not give the man a right to redundancy payment. Overtime might be reduced, for instance, by taking on more men: but that would not give the existing staff a right to redundancy payments. Also when overtime is reduced by a re-organisation of working hours, that does not give rise to a right to redundancy payment, so long as the work to be done is the same.

It seems to me that the problem in the case is whether this re-organisation—whereby the one long day shift plus overtime was altered into two day shifts for the machine setters—was done in the interests of efficiency or whether it was due to a drop in the amount of work required for the men employed in the factory. The employers gave evidence (which was not contradicted) that the amount of work coming into the factory and being done on the day shifts by all the direct operatives was just the same as before. There was no reduction in it. The night shift was done away with for want of work—and on that accord the night shift people would get redundancy payments. But the day shifts turned out the same amount of work by the same number of women operatives . . . .

. . . the re-organisation was not done because of less work but it was done in the interests of efficiency and to save the employers having to pay so much overtime . . . .

No doubt the men at work would not get as much overtime as they had done under the previous system. But the company had a scheme for alleviating the position. The men got compensation in that they received the basic wage plus $17\frac{1}{2}$ per cent. shift premium. It seems that on average a person who previously received £70 a week might now only be getting £54. So there was to that extent a saving in the money which the company spent on overtime.

An unrepentant Phillips J. still found a way to avoid the combined effect of the *Johnson* and *Lesney* cases.

Robinson v. British Island Airways Ltd.
[1977] I.R.L.R. 477
Employment Appeal Tribunal

Captain Robinson was employed as Flight Operations Manager reporting to the General Manager Operations and Traffic. The employers carried out a re-organisation which involved the replace-

> ment of the General Manager Operations and Traffic by an Operations Manager who absorbed the duties of the Flight Operations Manager. As Captain Robinson was adjudged not to have suitable qualities for the new post of Operations Manager, he was declared redundant.

PHILLIPS J.: Cases concerning redundancy arising out of a re-organisation always cause difficulties. Certain passages in some of the judgments in *Johnson* v *Nottinghamshire Combined Police Authority* [1974] I.R.L.R. 20 (see p. 80 above) and *Lesney Products & Co. Ltd.* v. *Nolan* [1977] I.R.L.R 77 (see p. 83 above) have been taken as suggesting that if a dismissal has been caused by a re-organisation the reason for the dismissal cannot be redundancy. We do not think that this is the meaning of the passages, or what was intended. In truth a re-organisation may or may not end in redundancy; it all depends on the nature and effect of the re-organisation. In *Johnson* v *Nottinghamshire Combined Police Authority* there was no redundancy because in the opinion of the Court of Appeal the change in the hours of work involved in that case did not change the particular kind of work being carried on. In *Lesney Products & Co. Ltd.* v. *Nolan* there was no redundancy because on the correct analysis of the facts (it was in the analysis of the facts that the Appeal Tribunal and the Industrial Tribunal were in error) there was no cessation or diminution of the requirement for employees to carry out work of a particular kind. The number of employees and the nature of the work remained the same, and all that changed was the ability to earn overtime. What has to be done in every case is to analyse the facts and to match the analysis against the words of [now EPCA, s.81]. In doing this it is of no assistance to consider whether as a matter of impression there was or was not a "redundancy situation." The question is whether the definition is satisfied . . . .

There is no doubt that Captain Robinson was dismissed. To what was his dismissal attributable? It seems to us that the work done by the flight operations manager was of a "particular kind" and that the work done by the general manager operations and traffic was of a "particular kind," and that each kind was different from the other. It seems to us that the work done by the operations manager was of a "particular kind" and of a kind different from that done by the general manager operations and traffic and different from that done by flight operations manager. Thus in our judgment it can truly be said that the dismissal of Captain Robinson was attributable to the fact that the requirements of the business for employees to carry out work of a particular kind had ceased or diminished and that each was redundant.

If this were wrong, we should be inclined to say that the circumstances constituted "some other substantial reason of a kind such as to justify the dismissal of an employee holding the position which that employee held." It seems to us that where there is a genuine re-organisation which has dislodged an employee who cannot be fitted into the re-organisation it must be open to the employer to dismiss him. But we prefer to think that in those circumstances he will usually be redundant, and thus entitled to a redundancy payment.

Other cases have reinforced the views of Phillips J. In *Carry All Motors Ltd.* v. *Pennington* [1980] I.R.L.R. 455 (E.A.T.), an employee was dismissed and his duties taken over by another employee. Waterhouse J. rejected the argument that there was no redundancy: "The effect of that interpretation would be to diminish quite drastically the protection afforded to employers (*sic*) by the redundancy provisions." Intentional or otherwise, the reference to protection of employers by the redundancy law is revealing, for it is acknowledged that redundancy payments are a major factor enabling employers to achieve reorganisations by undercutting resistance by the workforce (see below, *Quantity of Work*, at p. 113 *et seq.*) These policy considerations were explicit in another recent case.

Murphy v. Epsom College
[1983] I.R.L.R. 395
Employment Appeal Tribunal

> One of two plumbers was dismissed when the employer decided to dismiss one of them and appoint a heating technician to be responsible for all heating installations. An Industrial Tribunal held the dismissal was on grounds, *inter alia*, of redundancy.

BROWNE-WILKINSON J.: . . . if the College still required two general plumbers after the appointment of the new technician a much more difficult question arises. Can it be said that there is a reduction in the College's requirement for employees to do the work of a particular kind if there is neither a reduction in the number of employees required nor any reduction in the amount of work the employees have to do? On this basis, what happened was the mere re-allocation of the same quantity of work between the same number of employees, the new employee taking over some of the functions of the employee who was dismissed . . . .

. . . It is nowadays a common occurrence that employers need to re-organise so as to re-allocate functions between employees. If, for example, some new technology requires the introduction into the work force of an employee with a new skill, it may be a prudent and necessary management decision to include in the job of the new employee all or some of the functions previously performed by existing employees: in consequence, although there is no reduction in the overall work requirement of the business doing such work, the employer no longer requires the services of the employee who formerly carried out the functions which have been added to those of the new employee. In our judgment, the employee so dismissed may in some circumstances be dismissed by reason of redundancy flowing from that reorganisation.

[EPCA] s.81 does not refer to diminution in the requirements of a business for work of a particular kind: it deals with the diminution in the requirements of the business *for employees* to carry out work of a particular kind. In order to discover whether or not an employee is redundant, it is necessary first to identify what "particular kind" of work the employee was doing, and then to ask if there has been a diminution in the requirement for employees to do work of that kind. In the sort of case we are considering, the "kind of work" done by the old employee is the combination of the functions comprised in his job. If there are minor additions to, or subtractions from, those functions, then the particular kind of work he does will essentially remain the same. But if his job description is fundamentally changed by a re-organisation transferring substantial functions from him to another employee, if retained in employment he would no longer be doing work of the same "particular kind" as he had been doing hitherto. In each case it will be for the Industrial Tribunal to decide whether the re-organisation and re-allocation of functions is such as to change the particular kind of work he is employed to do.

In the present case, Mr Murphy, a plumber, was engaged on work of a kind involving a combination of general plumbing and heating (other than steam and industrial plant): he had no overall responsibility for heating. The requirement of the employers changed: their requirement was for a heating technician with overall responsibility for heating who could help out with the steam and industrial plant and also with general plumbing. In our judgment it was open to the Industrial Tribunal to hold that the re-organisation involved a fundamental change in the particular kind of work (being the combination of functions performed by Mr Murphy) required by the employers. If so, the employers ceased to require an employee to carry out work of the particular kind done by Mr Murphy and he was dismissed for redundancy . . . . [The E.A.T. then cited *Robinson*'s case [1977] I.R.L.R. 477 [above p. 83] as supporting their view and continued:]

. . . In [the *Butterwick*] case [1967] I.T.R. 299 [above p. 79] there was no suggestion that there was a new function to be performed by a new employee, such function not being previously covered by any employee. The case was simply concerned with a minor alteration in functions between existing employees . . . . Moreover, the decision of the Divisional Court was made soon after the concept of redundancy was first introduced into the law and before the complications of the subject had been appreciated . . . [If *Butterwick*] states a general proposition that attention has to be concentrated on the overall requirements of the business for work rather than on the requirements of the business *for employees* to do work of a particular kind, we must respectfully decline to follow it.

The Court of Appeal dismissed the appeal: [1984] I.R.L.R. 271.

The alleged distinction between minor job changes (no redundancy) and major changes and new job functions (redundancy) is undermined by the practice of express contractual job definitions of great breadth. It might then be argued that a major change in actual activity was merely another part of an employee's job as defined in the contract—and hence *not* a redundancy. The E.A.T. confronted this issue in the following case.

Cowen v. Haden Carrier Ltd.
[1982] I.R.L.R. 225; [1983] I.C.R. 1
Employment Appeal Tribunal

Mr Cowen's contract of employment provided that he would be required to undertake "any and all duties which reasonably fall within the scope of his capabilities." He was originally employed as a regional surveyor, but after a heart attack was given the new post of divisional contracts surveyor. When the company decided they could do without a divisional contracts surveyor, Mr Cowen was dismissed.

BROWNE-WILKINSON J.: If one simply reads the words of [EPCA] section 81(2) themselves, there is nothing in them which requires one to look at the terms of the particular claimant's contract of employment. What the Act on its face requires is that one should look at the business of the employer to see whether there is a diminution in the requirements of that business for employees to carry out work of a particular kind, unrelated to any definition

> of the work which the particular employee who is making the claim can be required to do. In practice, in the experience of all of us on this Tribunal a redundancy is accepted as having been shown where it is demonstrated that the actual job which the claimant was carrying out had ceased to exist. . . .
>
> [However, the E.A.T. was referred to two decisions of the Court of Appeal in *Nelson* v *B.B.C.* [1977] I.C.R. 649 and *Nelson* v. *B.B.C. (No. 2)* [1980] I.C.R. 110 and felt obliged to conclude as follows:]
>
> We are unable to treat the composite effect of those decisions of the Court of Appeal as being other than a decision binding on us that in considering section 81(2)(*b*) of the Act of 1978 it is not sufficient in order to establish redundancy to show merely that the requirements of the employers for employees to carry out work of the kind on which the employee was actually engaged had ceased or diminished: it is necessary to show such diminution or cessation in relation to any work that he could have been asked to do.

On appeal, the Court of Appeal in *Cowen* felt able to distinguish the two decisions in *Nelson* v. *B.B.C.*, but upheld the E.A.T.'s decision on different grounds. It nonetheless appeared to support the principle reluctantly endorsed by the E.A.T. that major changes in job functions, provided they fall within the contractual definition of job duties, do not constitute redundancy (*Haden Ltd.* v. *Cowen* [1982] I.R.L.R. 314 (C.A.)). Judicial control of the work obligation thus allows for considerable manipulation of the results of claims, as the *Cowen* case illustrates—the E.A.T. and the Court of Appeal each defined the employee's work obligation differently. But employers are able, by careful drafting of broadly phrased job descriptions, to impose changes on employees without risk of liability for redundancy payments. The irony is in that employers may often be only too glad to provide redundancy payments in order to secure employee co-operation in reorganisations. In both *Cowen* and *Nelson* the employer purported to make the employees redundant with appropriate payments. It was the employees who rejected these and claimed unfair dismissal. And in the case of broad and flexible job definitions, as Browne-Wilkinson J. put it in *Cowen*: "It will render it exceptionally difficult for employers to establish a case of redundancy" [1982] I.R.L.R. 225, para. 21).

The cases demonstrate that there is no consistent judicial policy on whether reorganisations will be facilitated by allowing employees dismissed to claim redundancy payments. The Court of Appeal under Lord Denning seemed reluctant to allow such claims, taking the view that it might obstruct change. Some judges in the E.A.T., more aware of employee resistance, have tended to favour allowing redundancy claims in the circumstances of changes or reorganisations at work, thus undermining employees' resistance.

It may be, however, that the changing industrial relations climate of the 1980s, in a context of high unemployment, would enable employers to impose changes and reorganisations even without the inducement of redundancy payments. A case in point is to be found in the contrasting judgments of the Industrial Tribunal, the E.A.T. and the Court of Appeal in *Gloucestershire County Council* v. *Spencer* [1985] I.R.L.R. 59 (E.A.T.); [1985] I.R.L.R. 393 (C.A.). To reduce costs, the employers proposed to reduce the number of school cleaners from five to four, and to reduce the hours of the remaining cleaners by three-quarters of an hour per week. The employers accepted that as a result the cleaning standards in the school would necessarily be lower. The employees who were offered alternative employment on the new terms refused on the ground that they did not think they could do a satisfactory job in the new conditions. The Industrial Tribunal, by a majority, upheld their claims to redundancy payments. The E.A.T. unanimously allowed an appeal: "It is not for an employee to determine what standard is appropriate for an employer to achieve" (*per* Popplewell J., p. 60). The Court of Appeal, while not dissenting from this view, allowed the employees' appeal that it was nonetheless reasonable on the facts "to refuse to work to the standards which the employer wishes to set" (*per* Neill L.J., p. 395).

Similar conflicts have arisen over whether employees dismissed following reductions in the workforce after transfer of an undertaking can claim redundancy payments despite Regulation 8(2) of the Transfer of Undertakings (Protection of Employment) Regulations (see above p. 73). In two cases (*Meikle* v. *McPhail (Charlston Arms)* [1983] I.R.L.R. 351 (E.A.T.), and *Canning* v. *(1) Niaz and (2) McLoughlin* [1983] I.R.L.R. 431 (E.A.T.), redundancy claims were rejected. In three others: *Gorictree Ltd.* v. *Jenkinson* [1984] I.R.L.R. 391 (E.A.T.); *(1) Anderson and (2) McAlonie* v. *Dalkeith Engineering Ltd.* [1984] I.R.L.R. 429 (E.A.T.); and *McGrath* v. *Rank Leisure Ltd.* [1985] I.R.L.R. 323 (E.A.T.); redundancy claims have been allowed.

(*B*) *Bilateral Changes Agreed Between Employers and Trade Unions*

Many organised workers have gained some control over changes at work by negotiating collective agreements whereby employers undertake certain obligations in cases of proposed changes, particularly where new technology is involved. These include provisions containing safeguards on the following matters.

(i) Anticipating changes

(*a*) *Advance notice and information*

An Agreement between APEX and the General Accident Fire and Life Assurance Corporation (237 Industrial Relations Review and Report 12)

1. The corporation will advise APEX of outline proposals to commence research on projects or feasibility studies which could include the consideration of new technologies.

2. The corporation will provide in writing to APEX, details of specific proposals for the introduction, extension or changing of applications involving new technologies which could affect working arrangements, skill requirements, job numbers, job levels or working conditions.

(b) Joint machinery: discussion, consultation, negotiation

An Agreement between ASTMS and the Scottish Provident Institution (234 Industrial Relations Review and Report 16)

(b) The productivity and new technology committee will discuss the general implications of any specific proposal following which the proposal will be the subject of departmental consultation. In many cases this will consist of the staff being given details of the proposals and their implications and the opportunity to ask questions and make comment. A departmental representative of the association appointed by the executive committee of the ASTMS/SPI Group will be involved in these discussions. Where a major application of new technology or new techniques is proposed or one which may present special difficulties, it will be open to the productivity and new technology committee to recommend that a departmental working party should be set up to investigate and report on specific aspects or applications. [ASTMS] would be represented on such working parties. The points to be investigated would normally include some or all of the following:

(i) the type of equipment or system and its siting;
(ii) the skills needed to operate or service or work with it;
(iii) manpower requirements;
(iv) any likely changes in job gradings;
(v) the expected introduction date of the new system and plan of expected progress during the time leading up to that date;
(vi) training and retraining requirements;
(vii) health and safety requirements.

(c) On completion of departmental consultation or when a copy of the working party report is available the proposal will be referred back to the productivity and new technology committee for further consideration.

(d) The management will then take a decision on the introduction of new technology and new techniques taking into account the views of the productivity and new technology committee and comments made during departmental consultation.

(ii) Introducing changes

(a) Status quo clauses

The TASS Model New Technology Agreement (246 Industrial Relations Review and Report 14)

(i) The introduction of all such new methods or equipment and any consequential changes in working conditions shall be the subject of mutual agreement between the company and the union.

(ii) Failing such agreement the *status quo* will prevail.

(iii) Before the introduction of any specific new method or equipment, detailed written agreement shall be reached and incorporated in this agreement as an appendix.

(b) Trial periods

The Code of Practice in the Electricity Power Supply Industry (236 Industrial Relations Review and Report 13)

(i) Where joint acceptance has been reached for the introduction of "equipment" [it] may be introduced for a trial period during which consultation shall continue to take place. If during the consultative process either party considers it necessary to invoke the disputes procedure this shall be done in sufficient time for it to be exhausted before the trial period ends.

(ii) If during the trial period it is accepted that the "equipment" can operate on a continuing operational basis any dispute subsequently arising shall be dealt with under the disputes procedure.

(c) Training and re-training

An Agreement between ASTMS and the Zurich Insurance Company (243 Industrial Relations Review and Report 14)

5.1. New technology will, in those areas where it is introduced, to some degree change the skills required by the company and, therefore both the company and [ASTMS] agree that retraining is a vital component in its introduction.

5.2. Priority will be given to those employees whose jobs are most directly affected by technological change.

5.3. During any period of retraining the salary of the individual will be maintained.

(d) Health and safety: operational conditions

An Agreement between APEX and the International Harvester Co. of Great Britain Ltd. (297 Industrial Relations Review and Report 15)

The company recognises that the environmental standards, location and use of new technological equipment is subject to continuous research. Improvements designed to safeguard the health and safety of the operators will be introduced at any appropriate time. . . .

Any complaints re working conditions should be raised by the employees concerned with their immediate supervisor and with the involvement of grade representatives and department manager, if necessary.

3.1 *Noise*: Noise levels will be controlled to avoid any irritating frequencies or continuous low frequency humming.

3.2 *Heating:* The minimum temperature required by legislation is to be maintained.

3.3 *Ventilation:* In all areas where electric/electronic/mechanical data process equipment is to be installed suitable air cleaning and air circulation equipment should be installed.

3.4 *Ergonomic Layout:* A minimum working area is to be determined for all employees operating new technological equipment, and where practicable the equipment should be adjustable to suit the requirements of the individual operator.

3.5 *Equipment:* The full manufacturer's specification of all equipment will be made available to the union during the joint discussions.

(iii) Monitoring changes

An Agreement between APEX and the Humber Graving Dock and Engineering Co. (232 Industrial Relations Review and Report 11)

The management agrees to provide sufficient information to the union to enable it to: monitor developments, changes in workflow, changes in working methods and the effects on jobs, assess the effect of any further proposed introduction of computer based systems, analyse health and safety effects and general working environment.

This information to include the management's long-term plans on the introduction of new technology. This information will be provided quarterly on a regular basis and as requested by the union where specific proposals are under consideration.

(iv) Job and income security

(a) Redundancies, redeployment and pay

See Chapter 4 on *Quantity of Work.*

(b) Job descriptions and satisfaction

An Agreement between APEX and Plessey Telecommunications (215 Industrial Relations Review and Report 15)

Staff operating the new system will not be given additional tasks which are not covered by the agreed systems without prior consultation with the trade union.

It is not the intention of the system to de-skill or fragment jobs, nor to introduce greater routine since these are not only harmful to job satisfaction, but may also be a self-defeating approach to improved productivity and the aims of the system.

The parties agree that the maximum flexibility shall exist to develop working methods that provide satisfying jobs and that an agreed positive programme of manpower and job development will be introduced with the object of increasing the responsibility and autonomy of job groups and employees, as well as seeking to enhance job content and enlarged personal status for employees covered by this agreement.

(v) Getting the benefits

(a) Reductions in work-time

The TUC New Technology Agreement Issues Checklist (240 Industrial Relations Review and Report 12)

c. Longer holidays, sabbaticals and early retirement on improved pensions can all be pursued in bargaining about new technology and attempting to reduce working time. The reduction or elimination of systematic overtime should be a bargaining priority.

d. Where new technology produces an increase in shift-working this should be accompanied by a reduction in hours worked. The flexibility associated with microelectronic technology can be used to change shift patterns to bring about a greater intensity of capital utilisation and shorter working hours.

(b) Pay and productivity

Changes at work are obviously an opportunity for re-negotiation of rates of pay and re-evaluation of jobs. Various methods can be found in collective agreements to extract some of the benefits:

(i) a percentage of the factory's wages bill is set aside for distribution over and above normal wages;
(ii) a proportional distribution of the benefits calculated as between employer and workers;
(iii) specific payments made against specific changes, lump-sum or regular periodic payments;
(iv) re-evaluation of jobs leading to up-grading or increments.

3. QUALITY CONTROL OF WORK

Various methods of quality control of work exist: through professional examinations and apprenticeship schemes; through management supervision enforced through sanctions of discipline and dismissal; through publicly enforced standards (*eg* licensing of heavy goods vehicle drivers). The law intervenes very substantially in each of these methods of control—not least through the national system of industrial training.

(A) Legislation on Industrial Training

B. Bercusson, "Labour Law" in MORE LAW REFORM NOW (A. Martin and P. Archer eds., 1983, pp. 261, 263)

Unlike its predecessors, the Industrial Training Act 1964 and the Employment and Training Act 1973, the Employment and Training Act 1981 was the subject of heated party political exchanges during its passage through Parliament. [The three statutes have now been consolidated into the Industrial Training Act 1982.] The 1964 Act was a response by the Conservative

Government to the problems of shortages of skilled labour and wide variations in quality and standards of training. The 1964 Act established a statutory framework: it empowered the Secretary of State for Employment to establish Industrial Training Boards (ITBs) with a view to resolving these problems. In 1973 the Conservative Government introduced the 1973 Act which established the Manpower Services Commission (MSC) with broad supervisory responsibilities. That Act amended the 1964 Act (s.1(1)) to provide that the Secretary of State may establish an ITB "if the MSC submits to him proposals that he should do so. . . ." The 1981 Act repealed that phrase and substituted a power of the Secretary of State to establish an ITB without any proposal from the MSC, but subject to certain procedures. More ominously, the 1981 Act conferred a similar enabling power on the Secretary of State with respect to abolition or changing the scope of an ITB . . .

Both the 1964 and the 1973 Acts were passed with bipartisan support in Parliament. The 1981 Act and the Conservative Government's use of it to abolish ITBs has destroyed this consensus. . . . The MSC's 1980 Review concluded (Chapter 8.6):

> The existing basic statutory framework for influencing training within industry has a number of important strengths which are relevant to all of our priority objectives for training in the 1980s. Those strengths have not been fully exploited in the particular arrangements set out in the 1973 Act or developed since. The right approach for the future is to build upon them and not to cast them aside.

One particular point needs attention. Up to 1981, the decision of an ITB to impose a levy on employers in the industry to finance its training activities was made by a majority of the "representative" members of the ITB (those representing either employers or employees, excluding independents). The 1981 Act changed this by providing that a majority of employer members must vote in favour. The decision as to the size of the levy and the level of training services is thus effectively in the hands of the employers.

(*B*) *Employer Control*

The contract of employment includes a warranty by the employee of his competence, which entitles the employer to control the quality of the work done.

Harmer v. Cornelius
(1858) 5 C.B. (N.S.) 236

> The defendant advertised in a newspaper for "two first-rate scene painters." The plaintiff replied enclosing a picture of an example of his work. He was engaged but dismissed within two days for incompetence. His claim for wrongful dismissal failed on the ground that his incompetence constituted a breach of an implied warranty of competence.

WILLES J.: When a skilled labourer, artisan or artist is employed, there is, on his part, an implied warranty that he is of skill reasonably competent to the task he undertakes—*spondes peritiam artis.* Thus if an apothecary, a watchmaker, or an attorney be employed for reward, they each impliedly undertake to possess and exercise reasonable skill in their several arts. . . .

It may be that, if there is no general and no particular representation of ability and skill, the workman undertakes no responsibility. If a gentleman, for example, should employ a man who is known to have never done anything but sweep a crossing to clean and mend his watch, the employer probably would be held to have incurred all risks himself. . . .

Misconduct in a servant is, according to every day's experience, a justification of a discharge. The failure to afford the requisite skill which had been expressly or impliedly promised is a breach of a legal duty, and therefore misconduct. . . .

The policy problems which confront judges in litigation concern which sanctions are available to employers to maintain the quality of their employees' work. A great deal of judicial authority exists on certain sanctions, such as fines, which are not much used in modern industry. There is also a developing common law on dismissal for incompetence (see Chapter 10 on *Termination of Work*). Other sanctions have so far attracted less judicial attention.

(i) Fines and deductions

The Truck Act of 1896 was concerned solely with the regulation of fines and deductions. The Act gave rise to arid questions of whether different ways of formulating systems of wage payment varying with the quality of the work avoided the statutory regulation of fines and deductions. One case dealing with these statutory provisions sheds considerable light on the once common method of control by fines for bad work.

Sagar v. Ridehalgh and Sons Ltd.
[1931] 1 Ch. 310
Court of Appeal

LAWRENCE L.J.: The employers based their contention on two alternative grounds: either that the established practice of making reasonable deductions for bad work in the defendants' mill was incorporated into the plaintiff's contract of service by reason of his having agreed to be employed upon the same terms as the other weavers in that mill, or else that the general usage of making reasonable deductions for bad work prevailing in the cotton weaving trade of Lancashire was so well known and understood that every weaver engaging in that trade must be taken to have entered upon his employment on the footing of that usage.

As regards the first of these grounds, it is clearly established by the evidence of Mr George Ridehalgh that the practice of making reasonable deductions for bad work has continuously prevailed at the defendants' mill for upwards of thirty years, and that during the whole of that time all weavers employed by the defendants have been treated alike in that respect. The practice was therefore firmly established at the defendants' mill when the plaintiff entered upon his employment there. . . .

In the result, I have come to the conclusion that the practice of making reasonable deductions for bad work prevailing at the defendants' mill was incorporated in the plaintiff's contract of service.

Further, I am of opinion that the second ground is also established by the evidence—namely, that the practice in the defendants' mill is in accordance with the general usage of making reasonable deductions for bad work prevailing in the weaving trade of Lancashire, which usage, in the absence of any stipulation to the contrary, would be incorporated into every contract of service as a weaver in a Lancashire cotton mill without special mention. . . .

. . . the Truck Act, 1896, is directed to regulating a practice recognized to be lawfully existing and is not directed to enabling something to be done which could not lawfully have been done previously.

Generally on the Truck Acts 1831–1940, see Chapter 7 on *Discipline at Work.*

(ii) Suspension

Suspension is an increasingly common sanction since it allows the employer time in which to make the enquiries which are often necessary if the employee's eventual dismissal is to be upheld as fair. In such circumstances, employees may be suspended on full pay. By contrast, the suspension of employees without pay may be a breach of the contractual obligation to pay remuneration in return for readiness to work: see Chapter 7 on *Discipline at Work.*

(iii) Dismissal

The ultimate sanction for lack of quality will be dismissal of the worker. The availability to employers of this sanction will generally nowadays depend on the remedy of unfair dismissal for alleged lack of competence. For detailed consideration of this question, see Chapter 10 on *Termination of Work.*

4. SAFETY AND JOB CONTENT

In this section we ask to what extent the pursuit of safety should limit the work obligation. Unfortunately this question can only be answered by looking at cases concerned with the assignment of blame for and the disposition of damages claims after an accident. The Health and Safety at Work Act 1974 indicates that rules can be developed to prevent injury separately from rules governing compensation.

(A) Assignment of Particular Work to Those Not Competent To Do It

Ross v. Associated Portland Cement Manufacturers Ltd.
[1964] 1 W.L.R. 768
House of Lords

Mr Ross was instructed to repair a badly dilapidated wire safety net, 22 feet above the ground. He was a steel erector and this was an unusual job for which he was given no instructions or proper equipment. To reach the job he leant a ladder on the netting. As he ascended the ladder, part of the netting collapsed and he fell to the ground.

LORD REID: I need not describe the circumstances in greater detail because the uncontradicted evidence of the only expert called was that it was obviously unsafe to use a ladder in this way. And it follows from that that there was a clear breach of what is now s.29 of the Factories Act, 1961. . . . Ross's working place was the place where he was working near the top of the ladder and there is nothing to show that it was not reasonably practicable for the respondents to provide the equipment which the expert says ought to have been used—a movable platform.

The respondents' case is that they were not at all to blame because they were entitled to leave it to Ross to decide what to do and to come to their chief engineer if he wanted further help or equipment. They say that the cause, and the sole cause of the breach and resulting accident was Ross's mistaken decision, or negligence, in using the ladder when he ought to have seen that it was unsafe. This defence was accepted by the learned trial judge and by the Court of Appeal, but it seems to me quite unrealistic;. . . .

. . . I have no doubt that the respondents cannot wholly escape liability. The owner of a factory who has given proper instructions and has provided proper equipment cannot make provision against disobedience either of his own servant or of the servant of a contractor who is working in the factory. But it is his responsibility to see that proper instructions are given and proper equipment is available. Where the work is to be done by a person fully skilled in that type of work he may say "go and plan out the work and come back and discuss the matter if you have any difficulty, or cannot find the equipment you need". But here Ross was only a chargehand, the respondents had no reason to suppose that he had ever done a job of this kind before, and there is nothing to show that the chief engineer gave him any encouragement to come back and discuss the matter. . . .

(B) Limiting the Work Obligation to Avoid Breach of Obligations as to Safety

Hamilton v. Western SMT Co. Ltd.
[1977] I.R.L.R. 439
Court of Session

The claimant was employed in the employer's cash room. One of her duties was to carry loaded boxes filled with money to a night safe 12 feet away. The boxes weighed about 85 pounds and were carried with the assistance of another female employee. On the day the accident in question occurred, the two women lifted such a box but the other dropped her end. This resulted in injury to Mrs Hamilton's back.

LORD MAXWELL: [The Offices, Shops and Railways Premises Act 1963] S.23(1) provides that "No person shall in the course of his work in premises to which this Act applies, be required to lift carry or move a load so heavy as to be likely to cause injury to him." Sub-section (2) empowers the Minister to make regulations laying down maximum weights in particular circumstances. I am informed that no such regulations were made under the section, which is no longer in force, though it was at the time of the accident. . . .

The absence of evidence of complaints or of prior injury is a matter to be taken into account, but cannot be fatal to the pursuer's claim. The fact that three women witnesses had all "managed" to do the job with varying degrees of difficulty or ease also must be taken into account but is not, I think, of much significance. The Act is not directed only against "impossible" loads. I suppose that in a case of this kind it might be possible to call expert opinion evidence, medical or otherwise, as to the danger of such loads, and that was not done in this case. But in my view it is open to the Court in a case under this section to approach the question in a "jury" fashion and to use its own judgment as to whether the load involved is of a kind likely to cause injury in the circumstances. Eighty-five pounds is a heavy weight—three-quarters of a hundredweight—even for two persons. In my opinion if women not particularly experienced or skilled in heavy work, being women of varying ages and physiques, are repeatedly required, acting in pairs to lift and shift boxes of this weight it is highly likely, that sooner or later one of them is going to suffer some kind of strain or other injury. I think that these boxes fully loaded were too heavy for female office staff working in pairs. I think that s.23(1) was breached and that that breach caused the accident. I shall accordingly find the defenders liable.

Contrast the following case:

White v. Holbrook Precision Castings Ltd.
[1985] I.R.L.R. 215
Court of Appeal

Mr White accepted a job as a grinder on higher wages than he was earning. After three years he complained of numbness in a finger and was diagnosed as having Reynaud's phenomenon. He was transferred to a less well-paid job, but claimed damages against his employers.

LAWTON L.J.: . . . what should an employer tell a prospective employee about the risks he will expose himself to if he takes the job? I have come to this conclusion. Generally speaking, if a job has risks to health and safety which are not common knowledge but of which an employer knows or ought to know and against which he cannot guard by taking precautions, then he should tell anyone to whom he is offering the job what those risks are if, on the information then available to him, knowledge of those risks would be likely to affect the decision of a sensible, level-headed prospective employee about accepting the offer.

Applying that test to the facts of this case I start with a finding of fact by the judge that the plaintiff did in fact take on the job, although he knew that his fellow workers were suffering from what they were describing as cold fingers or hot aches. There was nothing in the evidence to suggest that the plaintiff was not a sensible, level-headed young man. What was the position so far as the defendants knew or ought to have known on the information then available to them? It was that Raynaud's phenomenon caused minor discomfort which did not affect capacity for work at all in the vast majority of cases, and such inconvenience as it caused in the carrying on of hobbies was minor and trivial.

It seems to me that on the knowledge which would have been available to the defendants, had they had it, they would inevitably have come to the conclusion that the plaintiff whom they had been able to assess during the three months he worked as a labourer would have regarded Raynaud's phenomenon as something which was of no consequence at all when deciding to take on the job.

There is a difference between the work obligation and the various methods of carrying it out. If the work obligation is reasonably without risk, but the employee selects a risky method of carrying it out, the courts must decide whether the work obligation exposed the employee to the risk of injury or whether the risk was caused by the employee's free choice of a risky method. This uncertainty is well demonstrated in the opinions in the following case.

Black v. Carricks (Caterers) Ltd.
[1980] I.R.L.R. 448
Court of Appeal

Illness of other employees resulted in the plaintiff being left on her own at one of the defendants' bakers shops. She telephoned for instructions and was told to get on as best she could and, if she needed help, to ask a customer. She attempted to lift most of a pile of trays to disclose a loaf that a customer wanted, and in so doing injured her back.

MEGAW L.J. (for the majority): . . . the critical question is whether the defendants, via their acting supervisor, could reasonably have foreseen that the plaintiff's predicament in being temporarily deprived of assistance would bring about a situation in which, under some constraint imposed by her work, she would expose herself to the risk of the kind of injury she suffered in the circumstances which brought it about. . . . A number of uncertain factors combined to create the situation in which Mrs Black was imperilled. It was ill-fortune and not any negligence of the defendants which brought about her injury. . . .

PATRICK BROWNE L.J. (in the minority): I have found this a most difficult and anxious case, but in the end I have come to the conclusion that the defendants were in breach of their common law duty to the plaintiff. That duty was to take such care for her safety as was reasonable in all the circumstances. If the view I have taken of the evidence is right, the instructions given on behalf of the defendants to the plaintiff did expose her to a risk of injury, and a risk which did not exist in the ordinary course of her employment. I cannot regard this risk as trivial, since it involved a breach of the established system and practice of the shop, which was, no doubt, established for good reasons of safety. I accept that the defendants could not reasonably be expected to foresee the exact sort of accident which happened, but I think they ought to have foreseen the risk that the plaintiff might sustain some sort of accident and injury by handling the trays on her own. In the circumstances of this case, I do not see how this risk to the plaintiff could have been avoided except by telling her not to open the shop till help arrived. I can well understand the reluctance of the defendants not to open the shop, both for their own sake and the sake of their customers, but the fact that they were, as the judge said, providing a public service cannot exonerate them from their duty to their own staff. I can also understand that the defendants might have thought (if they had thought about it) that the chance of any injury to the plaintiff was slight but, in my view, they took the risk that such injury might happen and, when it did happen, they are liable.

(C) *Dismissal and Resignation on Grounds of Safety: When are they Justified?*

It is apparent from the above cases that the employer can enforce the work obligation if the employee receives proper instruction (see, *e.g. Horne* v. *Lec Refrigeration Ltd.* [1965] 2 All E.R. 898). If it is not possible to meet safety requirements, the employer must not impose the work obligation. In an extreme case, safety may justify termination of the relationship, by either party. In *Finch* v. *Betabake (Anglia) Ltd.* [1977] I.R.L.R. 470 (E.A.T.), Mr. Finch, an apprentice motor mechanic with defective eyesight, was dismissed following a medical report which stated that he could not be employed as a motor mechanic without "undue danger to himself and others." The E.A.T. agreed with an Industrial Tribunal which found the dismissal fair, holding: "The employers would be able to terminate . . . if they had good reason for believing that the apprentice was liable to cause injury to himself or to others through some form of incapacity." An employee who resigns on grounds of safety may be able to claim "constructive" dismissal by reason of the employers' conduct (as in *Pagano* v. *HGS* [1976] I.R.L.R. 9 (I.T.)).

Chapter 4

QUANTITY OF WORK

By quantity of work is meant the amount of work to be done by the worker. Three problems are addressed here: too much work, too little work and uniformity of working time.

1. TOO MUCH WORK

(A) Legal Control of Hours of Work

Working hours are a function of the contract of employment, often determined by collective agreements. The role of statute has historically been important: the campaign for the eight-hour day during the nineteenth century was a landmark in agitation for labour law. The common law, collective bargaining and legislation fixing hours of work must all confront the policy issues inherent in the conflicting interests of employers and employees in the intensity of work. Judicial choices are evident in the following cases.

Lake v. Essex County Council
[1979] I.R.L.R. 241; [1979] I.C.R. 577
Court of Appeal

A teacher's written terms of employment set out her hours of work as 19 hours, 25 minutes a week, including 3 hours and 40 minutes of "free time." She claimed she needed to, and actually did work more than these hours to carry out her duties properly, and that her contract provided for this.

LORD DENNING M.R.: Those were the terms of the contract. The question is whether there was an additional term in the contract whereby Mrs Lake was required to do extra work in the preparation of lessons or in the marking of pupils' work and the like so as to bring the hours she worked each week to more than 21. The Industrial Tribunal held that there was no implied term in the contract requiring her to work more than the 19 hours and 25 minutes.

She appealed to the Employment Appeal Tribunal. They allowed her appeal because they thought there was an implied term whereby she was "to do as much work outside the school hours specified in her contract as was reasonably necessary for the proper performance of her teaching duties in school hours." They therefore remitted the matter to the Industrial Tribunal to see whether, on the evidence, by reason of her out-of-school work Mrs Lake could prove that she had worked more than 21 hours a week. They said: "That Tribunal will have to satisfy itself on evidence in the ordinary way about how many hours Mrs Lake ordinarily worked outside her school hours in order to do her work in her school hours properly." Now there is an appeal to this Court.

We have heard all the arguments in this case: and I must say that I prefer the decision of the Industrial Tribunal. It seems to me that the "free" time of 3 hours and 40 minutes covered all that was required of her. That was the time allowed to her for preparation or marking. She was not required to do more. If she chose to do more, it was a voluntary act on her part outside her contractual obligations. This voluntary act was so unpredictable that it could not be regarded as contractual. One teacher might be able to do all the preparation and marking in the "free" time of 3 hours and 40 minutes. Another might not. It would depend on the subject which had to be taught, on the qualities of the teacher, and the knowledge she already had in her particular subject. There is so much personal variation in regard to the subject matter, the teacher, the pupils and everything else that it is completely impossible to lay down any guidance for a Tribunal to decide how much extra work an ordinary teacher would have to do. So much so that no implied term can be imported whereby Mrs Lake was required to work at any time over and above the 19 hours and 25 minutes.

There is also the question of payment. Mrs Lake was paid according to the number of hours she worked. She was paid for working 19 hours and 25 minutes a week. It is difficult to find any element in her salary which included her work out of school hours.

Seaboard World Airlines Inc. v. Transport and General Workers' Union
[1973] I.C.R. 458
National Industrial Relations Court

The complainants entered into a cargo handling contract with a foreign airline using London Airport. Clerical workers employed by them refused to undertake the extra work involved unless they were paid more.

SIR JOHN DONALDSON P.: These contracts normally would provide for the performance of broadly specified types of work for a specified period of working hours. It would not be a breach of contract by the employers to ask the clerical employees to do clerical work of any kind within those times. The fact that their actual work load increased over the working day because business improved would not be a ground for saying that the employers were in breach of contract. It might be a ground for an employee saying to the employers, "Well now, look, this job is getting a good deal harder. I am producing a good deal more. You ought to agree to pay me an increased wage." But there is no question of breach of contract in the employers asking the employee to do the work. It is what he has contracted to do. If the employee is unwilling to do the increased amount of work for the wage which he is being paid, his right then as an individual is to give notice terminating his contract and find another job.

The following extract highlights the problems of determining hours of work on a national industrial basis, akin to legislation, and considers the alternative of collective bargaining at lower levels.

M. White, *"Shorter Working Time Through National Industry Agreements,"* DEPARTMENT OF EMPLOYMENT RESEARCH PAPER No. 38 (September 1982), pp. 1–2

The 1970s were a decade of gradual inconspicuous reductions in working time. The 1980s have begun with a remarkable acceleration of this development. Before 1980 shorter working hours were introduced only by a small proportion of employers, acting in isolation. In 1981/82 it is estimated that about 3.5 million workers received reductions in their working week as a result of national agreements covering the majority of firms in their industries . . . .

The survey on which this report is based itself provides striking evidence that working hours are expected to continue shrinking, by both managers and unions. We asked whether further reductions (beyond the present industry agreements) were likely to take place within the next five years. About three-quarters, of both the managers and the senior shop stewards we interviewed, believed that they would . . . .

The platform from which reductions in working time have been advocated in recent years has been one of countering the growth in unemployment. If, as Beveridge said, we could all bring ourselves to take a little more leisure, then the number of the unemployed need not be so great. However, the findings from . . . studies on shorter hours . . . as well as findings from other sources . . . have shown that the equation between shorter hours and increased employment is not as simple or as reliable as it may seem at first sight. In particular, our studies showed that firms had been able in many cases to reduce hours substantially, without increasing either the numbers employed or the amount of overtime worked. Nor had the methods used to achieve these results been particularly sophisticated. Rather, the firms had relied upon relatively simple devices such as the reduction in tea-breaks or meal-breaks, or increases in the pace of working introduced through consultation with workers.

Accordingly, in our view of the development of shorter working time, the ability of firms to make productivity improvements to offset the potential costs of shorter hours is central . . . .

The issue of shorter working hours and productivity must also be seen against the background of economic and industrial developments in the 1970s. At the end of a decade which had witnessed great technological advances in many industries, industrial output was actually lower than at the beginning and, despite the large increase in labour productivity during 1981, the resulting level of productivity was merely on a par with the level of six years previously. Despite the waves of redundancies and closures of uneconomical factories which have taken place recently, it seems highly probable that there are still large reserves of unused industrial capacity and underemployed work-forces in some sections of industry. These circumstances must influence the response of management to shorter hours, making it easier to absorb the development without requiring a compensatory increase in the supply of manpower.

The arguments relating to the effect of productivity offsets must however be regarded with some caution. They are based on evidence concerning reductions in working before 1980 when such changes were confined to the plant or company level. It is by no means certain that they will hold good when shorter working time is being introduced through national industry agreements. Firms conforming to such an agreement may have less room to negotiate productivity offsets or less scope for timing the changes to fit in with advantageous circumstances. Although national agreements sometimes include clauses stipulating productivity offsets, firms may be unable to take advantage of them, either because they lack the skills or because they face strong opposition from workers. Indeed, the whole notion of making productivity improvements to offset the costs of shorter hours implies a degree of expertise in, or at least familiarity with, the methods of "plant bargaining", and these hardly exist in some industries.

It is natural and necessary, therefore, that a close examination of the steps taken to introduce productivity improvements should form a major part of the study reported here. We must also consider what happens if firms do not succeed in making such productivity improvements. It might be thought that, at this point, the employment effect re-emerges. In our view, it is still unlikely to do so, certainly not to the extent supposed in some estimates. Our previous studies indicated that increases in overtime were an alternative that seemed much more plausible to both managers and shop stewards. Anxiety about increases in overtime, paid at premium rates, constitutes one of the main reasons for employers' opposition to shorter hours. Moreover, even if recruitment takes place as a result of the reductions in hours, the costs of supplying a certain amount of manpower rise on the assumption that weekly wage rates (for fewer hours) remain the same as they were previously. Higher costs, whether resulting from increased overtime or increased recruitment at constant weekly wages, are likely, in a depressed economy and with fiercely competitive world trading conditions, to jeopardize future employment. Numerous macro-economic studies of the effects of shorter hours have, under the assumption of increased labour costs, forecast a net *decrease* in employment in the medium-term.

A policy to reduce working time has to consider the issues of recruitment of new employees, limitation on overtime, productivity and wages adjustments. Does the common law provide adequate, or any, tools for this task? Is the answer to be found in statutory regulation or an administrative scheme? What are the implications for collective bargaining and labour law? Contrast government policies on too little work: programmes such as the Temporary Employment Subsidy and the Temporary Short-Time Working Compensation Scheme (see below, pp. 111–112).

(B) Overtime Obligations

Overtime obligations too are determined by the contract of employment, which again often reflects collective agreements. As yet few national or company level agreements limit the amount of overtime worked. At most, there will be some general exhortation, or relatively high limits will be set, with some exemptions even then for emergencies allowing for overtime working. There are continuing efforts by trade unions at national level to limit overtime, but little local response. The TUC has called for legislation to be considered on the subject.

The problem of reconciling individual contractual and collectively negotiated rules on overtime is illustrated in the following case.

Camden Exhibition & Display Ltd. v. Lynott
[1966] 1 Q. B. 555; [1965] 3 All E. R. 28
Court of Appeal

Shop stewards, dissatisfied with wages, informed the employer that no employees would work overtime. The collective agreement applicable provided in working rule 6(a): "Overtime required to ensure the due and proper performance of contracts shall not be subject to restriction, but may be worked by mutual agreement between the employer and the operatives concerned." An injunction was sought alleging that the stewards were inducing breaches of contract by restricting overtime.

Lord Denning M.R. [in the majority]: What is the true interpretation of this working rule 6 (a)? I think it is clear that the unions agreed that when overtime was necessary to ensure the proper performance of contracts, the unions would not impose a restriction on overtime, and would not authorise their stewards, or anyone on their behalf, to impose a restriction on overtime. Overtime was to be arranged by mutual agreement and direct arrangement between the employers and the men.

Suppose that no authority is given by the unions for a ban on overtime, but some of the men seek together to restrict overtime, without any official sanction. Does this rule prevent it? Can the men put a collective unofficial embargo on overtime? This is a difficult point. On the whole I think this working rule means that the men will not, officially or unofficially, impose a collective embargo on overtime when it is required to ensure the due and proper performance of contracts. It follows that, if the defendants did induce the men to put a collective embargo on overtime, they were inducing them to break the working rules and hence their contracts of employment.

Russell L.J. [dissenting]: First of all, my present view of the construction of working rule 6 (a) is that it merely states that on the National Joint Council no ceiling is imposed by the working rules upon hours of overtime, the extent of overtime working being left to agreement between employers and operatives. As I see it, in my mind's eye, the parties of the Joint Council round the table said: "Are we in these rules going to fix a ceiling on the hours of overtime worked by any man?" Answer: "No." Hence the first part of rule 6 (a). They then proceeded to say, by way of addition: "It is to be left to agreement between operative and employer." If that be so, it certainly cannot import into the contract of any particular operative an agreement not to limit or refuse to work overtime save for a reason special to himself. Therefore, in my view, no breach of contract has been induced or procured.

Judicial policy on overtime requirements is inconsistent, as the following case demonstrates.

Martin v. Solus Schall
[1979] I.R.L.R. 7
Employment Appeal Tribunal

The employee was dismissed upon his refusal to work overtime.

LORD McDONALD: . . . we listened to a careful argument from (the appellant's) solicitor designed to establish that in law there was no obligation upon the appellant in terms of his contract of employment to work overtime.

This matter was not raised before the Industrial Tribunal. This is perhaps understandable in view of the fact that the appellant was not legally represented. The basis of the argument turns on an interpretation of the appellant's standard terms of employment, a copy of which he signed on 14.2.73. That document contains the following statement:

> "Your normal working week will be 40 hours per week made up as follows:–
> Eight hours per day Monday to Friday for employment in the United Kingdom. You will be expected to work such overtime as is necessary to ensure continuity of service."

It was argued that the word "expected" meant something less than a legal obligation. Our attention was directed to the case of *Pearson and Workman* v *William Jones Ltd* (1967) ITR 471 where it was held that for the purpose of calculating entitlement to redundancy payment, overtime hours worked fell to be disregarded notwithstanding that the contract of employment contained a clause to the effect that the employers had the right to decide when overtime was necessary. As that case deals with redundancy it is perhaps wise to apply it with caution to the circumstances of the present case. The appellant's solicitor relied upon a passage in the judgment of Waller J. which suggests that before overtime can be compulsory there must be an expressed statement to that effect in the contract of employment or at least it should be able to be read from it by implication. We were also referred to the Industrial Tribunal decision in *Deegan* v *Norman & Sons Ltd* [1976] IRLR 139 where the words "other hours as are necessary" appearing in a contract of employment were held not to connote a requirement to work overtime compulsorily. The wording there is very different and we do not gain assistance from that decision.

In our view in the present case the document signed by the appellant implies that he has accepted the need to work such overtime as was necessary to ensure continuity of service. If as was submitted on behalf of the appellant there was no obligation upon him whatsoever to comply with a request to work overtime, no meaning can be given to the very clear words contained in the written terms of his employment. It was suggested that this might impose an impossible burden upon the appellant and of course the extent to which the request by the respondents to perform such overtime work was reasonable will always be a vital question in considering the fairness or unfairness of any dismissal arising out of the operation of that clause.

Policy conflicts within the judiciary are evident when attempts by employers to introduce overtime are made, and employee resistance is met with dismissal. In such cases the courts confront clear policy choices in deciding whether to support employers' demands for overtime, or workers' resistance to them. Thus, in *Evans* v. *Elementa Holdings Ltd.* [1982] I.R.L.R. 143 (E.A.T.), an employee who refused to accept a new obligation to work overtime was held unfairly dismissed. The refusal was reasonable. In another case, however, a different division of the E.A.T. came to a different conclusion *(Chubb Fire Security Ltd.* v. *Harper* [1983] I.R.L.R. 311 (E.A.T.), *per* Balcombe J.):

> "We must respectfully disagree with that conclusion. It may be perfectly reasonable for an employee to decline to work extra overtime, having regard to his family commitments. Yet from the employer's point of view, having regard to his business commitments, it may be perfectly reasonable to require an employee to work overtime."

See generally on this point, Chapter 3 on *The Work Obligation*, pp. 41 *et seq*.

2. TOO LITTLE WORK

The problem of too little work may be dealt with by employers terminating contracts of employment with due notice. But the adverse consequences are not confined to workers. The loss of a cohesive work-force and the antagonism bred by such actions affect management's interests as well. One result has been the negotiation of collective agreements laying down detailed rules applicable in circumstances of too little work. These include rules on income maintenance (*eg* guaranteed pay) and work sharing (*eg* overtime bans).

The problem has gradations, beginning with relatively small reductions in work, rising to substantial amounts lost, and finally to wholesale loss of jobs. Each of these has been subject to statutory attention: respectively, the law on guarantee payments, the law on redundancy through lay-offs or short-time working, and the law on unfair dismissal, redundancy consultation and redundancy payments. Additional provision is made by social security law on unemployment benefits and subsidies to employers retaining workers on short-time. This area has been particularly fruitful in the establishment of links between legislation and collective bargaining.

(A) Too Little Work and Contract Law

The obligations of the employer under the contract of employment when there is too little work may be ambiguous. For example, what is the position where there is too little work, but there is a contract with an agreed wage for a 40-hour week?

Hanson v. Wood (Abingdon Process Engravers)
[1968] I.T.R. 46
Queen's Bench Division

> The employees were dismissed when they refused their employer's demand that they work and be paid for only 32½ hours instead of 40 hours weekly, because of a reduction in trade.

LORD PARKER C.J.: Represented by the union, (the appellants) urged that under the relevant trade agreement, which is the process trade agreement, there was a contract of employment for 40 hours per week on a day shift at £18.19s.0d., that accordingly Mr Wood was not entitled to require the men to work 32½ hours for a less sum . . . .

Mr Wood contended that he was fully entitled, despite this process trade agreement, to require the men to work less than 40 hours at a proportionately less rate, in other words, at an hourly rate calculated in accordance with the minimum wage for the week . . . .

. . . . There is no finding here as to what the exact contract was. It has been assumed in this court that the process trade agreement to which I have referred did form part of the contract. If so, it will be for the [Industrial] Tribunal to determine what the true effect of the contract is, invoking these terms, in other words: whether the contract is a contract by the week, for 40 hours a week with a minimum wage of £18.19s.0d. on day shift, or whether, as Mr Wood maintains, it was in effect a contract to work by the hour for such hours as he required at an hourly rate calculated in accordance with £18.19s.0d. for 40 hours.

Such ambiguities may be catered for by negotiations leading to collective agreements guaranteeing wages, but still giving rise to legal uncertainties as to the rights and obligations of employers and employees. Compare the following cases.

Powell Duffryn Wagon Company Ltd. v. House
[1974] I.T.R. 46
National Industrial Relations Court

> The employees were laid off, but the employer refused to pay the guaranteed minimum wage.

DONALDSON J.: When the boycott was imposed and, as a result, work ceased to be available, the men wanted to go on being employed and to receive this minimum wage. The employers wanted to go on employing them, but considered that in all the circumstances a payment of the minimum wage could not be justified. In passing we, like the Tribunal, can see no point in a guaranteed fall-back wage if it is not to be paid at the one time when it is needed, namely, when there is insufficient work to enable the men to earn more on time rates. The men accepted the fact that the employers were not prepared to pay the guaranteed wage and discussions ensued on two other possibilities, namely, that there should be short-time working for all—one week in three— or that all should be "laid off" until the work again became available. Under the "lay-off" alternative the men would all register at the employment exchange and draw unemployment benefit but their insurance cards would be retained by the employers until such time as they could resume work. The men elected to be laid off . . . .

. . . . In the course of giving evidence some of the men had very frankly stated that the lay-off was "negotiated", that their representatives had "accepted" it and even that it had been "agreed." It also emerged that during the lay-off period the men received holiday credits and payment for bank holidays. On this basis the employers contended that the men had agreed to be laid off and that accordingly there was no dismissal. The Tribunal rejected this argument . . . .

The Tribunal held that none of the men or their representatives was agreeing to forego their entitlement to guaranteed fall-back pay. Their negotiations and agreement were limited to choosing a lay-off rather than short-time working if, but only if, the employers refused to make the guaranteed payments. Accordingly the Tribunal held that the employers had unilaterally terminated the original contract of employment by refusing to pay the guaranteed minimum wage and had thereby dismissed all the applicants . . . .

A fall-back wage is intended to protect men in precisely the situation which was thought to have arisen, namely a temporary shortage of work. In such circumstances employers have to make up their minds whether to dismiss their employees and meet their obligation to make redundancy payments or to pay the guaranteed minimum wage. There is no reason why employees should forego their alternative rights and we should be very reluctant to conclude that the applicants had done so. Cogent evidence would be required to support any such conclusion and certainly it is not present in this case.

In our judgment as a matter of law the men were dismissed when the employers wrongfully refused to pay the guaranteed minimum wage and the applicants thereupon became entitled to redundancy payments.

Neads v. CAV Ltd.

[1983] I.R.L.R. 360
Queen's Bench Division

When a dispute occurred between Mr Neads' employer and employees in another department, the employers purported to lay off Mr Neads. Mr Neads nonetheless continued to work at part of his job unaffected by the dispute. The employer refused to pay him for the period he was purportedly laid off.

PAIN J.: I begin by referring to several authorities on the position at common law. The first one is *Devonald* v. *Rosser* [1906] 2 KB 728, which establishes that at common law there is no right to lay off without payment except in very limited circumstances. That is followed by *Hanley* v. *Pease & Partners* [1915] 1 KB 698, which shows that there is no right of suspension as a disciplinary measure at common law. In *Browning and Others* v. *Crumlin Valley Collieries* [1926] 1 KB 522, Greer J found that there was an implied term which entitled mine owners to lay off their miners without pay while repairs were done to the pit which was unfit through no fault of the mine owners. This decision rests upon the terms which were implied in the circumstances of that case and does not throw any doubt on the principle established in earlier authorities . . . .

It is therefore plain that there is no general right to lay off without pay at common law, but such a right exists only in very limited circumstances. It is now necessary to refer to a further collective agreement: "The Guarantee of employment for hourly rated manual workers," dated 22.12.64.. This was an agreement made between the Engineering Employers' Federation and the Confederation of Shipbuilding and Engineering Unions . . . . [The agreement provided for a guaranteed weekly wage, but also for the guarantee to be suspended in the event of dislocation of production.]

Mr Bennett [for the employers] developed a powerful argument that the collective agreement has in effect overtaken the common law position and he points to the decision of the Court of Session in *Burroughs Machines Ltd.* v. *Timmoney* [1977] I.R.L.R. 404, where the right of lay off was looked at purely in the terms of this collective agreement. Mr Goudie [for the employee] did not seek to dispute that the 1964 agreement might control the position where there is an industrial dislocation due to an industrial dispute in a federated establishment in consequence of which work is not available. But he contends that this agreement does not apply if work is available, and he points to the fact that, as far as Mr Neads is concerned, he was fully engaged on rectification which was part of his normal work for the two days in which the employers purported to lay him off. So he says the 1964 agreement does not apply and Mr Neads is entitled to rely on the implied undertaking of his employers to provide him with a reasonable amount of work so long as his employment lasted.

I think Mr Goudie's argument on this point is well founded. It seems to me to be plain that the 1964 agreement was intended to suspend the guarantee only where no work was available for a particular employee. I do not think it was intended to give an employer a general right of lay off wherever he could point to some dislocation of production by reason of an industrial dispute in a federated establishment.

Consider also the following statements as to contractual provisions allowing for lay-offs by Bristow J. in *A. Dakri & Co. Ltd.* v. *Tiffen* [1981] I.R.L.R. 567 (E.A.T.):

> "Unless a time was specified in the contract, then the law implies that the lay-off is to be for not more than a reasonable time. What is a reasonable time is a question of fact for the [Industrial Tribunal]."

Also by Lord McDonald in *Kenneth MacRae & Co. Ltd.* v. *Dawson* [1984] I.R.L.R. 5 (E.A.T.):

> "[Where] an employer has a contractual right to lay off indefinitely he is, in the normal case, not to be regarded [as being] in breach of his contract simply by virtue of the passage of time."

(B) *Too Little Work and Employment Subsidies*

The problem of too little work and consequent unemployment has led to government intervention, the main thrust of which has been to provide subsidies to those affected by too little work: employers and workers. A feature of this provision of significance to labour law is that judicial policy-making is largely ousted. Policy is implemented through administration of the social security system or other public agencies (usually the Manpower Services Commission or the Department of Trade).

(i) Guarantee payments for workers

Before 1975 an employee temporarily suspended from work (laid off) had to absorb the cost himself, except insofar as he could recoup something from the State (unemployment benefit) or from the employer (guaranteed pay, usually by virtue of a collective agreement). EPA, ss.22–28 altered this by placing some of the burden on the employer. An employer who lays off a worker or puts him on short-time must continue to pay his normal wages for a limited period. However, the wages payable are subject to a maximum, which is very low, and the maximum number of days for which it is payable is only five in any three-month period. Failure by the employer to pay allows for a complaint to an Industrial Tribunal (see now EPCA ss.12 *et seq.*). The operation of these provisions and their interaction with social security law are described in the following extract.

B. Bercusson, *Annotations to section 12 of EPCA* in THE EMPLOYMENT ACTS 1974–1980 (C. D. Drake and B. Bercusson, ed. 1981)

In the absence of any provisions for guarantee payments, workers laid off used to be entitled to social security payments, mainly unemployment benefit. During the first three days of lay-off, however, no benefit was payable. The enactment of provisions for guarantee payment might, therefore, seem a way of re-establishing the employee's benefit during these first three days (the three-day waiting period was a measure dropped by the National Insurance Act 1946, s. 11, but reintroduced by the Social Security Act 1971, s. 7—now the Social Security Act 1975, s. 14(3)). The amount of daily guarantee payment, in fact, is roughly equivalent (when taxed) to the daily unemployment benefit entitlement (untaxed). To summarise: the effect of the guarantee payment provisions could be to provide payment for the first three days of lay-off. Thereafter, any such payments would be effectively set-off against unemployment benefit (see s. 132(2)). But at least workers' earnings could have been protected to some extent during those first days of lay-off. (No doubt this could have been achieved in an infinitely simpler fashion by dropping the three-day waiting period for unemployment benefit).

Regulations make it clear that the protection of workers was far from the intention of these provisions. Reg. 7(1)(d)(i) of the Social Security (Unemployment, Sickness and Invalidity Benefits) Regulations (S.I. 1975 No. 564, as amended by S.I. 1976 No. 677) provides that "a day shall not be treated as a day of unemployment in relation to any person if it is a day in respect of which there is payable to that person—a guarantee payment" under s. 22 of the Employment Protection Act 1975 (now this section). The result is that workers who are entitled to guarantee payments from their employer *cannot receive unemployment benefit for the first eight days of the lay-off* (five days' guarantee payment plus three days' waiting period). Instead of the established and familiar machinery for collecting unemployment benefit, workers will now have to rely on their employers' willingness and efficiency in paying out five days' guarantee pay in any quarter. If the employer fails to comply, the worker has to process his claim through the Industrial Tribunal (or take collective action). He only qualifies for unemployment benefit after eight days of lay-off. Meanwhile he may have to subsist on supplementary benefit.

In practice, therefore, the procedure will be as follows: a worker is laid off. He may or may not be entitled to and claim and receive a guarantee payment. He should apply for one if there is the slightest chance. If refused, he should apply immediately for unemployment benefit. The insurance officer must then decide either that after the three-day waiting period is over benefit is to be paid; or he must decide that the employee is entitled to guarantee payment—so benefit is only to be paid after eight days' lay-off. The insurance officer will normally inquire of the employer about the position. If the employer says no payment is owed, then the officer must decide whether the employer is correct or not and dispose of the claim for unemployment benefit accordingly—within 14 days. If he takes the view that the employer is wrong in denying payment, he will refuse payment until eight days have elapsed. The employee's only course then is to claim the guarantee payment from the employer within three months of the lay-off (s. 17). The worker is thus made dependent on his employer's readiness to pay up at the time of the lay-off. The State can refuse to pay up and force the worker to take legal proceedings to get his due. In this way the State has effectively transferred the burden of paying unemployment benefit to the employer—and given the worker the arduous task of enforcing payment of the benefit through the Industrial Tribunal.

(ii) Wages subsidies for employers

The Temporary Employment Subsidy Scheme (TES), introduced on August 18, 1975 and closed on March 31, 1979, was by far the largest single special measure introduced to protect employment between 1975 and 1979. Gross spending on TES totalled over £500 million. The cumulative total of employees who had at any time been supported by TES represented over 6 per cent. of all employees in manufacturing and some 2.5 per cent. of all employees in Great Britain. During the three and a half years it was available, 8,787 applications were approved, involving 540,266 jobs. At any one time it was typically supporting around 150,000 jobs and keeping about 100,000 off the unemployment register. Under TES, provided the employer was prepared to defer an impending redundancy affecting 10 or more workers in an establishment, he might qualify for a subsidy of £10 a week for each full-time job maintained. The subsidy was payable for a maximum of one year. A requirement was introduced for all firms to present a restructuring plan if they wanted to receive the subsidy for more than six months. The industrial distribution of TES was remarkable: the textiles, clothing and footwear industries accounted for 43 per cent. of the jobs covered, although they comprise less than 4 per cent. of total employment in the United Kingdom and under 10 per cent. of private sector employees.

Concern expressed by the EEC Commission about the effect of TES on the competitive position of British firms in the textiles, clothing and footwear sectors led to restrictions on the level of support which could be offered to firms in these sectors under that scheme. To offset these limitations, new arrangements were introduced to enable employers in these industries to receive reimbursement for part-time working. This represented a move away from the idea of a subsidy paid for jobs preserved (TES) to one where the employer is encouraged to put workers on short-time working to avoid redundancies and to pay them at least 75 per cent. of normal pay for each day lost. The Government reimbursed the employer for such payments at 75 per cent. of the worker's normal pay plus National Insurance contributions. Under the new scheme covering textiles, 140 applications were approved, covering 8,432 jobs threatened with redundancy.

Due to continued concern at its effects on competition, the EEC Commission ordered Britain to end TES, and both it and the special scheme for the textiles sector came to an end on March 31, 1979. They were succeeded by the Temporary Short-Time Working Compensation Scheme (TSTWCS), introduced on April 1, 1979. Under TSTWCS employers prepared to introduce short-time working as an alternative to redundancies received compensation for payments made to employees affected. During the first year of its operation, the scheme was extremely modest: total public spending was only £24 million and in March 1980, the scheme was covering only 186,000 individuals sharing work, thereby reducing the unemployment register by 21,000. During 1980 and 1981, however, the numbers covered grew dramatically in line with the recession. At its peak in March 1981 firms were receiving compensation for 984,000 individuals sharing jobs. The number of full-time jobs supported was 219,000 and the unemployment register was thereby reduced by 148,000. The monthly cost of the scheme was over £50 million (for further details, see D. Metcalf, *Alternatives to Unemployment: Special Employment Measures in Britain* (1982)). The implications of schemes of this kind for labour law are explored in M. Freedland, "Leaflet Law: The Temporary Short-Time Working Compensation Scheme," (1980) 9 *ILJ* 254.)

More recently, large-scale wages subsidies have taken the form of training schemes for young people. The Youth Training Scheme (YTS) was introduced in April 1983 and offers training mainly to 16 and 17 year old school leavers. It consists of work experience and off the job training (of at least 13 weeks) provided in 1985/6 through some 5,800 managing agents (including employers, industrial training boards, employers' associations and private training companies) and sponsors (voluntary groups and local authorities). Managing agents are paid £2,050 per trainee (from September 1984) of which they pay £1,312.50 (£26.25 a week for 50 weeks) to the trainee as a tax free allowance, leaving £737.50 to cover training costs and the agent's fee. There were in 1985/6 nearly 400,000 young people on YTS schemes and cost the Manpower Commission in excess of £800 million annually. The extent to which this is subsidising employers' wages costs depends only partly on the extent to which employers are using YTS trainees as substitutes for employees who otherwise would be recruited in the normal way. In addition, where the employer takes on more 16 year olds than he otherwise would have done, he receives an MSC payment for all the trainees—though those employed in the ordinary way are generally paid more (in April 1984, the average gross weekly earnings for trainees under 18 was £58.10 for men and £47.50 for women; other employees under 18 earned £67.79 (male) and £62.00 (female)). The MSC payment thus subsidised a substantial proportion of employers' wages costs for trainees. Despite its title, the scheme is often perceived as a job creation exercise to compensate for the lack of employment for young people.

(C) *Too Little Work and Redundancy*

Redundancy resulting from too little work has not been the subject of comprehensive and systematic legal regulation. The legal rules dealing with different aspects of the problem of redundancy developed at different times and are to be found scattered over legislation and common law on redundancy payments, unfair redundancy dismissals, consultation procedures with trade unions and employees, time off to look for work in a redundancy situation, and so on. Here we organise these legal rules so as to set out the law on five key aspects of the redundancy problem encountered in practice usually in the following chronological order:

(a) preventing redundancy;
(b) redundancy consultations;
(c) selection for redundancy;
(d) redundancy notice and time off to look for work;
(e) redundancy payments.

The law on each of these aspects of redundancy will be contrasted with industrial practice manifest in collective agreements. This collective industrial practice in its immense variety and detail poses a great challenge to labour law. First, there is the policy question of whether such practice is best left alone untrammelled by legal supervision or enforcement procedures. But also, does labour law have the techniques and institutions adequate to play a constructive role? For example, is contract law flexible enough to cope with the obligations laid down in these agreements? Are courts and tribunals competent to deal with conflicts in this sphere involving not only individual workers and employers, but also trade unions, work groups and related employers? The collective agreements and judicial decisions presented below provide some insight into these issues. We begin, however, with a section on the legal definition of "redundancy" and its difficulties.

(i) The definition of "redundancy": EPCA, s. 81(2)

There is a statutory definition of redundancy in EPCA, s.81(2):

For the purposes of this Act an employee who is dismissed shall be taken to be dismissed by reason of redundancy if the dismissal is attributable wholly or mainly to—

(a) the fact that his employer has ceased, or intends to cease, to carry on the business for the purposes of which the employee was employed by him, or has ceased or intends to cease, to carry on that business in the place where the employee was so employed, or

(b) the fact that the requirements of that business for employees to carry out work of a particular kind, or for employees to carry out work of a particular kind in the place where he was so employed, have ceased or diminished or are expected to cease or diminish.

This definition is also applicable to unfair redundancies (s. 57(2)(*c*)) by virtue of section 153(2).

As a matter of policy, the decision of an employer to declare a redundancy could be challenged:

(a) the employer's motivation as a causal factor in the dismissal following cessation could be questioned; or

(b) where this motivation is linked, as it usually is, with a judgment of the economic "requirements of the business," the rationality of that judgment could be tested.

However, as in the case of terminations for misconduct and incapability (see Chapter 10 on *Termination of Work*), the subjective business discretion of the employer in declaring a redundancy is rarely questioned by the courts.

In *Moon* v. *Homeworthy Furniture (Northern) Ltd.* [1976] I.R.L.R. 298 (E.A.T.), employees declared redundant challenged the employer's assertion that the factory was not economically viable. The Industrial Tribunal queried whether they could go into policy decisions of a company's board of directors on trading and economic matters, and the E.A.T. (Kilner Brown J.) reiterated that "there could not and cannot be any investigation into the rights and wrongs of the declared redundancy." In *H. Goodwin Ltd.* v. *Fitzmaurice* [1977] I.R.L.R. 393 (E.A.T.) the Industrial Tribunal seemed to demand from the employer accounts or figures demonstrating lack of economic viability. The E.A.T. (Phillips J.) repudiated this approach: "there is no special obligation on the employers to establish the existence of some economic or accountancy state of affairs which would, as it were, justify the declaration of a state of redundancy."

The statutory definition, however, does assume the existence of a set of facts. On a claim for a redundancy payment, a statutory presumption exists that the reason for dismissal is redundancy: see EPCA, s.91(2). Unfair dismissal cases, where such a presumption does not operate, highlight the need for facts to be proved that a redundancy situation does exist.

In most cases, the closure of a plant is held to be a redundancy situation. But in less desperate circumstances the Industrial Tribunals have experienced some difficulties with the dismissal of one or more employees from an enterprise which continues in being.

Many such dismissals follow changes at work or major reorganisations which are alleged to cause redundancies (see above, *The Work Obligation*, pp. 67 *et seq.*). Others reflect the policy issues already referred to: challenges to the employer's motivation for the dismissals, particularly where this follows a judgment on the economic rationality of the business' requirements. The "fact that the requirements of that business for employees to carry out work of a particular kind . . . have ceased or diminished" involves a judgment weighing employment, wages, prices and profits. The following cases demonstrate the policy dilemmas the courts find themselves in when pushed to question employers' judgments. In the first case, the court had to decide whether the business was "overstaffed."

Hindle v. Percival Boats Ltd.
[1969] 1 W.L.R. 174; [1969] 1 All E.R. 836
Court of Appeal

The employee, a skilled wood craftsman, was employed by a firm of boat builders and repairers. In about 1965 some employees were dismissed because of a drop in demand for boat building. In 1966 he was dismissed when a costing carried out by the employers showed they could obtain no financial benefit from him because of the time taken by him to do his work.

Widgery L.J.: The issue presented to the Tribunal in this case was a very simple one. The applicant claimed that he was dismissed because the need for woodworkers had declined and he said that Mr Percival had told him this in terms. Mr Percival denied that he had given this reason and said that the appellant was dismissed because he spent so long on the job that his work was uneconomical. Although the Tribunal accepted Mr Percival as a truthful witness, it very properly went on to consider whether the business had become over-staffed lest Mr Percival had "deceived" himself in ignoring this factor. Its conclusion on the evidence as a whole was that the effects of the reorganisation in 1965 had spent themselves and that at the date of the appellant's dismissal the business was not overstaffed. It accordingly held that the dismissal was not attributable to redundancy, and like the Divisional Court I can see no error of law in this.

In the second case, the court was pushed to question whether the employer's wage rates were "fair."

Chapman v. Goonvean and Rostowrack China Clay Co. Ltd.
[1973] 1 W.L.R. 678; [1973] I.C.R. 310
Court of Appeal

As a result of a trade recession in the china clay industry, the employer decided that free transport for his workers to take them to work was no longer economical. The workers were unable to arrange other transport and left claiming redundancy payments. They were replaced by workers who lived near the workplace.

BUCKLEY L.J.: We are concerned, however, with a case in which it is said that the requirement of the employer's business for employees to carry out work of a particular kind was expected to cease or diminish. Whether such an expectation can justifiably be said to have existed must depend upon the circumstances in which it was supposed that the business would be conducted in the future. The test cannot, I think, be a purely subjective one, depending only upon the apprehensions, justified or unjustified, of the employer. The employer must, I think, justify his expectation by reference to objective circumstances relating to the commercial situation of his business and those commercial and economic conditions which exist generally at the relevant time or which could then reasonably be anticipated in the future. There seems to me, however, to be nothing in the language of the section to suggest that the employer should be treated as bound or likely to carry on his business in all, or indeed in any, respects in precisely the way in which he was carrying it on at the time when the facts have to be considered.

Suppose, for instance, that the employment is of a kind for which there is a recognised rate for the job, and that an employer in a period of affluence and in the interest of good staff relations has been paying his employees more than that rate. If a time comes when he can no longer afford to pay his employees more than the recognised rate for the job but he is prepared to continue to employ them at that rate, there is nothing in [what is now EPCA s.81(1)] to suggest that for the purpose of considering whether his requirement for employees to do that particular job is likely to cease or diminish he must be treated as an employer who is going to continue to pay the higher rate. This, however, as I understand Mr Pain's argument [for the claimants] would be the consequence of the view which he propounds. The facts would not, it seems to me, establish that the employer's need for employees to carry out work of the particular kind was expected to cease or diminish, but only that the employer was no longer able to pay his employees on so generous a scale as before. The position would be quite different if an employer dismissed his employees because he was no longer able to pay them either the recognised rate for the job, where one existed, or a fair wage at which he could secure the services of other employees in the labour market.

The policy conflicts inherent in defining "redundancy" are evident also where disputes arise between employers, workers and their organisations dealing with a redundancy situation.

(ii) Preventing redundancy

(*a*) *Collective bargaining*

The information on collective industrial practice concerning redundancy in this and subsequent sections is derived from the Labour Research Department's *Bargaining Report* No. 3 (July/August 1979) which surveyed 25 redundancy schemes; No. 14 (May/June 1981) which reviewed 175 redundancy agreements; No. 23 (November/December 1982) which analysed numerous redeployment practices; and No. 33 (May/June 1984) which surveyed 110 redundancy agreements and schemes.

Reviews of agreements containing *measures to avoid redundancy* in the surveys of 1981 and 1984 revealed the following:

	No. of agreements	
	1981	*1984*
Retirement of those over pension age	50	35
Limitation on recruitment	44	35
Limitation on overtime	44	32
Redeployment	39	48
Limitation on sub-contract work	26	12
Retraining	25	34
Replacement of casual and temporary labour	18	17
Short-time working	12	11

The following agreements were featured in the 1979 survey:

Ford Motor Company Ltd (Hourly Paid)

Where redundancy is anticipated, consultation will take place under the Procedure Agreement on:

restriction of overtime and recruitment, except where needed to clear bottlenecks etc.;

transfer of workers except where production would be adversely affected;

short-time working (usually not less than 4 normal days or shifts unless exceptional circumstances justify fewer).

International Computers Ltd (Staff)

The following measures apply except when it is jointly agreed that they are not practicable, have overriding legal obligations or are not directly related to the problem:

temporary or contract labour (on or off the premises) will be discontinued;

withdrawal of outside contracts;

suspension of overtime;

suspension of advertising and recruitment;

redeployment of craft, technician and student apprentices;

retirement of personnel on extension of service;

short term introduction of work-sharing/part-time working (up to 60 day maximum) in areas directly affected, neither to be introduced without trade union agreement.

Civil Service (Non-Industrial Staff)

Action required before redundancy is declared: redundancies are not to be declared until the following have been considered in full consultation with staff representation:

review of present and future departmental work patterns to see whether staff surplus is unavoidable;

transfer of staff within the department to other areas of work where there are suitable vacancies;

transfers to other Civil Service departments (or fringe bodies) where work is available;

if no suitable vacancies under the previous two options, staff outside the redundancy areas volunteering for early retirement to be considered as a further option;

cutting back or stopping recruitment/promotion in that department or

the rest of the Civil Service where similar work is being done—if this is agreed to be appropriate;
review of the department's retirement age policy;
retraining;
temporary blocking of posts vacant in junior grades in the same work category by senior staff—subject to agreement of trade union representation in that unit of redundancy.

Reviews of industrial practice of redeployment and offers of alternative work revealed the following:

Bargaining Report No. 23 (1982)

Redeployment may be defined as the transfer of workers either to a new place or to a new task, or both. Depending on the circumstances—whether the new work arises from the introduction of new technology, new working practices, or from proposed closures and redundancies—it may be voluntary or more or less compulsory: the workforce is faced with acceptance of new terms and/or location, or losing their jobs. . . .

Most well-organised workplaces will establish the right to negotiate redeployment terms. . . . A firm commitment to redeploy staff is obviously a major aim. Typical wordings from the public and private sectors are as follows:

> "Any employee whose job becomes redundant. . . . will be offered suitable alternative employment." (GEC Rectifiers–TASS new technology agreement) "Any surplus labour . . . will be dealt with by retraining or redeployment within the industry." (British Shipbuilders (Engineering and Technical Services)–APEX new technology agreement)

. . . 32 employers stipulate a firm undertaking to redeploy staff. . . .

Many employers, although unwilling or unable to agree to a *definite* promise of redeployment, are at pains to point out their willingness to make every effort to redeploy. Their good intentions are phrased in such terms as "will make every reasonable effort to obtain suitable alternative employment" . . . 62 organisations committed to making efforts to provide internal redeployment opportunities wherever possible . . .

Where redeployment opportunities may not be available in the immediate area of current work, it is important that wider opportunities be open to workers elsewhere in the company, group of companies, or in the geographical location. Management liaison can help here by contacting the Department of Employment, the Manpower Services Commission, or other firms in the area or associated companies. (There follow) details of 28 organisations which undertake to find redeployment outside the workplace immediately affected . . . (examples from redundancy agreements include):

> "to other sites if same site redeployment is impossible." (Cavenham Confectionery, Bristol)
> "will seek re-deployment throughout Dunlop group in the UK as a whole." (Dunlop)
> "will liaise with local employers and Dept of Employment." (London Brick)

"will arrange to notify employers in other parts of group in the geographical location and also within same product division." (Thorn Electrical Industries)

Bargaining Report No. 33 (1984)

Although the offer of alternative employment is an obvious (and popular) method of avoiding redundancies, it is necessary to ensure that members are protected from being forced into unsuitable jobs, and are given sufficient time and assistance to establish themselves in new posts. All offers should be made in writing. Those who are offered jobs not broadly similar to their existing ones are legally entitled to a four week trial period during which they are able to claim redundancy if the new position proves "unsuitable." 25 schemes improved on this trial period:

6 months—(8 schemes listed)
3 months—(15 schemes listed)
2 months—(1 scheme listed)
6 weeks—(1 scheme listed)

Although an employee is entitled to refuse an offer of alternative employment if it is unsuitable, it is not always clear what constitutes suitability, even where different rates of pay are concerned. [28 examples are then given] of agreements which provide protection of an individual's pay when transferring to a lower-paid job. . . .

Some schemes include definitions of what should be regarded as "suitable" alternative employment. The agreement between British Rail and the NUR includes a set of guidance notes for this purpose. These set out in detail a number of matters to be taken into consideration, stating:

"4. In determining whether the alternative offered is suitable in relation to the employee concerned, the offer should have regard to the skill, knowledge and experience of the grade in which the employee was previously employed, but consideration should also be given to the practicability of training the employee for work in other grades. The age of the employee will also be taken into account as will the hours of work compared with those in the employee's present post. Where it is evident that an employee's promotional prospects will be affected by the proposed offer, this will be regarded as a good reason for the employee to decline the alternative job offered to him."

The notes further state that if earnings are "materially below those of the employee's present post, the employee may, with good reason, decline the offer."

Also included are defined limits on acceptable additional travel. These are set at an additional $\frac{1}{2}$ hour each way, subject to the total travelling time not exceeding $1\frac{1}{4}$ hours each way.

Bargaining Report No. 23 (1982) provided even more detailed information of negotiated agreements protecting pay levels and other entitlements in the event of redeployment, as well as gradings, hours of work, and gave details of facilities in 27 agreements for time off to find accommodation, housing allowances, house removal expenses, disturbance allowances, travel allowances for those not moving house, and other miscellaneous relocation allowances. The following agreements were featured in the 1979 survey:

George Rose Printers Ltd (Printing and Related Staff)

Alternative employment;

Any workers transferred to another firm in the group after becoming redundant do so with full service and pension rights intact. In addition they are entitled to a "Change of Office Location" payment or an equivalent of 4 weeks severance pay—whichever is more.

The group management agrees to assist any worker wanting to transfer on these terms to find suitable alternative employment.

British Airways (Staff)

BA guarantees the current salary scale expectation (ie progression by increments to the top of the current scale, plus subsequent salary rises) of staff redeployed to jobs on lower pay and lower salary prospects.

Some redeployed staff may consequently be on a higher pay rate than the group they have been transferred to. This is jointly accepted in the agreement.

Staff redeployed within the area of the national agreement concerned can retain terms and conditions that are more favourable—*except* for shift pay rates/additional payments/allowances/uniforms and rank markings which must be those of the new job.

BA where necessary provides retraining with pay as laid down above.

National Freight Corporation (National Staff Council Grades)

Workers transferred to a lower grade are permitted to retain their previous grade on a personal basis, and receive wage increases etc appropriate for that grade.

Where alternative employment includes transfer to a different employing centre, the normal 4-week trial period can be extended to 13 weeks if it is agreed that the transfer is not reasonably practicable because of accommodation or other personal difficulties.

(*b*) *The law*

Laws helping to prevent redundancy began with the provision under the original Redundancy Payments Act 1965 whereby the employer could avoid liability to make a redundancy payment if he offered the employee "suitable alternative employment" (now EPCA, s.84). But there was no legal obligation on the employer to do so. The beginnings of such an obligation were introduced by the Industrial Relations Code of Practice 1972 (for its legal effect, see TULRA, Sched. 1, para. 3; EPA, Sched. 17, para. 4(1)). Tribunals are obliged to take the Code into account, and the Code (para. 45) encourages management to seek to avoid redundancies by such means as:

(i) restrictions on recruitment;
(ii) retirement of employees who are beyond the normal retiring age;
(iii) reductions in overtime;
(iv) short-time working to cover temporary fluctuations in manpower needs;
(v) re-training or transfer to other work.

The Code (para. 46) also advises management to:

. . . .
(ii) consider introducing schemes for voluntary redundancy, retirement, transfer to other establishments within the undertaking, and a phased rundown of employment; . . .
(iv) offer help to employees in finding other work in co-operation, where appropriate, with the Department of Employment, and allow them reasonable time off for the purpose. . . .

Redundancy dismissals can be held unfair unless employers act reasonably in the circumstances (EPCA, s.57(3)). It is open to tribunals and courts to adopt the policy laid down in the Code. Each case involves a policy choice: will the courts use the Code to require employers to take steps to prevent redundancies, or not. The following cases demonstrate the myriad of policy choices available.

Vokes Ltd. v. Bear
[1973] I.R.L.R. 363; [1974] I.C.R. 1
National Industrial Relations Court

Following a company takeover, Mr Bear was called into the chief executive's office, told that he was redundant, and asked to leave forthwith. An Industrial Tribunal found that the reason for dismissal had been redundancy, but that Mr Bear had been unfairly dismissed.

Griffiths J. [The judge quoted from para. 46(iv) of the Code (above) and the then equivalent of EPCA, s.57(3) requiring the employer to act reasonably in the circumstances, and continued]: The Tribunal are entitled to take into account all the circumstances affecting both the employer and the employee at the time of the dismissal. In the present case, no doubt the time would have come when the employer would have to dismiss Mr Bear for redundancy for the good of the company as a whole, but the Tribunal were fully entitled to take the view that that moment had not yet arrived by the 2nd March. The employer had not yet done that which in all fairness and reason he should do, namely, to make the obvious attempt to see if Mr Bear could be placed somewhere else within this large group. . . .

. . . . If the employer had made all reasonable attempts to place Mr Bear in the group and had failed, then the time might have come when it would be reasonable for him to regard the redundancy as a sufficient reason for the dismissal, but until that moment had come the Tribunal were entitled to take the view that it was not reasonable to dismiss for redundancy and accordingly that it was unfair.

Lloyd v. The Standard Pulverised Fuel Co. Ltd.
[1976] I.R.L.R. 115
Industrial Tribunal

The company operated a two-shift system and when a redundancy situation arose, the second shift was eliminated and the applicant dismissed. The remaining shift involved 12-hour work, normally seven days a week.

BIRMINGHAM TRIBUNAL (Chairman: H. Wilson) [The Tribunal quoted from para. 45(iii) and (iv) of the Industrial Relations Code of Practice 1972 on the avoidance of redundancies by reductions in overtime and by short-time working, and continued]: There are of course other ways in which it may be sought to avoid redundancies but those seem to us to be the material ones in this case because of the relatively large amount of overtime being worked on the shift system. . . .

. . . . the works manager, Mr Mason, said that there was no reason why one plant operator should not have worked the morning part of the shift and the other one the afternoon part of the shift. If this had been done the two men would have worked hours very closely approximating to their basic of 40 hours a week and when one takes account of the existence of £2 good time keeping bonus they would have received within about £3 of their basic wage. . . .

As it was, since the expedient was not thought of, it follows that it was not put to the men and therefore the men, and in particular the applicant, were deprived of the opportunity of accepting or refusing the offer. We are unanimously of the opinion that this failure on the respondent company's part to consider what really should be the first thing to come to mind tips the balance and makes this dismissal of the applicant statutorily unfair.

Modern Injection Moulds Ltd. v. Price
[1976] I.R.L.R. 172; [1976] I.C.R. 370
Employment Appeal Tribunal

A redundancy situation arose and the company proposed, instead of dismissing Mr Price, to offer him a position as shop foreman, with fewer shifts. No information was given to Mr Price about the overtime prospects of the new job and after giving it consideration, he rejected the offer and claimed that he had been unfairly dismissed.

PHILLIPS J. [After citing *Vokes Ltd.* v *Bear* see above p. 121, the judge continued]: In our judgment it can be said that inasmuch as there is this obligation on the part of the employers to try to find suitable alternative employment within the firm, it must follow that, if they are in a position, pursuant to their obligation, to make an offer to the employee of suitable alternative employment, they must give him sufficient information on the basis of which the employee can make a realistic decision whether to take the new job. It will, of course, depend upon the circumstances in every case, how much information, and information upon what subjects, must be given. Normally, at all events, and certainly in this case, it is necessary for the employer to inform the employee of the financial prospects of the new job. The test must always be (it has to be looked at from the point of view of the employee): has he been given sufficient information upon which he can make a realistic decision whether to take the job and stay, or whether to reject it and leave?. . . .

. . . we think the employer here failed in that obligation.

Gwent County Council v. Lane
[1977] I.R.L.R. 337; [1978] Q.B. 438
Employment Appeal Tribunal

Mr Lane was a lecturer employed on a fixed term contract. A tribunal found that he had been unfairly dismissed on grounds of redundancy, as the employers had not made sufficient efforts to find him alternative work when his appointment as lecturer expired.

PHILLIPS J.: While we accept that consideration for the needs of the employee should be given according to what is proper in the circumstances, it seems to us that there is a danger, if the duty is pitched too high, that the reasonable discretion of the appointing body or committee or sub-committee will be unduly hampered and that the recruitment of new blood will be unreasonably restricted. In particular, we feel that the Industrial Tribunal were not right when they said in para. 12 that before other posts were advertised the claims of the temporary employee, in this case Mr Lane, should be considered, and that if he were suitable he should have been engaged in preference to advertising the post generally. This appears to amount to a rule that a comparatively short-term temporary employee whose contract has not been renewed has some kind of right to priority of appointment to an available suitable post over and above any other suitable candidate. We think this is going too far. Certainly, we think that even if in a particular case the circumstances seem to justify such a conclusion, it would require careful examination of the evidence to see what the practical consequences of such a rule would be.

Hassall v. Fusion Welding & Construction (Birkenhead) Co. Ltd.
[1979] I.R.L.R. 12
Employment Appeal Tribunal

The employee was dismissed on grounds of redundancy. There was no implementation of a voluntary redundancy scheme or of short-time working.

SLYNN J.: It is clear that in considering redundancy it may very well be an important matter for an employer to consider whether either short-time [working] or voluntary redundancies can avoid the need to make people redundant who do not wish to be made redundant. . . .

. . . . It seems to us, having considered this matter with some anxiety, that here the size of the reduction which had to take place is such that short-time [working] could not in any event have produced any solution which could have affected the position of Mr Hassall. The question whether a scheme of voluntary redundancies could have been effected was considered and it appears to have been the view both of the union and of the employers that a scheme of voluntary redundancy here was not going to be an answer to the problem. It was only by adopting the principle of "last in first out" that the necessary reduction in the work force could take place.

Atkinson v. George Lindsay & Co.
[1980] I.R.L.R. 196
Court of Session

Mr Atkinson was dismissed from his job as a glazier on grounds of redundancy on the basis of the application of the last-in-first-out principle. An Industrial Tribunal held that his dismissal was unfair, on evidence which included statements at the hearing by several of Mr Atkinson's co-workers that if they had been consulted, they would probably have accepted an alternative scheme which did not require his dismissal, such as a reduction in the working week.

LORD EMSLIE: The evidence of "several" of the appellant's co-workers only, provides, too, a wholly inadequate basis on which to rest the Industrial Tribunal's inferential conclusion that consultation with the trade union would have induced the employers to adopt an alternative plan which did not involve any dismissals at all. The material to which the Industrial Tribunal had regard does not include any evidence that the alternative solution of a shorter working week was compatible with the requirements of the respondents' business, and it contains no evidence whatever of the attitude the respondents were likely to take to such a proposal . . . In the whole matter I am satisfied that the conclusion of the Industrial Tribunal owed everything to speculation and nothing to inference.

Williams v. Compair Maxam Ltd.
[1982] I.R.L.R. 83
Employment Appeal Tribunal

During 1980 a redundancy situation arose in the respondent company. The appellant and others were dismissed without warning or consultation.

BROWNE-WILKINSON J.: . . . there is a generally accepted view in industrial relations that, in cases where the employees are represented by an independent union recognised by the employer, reasonable employers will seek to act in accordance with the following principles: . . . 5. The employer will seek to see whether instead of dismissing an employee he could offer him alternative employment. . . .

Finally, the employers did not consider transferring employees to a different job involving demotion: such transfer was, as the majority found, "dismissed as a possibility" since it was thought to lead to bad industrial relations and dissatisfaction. If there had been any consultation with the union or the employees involved, there might well have emerged some ground for not considering such transfers. But in the absence of such consultation, simply to rule out the possibility seems to us unreasonable.

Barratt Construction Ltd. v. Dalrymple
[1984] I.R.L.R. 385
Employment Appeal Tribunal

Mr Dalrymple was dismissed because of redundancy. An Industrial Tribunal held the dismissal unfair as the employers could have done more to try to find him alternative employment.

LORD McDONALD: In the present case the evidence before the Tribunal was that the appellants' regional director had looked around within his own company but no other employment was available. Notwithstanding this the Tribunal seem to consider that the possibility of offering employment in a subordinate post such as general foreman ought to have been canvassed. Apparently in evidence the respondent said that he would have accepted such a post but there is no hint of this prior to his being asked about it at the Tribunal. The Tribunal take the matter further. They say that the regional director ought to have made enquiries as to whether there were vacancies in the other companies in the group, notwithstanding that these were autonomous. In this respect the Tribunal state that they consider that the appellants' regional director acted unreasonably, "and as there is no evidence to show that had such an enquiry been made it would have been fruitless, the applicant is entitled to the benefit of the doubt upon that question. The dismissal must therefore be found unfair."

In our opinion the Industrial Tribunal have erred in reaching this conclusion. . . . The evidence before [the Industrial Tribunal] disclosed that efforts were made to see if alternative employment was available within the appellants' company and that no suggestion was ever made by the respondent that he would be interested in a more junior appointment until he gave evidence before the Tribunal. Without laying down any hard and fast rule we are inclined to think that where an employee at senior management level who is being made redundant is prepared to accept a subordinate position he ought, in fairness, to make this clear at an early stage so as to give his employer an opportunity to see if this is a feasible solution.

It is well accepted that a reasonable employer will not make an employee redundant if he can employ him elsewhere, even in another capacity. This dates from the decision in *Vokes Ltd* v *D.C. Bear* [1973] I.R.L.R. 363, above p. 121. . . . The principle which [that case] decided still holds good. A reasonable employer will seek to see whether instead of dismissing for redundancy he can offer alternative employment (*Williams* v *Compair Maxam Ltd.* [1982] I.R.L.R. 83, above p. 124). It is not however, for an Industrial Tribunal to speculate as to what further steps ought to be taken and to draw an inference adverse to the employer because he has not taken them.

In the present case, in our opinion, the Tribunal have exceeded their function in postulating that the appellants should have canvassed the possibility of employment in other independent companies and, indeed, in the circumstances of this case, that there was an obligation upon them to offer employment, if available, in a junior capacity.

The cases above deal with the requirement to consider measures to avoid or prevent redundancies developed from the statutory "reasonableness" test in the law of unfair dismissal (EPCA., s.57(3)). Collective agreements requiring such measures were cited above (p. 117). A combination of the statutory requirements with those of collective agreements could be a powerful instrument of employment protection in redundancy situations. An agreed procedure could replace the Code of Practice as the legally required conduct in the event of redundancy, on pain of unfair dismissal claims. Such a combination of collective agreements and statute might seem to be indicated by EPCA, s.59(*b*), which declares a dismissal unfair if the employee "was selected for dismissal in contravention of a customary arrangement or agreed procedure relating to redundancy."

McDowell v. Eastern British Road Services Ltd.
[1981] I.R.L.R. 482
Employment Appeal Tribunal

MAY J.: . . . the brief facts of this case are, first, that there was in existence at the respondents' concern what one can describe as an agreed procedure in the case of redundancy. I need only refer to two sub-paragraphs. On p. 35 paragraph 1(a) reads:

> "There will be consultation with the trade unions at company or regional or appropriate committee level."

At p. 36, paragraph 1(b) is in these terms:

> "In declaring redundancy the principle of 'last in—first out', all things being equal, will be followed and regard will be paid to overall service with the organisation (and its predecessors). Substitution of volunteers may be permitted subject to suitability and following consultation between management and the trade unions."

Accepting for the purpose of deciding this appeal, but for no other purpose, that there were contraventions of that redundancy procedure in these respects, namely that there was no consultation with the trade unions at appropriate level and, secondly, that the question of calling for volunteers was not sufficiently investigated, Mr Goodchild, on the appellants' behalf, contends that the dismissals had to be regarded as unfair and there was no scope for the Industrial Tribunal to consider the matter under [EPCA] s.57. Mr Inglis, for the respondents, submits that on its proper construction, [EPCA] s.59 and, in particular, the words in sub-paragraph (b) only apply to contraventions of an agreed procedure, or customary arrangement if such there be, which are themselves relevant to the actual selection of the relevant employee for that particular redundancy. The point therefore is a narrow one. It depends upon first impressions as questions of construction so often do. Having considered the matter, we have no doubt that s.59 must be construed in the restricted way contended for by Mr Inglis and that it only applies where the actual selection of the relevant employee has itself been in contravention of an agreed redundancy procedure. For instance: where there is a redundancy agreement which provides without any qualification for the application of the "last in—first out" principle, then, if a redundancy situation thereafter develops and an employer chooses an employee to be redundant not upon that basis but upon the basis that his absenteeism record has not been good, or that his work is not quite up to the standard of his fellows, this would clearly be a breach of an agreed selection procedure; if the employee is dismissed as redundant for these reasons, then s.57 would have no application, the facts would fall under s.59, and the dismissal *ex hypothesi* would be unfair. It is, in our view, that type of situation to which s.59 is directed. If s.59(b), in particular, is to be given the wider construction for which Mr Goodchild contends, it is not easy to see the need for s.57 in a redundancy case. There are many decisions in the books where there have been fair selections for redundancy but breaches of procedural agreements in respects other than the direct selection of the person to be made redundant. These have gone to an Industrial Tribunal under s.57, it being contended under subsection (3) that although the selection may have been fair, the dismissal was unfair, having regard to all the circumstances of the case and to its merits. In our view, those are matters which are properly dealt with under s.57, not under s.59, which has, we think, to be a restricted meaning.

The E.A.T. in *McDowell* declined to adopt a policy of combining statutory requirements and collective bargaining. It preferred to retain the discretionary power of Industrial Tribunals to decide whether the employer has nonetheless acted reasonably, under EPCA, s.57(3), even when the collective agreement has been violated.

(iii) Redundancy consultations

There is a clear link between the taking of measures to avoid redundancy and redundancy consultation—for only consultation of the employees affected and their trade union representatives can ensure that alternatives to redundancy are thoroughly explored. Failure to consult thus means possible failure to prevent redundancies—which may make a dismissal unfair. As put by Bristow J. in *Abbotts and Standley* v. *Wesson-Glynwed Steels Ltd.* [1982] I.R.L.R. 51 (para. 16) E.A.T.:

> "If, as here, you dismiss a senior employee of long standing at a moment's notice with no consultation whatever, you are not simply treating him with discourtesy. . . . You are depriving yourself of the opportunity to explore together with him the possibility of finding another slot in which to place him, and upon this basis it would be open to the Industrial Tribunal to find your action in dismissing him in the circumstances to be unreasonable."

We begin by looking at collective industrial practice on the matter of consultation and then at the legal requirements included in EPA, s.99 and the law of unfair dismissal.

(*a*) *Collective bargaining*

Collective agreements have improved upon the statutory requirements in EPA 1975, which provide that employers should consult trade unions over redundancy proposals a minimum of 90 days before dismissals take place (if more than 100 redundancies are involved; 30 days if more than 10 redundancies are involved). *Bargaining Report* No. 33 (1984) refers to three agreements which feature regularly convened joint meetings which consider matters likely to affect staffing levels and seek to find methods of avoiding "staff surpluses." Reviews of agreements with guaranteed minimum consultation periods in the surveys of 1981 and 1984 revealed the following:

	No. of agreements	
	1981	*1984*
12 months	—	1
6 months before any redundancy	2	2
3 months before any redundancy	4	6
3 months before more than 50 redundancies	1	—
2 months before any redundancy	4	3
2 months before more than 10 redundancies	4	—
2 months before less than 10 redundancies	—	3

The following agreements were featured in the 1979 survey.

Williams & Glyns Bank Ltd (Bank staff)

> Redundancy Procedure:
>
> The Bank must inform the union of possible redundancies at least one month before the agreed two months' notice is given to staff concerned—unless there are "justifiable circumstances" for giving [shorter notice].
> There should be no general announcement until both sides have been able to consult fully on the implications of redundancy during the warning period.
> During this period the union must be consulted on management proposals to be made redundant. Any disagreement on the proposals can be referred to an internal joint redundancy appeals committee.
> During the consultation period the Bank will continue exploring the possibilities of redeployment and retraining for surplus staff, and inform the union of progress on this.

National Water Council (NJIC manual workers)

> Consultation:
>
> Employers will consult employees affected and the trade unions representing them on the appropriate negotiating body at the earliest opportunity, but in any event no later than 90 days before the implementation of the measures . . . to counteract employee surpluses.
> This requirement will normally exceed, both in scope of application and length of notice the minimum requirements imposed by Part IV of the Employment Protection Act 1975.

(b) The law

There are two principal legal sources requiring consultation before redundancies are implemented: EPA, s.99, and the law of unfair dismissal.

(i) Statutory consultation of trade unions: EPA, s.99. The origins of this legal obligation lie in the EEC Council Directive 75/129 of February 17, 1975. The U.K. gave effect to this Directive in EPA, s.99 *et seq.* Where the Act is ambiguous, the EEC Directive provides guidance as to the intention of Parliament (*e.g. GMWU (MATSA)* v. *British Uralite Ltd.* [1979] I.R.L.R. 409 (I.T.)).

The statutory provisions raise a number of difficulties when applied to complex industrial relations circumstances. Who are the trade union representatives who must be consulted when there is a multitude of representatives at different levels? What if the employer is not a single independent entity, but a unit in a complex organisation involving a holding company and a number of subsidiaries? At what level in the decision-making process of this larger economic unit does the obligation come into being? When is a trade union "recognised" so as to require the employer to consult it (see Chapter 12 on *Collective Bargaining*, p. 474). Each of these questions raises sensitive issues of policy which tribunals have to consider. The different policy choices open to tribunals are illustrated in the following cases.

(1) Which trade union representatives ought to be consulted?

General and Municipal Workers Union v. **Wailes Dove Bitumastic Ltd.**
[1977] I.R.L.R. 45
Industrial Tribunal

The employer consulted over proposed redundancies with the GMWU shop steward for their factory. The union complained that the consultation ought to have been with the union's appropriate full-time official, their Regional Organiser, Mr Porter.

NEWCASTLE TRIBUNAL (chairman: M.J. Goodman): . . . we hold that Mr Porter was not a trade union representative within the meaning of [EPA] s.99 who should have been consulted. Mr Porter had never himself carried on collective bargaining with the respondent company about the production workers at the Hebburn factory. There was no trade union representative who needed to be consulted other than Mr Madge the accredited GMWU shop steward at the Hebburn factory, who had held that position since December 1970. . . .

. . . s.99(1) and (2) require consultation with trade union representatives and then defines trade union representative in a way that exculpates the company if they dealt with Mr Madge alone, who was clearly willing to deal with this matter on his own without reference to Mr Porter. It may be that Mr Porter thinks that, within his own internal union structure, Mr Madge should refer such matters to Mr Porter. We make no comment about that. But all an employer has to do to discharge the onus laid upon him by s.99 is to show that he consulted a trade union representative or representatives and we are satisfied on the facts of this case that the employers did that for the reasons given above.

(2) At what stage in the decision-making process ought trade union representatives to be involved?

National Union of Teachers v. **Avon County Council**
[1978] I.R.L.R. 55; I.C.R. 726
Employment Appeal Tribunal

On October 28, 1976 the employers issued redundancy notices to a number of teachers. On the following day they began consultations over the redundancies with the recognised union.

PHILLIPS J.: The question, and really it is the only question we have to decide, is the fundamental question whether it is ever a compliance with the provisions of [EPA] s.99 to begin consultation after, rather than before, dismissing the employee for redundancy. . . . s.99(1) is talking about an employer proposing to dismiss and though "dismiss" may be ambiguous and mean either the giving of a notice, or the effective bringing into effect of that notice by its expiry, it seems to us that in the context it is the former which is in contemplation. Sub-section (4), similarly, is plainly talking about what is planned or proposed and not about what has been done. Sub-section (5) makes it even plainer because it requires a disclosure in writing to the trade union of matters such as the proposed method of selecting the employees who may be dismissed, and the proposed method of carrying out the dismissal; and the whole tenor of the enactment is that it is talking about what is planned or proposed to do but has (not) yet been done. . . . It seems plain to us that s.99 requires an employer who is proposing to dismiss to begin consultation. That really is in accordance with the practice, and the practice going back long before the Act came into operation. All that s.99 does is to give statutory force, in a case where a trade union is recognised, to the previous practice, but to give it teeth and to prescribe in far greater detail the way in which it is to be operated. . . . [The E.A.T. considered the case of the employer giving notice of dismissal one day *after* consultations begin, and concluded:] . . . it seems to us that the answer is this: that there is nothing to prevent it, but that, if it is done, it may well be the case that it will turn out that there has never been any meaningful consultation by the employer such as is required by s.99. . . .

Association of Patternmakers & Allied Craftsmen v. Kirvin Ltd.
[1978] I.R.L.R. 318
Employment Appeal Tribunal

In early 1977 the employers were in economic difficulties and by the end of April they decided to try to sell their company as a going concern. There was a real prospect of a purchaser being found until the end of June but, when the last prospective purchaser disappeared, they were forced to appoint a receiver. The receiver immediately gave notice of redundancy to the entire workforce.

Lord McDonald: It was argued on behalf of the appellants that an employer proposed to dismiss his employee as redundant not at the date when he decided to take this action but at the date when such a possibility entered or should reasonably have entered his contemplation. It was pointed out to us that the Directive of the European Economic Community [75/129] relating to collective redundancies, upon which [EPA] s.99 was said to be based, used the words "contemplating collective redundancies." In the present case the possibility of mass redundancy ought to have been within the contemplation of the respondents long before the end of June 1977.

In our opinion a proposal to make redundant within the meaning of s.99 connotes a state of mind directed to a planned or proposed course of events (*National Union of Teachers* v *Avon County Council* [1978] I.R.L.R. 55, above p. 129). The employer must have formed some view as to how many are to be dismissed, when this is to take place and how it is to be arranged. This goes beyond the mere contemplation of a possible event . . . [The Industrial Tribunal held as a matter of fact] that it was a reasonable hope for the respondents to entertain that they would be able to sell the business and avoid redundancies. Not only were potential purchasers genuinely in the field but the company was being subsidised by the Government right up until 30.6.77, no doubt with a view to preserving jobs. In these circumstances we cannot accept the appellants' argument that prior to that date they were "proposing" to dismiss as redundant members of their union. Even if they were, it would, in our view, have been fatal to the delicate negotiations for the sale of the business which were taking place if attempts were made at that stage to comply with s.99.

National and Local Government Officers' Association v. National Travel (Midlands) Ltd.

[1978] I.C.R. 598
Employment Appeal Tribunal

The employer was one of four regional subsidiaries of a London based parent company. On February 8, 1977, the parent company informed the employer-subsidiary that there would have to be redundancies.

KILNER BROWN J.: On February 11, because of rumours which were circulating, the appropriate representative of the National and Local Government Officers Association, the trade union, called on the general manager who informed him that the rumours were justified and that statements would be made on February 14. Before that announcement there was a meeting on that day with various trade union representatives. So they were informed. Were they consulted there and then? Was there a proposal at that time? Or was there a statement preparatory to a proposal? It was made clear at the meeting when the statement was read out that no detailed proposals had been considered, let alone made. It was arranged that there should be a meeting to discuss proposals on February 21. On February 18 the representative of the trade union sent off an application under [EPA] section 101(1) alleging a failure to comply with the provisions of section 99. We (and one of our number has many years of experience of trade union negotiation) find it difficult to understand why this step was taken so soon. In our judgment this legislation never envisaged a requirement for a trade union to be involved in preliminary policy considerations which are a managerial responsibility which most trade unions would wish to avoid. Secondly, it left the trade union wide open to the finding that the application was misconceived. By an allegation that the company were in breach of the statutory requirement by reason of the announcement of February 14 they were inviting the answer that they got from the Industrial Tribunal, which was that the company had done nothing wrong. . . .

(3) What is the content and nature of the consultation required?

Spillers-French (Holdings) Ltd. v. Union of Shop, Distributive and Allied Workers

[1979] I.R.L.R. 339
Employment Appeal Tribunal

Without prior consultation with the union, the employer announced on April 7, 1978 that 36 of their bakeries would be closed down on April 26, 1978.

SLYNN J.: Indeed the object of this legislation quite clearly is to give an opportunity for consultation between employer, trade unions and the Secretary of State. The consultation may result in new ideas being ventilated which avoid the redundancy situation altogether. Equally it may lead to a lesser number of persons being made redundant than was originally thought necessary. Or it may be that alternative work can be found during the period of consultation. So one has to bear in mind that at this first stage the duty is to give the "numbers and descriptions" of employees concerned. . . .

For example, one requirement of the [Employment Protection] Act [1975] is that necessary information shall be disclosed in writing. It might be that if all the information had been given orally to a trade union representative, a Tribunal would not take a very serious view of that as a failure to comply with a requirement. On the other hand, failure to give reasons at all, or failure to include one of the matters specified in s.99(5), might be more serious. A failure to consult at all, or consultation only at the last minute, might be taken to be even more serious.

General and Municipal Workers Union (MATSA) v. British Uralite Ltd.

[1979] I.R.L.R. 413
Industrial Tribunal

On February 5, 1979 the employers drew up proposals for redundancies. On February 14, 1979 the union was verbally informed that there would be redundancies. On February 15, 1979 notices of dismissal were despatched and the union was given a written memorandum with the details. On February 19, 1979 the employer met with the union officials who raised various questions about the redundancies. On February 26, 1979 the employer replied to these.

Ashford Tribunal (chairman: B.A. Hepple): . . . the respondent employers informed MATSA of actual dismissals rather than of *proposals*. Mr Panto (on behalf of the union) submits that this was a serious default because had MATSA been presented with proposals compromise would have been more readily available; the method of selection may have been different, particularly by voluntary redundancy; employees would have been kept in employment longer and consideration would have been given to longer notice periods. Mr Tabachnik (for the employer) on the other hand, submits that the default was one of language or form rather than substance, and that all the matters raised by Mr Panto were reasonably rejected by the respondent employers at the meeting on 26.2.79.

We accept Mr Panto's submission, insofar as he complains that this was a default of substance and not simply of form. It is obviously more difficult to have consultations with a view to reaching agreement after a decision has been communicated as an accomplished fact, instead of being given a genuine proposal open to discussion. In particular, it appears to us that had proposals been made there is a reasonable likelihood that voluntary redundancies could have been secured which might have averted the dismissals of some of the employees who form the subject of this complaint.

Transport and General Workers Union v. Ledbury Preserves (1928) Ltd.

[1985] I.R.L.R 412
Employment Appeal Tribunal

On September 23, 1983 the employers called a meeting at short notice and informed the shop stewards of the recognised union of 25 redundancies. The union representatives were asked for comments, but did not say much. Half an hour after the conclusion of the meeting, dismissal notices were given to the redundant employees. A subsequent meeting of October 20, 1983, requested by the union, produced no substantive changes. An Industrial Tribunal rejected the union's complaint.

Peter Graham J.: [After citing the *Avon County Council* and *Spillers-French (Holdings) Ltd.* cases (see p. 129 and p. 131 above)] it seems to us that these authorities are persuasive in support of the proposition that there must be sufficient meaningful consultation before notices of dismissal are sent out. The consultation must not be a sham exercise; there must be time for the union representatives who are consulted to consider properly the proposals that are being put to them. In the present case, we have already adverted to the fact that the meeting at which the consultation took place was called at short notice and that the union officials were somewhat taken by surprise. And yet, about half an hour after the meeting, the notices of dismissal were sent out.

The Tribunal appears to have placed considerable weight on the fact that there was a subsequent meeting on 20 October, that is to say long after the dismissal notices had gone out, and on the fact that the intentions of the employers were such that the dismissal notices themselves were not designed to shut the door on consultation. The dismissal notices were, however, in clear and unequivocal terms and did not invite consultation. We find it hard to see how a reasonable Tribunal could consider that those matters could have added to the meaningfulness or adequacy of the consultation required before the issue of the notices. True it is that the Tribunal find that at the time of the meeting on 23 September it was not too late for the union to make representations. But the union only had that meeting and half an hour thereafter to make representations before the dismissal notices were sent out.

In placing the weight that they did on opportunities to make representations after the issue of the dismissal notices, we think that the Tribunal erred in law.

(4) What are "special circumstances which make it not reasonably practicable for the employer to comply with any of the requirements" EPA, s.99(8)? In particular, to what extent can an Industrial Tribunal use its judgment in deciding that the employer's circumstances were or were not special?

Hamish Armour v. Association of Scientific, Technical and Managerial Staffs
[1979] I.R.L.R. 24
Employment Appeal Tribunal

In 1976 the employer, in financial difficulties, applied for a Government loan. It was granted, but too little and too late. In December 1977 another loan was applied for. On January 12, 1978 it was refused, but it was suggested that another Government department might help. On February 3, 1978 this hope was dashed. The employer thereupon laid off the entire workforce. On February 7, 1978 the receiver dismissed the workforce forthwith.

Lord McDonald: There are other findings, however, which we do not consider the Tribunal were entitled to make. These were that it should have been apparent to the company that the scales were weighted against a second loan being granted: that it should also have been apparent to them that even if granted it would afford only temporary relief to be replaced shortly by a further crisis; and that from the autumn of 1977 onwards the company was not entitled to indulge itself in hopes that it could survive. In reaching these conclusions the Tribunal have, with benefit of hindsight, substituted their own business and commercial judgment for that of the company and in effect decided for it when it should have gone into liquidation. It is not the function of a Tribunal to do this, and we do not consider that the present Tribunal were entitled to make these findings.

In light of the above has it been shown that there were special circumstances within the meaning of [EPA] s.101(2)(a)? It is settled that insolvency is not by itself a special circumstance, although it may be, It must be something out of the ordinary, something uncommon (*The Bakers' Union* v *Clarks of Hove Ltd.* [1978] I.R.L.R. 366). In our view an application for a government loan by a company in financial difficulties which had already received substantial financial help from government sources is a circumstance sufficiently special to make it not reasonably practicable to issue the formal written details required by s.99(5) until the outcome of the application was known.

(5) What is the remedy for a union representative whose right to be consulted has been violated by the employer?

The statute here pursues an unusual policy. The subject of the legal right—the trade union—is given the right to complain to an Industrial Tribunal. But the remedy is in the form of compensation to the employees who suffered as a consequence of the employer's non-compliance. This form of collective trade union right but individual employee remedy is also to be found in the other collective right in EPA: the right of a union to have information disclosed to it for collective bargaining purposes (see Chapter 12 on *Collective Bargaining*). The assessment of a remedy for employees in consequence of a wrong done to their trade union is an awkward exercise for Industrial Tribunals, hovering between the loss caused to the employees and the default of the employer. One can sympathise with their predicament, while still wondering at their solutions.

Spillers-French (Holdings) Ltd. v. Union of Shop, Distributive and Allied Workers
[1979] I.R.L.R. 339
Employment Appeal Tribunal

For the facts, see above, p. 131.

Slynn J.: Parliament has given to the Industrial Tribunals the power, if they so decide, also to make a protective award which involves the payment of money. It seems to us that when the decision is taken, the question which has to be looked at is not the loss or potential loss of actual remuneration during the relevant period by the particular employee. It is to consider the loss of days of consultation which have occurred. The Tribunal will have to consider, how serious was the breach on the part of the employer? It may be that the employer has done everything that he can possibly do to ensure that his employees are found other employment. If that happens, a Tribunal may well take the view that either there should be no award or, if there is an award, it should be nominal. It does not seem to us that the Tribunal has to be satisfied, before it can make an award, that the employees have been paid during the relevant period. Indeed, if the application is made before the dismissals take place, these facts may not be known. It might be quite impossible to know, until the end of the period, what is the position so far as earnings from the same employer or from other sources are concerned. . . .

This approach, looking to loss of days of consultation, was cited with approval in *E. Green & Son (Castings) Ltd.* v. *ASTMS* [1984] I.R.L.R. 135 (E.A.T.).

(ii) Failure to consult and unfair dismissal. The Industrial Relations Code of Practice 1972 (paras. 44–46) stipulated that management should consult employees or their representatives in redundancy situations. (*Cf*. the draft Code of Practice on Disciplinary Rules and Procedures 1986). In *Freud* v. *Bentalls Ltd.* [1982] I.R.L.R. 443 (E.A.T.), Browne-Wilkinson J. summarised the ambiguity of this requirement when he said that the Code "is the statutory statement of good industrial practice although the Code does not lay down rules of law."

The Code has been invoked as one source for interpreting the "reasonableness" obligation (EPCA, s.57(3)) in cases of dismissals as including an obligation to consult. Thus, failure to consult over redundancies may be so unreasonable as to make the subsequent dismissal unfair. The following case stated this is categorical terms.

Williams v. Compair Maxam Ltd.
[1982] I.R.L.R. 83
Employment Appeal Tribunal

For the facts, see p. 124 above.

BROWNE-WILKINSON J.: . . . there is a generally accepted view in industrial relations that, in cases where the employees are represented by an independent union recognised by the employer, reasonable employers will seek to act in accordance with the following principles:

1. The employer will seek to give as much warning as possible of impending redundancies so as to enable the union and employees who may be affected to take early steps to inform themselves of the relevant facts, consider possible alternative solutions and, if necessary, find alternative employment in the undertaking or elsewhere.

2. The employer will consult the union as to the best means by which the desired management result can be achieved fairly and with as little hardship to the employees as possible. In particular, the employer will seek to agree with the union the criteria to be applied in selecting the employees to be made redundant. When a selection has been made, the employer will consider with the union whether the selection has been made in accordance with those criteria.

The significance of industrial practice in educating the judges towards policy choices is illustrated by the following case.

Freud v. Bentalls Ltd.
[1982] I.R.L.R. 443
Employment Appeal Tribunal

In July 1980 a list of employees, including Mrs Freud, was drawn up whom it was proposed to make redundant. The decision to dismiss Mrs Freud was taken on January 22, 1981, however, and only five days later was she so informed, without prior warning or consultation. She claimed unfair dismissal. An Industrial Tribunal held the dismissal was not unfair by reason only of the absence of warning or consultation.

BROWNE-WILKINSON J.: Our reasons for holding this decision to be perverse hinge on the failure of the company to take any step to consult Mrs Freud during the period after 22.1.81. after the date when the board's decision to close the press office was final and Mrs Freud's redundancy became certain. It was perfectly possible for a reasonable Industrial Tribunal properly directing itself to reach the view that the failure to consult or warn Mrs Freud before 22.1.81 was not unreasonable. But in our view in the circumstances found by the Industrial Tribunal in their decision the failure to do so after 22nd January cannot be held to be reasonable. There are two main reasons for our view, the first a matter of law and the second relates to fair industrial practice.

The relevant point of law is that s.57(3) of [EPCA] (as amended) requires the Industrial Tribunal to consider whether *on the date on which the employers dismissed the employee* they were acting reasonably in treating redundancy as a sufficient reason for dismissing the employee. . . .

Turning now to considerations of industrial relations practice, consultation (as opposed to unilateral action by the employer) is one of the foundation stones of modern industrial relations practice. The statutory Code of Practice emphasises its importance in every aspect of industrial relations. In the particular sphere of redundancy, good industrial relations practice in the ordinary case requires consultation with the redundant employee so that the employer may find out whether the needs of the business can be met in some way other than by dismissal and, if not, what other steps the employer can take to ameliorate the blow to the employee. In some cases (though not this one) the employee may be able to suggest some re-organisation which will obviate the need for dismissal; in virtually all cases the employer if he consults will find out what steps he can take to find the employee alternative employment either within the company or outside it. For example, in present day conditions when so many people are unemployed many employees facing redundancy by reason of the disappearance of their existing job are prepared to take other jobs of lower status and commanding less pay. Only by consulting the employee can the employer discover whether such an option is open in any given case. Therefore good industrial relations practice requires that, unless there are special circumstances which render such consultation impossible or unnecessary, a fair employer will consult with the employee before dismissing him.

We must emphasise that we are not saying that good industrial relations practice *invariably* requires such consultation. There may well be circumstances (for example, a catastrophic cash flow problem making it essential to take immediate steps to reduce the wages bill) which render consultation impracticable. We are only saying that we would expect a reasonable employer, if he has not consulted the employee prior to dismissal for redundancy in any given case, to be able to show some special reason why he had not done so.

The views expressed in the last two paragraphs are those of the lay members of this Tribunal, although they accord with the Chairman's experience in seeing the approach of Industrial Tribunals to the very many cases on redundancy which come before this Appeal Tribunal.

Despite this recognition of industrial practice, the proper standard of reasonableness, the judges are reluctant to relinquish their discretion to decide upon the required timing and content of the consultations. This led another division (*A. Simpson & Son (Motors)* v. *Reid and Findlater* [1983] I.R.L.R. 401 (E.A.T.), *per* Lord McDonald at p. 402) of the E.A.T. to refer to the "guidelines" in *Williams* v. *Compair Maxam Ltd.* (see above p. 135):

> " . . . becoming overworked and increasingly misapplied . . . . It was certainly never intended that the five so-called principles [of good industrial practice] should be considered in each and every redundancy case, should be ticked off as in a shopping list, as to whether or not they had been complied with . . . ."

In each case the Tribunal measures what the employer has done against the sole legal criterion of "reasonableness." In an area as sensitive as redundancy, the Tribunals might well benefit from further guidance.

(iv) Selection for redundancy

When measures to avoid redundancy have not succeeded and consultations have not led to alternatives, the invidious task of selection for redundancy arises. Here once again we find collective industrial practice as well as legal rules regulating the process of selection.

(*a*) *Collective bargaining*

The review of 110 redundancy schemes and job security agreements in *Bargaining Report* No. 33 (1984) concluded that "while a number of schemes do mention factors such as timekeeping and attendance records as criteria for selection, the most common methods are volunteers, early retirement and last in first out." This was also reflected in the 1981 survey of 175 agreements (*Bargaining Report* No. 14). In 1981, 51 schemes accepted the principle of voluntary redundancy being preferable to compulsory dismissal, but many gave the management the right to reject individual applications. In 1984, nine schemes were specifically directed at volunteers, with no provision for compulsory redundancy; 48 schemes stipulated that the employer should first look for volunteers before introducing compulsion. In 1981, 15 schemes made provision for early retirement, but 53 made special provision for older workers to be made redundant. In 1984, 28 agreements provided for early retirement, mainly on a voluntary basis. The last in first out principle is widely accepted, with 52 schemes accepting it in 1981 and 27 in 1984. Some schemes reserve to management the right to alter the principle if an "unbalanced" workforce would result, with the agreement of the relevant trade union. The following agreements were featured in the 1979 survey (*Bargaining Report* No. 3).

London Co-operative Society Ltd. (Shop and Store Staff)

Selection Criteria:

When redundancy is unavoidable, selection for such redundancy will be in the following order:

persons beyond retirement age;
voluntary redundancy within the trade or grade where acceptable and practicable;
full and part-time staff within the trade or grade;
any such redundancies on a 'last in first out' basis, all other things being equal.

The Plessey Company Ltd (Staff)

Basis of selection:

The basis of selection of employees to be declared redundant is determined by 'the needs of business'. Particular attention is to be paid to the following—bearing in mind the need to maintain an efficient, balanced labour force:

part-time workers;
employees over normal retirement age;
voluntary redundancy;
short service rather than long service employees;

If an individual disagrees with his/her selection, there is an agreed procedure for dealing with this.

BBC (Weekly Staff)

Treatment of staff:

A main consideration in selection for redundancy will be the needs of the service. An example of this would be the need to maintain the balance of a reduced service. Subject to this, the following principles apply:

unestablished or temporary staff to be considered before established staff;
similarly, temporary staff to be considered before unestablished staff;
staff with short service to be considered for redundancy before those with longer service—subject to efficiency and any legal considerations;
staff under 65 have priority for retention over those over 65. Staff over 60 only to be retained in preference to younger staff in exceptional cases.

(*b*) *The law*

The rules governing the selection of employees for redundancy have two sources. One is the judicial development of the "reasonableness" requirement which the law of unfair dismissal imposes on the employer (EPCA, s.57(3)). The other is the provision in EPCA s.59 requiring adherence to "customary arrangement or agreed procedure."

(i) Customary arrangements or agreed procedures: EPCA, s.59. This provision could be read as supporting collective industrial practice, including measures to avoid redundancy, consultation procedures, provision for redundancy payments and time off entitlements—as well as selection procedures. But the view has been expressed that only contravention of *selection* procedures would allow a claim based on section 59 (*McDowell* v. *Eastern BRS Ltd.* [1981] I.R.L.R. 482 (E.A.T.), above, p. 126).

There is no definition of "customary arrangement or agreed procedure." The temptation to adopt common law conceptions of "custom" was apparent in the view of "customary arrangement" proposed by Donaldson J. in *Bessenden Properties Ltd.* v. *Corness* [1973] I.R.L.R. 365 (N.I.R.C.):

> "In our judgment what is contemplated by this section—though we do not seek to define it in this case—is something which is so well known, so certain and so clear as to amount in effect to an implied "agreed procedure" as contrasted with the express "agreed procedure" which is the alternative contemplated . . . ."

The common law approach was further evident in a decision of the Court of Appeal which disagreed with Donaldson J.'s view that agreed procedures need be *express*: "An agreement in English law, as is well known, can be made either expressly or by implication" (*Henry* v. *Ellerman City Liners Ltd.* [1984] I.R.L.R. 409, *per* O'Connor L.J. at p. 410). The problem of determining what amounts to a customary arrangement or agreed procedure raises questions of policy relating to collective bargaining structures and process, as the following cases illustrate.

Jackson v. General Accident Fire & Life Assurance Co. Ltd.
[1976] I.R.L.R. 338
Employment Appeal Tribunal

> In the summer of 1974 the employers began a reorganisation of aspects of their work. In August 1974 they wrote a letter to a trade union to which some of their staff belonged which said: "There will be no redundancies. The rundown is expected to take place over two years . . . ." In August 1975 the employee was selected for redundancy.

LORD MCDONALD: Whilst accepting that there was no customary arrangement within this industry in this respect, it was maintained on behalf of the appellant that the letter of 9.8.74 amounted to an agreed procedure relating to redundancy. It followed upon a meeting at which the re-organisation plans were explained to members of staff in July 1974. The letter, however, was written to only one trade union and not all employees of the respondents were members of that union. We do not therefore consider that it can be properly described as an agreed procedure within the meaning of [what is now EPCA, s.59(*b*)]. The natural meaning of that expression is that in a situation where it is known that redundancies are going to arise, agreement is reached between employers and employees as to the system to be adopted in selecting those who are to be made redundant. As already stated this letter is no more than an expression of intent on the part of the employers as to the manner in which they propose to re-organise their business without involving redundancy. It is not an agreed procedure regarding redundancy but a statement of policy as to how redundancy is to be avoided. We do not therefore consider that this argument on behalf of the appellant can succeed either.

Hassall v. Fusion Welding & Construction (Birkenhead) Co. Ltd.
[1979] I.R.L.R. 12
Employment Appeal Tribunal

On the first random list of employees to be made redundant, Mr Hassall's name was not included. But after meetings with union representatives, a new list was drawn up on which his name was included.

SLYNN J.: Mr Roberts [counsel for the applicant] contends that here Mr Hassall was selected for dismissal in contravention of a customary arrangement or agreed procedure, and that no special reason justifying the departure has been shown. What he says is that in the past the company itself chose the names of any of its employees who were to be made redundant. They did so, he says, initially and they were there following their approved, agreed procedure or practice. What happened after they had shown this to the union was that a new list on a different principle was worked out, and there is a suggestion that this change was to some extent influenced by some personal or other dispute between Mr Hassall and the other union representatives. We do not consider here that it has been shown that there was a customary arrangement or agreed procedure within the meaning of [EPCA, s.59(b)].

Cf. a case where criteria for redundancy selection were used by the employer for four years without objection by the union, this was held to be an "agreed procedure" (*Henry* v. *Ellerman City Liners Ltd.* [1984] I.R.L.R. 409 (C.A.)).

Tilgate Pallets Ltd. v.Barras
[1983] I.R.L.R. 231
Employment Appeal Tribunal

Despite the existence of a customary arrangement or agreed procedure of last-in, first-out ("LIFO") in the event of redundancy, the employers drew up lists based on their desire to retain what they considered to be a viable workforce. They defended their deviation from LIFO on the grounds of certain contacts with Mr Barras, the shop steward.

NEILL J.: As far as customary arrangement is concerned the decision of the Industrial Tribunal and their finding was this: that it was common ground that up until 1981 when redundancies had occurred they had been dealt with on a "last in, first out" principle and that that was, in the past, a customary arrangement as set out in EPCA s.59. Mr Valios [counsel for the employer] has no quarrel with that finding so far as it goes. But the Industrial Tribunal then went on to consider some discussions that had taken place with Mr Barras before this particular difficulty arose in August 1981, where there had been some mention by Mr Barras that in future some system other than "LIFO" would have to be applied. They expressed their conclusion in paragraph 3(b) of the reasons in these terms:

> "We find as a fact that Mr Barras at previous times had observed that it might be appropriate for there to be discussions about amending the manner in which future redundancies were to be handled [but] there was no formal commitment by the union through him, nor did he represent to the respondents more than that it was open to consideration and discussion."

Now, that was a clear finding that Mr Barras had not altered the agreed procedure. But Mr Valios relies upon the fact that also in [paragraph 3(b) of the Industrial Tribunal's decision] there is a reference to the belief of the employers that Mr Barras had agreed that "last in, first out" should not apply to any future redundancies including, what we may call, these "August" redundancies. It seems to us that where an agreed procedure or customary arrangement has been reached and there has been no alteration to it agreed by both sides that customary arrangement will continue: the mere fact that one party believes that some alteration has taken place is not enough. We are quite satisfied that the Industrial Tribunal were fully entitled to come to the conclusion that this first part of s.59 had been complied with. They put it as follows (paragraph 3(d)):

> "There was a customary arrangement or agreed procedure relating to redundancy namely that last-in, first-out would apply."

It seems to us that that finding is quite unassailable. [It is worth noting that, as in the case of EPA, s.99(8), there is in section 59 an escape clause whereby "special reasons" may justify a departure from the procedure or arrangement. This too was invoked in the *Barras* case above.] (Neill J.): . . . Mr Valios's argument was that the employers (whose evidence on this point was not really challenged) were saying "Well, we had sufficient reason not to apply 'LIFO' because it was necessary for us to find a viable nucleus to keep this factory going and if it had not been done in the way it was done, ie finding the best people, the factory would have had to be closed down"—as, indeed, was contemplated at the time of the board meeting on 21 August. . . .

. . . . Where it is sought to be said that there are—to use the words of the section—"special reasons to justify a departure from a customary arrangement or agreed procedure" it is for the employer by evidence to prove what those special reasons are which justify a departure from the procedure in the case of the person who is being made redundant. In that event it will usually involve the introduction of some objective criteria. It seems to us that employers are not entitled to come forward and say that they have departed from the "LIFO" principle and, simply by introducing an assertion by one witness, to seek to justify what they have done by saying that the particular individuals would not have been included in a viable workforce.

Whether the employers' evidence of their need for a "viable" workforce outweighs the contravention of an agreed procedure is a policy decision of the utmost delicacy. This was evident in the divisions within the Court of Appeal in *Cross International* v. *Reid* [1985] I.R.L.R. 387. An Industrial Tribunal held that the employer departing from an agreed procedure where a serious business reverse had led to redundancies did not have "special reasons justifying a departure." The E.A.T. and a majority of the Court of Appeal dismissed the employer's appeal. Neill L.J. rejected a submission which drew a parallel with EPCA, s.57(3) that "provided that the decision was within the range of reasonable responses of an employer in the situation predicated, it was not open to the Industrial Tribunal to rule that the dismissal was unfair" (p. 392). But Watkins L.J., dissenting, issued the following warning (p. 392):

> "But Tribunals must be careful, in endeavouring to observe the law which governs them, to avoid, albeit inadvertently, substituting their judgment for that of an employer who has manifestly striven with care to cope with the unwanted problem when the need to do so cannot be avoided of laying off employees in a manner contrary to agreed procedures. If employers are shown, as here, to have behaved reasonably under stress of harsh economic necessity, it is not surprising that they should feel aggrieved if, in carrying out their distasteful task, they are said to be guilty of unfairly dismissing employees. Moreover, an appellate court must not be too sensitive about overturning a decision founded on fact if it is so obviously wrong as to outrage common sense and is contrary to principle."

(ii) Unfair selection for redundancy. Where there is no customary arrangement or agreed procedure relating to selection for redundancy, the policy issue is whether there is to be any fetter on the management's subjective discretion in selecting from among the employees whom is to be made redundant.

EPCA, s.57(3) has again been invoked in two ways. The first to be dealt with here concerns the criteria used by the employer in making the selection. The second concerns the standard of "reasonableness" he is required to satisfy in applying these criteria. This latter: the "reasonable employer" standard, is that applied to cases of dismissal generally, not only redundancy dismissals, and is examined in Chapter 10 on *Termination of Work* (see below, p. 317).

The cases reveal a conflict of opinion as to how closely the Tribunals should examine the criteria used by the employer in the selection process. In the following case, the influence of collective industrial practice in the development of the legal rules is explicitly acknowledged.

Williams v. Compair Maxam Ltd.
[1982] I.R.L.R. 83
Employment Appeal Tribunal

During 1980 a redundancy situation arose in the respondent company. The department manager in the applicant employee's department, Mr Hennessy, drew up a list of those to be made redundant, retaining those he considered best to retain in the interests of the company in the long run, without regard to their length of service.

Browne-Wilkinson J.: It is not enough to show simply that it was reasonable to dismiss *an* employee; it must be shown that the employer acted reasonably in treating redundancy "as a sufficient reason for dismissing *the* employee", ie the employee complaining of dismissal. Therefore, if the circumstances of the employer make it inevitable that some employee must be dismissed, it is still necessary to consider the means whereby the applicant was selected to be the employee to be dismissed and the reasonableness of the steps taken by the employer to choose the applicant, rather than some other employee, for dismissal . . . .

. . . . It is accordingly necessary to try to set down in very general terms what a properly instructed Industrial Tribunal would know to be the principles which, in current industrial practice, a reasonable employer would be expected to adopt. This is not a matter on which the chairman of this Appeal Tribunal feels that he can contribute much, since it depends on what industrial practices are currently accepted as being normal and proper. The two lay members of this Appeal Tribunal hold the view that it would be impossible to lay down detailed procedures which *all* reasonable employers would follow in *all* circumstances: the fair conduct of dismissals for redundancy must depend on the circumstances of each case. But in their experience there is a generally accepted view in industrial relations that, in cases where the employees are represented by an independent trade union recognised by the employer, reasonable employers will seek to act in accordance with the following principles: . . . .

2. The employer will consult the union as to the best means by which the desired management result can be achieved fairly and with as little hardship to the employees as possible. In particular, the employer will seek to agree with the union the criteria to be applied in selecting the employees to be made redundant. When a selection has been made, the employer will consider with the union whether the selection has been made in accordance with these criteria.

3. Whether or not an agreement as to the criteria to be adopted has been agreed with the union, the employer will seek to establish criteria for selection which so far as possible do not depend solely upon the opinion of the person making the selection but can be objectively checked against such things as attendance record, efficiency at the job, experience, or length of service.

4. The employer will seek to ensure that the selection is made fairly in accordance with these criteria and will consider any representations the union may make as to such selection . . . .

The lay members stress that not all these factors are present in every case since circumstances may prevent one or more of them being given effect to. But the lay members would expect these principles to be departed from only where some good reason is shown to justify such departure. The basic approach is that, in the unfortunate circumstances that necessarily attend redundancies, as much as is reasonably possible should be done to mitigate the impact on the work force and to satisfy them that the selection has been made fairly and not on the basis of personal whim.

That these are the broad principles currently adopted by reasonable employers is supported both by the practice of the Industrial Tribunals and to an extent by statute. A very large number of appeals on cases of alleged unfair selection for redundancy come before this Appeal Tribunal. In the experience of all of us, without exception hitherto the approach of the Industrial Tribunals has reflected the canons of good industrial relations set out above. In *Greig v McAlpine* [[1979] I.R.L.R. 372] an Industrial Tribunal in Liverpool under a very experienced chairman found the dismissal to be unfair. The headnote accurately represents the Industrial Tribunal's views as follows:

> "The respondents had acted unreasonably in selecting the applicant for redundancy in that they had failed to show that they had an objective system of assessment for deciding that the applicant was not to be amongst those retained . . . .
>
> If an employer adopts criteria other than last-in, first-out for redundancy selection, however, he must be able to show both that the criteria adopted are reasonable and that he has applied those criteria rationally and objectively and, where large numbers are involved, on a reasonably structured and comparative basis. In a situation involving so many employees, it is not sufficient for a single person who makes the selection to say that he has done so on the basis of his management skill and judgment. When so many employees are involved, and a basis of selection is to be used which is open to the possibility of being influenced by over-subjective assessments, or even sheer prejudice, on the part of the person making the choice, it is important that management be able to show that they took sufficient steps to make their decision as objective and unbiased as possible . . . ."

If there had been consultation on the criteria, a reasonable employer would not have insisted on the criteria in fact adopted. The so-called criteria in this case lack any real objective element: the retention of those "who, in the opinion of the managers concerned, would be able to keep the company viable". Such a criterion is entirely subjective and, as Mr Hennessy in his evidence accepted, was applied subjectively. The purpose of having, so far as possible, objective criteria is to ensure that redundancy is not used as a pretext for getting rid of employees who some manager wishes to get rid of for quite other reasons, *eg* for union activities or by reason of personal dislike. The danger of purely subjective selection is illustrated in this very case. It was common ground that the relations between Mr Hennessy and one of the applicants, Mr H. Williams, were not good. Mr Hennessy accepted in evidence that he did not care for Mr H. Williams and thought him a bit belligerent. They did not "pass the time of day". Except in cases where the criteria can be applied automatically (eg last-in, first-out) in any selection for redundancy elements of personal judgment are bound to be required thereby involving the risk of judgment being clouded by personal animosity. Unless some objective criteria are included, it is impossible to demonstrate to an employee like Mr H. Williams who is not on good terms with the person making the selection that the choice was not determined by personal likes and dislikes alone: we would also have thought it was extremely difficult for an Industrial Tribunal to be satisfied on the point.

Although the criteria advocated are said to be "objective," this should not disguise the fact that they embody policy choices as to who should be selected, and that these policy choices will be made by the employer. The courts' support for employer prerogatives is evident in the following cases.

British Leyland Cars Ltd. v. Lewis
[1983] I.R.L.R. 58
Employment Appeal Tribunal

The employee, a senior shop steward with more than 20 years' service with the company, was selected for redundancy despite having been with the company longer than most other employees in his department. An Industrial Tribunal, by a majority, found the dismissal unfair on the grounds that the employer had given insufficient weight to his length of service, and instead relied on factors designed to leave the company with a balanced workforce.

BROWNE-WILKINSON J.: . . . the majority appear to attach "priority" to one of the factors to be taken into account in making the selection, ie length of service. They are saying, as it seems to us, that in order for the employers to select fairly they had to find major shortcomings in an employee's performance if that were to outweigh the factor of length of service. In our view, that is not a legitimate approach to these criteria. The overriding factor was the need to retain a balanced workforce. In making the selection for that purpose, there were to be taken into account (so far as we can see, on an equal basis) length of service, occupation and skill. There is no warrant for the approach of the majority that in making the selection in accordance with those criteria one long-serving employee is to be treated as having some 'priority' by reason of length of service . . . .

[The case was remitted to the Industrial Tribunal for re-hearing.]

. . . In approaching their decision, the Industrial Tribunal will have to consider the criteria that were adopted and whether the employers have demonstrated that they have fairly applied those criteria to this redundancy. (In the normal case of a large employer, that would normally involve the employers showing that in selecting Mr Lewis they had compared him in relation to his length of service, his job and his skills with those others who might be made redundant, namely, the other industrial engineers in the department. In the ordinary case, although not invariably, that would involve evidence from the person who made the selection indicating that the rating of each of the persons who might be made redundant had been made and that as a result it emerged fairly and genuinely that Mr Lewis was one of the two who rated worst on those heads.) Those are the matters for which we would expect the Industrial Tribunal to be looking when they reconsider the matter on the evidence which has already been heard.

Buchanan v. Tilcon Ltd.
[1983] I.R.L.R. 417
Court of Session

The employer's area contracts manager, Mr Grogan, selected employees for redundancy on the basis of factors such as skills, ability, length of service and maintenance of a balanced labour force. The dismissed employees complained and an Industrial Tribunal held the employer had to prove the accuracy of their information on the employees' relative skills, etc. The E.A.T. allowed the appeal, and the employees appealed further.

LORD EMSLIE: In the event the appellant, apart from throwing out the suggestion that he might have been victimised because of dislike, merely expressed his concern that others, with even less seniority than he and employed in the same work (labouring) had been kept on. In this situation where no other complaints were made by the appellant all that the respondents had to do was to prove that their method of selection was fair in general terms and that it had been applied reasonably in the case of the appellant by the senior official responsible for taking the decision. As was pointed out by Phillips J. in *Cox* v. *Wildt Mellor Bromley Ltd.* [1978] I.R.L.R. 157 it is quite sufficient for an employer in a case such as this to call a witness of reasonable seniority to explain the circumstances in which the dismissal of the employee came about and it was not necessary to dot every "i" and to cross every "t" or to anticipate every possible complaint which might be made. In our opinion, agreeing with the Employment Appeal Tribunal, it is quite unrealistic and unreasonable for an Industrial Tribunal, which is prepared to accept that the senior official who made the selection reached his decision fairly upon the basis of company information, the reliability of which he had no reason to question, to demand of the employer for the purposes of EPCA s.57(3), that he should set up the accuracy of that information by direct evidence of other witnesses speaking, perhaps, to records for which they had responsibility. The Industrial Tribunal, in our opinion, set for the respondents in this case a standard which was much too high. In so doing they misdirected themselves and we have no doubt that the Employment Appeal Tribunal was entitled to go on to hold that the only reasonable conclusion which was open upon the evidence led before the Industrial Tribunal was that the respondents had discharged the *onus* which rested upon them in terms of s.57(3) of [EPCA].

(iii) "Bumping." A redundancy situation can apply to a large or small unit of employees. If selection criteria are used, the unit of employees within which the criteria will be applied must be defined. For example, where the criterion is last-in, first-out (LIFO), if the unit of selection is *wider* than a department (or grade or skill), then an employee in one department may "bump" into redundancy a less senior employee in *another* department although the junior employee's post is not redundant, nor is there a redundancy situation in his department. The following cases illustrate the Tribunals' attempts to grapple with or evade this problem. In the first case, it was the practical problems that led the judge to support maximum discretion for employers and tribunals in allowing cross-department redundancies.

Thomas & Betts Manufacturing Co. Ltd. v. Harding
[1978] I.R.L.R. 213
Employment Appeal Tribunal

Mrs Harding was originally employed as a packer, but was then moved to other work concerned with the making of "fittings." She was dismissed, having been employed for two years, when a redundancy situation arose in the fittings section. A Tribunal upheld her claim of unfair dismissal on the grounds that there were people with less service in other parts of the business who were retained. In particular, there was one packer who had been employed for only five weeks.

PHILLIPS J.: The case has been argued as raising a question of principle. The way it is put is, that where a redundancy situation occurs in one section of a business an employer, when considering selection for redundancy, ought to consider only that section in which redundancies have been established and ought not to look to see whether a place can be found for the redundant employee in some other section of the business. So it is submitted that it was wrong in principle of the Industrial Tribunal here to have had any regard to what has been described as a "different" section of the business . . . .

. . . . The practical problem and difficulty which lies in the way of Mr Boswood's interesting submission [on behalf of the employer] is this, that it seems to us almost impossible to de-limit in any intelligent form the section or the grade or the area to which it would be legitimate to look if Mr Boswood's submission was well-founded. We are satisfied that there is no such proposition of law. Having said that, of course, we would stress the fact that such matters as these—that is to say the fact that a business may be divided into sections, or employees may be divided into different grades, or that the business may be carried on in more than one plant—are all matters of practical importance which the Industrial Tribunal will need to take into account when reaching its decision under [EPCA, s.57(3)]. All we are saying is that there is no rule of law which limits as such the area where an Industrial Tribunal may look or say that a reasonable employer ought reasonably to have looked.

Contrast the Court of Appeal's view: [1980] I.R.L.R. 255. In the second case, it was the legal difficulties which led the judge to a conclusion against cross-department redundancies.

Huddersfield Parcels Ltd. v. Sykes
[1981] I.R.L.R. 115
Employment Appeal Tribunal

Mr Sykes, a night driver/warehouseman was selected for redundancy after consultations with the union over the basis of selection. A Tribunal found the dismissal unfair because, *inter alia*, the employers did not offer or even discuss the possibility of alternative employment as a warehouseman.

WATERHOUSE J.: The second main criticism made by Mr Kirkbright [representing the employer] is that the Industrial Tribunal appears to have suggested that a reasonable employer would have offered to the respondent, or might have offered to him, work as a warehouseman on the footing that five of the warehousemen then employed by the appellants had entered their employ at a later date than the respondent. We have not been persuaded by Mr Ellis, on behalf of the respondent, that that was a conclusion that the Tribunal could properly draw in the circumstances of this case.

Mr Ellis has referred us to the recent decision of the Court of Appeal in *Thomas & Betts Manufacturing Ltd. v Harding* [1980] I.R.L.R. 255 . . . .

[The judge considered that the *Harding* case was distinguishable on its facts, and continued:] . . . here there was a series of discussions between the appellants and the respondent's trade union as to the basis of selection for redundancy. The discussions were not confined to selection within a category of employee because they embraced also the selection of the category. In these circumstances it would be difficult for an Industrial Tribunal to justify a finding that a reasonable employer, despite the discussions and agreement with the trade union, would have offered as alternative employment the job of another category of worker that had not been selected for redundancy. The obvious problem that would arise would be that the other person displaced could complain of unfair dismissal and that it would be difficult for the employer to show that the dismissal was for any admissible reason. In the instant case, if the decision of the employers was that their requirements for work of the kind carried out by night driver/warehousemen had diminished, and that was the reason for selecting the respondent for redundancy, it would be difficult for them to pray this in aid as an admissible reason for the dismissal of a warehouseman who was to be displaced in favour of the respondent.

In the last case, two possible criteria were canvassed as a basis for cross-department redundancy: similarity of terms of employment, and flexibility.

Powers and Villiers v. A. Clarke & Co. (Smethwick) Ltd.
[1981] I.R.L.R. 483
Employment Appeal Tribunal

The employer wished to reduce their fleet of five articulated lorries by two and their nine four-wheel vehicles by one, and to make consequent reductions in the workforce. They employed class 1 drivers to drive articulated vehicles who were also qualified to drive four-wheel vehicles, and class 3 drivers driving four-wheel vehicles who were not able to drive articulated lorries. In selecting for redundancy, the employers applied an agreed procedure of last-in, first-out to class 1 drivers and class 3 drivers as separate categories. Two class 1 drivers selected complained of unfair dismissal.

LORD MCDONALD: The issue before the Industrial Tribunal in the present case simplifies itself to a question as to whether the agreed procedure relating to redundancy laid down in the Joint Industrial Council Agreement (which was first-in, last-out) should apply across the board or whether it was proper to treat class 1 drivers and class 3 drivers as separate categories. The Tribunal have held that it was proper so to treat them. They based this upon the fact that different terms and conditions applied to each case; that there was a different level of earnings and that it was within the area served by the articulated lorries section that the redundancy situation arose . . . .

. . . . The whole argument here was that on the evidence class 1 drivers held positions similar to that held by class 3 drivers . . . [Reference was made, *inter alia*, to the *Harding* case p. 146 above.]

These cases however can clearly be distinguished from the present because of the nature of the employment involved. In both cases it was of an unskilled nature and a high degree of flexibility could therefore be expected. In the present case the difficulty for the appellants lies in the fact that it was only class 1 drivers who could drive articulated vehicles. There was perhaps a degree of flexibility as indicated by the position of Mr Lindsay in so much as a class 1 driver could competently drive a four-wheel vehicle. On the other hand that only worked one way and a class 3 driver could not drive an articulated vehicle. This distinction in our view makes it impossible to hold that class 3 drivers employed in the respondents' undertaking held positions similar to that held by the appellants who were class 1 drivers.

Subsequently, Lord McDonald deprecated even his own attempts to create guidelines for Industrial Tribunals, and fell back to the position that "two reasonable employers might follow a different course of action," but both would still be within the "band of reasonableness" required by the statute (*Green* v. *A. and I. Fraser (Wholesale Fish Merchants) Ltd.* [1985] I.R.L.R 55 (E.A.T.), at p. 57).

(v) Redundancy notice and time off to look for work

There is no special legal provision for redundancy notice: the statutory minimum of one week after four weeks' employment applies generally. Although this increases by one week for each year of employment to a maximum of 12 weeks' notice after 12 years (EPCA, s.49), both the 1981 and 1984 surveys of collective practice found 32 agreements which improved on this (*Bargaining Report* Nos. 14 and 33). Workers about to become redundant are entitled under statute to "reasonable" time off to look for work at the "appropriate" hourly rate (EPCA, s.31), but the maximum employer's liability is stipulated at two-fifths of a week's pay. The surveys of redundancy practice found a number of schemes which improved on this. The following agreements were featured in the 1979 survey (*Bargaining Report* No.3):

Pilkington Brothers Ltd.

Time-off—not exceeding 5 days/turns during this period— can be granted to workers seeking alternative jobs. If individuals fail to find work and want to attend more job interviews after these 5 days, management can grant further time off. Departmental managers must co-operate with employees who may need to leave work (*eg* for interviews) at a particular time of day. Payment for time off is at basic rate plus shift premium, if appropriate.

British Railways (Conciliation and Salaried Staff)

Time off arrangements: British Rail gives reasonable time off (up to a maximum of 5 days which need not be consecutive) at the hourly rate, plus free rail travel, where a redundant worker needs to visit a prospective employer—either to get a new job, or arrange training for future employment.

(vi) Redundancy payments

The redundancy payments legislation (EPCA, ss.81–120) requires employers to pay compensation to workers dismissed by reason of redundancy. Compensation is calculated as a multiple of a week's wages and number of years of continuous employment with the employer (up to a maximum of 20 years and $1\frac{1}{2}$ weeks' pay (the maximum weekly pay is fixed annually after a review by the Secretary of State: see EPCA, s.148 and Schedule 14, para. 8(1)(c) and (2))). Failure to make the payment entitles the employee to complain to an Industrial Tribunal. The original legislation also set up a Redundancy Fund financed through employers' National Insurance contributions whereby an employer making a redundancy payment could claim a rebate from the Fund. Part III of the Wages Act 1986, however, restricts the right to a rebate to those employers with nine or fewer employees.

Again, collective practice has greatly improved on the statutory scheme. The surveys of 1981 and 1984 revealed the following schemes:

Bargaining Report Nos. 14 and 33

	No. of agreements	
	1981	*1984*
Those paying at least 4 times statutory pay	15	17
" " " " 3 " " "	6	15
" " " " 2 " " "	33	31
" " " " $1\frac{1}{2}$ " " "	23	19
Those improving on statutory pay	15	15

Agreements often also omitted the minimum service requirement (two years), the maximum weekly pay limit, the maximum number of years (20) and the minimum hours limit (16 or 8). The 1984 survey revealed eight schemes which made payments to workers who remained unemployed after redundancy, supplementing state benefits. For example, those of NAAFI and Thorn EMI both provide that state benefits are made up to two-thirds weekly pay each week for those unemployed after a service-related "waiting period" (three weeks for those with one year's service, up to 12 weeks for 12 years service or more). Duration of the entitlement is one week per year of service up to a maximum of 25.

One major practical problem in obtaining a statutory redundancy payment is that presented by some employers' practice of giving long advance notice of redundancy. If, as a consequence, employees leave to find or take up other jobs, the legal question arises of whether they were dismissed for redundancy. Collective agreements would not fail to deal with this problem. Contrast the common law's solution.

Morton Sundour Fabrics Ltd. v. Shaw
[1967] 2 I.T.R. 84
Queen's Bench Division

The employers gave advance warning in March 1966 that they intended to close down the department in which Mr Shaw worked, but no date was fixed for the closure. Rather than wait for the department to close, Mr Shaw gave notice himself terminating his employment on April 22, well before the closure. He successfully claimed a redundancy payment from an Industrial Tribunal.

WIDGERY J.: As a matter of law an employer cannot dismiss his employee by saying "I intend to dispense with your services at some time in the coming months." In order to terminate the contract of employment the notice must either specify the date or contain material from which that date is positively ascertainable. It is, I think, evident from what the Tribunal has found that nothing which the employers in this case said to Mr Shaw in the early days of March could possibly be interpreted as specifying a date upon which he was to go, or as giving material upon which such a date might be ascertained. It was on its face not inappropriately described by Mr Henry [Counsel for the employers] in his argument to us as a warning of what was to come. If that is the true position, then nothing done by the employers at the beginning of March operated to terminate the contract of employment, and it would follow that the actual terminating event was the notice given by Mr

Shaw later that month and not any action taken by the employers. That is a result achieved by applying the strict principles of law to this case, as in my judgment they clearly must be applied . . . [Counsel for the employee suggested that] this is going to drive the proverbial coach and horses through the Redundancy Payments Act [now EPCA, Part VI]. He says that if the appellants are right, all that an employer need do if he knows that his factory is going to run down and that redundancy payments are in prospect, is to give a vague oral warning to his employees in the hope that they will then go off on their own and find other jobs before the moment of their dismissal arises. Again I find it quite impossible to go with Mr Waddington [Counsel for Mr Shaw] on this contention at all. It seems to me that however one looks at this case, the employee has the perfectly secure right if he thinks fit to wait until his contract is determined, to take his redundancy payment, and then see what he can do in regard to obtaining other employment. If he does, and one can appreciate that there may be compelling reasons, choose to leave his existing employment before the last minute in order to look for a new job before the rush of others competing with him comes, then that is up to him. The effect of the employer's warning is not in any way to derogate from his statutory rights but to give him an alternative which, if he is so minded, he can accept.

In *Dobie* v. *Firestone Tyre and Rubber Co. Ltd.* [1981] I.R.L.R. 300 (E.A.T.), Waterhouse J. described this decision as a "helpful warning" to employees.

3. UNIFORMITY OF WORK-TIME

The acceptance of the permanent, five-day, 35–40 hours week as the norm for work has come under increasing pressure.

Trade Union Research Unit, Ruskin College, Oxford, *"Working Time in Britain: The Effects of Changes in Pattern and Duration in Selected Industries"* (1981), p. 286.

The earlier analysis of the 1970s, and (with a few notable exceptions) much of the atmosphere of the plant and company level studies, reveals a world in which the main styles of working time are barely questioned, or only marginally changed. Indeed, in many cases the continuity of at least full-time patterns of working-time—length of basic week, propensity to overtime work, the nature of and extent of shift systems—appear as one of the few fixed elements in a fairly rapidly changing and sometimes markedly unstable economic environment . . . .

And yet it appears less and less likely that the perpetuation of "traditional" patterns of working time, combined with the passive acceptance of some of the new trends identifiable in the 1970s (not least the rise in part-time employment), can meet the new social and economic needs of the 1980s. Indeed, it is surprising that these traditional levels of working hours, and annual working time, could have co-existed with growing levels of persistent unemployment in the last decade without earlier meeting social challenge. Perhaps the high unemployment of the mid-1970s was seen for a while as largely cyclical, rather than the opening of a new phase in national economic development and management.

Some existing alternative patterns of work-time are summarised in the following extract

B. Bercusson, "Introduction," to THE EMPLOYMENT ACTS 1974–1980 *(C. D. Drake and B. Bercusson* ed. 1981), p.14

Patterns of working hours. Other patterns, where they exist, need also to be spelled out in the written statement [of particulars of terms of employment, EPCA, s.1]. For example, *flexible working hours*, an arrangement whereby employees may begin and end work at times of their choice provided they are all present at certain core-times and that within a settlement period of a week or month they work the total number of hours agreed. The spread of such arrangements has been remarkable. Thus, in the non-industrial Civil Service there were no such arrangements before 1972. By the beginning of 1980, 200,000 workers (40 per cent. of the total) were covered by flexible working hours, and the Civil Service negotiating body, the National Whitley Council, has urged their extension to all non-industrial staff.

The *compressed working week* is a work pattern in which the full complement of normal weekly hours are worked in fewer than five full days. It is most commonly found in practice among shift workers in the engineering industry. The EEF estimated in early 1980 that out of 220,000 workers in federated firms on night work, about 160,000 were on the system of four long nights and a short Friday night, and a further 35,000 worked four long nights only Monday to Thursday. The tendency to reductions in the working week to below 40 hours may lead to further attention being paid to cutting the number of working days among normal day workers.

Staggered working hours are sometimes adopted to alleviate traffic congestion problems (see, for example, the allowances paid to such workers in the cement industry of 7p. for each hour worked).

Finally, *job-sharing* is the practice whereby two people jointly fill one full-time post. The English clearing banks have systematically adopted this practice since the early 1960s when there was an acute shortage of clerical and secretarial staff in central London and it was sought to attract married women returners by splitting full time jobs into alternate week jobs. Various methods may be found: alternate weeks, alternate days, split weeks and even split days.

Legal support for the conventional approach to work-time is beginning to be questioned. The position of temporary and part-time workers has been scrutinised (see B.A. Hepple and B.W. Napier, "Temporary workers and the law" (1978) 7 I.L.J. 84 (see above, Chapter 2 on *Access to Work* p. 26). The legal problems of part-time workers (mainly female) have become a major concern of labour law concerned with discrimination (*Jenkins* v. *Kingsgate (Clothing Productions) Ltd.* [1981] I.R.L.R. 228 (E.C.J.), see below, Chapter 6 on *Discrimination and Inequality*, p. 218).

The problem of uniform working time is not one the judges can resolve. The challenge for labour law is whether the necessary changes will emerge from collective industrial practice or from legislation, or both. The following extract considers the problems of negotiating reductions in working time due to the sexual composition of the workforce.

Trade Union Research Unit, Ruskin College, Oxford, "*Working Time in Britain: The Effects of Changes in Pattern and Duration in Selected Industries*" (1981), pp. 281–282

The main distinction identified in the preferred form of reduced working time lay between men and women. The former overwhelmingly favoured reductions which would yield useful blocks of time—typically a whole day or series of extra days off. The latter, probably influenced by domestic considerations tended to favour earlier finishing times. The women's need to confine the working day was also emphasised by their resistance to overtime working, very few instances of which were uncovered in our case studies. By comparison overtime and weekend working were fairly common practices amongst men workers in the case studies.

Leaving aside for a moment the possible causes of this distinction, the implications for bargainers are significant. For example, in the context of a predominantly female workforce the demand for a 35 or a 30 hour week would probably win support, whereas additional holidays, whilst supportable, may be seen to be less of a priority. By comparison, in a male-dominated workforce negotiating longer holidays, particularly if workers experience the "locked-in-to-overtime" syndrome may prove the most effective bargaining strategy to reduce annual working time.

Plainly, then, the sexual make up of the workforce is an important characteristic in the pre-planning of shorter working time bargaining.

In the last extract of this chapter, consideration is given to some of the possibilities of changes in working time patterns through a combination of collective bargaining and legislation.

Trade Union Research Unit, Ruskin College, Oxford, "*Working Time in Britain: The Effects of Changes in Pattern and Duration in Selected Industries*" (1981), pp. 315–317

Redefining Full-Time Work

In bargaining for less working time can we bargain for the reshaping of working time to match more closely the changing needs of individuals for different combinations of work, study, leisure, and voluntary service? . . . .

One way of reviewing the possibilities that open up is to reflect that under "traditional" work weeks, the pattern of expected working hours is more tolerant of *extension* of working hours than of their *reduction*. Thus, while the basic hours are 40, the actual work week for manual men is likely to centre around 45 hours or more.

There would seem to be a number of ways of building a more flexible framework of full-time work around a lower level of "basic" weekly hours:

> There could be more recognition of the need for alternative forms of compensation for shift workers with their "unsocial" hours. This could involve priority in the reduction of the length of the basic week, limitation of overtime by re-manning shift teams and shift cycles, and shift of "compensation" for shift work towards increased access to paid rest days.
>
> More generally, time off in lieu could be used as recompense for temporary overtime working.
>
> Workers could have more opportunity of offering a range of weekly

hours (say, 30 to 35) while retaining the status, the job rights and working conditions and benefits, of full-time workers.

Workers who met agreed standards of attendance and work performance could build up entitlement to planned rest days with pay.

In all these ways planned manning to ensure the achievement of production schedules and the efficient use of capital can go along with reshaping of working time to meet a wider range of individual preferences and needs. If nothing else, the handling of full-time work might reverse the existing pattern; it could be more resistant to the extension of actual working time through persistent overtime, and more ready to accommodate a range of somewhat shorter hours planned and agreed in advance.

Redefining Part-Time Work

At the same time, there are a number of reasons to re-think the nature and character of part-time work.

There is no obvious necessity, in terms of the needs of enterprises for workers at a set retirement age to make as complete, abrupt and arbitrary an exit from full-time work to retirement as they do. The growing power, and potential flexibility of superannuation funds could allow a more flexible transition. This could include for workers nearing retirement access to planned blocks of leisure, sabbaticals, designed to help the adjustment to full retirement; or it could involve a period of half-time work.

Similarly, for many young workers a combination of part-time work or work experience, access to vocational training and further education, and help with constructive use of blocks of leisure time, may be socially and individually preferable to immediate entry into full-time work for some and unemployment for many others. Here, it is already accepted that public funds are deployed flexibly to assist in the varied needs of adaptation to the world of work. The shortened working time of young people under such admixtures of work and training does not have to involve inferior or casual status.

The redefinition of full-time work in a more flexible way would enable more women workers to undertake such work. But there is obvious scope for trade unions to bargain about the rights of part-time workers, their access to training, and the possibilities of exercising options to move between full-time and part-time work with an enterprise, and vice-versa.

In a similar way, bargaining—and government encouragement—might enable workers to reduce their paid work for periods of time in order to undertake voluntary social service, and representative (not merely trade union representative) commitments, without losing job security and without undue loss of income. One way in which this may naturally develop would be through negotiation of paid educational leave, and the connection of this training and education, for social service and voluntary activity.

In all of these ways bargaining over working time could move on from the immediate priorities of reducing the levels of working time, both normal and actual, to creating more flexible (but jointly determined) patterns of working time that *enable* the individual to express personal and social preferences and commitments without undermining the efficient planning and conduct of production and service of activities, and without weakening joint control of working time by trade unions and employers.

CHAPTER 5

PAY AND BENEFITS

1. INTRODUCTION: PAY AS AN ISSUE IN MODERN LABOUR LAW

The common law purports to regard payment as the contractual consideration for work, and no more. Applied literally to a case where a colliery had to close down while safety repairs were carried out (the unsafe condition of the mine was not the employer's fault), Greer J. held that the workers were not entitled to wages (*Browning* v. *Crumlin Valley Collieries Ltd.* [1926] 1 K.B. 522):

> "In business transactions such as this, what the law desires to effect by the implication [of terms as to wage payment] is to give such business efficacy to the transaction as must have been intended at all events by both parties who are business men. . . .
>
> . . . Were the perils of the transaction in that event to be all on one side, or must the consequences be divided between the two parties, the employers losing the advantages of continuing to have their coal gotten and being compelled to undertake expensive repairs, and the men on their part losing their wages for such

time as was reasonably required to put the mine into a safe condition? The latter, I think, must be presumed to have been the intention of both parties. . . ."

But for workers, pay is more than just an incident in a business transaction. A text of almost 500 pages on "Pay" in French labour law begins with the statement: "Labour law as a whole is constructed around the issue of pay" (G. Lyon-Caen, *Le Salaire* (2nd ed., 1981), p. 1). It continues with discussion of minimum wage-fixing, collective bargaining over pay, income security (*eg* during illness), holidays with pay, pensions and so on: "All labour law, as well as social security, can in simple terms be reduced to one issue: how is work to be remunerated." One indication of the significance of pay to workers is the fact that the vast majority of cases involving workers' industrial action arise from disputes over pay and pay-related issues.

Can modern labour law adhere simply to the common law view of pay as contractual consideration? The complex issues of pay in its economic, political and social context, and the currently *ad hoc* response of the common law, are illustrated in the following case.

Royle v. Trafford Borough Council
[1984] I.R.L.R. 184
Queen's Bench Division

The employer decided to reduce the number of teaching staff by two, and the employees' union responded by instructing its members not to accept additional pupils into their classes. When the employee-teacher refused to accept another five pupils into his class of 31, the employers allowed him to continue working, but refused to pay any salary. The judge considered on the one hand the employers' statutory duty to provide full-time education for all the children in its area, and said: "It does not seem to me that the unions, or their members, acted with such complete irresponsibility as to bring education within the defendant's area virtually to a standstill." On the other hand he considered the employees' claim to be paid in the light of the common law duty to obey orders, but in a situation where the employer had elected to accept the employee's defective performance, and concluded as follows.

PARK J.: . . . in my opinion the plaintiff is entitled to be paid his full salary only if he has properly and fully performed his duties under his contract of employment. For a period of nearly six months, in breach of his contract, he has failed to teach five children whom he otherwise would have taught. Thus, there is no reason why he should receive his full salary for that period. I think I am entitled to make a deduction representing the notional value of the services he has not rendered.

Miss Caws [counsel for the employer] suggested that, if I were minded to make such a deduction, the fraction 5/36ths of the salary over the relevant period, while being a far from perfect assessment, would probably represent the justice of the case, bearing in mind that the plaintiff carried out in full a number of extra-curricular activities.

Mr Peppitt [counsel for the teacher], while contending that the defendants are entitled only to nominal damages on the counter-claim, does not quarrel with that fraction.

The defendants have not suffered any financial loss by reason of the plaintiff's breaches of contract; for example, they have not incurred the cost of employing a teacher to teach the children whom the plaintiff had refused to teach; if they had done so, they might well have succeeded in recovering the cost of such employment (see *National Coal Board v Galley* [1958] 1 WLR 16); nor have they been required to meet any claim by a parent for their failure to educate a child. In those circumstances I have decided to follow the decision of Nicholls J. in the recent case of *Miles v Wakefield Metropolitan District Council* reported in *The Times* on 22.11.83 and to give judgment for the plaintiff for the amount of his salary between 7.1.79 and 30.6.79 less a proportion thereof amounting to 5/36th. . . .

(*Cf. Sims* v. *Rotherham Metropolitan Borough Council* [1986] I.R.L.R. 391 (Q.B.D.)). The Court of Appeal subsequently reversed Nicholls J.'s judgment in the *Miles* case relied on by Park J. in *Royle*.

Miles v. Wakefield Metropolitan District Council
[1987] 2 W.L.R. 795
House of Lords

The employers withheld 3/37ths of the salary of the holder of a statutory office of superintendent registrar who refused to perform marriage ceremonies on Saturday mornings on the instruction of his union, as part of industrial action. A majority of the Court of Appeal overruled Nicholls J., their decision turning upon a point of statutory interpretation rather than upon contractual obligations of work and pay. However, the following observations were made.

Parker L.J. (in the majority): I find it unnecessary to decide whether if the appellant had been an employee of the respondents, they would have been entitled to withhold part of his salary, but I do not accept that they would. Had that been the case, the respondents would no doubt have had a claim for any damages they could prove but, in the absence of a breach amounting to a repudiation accepted by dismissal or a specific right to suspend, there appear to me strong grounds for saying there is no right to withhold payment and take the benefit of all work in fact done during the period in which the refusal to perform a particular function was operative. *Gorse v Durham CC* [1971] 2 All ER 666 appears to me to be authority for the proposition that there is no such right. The right is asserted on the basis that an employee, in order to recover unpaid salary, must show that in the relevant period he was ready and willing to perform his contract and that, if he was not, he can recover nothing even if his unwillingness did not go to the root of the contract or, albeit that it did, it was not accepted as a repudiation. The validity of this proposition may have to be decided in the future. As it was not fully argued before us and does not require decision now, I say only that I regard the proposition as being of doubtful validity.

Eveleigh L.J. (dissenting): As to the right of an employer to withhold part of the salary when an employee does not work, I find it impossible to lay down a general rule other than there is no rule of law to prevent him from so doing. Each particular case, however, must depend upon the terms of the particular engagement. As I have said, the local scheme is to the effect that the salary is payable in respect of services rendered and I see nothing in this case to show that the council is required to pay when services were not rendered.

The House of Lords overruled the Court of Appeal holding that a worker can only claim remuneration if he proves he is ready and willing to perform the work which is the consideration for the remuneration claimed. Where the employer is unwilling to accept incomplete performance of a worker's obligation, the employer does not need to counter-claim for an amount equivalent to the worker's claim: the claim simply fails for lack of proof of an essential ingredient (*Miles* v. *Wakefield Metropolitan District Council* [1987] 1 All E.R. 118).

2. WHAT IS "PAY"?

"Pay" is not reducible to the cash payment made periodically to the worker. Recent research estimates that non-wage benefits of all kinds now make up between 10 and 30 per cent. of a company's labour costs on average. The major categories of fringe benefits are:

(a) private social welfare payments: superannuation, group life insurance, sickness payments, industrial accident payments, *ex gratia* and goodwill payments;
(b) payments in kind (net cost to employers for goods provided free or below cost), *e.g.* food, drink and fuel;
(c) subsidised services to employees (net cost to employers of medical services, canteens, housing, removal, transport to and from work, clothing and recreational facilities);
(d) provision for redundancy (statutory and voluntary payments to employees);
(e) paid holidays.

Problems of defining the concept of "pay" increase if one considers other non-monetary benefits from work: opportunities for travel, outlets for creativity, freedom from supervision, as well as benefits which are not immediately reducible to cash, but which have undoubted value, such as credit-worthiness, career prospects and security of employment.

These varied components of remuneration for work can create difficulties in areas of law where rights depend on a definition of pay. The following are illustrations.

(A) Itemised Pay Statements: EPCA, s.8

Cofone v. Spaghetti House Ltd.
[1980] I.C.R. 155
Employment Appeal Tribunal

In addition to his wages, a waiter kept tips, but out of them paid a weekly sum to the manager. He claimed under EPCA, s.11 that his itemised pay statement should include particulars of this sum as these payments were deducted from his pay.

TALBOT J.: To go back to the precise terms of [EPCA, s.8], what is required is that at or before the time any payment of wages is made an employee shall have the right to be given by his employer a pay statement containing the gross amount of his wages. It is plain from the facts, as contained in paragraph 8 of the Industrial Tribunal's decision that the employee kept his tips and the employers would not be in possession of information as to the amount that the employee received on any one day; they would not be in possession of the information of what he had received at or before the time at which the payment of wages had to be made. It would be impracticable, if tips are to be included in the word "wages," for an employer to carry out the obligation which is required of him under that section: he would be incapable of giving particulars. To comply with the obligation required of him it would be necessary for the tips, as we see it from the practicable point of view, to be paid by the employee to the employer so that he could then treat them as part of his wages, make the necessary deductions for tax purposes, and then pay that and the other moneys due to the employee at the specified weekly time. It seems to us, therefore, looking at the facts of this case—that is to say, the arrangement made between the parties in this case—that the practicalities of the situation do not allow the employee's tips to be described as "wages" within the section.

(B) Equal Pay: Article 119 of the EEC Treaty

Worringham v. Lloyds Bank Ltd.

[1981] I.C.R. 558; [1981] 2 All E.R. 434
European Court of Justice

> On a claim for equal pay, the European Court was asked whether contributions paid by an employer in the name of the employee to a retirement benefits scheme by way of an addition to the gross salary came within the concept of "pay" within the meaning of Article 119 of the EEC Treaty.

THE EUROPEAN COURT OF JUSTICE:

14. Under the second paragraph of article 119 of the E.E.C. Treaty, "pay" means, for the purpose of that provision:

> "the ordinary basic or minimum wage or salary and any other consideration, whether in cash or in kind, which the worker receives, directly or indirectly, in respect of his employment from his employer."

15. Sums such as those in question which are included in the calculation of the gross salary payable to the employee and which directly determine the calculation of other advantages linked to the salary, such as redundancy payments, unemployment benefits, family allowances and credit facilities, form part of the worker's pay within the meaning of the second paragraph of article 119 of the Treaty even if they are immediately deducted by the employer and paid to a pension fund on behalf of the employee. This applies *a fortiori* where those sums are refunded in certain circumstances and subject to certain deductions to the employee as being repayable to him if he ceases to belong to the contractual retirement benefits scheme under which they were deducted.

16. Moreover, the argument mentioned by the British Government that the payment of the contributions in question by the employer does not arise out of a legal obligation towards the employee is not in point since that payment is in fact made, it corresponds to an obligation by the worker to contribute and is deducted from his salary.

17. In view of all these facts, it is therefore necessary to reply to question 1(a) that a contribution to a retirement benefits scheme which is paid by the employer in the name of the employees by means of an addition to the gross

salary and which helps to determine the amount of that salary is "pay" within the meaning of the second paragraph of article 119 of the E.E.C. Treaty.

However, in *Newstead* v. *Department of Transport and H.M. Treasury* [1985] I.R.L.R. 299 (E.A.T.), Waite J. held that the *Worringham* case did not answer the question of whether compulsory deductions from the salary of male employees for the benefit of a future widow's pension could be called "pay" for the purposes of Article 119. He referred the question to the European Court, adding specifically (p. 304):

> "What precisely is the effect of the extended definition of 'pay' in Article 119 of the Treaty? What is the result of introducing into that definition the wide phrase 'any other consideration'? What intention is to be presumed from the emphasis 'which the worker receives'? What significance is to be attached to the fact that such remuneration may be received 'directly or indirectly'?"

(C) Loss of Earnings Compensation for Unfair Dismissal

Imperial London Hotels Ltd. v. Cooper
[1974] I.R.L.R. 199
National Industrial Relations Court

Mrs Cooper was unfairly dismissed. In calculating her compensation for loss of earnings, she argued that the weekly value of her free accommodation should have been taken into account.

DONALDSON J.: The question at issue is whether free accommodation which, as both sides concede, the employee is entitled and bound to occupy, is part of the employee's pay or remuneration . . . .

In our judgment the proposition sought to be made good by Mrs Cooper is not sustainable. The value of the accommodation which she was entitled and bound to occupy was not money or money's worth paid into her hands; all that can be said is that the value of such accommodation represented money which the nature of her employment saved her from having to spend. 104 weeks' free accommodation by Mrs Cooper of her flat cannot sensibly be described as part of "104 weeks" pay within the meaning of . . . [what is now EPCA, s.75].

Contrast damages for wrongful dismissal, where a company director was compensated for loss of private health insurance and the use of a car, including the provision of petrol and oil for private motoring (*Shore* v. *Downs Surgical plc* [1984] I.R.L.R. 17 (Q.B.D.). Yet in *TBA Industrial Products Ltd.* v. *Locke* [1984] I.R.L.R. 48, the E.A.T. contrasted the assessment of employee's loss for wrongful dismissal at common law with the same assessment under EPCA, s.74 for unfair dismissal by asserting that the premise in the latter differed by taking into account not only contractual obligations but also industrial practice (*per* Browne-Wilkinson J., p. 51). In that case the employee was compensated under the statutory provisions also for loss of use of a car and payment of telephone rental.

3. METHODS OF PAYMENT

The feature which most often marks the divide between what is variously described as white/blue collar, staff/manual or salaried/non-salaried employment is the method of payment.

Industrial Relations Review and Report No. *248 (May 1981), p. 2*:

> "As much as 26.1% of the male manual worker's weekly pay derives from supplements to the basic rate . . . .By contrast only 6.7% of the weekly earnings of male white collar workers come from such extras or supplements. Non-manuals generally receive the same sums of money week after week, or more normally month after month for their work. The pay packets of manual workers can fluctuate often wildly for those on PBR (payment by results) or bonus systems."

The differences in methods of payment between these categories of workers are linked to issues of inequality (discrimination) and security of pay during maternity, lay-off and sickness (discussed separately in other chapters). In the following extract, the argument is made that differences in methods of payment should be better appreciated in labour law.

M. R. Freedland, "The obligation to work and to pay for work" in CURRENT LEGAL PROBLEMS (1977) at pp. 181–2, 184–6

It seems to me that lawyers ought to look behind the facade they have set up, which is that of a single basic type of contract of employment whose terms can be varied by special agreement. Behind that facade stands a reality in which there are several fundamentally different types of contract of employment, differentiated according to the payment system used. There is no shortage of information about payment systems—it is simply that lawyers have not recognised them as representing fundamentally different types of contract of employment. The payment systems also change with time, far more rapidly than the common law does.

I suggest the main types at the present day are these. Firstly, systems of *fixed remuneration* where remuneration is related to the week, the months or the year and does not vary with the number of hours or the output within each such period. This corresponds roughly with the notion of "staff status" which used to be used very widely to distinguish administrative and clerical from production workers in industry. Such remuneration would also tend to be identified as "salary" rather than "wages," especially if it was on a monthly or longer time-basis. Such employees have been loosely described by the common law as paid for their readiness and willingness to work if of ability to do so, rather than for actual working. This is in a sense the classical form of the contract of employment, whereby the employee is paid for belonging to and being at the disposal of the employing organisation, rather than for the completion of specific agreed tasks. The system of fixed remuneration implies a relatively high degree of trust accorded to the employee and of discretion left to him that provides an instance of how the nature of the payment system tells us something about the nature of the work obligation. . . .

My second type of system is that of *time-rate* work where payment varies according to the number of hours worked within the week. This seems to me fundamentally different from the first type, although both types relate directly to time. The breaking down of time into units of hours within each week creates a type of contract where remuneration is far more closely related to specific work performed. It is a system typically applied to manual, rather than to intellectual, work, and to lower categories of work within a hierarchy. . . . In general, just as the fixed system of remuneration is identified with a whole set of assumptions about the nature of the employment concerned, so also is the hourly-paid system. The system of hourly pay (coupled with a fixed basic wage) gives the employer the opportunity to vary his labour costs in response to the demand for his products. The employee is less fully integrated into the organisation than a staff employee, in the sense that the organisation absorbs less of the risk of variation in demand—it passes more risk on to the employee. . . .

The next type of system I wish to consider is that of *payment by results*. I include in this, arrangements for piece-rates, commissions and any kind of relation of payment to output. Such arrangements are very widespread; and yet they are somewhat different from the standard theoretical model of the contract of employment and they exhibit some of the features of the relation between employer and independent contractor. Such arrangements are, in practice, drawn back towards the contract of employment model by the addition of provision for fixed or guaranteed weekly pay and, of course, by obligations upon the employee to work for fixed hours. Lawyers have tended not to become involved in the details of these schemes for payment by results. In fact, many such schemes are extremely sophisticated, with very intricate relationships between output and pay which are based on subtle theories as to how to get most out of employees for a given amount of payment. There are some schemes where remuneration is directly proportional to output; others, known as progressive schemes, where the rate of increase in remuneration proceeds more rapidly as output increases, and others, known as regressive schemes where the rate of increase slows down as output increases. . . .

I turn now to the last of the payment schemes I wish to consider, namely *measured day work*. You probably know of the introduction of this kind of system to replace piece work in wide sections of the motor industry. Measured day work is a hybrid between a fixed payment system and a system of payment by results. The idea is that fixed levels of remuneration are paid, but these are associated with pre-determined targets of output or productivity. In order to introduce a measured day work scheme, the employer will conduct a process of work study which enables high production standards to be set, while at the same time attempting to remain within the maximum output which the workers concerned can reasonably sustain over substantial periods of time. The aim is that by this scientific setting of standards, management can afford to dispense with the immediate relation of output to pay which is involved in payment by results. The point is that failure to achieve the targets is not directly reflected in the remuneration for the time concerned, but there are disciplinary sanctions or dispute resolution processes to deal with the shortfall against the targets. The worker does not lose pay for failing to achieve results, but the system reacts to his not doing so. It should be said that some systems described as measured day work lack this crucial characteristic of dissociating pay and output; where, for example, there is a fixed bonus which is withheld for failure to meet output targets such schemes are in my view still within the payment by results system. But when pay and measured output are dissociated, in a true measured day work scheme, the employment in a sense assumes a more fully contractual character than it has under any of the payment systems we have so far considered. The obligation to work becomes more concrete and specific than under other systems—the obligations are less diffuse than under fixed payment systems—and at the same time the obligation is more than just a measurement or condition of payment due, as it tends to become under payment by results systems. . . .

Measured day work systems depend, not only upon elaborate principles of work-measurement, but often also upon job evaluation—that is, the working out of the comparative values of different kinds of work. The kind of job evaluation scheme most widely used in this country is that of the points system, whereby numerical values are assigned to different factors such as skill, responsibility, effort and working conditions. The relative weights of the different factors are decided and each particular job is rated as to the different factors. The result is a points rating for each job as a whole, on which a scale of remuneration can be based. But although such a system may impose orderliness on, for instance, a payments by results system which has become chaotic over a period of time, it may well itself be hard to maintain intact against the differing demands and differing degrees of bargaining power of the various work-groups affected. Hence the principles of job-evaluation, whilst presenting a scientific appearance, often conceal very extensive value judgments, and accordingly raise policy issues which lawyers ought to be in a position to understand. For instance, it has become well-known that job evaluation schemes can contain in-built sex discrimination by attaching particular importance to qualities more likely to be possessed by one sex than the other, such as physical strength. There are many comparable underlying issues, connected with job evaluation which seem likely to surface as the Equal Pay Act case law develops.

Can I advance, on the basis of all this, something by way of general conclusion? I think that lawyers need to take a new look at the obligations to work and to pay for work. The factual material is there; the conceptual issues are there in plenty. The failure to take account of the factual situation has given the law of the contract of employment an outdated feeling which it would do well to shed.

Attempts are made by the courts to accommodate complex pay systems within a simple contractual framework. But in the following extract, the court refused to be limited to contractual characterisations of hourly pay when the reality was one of payment by results.

Ogden v. Ardphalt Asphalt Ltd.
[1977] 1 W.L.R. 1112; [1977] I.C.R. 604
Employment Appeal Tribunal

Kilner Brown J.: The way the employees were putting their case was "We are guaranteed eight hours' work a day. In the previous 12 weeks although the basic was 40 hours I was averaging between 70 and 80 hours a week for payment purposes." As the lay members of the Appeal Tribunal know, and have expressed their knowledge, this form of approach and this form of calculation is very well known throughout industry as a whole. In other words, if there is a 40-hour week and the basic pay is £1 per hour, that means that the basic pay at the end of the week is £40. But if in fact, through various means, the take-home pay of a worker is £80, instead of working out under the various heads whether it is overtime, whether it is an incentive or productivity bonus, or whatever allowance it might be, it has become common practice to say: "Well, if it is a 40-hour week and I took home £80, that means I worked 80 hours that week for payment purposes," because the basic pay is £1 per hour. It seems to us that this unfortunately put everybody on the wrong track. . . .

The argument which was put before the industrial tribunal, and which was put before us by Mr Crichton-Gold [counsel for the employers], is that the average hourly rate of remuneration should be the basic; in this case something of the order of 95p. Mr Crichton-Gold in support of his general argument (which was the one which appealed to the Industrial Tribunal) says that, where you have an incentive or productivity bonus built into the wage structure, that is really analogous to overtime; it is something which is additional; it is not within the hourly rate, and it is not within the ordinary weekly number of hours. This is a case, said Mr Crichton-Gold, before the Industrial Tribunal and here, which turned simply upon the normal working hours. And that is what the Tribunal in fact did: they multiplied the figure 40, which was the number of normal working hours, by the basic hourly rate of remuneration, something in the order of 95p. The point of law here which has been urged upon us, and which we accept as being correct, is that that is the wrong way of going about it. What the Industrial Tribunal should have done, in accordance with [the Redundancy Payments Act 1965, Sched. 1, para. 5(1) and the Contracts of Employment Act 1972, Sched. 2, para. 2(2)], parts of which I have read, was to determine the average hourly rate of remuneration which was in fact paid to the employees in respect of the four weeks ending with the last complete week.

Similarly, in the following case the court was not deterred by a complex commission payment system.

Weevsmay Ltd. v. Kings
[1977] I.C.R. 244
Employment Appeal Tribunal

Kilner Brown J.: Mr Miller's contention [for the employers] was that the commission was so variable in amount, and a commission which depended on the amount of effort which a man put into his collection—and that there was here a fairly solid, firm base in the basic wage of £20 a week—that, therefore, the commission ought not to be included for the purpose of assessing the remuneration upon which the redundancy payment was to be calculated.

On the other hand, of course, naturally enough, the employee who has appeared in person and put his case in a nutshell in one sentence, said: "Remuneration is what I pick up at the end of the week." . . . In our judgment the Industrial Tribunal were correct, and their method of calculation, namely, to average out not only the basic pay but also the amount of commission, was the proper way to do it.

Historical circumstances, attempts at measuring productivity, conflict over control of the work process between management and workers and technological developments may all contribute towards the evolution of a payment system. The development of legal concepts to reflect different methods of payment requires an appreciation of the economic and industrial relations reasons for different systems.

4. SYSTEMS OF PAY DETERMINATION

An historical perspective reveals many systems of wage-fixing. Centuries of Elizabethan statutory machinery; the beginnings of the industrial revolution in the late eighteenth century with laissez-faire individual contracts and the reality of employer dictation; the growth of craft union monopolies in the nineteenth century fixing rigid scales of prices for work; the spread of collective bargaining at the end of the nineteenth and during the twentieth centuries; State regulation during the World Wars and post-war incomes policies. These various systems of pay determination can be classified as follows:

(a) unilateral wage-fixing, whether by employer dictation or unions fixing rates for the job;
(b) bilateral bargaining between the employer and the individual worker;
(c) collective bargaining and the extension of collective agreements;
(d) wage-fixing involving third parties;
(e) State regulation.

The extracts which follow illustrate the encounters of different systems of pay determination with legal concepts and machinery.

(A) Unilateral Wage-Fixing

A modern example of unilateral wage-fixing can arise in company law with regard to payment of the managing director of a company, as provided for in the company's articles of association. Article 108 of the model set of articles in Schedule 1, Table A, to the Companies Act 1948 provided:

> "A managing director shall receive such remuneration (whether by way of salary, commission, or participation in profits, or partly in one way and partly in another) as the directors may determine."

(*Cf.* the current article 82 in the Companies Act (Tables A–F) Regulations 1985 (S.I. 1985 No. 805), Table A). Where adopted, this article may be incorporated into a contract of employment with the managing director—thus providing an instance of unilateral wage-fixing by the company's board of directors. The possible consequences are illustrated in the following case.

Re Richmond Gate Property Co. Ltd.
[1965] 1 W.L.R. 335; [1964] 3 All E.R. 936
Chancery Division

PLOWMAN J.: The effect of article 9 of the [company's articles of association] articles, coupled with article 108 of Table A, coupled with the fact that Walker was a member [*ie* shareholder] of the company, in my judgment, is that a contract exists between himself and the company for payment to him of remuneration as managing director, and that remuneration depends on article 108 of Table A and is to be such amount "as the directors may 'determine'; in other words, the managing director is at the mercy of the board, he gets what they determine" to pay him, and if they do not determine to pay him anything he does not get anything. That is his contract with the company, and those are the terms on which he accepts office.

. . . In the present case there was an express contract which relates to payment of remuneration, and the only question with which I am concerned is: according to the terms of that express contract, is any sum payable for remuneration? When one finds that the express contract is that the remuneration payable is such sum as the directors may determine that the managing director shall have, and that the directors have not determined that any sum is to be payable to the managing director, it seems to me to follow as a necessary consequence that no remuneration can be claimed.

(B) Bilateral Bargaining on an Individual Basis

The spread of bilateral bargaining on a *collective* basis has left less scope for *individual* bargaining. Nonetheless, such individual bargaining does occur, though it necessarily sometimes has uneasy relations with collective bargaining, as the following case illustrates.

Pepper & Hope v. Daish

[1980] I.R.L.R. 13
Employment Appeal Tribunal

TALBOT J.: At the beginning of December 1978, Mr Daish was approached by Mr Gasch, the production manager, and asked to undertake work on what was described as "4 star ware". That work had been transferred from a factory in Sheffield to the works where Mr Daish was employed. Mr Daish at that time—these facts which we are reciting, we take from the Reasons for the Industrial Tribunal's decision—was not content with his basic hourly rate and wanted to negotiate an increase. So he had what the Industrial Tribunal describe as "an important conversation" with Mr Gasch. His hourly rate at the time was £2.39 per hour for a normal forty hour week. Mr Gasch and Mr Daish talked about the rate for the new work, and it has to be emphasised that what they were talking about, according to the facts, was new work and new conditions of employment which were to apply to the work which Mr Daish was to undertake. He was working in a separate workshop. He was to have under him an apprentice and one other skilled man, whereas previously he had only had an apprentice working under him.

There was in the background, known both to Mr Daish and Mr Gasch, that at the beginning of January 1979, there was going to be a general increase in the hourly rate for the workforce of the company. As Mr Gasch put it in his evidence, that was to be paid to all except some of the employees who were to have a rise negotiated on a separate basis.

On the evidence, the Industrial Tribunal were satisfied that in the conversation that had taken place between Mr Gasch and Mr Daish in December no mention whatsoever was made of the general increase that was to take place in January 1979, but that the proposed increase which was to take effect, it was generally known, would take effect at the beginning of 1979.

In December 1978, according to paragraph 4 of the Reasons, Mr Gasch fixed the proposed increase which Mr Daish was to get at £2.65 an hour and he referred that matter to Mr Hope. The Industrial Tribunal were satisfied, on the evidence, that there was some conversation between Mr Gasch and Mr

Hope that satisfied Mr Hope that the 5% or the £5 general increase which was to take place had been taken into account so far as Mr Daish was concerned in fixing the £2.65. But the Industrial Tribunal were not satisfied, on the evidence, that Mr Daish was told that the increased rate to £2.65 took into account the prospective increase in January 1979.

What subsequently happened was this: Mr Daish started to work under the new arrangements, anticipating that in January he would receive, in addition to the additional increased rate he had negotiated, the general increase of £5 or 5%, but, to his dismay, he found on 12.1.79 that he was not receiving the general increase of 5%. So he had a discussion with Mr Gasch about it, and that took place probably, the Industrial Tribunal found, on 12.1.79. Having raised the matter with Mr Gasch, Mr Gasch said, 'Don't worry about it, leave it with me, there is no trouble'. That being the finding as to what Mr Gasch did say, it certainly seems to this Appeal Tribunal that if Mr Gasch had firmly fixed in his mind, as indeed Mr Hope had firmly fixed in his mind, that Mr Daish's additional rate included the 5%, it is very odd that he said what it was found that he did say.

Mr Daish was not satisfied because he did not receive the increase, so he approached Mr Gasch on two further occasions and then he was finally told he was not going to get it. That incensed Mr Daish. He went to see Mr Hope, whom we have mentioned, who was the managing director, on 17.1.79. As a result he was told he was not going to get it; he told them that they were not honouring his agreement and he would have no alternative but to work out his notice, which he did, and he left. On that basis, his claim was that his dismissal arose from the conduct of the employers in not honouring their agreement and paying him the general increase which all persons had who were not on a separate basis.

. . . What took place on the facts was, that Mr Daish negotiated for new work under new conditions [at] a new rate. We are quite unable to see that it was unreasonable, if unreasonableness is the test, that having so negotiated a new rate for new work under new conditions, that he should also receive the general increase to which all others were entitled except those who were on a separate basis. He was found, as we have indicated, on the facts not to have been on a separate basis, therefore, in our view, there is no reason why he should not have expected to receive the general increase. It was factually found that at the conversation with Mr Gasch, no question of the 5% ever arose, so it was not put to him that what he was then negotiating was including that which he would receive in January. To him, and without there being special mention of it, it was clear he was negotiating separately a new rate.

(C) Collective Bargaining

The dominance of collective bargaining (see Chapter 12 below) in pay determination varies between different sectors, between manual and non-manual workers, and among establishments. For example, although almost 100 per cent. of *non-manual* workers in *public* sector occupations are covered by collective agreements, engineering is the only *private* sector industry where more than half of *non-manual* workers are covered by collective agreements. On the other hand, the only industrial sectors with less than half their *manual* workers covered by collective agreements are agriculture, the distributive trades and miscellaneous services (and each of these is well covered by wages councils: see below). According to the 1978 New Earnings

Survey, 70 per cent. of full-time *workers* are covered by collective bargaining of arrangements. But a 1980 survey of 2,041 *establishments* of all sizes found that only in just over one half of the establishments in the sample (58 per cent. for manual workers, 50 per cent. for non-manual workers) were pay increases the result of collective bargaining at some level. In the great majority of the remainder, pay was not subject to collective bargaining (see W. W. Daniel and N. Millward, *Workplace Industrial Relations in Britain* (1983), p. 179).

(i) Pay bargaining structures and contracts of employment

The following extract describes the complex structure of collective pay bargaining.

LABOUR RESEARCH DEPARTMENT, LRD Book of Wage Rates, Hours and Holidays 1982, pp. 5–6

National Joint Industrial Councils

The commonest form of collective bargaining at national industrial level is through committees or councils consisting of equal numbers of representatives of the relevant employers' associations and officers of national trade unions. These bodies have a variety of different titles: National Joint Industrial Council (NJIC), National Joint Committee, or Council (NJC) or Joint Industrial Council (JIC). Some are very formal and have a full time secretariat while others rarely meet. Some take responsibility for a wide variety of industrial issues, pay, hours, holiday overtime rates, sick pay arrangements, maternity provision, disputes and grievance procedure etc, others concern themselves solely with minimum wage rates, hours and holiday entitlement. Some cover all the significant employers in an industry, others are not so comprehensive: the Chemical and Allied JIC, for example, does not cover Britain's largest chemicals employer, ICI.

Just as these NJIC's show wide variation in their responsibilities so there is a wide range in the importance of the wage rates that they establish. . . .

We have separated the NJIC rates into 3 categories.

(1) NJIC with local rate bargaining

In many industries national minimum rates are agreed. Although strictly speaking there is not an NJIC for the engineering industry, what happens in that industry is typical of this category of agreements. National minimum rates are agreed annually by the Confederation of Shipbuilding & Engineering Unions and the Engineering Employers' Federation. Second and in some cases third tier bargaining then takes over. New basic rates are negotiated in the different companies and areas covered by the agreement. Either the same agreed percentage is added on or new rates are worked out at company or plant level. In addition new local bonus rates may be negotiated.

In practice, therefore, the national minimum rates are not likely to be applied in any but a few poorly organised backwood workplaces. The rates either act as a fall-back position or the percentage increase that is obtained is the figure that matters for the purposes of increasing local rates in other federated companies. Firms which are not members of the employers' associations that sign the agreement are not required to pay even these 'minimum' rates. . . .

(2) NJIC with local bonus bargaining

Many NJIC's set wage rates which are applied in all federated organisations throughout the country, but provide considerable scope for company or plant level bargaining over bonus payments. These may be piece rates, shift rates, overtime rates, commission etc. This is a feature of local authority manual agreements for example. The extent of this bonus bargaining varies from industry to industry in the private sector and its significance in individual workplaces is obviously a reflection of local trade union negotiating strength. . . .

(3) NJIC substantive basic rates

In some NJIC's the rate that is agreed nationally is the rate that is applied locally—there is no local rate bargaining or bonus bargaining. With these agreements, therefore, the national rate comes nearest to representing the actual wage rate received.

Industries dominated by a small number of very large employers are much more likely to fall into this tightly controlled category than industries with a much larger number of small employers. . . .

Company/Corporate Basic Rates

Although it may be interesting to know the minimum rates an NJIC has agreed in an industry which has considerable second tier bargaining, or what wages councils rates may be in different industries, the actual basic rates that employers in those industries pay give a much clearer view of conditions in the industry . . . wage rates paid by companies or corporations in each of the different groups in the economy . . . correspond more closely than the NJIC rates above to what workers can expect to receive from major employers in those industries. . . .

Non-manual agreements

The pay rates, holidays and hours in non-manual agreements correspond almost exactly to the conditions that some workers covered by the agreement will receive. This is particularly true of public sector national agreements and private sector company agreements. . . .

It is a common characteristic of clerical and professional rates to have an incremental scale, where workers in the same grade will receive annual rises for a number of years (3–10 years is the common time scale) in addition to any annual percentage wage increase that all those covered by the agreement may receive.

Workers on these incremental scales, therefore, effectively receive 2 increases per year; one as part of the annual wage review and the second as "experience money". Incremental scales are very uncommon in manual occupations, but not unknown. . . .

A second major difference between the non-manual and the manual wage rates concerns "other payments". The wage rate (plus increments) of a particular job is largely what the holder of that job can expect to earn as a gross salary in a non-manual occupation. . . .

. . . the vast majority of white collar workers receive little or no paid overtime or bonus payments or shift work premiums.

The impact of complex collective bargaining structures on the contract of employment is illustrated by the following case.

(1) Bond v. CAV Ltd.; (2) Neads v. CAV Ltd.
[1983] I.R.L.R. 360
Queen's Bench Division

Peter Pain J.: The terms of service of both plaintiffs derived from four different sources: (1) national agreements made between the Engineering Employers Federation and the Confederation of Shipbuilding and Engineering Unions (the plaintiffs were both members of the Transport and General Workers Union, which is a member of the Confederation); (2) agreements made at factory level between the defendants and various unions representing their employees, including the Transport and General Workers Union; (3) departmental agreements made by the shop stewards in their departments with the management; and (4) individual agreements made between the plaintiff and those immediately in charge of him.

The weekly wage had four constituents: (1) the basic wage deriving from the national agreement; (2) a fixed sum arising out of the actual factory negotiations; (3) a piece-work bonus; and (4) a monthly factory bonus.

As will be seen from the above, this was a factory where conditions of employment were regularly negotiated between the management and trade union representatives. The defendants belonged to the Engineering Employers Federation.

Mr Bond was issued with a statement of terms and conditions of his employment pursuant to [E.C.P.A., s.1], but this is somewhat cryptic as to remuneration, since it tells one only that, "Your rate of pay and total earnings are shown on your pay slip". Mr Neads was not issued with such a notice. Both plaintiffs were issued with a copy of the Workshop Rules, which provide by paragraph 3, "Working conditions and arrangements are to a large extent the outcome of national, local, and domestic agreements currently in force and made from time to time between the Engineering Employers' Federation, East Anglian Association, or the Company and Trade Unions (registered or unregistered). Few, if any, of these agreements are enforceable by law but the willingness of all the parties, on whose behalf they are made, to observe them is fundamental to orderly relationships between employer and employee. The acceptance of this attitude is implicit in contracts of employment".

Despite these rather tentative terms, counsel were agreed that the terms of the various collective agreements as they affected each plaintiff were imported into the plaintiff's contract of employment.

The calculation of Mr Bond's piece-work bonus was provided for in an agreement called "The Incentive Scheme for Multi-Spindle Bar Automatics in 601 Department". This provided for the level of manning of machines and for the method of bonus calculation. The payment scale was set out in Appendix 1. Thus it was envisaged that in the ordinary way Mr Bond and his fellow setters would be operating on the Appendix 1 scale. . . .

. . . (However) there were occasions on which the management required a setter to continue operating a machine even though it was below normal efficiency. . . . In order to cope with this there was a further agreement called the "Sign Up Procedure". . . .

It soon became apparent that this agreement did not cover the position adequately. . . .

. . . accordingly (there was) devised a scheme which was referred to in evidence as the "Ad Hoc Arrangement", which provided for certain additional payments so as to maintain the actual piece-work bonus. This was intended to be a purely temporary arrangement . . . but, despite a certain amount of grumbling from the setters, it continued in operation. . . .

Further disputes led finally to a refusal by the setters to operate machines which were on sign up or under the ad hoc arrangement. The employer claimed they were in breach of contract and refused to pay any wages. On a claim for wages, the court held that the supplemental agreements were incorporated into the contracts of employment, but were only temporary and could be terminated by the employees on reasonable notice without affecting the main employment contract.

Collective agreements determining pay are not usually legally enforceable as between the collective parties (trade unions and employers) which negotiate them (on legal enforceability, see Chapter 12 on *Collective Bargaining*). However, they do have legal effects. Most commonly, this is as a result of their *de facto* incorporation into individual contracts of employment, emphasised in a recent judgment of the European Court of Justice, which required the United Kingdom government to secure that collective agreements complied with EEC law's provisions on equal treatment (*Commission of the European Economic Communities* v. *U.K.* [1984] I.R.L.R. 29). The recognition of the *de facto* effects of collective agreements highlights the gulf between the reality of pay determination through collective bargaining and British labour law's focus on the individual contract of employment. The startling contrast with the law of other European countries was pointed out by Kahn-Freund in the following extract.

P. Davies and M. Freedland, KAHN-FREUND'S LABOUR AND THE LAW (3rd ed., 1983), p. 177

More than thirty years ago, in *Hulland v Saunders & Co.* [[1945] K.B. 78 (C.A.)] the Court of Appeal assumed (there was no need to decide the point) that if the worker agreed to less than the collective wage, he could not claim the difference; that is, that the employer can validly contract out of the collective agreement. What is remarkable is that the trade unions never seem to have pressed for legislation to change this. . . .

This is remarkable and all the more so because this is an almost unique feature of British law. In most Continental countries the terms of collective agreements are legally binding. This means that they are mandatory law; and that an employer who is a party to the agreement, or member of an organisation which is, cannot to the detriment of his employees validly contract out of its terms; and in many countries it does not matter whether the employee concerned is or is not a union member. Thus the bilateral rule-making power of the parties to the collective agreement does not only influence but restrains the unilateral rule-making power of management. A term of the contract of employment which is less favourable to the worker than the corresponding collective term is automatically void, and the collective term is deemed to have been agreed by the parties to the individual contract. It is a compulsory effect which is automatic (in most Continental countries) as regards employers who are parties or members of parties to the agreement, but not as regards "outsiders", "non-federated firms". They can also be subjected to this compulsory effect, but this is not automatic. To "extend" it to them an order of some authority is needed, generally the Ministry of Labour.

(ii) Fair wages policy and collective bargaining

A "fair wages" policy, whereby pay standards in collective agreements in the U.K. could be made legally binding on employers, had its origins in the Fair Wages Resolutions of the House of Commons dating from 1891 (and earlier in many local authorities). These Resolutions required employers who contracted with public authorities to agree to observe "fair" wages standards—including those embodied in collective agreements. In effect, collectively agreed pay standards were to be mandatory on public contractors. These employers became indirectly legally bound by collective agreements. This policy was taken up in wartime and made applicable to British industry as a whole in Order 1305 of 1940, and again in 1951, 1959 and lastly, in Schedule 11 to the EPA 1975. It was again made specifically applicable to public contractors in the Fair Wages Resolution of 1946. The fair wages policy is now in eclipse due to the repeal of Schedule 11 by the Employment Act 1980, and the revocation of the 1946 Resolution in September 1983.

A major problem for a policy of legal enforcement of a system of pay determination by collective bargaining is posed by the existence of complex bargaining structures. As the extract from the *LRD Book* (see above, p. 168) shows, pay bargaining is common on at least three levels: national, local and company. Which of many collective agreements is to be enforced? There can be a variety of wage rates negotiated at the industry, occupational, enterprise, establishment and work-group levels. The relation between a legal policy of enforcement of collectively negotiated pay standards, and a constantly changing system of collective bargaining, was the theme of a study of the Fair Wages Resolutions of 1891–1946.

O. Kahn-Freund, a book review of B. Bercusson's "Fair Wages Resolutions" (1978) in (1979) 8 I.L.J. 188 at 189–190

. . . the dominant theme of his work . . . is the relation between the standards "established" by the fair wages policy as crystallised in the [Fair Wages] Resolutions and the relevant legislation, and those resulting from collective bargaining . . . The link was not formed until 1946 when the Resolution of that year, influenced by the war time Order 1305 of 1940, referred to wages, hours and conditions "not less favourable than those established by machinery of negotiation or arbitration." Until then the government departments concerned always distinguished between the two standards and took the view that a contractor complied with the fair wages clause if he paid what was generally paid in the district even if it fell short of what ought to have been paid under a relevant collective agreement. With an abundance of evidence Dr. Bercusson demonstrates that the civil servants administering the Resolutions of 1891 and 1909 deliberately refused to use them in order to promote the observance of collective agreements. . . .

Until the early 1940s the standards actually observed tended not to exceed, and all too often to fall short of, those laid down in negotiated agreements. In a labour market in which generally supply exceeded demand, the interpretation placed by both the government departments and the arbitration authorities on the earlier Resolutions was unfavourable to the unions and to the worker. In this respect—as brought out very clearly in the concluding parts of this book—the situation has changed radically since the Second World War. To some extent this was due to the deliberate amendment of the Resolution in 1946. What is far more important is that, owing to change in the relation of labour demand and supply, national or district wage bargaining was largely superseded by plant bargaining. "Wage drift" dominated the scene, and the wages actually paid tended to exceed, sometimes drastically, those "established" by "recognised terms and conditions." Thus it was now in the interest of the unions to insist on the observance of what was generally done rather than on what national or district agreements provided: like two sporting teams the two sides of industry have "changed places". . . .

In *Racal Communications Ltd.* v. *Pay Board* [1974] I.C.R. 590 (Ch.D.) the court held that the 1946 Resolution required adherence to nationally agreed pay standards, although these standards had become unrealistically low due to increased collective bargaining over pay at local level. In *Crittall-Hope Ltd.* v. *Pay Board* (Award 3290/1974), however, the Industrial Arbitration Board (predecessor to the Central Arbitration Committee) refused to accept national agreements as "fair wage" standards, in the light of changes towards local collective bargaining over pay. A similar dispute under the statutory embodiment of fair wages policy in Schedule 11 to EPA led to another court decision which again upheld the admittedly unrealistic national agreement (*R.* v. *Central Arbitration Committee, ex p. Deltaflow Ltd.* [1978] I.C.R. 534 (Q.B.D.)).

The courts in both *Racal* and *Deltaflow* recognised the conflict between the legally enforced standard and the changing system of collective bargaining that rendered it unrealistic, but felt unable to adapt the law to the changing social reality. The success of a "fair wages" policy based on collectively bargained pay determination depends on whether statutory policy can be made flexible enough to cope both with complex bargaining structures and overcome strict construction of statutory language.

(D) Third-party intervention: arbitration

Third-party intervention in the process of pay determination takes various forms in the United Kingdom. At one level, ACAS provides an ad hoc service of conciliation, mediation and arbitration in industrial disputes. In 1985, pay and other terms of employment were the most frequent issues in disputes in which ACAS conciliated on a collective basis (854 (59 per cent) of disputes; *cf.* 1,003 and 53 per cent. in 1980). Of 202 cases referred to ACAS for arbitration or mediation in 1985, 66.3 per cent. involved disputes over pay and terms of employment (*cf.* 323 and 76 per cent. in 1980). The arbitration process is described as follows.

ACAS, *The ACAS Role in Conciliation. Arbitration and Mediation* (1979), pp. 17–19

18 There is no prescribed form for initiating a request for arbitration but it is usually convenient for representatives of the parties to sign a joint application setting out the relevant details of their names and addresses and the agreed terms of reference. . . .

19 ACAS then appoints a suitable arbitrator (or board as the case may be) after confirming that he is able and willing to arbitrate on the dispute and sends a signed minute of appointment to him.

20 The time and place of the hearing is arranged so far as possible to suit the convenience of all those taking part. . . .

21 [Following a joint application] The parties are notified in writing of all the details, with a request to send their written statements of case to the arbitrator and to exchange them in advance of the hearing. . . .

22 The arbitrator meets the parties at the hearing about a week after he has received their written statements of case. The hearing is held in private, unless both parties wish otherwise, and is conducted in an informal atmosphere. Each party is free to bring along such advisers and witnesses as are necessary to the presentation of its case. Representation by counsel or by solicitor is very unusual and requires the consent of the arbitrator or board who will offer the other party the same facility. Detailed procedure is decided by the individual arbitrator or chairman of the board. The arbitrator normally meets both parties together and, in order to obtain the relevant information, he usually first asks the claimant party to state its case in the presence of the other party who is then invited to reply. The arbitrator usually then questions both parties about their case and finally invites them to make any closing statements.

23 The arbitrator submits his report and award to ACAS for distribution to the parties usually about a week after the hearing. Awards of boards of arbitration can be expected about two or three weeks after the hearing. All awards are regarded as the confidential property of the parties and are not published by ACAS. The parties themselves may however decide to make awards public.

24 Parties to arbitration sometimes seek a clarification or interpretation of an award. Any such requests are examined to ensure that no new question is being raised which might require fresh terms of reference. ACAS also requires the agreement of all the parties to the original arbitration before proceeding to invite the arbitrator to give an interpretation. Sometimes a further hearing may be required but more often the question can be resolved by correspondence.

A more institutionalised form of voluntary arbitration is described in the following extract.

ACAS ANNUAL REPORT 1981, Appendix B, *ACAS evidence to the Megaw Committee of Inquiry into Civil Service Pay,* paras. 24–26, 28–29

. . . Arbitration is the process whereby both parties agree in advance to be bound by the award and this has clear advantages in certain circumstances. Mediation produces recommendations of a non-binding nature which can be either accepted without reservation by both parties or serve as a basis for further negotiations between them. Mediation, was, for example, the means whereby an independent committee of inquiry in the steel industry dispute in 1980 arrived at recommendations and sought and secured acceptance by the parties. Misunderstandings of the two terms often arise and can be dangerous, but it is entirely possible to devise a procedural agreement which has the advantage that it provides for both in a flexible way. Such a provision avoids a common criticism that where arbitration is written in as an obligatory final step in an agreement, it weakens the resolve of the negotiators to reach a settlement on a voluntary basis.

Many public authorities provide for arbitration as the last stage in their disputes procedure. The Post Office and Police are two examples of bodies which have standing voluntary arbitration arrangements to which independent chairmen are appointed (with the advice or assistance of ACAS where necessary) and for which ACAS provides secretarial services. Standing arbitration of this kind has the advantage of allowing the arbitration body to develop considerable expertise and knowledge of the particular industry or service concerned; this enables it to understand clearly the industrial relations and commercial/industrial context in which its awards have to be implemented and to ensure that awards are consistent with each other. Normally the chairman of standing arbitration boards are also on the ACAS panel of arbitrators so that they have also a continuing experience of conditions in other industries.

One particular area of the public sector, the railways, is noted for the flexible procedure which it has effectively operated since 1936. It provides for both unilateral access to mediation and jointly agreed access to arbitration. Thus, the procedure providing for ultimate resort to the Railways Staffs National Tribunal, allows, on the one hand, one party to initiate a reference to mediation (with which the other party has to be associated, albeit reluctantly at times) leading to a Tribunal decision which is tantamount to a recommendation, and on the other permits parties to make a joint reference to arbitration in which the Tribunal's decision is an award which is traditionally morally binding on all parties. A total of 75 decisions have been issued so far in the 45 years of the existence of the RSNT in its present form and difficulties in implementing the awards have been rare. The Tribunal is serviced by a secretary who is an ACAS official seconded to the Tribunal on a part-time basis.

The arbitration agreement in the Civil Service provided that arbitration should be available "on application by either party" for issues on grades up to and including Principal. Above that arbitration was available by mutual agreement. If there is to be a new arbitration agreement, there are three choices:

(*i*) automatic arbitration, that is, any failure to agree proceeds to arbitration;
(*ii*) unilateral arbitration, that is, provided at the wish of one party;
(*iii*) voluntary arbitration, that is, by joint agreement of both parties.

Automatic arbitration in industrial relations is normally undesirable because it is inflexible and could encourage parties not to seek negotiated settlements. Unilateral arbitration can provide an acceptable alternative to industrial action in many circumstances although, if recourse to arbitration becomes too frequent, the willingness or ability of the parties to reach agreement in direct negotiation could be affected. It is not conducive to effective bargaining to have one party or the other taking the view that matters more appropriate for resolution at the bargaining table are increasingly being taken out of their hands. Many unions and employers also often hesitate to give *carte blanche* as to what issues can be taken to arbitration by the other party. Voluntary arbitration provides the most flexible option, a means of resolving the issue short of industrial action when all other means have failed, but where both parties retain choices over invoking the option.

The most extensive mechanism for third-party intervention in the United Kingdom is the Wages Council system, first established in 1909. After the coming into operation of the Wages Act 1986 about two and a quarter million workers were covered by wages councils. The Wages Act 1986, Pt. II now allows these bodies to fix only a single minimum hourly rate, a single overtime rate, and a limit on charges for any accommodation provided by employers. Each wages council comprises equal numbers of members representing employers and workers, and not more than five independent members, one of whom acts as chairman. The process of fixing minimum pay in these councils is described in the following extract.

"Wages Councils Parts 1 and 2" in INDUSTRIAL RELATIONS REVIEW AND REPORT No. 284 (November 1982), p. 8 and No. 290 (February 1983), p. 8

Meetings of Wages Councils to improve pay and conditions are instigated—usually by the workers' side—by the submission of a motion to the Council. Copies of the motion are then distributed to the parties by the Office of Wages Councils and a meeting is arranged. Most Wages Councils meet at the Department of Employment's Steel House offices in London.

In recent years it has become common practice in some of the larger Councils for the workers' side to issue a detailed written claim with supporting arguments well before the meeting takes place. This gives employers the opportunity to work out their response in advance. Often they, too, circulate a written statement of their position. In some sectors—notably the clothing industry—extensive negotiations take place before the Wages Council formally convenes.

Because the parties are generally aware of each others' respective positions in advance, the formal proceedings of deciding on a Proposal are generally completed within a single day—or two days in the case of the larger Councils such as those for retailing. This marks a considerable change from the procedure common ten years ago when several meetings on separate occasions were the norm.

A Wages Council meeting begins with the workers' side making a formal presentation of its claim. This may already have been revised from its original form in the light of the employers' response received before the meeting. The employers then follow by giving their reply to the claim and the meeting is adjourned for the independents to consider their views.

Sometimes the two sides reach agreement without the intervention of the independent members. More commonly, the final Proposal is drafted after the disagreements between them are narrowed down in a series of separate informal, unminuted meetings between each side and the independent members. Ultimate power lies with the independents because they can use their casting votes to decide the outcome of the negotiations. But their main role is to act as conciliators between the parties, encouraging them to reach an agreed compromise.

At these meetings the independents are also able to make their own assessment of the merits of each side's case. This means that, as well as acting as go-betweens, the independents can indicate what they would be prepared to support.

The need to gain the support of the independents, in the event of a deadlock in the negotiations, in itself, encourages each side to moderate its position, making agreement easier to reach. Frequently, however, no agreement is possible, even though both sides may have shifted substantially from their original positions. In these circumstances the terms of the Proposal are determined by a majority decision in which the casting votes of the independents are decisive. . . .

To gauge the views of the independents, we spoke to four experienced Council chairmen (all of whom served on a number of Councils). Sir John Wordie, Mr Monaghan and Mr Sim emphasised that their main function was to act as conciliators, with the job of helping the two sides to reach a mutually acceptable compromise. As Sir John Wordie pointed out, a detached person can often see areas of agreement and ways of minimising the points of disagreement that are unclear to the parties immediately involved. Because of this, he thought that independents played a useful role as "catalysts", smoothing the path to an eventual settlement. In a similar vein, Mr Monaghan felt that the use of the casting vote represented a failure by the independents. He stressed, however, that outside the retail Councils, he was rarely called upon to use this vote. This point was taken up by Sir John Wordie and Mr Sim who saw no sign of a breakdown in the system, because, in their experience, they were not required to use their casting vote any more frequently now than in the past. Mr Sim also commented that, even where the independents do have to support one side or the other, in practice the "losing" side may be reasonably satisfied with the outcome. Often they are voting "for the record", knowing that the award will be passed by the combined votes of the independents and the other side.

The Wages Act 1986, s.14(6)(*a*) now provides that before a Wages Council makes an order it shall have regard to its effects on the level of employment among workers to whom it will apply, particularly as regards those workers whose remuneration is below the national average for such workers, thus providing an intentional downward pressure on wages.

A major problem of third-party intervention arises when the third-party's role is governed by rules or policy dictated not by the parties, but by someone else. The case of arbitration subject to public policy has been called by Rideout "regulated arbitration" (R. W. Rideout, "Arbitration and the public interest: regulated arbitration" in *Labour Law and the Community*, (Lord Wedderburn and W. T. Murphy eds. (1982), pp. 49 and 51):

> " . . . the resolution of an industrial dispute within a framework of rules which, in a sense, take the place of terms of reference. . . .
>
> Inevitably, therefore, one would expect arbitration to occur where an independent body regulates a pay policy. This is clearly arbitration in the public interest and it will clearly involve policy."

Would a system of pay determination by regulated arbitration work better under a loose framework of policy for the guidance of arbitrators (as in fair wages policy), or a tightly defined set of rules which, by ad hoc interpretations, could allow for loopholes (as in the Heath Government's pay policy of 1972–74, see below p. 184).

(E) State Intervention

The State intervenes in the system of pay determination indirectly, for example, by providing legal machinery to enforce contractual claims for pay, or for the extension of collective agreements (fair wages policy), or to support third-party intervention, as in the case of ACAS or the Wages Inspectorate, which is charged with ensuring that the minimum rates of pay laid down by wages councils are adhered to. More directly, the State, through taxation (Pay-As-You-Earn) and the social security system (National Insurance contributions) regulates the take-home pay received by employees. Again, as the employer or paymaster in the public sector the State becomes a direct participant in the process of pay determination. In this section, we focus on two principal areas of State intervention: low pay policy and pay restraint.

(i) Low pay policy

Policy to combat low pay often adopts the method of fixing minimum levels of pay. A recent book (G. Starr, *Minimum Wage Fixing*, (1981) I.L.O.) identified four basic roles played by minimum wage fixing in countries which have adopted such machinery. They were summarised in the following extract.

B. Bercusson, "*The future of fair wages policy*" (1982) 11 I.L.J. 271

(i) To protect a small number of carefully delineated low-paid workers who, because of their special characteristics, are considered to occupy an especially vulnerable position in the labour market. In the United Kingdom this role has been adopted *vis-à-vis* certain low-paid industries (Wages Councils), women (the Equal Pay Act 1970) and to some extent economically vulnerable industries/sectors (subsidies).

(ii) To reduce poverty by providing a basic floor to the wage structure. In the United Kingdom there is no national minimum wage, though there was an inter-departmental working party report on the subject in 1969.

(iii) To secure "fair wages" by fixing separate minimum wages for particular groups, those not being necessarily confined to lowest-paid or most vulnerable, but include those for whom it is judged necessary to ensure the maintenance of wages at "appropriate levels." In the United Kingdom there has been a myriad of instruments and measures: Fair Wages Clauses in government contracts, extension of collective agreements (Sched. 11 to the E.P.A. 1975), arbitration provisions (*eg* Order 1305 of 1940 and its successors up to the Terms and Conditions of Employment Act 1959). One objective of these various measures seems broadly to avoid disparities based on establishment or geographical position in an industry. . . .

(iv) To achieve broad national objectives, *eg* major shifts in the distribution of income, or economic stability and growth. Every incomes policy during the late 1960s and 1970s stressed the specific problem of low pay and catered for it by various methods, *eg* exceptions to the limits or flat-rate increases.

It is increasingly recognised, however, that minimum wage *fixing* has only a partial role to play in combatting low pay. Recent theories about the causes of low pay locate the problem in the industrial structure: a limited number of relatively high paying jobs in the "primary" sector, large firms using modern technology with a stable product market and strong market power and a low paid "secondary" sector, small firms using traditional technology with competitive or declining product markets. To this division in the industrial structure there corresponds a segmented labour market. The "secondary" labour market comprises workers who are confined to, yet are available for, work at low rates of pay. Factors such as sex or race, family structure and responsibility, and possession of restricting skills may create such "non-competing" segments of the labour force. The focus of this "segmentation theory" on the role of specific low paying industrial sectors and occupations and specific low paid disadvantaged groups of workers means that a policy to combat low pay must look to more than minimum wage-fixing for a solution. Policies aimed at specific industries and at particular groups (a combination of industrial policy and labour market policies) are required. This is one conclusion of a study which applied segmentation theory to low paying industries in the United Kingdom.

C. Craig, J. Rubery, R. Tarling, F. Wilkinson, LABOUR MARKET STRUCTURE, INDUSTRIAL ORGANISATION AND LOW PAY (1982), p. 141

The analysis of the causes of low pay—showing that these are rooted in the economic and technical conditions of production and in the institutional and social structure—suggests that minimum wage control could *not* be a major vehicle for reducing the degree of pay inequality. A move towards a high wage economy, from the present wide dispersion of earnings based on low productivity employment areas, can only be achieved through an extension of effective trade union organisation and collective bargaining combined with an active macro-economic and industrial policy, and cannot be effected by minimum wage protection alone. However, we would hope that minimum wage policy would not be taken in isolation but would form part of a policy programme designed to extend protection in the labour market and to improve the distribution of income, thus reducing the supply of low-paid labour to the labour market.

One long-standing mechanism in the United Kingdom for combatting low pay was a fair wages policy, embodied in the Resolution of 1946 and Schedule 11 to the EPA 1975 (see above, pp. 172 *et seq.*). In the four years of its most intensive operation (1977–1980), there were 2,804 claims (759 withdrawn) and 1,768 awards under these two instruments. The fair wages policy embodied two standards to which low paid workers might aspire: "recognised" terms and conditions in collective agreements; and a "general level" of terms and conditions. The use of Schedule 11 and the 1946 Resolution as instruments of low pay policy was emphasised by the body hearing claims, the Central Arbitration Committee, in the following extract:

Central Arbitration Committee ANNUAL REPORT 1982, para. 3.7

An interesting issue which has given rise to considerable discussion has been whether machinery of this type is intended to protect against absolute or relative low pay. That is to say does it aim to take care of only those whose pay levels fall below a set figure or does it also serve to assist those whose pay, although above this level, falls seriously below the rate for the job? The drafting of the Resolution over 30 years ago reflects the decision that it should deal with relatively low pay. Indeed in principle it would appear that, if the intention had been to protect actual low pay, the appropriate system would have been a national or industry minimum wage system.

The CAC's reference to "absolute" or "actual" low pay (in contrast to "relatively" low pay) raises the question of how these standards could be determined, and the role of legal rules and institutions in low pay policy. The merits of the fair wages instruments as part of a low pay policy—claims by both trade unions (Schedule 11) and workers (the 1946 Resolution) went to a specialised tribunal (the CAC), and their deficiencies (the ad hoc nature of claims, their applicability only to specific individual enterprises and groups of workers, the uncertainty of the standard required, its relation to a changing system of collective bargaining)—illustrate the problems of devising standards and machinery for a low pay policy.

(ii) Pay restraint

All proposals for Government action on pay restraint start from the assumption that there is some connection between the pay bargaining system and inflation (see F. T. Blackaby ed., *The Future of Pay Bargaining* (1980), p. 64). The following extract charts, *inter alia*, the legal and institutional elements of post-Second World War policies up to 1977.

S. Brittan and P. Lilley, THE DELUSION OF INCOMES POLICY (1977), pp. 154–155

A Summary of UK Incomes Policies 1948–1976

Period	Name	Government	Voluntary/ Compulsory	TUC Co-operation	Institutions
Feb 48– Oct 50	Cripps-TUC	Labour	Voluntary but wage rises not allowed for cost pass through under margin controls	Yes	None

Period	Name	Government	Voluntary/ Compulsory	TUC Co-operation	Institutions
Jul 61– Mar 62	Selwyn Lloyd's pay pause	Conservative	Voluntary but imposed in public sector	No	None
Apr 62– Oct 64	Guiding light	Conservative	Voluntary	No refused to co-operate with NIC	National Incomes Commission (NIC)
Dec 64– Jul 66	Statement of Intent	Labour	Voluntary	Yes	National Board for Prices & Incomes (NBPI)
Jul 66– Dec 66	Freeze	Labour	Statutory	Acquies-cence	NBPI retained
Jan 67– Jun 67	Severe restraint	Labour	Statutory	Acquies-cence	NBPI retained
Jun 67– Apr 68	Relaxation	Labour	Statutory	Acquies-cence	NBPI retained
Apr 68– Jun 70	Jenkins: renewed restraint	Labour	Statutory	Acquies-cence	NBPI retained
Nov 72– Jan 73	Stage I Freeze	Conservative	Statutory	Hostile compliance	
Feb 73– Oct 73	Stage II	Conservative	Statutory	Hostile compliance	Pay Board Price Commission
Nov 73– Feb 74	Stage III	Conservative	Statutory	Hostile compliance	Pay Board Price Commission
Mar 74– Jul 74	Social Contract	Labour	Voluntary		
Aug 75– Jul 76	£6	Labour	Compulsory (not statutory)	Yes	None
Aug 76– Jul 77	$4\frac{1}{2}$%	Labour	Compulsory (not statutory)	Yes	None

Period	Wage norm	Actual* wage increases†	Actual price increases†	Associated conditions and concessions	How ended
Feb 48– Oct 50	None	2.4%	3.1%	(i) prices on controlled goods frozen (ii) dividends frozen (iii) voluntary price and profit restraint by FBI etc.	TUC Congress voted to abandon wage restraint

* Increase in the index of basic hourly wage rates

† At annual rate

Period	Wage norm	Actual* wage increases†	Actual price increases†	Associated conditions and concessions	How ended
Jul 61–Mar 62	Zero for new agreements	4.3%	4.6%	None	Breached by Electricity Council in November 1961
Apr 62–Oct 64	2–2½% p.a. adjusted to 3½% p.a. in 1963	4.3%	2.7%	(i) "Neddy" indicative planning apparatus (ii) 4% growth rate	Faded away
Dec 64–Jul 66	3–3½% p.a.	7.4%	4.2%	(i) National plan (ii) 4% growth target	"Blown off course" by seamen's strike May/June 1966
Jul 66–Dec 76	Zero, roll back of previous agreements	0.1%	3.5%		
Jan 66–Dec 66	"Severe restraint"	4.0%	2.7%		
Jan 67–Jun 67	"Continued restraint"	8.6%	4.9%		
Jun 67–Apr 68	3½% plus productivity agreements raised to 3½–4½% at end 1969	7.1%	5.4%	(i) Abandonment of "In place of Strife"	"Dirty Jobs" pay explosion 1969/70
Nov 72–Jan 73	Zero	1.1%	7.3%	(i) Effective non-implementation of Industrial Relations Act (ii) 5% growth target? (iii) Subsidies to State industries	
Feb 73–Oct 73	£1 per week plus 4%	14.1%	11.0%		
Nov 73–Feb 74	7% plus partial indexation	12.8%	18.9%		Miners dispute and February election defeat
Mar 74–Jul 75	Wages to move in line with cost of living index	32.0%	24.4%	Repeal of Industrial Relations Act, food subsidy, gift tax, etc.	Sterling crisis provokes compulsory policy
Aug 75–Jul 76	£6 per week flat rate	17.5%	12.9%	Renewed commitment to egalitarian plans	
Aug 76–Jul 77	£2.50–£4 per week			(i) Reductions in tax (ii) National-isation of Aircraft and Ship-building industries	

The implications for labour law of these multiple interventions are varied. The following extracts explore some of them.

(a) Statutory pay restraint

Statutory interventions restraining pay must obviously be central to labour law. The following extract describes one such early intervention: the Prices and Incomes Act 1966.

K. W. Wedderburn, *The Worker and the Law* (2nd ed., 1971), pp. 212–214

. . . the Act did mainly three things which have remained the chief headings of discussion about legislation ever since. Since we have not heard the last of incomes policy, a summary of them is worth-while.

First, Part I established the N.B.P.I. [National Board for Prices and Incomes] on a statutory basis, allowing the Government to refer any "question" on incomes, employment terms, or prices to it. The statute gave the N.B.P.I. powers to compel testimony on pain of a fine which, although a big union did once threaten not to appear, have never had to be used. The job of the Board as set out in Part I was to examine the "question" with reference to the current White Paper expressing Government incomes policy.

Secondly, the core of the Act was Part II, to be brought into effect by Order for twelve months (first done in August 1967). Its sections give to the Secretary of State a set of "weapons" which he can fire off; but, contrary to popular belief, until he pulls the relevant trigger, by Order or directive, no *legal* obligation rests on anyone (either to abstain from, or even to report, wage increases). Thus, he can by Order enforce the reporting of any "claims" about pay or other conditions of employment. Under Section 14 he can order that future awards and settlements be reported within seven days, in which case they must not be implemented until notified and for a further "standstill" period of thirty days or longer if referred to the N.B.P.I. In practice, what was used was neither of those sections, but Section 15 under which he can give a "direction" putting a legal "standstill" on the implementation of an award or settlement referred to the N.B.P.I. as a "question" under Part I. This basic structure was parallel to a set of sections on prices and charges.

How long could this "standstill" last? Under the 1966 Act the maximum period was three months (or four under Section 14, the extra thirty days normally applying to that section). But the 1967 and 1968 Acts, apart from extending control over dividends, also extended the basic standstill period first to six months and then to eleven months from *reference* to the Board where the N.B.P.I. made an "adverse recommendation" in regard to the increase. . . .

Thirdly, what was the sanction for breach of a standstill? The civil consequences were for a while obscure, but the 1967 Act made it clear that a contract of employment became invalid only in respect of the amount of the remuneration "in excess of the restriction", no right to which could exist. Also, it is noticeable that disputes about "standstill" restrictions or differences of opinion about their effect were always stated to be included within the legal concept of "trade dispute". . . .

. . . and that Section 16 of the 1966 Act was stated not to give rise (except for the liabilities next set out) to "criminal or tortious liability for conspiracy or any other liability in tort" (a material point on strikes. . . .) That Section made it a crime for (a) an employer to implement the wage-increase during a standstill, and (b) any person or trade union to take any action, including strike action, "with a view to compel induce or influence" an employer so to do. The penalty was a fine of £100 (or for companies £500). Proceedings, however, could not be brought without the consent of the Attorney-General.

Reflecting on this experience, one commentator wrote the following.

H. Clegg, HOW TO RUN AN INCOMES POLICY (1971), p. 58

Legal regulation has yet another shortcoming. There has to be a reasonable chance of detecting offenders. Laws against fornication do not work very well. Pay increases can easily be detected if they are granted by industry agreements, or throughout a great company such as I.C.I. or Ford. But the thousands of workshop decisions about piece-rates, allowances, overtime and plus rates are quite another matter. They may follow the policy if managers and foremen, shop stewards and workers understand it and choose to apply it. But it is impossible to stop them increasing earnings if they choose to make earnings rise, and rising earnings can undermine a pay policy.

Consequently, the function of the law in an incomes policy is not to force the country to conform to a policy that would otherwise be unacceptable. It can do little for an unpopular policy. Where a policy has widespread support, however, the government can take powers in order to reassure the country that the policy will not be undermined by self-seekers trying to turn the sacrifice of others to their own advantage.

The next statutory policy, imposed by the Heath Government on November 6, 1972, was described as having the most detailed pay controls in the history of British incomes policy (B. Towers "British Incomes Policy" in *Occasional Papers in Industrial Relations* (Universities of Leeds and Nottingham (1978)), p. 15):

> "Not surprisingly, given their complexity, precise guidance on the controls was contained in a Price and Pay Code. The pay controls, implemented by the [Pay] Board, descended in stages of severity by size of company from requiring approval to simply an expectation that the Code would be observed. Thus real control was reserved for companies employing 1,000 or more in which pay settlements required approval before implementation. It was hoped that detailed control of the top slice would have a demonstration effect at lower levels."

The statutory imposition of a simple wage freeze or period of delay need not pose problems of legal complexity; but once the statutory policy contains detailed rules to be applied, familiar problems of interpretation arise. This was the position under Stages 2 and 3 of the Heath policy mentioned above.

R. W. Rideout, "Arbitration and the public interest: regulated arbitration" in LABOUR LAW AND THE COMMUNITY (Lord Wedderburn and W. T. Murphy eds., 1982), at pp. 52–3

The pay policy first introduced by the Counter Inflation (Temporary Provisions) Act 1972 was presented as the application of a set of rules contained in the counter-inflation Code. For most of the life of the policy the Press and the public appeared to accept this. In fact, a glance at any of the supposed rules will reveal that a decision either way was possible in many cases. There was therefore, ample room for arbitration. To take but two examples of the supposed rules:—

> "No group may receive an increase in pay under a settlement . . . less than twelve months after the group last received a principal increase."
> "Where the Code refers to a group, the group will normally be the same as that used for the purpose of determining pay in the preceding twelve months. It will, however, remain open to those concerned to vary the composition of their group."

The Pay Board had no wish to acquire a reputation as a creator of strife. On at least one occasion when a small employer was threatened with renewed strike action if he included the terms of a dispute settlement in his pay bill for the year the Board was prepared to conclude that what every industrial relations expert would call a settlement was, instead, the compromise of a potential claim for damages in contract. Surprisingly few agreements took advantage of the open invitation to change the composition of last year's groups but the decision in *British Leyland (UK) Ltd. v The Pay Board* [1984] I.C.R. 134 reveals that, apart from its likely devastating effect on established bargaining patterns, this was so easy that it might well have formed the basis for many solutions to the restraint.

(b) Voluntary pay restraint

The implications for labour law of a voluntary policy of pay restraint are less obvious. They are nonetheless real, as was pointed out in the following extract.

"Introduction" (P. Davies and M. Freedland eds.) to Kahn-Freund, LABOUR AND THE LAW (3rd ed., 1983), at pp. 7–8

[One] strategy to develop out of incomes policy is that whereby it is sought to achieve the effect of income restraint by agreement essentially between the government and the trade unions. The main example has been the Social Contract of 1975–77, but it was a strategy also attempted in 1972 when the Conservative government engaged in (abortive) negotiations with the unions in which terms were sought for the suspension of the operation of the Industrial Relations Act. Such a strategy may have an impact upon labour law traditionally so called if the passing of labour legislation is part of the *quid pro quo* for acceptance by the unions of wage restraint. That this was the main function of the Employment Protection Act 1975 may serve to explain its rather incoherent nature. . . .

Moreover, the Social Contract of 1975 was more than simply an agreed form of incomes policy. It had the potentiality, and to some extent the actuality, of enlarging the scope of labour law at a more fundamental level, because of its aim of involving the union movement, through the T.U.C., in a much wider range of government social and economic policies than just incomes on the one hand and labour legislation in a traditional sense on the other. Social contract philosophy involved acceptance of the fact of union power in a high employment economy but it coupled acceptance with an attempt to redirect it away from simple wage-bargaining and into a wider range of social, political and economic objectives. One can see industrial democracy of the kind advocated by the Bullock Committee Report as an attempt to repeat the process at the level of the employing enterprise. The Social Contract was short-lived and the Bullock initiative was stillborn. Had they or either of them become permanent parts of the landscape, they would have tended towards the development of new levels of bargaining—between T.U.C. and government and between enterprises and unions—in addition to the traditional national industry-level and establishment level bargaining. The T.U.C. and government level bargaining would have involved a greater commitment by the T.U.C. to the method of political action as against the method of industrial action, with consequent changes for relations between the T.U.C. and its affiliated unions. To the extent that these developments were even put on the map of labour law as potentialities in the Social Contract period, this represents a change in the discourse of labour law which is indirectly attributable to the central concern of governments with the control of wage inflation.

(c) Pay policy in the public sector

The enormous size of the public sector means that State determination of the pay of public sector employees offers a temptation to governments pursuing policies of pay restraint. The history of this process is described in the following extract.

B. A. Hepple, "Labour law and public employees in Britain" in LABOUR LAW AND THE COMMUNITY (Lord Wedderburn and W. T. Murphy eds., 1982), at pp. 67, 71–2, 77–78

Over one-third of British workers are in the public sector: $1\frac{1}{2}$ million in central and local government, $\frac{1}{2}$ million in the police and armed forces; $1\frac{1}{2}$ million in education; $1\frac{1}{2}$ million in the health services and 2 million in the public corporations. Despite the dramatic recent contraction of the public corporations and the abrupt decline since 1979 in civil service employment—a drop of 66,000 (9%) over one-third of whom were in industrial employment—the sector as a whole has grown by a quarter in the past 20 years. More significant than numbers is the highly visible place of the public sector as pacesetter for the rest of the economy and a testing ground for direct and indirect government intervention in labour relations. . . .

After 1919 changes in civil service pay were determined first through movements in the cost of living index, then, following the recommendations of the Tomlin Royal Commission on the Civil Service (1923–31) [Cmd. 3909], by using comparisons with pay in the private sector on the basis of long-term trends. During the Second World War flat-rate increases were paid and then there was a return to centrally negotiated agreements with a cost of living "addition" for the lower paid. The Priestly Commission (1953–55) [Cmd. 9613] recommended as the "primary principle" fair comparison with current remuneration of outside staffs employed on broadly comparable work, taking account of differences in other conditions of service. Internal relativities were to supplement fair comparison. These recommendations were put into effect by agreement in 1956 and a Pay Research Unit was set up the same year. For the next 25 years some 70% of the home civil service were covered by a system in which the PRU undertook fact-finding, followed by negotiations in which the PRU evidence was used and other relevant factors brought into account . . . on various occasions since 1956 governments have overridden, suspended or paid in stages, agreed settlements on grounds of public policy. The "cash limits" policy led, in 1979–80, to staged or deferred settlements to contain the cost within those limits; in 1981–82 the government unilaterally suspended and then withdrew from civil service pay agreements, leading to the dispute and industrial action of March-July 1981. . . .

The Megaw Inquiry into Civil Service Pay, established after the 1981 dispute, reported in July 1982 and suggested a new system [not yet implemented as at April 1987] in which comparisons "should have a much less decisive influence than in the past", [Cmnd. 8590, pp. 113–114] with significant changes in the type of comparisons and the way in which data are collected. . . .

The Megaw report envisages that "market forces" will be used in ways which are bound to depress relative levels of pay in the civil service. For example, only private sector companies will be used as a basis of comparison, thus excluding the largest groups of organised white collar workers who are in the public corporations, local government and health services. The comparisons are to be only with those private sector employees settling in the August–February period of the pay round. This will have the effect of excluding two of the largest private sector groups of organised workers, in banking and the chemical industry. The new [Pay Information Board] will no longer be required to compare with "good" employers as the old PRU did, but will have to ignore the top and bottom rates it discovers and take market forces and job security into account. The right, which has existed since 1925, to unilateral access to arbitration would be withdrawn and arbitration would be available only if both sides (ie in practice, the government) agreed. There would be a "cooling off" period in the new arbitration agreement before any industrial action could be taken after the breakdown of negotiations, and protracted action would be inhibited by a provision that back pay following a dispute would be limited to three months.

All of this marks a very different system from that which resulted from earlier Reports such as those of the Tomlin and Priestly Commissions and it may be of great importance as a model for other public sector workers outside the non-industrial civil service.

5. PAY AND INFLATION

For workers, the problem of inflation requires solutions which are not reducible to simple pay restraint. Maintenance of living standards when prices are rising means that pay must rise commensurately. Incomes policy is not necessarily responsive. Collective bargaining has in some cases tied pay increases to movements in the Retail Price Index (RPI). Examples include a "reopener clause"—pay negotiations will be reopened before the agreement is due to end if the RPI exceeds a certain value; direct indexation, by which pay is adjusted as the RPI rises, and threshold clauses: pay increases are promised if the RPI reaches a certain value, known as the threshold, and further payments follow as the RPI reaches agreed "trigger" values.

Collective bargaining can interact with legal pay restraint at a time of inflation. One example is the exception to the legal limitations of pay increases granted to "productivity agreements," described as follows:

> "The essential characteristic of the practice of productivity bargaining was the negotiation between management and workers'

representatives of changes in working practices leading to more efficient working, at the same time as the re-negotiation of levels of earnings to give workers a share of the savings brought about by the changes."

The experience of the "productivity" exception to pay restraint highlights two approaches which labour law could take to the problem of pay and inflation. One is a regulative framework which allows for collective bargaining to develop through exceptions to the legal limits. This approach, by way of "regulated bargaining," reveals a paradox which emerged in the study from which the above description of productivity bargaining was taken.

W. W. Daniel and N. McIntosh, *"Incomes Policy and Collective Bargaining at the Workplace: a study of the productivity criterion cases"* PEP BROADSHEET 541 (May 1973), p. 65

In principle . . . a national incomes policy contradicts the trend towards decentralisation of collective bargaining. It suggests that earnings are settled at a level even more centralised than the industry agreement. Moreover, one of the chief fears and criticisms of incomes policy is that it is totalitarian and destroys free collective bargaining which is a touchstone of democracy. In view of this it is a nice paradox that in the agreements we looked at as part of the last incomes policy, local union officials and particularly lay officers were more heavily involved in collective bargaining over a wider range of issues than ever before. Stewards reported that the main effect of the agreements for them was that they had more influence and responsibility. This paradox highlights how there is a means of accommodating the needs for plant bargaining and greater influence on the part of workers and stewards over decisions with the need for greater control at the centre over movements in earnings. And this means conceiving a national incomes policy as a framework. The national framework agreement at company level, and indeed at industry level within nationalised industries, was a feature of the productivity bargaining phase and often very successful. The framework agreement did provide a mechanism whereby local autonomy could be accommodated within central control. Scope was provided for people at plant level still to influence events, even exercise a greater influence over events, within a regulated context.

Labour law takes on the appearance of a national framework with room for local autonomy.

In contrast, the second approach by way of "regulated arbitration" was described by Rideout in the context of the 1972 pay policy (see p. 177 above). In a system of regulated arbitration the emphasis would be on adapting a centralised pay policy through an arbitration process (whether or not it bears that name). The distinction is one of emphasis: a system could incorporate incentives to bargainers together with an arbitration body to resolve hard cases (or "difficult" claims).

The significance of "regulated bargaining" has been noted by various studies of collective bargaining under incomes policy. The conclusion of one such was as follows.

P. Willman, FAIRNESS, COLLECTIVE BARGAINING AND INCOMES POLICY (1982), at pp. 148, 152

Put at its simplest, the argument claims that the co-ordination of collective bargaining is a sufficient condition for the establishment of a long-term incomes policy. Previous policies collapsed since they failed to control earnings increases because of a mismatch between their policing mechanisms and the structure of collective bargaining: as the structure of bargaining is rationalized, successful policies become attainable. . . .

In summary, then, a successful long-term incomes policy would be designed and implemented so as to incorporate trade union organisations in its administration and would support trade union leadership to the extent of satisfying members' requirements about fairness.

The neo-corporatist implications of this view were implicit in Daniel and McIntosh's study of the pay policy of the later 1960s.

W. W. Daniel and N. McIntosh, *"Incomes Policy and Collective Bargaining at the Workplace: A study of the productivity criterion cases"* PEP BROADSHEET 541 (May 1973), p. 66

. . . a national incomes policy that seeks to represent anything more than a short-term freeze stands very much more chance of achieving its different objectives, and accommodating obstacles, if it is conceived of as a framework which not only permits, but positively encourages, company and plant agreements seeking to reform degenerated systems of payments, bring overtime under control, improve the utilisation of plant and labour, and reform labour relations institutions and procedures. Implicit in this prescription is the idea that trade unionists will be more than compensated for any apparent decline in their freedom to negotiate wage rates (though the extent to which trade unions have ever influenced the level of earnings through collective bargaining remains a matter of academic debate) by the greater scope they have to influence "control" or organisation issues as opposed to "wage" issues through an extension of joint regulation at the work place.

We have seen through our analysis of these cases how the last incomes policy, through the productivity criterion, did give a considerable boost to reform and change at plant level in a way that increased rather than reduced worker and trade union influence. It is clear from our findings that an incomes policy can be a powerful force in encouraging good practice or at least pushing people more quickly in the direction in which they are already going or know they should be going.

The neo-corporatist tendencies of regulated bargaining were made explicit in the following extract from a study of West Germany, which also, however, points out the potential problems.

W. Streeck, *"Qualitative demands and the neo-corporatist manageability of industrial relations"* (1981) 19 B.J.I.R. 149 at 149, 151–2

By the mid-seventies, it had become clear that economic growth rates were to remain for a long time below those to which unions and employers had grown accustomed in the past one and a half decades. If future wage settlements were to conform to the national goal of curbing inflation, therefore, they had to be significantly lower, both in real and in nominal terms, than in previous years. In the past, high growth rates had made it possible for the unions to get high wage increases for their members, and for the employers to make relatively generous concessions in wage negotiations. In so far as this was why the German pattern of "co-operative conflict resolution" had functioned so effectively, lower economic growth seemed to present a threat to institutional stability. Among the anticipated consequences of lower growth were dissatisfaction among union members, unofficial strikes, "irresponsible" union behaviour, and a declining governability of the system of industrial relations from the perspective of macro-economic management. . . .

[The author then recounts how the trade unions in West Germany in the early 1970s began to place emphasis on the issues of "humanisation of working life", protection against the impact of rapid technological change and reductions in working time.]

Unlike pay claims, union demands for improvement of working conditions, protection of workers against technological change and reduction of working time relate, albeit to different degrees, to the organisation of work and to the range and exercise of managerial prerogatives. On this account they have frequently been referred to as "qualitative" demands, as distinct from "quantitative" demands for higher wages. While it is impossible to say how significant the events in the late seventies were for future developments, it cannot be denied out of hand that qualitative matters will be more important in the eighties as subjects of joint regulation than they were in the past. One factor contributing to this may be reduced economic growth. Since trade unions in a low-growth economy have not much to offer to their members in terms of quantitative wage increases, they may have to turn to other, qualitative subjects. (In this sense, a heightened level of industrial conflict associated with non-quantitative union demands would be an indirect consequence of low growth.) Hence system stability may increasingly become a question of whether existing institutions will be able to regulate qualitative conflicts as effectively and legitimately as they have regulated quantitative conflicts in the past.

Qualitative demands of trade unions may relate to a wide variety of subjects. Their common element is that they attempt to impose limits on managerial discretion. Successful representation of qualitative demands creates rigidities for the organisation of work. Examples of qualitative regulations are rules on safety, job content, working hours, job classification, mobility of labour, employment security, etc. Union demands for qualitative improvements can be expected to be particularly strong in periods of rapid industrial change. Under conditions of economic prosperity, they tend to be phrased in terms of "job enlargement", "humanisation of working life" and the like. In situations of low growth and unemployment, they usually focus on statutory security, job protection, and employment rights. From the perspective of management, qualitative regulations generally represent impediments to managerial efforts to increase productivity and are therefore often heavily resisted. . . .

The problems of pay thus affect trade union structures and functions, issues of job control, employment security, and so on. Pay is becoming ever more central to labour law.

CHAPTER 6

DISCRIMINATION AND INEQUALITY

One meaning of discrimination is unequal treatment. Unequal treatment is the norm at work. Workers are paid different salaries, work different hours, are permitted more or less freedom in the performance of their work and have access to different benefits. Inequalities at work are so much taken for granted that the justifications for them are rarely debated. This chapter focuses on the policy issues which arise when the law requires unequal treatment of workers to be justified.

Inequalities in treatment at work are often justified on the basis that they reflect differences in the work being performed by different workers: they are "work-related." Much of the present law on race and sex discrimination builds on this foundation: there may be differences between work performed by two workers, of a different race or sex or married status, which justify inequality in treatment.

This chapter starts by looking first at the legislation prohibiting inequality (the Sex Discrimination Act 1975 and the Race Relations Act 1976); then at the legislation requiring workers to justify claims to equality (the Equal Pay Act 1970); and then at the law which allows employers to justify inequality (a "material difference" justifying unequal pay; the "justification" defence for sex or race discrimination).

1. PROHIBITING INEQUALITY: RACE AND SEX DISCRIMINATION

(A) Direct Discrimination

The following cases illustrate the operation of the prohibition on direct discrimination in the Sex Discrimination Act 1975, s.1(1)(*a*) and in the Race Relations Act 1976, s.1(1)(*a*).

Saunders v. Richmond Upon Thames Borough Council
[1977] I.R.L.R. 362; [1978] I.C.R. 75
Employment Appeal Tribunal

Mrs Saunders applied unsuccessfully for a job as a golf professional. She appealed to the E.A.T. contending that certain questions asked during her interview were in themselves discriminatory.

PHILLIPS J.: Mr Beloff [counsel for Mrs Saunders] stressed the fact that since the enactment of the Sex Discrimination Act 1975 it is necessary for everyone, and in particular employers, to reconsider their approach to such matters and to rid themselves of (what are now) out-of-date ideas and prejudices. It is thus essential for an appointing committee to realise (unless in exceptional cases) that the sex of the applicant is totally irrelevant considered as a qualification or disqualification for a particular employment. If strength is a necessary qualification for appointment it is permissible to reject a woman because she is weak, but not because she is a woman. No doubt, this approach requires a difficult re-adjustment of mental attitudes among many people, and it is now entirely improper to regard a particular job as being "suitable" or "unsuitable" for a man or for a woman as the case may be. There is probably not much doubt that such questions as . . . "Are there any women golf professionals in clubs?" or . . . "Do you think men respond as well to a woman golf professional as to a man?" reflect, in part at least, what is now an out-of-date and proscribed attitude of mind. That such questions were asked may be very relevant when it comes to be determined . . . whether there has been discrimination in not appointing a woman. . . .

. . . But we do not think that it is unlawful to ask such questions, or that Mr Beloff is right when he says that it is now unlawful to ask a woman (or a man) any questions which would not be asked of a man (or a woman). Indeed it may be desirable to do so. To take the example cited in the course of argument: suppose a man be considered as an applicant for the headship of a single sex girls' boarding school. If appointed it is obvious that in practice he might have problems with the girls which would be different from those which a female head would have. An appointing committee might well think it proper to enquire whether he had insight into this problem, and was prepared, and was the sort of man who would be able, to deal with it. For that reason they might well wish to enquire whether he had given consideration to his ability as a man to deal with pupils all of whom were girls. It would be absurd to regard such a question as in itself and by itself discriminatory.

Owen & Briggs v. James
[1981] I.R.L.R. 133
Employment Appeal Tribunal

Miss James, a coloured English woman, was twice unsuccessful in applying for a job as a shorthand typist. A white girl with a slower shorthand speed was appointed. Miss James's complaint was upheld by an Industrial Tribunal.

SLYNN J.: Then it is said, in the second group of grounds to be found scattered throughout the 22 grounds of appeal in the notice of appeal, that this decision of the Industrial Tribunal imposes on an employer the duty of taking on somebody with no experience; that it imposes on an employer the standards of an Industrial Tribunal as to how he should interview applicants and what qualifications he should look for; that it imposes on an employer the duty to speak at length to an interviewee, to require tests and to conduct the interview in a way which really it is for the employer to decide upon. Now plainly it *is* for the employer to decide how he will conduct the interview and what criteria he wishes to adopt in selecting from the candidates, as long as he is not in breach of the provisions of the Race Relations Act 1976 or the Sex Discrimination Act 1975. We find it quite impossible to say that this Tribunal has imposed on this employer any kind of duty or obligation such as that which is contended for. If the decision and reasons are read as a whole, it is quite plain that what the Industrial Tribunal was doing was to analyse the reasons put forward by the potential employer and, because of the matters to which we have returned, to conclude that these were not the only reasons why Miss James was not really considered at all for this appointment. . . .

It is for the Industrial Tribunal to investigate all the reasons which are put forward and to see whether there has been discrimination. If the Tribunal finds that a substantial reason for what has happened is that a candidate has not been considered for a post, or has been refused an appointment because of his or her race, then it seems to us that the Tribunal is entitled to say that there has been a breach of the legislation. If there are other grounds put forward which may also have been a factor, it is for the Tribunal to consider whether, at the end, the candidate has, because of discrimination, lost the chance of or lost the appointment.

The decision of the E.A.T. was affirmed by the Court of Appeal: [1982] I.C.R. 377.

Horsey v. Dyfed County Council

[1982] I.R.L.R. 395
Employment Appeal Tribunal

Mrs Horsey lived in Aberystwyth and worked as a social worker. When her husband got a job in London, she applied to her employer to pay for a two-year secondment to a social service course in Maidstone, so as to be able to live with her husband in the London area. She undertook to return to Wales at the end of the two-year course. She was refused secondment on the grounds that she would probably not return to Wales.

BROWNE-WILKINSON J.: We have not found this an easy case to decide. Before dealing with these specific submissions made by the parties, there are certain general considerations which apply to discrimination under either s.1 or s.3 of the [Sex Discrimination Act 1975]. Under both ss.1 and 3 of the Act (and also the corresponding provisions of s.1 of the Race Relations Act 1976) unlawful discrimination consists in treating someone less favourably 'on the ground of' sex, marital status or race. Do these words cover only cases where the sex, marital status or race of the complainant in isolation is the reason for the decision, or do they extend to cover cases where the alleged discriminator acts on the basis of generalised assumptions as to the characteristics of women or married or coloured persons? In our view it is now established by authority that those words do not only cover cases where the sole factor influencing the decision of the alleged discriminator is the sex, marital status or race of the complainant. The words "on the ground of" also cover cases where the reason for the discrimination was a generalised assumption that people of a particular sex, marital status or race possess or lack certain characteristics, *eg* "I like women but I will not employ them because they are unreliable"; "I will not lend money to married women because they are not wage earners"; or "I will not employ coloured men because they are lazy". Most discrimination flows from generalised assumptions of this kind and not from a simple prejudice dependent solely on the sex or colour of the complainant. The purpose of the legislation is to secure equal opportunity for individuals regardless of their sex, married status or race. This result would not be achieved if it were sufficient to escape liability to show that the reason for the discriminatory treatment was simply an assumption that women or coloured persons possessed or lacked particular characteristics and not that they were just women or coloured persons.) The decision of the Court of Appeal in *Skyrail Oceanic Ltd v Coleman* [1980] I.R.L.R. 226 establishes that generalised assumptions of this kind constitute discrimination under the Acts: see also *Hurley v Mustoe* [1981] IRLR 208.

We turn to consider the particular submissions of the parties. In our view it is necessary to analyse the factors which led Mr Evans [the respondent's deputy director for social services] to refuse Mrs Horsey's secondment. They were as follows:

a) the fact that she was married;
b) the fact that her husband had a permanent job in London;
c) the assumption that married persons will want to live together;
d) the assumption that, in order to be able to live together, the husband would not move and seek a different job in Wales but the wife would follow her husband's job and live in London;
e) Mrs Horsey would not honour her undertaking.

If that analysis is correct, it seems to us that Mr Evans's decision was at least in part based on the generalised assumption that married women follow their husbands' jobs. In our view, [the Sex Discrimination Act 1975] s.5(3) does require that, when considering the claim under s.1, the Tribunal has to compare the treatment of Mrs Horsey with the treatment which would have been afforded to a married man. . . .

As to the submission that there was no evidence that Mr Evans would have treated a married man differently from the way he treated Mrs Horsey, it is true that there was no direct evidence to that effect. However, in our view it is an inescapable inference from his approach to Mrs Horsey's case. Mrs Horsey had a permanent job with the County Council in Wales; her husband had a permanent job at the House of Commons in London. Mr Evans assumed that Mr. Horsey would not give up his job to join his wife, but that Mrs Horsey would give up her job to join her husband, i.e. he had made a general assumption on the basis of her sex that she would follow her husband's job and not *vice versa*. If Mr Evans had looked at the facts of this particular case instead of making that assumption he would have discovered a different pattern, namely that on two occasions Mr Horsey had followed his wife, ie he left Cardiff to join her at Stirling and left Stirling to join her at Aberystwyth.

In our view, therefore, the position is as follows. Under s.1(1) one has to see whether on the ground of sex Mr Evans treated Mrs Horsey differently from the way he would have treated a comparable man. Mrs Horsey, being married, under s.5(3) the comparable man must also be taken to be a married man. Having assumed that Mrs Horsey would give up his permanent job to join her husband and that a married man (*eg* Mr Horsey) would not give up his permanent job to join his wife, Mr Evans had made a different assumption dependent upon the sex of the person under consideration. Therefore he has discriminated against Mrs Horsey on the grounds of her sex.

(B) Indirect Discrimination

The policy of eliminating discrimination on grounds of sex or race extends to situations, where these non-work-related criteria indirectly affect employment (the Race Relations Act 1976, s.1(1)(*b*); the Sex Discrimination Act 1975, s.1(1)(*b*)).

Price v. (1) The Civil Service Commission (2) The Society of Civil and Public Servants

[1977] I.R.L.R. 291; [1978] 1 All E.R. 1228
Employment Appeal Tribunal

To be eligible for appointment as an executive officer in the Civil Service, candidates had to be under 28 years of age. Miss Price, a woman of 36, claimed indirect discrimination on grounds of sex.

PHILLIPS J.: The test is whether the condition is such that the proportion of women who can comply with it is considerably smaller than the proportion of men who can comply with it. Examples usually given are of physical attributes such as height or strength or weight. But the sub-paragraph [s.1(1)(*b*)(i)] of the Sex Discrimination Act [1975] goes much farther than that, and would extend to educational or professional qualifications, if they are of a kind which few women but many men possess. Thus an advertisement which required as a condition for appointment to a post a degree in engineering, or the status of a barrister-at-law, would seem to be prima facie discriminatory in that the proportion of women who can comply with the condition is considerably smaller than the proportion of men who can comply with it.

Experience shows that when considering s.1(1)(b) it is necessary to define with some precision the requirement or condition which is called in question. Even when the facts are not in dispute it is possible to formulate the requirement or condition, usually at all events, in more than one way; the precise formulation is important. . . .

A fair way of putting it in the present case seems to be that candidates for the post of executive officer must not be over 28 years of age. We do not accept the submission of counsel for the Civil Service Commission that the words 'can comply' must be construed narrowly, and we think that the Industrial Tribunal were wrong to accept this submission. In one sense it can be said that any female applicant can comply with the condition. She is not obliged to marry, or to have children, or to mind children; she may find somebody to look after them, and as a last resort she may put them into care. In this sense no doubt counsel for the Civil Service Commission is right in saying that any female applicant can comply with the condition. Such a construction appears to us to be wholly out of sympathy with the spirit and intent of the Act. . . .

"Can" is defined (Shorter Oxford English Dictionary) as "to be able, to have the power or capacity". It is a word with many shades of meaning, and we are satisfied that it should not be too narrowly—nor too broadly—construed in its context in s.1(1)(b)(i). It should not be said that a person "can" do something merely because it is theoretically possible for him to do so: it is necessary to see whether he can do so in practice. Applying this approach to the circumstances of this case, it is relevant in determining whether women can comply with the condition to take into account the current usual behaviour of women in this respect, as observed in practice, putting on one side behaviour and responses which are unusual or extreme.

Knowledge and experience suggest that a considerable number of women between the mid-twenties and the mid-thirties are engaged in bearing children and in minding children, and that while many find it possible to take up employment many others, while desiring to do so, find it impossible, and that many of the latter as their children get older find that they can follow their wish and seek employment. This knowledge and experience is confirmed by some of the statistical evidence produced to the Industrial Tribunal (and by certain additional statistical evidence put in by consent of the parties on the hearing of the appeal). This demonstrates clearly that the economic activity of women with at least one "A" Level falls off markedly about the age of 23, reaching a bottom at about the age of 33 when it climbs gradually to a plateau at about 45.

Basing ourselves on this and other evidence, we should have no hesitation in concluding that our knowledge and experience is confirmed, and that it is safe to say that the condition is one which it is in practice harder for women to comply with than it is for men. We should be inclined to go further and say that there are undoubtedly women of whom it may be properly said in the terms of s.1(1)(b)(i) that they "cannot" comply with the condition, because they are women, that is to say because of their involvement with their children. But this is not enough to enable Miss Price to satisfy the requirements of sub-para. (i). The difficulty we have is in saying whether the proportion of women who can comply with the condition is *considerably smaller* than the proportion of men who can comply with it. It follows from what we have said earlier that we do not agree with the approach of the Industrial Tribunal to this question, and it follows that there has never been a finding of fact based upon the evidence correctly approached and interpreted.

At one stage of the hearing we thought that it might be in order for us to make a finding ourselves on the basis of the evidence given to the Industrial Tribunal, together with that put in by consent on the hearing of the appeal. At the end of the day we have come to the conclusion that we ought not to do so. The difficulty is that most of the evidence is statistical and is of a kind which needs to be analysed and interpreted since it is designed for other purposes, and it is not entirely easy to draw relevant conclusions. We think it *does* confirm the likelihood that women are put into difficulties by the condition, and that there are women who would wish to apply to be an executive officer and could do so in (say) their thirties, but cannot do so in their late twenties. The difficulty is to quantify this in the terms of a "considerably smaller" result. We find that it would be unsafe for us to reach a conclusion without having had the benefit of hearing the statistician give evidence and be subjected to cross-examination upon the proper analysis and inferences to be drawn from the statistics.

Accordingly we propose to allow the appeal and to remit the case to be heard afresh, bearing in mind the terms of this judgment and such guidance as we have been able to give. It may perhaps be helpful to mention one other matter. The Industrial Tribunal, in paragraph 12, rightly point out that when considering s.1(1)(b)(i) and considering the proportion of women and the proportion of men, it may be proper to consider as the "pool" of women or men available for the purpose something less than the total female and male population. We agree with that, though, as we have pointed out, the Industrial Tribunal itself in the present case proceeded on the footing that it was appropriate to take into account the whole population, male and female respectively. We doubt whether that was the right approach, though we do not wish to lay down a proposition binding upon the Industrial Tribunal which will hear the remitted case. It seems to us, as at present advised, there would be a good deal in the present case for saying that the appropriate 'pool' is that of qualified men and qualified women as the case may be.

The selection of the "pool" of persons to whom the requirement or condition is applied will often determine whether a smaller proportion of, for example, women or married women in that pool can comply with that condition. This selection was held to be one of fact for the Industrial Tribunal in the following case.

Kidd v. DRG (U.K.) Ltd.
[1985] I.R.L.R. 190
Employment Appeal Tribunal

In a redundancy situation, part-time workers were selected for redundancy before full-time workers. Mrs Kidd, a married women with two children and a husband who worked full-time, was dismissed from her job as a part-time worker.

WAITE J.: The choice of an appropriate section of the population is in our judgment an issue of fact (or perhaps strictly a matter for discretion to be exercised in the course of discharging an exclusively fact-finding function) entrusted by Parliament to the good sense of the [Industrial] Tribunals, whose selection will be influenced by the need to fit it as closely as possible to the varying circumstances of each case. Of course in those exceptional cases where it can be shown that good sense has not prevailed, and the Tribunal has chosen to make the proportionate comparison within an area of society so irrationally inappropriate as to put it outside the range of selection for any reasonable Tribunal, then the Tribunal would have fallen into an error of law which could be corrected in the appellate jurisdiction.

No such error . . . has in our judgment occurred in this case. On the contrary, by limiting the range of comparison to the section of the population for whom the need to provide care for children at home represents a potential obstacle to a parent's acceptance of full-time employment, the Tribunal in our view adopted a fair and sensible way of ensuring that the requirements of relevance and similarity of circumstance in [the Sex Discrimination Act 1975] s.5(3) were complied with. The judge therefore dismissed the appeal and approved the Industrial Tribunal's rather remarkable conclusion:] . . . they were not prepared to accept without evidence that within this section of society a requirement to be in full-time employment (as a condition of ranking for redundancy selection on a seniority basis) was one with which a considerably smaller proportion of married than of unmarried women could comply. It was implicit in their decision (though understandably in a case where the workforce was all female they did not give it equal emphasis) that they were similarly unprepared to accept without evidence that within the same section the same requirement was one [with] which a considerably smaller proportion of women than of men could comply.

Cf. Clarke and Powell v. *Eley (IMI) Kynoch Ltd.* [1982] I.R.L.R. 482

which came to a different conclusion on similar facts (see p.198 below). Contrast *Turner* v. *The Labour Party* [1987] I.R.L.R. 101 (C.A.) where a single divorced parent was held not to be discriminated against on the ground that she "cannot" comply with a condition *i.e.* marriage.

Indirect discrimination is identified through the effects of a requirement or condition. One difficulty is that there may be no formalised testing—no clear specification of a requirement or condition the effects of which can be assessed. The extent to which Tribunals are prepared to formulate "requirements or conditions" and ask whether they indirectly discriminate on non-work related grounds is illustrated by the following cases.

Clarke and Powell v. Eley (IMI) Kynoch Ltd.
[1982] I.R.L.R. 482
Employment Appeal Tribunal

The two women applicants were among 60 part-time women to be made redundant in accordance with the company's redundancy selection procedure of dismissing part-timers first before applying the last-in, first-out criterion to full-timers.

BROWNE-WILKINSON J.: The Industrial Tribunal accepted that the company had applied the following requirement or condition in this case:

"The requirement or condition that, to rank in selection for redundancy by virtue of service in unit and the principle of last-in, first-out, the applicant had to be employed full-time."

In our view it is not right to give these words a narrow construction. The purpose of the legislature in introducing the concept of indirect discrimination into the [Sex Discrimination Act 1975] and the Race Relations Act 1976 was to seek to eliminate those practices which had a disproportionate impact on women or ethnic minorities and were not justifiable for other reasons. The concept was derived from that developed in the law of the United States which held to be unlawful practices which had a disproportionate impact on black workers as opposed to white workers: see *Griggs v Duke Power Company* (1971) 401 US 424. If the elimination of such practices is the policy lying behind the Act, although such policy cannot be used to give the words any wider meaning than they naturally bear, it is in our view a powerful argument against giving the words a narrower meaning thereby excluding cases which fall within the mischief which the Act was meant to deal with.

Watches of Switzerland Ltd. v. Savell
[1983] I.R.L.R. 141
Employment Appeal Tribunal

The employee was not promoted when there were two more senior vacancies.

WATERHOUSE J.: The context of the alleged indirect discrimination in the present case was access to promotion within the terms of [the Sex Discrimination Act 1975] s.6(2)(a). . . . Thus, Mrs Savell had first to establish the relevant requirement or condition which was alleged to be discriminatory. Counsel on her behalf has formulated it as a requirement or condition that in order to be promoted in a London branch of the employers' organisation she had to satisfy or comply with a promotion procedure that was discriminatory in its impact upon women. In the answer to the notice of appeal the requirement or condition was phrased as follows:

> "that to be promoted to the post of manager in a London branch of the retail business owned by the appellant one must satisfy the criteria of a vague, subjective, unadvertised promotion procedure which does not provide any or any adequate mechanisms to prevent subconscious bias unrelated to the merits of candidates or prospective candidates for the post of manager."

The Industrial Tribunal found that there was a requirement or condition within the meaning of [the Sex Discrimination Act 1975] s.1(1)(b), and they put their finding in the following words:

> "In examining the allegations of indirect discrimination by the company against Mrs Savell we find that the company applied to her a system or requirement implied, if not expressed, and they operated the system so that there was a requirement or condition within the meaning of s.1(1)(b) of the Act in the way the company afforded 'her access to opportunities for promotion, transfer or training or any benefits, facilities or services' within the meaning of s.6(2)(a) of the Act and that she was indirectly discriminated against contrary to the Act. The system of promotion for a manager at the time of the promotions of Mr Butcher for the Poultry Branch and Mr Benn to the Royal Exchange Branch were mainly subjective and contained criteria of which Mrs Savell was unaware, and therefore she was unable to comply with them, such as flexibility, co-operative attitude, mobility and willingness to work on Saturdays, whether or not required for a specific post."

We think that that paragraph and the two paragraphs that follow, which I have already quoted in this judgment, show some confusion on the part of the Industrial Tribunal in their application of s.1(1)(b); and they have been criticised strongly by counsel for the employers on a number of grounds. The first ground is that it was wrong in law for the Tribunal to accept that any relevant requirement or condition had been established by Mrs Savell. The Tribunal did not formulate the requirement or condition as counsel for Mrs Savell framed it, and it is submitted that they confused the system to which they referred with a requirement or condition. The employers argue that a promotion procedure cannot constitute a requirement or condition for the purposes of ss.1(1)(b) and 6(2)(a) and that the matters particularised as requirements within which Mrs Savell could not comply emphasised an illogical process of thought by the Tribunal. In the end it is suggested that the Tribunal further confused themselves by failing to distinguish between the possible adverse impact of various aspects of the procedure and the alleged requirement or condition itself.

In answer to this, counsel for Mrs Savell submits that his formulation of the requirement or condition fits the structure of s.1(1)(b) when read with s.6(2)(a). He suggests that, in the light of the wording of s.6(2)(a) in particular, it must have been the intention of Parliament to render unlawful a promotion procedure with disparate impact and his formulation does not involve any misapplication of ordinary words within the statutory framework. . . .

In the end, our decision in this appeal does not turn directly on the interpretation of the words "requirement or condition" in s.1(1)(b) of the Sex Discrimination Act 1975; but we think that it is right for the purposes of this appeal to accept that a requirement or condition of the kind formulated on behalf of Mrs Savell is capable of being a requirement or condition to which the Act applies, and that there was evidence before the Industrial Tribunal to justify a finding that the employers applied the requirement or condition to Mrs Savell and men in line for promotion equally in the present case. We respectfully agree also with the dicta of Phillips J. and Browne-Wilkinson J. [in *Steel v Union of Post Office Workers* [1978] I.R.L.R. 288, 291 and *Clarke v. Eley (IMI) Kynoch Ltd* (see above p. 198)] to the effect that the statutory words should be given a liberal interpretation in order to implement the object of the legislation.

Perera v. (1) The Civil Service Commission, (2) The Department of Customs and Excise

[1983] I.R.L.R. 166

Court of Appeal

Mr Perera complained that his rejection for jobs in the Civil Service was a result of indirect discrimination by interviewers.

O'Connor L.J.: Mr Perera has submitted that because the Civil Service Commission asked the interviewing board for their opinion on certain attributes of the candidates, those amounted to requirements or conditions.

For my part, I cannot accept that. It is only necessary to look at the request made by the Commission to the interview board in making their assessment; they were asked to give their opinion, individually, of the personal qualities of the applicant, his ability to communicate, his intellectual capacity and his potential, and in order to help the members of the board to form an opinion, the four categories were further particularised. For example, in considering their opinion on personal qualities they were asked to apply their minds to maturity, commonsense and ability to get on with people; and, in expressing their opinion, limiting it to whether it was very good, good, fair or poor.

In my judgment it is quite impossible to say that that exercise was imposing any condition or requirement on the board in making up its mind or in giving its opinion. The evidence before the Industrial Tribunal from the two members of the interview board who gave evidence, as reflected in the judgment of the Employment Appeal Tribunal, shows that in their general look at the applicants, and perhaps particularly at those applicants from overseas they directed themselves that they should ask themselves whether the applicant had experience of the United Kingdom, whether the applicant had a good command of the English language, whether the applicant had British nationality or intended to apply for it, and the age of the applicant. Once again, it seems to me that none of those is a condition or a requirement; they are merely further examples of the means by which the individual members of the interview board were forming their opinion of an applicant. The fact that some applicants had opinions expressed about them which led to their not going forward on the short list is one of the facts of life; it is the whole purpose of an interview board and it is not the application of any condition or requirement within the meaning of s.1(1)(b) of the Race Relations Act of 1976.

2. JUSTIFYING EQUALITY: EQUAL PAY FOR WOMEN

The extracts above show how the law has sought to prohibit discrimination in employment opportunities based on non-work-related factors such as sex and race. However, discrimination on grounds of sex in contractual terms of employment is not covered by this legislation (see sub-sections 6(2), (6) and 8(5) of the Sex Discrimination Act 1975). Sex discrimination in that aspect of employment is covered by the Equal Pay Act 1970. However, the 1970 Act does not explicitly prohibit discrimination in terms of employment. Rather, it allows a claim for equality to be made, but only when specified work-related grounds can be shown. The emphasis is on banning work-related discrimination rather than on banning sex discrimination. Equal treatment is achieved by the mandatory inclusion of an equality clause in the contract of employment. However, this clause only operates in three circumstances specified in the Act. Either:

(a) the woman and the man are doing "like work" (section 1(2)(a)); or
(b) the woman is employed on "work rated as equivalent" (section 1(2)(*b*)); or
(c) the woman is employed on work "of equal value" (Equal Pay (Amendment) Regulations 1983, adding section 1(2)(*c*)) to the Equal Pay Act 1970.

In other words: inequality based on sex is not banned, rather equality needs to be justified on work-related grounds.

(A) "Like Work"

The definition of "like work" in the Equal Pay Act, s.1(4) makes clear how much claims for equal pay are seen as justified only by work-related factors. Non-work-related factors, such as sex, are implicitly denied legitimacy. This emerges because the law does permit work-related discrimination, even when this results in inequality for women. In the following cases, the Tribunals confronted the dilemma of legislation, ostensibly committed to combatting inequality based on sex, which nonetheless allows inequality based on work.

Capper Press Ltd. v. Lawton
[1976] I.R.L.R. 366; [1977] Q.B. 852
Employment Appeal Tribunal

Mrs Lawton worked as a cook in the kitchen from which the company's directors were served. She claimed equal pay with male employees who worked as assistant chefs in the kitchen serving the factory canteen.

PHILLIPS J.: Equality of treatment is required where the woman is employed on "like work" with the man. And "like work" is work which is of the *same* nature as, or of a broadly *similar* nature to, the man's work.

In cases of dispute this test, imposed by [the Equal Pay Act 1970] s.1(4), requires the Industrial Tribunal to make a comparison between the work done by the woman and the work done by the man. It is clear from the terms of the sub-section that the work need not be of the *same* nature in order to be like work. It is enough if it is of a similar nature. Indeed, it need only be broadly similar. In such cases where the work is of a broadly similar nature (and not of the *same* nature) there will necessarily be differences between the work done by the woman and the work done by the man. It seems clear to us that the definition requires the Industrial Tribunal to bring, to the solution of the question whether work is of a broadly similar nature, a broad judgment. Because, in such cases, there will be such differences of one sort or another it would be possible in almost every case, by too pedantic an approach, to say that the work was not of a like nature despite the similarity of what was done and the similar kinds of skill and knowledge required to do it. That would be wrong. The intention, we think, is clearly that the Industrial Tribunal should not be required to undertake too minute an examination, or be constrained to find that work is not like work because of insubstantial differences.

It seems to us that in most cases the enquiry will fall into two stages. *First*, is the work of the same, or, if not, 'of a broadly similar' nature? This question can be answered by a general consideration of the type of work involved, and of the skill and knowledge required to do it. It seems to us to be implicit in the words of sub-section (4) that it can be answered without a minute examination of the detail of the differences between the work done by the man and the work done by the woman. But, *secondly*, if on such an examination the answer is that the work is of broadly similar nature, it is then necessary to go on to consider the detail and to enquire whether the differences between the work being compared are of practical importance in relation to terms and conditions of employment. In answering that question the Industrial Tribunal will be guided by the concluding words of the sub-section. But again, it seems to us, trivial differences, or differences not likely in the real world to be reflected in the terms and conditions of employment, ought to be disregarded. In other words, once it is determined that work is of a broadly similar nature it should be regarded as being like work, unless the differences are plainly of a kind which the Industrial Tribunal in its experience would expect to find reflected in the terms and conditions of employment. This last point requires to be emphasised. There seems to be a tendency, apparent in some of the decisions of Industrial Tribunals cited to us, and in some of the arguments upon the hearing of this appeal, to weigh up the differences by reference to such questions as whether one type of work or another is or is not suitable for women, or is the kind of work which women can do, or whether the differences are important, and so on. These are not the tests prescribed by the Act. The only differences which will prevent work which is of a broadly similar nature from being 'like work' are differences which in practice will be reflected in the terms and conditions of employment.

Mrs Lawton's claim was successful.

Despite manifest inequality, sexual segregation of women in different jobs prevents a claim succeeding under the "like work" criterion. The woman claiming must find a male comparator doing "like work." As put in *Meeks* v. *National Union of Agricultural & Allied Workers* [1976] I.R.L.R. 198 "There is a resultant gap in the case of indirect discrimination where there is no comparable employee in employment with the same or an associated employer."

The principle of work-relation is also applied to permit differences related to work to justify unequal pay.

Noble v. David Gold & Son (Holdings) Ltd.
[1980] I.R.L.R. 252; [1980] I.C.R. 543
Court of Appeal

The three women concerned in this case were all employed in the company's warehouse. Their job was to unpack, sort, arrange, price, label and repack books which came into the warehouse. All those employed on this particular work were women. Men also worked in the warehouse, but they did the heavier tasks of unloading, carrying and lifting.

LAWTON L.J.: On the state of the evidence the question is, when the employers allocated the light work to the women and the heavy lifting work together with some light work to the men, whether they were making any discrimination on the grounds of sex. For the reasons which I have indicated on the evidence, it seems to me that the Industrial Tribunal were justified in coming to the conclusion that there was a division of work, that it was not based on sex but on practical experience of organising the work in the warehouse. If that is so, in my judgment everything else follows, because the women were doing a different kind of work from that done by the men. It follows from that that they could not be expected to be paid the same as the men.

The principle that equal work justifies equal pay in Article 119 of the EEC Treaty led to Council Directive 75/117/EEC of February 10, 1975 which interpreted it as meaning "the elimination of all discrimination on grounds of sex with regard to all aspects and conditions of remuneration." As the following extract shows, emphasis can be placed *either* on the policy that equal work warrants equal pay (see the judgment of Orr L.J.), *or* on the policy of prohibiting sex discrimination (see the judgment of Lord Denning).

Shields v. E. Coomes (Holdings) Ltd.
[1978] I.C.R. 1159; [1979] 1 All E.R. 456
Court of Appeal

A female counterhand in a betting shop was paid less than a male counterhand because he was employed to act as a deterrent and to render immediate physical assistance in case of robbery or customers causing trouble. There had been no trouble of the kind feared since the employers took over the shop. The Industrial Tribunal dismissed the women's claim for equal pay; the E.A.T. allowed her appeal. The employers appealed.

LORD DENNING M.R.: I confess, however, that I have felt great difficulty in overcoming the finding of the Industrial Tribunal that the differences, especially the protective role of the man, were "real and existing and of practical importance." I thought for some time that this protective role should be rewarded by some additional bonus or premium. But my difficulties on this score have been resolved by giving supremacy to Community law. Under that law it is imperative that "pay for work at time rates shall be the same for the same job . . . " ([EEC Treaty, article 119): and that all discrimination on the grounds of sex shall be eliminated with regard to all aspects and conditions of remuneration: see Council Directive 75/117/EEC, article 1. The differences found by the majority of the Industrial Tribunal are all based on sex. They are because he is a man. He only gets the higher hourly rate because he is a man. In order to eliminate all discrimination, there should be an equality clause written into the woman's contract.

ORR L.J.: The sub-section by its terms requires that, in comparing her work with his, regard should be had to the frequency with which any such differences occur in practice as well as the nature and extent of the differences, and it is abundantly clear, in my judgment, that the comparison which the sub-section requires to be made is not between the respective contractual obligations but between the things done and the frequency with which they are done. But it is equally clear from the terms of the decision of the Industrial Tribunal that the majority of the members misdirected themselves in this respect by paying too great attention to the contractual obligations and too little to the acts in fact done and their frequency, and in particular to the fact that [the male counterhand] had never, on the evidence, had to deal with any disturbance or attempted violence.

(B) "Work Rated as Equivalent"

The emphasis that claims for equality in pay need to show equal work, rather than sex discrimination, is evident in the ground allowing for insertion of an equality clause where the woman's work has been rated as equivalent to a man's under a job evaluation scheme (Equal Pay Act, s.1(5)). The application of this provision illustrates the policy choice before the courts of allowing claims based on sex discrimination, or of only allowing claims based on work-related similarities. The issue was posed in cases involving allegedly discriminatory job evaluation schemes.

England v. Bromley London Borough Council
[1978] I.C.R. 1
Employment Appeal Tribunal

PHILLIPS J.: [Counsel for the employee's] primary contention was that the evaluation study . . . is not a valid evaluation study, that is to say, is not a valid study for the purposes of section 1(5) of the Equal Pay Act 1970. He relied on some observations of the Appeal Tribunal in *Eaton Ltd.* v *Nuttall* [1977] I.C.R. 272. The passage upon which he primarily relied is on p. 277 . . . the effect of it is to set out certain conditions which an evaluation study must satisfy in order to be able to say of it that it is an evaluation study for the purposes of section 1(2)(*b*) and section 1(5) of the Act. In effect and in particular, it should be complete and objective and by its application enable all factors of importance in relation to the work to be taken into account, making it unnecessary for the employers to make subjective judgments upon the work content.

He further referred in this connection to . . . *Greene* v *Broxtowe District Council* [1977] I.C.R. 241, relying upon that part of it which specifies the circumstances in which the Appeal Tribunal or an Industrial Tribunal can look into the details of an evaluation study for the purpose of saying whether or not it is a satisfactory study. Putting those two excerpts from those two cases together, he submits that if one examines the study in this case . . . one finds that it was basically unsatisfactory . . . it was impossible to say of it that it was an evaluation study which satisfied the conditions necessary to be accounted an evaluation study for the purpose of section 1(5) . . . the difficulty, it seems to us, in the way of the employee's case as so put is this. If it be assumed (without deciding) that the evaluation study . . . was not an evaluation study within the meaning of section 1(5), what is the consequence from the point of view of the employee's claim? It seems to us that it really carries his case no further forward . . . putting it at its simplest, there does not exist an evaluation study in force which produces an answer favourable to his case. So really at the end of the day [counsel for the employee's] way of putting it, although more elegantly, powerfully and clearly presented, does not carry the case any further forward than the employee's own argument on the same lines. Just as we said of the employee's argument that his complaint in reality is (though not so expressed) that the evaluation study was incompetently or improperly carried out, be that as it may, it was the only study which existed at the appropriate time and his claim under this head must stand or fall upon it, so equally, it seems to us, the same remark may be made of the case as presented by Mr Tabachnik.

Alternatively, or cumulatively, Mr Tabachnik puts it in a slightly different way. He says that the Appeal Tribunal should apply the "blue pencil" test and cross out or discard the objectionable element of the study. . . .

It follows that from what we have already said, that it does not seem to us that there is any warrant for such a proceeding. Indeed, one can test it by the language of section 1(5). . . . And so the employee has to find (and it is only if he can find it, that he can rely on it) a study undertaken with a view to evaluating, etc. which produces the result and the jobs which he seeks to compare have been given an equal value. The answer is that there is no such study, and it is the function of the Appeal Tribunal, as it were, to do over again the evaluation study in fact done by and on behalf of the Council.

So a challenge that a job evaluation scheme is discriminatory, even if successful, can only have the effect of removing any grounds for a claim—as no valid scheme demonstrating equal work exists. Discrimination on its own does not require equal pay; the complainant must show equal work to get it.

(C) Work "Of Equal Value"

The Equal Pay Act 1970 did not require employers to carry out job evaluation schemes. This was the basis of a ruling by the European Court of Justice that the United Kingdom had not complied with its obligation to implement Article 119 of the EEC Treaty and Council Directive 75/117/EEC.

Commission of the European Communities v. United Kingdom of Great Britain and Northern Ireland

[1982] I.R.L.R. 333; I.C.R. 578

Court of Justice of the European Communities

(IV) **Written replies submitted by the Commission in response to the questions asked by the Court**

In the first place the Commission observes that "in order to be able to determine whether two (different) jobs have an equal value, they must be compared one with the other or evaluated against a common standard". That being so, Member States have a duty to set up a system whereby employees are able to obtain, if necessary by recourse to the courts, equal pay for work of equal value. This means that it is not necessary to oblige all employers to adopt job evaluation schemes, but that at the same time enabling employers to choose whether or not to introduce such schemes without making any provision for equal pay in respect of jobs of equal value where they do not, is inadequate.

Hence in many cases work of equal value will be compared within the framework of a collective agreement, or under a job evaluation scheme, or even more informally, without any detailed study having been undertaken. The State may also set up a system of official surveillance or less formal conciliation.

What is essential, in the view of the Commission, is that, in the final count, individuals should have the possibility of succeeding in the argument that the two jobs in question are of equal value.

The Commission then reviews the different systems adopted by the Member States, relying for the most part on its report. In Belgium, France, Italy and Luxembourg, as also in the Federal Republic of Germany, many problems are resolved by works inspectorates, and where a question falls to be resolved by the courts, the latter are not necessarily bound by the results of job evaluation schemes. In the Netherlands the question whether work is of equal value is assessed on the basis of a reliable system of job evaluation. Under the Irish legislation—which the Commission believes to be an example of how the United Kingdom could comply with its obligations under Directive No. 75/117—any dispute on the subject of equal pay may be referred to one of the three Equality Officers who, after investigating the matter, will issue a recommendation. Since such recommendations are not legally binding, it is ultimately for the courts to decide the matters referred to them.

The Commission concludes from the foregoing that, on a technical level, there are several possible ways in which the Equal Pay Act [1970] might be amended in order to make it comply with Community law. In this respect it emphasises that in the United Kingdom itself the Equal Opportunities Commission and the Trades Union Congress have drafted proposals along those lines. . . .

Decision

[After giving the text of the first article of the Council Directive and of s.1(5) of the 1970 Act, the Court continued:]

. . . British legislation does not permit the introduction of a job classification system without the employer's consent. Workers in the United Kingdom are therefore unable to have their work rated as being of equal value with comparable work if their employer refuses to introduce a classification system. . . .

. . . [This] amounts to a denial of the very existence of a right to equal pay for work of equal value where no classification has been made. Such a position is not consonant with the general scheme and provisions of Directive No 75/117. The recitals in the preamble to that Directive indicate that its essential purpose is to implement the principle that men and women should receive equal pay contained in Article 119 of the Treaty and that it is primarily the responsibility of the Member States to ensure the application of this principle by means of appropriate laws, regulations and administrative provisions in such a way that all employees in the Community can be protected in these matters. . . .

. . . a worker must be entitled to claim before an appropriate authority that his work has the same value as other work and, if that is found to be the case, to have his rights under the Treaty and the Directive acknowledged by a binding decision. Any method which excludes that option prevents the aims of the Directive from being achieved. . . .

In this instance, however, the United Kingdom has not adopted the necessary measures and there is at present no means whereby a worker who considers that his post is of equal value to another may pursue his claims if the employer refuses to introduce a job classification system.

The United Kingdom has emphasised (particularly in its letter to the Commission dated 19.6.79) the practical difficulties which would stand in the way of implementing the concept of work to which equal value has been attributed if the use of a system laid down by consensus were abandoned. The United Kingdom believes that the criterion of work of equal value is too abstract to be applied by the courts.

The Court cannot endorse that view. The implementation of the Directive implies that the assessment of the "equal value" to be "attributed" to particular work, may be effected notwithstanding the employer's wishes, if necessary in the context of adversary proceedings. The Member States must endow an authority with the requisite jurisdiction to decide whether work has the same value as other work, after obtaining such information as may be required.

Accordingly, by failing to introduce into its national legal system in implementation of the provisions of Council Directive No 75/117/EEC of 10.2.75 such measures as are necessary to enable all employees who consider themselves wronged by failure to apply the principle of equal pay for men and women for work to which equal value is attributed and for which no system of job classification exists to obtain recognition of such equivalence, the United Kingdom has failed to fulfil its obligations under the Treaty.

In order to comply with this judgment, Parliament enacted the Equal Pay (Amendment) Regulations 1983, which added section 1(2)(*c*) to the 1970 Act, allowing a woman to claim the benefit of an equality clause where she is "employed on work of equal value to that of a man in the same employment."

This principle of equal pay for work of equal value, measured in terms of demands on the worker, embodies less a ban on sex discrimination than a justification of equality based on work-related similarities. As such, it raises a further major policy issue. Should not a worker, regardless of sex, be able to claim equal pay with another worker who is doing work of equal value?

In *Hayward* v. *Cammell Laird Shipbuilders Ltd.* [1984] I.R.L.R. 463 (I.T.), the Industrial Tribunal accepted the report of an independent expert which compared the applicant's jobs with others, taking no account of sex difference.

INDUSTRIAL RELATIONS REVIEW AND REPORT No. 332 (November 20, 1984), pp. 20–23

Report of the independent expert

Background notes, conclusions and decision

Miss J A Hayward v Cammell Laird Shipbuilders Ltd

Requirement

The question I am required to report on is: "whether or not the applicant is employed on work of equal value to Mr Paul Brady (painter), Mr Derek Gilbert (thermal insulation engineer) or Mr Tim Cox (joiner)".

The requirement stipulates that the expert shall—

(a) take account of all such information and all such representations made to him as have a bearing on the question;
(b) before drawing up his report, produce and send to the parties a written summary of the said information and representations and invite the representations of the parties upon the material contained therein;
(c) make his report to the tribunal in a document which shall reproduce the summary and contain a brief account of any representations received from the parties upon it, any conclusion he may have reached upon the question and the reasons for that conclusion or, as the case may be, for his failure to reach such a conclusion;
(d) take no account of the difference of sex and at all times act fairly.

Equal value

The equal value provision is defined by the [Equal Pay (Amendment)] Regulations [1983] as applying "where a woman is employed on work which . . . is in terms of the demands made on her (for instance, under such headings as effort, skill and decision), of equal value to that of a man in the same employment". In this respect the statutory language derives from principles used in analytical job evaluation. I have interpreted this as requiring that the jobs in question be assessed by job evaluation methods to determine the level of demand under different headings or factors. Equal value means that the applicant's job has been assessed in terms of its demands as being at least equivalent to one or more of the comparator jobs.

Background

The applicant and the comparators are employed by the respondent at Cammell Laird Shipyard, Birkenhead, and are all members of the General, Municipal, Boilermakers and Allied Trades Union (GMBATU). The applicant is a cook in the works cafeteria working Mondays to Fridays from 07.30am to 15.30pm. Her main duties occupying approximately 80% of her time, consist of preparing and cooking meals, with a further 15% spent on cleaning, and serving and miscellaneous work making up the remainder. She holds a City and Guilds qualification in catering—Course 706, Cookery for the Catering

Industry, Parts I and II. Her claim for equal pay is supported by the GMBATU and by the comparators, who are all shop stewards.

The comparators are engaged in shipbuilding outfitting trades and are also required to work in the workshops and undertake maintenance duties about the yard. They work from 07.30am to 16.30pm on 4 days per week and 07.30am to 15.30pm on Fridays, and are paid a common craft rate. Mr Gilbert holds a City and Guilds qualification—Course 216, Sheet Metal and Thin Plate Craft Studies, Parts II and III. During my investigations, work was proceeding on two contracts, a type 42 destroyer and an accommodation rig for gas exploration. Both were at an advanced stage, the destroyer having been in the yard for over 4 years and the rig for nearly 2 years.

Methods of investigation

I have held separate discussions and consultations with both parties and their representatives, and the comparators. Some meetings have been in the workplace, where I conducted observational studies of the jobs under consideration.

One of the difficulties encountered was that Mr Paul Brady had ceased employment with Cammell Laird, and my investigations were further complicated by the position of Mr Tim Cox as a full-time shop steward. I, therefore, requested the nomination of some additional comparators, and Mr Joe Morrisey (painter), Mr George Buckley and Mr Paul McCarthy (joiners) were named.

Conclusions

Job comparison methods

Job factors—The jobs under consideration can be viewed as the source of a number of key "demands" upon those who do them. In order to reflect these, unweighted factors have been selected, each having some relationship to job difficulty or value. Consideration has been given to ensure no overlap of factors, to prevent double-counting features of the jobs. To reach a decision, when comparing the applicant's job with a comparator job, judgments have been made in terms of whether demand under each factor is at one of three levels, low, moderate and high.

The factors are:

(a) Physical demands—the need for physical effort and stamina and the application of human energy in applying the skills necessary to the performance of the tasks.

(b) Environmental demands—which arise from the physical conditions of the work station, and the general conditions of work which apply to the job holder in that job, for example noise, cold, dust, fumes, wetness, heat and humidity.

(c) Planning and decision-making demands—the dynamic element in carrying out the decisions related to the work tasks, including reasoning, thinking and judgment, the level of discretion, the level of supervision received.

(d) Skill and knowledge demands—the depth and breadth of knowledge required for doing the actual job as indicated by possession of recognised training and qualifications.

(e) Responsibility demands—for tools, equipment and materials.

Physical demands

Two general considerations have been borne in mind when making judgments under this heading. First, two jobs may require similar effort, though the effort may be exerted in different ways. Secondly, the occasional, or sporadic performance of an activity which may require extra physical exertion would not in itself justify a finding of dissimilar effort.

The evidence received from the respondent has not indicated significant differences in the overall physical demands made on each comparator job, compared to the applicant's job. "Taking averages of all the work carried out there appears to be little difference in the amount of basic effort and stamina expended by the cook or by each of the comparator jobs, . . . although tradesmen are subjected to more work in awkward postures." The applicant's evidence does not differentiate sufficiently between physical and environmental demands to pinpoint its conclusions. The contention that the applicant's job is physically more demanding than each of the comparator jobs is, however, implicit in the applicant's submission.

Joiner and cook

The cook stands when preparing and cooking meals and snacks. She exerts low levels of effort when mixing, cutting and slicing ingredients, with moderate levels of effort needed for lifting, carrying and sliding items of equipment, foodstuffs, semi-prepared and finished dishes. She has routine daily and weekly cleaning duties, which involve moderate levels of effort.

The joiner works on a vessel, in the joinery shop, or about the yard, as required. Much of his activity in cutting, shaping and fixing involves low levels of effort although these tasks can require moderate and sometimes high levels of effort when working in awkward postures on board a vessel. The higher level of effort required on occasions by the joiner is, in my judgment, counter-balanced by the extra stamina required, by the applicant, each day, during the period of increased working pace and level of activity preceding the mealtime deadline.

Level of demand

Cook—moderate

Joiner—moderate

Painter and cook

Some of the painter's work involves high physical effort, for example, when required to work in awkward postures and when erecting trestles, ladders and staging, plus some of the work relating to the removal of wall-coverings and old paint. These bouts of heavy work have to be balanced against his more routine work where low levels of effort are expended, materials, tools and other painting and scraping equipment being generally light in weight and easy to use. Comparing his work overall with the cook's, there is little difference in the physical effort and stamina demanded.

Level of demand:

Painter—moderate

Cook—moderate

Thermal insulation engineer (TIE) and cook

Most of the materials used by the TIE are light in weight and easy to handle. The work involves using small hand tools for cutting, shaping, stitching and fitting insulation material. Some high physical effort and stamina is required when plastering and working with large amounts of heavy insulation material although fitting and cutting on this scale is done in co-operation with others. In general, the TIE exerts low levels of effort but it can increase significantly when work is undertaken in awkward positions, in confined spaces. Balancing out the physical and stamina demands, and comparing the cook with the TIE suggests an equal level of demand in each job.

Level of demand:

TIE—moderate
Cook—moderate.

Environmental demands

In the evidence presented under environmental hazards the respondent has concluded that, "the cook and all three tradesmen are exposed to some degree to unpleasant environmental conditions and unavoidable hazards. The range of conditions are probably equivalent, with the exception of exposure to outside elements by the tradesmen. The hazards to which each of the tradesmen are exposed . . . leads to greater risk of minor injury." The applicant's submission places repeated emphasis on "the hot and sometimes humid conditions" in the kitchen, when comparing the environmental conditions of the jobs.

Painter and cook

The painter has to cope with a wide range of environments and can be subject to noise, heat, fumes, dust, cold and wetness. The frequency of the exposure varies between and within the work locations, ie the vessel, the yard and the paint shop. The number of hazards faced at any one time also varies, and can include floor hazards, eg cables and hoses.

The environmental hazards confronting the cook constitute a more enduring and permanent feature of her work station. Whilst she does not experience the more extreme conditions which can exist on board a vessel under construction, she spends her working time in close proximity to ovens, hot plates, boiling fats and liquids, in a kitchen which is usually hot and humid.

Much of the painter's time is spent outside, exposed to the elements, and I have had to take this into account. There is no strict comparison between working outside and working inside except in terms of weighing the advantages against the disadvantages.

On balance, I conclude that the environmental demands in both jobs are the same.

Level of demand:

Painter—moderate
Cook—moderate.

Joiner and cook

The joiner has to contend with a range of environmental difficulties when working; dust, heat, cold, noise and paint fumes being the main ones. Working conditions vary on a vessel, although in the joinery shop they are generally good. In comparing the joiner's environment with that of the cook, I have taken into account the slightly more limited range, but more permanent nature, of the environmental hazard faced by the cook. Also noted is the level of work pressure, which is greater for the cook, and the relationship of this to environmental demands.

I conclude, on balance, that the level of demand under this heading is equal.

Level of demand:

Joiner—moderate
Cook—moderate

Thermal insulation engineer (TIE) and cook

The TIE spends 80% of his time working on vessels, and is intermittently exposed to the full range of hazards associated with shipbuilding, viz, noise, heat, cold, dust and wetness. He also has to contend with various floor hazards, such as hoses, welding cables, temporary walkways and lighting cables, which are a feature of ship construction. Conditions are generally good when working in the workshop. The TIE is subject to considerable variation in environmental demands, depending on where he is working, but overall I do not feel that his environment is any more arduous than the cook's.

Level of demand:

TIE—moderate
Cook—moderate.

Planning and decision making demands

General instructions are given by supervisors to the comparators and the cook normally on a daily basis. The planning and decision making demands are as follows.

Painter/joiner/TIE

Planning relating to:

The sequence of operations required to complete a task.

Decisions relating to:

(i) the appropriate methods of working;
(ii) the economical and proper use of materials;
(iii) safe working practices;
(iv) quality of work;
(v) co-ordination with other trades.

Cook

Planning relating to:

(i) deadlines to ensure menu items are ready on time;
(ii) preparation of menu items ahead of time, eg for use the following day.

Decisions relating to:

(i) portions and mixes;
(ii) optimal use of equipment;
(iii) presentation and taste of food;
(iv) hygiene requirements;
(v) safe working practice;
(vi) economical and proper use of ingredients.

I have not accepted that the cook is more closely supervised than the painter, the joiner or the thermal insulation engineer. Given the critical importance of pace and timing in the cook's job detailed supervision would not be practical, irrespective of how close the supervisor is in physical terms.

Much of the planning and decision-making is of a limited kind and common to all four jobs. But in one respect the planning responsibilities of the cook are greater. She has to meet, in organizing and deciding her priorities and methods of working, a daily deadline. Her planning decisions are made in the context of greater work pressure. The comparators' work without this pressure—any deadline relating to the completion of a shipbuilding or refitting contract, given the long cycle times, is too remote to affect the day to day decision-making of the tradesmen.

Level of demand:

Cook—moderate
Painter—low
Joiner—low
TIE—low.

Skill and knowledge demands

The respondent has presented in evidence details of the Local Agreement for the revision of working practices negotiated with the constituent unions of the Confederation of Shipbuilding and Engineering Unions (CSEU) known as the Phase V Agreement. I have not been able to take this agreement into account in reaching my conclusions, because it is not yet fully implemented and it is unclear exactly how the agreement is affecting the demands of the jobs under consideration.

In order to reach conclusions about skills and knowledge I applied a test to determine the level of demand, ie. whether or not the job-holder is in possession of recognised qualifications or training to that level. The applicant and each of the comparators has either the recognised City and Guilds qualification or training to that level of skill and knowledge.

Responsibility demands

In summarising the position after presenting evidence relating to this factor, the respondent states, "A comparison between the actual potential costs caused by failure to carry out work efficiently, in terms of damage to plant or equipment, or in the use of materials, indicates that the cook's work is probably similar to the thermal insulation engineer, but less likely to lead to losses than the work of the joiner or the painter if not carried out efficiently." The applicant's submission uses a factor headed "tools and equipment," but no mention is made of materials. It is accepted in the submission that the joiner is responsible for a larger number of tools than the cook and that his responsibility for maintaining them is more demanding than that required of the cook. It is further contended that the cook uses a wider range of tools and equipment than the painter . . . "but the use of ladders and platforms probably makes as much demand as the wider range of the equipment in the kitchen".

Joiner and cook

The joiner has a personal kit of tools and receives a tool allowance to cover provision and maintenance. In the course of his work he uses some of the general woodworking equipment provided in the joinery, for example, drilling machines and circular saws.

The cook provides some of her own hand tools and used a range of catering equipment, for example, mixers and slicing machines. Although the cook uses ingredients including large quantities of perishable foodstuffs, the value of the materials used by the joiner is, on balance, greater if the full range of work is compared.

Level of demand:

Joiner—moderate
Cook—low.

Painter and cook

The painter uses a range of hand tools which, in terms of value, are not dissimilar to those used by the cook. Some of the paints and wall-covering would, also, compare in value to some of the ingredients and food prepared by the cook. However, there is more likelihood that the painter will be called upon to work with materials of greater value than those used by the cook.

Level of demand:

Painter—moderate
Cook—low.

Thermal insulation engineer (TIE) and cook

The hand tools used by the TIE are basic and the materials used, on the whole, are low in value.

Level of demand:
TIE—low
Cook—low.

Decision

The applicant is employed on work of equal value to—

Mr Paul Brady (painter)
Mr Derek Gilbert (thermal insulation engineer)
Mr Tim Cox (joiner).

Subsequently, the Court of Appeal reduced the advantage of a successful equal value claim by holding that in comparing terms of a claimant with a comparator, regard should be had to the parties' terms and conditions of employment as a whole. So holiday and sick pay entitlements and free meals could balance out a comparator's more favourable basic pay and overtime rates (*Hayward* v. *Cammell Laird Shipbuilders Ltd.* (1987) 390 I.R.R.R.).

The expert's conclusion that Miss Hayward was employed on work of equal value enabled her to claim equal pay, but only because of her sex. Paradoxically, the use of work-related factors to enable women to combat sex discrimination also appeared to be about to produce another form of discrimination or inequality. In *Pickstone* v. *Freeman* [1986] I.C.R. 886 the E.A.T. held that the law precludes claims by a man, where a woman could claim for equality based on work of equal value. A man in Miss Hayward's position could not have used the same factors as she did to justify a claim for equal pay with another man doing work of equal value. This is apparent from a useful summary table of the scoring used by the expert in *Hayward*'s case, reproduced from *Industrial Relations Review and Report* No. 332 (November 20, 1984), p. 23:

Factor heading	Cook	Painter	Joiner	Thermal insulation engineer
Physical demands	Moderate	Moderate	Moderate	Moderate
Environmental demands	Moderate	Moderate	Moderate	Moderate
Planning and decision-making demands	Moderate	Low	Low	Low
Skill and knowledge demands	Equal	Equal	Equal	Equal
Responsibility demands	Low	Moderate	Moderate	Low

Note: The applicant's job (cook) was measured against each comparator job in terms of whether the demand under each factor was at one of three levels: low, moderate or high.

As this table shows, despite their identical scoring, a male painter could not use the law to claim that he was entitled to equal pay with a male joiner even though their work is of equal value, or even "more equal" than that of the female cook. However, the Court of Appeal has now held that Article 119 of the EEC Treaty and the Council Directive on equal pay 75/117 permit a woman, who is paid the same as men doing the same work, to make a successful claim in relation to work which is different but of equal value, done by another man.

3. JUSTIFYING INEQUALITY: SEX AND RACE DISCRIMINATION

(A) A "Material Difference" Justifying Unequal Pay

Equal pay legislation gives priority to the question of whether work-related factors justify a claim for *equality*. The Tribunal must simultaneously answer the opposite question: do work-related factors justify *inequality*? For, even where the woman *is* employed on like work the Equal Pay Act 1970, s.1(3) states:

> "An equality clause shall not operate in relation to a variation between the woman's contract and the man's contract if the employer proves that the variation is genuinely due to a material difference (other than the difference of sex) between her case and his."

The development of "material" differences justifying inequality illuminates how the policy of *combatting* inequality between the sexes at work comes into conflict with policies *supporting* work-related inequality.

National Vulcan Engineering Insurance Co. Ltd. v. Wade
[1977] I.R.L.R. 209 (E.A.T.); [1978] I.R.L.R. 225 (C.A.)
Employment Appeal Tribunal and Court of Appeal

Mrs Wade claimed she was employed on like work with a male employee receiving a higher rate of pay. The company argued that the differential was due to the normal application of the salary structure, and thus fell within the exception in section 1(3) of the Equal Pay Act 1970.

PHILLIPS J. (in the E.A.T.): Although it is not spelt out in terms of the [Equal Pay] Act [1970], once a woman has established that she is being paid less than a man in the same employment employed on like work with her it is presumed that the variation between her contract and his contract is due to the difference of sex. The Act, which is entitled "An Act to prevent discrimination, as regards terms and conditions of employment, between men and women" forms one code with the Sex Discrimination Act 1975 (see especially s.6) and is the performance in municipal law of this country's obligations under Article 119 of the Treaty of Rome. Thus when an Industrial Tribunal comes to consider the claim of an employer that s.1(3) of the Act is satisfied, the prima facie position has been established that the woman is entitled to the relief claimed and that the variation is due to the difference in sex. In applying s.1(3) it will no doubt be material to consider whether the claimant has succeeded in establishing direct evidence of sex discrimination, but it is not necessary for the claim to succeed that she should be able to do so; for so much is presumed once it is established that a woman employed on like work with a man in the same employment is paid less than he is.

It is against this background that an assertion by an employer under s.1(3) that the variation is due to the operation of some scheme or arrangement for the payment of wages, must be judged. Where the employer can point to the existence of a fully developed scheme, especially one jointly negotiated and in which the last word does not rest with the management alone, in accordance with which the man and the woman have been assessed and that the scheme has been fairly and reasonably operated, the employer's claim may very well succeed. The question which arises in this case, and has arisen in others, is how the Industrial Tribunal should approach the question. . . .

. . . We reject the view that it is enough for the employer to establish that there is in force some scheme for the fixing of wages and that the woman's wages were fixed in accordance with it. There may well be circumstances about the nature of the scheme, or its method of operation, which leave a doubt in the mind of the Tribunal in which case the woman's claim will succeed. Such a doubt of course must not be fanciful, and the Industrial Tribunal should consider all the circumstances. Amongst them will be the following: Was the scheme unisex? Was it jointly negotiated? Did it leave the final say invariably to the management? If it was unisex, had it succeeded a discriminatory scheme; and, if so, how long ago? What were the criteria applied for personal assessment? Did the scheme appear to have been fairly operated in relation to the persons sought to be compared with the claimant? There will be many other considerations. It should be emphasised that it is right for the Industrial Tribunal to consider these matters not because it is its function to prescribe the contents of such schemes but because it is only by looking to see what happened in practice that it is possible to see whether the employers have really established that the variation is genuinely due to a material difference (other than the difference of sex) between her case and his.

[The E.A.T. agreed with the Industrial Tribunal's upholding of the claim, but the Court of Appeal set aside the E.A.T.'s decision.]

LORD DENNING M.R.: [The employers] say that this variation is genuinely due to the difference in the skill, capacity and experience of the individual. It has nothing to do with the sex. A better person, whether he be man or woman, is given a higher grading and more pay than a worse man or a worse woman. They say that the difference is due to the employee's skill, capacity and experience and is not due to their sex at all. . . .

I must say that the consequences of any other decision would be most serious for any business. It would mean that in a department where all were doing like work, any low-paid woman amongst, say, 18 people could put in a claim and say that she ought to be paid the same amount as the highest paid man, or *vice versa*. In other words, everyone in the department, men and women, where both are employed, would have to be raised up to the highest wage paid to anyone in the department. Alternatively, it might operate very badly for the employees eventually because they all might be paid at the lowest rate so that none could claim higher than the other. If it were to go forth that these grading systems are inoperative and operate against the Equal Pay Act, it would I think be disastrous for the ordinary running of efficient business. It seems to me that a grading system according to ability, skill and experience is an integral part of good business management: and, as long as it is fairly and genuinely applied irrespective of sex, there is nothing wrong with it at all. It ought not to be challenged and made inoperative by reason of the Equal Pay Act. The contrary view would leave these grading systems open to challenge.

ORMROD L.J.: Here the employers said that they were operating a differential scheme based on performance or personal assessment. That in itself I would have thought, was enough, provided only that they can show that they were genuinely operating the scheme. It could be, of course, that an employer had so set up a scheme to conceal an underlying sex discrimination in rates of pay. If so, he fails under sub-section (3). But, with respect to the Employment Appeal Tribunal, the complexity which they appear to have found in this case astonishes me. I cannot think that many of the considerations mentioned by the learned judge below in the course of his judgment are anything but entirely neutral when it comes to the question of deciding whether or not the employers have been genuinely operating a grading scheme. The fact that they formerly operated a discriminatory scheme before they changed their policy must be wholly neutral. The fact that they, like very many other employers, paid women a lower rate than men for comparable work in the past adds absolutely nothing to the question as to whether this is a genuine scheme. Although I do not wish to go through them in detail, the same comment would apply to the criticisms of the fact that this was a subjective scheme which had not been negotiated. The only question is, was it genuinely operated?

GEOFFREY LANE L.J.: I should add this. It is not for the Tribunal to examine the employers' system with the object of seeing whether it is operating efficiently or even fairly. The only enquiry is whether it is genuine—that is to say, designed to differentiate between employees on some basis other than the basis of sex.

Two categories of "material difference" illustrate the judicial quandary over whether work-related inequalities take priority over equal treatment of the sexes.

(i) "Market forces"

There is currently a division of opinion as to whether "market forces" or "economic reasons" justify inequality even where the result is unequal treatment of women as compared to men. Despite the Court of Appeal's view of Article 119 of the EEC Treaty, the European Court of Justice interpreted it in *Jenkins* v. *Kingsgate* [1981] I.R.L.R. 228 as allowing economic factors to justify inequality, even when women are the victims.

Rainey v. Greater Glasgow Health Board
[1987] I.R.L.R. 26
House of Lords

The National Health Service in Scotland decided to establish an artificial limb fitting service in place of the "prosthetic" services previously supplied by private contractors. It was decided that NHS prosthetists should be paid on an appropriate Whitley Council scale. However, in order to attract experienced prosthetists from the private sector, it was agreed that the NHS would employ such prosthetists at the same level of pay that they had enjoyed while in private employment.

The appellant, a prosthetist who had been appointed to the NHS prosthetic service immediately after training, complained of the disparity between her pay and that of Mr Crumlin, a prosthetist previously employed in the private sector. All the prosthetists appointed by the NHS from the private sector happened to be male.

The House of Lords upheld the decisions of the courts below, dismissing the applicant's claim, on the ground that there was a material difference between the applicant's and Mr Crumlin's cases, which was objectively justified.

LORD KEITH: Counsel for the appellant argued that nothing can constitute [a "material difference" (other than the difference of sex) between the woman's case and the man's within the Equal Pay Act 1970, s.1(3)] which is not related to the personal circumstances of the two employees, such as their respective skills, experience or training. Reliance was placed upon the decision of the Court of Appeal in *Clay Cross (Quarry Services) Ltd* v *Fletcher* [1978] IRLR 361. In that case a woman sales clerk was employed at a lower wage than a male sales clerk who had been engaged at a later date. The employers relied, as being the material difference between her case and his, on the circumstance that the male clerk had been the only suitable applicant for the post and that he had refused to accept it unless he was paid the same wage as he had received in his previous job. The Employment Appeal Tribunal had accepted this as discharging the onus on the employers under s.1(3) of the Act of 1970, but their decision was reversed by the Court of Appeal. Lord Denning MR said, at p.363:

> "The issue depends on whether there is a material difference (other than sex) between her case and his. Take heed to the words 'between her case and his'. They show that the Tribunal is to have regard to *her* and to *him*—to the personal equation of the woman as compared to that of the man—irrespective of any extrinsic forces which led to the variation in pay. As I said in *Shields v E Coomes (Holdings) Ltd* [1978] IRLR 263/266, s.1(3) applies when 'the personal equation of the man is such that he deserves to be paid at a higher rate than the woman'. Thus the personal equation of the man may warrant a wage differential if he has much longer length of service, or has superior skill or qualifications; or gives bigger output or productivity; or has been placed, owing to down-grading, in a protected pay category, vividly described as 'red-circled'; or to other circumstances personal to him in doing his job. But the Tribunal is not to have regard to any extrinsic forces which have led to the man being paid more. An employer cannot avoid his obligations under the Act by saying: 'I paid him more because he asked for more', or 'I paid her less because she was willing to come for less'. If any such excuse were permitted, the Act would be a dead letter. Those are the very reasons why there was unequal pay before the statute. They are the very circumstances in which the statute was intend to operate.
>
> Nor can the employer avoid his obligations by giving the reasons why he submitted to the extrinsic forces. As for instance by saying: 'He asked for that sum because it was what he was getting in his previous job', or 'He was the only applicant for the job, so I had no option'. In such cases the employer may beat his breast, and say: 'I did not pay him more because he was a man. I paid it because he was the only suitable person who applied for the job. Man or woman made no difference to me'.

> Those are reasons personal to the employer. If any such reasons were permitted as an excuse, the door would be wide open. Every employer who wished to avoid the statute would walk straight through it. . . ."

In my opinion these statements are unduly restrictive of the proper interpretation of s.1(3). The difference must be "material", which I would construe as meaning "significant and relevant", and it must be between "her case and his". Consideration of a person's case must necessarily involve consideration of all the circumstances of that case. These may well go beyond what is not very happily described as "the personal equation", i.e. the personal qualities by way of skill, experience or training which the individual brings to the job. Some circumstances may on examination prove to be not significant or not relevant, but others may do so, though not relating to the personal qualities of the employer. In particular, where there is no question of intentional sex discrimination whether direct or indirect (and there is none here) a difference which is connected with economic factors affecting the efficient carrying on of the employer's business or other activity may well be relevant.

This view is supported by two decisions of the European Court of Justice upon the interpretation of Article 119 of the Treaty of Rome, requiring the application "of the principle that men and women should receive equal pay for equal work," and to the implementation of which the Equal Pay Act 1970 is directed. The first of these decisions is *Jenkins v Kingsgate (Clothing Productions) Ltd.* (Case 96/80) [1981] IRLR 228, which originated in the Employment Appeal Tribunal in England. A company employed full-time and part-time workers on like work, but paid the latter, almost all of whom were female, less than the former, who were predominantly male. The company claimed that it did so in order to encourage full-time work and hence achieve fuller utilisation of machinery, and this was accepted by an Industrial Tribunal as discharging the onus under s.1(3). The Employment Appeal Tribunal referred to the European Court questions directed to ascertaining whether the employers' policy constituted a contravention of Article 119. The court's answer was at p. 234:

> "9. It appears from the first three questions and the reasons stated in the order making the reference that the national court is principally concerned to know whether a difference in the level of pay for work carried out part time and the same worked carried out full time may amount to discrimination of a kind prohibited by Article 119 of the Treaty when the category of part-time workers is exclusively or predominantly comprised of women. 10. The answer to the questions thus understood is that the purpose of Article 119 is to ensure the application of the principle of equal pay for men and women for the same work. The differences in pay prohibited by that provision are therefore exclusively those based on the difference of the sex of the workers. Consequently the fact that part-time work is paid at an hourly rate lower than pay for full-time work does not amount per se to discrimination prohibited by Article 119 provided that the hourly rates are applied to workers belonging to either category without distinction based on sex. 11. If there is no such distinction, therefore, the fact that work paid at time rates is remunerated at an hourly rate which varies according to the number of hours worked per week does not offend against the principle of equal pay laid down in Article 119 of the Treaty in so far as the difference in pay between part-time work and full-time work is attributable to factors which are objectively justified and are in no way related to any discrimination based on sex. 12. Such may be the case, in particular, when by giving hourly rates

of pay which are lower for part-time work than those for full-time work the employer is endeavouring, on economic grounds which may be objectively justified, to encourage full-time work irrespective of the sex of the worker. 13. By contrast, if it is established that a considerably smaller percentage of women than of men perform the minimum number of weekly working hours required in order to be able to claim the full-time hourly rate of pay, the inequality in pay will be contrary to Article 119 of the Treaty where, regard being had to the difficulties encountered by women in arranging to work that minimum number of hours per week, the pay policy of the undertaking in question cannot be explained by factors other than discrimination based on sex. 14. Where the hourly rate of pay differs according to whether the work is part time or full time it is for the national courts to decide in each individual case whether, regard being had to the facts of the case, its history and the employer's intention, a pay policy such as that which is at issue in the main proceedings although represented as difference based on weekly working hours is or is not in reality discrimination based on the sex of the worker. 15. The reply to the first three questions must therefore be that a difference in pay between the full-time workers and part-time workers does not amount to discrimination prohibited by Article 119 of the Treaty unless it is in reality merely an indirect way of reducing the level of pay of part-time workers on the ground that that group of workers is composed exclusively or predominantly of women."

The European Court had occasion to consider the question afresh in *Bilka-Kaufhaus GmbH v Weber von Hartz* (Case 170–84) [1986] IRLR 317. A German department store operated an occupational pension scheme for its employees, under which part-time employees were eligible for pensions only if they had worked full time for at least 15 years over a total period of 20 years. That provision affected disproportionately more women than men. A female part-time employee claimed that the provision contravened Article 119 of the Treaty. The employers contended that it was based upon objectively justified economic grounds, in that it encouraged full-time work which resulted in lower ancillary costs and the utilisation of staff throughout opening hours. The European Court by its decision made it clear that it was not sufficient for the employers merely to show absence of any intention to discriminate, saying, at pp. 320–321:

"It is for the national court, which has sole jurisdiction to make findings of fact, to determine whether and to what extent the grounds put forward by an employer to explain the adoption of a pay practice which applies independently of a worker's sex but in fact affects more women than men may be regarded as objectively justified economic grounds. If the national court finds that the measures chosen by Bilka correspond to a real need on the part of the undertaking, are appropriate with a view to achieving the objectives pursued and are necessary to that end, the fact that the measures affect a far greater number of women than men is not sufficient to show that they constitute an infringement of Article 119. The answer [to question 2(a)] must therefore be that under Article 119 a department store company may justify the adoption of a pay policy excluding part-time workers, irrespective of their sex, from its occupational pension scheme on the ground that it seeks to employ as few part-time workers as possible, where it is found that the means chosen for achieving that objective correspond to a real need on the part of the undertaking, are appropriate with a view to achieving the objective in question and are necessary to that end."

It therefore appears that the European Court has resolved the doubts expressed by Browne-Wilkinson J in *Jenkins v Kingsgate (Clothing Productions) Ltd.* [1981] IRLR 228 and established that the true meaning and effect of Article 119 in this particular context is the same as that there attributed to s.1(3) of the Act of 1970 by the Employment Appeal Tribunal. Although the European Court at one point refers to "economic" grounds objectively justified, whereas Browne-Wilkinson J speaks of "economic or other reasons," I consider that read as a whole the ruling of the European Court would not exclude objectively justified grounds which are other than economic, such as administrative efficiency in a concern not engaged in commerce or business.

The decision of the European Court on Article 119 must be accepted as authoritative and the judgment of the Employment Appeal Tribunal on s.1(3) of the Act of 1970, which in my opinion is correct, is in harmony with it. There is now no reason to construe s.1(3) as conferring greater rights on a worker in this context than does Article 119 of the Treaty. It follows that a relevant difference for purposes of s.1(3) may relate to circumstances other than the personal qualifications or merits of the male and female workers who are the subject of comparison.

In the present case the difference between the case of the appellant and that of Mr Crumlin is that the former is a person who entered the National Health Service at Belvidere Hospital directly while the latter is a person who entered it from employment with a private contractor. The fact that one is a woman and the other a man is an accident. The findings of the Industrial Tribunal make it clear that the new prosthetic service could never have been established within a reasonable time if Mr Crumlin and others like him had not been offered a scale of remuneration no less favourable than that which they were then enjoying. That was undoubtedly a good and objectively justified ground for offering him that scale of remuneration. But it was argued for the appellant that it did not constitute a good and objectively justified reason for paying the appellant and other direct entrants a lower scale of remuneration.

The position in 1980 was that all National Health Service employees were paid on the Whitley Council scale, and that the Whitley Council negotiating machinery applied to them. The prosthetic service was intended to be a branch of the National Health Service. It is therefore easy to see that from the administrative point of view it would have been highly anomalous and inconvenient if prosthetists alone, over the whole tract of future time for which the prosthetic service would endure, were to have been subject to a different salary scale and different negotiating machinery. It is significant that a large part of the difference which has opened up between the appellant's salary and Mr Crumlin's is due to the different negotiating machinery. Accordingly, there were sound objectively justified administrative reasons, in my view, for placing prosthetists in general, men and women alike, on the Whitley Council scale and subjecting them to its negotiating machinery. There is no suggestion that it was unreasonable to place them on the particular point on the Whitley Council scale which was in fact selected, ascertained by reference to the position of medical physics technicians and entirely regardless of sex. It is in any event the fact that the general scale of remuneration for prosthetists was laid down accordingly by the Secretary of State. It was not a question of the appellant being paid less than the norm but of Mr Crumlin being paid more. He was paid more because of the necessity to attract him and other privately employed prosthetists into forming the nucleus of the new service.

I am therefore of the opinion that the grounds founded on by the board as constituting the material difference between the appellant's case and that of

Mr Crumlin were capable in law of constituting a relevant difference for purposes of s.1(3) of the Act of 1970, and that on the facts found by the Industrial Tribunal they were objectively justified.

(ii) Personnel practices: the "red-circle" cases

Personnel practices adopted by employers at work may lead to inequalities in pay between men and women, yet may be held to be "material differences" justifying inequality. The policy arguments were carefully weighed in the following case.

Snoxell and Davies v. Vauxhall Motors Ltd.
[1978] Q.B. 11; [1977] I.R.L.R. 123
Employment Appeal Tribunal

Miss Snoxell and Mrs Davies worked as inspectors alongside male inspectors who included a group—the "red-circle" group—which was paid at a higher rate, having been down-graded to the women's category in a pay structure revision some years earlier. Their former grade had been exclusively male, so no women were in the "red circle."

PHILLIPS J.: . . . the principal issue concerns the correct treatment of the practice known as "Red Circling" or "Red Ringing." It is sometimes necessary to protect the wages of an employee, or a group of employees, moved from a better paid type of work to a worse paid type of work, perhaps because the first is no longer being undertaken. There may be all sorts of reasons why such a course of action is desirable; in particular, it would otherwise be necessary to reduce the employee's wages. Nonetheless, it gives rise to an anomaly when contrasting the transferred employee's wages with those of the existing, or new, employees doing the same work, and who will be paid less. It is customary when arranging schedules or tables of wages to distinguish such transferred employees by circling or ringing them in red. Hence the phrase "Red Circling" or "Red Ringing". Because until recently women were customarily paid less than men it can often happen (and has in the cases the subject of these appeals) that where men and women are engaged on like work all the women will be paid less than any of the men, and it will be sought to justify the discrimination on the ground that the men are all "Red Circle" cases. . . .

The question which arises in these appeals is, what is the proper approach to be adopted in such cases? It is a situation which gives rise to much feeling and difficulty. Because women's wages have customarily been lower than men's it is usually the women whose claim to equal pay is confronted with the answer that the payment of the higher wages to the men is the result of a "Red Circle" anomaly. This causes much bitterness.

On the employer's side there are problems also. It is seldom right or desirable (or, indeed, permissible) to reduce the wages of employees who are being asked to move, for reasons of economy or re-organisation or otherwise, from one sort of work to another. But if in such a case the women succeed in having their wages uplifted to be on an equality with the "Red Circle" men, other male employees, not being "red-circled," may then make a claim under the Equal Pay Act 1970 to have their wages uplifted to that of the women doing the same work as themselves (s.1(3)). . . .

The present cases are ones in which the claimants have satisfied the condition that they were engaged upon like work with the men. Therefore they are entitled to succeed in their claim unless the employers can establish that their case falls within s.1(3). . . .

At the end of the day, then, the Industrial Tribunal must be satisfied that the employers' answer has shown that the *prima facie* discrimination in the field of pay is genuinely due to a material difference (other than the difference of sex) between the woman's case and the man's case. At the extremes it is easy enough. Suppose the case of a single employee approaching retirement in a few months' time, whose job has ceased to exist and who is temporarily transferred at his old wages to a lesser paid job. We would not expect a woman's claim based on a comparison with him to succeed. Suppose the case of men and women doing the same work before the coming into operation of the Equal Pay Act 1970, the women being paid less than the men. If the women were put into a special category, and "red-circled," we should expect the women's claim to succeed.

The difficulty is in the cases in between; and, in particular, in establishing the principle to be applied. For example, is it relevant to consider whether the "red-circling" is permanent or temporary, being phased out; whether the origin of the anomaly enshrined in the "red-circling" is to be found in sex discrimination; whether the group of "red-circled" employees is a closed group; whether the "red-circling" has been the subject of negotiations with the representatives of the work people and the views of the women taken into account; or whether the women are able equally with the men, to transfer between grades?. . . .

. . . The onus of proof under s.1(3) is on the employer and it is a heavy one. Intention, and motive, are irrelevant; and we would say that an employer can never establish in the terms of s.1(3) that the variation between the woman's contract and the man's contract is genuinely due to a material difference (other than the difference of sex) between her case and his when it can be seen that past sex discrimination has contributed to the variation. To allow such an answer would, we think, be contrary to the spirit and intent of the Equal Pay Act 1970. . . .

The effect of allowing the appeals of Miss Snoxell and Mrs Davies will be that they (and the other two women) will be placed within the red circle. It is easy to see that this could give rise to important practical problems, for male inspectors [outside] the red circle, doing the same work as they do, may make a claim to be treated with equality with them: see s.1(13). The effect upon a delicately poised wages structure is likely to be far-reaching, though that fact could not influence the outcome of such claims if well founded.

In certain circumstances, an employer's personnel practice can justify inequality despite "like work" being performed (see *Farthing* v. *Ministry of Defence* [1980] I.R.L.R. 402 (C.A.)). A "material difference" justifying inequality can include an employer's view of desirable personnel practice. The question is whether the courts will limit this subjective justification of inequality. In the cases above, the policy of combatting sex discrimination was one such limitation explicitly considered. This policy was given less emphasis in the cases which follow.

(B) The "Justification" Defence for Race and Sex Discrimination

The clearest manifestation of a policy permitting work-related inequality over the policy prohibiting inequality between sexes or races is the so-called "justification" defence for indirect discrimination (Sex Discrimination Act 1975, s.1(1)(*b*)(ii); Race Relations Act 1976, s.1(1)(*b*)(ii)). In the following case, the "work-relatedness" of the justification defence was clearly delineated.

Steel v. (1) The Union of Post Office Workers, (2) The General Post Office

[1977] I.R.L.R. 288; [1978] 2 All E.R. 504
Employment Appeal Tribunal

> Though employed as a postwoman since 1961, Mrs Steel only achieved "permanent full-time" status in 1975, when a rule banning women from such status in the Post Office was abolished. In March 1976 she applied for a vacant "walk," allocated according to seniority. She did not get it; instead it was allocated to a Mr Moore, who had become permanent full-time in 1973, though he had less continuous service than Mrs Steel.

PHILLIPS J.: The difficult question is whether the Post Office can show the requirement or condition of seniority to be justifiable irrespective of the sex of the person to whom it is applied, within [the Sex Discrimination Act 1975] s.1(1)(b)(ii).

The purpose of paragraph (ii) is clear enough. There may be discrimination by indirect means by requiring a condition equally of men and women, but one which few women but most men can satisfy. A requirement that a candidate should be six foot high, or capable of lifting 200lbs., or have a degree in engineering in practice would rule out more female applicants than male. It is discriminatory unless the employer (in this case) can show it to be justifiable irrespective of sex. There is no doubt that the onus of proof here lies upon the employer and that it is a heavy onus in the sense that before it is discharged the Industrial Tribunal will need to be satisfied that the case is a genuine one; somewhat in the way that it must when a not dissimilar case is made by an employer under s.1(3) of the Equal Pay Act 1970 (as amended). The question is what considerations are relevant and proper to be taken into account when determining whether the requirement or condition was justifiable; in particular, is it sufficient merely to take into account the needs of the enterprise for the purpose of which the requirement or condition has been imposed, or is it necessary to look at all the circumstances including the discriminatory effect of the requirement or condition? We are satisfied that the latter is the case and that the Industrial Tribunal has to weigh up the needs of the enterprise against the discriminatory effect of the requirement or condition. Were it not so many acts *prima facie* discriminatory would be allowed when there was no overriding need. . . .

It may be helpful if we add a word of detail about what we consider to be the right approach to this question. First, the onus of proof lies upon the party asserting this proposition, in this case the Post Office. Secondly, it is a heavy onus in the sense that at the end of day the Industrial Tribunal must be satisfied that the case is a genuine one where it can be said that the requirement or condition is necessary. Thirdly, in deciding whether the employer has discharged the onus the Industrial Tribunal should take into account all the circumstances, including the discriminatory effect of the requirement or condition if it is permitted to continue. Fourthly, it is necessary to weigh the need for the requirement or condition against that effect.

Fifthly, it is right to distinguish between a requirement or condition which is necessary and one which is merely convenient, and for this purpose it is relevant to consider whether the employer can find some other and non-discriminatory method of achieving his object.

Turning to the facts of this case, it will be right to enquire whether it is necessary to allot walks by seniority or whether some other method is feasible, to consider whether the seniority roll could not be revised so as to give the women some credit for their part-time service, and to consider the extent of the disadvantage which the women suffer under the present system in terms of numbers and likely duration. Assistance may be obtained from the judgments in the Supreme Court of the United States in *Griggs v Duke Power Co* 401 US 424. Although the terms of the Act there in question are different from those of the Sex Discrimination Act 1975, it seems to us that the approach adopted by the Court is relevant. In particular, the passage at page 431 is helpful where it is said:

> "Congress has now provided that tests or criteria for employment or promotion may not provide equality of opportunity merely in the sense of the fabled offer of milk to the stork and the fox. On the contrary, Congress has now required that the posture and condition of the job-seeker to be taken into account. It has—to resort again to the fable—provided that the vessel in which the milk is proffered be one all seekers can use. The Act proscribed not only overt discrimination but also practices that are fair in form, but discriminatory in operation. The touch-stone is business necessity. If an employment practice which operates to exclude Negroes cannot be shown to be related to job performance, the practice is prohibited."

A similar approach seems to us to be proper when applying s.1(b)(ii) of the Sex Discrimination Act 1975. In other words a practice which would otherwise be discriminatory—which is the case here—is not to be licensed unless it can be shown to be justifiable, and it cannot be justifiable unless its discriminatory effect is justified by the need—not the convenience—of the business or enterprise.

The stringency of the test that the requirement or condition be "necessary" to the work has been watered down. In *Ojutiku and Oburoni* v. *Manpower Services Commission* [1982] I.R.L.R. 418, the Court of Appeal transformed it into a test of whether the employer's need for the requirement was reasonable. It must still be work-related, but if the employer's needs reasonably require it, it is justifiable. The change is described in the following case.

Clarke v. Eley (IMI) Kynoch Ltd.
[1982] I.R.L.R. 482
Employment Appeal Tribunal

For the facts, see above, p. 198.

Browne-Wilkinson J.: Once the applicants have shown that there has been applied to them a "requirement or condition" within [the Sex Discrimination Act 1970, s.1(1)(*b*) para. (i) and a detriment within para. (iii), the discrimination will be unlawful unless the employer shows that the requirement is "justifiable" within para. (ii). Parliament has given no guidance either in the 1975 Act or in the Race Relations Act 1976 as to the circumstances in which other factors are to be held to justify an otherwise discriminatory practice.

The decisions of the Court of Appeal and of this Appeal Tribunal disclose a steady decline in the strictness of the requirements which an employer has to satisfy in order to show that a discriminatory condition is "justified". In *Steel v The Union of Post Office Workers* [1977] IRLR 288 [above p.198] this Appeal Tribunal, following the approach of the US Supreme Court in *Griggs v Duke Power Company*, indicated that a requirement could not be justified unless it was "necessary" for some other purpose of the employer. This test of necessity was slightly eroded in *Singh v Rowntree Mackintosh Ltd* [1979] IRLR 199 which, while stating that the test was "necessity," indicated that that test had to be applied "reasonably and with common sense". . . .

Finally, since the conclusion of the argument in this case we have received the transcript of the judgments of the Court of Appeal in *Ojutiku v Manpower Services Commission* delivered on 26.5.82 ([1982] IRLR 418). In that case the question arose whether the Manpower Services Commission could justify a requirement that those they accepted for certain management courses should have previous managerial experience. It was accepted that such requirement indirectly discriminated against coloured immigrants. The Court of Appeal upheld the decision of the Industrial Tribunal and the Employment Appeal Tribunal that such requirement was justified. All the members of the Court of Appeal rejected the test of necessity laid down in the *Steel* case. Eveleigh L.J., though reluctant to lay down any interpretation of the word "justifiable," said:

> "It seems to me that if a person produces reasons for doing something, which would be acceptable to right-thinking people as sound and tolerable reasons for so doing, then he has justified his conduct."

Kerr L.J., also declined to put any gloss on the word "justifiable" but said that it clearly applied a lower standard than the word "necessary". Stephenson LJ, took a rather more stringent approach. He adopted the approach in the *Singh* case and said this of the decision in the *Steel* case:

> "What Phillips J. there said is valuable as rejecting justification by convenience and requiring the party applying the discriminatory condition to prove it to be justifiable in all the circumstances on balancing its discriminatory effect against the discriminator's need for it. But that need is what is reasonably needed by the party who applies the condition. . . . "

In case this or some other matter goes to the House of Lords, we would express some apprehension as to the direction in which the decision of the courts are going on this issue. To decide whether some action is "justifiable" requires a value judgment to be made. On emotive matters such as racial or sex discrimination there is no generally accepted view as to the comparative importance of eliminating discriminatory practices on the one hand as against, for example, the profitability of a business on the other. In these circumstances, to leave the matter effectively within the unfettered decision of the many Industrial Tribunals throughout the country, each reflecting their own approach to the relative importance of these matters, seems to us likely to lead to widely differing decisions being reached. In our view, the law should lay down the degree of importance to be attached to eliminating indirect discrimination (which will very often be unintentional) so that Industrial Tribunals will know how to strike the balance between the discriminatory effect of a requirement on the one hand and the reasons urged as justification for imposing it on the other.

Browne-Wilkinson J.'s apprehension as to the danger of widely differing decisions being reached by Tribunals applying independent approaches to the justifiability of discriminatory practices was not shared by Waite J. in *Raval* v. *DHSS and the Civil Service Commission* [1985] I.R.L.R. 370 (E.A.T.) (p. 375):

> "The issue of justifiability, being a question of fact, is one that has been left by Parliament to the Industrial Tribunals, whose function it therefore is to reflect the attitude of society as a whole regarding the degree of justification required to make distinctions of race or sex tolerable in an employment context."

Waite J. accepted with equanimity the prospect that, on the same facts as those in which an Industrial Tribunal had found justifiable discrimination, "another Tribunal might perfectly reasonably have taken a contrary view" (p. 375).

Subsequently, however, the House of Lords has ruled that, consistent with the objective standards that it has ruled are to be applied to "genuine material differences" in section 1(3) of the Equal Pay Act 1970, in the light of the EEC case-law and legislation, justification of indirectly discriminatory conditions under the Sex Discrimination Act 1975, s.1(1)(*b*) is also to be objectively applied. (*Rainey* v. *Greater Glasgow Health Board* [1987] I.R.L.R. 26 (H.L.) *per* Lord Keith at para. 25):

> Counsel for the appellant put forward an argument based on s.1(1)(*b*) of the Sex Discrimination Act 1975 (with which the Act of 1970 is to be read as one: *Shields v E Coomes (Holdings) Ltd.* [1978] IRLR 263), which is in these terms:
>
> > "(1) A person discriminates against a woman in any circumstances relevant for the purposes of any provision of this Act if—. . . (*b*) he applies to her a requirement or condition which he applies or would apply equally to a man but—(i) which is such that the proportion of women who can comply with it is considerably smaller than the proportion of men who can comply with it, and (ii) which he cannot show to be justifiable irrespective of the sex of the person to whom it is applied, and (iii) which is to her detriment because she cannot comply with it."
>
> This provision has the effect of prohibiting indirect discrimination between women and men. In my opinion it does not, for present purposes, add anything to s.1(3) of the Act of 1970, since, upon the view which I have taken as to the proper construction of the latter, a difference which demonstrated unjustified indirect discrimination would not discharge the onus placed on the employer. Further, there would not appear to be any material distinction in principle between the need to demonstrate objectively justified grounds of difference for purposes of s.1(3) and the need to justify a requirement or condition under s.1(1)(*b*)(ii) of the Act of 1975.

It remains to be seen what the Courts will decide represent objective standards of justification.

4. PROBLEMS OF WORK-RELATED DISCRIMINATION

Employers may, at one and the same time, treat races or sexes unequally, and yet their action may be clearly dictated by work-related factors. The same problem will be noted in the case of discrimination on trade union grounds (see Chapter 11 on *Organisations of Workers*, pp. 437 *et seq*.). In practice it is frequently impossible to distinguish a shop steward's militant defence of his or her members' interests from conduct which (from the employer's point of view) is detrimental to the interests of the business. The steward may leave his workplace and spend time contesting managerial discipline, changes in work practices, the calculation of pay, and so on. If management takes action against the steward, is this work-related lawful discipline, or unlawful discrimination?

One approach to this conflict of policies (support for managerial prerogative and also for union activities) involves a weighing up of the conflicting interests (as in *The Post Office* v. *Crouch* [1974] 1 W.L.R. 89 (H.L.)). There is a danger, however, that the policy conflicts will be ignored, for example, by denying that any discrimination has occurred at all (as, for example, in *Stokes and Roberts* v. *Wheeler-Green Ltd.* [1979] I.R.L.R. 211 (I.T.), see below, Chapter 11 on *Organisations of Workers*, p. 442), distinguishing the "motivation" of the employer from his "intention," and legitimising the latter by characterising the former as work-related and not discriminatory. The problem of such work-related discrimination arose in an early case where a man complained that the employers' practice of permitting women employed on the same shift as him to leave work five minutes early each day constituted unlawful discrimination on grounds of sex. Lord Denning held (*Peake* v. *Automotive Products Ltd.* [1977] I.R.L.R. 365 (C.A.)):

> ". . . that arrangements which are made in the interests of safety or in the interests of good administration are not infringements of the law even though they may be more favourable to women than to men; or conversely more favourable to men than to women."

(Lord Denning later reconsidered his view in *Jeremiah* v. *Ministry of Defence* [1979] I.R.L.R. 436 (C.A.).)

In a subsequent case involving race, the question was whether the employer's hiring practice was racially discriminatory, or merely a cheap and efficient method of recruiting workers.

Pel Ltd. v. Modgill
[1980] I.R.L.R. 142
Employment Appeal Tribunal

Mr. Modgill and 15 other African Asians complained that they had been segregated from other persons in the factory on racial grounds.

SLYNN J.: [The Tribunal] had evidence which they appear to have accepted, in the body of their decision, that when vacancies arose in the paint shop they were filled by persons introduced by those who were already working there or those who were leaving. . . .

. . . the facts appear to be that here, for a period of something like two years, the personnel department of the company had not had to select or interview persons for employment in this particular area. Those who worked there had produced candidates for appointment to Mr. Barron [the manager of the paint shop] and he had found men who were able and willing to take on the job. It seems to us that the Tribunal accepted that there arose a situation, really by the acts of those working in the paint shop itself, that all the workers were in fact Asian. This had not always been the position. A few years ago there had been a number of white men working there, and there had been some coloured, non-Asian workers there as well. But over a period the position had changed and, by the introduction of cousins and friends, Asians alone worked there.

The Tribunal, as we read their decision, really decided the case on the basis that there had been what they called "indirect" or "secondary" discrimination because the company had not had a more positive employment policy which would have removed any element of factual segregation, or suspicion of it, arising in the paint shop. This appears to suggest that it was the opinion of the Industrial Tribunal, not so much that the company had by its own acts segregated these men in this particular area away from others, but that it had not prevented the men themselves from coming together in this way. What appears to be suggested is that the company ought to have taken steps to ensure that for some of these jobs, white or non-Asian or coloured men were put in, and that Asians were not allowed to take on these jobs on the grounds of their colour, in order to prevent this segregation in fact arising. We repeat that had there been here evidence of a policy to segregate, and of the fact of segregation arising as a result of the company's acts, that might well have constituted a breach of the legislation; but it does not seem to us that there was evidence to support that position. We do not consider that the failure of the company to intervene and to insist on white or non-Asian workers going into the shop, contrary to the wishes of the men to introduce their friends, itself constituted the act of segregating persons on racial grounds within the meaning of [the Race Relations Act 1976] s.1(2) of the Act.

Paradoxically, in a subsequent case involving hiring through relatives and friends of existing employees, an employer who deliberately attempted to avoid the discriminatory consequences, and was then forced to withdraw by threats of industrial unrest, was held to be guilty of unlawful discrimination (*R.* v. *Commission for Racial Equality ex p. Westminster City Council* [1985] I.R.L.R. 426 (C.A.))]. Contrast the following cases: was the employers' action racially discriminatory, or merely a desire to prevent dissension at the workplace?

Seide v. Gillette Industries Ltd.
[1980] I.R.L.R. 427
Employment Appeal Tribunal

After a number of incidents involving anti-Semitic remarks directed by an employee, Mr Garcia, towards Mr Seide, Mr Seide was moved to another shift near a Mr Murray. When Mr Murray complained that Mr Seide was trying to involve him in the antagonism with Mr

Garcia, the management moved Mr Seide yet again. Mr Seide complained of racial discrimination.

Slynn J.: Mr Beloff [counsel for the company] I think, would accept that there can be more than one ground for a particular step being taken by an employer and if one of those—a substantial and effective cause for the employer's action—is a breach of the statute [the Race Relations Act 1976] then that might well be enough. He says here that the Tribunal have effectively decided, as they were entitled to do on the evidence, that the only course here at the end of the day was the reaction of Mr Murray to the situation which had arisen on May 15 1978.

Mr Macdonald [counsel for Mr Seide] says that is not enough. If the fact of Mr Seide's being Jewish is still here in the background, is still there as a factor and has not, as he put it, entirely been snuffed out as the link in the causation, then it must be taken by the Tribunal as a matter of law to be one of the grounds on which the company acted.

We consider that on this Mr Beloff is right in his submissions as a matter of law. It does not seem to us to be sufficient merely to consider whether the fact that the person is of a particular racial group within the definition of the statute is any part of the background, or is (as is said in other cases) a *causa sine qua non* of what happens. It seems to us that the question which has to be asked is whether the activating cause of what happens is that the employer has treated a person less favourably than others on racial grounds.

Din v. Carrington Viyella Ltd. (Jersey Kapwood Ltd.)
[1982] I.R.L.R. 281; [1982] I.C.R. 256
Employment Appeal Tribunal

Mr Din was not re-engaged when he returned from a period of extended leave to his home country of Pakistan. He had previously been involved in an incident with a technical foreman which had led to unrest among Mr Din's Pakistani workmates, after management refused to take any action.

Browne-Wilkinson J.: . . . what the Tribunal have done is to say that you can draw a line immediately before the decision in September not to re-engage and that the Tribunal was properly taking the view that the reason for not re-engaging Mr Din was the unresolved and potentially explosive situation arising out of the episode in July 1980. The decision not to re-engage, it is said, can be looked at in isolation since the reason for the non-re-engagement was an industrial reason and [the Production Manager's] reasons for his decision [not to re-engage Mr Din] were not on that occasion racial. The Tribunal sought to justify such an approach in reliance on *Seide v Gillette Industries Ltd* [above p.229]. . . .

In this case the Industrial Tribunal said that the decision not to re-engage was made on the grounds of the potential unrest which a re-engagement would involve and that therefore they were not concerned with any racial discrimination which lay behind that unrest.

We think that is an unacceptable extension of the decision in the *Seide* case. In our view, if an act of racial discrimination gives rise to actual or potential industrial unrest, an employer will or may be liable for unlawful discrimination if he simply seeks to remove that unrest by getting rid of, or not re-employing, the person against whom racial discrimination has been shown.

In *R.* v. *Commission for Racial Equality, ex p. Westminster City Council* [1984] I.R.L.R. 230 (Q.B.), Woolf J. confirmed that: "It is not a justification for what would otherwise be an unlawful discrimination to rely on the fact that the alternative would be possible industrial unrest."

The exercise of judicial discretion is made possible by drawing a distinction between work-related motive and discriminatory intention, or discriminatory motive and work-related intention. In the *Westminster City Council* case, Woolf J. stated:

> "Motive may often be substantial evidence of why an action was taken and therefore indicate the grounds on which it was taken. However, I fully accept that you can have discrimination on racial grounds without there being an intention to discriminate on those grounds."

The non-discriminatory motive of the Council did not preclude a finding that the act was done on discriminatory grounds. The Court of Appeal upheld Woolf J. by a majority, but contrast the dissenting judgment of Sir Denys Buckley ([1985] I.R.L.R. 426 (C.A.) at p. 432):

> "Under [the Race Relations Act 1976] s.1(1)(a) there can be no relevant discrimination unless the alleged discriminatory act was done 'on racial grounds.' The grounds relied on must, in my judgment, constitute an activating cause of the alleged discrimination. They need not, I think be the sole activating cause. A discriminator must [*sic*] discriminate for mixed motives, that is, on a combination of distinct grounds, but at least one significant cause must be shown to have been a racial ground."

He concluded that the evidence was indisputable that the Council was "not motivated by any racial reason, but only by the fear of jeopardizing" industrial relations. In contrast, in the following case, the distinction between motive and intention was invoked to preclude such a finding. Intention was essential. Evidence of malice (discriminatory motivation) would not suffice to find unlawful discrimination.

Armagh District Council v. The Fair Employment Agency for Northern Ireland

[1984] I.R.L.R. 234
Northern Ireland Court of Appeal

The Northern Ireland Fair Employment Agency concluded that an appointment of a wages clerk by the Council was discriminatory when 11 councillors (all Unionists) voted for one Protestant candidate (Mrs. Wakenshaw). By prior agreement councillors voting for another Protestant candidate, Miss McFarland, had agreed to change their votes, and 8 councillors (all members of the SDLP and one Independent councillor) voted for the Catholic candidate.

Lord Lowry L.C.J.: An action may be deliberate without being malicious. Most acts of discrimination are both, but the only *essential* quality is deliberation. If a Protestant employer does not engage a Roman Catholic applicant because he genuinely believes that the applicant will not be able to get on with Protestant fellow workmen, he is discriminating against the applicant on the ground of his religious belief, although that employer's motives may be above reproach. If women are allowed to stop work five minutes early in order to avoid being endangered when the day's work ends, it has been decided that the men in the workforce are discriminated against on the ground that they are men. The employer's decision to keep the men at work longer, though reached in good faith, was deliberately based on the fact that they were men.

Accordingly, it can be stated that, although malice (while often present) is not essential, deliberate intention to differentiate on the ground of religion, politics, sex, colour or nationality (whatever is aimed at by the legislation) is an indispensable element in the concept of discrimination. The distinction is sometimes expressed as one between motive and intention. In *Peake v Automotive Products Ltd* [1977] IRLR 365, the case about releasing women early from their work, Phillips J stated:

> "It seems to us that counsel is confusing the motive or the purpose of the act complained of with the factual nature of the act itself. [The Sex Discrimination Act 1975] s.1(1)(a) requires one to look to see what in fact is done amounting to less favourable treatment and whether it is done to the man or the woman *because he is a man or a woman*. If so, it is of no relevance that it is done with no discriminatory motive."

This idea runs through all the cases.

Once this proposition is understood, it can be seen that there was no evidence of discrimination against the complainant. . . .

. . . the factual basis found by the learned judged [was] that Mrs. Wakenshaw was "the most suitable candidate for the post". The supporters of this candidate and Miss McFarland know that the eight non-Unionist councillors are all going to vote for the complainant; whether because they think she is the most suitable candidate or because they intend to support her in any event does not matter. It is then only common sense for the supporters of Miss McFarland to give their vote to Mrs Wakenshaw whom, (if they adopt the judge's criteria of qualifications and experience), they are bound to consider better suited for appointment than the complainant, even if (in their opinion) less well suited to the job than Miss McFarland. Indeed, because the qualifications and experience of Mrs Wakenshaw and Miss McFarland were similar in nature, it would be almost inevitable, on genuine grounds of suitability, for a supporter of one to put the other second in front of the complainant.

These cases demonstrate, first, that statutory policy prohibits direct and intentional discrimination, but, second, that some judges may find even this policy difficult to accept when work-related grounds are put forward to justify the employer's action. Ways may be found to avoid a conclusion of indirect illegitimate discrimination: by referring to activating versus other reasons (*Seide v. Gillette Industries Ltd.* (see p.229 above), approved by May L.J. in *Kingston* v. *British Railways Board* [1984] I.R.L.R. 146 (C.A.), at p. 152); by distinguishing motive from intention (*Armagh District Council v. The Fair Employment Agency for Northern Ireland* (see p.231 above) or justifying passive acquiescence rather than action (*Pel Ltd. v. Modgill* (see p.228)). This judicial tendency to justify inequality on work-related grounds has its roots, or rather its unarticulated premises, in a rationale of industrial "efficiency." The following extract describes this policy and the alternatives which could be adopted by the judges.

L. Lustgarten, LEGAL CONTROL OF RACIAL DISCRIMINATION (1980), pp. 53–55

Job relatedness—"a manifest relationship to the employment in question"—means above all that the requirements of the job itself . . . must provide the guidelines. . . .

Only requirements inherent in the job may be regarded as justifiable. This seemingly abstract concept is in fact quite realistic, for it forces employers at first instance and then tribunals to make a practical appraisal of job content, cocking a sceptical eye at traditional restrictions and the more recent, albeit limited, vogue for credentials and testing. The result will surely be to eliminate many practices that have excluded able people and have been carried on primarily through habit and neglect; in numerical terms more whites than non-whites will be the gainers. An effective anti-discrimination law is a powerful source for what is truly "rationalisation" of industry—the clearing away of mythologies surrounding employment practices, and their replacement by prerequisites that demonstrably help select the most competent people.

The key legal issue is developing a workable test of job-relatedness. The one standard that must be ruled out at the start is that of good-faith belief in the validity of a qualification. The test must be objective, for the issue is not the intention of the employer but the effect of the practice. Concretely this means that the challenged requirement must demonstrably and significantly contribute to industrial efficiency or safety, a test that cannot be satisfied by belief, good faith or otherwise, but only by empirical evidence. This may be hard to come by, but that argues for abandonment of the discriminatory practice, not acceptance of prevailing dogma. . . .

If this approach is rejected as being too vague there would seem to be but two alternatives, each even less attractive. The first is unbridled judicial law-making: giving meaning to the phrase by infusing the policy preferences of the interpreters themselves. The second, and more likely, is adoption of the attitude of extreme deference the courts continue to take when administrative decisions are challenged by persons asserting personal or political rights . . . the familiar test of reasonableness: only if the policy were adopted on "unreasonable, capricious or irrelevant" grounds would it be regarded as *ultra vires* . . . and affirmatively demonstrating that something is justified, and if the tribunals and courts are to be faithful to the [Race Relations Act 1976], ensuring that the responsibility it imposes on the employer is a real one, they can only draw upon the policies and perspectives of the Act itself.

It should be recognised that the task placed upon tribunals and courts hearing such cases is an unusual one. . . . These bodies must make substantive judgments about the appropriateness of private decisions, drawing upon evidence and supported by a mode of interpretation, both of which are outside the ordinary compass of English jurisprudence.

The argument that capitalist "efficiency" can justify inequalities at work requires critical examination. At what point does inequality in treatment at the workplace, even for work-related reasons, become counter-productive? If many disputes arise as a result of unequal treatment between groups or individuals, even the alleged efficiency of such practices can be questioned. Ultimately, rational production may entail the need for justification of any inequalities between workers. And even then, the factor of increased efficiency needs to be weighed in the political balance with the inequality remaining.

5. THE PRACTICAL OPERATION OF THE LAW ON DISCRIMINATION

The problem of enforcement of laws against discrimination has met with various answers: the creation of institutional machinery (the Equal Opportunities Commission, the Commission for Racial Equality), the promulgation of Codes of Practice and the use of procedural devices to help complainants (shifts in the evidential burden of proof, requiring employers to complete forms of questions, imposing extensive discovery obligations to obtain documentary evidence).

Whatever other effects these measures may have had, they have not produced many complaints to Industrial Tribunals. The figures for applications under the Sex Discrimination Act 1975 in the years since 1976 are as follows (*Employment Gazette*, April 1983, p. 167):

1976	243	1981	256
1977	229	1982	150
1978	171	1983	265
1979	178	1984	310
1980	180	1985*	26

*Jan 1—March 31 only

The outcome of Tribunal applications does not present an image of effective enforcement: (*Employment Gazette*, February 1986, p. 54, Tables 4–5)

Table 15 Outcome of applications (1982–1984 and January–March 1985)

	Male	Female	All
Cases cleared without a tribunal hearing			
Conciliated settlements	37	181	218
Withdrawn by applicant			
private settlement	4	26	30
reasons not known*	57	153	210
Tribunal decisions			
Order declaring rights*	1	8	9
Awards of compensation	15	46	6
Recommended course of action	5	68	73
Complaint dismissed	34	122	156
All	153	604	757

* Including cases where the parties reached a private settlement but ACAS were not informed and cases where the applicant found the complaint to be out of scope.

Table 16 Compensation (1984 and January–March 1985)

	Agreed at conciliation	Awarded by tribunal
£1–£49	4	0
£50–£99	7	1
£100–£149	14	6
£150–£199	7	0
£200–£299	13	0
£300–£399	11	1
£400–£499	6	1
£500–£749	10	3
£750–£999	8	0
£1,000 and over	16	6
All	96	18

The position appeared even less satisfactory in equal pay claims (*Employment Gazette,* April 1983, pp. 165–167, as partially updated *cf.* EOC Annual Report Appendix 3) although the improved success rates of applicants in 1983 and 1984, even if based on small numbers of hearings, seems to bear testimony to the possibilities opened up by "equal pay for equal value" claims.

Year	Applications	% conciliated or withdrawn	No. heard by tribunal	No. in favour of applicant	% in favour of applicant
1976	1742	55	709	213	30
1977	751	52	363	91	25
1978	343	71	80	24	30
1979	263	70	78	13	17
1980	91	71	26	4	15
1981	54	50	27	6	22
1982	39	67	13	2	15
1983	35	—	15	9	60
1984	70	—	24	11	46

A report published in March 1986 on the progress of claims for equal pay for work of equal value under the Equal Pay (Amendment) Regulations 1983, in force since January 1984, described 40 claims at Industrial Tribunals and another 25 claims being taken through negotiations (Labour Research Department, *"Women's Pay: Claiming Equal Value"* (1986)).

As in many other areas of labour law, the legal policy against discrimination has been implemented largely through the autonomous action of those involved. Policies and practices can be developed at the workplace to achieve the objectives desired by the legislation, but not enforced by it. Below we produce the results of a report prepared by trade unionists at one workplace. This report resulted in a number of practical measures being implemented which appear to have had some impact on inequalities at work (see *Industrial Relations Review and Report,* No. 228 (July 1980), p. 6).

Camden NALGO EQUAL RIGHTS WORKING PARTY REPORT (August 1976) Summary of Recommendations

Position of Men and Women in the Job Structure

1. To enable more detailed conclusions to be drawn on the position of men and women in Camden, regular data on the grade, age, length of service and qualifications of all Department's staff, analysed by sex, should be produced by the Council, and supplied to the unions and other interested parties.

Women's Work and Men's Work

2. The Council should investigate fully all types of work heavily dominated by one sex to check whether any unnecessary discrimination is taking place, and should propose measures to attract both sexes into these jobs.

3. The Branch [of NALGO] should help to improve pay and conditions for lowly paid jobs including campaigning to raise the status of under-graded jobs held by women, particularly in Social Services, should seek the integration of specialist pay scales into basic ones, and should insist management examines regularly the grading of the lower paid jobs.

4. Positive action needs to be taken towards specific areas where women are concentrated in low paid jobs. We have identified these as follows: clerical and lower administrative grades, telephonists, typists, child care officers, day care staff, residential staff, social workers and librarians. The Council should apply an intensive policy of training and broadening opportunities for staff in these lower paid jobs.

5. In many departments there are very low numbers of women in [Senior Officer] and [Principal Officer] grades compared with the number of women in the department as a whole. The Council should be prepared to positively discriminate in these areas and should, in conjunction with the Branch, closely monitor future appointments to these jobs and report progress on securing a more equitable representation.

Training and Career Development Opportunities

6. Much better monitoring of career progression and access to training is required, including regular data by sex and grade of staff attending various types of training and staff who apply but are refused.

7. Departmental management and the Directorate of Central and Management Services ["DCMS"] should regularly carry out career counselling with less qualified staff and give them particular assistance if they wish to train for higher graded or more interesting jobs. Some form of regular appraisal interview might be appropriate.

8. The Council should investigate the special problem of married women returning to work after raising a family, whether or not they worked for Camden previously, and assist then to train or retrain.

9. Both the Council and the Union should develop a much better education programme for promoting job and training opportunities aimed especially at lower graded staff, particularly women who are lacking in the motivation or courage to take the initiative themselves.

10. There should be careful monitoring of career grade schemes and basic qualification requirements that are introduced, to ensure that less qualified staff still have adequate avenues for promotion.

11. If training is to be restricted in the next few years in any way, special

consideration should be given to the types of training that benefit women eg day release rather than evening courses.

12. All the training and career development proposals outlined above should be applied intensively to staff in jobs which have traditionally given them little opportunity for further promotion, and particularly to those areas identified in recommendation 4.

Opportunities for more flexible work arrangements

13. That the Council look at the possibility of employing more part-time staff in office jobs in general, particularly in clerical situations. Job adverts could be worded flexibly to suggest that full or part-time staff would be considered.

14. That the Council be considerably more flexible in allowing staff in higher grade jobs to work part-time, particularly if they are women returning after having a child or single parents, and if they are prepared to work over 16 hours per week.

15. That the Council should consider employing staff on "twinning" arrangements as is common in banks and other commercial offices.

16. The Council should at least look into the demand for, and feasibility of, employing women or single parents on a school term basis, particularly in areas with a "seasonal" workload.

17. Middle management should be encouraged to take a sympathetic view of working at home in situations where little supervision is required on a job, or when work could be done on a "contract" basis by women on maternity leave, or by parents with a sick child to look after. This recommendation could only be applied on a highly selective basis and both the Branch and the Council would need to ensure that it was not being abused by establishing regular or full time working as a substitute for office based jobs.

Facilities for Parenthood

18. The Council should apply immediately the provisions of the Employment Protection Act [1975] on maternity leave.

19. All maternity leave provisions should apply equally to part-time staff who work more than 16 hours per week.

20. The Branch should seek further improvements to maternity leave provisions:

(a) the right to return to work for up to 52 weeks after the birth with no loss of rights or seniority;
(b) fully paid leave for EPA period ie up to 29 weeks after the birth, and half-pay for the remainder;
(c) there should be paid leave for ante-natal care, and a right to a reduction in hours if required before the birth.

21. The demand for maternity leave provisions should be monitored by the Council to discover under what conditions a higher percentage of staff might return to work.

22. There should be a better system of contact with staff during maternity leave, both by departments and DCMS staff, particularly to help organise or ease the return to work.

23. That the Council should consider granting at least 5 days paid leave to fathers around the time of the birth of a child.

24. That the forthcoming birth of a child should entitle a parent to carry over as much annual leave as he or she requires.

25. The Branch should encourage the Council to consider the possibility of several creche facilities in the borough, open to Council staff but shared with

other interested local employers. The Branch could canvass support for this in the near future.

26. The Branch should add its weight to the cause of extending Council provision for resident under-5's in the borough.

27. That the Branch should press the Council to consider granting at least 3 weeks' paid leave a year to attend to a sick child for single parents or where both parents of a family are at work.

Job Adverts and Application Forms

28. All job adverts for the next few years should state that the job is open to both sexes.

29. Outside adverts should be directed towards gaining a high response rate from women, and media should not be employed solely with the objective of gaining a large number of suitable applicants, irrespective of sex, particularly where women fill few posts at present.

30. Job application forms should be redesigned to eliminate reference to marital status.

31. The Council should set up an experimental scheme using a "sexless" application form ie where all reference to the sex of the applicant is omitted and Christian names are shown by initial only, with close monitoring to see how this affects short-listing.

Interview Code of Conduct

32. It is essential that an interview code of conduct is drawn up which is sent to all those called for interview, pointing out their right to complain (to Central Personnel or NALGO) if it is breached. It would be improper to enquire about marital status or parental status, family intentions or home responsibilities, unless such matters are central to the job in which case all applicants should be asked.

A pessimistic assessment of the practical effects of such policies was the conclusion reached in a report published by the Department of Employment.

T. Hitner, D. Knights, E. Green and D. Torrington, "*Racial Minority Employment: Equal Opportunity Policy and Practice*" DEPARTMENT OF EMPLOYMENT RESEARCH PAPER No. 35, (January 1982), pp. 1–2, 23–24

As the study proceeded, it became increasingly evident that the existence of an equal-opportunity policy or statement was an imperfect guide [to] good practice in relation to the employment of racial and ethnic minorities. Drawing upon a provisional list of companies known to have adopted equal-opportunity policies or statements, preliminary interviews raised certain anomalies in that:

(1) personnel departments were often unaware of even the existence of their written policies;
(2) where the existence of a policy was established, many personnel managers had some difficulty in locating the actual document; and
(3) an initial examination of recruitment and promotion procedures indicated that the policy had little or no impact. . . .

. . . equal-opportunity practice often emerged as an unintended consequence of dealing with multi-racial problems at the workplace. . . . It is the central conclusion of this research that the development of equal-opportunity practices is *more likely to occur* when:

(1) equal-opportunity policies and procedures are the actual outcome of a response to work-place issues concerning the employment of racial minorities in given situations;
(2) there is a general involvement in developing and operating equal-opportunity policies and procedures by those who are to be affected by them; and
(3) equal opportunity is not hived off but seen as an integral part of employment policy and practice in general.

What we are suggesting in this report is that success in developing equal-opportunity policy and practice in employment is dependent upon organizations meeting these three conditions . . . equal-opportunity policies which are conceived independently of these three issues are likely to prove ineffective.

To illustrate this conclusion, we turn to "Foundries Ltd." which is part of a large corporation with a highly centralized administration. As a leading exponent of equal opportunity, the corporation head office first introduced a formally written policy in 1970 in response to the 1968 Race Relations Act. This first policy was somewhat defensive in that it was orientated toward instructing managers on how to avoid trouble, but it established a system of monitoring and record-keeping whereby the racial composition of the work-force was to be audited. In 1980, the corporation re-issued the equal-opportunity policy. The emphasis this time was on recognizing the company's responsibility to its multi-racial work-force; communicating the corporate philosophy on equal opportunity to all members of the organization; and assigning overall responsibility for the policy to a senior executive within the corporation's head office. To this end:

(1) all managers and supervisors received a copy of the policy and were briefed as to its contents and application;
(2) sufficient copies of the policy were printed to make possible organization-wide distribution;
(3) the policy was published in the corporation's newspaper which is, in principle, available to every employee; and
(4) the corporation allowed its commitments to equal opportunity to be publicized more generally by the media.

Here, then, is an organization whose activities in the field of equal-opportunity promotion would lead one to describe it as a model employer. Not only has it implemented many of the recommendations of the agencies concerned with promoting equal opportunity in employment, but also has gone further than most in providing the formal framework for alleviating racial discrimination at work. Indeed, this equal-opportunity policy was the most elaborate of all those examined in the course of our case-study research.

An investigation of "Foundries Ltd.", however, came up with the surprising information that despite the intensive communication campaign, none of the hourly paid staff interviewed, including the works convenor, knew anything about the equal-opportunity policy. Furthermore, there seemed to be considerable doubt amongst personnel and training staff that they had ever received a copy—a typical response was "we get so much stuff from head office, it's probably on file". Certainly, no one remembered having been consulted, briefed or advised about the policy even though it included a directive that all employees and job applicants be notified of its contents.

How is it then when so many resources had been deployed to ensure communication of the equal-opportunity policy, so few people at plant level were aware either of its existence or of their obligations under it? One might conclude that either the head office system of communication was inefficient, or the imposed prescriptions were seen as irrelevant to the productive operations of "Foundries Ltd." Our empirical data suggests that it is difficult to separate out issues of relevance from problems of communication, for when the contents of a policy are seen as irrelevant, no matter how advanced the communication system, it will be ineffective. This was the case in "Foundries Ltd." Since senior management in the plant were not involved in the formulation of the policy, their feeling that it had nothing to do with them resulted in a breakdown of communication and the consequent ineffective translation of policy into practice. It was revealed, for example, that the policy directive of communicating equal-opportunity information to job applicants was ignored and that recruitment and promotion practices were largely unaffected by the policy. Furthermore, apart from two senior managers, no one else was aware that ethnic records were kept to monitor the effectiveness of the policy.

Perhaps the most damaging indictment of this elaborate equal-opportunity policy is that since 1975, there is virtually no evidence to suggest that the policy has had any effect on the employment and promotion prospects of ethnic minorities. Although labour turnover had averaged 8 per cent a year over the last five years, the occupations distribution of ethnic minorities within the unskilled and semi-skilled hourly paid grades had hardly changed. Furthermore, although there has been a 17 per cent increase in employment in the top skilled grade, none of the ethnic minorities have been promoted or recruited into this highest grade.

To what must this be attributed? First, the policy was unilaterally imposed upon "Foundries Ltd.", thus denying management and employees any involvement in its formulation. Second, as a consequence, it was seen not to be relevant to the daily concerns of production. And, third, insofar as it was seen as having little to do with them, management failed to incorporate the contents of the policy into their general employment practices. This case study clearly illustrates the importance of developing equal-opportunity policy through (1) involving management and employees in its formulation, implementation and monitoring; (2) relating it to work-place issues, problems and concerns; and (3) integrating it with general employment practice. It is only when these three conditions are met that sufficient commitment will be generated to ensure the successful development of equal opportunity.

The conclusions in the above study shed light on the lack of impact of the even more remote, abstract and non-participative legal standards and machinery established by the anti-discrimination legislation.

CHAPTER 7

DISCIPLINE

1. DISCIPLINARY RULES

The common law perspective on discipline at work is based on employer control through contractual obligation and property ownership. Whether discipline is a necessary incident of work may be addressed from other perspectives. The organisation of work may entail rules, and breach of rules may require remedial measures, for which corrective or punitive approaches may be adopted. In any case, questions arise of who does the correction or punishment: management, workers, union or jointly regulated discipline, to mention only some of the options. The common law perspective on discipline, rooted in employer control, creates difficulties when legislation purports to remove its underpinnings, and judges struggle to accommodate statutory provisions within their common law tradition.

The basis of the common law view of disciplinary power is the employee's contractual duty to obey reasonable lawful orders. It is highly unlikely that the common law would ever fail to imply such a term, and if it were expressly excluded, doubt would be cast on the status of the contract as one of employment. The courts have always assumed that the ultimate authority of the employer (from whom management derive their authority) is inherent in the concept of employment.

The introduction of a statutory requirement that dismissal be fair and reasonable has eroded absolute employer prerogative. Now, an unreasonable exercise of authority can be challenged, although the practical significance of such a challenge will depend on the effectiveness of the remedies available to the employee against an unreasonable exercise of discipline. To the extent that reinstatement is not available, management still dominates. Also, the statute, EPCA, only applies to discipline by way of dismissal, though other forms of discipline may be inhibited if they constitute a breach of contract upon which the employee may have a claim for constructive unfair dismissal (see p. 307 below).

The way labour lawyers perceive discipline at work needs to be shaped not only by the legacy of the common law and new statutory developments, but by the reality of the industrial practice of discipline.

M. Mellish and N. Collis-Squires, "*Legal and social norms in discipline and dismissal*" in (1976) 5 I.L.J. 164, at pp. 168–176

. . . the formalising of disciplinary practice has been a widespread result of unfair dismissal law, and for many employers the new duties to ensure that records are kept, warnings given, and hearings recorded, are what they understand as the law's requirements. But it is equally clear that while employers see this as an extra administrative burden, most do not see it as otherwise changing their previous practice. Of itself there seems no good reason why formalisation—"the codifying" of disciplinary rules . . . should change the attitudes of either management or employees. In fact, there are several possible types of relationship between formal rules and procedures on the one hand and informal rules and practice on the other, and those who urge formalisation should be aware of these.

. . . formality should not be pursued at the expense of flexibility, and in a similar vein tribunals have ruled that employers should exhibit both consistency in their action and a concern for mitigating circumstances in individual cases. This indicates one possible set of relationships between formal and informal rules, what we may term *supplementary*. Most formal rules allow for the exercise of discretion. . . .

But there are other possible relationships between formal and informal rules. William Brown's study, *Piecework Bargaining* (1973), shows how informal rules—as well as wages—may "drift," in other words the number of informal rules may grow and their leniency towards worker control and behaviour may be enhanced. In Brown's study this often happened where there were no formal *agreements* but the drift of informal rules nevertheless subverted formal management *rules*:

> "A ratefixer who regularly fails to prevent workers slowing down their machines before a work study is likely to find a strike on his hands when he starts trying to dictate how fast they should be run, even if he is officially supposed to do that. A foreman who overlooks the misrecording of work or the pilfering of components for a period of time will find it difficult to tighten up his controls on these matters."

Informal rules here do not supplement formal rules, they govern behaviour, often in the absence of formal agreements. In so doing they may *supplant* formal rules. It is clear from the Brown study that such informal rules do not arise randomly. Workers have a natural bias towards rules which enhance their own control of the working environment and towards rules which are lenient to their own behaviour. Lower levels of management may have few sanctions against employees and must use concessions in order to get co-operation in achieving production targets. Individual concessions quickly become precedents and may then be established as informal, custom and practice rules. In this situation attempts by senior management to "tighten up"—for example in the area of timekeeping . . . may flounder because of the relationships of informal co-operation and interdependence between foremen and employees . . . when a company introduced a new formal agreement on timekeeping. The standards of lateness and the procedure for dealing with cases of lateness set by this agreement were quickly replaced by informal rules established by foremen under pressure from workers.

Finally on formality one other possibility must be observed. We have seen that informal rules can supplement or supplant formal rules. It can also happen that formal rules or agreements represent "no more than 'snapshots' of the current state of the (informal) transactional rules already in being." If the rules which govern behaviour are effectively those established by custom and practice and these rules originate in the bargaining strengths and weaknesses of management and workers on the shopfloor, then "outside" attempts by senior management to codify rules and formalise procedures are not, in themselves, likely to have much effect on behaviour. . . .

Broadly our view is that what is a disciplinary issue depends in part on what management care to treat as such. This itself will depend on the interest they have in controlling any particular aspect of employee behaviour and on their use, habitual or otherwise, of disciplinary rules to control behaviour. But it will also depend on whether employees collectively allow an issue to be treated as an individual one. This in turn will depend in part on their bargaining interests, strength and history.

We can illustrate this view by giving some examples from our current research. In particular these concern absenteeism and timekeeping and involve port transport employers whom we visited. Most of them had employed the majority of their workers in gangs on a casual basis until 1967, and most had traditionally paid them according to the amount of tonnage the gang cleared. The combination of casual working, a gang system and piecework, together with the collective bargaining strength of dockers, had meant that many aspects of operational control were, by 1967, exercised by the gangs themselves. They were presented with the jobs and left to decide how best and how quickly to do them. One particular firm we visited . . . had formal rules on timekeeping and unauthorised absence which were not exceptional. For all that various informal practices were noticed. One of these was called the "hop system." It involved shipworkers taking time off and being covered by their mates. It was called a system because the practice was done regularly and members of the gang had their own informal rotas for deciding whose day off it was. It goes without saying that this system relied on individuals not being reported absent. Generally they were not reported, but very occasionally reports were made, and when this occurred—it was suggested—it was because such reports were one way gang members had of "keeping in line" an individual who was not pulling his weight in the gang.

The "hop system" of shipworkers was not possible for other work at this firm because gangs were of a much smaller size. But here regular overtime was expected. This was ensured by dockers working a "quiet period" for a time in the early afternoon. This was a period of anything up to an hour or more when little or no work was done in order that the employer would "order" overtime for the two-hour period between 5 p.m. and 7 p.m. Once such orders were given it was then custom and practice to work what was called a "job and finish," a system by which employees went home as soon as their given task was completed. In practice this meant that workers would often go home at 6 o'clock or even earlier, although two hours overtime had been "ordered" and was paid for. . . .

. . . The docks' examples indicate a number of points. First, they show features of management's control system. Whatever rules management had about timekeeping and absenteeism, it had decided—at least on shipwork—to rely on incentive bonus schemes to ensure that work was done and, by default, to allow men themselves to decide how many men in the gang should be present and when work should start. On the other work mentioned management had been subject to not unusual pressures aimed at stabilising and enhancing earnings, and again in endorsing "job and finish" it accepted workers' right to determine the pace of the job and the time when it should end. Whatever the benefits for workers such control brought them, it did give them responsibility for controlling the behavior of their own members. Generally this would be done by informal work group pressures, but occasionally it would involve the use of formal procedures which could result in fines or worse by management. Workers' control over the time of work was not complete. There were some limits beyond which overtime would not be ordered, and on shipwork overtime orders generally required the approval of the relevant shipping company's agent, which was not always forthcoming. But if management wanted to control absenteeism or change timekeeping practices, it could not simply rely on formal rules. It would have to negotiate new manning standards and probably a new payment system as well. The issues were collective ones which would only become individual if workers themselves reported the absence of a colleague or acquiesced in action taken against an individual. . . .

Our studies convince us that discipline is not a special area of industrial relations because of the individual nature of the issues involved. . . . What makes a matter an individual disciplinary issue rather than a collective bargaining issue is firstly the extent to which management tries to control any given feature of the behavior of their employees (whether it be timekeeping, output, respect for supervisors, or whatever). It will also depend on the manner in which such a control is sought. For example, increased effort from workers can be sought either by enforcement of a given set of rules by management personnel or else by reliance on incentive payment schemes, in which management-initiated discipline will not be involved. . . .

As well as management initiatives, what determines the status of an issue is the collective response of employees. This will depend on their organisation and also on the bargaining strength which they think they have and their history of using this strength. It will depend on whether they can identify with the individual concerned and whether they support or are indifferent to any action taken against him by management.

The problems of Industrial Tribunals in adapting to this complex reality are reflected in cases of unfair dismissal claims. Management may attempt to enforce a provision in the work's rules which nobody on the shop floor considers to be binding—it having been waived, or fallen into disuse, or "interpreted" into something quite different in practice. Tribunals occasionally realise this, but rarely stipulate the "real" rule. They prefer to uphold the "formal" rule, and condemn management for applying it arbitrarily or capriciously in the past. Tribunals thus do not usually challenge the content of rules, only the procedure of applying them.

The following case illustrates a Tribunal's attempt to grapple with the reality of industrial discipline.

Ayub v. Vauxhall Motors Ltd.
[1978] I.R.L.R. 428
Industrial Tribunal

The applicant had been employed for over seven years as a production operator. He was dismissed after he had been caught sleeping in a "bed" whilst he was employed on the night shift. He had by that time finished his quota for the shift. The applicant claimed unfair dismissal.

BEDFORD TRIBUNAL (chairman: W. B. Carruthers): We are also satisfied that sleeping on the night shift amounts to misconduct. Although the applicant's case at one stage looked as though one of its arguments was the fact that there was custom and practice that one was able to sleep after one had done one's work at the end of the day, Mr Lynn [counsel for the applicant], very sensibly in the view of the Tribunal, did not pitch his case on such a plane. Clearly it would be contrary to common-sense that it would be custom and practice that employees be allowed to make up "beds" in such circumstances as have come out in the present case. . . .

Some three days previously, another employee at Vauxhalls, Mr Majid, had been caught in similar circumstances to the applicant. He had been dismissed; he had then appealed under the respondent company's internal appeal procedure and succeeded on appeal in having the dismissal turned into a three-day suspension. The basis for his appeal succeeding was the plea in mitigation that was put on his behalf. As we understand it there had been some talk after Mr Majid's case of the respondent company putting up notices to the effect that sleeping on the night shift was a matter of misconduct. However, nothing to this effect had been done. The applicant in evidence said that he was unaware of Mr Majid's case at the time and was only told of it by the shop steward after he had been caught and during the process of disciplinary hearings. The rule book of the company has a section 20 on page 17 dealing with penalties. It distinguishes between misdemeanours and misconduct. Further some types of misconduct are obviously more serious than others. For instance the works rules provide that pilfering would almost certainly result in the dismissal of an employee. It is implicit that other types of offence, although sufficiently serious to count as misconduct, would not almost certainly result in the dismissal of an employee. The general description of misconduct is

> "Misconduct is an action of a kind calculated to defraud the company or likely to affect adversely either other employees or the work situation."

One of the witnesses for the company was Mr Casey who was the industrial relations manager. He held the appeal meeting when it was decided Mr Majid's dismissal would be rescinded and a sentence of suspension imposed. He gave evidence that at the appeal meeting he made it clear that the company's view was that sleeping was a matter of misconduct as opposed to a misdemeanour and that this was accepted by the union officials present. One of the matters which the respondent company has brought out in connection with the act of an employee going to sleep is that it is likely to cause him to hurry up with his work to such an extent that the quality would deteriorate. . . .

There are two particular reasons why we find the dismissal to be unfair and the penalty of dismissal out of proportion to the offence. The first one is that leaving aside completely the question of Mr Majid, sleeping after one has finished one's work is not gross misconduct. We would go further than that, we are satisfied that no reasonable employer would consider it gross misconduct. On the facts of this present case we accept that sleeping is an infrequent matter. There has been a reference by the respondents to a security guard who was dismissed for it and a statement by the applicant's representative that he recalled employees in the past who had been suspended for it. Clearly it is not a matter which has come up frequently. We are satisfied that unless something had been done to draw to the applicant's attention that this was regarded as a serious matter of gross misconduct, then on the facts of the present case it was not gross misconduct. Obviously if the respondents formed the view that the quality of the work was suffering through persons on the night shift skipping their work so that they could make a "bed" and they put up notices advising employees that a very serious view would be taken of sleeping and that it would be regarded as a dismissible matter, then different considerations would apply. However, nothing of this sort had been done. We are satisfied that there had been some talk after the Majid case of notices being put up but nothing had been done. We accept the applicant's evidence that he was not aware of the Majid case and certainly nothing had been done to draw his attention to the fact that making a "bed" was regarded as of such a serious nature that dismissal might follow.

Mr Lynn in one of his arguments, or so the Tribunal understood it, was making the point that the company were trying to change the rules. We are not basing our decision on this argument. We are satisfied that they were not changing the rules. However, if one looks at section 20 there is no rigid definition of misconduct, it gives considerable latitude. If notices were put up by the respondents as regards sleeping on the night shift being regarded as a serious matter we do not see that this would be a question of changing the rules, it would be a matter of applying the existing rules. Therefore if the respondents did put up notices they would in our view put a different complexion on the matter. However, they had not done so and accordingly we are satisfied that the applicant was not guilty of gross misconduct irrespective of Mr Majid's case.

However, there is an additional reason for finding the dismissal to be unfair and that arises out of the consideration of Mr Majid's case. Mr Majid had his dismissal set aside and a three day suspension put in its place. It is common ground between the parties that the basic facts so far as sleeping are approximately similar between the two cases. Mr Majid had marginally longer service than the applicant. It is clear that Mr Majid through his trade union representatives put up a good plea in mitigation when his case came up on appeal. However, in our view, the difference between the two cases is not so substantial as to justify the difference in punishment between the two. A reasonable employer, if he felt the applicant had not put up such an effective plea in mitigation might have suspended him for a little longer. However, to this Tribunal it seems quite unfair to the applicant that he be dismissed and Mr Majid not be dismissed. To treat employees who commit the same type of offence in completely different ways creates ill-feeling and understandably so. We are satisfied that this in itself would be a reason for finding the dismissal to be unfair. It should be borne in mind that there was no evidence before the respondents when they dismissed the applicant that he knew anything about Mr Majid's case or of any communication from the company that sleeping would be regarded as a serious matter thereafter. . . .

Although the shop stewards present in the case of Mr Majid may have agreed with the respondents that sleeping was to be regarded as a case of misconduct, we do not see how this affects the present case unless the applicant had been told either by shop stewards or by the respondents of the seriousness of the position so far as sleeping is concerned.

For another illustration, *cf. Martin* v. *Yorkshire Imperial Metals Ltd.* [1978] I.R.L.R. 440 (E.A.T.).

2. DISCIPLINARY PENALTIES

A hierarchy of disciplinary penalties can develop haphazardly. Management may impose penalties other than dismissal where mitigating circumstances exist or the offence is considered insufficient to merit the sack. The application of lesser penalties may be the subject of negotiation through which trade unions limit the discretion of an employer. A hierarchy of disciplinary penalties can be progressively rationalised by the shared experience of unions spanning more than one industry, or by the national influence of a trade union on local bargaining. Statute can control the imposition of disciplinary penalties. For example, most recently EPA ss. 53–58 introduced a general statutory restriction on using disciplinary action, short of dismissal, whatever the ostensible reason, where the real reason is prevention or deterrence of union membership (or non-membership or of union activities (now *cf.* EPCA, s.23, as amended; see below, pp. 438).

(A) Fines and Penalties

Before its repeal by the Wages Act 1986, Sched. 1 to the Truck Act 1831 restricted the payment of wages otherwise than in cash and was held by the House of Lords to preclude an employer from making any deductions from wages (*Williams* v. *North's Navigation Collieries (1889) Ltd.* [1906] A.C. 136). Following a restrictive interpretation of the 1831 Act in *Redgrave* v. *Kelly* [1889] 5 T.L.R. 477 (Div.Ct.), the Truck Act 1896 (also repealed in 1986) explicitly prohibited both deductions from pay "for or in respect of any fine" (section 1(1)), and deductions "in respect of bad or negligent work" (section 2), unless stringent conditions were fulfilled. Neither of these statutory provisions prevented judges interpreting them so as to allow management to continue to exercise disciplinary powers through the pay packet. The following case illustrates the approach to the 1831 Act.

Hart v. Riversdale Mill Co.
[1928] 1 K.B. 176
Court of Appeal

The employers had a price list for the weaving of "good merchantable" cloth. It was customary to pay less for bad or negligent work.

LORD HANWORTH M.R.: An admission is made for the purposes of the case that the deduction of 6*d.* made in the present case for bad work was fair and reasonable, and was, indeed, less than the actual loss caused to the employers. It is also found that:

"Deductions for bad work are, and have been for many years, the usage and custom in the cotton weaving trade of Lancashire and have always been, and are, an incident of a weaver's contract of service, and have always been and are taken into account in calculating the correct wages. . . ."

. . . It appears, therefore, that, upon this list of prices and upon the facts found by the justices, this contract of service between the workman and her employers provided that deductions for bad work are to be taken into account in calculating the correct wages. . . .

It is argued that in the present case the employers have deducted *6d.* in respect of this negligent work from the wages payable to Nellie Hart, and the point is put that, if they have deducted *6d.*, they have not then and there paid the entire amount of the wages earned or payable to the artificer, and have committed a breach of s.3 of the Truck Act [1831]. If, however, before the wages are ascertained a calculation is to be gone through which involves the possibility of a deduction being made in respect of bad work, or an enhancement of the wages being paid in respect of bad material, unless and until that calculation has been made, it is impossible to determine what is the entire amount of the wages earned. It is said that this incident is contrary to the Truck Act [1831]; that the wages must be determined according to this standard list, which will give a particular fixture, or the basis of a particular figure, to the workman, whereas if there are to be deductions it would be difficult for the workman to know what are the wages to be paid;. . . .

. . . but I have to come back to the facts that implied as a term of the contract of service individually made by the workman with her employer, there was this system of making deductions for bad work, and those deductions are taken into account in calculating the correct wages. In other words, although you have a standard of price set out on the standard list, before you get to the entire amount of the wages earned you have to calculate the hours worked, or if it is piecework the amount done, and you have to take the basic standard on which the rate depends, and even then you have not completed your calculation, for you must also decide whether there is any deduction to be made in respect of bad work, just as you must determine whether there is to be any addition made in respect of bad material supplied by the employer. Unless and until you have gone through that process and come to a conclusion what is the true figure on the calculation of those several matters, you do not get to the entire amount of the wages earned.

. . . For the reasons which I have given and on the facts of this case, it appears to me quite clear . . . that the sum of which Nellie Hart has been deprived is not a sum deducted from the wages which were first found to be due to her, but is a loss which she has sustained in the course of the proper and just ascertainment of what is the right sum to be paid to her as wages after appropriate and proper calculations have been made. If that be the true nature of this loss which she has suffered, it is not a deduction and the employers have not offended against s.3 of the Truck Act, 1831.

A lower rate for bad work is a deduction from the rate for good work—which may be assumed to be the norm. The rate for bad work is, therefore, the good work rate less a fine or penalty. To characterise it as a "loss" in calculating damages is to play with words with a view to evading the Act's objectives. *Hart*'s case was affirmed nonetheless in *Sagar* v. *Ridehalgh* [1931] 2 Ch. 310 (see above, p. 94).

The repeal of the restrictions on deduction from wages contained in the series of Truck Acts by the Wages Act 1986 implicitly restores the common law position that the contractual wages due should be paid. It follows that disciplinary deductions from wages are not permitted unless provided for by the contract of employment or some ancillary agreement. The Wages Act constructs the freedom to contract in this respect only by requiring that the deduction be authorised by a *written* contractual term or the worker's written consent given prior to the deduction. Deduction arising from disciplinary proceedings held by virtue of statutory provisions is permitted regardless of those limitations; nor does the Act apply to deductions in regard to overpayments of wages, or to tax or national insurance payments, to third parties expressly authorised in writing (such as the payment of trade union subscriptions by "check-off"), any deductions made with the worker's prior written consent in satisfaction of a court order in favour of the employer or any deductions "where the worker has taken part in a strike or other industrial action and the deduction is made . . . by the employer on account of the worker's having taken part in that strike or other action" (s.1(5)). Coincidentally, a few months before the Wages Act 1986 came into operation, it was held that an employer can by reference to the equitable doctrine of set-off justify a deduction from an employee's wages in respect of a breach of his contract of employment occasioned by his participation in industrial action (*cf. Sim* v. *Rotherham Metropolitan Borough Council* [1986] I.R.L.R. 391). In the words of Scott J.: "If an employee, in breach of contract, fails or refuses to perform his contractual services, his right or title to recover his salary for the period during which the failure or refusal occurred is impeached by the employer's cross-claim for damages" (*ibid.* para. 136). The House of Lords judgment in *Miles* v. *Wakefield Metropolitan District Council* [1987] 2 W.L.R. 795, above p. 158, however, rules that such counterclaims are unnecessary.

Section 2 of the Wages Act 1986 adds the further limitation on deductions from wages of workers in retail employment in respect of cash shortages or stock deficiencies that they must not exceed one-tenth of a worker's gross pay on a pay day except in the case of a worker's final instalment of wages prior to the termination of his or her contract or money paid in lieu of notice.

(B) Demotion

The common law is almost certainly responsible for the absence of widespread use of demotion as a form of discipline. Demotion involves an infringement of the employee's contractual right only to be required to undertake his proper contractual work. The power to discipline by demotion, therefore, may be challenged unless it is formally contained in the contract.

Ford v. Milthorn Toleman Ltd.
[1980] I.R.L.R. 30
Court of Appeal

When Mr Ford gave three months' notice of resignation to join a competing firm, his employers wrote to him that he was to be replaced as sales manager and assigned to other sales duties, that he was not to call on customers, who would be advised that he was leaving, and that he was to exchange offices with his replacement. Mr Ford regarded this as a demotion and claimed unfair dismissal. The E.A.T. upheld the Industrial Tribunal's finding that the employers' actions amounted to a repudiation of the contract and that the dismissal was unfair.

Stephenson L.J.: . . . in the majority view [of the Industrial Tribunal] the applicant did suffer a measure of demotion, inasmuch as Mr Porrett, who was at that time Sales Administrator, took over the applicant's duties and his office as Sales Manager. This in the majority view was a fundamental variation in the applicant's contract of employment. The applicant was not obliged to accept it and did not do so. He was entitled to serve out his three months' notice or in the alternative to receive three months' wages in lieu. The minority view of Mr Upcroft [in the Industrial Tribunal] is that the element of demotion was relatively minimal. But even if it was not, Mr Upcroft's view is that the element of demotion was a perfectly reasonable imposition having regard to the paramount necessity of the respondents to safeguard the interests of their business during the period of the applicant's notice'. . . .

As to the demotion, I would have thought that even without firsthand experience of industrial relations, it would be extremely difficult to say there was no demotion in the restrictions imposed on him by his employers. I note that one member of the Tribunal thought that it was minimal and I express no opinion about that, but I cannot see that there was not ample material for the Tribunal finding there was not only demotion, but demotion which was not minimal, which demotion Mr Ford was entitled to complain about and which could properly be treated, not only by Mr Ford but by a Court of Law, as a repudiation by the employers in effect, if not in intention. Of course, it is the effect of their conduct which one has to consider at common law.

Theedom v. British Railways Board

[1976] I.R.L.R. 137
Industrial Tribunal

The applicant was a signalman and branch secretary of the Union of Railway Signalmen, which carried out a series of unofficial strikes in late 1974 and early 1975. Part of his job was to instruct other signalmen, and on April 10, 1975 he was asked to instruct a signalman who had not taken part in the industrial action and had worked extra hours during it. When the applicant refused to instruct him, disciplinary proceedings were taken. The applicant was demoted to the position of railman, later mitigated to demotion to leading railman. This involved, according to the respondents, a reduction in average weekly earnings from a previous £94 per week to £59 per week. The applicant resigned and claimed that he had been dismissed in law.

London Tribunal (chairman: O. Lodge): On any view the punishment imposed was a severe one, both in loss of status and in loss of pay. The transfer to Liverpool Street would moreover involve the applicant in considerably more travelling to and from work. The transfer was however not intended as an additional punishment but was directed because Mr Calvert [the Divisional Operating Officer] considered that it would be undesirable for the applicant to perform the duties of a shunter among the same people as those with whom he had worked as a signalman. As we have already indicated, the demotion was not necessarily permanent, although it was for an indefinite period.

In determining what punishment was appropriate, Mr Calvert took into account the applicant's previous record. Between 1958 and 1973 the applicant had received recorded punishments on seven occasions. On two of those occasions (once in 1968 and once in 1970) the punishments had included "final warnings". Mr Calvert described the applicant's service record as the worst he had seen in 12 years' experience. Mr Calvert also considered that the punishment should be such as would deter other signalmen from acting as the applicant had done.

By letter dated 16.6.75 the applicant resigned from the service of British Rail with effect from 23.6.75.

The applicant contends that the punishment inflicted on him was so severe as to amount to conduct by the respondent entitling him to terminate his contract of service without notice. If that were right he would, by virtue of [what is now EPCA, s.55(2)(*c*)] . . . be treated for the purposes of that Act as having been dismissed.

Reduction in grade is one of the normal types of recordable punishment under the railways disciplinary procedure. It is an accepted custom and practice in the railway service that an employee is subject in appropriate circumstances to reduction in grade and also to transfer from one place of work to another. We are satisfied that this custom and practice was an implied term of the applicant's contract of service. The punishment imposed therefore was not a repudiation of the applicant's contract of service unless it was either grossly out of proportion to the offence or it was imposed from improper motives . . . .

For our part we think that the punishment imposed was in the circumstances more severe than we ourselves would have thought fit to impose. Nevertheless we do not think that it can be said to have been so excessive as to have left the applicant with no real option but to resign. There is no evidence that it was imposed from any improper motive. We find that the punishment was a legitimate one imposed in good faith and did not amount to repudiatory conduct by the respondents. Its imposition did not entitle the applicant to terminate his contract of service.

Theedom was approved in *B.B.C.* v. *Beckett* [1983] I.R.L.R. 43 (E.A.T.), but Neill J. confirmed that "the imposition of a punishment which is grossly out of proportion to the offence can amount to a repudiation of a contract of service" (p. 46), and upheld an Industrial Tribunal's finding to that effect. In *Cawley* v. *South Wales Electricity Board* [1985] I.R.L.R. 89 (E.A.T.), it was held that demotion amounting to repudiation would allow the employee to claim constructive dismissal and, save for rare cases, would be held to be an unfair dismissal.

(C) Suspension

Suspension as a form of discipline is used for different purposes. Suspension on full pay may appear as part of a disciplinary procedure during which a full enquiry is to be carried out (ACAS Code of Practice on Disciplinary and Related Procedures, para. 10). Suspension without pay as a disciplinary measure in itself is normally regarded as a minor penalty and rarely extends over more than two or three days. All forms of suspension, however, raise two difficult questions. First, is there power to suspend? Secondly, whether the contract of employment can be said still to be in existence during suspension? If suspension does not involve termination of the contract, which, if any, obligations remain in force?

Hanley v. Pease and Partners Ltd.
[1915] 1 K.B. 698
King's Bench Division

When the plaintiff employee was absent without permission for one day, the employers suspended him without pay for one day.

Lush J.: Assuming that there has been a breach on the part of the servant entitling the master to dismiss him, he may if he pleases terminate the contract, but he is not bound to do it, and if he chooses not to exercise that right but to treat the contract as a continuing contract notwithstanding the misconduct or breach of duty of the servant, then the contract is for all purposes a continuing contract subject to the master's right in that case to claim damages against the servant for his breach of contract. But in the present case after declining to dismiss the workman—after electing to treat the contract as a continuous one—the employers took upon themselves to suspend him for one day; in other words to deprive the workman of his wages for one day, thereby assessing their own damages for the servant's misconduct at the sum which would be represented by one day's wages. They have no possible right to do that. Having elected to treat the contract as continuing it was continuing. They might have had a right to claim damages against the servant, but they could not justify their act in suspending the workman for the one day and refusing to let him work and earn wages.

Atkin J.: On the other point I entirely agree that in the circumstances of this case the master had no power to suspend the contract in the sense which really means the fining of the employee in the sum of one day's wages for his previous default. If he had such a power by the contract or otherwise I think it would have to be very carefully considered in the light of the more recent Truck Acts.

Wallwork v. Fielding
[1922] 2 K.B. 66; [1922] All E.R. Rep. 287
Court of Appeal

A police sergeant had been demoted to constable. He refused to parade as a constable and was suspended without pay. He sued to recover damages.

Warrington L.J.: It is said that the power to suspend does not involve the power to abstain from payment of salary. In my opinion that argument is unfounded for this reason. The relations are those of employer and employed. If the employed is suspended from his functions as an employed person, it seems to me that the effect of that is to suspend the relation of employer and employed for the time being; to excuse the servant or the employed person from performing his part of the contract, and at the same time to relieve the employer from performing his part of the contract. It would be a most extraordinary thing if suspension (assuming that there is power to effect suspension) were to be so one-sided that the servant were to be excused from performing his part of the contract while the employer was to remain liable to perform his. It seems to me that suspension suspends for the time being the contractual relation between the parties on both sides; the suspension, therefore, by the Watch Committee [ie the employer] does involve suspension of payment by them, as well as of the performance of the duty by the police constable.

Bird v. British Celanese
[1945] 1 K.B. 336; [1945] 1 All E.R. 488
Court of Appeal

The plaintiff's contract permitted temporary suspension for misconduct or breach of an order. He was suspended for two days and sought damages for loss of wages.

Scott L.J.: The very nature of the [employer's] right [to suspend] shows that its object is, on the one hand, to enforce discipline by a reasonable exercise of pressure, and, on the other, to relieve both employer and workman of the burden of actual dismissal, by the agreed substitution of a milder sanction . . . the learned judge gave a considered judgment in favour of the workman because of his interpretation of the Truck Act [1896].

. . . The consequences of this suspension, namely, the agreed absence of any right to receive, or duty to pay wages during the suspension, does not, in my opinion, come within the ambit of s.1 [of the Truck Act 1896]. . . . There are only two types of contractual stipulation within the provisional prohibition [of the 1896 Act]—(1) deductions from wages; and (2) payments made by the workman unconnected with his wages. Both are, I think, qualified by the last seven words "for or in respect of a fine." Those words are an essential limitation on both prohibitions, because without that limitation all deductions from wages, and also all payments by the workman out of his own pocket would be brought within the ban—for example, subscription to a pension or welfare or sports fund. It is quite clear that the "suspense" clause in the particular contract of employment before the court is not within the second category of prohibited stipulations: no payment by the workman was called for by it. Is it within the first? Clearly not, because you cannot deduct something from nothing. The suspense clause may act in two ways. It may be a merciful substitute for the procedure of dismissal, and a possible re-engagement. Under the suspense clause the right to wages ceases and the wages are not earned, and no deduction can be made from wages which are not payable. In the present case, as the workman was adjudged guilty of serious misconduct, the operation of the clause was merely merciful. It enabled the workman, when the suspension ended, to claim as of right to continue in his old job. The clause operates in accordance with its terms; the whole contract is suspended, in the sense that the operation of the mutual obligations of both parties is suspended; the workman ceases to be under any present duty to work, and the employer ceases to be under any consequential duty to pay. That is the natural meaning of the word "suspend" when applied to a contract of employment, and I think it is also its legal meaning. If so, this suspense clause is not obnoxious to the veto of s.1 of the Act. . . . where there is a suspension in accordance with the terms of the contract, there are no wages so to become payable. For these reasons I think the Truck Act veto is inapplicable. . . .

Marshall v. English Electric Co. Ltd.

[1945] 1 All E.R. 653; 61 T.L.R. 379
Court of Appeal

LORD GODDARD L.C.J.: [The respondent employers] contend that if they merely suspend and do not give a man notice they do not dismiss him but merely tell him that he is not to work for a specified time and they are not going to pay him during that time. What then is left of the contract of service during that time? Everything, say the respondents, except the obligation to work on the one side and to pay on the other. But in the case of an hourly servant are there any rights or obligations left except possibly the obligation to pay for one hour? It was suggested there might be pension rights, but there was no evidence that the appellant had any right to a pension, nor would one expect that a pension was secured as of right to a man subject to dismissal at one hour's notice.

In my opinion what is called suspension is in truth dismissal with an intimation that at the end of so many days, or it may be hours, the man will be re-employed if he chooses to apply for re-instatement. This indeed seems to be the effect of the evidence as the witnesses called for the respondents appear to agree that a suspended man can go off and seek employment elsewhere if he chooses to do so; he is under no obligation to return if he does not wish to submit to suspension. . . .

DU PARCQ L.J.: The [trial] judge found that "there was in the defendants' [respondents'] works at Stafford a well established and well recognised practice of suspending workmen" for breaches of discipline, disobedience to orders and offences against good conduct in general. Those included (he said) "negligence in the performance of work or carelessness in carrying out work." I am prepared to accept this finding, but it is not in my opinion conclusive. Such a practice as the judge finds to have existed may imply the existence of a rule empowering the employer to make, and compelling the workman to submit to, an order suspending the workman. On the other hand, it may be accounted for by the facts that a workman is in most cases willing to submit to suspension lest a worse fate befall him, and that in a number of instances workmen have so submitted not as a matter of legal obligation but of their own choice. In the former case it may well be true that every man who takes employment in the factory impliedly binds himself to submit to the rule. It may be said either that he knew of the rule and by accepting employment agreed to be bound by it, or that, without particular enquiry, he impliedly bound himself to observe whatever rules prevailed in the factory. If, however, all that is proved is a practice under which the workman elects whether he will be suspended or not, it is in my opinion impossible to say, when he does so elect, that he is being suspended "in accordance with the conditions of his service." The master's right to offer him the alternative of suspension, and the workman's right to accept or refuse the offer at his own pleasure, form no part of the conditions of the service. Any contract may be varied by agreement between the parties, not because there is an implied term in the contract under which they are empowered to vary it, but because the parties remain free to make what new bargain they please. A workman who knows of a so-called practice according to which he may enter into a new bargain, is certainly not binding himself to make a new bargain. The distinction between a practice which can be said to import a condition into contracts made with reference to it, and a practice which is no more than a series of fresh bargains seems to me to be of radical importance for the present purposes. . . .

The respondents were faced with a difficulty inherent in the nature of the practice alleged. If one is to judge from conduct alone, it is difficult, if not impossible, to say whether a workman is accepting a sentence of suspension because it is a term of his employment that he must accept it and the penalty for refusal to accept it is dismissal, or is accepting it because in the circumstances it suits him to accept it. Faced by such a problem it is natural to look for some documentary record of the contract between the parties. The only record we have here is the booklet to which I have referred, and it contained no reference whatever to suspension. The judge was perhaps right in saying that this omission is not conclusive, but it seems to me to be of much greater significance than he thought, and considerably to weaken the respondents' case. After a careful consideration of the evidence I cannot find that the respondents have proved that they had a contractual right to suspend the appellant.

Gorse v. Durham County Council
[1971] 2 All E.R. 666
Queen's Bench Division

> The plaintiffs were school teachers who had refused for three and a half days to participate in the supervision of school meals. Clause 11 of the plaintiffs' contracts of employment provided that the district education officer in one case and the director of education in the other: " . . . shall have power to suspend the Teacher from the performance of all duties connected with the school for misconduct or other good and urgent cause but shall at once make a full report to the Council and the [Durham County Education] Committee. The suspended Teacher shall have the right of a personal hearing (with the assistance of a friend if he/she desires) at any meeting of the Council and the Committee at which the confirmation or otherwise of his/her suspension is to be considered and shall be given not less than seven days' notice of such meeting. If the Teacher be reinstated he/she shall not suffer any loss of salary during the period of suspension, and if he/she be not reinstated he/she shall be deemed to have been dismissed for misconduct or for good and urgent cause as at the date of suspension and it shall be in the discretion of the Council or the Committee either to pay or withhold salary for the period of suspension."
>
> The defendants' education officer had warned the plaintiffs in advance that their action would be regarded as repudiation of their contracts of employment, that they would not be allowed to attend school until they resumed their full duties, and that in the meantime they would not be paid.

CUSACK J.: The defendant councils say that this refusal to pay the salary for three and a half days was justified because the plaintiffs, by their action of 27th November 1967, had repudiated their contracts and that they, ie the councils, had accepted such repudiation. The effect of this would be that for the three and a half days in question the plaintiffs and the defendant councils were not in any contractual relations at all, and that when the plaintiffs returned to duty they would have to be re-engaged by means of a new agreement in the same terms as their original agreement, or I suppose in different terms, if it was thought right. In fact no new agreement in writing was entered into, and the suggestion of such an agreement did not emerge as between the plaintiffs and the defendant councils until, long after the return to school, when it was referred to in correspondence between the first plaintiff and Mr Dormand, the district education officer, in the months of February and March 1968.

The plaintiffs say, first, that their conduct, viewed in its proper setting, did not amount to a repudiation. Secondly, they say that even if it did amount to a repudiation the defendant councils had no power to act on it without going through the prescribed procedure for terminating their employment, as set out in the agreements under which they were employed. Thirdly they say that what really happened is that they were suspended, but suspended without observing the required procedure, or observing subsequently the rule that payment of salary must be made for a period of suspension if that suspension is followed by reinstatement. . . .

[The judge quoted from a letter of November 21, 1967 from the employers to the teachers concerning their refusal to perform certain functions:]

> "If you refuse to do so you will have in fact repudiated your contract and your attendance at school cannot be permitted until such time as you are prepared to carry out the whole of your duties and in the meantime no further salary will accrue to you."

There is no clear statement there that the contract is going to be regarded as terminated. If one refers to the last paragraph of the letter of 28th November 1967, which it will be remembered was issued after the teachers had made their decision, it again is worthy of consideration because it reads:

> "I hope you will find it possible to decide to undertake all the duties of your employment at an early date when you will be reinstated."

It is not of course conclusive by any means, but it is not without interest that that word "reinstated" is the very word used in para. 11 of the plaintiff's individual contracts when reference is being made to what happens when a teacher is suspended and suspension is not upheld. . . .

I do not think it necessary for me to deal further with the documents or the oral evidence. My finding is that the defendant councils did not act on the repudiation by the plaintiffs of their agreements. The evidence convinces me that at the material time the councils did not regard the agreements as at an end, but merely regarded individuals as temporarily excluded, a wording which in the circumstances it is impossible, as Mr Metcalfe [the Director of Education] himself found in the witness box, to distinguish from being suspended. It merely begs the question to say that it could not be suspension because the proper machinery for suspension was not observed. The fact is that it was suspension, but the suspension procedure was not used. No doubt it would have been most inconvenient administratively, but that is not the point. What the councils desired to do was to suspend the plaintiffs, and indeed the others involved, without the necessity of restoring their salaries on reinstatement. It may be that it was hoped that thereby the threat of loss of salary would either act as a deterrent to action being taken, or perhaps if action were taken, that it would secure a more speedy return of those who had taken the action. There is, therefore, no valid ground on which the plaintiffs can be deprived of their salaries for the three and a half days when they were excluded, and they are accordingly entitled to succeed in this action.

(D) Warnings

See below, Chapter 10 on *Termination of Work*, pp. 346.

3. DISCIPLINARY PROCEDURES

In Chapter 10 on *Termination of Work*, a number of themes relating to disciplinary procedures are developed:

(a) the inability of the common law to develop standards of procedural justice (analogous perhaps to the rules of natural justice) in the sphere of employment;
(b) the existence of detailed disciplinary procedure agreements negotiated by trade unions;
(c) the view of the disciplinary process as more akin to a negotiating than an adjudicatory model;
(d) the changing attitude of the courts and tribunals towards failures by employers to adhere to procedure—whether collectively agreed, unilaterally adopted, or derived from the ACAS Code of Practice.

The implications of legal intervention in the internal discipline of an enterprise, even that limited to requiring adherence to disciplinary procedures, are described in the following extract (which discusses the problem in the context of unfair dismissal legislation).

H. Collins, *"Capitalist discipline and corporatist law"* (1982) 11 I.L.J. 78 and 170, at 87–88, 173–175

There was a crisis of industrial discipline in the late 1960s Because of the high levels of employment, the power of the shop floor workers was strong. A small group of employees could insist on their demands through quick, unofficial, "wildcat" strike action in the face of opposition from both management and union. . . .

It was in response to this challenge that the Donovan Commission and then successive governments proposed legislation on unfair dismissal. There was evidence that many unofficial stoppages were against dismissals, and it was hoped that the alternative legal mechanism would defuse these conflicts and discourage the use of unofficial shopfloor power to secure reinstatement. . . .

Thus the law of unfair dismissal was conceived in order to manage a crisis in industrial relations. The courts were broadly in sympathy with the purpose of this legislation, and they quickly stressed the importance of restoring order to industrial relations by insisting that proper procedures should be followed by employers before dismissing the employee. Warnings had to be given, an opportunity to improve was usually required, and the employee was entitled to a chance to explain his behaviour and so set the record straight. Failure by an employer to observe such procedural steps was penalised by a finding of unfair dismissal and an award of compensation. This emphasis upon procedures is not to be found in the words of [what is now EPCA, which] . . . only set out a broad standard of reasonableness. The courts obviously chose to stress this dimension of fairness because it fitted into the main purpose of the legislation from their point of view. It was hoped that if employers were induced to adhere to more elaborate procedural norms then there would be opportunities for second thoughts and conciliation, and thereby the incidence of industrial conflict might be reduced. . . .

The attention to procedural matters was perceived as less of an intrusion into industrial relations than the invasion which was threatened by a full-scale judicial review of the substantive merits of the management's decision to dismiss the employee. This interpretation of the concept of fairness was therefore also attractive because it minimised the extent of the departure from the traditional policy of legal abstentionism in the relations between capital and labour. At the same time as fulfilling the legislative aim of restoring order to industrial relations, the emphasis on procedure avoided the introduction of more penetrating interventionist reviews of managerial discretion to test whether their decisions accorded with broader ideals of industrial justice. . . .

Inevitably, a conflict develops between these procedural rights and the abstentionism of the tribunals over the general question of reasonableness. In a case where, in a tribunal's view, an employer acted within the range of reasonable responses of employers, but has in so doing ignored the accepted procedural standards, the tribunals are placed in a quandary. If they insist upon attention to procedural due process, their actions would amount to considerable interference with management and so compromise their pursuit of neutrality. On the other hand, if procedural requirements are ignored, there is a danger that the main purpose of the Act to restore order to industrial relations will be subverted because opportunities for compromise and conciliation may be lost. It is well-known that increasingly the courts have discounted the importance of fair procedures. . . .

The Court of Appeal held that a fair procedure is only one of the factors to be taken into account when assessing the reasonableness of the dismissal. Thus, even though there may be inadequate consultation or no warning at all, a dismissal will be fair provided that the management's response was within the range of reasonable reactions. . . .

The reason why the courts are currently choosing to resile from strict procedural requirements is . . . because there is a real conflict between the imposition of strict procedural standards and the general abstentionist approach to questions of fairness. The courts cannot on the one hand refuse to interfere with the decision within a range of reasonable responses and on the other rigorously test the fairness of the procedures according to the minutiae of the principles of natural justice. This contradiction in the reasoning of the courts is caused by their attitude towards the law of unfair dismissal as a piece of corporatist legislation. Whilst the judges approve of the ends of the law and so promote procedural fairness and sophisticated management techniques, at the same time they are uneasy about the means which are used because they lead to considerable state intervention in industrial relations and managerial discretion.

4. MUTUALITY IN DISCIPLINE: CONTROLLING EMPLOYER MISCONDUCT

Once the common law perspective of employer control is set aside, the problem of discipline is perceived as involving the control of behaviour at work. Equally, therefore, management behaviour may be subject to control. As there is no need for an employer monopoly over discipline (as demonstrated with regard to industrial practice, see above pp. 242 *et seq.*), workers may seek to discipline management.

An examination of the American experience of grievance arbitration illuminates this possibility. In the United States collective agreements almost invariably expressly prohibit unjust disciplinary action by the employer—and provide for arbitration by outside professionals of disputed cases. The system, moreover, also allows for complaints to be lodged concerning the behaviour of management: grievance arbitration.

H. Shulman, "*Reason, contract and law in labor relations*" (1955) 68 HARVARD LAW REVIEW 999 at 1007–8

While the details of the grievance procedure differ from one enterprise to another, its essence is a hierarchy of joint conferences between designated representatives of the employer and the union. But joint conferences even at the highest levels of authority may not, and frequently do not, result in agreement. In the absence of provision for resolution of stalemate, the parties are left to their own devices. Since grievances are almost always complaints against action taken or refused by the employer, a stalemate means that the employer's view prevails. Of course, in the absence of some restraint by contract or otherwise, the union is free to strike in order to reverse the employer's choice. But the union can hardly afford an all out strike every time it feels that a grievance has been unjustly denied. The consequence is either that unadjusted grievances are accumulated until there is an explosion, or that groups of workers, less than the entirety, resort to job action, small stoppages, slowdowns, or careless workmanship to force adjustment of their grievances.

The method employed by almost all industry today for the resolution of stalemates in the adjustment of grievances under the private rule of law established by the collective agreement is private arbitration by a neutral person. The largest enterprises provide for a standing umpire or arbitrator to serve for a stated period of time or so long as he continues to be satisfactory to both sides. The great majority of agreements provide for separate appointment of an arbitrator in each case. And the appointments in any case are made by the parties or by a method agreed upon by them.

The development of a system of grievance arbitration reflects the balance of power as well as the interests of the parties involved.

J. G. Getman, "*Labor arbitration and dispute resolution*" (1979) 88 YALE LAW JOURNAL 916, note 32 at 925–6, 933–4

Arbitration is provided for in over 94% of collective agreements. This fact, however, does not provide a total measure of its overall success. To some extent the prevalence of arbitration reflects the lack of acceptable alternatives and the potential usefulness of arbitration in achieving productivity when relations are acceptable. . . . Unions want an external check on management. It would be costly to bring suit each time they believed management violated the agreement, since this would require the constant use of lawyers and courts. Moreover, for various economic, historic and ideological reasons, unions seek to minimize the use of these institutions. Regular strikes would be tumultuous and costly. The National Labor Relations Board does not have jurisdiction over most breaches of contract. Of course, if unions were totally dissatisfied with arbitration they might agitate for special courts, but special courts would require a reversal of labor's historic distrust of government involvement and would be unlikely to solve the problems that unions experience with the grievance machinery. Besides, the fact that arbitration offers another technique for exerting bargaining pressure makes it at least as attractive, from a union's perspective, as other means of adjudication. Thus, it is easy to see why arbitration is liked by unions, whether or not it reduces strikes.

From management's perspective, the issue is more doubtful. If arbitration does not reduce strikes but instead gives the union a new source of pressure, why should management accept it so routinely? The fact that management regularly accepts arbitration does not mean that management always favors it. Provision for union security and limits on discipline, work assignment, and promotion, when lawful, are pervasive in collective agreements not because they are desired by management, but because they are sufficiently important for the union to insist on them as a precondition to agreement. The union will moderate other proposals to achieve such provisions. In addition, for management, most other techniques of dispute resolution have substantial drawbacks: court cases may be costly and may involve long delays during which the law of the shop may be confused; agencies or special courts involve government interference or oversight of managerial decision-making. Arbitrators partial to employers can be carefully selected and their role at least partially controlled. Moreover, if the parties do not pay for the dispute-resolution mechanism, the union may be motivated to pursue many more grievances. . . .

Disparities of power in the relationship that is the focus of a dispute are bound to be reflected in the mechanism used to resolve the dispute. When labor arbitration has been successful, it is because collective bargaining has established a rough equality and mutual respect between the parties.

In Britain, too, there are industrial relations procedures through which workers seek to control management behaviour. These reflect the unsystematic nature of British industrial relations, the conflict of formal and informal systems, and, in particular, the refusal to distinguish individual grievances and collective disputes as requiring different procedures.

N. Singleton, *"Industrial Relations Procedures"* DEPARTMENT OF EMPLOYMENT MANPOWER PAPER No. 14, (1975)

44 . . . A grievance procedure is commonly thought of as the method by which an individual raises some query or complaint about his or her pay or working conditions and the steps which are laid down for dealing with the matter. But a grievance can affect a group of individuals either in relation to working conditions *eg* the temperature in the workroom or in relation to matters affecting pay, such as the allocation of overtime or the grading of a group of employees. . . .

46 An unsettled grievance can clearly give rise to a dispute and it was no doubt with this evolution in mind that grievances and disputes procedures were grouped together in the terms of reference. Disputes also occur however through failure to agree on matters which originate in the negotiating procedure. Negotiating procedures . . . commonly provide for the steps to be taken in the event of failure to agree in negotiation, *ie* they may include a disputes procedure. A disputes procedure can therefore be a feature or element

of both a grievance and a negotiating procedure though some joint factory committees with negotiating functions do not make specific provision for the resolution of disputes. In some cases negotiating and grievance procedures with their associated disputes provisions are kept separate; in others the disputes procedure is used to process issues arising either from general negotiations or from the operations of the grievance procedure. Sometimes no distinction is made between a negotiating procedure and a grievance procedure where all dealings with union representatives are regarded as a form of negotiation or alternatively where all such business, including the response to wage claims, is regarded as dealing with grievances. Where there is a recognised distinction between negotiating and grievance procedures it may not be clear-cut in cases where the negotiating machinery is embodied as a stage in the grievance procedure or where an issue arising as a sectional grievance is adopted as the subject of a formal claim. . . .

49 In some of the cases studied the employee was expected in the first instance to go alone to his supervisor. If satisfaction was not obtained his shop steward could take the matter up with the supervisor, or perhaps with the next level of management. In some cases the employee would go on to the second level of management before the shop steward was involved. In some cases it was intended that the shop steward would only be involved if the employee so wished. At the other extreme it was accepted that the steward would make the first approach to management on behalf of the employee. In some cases the steward would go first not to the supervisor but to whichever representative of management he felt would be most likely to solve the problem quickly. Where written procedures existed it was rare indeed for the prescribed procedure to be consistently or universally followed. In particular, a provision precluding any form of shop steward involvement at the first stage of procedure, that is in the initial approach to the employee's immediate superior, was often disregarded. . . .

58 In some cases it was accepted practice for the union to make the approach first to management on behalf of the employee, for example in the printing industry. Generally, however, the normal practice—at any rate in theory—was for the individual to make his own first approach and this was widely reflected in written procedures. Here is an example from a chemical company:

> "If an employee wishes to make a complaint he should approach his supervisor before reporting to his shop steward. If no satisfactory agreement can be reached he should either see his manager or his shop steward who will try to reach a settlement with the supervisor, or if necessary, take the matter to higher authority."

This example reflects in writing the uncertainty which commonly exists as to what happens after failure to resolve [a complaint] at the first level of management. The language setting out the procedure is also more tentative than that used, for example, in the following extract from an engineering company's procedure, jointly agreed by management and the unions concerned:

> "In the event of a grievance arising in matters directly affecting work or conditions of work the employee concerned will take the matter up with his supervisor. At this stage the grievance concerns only the individual and it is expected that normally it will be resolved at this level. . . . "

61 Different considerations arise when a grievance affects a group of employees. A group needs a spokesman and, in a unionised establishment, the job will normally fall naturally to a union representative. In the case of a grievance affecting a group of employees responsible to the same supervisor,

the steward may approach the supervisor. In the case of a grievance affecting employees in more than one department, the first approach will probably be to a member of middle or senior management whose span of control extends to all the employees concerned, which may raise some problems in defining responsibilities. Many procedures, however, take no account at all of collective issues, having been constructed entirely round the handling of individual grievances, on the apparent assumption that such collective issues as do arise will be dealt with at the appropriate level. In only half of the domestic procedures analysed was there provision for a collective issue to be referred in the first instance to a stage in procedure beyond the first stage.

62 From the point of view of a steward or convenor, the "appropriate level" will be the level at which he considers he can most effectively negotiate and obtain speedy satisfaction for his members. Senior managers may disagree with the union representatives on what the appropriate level is, but through lack of clarity in the definition of responsibilities and through unwillingness to delegate responsibility they may find themselves in a weak position to challenge an over-centralised and top-heavy arrangement that has become established by custom and practice. In these situations the personnel department often bears a heavy burden in dealing with union representations on matters which could have been cleared with line management.

63 Many written procedures provide for a joint management–union committee as a stage in procedure. Most of the committees whose operation was examined in field inquiries took the form of a standing body, made up of equal numbers of management and trade union representatives, which met at regular intervals. . . .

64 Where a grievance procedure includes collective issues within its scope grievance handling readily merges into negotiation on claims and the existence as a stage in procedure of a joint body which is also the established negotiating body provides an integrated agency for resolving the matters at issue.

As with the American procedures, British procedures reflect the balance of power and the interests of different parties. The following extract indicates that pressure for the acceptance of grievance procedures can come from either management or workers, depending on the balance of power and interests.

B. Weekes, *et al.*, INDUSTRIAL RELATIONS AND THE LIMITS OF LAW (1975), pp. 172–174

The nature and function of procedures depend on traditional practice and the existing power relationship. In establishments where there is no kind of employee organization or representation, procedures are part of the managerial decision-making function and provide a method for dealing with personnel problems. A typical grievance procedure in such an establishment states: "If you feel you have a grievance, raise it verbally with your Department Head or Manager. He will investigate your complaint and report his findings to you. If not satisfied, you have a right of appeal to your area supervisor, verbally, who will communicate his findings to you." An employee with a grievance in a plant or office where there is no representation faces a number of difficulties if he wishes to prosecute his case with vigour. Management will be unaccustomed to the give and take which is implicit in a collective bargaining process. The employee will have no detailed information about how previous grievances have been handled. Finally, in the majority of cases, if management refuses to concede, the employee's only "sanction" will be to move to another job. Only where a disciplinary procedure, in an unorganized establishment, deals with a dismissal case covered by statutory unfair dismissal provisions, does the possibility of a sanction arise if the procedure is defective or unfairly operated.

Where a trade union or staff association has little bargaining power (perhaps because white-collar workers are involved) procedures may be a necessary prerequisite for the establishment of collective bargaining; for without these the employee organization has no obvious means of processing a grievance or claim beyond the first stage of negotiation. A union weakly organized at the work-place may seek procedures with an external final stage (probably involving [now ACAS]).

In establishments where trade union or work group bargaining strength is considerable there is no *a priori* reason for workers to support the introduction of procedures to deal with disputes, discipline or grievances. Shop-floor bargaining power is the effective limitation on managerial prerogative. Procedures have nevertheless been introduced into highly organized workplaces. Management may, for example, persuade union officials and work groups that the avoidance of disputes is in the interest of both sides and that a procedure in no way limits union or workers' power. Moreover, management may concede facilities for shop stewards, or include procedural reform as part of a general agreement on wages and conditions. Procedural reform in a well-organized establishment has therefore to emerge from the bargaining process.

In work-places where there exists a high level of trade union organization the character and operation of procedures vary considerably. We were told by some senior managers working at the centre of companies that they had only the vaguest impression of the actual operation of procedures in plants and offices. A number of trade union officers have told us that company-wide procedures are frequently ignored by plant managers. We have not looked in detail at how procedures operate at establishment level, but such evidence as we have suggests that many formal company-wide procedures are model procedures which establishments may or may not apply in detail. Alternatively, where company-wide procedures are expected to be effective, they are not necessarily followed in practice.

Informality plays an important part in procedural arrangements. There are national procedures which are unwritten and depend on the existence of a customary method of handling problems and disputes without immediate recourse to industrial action (*eg* in the wool industry). Full-time trade union officers, shop stewards and managers may work closely together, developing means of resolving disputes without using formal machinery. Once formal machinery is used it may mean that the immediate parties to a dispute lose control, either to a more senior level within the company or to the trade union hierarchy, or both.

In many of the companies we interviewed, it was management policy that procedures should be negotiated with trade union representatives (although in some companies unions refused to negotiate procedures), but the decision on particular questions in the last resort (after the unions had presented their case) rested with management (*ie* at each stage decisions of lower-level management were reviewed by other, more senior managers). Some employers' associations and nationalized industries have joint union/management panels at all procedural stages beyond the work-place. In effect this may mean that a settlement depends upon union concurrence. It may be argued that where trade unions exercise considerable power, management must have the consent of the union organization, or face industrial action. What this means in practice is that where unions are powerfully organized, and the issue is important to the unions, management's decision has to take account of the likely response by workers.

We conclude this section with two cases which illustrate an attempt by the Employment Appeal Tribunal to respond to workers protesting against management behaviour by developing a catalogue of employer misconduct which entitles workers to terminate the contract of employment and claim unfair dismissal (EPCA, s.55(2)(c): "constructive" dismissal). Unfortunately for workers, the use of the law has the enormous disadvantage that they will most probably never get their jobs back. So, faced with employer misconduct, workers must choose between job and justice. But these cases do illustrate the genesis of a law of discipline applicable to employers.

The Post Office v. Roberts
[1980] I.R.L.R. 347
Employment Appeal Tribunal

> The employee's application for a transfer was rejected on the grounds that there were "no available vacancies." Upon investigation, however, she discovered that the real reason for the rejection of her application was a negative assessment of her by a senior officer, which differed from other appraisals of her performance. She resigned and claimed "constructive" unfair dismissal.

TALBOT J.: [Counsel] cited a number of authorities: the first was *Isle of Wight Tourist Board v Coombes* [1976] IRLR 413. In that case the respondent had been a personal secretary to the appellant's director and in the course of an argument that director had spoken to another employee about her, saying that she was an "intolerable bitch on a Monday morning". The Employment Appeal Tribunal held that the relationship between the director and his personal secretary must be one of complete confidence and they must trust and respect each other, that in calling his secretary a "bitch" the employer's director had shattered that relationship. Thus, they confirmed the Industrial Tribunal's decision that there had been a constructive dismissal. . . .

The next case was *Courtaulds Northern Textiles Ltd v Andrew* [1979] IRLR 84. Again this was a case where words had been spoken in an argument. The words spoken by the assistant manager of the respondent were "You can't do the bloody job anyway." Again the Employment Appeal Tribunal, in this case Arnold J. presiding, referred to the implied term of the contract of employment that "the employers will not without proper reason and cause conduct themselves in a manner calculated or likely to destroy or seriously damage the relationship of confidence and trust between the parties". . . .

The next authority was *F C Gardner Ltd v Beresford* [1978] IRLR 63. In substance, the complaint in that appeal was that there had been no increase in pay for two years. Phillips J., giving the judgment of the Employment Appeal Tribunal, referred to the obligation on an employer not to behave arbitrarily, capriciously, or inequitably in matters of remuneration. . . .

Then there was the authority of *Robinson v Crompton Parkinson Ltd* [1978] IRLR 61. In that appeal Kilner Brown J. referred to this obligation of mutual trust and confidence. He said, in his judgment:

> "It seems to us, although there is no direct authority to which we have

been referred, that the law is perfectly plain and needs to be re-stated so that there shall be no opportunity for confusion in the future. In a contract of employment, and in conditions of employment, there has to be mutual trust and confidence between master and servant. Although most of the reported cases deal with the master seeking remedy against a servant or former servant for acting in breach of confidence or in breach of trust, that action can only be upon the basis that trust and confidence is mutual. Consequently where a man says of his employer, "I claim that you have broken your contract because you have clearly shown you have no confidence in me, and you have behaved in a way which is contrary to that mutual trust which ought to exist between master and servant," he is entitled in those circumstances, it seems to us, to say that there is conduct which amounts to a repudiation of the contract."

Mr Barry brought to our attention an authority on this matter, *British Aircraft Corporation Ltd v Austin* [1978] IRLR 332. In that case goggles, which were necessary for the work, had been provided for the respondent. She was unable to wear them because of her spectacles. She made complaints and they were not heeded or investigated and constructive dismissal was found. At paragraph 13 of the judgment of Phillips J, having referred to the case of *Western Excavating (ECC) Ltd v Sharp* [1978] I.C.R. 221, he said:

> "First of all, before looking at that case, it is desirable perhaps to say that that case and *Scott v Aveling Barford Ltd* [1977] I.R.L.R. 419 are by no means in total opposition, and if employers do behave in a way which is not in accordance with good industrial practice to such an extent—and this is how it was put in that case—that the situation is intolerable or the situation is that the employee really cannot be expected to put up with it any longer, it will very often be the case, that by behaving in that way the employers have behaved in breach of contract because it must ordinarily be an implied term of the contract of employment that employers do not behave in a way which is intolerable or in a way which employees cannot be expected to put up with any longer. That is an aside, and we certainly do not wish Industrial Tribunals to guide themselves otherwise than in accordance with the judgment in *Western Excavating (ECC) Ltd v Sharp*."

We would agree with Phillips J.'s statement that there may be conduct so intolerable that it amounts to a repudiation of contract. There are threads then running through the authorities whether it is the implied obligation of mutual trust and confidence, whether it is that intolerable conduct may terminate a contract, or whether it is that the conduct is so unreasonable that it goes beyond the limits of the contract. But in each case, in our view, you have to look at the conduct of the party whose behaviour is challenged and determine whether it is such that its effect, judged reasonably and sensibly, is to disable the other party from properly carrying out his or her obligations. If it is so found that that is the result, then it may be that a Tribunal could find a repudiation of contract.

Finally, therefore, we have to consider whether the conduct relied upon by the Industrial Tribunal was such that it was capable in law of amounting to repudiation by the Post Office. . . .

The Industrial Tribunal had evidence that the respondent's appraisal was that she was a capable worker. There was then the fact that Mr O'Keefe, without proper consideration (so the Industrial Tribunal found), had given her a bad report. There followed the refusal of her transfer, the reason given being that she was entitled to think meant that there were no vacancies for her job, when, in fact, it was because of Mr. O'Keefe's report. Finally, after some six weeks of inquiry she discovered fully the true reason for the refusal to transfer her. In our judgment, on those facts the Industrial Tribunal were entitled to come to the conclusion that the conduct of the employer had broken the vital trust and confidence that must exist, and entitled her to terminate the contract. That being something which, in our view, the Industrial Tribunal on the facts of this case were entitled to find, this appeal must be dismissed.

Woods v. WM Car Services (Peterborough) Ltd.
[1981] I.R.L.R. 347; [1982] I.C.R. 693
Employment Appeal Tribunal

Following a takeover of the firm for which she had worked for 28 years, the employee was subjected to persistent attempts by her new employers to alter the terms and conditions of her employment. She resisted successfully, but in the end resigned and claimed "constructive" unfair dismissal.

BROWNE-WILKINSON J.: In our view it is clearly established that there is implied in a contract of employment a term that the employers will not, without reasonable and proper cause, conduct themselves in a manner calculated or likely to destroy or seriously damage the relationship of confidence and trust between employer and employee: *Courtaulds Northern Textiles Ltd v Andrew* [1979] IRLR 84. To constitute a breach of this implied term, it is not necessary to show that the employer intended any repudiation of the contract: the Tribunals' function is to look at the employer's conduct as a whole and determine whether it is such that its effect, judged reasonably and sensibly, is such that the employee cannot be expected to put up with it: see *BAC Ltd v Austin* [1978] IRLR 332 and *Post Office v Roberts* [1980] IRLR 347 [see above p. 264]. The conduct of the parties has to be looked at as a whole and its cumulative impact assessed: *Post Office v Roberts* [at] paragraph 50.

We regard this implied term as one of great importance in good industrial relations. Quite apart from the inherent desirability of requiring both employer and employee to behave in the way required by such a term, there is a more technical reason for its importance. . . .

[The judge explained how it was only by demonstrating that it was employers' repudiation of the contract of employment that led to the employee leaving that an employee could claim "constructive" unfair dismissal.]

It is for this reason that we regard the implied term we have referred to as being of such importance. In our view, an employer who persistently attempts to vary an employee's conditions of service (whether contractual or not) with a view to getting rid of the employee or varying the employee's terms of service does act in a manner calculated or likely to destroy the relationship of confidence and trust between employer and employee. Such employer has therefore breached the implied term.

Any breach of that implied term is a fundamental breach amounting to a repudiation since it necessarily goes to the root of the contract: see *Courtaulds Northern Textiles Ltd v Andrew* (*supra*) at paragraph 11.

Applying those principles to the facts of this case, if the matter were for us to decide we would hold that the conduct of the company in this case did amount to a breach of the implied term. Although it may not be fair to describe the company's behaviour as unscrupulous, its actions were directed to inducing Mrs Woods to accept a change in her terms of service. Starting immediately after the takeover and for a period of four months thereafter the company tried unilaterally to reduce Mrs Woods' wages, to increase her hours of work, to change her job title, to change her contract of service, to change her job content fundamentally and to impose a job description which she considered to be more than she could manage. In the face of her protest, on each occasion (save the last) the company withdrew from its original requirement only to make a fresh requirement of a different kind. In the same period, the company gave her a verbal and written warning relating to her conduct which the Industrial Tribunal found to be unnecessary. All this was against the background that management was "gunning" for Mrs Woods, not to get rid of her but to get her to agree to a change in the terms of her contract which they desired, notwithstanding the fact that they had agreed to employ her on terms not less favourable in any respect than her previous employment with Mr Todd. The fact that such conduct was calculated or likely to damage seriously the relationship of confidence and trust between Mrs Woods and the company seems to us to be shown by the actual breakdown in the normal relationship between employer and employee that in fact occurred.

In the event the EAT found itself unable to overrule the Industrial Tribunal's decision in favour of the employers that their conduct did not amount to construction dismissal, a view which was upheld by the Court of Appeal (*cf.* p. 309 below).

Chapter 8

WORK AND FAMILY

In this chapter, we are concerned with the policy considerations underlying the law's treatment of workers: men and women, with families.

1. WORK AND FAMILY LIFE

We begin with an extract on the impact of family life on different workers, and particularly, as between men and women workers.

L. Rimmer and J. Popay, *"The Family at Work"*, EMPLOYMENT GAZETTE (June 1982), p. 255

Family responsibilities can affect an individual's ability to work, or their choice of employment. But there are currently substantial differences between the impact of family responsibilities on the employment of men and that of women.

For men a typical employment profile is to enter the labour force at the end of full-time schooling or training and to participate full-time until retirement. Only a very small proportion of men work part-time and they are most likely to do so as a prelude to retirement. For women, on the other hand, the employment profile is quite different. . . . [there is a] lower level of labour force participation of women in the 25–34 year age group and . . . the employment behaviour of non-married women is more like that of men than their married counterparts. What explains the differences in the employment profiles presented here?

It is clearly the case, supported by much research evidence, that women's employment behaviour is largely explained by their responsibility for young children. The presence of children affects the likelihood that a woman will work outside the home, whether or not she works "part-time" (or more generally the hours that she can work), and even the type of work she feels able to undertake. Mothers are far less likely to work than women without children. In 1979, 69 per cent of women without dependent children were working compared with only 52 per cent of those with dependent children. When mothers do work they are far more likely than other women to be working part-time. In 1979, 70 per cent of working mothers worked part-time compared with only 26 per cent of working women without dependent children.

Both the number of children for whom a woman is responsible and their ages affects her participation. But overall it is the age of the youngest child, and particularly the presence of a child under five, which is the main determinant of whether or not women work outside the home and whether or not they work full time. In 1979 only 28 per cent of women whose youngest child was under five were working; three-quarters of these mothers worked part-time. Despite a widespread assumption to the contrary, it is therefore still very rare for mothers with pre-school children to work full-time—indeed only six per cent of such mothers do so.

In addition to determining both the likelihood and the hours of work, it has also recently been suggested that home responsibilities influence the type of work undertaken. A study of female factory workers, for example, noted that "employment has to be fitted in with their household duties and child care arrangements which they and their families regard as unquestionably their responsibility. Factory work is often seen as the only job possible in the circumstances and entered into more from necessity than from choice. Similarly, a study of homeworkers concluded that "many mothers gave as their reason . . . the flexibility it gave them to work when it was convenient to them". . . .

. . . the proportion of fathers in work does not seem to vary with the age of their youngest child, nor with the number of dependent children in the family. In addition, whereas women with children tend to work fewer hours than those without, the majority of fathers work full-time and fathers of large families, who tend to have lower hourly earnings, work longer hours on average than fathers in small families. Equally a number of studies suggest that paid overtime is most common among younger married men especially those with dependent children whose financial commitments are often high: one study showed that married men under 30 with children worked four times as much paid overtime as similarly aged childless husbands. And men with children are similarly more likely to work shifts.

The General Household Survey of 1984 showed that only a quarter of working wives were in full-time employment, while men formed 71 per cent. of the full-time workforce. Among couples of working age, 57 per cent. of wives worked, compared with 84 per cent. of husbands. Both partners worked in 53 per cent. of the couples of working age surveyed. Only 15 per cent. of wives with dependent children worked full-time, compared with 74 per cent. of wives under 34 years old without children. Married women made up 27 per cent. of the total labour force, but in 1979 78 per cent. of all part-time workers. The notionally average man, married with two children and a non-working wife, in fact represented in 1979 only 5 per cent. of the total labour force, according to the survey.

Slightly less than half of all children under five (according to the 1979 Survey) attended play groups, day nurseries or school, or were regularly looked after by someone other than their parents. Few children less than a year old (12 per cent.) fell into this category, but the vast majority of four year olds (89 per cent.) did. Children of single parents were more likely to be looked after by a child-minder, relative or friend than to attend nursery school or a play group. Almost 40 per cent. of the children of full-time working mothers were regularly looked after by a relative outside the household. According to the survey, 58 per cent. of working mothers said that if their arrangements for having their children looked after fell through, they would have to give up work. And in the 12,000 households on which information was collected, only four children were in a day nursery, creche or play group provided by an employer (*Employment Gazette* (February 1982), p. 48).

Workers with families, therefore, have two alternatives. Either one member of the family has to give up full-time work—with consequent financial loss, or provision has to be made for child care and the performance of various family responsibilities. The cost of these latter has been variously estimated, as in the following extract.

EMPLOYMENT GAZETTE, *"Housework worth at least £7,000 a year"* (March 1982), p. 85

A conservative estimate of the annual value of housework was £7,000, said Dr Ellen Derow of the Policy Studies Institute at a symposium on women's work, paid and unpaid, organised by the Fawcett Society.

Her estimate was based on a comparison with the skills needed for jobs listed in the *New Earnings Survey* and was lower than some estimates, by a women's magazine and by insurance companies, by £4,000.

She based her costing for the childcare element of housework on the wages paid to nannies, which she found to be between £90 and £120 a week take home. At 14½ hours of childcare per week, a houseworker is worth £26.40 a week.

Home and domestic helpers earned 187.7p per hour, according to the NES, and Dr Derow calculated that the average houseworker spends 5 hours on laundry and clothes care.

On a basis of four hours shopping per week, at a rate of 194.7p per hour for comparability with a shop assistant, a houseworker could earn over £7 per week.

At six hours cleaning and gardening per week, rated at £2.18 per hour on a comparison with women caretakers and cleaners, a houseworker earns £13.80.

Travel, which included taking children to and from school, was compared with transport operatives and materials moving which at £2.05 per hour would give a weekly rate of £10.28.

Management and administration, which included tasks such as budgeting and planning, was estimated at 3½ hours per week at a rate of £3.34 per hour.

The total weekly earnings of a houseworker claiming comparability with women workers in different jobs would be £138.08, which gives an annual earning of £7,180.

But if a houseworker claimed comparability with a man in costing the various tasks involved in housework, the annual rate would rise to £8,393.

2. MATERNITY RIGHTS

Labour law has heretofore made little attempt to address the problems specific to workers with families. These issues are considered to be within the province of revenue law or social security law.

(A) The Common Law

The capacity, or lack of it, in the common law to develop rules to assist working mothers is revealed in the following case.

Lawrence v. Newham London Borough Council
[1977] I.R.L.R. 396; [1978] I.C.R. 10
Employment Appeal Tribunal

BRISTOW J.: In June 1974 Mrs Michele Lawrence, in response to an advertisement on behalf of the Council of the London Borough of Newham, applied for a job as cleaner at the Monega Road Infant School. She was seen by Mr Marsh, the caretaker, who had authority from the Council to engage cleaning staff for the school. She had a baby son, Jason, then four months old. She explained her position to Mr Marsh and made it clear that she could not take the job unless she could bring Jason with her.

Mr Marsh said that he would have to find out if she could bring the baby with her. He referred to higher authority and after doing so told Mrs Lawrence that she could start with the baby as long as it did not interfere with her work.

Mrs Lawrence worked at the school until February 1976. Her hours were 0630 to 0830 and 1530 to 1830 Monday to Friday in term time, and 0630 to 1200 in the holidays. As the months went by Jason ceased to be a baby horizontal in a pram. He became mobile first with the help of a 'baby walker,' and then on his own. He had a minor accident at the school and then, after Mr Marsh had retired and been succeeded by Mr Jones, a nasty fall after which he was taken to hospital. The structure and some of the appurtenances of the school included sources of potential danger to an active two-year-old.

Mr Jones in February 1976 came to the conclusion that Mrs Lawrence must be asked to make other arrangements for Jason to be looked after when she was at work. He was not prepared to accept the responsibility in case Jason was involved in an accident on the school premises. He did not consider that Mrs Lawrence could pay proper attention to her work if she had to have Jason with her at the different places and floors where she cleaned. He was not prepared to let Jason wander about unsupervised as he pleased. So he asked Mrs Lawrence to make other arrangements for Jason.

Mrs Lawrence refused to do so and said that Mr Jones did not have the authority to ask her. On 5.2.76 she was asked in writing to arrange at once to stop bringing Jason. She refused. On 16.2.76, after a final warning and a meeting in the presence of a representative of NUPE, her union, and of Mr Jones's union, GMWU, Mrs Lawrence was dismissed. She resorted to the appropriate Council appeal procedures and on 7.4.76 she was informed that her appeal had been disallowed. . . .

When you try to express in the terminology of the law of contract the effect of the conversation in June 1974 between Mrs Lawrence and Mr Marsh, you have to do so in its context. Jason was then a four months' old baby. Mrs Lawrence would not have taken the job had she not been able to have him with her. While he was a baby in his pram, horizontal and immobile, his presence on the job would be very unlikely to interfere with his mother's work or that of the other cleaners, and he would be reasonably safe. Mr Marsh made it clear to Mrs Lawrence that he had to refer the Jason question to higher authority: and that the answer was, she could start with Jason so long as he did not interfere with her work.

But everyone concerned must have realised that the time would come when Jason, mobile, must inevitably interfere with his mother's work in an environment containing hazards to the safety of small children. The proposition that Mrs Lawrence was entitled to insist on bringing him with her until he became an interference immediately poses the problem, how and by whom is the question, has be become an interference, to be decided? Is it to be by Mrs Lawrence herself, or the caretaker, or someone higher up the Council hierarchy, or her union shop steward, or by whom?

There was evidence before the Tribunal that other members of the school staff brought their children to work from time to time, and it was submitted that this was something from which the Tribunal should have drawn the inference that Mrs Lawrence had the contractual right, for which she contended, to bring Jason. We do not agree. Any humane employer in this field might well in emergency be ready to put up temporarily with the reduction of efficiency involved in allowing a young child to accompany his mother to work. That would not mean that the mother had a contractual right to do so.

In addition to these considerations, in this case, even if the contract were as Mr Hendy [counsel for Mrs Lawrence] contends, the Tribunal found as a fact that by February 1976 Jason's presence must have been a distraction to his mother at work. Even on Mrs Lawrence's case therefore the Council was entitled as a matter of law to require her to cease bringing him, and the Tribunal was on this basis also fully entitled to find, as it did, that her dismissal for insisting that she had the right to go on bringing him was not unfair.

(B) Statutory Provisions

The only area of intervention by statute so far, has been when a working woman takes time off work to have a child and provide for:

- (i) the right to take paid time off for ante-natal care;
- (ii) the right to maternity pay (prior to April 6, 1987 nine-tenths of a week's pay less maternity allowance, payable for a maximum six weeks);
- (iii) the right to return to work within 29 weeks of the birth; and
- (iv) the right not to be dismissed because of pregnancy or reasons connected with it (EPCA, ss. 31A and 60, Pt. III, and Sched. 2 and the Sex Discrimination Act 1975).

Prior to April 1987 these provisions overlapped with social security law which provided that a working woman was eligible for a maternity allowance of £27.25 for 18 weeks beginning with the 11th week before the date on which the baby was expected to be born, provided she had made appropriate national insurance contributions. The following extract explains how the provisions on maternity pay in labour law co-existed with social security provisions.

R. Upex and A. Morris, *"Maternity rights—illusion or reality?"* (1981) 10 I.L.J. 218

Whilst the employment and the social security legislation clearly aim to provide a minimum level of protection and benefits for pregnant employees, it is also clear that low-paid women in part-time employment are amongst those who fail to satisfy the qualifying conditions. In addition, the very existence of the dichotomy between the two schemes results, inevitably, not only in divided responsibilities between the Department of Employment (DE) and the Department of Health and Social Security (DHSS), but also in increased problems for the employer and employee seeking to comply with the qualifying conditions. The unfortunate results of having two separate systems working on different, complex qualifications will not be avoided until the whole scheme of maternity provision has been withdrawn and co-ordinated.

Who benefits? (i) Numbers of working women

Much has been said about the problems created for employers by protective employment legislation, and in particular about the administrative problems related to maternity pay and reinstatement. Apart from those few disputes which reach a tribunal, how far has the scheme added to the burdens of the employer? In December 1980, the number of people in employment in the United Kingdom was 21,812,000 of whom 9,168,000 were women. It has been calculated that, each year, 3.6 per cent. of working women stop work to have a baby (*ie* 330,000). Since approximately 760,000 women have babies each year, 43 per cent. of all women who have babies were working when they became pregnant. These are the women who comprise the prospective beneficiaries, or viewed another way, the potential problems. It is, however, instructive to compare the above figures with what may be termed the "take up" figures. Two questions arise: how many women qualify for the benefits and, of those, how many actually take advantage of them?

(ii) Numbers benefiting

In relation to the financial benefits alone, ie maternity grant, maternity allowance and maternity pay, the DHSS has calculated that, of all the women who have babies in a year (*supra*), 60,000 (7.9 per cent.) qualify for no benefit at all; 310,000 (40.9 per cent.) qualify for only the maternity grant; 270,000 (35.5 per cent.) may claim the grant and the allowance; 40,000 (5.26 per cent.) the grant and maternity pay, whilst only 80,000 (10.53 per cent.) qualify for all three payments. These figures are reflected in the findings of the EOC that, since the introduction of the right to maternity pay in April, 1977, only 202,776 women have taken it up, *ie* 3.1 per cent. of the total female working population of child-bearing age. . . . In our view, piecemeal reform or the clarification of unclear provisions are insufficient to remedy the defects which we hope we have illustrated. We would suggest that the whole system should be re-drawn and put into a single code, so that the overlap between social security and employment legislation is eliminated and the differences in the interpretation of words and phrases in the present set-up are ironed out.

Since April 6, 1987 a two-tier "statutory maternity pay" (SMP) for 18 weeks replaces maternity allowances, provided by Social Security and maternity pay provided by employers except in the case of self-employed women and women without the 26 weeks service with the employer by the 14th week before the week of expected confinement, which is a prerequisite to entitlement to SMP (Social Security Act 1986, ss.46–50, *cf*. 377 I.R.R.R. 9). The operation of the pre-1987 maternity leave provisions in practice was explored in a survey covering 41 public sector organisations and 220 private sector firms employing 1,247,000 people, 407,000 of whom were women.

INDUSTRIAL RELATIONS REVIEW AND REPORT, No. 217 (February 1980), p. 8

Take-up rates

Our survey shows that the take-up rates for maternity pay (1.9% of the women covered in the survey) is roughly in line with the national figures (2.2% of working women). However, of that 1.9% only 0.3% took maternity leave and returned to work.

These figures are relatively low and could be accounted for by a number of factors such as the fact that the proportion of the total labour force leaving work because of pregnancy is probably fairly small, the fact that some women leaving because of pregnancy will not have served two years with one employer and will not therefore be entitled to the statutory maternity provisions and the lack of State or company child-care facilities which may make it impossible for many women to return to work after the birth of their child.

More interesting are the figures . . . which show that of the 7930 women taking maternity pay, 60% indicated that they intended to return to work, whereas only 15% *actually* returned. . . .

Status of contract of employment

The Employment Protection (Consolidation) Act 1978, s.33(3) states that a woman who fulfills the stipulated qualifications is entitled to maternity pay and maternity leave *"whether or not a contract of employment subsists during the period of absence"*.

The dilemma facing many employers when the maternity provisions first came into force, was how to deal with the contract of employment of a woman who was now to take (for the first time in many cases) paid maternity leave with a contractual right to return to her job up until 29 weeks after the birth. Should the personnel department terminate the contract and re-issue a new one if the woman actually returned? Or should the woman be "kept on the company's books" and be treated as an employee on extended unpaid leave, with the contract of employment merely suspended, until it was actually known whether or not she was coming back? In some companies the policy decision was taken that the contract should be terminated and a new one issued in the "rare" event (it was thought) that the woman returned to work. This, it was felt, would be far easier than having a number of "ghost" employees still technically employed by the company. It was feared that the time span that could elapse—some 40 weeks—might induce errors in administration which could result in a total failure to actually terminate the contract.

With over three years' experience of the provisions, employers have been able to sort out these difficulties and our survey reveals that a substantial proportion of employers—88% of respondents to our question on the status of the contract of employment during maternity leave—said that they treated the contract of employment as "suspended" until the woman returns to work—as if she is on extended unpaid leave. . . .

Only 12% terminate the contract and re-issue the contract if the woman returns. In either case, the law provides that whether or not the contract of employment subsists during this time, the period of absence will count for computation of statutory rights such as redundancy, notice and unfair dismissal and the woman will be treated as if she was never away. Contractual rights such as holidays, pension, seniority and other service-related benefits are "frozen" during maternity leave—the period(s) of employment prior to the leave and after the leave are in effect joined for computation purposes but the period of absence is disregarded.

Some companies, eg the Intercontinental Hotel and Cadbury Schweppes (Bournville site) permit contractual rights to accrue (excluding holiday entitlement) during the period of absence.

Cover during leave

A genuine concern of employers was how they would cope whilst their employees were absent. There are basically four options open to employers:

—to hire temporary replacements—77% respondents to our question on how employers cover during maternity leave did this;

—to hire permanent replacements—35% did this;
—to temporarily upgrade existing staff—43% did this; and
—to re-allocate work amongst existing staff—19% did this.

Many respondents to this question said that they were able to cover for absent employees on maternity leave by employing a combination of these options depending on the nature of the work to be covered, the size and location of the unit, the availability of staff and company attitudes.

Another survey of the operation of the maternity legislation made the following finding specifically on the right to return to work.

W. W. Daniel, "*Women's experience of maternity rights legislation*" DEPARTMENT OF EMPLOYMENT GAZETTE (May 1980), p. 468

A very substantial minority of women were back in work eight months after they had the baby. The proportion represented a marked increase in the level less than ten years previously. Data from the 1971 census suggested that nine per cent of recent mothers were economically active as long as 12 months after having had the baby. Our survey showed that, of all women who had babies in February or March of 1979, 15 per cent were in paid work around eight months later and a further nine per cent were looking for some kind of work. Of recent mothers who worked during pregnancy, 24 per cent were in work about eight months after the baby. The difference between the census figures and our survey findings represents a marked change in the nature of the labour market which has wide implications. The right to reinstatement was introduced in the middle of the period to which the difference relates. We were not able, however, to attribute that difference to the right.

First only one-fifth of all women who returned to work went back to jobs on a basis that conformed with the statutory requirements.

[This is particularly significant as compliance with statutory rights has been rigidly required even where the woman is seeking to rely on a *contractual* right to return: see *Lavery* v *Plessey Telecommunications Ltd.* [1983] I.R.L.R. 202 (C.A.); *Kalfor Plant Ltd.* v *Wright* [1982] I.R.L.R. 311 (E.A.T.); *McKnight* v *Adlestones (Jewellers) Ltd.* [1984] I.R.L.R. 483 (N.I.C.A.).]

Only one-third of those who returned to the same employer went back to the same job, working the same hours, after having given notice of return. Most women returned to work on the basis of reduced weekly hours. Secondly, and more importantly, we were not able to identify, in our analysis of the sources of variation in the extent to which women returned to work, any effect from the reinstatement right. The chief sources of variation in whether women returned to work, and indeed whether they remained with the same employer, were associated with the hours they had worked previously, the level of job they had done, the level of pay they had received and the type of employer for whom they had worked. . . .

It appeared to be women's level of involvement in work, and the convenience or practicalities associated with working, that influenced the extent to which they returned. When we asked women what changes they would like to see to make it easier for mothers to work they gave overwhelming priority to improved child-care facilities, especially nurseries or creches at the place of work. Secondly, they sought more flexible working hours to enable them to combine the demands of motherhood with those of working.

The maternity rights legislation in the EPCA gives little attention to either the desire for child-care facilities or for greater flexibility of working hours. EPCA, s.48 sought, apparently, to render the statutory right to return to work more flexible by embracing any contractual right to return to work and providing that the employee "may in returning to work take advantage of whichever right (contractual or statutory) is, in any particular, the more favourable." The first E.A.T. decision on the provision is analysed in the following extract.

B. Bercusson, Annotation to EPCA, s.48, in THE EMPLOYMENT ACTS 1974–1980 (C. D. Drake and B. Bercusson, ed. 1981)

In *Bovey* v *The Board of Governors of the Hospital for Sick Children* [1978] I.R.L.R. 241 (E.A.T.) a *full-time* physiotherapist Grade 1 took maternity leave, but before going on leave she *agreed* to return to work as a *part-time* physiotherapist on the *basic* grade. On her return she sought to select the most favourable aspects of her statutory and contractual rights—to return to her original job (Physiotherapist Grade 1), as per the statute; and to work part-time, as per the agreement. The E.A.T. denied her this right on a number of grounds: (1) "a contract of employment" in s.48(1) means the contract under which she worked when she departed, so the agreement to return is not covered by this subsection—but there is no warrant for such a narrow interpretation; (2) anyway, the agreement to return to work part-time was "merely a collateral agreement," again not within the terms of the Act—but collateral agreements may be legally enforceable, and Mrs Bovey did in fact return to work under it; (3) "There must be a limit to the extent to which the right in question, to return to work, can be sub-divided so as to identify the particular respects in which it is more favourable." Here the right to work part-time on the basic grade was held indivisible—but it is submitted that there is nothing to support the principle—the Act does say "in any particular respect," and here the facts were eminently suited to such sub-division.

The real reason for the decision is the E.A.T.'s view that it would "produce an absurdity." This seemed to rely on two approaches. First, and somewhat peculiar, was eugenics. Phillips J. repeatedly referred to the "strange" result of the combination of rights, a "mulish" and "illegitimate" progeny. Maternity rights provoke peculiar responses.

But secondly, it was stated that the two lay members of the Tribunal were "convinced that if assent were given to this proposition and it were applied generally in industry, it would have most unfortunate and inconvenient consequences." The E.A.T. did not elaborate, but clearly referred to the conclusion of the Industrial Tribunal at first instance that if the employee was to be allowed to utilise a composite right "no employer could ever safely offer a woman the opportunity of employment on a part-time basis on different terms as to remuneration as this might lead to a claim similar to that now advanced on behalf of Mrs Bovey. The Tribunal would be extremely reluctant unless compelled by the clear language of the statute to come to a decision which might deprive a mother who had previously filled a full-time appointment of the opportunity of an offer of part-time employment which might be beneficial to her" ([1977] I.R.L.R. 417).

The result is, in true paternalist fashion, that the E.A.T. has denied women statutory rights to allow for the *possible* exercise of employers' benevolence. So long as they cannot demand their rights, they may be allowed to benefit from employers' goodwill. Perhaps the E.A.T. should have noted the agreed facts before the Industrial Tribunal at first instance, which included the statement that the employers here "for reasons which *seem good and sufficient to them*, do not employ Senior Physiotherapists Grade 1 on a part-time basis at Great Ormond Street Hospital, although there *are* part-time physiotherapists *on that grade* at other hospitals within the N.H.S., and there is an established national hourly rate of pay for *part-time* staff *on that grade*" (my italics). Rather than resort to dubious statutory interpretation to avoid what they characterised as an absurdity, the E.A.T. might have backed up the woman here in her battle against the absurdity—by requiring the hospital to do what other hospitals had done and follow established practice.

A final point made by the E.A.T. will confirm doubts as to the capacity of all-male Tribunals to decide questions of maternity rights. Referring to the woman's right to take advantage of whichever right is in any particular respect the *more favourable* the E.A.T. asked "who is to judge what are 'the more favourable' (terms); that is to say, is it objective or is it according to the circumstances of the employee. For example, is part-time employment more favourable? And so on; it depends on what one wants, one supposes." One awaits with trepidation a Tribunal's view of what is "objectively" more favourable to women seeking to return to work.

The inadequacy of the specific legislation on maternity rights in EPCA may be compensated for, to some extent, by a liberal interpretation of the Sex Discrimination Act 1975. In a subsequent case, the E.A.T. referred to the "limited and special rights afforded to mothers over the period of confinement, and shortly thereafter, by the Act of 1978" as not precluding mothers seeking to return to work from complaining under the Sex Discrimination Act 1975 (*The Home Office* v. *Holmes* [1984] I.R.L.R. 299 (E.A.T.), at p. 301). While careful to emphasise that each case would depend on its facts, the E.A.T. was prepared to find that an employer who required a mother to return to work full-time after the birth of a child had indirectly discriminated against women without justification (see above, Chapter 6 on *Discrimination and Inequality*).

The Home Office v. Holmes
[1984] I.R.L.R. 299
Employment Appeal Tribunal

Ms Holmes was one of 250 employees (men and women), all of whom were required by the terms of their engagement to work full-time. Following the birth of her first child, she had great difficulties in fulfilling her duties as an employee and as a mother. In the two years and eight months following the birth she was forced to take two years and two months unpaid leave before she could resume normal working. After the birth of her second child, she requested that she be allowed to come back on a part-time basis; her request was refused.

WAITE J.: The first question the Tribunal members asked themselves was this: did the requirement of full-time service in Ms Holmes's contract of employment amount to a requirement or condition? There was no dispute that if it did, it was one which applied or was applicable within her grade and her department equally to a man. The Tribunal took the view, in answer to that question, that her obligation to serve full-time was, indeed, a condition or requirement within the terms of [the Sex Discrimination Act 1975] s.1(1)(b). They said it was an essential term of her engagement because unless she went on working full-time she would not be allowed to continue in her job.

The second question they asked themselves was whether this requirement or condition (*ie* the requirement of full-time service) was such that the proportion of women who could comply with it is considerably smaller than the proportion of men who could comply with it. They reached the answer to that one unhesitatingly. It was yes; and the reason was that despite the changes in the role of women in modern society, it is still a fact that the raising of children tends to place a greater burden upon them than it does upon men.

Next, they posed for themselves the question whether the Home Office had been able to show the requirement or condition to be justifiable irrespective of the sex of the person to whom it was applied. This question brought them into the area of detailed evidence . . . . They very carefully considered departmental reports and other relevant data and statistics including the recommendations emanating from a joint review group established by the Civil Service National Whitley Council. They heard on this same issue, too, the oral evidence on the Home Office side of two senior representatives; and on Ms Holmes' side the evidence of her union representative and herself. Their finding was that, in all the circumstances, they had no hesitation in preferring the evidence on those issues put forward on behalf of Ms Holmes, and they therefore found that the Home Office had been unable to show the requirement or condition of full-time service to be a justifiable one.

Then the Industrial Tribunal turned to the last of the questions demanded of them by s.1 of the Act. They asked themselves whether the requirement or condition of full-time service was to her detriment because she could not comply with it. That was an issue on which very little evidence was required, and they expressed their finding briefly. They took the view that the requirement was to her detriment and that she could not comply with it, adding the comment that her parental responsibilities prevented her carrying out a normal full-time week's work, and that in trying to fulfil all of these at the same time she had had to suffer excessive demands on her time and energy.

But that did not exhaust the line of self-interrogation imposed upon the Tribunal by the Act, for having been satisfied as to the matters raised by s.1, they were then required to turn to s.6 of the Act which contains the definition of unlawful discrimination within an employment context. Subsection (2) of that section renders it unlawful for a person, in the case of a woman employee, to discriminate against her in a number of ways which, it is common ground, are not applicable to this case, but then goes on to say "by dismissing her, or subjecting her to any other detriment".

Ms Holmes, of course, was never dismissed. So the Tribunal had to ask whether the Home Office had, within the terms of the section, subjected her to any other detriment. Again without hesitation, they answered that question by saying that she had been so subjected. They said it was all one and the same detriment. She was being compelled to do a duty with which she could not, in the circumstances, comply.

Having thus arrived at an affirmative answer to all the questions they posed themselves down the line of self-enquiry [*sic*], the Industrial Tribunal came to the conclusion that a case of unlawful discrimination on the ground of Ms Holmes' sex was made out. . . .

The scheme of the anti-discrimination legislation involves casting a wide net throwing upon employers the onus of justifying the relevant requirement or condition in particular instances. One must be careful, however, not to fall into the error of assuming that because the net is wide, the catch will necessarily be large. Mr Goldsmith [counsel for the Home Office] eloquently invited us to envisage the shock to British industry and to our national and local government administration which, he submitted, would be bound to be suffered if, in addition to all their other problems, they now had to face a shoal of claims by women full-time workers alleging that it would be discriminatory to refuse them part-time status. In answer to that we emphasise, as did the Industrial Tribunal in the last sentence of their decision, that this one case of Ms Holmes and her particular difficulties within her particular grade in her particular department stands very much upon its own. It is easy to imagine other instances, not strikingly different from hers, where the result would not be the same. There will be cases where the requirement for full-time staff can be shown to be sufficiently flexible as arguably not to amount to a requirement or condition at all. There will be cases where a policy favouring full-time staff exclusively within a particular grade or department is found to be justified. There will be cases where no actual or no sufficient detriment can be proved by the employee. All such cases will turn upon their own particular facts. We only decide today that in this case the Industrial Tribunal were right, in our view, in saying that a case of unlawful discrimination had been made out.

The cautionary words of Waite J. in the final paragraph quoted above were borne out by his decision in *Kidd* v. *DRG (UK) Ltd.* [1985] I.R.L.R. 195 (E.A.T.), which dismissed an appeal by a part-time woman selected for redundancy for that reason. He upheld the Tribunal which dismissed her claim on the grounds, *inter alia*, that evidence was not presented to show (at p. 192):

> " . . . that a considerably greater proportion of women than of men, or (amongst women) or married than of unmarried women, regularly undertake a child-caring role precluding their acceptance of full-time employment."

As to the apparent conflict with *The Home Office* v. *Holmes* (and also with other cases concerning dismissal of part-time women in redundancy situations: *Clarke and Powell* v. *Eley (IMI) Kynoch Ltd.* [1982] I.R.L.R. 482—see above, Chapter 6 on *Discrimination and Inequality*, p. 198), Waite J. was content to observe that "a degree of uncertainty as to how a particular Tribunal will react to particular circumstances is . . . inevitable," but that it was preferable to (p. 196):

> " . . . enunciating broad principles of universal application whose enforcement would run the risk of leading in some cases to injustice and in others to the important aims of anti-discrimination becoming exposed to criticism or even ridicule as a result of discrimination being held to have occurred in trivial or absurd instances far outside the spirit of the legislation."

The uncertainty is highlighted by the case law on dismissal by reason of pregnancy. An E.A.T. decision of 1980 (*Turley* v. *Allders Department Stores Ltd.* [1980] I.R.L.R. 4 (E.A.T.)) which held that dismissal because of pregnancy was not sex discrimination was only dissented from in 1985, when Waite J. determined that it should not be treated as authority ((1) *Hayes* v. *Malleable Working Men's Club and Institute, (2) Maughan* v. *North East London Magistrates' Court Committee* [1985] I.R.L.R. 367 (E.A.T.)).

CHAPTER 9

SICKNESS AND INJURY

The problem of sickness and injury (for workers) primarily concerns security of earnings during their absence from work (the problem of security of employment is dealt with in Chapter 10 on *Termination of Work*, below, pp. 365 *et seq*.). To some extent this problem was instrumental in the formation of mutual assistance schemes which gave rise to the early trade unions which provided such benefits (see below, Chapter 14 on *Internal Affairs of Trade Unions*, pp. 691 *et seq*.). Later still, it gave rise to social legislation which sought to compensate workers for illness and injury—and slowly and unevenly, there developed collective bargaining which established many of today's occupational sick pay schemes. The common law's treatment of sick pay is particularly fascinating as the judges have sought to accommodate classical concepts of contract law with different labour market conditions and changes in social legislation. The fluctuations in judicial attitudes are evident in the cases, all the more so when contrasted with industrial practice.

1. INDUSTRIAL PRACTICE

Income during absence from employment due to sickness or injury is not available equally to all workers. Employees in the public sector and white-collar employees are more likely to be covered, and to be covered by less restrictive schemes than are private sector and manual employees respectively. So while some industrial processes are noticeably more apt to cause ill-health and injury, these industries, do not (with the exception of mining) enjoy the most beneficial sick pay schemes.

The overall percentage of full-time male employees covered by an occupational sick pay scheme is reported to have risen from 57 per cent. in 1961 to 80 per cent. in 1976, but considerable variations by industry have occurred. The highest coverage for both men and women occurred in public administration followed by public utilities, banking and professional employment. Mining formed an exception among labour intensive industries which otherwise revealed considerably lower coverage with shipbuilding, textiles and leather around 50 per cent.

(A) Short-term Illness

The following extract is from a review of 53 public and private sick pay schemes.

INDUSTRIAL RELATIONS REVIEW AND REPORT No. 273 (June 1982), p. 2

According to the DHSS, almost 90 per cent. of full-time employees are covered by an occupational sick pay scheme. Some schemes are completely discretionary, in that management makes a decision on each occasion whether or not to pay employees who are off sick and how much to pay them. Most schemes, however, form part of an employee's contract of employment and there are fixed scales which determine how much a sick employee is paid and for what period. But even when this is the case, management usually retains discretion to withhold payment if it is suspected that an employee is not genuinely ill, and to make additional payments after an employee's entitlement has been exhausted.

Who qualifies for sick pay?

Most of the schemes require employees to serve a qualifying period before they become entitled to sick pay. Three months is a common qualifying period. . . .

While some companies have a single sick pay scheme which applies to all employees others have two or more schemes applying to manual workers, white collar workers and senior staff. Where this is the case the qualifying period for manual workers is generally longer than that for staff. . . .

Turning to the public sector, there is no clear pattern. No qualifying service is required in the Civil Service, the BBC or at British Aerospace. IBA employees do not qualify unless they have a year's service and in the local authorities staff qualify immediately while manual workers do not qualify until they have six months' service. . . .

Duration of sickness payments

One of the key questions arising when negotiating a sick pay scheme is: for what period of sickness absence will employees be paid? The range of annual entitlements . . . is considerable, and in almost all organisations long-serving employees are entitled to receive sick pay for longer periods than short-serving employees. . . .

What is [the sick pay] year?

Most schemes define sick pay entitlement in terms of benefit payable per year. The definition of a year for these purposes varies between companies. In some instances the calendar year is used, in others it is the tax year, the holiday year (however defined), the year starting with the date an employee began work with the company, or a rolling 12 month period.

It is very important that the "year" is clearly defined in any sick pay scheme as it can significantly affect the length of time for which an employee receives sick pay. For example, a company scheme might entitle employees to full pay for two months a year, and a particular employee may be off work for the whole of February and March and for the whole of May and June. If the entitlement year ran from January to December, the employee would only be paid for February and March, but if the entitlement year equalled the tax year, the period of absence would fall in different years and the employee would be entitled to payment for both periods. . . .

How soon do payments start?

. . . Generally speaking, . . . occupational sick pay schemes no longer require employees to serve waiting days, but pay sick pay for all days of sickness absence. (A DHSS survey in 1974 found that 70 per cent. of full-time men and 86 per cent. of full-time women qualify for sick pay from the first day of sickness absence.)

Nearly all the sick pay schemes in our survey provide for payments to begin on the first day of absence and for payments to be made even where the absence lasts for only one or two days. . . .

It is very rare for white collar staff to be required to serve waiting days, but some schemes do stipulate that manual workers are not paid for their first three days off work. . . .

How much sick pay?

Most of the company and public sector sick pay schemes . . . base the level of payment for initial periods of sickness absence on normal wages. But four of the five industry-wide agreements set a weekly cash sum and in each case the figure is substantially below normal earnings.

Where it is agreed that employees should be no worse off, and no better off, when they are sick than when they are at work, the most obvious course is to award normal pay less an amount equal to the State sickness benefit being claimed by the employee. However this raises two questions: how much is "normal pay" and how much should be deducted from this to offset the benefit being claimed?

Where an employee receives only a basic wage or salary, and this does not fluctuate from week to week, there is no problem in defining normal pay. But many employees receive productivity-related bonuses, payments for working shifts or overtime and allowances of some kind. Some employers argue that there is no reason to pay overtime rates to employees who are not working, but this is countered by the union response that where overtime is worked regularly, employees come to count upon the overtime pay. Some of the schemes in our survey stipulate that sick pay is calculated on the basis of normal earnings or full pay. Elsewhere basic pay is taken. . . .

Sickness during holidays

In devising a sick pay scheme consideration should be given to what will happen when an employee is sick while off work on holiday. So far as public holidays are concerned, the usual practice is for employees to receive the normal rate of public holiday pay—rather than sick pay—and not to be allowed to take a lieu day later in the year. (This means that if a public holiday falls in the middle of a period of sickness absence, holiday pay is given for that day and sick pay is paid for the other days.)

However, where sickness coincides with a period of annual holiday, employees are usually allowed to take their holiday at some other time, provided the illness is certificated, and they receive sick pay rather than holiday pay for the period of sickness. . . .

Comparing the schemes

It is difficult to make direct comparisons between the schemes covered by our survey. Some schemes clearly provide better cover than others, but many of the schemes have one good feature—a short qualifying period, a long period of entitlement or a high level of payment but are less generous as far as the other elements are concerned.

(B) Long-term Illness

Most schemes provide for some form of examination in the case of long-term sickness. This may simply take the form of a requirement to submit to independent medical examination.

Calor Gas

> "In cases of prolonged or recurring periods of sickness absence the company may require an independent medical examination by a company doctor."

Many employers supplement medical examination with a system of sick visiting partly designed to detect misconduct likely to impede recovery.

Alcan Booth Sheet Ltd.

> "In the case of a long absence sickness visiting will take place. The company may, in certain circumstances, request [that] the individual is examined by the works doctor."

Dismissal may be avoided by schemes which provide for transfer to some form of holding list.

Associated Octel Company Ltd.

> "In the 25th week of service the company would write advising the employee that the benefit entitlement is about to expire. After the 26th week benefit stops, but the employee is placed on the "special leave without pay" register and stays there for 18 months; if unable to return during that time the employee's GP would be contacted by the company's chief medical officer who might then recommend early retirement depending on the circumstances."

Others provide forms of early retirement pensions.

Gulf UK Ltd.

> "An employee who sustains a very serious or long term disability and has completed one year's service may be eligible for a disability pen-

sion—normal retirement pension calculated at what would have been normal retirement date at current rates of pay. This would be dependent on medical evidence and the amount of State benefit received."

Six of the schemes covered by the survey:—

> "provide for employees to be covered by a permanent health scheme after their entitlement to sick pay has been exhausted. These schemes are arranged with insurance companies and provide for employees to continue to receive payments for a long period—for example, until recovery, retirement or death. The level of payment depends upon the premium paid by the employer."

Although "holding schemes" were commended in the following case, it is not clear from the judgment's brief analysis of the legal position that in themselves they offer the employee any security.

Marshall v. Harland and Wolff Ltd.
[1972] I.C.R. 101; [1972] 2 All E.R. 715
National Industrial Relations Court

Sir John Donaldson: We have been caused some concern by Mr Bingham's (counsel for the Department of Employment) suggestion that our decision could lead to employers abandoning the admirable practice of keeping sick employees "on the books," thus giving them assurance that, other things being equal, they will be able to get work as soon as they have recovered. We see no reason why this practice should be disturbed. If employers are worried that in the event of a redundancy situation arising a very long time after the employee has left the active list, they will thereby expose themselves to an unintended liability and so be tempted simply to dismiss [employees], an alternative exists. They can (and it is a much better approach to the problem) transfer such an employee to a "holding department" as was done in *O'Reilly v Hotpoint Ltd.* (1969) 7 K.I.R. 374. The effect of such a transfer is that the employee ceases to be employed in any legal sense, but [is put] on a list of men in respect of whom there is a voluntary arrangement between the employers and any relevant union, or the employees themselves, that all concerned will do their best to provide them with work as soon as they are again fit. In putting forward this suggestion we should like to stress that is it only made in relation to the long-term sick. Those who are absent for shorter periods should, in accordance with good industrial practice, be maintained in employment, whether or not in receipt of full wages or sick pay.

See also *Hart* v. *A. R. Marshall & Sons (Bulwell) Ltd.* [1977] I.R.L.R. 51 (E.A.T.) (see below Chapter 10 on *Termination of Work*, p. 369).

2. THE COMMON LAW

The enormous variety of arrangements for sick pay in industrial practice (though many are of recent origin) contrasts with the limited involvement of the common law on this subject. Such involvement as there is finds expression in decisions which debated, first, whether there was a general presumption as to entitlement to sick pay in a contract of employment; and secondly, whether the receipt of other payments (workers' compensation or national insurance) disentitled the employee from claiming sick pay under the contract. The common law policy perspective often seems to mirror the economic and labour market conditions and social preoccupations of the times when the cases were decided. The first case below draws a parallel with other commodity transactions, but distinguishes the contract of employment as different in this particular respect.

Cuckson v. Stones
(1858) 1 E. and E. 248

> The plaintiff had agreed to serve the defendent for a term of 10 years as a brewer. Some years into the term the plaintiff became ill, although he continued at the defendant's request to instruct him in the art of brewing. The defendant refused to pay wages for the period of illness.

Lord Campbell C.J.: Whether when issue is joined on such a plea, the want of ability to do the act proves, in point of law, a want of readiness and willingness, depends upon whether the want of ability is necessarily a breach of the contract to perform a condition precedent, or the consideration for the promise sued upon. In an action for not accepting goods purchased, issue being joined on a plea that the plaintiff was not ready and willing to deliver them, the defendant would be entitled to a verdict, on proof that the plaintiff never was in possession of the goods he undertook to deliver. But looking to the nature of the contract sued upon in this action, we think that want of ability to serve for a week would not, of necessity, be an answer to a claim for a week's wages, if in truth the plaintiff was ready and willing to serve had he been able to do so, and was only prevented from serving during the week by the visitation of God, the contract to serve never having been determined.

The next reported case, almost 50 years later, reflects a less relaxed laissez-faire attitude, an uneasy awareness of social legislation not wholly welcome. The judgment appears to proceed on the basis that the provision of statutory compensation for injury at work was made on the assumption that the salaried workman in the case would not be entitled to wages whilst absent from work.

Elliott v. Liggins
[1902] 2 K.B. 84; 71 L.J.K.B. 483
King's Bench Division

Darling J.: The right of a workman to make a claim for compensation under the [Workman's Compensation] Act [1897] is founded on the basis that, when his capacity to earn his wages has ceased because of the injury which he has sustained, money becomes payable to him calculated on a consideration of his weekly earnings which he has been receiving before he sustained the injury. The compensation is, therefore, payable in lieu of the wages which he has lost. If the contention of the plaintiff were correct, he would logically be able to sue for the whole of his wages during the time of his incapacity and not merely for the balance after deducting the amount paid to him each week by way of compensation, for, according to the argument on his behalf, he is entitled to compensation for the injury he sustained, and also to his wages although he was incapacitated from earning them.

I think that the construction that we are putting upon the Act is not opposed to the interests of workmen in general, for, if the opposite construction were to prevail, the first act of every employer on hearing of an accident to a workman would be to discharge that workman from his employ, so as to prevent him from setting up a claim to his wages in addition to his claim for compensation for the injury.

The changes in social legislation over the following decades are reflected in often conflicting judicial attitudes, as manifest in the judgment in the next case.

Marrison v. Bell
[1939] 1 All E.R. 745; [1939] 2 K.B. 187
Court of Appeal

Scott L.J.: In this case, a workman appeals from the decision of His Honour Judge Essenhigh, sitting at Sheffield, who dismissed his claim for arrears of wages during a period of incapacity by illness. The judge decided, without considering any of the decided authorities bearing on the matter, in favour of the defendant, on the ground that, in a case where the National Health Insurance Act [1936] gives the workman rights to various benefits under that Act during any period of incapacity by illness entitling him to those benefits, there is a term implied in the contract of service that, whilst in receipt of benefit, the workman's contract, under which he has the right to receive wages, is modified by an implied term that the right to wages is wholly suspended. In my view, there is no such implied term. . . .

A long series of decisions has been given in our courts, making it quite clear that the common law of this country does not recognise any such rule in contracts of service as is suggested by the county court judge. On the contrary, those cases say, in my opinion quite clearly, that, under a contract of service, irrespective of the question of the length of notice provided by that contract, wages continue, through sickness and incapacity from sickness to do the work contracted for, until the contract is terminated by a notice by the employer in accordance with the terms of the contract . . . the law, I think, is quite clear, and to the effect that I have stated. The first and leading case on the subject is *Cuckson v Stones*. [above p. 286] . . .

As in the contract of employment . . . one may imply a term of the contract suspending wages during the receipt of the benefit which those rules contemplate shall take the place of wages, so, in my view, it also results from the cases that, where, under the Workmen's Compensation Act, a man is getting half his wages in the form of compensation, it is right to interpret that Act as suspending the right at common law to the receipt of full wages during incapacity from accident or from a disease within that Act. I think that that is the true ground upon which to base the suspension of wages where, by reason of incapacity, a man is receiving compensation under the Workman's Compensation Act.

It is sought to say that that same principle which applies in the case of the Workmen's Compensation Act ought also to apply where a servant is in receipt of benefit under the National Health Insurance Acts, the Act in question being the Act of 1936, which is the last of the series of statutes which began with the Act of 1911. The first comment on that argument is that the benefits conferred by that last Act and by its predecessors are in their nature additional benefits conferred on the classes who come within the scope of those Acts, being mostly persons engaged as workmen. Those benefits are intended to be an addition to such financial emoluments as the workman may have during his life, to improve his position by giving him medical assistance, disablement benefit and others of a long list of additional benefits which will improve his lot. Those benefits are, in their nature, irrespective of the amount of wages as determined by the workman's individual contract of service. Rights are given independently of any relation between the rights and the wages as a general principle through the Acts, and there is absent—at any rate, from most of the earlier Acts, and certainly from the Act of 1936—any such ground as there is in the Workmen's Compensation Act for supposing that Parliament intended by the Act which conferred the benefits of health insurance to take away from the workman any right to wages that he might have. I suppose that the great majority of employed persons in this country are employed on terms of a week's, or at any rate, a month's, notice—mostly a week's notice—and consequently there is no social need for protecting the employer from the liability of having to go on paying wages, since he can always terminate that liability within a short time.

The link between dismissal for illness and sick pay entitlement was referred to in a note by A.T. Denning (later Lord Denning M.R.) in (1939) 55 L.Q.R. 353, where he contended that the presumption that wages were payable during sickness would be progressively less likely to triumph over the contrary implication as the term within which the contract could be terminated became shorter. Scott L.J.'s judgment, above, proved a rare case of a judicial invitation to workers to claim wages when absent through illness. It was readily taken up by employees who had heretofore been denied payment when ill. However, they were quickly to discover that other judges were equally ready to withdraw Scott L.J.'s invitation (*cf. Petrie* v. *MacFisheries Ltd.* [1940] 1 K.B. 258; *Hancock* v. *BSA Tools Ltd.* [1939] 4 All E.R. 538). It is the following case, however, which reveals most clearly the degree of judicial discontent with Scott L.J.'s initiative. It displays unwillingness to accept that the employer possessed superior economic power in the context of the Great Depression of the 1930s, and an equally astonishing readiness to regard employee acquiescence as free consent—even when this is recognised explicitly as being a consequence of employer threats of dismissal. The judge in the following case is keen to protect helpless employers from the claims of unhealthy workmen.

O'Grady v. M. Saper Limited
[1940] 2 K.B. 469
Court of Appeal

MacKinnon L.J.: This is an appeal from Bow County Court. In my view it is a disastrous example of the results of the misapplied industry of the compilers of law reports. A decided case is only worthy of report if it decides some principle of law and it is only deserving of citation in a later case if the same principle of law is involved. Unhappily very many cases are reported unnecessarily, and the practice has arisen, in a case involving no principle of law but purely a question of fact, of saying: "Here is a report of another case rather like this, so please decide it in the same way."

In this case the plaintiff was a commissionaire who had been employed by the defendants to attend to a gate at their works. He was engaged in December 1936, first at a wage of £2 15s. a week and then it was raised to £3 a week. He continued in their employment for more than three years. During the time when he was working for them he was away ill for four weeks in 1938, and during his absence he did not receive any wages. Again in 1938, later on, he was away ill for nine weeks and again he was not paid any wages during his absence. In 1939 he was away through illness for two weeks and again he did not receive any wages. He said in his evidence that at these times he never expected to be paid and it never occurred to him that he had any claim for wages whilst he was not working. Then he went on to say: "Till I saw the piece of paper I neither asked for payment during illness nor expected it." Now the piece in the paper was, one may gather, some journalistic summary of a recent decision in the Court of Appeal in the case of *Marrison v Bell* [[1939] 2 K.B. 187, above p. 287]. Unhappily that is one of the cases which, as I think, was unnecessarily reported and, more unhappily, the headnote of the case—which I cannot think can be justified by anything which was decided by the Court—reads thus: "Illness of a servant, which, while it lasts, incapacitates him for the performance of his duties, but is not so long-continued or so serious as to terminate the contract of service, does not at common law suspend his right to wages under the contract." That, in terms, appears to be a statement of a principle of common law, but it is not and cannot be any statement of any principle of the common law. The whole question in such a case as this is: what were the terms of the contract between the employer and the servant and what did those terms provide in regard to payment of wages to him during his absence from the service by reason of illness?

Now the sort of contract which is involved is usually concluded orally be people who rarely think out, and still more rarely, express any terms. The whole difficulty in such a case is to ascertain what in truth were the terms of the contract. Where the thing is not expressed it may be that you have to ascertain the terms as a matter of implication, but in any case, it is a question upon the evidence in the case. What were the terms of the employment? Were they an agreement that the man should be paid when ready and willing to work, and that he should only be paid when he was actually working? It depends upon the evidence what the terms were. In this case, as it seems to me, there was abundant evidence that the terms, not expressed but no doubt implied upon which this man was employed were that he should not be paid wages whilst he was sick. The conclusive evidence of that is that on at least three occasions, during the time he had been employed, when he was away sick he was not paid wages, and he acquiesced in that position and, as he said: "Till I saw the piece in the paper I neither asked for payment during illness nor expected it." As was rightly pointed out [during argument] if you are to ascertain what the implied terms are you have got to ask yourself: if somebody had raised the question when they were originally making the bargain what would they both have said about it? What in this case they would both have said about it is best proved, and I think is conclusively proved, by what the parties did when the event arose. When the event arose, and he was away ill, and he was not paid, he acquiesced in it, and, as he said, he did not think he ought to have it; he did not expect to get it. I come without hesitation to the conclusion that the terms of the contract between these parties were that he should be paid not during the period when he was ready and and willing to work but only during such period as he did work, and I regard it as most unfortunate that the headnote in *Morrison v Bell* should have purported to state as a principle of common law that a man who is incapacitated through illness is entitled to his wages during that illness. What the results may be I do not know, but this case is not at all a bad example of the effect of that unhappy report filtering down through the ordinary newspapers. It may be that county courts are now being deluged with stale claims by workmen for wages during the periods when in the past six years they were away from work through sickness. The result of that it is easy to imagine; subject to the Statute of Limitations an unhealthy workman might now, if there was any such principle of common law, claim for frequent periods of absence through illness during six years, and if that was the rule of common law the employer would have no answer to the claim. Whereas, obviously, if any such claim had been made on the first occasion when he was ill at the beginning of the six years and the man had said: "I ought to be paid although I was away sick," the employer would have said: "Good gracious, if that is your idea of the terms of your engagement it is not mine, and you will take a week's notice to end our contract." The learned [trial] judge, misled, as I think, and perhaps very reasonably misled, by the headnote in *Marrison v Ball*, said: "In the absence of evidence as to what were the terms agreed when the man was engaged in 1936 in my view there was no express and no implied term to prevent the normal rule applying." I understand that to mean that he accepted as the normal rule of common law that which is stated in that misleading case. It is nothing of the sort; it is a pure question of fact in every case. In this one I am quite satisfied that the agreement was that he should not be paid during illness and that therefore the claim ought to have been dismissed.

As a result I think the appeal should be allowed and judgment entered for the defendants with costs here and below.

Twenty years later, at the height of the post-war boom which eliminated high unemployment, the labour market tables had turned, and, the judge in the following case recognised the power which enabled workers to insist on payment during ill-health.

Orman v. Saville Sportswear Ltd.
[1960] 1 W.L.R. 1055; [1960] 3 All E.R. 105
Queens Bench Division

The plaintiff was employed as production manager at a weekly salary plus bonus on items manufactured. There was no express provision concerning payment during sickness. The plaintiff was absent for two months due to coronary thrombosis and he was dismissed when he informed his employers that he was fit to return to work.

PILCHER J.: [Having considered *Morrison v Bell* (above p. 287) and *O'Grady v Saper Ltd.* (above p. 288) *inter alia*, the judge concluded:]

Having considered all these cases and the careful argument addressed to me by counsel, it seems to me that they establish the following proposition. Where the written terms of the contract of service are silent as to what is to happen in regard to the employee's right to be paid whilst he is absent from work due to sickness, the employer remains liable to continue paying so long as the contract is not determined by proper notice, except where a condition to the contrary can properly be inferred from all the facts and the evidence in the case. If the employer seeks to establish an implied condition that no wages are payable, it is for him to make it out, and the court, in construing the written contract, will not accept any implied term which will not pass the test laid down by Scrutton, L.J., in *Reigate v Union Manufacturing Co. (Ramsbottom)* [1918] 1 K.B. at p. 605: the business efficiency test]. . . .

In my view, it is clear from the evidence in this case that if the matter had been mooted when the contract of service was made between the plaintiff and Mr Saville, the situation envisaged by Scrutton L.J., in the *Reigate* case namely, that the plaintiff and Mr Saville would at once have disagreed, would have obtained. I am accordingly of the opinion that in this contract no implied term in regard to payment during the period of illness can properly be introduced at all. It follows, therefore, that on the authorities the defendants remain liable to pay the plaintiff from the time when he ceased work until the contract of service was determined.

Two decades later, the economic decline was having its effect on the labour market, and another judge made his misgivings plain in a case which also looked to changes in social legislation as influencing the terms to be implied as to sick pay in a contract of employment.

Mears v. Safecar Security Ltd.
[1981] I.R.L.R. 99
Employment Appeal Tribunal

The appellant was employed as a security guard. His statutory statement of terms and conditions of employment contained no provisions as to payment during sickness. He applied for a declaration as to the particulars which should have been included. An Industrial Tribunal, following *Orman*'s case (above p. 290), assumed that a term for the payment of wages during sickness should be implied unless it could be shown that there was a contrary term.

SLYNN J.: We, of course, attach great weight to the judgment of Pilcher J. in *Orman v Saville Sportswear Ltd.* although, strictly, it is not binding upon us, but it seems to us quite clearly that what is said in that case must be seen against the background of what had been said in the other cases following *Marrison v Bell* [above p. 287].

In the result, it seems to us that it is not a correct approach to begin with the presumption that, if nothing is expressly said in the contract, wages are to be payable unless the employer satisfies the burden of showing that some other term is to be implied. In our judgment the proper approach is to look at all the facts and the circumstances to see whether a term is to be implied that wages shall or shall not be paid during periods of absence through sickness. Such a term, as the cases show, may be implied from the custom or practice in the industry. It may be implied from the knowledge of the parties at the time when the contract is made. The implication may depend upon whether the contract is one where the payment is due if the servant is ready, willing and able to work. It may depend, as was suggested in an article in volume 219 of the *Law Quarterly Review* at page 353, not so much as to whether the employee is willing and ready, or willing and able to work, but on whether payment of the wages is the consideration for faithful service at other times during the contract than during the period of absence rather than for a particular week's work actually performed. These are all matters which will have to be taken into account. So will the nature of the contract itself. The implication to be drawn in a case where a man is employed on a daily basis may be different from one to be drawn in a case where a man is employed for a fixed term of years, such as five or ten years, as has been referred to in some of the cases. It seems to us on the basis of what was said by MacKinnon L.J. in *O'Grady v Saper* [above p. 288] that it is also permissible on occasions to look at what the parties did during the performance of the contract. We, of course, recognise the dangers which are inherent in such a course, because evidence of what the parties did is generally inadmissible evidence in construing the terms of a contract, but in *Wilson v Maynard Shipbuilding Consultants AB* [1977] I.R.L.R. 491 Megaw L.J. having regard to the general rule, said this at page 493: "There would seem, however, to be an exception to the strictness of that doctrine where there must be a relevant term, but what that term is cannot be ascertained otherwise than by looking at what the parties did."

That seems to us to be in accordance with what was said in *O'Grady v Saper*, and so it seems to us that, contrary to the approach of the Industrial Tribunal in this case, and contrary to the approach which we understand Pilcher J. to have taken [in *Orman v Saville Sportswear Ltd.*] the right approach is to ask, on all the facts and circumstances of the case to which it is proper to have regard, what term is to be implied. One does not begin by assuming the term as to payment is to be implied unless the employer displaces it. On the facts of the present case it is clear that nothing was said at the time when the contract was made, but the Industrial Tribunal were quite satisfied that had the employer been asked he would have said that no wages would be paid to an employee like Mr Mears if he was away ill. He would, on the findings of the Tribunal, have said that it was their policy not to pay. We understand that to mean also that it was their practice not to pay. There was evidence that Mr Mears, who was ill some six months after he began working, did not ask for any payment—did not, apparently, send in the sort of sick notes regularly from the beginning which one would have expected had he considered that he was entitled to his wages. He was told by his colleagues that he would not get any sick pay from the company.

It seems to us, accordingly, in this case, if one adopts the approach which we consider it is right to adopt in these cases, that here the term to be implied into this contract is that wages would not be paid during periods of absence during sickness. In our judgment the Industrial Tribunal in the present case erred in their approach and they refused to imply a term which really ought to have been implied. . . .

. . . The second question arises as to whether there is to be implied a term that wages shall be paid regardless of whether benefits are received under the Social Security Act 1975. It seems to us to be quite clear that *Marrison v Bell* did not decide that in every case where any money was received under the National Insurance Act [1936], wages were also to be paid in full. The cases to which we have referred make it plain that the receipt of benefit under the legislation does not take away the man's right under his contract, but that of itself does not determine what the rights under the contract are, and the first question has to be decided as to what are the rights under the contract.

In our judgment it is clear that in deciding the implied term it is right to have regard to the nature of the payment which is made under the provisions of the Social Security Act 1975 if someone is away from work through illness. It is right, in our judgment, to take into account the differences between payments under that Act and under the National Insurance Act

1936, to the fact that both employer and employee make contributions, the fact that for a period earnings related supplements are paid to someone who is away ill, in addition to the flat rate benefit, which may provide for as much as 85 per cent. of the employee's contractual wages, subject to the upper limit provided from time to time under the legislation. If regard is had to those matters, and to the terms and conditions of employment on the facts of this case, it seems to us that quite plainly the term which would have to be implied as to the payment of wages, if one were implied, would have regard to the monies which would be payable to the workman under the 1975 Act.

Mr Mears himself accepted in his evidence that he could not have it both ways, and that he would have to give credit for any monies received under the 1975 Act. It is quite plain that the employers would have said the same thing. Reliance has, however, been placed by Mr Mears on *Marrison v Bell.* In our judgment, *Marrison v Bell* does not say, as is contended on behalf of Mr Mears, that these monies under the legislation are always payable in addition to the payment of full wages. One has to look at what is the implied term in any case.

The Court of Appeal affirmed the E.A.T.'s decision and expressly adopted the first four paragraphs of Slynn J.'s judgment quoted above ([1982] I.R.L.R. 183, *per* Stephenson L.J.).:

> " . . . I agree with the passage as a correct statement of the law relating to payment of wages during absence through sickness as it emerged, not without some judicial stretching and straining in 1940, and I could not improve it if I were to embark upon any detailed commentary on those cases. . . .
>
> . . . I should like to comment [that the E.A.T.'s] decision disapproves the conclusion of Pilcher J. as expressed in the proposition cited from *Orman's* case [1960] 3 All E.R. 105 and substitutes an approach to the facts and evidence in each case with an open mind unprejudiced by any preconception, presumption or assumption. With this I respectfully agree. . . .

3. STATUTORY SICK PAY

Inequality among different classes of workers and among employers is also reflected in the new Statutory Sick Pay scheme (SSP), under the Social Security and Housing Benefits Act 1982. This scheme set rates of statutory sick pay at three different levels, depending on earnings. The following extract describes the position before and after the new scheme came into effect, with interpolations for subsequent amendments made in 1985 and 1986 (see SIs 1985 No. 1694, 1986 Nos. 318, 477 and 478 and 366 I.R.R.R. 303 I.R.L.I.B. 15).

INDUSTRIAL RELATIONS REVIEW AND REPORT No. 275 (July 1982), p. 2

[*Position prior to introduction of SSP*] Sick pay [fell] into two main categories—benefits payable under occupational sick pay schemes and State sickness benefit. . . .

In addition to any entitlement to occupational sick pay, employees who have satisfied the contribution conditions are entitled to State sickness benefit. . . . This is not taxed and lasts for a maximum of 28 (six day) weeks; Sundays do not count for State benefit purposes.

Since some sick pay schemes pay normal wages minus State sickness benefit claimed by the employee, some employees are better off when sick than at work. This is because taxable pay is less, National Insurance contributions are less and State sickness benefit is not taxed.

Employer's liability to pay SSP

From 6.4.83 employers will be responsible for paying SSP to their employees for the first [twenty-] eight weeks of sickness [or for two periods of sickness or incapacity separated by no more than eight weeks . . .]. There are three different rates of SSP according to the "normal weekly earnings" of the employee (see below for explanation). These are flat rates and there will be no extra allowances for dependants or for married workers. SSP will be taxed and both employers and employees will have to pay NI contributions on the SSP payments. Employees do not have to satisfy any contribution conditions in order to become eligible for SSP. . . .

Decision not to pay

Employers are entitled to withhold SSP until they have received the evidence of incapacity they require. If this evidence is not considered satisfactory or if the evidence is not produced, the employer is entitled to withhold payment altogether. The decision whether or not to pay lies initially with the employer and not with the DHSS, but if payment is refused and the employee is not satisfied, the employee may appeal through the normal insurance appeals system.

The appeal at first instance is to the Insurance Officer (IO). Only the employee may appeal at this stage and only written representations (from both sides) may be made. There is no burden of proof. The IO will weigh up the evidence of both parties and will make a decision that SSP should or should not be paid. Either side can then appeal to a National Insurance Tribunal (made up of a legally qualified chairman, and representatives of employer and trade union). Only appeals on a point of law can then be made to a Social Security Commissioner, whose decisions make precedent. In most cases, this is the final level of appeal.

Where an employer refuses to pay SSP the employee may ask for certain written information from the employer within a reasonable time, which must include the following information:

> The days in the past period of sickness for which the employer considers he is liable to pay SSP to the employee;
> the reasons why the employer considers there is no liability to pay SSP for other days in the period; and
> the amount of SSP during that period for which the employer considers himself liable. . . .

Offsetting company sick pay

The Act (Schedule 1 para. 2) makes it clear that any contractual payment to an employee on a day of sickness, whether it is holiday pay or sick pay, offsets any SSP due, so that employers do not have to pay SSP on top. The only requirement is that the amount paid to an employee is at least the amount of SSP due. Similarly, any SSP paid on a day of sickness offsets any liability an employer may have to pay contractual pay [for] that day. So for example, an employer pays only a flat rate amount of sick pay (eg £10 for a five day week). In this case, if an employee were entitled to £7·40 a day SSP, the employer would legally be free to pay just that sum (which could be reclaimed) and not pay the £2·00 per day company sick pay on top. This would also be the case, where sick pay is based on a percentage of wages, *eg* half pay for a number of weeks. It is of course up to every employer to decide (or negotiate) how or if company sick pay will be offset.

The introduction of statutory sick pay illustrates the fluid boundary between social security law and labour law. At a stroke, conflict between citizen and the State over social security provision during illness have been transferred to the sphere of employer/employee relations. The following extract reveals the extent of the potential conflict in terms of the costs to both sick employees and their employers.

R. Lewis, "*The privatisation of sickness benefit*" (1982) 11 I.L.J. 145

. . . cut in provision for some sick people will occur as a result of transferring responsibility from the State to employers. One of the main aims of the legislation is to ensure that the benefit paid by employers under occupational sick pay (O.S.P.) agreements negotiated by individual trade unions will be brought into account in assessing the need for and proper extent of State provision for sickness. Where previously some sick people have obtained both sickness benefit and payments under O.S.P. they may now in effect only be paid O.S.P. for this will be payment by an employer which will also satisfy the requirements for S.S.P. This means that unless the level of O.S.P. is raised the income of employees in these few cases will have been reduced from its present level by the full amount of current sickness benefit. If such a cut is to be avoided individual trade unions must renegotiate O.S.P. for otherwise these members will be substantially worse off. . . .

. . . employers are allowed to deduct all payments of S.S.P. from their [National Insurance] contributions. However, the transfer of responsibility for sickness to employers will still cost them dear: they must now pay N.I. contributions on S.S.P. where previously they did not when sickness benefit was claimed: if their O.S.P. schemes make up D.H.S.S. benefits to full pay those schemes will have to pay more where S.S.P. is lower than present sickness benefit: they face pressure to improve existing O.S.P. schemes so as to compensate, for example, for the taxation of S.S.P., and to harmonise the position of white and blue collar workers who are treated equally by S.S.P. but very differently by O.S.P.; and finally, employers must meet the costs of administering S.S.P. themselves. The specialist advice required and paperwork costs could be substantial especially for a small firm not presently operating an O.S.P. scheme. Detailed records must be kept, for example. The C.B.I. estimate these additional costs to employers as amounting to well over £130 million. This is in addition to the transaction costs of the negotiations with trade unions in order to implement the new scheme. Sick pay may now prove to be a more fruitful area for industrial disputes than previously has been the case.

CHAPTER 10

TERMINATION OF WORK

1. RULES ON TERMINATION: SOURCES AND STRUCTURE

In this chapter "termination of work" is taken to mean the ending of the link between the worker and the work. The common law of termination of the contract of employment has been supplemented by a complex body of statutory provisions on termination of work (*eg* unfair dismissal, redundancy, insolvency, transfer of employment, and so on). In addition, legal obligations, both statutory and contractual, are moulded by collective agreements and industrial practice. The result is a very unsystematic body of legal rules applicable to termination of work.

There are two ways of organising this subject-matter. First, all rules dealing with termination can be gathered together. But to do so tends to give "termination" an unfortunate prominence. Workers who are ill, incompetent, redundant, insubordinate and so on are all dealt with under the same legal principles that govern termination. Alternatively, the situations which may result in termination can be studied. The rules on termination can then be viewed in the context of each situation as only one of a number of possible responses. It is arguable that the principles dealing with workers who are ill, incompetent, redundant, insubordinate and so on are different. Termination would be only one part of the body of rules dealing with such situations.

Both of these methods of organising the rules on termination in labour law are reflected in this book. In this chapter on *Termination of Work* we have concentrated on the rules governing termination by reason of misconduct, ill–health and incompetence. These are treated here because they illustrate, particularly on the procedural side, the wide differences between the principles which govern termination in these cases. Other situations which often give rise to termination (redundancy and reorganisations) are treated elsewhere, because they involve a range of matters over and above termination, for example, in the case of redundancy, measures to avoid redundancy, short-time working, redundancy payments, consultation of unions (see Chapter 4 on *Quantity of Work*); in the case of reorganisations, trial periods and the general issue of change at the workplace (see Chapter 3 on *The Work Obligation*). Our proposed structure is by no means the only one possible. Thus, Chapter 9 on *Sickness and Injury* ought perhaps to include the rules governing termination for ill-health; and Chapter 3 on *The Work Obligation* could include the rules governing termination for incompetence. Such overlaps should be the subject of debate when legislation on these problems is considered.

The existence of a body of statutory provisions on unfair dismissal (EPCA, Pt. V) has led to attention being focussed on the employer's attitudes. Everything depends on the employer's reasons for either terminating the contract or justifying the termination. Since one premise of this book is that the subject-matter of labour law is work and workers, the employer's subjective opinions should not form the basis for our analysis of the rules on termination of employment. Given the present dominance of statutory provisions on "unfair dismissal" in the case law, however, it is necessary to explain why a different analysis is adopted in this book. There are three principal reasons.

First, although there are obviously cases of dismissal in the sense of personal termination by the employer, termination in that sense alone is a very misleading guide to industrial reality. Termination in any personal sense is derived from common law concepts of a personal employment relationship. At a time when most workers are employed in establishments of over a 100 employees, such personal relationships do not exist in any real sense (particularly where the employer is a corporate body of some size). Termination is a bureaucratic exercise. There are structures of authority which operate to produce termination in various ways (ranging, according to the status of workers, from personal interviews, the operation of lengthy procedures, the "dishing-out" of anonymous pink slips, to shouted sackings). In large organisations, indeed, termination is often avoided by alternative measures (transfer, suspension, demotion, retraining) which are often not possible in small establishments. The worker's response may be to terminate work himself. Rules based on the concept of personal termination by an employer are not appropriate for the large organisations in which most people work. "Dismissal" is, therefore, twisted by statute and the courts in an attempt to accommodate this reality. "Dismissal" can be seen as a shorthand description for the ending of the employment relationship (which lawyers express as the termination of the contract of employment). It is not a single concept at all, but must cope with innumerable different situations.

The analysis proposed here, therefore, drops the concept of "dismissal" as a criterion for application of the rules. Instead, the "voluntariness" of the termination from the worker's viewpoint is the factor which determines the rules applicable to various situations of termination of work.

A second reason for our divergence from the statutory framework is because that framework is organised around explicit "fair" reasons for dismissal, mainly misconduct, incapability and redundancy. The statute fails, however, to explain what these generalisations mean. Specifically, the relation between them and existing rules and practices in industry is not spelled out. One danger is that traditional common law concepts of master and servant supply the missing definition, for example, of the conduct expected of a modern unionised worker. Furthermore, terminations are often the result not of misconduct, incapability or redundancy, but are rather caused by reorganisations, transfers of assets, introduction of new technology, and, not least, deficiencies in management behaviour and policy. The attempts by the courts to accommodate part of this reality in the statutory category of "some other substantial reason" justifying dismissal (EPCA, s.57(1)(*b*)) may be admired for their creativity and criticised for their policy at one and the same time. The judges' recognition, in the development of "constructive dismissal," that employers' behaviour may be the cause of a termination is also open to critical approval. Nonetheless, the statutory framework of unfair dismissal is misleading. The classification of a few generalised categories and one miscellaneous category conceals the fact that the latter will include every other conceivable reason for dismissal, and yet affords no indication of the different considerations that must be applied in such individual cases.

The structure adopted in this book elaborates the meaning of termination for misconduct and lack of capability in their industrial context in detail. The problem of employer-induced termination is analysed separately. Consideration of redundancies and reorganisations is provided in other chapters, where their context is better appreciated and where it can be seen that the courts are actually dealing with totally different problems.

The third premise underlying our analysis of the rules on termination is the recognition that adherence to procedures is all important in the practical experience of workers. Yet the statute contains little reference to procedures, and nothing to suggest that procedures must differ according to the cause of a specific dismissal. There is statutory ackowledgement of procedures (already in existence) in redundancy situations (EPCA, s.59(*b*)); and judicial activism has led to widespread utilisation of the Code of Practice on Disciplinary Practice and Procedures in misconduct cases, but procedures in cases of ill-health and incompetence need equal emphasis.

In our analysis the centrality of procedures is recognised. We seek to illustrate the variety of collective industrial practice and the important ways in which procedures required in misconduct, ill-health and incompetence cases differ. Further, we consider two different models of procedures in circumstances where termination is a possibility: the "trial" model of adjudication, and the "bargaining' model of negotiation.

2. DISMISSAL VERSUS VOLUNTARINESS OF TERMINATION

Our analysis of the rules on termination of work looks not to the statutory framework of unfair dismissal law, but to the *voluntariness* of the termination: did the worker leave, or was he or she sacked? As put by Stephenson L.J. in *Sothern* v. *Franks Charlesly & Co.* [1981] I.R.L.R. 278 (C.A.):

> "Did he trip or was he pushed? Was it murder or was it suicide? I know that such a simple consideration of starkly contrasted alternatives is too often outlawed by authority in deciding the issue of dismissal [or not]. Even if the question, 'Was the employee dismissed?' cannot always be answered, by answering the question, 'Who really terminated his contract?' the right answer to the second question gives the right answer to the first question in this case."

Such a classification is desirable for three reasons. First, it is consistent with the way termination is perceived by workers. The key question is: did the worker want to go, or was he sacked or forced to leave? Secondly, it is consistent with the way termination is handled in industrial practice: rules and procedures are invoked when involuntary termination occurs or appears likely due to the employer's conduct or policy. Thirdly, it avoids a major defect of the statutory structure: the concept of dismissal. In an approach based on "voluntariness," it does not matter whose action terminates the employment, let alone the contract of employment. Termination is seen merely as a matter of fact, not of law.

In the event of termination of work, it needs to be established, again as a matter of fact, whether it was voluntary on the part of the worker. If so, were the rules on voluntary termination complied with? If not, were those governing involuntary termination violated? The issue of voluntariness is a problem of fact. Who terminates is not a clear sign: a worker may terminate his or her employment, or have it terminated voluntarily or involuntarily. There may be a dispute: the worker claiming he left involuntarily and the employer claiming it was voluntary. Since in our proposed classification, the voluntariness of termination is simply a matter of fact, one might start with a presumption that, on a complaint by a worker, termination is deemed involuntary unless the contrary is proved.

By way of contrast, under the statutory law of unfair dismissal (EPCA, Pt. V), the key practical and factual question of the voluntariness of the termination is masked by the need to show a *dismissal,* as defined in section 55(2)(*a*)–(*c*). This focuses attention on the question: who terminated the contract of employment, the employer or the employee? The following are some categories of cases which reveal the substantive and factual issue of voluntariness of termination underlying the formal and legal question of "dismissal," *ie* who terminated the contract.

(A) "Resign or be Dismissed"

In these cases, the undisputed "resignation" (termination) by the employee has been attacked on the grounds of its "voluntariness," and said to be a "dismissal" (termination by the employer). The following extract illustrates this problem.

Martin v. MBS Fastenings (Glynwed) Distribution Ltd.
[1983] I.R.L.R. 198; [1983] I.C.R. 511
Court of Appeal

When the employee severely damaged his employer's mini-bus while driving under the influence of drink, he was advised by the employer's regional director that it would probably be in his own interest to resign. The employee then proceeded to write a letter of resignation. He subsequently complained that he had been unfairly dismissed. An Industrial Tribunal concluded that this was not a dismissal but a voluntary termination. A majority in the E.A.T. allowed an appeal on this point. The Court of Appeal restored the decision of the Industrial Tribunal.

Sir John Donaldson M.R.: The Industrial Tribunal had to make up its mind whether on the evidence, the reality of the situation was that the employer terminated Mr Martin's employment or that Mr Martin did. Plainly the fact that Mr Martin signed a letter of resignation is a factor and an important factor in reaching a conclusion on this issue, but it cannot be conclusive. . . . It is tempting to give other examples of circumstances in which either the only conclusion, or a possible conclusion, is that it was really the employer who was terminating the contract and not the employee, notwithstanding that the employee went through the motions of resigning. However experience shows that Industrial Tribunals tend to treat illustrations as being what they are not—an explanation or qualification of the parliamentary definition. Whatever the respective actions of the employer and employee at the time when the contract of employment is terminated, at the end of the day the question always remains the same, "Who really terminated the contract of employment?"

SIR DENYS BUCKLEY: . . . the findings of the Industrial Tribunal that "in our view this was not a dismissal" was a pure finding of fact. It was not a decision on a point of law or on a point of mixed fact and law. It was a finding upon the question whether on the primary facts the applicant in choosing to resign was in fact exercising his own right to choose whether to resign or to submit to an inquiry, or whether he was induced to resign by the conduct of the regional director.

(B) Termination "By Agreement"

In such cases, the employee's apparent agreement to terminate may be vitiated by the involuntariness in fact of the agreement, and the termination will be held to be a "dismissal." The following case is an illustration.

Thames Television Ltd. v. Wallis
[1979] I.R.L.R. 136
Employment Appeal Tribunal

> The employee was told her contract would come to an end on January 1, 1978. Following negotiations with her union representative, the employers offered her either alternative employment, or an *ex gratia* payment. She chose the latter, and then claimed unfair dismissal. The E.A.T. held that she had been dismissed.

TALBOT J.: In the view of this Appeal Tribunal it is difficult to see how the agreement which the Industrial Tribunal found was made could have been said to vary what was already an accomplished fact, namely the contract was to end at its date of termination. It is difficult to comprehend a contract whereby the employee, who has been told "Your contract will end on the fixed date," then agrees that it will end on the fixed date, and that he will receive a sum of money, so that it can be said that the termination [of the Contract] was not [due to its] expiry on the fixed date but [to] an agreement that it should expire on the fixed date. This difficulty, presented itself to the National Industrial Relations Court in *McAlwane v Boughton Estate Ltd* [[1973] I.C.R. 470. The facts of the decision are not important, but what was said *per curiam* in our view is. Sir John Donaldson said:

> "We would further suggest that it would be a very rare case indeed in which it could properly be found that the employer and the employee had got together and notwithstanding that there was a current notice of termination of the employment, agreed mutually to terminate the contract, particularly when one realises the financial consequences to the

employee involved in such an agreement. We do not say that such a situation cannot arise; we merely say that, viewed in a real life situation, it would seem to be a possibility which might appeal to a lawyer more than to a personnel manager."

The confusion into which the law of unfair dismissal has descended is illustrated by the decision in *The University of Liverpool* v. *(1) Humber and (2) Birch* [1984] I.R.L.R. 57 (E.A.T.), which asserted, first, that: "the fact that an employee has no objection to being dismissed, or even volunteers to be dismissed, does not prevent his dismissal, when it occurs, from being a dismissal within the meaning of (EPCA)," but went on to find that employees who were approached by the employer to take early retirement, and whose offers to take this up were accepted by the employer, were not dismissed. Rejecting the appeal, Slade L.J. in the Court of Appeal quoted Sir John Donaldson M.R. in *Martin's* case (p. 301 above) that the question was who really terminated the contract, but concluded that on the facts, the contract "was terminated not by the employer but by the freely given mutual consent of the employer and employee" ([1985] I.R.L.R. 165, at 172).

(C) Fixed-term Contracts

Statute designates expiry of a fixed-term contract as a dismissal (EPCA, s.55(2)(*b*)). It is recognised that such contracts are usually in the interests of the employer, and that expiry is effectively an involuntary termination from the employee's point of view, as the following case illustrates.

Terry v. East Sussex County Council
[1976] I.C.R. 536; [1976] I.R.L.R. 332; [1977] 1 All E.R. 567
Employment Appeal Tribunal

When the employee's fixed-term contract was not renewed, he claimed unfair dismissal.

PHILLIPS J.: What an Industrial Tribunal must do is to ensure that the case is a genuine one where an employee has to his own knowledge been employed for a particular period, or a particular job, on a temporary basis. We accept Mr Gibson's suggestion [on behalf of the County Council] that there may be a wide scale in what can ordinarily be described as "temporary" jobs. At one end is the plain case where a person (for example, a school teacher) is employed to fill a gap where somebody is absent, and it is made plain at the moment of engagement that he is only being employed during the period of the absence of the person he is temporarily replacing. At the other end is the case of the employee who is engaged on a short fixed-term contract, perhaps described as "temporary," in an employment where as a general rule the employees are engaged on a weekly basis and where there is no particular end served by the employment being arranged in the manner in which it has been. In between, there will be every possible variety of case. . . .

. . . The great thing is to make sure that the case is a genuine one, and for

Industrial Tribunals to hold a balance. On the one hand, employers who have a genuine need for a fixed-term employment, which can be seen from the outset not to be ongoing, need to be protected. On the other hand, employees have to be protected against being deprived of their rights through ordinary employments being dressed up in the form of temporary fixed-term contracts. What we are saying in this judgment is that there is no magic about fixed-term contracts; that they are not, except where otherwise provided, excluded from the provisions of [E.P.C.A.], and that the rights of those employed under them are to be judged by the good sense of Industrial Tribunals.

Terry was approved by the Court of Appeal in *North Yorkshire County Council* v. *Fay* [1985] I.R.L.R. 247.

(D) Performance Contracts

The contract may specify that it is to be terminated by completion of a task or the occurrence of an event. This may be agreed by the worker, but, as with fixed-term contracts, it should not usually be regarded as voluntary. Nonetheless, the Court of Appeal held in the following case that the voluntariness of such terminations could not be challenged by way of a claim for unfair dismissal because of a technical construction of the statutory language.

Wiltshire County Council v. National Association of Teachers in Further and Higher Education and Guy

[1980] I.C.R. 455; [1980] I.R.L.R. 198
Court of Appeal

From 1969 the employee was engaged each year to teach specific subjects for the academic session. Her classes did not necessarily continue to the end of the session and she was paid only for the hours taught. She was not offered a new contract at the end of the 1976/77 session, and claimed unfair dismissal. The Court of Appeal rejected her claim.

Lord Denning M.R.: I would also mention an interesting paragraph in the report of Lord Donovan's *Royal Commission on Trade Unions and Employers' Associations* 1965–1968 (Cmnd. 3623). Paragraph 558 says:

> "Most employers have contracts of employment for an indefinite period. However the need for protection against unfair deprivation of employment may also arise when the contract of employment has been entered into for a fixed period or for a particular purpose and its renewal is refused by the employer."

Although the Royal Commission recommended "a particular purpose" the legislature did not accept that recommendation. It limited the protection to contracts for a "fixed period." It did not extend the protection to a contract "for a particular purpose."

If I may seek to draw the matter together, it seems to me that if there is a contract by which a man is to do a particular task or to carry out a particular purpose, then when that task or purpose comes to an end the contract is discharged by performance. Instances may be taken of a seaman who is employed for the duration of a voyage—and it is completely uncertain how long the voyage will last. His engagement comes to an end on its completion. Also of a man who is engaged to cut down trees, and, when all the trees have been cut down, his contract is discharged by performance. In neither of those instances is there a contact for a fixed term. It is a contract which is discharged by performance. There is no "dismissal." A contract for a particular purpose, which is fulfilled, is discharged by performance and does not amount to a dismissal.

In *Ford* v. *Warwickshire County Council* [1983] I.R.L.R. 126 (H.L.), Lord Brightman appeared reluctant to distinguish contracts for a fixed-term measured in time, and those for a fixed-term measured in work: "There is no essential difference in my view where the contract of employment is for a fixed-term, the term being fixed by reference to the anticipated availability of work."

(E) Employee/Employer Repudiation

The common law's confusion as to whether one party's fundamental breach of contract (repudiation) automatically terminates the contract of employment has disastrous consequences when statutory protection is dependent upon the identity of the person who terminates the contract. The differences of view among the judges reflects the different weight they attach to the voluntariness of the employee's termination. In the extracts below, in Lord Denning's view, if the worker repudiating the contract intended to terminate his employment (voluntary termination), he cannot claim unfair dismissal. In the opinion of Templeman L.J., if he wants to return (involuntary termination), the question of unfair dismissal has to be addressed.

London Transport Executive v. Clarke
[1981] I.C.R. 355; [1981] I.R.L.R. 166
Court of Appeal

> The employee was refused unpaid leave of absence to go to Jamaica. He went nonetheless. His employers wrote on March 5, 1979 asking for an explanation for his absence and saying that, if no reply was received within 14 days, it would be assumed he did not wish to continue in their employment. On March 26, 1979 the employers removed his name from their books and wrote to the employee to that effect. On his return on April 14, 1979 the employee claimed unfair dismissal.

LORD DENNING M.R.: Under our modern legislation a new question arises. It arises under s.54 of the Employment Protection (Consolidation) Act 1978, re-enacting earlier sections going back to 1971. When an employee is dismissed for misconduct, we have to ask—and to answer—the question: who "terminates" the contract? If the employer "terminates" it, it is taken to be unfair unless the employer proves that it was fair. But, if the employee "terminates" it by his own misconduct, he gets nothing. . . .

. . . The cases fall into two groups . . .

The first group is when the misconduct of the employee is such that it is completely inconsistent with the continuance of the contract of employment.

So much so that the ordinary member of the Tribunal would say of him: "He sacked himself." In these cases it is the employee himself who "terminates" the contract. His misconduct itself is such as to evince an intention himself to bring the contract to an end. Such as when an employee leaves and gets another job: or when he absconds with money from the till: or goes off indefinitely without a word to his employer. If he comes back and asks for his job back, the employer can properly reply: "I cannot have you back now." There is no election in that case. The man dismisses himself. In the words of Lord Justice Shaw in *Gunton v Richmond-Upon-Thames London Borough Council* [1980] I.R.L.R. 321 at page 324, there is a "complete and intended withdrawal of his service by the employee." . . .

The second group is where the misconduct of the employee is bad enough to justify the employer at common law in dismissing him, but leaves it open to the employer whether to dismiss him for it or not. His misconduct is such as to show that he is not going to fulfil his duties as he ought to do: but nevertheless it is not such as to be entirely disruptive of the contract. He does not "sack" himself: but he is guilty of a breach which entitles the employer at common law to dismiss him. If the employer does elect to dismiss him, it is the employer who "terminates" the contract . . . to my mind this man dismissed himself. He himself terminated the contract of employment when he "took off" for a seven-week holiday in Jamaica—just as much as if he "took off" for a highly paid seven-week job there—or if he "took off" for another job, but after seven weeks disliked it and returned asking to be taken back. The employer could not be expected to keep his job open for him after conduct of that kind.

TEMPLEMAN L.J.: . . . If a worker walks out of his job and does not thereafter claim to be entitled to resume work, then he repudiates his contract and the employer accepts that repudiation by taking no action to affirm the contract. No question of unfair dismissal can arise unless the worker claims that he was constructively dismissed. If a worker walks out of his job or commits any other breach of contract, repudiatory or otherwise, but at any time claims that he is entitled to resume or to continue his work, then his contract of employment is only determined if the employer expressly or impliedly asserts and accepts repudiation on the part of the worker. Acceptance can take the form of formal writing or can take the form of refusing to allow the worker to resume or continue his work. Where the contract of employment is determined by the employer purporting to accept repudiation on the part of the worker, the Tribunal must decide whether the worker has been unfairly dismissed.

In the *Clarke* case, Dunn L.J. while otherwise agreeing with Templeman L.J. that the employer's acceptance of the employee's repudiation was necessary, differed from him in the case of the need for the employee's acceptance of the employee's repudiation. The position was described in the following extract.

Robert Cort & Son Ltd. v. Charman
[1981] I.R.L.R. 437
Employment Appeal Tribunal

The employee was summarily dismissed by a letter of September 26, with one month's pay in lieu of notice.

BROWNE-WILKINSON J.: There have been two views as to how repudiation affects a contract of employment and there is a long-standing difference of judicial opinion on the point. The first view (which we will call the "unilateral view") is that contracts of service provide an exception to the general law and that a repudiation of a contract of employment puts an end to the contract at once without any acceptance of the repudiation by the other party. The other view ("the acceptance view") is that the general law applies and acceptance of repudiation is necessary to put an end to a contract of employment. In our judgment, it is still not established which of these two views is the correct one. In *Gunton v Richmond-upon-Thames Borough Council* [1980] I.R.L.R. 321 the majority of the Court of Appeal held that the acceptance view was correct; even so, they indicated that even before the repudiation was accepted, for all practical purposes the employment is at an end: see per Buckley L.J. at p. 325 and per Brightman L.J. at p. 329. But the decision of the Court of Appeal in *London Transport Executive v Clarke* [1981] I.R.L.R. 166 indicates that the matter is still unresolved. In that case Lord Denning M.R. (dissenting) favoured the unilateral view and Templeman L.J. the acceptance view; Dunn L.J. basically adopts the acceptance view but at paragraph 49 says this:

> "But there may be cases in which there has been no repudiation by the employee, and the employer has given notice of dismissal either in accordance with the terms of the contract or in breach of them (see *Gunton v Richmond-upon-Thames Borough Council* and cases there cited). Such cases where the employee has no option but to accept the notice I would regard as an exception to the general rule as stated in *Ansell v. Boston Deep Sea Fishing* (1888) 39 Ch.D. 339). In these cases the contract is terminated by the notice of the employer."

Therefore, in the view of Dunn L.J., in the present case the letter of September 26 would have produced an immediate termination of the contract.

On this view, the employee can claim unfair dismissal whether his own or the employer's breach results in an involuntary termination. In *R.* v. *East Berkshire Health Authority ex p. Walsh* [1984] I.R.L.R. 278 (C.A.), May L.J. agreed with Browne-Wilkinson J. that the question was still unresolved, but aligned himself with the dissenting view of Shaw L.J. in *Gunton* favouring the unilateral approach. In *Irani* v. *Southampton and South-West Hampshire Health Authority* [1985] I.R.L.R. 203 (Ch.D.), Warner J. referred to May L.J.'s view, but also to the "powerfully-reasoned judgment of Sir Robert Megarry V.C., in *Thomas Marshall (Exports) Ltd.* v. *Guinle* [1978] I.R.L.R. 174 at p. 207, in which he came down firmly in favour of the acceptance view" (see p. 314 below).

(F) "Constructive" Dismissal

The statutory definition of what has become known as "constructive" dismissal in EPCA, s.55(2)(*c*) (see p. 309 below: *Termination, Voluntariness and Employer Conduct*) focuses on employee termination, but looks also to the circumstances: whether the conduct of the employer entitles the employee to terminate. The apparent voluntariness of the employee terminating may be vitiated by the employer's conduct. Employee termination is construed as an employer's dismissal. The problem is to decide when an employee's apparently voluntary termination is to be treated as a "constructive" dismissal.

The tests are variously described as the "contract" test and the "reasonableness" test. These tests and the problems they give rise to are outlined in the following extract.

Woods v. W.M. Car Services (Peterborough) Ltd.
[1981] I.R.L.R. 347
Employment Appeal Tribunal

Browne-Wilkinson J.: The statutory right of an employee who ceases to be employed to complain that he has been unfairly dismissed is wholly dependent on his showing that he has been "dismissed." In the ordinary case, where an employer in fact dismissed the employee (ie cases falling within [EPCA] s.55(2)(a) and (b)) this normally presents no difficulty. The difficulty arises in cases of constructive dismissal falling within s.55(2)(c) where the employee has resigned due to the behaviour of the employer. As is well known, there used to be conflicting decisions as to whether, in order to constitute constructive dismissal, the conduct of the employer had to amount to a repudiation of the contract at common law or whether it was sufficient if the employer's conduct was, in lay terms, so unreasonable that an employee could not be expected to put up with it. In *Western Excavating (ECC) Ltd v Sharp* ([1978] I.R.L.R. 27 (C.A.)) this conflict was resolved in favour of the view that the conduct of the employer had to amount to repudiation of the contract at common law. Accordingly, in cases of constructive dismissal, an employee has no remedy even if his employer has behaved unfairly, unless it can be shown that the employer's conduct amounts to a fundamental breach of the contract.

The same considerations apply to claims for redundancy payments, eg an employee who resigns because of his employer's conduct is not entitled to any redundancy payment unless he can show that such conduct amounts to a repudiation of the contract at common law: see [EPCA] s.83(2)(c).

Experience in this Appeal Tribunal has shown that one of the consequences of the decision in the *Western Excavating* case has been that employers who wish to get rid of an employee or alter the terms of his employment without becoming liable either to pay compensation for unfair dismissal or a redundancy payment have had resort to methods of "squeezing out" an employee. Stopping short of any major breach of the contract, such an employer attempts to make the employee's life so uncomfortable that he resigns or accepts the revised terms. Such an employer, having behaved in a totally unreasonable manner, then claims that he has not repudiated the contract and therefore that the employee has no statutory right to claim either a redundancy payment or compensation for unfair dismissal.

This decision was reversed on the facts by the Court of Appeal: [1982] I.R.L.R. 413, see below, p. 309).

The involuntariness of the employee's termination springs from the employer's conduct. Analysis of this conduct could be along similar lines to the statutory test of "fairness" (*cf.* EPCA, s.57), so a decision that the employer's conduct was unreasonable and a "constructive" dismissal would parallel the same lack of fairness found in ordinary cases of unfair dismissal. For an illustration, see *Dutton & Clark Ltd.* v. *Daly* [1985] I.R.L.R. 363 (E.A.T.), which held that the test of fundamental breach by the employer of the contract of employment was identical to the "reasonable employer" standard of unfair dismissal. However, the prevailing doctrine of "constructive" dismissal looks only to conventional common law contractual doctrines of repudiation.

3. TERMINATION, VOLUNTARINESS AND EMPLOYER CONDUCT

It was remarked on p. 299 above that one defect of the statutory law of unfair dismissal was its failure to address the problem of terminations caused by employers' action (*eg* reorganisations, misbehaviour, etc.,). This omission is only partly remedied by judicial attempts to develop the law of constructive dismissal to impose standards of behaviour on employers whose conduct leads employees to terminate their employment (see also Chapter 7 on *Discipline*, section 258 on *Mutuality in discipline: controlling employer misconduct*, and in particular the *Woods* case, p. 266).

The vagaries of the current standard of employer conduct entitling the employee to statutory protection against unfair dismissal are amply illustrated by *Woods* v. *W.M. Car Services (Peterborough) Ltd.* [1981] I.R.L.R. 347 (E.A.T); [1982] I.R.L.R. 413 (C.A.). The Industrial Tribunal held that the employer's conduct in persistently attempting to alter the employee's terms of employment was not constructive dismissal. The E.A.T. took the view that it was (though it would not overrule the Tribunal on this "question of fact"). In the Court of Appeal, Watkins L.J. opined that:

> "The obdurate refusal of the appellant to accept conditions very properly and sensibly being sought to be imposed upon her was unreasonable. Employers must not, in my opinion, be put in a position where, through the wrongful refusal of their employees to accept change, they are prevented from introducing improved business methods in furtherance of seeking success for their enterprise."

The use by Watkins L.J. of words like "obdurate," "unreasonable" and "wrongful" with respect to the employee, and "properly," "sensibly," "improved" and "success" with respect to the employer indicate how value judgments intrude in the question of constructive dismissal whenever employers' conduct is being assessed.

The policy views of the Tribunals appear even more significant if the question of constructive dismissal is treated as one of fact, not law, precluding appeals.

Woods v. W.M. Car Services (Peterborough) Ltd.
[1982] I.R.L.R. 413
Court of Appeal

An Industrial Tribunal held that the employee's resignation because of her employer's persistent attempts to alter her terms of employment was not a "constructive" dismissal. The E.A.T dismissed the appeal.

Lord Denning M.R.: In modern times an employer can be guilty of misconduct justifying the employee in leaving at once without notice. In each case it depends on whether the misconduct amounted to a repudiatory breach as defined in *Western Excavating (ECC) Ltd v Sharp* [1978] I.R.L.R. 27.

The circumstances are so infinitely various that there can be, and is, no rule of law saying what circumstances justify [the employee leaving his employment without notice] and what do not. It is a question of fact for the tribunal of fact—in this case the Industrial Tribunal. Once they come to their decision, the Employment Appeal Tribunal should not interfere with it.

Fox L.J.: The question where there has been repudiation is, I think, one of mixed law and fact. But for the present purposes it does not, I think, matter whether that characterisation is correct or whether the question should be regarded as one of law. Let it be supposed that it is a question of law. The law provides no exhaustive set of rules for determining whether a particular set of facts does or does not constitute repudiation. The law provides some general principles and numerous examples of the working of those principles in the reported cases. But the boundaries of the law, as thus stated and exemplified, are imprecise. There are, therefore, many set of circumstances in which it cannot be said that the initial Tribunal would be wrong to decide the case one way or the other. It is essentially a matter of degree. If there are grounds upon which the Tribunal could reasonably have reached the conclusion which it did, then the appellate Tribunal cannot reverse its determination as having been wrong in law whatever the views of the Appellate Tribunal themselves.

Watkins L.J.: . . . it undoubtedly seems to me, essentially to be a question of fact for the Industrial Tribunal.

The courts have placed themselves in a position where they acknowledge that views may differ as to whether an employer in given circumstances is repudiating a contract of employment. They appear to have accepted that there is no legal standard applicable beyond that of "reasonableness." That issue is a matter for the Industrial Tribunal deciding the case.

Treating contractual repudiation as a mere question of fact makes the problem for workers of how to respond to employer misconduct less legalistic, but still uncertain and arbitrary. Moreover, judicial insistence that the test is derived from contract pulls in its wake other common law rules. Workers faced with an employer's repudiatory misconduct need to know not only *whether*, but also *when*, they can leave. This problem was discussed in *W.E. Cox Toner* (*International*) *Ltd.* v. *Crook* [1981] I.R.L.R. 443 (E.A.T.), which considered the normal application of common law doctrine concerning repudiation of contracts requiring either acceptance by the employee (who leaves) or waiver of the employer's breach by the employee (who stays). The uncertainties are well illustrated in the following case.

Lewis v. Motorworld Garages Ltd.
[1985] I.R.L.R. 465
Court of Appeal

Mr Lewis was demoted in November 1981 with detrimental consequences to his terms and conditions of employment. However, he did not resign. Following further criticisms of his performance by management, he was given a final warning in July 1982. He considered these criticisms, and his earlier demotion unjustified, and resigned in August 1982, claiming constructive dismissal. The Industrial Tribunal dismissed his complaint and the E.A.T. dismissed his appeal.

GLIDEWELL L.J.: The principles to be found in the relevant authorities can, I believe, be summarised as follows:

(a) In order to prove that he has suffered constructive dismissal, an employee who leaves his employment must prove that he did so as the result of a breach of contract by his employer, which shows that the employer no longer intends to be bound by an essential term of the contract: *Western Excavating Ltd v Sharp* [1978] I.R.L.R. 27.

(b) However, there are normally implied in a contract of employment mutual rights and obligations of trust and confidence. A breach of this implied term may justify the employee in leaving and claiming he has been constructively dismissed: see *Post Office v Roberts* [1980] I.R.L.R. 347 and *Woods v W.M. Car Services Ltd* [1981] I.R.L.R. 347 per Browne-Wilkinson J. at 350.

(c) The breach of this implied obligation of trust and confidence may consist of a series of actions on the part of the employer which cumulatively amount to a breach of the term, though each individual incident may not do so. In particular in such a case the last action of the employer which leads to the employee leaving need not itself be a breach of contract; the question is, does the cumulative series of acts taken together amount to a breach of the implied term? see *Woods v W.M. Car Services Ltd.* This is the "last straw" situation.

(d) The decision whether there has been a breach of contract by the employer so as to constitute constructive dismissal of the employee is one of mixed law and fact for the Industrial Tribunal. An appellate court, whether the Employment Appeal Tribunal or the Court of Appeal, may only overrule that decision if the Tribunal has misdirected itself as to the relevant law or has made a finding of fact for which there is no supporting evidence or which no reasonable Tribunal could make: see *Pedersen v Camden LBC* [1981] I.R.L.R. 173 and *Woods v W.M. Car Services Ltd* [1982] I.R.L.R. 413 applying the test laid down in *Edwards v Bairstow* [1956] A.C. 14.

This case raises another issue of principle which, so far as I can ascertain, has not yet been considered by this Court. If the employer is in breach of an express term of a contract of employment, of such seriousness that the employee would be justified in leaving and claiming constructive dismissal, but the employee does not leave and accepts the altered terms of employment; if subsequently a series of actions by the employer might constitute together a breach of the implied obligation of trust and confidence, is the employee then entitled to treat the original action by the employer which was a breach of the express terms of the contract as a part—the start—of the series of actions which, taken together with the employer's other actions, might cumulatively amount to a breach of the implied terms? In my judgment the answer to this question is clearly "yes."

It follows, in my judgment, that in the present case the Industrial Tribunal should have asked themselves the question whether the respondent's treatment of Mr Lewis starting with the demotion in November 1981 and including the reduction in pay, the loss of the use of an office and the various memoranda of complaint in 1982, culminating in that of 2.8.82, cumulatively constituted a breach of the implied obligation of trust and confidence of sufficient gravity to justify Mr Lewis in leaving his employment on 2.8.82 and claiming that he had been dismissed.

An employee who terminates his employment by reason of the employer's repudiation might well be considered to have established a case for unfair dismissal, since EPCA, s.57, requires the employer to act reasonably given the existence of a reason which he has established. There are, as Browne-Wilkinson J. pointed out in *R.F. Hill Ltd.* v. *Mooney* [1981] I.R.L.R. 258 (E.A.T.) para. 11: "semantic difficulties attaching to any attempt to apply the provisions of section 57 to cases of constructive dismissal"—for how are a reason for, and reasonableness of, dismissal to be shown "where the actual termination of the contract has not been a dismissal by the employer at all, but conduct by the employer, not amounting to a dismissal which has given rise to a termination of the contract by the employee". Similar considerations led the E.A.T. to reject the notion of employee contribution to an employer's constructive dismissal, and consequently to refuse normally to allow for reduction of unfair dismissal compensation (*Holroyd* v. *Gravure Cylinders Ltd* [1984] I.R.L.R. 259 (E.A.T.)).

Nonetheless, citing two previous decisions of the E.A.T., it was held in *Mooney* that section 57 was applicable even in cases of constructive dismissal. This view was later sustained by the Court of Appeal in *Savoia* v. *Chiltern Herb Farms Ltd.* [1982] I.R.L.R. 166. The actions which have been held to constitute "constructive" dismissal must go on to be judged by the statutory standards of "fairness." The dilemma was faced in the following case.

Cawley v. South Wales Electricity Board
[1985] I.R.L.R. 89
Employment Appeal Tribunal

The appeal was against an Industrial Tribunal's finding that an employer's offer of re-engagement was sufficiently unreasonable to amount to a constructive dismissal, but was nonetheless a reasonable fair dismissal.

WAITE J.: We are indeed faced by a Tribunal which on the face of it has reached inconsistent findings. How are they to be reconciled? The solicitors for each side, in the course of submissions which have been of the utmost help to us and most ably urged, agree that considerations of fairness on the one hand and the considerations affecting constructive dismissal on the other hand are two sides of the same coin. In some curious way the Tribunal appears to have persuaded itself that two coins can be made out of one: that the same offer can be an unreasonable offer when looked at from the standpoint of whether or not it amounts to a repudiation of the contract of employment, and at the same time be a reasonable offer when looked at from the standpoint of fairness—or *vice versa*. We have found that an over-sophisticated approach. In ordinary life and in reality you cannot say that a re-engagement offer is reasonable for one purpose and not reasonable for the other.

If, as the E.A.T. held, it was an error to think "that there were two different sets of rules for reasonableness for the purposes of constructive dismissal on the one hand and for the purposes of dismissal on the other" (p. 92), one is driven full circle towards the conclusion (as *per* the Court of Appeal in *Woods*, above p. 309) that both are to be treated as questions of *fact*. In such a case, one wonders what is left of the *law* of unfair dismissal!

One alternative to a double test of fact would be to adopt as the test of involuntary leaving substantive rules of employer conduct, violation of which would lead to a conclusion of unfair dismissal, a question of law. In this context, it is suggested that it would be worth exploring the potential of Browne-Wilkinson J.'s "floating" rules founded on good industrial relations practice, which he put forward in *Williams* v. *Compair Maxam Ltd.* [1982] I.R.L.R. 82 (E.A.T.) (below p. 322).

4. VOLUNTARY TERMINATION

The limits placed by law on a worker seeking voluntarily to terminate work have varied over time from criminal restraints (*eg* the Master and Servant Acts, in force until 1867, made breach of contract of employment a criminal offence so that termination without notice could, therefore, lead to criminal penalties), to provisions in the contract of employment and social security law. A number of the more prominent restraints are examined in the sections which follow.

(A) Contractual Restraints

(i) Notice

EPCA, s.1(3)(*e*) requires that the written statement of particulars of contractual terms given to the employee must state "the length of notice which the employee is obliged to give . . . to determine his contract of employment." Provided the employee gives due notice, he or she is acting lawfully. In the absence of express provision, the period of notice may be implied from trade custom. In other situations, the courts usually imply a requirement that a "reasonable period of notice" be given. Breach of this requirement entitles the employer to sue, but only to recover damages. In practice, the difficulty of proving loss, the relative expense of legal action, and the likely effect on industrial relations mean there is rarely an attempt to enforce notice provisions against employees (for an exception, see *Payzu Limited* v. *Hannaford* [1918] 2 K.B. 348).

Section 49(2) of EPCA requires the employee, after four weeks' employment, to give a minimum of one week's notice of termination to the employer. Nothing is said, however, as to the consequences of an employee giving less than the statutory minimum period. The relaxed attitude of the law towards workers who wish to terminate their employment is illustrated by *Ready Case Ltd.* v. *Jackson* [1981] I.R.L.R. 312 (E.A.T.), paras. 22–25.

(ii) Fixed-term and performance contracts

Employment is usually undertaken for an indefinite period, with express or implied provision for termination by notice. But the parties may agree that termination is to occur only when a fixed period has expired or a specified task has been performed. If so, the employee will be breaking the contract if he leaves earlier. One view of the consequences is spelt out in the following extract.

Thomas Marshall (Exports) Ltd. v. Guinle
[1978] 3 All E.R. 193; [1978] I.R.L.R. 174
Chancery Division

The employee was managing director of a company under a 10-year fixed-term contract commencing on September 2, 1972. At a meeting on December 5, 1977, he purported to resign. The company insisted that the contract of employment remained in being, and in particular, the obligations as to not working in other businesses or disclosing confidential information.

MEGARRY V.-C.: I shall take first Mr Hutchison's submissions on behalf of the defendant that his service agreement was terminated by his unilateral repudiation of it on 5.12.77, even though the Company never accepted it as ending the agreement. This is a striking contention. It means that although the defendant and the Company contractually bound themselves together for ten years from the 2.9.72, so that the agreement still had over $4\frac{1}{2}$ years to run, the defendant and also the Company, was able at any time, without the consent of the other, to bring the contract to an end simply by saying so; and that is just what the defendant has done. Mr Hutchison accepted that the general rule was that a contract was not determined merely by the wrongful repudiation of it by one party, and that it was for the innocent party to decide whether to treat the contract as having determined or as continuing in existence. That rule, however, did not apply to contracts of employment, for they were subject to a special exception. Under the exception, any contract of employment could at any time be brought to an end by either party repudiating it.

I think the courts must be astute to prevent a wrongdoer from profiting too greatly from his wrong. If without just cause a servant who has contracted to serve for a term of years refuses to do so, it is easy to see that the Court is powerless to make him do what he has contracted to do: neither by decreeing specific performance nor by granting an injunction can the Court make the servant perform loyally what he is refusing to do, however wrongfully. If such an order were to be made, the ultimate sanction for disobedience is committal to prison; and this, far from forcing the servant to work for his master, will effectively stop him from doing this. But why should the court's inability to make a servant work for his employer mean that as soon as the servant refuses to do so the court is forthwith disabled from restraining him from committing any breach, however flagrant, of his other obligations during the period of his contract? I would wholly reject the doctrine of automatic determination, whether in its wide form or in its narrowed version.

I accept, of course, that there are difficulties in almost any view that one takes. To say that a contract of service remains in existence despite the servant's resolute refusal to do any work under it produces odd results. Here, however, I am concerned only with the issue whether the servant's wrongful refusal to serve has set him free of his obligations which bound him while his contract of service continued. . . .

First, in my judgment the service agreement between the parties has not been determined but remains still in force. Second, the defendant is subject to all the obligations that flow from his being bound by the service agreement. Third, as the service agreement is still in force, clause 12, which provides for the defendant to be free from restrictions when he ceases to be managing director, has not come into operation, and that is so whether or not the two provisos are satisfied. Fourth, there is ample jurisdiction in the Court to grant an injunction to restrain the defendant from doing acts contrary to his obligations under the service agreement, subject always to the exercise of the Court's discretion whether to grant an injunction at all, and, if so, in what width.

(iii) Restrictive covenants

A substantial inhibition on voluntary termination by the worker may be found in restrictive covenants in the contract concerning future employment. For two contrasting illustrations, see *Greer* v. *Sketchleys Ltd.* [1979] I.R.L.R. 445 (C.A.), and *Spafax Ltd.* v. *Harrison* [1980] I.R.L.R. 442 (C.A.); also *The Marley Tile Co. Ltd.* v. *Johnson* [1982] I.R.L.R. 75 (C.A.).

(iv) Benefits restricting mobility

Many contractual benefits (and statutory rights) are contingent upon continued employment with the same employer. Among such benefits are pensions, housing (tied cottages) and redundancy payments. Such contingent entitlements may inhibit voluntary termination more effectively than formal legal obligations. For a modern illustration, see *Strathclyde Regional Council* v. *Neil* [1984] I.R.L.R. 11.

(B) Social Security Rules

As work is the primary source of income for most workers, termination of work means termination of income. If, on cessation of work, unemployment benefit was immediately forthcoming, loss of income might not restrain voluntary termination. But one ground of temporary disqualification for unemployment benefit is precisely that the claimant "has voluntarily left such employment (as an employed earner) without just cause" (see the Social Security Act 1975, s.20(1)(*a*)).

Crewe v. Social Security Commissioner

[1982] I.R.L.R. 295
Court of Appeal

The employee retired as a school teacher at the age of 61 under a scheme encouraging early retirement. He was held disqualified from receiving unemployment benefit for six weeks.

LORD DENNING M.R.: Mr Crewe is, of course, not guilty of any misconduct: but he did voluntarily leave his employment. The question is whether he left it "without just cause." At first sight it would look as if Ernest Crewe had "just cause" for leaving his employment. His employers wanted him to go—not for his own sake—but for their own sake. That is shown by the regulations about premature retirement. They apply only when his employer is satisfied that his services have been terminated "in the interests of the efficient discharge of his employer's function." The education authority here were so satisfied because the educational system would be more efficient if he retired and was replaced by a younger man.

But this simple approach is contrary to a long line of decisions by the commissioners. . . .

They warrant the following propositions:

1. When a man voluntarily leaves his employment, he is disqualified from receiving unemployment benefit for six weeks, unless he proves—and the burden is on him to prove—that he had "just cause" for leaving his employment.

2. It is not sufficient for him to prove that he was quite reasonable in leaving his employment. Reasonableness may be "good cause," but it is not necessarily "just cause."

3. "Without just cause" means without any just cause for throwing on to the unemployment fund the payment of unemployment benefit. If he voluntarily retires on pension, he is getting a substantial financial benefit for himself, and it is not fair or just to the unemployment fund that he should also get unemployment benefit for the six weeks.

To which I would add this. Even though the employer wants him to retire—and offers him inducements to do so—for the employer's benefit, nevertheless he is still getting a substantial financial benefit for himself and is disqualified from obtaining unemployment benefit.

I would, therefore, dismiss this appeal.

5. INVOLUNTARY TERMINATION

Terminations which are involuntary on the part of the worker are the most fertile source of disputes. Until the Industrial Relations Act 1971, workers could be required to leave involuntarily subject only to a few legal and practical restraints (notice, agreed disciplinary procedures, etc.). It was only by the law of unfair dismissal, enacted in 1971, that an involuntary termination was declared unfair, unless fair reasons for it could be shown to exist.

The resulting case law is organised below around three central practical problems: involuntary termination for alleged misconduct, ill-health and incompetence. In each case we ask, first, the substantive questions: what is misconduct, ill-health or incompetence which justifies termination. Secondly, what are the procedural requirements in such situations.

Two general points need to be made. First, *termination* is the solution to problems of misconduct, ill-health and incompetence primarily from the *managerial* viewpoint, not from that of the worker who misbehaves or is ill or incompetent. The legal rules should be evaluated in terms of their appreciation and successful balancing of this conflict of interest between employer and employee. Secondly, as with redundancy and reorganisation, termination is only one solution to the problem. Collective bargaining, as we have shown elsewhere, often provides other answers. The legal rules can thus be evaluated also by comparison with industrial practice.

The sources of the legal rules are to be found in the common law, in industrial practice, and in statutory provisions. Below we give extracts illustrating the rules derived from each source. These demonstrate considerable cross-fertilisation, *e.g.* contractual rules and statutory provisions in some cases rely on industrial practice. However, it is the case law on unfair dismissal which provides most of our illustrations based on all three sources. In it, two major issues emerge which underlie the legal rules on involuntary termination as interpreted and applied by the courts. First, what is the substantive standard of fairness; and second, what is the significance of procedure?

(A.) The Legal Standard of Fairness

Legal protection against unfair dismissal under EPCA requires that the employer should have a sufficient reason for dismissing the employee and that he should act reasonably in the circumstances. This raises the issue of whether Tribunals and Courts are prepared to challenge the actions of management in dismissing employees; and, if so, what standards will they invoke to assess management behaviour.

Watling & Co. Ltd. v. Richardson
[1978] I.R.L.R. 255
Employment Appeal Tribunal

An employee, dismissed for redundancy, complained of unfair dismissal because his employers had hired two other employees shortly before his dismissal. The Industrial Tribunal upheld the complaint.

Phillips J.: One view—now rejected in the authorities, and to be regarded as heretical—is that all the Industrial Tribunal has to say to itself, reciting the words of [EPCA, s 57(3)], "Was the dismissal fair or unfair"; that having done this it has arrived at an unappealable decision; and that in answering that question it is not required to apply any standard other than its own collective wisdom. What the authorities, including *Vickers v Smith* [1977] I.R.L.R. 11 (E.A.T.), have decided is that in answering that question the Industrial Tribunal, while using its own collective wisdom, is to apply the standard of the reasonable employer; that it is to say, the fairness or unfairness of the dismissal is to be judged not by the hunch of the particular Industrial Tribunal which (though rarely) may be whimsical or eccentric, but by the objective standard of the way in which a reasonable employer in those circumstances, in that line of business, would have behaved. It has to be recognised that there are circumstances where more than one course of action may be reasonable. In the case of redundancy, for example, and where selection of one or two employees to be dismissed for redundancy from a larger number is in issue, there may well be and often are cases where equally reasonable, fair, sensible and prudent employers would take different courses, one choosing "A", another "B" and another "C." In those circumstances for an Industrial Tribunal to say that it was unfair to select "A" for dismissal, rather than "B" or "C," merely because had they been the employers that is what they would have done, is to apply the test of what the particular Industrial Tribunal itself would have done and not the test of what a reasonable employer would have done. It is in this sense that it is said that the test is whether what has been done is something which "no reasonable management would have done." In such cases, where more than one course of action can be considered reasonable, if an Industrial Tribunal equates its view of what it itself would have done with what a reasonable employer would have done, it may mean that an employer will be found to have dismissed an employee unfairly although in the circumstances many perfectly good and fair employers would have done as that employer did.

Rolls-Royce Ltd. v. Walpole
[1980] I.R.L.R. 343
Employment Appeal Tribunal

> The employee was dismissed because of his poor attendance record, due to certified illness. The Industrial Tribunal upheld his complaint of unfair dismissal. A majority of the E.A.T. including May J. allowed the appeal.

MR. J. D. HUGHES: The other two members of this Appeal Tribunal, however, take the view that this appeal should be allowed. Each of them accepts, as they must, the principle laid down in many cases, including those to which we have referred earlier, that not only is it not for an Industrial Tribunal to substitute its own view of the circumstances of a dismissal for that of the particular employer, but, even more, it is not for this Appeal Tribunal to substitute its own view, in its turn, of the circumstances of a particular case for that of an Industrial Tribunal. They have in mind the dicta of the members of the Court of Appeal in the *Retarded Children's Aid Society case* [1978] I.R.L.R. 128 and that, for instance, of Lord Widgery C.J. in *Global Plant Ltd v Secretary of State for Social Services* [1972] 1 Q.B. 139 at page 155. Nevertheless, the exercise of good industrial relations is not an exact science. As this Appeal Tribunal pointed out in the judgment in *Watling's* case [above p. 317] in a given set of circumstances it is possible for two perfectly reasonable employers to take different courses of action in relation to an employee. Frequently there is a range of responses to the conduct or capacity of an employee on the part of an employer, from and including summary dismissal downwards to a mere informal warning, which can be said to have been reasonable. It is precisely because this range of possible reasonable responses does exist in many cases that it has been laid down that it is neither for us on an appeal, nor for an Industrial Tribunal on the original hearing, to substitute our or its respective views for those of the particular employer concerned. It is in those cases where the employer does not satisfy the Industrial Tribunal that his response had been within that range of reasonable responses, that the Industrial Tribunal is enjoined by the statute to find that the dismissal of the relevant employee has been unfair. Nevertheless, insofar as this Appeal Tribunal is concerned even though it, too, must not, as we have said, substitute its views for those of the Industrial Tribunal, where it is satisfied, on the facts found by the Industrial Tribunal, that the action taken by an employer in a particular case was without question within the range of reasonable responses, but the Industrial Tribunal have held the dismissal to be unfair, then the Appeal Tribunal should interfere. Equally, when the Appeal Tribunal takes the view that before the Industrial Tribunal the employers did not show that the action which they had taken was within the range of normal responses, but nevertheless the Industrial Tribunal have held the dismissal to be fair, then again we think that the Appeal Tribunal should interfere and allow an appeal. In neither of these cases is this Appeal Tribunal substituting its own view for that of the Industrial Tribunal from whom the appeal is brought, nor, indeed, for that of the employers whose dismissal of the employee is being called in question. All that the Employment Appeal Tribunal is saying in such circumstances is that, in reaching the conclusion which it did, the Industrial Tribunal must have misdirected itself as to the extent of the range in the particular circumstances in which a fair and reasonable response by an employer could lie; that it was thus a decision to which no Industrial Tribunal [which had] properly directed itself upon the facts could have come, and that it was thus perverse.

British Leyland UK Ltd. v. Swift

[1981] I.R.L.R. 91
Court of Appeal

> The employee was dismissed after 18 years' service when his own vehicle was found with a road fund licence belonging to his employer's vehicle. An Industrial Tribunal found the dismissal unfair as dismissal was too severe a penalty, and this was upheld by a majority of the E.A.T.

LORD DENNING M.R.: The first question that arises is whether the Industrial Tribunal applied the wrong test. We have had considerable argument about it. They said: " . . . a reasonable employer would, in our opinion, have considered that a lesser penalty was appropriate." I do not think that that is the right test. The correct test is: was it reasonable for the employers to dismiss him? If no reasonable employer would have dismissed him, then the dismissal was unfair. But if a reasonable employer might reasonably have dismissed him, then the dismissal was fair. It must be remembered that in all these cases there is a band of reasonableness, within which one employer might reasonably take one view, another quite reasonably take a different view. One would quite reasonably dismiss the man. The other would quite reasonably keep him on. Both views may be quite reasonable. If it was quite reasonable to dismiss him, then the dismissal must be upheld as fair, even though some other employers might not have dismissed him.

Iceland Frozen Foods Ltd. v. Jones

[1982] I.R.L.R. 439
Employment Appeal Tribunal

> In the next extract the E.A.T. quoted from all the above cases, and concluded as follows.

BROWNE-WILKINSON J.: Since the present state of the law can only be found by going through a number of different authorities, it may be convenient if we should seek to summarise the present law. We consider that the authorities establish that in law the correct approach for the Industrial Tribunal to adopt in answering the question posed by s.57(3) of EPCA is as follows:—

(1) the starting point should always be the words of s.57(3) themselves;

(2) in applying the section an industrial tribunal must consider the reasonableness of the employer's conduct, not simply whether they (the members of the industrial tribunal) consider the dismissal to be fair;

(3) in judging the reasonableness of the employer's conduct an Industrial Tribunal must not substitute its decision as to what was the right course to adopt for that of the employer;

(4) in many (though not all) cases there is a band of reasonable responses to the employee's conduct within which one employer might reasonably take one view, another quite reasonably take another;

(5) the function of the Industrial Tribunal, as an industrial jury, is to determine whether in the particular circumstances of each case the decision to dismiss the employee fell within the band of reasonable responses which a reasonable employer might have adopted. If the dismissal falls within the band the dismissal is fair; if the dismissal falls outside the band it is unfair.

The characterisation of judges viewing dismissal issues through the eyes of management has been deemed "obvious but perhaps simplistic" (P. Davies and M. Freedland, *Labour Law: Text and Materials*, (1st ed., 1979), p. 370. Davies and Freedland go on to elaborate the different kinds of "good employers" the judge could identify with. They equate the "substantive" justice applied by the judges with "distributive notions of justice" (p. 355), which is translated into "a fair balance" between the interests of the employing enterprise and those of the employee (p. 361). Hugh Collins perceives judicial ideology as characterised by neutrality in employment relationships ("Capitalist discipline and corporatist law" (1982) 11 I.L.J. 78, 170). Is it the case that the employer's or management's view adopted by judges can be relied upon to achieve a fair balance, or represents a kind of "neutrality"? The following extract argues to the contrary.

B. Bercusson, Annotation to EPCA, s.57(3), in the *Encyclopedia of Labour Relations Law* (B.A. Hepple and P. O'Higgins ed.)

What most lawyers declared to be the law was as follows. Under this subsection, far from tribunals being empowered to pass judgment on the employer's actions, they must *take the part of the employer* and ask if, *as the employer*, the action was reasonable. *Not* whether the Tribunal as an independent arbiter thinks it was reasonable but whether an *employer* would think it was. As put by Browne-Wilkinson J. in the context of an employee dismissed for suspecting dishonesty who is in fact innocent: "The choice in dealing with [EPCA, s.57(3)] is between looking at the reasonableness of the employer or justice to the employee. *Devis v Atkins* [1977] I.R.L.R. 314 (H.L.) shows that the correct test is the reasonableness of the employer" (*Sillifant v Powell Duffryn Timber Ltd.* [1983] I.R.L.R. 91 (E.A.T.) para. 31). Another decision of the E.A.T. similarly held that the ratio of the House of Lords' decision in *Devis v Atkins* was to be found in Lord Dilhorne's stressing "that the Tribunal is to focus its attention on the employer, and not on whether the employee has suffered injustice" (*West Midland Co-operative Society Ltd. v Tipton* [1983] I.R.L.R. 276 (E.A.T.) para. 14). In a subsequent case, the Court of Appeal referred to Lord Dilhorne's words as being "spoken in a special context" (Slade L.J. in *Dobie v Burns International Security Services (U.K.) Ltd.* [1984] I.R.L.R. 329, para. 21). But the context of the judge's statement made it seem that the injustice to the employee is a matter that the *employer* has to take into account in deciding on dismissal—not the tribunal (see Sir John Donaldson M.R., at para. 14).

The standard of reasonableness was thus turned into that of a reasonable employer, as if the seriousness of a dog's bite should be judged by the standard of a reasonable dog. There is nothing objective about the standard of reasonableness thus put forward—unless, that is, one subscribes to the unitary view of industrial relations—that employer and employees are united in their common interest in the business enterprise and share common industrial standards. But, it need hardly be said, such a view is extremely politically contentious and has been criticised as such by industrial relations pluralists, not to mention many others.

One danger of such an approach is that it can openly conflict with the purpose of a statute intended to protect individual employees from unfair dismissal. A clear illustration is to be found in dicta by Ackner L.J. in *British Leyland UK Ltd. v Swift* [1981] I.R.L.R. 91 (C.A.). Discussing the options open to *reasonable* employers faced with misconduct by an employee, he said: "An employer might reasonably take the view, if the circumstances so justified, that his attitude must be a firm and definite one and must involve dismissal *in order to deter other* employees from like conduct. . . . " (para. 17) (emphasis added). The law protecting employees from unfair dismissal is here perverted to accomodate the employer's management policy.

Even when a Tribunal takes the view that a reasonable employer would not have acted as the employer in question did, they may still be precluded from interfering with the management's decision. The judges are divided over the extent to which, even then, the Tribunal's views can override those of the employer in question. The less management-minded—*less*, mind you, have held that there may be differences between the actions of different reasonable employers. Management has discretion—some may be harsh, others lenient—but it is not for Tribunals to condemn the former by saying they are acting unreasonably. It is harsh—but fair, and not unreasonable. It is not for the Tribunal to substitute its judgment for the employers'. So many Tribunals have been overruled by the EAT and higher courts when they condemn management's actions as unreasonable, that they will now only rarely interfere with management's substantive decisions.

This tendency is reinforced by the more management-minded judges' views on the matter. These judges apparently find it conceivable that the law will interfere only with the most extreme cases of unreasonable behaviour by management. As stated by Cumming-Bruce J. in *Vickers Ltd. v Smith* [1977] I.R.L.R. 11 (EAT), Industrial Tribunals may overrule management decisions not where management's decision was merely wrong, but only where: "It was so wrong, that no sensible or reasonable management could have arrived at the decision at which the mangement arrived." It is here seriously suggested that the law will hold as unfair only the most extremely unreasonable sorts of management action. Many judges have been wary of too firmly endorsing this extreme position, and have continued to allow Industrial Tribunals to intervene where management's action is very unfair, and not only positively outrageous.

The reluctance of the law to challenge managerial discretion, by the courts designating a range of (even contradictory) managerial decisions as "reasonable" is, perhaps, subject to one qualification. The courts may be prepared to assess management behaviour in terms of what is called "good industrial relations practice." This may be a way of introducing an agreed, rather than a one-sided management standard. The following extracts explain how Industrial Tribunals are expected to apply this standard.

Williams v. Compair Maxam Ltd.

[1982] I.R.L.R. 83
Employment Appeal Tribunal

An Industrial Tribunal held a redundancy dismissal to be fair.

BROWN-WILKINSON J.: . . . In considering whether the decision of an Industrial Tribunal is perverse in a legal sense, there is one feature which does not occur in other jurisdictions where there is a right of appeal only on a point of law. The Industrial Tribunal is an industrial jury which brings to its task a knowledge of industrial relations both from the viewpoint of the employer and the employee. Matters of good industrial relations practice are not proved before an Industrial Tribunal as they would be proved before an ordinary court: the lay members are taken to know them. The lay members of the Industrial Tribunal bring to their task their expertise in a field where conventions and practices are of the greatest importance. . . .

[The E.A.T. elaborated five steps which good industrial practice required in a redundancy situation. It then assessed that behaviour of the employer in question and the Industrial Tribunal's favourable view of it.]

. . . we consider that the majority decision was not merely wrong, but so wrong that no Industrial Tribunal properly directing itself could have reached it. To anyone versed in industrial relations, the decision offends common sense.

We must add a word of warning. For the purpose of giving our reasons for reaching our exceptional conclusion that the decision of the Industrial Tribunal in this case was perverse, we have had to state what in our view are the steps which a reasonable and fair employer at the present time would seek to take in dismissing unionised employees on the ground of redundancy. We stress two points. First, these are not immutable principles which will stay unaltered for ever. Practices and attitudes in industry change with time and new norms of acceptable industrial relations behaviour will emerge. Secondly, the factors we have started are *not* principles of law, but standards of behaviour. Therefore in future cases before this Appeal Tribunal there should be no attempt to say that an Industrial Tribunal which did not have regard to or give effect to one of these factors has misdirected itself in law. Only in cases such as the present where a genuine case for perversity on the grounds that the decision flies in the face of commonly accepted standards of fairness can be made out, are these factors directly relevant. They are relevant only as showing the knowledge of industrial relations which the industrial jury is to be assumed as having brought to bear on the case they had to decide.

Insofar as the E.A.T. here expounds principles of "good industrial practice" and holds Industrial Tribunals, and employers, to them, there could emerge some more explicit legal limits to the unrestrained discretion of the "reasonable employer."

But the courts are still very reluctant to allow standards of good industrial practice to be regarded even as variable guidelines if their effect would seem to them to interfere with the overriding test of reasonableness (as in *A. Simpson and Son (Motors) Ltd.* v. *Reid and Findlater* [1983] I.R.L.R. 401 (E.A.T.). Other judges are even more forthright. In *Gray* v. *Shetland Norse Preserving Co. Ltd.* [1985] I.R.L.R. 53 (E.A.T.), Lord McDonald, while acknowledging the E.A.T.'s power to lay down guidelines, welcomed the opportunity to point out "yet again how very limited the scope of the (*Williams*) principles is" (p. 54). In *Rolls-Royce Motors Ltd.* v. *Dewhurst* [1985] I.R.L.R. 184 (E.A.T.), Popplewell J. opined that:

> "No decision of this court seems to give greater trouble than the decision in *Williams* v. *Compair Maxam*" (p. 186), and went on to elaborate the limitations on the principles enunciated there, including that for an Industrial Tribunal to direct itself "that an act contrary to *any* of the principles enunciated in *Compair Maxam* leads to the conclusion, even *prima facie*, that the dismissals are unfair—is not, in our judgment, a proper direction" (p. 187).

Despite these views, other attempts are to be found to encourage Industrial Tribunals to have regard to good industrial practice, as is evident in the following case.

Neale v. County Council of Hereford and Worcester
[1985] I.R.L.R. 281
Employment Appeal Tribunal

> Mr Neale, a teacher, noticed that a particular exam question might confuse a student by requiring information unrelated to her studies, and so he wrote the information on her paper. He was reported and, after an inquiry, dismissed.

WAITE J.: It is, of course, an inevitable part of every Tribunal's thought process, as they set about fixing the parameters of reasonable response to a given set of circumstances, that they should develop within their minds a picture of a hypothetical employer endowed with the attributes of reasonableness; and should ask themselves what range of response, in the same circumstances, would have been tolerable to him. The building up of that mental picture will normally be a gradual process to which many influences will have contributed—not least the impact made upon their minds by the experience (which is uniquely theirs) of seeing and hearing the parties and witnesses. The law protects that process by insisting that this delicately formed mental image is not to be shattered by applying to the case any less informed view of the facts or merits that may happen to occur to the minds or sympathies of an appellate Tribunal. When the time comes, however, for an Appeal Tribunal in its own turn (for the purpose of posing and answering the question: was the verdict one at which any reasonable Tribunal could have arrived?) to build a mental picture of the hypothetical reasonable Tribunal, it is permissible, and indeed essential, that we should ask ourselves whether there are any attributes of reasonableness so obviously called for by the circumstances as to make it inevitable that any reasonable Tribunal would be bound to include them in the picture of the reasonable employer developing in their minds' eye.

Any reasonable Tribunal required to sketch for itself the lineaments of the reasonable employer within a teaching context would in our judgment remind itself that such an employer is called upon to demonstrate special qualities appropriate to the vocational character of the employment, and that such qualities may well differ from those which it would be right to attribute to a reasonable employer within an industrial or commercial context. There will be times when the need to maintain professional standards generally and the quality of teaching within the particular school or college for which he is responsible may require him to be more severe than his counterpart in industry. There will be other times when account has to be taken of the stress and anxiety which are paid by many teachers as the price of dedication; and of the fact that the very qualities of intuition and enthusiasm which make for a good teacher may sometimes be manifested in behaviour more emotional (and possibly even less mature) than it would be normal to expect of those in more hard-headed occupations. Occasions of that kind may require him to show a lenience that it would be surprising to experience on the shop-floor. A reasonable Tribunal would remind itself that the necessity to make a right and fair choice between those opposing approaches in the particular circumstances of each case calls for the exercise of qualities amongst which sensitivity, deliberation, a sense both of proportion and humour, and a desire at all times to maintain not only the substance but also the appearance of fairness, must rank high.

Would an educational employer possessing those essential qualities of reason be capable, in the eyes of any reasonable Tribunal, of responding in the way that the Council did in the present case to the problem presented by Mr Neale's misconduct? We think not. When their total response is regarded in the round, there was too much haste about it, too much stubbornness and secrecy, and too little concern for the appearance of fairness as well as its substance, for their reaction generally to be seen in the eyes of any reasonable Tribunal as conduct which would have commended itself to a reasonable employer in their position.

The E.A.T.'s attempts to lay down guidelines of good industrial practice for Industrial Tribunals contrasts sharply with the Court of Appeal's approach to Industrial Tribunal decision-making. The primary test of the "reasonable range of employer responses" which cannot be condemned by an Industrial Tribunal has been invoked by the higher courts to curb the E.A.T.'s overruling of Tribunal decisions. As an appellate Tribunal only on points of law, the E.A.T. has been restrained from overruling an Industrial Tribunal unless the Tribunal has itself moved outside the range of reasonable decisions open to a reasonable tribunal (*Spook Erection* v. *Thackray* [1984] I.R.L.R. 116 (Ct. Sess.); *cf.* the willingness, nonetheless, of the E.A.T. to overrule an Industrial Tribunal decision as perverse in the light of good industrial practice in a case involving the same company less than one year later: *Payne* v. *Spook Erection Ltd.* [1984] I.R.L.R. 219 (E.A.T.).)

This is compounded by the oft-reiterated preference of the Court of Appeal for Industrial Tribunal decisions with a minimal recital of facts and a statement of law going little further than reference to appropriate statutory provisions (*UCATT* v. *Brain* [1981] I.R.L.R. 225 (C.A.), *per* Donaldson L.J.; *Kearney and Trecker Marwin Ltd.* v. *Varndell* [1983] I.R.L.R. 335, *per* Eveleigh L.J.). This call has been taken up by the E.A.T. President, Waite J. (*Anandarajah* v. *Lord Chancellor's Department* [1984] I.R.L.R. 131 (E.A.T.).

Accordingly, the enforcement of guidelines of good industrial relations practice is rendered extremely difficult, as only the most unreasonable Industrial Tribunal will be subject to review. So both employers and Industrial Tribunals are given free rein. The result may prove chaotic, as Industrial Tribunals could intervene to strike down employer decisions, but the E.A.T. would find it difficult to intervene, even where there is glaring inconsistency among Tribunals applying the same substantive standard of fairness. This prospect was nonetheless viewed with equanimity by the Court of Appeal in the following case.

Kent County Council v. Gilham
[1985] I.R.L.R. 17
Court of Appeal

An employer appealed against an Industrial Tribunal decision which took the opposite view from that of two other tribunals as to the fairness of a dismissal for economic reasons.

Griffiths L.J.: The facts were of course not identical in the three cases, but the issue was undoubtedly broadly the same, namely whether the Councils were acting unfairly because they dismissed school meals staff in order to impose upon them new and less favourable conditions of service in breach of the National Conditions, for the purpose of effecting economies in their budgets. In very carefully reasoned decisions both these Industrial Tribunals concluded that the need to effect economies was a "substantial reason," and that the local authority had acted reasonably in regarding it as a sufficient reason for the dismissals.

Mr Harvey [counsel for the County Council] therefore submits that those decisions are a powerful indication that this Tribunal must have misdirected itself in law in order to arrive at an opposite conclusion. This court must not allow itself to be seduced by this beguiling argument. Parliament has determined that there shall be no appeal from an Industrial Tribunal on a question of fact. No doubt one of the parties is often very fed up when an Industrial Tribunal has found the facts against him, but that is just too bad; there is nothing he can do about it; he has had his hearing and that is an end of the matter. This was a policy decision taken by Parliament, presumably because it is obvious that he country's legal resources would not run to providing for the vast numbers of appeals that would result from allowing an appeal on fact.

Now whether or not an employer has behaved reasonably in dismissing an employee is a question of fact, and it is a question upon which different people, looking at the same set of circumstances, may reasonably come to different conclusions. It is therefore endemic in a system where there is no appeal on fact that from time to time different Industrial Tribunals will give different answers to broadly similar situations, and neither decision can be challenged. It is therefore important that this court should resist the temptation to seek to overturn a factual decision with which it may not agree by searching for some shadowy point of law on which to hang its hat for the purpose of bringing uniformity to the differing decisions. If we were to take this course, it would have the very undesirable effect of encouraging innumerable appeals which raised no point of law, but depended upon comparative findings of fact.

For the extension of this pyramid of uncontrolled discretion upwards to include judicial review (or lack of it) of public employers, see *R.* v. *Hertfordshire County Council, ex p. NUPE* [1985] I.R.L.R. 258 (C.A.) above, Chapter 3 on *The Work Obligation*, p. 72.

(B) The Significance of Procedure

In practice, termination as a solution to problems of misconduct, ill-health or incompetence (as well as redundancy, reorganisations, and so on) is often avoided by the use of procedures. Inquiries, investigations, hearings, a search for alternatives or substitution of other measures frequently renders termination unnecessary. Hence the significance of procedure in industrial practice. Its significance in law is less clear. Does a failure to adopt or comply with procedures prior to termination make the termination unfair?

In *Charles Letts & Co.* v. *Howard* [1976] I.R.L.R. 248 (E.A.T.), the E.A.T. put the onus on the employer to satisfy the Tribunal that even if the proper, fair procedure had been carried out, it would not have made any difference. Cumming-Bruce J. held that "the employers had failed to show that, if they had followed the appropriate procedure when contemplating dismissal, the result would inevitably have been the same" (para. 25). But in *British Labour Pump Co. Ltd.* v. *Byrne* [1979] I.R.L.R. 97 (E.A.T.), Slynn J. while acknowledging that the *Charles Letts* case was frequently cited in appeals, nonetheless sought to modify the impact of that case by proposing his own standard (para. 17):

> "We doubt whether in that case the Tribunal was really laying down as an absolute rule that an employer cannot succeed unless he can show that inevitably it would have made no difference. It seems to us that the right approach is to ask two questions. In the first place, has the employer shown on the balance of probabilities that they would have taken the same course had they held an inquiry, and had they received the information which that inquiry would have produced? Secondly, the employer must show—the burden is on him—that in the light of the information which they would have had, had they gone through the proper procedure, then would they have been behaving reasonably in still deciding to dismiss."

This apparent "change of view of the EAT in those cases where there has been a failure of procedure" was commented upon in *W & J Wass Ltd.* v. *Binns* [1982] I.R.L.R. 283 (C.A.) quoting the Industrial Tribunal which had stated that one result was dictated by *Charles Letts*, but another by "more recent authority" (quoted at para. 18). The Court of Appeal in *Binns* upheld the Industrial Tribunal's decision, saying that "the *British Labour Pump* case provides useful guidelines" (Waller L.J. at para. 16). The Court of Appeal did not see that case as conflicting with *Devis* v. *Atkins* [1977] I.R.L.R. 314 (H.L.).

Just before the Court of Appeal's decision in *Binns*, in *Dunn* v. *Pochin (Contractors) Ltd.* [1982] I.R.L.R. 449 (E.A.T.), Browne-Wilkinson J. had remarked on the "difference of emphasis in the authorities" between the support of *Charles Letts & Co. Ltd.* and *British Labour Pump Co. Ltd.*, adding: "At some stage we think it will be necessary for the assistance of Industrial Tribunals in approaching this kind of case to indicate what are the circumstances which justify a finding of fair dismissal even though no opportunity to explain has been given" (para. 14). The decision in *Binns*, however, was plainly not to his liking. In the following case he expressed his views.

Sillifant v. Powell Duffryn Timber Ltd.
[1983] I.R.L.R. 91
Employment Appeal Tribunal

BROWNE-WILKINSON J.: This appeal raises a point of considerable practical importance in the law of unfair dismissal. In general, it is established law that in deciding whether or not a dismissal is fair for the purposes of s.57 of the Employment Protection (Consolidation) Act 1978 attention has to be concentrated on the reasonableness of the employer's decision to dismiss judged in the light of the facts known to the employer at the time of dismissal and his conduct at that time. There has become engrafted onto that approach the principle that even if, judged in the light of the circumstances known at the time of dismissal, the employer's decision was not reasonable because of some failure to follow a fair procedure yet the dismissal can be held fair if, on the facts proved before the Industrial Tribunal, the Industrial Tribunal comes to the conclusion that the employer could reasonably have decided to dismiss if he had followed a fair procedure. For example, if an employer has dismissed an employee for dishonesty without giving the employee an opportunity to state his case (which would normally be held to be unfair conduct) an Industrial Tribunal could properly hold the dismissal to be fair if satisfied on the evidence before it (the Industrial Tribunal) that the employee's explanation if it had been given to the employer would have made no difference. This engrafted principle known as the *British Labour Pump* principle since its latest statement is contained in *British Labour Pump Co. Ltd. v Byrne* [1979] I.R.L.R. 94. . . .

[This principle] requires the Industrial Tribunal to consider two separate points each involving distinct evidence in reaching a conclusion whether the dismissal was fair. First, looking at the matter in the light of the circumstances known at the time of the dismissal, was the employer acting reasonably? Secondly, did the procedural shortcomings make any difference to the outcome, this second question being judged in the light of the evidence before the Industrial Tribunal and by definition not known to the employers at the time of dismissal. . . .

The correct approach to the question posed by s.57(3) has been established by the decision of the House of Lords in *Devis v Atkins* [1977] I.R.L.R. 314 (H.L.). In that case, the employee had been dismissed for refusing to carry out instructions but without the employer having given him fair prior warning. After the date of dismissal, the employer discovered that the employee had been guilty of dishonesty. Before the Industrial Tribunal, the employer sought to lead evidence of such dishonesty. The Industrial Tribunal refused to admit such evidence on the grounds that the employer did not know of the dishonesty at the time of dismissal. The House of Lords upheld that decision. The leading speech was given by Lord Dilhorne.

At page 318 he said this:

> "In my opinion it is not the case that an employer can establish that a dismissal was fair by relying on matters of which he did not know at the time but which he ought reasonably to have known. T.U.L.R.A., Sched. 1, para. 6(8) [now EPCA, s.57(3) as amended] does not so provide."

At first sight the decision in *Devis* v *Atkins* is wholly inconsistent with the

British Labour Pump principle. The reasonableness of the employer's conduct cannot be affected by facts which he ought to have discovered by holding a proper investigation which in fact he did not hold.

[Browne-Wilkinson J. then reviewed and rejected opposing arguments based on a different view of *Devis v Atkins*, and concluded:]

Therefore, apart from authority we would hold that the *British Labour Pump* principle is logically inconsistent with the provisions of s.57(3) as construed in *Devis v Atkins*. . . .

We also agree with Mr Tabachnik [counsel for the employee] that the application of the *British Labour Pump* principle has given rise to practical difficulties. Industrial Tribunals apply the principle in widely different types of case. If the procedural failure by the employer is truly procedural only, there is not much difficulty. Thus, for example, if the failure consists in holding an otherwise full investigation in the absence of a representative for the employee whose presence is required by an agreed procedure, it is not unduly difficult for an Industrial Tribunal to decide whether the absence of the representative made a substantial difference. But in practice Industrial Tribunals have come to apply the principle to cases where the error, although in one sense procedural, goes to the very substance of the employer's decision. So, as in the present case, it is frequently applied to cases where the "procedural" error consists of the failure to give the employee an opportunity to give an explanation of his conduct or draw attention to mitigating circumstances. Such "procedural" error will normally (although not invariably) be unfair because by failing to hear the employee's version the employer will have failed to investigate the allegation properly in the absence of hearing the employee's version of the events. In this type of case, the *British Labour Pump* principle causes great evidential problems. The Industrial Tribunal has to make a decision as to what facts would have emerged if a proper investigation had taken place and what would have been the employer's attitude in the light of those facts. Such hypothetical findings of fact as to what would have happened in a hypothetical event have given rise to a number of appeals before us. In practice, it is difficult in such a case to distinguish between fair inferences drawn from evidence and pure guesswork. What evidence is required to prove what would have happened if an event had occurred which *ex hypothesi*, did not occur?. . . .

In our judgment, apart from the authority to which we are about to refer, the correct approach to such a case would be as follows. The only test of the fairness of a dismissal is the reasonableness of the employer's decision to dismiss judged at the time at which the dismissal takes effect. An Industrial Tribunal is not bound to hold that *any* procedural failure by the employer renders the dismissal unfair: it is one of the factors to be weighed by the Industrial Tribunal in deciding whether or not the dismissal was reasonable within s.57(3). The weight to be attached to such procedural failure should depend upon the circumstances known to the employer at the time of dismissal not on the actual consequence of such failure. Thus in the case of a failure to give an opportunity to explain, except in the rare case where a reasonable employer could properly take the view on the facts known to him at the time of dismissal that no explanation or mitigation could alter his decision to dismiss, an Industrial Tribunal would be likely to hold that the lack of "equity" inherent in the failure would render the dismissal unfair. But there may be cases where the offence is so heinous and the facts so manifestly clear that a reasonable employer could, on the facts known to him at the time of dismissal, take the view that whatever explanation the employee advanced it could make no difference: see the example referred to by Lawton L.J. in *Bailey v BP Oil (Kent Refinery) Ltd.* [1980] I.R.L.R. 287. Where, in the circumstances known at the time of dismissal it was not reasonable for the employer to dismiss without giving an opportunity to explain but facts subsequently discovered or proved before the Industrial Tribunal show that the dismissal was in fact merited, compensation would be reduced to nil.

[Having reviewed the authorities, however, Browne-Wilkinson J. concluded that the *Binns* decision ([1982] I.R.L.R. 283 (C.A.)) required him to follow the *British Labour Pump* principle:)]

The position therefore is that, contrary to our own view of what the law was and should be, we are bound by authority to hold that the *British Labour Pump* principle is good law and that the Industrial Tribunal in this case has not erred in applying it. Unless and until a higher court rules to the contrary, Industrial Tribunals can continue properly to approach cases of procedural failure (whether in cases of suspected misconduct or selection for redundancy) in accordance with the principle set out in the *British Labour Pump* case.

In *Siggs & Chapman (Contractors) Ltd.* v. *Knight* [1984] I.R.L.R. 83 (E.A.T.), Waite J. confirmed that the *British Labour Pump* principle "is beyond challenge," though not "automatically applicable to every case" (p. 85). He expressed a preference for simple statutory formulas over "authorities which, by frequency of citation, have attained a status as hallowed, for example, as that of (*British Labour Pump*)" (*Anandarajah* v. *Lord Chancellor's Department* [1984] I.R.L.R. 131, at p. 132).

We turn now to examine the standard of fairness and the significance of procedure in each of three areas: misconduct, ill-health and incompetence.

6. MISCONDUCT

The definition of misconduct warranting termination is a policy exercise concerning control of behaviour at the workplace. There is a spectrum from freedom to subordination. The narrower the definition of misconduct, the greater the freedom of the worker. The wider the definition, the greater his subordination to authority. Sometimes, attempts are made to deny this policy choice by appealing to concepts of "labour discipline," "organisational necessity" or "efficiency." These are said to require certain behaviour (*e.g.* co-operation) and to disallow various broad categories of conduct without any necessary connotations of authority and subordination. But from the point of view of the worker, it is still a matter of extending, or circumscribing, the conduct he may engage (or indulge) in.

(A) Substantive Rules

(i) Common law

At common law, the conduct required of the worker is a function of the obligations in the contract of employment. The contract may explicitly define misconduct, *eg* by incorporating works rules. Or the courts may imply obligations of obedience, honesty, loyalty, and so on, so that breach of these obligations amounts to misconduct. The first step is to determine whether the conduct in question breaks any contractual obligation.

Dairy Produce Packers Ltd. v. Beverstock
[1981] I.R.L.R. 265
Employment Appeal Tribunal

The employee was dismissed for drinking in a public house when he should have been working. The company argued that drinking in a pub during working hours was a more serious offence than drinking on factory premises because it involved a breach of trust.

LORD MCDONALD: . . . a reasonable employer may require to impose differing standards with regard to the question of alcohol dependent upon a number of factors, such as the nature of his business, the extent to which other personnel may be put at risk and the effect which conduct of this nature may have upon public opinion. Where it is considered necessary to have specific penalties attached to the misuse of alcohol in a particular enterprise then it is proper, as the Industrial Tribunal have pointed out, that this should be clearly laid down and made a term of the contract of employment.

In the present case there is no such clear term contained in the contract of employment: it was argued on behalf of the appellants that the view which a reasonable employer would take would be that in the circumstances of the present case the offence of drinking during working hours outside the factory was more serious than similar drinking within the factory premises.

. . . In our opinion this is an argument which seeks to add yet another category [to the list of offences] of offence relating to alcohol and certainly if it had been the intention of the appellants that such a distinction fell to be made they should have had this clearly spelt out in the contracts of employment which they entered into with the employees.

At common law, the employer is entitled to terminate the contract of employment with due notice, whatever the conduct of the worker. Termination without notice (summary dismissal), however, may amount to a breach of contract (wrongful dismissal), but serious misconduct by the workers can justify even summary dismissal. Attitudes towards what constitutes serious misconduct fluctuate with time and circumstances, as the following case shows.

Wilson v. Racher
[1974] I.R.L.R. 114
Court of Appeal

A head gardner was summarily dismissed following an argument with his employer in which he used obscene language in the presence of the employer's wife and children.

EDMUND DAVIES L.J.: There is no rule of thumb to determine what misconduct on the part of a servant justifies summary termination of his contract. For the purpose of the present case, the test is whether the plaintiff's conduct was insulting and insubordinate to such a degree as to be incompatible with the continuance of the relation of master and servant (per Hill J. in *Edwards v Levy* (1860) 2 F and F p. 94 at p. 95). The application of such test will, of course, lead to varying results according to the nature of the employment and all the circumstances of the case. Reported decisions provide useful, but only general guides, each case turning upon its own facts. Many of the decisions which are customarily cited in these cases date from the last century and may be wholly out of accord with the current social conditions. What would today be regarded as almost an attitude of Czar-serf, which is to be found in some of the older cases where a dismissed employee failed to recover damages, would, I venture to think, be decided differently today. We have by now come to realise that a contract of service imposes upon the parties a duty of mutual respect. . . .

The present case, too, has to be looked at against the whole background. On the judge's findings, here was a competent, diligent and efficient gardener who, apart from one complaint of leaving a ladder against a yew tree, had done nothing which could be regarded as blameworthy by any reasonable employer, applying proper standards. Here, too, was an employer who was resolved to get rid of him, an employer who would use every barrel in the gun that he could find, or thought available, and an employer who was provocative from the outset and dealt with the plaintiff in an unseemly manner. The plaintiff lost his temper. He used obscene and deplorable language. He was therefore deserving of the severest reproof. But this was a solitary occasion. Unlike *Pepper v Webb* [1961] 1 W.L.R. 514 there was no background either of inefficiency or of insolence. The plaintiff tried to avert the situation by walking away, but he was summoned back and the defendant continued his gadfly activity of goading him into intemperate language. Such are the findings of the county court judge.

In those circumstances, would it be just to say that the plaintiff's use of this extremely bad language on a solitary occasion made impossible the continuance of the master and servant relationship, and showed that the plaintiff was indeed resolved to follow a line of conduct which made the continuation of that relationship impossible? The learned judge thought the answer to that question was clear, and I cannot say that he was manifestly wrong. . . .

[The employee's claim was upheld.]

(ii) Industrial practice

At the workplace, there are a multitude of sources: employers' works rules, collective agreements, and custom and practice may contribute to defining the conduct required or prohibited. In Chapter 7 on *Discipline*, we looked at the problems raised by the conflict between formal concepts of disciplinary rules and the fluidity of industrial practice (see above, pp. 242 *et seq*. and 262 *et seq*.). The following case illustrates how industrial practice can infiltrate strict contractual definitions of misconduct.

Wallace v. Guy Ltd.
[1973] I.R.L.R. 175
National Industrial Relations Court

Mr Wallace had been employed as a semi-skilled worker since 1966, but did a number of different types of job in the course of his service. When he was asked to do pipe bending he refused unless he were paid an additional 2p. an hour. He was thereupon dismissed.

BRIGHTMAN J.: The Tribunal dismissed Mr Wallace's claim on the simple ground that he had refused to do his job and that the employer therefore had no option but to dismiss him. The Tribunal reasoned that by declining to do pipe bending unless paid extra money, which the employer was unwilling to pay, Mr Wallace was declining to perform his contract; and that, they considered, was conduct which justified his dismissal. In our judgment, the approach of the Tribunal paid insufficient attention to the conditions which prevailed in this factory. The Tribunal found as a fact that it was customary for men to negotiate bonus rates individually, in other words, pay would or might vary according to the type of work to be done. There was no trade union recognition, at least in relation to pay negotiations.

There was no set procedure for negotiating rates of pay. The rate was bargained between the foreman or works manager and the employee. Where the precise rate of pay for the job is by custom left open to negotiation between management and individual worker, it seems to us imperative that management should allow negotiation to take place. If a job is presented to an employee and the employee asks for a certain rate of pay for that job, it is not "negotiation" for management to decline that rate of pay and forthwith dismiss the employee.

According to the unchallenged evidence of Mr Wallace that is what happened in this case. Of course, management is not bound to agree to the employee's demand, but at least management should tell the employee that the rate demanded is not acceptable and explain to the employee that the employee is faced with the option of accepting management's rate for the job or being served with notice of dismissal. The employee must be clearly given to understand what the choice is and must be given a reasonable opportunity to consider his position and decide what to do. That was not done in Mr Wallace's case. The position was rendered even less satisfactory because, according to his evidence, Mr Wallace thought that pipe bending was outside the contractual scope of his employment, and management knew that he laboured under that error.

In the circumstances, we find that the dismissal was unfair and we allow the appeal.

(iii) Statutory provisions

Under the legislation allowing a worker to complain to an Industrial Tribunal of unfair dismissal (EPCA, Pt. V), one specified reason for dismissal is the employee's conduct (section 57(2)(*b*)). Unlike common law claims of wrongful dismissal for alleged misconduct, however, the word "conduct" in the legislation has not been defined by reference to the contract of employment: (*Redbridge London Borough Council* v. *Fishman* [1978] I.C.R. 569 (E.A.T.) *per* Phillips J.)

> "The jurisdiction based on [EPCA, s.57(3)] has not got much to do with contractual rights and duties. Many dismissals are unfair although the employer is contractually entitled to dismiss the employee. Contrariwise, some dismissals are not unfair although the employer was not contractually entitled to dismiss

the employee. Although the contractual rights and duties are not irrelevant to the question posed by [s.57(3)], they are not of the first importance."

So what *is* "conduct" justifying dismissal for statutory purposes? It has been said to mean that "the idea that the employer can reasonably seek to maintain an efficient and disciplined work force . . . (is) implicit in the legislation" (P. Elias, (1981) 10 I.L.J. 201 at 211). But concepts of "discipline" and "efficiency" mean different things to employers and workers. For example, fighting at work may be indiscipline to an employer, but self-defence to a worker; refusal to do more work may be inefficient for the employer, but efficient for the worker.

In accordance with the legal standard of fairness described above (pp. 317, *et seq.*), the Courts and Tribunals have chosen to interpret "conduct" from the point of view of the employer: the "reasonable employer" standard of fairness. As stated in *UCATT* v. *Brain* [1981] I.R.L.R. 224 (C.A.) (*per* Donaldson L.J.):

> " . . . this approach of Tribunals, putting themselves in the position of the employer, informing themselves of what the employer knew at the moment, imagining themselves in that position and then asking the question, 'Would a reasonable employer in those circumstances dismiss,' seems to me a very sensible approach—subject to one qualification alone, that they must not fall into the error of asking themselves the question 'Would we dismiss,' because you sometimes have a situation in which one reasonable employer would and one would not. In those circumstances, the employer is entitled to say to the Tribunal, 'Well, you should be satisfied that a reasonable employer would regard these circumstances as a sufficient reason for dismissing,' because the statute does not require the employer to satisfy the Tribunal of the rather more difficult consideration that *all* reasonable employers would dismiss in those circumstances."

In the following extracts, we examine the courts' views on "conduct" in four main areas: employers' works rules, "co-operation," potential misconduct and subordination.

(a) Employers' works rules

Industrial practice reveals a distinction in employers' works rules between different degrees of misconduct: gross misconduct, minor misconduct, and unclassified disciplinary offences. The Code of Practice on Disciplinary Practice and Procedures in Employment (1977) reflects this difference in paragraph 10(h). Despite this recognition in employers' works rules and the ACAS Code of distinction between gross (or serious) and other lesser forms of misconduct, the judges appear reluctant always to be bound by the stated consequences of these categories. The following extract illustrates their attitude.

Taylor v. Parsons Peebles NEI Bruce Peebles Ltd.

[1981] I.R.L.R. 119
Employment Appeal Tribunal

The employee worked for the company for over 20 years before being dismissed after he was involved in a fight with another employee.

LORD MCDONALD: The Tribunal have expressly stated that they were satisfied that the policy of the respondents was that in such circumstances the only possible penalty was dismissal and that this penalty was justly enforced when they dismissed both the appellant and Henderson. So expressed this does not in our view state the proper test. The proper test is not what the policy of the respondents as employers was but what the reaction of a reasonable employer would have been in the circumstances. That reaction would have taken into account the long period of service and good conduct which the appellant was in a position to claim. It is not to the point that the employee's code of disciplinary conduct may or may not contain a provision to the effect that anyone striking a blow would be instantly dismissed. Such a provision no matter how positively expressed must always be considered in the light of how it would be applied by a reasonable employer having regard to circumstances of equity and the substantial merits of the case. In the present case the Tribunal do not seem to have approached the problem from this point of view. They have been apparently influenced by what they held to be the policy of the respondents and left the matter at that. We accordingly feel that it is open to us to approach the question of whether or not, having regard to the history of the appellant, a reasonable employer would have dismissed him in the circumstances. Our conclusion is that he would not. This is not to say that the conduct can be condoned but to apply a rigid sanction of automatic dismissal in all circumstances is not in our view what a reasonable employer would have done:

Ladbroke Racing Ltd. v. Arnott

[1983] I.R.L.R. 154
Court of Session

An investigation of employees suspected of dishonesty did not disclose such instances, but it did emerge that Mrs Arnott had placed bets on behalf of old age pensioners. The employers' disciplinary rules specifically stated that placing bets by staff was prohibited and that breach of the rule would result in immediate dismissal.

LORD WEATLEY: What is said by the appellants in their Notices of Appearance to the Industrial Tribunal is that the respondents were guilty of misconduct by breaking the relevant rule in each case. While the appropriate rule in each case specifically stated that a breach of the rule would result in dismissal that cannot in itself necessarily meet the requirements of TULRA, Sched. 1, para. 6(8); [now EPCA, s.57(3) as amended] which calls for the employer satisfying the Tribunal that in the circumstances (having regard to equity and the substantial merits of the case) he acted reasonably in treating it as a sufficient reason for dismissal. This seems to me to predicate that there may be different degrees of gravity in the admitted or proved offence, and, as each case has to be considered on its own facts, consideration has to be given *inter alia* to the degree of culpability involved. This is something which Mr

McGuigan [the area manager who took the decision to dismiss Mrs Arnott] appears not to have done. He simply branded as gross misconduct the breaking of the relevant rule, and if that was a legitimate approach it would follow that any breach of rules so framed would constitute gross misconduct warranting dismissal irrespective of the manner in which the breach occurred.

In the instant case there were several factors which seem to me to have called for consideration as mitigation of the respective offences to an extent which could have affected the justification for dismissal when the standard test was applied. . . .

These were all matters which in my view would have been considered by a reasonable employer in this line of business in the circumstances which prevailed and if that had been done I do not consider that such an employer would have branded the acting of the respondents as gross misconduct warranting dismissal despite the terms of the rules. The failure of Mr McGuigan to take these matters into consideration confirms my view that he simply proceeded on the simple fact that there were admitted breaches of the rules and, because of the philosophy and policy underlying the rules, that in itself warranted dismissal without any regard to the requirements which TULRA, Sched. 1 para. 6(8) [now EPCA, s.57(3), as amended] imposed.

(b) Non-co-operation

An employee who refuses to co-operate with the employer, regardless of any contractual obligation, may be dismissed as a consequence. The following case illustrates how the "reasonable employer" standard can be relied upon to hold such a dismissal fair.

Horrigan v. Lewisham London Borough Council
[1978] I.C.R. 15
Employment Appeal Tribunal

After 10 years' employment during which he regularly worked overtime, the employee decided he was not obliged to do so and refused to. He was dismissed.

Arnold J.: [The Industrial Tribunal held:] . . . even if [the employee] had not been in breach of his contract in refusing to do the overtime as required by the Council, it seems to [the majority of the Tribunal] that, as it was impracticable for the Council to carry on the services they were providing unless the drivers were prepared to work this essential overtime, it would, in any event, have been reasonable for them to dispense with [the employee's] services and to replace him with another employee who was prepared to co-operate in the existing system . . . [the employee] had made it perfectly clear that he was no longer prepared to co-operate in the Council's existing system. As matters now stand, it seems to us that the Council are unable to provide the service they need to provide for handicapped people, unless their driver/attendants are prepared to co-operate with the existing system. That being so, we think that it was reasonable to treat [the employee's] refusal to co-operate as a sufficient reason for dismissal, whether it involved any breach of his contract or not. In our view the Council could not be expected to tolerate a situation where they would not know from day to day whether one of their driver/attendants was or was not going to be available to work the essential overtime required to complete his rounds . . . we can find no flaw in any of that reasoning which can be characterised as a mistake of law as that phrase is used in the deliberations of the Appeal Tribunal.

(c) Potential misconduct

The requirement to show "conduct" justifying dismissal has been deemed to include cases where there is a risk to the employer of future potential misconduct by the employee. The dangers of such "anticipatory" terminations are illustrated in the following case.

Saunders v. Scottish National Camps Association
[1980] I.R.L.R. 174
Employment Appeal Tribunal

The employee was a maintenance handyman at a children's camp. He was dismissed on the grounds of being a homosexual.

LORD MCDONALD: It was argued on behalf of the appellant that the Tribunal had made illegitimate and misinformed use of their knowledge and experience of how a reasonable employer would react. They had assumed, it was argued, in the teeth of the evidence that homosexuals created a special risk to the young. This does less than justice to their finding which is that a considerable proportion of employers would take the view that the employment of a homosexual should be restricted, particularly when required to work in proximity and contact with children. Whether that view is scientifically sound may be open to question but there was clear evidence from the psychiatrist that it exists as a fact. That evidence the Tribunal were entitled to accept and it appears to have coincided with their own knowledge and experience. . . .

(d) Disobedience

The policy nature of terminations for conduct is demonstrated most clearly in those cases involving refusal to obey orders and insubordination. Here the struggle for control over the workplace is apparent. The courts must determine whether the employer's control is to be maintained, and to what extent challenges to it by employees may be penalised by dismissal. By applying the standard of a "reasonable employer," the result is usually a foregone conclusion.

St. Anne's Board Mill Co. Ltd. v. Brien
[1973] I.R.L.R. 309
National Industrial Relations Court

The employees were dismissed because they refused to act as mates to an electrician whom they believed had been responsible for an accident. The employer, following an inquiry, had concluded that another electrician had been responsible for the accident.

GRIFFITHS J.: . . . These men were quite clearly dismissed because the refused to obey the employer's instruction to act as a mate to Mr White. That was a reason which related to the conduct of the employees within the meaning of s.24(2)(b) [of the Industrial Relations Act 1971, now EPCA, s.57(2)(*b*)] and the Tribunal should have so concluded. If the Tribunal had approached the matter in that way, as it should have done, the next question that its members should have asked themselves was . . . was [the employer] behaving reasonably in regarding their refusal to work with White as a sufficient reason for dismissing them in the circumstances that existed at that date?. . . .

The history of events shows that the employers made a very careful enquiry into the circumstances of this accident and were as a result faced with two wholly irreconcilable bodies of evidence. One the one hand they had the three men involved in the tracing of the cables, all of whom said that it was Randall who was responsible for the mistake—including Randall himself. On the other hand they had four men who were refusing to work with White, who said that it was White's fault. The employers accepted the evidence of the electricians, and in the view of this Court it would be quite impossible to say that they acted unreasonably in so doing. The employers tried to resolve the dispute through the intervention of union representatives. They failed. There was no course that remained open to them other than to dispense with the services of White, on the one hand, or of the cable-pullers on the other. As they had formed the *bona fide* view that White was in no way to blame for the accident, upon cogent evidence, it would have been manifestly unfair for them to have victimised White, who they genuinely believed to be innocent of fault. In these circumstances it cannot be said that the employers behaved unfairly in dismissing the men who refused to work with White.

Lindsay v. Dunlop Ltd.
[1980] I.R.L.R. 93
Employment Appeal Tribunal

> Following the refusal of employees to work where there was a health hazard from hot rubber fumes, the company suggested as a temporary measure the use of masks. The unions and men, by a large majority, agreed, but Mr Lindsay continued to refuse to work in the area and was eventually dismissed for refusing to work normally.

Lord McDonald: The Industrial Tribunal held, correctly, that the reason for dismissal was shown to be the conduct of the appellant in refusing to comply with an instruction from the respondents to resume work. The question which they had to decide was whether such instruction was one which the respondents were entitled to give and whether they acted reasonably in dismissing the appellant because he did not comply with it.

Upon the evidence the Tribunal held that working conditions in the respondents' factory were far from ideal. The factory was old and required to be modernised. The concentration of fumes exceeded the threshold recommended by the British Rubber Manufacturers' Association, but the Tribunal held that in the present state of medical knowledge it cannot be stated whether this represents a serious threat to the health of operators exposed to it. There was no evidence before them to enable them to conclude whether the masks provided were or were not adequate protection. Their conclusion on the evidence presented to them is neatly summarised in one sentence as follows:

> "The whole picture, as presented in the evidence, was a picture of management belatedly but nevertheless with some determination pursuing a policy of guarding against a danger to health which is suspected but not proved, in a factory which can only be radically altered at enormous cost."

Technical evidence before the Tribunal was that a proper system would involve the extraction of fumes at source and that in modern factories this was done. They felt however, that viewing the matter practically, the respondents had acted reasonably in requiring men to work in the affected area wearing masks following upon full discussions with the unions, with the men and indeed with the Health and Safety Executive. They therefore concluded that it was reasonable to dismiss the appellant for refusing to comply with this requirement. They commented that the appellant's fear of injury to his health struck them as genuine but not necessarily realistic.

Contrast the extracts above with the following cases.

Morrish v. Henlys (Folkstone) Ltd.
[1973] I.R.L.R. 61
National Industrial Relations Court

The employee was dismissed after he refused to accept book entries recording that he had drawn quantities of fuel for his vehicle which had not in fact been put into the vehicle.

GRIFFITHS J.: Henlys contended that as there was evidence before the Tribunal that it was a common practice to alter the records in this way to cover deficiencies, it was unreasonable of Mr Morrish to object, and he should have accepted the manager's instructions. Accordingly his refusal to do so was an unreasonable refusal to obey an order, which justified dismissal.

We cannot accept this submission. It involves the proposition that it is an implied term of an employee's contract of service that he should accept an order to connive at the falsification of one of his employers' records. The proposition only has to be stated to be seen to be untenable. In our view, Mr Morrish was fully entitled to refuse to be in any way party to a falsification of this record and the Tribunal was manifestly right in holding that he had been unfairly dismissed.

Union of Construction and Allied Trades and Technicians v. Brain
[1981] I.R.L.R. 224
Court of Appeal

The employee, a publications officer, was sued for libel following an article in one of the employers' publications. The matter was handled by the employers' solicitors and terms of a settlement were agreed which included an undertaking by the employee not to publish further libels. The employee had not been consulted about the settlement and refused to give the undertaking. He was summarily dismissed.

LAWTON L.J.: First the problem arises—and it is a fundamental problem, in my judgment—whether the employers acted reasonably in giving Mr Brain an order to sign the undertaking. I have no hesitation myself in saying that they were acting most unreasonably in giving that order to Mr Brain. They had intermeddled in Mr Brain's action. It is true that they had done so as good employers and in what they thought were Mr Brain's best interests. But it was Mr Brain who was the defendant in the action, it was Mr Brain who was going to have judgment given against him for libel if the case was not settled; it was Mr Brain whose name had been bandied around in the statement made in open court; and it was Mr Brain who, in the apology to be printed in "Viewpoint" was going to be held up as a journalist who had published defamatory statements. In these circumstances, it seems to me that the employers should have appreciated, and they would have done so had they had some legal advice, that what they were asking Mr Brain to do was something which they had no right to ask him to do. What they could have done was to have pointed out to him that if he behaved unreasonably they would not support him financially; but they had no business, in my judgment, to order him to sign an undertaking to the plaintiffs.

So the case started with a misconception by UCATT as to their rights and the Industrial Tribunal, in my judgment, misdirected themselves by saying, as they did say in paragraph 12 of their award, that the order was a "reasonable and lawful instruction." But assuming for the moment that it was a reasonable and lawful instruction, having regard to the fact that Mr Brain had never been consulted about the terms of settlement and he was being asked to do something about which he had no background knowledge at all, it seems to me, in these circumstances, looking at it from the employers' point of view and what they knew at the time, they were acting unreasonably in asking him to sign when they knew that the negotiations related to his position as defendant and not the union's.

(B) Procedures

(i) Common law

At common law procedural requirements relating to termination for misconduct are derived from contractual provisions: *eg* the employer may terminate the contract on giving the contractually agreed length of notice. Where the contract does not expressly provide for a period of notice, the common law will imply a "reasonable" period. Apart from this, however, the common law fails to require any other procedural safeguards as regards dismissal for misconduct, such as warnings of termination, the giving of reasons for termination, hearings on, or appeals against, decisions to terminate, or as regards the proportionality of the sanction of termination of employment to the degree of misconduct (see M.R. Freedland, *The Contract of Employment* (1976) p. 227).

If the contract of employment does contain procedural requirements, however, these must be observed. In the following case, the remedy for an employer's failure to adhere to contractual procedures was an injunction.

Jones v. Lee and Guilding
[1980] I.R.L.R. 67
Court of Appeal

> Mr Jones applied for an injunction restraining his employer from purporting to dismiss him except with the consent of the County Council, following a hearing by the appropriate committee of the Council, as provided in his terms of employment.

LORD DENNING M.R.: I turn to the important matter in this case. It is whether under the contract by which Mr Jones was employed he was entitled

(1) to a hearing by the County Council and (2) was not to be dismissed unless the county council consented. His appointment was in writing. . . .

[The judge quoted from the documents.]

So there is that whole page (page 29) setting out the conditions relating to dismissal. It is clear that anyone reading it would believe—and certainly Mr Jones would believe—it applied to him. He would believe that, before he could be dismissed, he would be entitled to a hearing before the Gloucestershire County Council, and that their consent would have to be given. Any ordinary head teacher—or anyone reading those conditions of tenure—would, I am quite sure, take the view that they applied to him and would act on that belief. We have heard all sorts of legal niceties to escape that result, but I would brush them all aside. This document should be interpreted in the sense it would convey to the ordinary reader of it. So read, Mr Jones is right: . . . .

I would say that this contract is binding upon the managers. The consent of the County Council is required. The head teacher, before dismissal, is entitled to a hearing and to have all the protection of those conditions. They were certainly not complied with in this case. . . .

I would, therefore, allow the appeal and grant the injunction accordingly.

The prevalence of procedures in the context of employment protection legislation may lead to a reconsideration of the common law's refusal to impose procedural standards in employment termination cases.

R. v. British Broadcasting Corporation, ex p. Lavelle
[1982] I.R.L.R. 404
Queen's Bench Division

The employee was charged with misconduct. On the grounds that she was given only one hour's notice of the disciplinary interview, she asked the court for an injunction to stop the employer from violating the disciplinary procedure applicable.

WOOLF J.: It was contended on behalf of the BBC that in relation to the dismissal of a servant, the ordinary courts would not interfere by way of injunction. There was no duty, in the case of tribunals under the disciplinary appeal procedure set up by the BBC, to act fairly which was enforcable by the courts. The procedure was purely domestic, and if it resulted in a wrongful dismissal, the remedy was the common law remedy of damages.

[The judge quoted from Lord Reid's judgment in *Ridge v Baldwin* [1964] A.C. 40, which distinguished ordinary common law cases of master and servant from cases of dismissal of the holder of an office.]

When one has regard to the framework of this employment, one finds that the BBC has engrafted onto the ordinary principles of master and servant an elaborate framework of appeals. This framework restricts the power of the BBC as an employer to terminate the employee's employment. It clearly presupposes that the employee should have more than one opportunity of being heard. It may be right, as was submitted, that the reason this is done is to avoid any question of the dismissal being regarded as being unfair. However, here I would adopt the argument advanced by Mr Evans, on behalf of the applicant, that the employment protection legislation has substantially changed the position at common law so far as dismissal is concerned. In appropriate circumstances the statute [ie EPCA] now provides that an Industrial Tribunal can order the reinstatement of an employee. It is true that the order cannot be specifically enforced. However, the existence of that power does indicate that even the ordinary contract of master and servant now has many of the attributes of an office, and the distinction which previously existed between pure cases of master and servant and cases where a person holds an office are no longer clear. . . .

In this case it seems clear to me that Miss Lavelle had a right to be heard and that there was a restriction as to the circumstances in which she could be dismissed. Although the restriction was largely procedural, as the respondent contends, it did alter her rights substantially from what they would have been at common law. In my view, this had the consequence of making her's a contract of employment different from those referred to by Lord Reid where in the past the sole remedy was one of damages. I have therefore come to the conclusion that in the appropriate circumstances, in the case of employment of the nature here being considered, the court can if necessary intervene by way of injunction and certainly by way of declaration.

Although Woolf J. was prepared to intervene in appropriate cases when an action was begun by way of a writ for breach of contract, he rejected an application for judicial review under Order 53, rule 1(1) of the Rules of the Supreme Court as the prerogative remedies of mandamus, prohibition or certiorari are not available to enforce private rights, but are public law remedies: "The disciplinary appeal procedure set up by the B.B.C. depends purely upon the contract of employment between the applicant and the B.B.C., and therefore it is a procedure of a purely private or domestic character" (p. 408). The policy behind his view was expressly succinctly: "An application of judicial review has not and should not be extended to a pure employment situation," but this opinion is difficult to reconcile with his willingness to hear the application on the basis that it might have been commenced by way of writ. The inappropriateness of judicial review by way of Order 53 was reiterated in the following case, which demonstrated both the fragility of the attempt to distinguish public and private law remedies, and the policy grounds for the decision.

R. v. East Berkshire Health Authority, ex p. Walsh
[1984] I.R.L.R. 278
Court of Appeal

Mr Walsh was dismissed for serious misconduct following disciplinary procedures. He applied for judicial review under Order 53 of the R.S.C. to quash the purported dismissal. Hodgson J. in the Divisional Court held that although there is no "public law" element in the ordinary relationship of master and servant which would make a remedy of judicial review available, Mr Walsh's case was not "ordinary" since he held office in a public service and "the public is concerned that the nurses who serve the public should be treated lawfully and fairly by the public authority employing them."

Sir John Donaldson M.R.: The ordinary employer is free to act in breach of his contracts of employment and if he does so his employee will acquire certain private law rights and remedies in damages for wrongful dismissal, compensation for unfair dismissal, an order for reinstatement or re-engagement and so on. Parliament can underpin the position of public authority employees by directly restricting the freedom of the public authority to dismiss, thus giving the employee 'public law' rights and at least making him a potential candidate for administrative law remedies. Alternatively it can require the authority to contract with its employees on specified terms with a view to the employee acquiring "private law" rights under the terms of the contract of employment. If the authority fails or refuses to thus create "private law" rights for the employee, the employee will have "public law" rights to compel compliance, the remedy being mandamus requiring the authority so to contract or a declaration that the employee has those rights. If, however, the authority gives the employee the required contractual protection a breach of that contract is not a matter of "public law" and gives rise to no administrative law remedies. . . .

I therefore conclude that there is no "public law" element in Mr Walsh's complaints which could give rise to any entitlement to administrative law remedies. I confess that I am not sorry to have been led to this conclusion, since a contrary conclusion would have enabled *all* National Health Service employees to whom Whitley Council conditions of service apply to seek judicial review. . . .

May L.J.: I think that at the present time in at least the great majority of cases involving disputes about the dismissal of an employee by his employer, the most appropriate forum for their resolution is an Industrial Tribunal. In my opinion the courts should not be astute to hold that any particular dispute is appropriate for consideration under the judicial review procedure provided for by Order 53. Employment disputes not infrequently have political and ideological overtones, or raise what are often described as "matters of principle"; these are generally best considered not by the Divisional Court but by an Industrial Tribunal, to the members of which, both lay and legally qualified, such overtones or matters of principle are common currency. . . .

. . . certainly the appellants are a public authority. I doubt, however, whether one should properly say, in the present context, that as a senior nursing officer Mr Walsh held a public position: whether he did or not, it was only "fortified by statute" to the extent I have indicated. Having regard to the detailed terms of Mr Walsh's contract with the appellants, I do not think that the considerations which determine whether he was validly dismissed do go beyond that contract. I respectfully see no reason why those considerations in the circumstances of the instant case require to be tested broadly on arguments of public policy. The fundamental issues are whether the appellant had grounds to dismiss Mr Walsh summarily and whether they did so in accordance with his detailed terms and conditions of service.

For all these reasons I am driven to differ respectfully from the conclusion of the learned judge below. I do not think that there is any element of "public" or administrative" law in this case rendering it susceptible to or suitable for proceedings for judicial review under Order 53. On the contrary, there is in my opinion nothing in this case which takes it out of the "ordinary" (by which one intends no disrespect to either side) employer/employee unfair dismissal dispute, one which could and should long ago have been relatively cheaply determined by an experienced Industrial Tribunal. It follows that in my opinion Mr Walsh's application was a misuse of Order 53.

Purchas L.J.: However, in my judgment, the relationship between the applicant and the Health Authority was one which fell within the category of "pure master and servant" although the powers of the authority to negotiate terms with their employees was limited indirectly by statute and subordinate legislation. Any breach of those terms of which Mr Walsh complains related solely to the private contractual relationship between the Health Authority and him and did not involve any wrongful discharge by the Health Authority of the rights or duties imposed upon it *quā* Health Authority. The rules of natural justice may well be imported into a private contractual relationship, *vide* the category of employee/master relationship envisaged in the first of three categories described by Lord Reid in *Ridge v Baldwin* [1964] A.C. 40 to which the Master of the Rolls has already referred but in such circumstances they would go solely to the question of rights and duties involved in the performance of the contract of employment itself. The manner in which the authority terminated, or purported to terminate, Mr Walsh's contract of employment related to their conduct as employers in a pure master and servant context and not to the performance of their duties, or exercise of their powers as an authority providing a health service for the public at large. The importation by direct reference or by implication into a context of employment of the rules of natural justice does not of itself import the necessary element of public interest which would convert the case from the first category envisaged by Lord Reid into one in which there was an element of public interest created as a result of status of the individual or the protection or support of his position as a public officer.

The policy that led Hodgson J. in *Walsh* to conclude that there was a sufficient "public law" element to allow for judicial review appears to have survived his reversal by the Court of Appeal, as the following case shows.

R. v. The Secretary of State for the Home Office Department, ex p. Benwell
[1985] I.R.L.R. 6
Queen's Bench Division

Mr Benwell was dismissed from his post as a prison officer for disobedience to orders, having regard to his disciplinary record which contained information which should not have been recorded under the Code of Discipline for prison officers.

Hodgson J.: (after noting his reversal by the Court of Appeal in *R.* v *East Berkshire Health Authority, ex p. Walsh* (above p. 341). The question whether the applicant's complaints in this case give rise to any right to judicial review is, as I have indicated, of great general importance. The reason is this: because of the status of the constable a prison officer cannot resort to the Industrial Tribunals under the Employment Protection (Consolidation) Act 1978 (see *Home Office v Robinson* [1981] I.R.L.R. 524). Save to the extent that Parliament has by statute provided a Crown servant with some special entitlement, he is dismissible at pleasure and has no private law remedy. It follows that, unless a prison officer can seek leave to move for judicial review, he is without remedy if he is unlawfully dismissed unless as Mr Lester [counsel for the applicant] points out in certain circumstances the officer is black or a woman). But these disadvantages go only, it seems, to the question whether this court should exercise its discretion to grant relief. They do not directly affect the jurisdiction point (see Sir John Donaldson MR in *Walsh* at page 280). So the position is that, unlike Mr Walsh (who can now start proceedings by writ with all the procedural advantages he thereby gains) the applicant, if he is turned away empty-handed from this court, has nowhere else to go in this country.

At first sight, at any rate, the position of a nurse and a prison officer have much in common. . . .

There are, however, differences between nurses and prison officers. Nurses enter into a contract of employment with health authorities whereas prison officers are appointed by the Home Secretary (Prison Act 1952, s.4(1); Prison Commissioners Dissolution Order 1963, Article 3(2) Schedule 1). It seems to me that this may point the way I should go. Second, as I have said, nurses have remedies in civil law which are not available to prison officers and, although this fact only goes directly to discretion, it may be some indication that Parliament intended questions of the exercise of the Home Secretary's powers and duties under the Code [of Discipline applicable to the Prison Service] to be in the public sector. It was under and purportedly in compliance with that Code of Discipline that the Department issued the applicant with notice of its intention to dismiss him and the Home Secretary decided to implement that decision. The question is whether that is a sufficient statutory under-pinning to inject the element of public law into this application (see Sir John Donaldson MR in *Walsh* at page 281). . . .

It seems to me that the reason why the Court of Appeal came to the conclusion it did in *Walsh* was that the disciplinary procedures in section XXXIV were incorporated into the contract of service and that it was this incorporation which deprived the procedures and compliance with them of any possible public law character (see Sir John Donaldson MR at page 281 Lord Justice May at page 282, and Lord Justice Purchas at page 285 *et seq*. The applicant in this case was a Civil Servant appointed by the Home Secretary whose employment was governed by the Code of Discipline and, no doubt, by the standing orders formulated by the Prison Department of the Home Office and circular instructions amending standing orders and making provision for matters of detail (see generally Halsbury's Laws of England fourth Edition, paragraphs 1101 and 1121). In *Walsh* Lord Justice Purchas said this: "There is a danger of confusing the rights with their appropriate remedies enjoyed by an employee arising out of a private contract of employment with the performance by a public body of the duties imposed upon it as part of the statutory terms under which it exercises its powers. The former are appropriate for private remedies *inter partes* whether by action in the High Court or in the appropriate statutory tribunal whilst the latter are subject to the supervisory powers of the court under Order 53." Clearly, the Court of Appeal in *Walsh* did not consider the purported dismissal on disciplinary grounds of Mr Walsh to be the performance of any duty imposed upon the authority as part of the statutory terms under which it exercised it powers.

In this case, however, it is my opinion that in making a disciplinary award of dismissal, the Home Office (to use a comprehensive term to include the Department and the Secretary of State so distinguished by the respondent itself in this case) was performing the duties imposed upon it as part of the statutory terms under which it exercises its power. I conclude there that this court in the exercise of its supervisory jurisdiction can come to the aid of the applicant in this case and I am glad that it can. I can only hope that my gladness is longer than the gladness I was foolhardy enough to express in *Walsh*.

Contrast Sir John Donaldson's haste to rebut Mann J.'s conclusion that "officer" could cover the whole range of local authority employees, by reiterating that "it is at least arguable that no employee of a local authority can properly be described as an 'officer,' unless he fills an office which has an existence independent of the person who for the time being fills it" (*R.* v. *Hertfordshire County Council ex p. NUPE* [1985] I.R.L.R. 258 (C.A.), p. 260).

On the other hand, the view of Woolf J. in *Lavelle* (above p. 340) that there remained a judicial power to intervene where the action was other than by way of Order 53 was not contradicted by the Court of Appeal in *Walsh* (above p. 341), and was reinforced in the following case.

Irani v. Southampton and South West Hampshire Health Authority

[1985] I.R.L.R. 203
Chancery Division

> Mr Irani was given six weeks' notice of dismissal, but complained that the employers had failed to follow the disputes procedure laid down by the Whitley Councils (joint trade union/employer machinery) for the Health Services. He asked for an injunction requiring his employer not to implement the dismissal notice without first exhausting the procedures.

WARNER J.: . . . what was decided in *R.* v *East Berkshire Health Authority, ex p. Walsh* [above p. 341] was no more than that the contract between a National Health Service practitioner and his employer, the health authority, was not one that conferred on him rights enforceable by the judicial review procedure under Order 53 of the Rules of the Supreme Court. That was because any rights that it conferred on him were rights governed by what it has become fashionable in this country to call "private" law and not rights which, according to the same fashion, are governed by what is called "public" law. Therefore such a practitioner is not entitled to the administrative law remedies available under Order 53. The case decides nothing at all about what remedies such a practitioner may be entitled to under the court's normal equitable jurisdiction, which is the jurisdiction that I am exercising. . . .

If I were to decline to grant the injunction sought by Mr Harwood-Stevenson [counsel for the plaintiff], I would in effect be holding that without doubt, an authority in the position of the defendant is entitled to snap its fingers at the rights of its employees under the blue book [which incorporated statutory terms and conditions of employment into the plaintiff's contract of employment]. Indeed, that is what Mr Clifford [counsel for the defendants] invites me to hold. He invites me to hold that, despite the existence in the blue book of sections 33 and 40 [providing respectively a procedure for settling disputes between the employer and employees and a disciplinary procedure], a health authority is entitled to dismiss a medical practitioner summarily and to say that, if and in so far as his rights under those sections are infringed, his remedy lies in damages only. . . .

It means that for the price of damages—and the authorities show that damages at common law for wrongful dismissal are not generous—a health authority may, among other things, ignore the requirement at the end of clause 190 [of the National Health Service Hospital Medical Terms and Conditions of Service which, it had been conceded, were incorporated into the plaintiff's contract of employment] that:

> "where the Secretary of State's decision cannot be given before the expiry of a notice given, such notice shall be extended for a month or longer period by the authority until the Secretary of State's decision is given."

The development of the law since the decision in the *Barber v Manchester Regional Hospital Board* [1958] 1 W.L.R. 181 case leads me to the conclusion that it is open to question whether that is right. If it is not right, nor can it be right, in my view, that, in the case of a more junior practitioner, the employing authority can ignore the rules in the blue book.

There is evident here a severe conflict between judicial policies in favour of and against allowing judicial review of dismissal decisions by public employers. It is unfortunate that the search for an elusive "public" element should be the criterion for Order 53 proceedings, whereas it is irrelevant for claims invoking other procedural bases for judicial intervention. Beyond requiring adherence to agreed procedures and to principles of natural justice, the common law of public employee dismissals remains to be developed by judges. It remains to be seen whether the experience of the Industrial Tribunals and the E.A.T. in developing the statutory law of unfair dismissal will infiltrate this new common law.

(ii) Industrial practice

In stark contrast to the poverty of common law procedural safeguards, there has developed a rich and varied industrial practice with regard to procedures for dealing with misconduct at work. The following extract presents the results of a survey of disciplinary procedures in one hundred organisations in Britain.

Bargaining Report No. 15 (July/August 1981) LABOUR RESEARCH DEPARTMENT

Warning systems

. . . a warning system can control management action—for example by providing that no one shall be dismissed unless she/he has been adequately warned. . . .

The ACAS Code of [Disciplinary Practice and Procedures in Employment 1977] recommends an oral warning (minor offences) or a written warning for serious offences and a final written warning.

For less serious offences the majority of procedures provided for a three stage warning system. . . .

Most of the procedures with more than three stages include an extra informal warning or additional verbal (recorded) warning. . . .

36 agreements allowed for a basic three stage warning system, providing for an oral, and two written warnings, although stages can usually be skipped where serious offences are involved. . . .

A further 20 procedures indicated only two stages in the warning system—usually a verbal and written warning. . . .

The question of the oral warning poses a problem for disciplinary procedures. If it is to be exactly as it says, oral, it cannot be in writing. But if it is not in writing there is no record of it and so it is difficult to establish whether the correct procedure (oral warning, written warning, final warning, for example) has been followed. If there is never any record that an oral warning has been given there is considerable room for argument if management wishes to invoke further steps in the disciplinary procedure.

Some agreements state quite categorically that oral warnings shall be recorded but others invoke a variety of different methods which have the effect of making the procedures more informal and effectively adding an additional stage to the disciplinary procedure. A typical approach is to say that there shall be two oral warnings the first recorded by the line management and the second by the personnel department. We have identified 14 variations on this theme.

Investigation procedures

The [1977] ACAS Code of Practice [para. 11] states:

> "When a disciplinary matter arises, the supervisor or manager should *first establish the facts promptly* before *recollections fade*, taking into account statements of any available witnesses. In serious cases consideration should be given to a *brief period of suspension* while the case is investigated and the *suspension should be with pay*. Before a decision is made or penalty imposed the *individual should be interviewed and given the opportunity to state his or her case* and should be advised of any rights under the procedures, including the right to be accompanied" [emphasis added]

Over 40 procedures included at least one of the following provisions:

(i) there would be an investigation into allegations;
(ii) a formal disciplinary interview would be held before action was taken;
(iii) the right for workers to state their cases;
(iv) the right for a worker and/or his representative to call witnesses.

One procedure—E. Green & Sons not only provided for an investigation, but also said that full facilities would be provided for the shop steward to carry out an investigation "including paid leave" if necessary so that she/he could interview witnesses etc.

Amongst the private sector agreements only two contained any detailed provisions about how disciplinary hearings should be carried out.

In the public sector seven agreements contained very detailed procedures which read more like a set of court rules than a domestic hearing. The British Waterways procedure, for example, covers eleven paragraphs outlining who shall have the right to do what at every stage of the hearing.

Formal procedures can seem a bit daunting at first glance. In fact they only describe what would generally be accepted as a sensible and fair way of hearing a case:—

—each side is able to put its case;
—it allows for witnesses to be called—they may be able to add support to each side's case;
—it allows for questions to be asked;
—it allows the worker who has been "accused" or his/her representative to have the last word.

The advantages of putting everything down in writing is that it provides a clear guide; the employer must abide by the procedure and the employee is therefore assured of the proper hearing.

The disadvantage of such a procedure is that it can result in proceeding being very legalistic and formal. This can be intimidating and may make it more difficult for a worker or his/her representative to present the case.

Union involvement

The overwhelming majority of agreements give workers the right to be represented or accompanied by "a friend" in disciplinary proceedings and most workers would choose as the friend a trade union representative. What is the position of the union if the worker chooses not to have a union representative or fails to notify the union that disciplinary action is pending or has taken place?

Views differ. Some believe that individuals should have the right to conceal the fact that they are being disciplined. Others would argue that disciplinary action against an individual always affects other workers' terms and conditions (*eg* by setting a precedent: "I gave Mr Sleepy a written warning for being late, so I must give Ms Dopey a warning too . . . "). The argument here is that the union can only protect its members' interests properly if it knows what standard management is enforcing.

A number of agreements recognise trade union rights in disciplinary matters and make provision for union involvement or at least notification in all circumstances. Three main approaches can be identified: all discussions must take place in the presence of union officials or representatives [ten agreements]; trade union reps are informed of all disciplinary action [six agreements]; and trade union reps are given copies of all documents of a disciplinary nature [seven agreements]. . . .

Appeals procedure

In most cases appeals are internal, usually to the next higher level of management. . . . Other agreements envisage an appeal being pursued through the grievance procedure. . . . Since grievance procedures normally contain "status quo" clauses and put management on the defensive, agreements with this provisions have major advantages. Independent judgment, free of company prejudice, can be obtained by appeals to external bodies. . . . Some procedures make specific reference to ACAS as a body to which an appeal can be addressed. . . . In cases of dismissal, of course, workers have the option of appealing to an Industrial Tribunal. . . .

In the procedures we looked at 54 had provision for an investigation and/or a hearing before someone could be "instantly" dismissed. Because of the way in which the procedures were worded it was not always clear whether or not an investigation or hearing would always be held before a dismissal.

In addition 32 of the procedures allowed for the worker to be suspended on full or basic pay whilst an investigation was being conducted. In another 5 of the procedures workers could be suspended without pay during an investigation. Again, in practice there may be others which allow for suspension on full pay, although this is not explicitly stated in the procedure.

There are two ways in which the courts could incorporate industrial practice on the matter of disciplinary procedures into the law. First, adherence to procedures could be taken as a standard of "reasonableness" required of an employer in the law of unfair dismissal.

Gunton v. The Mayor, Aldermen and Burgesses of the London Borough of Richmond-Upon-Thames
[1980] I.R.L.R. 321
Court of Appeal

The employee's letter of appointment provided that the appointment would be terminable by one month's notice in writing on either side and subject to "the National Scheme of Conditions of Service" and "to any regulations which may be made by this Council from time to time." Subsequently, the Council adopted a disciplinary procedure, entitled "Regulations as to Staff Discipline." In dismissing the employee, the employers by-passed the introductory steps prescribed by this procedure.

SHAW L.J.: I think it as well to indicate at the outset the view which I have formed as to the interaction of the stated contractual term of notice, and the procedure in relation to dismissal for breaches of discipline which it is accepted forms part of Mr Gunton's contract of employment. For myself, I do not consider that the regulations as to staff discipline were designed to deprive the Borough of its contractual power to determine the contract of service by one month's notice; nor in my view did they have that result. If, however, the Borough exercised that right and was called upon before an Industrial Tribunal to justify a dismissal on some disciplinary ground as being fair it might be very difficult for the Borough to establish that the dismissal was not unfair if the code had not been followed. Mr Gunton would then be accorded appropriate redress by the Industrial Tribunal pursuant to the statutory provisions in that regard. On the other hand, if the code had been fully observed, the onus on the Borough to demonstrate that the dismissal was fair would be relatively easy to discharge.

Secondly, using contract law, the industrial practice could be incorporated into the contract of employment and made obligatory on the employer (*cf.* Lord Denning M.R. in *Jones*, above p. 339). But all depends on the courts' willingness to acknowledge industrial practice and on the significance they attach to it as a matter of policy. The policy choices are evident in the opinions of the E.A.T. and of the Court of Appeal in the following case.

Bailey v. BP Oil (Kent Refinery) Ltd.
[1979] I.R.L.R. 150 (E.A.T.); [1980] I.R.L.R. 287
Employment Appeal Tribunal and Court of Appeal

The employee, dismissed for misconduct, complained that the agreed disciplinary procedure had not been followed, in particular paragraph C4 which stated: "The company will inform the appropriate full-time official as soon as possible of any case in which the employee's dismissal or down-grading is contemplated." An Industrial Tribunal held the dismssal fair.

ARNOLD J. (in the E.A.T.): It seems to us that on its true construction paragraph C4 requires the appropriate full-time official to be informed *in every single case in which dismissal is contemplated* of that contemplated dismissal before the dismissal is effected, except when it is impossible so to do. There is no evidence upon which the Tribunal could, in our judgment, have come to the conclusion that it was impossible in this case.

Now it is argued that that should not be regarded as fatal to the conclusion that the mode of this dismissal was fair, because it is said, that, in overwhelming probability, if Mr Barr [the relevant full-time union official] had been informed it would have made no difference in the event. It is, we think, plain that the purpose of the prescription of paragraph C4 is to enable the full-time official to take whatever steps (if any) he considers appropriate at the stage when the dismissal remains in a state of contemplation. If Mr Barr had been informed when the dismissal was still in the state of contemplation, it cannot be certain what he would have done. Obviously it is possible having ascertained the relevant facts (which included the circumstances that Mr Bailey was an employee of very long standing) he might have made representations to the employers that some punishment (for punishment was plainly merited) less severe than dismissal would meet the facts of the case. It does not seem to us that it is impossible that those representations might have succeeded. . . .

LAWTON L.J.: (in the C.A.): . . . We are unable to accept [Arnold J.'s] reasoning for two reasons: first, we do not construe safeguard C4 as creating a condition precedent which has to be complied with before an employee could be dismissed; and secondly, and more importantly, the Employment Appeal Tribunal did not apply the relevant statutory provisions which were contained in Part II of Schedule 1 of the Trade Union and Labour Relations Act 1974, now re-enacted in the Employment Protection (Consolidation) Act, 1978 [s.54 *et seq.*].

Safeguard C4 can only be construed as providing a condition precedent to dismissal if further words are read into it; but if it is read literally it provides no safeguard for an employee because he could be dismissed as soon as the trade union official had been informed. Doing the best we can with a badly drafted provision of the agreement, we construe it, not as creating a condition precedent but as meaning that the employers have to keep the employee's trade union official informed of what they are thinking of doing so that he can take such action as he thinks fit, including, if there is a dismissal, having the case referred to arbitration.

The relevant statutory provisions contain no reference to procedures agreed with trade unions. . . .

. . . In most unfair dismissal cases Industrial Tribunals are likely to be critical, and justly so, of an employer who has dismissed a man without giving him an opportunity of explaining why he did what he did; but cases can occur when instant dismissal, without any opportunity for explanation being given, would be fair, as for example when on the shop floor a worker was seen by the works manager and others to stab another man in the back with a knife. The dismissal in such a case would not be any the less fair because the employers did not follow a disciplinary procedure agreement with a number of trade unions containing the kind of provisions which are under consideration in this appeal. In most cases, if not all, a failure to comply with such an agreement would be a factor to be taken into account; but the weight to be given to it would depend on the circumstances. An Industrial Tribunal should not base its decision on reasoning to the effect that because there has been a failure to comply, the dismissal must have been unfair.

(iii) Statutory provisions

EPCA, s.49 entitles the employee to a minimum period of notice (subject to repudiatory misconduct on his part—subsection (5)), and EPCA, s.53 entitles him to be provided with a written statement of reasons for his dismissal within 14 days (though what constitutes an unreasonable refusal by the employer to provide such a statement is, it seems, a question of fact: *Newland v Simons and Miller (Hairdressers) Ltd.* [1981] I.R.L.R. 359 (E.A.T.)). But the main procedural safeguard derives from the requirement of "reasonableness" in the law of unfair dismissal: EPCA, s.57(3). Before examining the precise content of the statutory provisions, we consider two procedural models on which safeguards for workers charged with misconduct may be based.

(a) Procedural models for termination for misconduct

The two procedural models to be considered derive from law on the one hand and industrial relations on the other. The legal model is that of the trial, and the standards are those of the rules of natural justice. The second model is that of negotiation, and its standards are derived from collective bargaining practice.

(i) The trial model and natural justice. The possibility of a statutory standard of "procedural justice" under the rubric of "reasonableness" in EPCA, s.57(3) provides a standing temptation to labour lawyers to adapt to the workplace "a trial process and the procedural criteria [of] the principles of natural justice familiar to administrative lawyers generally" (P. Davies and M. Freedland, *Labour Law: Tax and Materials* (1979) p. 363). As Kilner Brown J. put it in *Haddow* v. *Inner London Education Authority* [1979] I.C.R. 202 (E.A.T.):

> "Although domestic tribunals are not expected to apply and follow the strict procedures appropriate to judicial tribunals they must in these days avoid a fundamental breach of the rules of natural justice. This is essential where a man's job is at stake."

The fundamental problem in using the "trial process" or "natural justice" as a model for procedural justice in employment is the authoritarian nature of the workplace: the employer is usually both judge and prosecutor and appeal tribunal. There is no impartial adjudicator. This quality of the employment context overshadows the requirements of procedural justice, as the following extracts illustrate.

The Royal Naval School v. Hughes
[1979] I.R.L.R. 383
Employment Appeal Tribunal

The employee, a housemistress in a girls' public school, was dismissed by the headmistress. A majority in the Industrial Tribunal found the dismissal unfair.

BRISTOW J.: Above the headmistress there is only the board of governors. The majority of the Tribunal criticised them as wanting in impartiality and biased in favour of supporting the decision of the headmistress. But, other than in the exceptional cases in which a grievance procedure provides for a neutral arbitrator from outside, this is to a greater or less extent inherent in any grievance procedure in which you appeal up the chain of command towards the top, and the fewer links there are in the chain the less likely is higher authority to reverse a subordinate authority disciplinary decision. "Natural justice," in this field, does not mean you must have a neutral tribunal; only that you must know what is said against you; you must have the opportunity to be heard; and the tribunal must act honestly.

Mrs Hughes did know what was said against her in June 1977. She at all times had access to the governors. In October she and they fully discussed what was said against her. It is not suggested that the decision to support the headmistress was other than honest. In the following April, Mrs Hughes, no doubt realistically, did not seek to involve the governors again.

The majority of the Tribunal went so far as to comment (we think, as a matter of criticism) on the absence of an appeal procedure against the governors. How could there be one? The governors were the top; and you have only to postulate calling in a neutral arbitrator to resolve this kind of dispute, possibly through the good offices of ACAS, to appreciate how far the majority had allowed themselves to stray from reality into a legalistic approach not shared by their legally qualified chairman. In our judgment, the majority approach to the procedural aspect of the matter involved error of law in thinking that . . . grievance procedures must include some kind of neutral decision-making body.

Rowe v. Radio Rentals Ltd.

[1982] I.R.L.R. 177
Employment Appeal Tribunal

> The employee was dismissed for misconduct by his immediate superior, the area manager. He appealed to the regional controller, who upheld the dismissal. The Industrial Tribunal held the dismissal fair.

Browne-Wilkinson J.: It is very important that internal appeals procedures run by commercial companies (which usually involve a consideration of the decision to dismiss by one person in line management by his superior) should not be cramped by legal requirements imposing impossible burdens on companies in the conduct of their personnel affairs. There may be some exceptional case (which we cannot now think of) in which the rule that justice must appear to be done might apply to the full extent that it applies to a judicial hearing. But, in general, it is inevitable that those involved in the original dismissal must be in daily contact with their superiors who will be responsible for deciding the appeal: therefore the appearance of total disconnection between the two cannot be achieved. Moreover, at the so-called appeal hearing (which in this and many other cases is of a very informal nature) the initial dismisser is very often required to give information as to the facts to the person hearing the appeal. It is therefore obvious that rules about total separation of functions and lack of contact between the appellate court and those involved in the original decision simply cannot be applied in the majority of cases. It seems to us that the correct approach is that indicated by Lord Denning M.R. in *Ward v Bradford Corporation* (1971) 70 LGR 27 at p. 35:

> "We must not force these disciplinary bodies to become entrammelled

in the nets of legal procedure. So long as they act fairly and justly, their decision should be supported."

On the facts of this case, the majority of the Industrial Tribunal have come to the conclusion that the appeals procedure was proper and that justice was done. In those circumstances, it would be wrong for us to say that the rules of natural justice had been breached simply because justice might not appear to have been done. In the context of these internal appeals from one man in line management to another, it must be difficult to show that rules of natural justice have been infringed if the person hearing the appeal in fact took the decision, the employee having been given the opportunity to deal with the case against him, and having been heard.

(ii) The negotiation model and collective bargaining. In contrast to the trial model, industrial practice suggest that in dismissal procedures what purports to be a "trial of law" is often a "trial of strength." Particularly in cases where the worker concerned is a trade unionist, the nature of the disputes procedure involving misconduct is not legalistic, it is confrontational. Negotiation, not adjudication, is the essence of the procedure. This point is made in the following extract.

M. Mellish and N. Collis-Squires, "*Legal and Social Norms in Discipline and Dismissal*" (1976) 5 I.L.J. 164 at 172, 176–7

. . . The D.E. Study *In Working Order, A Study of Industrial Discipline*" Paper No. 6 (1973) Department of Employment Manpower found evidence of disciplinary issues being bargained over like any other. In joint disciplinary committees it noted a tendency for management to suggest a more severe penalty than it thought necessary "in order to allow a margin to bargain over." Employee representatives as a result nearly always sought a reduction in the penalty. "In other words, the joint committee institutionalised a fairly straightforward bargaining process rather than formalised a judicial process."

Discipline is not always an individual issue, it can be a collective one. Moreover, the distinction in many situations lies not, as the [Department of Employment] suggests, in the intrinsic nature of the issue, but rather in the values, goals and power of parties in respect of *any* issue. This may be seen by contrasting two phenomena common enough in their own industries, piecework "fiddling" in engineering and the shop assistant caught with a hand in the till. . . .

[The latter] is normally viewed and treated as an individual issue by a judicial or quasi-judicial method of settlement. In contrast, piecework "fiddling" is more often and more easily seen as raising collective issues which have to be dealt with—if at all—by straightforward bargaining.

. . . Tribunals operate on very different principles to those of organised groups of employees. Following through our examples of absenteeism and timekeeping, a typical Tribunal might act as follows. It would ensure that the factual case against an employee was proven; it might insist that an employer inquired into the circumstances of the individual's offence before dismissing him; it would probably insist that an employer warned an employee prior to dismissal; and it might decide that an individual should be given the right to explain any transgression and appeal against any decision to dismiss to more senior management. What a typical Tribunal would *not* do is question the appropriateness of a rule on absence or time-keeping as organised employees might.

More than this, though, the Tribunal has a duty to settle the individual complaint it receives and so it necessarily treats it in relative isolation from the bargaining context whence it came. Tribunals in effect individualise what can be collective disputes . . . Since [the Report of the] Donovan [Committee 1965–1968 Cmnd. 3623] the intention of unfair dismissal law has been to take dismissal questions out of the area of collective industrial disputes by providing an alternative individual remedy.

Earlier field research on procedures had highlighted the extent to which discipline was dealt with by negotiation rather than adjudication, even where, as in the following extract, the formal rules did not mention it.

W.E.J. McCarthy, *"The Role of Shop Stewards in British Industrial Relations"* in ROYAL COMMISSION ON TRADE UNIONS AND EMPLOYERS' ASSOCIATIONS *Research Paper No. 1 (1967), para. 23*

We also found that in every establishment with shop stewards they acted as spokesmen for those facing disciplinary charges, and here the aim was to secure removal or reduction of the sanctions proposed. Thus examples were given where dismissals were changed to suspensions, suspensions to admonitions, and admonitions to apologies—all following the intervention of a steward. Naturally, they were not always successful, and occasionally, usually in the case of proved theft, they informed members in advance that nothing could be done. In general, shop steward efforts to reduce or eliminate penalties were based on the establishment and acceptance of various precedents. If they could show that penalties suggested in a particular instance were not justified by past precedents they could usually secure some measure of success. Alternatively if management could show—say—that proved theft had been accepted in the past as a justification for dismissal nothing much could be done.

Bargaining may even predominate where, as in the next extracts, the procedure was formally institutionalised in a quasi-judicial process.

K.W. Wedderburn and P.L. Davies, EMPLOYMENT GRIEVANCES AND DISPUTES PROCEDURES IN BRITAIN (1969), pp. 143–144

Account of the internal "Misconduct Committee" at the Firestone Tyre and Rubber Co. Ltd.

But it has been suggested that what happens on such a joint participative committee is something in the nature of a "judicial" proceeding, and that its decisions come to build up a body of "case law." Such legalistic notions need reconsideration when the operation of the procedure is more closely considered, though no doubt the actual decisions come to be regarded as "precedent". . . .

[There follows an account of the discussions between the labour and management representatives in the committee under the "impartial" chairman.]

From this account emerges the authentic flavour not so much of a quasi-judicial body, but of a negotiating or bargaining body using a pre-agreed set of principles and procedures invoking some semi-legal processes. The bargaining functions of the stewards are translated from the shop floor to a higher level where they have both greater power and greater responsibility. The process is less that of adjudication than of joint bargaining and decision-making. Though these participative committees are still rare in the British experience, it was thought worthwhile to examine the best-known example in some detail to see just what happens at its hearings. Some commentators have used the precedent of such participative bodies to suggest a system of labour courts to deal with discipline. It would be a gross error to see the germ of the matter in the former unless it be remembered that a labour court, as in the French experience, may ordinarily exclude lawyers altogether and concentrate on conciliation and compromise, rather than on the judicial process. Furthermore, the "judges" in this participative system are closely associated with the very parties to the dispute. No labour court tolerates that.

R. Hyman, DISPUTES PROCEDURES IN ACTION (1972) pp. 3, 38–39

. . . disputes procedure is often viewed as a form of judicial process; in fact it is best conceived as a type of bargaining. . . .

. . . the agreements which specify the institutions of procedure offer no precise guidance as to the nature of the resolution process. Are workplace differences to be resolved through a process of adjudication, conciliation, or bargaining?

The judicial model is suggested by many of the accoutrements of engineering procedure: the formalized terms of reference and findings, the process of multi-stage hearings, the culmination at the several "courts" at Central Conference. A judicial analogy is also apparent in some official accounts of the operation of procedure: the aim of "bringing out all the underlying facts" as a basis for "judging the merits of the trade union claim." Yet the model is fundamentally unsatisfactory: first because the proceedings are conducted by representatives—however detached from the immediate focus of the dispute—of one of the parties; second, because a positive outcome requires some formula acceptable to both parties; third, because of the fervent insistence (in theory at least) that no decision may set a precedent for any future case. . . .

The case law on termination of work displays two areas of tension: first, between the conflicting models of negotiation and adjudication processes; and secondly, the problematic quality of a "trial" model and of the requirements of natural justice in a context where the common law has traditionally upheld managerial prerogatives. The Code of Practice on Disciplinary Practice and Procedures in Employment manifests an uneasy and unsatisfactory resolution of these tensions.

To adherents of the "trial" concept, the Code of Practice would fail on the grounds of there being no impartial judge (the employer being the adjudicator); also, because of the lack of regulation of the hearing (indeed, the word "hearing" does not appear—only that the worker accused must be allowed to state his case, with nothing said as to the witnesses, cross-examination, evidence, etc.). The "trial" model closest to the Code, with its emphasis on investigation and inquiry by the employer (para. 11–12), would seem rather to be that of an inquisitorial system, not the adversarial system of the common law.

To adherents of the "bargaining" model, a trade union presence is essential. Their emphasis on agreed procedures, on union involvement and negotiation is not adequately reflected in the Code. McCarthy's finding that shop stewards are mainly engaged in disputing *penalties*—not facts—is not reflected in any emphasis in the Code on this element, which in practice appears more important than fact-finding (*cf.* dismissals involving alleged incompetence, when the fact-finding stage may be more central and contentious).

(b) Reasonableness and procedures under EPCA, s.57(3)

The case law on unfair dismissal concerned with procedures in misconduct dismissals identifies three stages of procedure:

(1) establishing facts;
(2) holding a hearing; and
(3) deciding appropriate penalties (including elements of employer responsibility, warnings, inconsistency and alternative employment).

Each of these stages will be examined below in extracts which illustrate the tension between the "bargaining" and the "trial" models, and the problems of applying "natural justice" in the employment context.

(1) Establishing facts. The employer must show that he had a fair reason in his mind at the time of dismissal (*Devis & Sons Ltd.* v. *Atkins* [1977] I.R.L.R. 314 (H.L.)). Problems arise where an employer dismisses for a reason genuinely held, but which is in fact incorrect, *ie* the facts of the situation do not support his belief. The Code of Practice on Disciplinary Practice and Procedures in Employment provides guidance aimed at avoiding this discrepancy between belief and facts in paragraph 10(i) and 11. The following case elaborates this guidance.

British Home Stores Ltd. v. Burchell
[1978] I.R.L.R. 379; [1978] I.T.R. 560
Employment Appeal Tribunal

The employee was dismissed for alleged involvement in acts of dishonesty.

ARNOLD J.: The case is one of an increasingly familiar sort in this Tribunal, in which there has been a suspicion or belief of the employee's misconduct entertained by the management, it is on that ground that dismissal has taken place, and the Tribunal then goes over that to review the situation as it was at the date of dismissal. The central point of appeal is what is the nature and proper extent of that review. We have had cited to us, we believe, really all the cases which deal with this particular aspect of the recent history of this Tribunal over the three or four years; and the conclusions to be drawn from the cases we think are quite plain. What the Tribunals have to decide every time is, broadly expressed, whether the employer who discharged the employee on the ground of the misconduct in question (usually, though not necessarily, dishonest conduct) entertained a reasonable suspicion amounting to a belief in the guilt of the employee of that misconduct at that time. That is really stating shortly and compendiously what is in fact more than one element. First of all, there must be established by the employer the fact of that belief; that the employer did believe it. Secondly, that the employer had in his mind reasonable grounds upon which to sustain that belief. And thirdly, we think, that the employer, at the stage at which he formed that belief on those grounds at any rate at the final stage at which he formed that belief on those grounds, had carried out as much investigation into the matter as was reasonable in all the circumstances of the case. It is the employer who manages to discharge the onus of demonstrating those three matters, we think, who must not be examined further. It is not relevant, as we think, that the Tribunal would itself have shared that view in those circumstances. It is not relevant, as we think, for the Tribunal to examine the quality of the material which the employer had before him, for instance to see whether it was the sort of material, objectively considered, which would lead to a certain conclusion on the balance of probabilities, or whether it was the sort of material which would lead to the same conclusion only upon the basis of being "sure" as it is now said more normally in a criminal context, or, to use the more old-fashioned term, such as to put the matter "beyond reasonable doubt." The test, and the test all the way through, is reasonableness; and certainly, as it seems to us, a conclusion on the balance of probabilities will in any surmisable circumstance be a reasonable conclusion.

In *Weddel & Co. Ltd.* v. *Tepper* [1980] I.R.L.R. 96 (C.A.), Stephenson L.J. supported the *Burchell* approach:

> "Employers suspecting an employee of misconduct justifying dismissal cannot justify their dismissal simply by stating an honest belief in his guilt . . . they must act reasonably in all the circumstances, and must make reasonable inquiries appropriate to the circumstances. If they form their belief hastily and act hastily upon it, without making the appropriate inquiries or giving the employee a fair opportunity to explain himself, their belief is not based on reasonable grounds and they are certainly not acting reasonably."

But in *Monie* v. *Coral Racing Ltd.* [1980] I.R.L.R. 464 (C.A.), Sir David Cairns, while acknowledging that the Court of Appeal in *Tepper* found the *Burchell* approach "helpful," declared:

> "But as I understand the judgments none of the Lord Justices were saying that the passage contained a test of universal application. Ultimately the test must be that laid down in [EPCA, s.57(3)] which I have already read. While guidelines such as those

provided by Arnold J. are helpful, each case must in the end depend on its own facts. . . ."

On the facts of the case before him, Sir David was prepared to say: "Looking at the matter as an ordinary businessman would look at it . . . (it was correct to ask) whether there were solid and sensible grounds on which the employer could reasonably infer or suspect dishonesty."

It is important to distinguish the *Burchell* principle from that in the *British Labour Pump* case (see pp. 326 above). The *Burchell* principle involves a judgment on known facts. If they are inadequate for the basis of a reasonable belief, the failure of proper procedures actually destroys the alleged reason. The *British Labour Pump* principle assesses reasonableness after a hypothetical guess at what action following proper procedures would have produced. Under the *Burchell* principle, failure to carry out a proper investigation may demonstrate an absence of facts sufficient to provide reasonable grounds for any belief the employer may have had. If so, there is no fair reason for dismissal established at all, and the *British Labour Pump* principle never comes to be applied.

This contrast between the two principles demonstrates what Browne-Wilkinson J. called the "danger of seeking to make a clear-cut division between substantive and procedural matters in industrial relations cases" (*Grundy (Teddington) Ltd.* v. *Plummer and Salt* [1983] I.R.L.R. 98 (E.A.T.) para. 21). The same point was made in *Henderson* v. *Granville Tours Ltd.* [1982] I.R.L.R. 494 (E.A.T.), where a coach driver was summarily dismissed following a brief interview concerning a complaint by one of his passengers. An Industrial Tribunal held by a majority that the dismissal was fair, that had further investigation been made, the result would have been the same. On appeal, Waterhouse J. stated:

> "There are, of course, many cases in the employment field involving dismissal in which it is appropriate for Tribunals to consider what would have happened if procedural defects had not occurred. . . . But the Tribunal here were not concerned simply with a procedural defect. They were concerned with the employers' state of mind at the moment of dismissal and the sufficiency of information to justify that state of mind. That is not simply a procedural question, it goes to the heart of the fairness of the dismissal and to the question whether or not the test contained in [EPCA] s.57(3) (as amended) has been fulfilled."

(2) Holding a hearing. The common law never required natural justice to be applied to termination of employment. The statutory protection against unfair dismissal introduced in 1971 did not provide any procedural requirements. It was only the Code of Industrial Relations Practice of 1972 which gave rudimentary guidance drafted in terms of disciplinary termination (see the Code, para. 10(f) and (g)). The controversy over the significance of procedure in unfair dismissal cases (see above, pp. 326 *et seq.*) focussed on the "hearing" stage in the following extract.

Dunn v. Pochin (Contractors) Ltd.
[1982] I.R.L.R. 449
Employment Appeal Tribunal

The employee was dismissed for failing to clean his machine without having been given any opportunity to offer an explanation. An Industrial Tribunal dismissed his claim for unfair dismissal on the grounds that, even if given such an opportunity, the employer would still have dismissed him.

BROWNE-WILKINSON J.: We have not found this a very easy point primarily because of the state of the authorities. Before an employee is dismissed, an employer has to satisfy himself by proper investigation as to the facts of the matter and the nature of the employee's conduct. In the ordinary case, such investigation will necessarily involve finding out from the employee himself what is his account of the matter, his explanation of the events that occurred and any mitigating factors there may be. It is for that reason that in the vast majority of cases a dismissal of an employee without giving him an opportunity to explain his conduct is going to be held unfair. As the Court of Appeal has expressed it recently in *W. Weddell & Co. Ltd. v Tepper* [1980] I.R.L.R. 96 at p. 101:

"Employers suspecting an employee of misconduct justifying dismissal cannot justify their dismissal simply by stating an honest belief in his guilt. There must be reasonable grounds and they must act reasonably in all the circumstances having regard to equity and the substantial merits of the case. They do not have regard to equity, in particular, if they do not give him a fair opportunity of explaining before dismissing him."

That is undoubtedly the starting point.

However, it is clear from at least one other decision in the Court of Appeal that the rule is not an absolutely invariable one. There may be cases of a kind where the failure to give the employee an opportunity to explain is not fatal to an employer's claim that the dismissal was fair. The example given by Lawton L.J. in [*Bailey v BP Oil (Kent Refinery) Ltd.*] [1980] I.R.L.R. 287 at p. 289] was a case where, on the shop floor, a worker was seen by the works manager and others to stab another man in the back with a knife. He gave that as an example where failure to give him an opportunity to explain his conduct could not have rendered the dismissal unfair. What at present is not clear is where the borderline runs between those cases where a failure to give an opportunity to explain renders the dismissal unfair and those where it does not.

Certainly, there is no hard and fast line; it must depend on the circumstances of each case. But there does appear to be a difference in emphasis in the authorities. On the one hand, there is the test propounded by Sir John Donaldson sitting in the National Industrial Relations Court in *Earl v Slater & Wheeler (Airlyne) Ltd.* [1972] I.R.L.R. 115 at p. 117 where he says this:

"Whilst we do not say that in all circumstances the employee must be given an opportunity of stating his case, the only exception can be the case where there can be no explanation which could cause the employer to refrain from dismissing the employee. This must be a very rare situation."

The same approach is echoed by the Employment Appeal Tribunal in *Charles Letts & Co. Ltd. v Howard* [1976] I.R.L.R. 248 where it is suggested that a failure to give an opportunity to explain will only be capable of being justified by the employer if he can show that even if an opportunity had been given the result would "inevitably have been the same." On the other hand in *British Labour Pump Co. Ltd. v Byrne* [1979] I.R.L.R. 94 (in which *Earl v Slater & Wheeler (Airlyne) Ltd.* was not cited) the Employment Appeal Tribunal laid down the test as being whether, on the balance of probabilities, the employer had shown that the same result would have ensued.

At some stage we think it will be necessary for the assistance of Industrial Tribunals in approaching this kind of case to indicate what are the circumstances which justify a finding of fair dismissal even though no opportunity to explain has been given. But this case is on any view wholly exceptional. There was here no direct evidence as to what would have been the employers' attitude had they heard the explanation which Mr Dunn gives in his form of application to the Industrial Tribunal. . . .

In those circumstances, we do not think it right for the Industrial Tribunal to draw an inference, unprompted by the parties and without direct evidence, as to what the outcome would have been if an opportunity to explain had been given. In our view, it must be a rare case in which a Tribunal can be satisfied without direct evidence that, if an opportunity to explain had been given which had not been given, a hypothetical decision, identical to the one actually reached, would have followed. One is building hypotheses—a notoriously difficult matter to adjudicate on with any certainty. In the circumstances of this case, we do not think there was evidence justifying this Tribunal in reaching the conclusion that it did, namely that the outcome would have been the same in any event.

If it is held that a hearing is necessary, there remains the problem of the extent to which procedural niceties have been observed, *e.g.* as to the right of cross-examination (see *Khanum* v. *Mid-Glamorgan Area Health Authority* [1978] I.R.L.R. 215 (E.A.T.); *Bentley Engineering Co. Ltd.* v. *Mistry* [1978] I.R.L.R. 436 (E.A.T.); written confessions (*Ladbroke Racing Ltd.* v. *Arnott* [1979] I.R.L.R. 192 (E.A.T.), [1983] I.R.L.R. 154 (Ct. Sess.)); refusal of the employee to participate (*Harris and Shepherd* v. *Courage (Eastern) Ltd.* [1981] I.R.L.R. 153 (E.A.T.), [1982] I.R.L.R. 509 (C.A.)) etc.

In the section on *Industrial Practice* (pp. 346 *et seq.*) there was much emphasis on the role of trade union representatives. The bargaining model of disciplinary procedure (above pp. 353 *et seq.*) recognises the negotiating role of union representatives where employee discipline has implications for a group of employees. This role of the union representative is sometimes recognised in the case law.

Pirelli General Cable Works Ltd. v. Murray
[1979] I.R.L.R. 190
Employment Appeal Tribunal

The employee was dismissed for refusing to comply with his foreman's instruction. At the disciplinary hearing he was represented by his shop steward, but, having given his version of events, he was not thereafter personally present at the hearing. Nor was he present at the appeal hearing, which was again attended by his union representatives. An Industrial Tribunal held his dismissal unfair.

BRISTOW J.: In our judgment the Tribunal were plainly wrong in law in holding, as they did, that at the hearing on 14 March the principles of natural justice were not observed, or that the fact that Mr Murray was not told that he could personally attend the hearing of the appeal at which he was represented by a union official and his two shop stewards in some way was a denial of natural justice. The shop stewards who dealt with the matter on Mr Murray's behalf were present when Mr Terry Davis and the other shift workers gave their versions of what had happened, and could ask them any questions they wished. The concept of natural justice does not include the right to be personally present throughout. If Mr Murray felt that things were being said behind his back which he did not have a proper opportunity to contradict it does not follow that the principles of natural justice were not observed. In the way in which this "disciplinary hearing" was conducted nothing was done behind the back of his shop steward representatives, and they had every opportunity to ensure that his side of the question was heard.

On the other hand, consider the following case, in the light particularly of the view that union representatives negotiate less about facts than about penalties (see the extract from McCarthy on p. 354 above).

Dacres v. The Walls Meat Co. Ltd.
[1976] I.R.L.R. 20
Queen's Bench Division

Following a fight, the employee was dismissed. He complained that he was not given a fair chance of being heard and did not have the advantage of being assisted by his stop steward or other union representative, contrary to the Industrial Relations Code of Practice 1972.

PHILLIPS J.: So, I turn to the next ground of appeal, which is that Mr Dacres was not given a proper opportunity of explaining himself to Mr Richardson, who dismissed him, and was not accompanied by his own representative. As to the first point, it is perfectly plain that he had every opportunity of explaining his part in the matter. The trouble was that Mr Richardson did not accept what the appellant was saying, any more than the Tribunal did later on. As to the second point, the lack of a representative, it is true that the shop steward or other representative did not accompany him. There is no doubt that a representative could have accompanied him. There is no doubt that Mr Richardson was at fault in not seeing that that happened, because it was in accordance with the domestic procedure that Mr Dacres should have that advantage. But that is a view, too, which the Tribunal took. They then went on to say, in paragraph 8: "We do not think that this particular matter in all the circumstances amounts to such a defect in procedure as to render the dismissal itself unfair." And so they have directed themselves quite correctly. They have realised that the Code of Practice is not binding, although it is very important. It is only a guide, although it is a guide which ought in ordinary circumstances to be followed. The Tribunal go on: "Nor could we in any event have held that Mr Dacres was not involved in the fight, and should not have been dismissed. We think that it is regrettable that Mr Richardson did not take the precaution of waiting until the shop steward or some other union officer was available to attend his meeting; and this should be watched in the future." In effect what the Tribunal are saying is, that this was an error, but that in the circumstances of the case it caused the appellant no injustice.

The reason it caused him no injustice is this: he, as follows from the passage which I read from page 22, had a perfectly good opportunity of saying that he was not fighting. Mr Richardson did not believe him. The Tribunal thought that Mr Richardson was right and did not believe the appellant either. So, the only question upon which the shop steward or union representative could have assisted was the simple question, "fighting or not fighting?" It really could have made no difference, because there were no other, more complicated questions. I say this because it appears that Mr Dacres himself, when giving evidence to the Tribunal, said: "Fighting is against the company rules, I agree, not only there but anywhere. I myself never fight. If I fought then my dismissal would be right." And so it was the simplest possible question: had he been fighting, or hadn't he? Although I accept that it was regrettable that a union representative was not present, the Code of Practice, is, as I say, but a guide, notwithstanding that it ought usually to be followed. But the failure to follow it in this particular case made really no difference at all.

(3) Appropriate penalties. The first two stages of procedure, investigation and hearing, are aimed at determining the facts and assessing the surrounding circumstances so that a decision can be taken. In practice, the facts are frequently not as controversial as a reading of the cases might lead one to expect. Consensus is often reached fairly quickly on what actually happened. The third stage of procedure, what to do about it, is often the crucial one in practice. The hearing may be more concerned with negotiating penalties than assessing facts. Trade Union representatives play an especially active role in negotiations over what, if any, penalty is appropriate.

It is implicit in a claim of unfair dismissal that termination was not the appropriate penalty. The ACAS Code of Practice gives guidance to Industrial Tribunals on this issue in paragaphs 10(h), and 12. As paragraph 10(h) indicates, the sanction of dismissal, even without prior warning, is deemed appropriate for *gross* misconduct. The difficulties of defining gross misconduct, and the extent to which Tribunals are prepared to challenge employer definitions were illustrated above (pp. 329 *et seq.*). Where the misconduct is not gross, repetition of lesser misconduct may lead to termination. The question, on which the Code provides little guidance, is whether other sanctions are appropriate for such misconduct, particularly when other penalties have been used by the employer in the past, for such past experience provides concrete evidence that penalties short of dismissal may be adequate. Inconsistency is a frequent ground on which trade union representatives negotiate in disciplinary cases (see the extracts from McCarthy, and Wedderburn and Davies on p. 354 above). The following cases illustrate the courts' varying attitudes towards inconsistency by employers.

The Post Office v. Fennell
[1981] I.R.L.R. 221
Court of Appeal

The employee was summarily dismissed after assaulting another employee in the works canteen.

BRANDON L.J.: It was conceded by Mr Carr on behalf of the Post Office—very properly, in my view—that, if the facts were that the Post Office had adopted a course of conduct in relation to comparable cases by abstaining from ever inflicting the final punishment of summary dismissal, and without giving any warning of any change in their policy on the matter, dismissed the applicant for similar behaviour, then it would be open to an Industrial Tribunal to find that they had not acted fairly. It seems to me, therefore, that the question in this case boils down to this, whether there was any evidence upon which the Industrial Tribunal could find that there had been such a course of conduct by the Post Office, and that there had been a departure from it without any warning, and that that was unfair.

The relevant statutory provision is now contained in s.57 of the Employment Protection (Consolidation) Act 1978. Under that section, what the employer has to prove is, first of all, his reason for dismissal, and he did that. Then he has to satisfy the court that in the circumstances, having regard to equity and the substantial merits of the case, he acted reasonably in treating it as a sufficient reason for dismissing the employee. I would stress in sub-section (3) of s.57 the words in brackets "having regard to equity and the substantial merits of the case." It seems to me that the expression "equity" as there used comprehends the concept that employees who misbehave in much the same way should have meted out to them much the same punishment, and it seems to me that an Industrial Tribunal is entitled to say that, where that is not done, and one man is penalised much more heavily than others who have committed similar offences in the past, the employer has not acted reasonably in treating whatever the offence is as a sufficient reason for dismissal.

Hadjioannou v. Coral Casinos Ltd.
[1981] I.R.L.R. 352
Employment Appeal Tribunal

The employee was dismissed for fraternising with the casino's customers contrary to rule 13 of the employer's work rules. He claimed unfair dismissal, arguing, *inter alia*, that in the past other employees had broken rule 13 but had not been dismissed.

WATERHOUSE J.: In resisting the appeal, counsel for the respondents, Mr Tabachnik, has submitted that an argument by a dismissed employee based upon disparity can only be relevant in limited circumstances. He suggests that, in broad terms, there are only three sets of circumstances in which such an argument may be relevant to a decision by an Industrial Tribunal under s.57 of [EPCA]. Firstly, it may be relevant if there is evidence that employees have been led by the employer to believe that certain categories of conduct will be either overlooked, or at least will not be dealt with by the sanction of dismissal. . . .

Thirdly, Mr Tabachnik concedes that evidence as to decisions made by an employer in truly parallel circumstances may be sufficient to support an argument, in a particular case, that it was not reasonable on the part of the employer to visit the particular employee's conduct with the penalty of dismissal and that some lesser penalty would have been appropriate in the circumstances.

We accept that analysis by counsel for the respondents of the potential relevance of arguments based on disparity. We should add, however, as counsel has urged upon us, that Industrial Tribunals would be wise to scrutinize arguments based upon disparity with particular care. It is only in the limited circumstances that we have indicated that the argument is likely to be relevant and there will not be many cases in which the evidence supports the proposition that there are other cases which are truly similar, or sufficiently similar, to afford an adequate basis for the argument. The danger of the argument is that a Tribunal may be led away from a proper consideration of the issues raised by s.57(3) of [EPCA]. The emphasis in that section is upon the particular circumstances of the individual employee's case. It would be most regrettable if Tribunals or employers were to be encouraged to adopt rules of thumb, or codes, for dealing with industrial relations problems and, in particular, issues arising when dismissal is being considered. It is of the highest importance that flexibility should be retained, and we hope that nothing that we say in the course of our judgment will encourage employers or Tribunals to think that a tariff approach to industrial misconduct is appropriate. One has only to consider for a moment the dangers of the tariff approach in other spheres of the law to realise how inappropriate it would be to import it into this particular legislation.

The use of warnings as a form of penalty is highlighted in the Code of Practice and is much in evidence in industrial practice (see above p. 346). If the employers are given latitude with respect to adherence to procedures where dismissal occurs, however, it is not surprising that the Tribunals display a similarly lenient attitude when employers issue warnings without adhering to procedures. The following case is an illustration.

Wood v. Kettering Co-operative Chemists Ltd.
[1978] I.R.L.R. 438
Employment Appeal Tribunal

On March 14, 1977, the employee received a warning in relation to complaints about his behaviour. The warning was issued without hearing what he had to say, and though he wrote a letter protesting at its issuance, the employers never replied to the letter. On May 17, 1977 he was dismissed following an incident of misbehaviour.

PHILLIPS J.: It is said that the circumstances surrounding the warning were such that it could not be regarded as a valid warning for the purpose of disciplinary procedure, or indeed for any purpose at all; that therefore it must be disregarded; that therefore there was no valid prior warning; that therefore it was unfair to dismiss. We have given careful consideration to that submission, but we find that we cannot accept it. It is perfectly true that the making of the warning of 14.3.77 was in many respects unsatisfactory, and the proper procedures were not complied with. In the first place it was issued without first hearing what Mr Wood had to say. That is not good procedure and indeed was contrary to the procedure followed by these employers in other cases. Secondly, Mr Wood, on 4 April, having written what may be described as partly a protest and partly a request for further information, the employers through Mr McGain or anybody else never replied to the letter. The Industrial Tribunal censure them correctly for that, and say that at best not to have replied was an act of discourtesy. Other less important criticisms have been made. As we have said, we accept the validity of the criticisms; and we would further accept that had Mr Wood been dismissed for those offences in a similar way the dismissal plainly would have been unfair. But we cannot accept the submission that precisely the same considerations apply in deciding whether a dismissal was unfair, as apply in considering whether a warning is a warning which it is proper to take into account on a later occasion.

We accept entirely what Mr Martin Reynolds [counsel for the employee] says, that caution is necessary, because if warnings given today are to be the foundation of a dismissal a month later, it is very unsatisfactory if warnings are given as a result of bad procedure. That we entirely accept. We also entirely accept that the matter needs critical examination, if the way in which the warning is given is open to criticism of disapproval. . . .

Our view of the matter is that it is necessary to examine the prior warning of 14 March, not as it were as a technical exercise, but having regard to the merits and reality of the case. That is, that there had been a deputation, serious complaints had been made, the letter . . ., whatever else can be said about it, is perfectly clear in the sense that it gives a perfectly clearly expressed warning. There cannot be any doubt at all that Mr Wood must have so understood it. Although he protested, he had the advice of his union, who could not because of other commitments take it up for him. He knew it was urgent to pursue the matter if he wanted to get it off his record. Although he wrote the letter of protest, and the letter (if one wishes) of further inquiry, he let the matter rest there. He must have known he was still, and continued to be, under this warning; and, if not content, he did nothing more to have it removed. It seems to us that in those circumstances the employers, and indeed the Industrial Tribunal, if they are going to deal with the substance of the matter rather than mere technical compliance with sets of rules, were plainly entitled on the merits to take that earlier warning into consideration.

7. ILL-HEALTH

Incapacity due to illness or injury may be caused by the work performed by the worker, or it may originate in other ways. In either event the incapacity leads to absence from work, either temporarily or permanently. The worker's incapacity, whether work-related or not, temporary or permanent, is of varying importance to the law on termination. At common law, all depends on the obligations undertaken in the contract of employment. Under statute, other considerations apply as well.

(A) Substantive Rules

(i) Common law

As with misconduct, the employer's power to terminate at common law is a function of notice requirements. If he terminates *with* notice by reason of the ill-health of the employee, the common law does not question his judgment. But termination *without* notice due to ill-health is only justifiable if the employee has broken his contractual obligations in a way that allows the employer to treat the contract as at an end. Illness which is temporary in nature would seem to preclude the employer treating the contract as at an end (see *Cuckson* v. *Stones* [1858] 1 E. & E. 248, Chapter 9 on *Sickness and Injury*). Illness which is uncertain in duration or permanent (even though caused by the employee's work) may allow for termination.

Condor v. The Barron Knights Ltd.
[1966] 1 W.L.R. 87
Queen's Bench Division

> The plaintiff, aged 16, was employed in December 1962 as a drummer in a band on condition that he performed seven nights a week. In January 1963 he collapsed and the doctor's report indicated he could not perform more than four nights a week. He was dismissed.

THOMPSON J.: That brings one accordingly to the question whether at that date the plaintiff was capable of and available to work as the contract contemplated, that is to say, not merely to play drums, but to play drums on seven nights a week, if need be travelling from one one-night stand to another. The plaintiff thought he was and the plaintiff said that at a later date in the year he did, but I am satisfied that at the time when the defendants had to consider the situation, not merely was it a reasonable view for them to take that he was not then fit, but that he was not in fact fit, that is to say, fit to work, as the contract contemplated, seven days a week. In my judgment for this purpose fitness involves not merely being able to do the work, though with the virtual certainty that at the end of a week or a very short period such as a month there will be a breakdown of a worse kind, but it does involve the ability to do it without the likelihood of such damage to health and so as, within the contract, to continue with the continuity which the contract contemplated. I am satisfied that (at the relevant date) . . . the situation was that the plaintiff was not fit to perform his part of the contract and at that date there was no reasonable likelihood that he would in the near future become so able.

Accordingly in my judgment . . . [seven nightly performances a week] had in a business sense made it impossible for him to continue to perform or for the defendants [to] have him perform the terms of the contract as a member of the group. It follows that in my judgment there was no wrongful dismissal in this case. . . .

Termination by reason of ill-health may occur automatically at common law through "frustration." A contract is "frustrated" as the consequence of events which are, the courts hold, not intended by either party. Frustration affects other cases of termination, but ill-health may well be the most frequent.

In employment cases, the doctrine of frustration has been applied in three different ways, depending on the type of contract concerned:

(a) short-term contracts for a specific purpose;
(b) fixed-term contracts of employment;

(c) contracts for an indefinite period terminable by notice (M.R. Freedland, *The Contract of Employment* (1976), pp. 303–310).

These considerations were reflected in the following cases.

The Egg Stores (Stamford Hill) Ltd. v. Leibovici
[1977] I.C.R. 260; [1976] I.R.L.R. 376
Employment Appeal Tribunal

The employee was absent from work following an accident from November 28, 1974, though he continued to be paid until January 1975. In April 1975 he asked for, but was refused, his job back, on the ground that somebody else was doing it. The employer claimed that the contract of employment had been frustrated. The employee claimed that he had been unfairly dismissed.

PHILLIPS J.: . . . there is no doubt that difficulties in applying the doctrine [of frustration] do occur in the case of those contracts of employment which can be determined at short notice. In the case of a fixed term contract of substantial length, no question can arise of the employer's terminating the contract and the doctrine of frustration is necessary if it has become impossible for the employee to continue to perform the contract. In the case of short-term periodic contracts of employment different considerations apply. Subject to the provisions of [what is now EPCA, s.49] the employer can terminate the contract of employment at short notice, and, if he does so, the only question will be whether in the circumstances such dismissal was unfair. . . . It is possible to divide into two kinds of events relied upon as bringing about the frustration of a short-term periodic contract of employment. There may be an event (*eg* a crippling accident) so dramatic and shattering that everyone concerned will realise immediately that to all intents and purposes the contract must be regarded as at an end. Or there may be an event, such as illness and accident, the course and outcome of which is uncertain. It may be a long process before one is able to say whether the event is such as to bring about frustration of the contract. But there *will* have been frustration of the contract, even though at the time of the event the outcome was uncertain, if the time arrives when, looking back, one can say that at some point (even if it is not possible to say precisely when) matters had gone on so long, and the prospects for the future were so poor, that it was no longer practical to regard the contract as still subsisting. Among the matters to be taken into account in such a case in reaching a decision are these:

(1) the length of the previous employment;
(2) how long it had been expected that the employment would continue;
(3) the nature of the job;
(4) the nature, length and effect of the illness or disabling event;
(5) the need of the employer for the work to be done, and the need for a replacement to do it;
(6) the risk to the employer of acquiring obligations in respect of redundancy payments or compensation for unfair dismissal to the replacement employee;
(7) whether wages have continued to be paid;
(8) the acts and statements of the employer in relation to the employment, including the dismissal of, or failure to dismiss, the employee; and
(9) whether in all the circumstances a reasonable employer could be expected to wait any longer.

Harman v. Flexible Lamps Ltd.
[1980] I.R.L.R. 418
Employment Appeal Tribunal

The employee began work as a quality control inspector in October 1977. In 1978 she was absent for 13 weeks due to ill-health. From February 16 to March 12, 1979 she was off sick, returned for one day and on March 13, was sent home because of abdominal pains, remaining absent for the rest of March and all of April. On May 3, she was sent a letter stating that her termination was being considered. On May 8, she and her mother met the company's personnel manager. She was then given a letter stating it was assumed she had left employment and would be given one week's pay in lieu of notice. She claimed unfair dismissal.

BRISTOW J.: Before the Industrial Tribunal two additional lines of defence to the claim were raised. One was that in the light of her illness and having regard to the importance of her job and the length of her service in that job, her contract had come to an end by operation of law by the process known to lawyers as "frustration". . . .

. . . . In our judgment, the circumstances of this case are a very long way in deed from any situation in which a contract of employment is discharged by operation of law because the basis of the contract has been destroyed by supervening ill-health on the part of the employee. This contract was in any case terminable at a week's notice, and once the employer decided that the ill-health of Miss Harman made it necessary to replace her, nothing was easier than to give her notice determining her job and to employ and train a replacement. In the employment field the concept of discharge by operation of law, that is frustration, is normally only in play where the contract of employment is of a long term which cannot be determined by notice. Where the contract is terminable by notice, there is really no need to consider the question of frustration and if it were the law that, in circumstances such as are before us in this case, an employer was in a position to say "this contract has been frustrated" then that would be a very convenient way in which to avoid the provisions of the Employment Protection (Consolidation) Act [1978]. In our judgment, that is not the law in these sort of circumstances. So, in our judgment, the Industrial Tribunal was wrong to find against Miss Harman on this head.

There has been a similar reluctance to impute frustration where termination procedures exist in cases of termination following imprisonment of the employee (*cf F.C. Shepherd & Co. Ltd.* v. *Jerrom* [1985] I.R.L.R. 275 (E.A.T.)). However, this hesitancy to apply the common law doctrine of frustration in unfair dismissal cases must now be qualified in the light of the Court of Appeal's decision in *Notcutt* v. *Universal Equipment Co. (London) Ltd.* [1986] I.R.L.R. 218 where Dillon L.J. said (para. 14):

"For my part, as a periodic contract of employment determinable by short or relatively short notice may none the less be intended in many cases by both parties to last for many years and as the power of the employer to terminate the contract by notice is subject to the provisions for the protection of employees against unfair dismissal now in [EPCA], I can see no reason in principle why such a periodic contract of employment should not in appropriate circumstances be held to have been terminated without notice by frustration according to the accepted and long established doctrine of frustration in our law of contract. The mere fact that the contract can be terminated by the employer by relatively short notice cannot of itself render the doctrine of frustration inevitably inapplicable. Accordingly, the words of Bristow J. cited earlier in this judgment [in *Harman* v. *Flexible Lamps Ltd.*, see above p. 368] must be taken as no more than a warning that the Court must look carefully at any submission that a periodic contract of employment has been discharged by frustration if that submission is put forward to avoid the provisions of the Act; if Bristow J. intended to go further than that I cannot agree with him."

(ii) Industrial practice

Most periods of ill-health are short, and are covered by sick pay schemes and the statutory sick pay system (see Chapter 9 on *Sickness and Injury*). In cases of serious long-term illness, however, problems of termination may arise, even before sick pay is exhausted, where the employer thinks the worker is incapacitated and likely to remain so for a considerable time. Various arrangements exist in practice to avoid loss of their jobs by workers who are ill. The judges have found some difficulty in adapting legal concepts of termination of contract to the realities of industrial practice, as the following case illustrates.

Hart v. A.R. Marshall & Sons (Bulwell) Ltd.
[1977] I.R.L.R. 51; [1977] 1 W.L.R. 1067
Employment Appeal Tribunal

The employee, one of two fitters, contracted industrial dermititis in April 1974, and thereafter periodically sent the employers sickness certificates. In August 1974 the employers took on a permanent replacement. In January 1976 the employee recovered and presented himself for work. He was told there was no work for him and given his P45. He claimed unfair dismissal.

PHILLIPS J.: However, experience shows that in a surprisingly large area of industry contracts of employment, and standard terms and conditions, still do not exist or if they do, make no provision for the rights of the parties during a prolonged period of illness of an employee. Very often, as in the present case, no wages are paid during sickness nor are any other formal arrangements made. In such cases the employee is in a sort of limbo. It seems that from the employer's point of view there is a reluctance to dismiss an employee when he is away sick because to do so may seem harsh. From the employee's point of view it may seem preferable not to be dismissed, albeit that no wages are being paid, because there is a hope that one day he will be able to return to work, though not necessarily to the same job. Experience in such cases shows that the parties very often drift along in this situation for long periods of time during which the employee has ceased to do any work, or to be able to do any work, but has not been formally dismissed. The legal position seems to be that the employee is still employed although he is not in receipt of wages, and that his employment continues until he is dismissed or the contract is frustrated and comes to an end by operation of law. In these circumstances, while we think it right to attach considerable importance in a case of this kind to the failure by the employer to dismiss the employee, it is, we think, impossible to say that unless the employee is dismissed the contract must always be taken to be continued. To do so would be tantamount to saying that frustration cannot occur in the case of short-term periodic contracts of employment. We do not read the judgment of Sir Hugh Griffiths in *Hebden v Forsey & Son* [1973] I.R.L.R. 344 (National Industrial Relations Court) as going as far as that in the passage at pages 345 to 346. In truth the employers are in a difficulty in this connection. First of all, if they dismiss the employee prematurely they may be said to have dismissed him unfairly; here we have suggested that the test is whether the employer can reasonably be expected to wait any longer (*K Spencer v Paragon Wallpapers Ltd* [1976] I.R.L.R. 373). Secondly, if the employer takes on a temporary replacement pending the recovery of the sick employee, there is a risk that he will be obliged to pay him compensation if he dismisses him when the sick employee has recovered; and even if he guides himself by our decision in *Terry v East Sussex County Council* [1976] I.R.L.R. 332 he is probably buying litigation.

Furthermore, we are very conscious of the fact—and attach much importance to it—that if frustration can never occur in such cases employers will feel obliged to dismiss employees in cases where they at present do not do so. In the long run, it is the employees who would be the losers.

In our judgment it comes to this. The failure of the employer to dismiss the employee is a factor, and an important factor, to take into account when considering whether the contract of employment has been frustrated. But it is not conclusive. The important question, perhaps, is to look to see what was the reason for the failure. It may be due to the fact that the employer did not think that the time had arrived when he could not reasonably wait any longer, in which case it is a piece of evidence of the greatest value. Or it may be a case where the failure to dismiss is attributable to the simple fact that the employer never applied his mind to the question at all. It is quite obvious that in the present case the employers felt—and the Tribunal found correctly—that they could not wait any longer, for they engaged Mr Twells to do the work previously done by Mr Hart, and the Tribunal have found that this was not key work. It seems to us that the reason why the employers never dismissed Mr Hart was that the relationship after he fell sick was being conducted in the casual manner which, we have indicated earlier in this judgment, is not uncommon in such cases.

(iii) Statutory provisions

One of the reasons said to make a dismissal "fair" is "capability . . . of the employee for performing work of the kind he was employed by the employer to do" (EPCA, s.57(2)(*a*)), and " 'capability' means capability assessed by reference to . . . health or any other physical or mental quality" (EPCA, s.57(4)(*a*)). The key question is: what is the standard adopted by tribunals in determining when ill-health justifies dismissal? Initially, there was an attempt to strike a balance between the interests of employers and employees (see *Luckings* v. *May & Baker Ltd.* [1974] I.R.L.R. 151 (N.I.R.C.)). But it was not long before the general standard of fairness, that of the "reasonable employer," was adopted. Termination for reasons of the employee's ill-health is said to be fair if a "reasonable employer" would terminate in the circumstances. As the E.A.T. has said: " . . . we agree with the view of the Industrial Tribunal that this applicant's absence had reached a volume which no reasonable employer could countenance. . . . " (*Townson* v. *The Northgate Group Ltd.* [1981] I.R.L.R. 382 (E.A.T.)).

The problem of workers' ill-health can arise in different circumstances giving rise to solutions other than termination. The standard of "fairness" might be thought to apply differently as between illness caused by the employee's work and that having other origins; and as between temporary and permanent ill-health. Below we give illustrations from each of these categories.

(a) Ill-health caused by work

McPhee v. George H. Wright Ltd.
[1975] I.R.L.R. 132
Industrial Tribunal

> An employee with over seven years' service was dismissed from his job as a warehouseman following some three and a half months off work due to an "anxiety state" connected with incidents which took place at work. He claimed unfair dismissal.

Colwyn Bay Industrial Tribunal (chairman: H.C. Easton): . . . The employers in this case satisfied us beyond a doubt that [the employee's] dismissal was reasonable in all the circumstances. His position had to be filled, and was filled. He was offered another, but was unable for medical reasons to take it up, so that the company could not keep it open for him any longer. Cases where an employee is dismissed because of absence, where that absence is unquestionably due to medical reasons, are always difficult. At the same time a firm cannot wait indefinitely for an employee to return when his work has to be done, and there is a need for a replacement. By waiting as long as they did we consider that the firm acted as reasonably as could possibly have been expected. The more true it is the that his illness was occasioned by incidents or attitudes at his place of work, the more reasonable it becomes for the company to reach a decision that they can no longer employ him. In reaching this decision we take into account the length of his service; but we also bear in mind the fact that his work simply had to be done by somebody, and that at no time was any indication ever given to the company of a possible date on which he might be available to work again. It was reasonable to say that they could not put him back into his original position because it had been filled; and when one vacancy which might possibly have been suitable for him had necessarily been filled in turn because of Mr McPhee's continued illness, we feel that enough had been done by the company to make this decision a reasonable one. It has to be borne in mind that TULRA, Sched. 1 [now EPCA, Pt. V], like the Redundancy Payments Act [now EPCA, Pt. V], is designed to provide compensation for certain specific matters, and cannot be used, nor was it intended, to provide an additional source of compensation for any illness, sickness or injury.

See also the unreported decision of the E.A.T. in *Davies* v. *Odeco (UK) Incorp.* (E.A.T. 702/79, April 1980, in (October 1980) 58 Health and Safety Information Bulletin 5). The employee sustained an injury whilst working on an oil rig. The E.A.T. considered that the:

> " . . . onus which rests upon an employer under [EPCA, s.57(3)] is simply to satisfy the Tribunal that they have acted reasonably. The manner in which the ill-health has come about may or may not be a matter which falls to be taken into account. It is not, however, a matter which can increase the burden of proof."

(b) Ill-health originating elsewhere than work

O'Brien v. Prudential Assurance Co. Ltd.
[1979] I.R.L.R. 140
Employment Appeal Tribunal

> The employee was dismissed from his job as district agent of the insurance company when it was discovered that he had a long history of mental illness.

SLYNN J.: . . . it is [the company's] practice not to appoint someone to the job of a district agent with this kind of illness. It is said that the reason for that is plain, namely that a district agent will frequently find himself visiting people's homes and if there were any possibility of a recurrence that might lead, with people alone or old people or young children, to difficulties and even to some dangers. So it is for that reason that this practice or policy of the company has been adopted.

Mr O'Brien then began his work and, in fact, he proved to be completely satisfactory. Some of his colleagues and superiors spoke highly of the way in which he had carried out his duty and no possible criticism was made of any lack of integrity in the way in which he did his actual work. . . .

. . . it would have seemed to us here that the Tribunal would have been entitled, on the facts which they found, to classify this as a reason relating to Mr O'Brien's capabilities for performing the work which he was employed to do. . . .

. . . It must depend upon the facts of the case as to whether for a particular employment, the employer behaves reasonably in stipulating the conditions which he seeks to establish. Here the Tribunal clearly, having heard all the evidence, were quite satisfied, as we read it, that this was a reasonable condition for this work, but not only for the company to impose in the beginning, but also for it to enforce in the case of someone who had misled them as to facts which they regarded as being important. It is necessary to stress that this practice or policy is, it appears, one limited to appointment as a district agent, with the particular features of the employment to which we have referred. What the position would be in relation to some other category of employment, where a person has a history of mental illness, is a different question and would always need to be looked at on the particular facts of the case.

Harper v. National Coal Board
[1980] I.R.L.R. 260
Employment Appeal Tribunal

The employee, an epileptic, had for a number of years worked without any problems alongside other disabled employees. But after two epileptic fits within two years, during which he unknowingly attacked and displayed violence to other employees, he was dismissed.

LORD McDONALD: On behalf of the appellant it was argued before us that the Industrial Tribunal were not entitled to conclude that the reason for dismissal related to capability in view of the fact that there was no evidence to suggest that the appellant's disability in any way interfered with his capacity to perform the work of a dust mask cleaner, except perhaps for the very brief period during which an attack was taking place. This is probably correct insofar as Dr. Mackinnon [the National Coal Board's Area Medical Officer's] view was that the job concerned was one which was entirely suited to a person suffering from the appellant's disability. At the same time, if by reason of ill health, an employee, however involuntarily, may be from time to time a source of danger to fellow employees, this in our view reflects upon his capability for performing work of the kind which he was employed to do. We are not therefore prepared to hold that the Industrial Tribunal fell into error in relating the reason for dismissal to the capability of the appellant. . . .

(c) Temporary incapacity through ill-health

Spencer v. Paragon Wallpapers Ltd.
[1976] I.R.L.R. 373; [1977] I.C.R. 301
Employment Appeal Tribunal

The employee, off work with back trouble, was dismissed although his doctor informed the employer that he might be able to return to work in four to six weeks. Due to a sudden increase in work, however, the company judged that their whole work force was needed, and dismissed the employee in order to fill his position.

PHILLIPS J.: There is no doubt that the Industrial Tribunal directed their minds to the correct question in this case. . . . They took into account the nature of the illness, the likely length of the continuing absence, the need of the employers to have the work done which the employee was engaged to do, the circumstances of the case, and concluded that the employers had discharged the onus put upon them under [TULRA, Sched. 1, para. 6(8), now contained in amended form in EPCA, s.57(3)]. Nothing has been shown to us which would justify us in interfering with that conclusion. In the first instance, the decision how to act in circumstances such as the present is that of the management. Secondly, it is the function of the Industrial Tribunal to determine whether the management has satisfied them that in the circumstances (having regard to equity and the substantial merits of the case) they acted reasonably in treating it as a sufficient reason for dismissing the employee. It is not the function of the Industrial Tribunal to take the management's decision for it, but only to decide whether the decision taken by the management passes that test. The Industrial Tribunal found that it did. . . .

We would merely add one caution. It is obviously a hardship to any employee to be dismissed when he has been absent due to illness for only a few weeks . . . and this case should not be interpreted as laying down any rule, applicable to other cases, that employees may be dismissed when they are absent, and are likely to continue to be absent, for another four to six weeks. Every case depends on its own circumstances. The basic question which has to be determined in every case is whether, in all the circumstances, the employer can be expected to wait any longer and, if so, how much longer? Every case will be different, depending upon the circumstances.

(d) Permanent incapacity through ill-health

Kyte v. Greater London Council
[1974] I.R.L.R. 8
National Industrial Relations Court

The employee broke his leg during the course of his work. On his return he was certified as only fit for light work and was given such work. Ten years later he was asked to do other work. He refused on grounds that he was not fit, though the employer's doctor said he was. He was dismissed.

GRIFFITHS J.: This is the ordinary case of a man returning to work, the employer waiving his entitlement to insist upon the performance of the full service and giving the man every opportunity to return to full fitness. Unfortunately, that did not occur in this case and, in the end, the employer, having no further work which the employee could perform, had no alternative but to dismiss him.

Finch v. Betabake (Anglia) Ltd.
[1977] I.R.L.R. 470
Employment Appeal Tribunal

The employee was dismissed when the employers became increasingly disturbed about his eyesight and after an opthalmic surgeon stated that it was dangerous to continue to employ him.

PHILLIPS J.: There was here very strong evidence indeed leading to the conclusion that because of his defective eyesight Mr Finch could not continue to be employed with safety to himself and others. In those circumstances it seems to us inevitable that the employers—who, it should be said, acted considerately—should have acted in the way they did. It is perfectly true that he was taken on when his eyesight was defective. It is perfectly true that he completed his probationary period. It is perfectly true that in the early days, although they had doubts about his ability, he got by—only just got by, perhaps, but still, got by. All those matters were matters properly to be taken into account in coming to a decision under [TULRA, Sched. 1, para. 6(8), now EPCA, s.57(3)]. It seems to us that the Industrial Tribunal did not take them into account.

(iv) Common law and statutory standards compared

The cases above demonstrate that the modern law of unfair dismissal, which applies a standard based on the needs of the "reasonable employer," is linked with the older common law notions of a mutual exchange of undertakings through contracts of employment. This is evident in a dictum of Phillips J. in *The Egg Stores (Stamford Hill) Ltd.* v. *Leibovici* [1976] [above p. 367] where he compared the common law doctrine of "frustration", an extreme situation operating as termination, and the statutory law of unfair dismissal (para. 9):

> "It seems to us that an important question to be asked in cases such as the present—we are not suggesting that it is the only question—is: has the time arrived when the employer can no longer reasonably be expected to keep the absent employee's post open for him? It will thus be seen that the sort of question which has to be considered when it is being decided whether a dismissal in such circumstances was unfair, and that which has to be considered when deciding whether the contract has been frustrated, are not dissimilar."

Compare *Tan* v. *Berry Bros. and Rudd Ltd.* [1974] I.R.L.R. 244 (N.I.R.C.) where Donaldson J. was careful to distinguish the two tests.

That the standard of fairness in ill-health cases leans towards the employers' interest is illustrated by cases allowing absence due to ill-health to be treated as a form of misconduct, or some other reason justifying dismissal.

International Sports Co. Ltd. v. Thompson
[1980] I.R.L.R. 340
Employment Appeal Tribunal

The employee was dismissed for persistent absenteeismugh most of the absences were covered by medical certificates.

WATERHOUSE J.: The appellant had a code of disciplinary procedure which has been agreed with all the trade unions represented at the Goldthorpe factory, including the respondent's own trade union. This code refers to two classes of "offences." Class I is described as serious misconduct, and Class II is defined as unsatisfactory performance, attendance or conduct. The extended definition of Class II is:

> "Unsatisfactory performance, attendance or conduct, ie an offence which warrants reprimand by an official of the company and which, after repetititon, could lead to either suspension (where applicable) or dismissal."

Among the examples cited for guidance appear "persistent absence and lateness beyond agreed levels." There was also evidence before the Tribunal (which they accepted) that the level of absence for this purpose, agreed with the trade unions, was 8 per cent.

The essence of the appellants' case should however have been reasonably clear. Their submission was that the reason for the respondent's dismissal was her persistent absence from work within the terms of Class II of the agreed disciplinary procedure. They did not allege that the dismissal was on a ground related to the respondent's capability, and they did not seek to establish that she was deliberately malingering. Their case was that her level of attendance at work over a long period was unacceptable, and that she had

> been given repeated formal warnings about the consequence of continued absences.
>
> In our judgment this was a reason related to the conduct of the respondent within the terms of s.57(2)(b) of the Employment Protection (Consolidation) Act 1978. If this were to be regarded as incorrect, however, it would in our view be some other substantial reason of a kind such as to justify the dismissal of an employee holding the position which the respondent held within the terms of s.57(1)(b).

The Industrial Tribunal in *Thomson* attempted to apply principles derived from cases of absence on grounds of ill-health. The E.A.T. did not accept this: "Here, however, the employer did not purport to dismiss the employee on the grounds of incapability. They were concerned with the impact of an unacceptable level of intermittent absences due to unconnected minor ailments" (para. 14). See for a similar view: *Rolls-Royce Ltd.* v. *Walpole* [1980] I.R.L.R. 343 (E.A.T.).

(b) Procedures

(i) Sick pay schemes and termination

In practice termination for ill-health reasons is affected by the terms of occupational sick pay schemes: "The most common way for schemes to deal with long term sickness is the extension of entitlement to a period of leave on (*e.g.*) half pay. Under some circumstances, however, the employer may be able to dismiss workers once they are clearly no longer able to do the.job. . . . " (*Sick Pay: A Negotiators' Guide* (1985), Labour Research Department).

In cases involving statutory unfair dismissal claims, some Tribunals appear to accept the possibility of dismissal even during the period of sick pay entitlement (*Coulson* v. *Felixstowe Dock & Railway Co.* [1974] I.R.L.R. 11 (I.T.)). Others regard such entitlement as precluding termination for its duration (*Kerr* v. *Atkinson Vehicles (Scotland) Ltd.* [1974] I.R.L.R. 36 (I.T.)), and even after it has expired (*Hardwick* v. *Leeds Area Health Authority* [1975] I.R.L.R. 319 (I.T.)). In the last-mentioned case the Tribunal opined: "It seems to us to be quite outmoded at the present day for a rule to exist that employees on exhaustion of sick pay should be automatically dismissed irrespective of the circumstances as if it was one of the laws of the Medes and Persians and it is not a reasonable one to apply" (chairman of Leeds Tribunal: G.M. Smailes, para. 6).

To the extent that sick pay entitlement makes dismissal unreasonable for at least its duration, it acts as a procedural safeguard for employees in ill-health. This much seems to be implicit in the following dictum in *Marshall* v. *Harland & Wolff Ltd.* [1972] I.C.R. 101 (N.I.R.C.), *per* Donaldson J.:

> "When the contract provides for sick pay, it is plain that the contract cannot be frustrated so long as the employee returns to work, or appears likely to return to work, within the period during which such sick pay is payable. But the converse is not necessarily true, for the right to sick pay may expire before the

incapacity has gone on, or appears likely to go on, for so long as to make a return to work impossible or radically different from the obligations undertaken under the contract of employment. . . . "

On the industrial practice regarding sick pay schemes, see Chapter 9 on *Sickness and Injury*. There is also now to be taken into account the Statutory Sick Pay Scheme effective from April 6, 1983 (see above pp. 293 *et seq.*).

(ii) Statutory provisions

The provisions of EPCA requiring notice and written reasons (sections 49 and 53) apply equally to cases of termination for ill-health. But the procedure developed from the statutory requirement of "reasonableness" in EPCA, s.57(3) in cases of ill-health terminations is, for practical reasons, quite different in principle from the procedure required in misconduct cases described above (pp. 351 *et seq.*). This is so despite the fact that statute and Code of Practice do not in terms recognise this. There is no code on ill-health practice and procedure to guide employers, as there is in disciplinary cases. The three stages of the procedure for dealing with misconduct developed from EPCA, s.57(3): (a) establishing facts; (b) holding a hearing; and (c) determining appropriate penalties—are not easily applicable to cases of ill-health.

(a) *Facts*, not beliefs, are more clearly at issue because the facts in ill-health cases are not solely matters for the employer to establish. A professional medical opinion is involved. The question of whether termination for ill-health should be a business or medical judgment is raised.

(b) A *hearing* may not be feasible given the absence and incapacity of the worker. The "trial" model of adversary proceedings is even less appropriate here than in the case of misconduct.

(c) The concept of *penalties* is arguably irrelevant where no fault is involved. Since power relations are not being directly challenged, and the notion of subordination is not paramount, it becomes possible to consider continuation of employment in some form. Hence new alternatives are available to termination, which are not themselves simply lesser sanctions, but genuine alternatives. Further, the role of union officials negotiating alternatives may be supplemented by agreed sickness schemes designed to deal with ill-health cases on a long-term basis.

(a) Establishing facts, not beliefs

Unlike misconduct, the existence of ill-health is seldom a matter of the subjective belief of the employer. In misconduct cases, following *Burchell's* case ([1978] I.R.L.R. 379 (E.A.T.)) (above, p. 356), the employer has to show primarily the fact of his belief that misconduct has occurred, and secondarily, that there are reasonable grounds for such a belief. In ill-health cases, a doctor's opinion is usually readily available as to the facts. Two issues need to be resolved: (a) is the employer required to ascertain the facts by obtaining medical opinion; and (b) to what extent is the employer bound by such medical opinion?

(1) Need the employer obtain a medical opinion? The cases do not appear to have established any rule on this point. The following case indicates the desire to emphasise the need for facts, but without removing the determination of them from the employer.

Patterson v. Messrs. Bracketts
[1977] I.R.L.R. 137
Employment Appeal Tribunal

Shortly after a heart operation, for which he had been given three months' leave, the employee attended an office party at which his behaviour was such that his employers thought he was likely to endanger his health. He was dismissed shortly thereafter.

PHILLIPS J.: And so we come to the ground on which we reach the conclusion that this decision cannot stand. It seems to us that the Industrial Tribunal failed to apply their mind to the fact that, so far as we can see, little or no consideration was given by the employers to the state of Mr Patterson's health in such circumstances that he could say something about it and they could find out from an informed source what the true situation was. Generally speaking, in a case such as this, it seems to us that the approach should be that which was indicated—in somewhat different circumstances it is true—in *Spencer v Paragon Wallpapers Ltd.* [1976] I.R.L.R. 373 which is that there should be an opportunity for the employer to inform himself about the true situation of the employee's health; and that should be arranged in such a way that the employee can have an opportunity to contribute to it. What is required in a particular case will, of course, depend on the circumstances, but the principle is twofold: first, that there should be consultation or discussion with the employee; and secondly, that such other steps as are necessary should be taken to enable the employer to form a balanced view about the employee's health. In some cases that will require consultation with the doctors; in other cases it will not. It seems to us that the Industrial Tribunal here never really considered this question at all.

See also *Grootcon (UK) Ltd.* v. *Keld* [1984] I.R.L.R. 302 (E.A.T.) for a case where the absence of medical evidence led the E.A.T. to reject an employer's assertion that the reason for the dismissal was that the employee was not medically fit for work.

(2) Is the employer bound by medical opinion?

East Lindsey District Council v. Daubney
[1977] I.C.R. 566; [1977] I.R.L.R. 181
Employment Appeal Tribunal

The employers' decision to dismiss the employee was reached upon the report of the district community physician, Dr. Haigh, whose advice was based upon an examination of the employee by a Dr. O'Hagen.

Phillips J.: The actual ground of the Industrial Tribunal's decision seems to be set out in paragraph 12. They say that the manner of the dismissal was "patently open to criticism." In substance they give two reasons for this view: first, the District Council had failed to obtain the information which they ought reasonably to have obtained before taking such an important step as dismissal (*ie* a full medical report); and, secondly, they had dismissed Mr Daubney without giving him the elementary right either to contend against such a step or at least to seek an independent medical opinion.

The first of these reasons had caused alarm to the District Council for it has been interpreted as requiring employers in their position to undertake a medical assessment of their own, and disentitling them from relying upon the opinion of their medical advisers. We are prepared to accept Mr Yorke's submission [on behalf of the employers] that it is not the function of employers, any more than it is of Industrial Tribunals, to turn themselves into some form of medical appeal tribunal to review the opinions and advice received from their medical advisers. And on the whole we think that the District Council would have been entitled to act here on the opinion of Dr Haigh, brief as it was if they had consulted Mr Daubney and discussed the matter with him. We would merely add this caution. While employers cannot be expected to be, nor is it desirable that they should set themselves up as, medical experts, the decision to dismiss or not to dismiss is not a medical question, but is a question to be answered by the employers in the light of the available medical advice. It is important therefore that when seeking advice employers should do so in terms suitably adjusted to the circumstances. Merely to be told, as the District Council were told, because that is the question they asked, that an employee "is unfit to carry out the duties of his post and should be retired on grounds of permanent ill health," is verging on the inadequate, because the employer may well need more detailed information before being able to make a rational and informed decision whether to dismiss. Nonetheless, it seems to us on the whole that the Industrial Tribunal required overmuch of the District Council when saying that they should have demanded a detailed medical report, and should have questioned Dr. Haigh about it.

(b) Enquiry, consultation or hearing

The adversarial process of disciplinary hearings in misconduct cases is certainly inappropriate for cases of ill-health. The model developed for ill-health cases owes nothing to "trial" precedents; insofar as any model is relevant, it is that of personal consultation by paternalist employers.

Spencer v. Paragon Wallpapers Ltd.
[1976] I.R.L.R. 373; [1977] I.C.R. 301
Employment Appeal Tribunal

For the facts, see above, p. 373.

Phillips J.: Obviously, the case of misconduct and the case of ill-health raise different considerations, but we are clearly of the view that an employee ought not to be dismissed on the grounds of absence due to ill-health without some communication being established between the employer and the employee before he is dismissed. The word "warning" perhaps is not appropriate, for by its association with cases of misconduct it carries with it a suggestion that the employee is being required to change or improve his conduct. That is not the case where the absence is due to ill-health, and it is possible to imagine cases of ill-health where some damage could be done by a written warning unaccompanied by a more personal touch. What is required will vary very much indeed according to the circumstances of the case. Usually what is needed is a discussion of the position between the employer and the employee. Obviously, what must be avoided is dismissal out of hand. There should be a discussion so that the situation can be weighed up, bearing in mind the employer's need for the work to be done and the employee's need for time in which to recover his health.

East Lindsay District Council v. Daubney
[1977] I.R.L.R. 181; [1977] I.C.R. 566
Employment Appeal Tribunal

For the facts, see above, p. 378.

PHILLIPS J.: Unless there are wholly exceptional circumstances before an employee is dismissed on the ground of ill-health it is necessary that he should be consulted and the matter discussed with him, and that in one way or another steps should be taken by the employer to discover the true medical position. We do not propose to lay down detailed principles to be applied in such cases, for what will be necessary in one case may not be appropriate in another. But if in every case employers take such such steps as are sensible according to the circumstances to consult the employee and to discuss the matter with him, and to inform themselves upon the true medical position, it will be found in practice that all that is necessary has been done. Discussions and consultation will often bring to light facts and circumstances of which the employers were unaware, and which will throw new light on the problem. Or the employee may wish to seek medical advice on his own account, which, brought to the notice of the employers' medical advisers, will cause them to change their opinion. There are many possibilities. Only one thing is certain, and that is that if the employee is not consulted, and given an opportunity to state his case, an unjustice may be done.

In the present case, Mr Daubney was never consulted and the matter never discussed with him. Mr Yorke [on behalf of the employers] submits that consultation and discussion is unnecessary where it can be seen that it will yield no useful result. In the first place, it is only in the rarest possible circumstances that it is a good answer to a failure to consult and discuss that discussion and consultation would have been fruitless. Secondly, it does not seem to us to be in the least clear that this is such a case. Mr Daubney had had long service in local government, and had reached a high position. Local government reorganisation had resulted in his being employed in a subordinate capacity. It is plain that he was not happy in the circumstances in which he found himself, although he wished to remain in the employment of the District Council. It appears from the documents exhibited to the case that his illness was, in part at least, functional in nature and it is probable that the illness and his conditions or work were connected. This seems to us to be precisely the kind of case where sensitive consultation and discussion might — nobody can say that it would — have resulted in some solution being found to his position consistent with continued employment by the District Council. It is true that his recovery, which followed his departure from the District Council, may have been connected with that departure; but it is not in the least sure that had the matter been dealt with in the way we should have expected it to have been, no way out of the problem could have been found. It is not necessary to say that it would have been, but it might; and we are abundantly satisfied that this is not a case where it can be said that discussion and consultation would have been superfluous.

For an ill-health dismissal where lack of consultation was excused on the ground that "it has been proved that no difference would have been made," (see *Taylorplan Catering (Scotland) Ltd.* v. *McInally* [1980] I.R.L.R. 53 (E.A.T.) *per* Lord McDonald).

(c) Penalties or alternatives

As the objective is not to punish, no fault being involved, a different range of alternatives to termination comes into view. The requirement of reasonableness in E.P.C.A., s.57(3) does not appear to extend to imposing an obligation on the employer to create a job for the employee rather than dismiss him or her. This was ruled out by O'Connor J. in *Merseyside & North Wales Electricity Board* v. *Taylor* [1975] I.R.L.R. 60 (Q.B.D.). He did, however, add the following comment (para. 25):

> "The circumstances may well be such that the employer may have available light work of the kind which it is within the capacity of the employee to do, and the circumstances may make it fair to at least encourage him or to offer him the chance of doing that work, even if it be at a reduced rate of pay."

The point was reiterated in *Spencer* v. *Paragon Wallpapers Ltd.* [1976] (above p. 373), and again by Slynn J. in *O'Brien* v. *The Prudential Assurance Co. Ltd.* (above p. 372) (para. 28):

> "We have said on a number of occasions that although an employer does not have a duty to create a new job there may be circumstances in which it is right that an employer who is dismissing a man from one post should consider whether there are other posts in his organisation which could be offered to the man. Thus somebody who suffers a physical disability which prevents him from doing his particular job may, if the employer behaves reasonably, expect an offer of some work which is available."

In addition, employers may be required to take measures to enable employees suffering ill-health to remain in their present jobs; see *Garricks (Caterers) Ltd.* v. *Nolan* [1980] I.R.L.R. 259 (E.A.T.) and the following case.

Jagdeo v. Smiths Industries Ltd.
[1982] I.C.R. 47
Employment Appeal Tribunal

The employee, after ten years' employment as an assembler, was moved to soldering work. She became ill due to the fumes, and masks did not help. She was given notice of dismissal, but before it expired the company was notified by Mr Kemball of the Health and

> Safety Executive that extractor fans had been installed at one of the company's factories situated nearby in order to deal with a similar problem, and that portable extractor fans were also available. An Industrial Tribunal found the company had acted reasonably in dismissing the employee for her inability to perform her work on medical grounds.

BROWNE-WILKINSON J.: The company is a substantial concern in a large way of business. The only evidence presented to the Industrial Tribunal indicated that, before the date of dismissal, the risk to the health of the employee from the soldering fumes had been drawn to the attention of the company by Mr Kemball; indeed, another branch of the company had installed extractor fans. The only evidence before the Tribunal indicated that portable extractor fans were available (or appear to have been available) and that Mr Kemball thought them desirable. We must be careful to confine ourselves to the state of facts as they were before the dismissal. Later on Mr Kemball required fans to be installed; before the dismissal he merely advised that they were desirable. That was the only evidence, except for the fact that there had been subsequent discussions and correspondence of some kind between the company, on the one had, and the Health and Safety Executive, on the other. We find it difficult to understand, on that evidence, why it was not practicable, before dismissing the employee, to try the use of locally situated extractor fans. Equally we find it difficult to see how, on that state of the evidence, and without having heard anything from the company as to what steps they took in response to Mr Kemball's initiative, the Industrial Tribunal could have come to any conclusion as to whether the company had acted reasonably or not. There was a step which had been suggested by a public body as being possibly capable of meeting the position: the Industrial Tribunal were not told what response had been made to that suggestion. It seems to us that if it had been shown that it was not practicable to deal with the employee's position, the Industrial Tribunal's decision would have been impeccable; but in the absence of any explanation from the company as to what, if any, steps had been taken, there is a vital fact missing which must be ascertained before it can be decided whether or not the company's behaviour in dismissing the employee without trying extractor fans was or was not reasonable. We therefore think that there was here a critical matter of fact which was not ventilated and needed to be ventilated before a proper decision could be reached on the issue.

In those circumstances—although we do so with great regret—we think the fair course to both parties is to remit the matter to the Industrial Tribunal for them to hear evidence as to what steps the company did take prior to the dismissal to consider and utilise Mr Kemball's suggestion that extractor fans of some kind could be employed. In the light of that evidence, the Industrial Tribunal will have before it the evidence necessary to decide whether, before dismissing the employee from the position to which the company had transferred her, they had taken reasonable steps to ensure that she could not continue to hold that job.

8. INCOMPETENCE

Incapacity due to lack of competence or qualifications relates to the work obligation undertaken by the employee. It needs to be distinguished from incapacity which results from changes in the nature of the work obligation (*eg* through technological change), or in the quality of the work required (on these problems see Chapter 3 on *The Work Obligation*).

(A) Substantive Rules

(i) Common law

As with misconduct and ill-health, the employer can terminate the employee's contract of employment by simply giving notice. Additionally, proved incompetence in the job originally undertaken is usually considered a repudiatory breach justifying dismissal without notice.

Harmer v. Cornelius
(1858) 5 C.B. (N.S.) 236.

Two scene painters, engaged on a term of at least a month, were dismissed on the second day on grounds that they were incompetent.

WILLES J.: . . . supposing that, when the skill and competency of the party employed are tested by the employment, he is found to be utterly incompetent, is the employer bound nevertheless to go on employing him to the end of the term for which he is engaged, notwithstanding his incompetency? This is a question upon which we have been furnished by the Bar with no authority, probably because, such labour being seldom retained for a long time certain, the question has not often arisen. But it seems very unreasonable that an employer should be compelled to go on employing a man who, having represented himself competent, turns out to be incompetent. An engineer is retained by a railway company, for a year, to drive an express-train, and is found to be utterly unskilful and incompetent to drive or regulate the locomotive—are the railway company still bound, under pain of an action, to intrust the lives of thousands to his dangerous and demonstrated incapacity? A clerk is retained for a year to keep a merchant's books, and it turns out that he is ignorant, not only of book-keeping, but of arithmetic—is the merchant bound to continue him in his employment?

Misconduct in a servant is, according to every day's experience, a justification of a discharge. The failure to afford the requisite skill which had been expressly or impliedly promised, is a breach of legal duty, and therefore misconduct.

The existence of an implied obligation to perform with competence was confirmed in *Lister* v. *Romford Ice & Cold Storage Co. Ltd.* [1957] A.C. 555 (H.L.) as a characteristic term of the contract of employment.

(ii) Statutory provisions

EPCA, s.57(2)(*a*) allows that a reason for dismissal can be "related to the capability or qualifications of the employee for performing work of the kind which he was employed by the employer to do," and further: " 'capability' means capability assessed by reference to skill, aptitude . . . or any other physical or mental quality; 'qualifications' means any degree, diploma or other academic, technical or professional qualification relevant to the position which the employee held'' (section 57(4)). But this is merely a broad descriptive head of what may in fact be a reason for termination. It does not assist resolution of a dispute as to whether a particular employee is so incompetent as to justify dismissal.

As with misconduct and ill-health, the law takes the ''reasonable employer'' as setting the standard of incompetence which justifies dismissal. In certain employments, a single failing has been held sufficient to justify dismissal for incompetence (*eg* a negligent gambling inspector in *Turner* v. *Pleasurama Casinos Ltd.* [1976] I.R.L.R. 151 (Q.B.D.); a pilot's error in *Taylor* v. *Alidair Ltd.* [1978] I.R.L.R. 82 (C.A.)). But the assessment of capability outside these specialised occupations is no less subjective and often more difficult. For example, in *Blackman* v. *The Post Office* [1974] I.R.L.R. 46 (N.I.R.C.), the Court found that as a matter of common sense, a Post Office employee had proved his capability over five years' work, but by failing to pass a special aptitude test, which was a requirement of his job, the employer could argue that the employee was incapable within the meaning of the statute.

In applying the ''reasonable employer'' standard, the fairness of the dismissal often hangs in the balance between the subjective assessment of the employer and the objective evidence of incapability. The Tribunals have found it difficult to maintain this balance. A subjective assessment of incompetence by the employer is necessary to satisfy the need for genuine belief in the reason. But there are conflicting views as to whether it is sufficient, and whether the employer's assessment needs to be supported by objective evidence. The following cases illustrate the position.

Cook v. Thomas Linnell & Sons Ltd.
[1977] I.R.L.R. 132
Employment Appeal Tribunal

The employee worked as manager of a ''non-food'' depot from 1966 to 1974. He was then promoted to manager of a food depot, though he had no experience of that side of the business. In May 1976 he was dismissed on grounds of poor performance.

PHILLIPS J.: A central theme in Mr Tabachnik's submission [on behalf of the employee] was that although there was plenty of contemporary evidence to show that the employers had lost confidence in the ability of Mr Cook as a manager there was no hard factual evidence of a particular kind to support that judgment. Criticism and exhortation, he submitted, however strong, do not by themselves provide evidence of incapacity. It amounts to no more than the assertion of an opinion. It seems to us that this goes too far, although we accept that there is something in the point. When responsible employers have genuinely come to the conclusion over a reasonable period of time that a manager is incompetent we think that it is some evidence that he *is* incompetent. When one is dealing with routine operations which may be more precisely assessed there is no real problem. It is more difficult when one is dealing with such imponderables as the quality of management, which in the last resort can only be judged by those competent in the field. In such cases as this there may be two extremes. At on extreme is the case where it can be demonstrated, perhaps by reason of some calamitous performance, that the manager is incompetent. The other extreme is the case where no more can be said than that in the opinion of the employer the manager is incompetent, that opinion being expressed for the first time shortly before his dismissal. In between will be cases such as the present where it can be established that throughout the period of employment concerned the employers had progressively growing doubts about the ability of the manager to perform his task satisfactorily. If that can be shown, it is in our judgment some evidence of his incapacity. It will then be necessary to look to see whether there is any other supporting evidence. . . .

It is important that the operation of the legislation in relation to unfair dismissal should not impede employers unreasonably in the efficient management of their business, which must be in the interest of all. Certainly, employees must not be sacrificed to this need; and employers must act reasonably when removing from a particular post an employee whom they consider to be unsatisfactory.

The policy of supporting managerial prerogative in this area was emphasised in *The Post Office* v. *Mughal* [1977] I.R.L.R. 178 (E.A.T.). When the dismissal of a probationer was at issue, Cumming-Bruce J. accepted the following two propositions:

> "In recruiting the established staff in the Post Office, it is important that the management should set the standards of capability and efficiency that are required. This inevitably involves an element of subjective judgment when individual probationers are assessed. . . .
>
> The question for the Industrial Tribunal is not the same as the question for the employer. This cannot be emphasised too strongly, as it would be a public disaster if it were thought that Industrial Tribunals had usurped the employer's responsibility for selecting probationers."

The balance between subjective and objective elements was formulated in a definitively ambiguous way by Lord Denning M.R. in *Taylor* v. *Alidair Ltd.* [1978] I.R.L.R. 82 (C.A.) (para. 20):

> "Whenever a man is dismissed for incapability or incompetence it is sufficient that the employer honestly believes on reasonable grounds that the man is incapable or incompetent. It is not necessary for the employer to prove that he is in fact incapable or incompetent."

The test was applied in the following case.

Grant v. Ampex Great Britain Ltd.
[1980] I.R.L.R. 461
Employment Appeal Tribunal

The employee was dismissed after many complaints about his work.

Slynn J.: Mr Wilkie, to whom we are indebted for a very able argument on behalf of Mr Grant, has submitted that the Tribunal have gone wrong in a number of respects. In the first place, he says, they have failed to carry out the exercise which the Court of Appeal in *Taylor v Alidair Ltd.* [1978] I.R.L.R. 82 required that they should carry out. That was a decision where the Court of Appeal really said that there were two questions to be asked: (1) did the employer honestly and reasonably believe that the employee was not competent? (2) Were there reasonable grounds for that belief? Mr Wilkie says here that in the sense that the respondents made out their reason for Mr Grant's dismissal on the grounds of lack of capacity, they had not really gone through that exercise and, in effect, what the Tribunal have done is to really look at the evidence themselves and come to a conclusion as to whether there was lack of capacity. Mr Wilkie is quite right. It is not for the Tribunal to decide afresh whether a man is competent or not. It is for the Tribunal to decide whether there was material before the employers which the employers believed and upon which the employers could reasonably have decided to dismiss. It would, it seems to us, have been very much better if the Industrial Tribunal in their decision here had dealt specifically with the two factors which are referred to in *Taylor v Alidair Ltd.* But at the end of the day we are quite satisfied here that from the decision as a whole the Tribunal really were accepting the evidence which was given by the witnesses for the company that they did genuinely hold the view that Mr Grant was not complying with his duties, was not capable of the work because of slowness and because of the quality of the work. They accepted that evidence and it seems to us that when they say in a shorthand way, "the respondents have made good their reason for Mr Grant's dismissal, on the grounds of lack of capacity" what they were really saying was that they accepted that the facts which were relied upon were sufficient to constitute reasonable grounds upon which a reasonable employer would have decided that an employment should be determined.

(B) Procedures

(i) Assessment procedures and termination

Employee assessment procedures may be incorporated into contracts of employment, and requirements of industrial practice may determine a Tribunal's attitude to the fairness of dismissal. For example, in the case of a probationer in *The Post Office* v. *Mughal* [1977] I.R.L.R. 178 (E.A.T.), *per* Cumming-Bruce J.:

> " . . . the Post Office had not applied to the case the procedure set out in their own memorandum upon supervision of trial [*sic*] on first appointment, and that thus they had failed to discharge the onus of showing that the manner of the dismissal was fair, even though, had the procedure been followed, the same result might possibly have been reached."

(ii) Statutory provisions

As with ill-health and misconduct dismissals, termination for reasons of incompetence also requires notice and written reasons (EPCA, ss. 49 and 53). But the "reasonableness" requirement of the law of unfair dismissal (EPCA, s.57(3)) has produced distinctive rules on procedures to be followed in a case of termination for incompetence. These reflect a perception of incompetence as being somewhere between the deliberate and intentional quality of misconduct, and the no-fault aspect of ill-health. The procedures applicable to termination for incompetence thus differ from the others. The main element, not really present in the cases of ill-health or misconduct dismissals, is a recognition of employers' responsibility. This has implications for the three stages of procedure described below.

(a) Evidence of incompetence: facts and beliefs

The standard of competence expected is a balance between the subjective assessment of the employer and objective evidence of capability (above pp. 356 *et seq.* and 377). If the employer has not accumulated sufficient evidence to sustain an assessment of incompetence, this may count as a procedural failure. The process of assembling evidence, and its nature, are different in cases of incompetence from those of misconduct and ill-health. The following case illustrates what Tribunals may require.

The Post Office v. Mughal
[1977] I.R.L.R. 178
Employment Appeal Tribunal

The employee was dismissed for unsatisfactory performance when her one year period as a trainee clerical officer ended.

CUMMING-BRUCE J.: In relation to [the employee's] paper work she was criticised for inefficiency, because she was not sufficiently scrupulous to complete properly the documents known as Memoranda, though her facing sheets were up to standard, and because her advice notes showed errors of omission and commission. We wish to make it plain that we do not agree with the approach of the Industrial Tribunal to the evidence of these failures in her paper work. They were influenced by the fact that there was no adverse consequence from the probationer's shortcomings, no customer gave evidence of dissatisfaction about her telephone manner, and there was no evidence that any engineer had been set on the wrong work. It is in our view quite wrong to accept such evidence when the question is whether the employer has fairly and reasonably decided that a probationer is not up to the employer's standards. The superior officers have to arrange for supervision and make known to the employee the standard of performance that is set. The employer discharges the onus that [E.P.C.A., s. 57] imposes upon him if he satisfies the Industrial Tribunal that the supervising staff took proper trouble to assess conduct and capacity and warned of shortcomings when appropriate; and that the officer responsible for dismissal took proper steps to review the capacity and conduct of the probationer over the period before dismissal by examining written reports and, if necessary, discussing the history with the individual supervising officer or officers before deciding whether the probationer was someone whom the employer should take on the established staff. It would place an impossible burden on an employer to require him to call as witnesses dissatisfied members of the public or aggrieved members of the technical staff in order to satisfy a Tribunal that an assessment of capability or efficiency was made fairly and reasonably.

(b) Warnings, explanations and opportunities to improve

The procedure to be followed in cases of termination for incompetence falls between the adversarial hearing required in misconduct cases and the paternalist consultation of employees who are ill. What emerges from the case-law is an emphasis on the desirability of warnings and opportunities for the employee to explain and to improve his performance. This was spelled out by Donaldson J. in *James* v. *Waltham Holy Cross U.D.C.* [1973] I.R.L.R. 202 (N.I.R.C.), adding the familiar qualifications (para. 23):

> "An employer should be very slow to dismiss upon the ground that the employee is incapable of performing work which he is employed to do, without first telling the employee of the respects in which he is failing to do his job adequately, warning him of the possibility or likelihood of dismissal on this ground and giving him an opportunity of improving his performance. But those employed in senior management may by the nature of their jobs be fully aware of what is required of them and fully capable of judging for themselves whether they are achieving that requirement. In such circumstances, the need for warning and an opportunity for improvement is much less apparent. Again, cases can arise in which the inadequacy of performance is so extreme that there must be an irredeemable incapability. In such circumstances, exceptional though they no doubt are, a warning and opportunity for improvement are of no benefit to the employee and may constitute an unfair burden on the business.

Similarly, Kilner Brown J. in *Sutton & Gates (Luton) Ltd.* v. *Boxall* [1978] I.R.L.R. 486 (E.A.T.):

> "It is our unanimous view, in accordance with views which have been expressed by the Employment Appeal Tribunal and our predecessor, the National Industrial Relations Court, that these cases have to be approached along some such lines as these. A man is falling down in his work to the extent that it is detrimental to the employer's business. In those circumstances, because it is something over which he himself has control, he should be warned of it, probably several times, and given plenty of opportunity to improve his performance. If it reaches the stage that it becomes obvious that he is incapable—perhaps due to some illness or disability—of reaching his former standard, the employer, provided he handles the matter sensibly, is entitled to say to the man. 'We cannot keep you any longer. You are a liability.' But the employer should not dismiss the man at sight [*sic*] once he has made up his mind that that is the position. Still more so where the employer is satisfied that it is sheer idleness or sheer negligence on the part of the employee, should he dismiss him without giving him some opportunity and, it may well be, a final opportunity [to improve his performance]."

And in the following case.

Grant v. Ampex Great Britain Ltd.
[1980] I.R.L.R. 461
Employment Appeal Tribunal

The employee was dismissed after many complaints about his work.

SLYNN J.: Sometimes the degree of inadequacy is such that a warning is really not necessary although in the majority of cases, if the complaint of capability which is made is one that could or might lead to an improvement, then clearly it is right that a warning should be given. We desire to do nothing to cut down what has been said in any of the previous cases as to the desirability of giving an appropriate warning bearing in mind what was said by this Tribunal in *Mansfield Hosiery Mills Ltd. v Bromley* [1977] I.R.L.R. 301 [below p. 390], that even if a warning would have made no difference, it may still be that a dismissal in all the circumstances was unfair. But it seems to us here that the Tribunal is not simply relying upon what Mr Grant said in his evidence. They found as a fact that Mr Grant really would not admit any of the shortcomings which were drawn to his attention, and it seems to us that the Tribunal is taking that into account as well as Mr Grant's own evidence. It seems to us that in this case they were entitled to have regard to both of those [factors] and to come on the basis of both those factors to their conclusion that a warning would not have made any difference.

(c) Employer responsibility displacing penalties

The giving of warnings is often coupled with other requirements which carry with them employer responsibilities. The employer may be called upon to provide training, supervision or even alternative employment.

Tiptools Ltd. v. Curtis
[1973] I.R.L.R. 276
National Industrial Relations Court

After 19 years' service, the employee was dismissed for failing to complete an important order to the required standard.

GRIFFITHS J.: The Tribunal concluded that this was an unfair dismissal. Its principal reason for so concluding was that this man was dismissed after spending his whole working life to date with this company without ever having been given any serious personal warning, either orally or in writing, that if he did not improve his standards he would have to leave. If such a personal warning had been given it may well be that Mr Curtis would have been able to lift his standards and discharge his work to the satisfaction of his employers as he had done for many years previously. Alternatively the matter might have been investigated and, if he was being given work which was truly beyond his capabilities, arrangements might have been made to see that rather simpler work was directed his way, or he might have been accommodated in some other job within the framework of the company's two factories. One would surely have expected that some special consideration would have been given to a man who had been employed with the company since the age of 15. Against that background, small wonder that the Tribunal concluded that this was an unfair dismissal by virtue of the lack of any particular warning.

Mansfield Hosiery Mills Ltd. v. Bromley
[1977] I.R.L.R. 301
Employment Appeal Tribunal

The employee was dismissed following a series of complaints about his poor work performance.

PHILLIPS J.: It seems to us that it is important to bear in mind that Mr Bromley had not received the instruction which he had expected when he was first employed; that although there were complaints about him, which are summarised, they were complaints and failings of a kind in respect of which warnings, encouragement and urgings-on to better performance could have been effective. And, although the Industrial Tribunal in paragraph 10 do not spell out very clearly and precisely what they had in mind, it seems to us that what they were saying was this: that although there had been one verbal warning and one written warning, looking at the whole of the evidence and the whole of the circumstances and bearing in mind, in particular, the ultimate failure which led to his dismissal, they were of opinion that there was a failure on the part of the employers to give that measure of supervision and encouragement for improvement which is required of the reasonable employer in circumstances of that kind. . . .

There are cases, as we have indicated, where an Industrial Tribunal may say that "There has been a failure in supervision or procedure, but the case is such an obvious one and the misbehaviour is so extreme that we think that the failure of procedure can be excused." The fact that it can be said in some very plain circumstances does not mean, as it seems to us in the circumstances of this case, that this is a case where the Industrial Tribunal were bound to have said it. What the situation would have been had they said it is another matter. In effect, then, what they are saying is, that "In all the circumstances, Mr Bromley was entitled to a further chance and further warnings. Maybe and probably it would not have done any good, but at least he is entitled to compensation attributable and limited to what flows directly from that failure."

Bevan Harris Ltd. v. Gair
[1981] I.R.L.R. 520
Employment Appeal Tribunal

A 61 year old employee was dismissed after 11 years' service after having been warned four times in his last eight months' work about his poor performance. An Industrial Tribunal held the dismissal unfair because a reasonable employer would have demoted rather than dismissed him.

LORD MCDONALD: In any event we do not consider that there is necessarily an obligation upon every employer who dismisses an employee on the grounds of capability to offer him employment in a subsidiary or another position. Every case must depend upon its own circumstances. Different considerations may apply to dismissals for other reasons. For instance where an employee is dismissed because he is redundant there may be in certain situations an obligation upon his employer to do his best to attempt to fit him in in some other capacity within his own enterprise (*Vokes Ltd v Bear* [1973] I.R.L.R. 363 [above p. 121]; *Thomas & Betts Manufacturing Co Ltd v Harding* [1978] I.R.L.R. 213 [above p. 146]). Where however the reason for dismissal is shown to be capability and where is it shown that the employee received adequate warning as to his shortcomings and adequate opportunity to improve and has failed to do so we do not think that there is the same obligation upon an employer to attempt to fit him in in a subordinate capacity. Even if there is this must to a very great extent be influenced by the size and administrative resources of his undertaking. These words were incorporated into s.57(3) of the Employment Protection (Consolidation) Act 1978 by the Employment Act of 1980 and they are of particular relevance in our view to the present case. The small scale of the appellants' business and the circumstances of the respondent's proposed demotion were such as would, in our opinion, entitle a reasonable employer to conclude that even if he had a job to offer it would not be to the advantage of his business that the employee should continue in it. We certainly cannot accept the Tribunal's reasoning that the alternative job, if one was available, should have been offered on the view that if the respondent proved unsuitable or, as the Tribunal describe it, caused trouble, the appellants would have then been entitled fairly to dismiss him. Nor can we accept their observations that the respondent being well aware of his precarious position, if offered a job of shaver operator might well have accepted it and remained in the employment of the appellants until the end of his working days. This is at best speculation and there was no evidence before the Tribunal to entitle them to make such a finding.

The Court of Session dismissed the employee's appeal: [1983] I.R.L.R. 368.

9. THE PROCESS OF DISPUTING A TERMINATION

Where involuntary termination is disputed by the employee, two problems need to be addressed. First, what is the immediate effect of the disputed termination upon the employment relationship? Secondly, what is the subsequent procedure for resolving the dispute?

(A) The Effect of a Disputed Termination on the Employment Relationship

A disputed termination can have a number of alternative effects on the employment relationship:

(i) The status quo is maintained. The purported termination is not effective if challenged. The worker remains employed while the dispute is resolved.

(ii) The purported termination is effective, at least until the dispute is resolved, and perhaps even afterwards.

(iii) A compromise of (i) and (ii): some attributes of the employment relationship are terminated (*e.g.* attendance at work) while others (*e.g.* payment of wages) continue until the dispute is resolved.

Rules may be found which embody each of these alternatives. In the section 6(B) on Industrial Practice on procedures in cases of misconduct we referred to appeals procedures many of which contain *status quo* clauses (see above p. 6(B)), which could be incorporated into contracts of employment. In the case-law so far, much seems to depend on the precise wording of the provisions (see *Savage* v. *Sainsbury Ltd.* [1980] I.R.L.R. 109 (C.A.); *Howgate* v. *Fane Acoustics Ltd.* [1981] I.R.L.R. 161 (E.A.T.); *The Board of Governors, The National Heart & Chest Hospitals* v. *Nambiar* [1981] I.R.L.R. 196 (E.A.T.)). The question whether a purported termination is *effective* has been the subject of much judicial controversy in cases of employer repudiation (see *Gunton* v. *London Borough of Richmond* [1980] I.R.L.R. 321 (C.A.); *Jones* v. *Lee and Guilding* [1980] I.R.L.R. 67 (C.A.)) and employee repudiation (see *Thomas Marshall (Exports) Ltd.* v. *Guinle* [1978] I.R.L.R. 174 (Ch.D.) (see above p. 314); *London Transport Executive* v. *Clarke* [1981] I.R.L.R. 167 (C.A.)) (see above p. 305). Many statutory provisions adopt the solution that a disputed termination is effective, but some allow for a compromise (*e.g.* that of interim relief, EPCA, ss. 77–79).

It is of paramount importance to realise that the practical effects of these different alternatives may overshadow the substantive rules of permissible termination. The first alternative (maintenance of the *status quo*) means that the worker stays at work for however long it takes to resolve the dispute over the purported termination. The realities of industrial relations practice in the United Kingdom militate against subsequent termination if the *status quo* is maintained (tempers cool, alternatives are found). The second alternative (effective termination) means the worker will remain away from the workplace until the dispute is resolved. In practice, day to day operations militate against subsequent re-employment once termination is effective and the worker is absent (production adjusts, replacements are found). In other words, what happens immediately when a purported termination is disputed in many cases determines the outcome, regardless of whether the rules have been broken. Whether termination of work occurs or not depends more on what happens immediately than on whether what happens is permissible.

Recent research on the remedy of re-employment in unfair dismissal claims demonstrates this point (see below p. 394). It is an indictment of the law on termination of work that so little has been achieved on the vital question of the immediate effects of a disputed termination.

(B) Procedures for Resolving Disputed Terminations

Regardless of the immediate consequences, the dispute needs to be resolved as to whether the termination complies with or violates the rules. In the United Kingdom, dispute settlement mechanisms include negotiation between the parties: workers and/or their representatives and management; autonomous procedures unilaterally adopted by employers or collectively agreed; official conciliation (ACAS officials); complaints to Industrial Tribunals; and litigation in civil courts.

Two stages may be distinguished in dispute settlement. First is the stage in which the dispute is brought to, or injected into, the machinery: *access*. This happens in two main ways: either the machinery is invoked by the worker when work is terminated; or by somebody else, *e.g.* his union, shop steward or workmates, or another third party.

Rules derived from industrial practice will often treat termination as a collective issue. Before a worker is terminated, his group representative becomes involved in negotiations or procedure, often jointly with the worker concerned. This greatly increases the likelihood that terminations will become subject to the formal dispute-resolving machinery, and that the permissibility of the termination will be examined. On the other hand, isolated workers, those not in unions or out of favour with them may be prejudiced.

Rules derived from statutory provisions and common law adopt a private law model in accordance with which *only* the worker whose work is terminated may invoke the machinery. In practice this tends to mean that many workers, unaware of the law, uncertain of, or intimidated by it, or ill-equipped to use it (*e.g.* those lacking access to advice or organisational time and resources) will not invoke the machinery. Such rules also often exclude certain categories of workers or impose formal qualifications which must be satisfied. As a result, many terminations which are disputed never come to be subject to rules at all as they never reach the machinery.

The second stage in dispute settlement, assuming access has been gained to the mechanism, is the practical operation of the machinery. If the cost, in terms of time, effort and expense outweighs the benefits of going through the machinery, the worker or employer may regard the rules as to what is permitted as irrelevant. Regardless of them, the employer may prefer to pay up rather than fight a claim of unfair dismissal; a worker may acquiesce in the termination rather than undergo the ordeal of proceedings. Industrial Tribunals were established in an attempt to meet objections regarding the expense, delays and formality of the civil courts. Whether they have succeeded is a matter of some difference of opinion.

As with the immediate effect of disputed terminations, the issues of access to, and operation of, the dispute resolution machinery can overshadow in practice the substantive rules on termination of work.

10. REMEDIES

The obvious remedy for unjustified ("unfair") involuntary termination is re-employment, if the employee so wishes, and otherwise compensation. The first remedy is not available at common law. The essentially reciprocal nature of contractual obligations means that it is impossible to force an unwilling party to remain bound to a contract against his will. This in effect gives a veto to either side to prevent the continuance of a contract of employment notwithstanding the possible merits of the other party's case for maintaining the contractual relationship. Compensation at common law is minimal, being confined to the precise contractual loss suffered, namely, any loss inflicted by the employer's termination of the employment with less than the employee's due period of notice. Statute, as will be seen, has only partially overcome these limitations.

(A) Re-employment

Statutory protection against unfair dismissal purports to offer first a remedy of reinstatement or re-engagement which is seldom available in practice, *cf.* Dickens, Jones, Weekes and Hart *Dismissed* (1985) p. 108:

> "Although reinstatement is clearly the primary remedy for unfair dismissal provided by law, very few successful applicants are awarded it. The usual remedy for successful applicants is compensation [which] has accounted for at least two-thirds of the successful tribunal outcomes each year since 1972 with the exception of 1981 and 1982 when the proportion of 'other remedies' increased. This increase appears to reflect an increasing tendency of tribunals, having found dismissal unfair, to leave the remedy to be agreed by the parties. This is more likely to happen where both sides are legally represented and the increase probably reflects the increasing use of legal representation . . . The level of re-employment awarded by tribunals has always been low. In 1980 re-employment made up only 2.8 per cent of the remedies awarded by tribunals, the lowest proportion ever. In 1981 there was an increase in the frequency of this remedy and for the first time since 1976 it constituted almost 5 per cent of all the awards made by tribunals but this level was not sustained in 1982."

There has been a lively debate as to the reasons for and possible solution to the absence of re-employment as a practical remedy for unjustifiable involuntary termination. The following extracts are taken from that debate.

(i) Employee choices

P. Lewis, "*An analysis of why legislation has failed to provide employment protection for unfairly dismissed employees*" (1981) 19 B.J.I.R. 316 at 317, 319–320

What applicants in Unfair Dismissal cases want has been until recently a matter of conjecture. A committee of the [National Joint Advisory Council] in 1967 thought that "reinstatement is often what the worker wants," but Donovan, implicitly perhaps, had some doubts about this, and cited this doubt as one of the arguments against reinstatement being the sole remedy. It went on: "Often however, reinstatement does not offer a satisfactory solution when an employee is found to have been unfairly dismissed because the circumstances of the dismissal have opened up a permanent rift between employer and employee." G. de N. Clark said that opponents of giving the

Tribunals the power to force reinstatement have argued that applicants do not want it, though he could see little or no evidence to support this argument. More recently . . . research evidence [goes] . . . to show that most applicants in fact do not want "re-employment."

In the author's view the question of the wishes of the applicant is influenced by the crucial factor of time. The first thing to establish, therefore, is whether or not the applicant's choice is the same after the dismissal as it is some two and a half months or more later at the time of the hearing.

Since the [statutory amendments effective] from 1 June 1976 the originating application form (IT 1) has contained a question asking the applicant which remedy he or she prefers (viz: "reinstatement," "re-engagement" or compensation).

It is information based on the IT 1 forms and the applicant's choice as stated at the hearing (and reported in the written decision) upon which the author's research is dependent. . . .

. . . at the application stage [the information makes it] clear that a substantial majority [71·5 per cent.] are seeking "re-employment" . . .

. . . [However] the crucial choice is made at the hearing, not on the IT1. [The data] shows that by the time the case has reached the stage of a Tribunal hearing, the vast majority of applicants (four out of five) want cash compensation. . . .

. . . [The Table below] shows a fundamental difference in choice of remedy at the hearing from that two and a half months earlier when the application form was completed. In fact, about half the applicants have changed their choice of remedy from "re-employment" to compensation. Columns 2 and 3 show that the postal questionnaire responses were reasonably typical of the whole group of 350 in their choice.

TABLE 3

Comparison of Applicants' Choice of Remedy at the Different Stages

Remedy sought	1 *IT1 Stage (National figures)*	2 *Hearing stage (all Northern Region 'successful' cases)*	3 *Hearing stage (Northern Region postal respondents)*
Compensation	28·5	79·0	79·1
"Re-employment"	71·5	21·0	20·9
Total	100	100	100

Perhaps the most outstanding conclusion to be drawn from Table 4 is the prevalence of factors which in one way or another relate to the breakdown of the employment relationship. If the postal questionnaire respondents were typical, it would suggest that breakdown of employment relationship is the reason for 80 per cent. of the cases choosing compensation. It is concluded that this is the key factor in explaining the choice of compensation by so many applicants.

The general picture is that at the stage of completion of the application form most applicants seek job security. But by the time the hearing takes place, most are seeking cash compensation. We have examined why compensation is preferred to reinstatement at this latter stage. These explanations of choice of remedy are also very much the factors operating to *change* the choice of a large proportion of applicants in the period of waiting for the Tribunal hearing.

TABLE 4

Reasons for Choosing Compensation

	No.	%
Relationship with employer had broken down irreconcilably	23	27·7
Employer's behaviour was so bad that applicant would not work for that employer again	23	27·7
Fear of possible victimisation	18	21·7
Job had disappeared (including where workplace had closed)	7	8·4
Had obtained another job	3	3·6
Company made it clear they would not "re-employ"	3	3·6
Company unstable and likely to close	2	2·4
Other	4	4·8
Total	83	100·0

Some of the information which changes the applicant's mind in these cases may well come out, wholly or partly, during the hearing. Some will have come out in any dealings with the employer after the dismissal but before the hearing. For example, the applicant begins to recognise just what the employer's attitude towards him is—how he feels towards him, the degree of hostility etc. This has the effect of dissuading the employee from going back because he realises that the employment relationship has irretrievably broken down, or because he fears victimisation. Or, secondly, the employee comes to realise just how objectionable his employer is, and decides that he wouldn't be prepared to work for him again.

A third factor is that the applicant may have obtained another job during the period between dismissal and the hearing. The need to minimise losses (required by the statute) encourages this, although a more important force may be the economic circumstances of the applicant. A fourth factor is that the employer may have filled the job or re-organised the work in some way so that the job does not exist any more, and the applicant comes to know of this. Finally, the mere passage of time probably hardens attitudes on both sides.

The evidence of change of remedy cited here, and the tentative suggestions above as to the reasons for it, might support the theory that it is in fact the administrative delay, a feature of the Tribunal system itself, which is at least part of the reason for such a very low proportion of "successful" applicants being "re-employed." This suggests that tinkering with the legislation (as was done with the 1 June 1976 alterations) will not really lead to any dramatic, or indeed any, improvement in job security.

(ii) Employer attitudes

K. Williams and D. Lewis, *"The Aftermath of Tribunal Reinstatement and Re-engagement"* DEPARTMENT OF EMPLOYMENT RESEARCH PAPER No 23 (June 1981) pp. 35–37

Unfair dismissal hearings are generally broadly accusatorial in character and normally entail irrecoverable costs and the possibility of adverse publicity. It might be supposed therefore, that by the time this stage was reached, attitudes would have hardened to such an extent that few unsuccessful employers would be prepared to take anything other than an adverse view of the Tribunal's conclusions. Such employers may be particularly hostile to any proposal which could revive or create potentially difficult supervisory problems. . . .

. . . the attitude of employers has been crucial to the way in which the re-employment provisions have operated. Substantial employer opposition is likely to mean either that Tribunals will decline to make an order or, if one is made, that it will not be put into effect. . . .

Whether a particular re-employment is seen as an unacceptable challenge to managerial authority may depend upon a number of considerations, including the circumstances of the dismissal, the cost of non-compliance with the Tribunal ruling, and the characteristics and experience of the employer in question. The larger the company, the more likely it is to employ industrial relations or personnel staff, to operate more impersonal procedures and, therefore, to be more dispassionate in its judgment of any re-employment proposal. . . .

. . . larger organizations are more likely to have had prior experience of resolving disciplinary problems by means of reinstatement or re-engagement, albeit that this experience will usually have been gained via voluntary procedures. Eleven of the 37 employers questioned (29·7 per cent.) had experience of this kind and it is hardly coincidental that they were the larger organizations with developed personnel functions and a relatively strong trade union presence. On the other hand eight of the nine employers involved in non-return cases had no prior experience of the remedy and six employed fewer than 100 workers.

To what extent do the circumstances of dismissal influence employers' attitudes towards re-employment? Some reasons, such as redundancy or ill-health absenteeism, may be thought less likely than others, such as trade union activity, incompetence or certain sorts of misconduct (especially perhaps by senior staff) to inspire strong feelings of hostility or resentment. Different employers, however may react differently and occasionally the agreement to re-employ may have little to do with individual circumstances. . . .

. . . Similarly, while smaller organizations usually have greater difficulty coping with absences, retraining or re-allocating job duties, these may be less important considerations than finding a suitable replacement. Thus six of the 28 employers questioned (21·4 per cent) said that they agreed to re-employ largely because the employee in question was a "good worker" a "skilled man" or "difficult to replace." Clearly an unsatisfied demand for labour may constitute an important element in an employer's calculations yet here again the impact of external forces upon the two parties may underline their conflicting interests. High unemployment may cause more unfair dismissal applicants to view re-employment favourably but may have the opposite effect upon employers, either because the applicant can be more readily replaced or because the low levels of economic activity associated with high unemployment may mean that no replacement will be sought. . . .

The decision whether to re-employ frequently involved the balancing of various factors, one of these being the employer's perception of the cost of the alternative remedy of compensation and the sanction for non-compliance. Amongst the group of 28 employers who put into effect a Tribunal order, nine (32 per cent.) gave as their reasons for doing so the desire to avoid paying compensation. That re-employment was the cheaper alternative was the commonest single reason given to explain its acceptance. As one bluff pragmatist who had denied dismissing in the first place declared "the

Tribunal told us that compensation for a man of 58 could be very high and anyway we weren't going to pay him money for nothing—he could work for it."

Conversely, where a Tribunal told an employer in advance that the cost of not complying with the order would be £138 it was promptly accepted as a bargain.

(iii) ACAS's role

L. Dickens, M. Hart, M. Jones, B. Weekes, "*Re-employment of unfairly dismissed workers: the lost remedy*" (1981) 10 I.L.J. 160 at 171–173

Although conciliation did at first achieve more re-employment than was being awarded by Tribunals, the gap has narrowed over the years and reinstatement and re-engagement accounted for only 3·5 per cent. of the remedies obtained through conciliation in 1979. The statute is clear and ACAS's duty is to give priority to the settlement of unfair dismissal claims on the basis of re-employment rather than compensation. The evidence from our research and from Williams and Lewis [see above p. 396] suggests that, other than in a fairly perfunctory way, this is not done. The statute instructs ACAS to attempt to achieve settlement on the basis of compensation only "where the complainant does not wish to be reinstated or re-engaged or where reinstatement or re-engagement is not practicable" [EPCA, s.134(2)]. It is here that the beliefs examined above that applicants do not want re-employment, and that employers will not accept it, are influential. As noted, while these statements may be true generalisations at one level, it is not sufficient to accept the stated preference on the IT1 as evidence of the applicants' wishes nor to interpret employer hostility towards re-employment as automatically rendering it "not practicable." However, it appears that ACAS conciliation officers readily do this and then proceed to explore the easier option of settlement for money. . . .

. . . If there is any pressure on the conciliation officers it comes from an appreciation of the pragmatic considerations underlying the conciliation stage. That is to say, ACAS officers are aware that the efficient operation of the Tribunal system requires that a certain proportion of cases be filtered out without the need for a Tribunal hearing. ACAS, relying on section 134(1), interprets its duty as being, foremost, to endeavour to promote settlements. The nature of the settlement—re-employment or compensation—is of secondary importance. Although an ACAS conciliation officer may pursue re-employment positively where both sides appear spontaneously receptive or where the applicant or his/her representative insists on it (and this would apply to union representatives more than others), he or she is unlikely to jeopardise the chance of obtaining a speedy settlement, which after all is "voluntarily agreed to" by the parties, by resolutely attempting to give effect to the intention of the statute in section 134(2)(*a*). To pursue re-employment at conciliation would, generally speaking, take longer and use more resources.

A further inhibiting factor appears to be ACAS's worry about how it is likely to be perceived by employers should it be more active in pursuing the specific remedies. Although the primacy of re-employment in the statute is indisputable, ACAS nonetheless fears its neutrality may be questioned if it were pursued with vigour. It also feels that in pursuing re-employment conciliation officers imply that they have taken a decision on the fairness or otherwise of the dismissal. The specific remedies, therefore, ACAS argues, can be pursued only when the employer has realised his actions were to some extent unfair. It is difficult to see how a decision to pursue settlement on the basis of re-employment implies that the conciliation officer has taken a view of the fairness or otherwise of the dismissal while a decision *not* to pursue re-employment carries no such implication. Indeed, given the clear statutory duty to pursue settlement on the basis of re-employment, not to do so surely carries the greater implication and appears to sanction the employer's view as the objective or "neutral" one.

Cf the judicial viewpoint: in *Slack* v. *Greenham* (*Plant Hire*) *Ltd.* [1983] I.R.L.R. 271 (E.A.T.), where Tudor Evans J. declared (para. 18):

> "In a case such as the present where, on the findings of the Tribunal, the appellant was anxious for an immediate [conciliated] monetary settlement, it might defeat the officer's very function if he were obliged to tell [the appellant], in effect, that he might receive considerably more money because of his right to claim future loss of wages [in a successful claim for unfair dismissal]. If the appellant were to be deflected from his wish for an immediate settlement by such prospects, he would no doubt be the first to complain if, in due course, he lost not only his right to future earnings but received nothing or less than he would have received in the settlement."

(iv) Industrial Tribunal attitudes

Once the employee has been held to be unfairly dismissed, and expresses the desire to be re-employed, the Industrial Tribunal has to "take into account" whether it is "practicable," and if there is contributory fault, whether it is "just" so to order re-instatement or re-engagement (EPCA, s.69(5) and (6)).

P. Lewis, *"Interpretation of 'practicable' and 'just' in relation to 're-employment' in unfair dismissal cases"* (1982) 45 M.L.R. 384 at 386–389

. . . in a series of major cases, the courts have established a number of principles on the question of "practicability." These are as follows:

(i) *"Practicable" is narrower than "possible"*

The mere fact that the job has not been filled by the time of the hearing is not sufficient to make "re-employment" "practicable."

(ii) *The likely consequences of "re-employment" should be looked at by Tribunals*

If serious industrial strife is likely to result, "re-employment" will not be possible."

(iii) *There is no automatic right of "re-employment" for the unfairly dismissed employee who is blameless*

The approach that if the employee was not to blame for his dismissal he should be "re-employed" was faulty. It would not give the Tribunals sufficient discretion. "Practicable" ought to be looked at in a "common-sense" and "pragmatic" way, "bearing in mind the particular circumstances of the case."

(iv) *Reinstatement will be "practicable" in small firms only in exceptional cases*

This is because of the "close personal relationship" which exists between employer and employee.

Another case raised the issue of whether "re-employment" was "practicable" where the dismissal was unfair but the employee was to some extent not competent. In *Oliso-Emosingoit v Inner London Education Authority* [(1977) E.A.T. No. 139/77] there was no recommendation for "re-employment."

Finally, further reluctance of the courts and tribunals to grant specific performance was evident in *Chromation Electroplating Co. Ltd. v Finlay* [151 I.R.L.I.B. 10] where the E.A.T. said that if the employer does not attend the hearing and there is therefore no evidence on the question of the "practicability" of "re-employment," the Tribunal can still order "re-employment" if it thinks fit. But, went on the E.A.T., it is always unsatisfactory for courts to grant specific performance unless they are satisfied it can be reasonably implemented, and compensation may be preferable.

It can be seen from this survey of cases that the courts and the E.A.T. have narrowed what is "practicable" very considerably. It is contended here that this is one of the factors explaining why so few recommendations or orders for "re-employment" have been made. Indeed, this view is shared by the authors of the two recent studies to which reference has already been made, *viz.* Williams and Lewis, and Dickens *et al.* [see above, pp. 396 and 398] The former suggest that tribunals tend to award "re-employment" in very limited circumstances, and notably where both parties are prepared to agree to it, and where there is a general absence of controversy. Both studies argue that Tribunals should be influenced less by employers' arguments. In the view of Williams and Lewis they ought to be examining organisational aspects (eg the work group; supervisory relationships) and personal factors (such as length of "service"). Tribunals should also be less passive, and not assume that the parties have made informed judgments on the matter. They ought to actively encourage "re-employment" since not only is it the primary remedy in the statute, but the Williams and Lewis study suggests that it might be viable in practice on quite a large scale.

However, the picture is not uniform, and the research by Williams and Lewis tells us something about the conditions under which "re-employment" orders are more likely to be made. For example, such orders are more likely in some Tribunal regions than others, and particularly in those regions with relatively high rates of unemployment. "Re-employment" also seems to be quite frequently associated with certain characteristics of the applicant, such as: union membership; representation at the Tribunal; employment in a firm with 100 or more employees; disablement; apprenticeship.

Having surveyed the court and Appeal Tribunal interpretation of "practicable," and briefly described recent research evidence showing some of the characteristics of "re-employment" cases, we now turn to investigate the interpretation of "just."

(b) *Interpretation of "just"*

Three main principles have been established, *viz.*

(i) *Decision on extent of contributory fault should precede decisions on type of remedy*

The purpose would be to see if "re-employment" was still a "just" remedy.

(ii) *Contributory fault in relation to "re-employment" is different from that in relation to compensation*

It appears that contributory fault in relation to "re-employment" has a qualitative aspect as well as a quantitative one, whereas in compensation cases it has merely the latter.

(iii) *A "high" percentage of contributory fault is likely to make re-employment "unjust."*

Contrast may be made between the notion of "practicability" of re-employment in EPCA section 69(5) and (6) and in section 71(2)(*b*) which concerns an employer's refusal to comply with a Tribunal's order of re-employment on grounds of impracticability. The latter would seem to be a more stringent standard. Yet, as interpreted in *Times Corporation* v. *Thomson* [1981] I.R.L.R. 522 (E.A.T.) and *Freemans plc* v. *Flynn* [1984] I.R.L.R. 486 (E.A.T.), this more stringent requirement did not mean the employer had to fit the unfairly dismissed employee in regardless of vacancies. Apparently, if the employee is not suitable for such vacancies as exist, it may not be "practicable" to comply with the order of re-employment.

(v) Reforms

L. Dickens, M. Hart, M. Jones, B. Weekes, *"Re-employment of unfairly dismissed workers: the lost remedy"* (1981) 10 I.L.J. 160 at 175

The need for re-employment arises only because the employment contract is terminated. A new approach would provide that no dismissal decision, if challenged by the employee or the union, could be implemented until and unless the reasons put forward by the employer were upheld by a Tribunal as justifying a fair dismissal. The outcome would be that the notice of dismissal is declared invalid by a Tribunal or is voluntarily withdrawn or, if the proposed dismissal is sanctioned by the Tribunal, it takes effect with or without compensation. Because the employment contract continues the employee would have a continuing right to wages despite any employer reluctance actually to provide work. Clearly this approach is not without its problems but arguably it does provide a more positive way of attempting to give effect to the right not to be unfairly dismissed.

(B) Compensation

In establishing the compensation due to an employee found to have been unfairly dismissed, EPCA, s.74 directs attention to loss attributable to the employer's action (effectively, lost earnings). There are established heads of compensatable damage, and often detailed rules governing assessment (*e.g.* for loss of pension rights). Despite this, it has been conceded that "the assessment of compensation is essentially a rough and ready matter" (*Manpower Ltd.* v. *Hearne* [1983] I.R.L.R. 281 (E.A.T.) at 284, *per* Browne-Wilkinson J.). Further, all careful and precise assessment criteria are subject, as put by May J. in *Townson* v. *The Northgate Group Ltd.* [1981] I.R.L.R. 382 (E.A.T.), to the function of the Industrial Tribunal as an "industrial jury to come to a conclusion of what is just and equitable compensation in all the circumstances." Here we examine the exercise by the Industrial Tribunal of this discretion with respect to the key problem of the employee's contribution to an unfair dismissal as a factor going towards a reduction of compensation (EPCA, s.74(6)).

(i) Reduction for employee's contribution

In deciding whether to reduce compensation for contributory fault, the Court of Appeal in *Nelson* v. *B.B.C.* (*No.* 2) [1979] I.R.L.R. 346, said three findings must be made: first, a finding that there was conduct of the employee in connection with the unfair dismissal which was culpable or blameworthy; secondly, that the unfair dismissal was caused or contributed to some extent by that conduct; thirdly, that it was just and equitable, having regard to the first and second findings, to reduce the assessment of compensation by a given percentage (*per* Brandon L.J. at paras. 43–45). In *Pirelli General Cable Works Ltd.* v. *Murray* [1979] I.R.L.R. 190 (E.A.T.), Bristow J. said Industrial Tribunals should spell out the reason for a reduction in a case where the reduction is less that 100 per cent.; and in *Savoia* v. *Chiltern Herb Farms Ltd.* [1981] I.R.L.R. 65 (E.A.T.), Slynn J. said this applied *a fortiori* to cases of 100 per cent. reduction. In *Hutchinson* v. *Enfield Rolling Mills Ltd.* [1981] I.R.L.R. 318 (E.A.T.), Browne-Wilkinson J. reiterated the need for a "causal link between the actions of the employee and the dismissal. You cannot simply point to some bad behaviour of the employee and say, 'By reason of that matter we are going to reduce the amount of the compensation' " (para. 9).

The extent to which this guidance should be followed is rendered doubtful, however, as a result of the Court of Appeal's decision in the following case.

Hollier v. Plysu Ltd.
[1983] I.R.L.R. 260
Court of Appeal

The employee was dismissed following the discovery of stolen goods in her home. The Industrial Tribunal held the dismissal unfair because the company had not carried out adequate investigations before deciding to dismiss, but reduced her compensation by 75 per cent., the degree to which they held she was to blame. A majority of the E.A.T. allowed an appeal on the level of employee contribution and altered it to 25 per cent. The Court of Appeal allowed the appeal and restored the Industrial Tribunal's assessment.

Stephenson L.J.: In reaching their conclusion about [the employee's contributory fault] [the E.A.T.] took the broad approach which, as I have indicated, is correct. They appreciated that it was not their function to tinker with the apportionment of the Industrial Tribunal in a matter which was, to a large extent, in the discretion of that Tribunal. Mr Justice Kilner Brown, giving the decision of the Appeal Tribunal, divided the cases under the statutory provisions into four general categories: first, when the employee was wholly to blame and the reduction could be 100%; second, when the employee was largely responsible, and in the case, said the judge, nobody would quarrel with the figure of 75%. Third, there was the case in which both parties were equally to blame, and that was obviously his view when he gave his opinion that the reduction should be 50%. The fourth category was the one into which the majority of the Appeal Tribunal put this case, namely, the case in which the employee is to a much lesser degree to blame.

. . . The Industrial Tribunal were, I think, entitled to their opinion, both on the particular matter and on the general result, as within the band of opinions which different men and women might hold without being called unreasonable. The Appeal Tribunal were not entitled to substitute their percentages for those of the Industrial Tribunal.

. . . In a question which is so obviously a matter of impression, opinion, and discretion as is this kind of apportionment of responsibility, there must be either a plain error of law, or something like perversity, to entitle an appellate Tribunal to interfere with the decision of the Tribunal which is entrusted by Parliament with the difficult task of making the decision.

This reluctance to interfere was reiterated in *Warrilow* v. *Robert Walker Ltd.* [1984] I.R.L.R. 304 (E.A.T.): "the proportion of culpability is very much a matter for an Industrial Tribunal" (*per* Tudor Evans J., at p. 306).

(ii) Future loss of wages

One of the most important and most difficult of the elements of the compensatory award to assess is the employee's loss of future earnings. At a time of high unemployment, when a dismissed worker may have to remain unemployed for a considerable time before finding another job, the Tribunal's task of assessing his future loss is a daunting one. This difficulty is increased since the Tribunal has to take as its basis the position as it stands at the date of the hearing (*Qualcast (Wolverhampton) Ltd.* v. *Ross* [1979] I.R.L.R. 98 (E.A.T.)).

The problem of estimating future loss of wages may be met, however, by an interesting precedent set in *Ladup Ltd.* v. *Barnes* [1982] I.R.L.R. 7 (E.A.T.). An appeal was allowed against a refusal by an Industrial Tribunal to *review* its findings of no contributory fault when subsequent to the hearing the employee in question was convicted for the offence on suspicion of which he was dismissed. The E.A.T. held that the interests of justice (see rule 10(1)(*c*) of the Industrial Tribunals (Rules of Procedure) Regulations 1980) required a review of the finding of nil contribution. They proceeded then to assess a 100 per cent. contribution.

Should this precedent be followed, it would appear to allow for review of Industrial Tribunal awards whenever subsequent events or circumstances indicate that the tribunal's original assessment of compensation (albeit correct when it was made, as was held in *Barnes*), requires adjustment. And there would seem no reason to restrict such reviews to cases for reduction by way of employee's contributory fault. Hence an employee might ask for review where compensation awarded turns out to be inadequate, *eg* where future loss of earnings is estimated at X weeks but after X weeks have passed the complainant is still unemployed. The interests of justice would seem to apply equally to such cases.

11. THE IMPACT OF THE LAW OF UNFAIR DISMISSAL

S. Evans, J. Goodman, L, Hargreaves, *"Unfair Dismissal Law and Employment Practice in the 1980s,"* DEPARTMENT OF EMPLOYMENT RESEARCH PAPER No. 53 (July 1985), p.71

. . . It is easy to exaggerate the influence that unfair dismissal legislation, and changes in it, have on the day-to-day operation of companies' employment decisions, policies and practices. This is especially so in the case of small businesses. . . . Although, hypothetically, the law's introduction and its amendment "should" cause behavioural changes, our evidence suggests that in many cases it either made little substantial difference, or was simply one consideration (and often a minor one) to be weighed against other factors.

One of the main qualifications to this general statement concerns the introduction of formal disciplinary procedures . . . most were introduced as a direct consequence of the legislation, had induced more care and caution, and sometimes had the effect of slowing down the process of dismissal. Many small firms regarded formal disciplinary procedures as alien to their preferred informal style of management, and had not introduced them, though some of these took care to act "procedurally" when dismissal appeared very likely or inevitable.

For the great majority of the sample companies unfair dismissal legislation was an issue of only occasional rather than continuous significance. Very few firms felt strongly inhibited from dismissing because of the legislation, though many now felt constrained to do it "properly," in order to reduce the risks of facing or losing a Tribunal case. . . .

The general operation of firms' employment policies revealed little evidence of the law's alleged inhibiting influence. . . .

Such antagonism as employers expressed towards the legislation was generally derived from their awareness of the potential costs it held for them, or, in the case of the smaller firms, of proprietorical principle . . . .

Overall, the evidence of this study indicates that the current unfair dismissal legislation is relatively marginal among the factors influencing management's employment decisions whilst the law's potential ability to protect individuals is something of which many employees are, in a routine sense, only vaguely aware.

CHAPTER 11

ORGANISATIONS OF WORKERS

In most circumstances employers have greater economic power than workers due to their ownership of the means of production and their power to hire and fire. The Industrial Revolution, by bringing together in one workplace unprecedentedly large numbers of workers, paradoxically both increased the degree of exploitation and also produced the conditions in which workers could most effectively challenge employers' superiority. Henceforth, workers, by concerted withdrawal of their labour, commanded a collective sanction with which to reinforce their demands. Appreciation of this collective power led to the gradual recognition of organisations of workers (trade unions) by employers during the latter half of the nineteenth century. The emergence of trade unions in the United Kingdom, therefore, occurred relatively early and with little dependence on the enactment of favourable legislation.

The success of trade unions in establishing themselves largely by their own efforts bequeathed a unique legacy to British industrial relations. To this day the British trade union movement remains suspicious of interference with its traditional autonomy, and especially of intervention from a judiciary reared on the very different legacy of the common law with its antipathy to collective action. Hence, even after the Employment Acts of 1980 and 1982 and the Trade Union Act 1984, legislation in the United Kingdom plays at best a supplementary role in shaping the structure, government and activities of workers' organisations.

1. THE STRUCTURES OF TRADE UNIONS: CONCEPTS AND DEFINITIONS

(A) Industrial Relations Concepts

ACAS, *Industrial Relations Handbook* (1980), pp. 39–47

Trade unions are organisations of workers set up to improve the status, pay and conditions of employment of their members. The Trade Union and Labour Relations Act 1974 (TULRA) defines a trade union at law, and any organisation which fits this definition may apply to have its name included in the statutory list of trade unions which is maintained by the Certification Officer . . . . Entry on the list is an essential preliminary to applying for a certificate of independence, and also entitles trade unions to tax relief for expenditure on provident benefits. . . . The long-term trend has been in the direction of a reduction in the number of unions. In 1938 there were 1024, in 1958, 660 and in 1968, 586. [In December 1985 there were 409 unions on the statutory list.]

Any classification of British trade unions is difficult since the long and complex evolution of the present structure of organisation has led to a number of exceptions to every generalisation. The most commonly used classification, however, is into "general," "craft," "industrial," and "white-collar" unions.

(i) General unions do not restrict their membership to workers in any one industry or occupation or to those possessing specific skills. In practice this is true of the majority of major trade unions, although few set out to recruit on this basis. The largest general unions are the Transport and General Workers' Union (TGWU) and the National Union of General and Municipal Workers [now the General, Municipal, Boilermakers and Allied Trades Union, GMBATU].

(ii) Craft unions are based on the possession of specific skills, usually associated with the serving of an apprenticeship. Some medium-sized and small unions still restict entry to skilled craftsmen and apprentices as was common practice in the nineteenth century. A number of the larger unions have a strong craft tradition, for instance the Amalgamated Union of Engineering Workers (AUEW) [now the Amalgamated Engineering Union], the Electrical, Electronic, Telecommunication and Plumbing Union (EETPU), and the Union of Construction, Allied Trades and Technicians (UCATT).

(iii) Industrial unions restrict their membership to a single industry and aim to recruit all or most grades of workers within it. The National Union of Mineworkers (NUM) comes nearest to the model of an industrial union; but even in mining, certain supervisory workers and management staff have their own (respective) unions. Other examples of industrial unions are the National Union of Railwaymen (NUR) and the National Union of Agricultural and Allied Workers (NUAAW).

(iv) White-collar unions restrict their membership to clerical, administrative or professional workers. Some, such as the Association of Scientific, Technical and Managerial Staffs (ASTMS) and the Association of Professional, Executive, Clerical and Computer Staff (APEX) recruit amongst employees in many occupations and in a wide range of manufacturing and service industries. Some such as the National Union of Journalists (NUJ) and the National Union of Teachers (NUT)—organise on an occupational basis. Others—such as the National and Local Government Officers' Association (NALGO) or the Transport Salaried Staffs' Association (TSSA)—operate in specific industries or parts of the public sector. A number of the general, craft and industrial unions also have white-collar sections.

It is apparent that few trade unions conform easily to this typology. Some unions, such as the Union of Shop, Distributive and Allied Workers (USDAW), bear little relation to any of the stereotypes. Mergers and changes in recruitment boundaries keep the pattern constantly changing. A recent development has been the recruitment of managerial and senior staff in the private sector into trade unions. At the end of [1985] membership of the largest 24 unions [with memberships in excess of 100,000] numbered over [8.6] million. . . .

Trade unions are autonomous associations of individuals. They are governed by a mixture of lay and full-time officials variously elected and appointed.

Policy is usually determined at a conference, normally held annually, attended by elected delegates. Policy is carried out between conferences by an executive body—usually called a committee or council—which may be elected at the conference by branches, on a regional or industrial basis, or occasionally by ballot of the membership. The executive body may consist entirely of lay members, of full-time officials or of a mixture of the two.

All but the smallest unions have a full-time "chief officer" who is usually the general secretary. He may be appointed by the executive body, by the conference, or by ballot of the members, usually until retirement. In a few unions, the chief officer and other full-time officials are elected for a limited period. The president of a union may be a lay member elected periodically or may, like the general secretary, be a full-time official. Sometimes the president, not the general secretary, is the chief officer of the union.

Below the chief officer, the national full-time officers and the national executive body, is a network of divisional, regional, district and branch officials and committees. The number of officials and the complexity of the network depend mainly on the size of the union. Branches may—as in the mining industry—be based on the workplace. More typically a branch is based on a locality and may draw its members from more than one industry. Within an individual factory or office, members of trade unions commonly elect workplace representatives, known as shop stewards in most industries or, in white-collar areas, staff representatives. Their election to office must be approved by the union, and among their duties may be the recruitment of new members, the collection of union subscriptions (when check-off facilities, where subscriptions are automatically deducted by the employer, do not exist) and generally to look after the interests of "constituents," including local negotiations on pay and conditions. There has been an increase in the importance of plant bargaining since the last war and this has meant a greater involvement of shop stewards in negotiations over pay as well as making representations over individual grievances.

The law has not heretofore directly determined union structure. But some aspects of the present structure (closed shops, demarcation and jurisdiction disputes) may be or become the subject of legal regulation, and this could indirectly affect trade union structure. The following extract analyses the present structure of British trade unions from a different perspective.

H.A. Turner, *"The morphology of trade unionism,"* in TRADE UNIONS, (W.E.J. MacCarthy ed. 1972), pp. 89 *et seq*.

One clue to the structure of British trade unionism is the concentration of membership in a few very large trade unions. . . . Another clue, however, is the apparently comfortable survival, despite this century's general trend to merger and amalgamation among unions, of a number of relatively small organizations, like the Tapesizers in cotton and the Patternmakers outside.

The larger unions are "open," at least in the sense that they are able to impose no restrictions on entry into many of the occupations that they organize, but are content to recruit all workers in those occupations whom the employers themselves engage. Such unions are almost inevitably expansionist in tendency. Since an open union is usually unable to bring pressure to bear on employers through controlling the supply of labour to a key stage in the production process, it is bound to rely on strength of numbers for its bargaining power instead . . . .

The smaller stable unions, however, will generally be found to be predominantly closed. They are also restrictionist, not merely in the sense that they base themselves on a capacity to control the supply of labour to particular occupations and maintain an exclusive claim to employment within those occupations, but also in the sense that they have little intrinsic interest in increasing their merely numerical strength. Indeed, their interest lies rather in the opposite direction—of limiting the intake of labour to the jobs that they control and thereby restricting also the membership of the union itself. Thus the shape of British trade unionism in general might be described as one in which open, expansionist unions have spread around islands of stable closed unionism. . . .

The distinction between closed and open unionism, therefore, pretty adequately explains . . . the general pattern of British trade union organization. It also, however—and this is something that the customary typologies of trade union external structure certainly fail to do—explains some important differences in the normal behaviour and preoccupations of various unions.

One would naturally expect, for instance, that open unions should be rather more preoccupied with wage questions, while closed unions will be concerned with issues affecting their control of labour supply and employment? . . . .

The distinction between closed and open unions also means a good deal in terms of detailed inter-union relationships. Thus, the typical inter-union problem of open trade unionism is the "jurisdiction" dispute—about which union should have what members? . . . .

The typical inter-union conflict of closed trade unionism, however, is the "demarcation" dispute—about which union's members should have what jobs? . . . .

Similarly there is a difference in attitude to union membership. The closed union is identified with the "closed shop"—that is, the insistence on acceptance into the union as a prior condition of employment. The open union is characteristically associated with the form of compulsory union membership best described as the "union shop" (but sometimes improperly called "100 per cent. trade unionism"), involving a requirement that entry into a job which the union organizes shall be followed by joining the union. And it is probably true that there is a considerable difference between the attitudes of closed and open unions to employers. Since the essential technique of closed trade unionism is a system of "autonomous regulation," it is with unions of this type that trade rules and customs of a kind which are often described by managements as "restrictive practices" are largely associated. The open union's dependence on collective bargaining, however, involves at least the employers' acquiescence in that, and preferably their co-operation . . . .

But, of course, the frontier between open and closed unionism is not rigid and permanent. So a closed union may become open—or develop open sections within its membership. Since the general conditions of effective closed unionism are an occupational stability on the part of the workers it organizes and a system of restricting entry to their jobs, the most obvious cause of such a transformation in a closed union's character is a technical change which undermines the permanence or blurs the identity of its members' occupation. Whether the union will in fact then modify itself depends on the pace of the technical revolution with which it is confronted.

Application of Turner's analysis to professional organisations (of lawyers, doctors, architects, engineers, nurses, teachers, etc.), many of which have the same objectives as trade unions, may help to correct the impression that trade unions are unique organisations.

Apart from organisations of workers based on industries, skills, general labour and so on, we need to attend to the pattern of organisational practice based on the workplace. Clegg's study seeks to provide a view of British industrial relations based on the work of sociologists during the past two decades. This extract highlights the contrast between the formal and informal organisation of industrial relations.

H.A. Clegg, *The System of Industrial Relations in Great Britain* (1972), pp. 1 *et seq.*

There are three well-known ways in which employment rules can be made and administered. It can be done by managers. It is widely supposed that in the early days of industrialisation factories, mines, railways and offices were run by autocratic managers whose word was law. This is generally called *employer regulation*. When a union (or unions) establishes a foothold some of the rules may be made by agreement between manager and unions, with joint arrangements for revision and interpretation. This is called *collective bargaining*, or sometimes bilateral or joint regulation in contrast to the unilateral regulation of managers acting on their own. Firms may join together in an employers' association to bargain with unions, and the resulting agreements will then apply to all the firms in the association, but this is still collective bargaining. The third method is *statutory regulation*. The state can intervene by laying down legal rules governing aspects of employment in particular classes of undertaking, or throughout the country. These rules can prescribe rates of pay, hours of work, standards of safety and so on, and statutory arrangements may be made for their enforcement and interpretation . . . .

. . . in recent years it has become evident that there is another important method of regulating employment which has no accepted name, but may perhaps be called 'worker regulation'; and another type of organisation which plays an important part in the making and administration of rules affecting employment, namely the work group. In order to describe and analyse the British system of industrial relations, therefore, it is necessary to explain what worker regulation means, and to say what work groups are. . . .

. . . . Men and women form groups at work, as they do outside it, for all manner of purposes. They chat together, take tea-breaks and meal breaks together, exchange cigarettes and newspapers, lend each other money and help each other with their work. If work groups have no other objectives but these they are of no direct interest to the student of industrial relations. It is when they act together to make or to influence rules governing their employment that work groups enter into the field of industrial relations . . . .

. . . The preference of managers for dealing with shop stewards can be understood if the stewards are seen as the representatives of their constituents rather than as the agents of their unions; for these constituents are the employees whom managers have to manage. If the shop steward acts on their behalf with no more than relaxed and general guidance from his union and from formal agreements then the manager is likely to see his advantage in securing a settlement with the shop steward.

Circumstances and personalities make for wide variations in the relationship between the shop steward and his constituents, but the evidence suggests that the shop steward is mainly dependent on them for his authority in collective bargaining. In some instances, such as the docks and coalmining in the past, the work group's part in collective bargaining has not been recognised by the union and the group has operated outside the union machinery. Elsewhere the shop steward provides a link between the group and the union, but even so it is not the union which gives the steward his position in collective bargaining. Accordingly the important position of the steward in collective bargaining in Britain is evidence of the importance of the work group in collective bargaining.

However, all this assumes that the shop steward is the representative of a single and clearly defined group of workers who are in the habit of acting together over a whole range of matters affecting their work. This can happen, but it is by no means universal, perhaps not even general, for two reasons. The first is that even where such "primary" work groups can be clearly identified, the shop steward's constituency may include several of them. A study by J. F. B. Goodman and T. G. Whittingham found that in a sample of nineteen stewards the median number of groups per steward was five. "One steward represented ten different primary groups and another nine and, excluding those, the mean average was three." The second reason is that it is not always possible to pick out clearly defined work groups.

Take a bus garage. Normally a driver and conductor work together as a team but both of them are also part of larger groups. Drivers have interests in common and for some purposes all the drivers may be said to constitute a single work group, and all the conductors another. Alternatively, since many busmen work on shifts, the drivers and conductors on one shift may have their own view of a particular issue. At other times the whole of the road-operating staff may act as a single unit. There is still the inside staff, consisting of skilled mechanics, semi-skilled workers, cleaners and so on, each forming a group of their own for some purposes, perhaps coming together for others. Usually there is a single union delegate or representative for the operating staff, and one or more shop stewards for the inside staff.

As Goodman and Whittingham observe, "it is more plausible to count shop stewards as leaders of work *groups* rather than as work group leaders."

Perhaps it is even more apt to see them as leaders of complexes or coalitions of work groups. Thus individual groups may act on their own, perhaps contrary to the advice of their steward and the wishes of other groups within his constituency, or all the groups may act together under his leadership, while for other purposes many work groups may coalesce behind a committee of stewards, or even contrary to the wishes of the stewards' committee. Where worker regulation extends over a considerable area of employment without any direct support from trade unions, as with welting or spelling in the docks, it seems sensible to regard the practice as the product of a coalition of work groups each following the same custom. Unofficial strikes of any size might also be regarded as evidence of work group coalition, as could shop stewards' committees formed without union backing—for example the "combine" committees which bring together shop stewards from the several factories of a major company . . . .

The following extract draws a parallel between the law and collective bargaining by trade unions as ways of securing rights for workers. It also highlights how trade unions go beyond protection of their members' interests to allow for participation in decision-making, a function which may not be easily fulfilled by the law. Finally, it points to workplace bargaining as a potential force for further democratisation.

A. Flanders, *"What are trade unions for?,"* in *TRADE UNIONS* (W.E.J. MacCarthy ed. 1972) p. 17

. . . one of the principal purposes of trade unions in collective bargaining is regulation or control. They are interested in regulating wages as well as in raising them; and, of course, in regulating a wide range of other issues appertaining to their members' jobs and working life.

Why do they have this interest in regulating employment relationships and what social purpose does such regulation serve? It is certainly not a bureaucratic interest in rules for their own sake. Unions and their members are interested in the effect of the rules made by collective bargaining, which is to limit the power and authority of employers and to lessen the dependence of employees on market fluctuations and the arbitrary will of management. Stated in the simplest possible terms these rules provide protection, a shield, for their members. And they protect not only their material standards of living, but equally their security, status and self-respect—in short, their dignity as human beings.

One can put the same point in another way. The effect of rules is to establish rights, with their corresponding obligations. The rules in collective agreements secure for employees the right to a certain rate of wages; the right not to have to work longer than a certain number of hours; the right not to be dismissed without consultation or compensation and so on. This surely is the most enduring social achievement of trade unionism; its creation of a social order in industry embodied in a code of industrial rights. This, too, is the constant service that unions offer their members: daily protection of their industrial rights.

Such rights could be, and to some extent are, established by law. But collective bargaining serves yet another great social purpose. Apart from providing protection, it also permits participation. A worker through his union has more direct influence on what rules are made and how they are applied than he can ever exercise by his vote over the laws made by Parliament. We hear a lot these days about participation, including workers' participation in management. I have yet to be convinced that there is a better method than collective bargaining for making industry more democratic, providing its subjects and procedures are suitably extended. Putting a few workers or union officials on boards of directors only divorces them from the rank and file. In collective bargaining, trade unions must continually respond to and service their members' interests . . . .

. . . over the post-war years there has been at the same time a great upsurge of union activity *in the workplace*. Bargaining between shop stewards and management has developed on a scale previously unknown. This bargaining is not only about money, though that is an important feature. It is equally associated with demands for a greater say in managerial decisions in such matters as discipline and redundancy, control of overtime and fringe benefits. In general, for a variety of reasons, workers are raising their sights; their level of aspirations and expectations is rising. The increase in workplace bargaining has undermined the regulative effect of industry-wide agreements in many industries, so that much of the old formal system of collective bargaining has become a pretence and is in a state of decay.

This has very important implications for trade unions. In terms of their basic social purpose the upsurge of workplace bargaining represents at once a danger, an opportunity and a responsibility. It is a danger because, although they now rely heavily on the workplace activity of their stewards, this activity in its present form threatens their discipline, cohesion and strength. At the same time it is an opportunity for the trade unions to make the most of a movement already in being. Properly led and directed it could result in a considerable extension of the subjects of collective bargaining and, therefore, a greater fulfilment of their basic purpose of job regulation. Their responsibility is self-evident once the danger and opportunity has been stated.

The tension between union members at their workplace and full-time officers employed by unions was the subject of the study from which the following extract is taken. It emphasises various factors which could reinforce or weaken internal workplace, in contrast to external trade union, structures. While the law is not explicitly referred to, legal regulation of internal trade union constitutional structures, legal provision of resources for workplace representatives and legal control of the scope and content of collective agreements clearly have the potential to influence workplace organisation.

I. Boraston, H.A. Clegg and M. Rimmer, WORKPLACE AND UNION: A STUDY OF LOCAL RELATIONSHIPS IN FOURTEEN UNIONS (1975), pp. 186–88, 199

The argument can now be summarised by enumerating the influences on the relationship between union organisation in the workplace and the union outside. . . .

The most general influence on dependence is the size of the workplace organisation. The larger the workplace organisation, the greater the resources at its disposal, and the more independent its behaviour. But the size is not the only influence at work. The greater the unity within a workplace organisation, the trade union experience of its members and their status as employees, the larger will be the resources at its disposal, and the more it will tend to act on its own. Close association with a powerful workplace organisation in the same plant can also help a relatively small workplace organisation to act independently of its full-time officer.

It follows that a workplace organisation may not achieve the independence which its potential membership would seem to support because the potential members have not all joined the union, or because they have not formed the habit of united action, or because they lack trade union experience. Consequently the trade union outside can encourage or discourage workplace independence by promoting or hindering organisation, unity and experience. Managers can also encourage or discourage workplace independence. Many of the resources commonly enjoyed by independent workplace organisations—facilities for shop stewards' meetings and mass meetings, time off for shop stewards', sinecures for senior stewards or convenors, an office, a telephone—are concessions which mangers can make or try to withhold. Besides that, union and management can co-operate in developing and sustaining a style of bargaining in the workplace which fosters independence, or they can adopt a style of bargaining designed to keep a workplace organisation in subjection. The availability of the full-time officer is for the union to determine and within limits the lack of a full-time officer to whom its representatives can turn may push a workplace organisation towards independence, whereas the ready availability of a full-time officer may hold it back.

In a non-federated single plant firm the scope for workplace bargaining is as wide as the participants choose to make it. Elsewhere it is limited by such agreements as its association or parent company have signed. Nearly all these external agreements are either at industry or company level and can be ranged from "tight" to "loose" according to the scope they give for workplace bargaining. Tight or relatively tight agreements are associated with centralised managerial structures, especially in the public services, and loose or fairly loose agreements with decentralised managerial structures. Trade unions can influence the scope for workplace bargaining only by agreement with the managers with whom they negotiate and only within the limits imposed by the structure of managerial organisation.

The power of management to influence workplace organisations has been particularly evident since 1979.

M. Terry, *"Shop steward development and managerial strategies"* in INDUSTRIAL RELATIONS IN BRITAIN (G. Bain ed. 1983) p. 67 at 90

. . . . A combination of growing economic crisis and a government more hostile to the organised labour movement than any of its predecessors has made available to managements a strategy frequently contemplated but not often adopted since World War II—that of a major assault on union organisation in general and shopfloor organisation in particular. Helped by the debilitating effects of unemployment and recession on trade union power and organisation (and to some extent by law) a few employers, of whom British Leyland are often held to be the best example, have tried to undermine the traditional strengths of shopfloor organisation. Their strategies have made a combined attack on shopfloor organisation by reducing the number of full-time shop stewards and restricting the mobility of others, by attempts to "by-pass" them by obtaining workforce opinions directly through ballots and referenda, and by the unilateral imposition of sets of working agreements designed to reduce or elimate "restrictive practices."

The majority of employers have not adopted such tough tactics, but have exploited the weakening of trade union bargaining power within a framework of continued union rights. One interesting finding is the evidence of recent increase in the use of formal joint consultation procedures involving shop stewards in discussions with management about a range of company issues . . . . Such bodies, which give shop stewards a degree of involvement without any formal rights to negotiation, were rejected as useless by stewards throughout the 1950s and 1960s . . . . Employers adopting these strategies hope to be able to obtain radical change through agreement with a weakened labour force while at the same time preserving forms of union representation as the best guarantee of future order and stability should the balance of bargaining power shift again.

(B) The Legal Definition of a Trade Union

The current statutory definition of a trade union (TULRA, s.28(1)) stresses that a trade union is an organisation of workers, whether permanent or temporary, whose principal purposes include regulating relations between employers and workers. The difficulty of applying even such a broad definition in a system of proliferating organisations of workers, formal and informal, are illustrated by the following cases. In the first, the court considered the legal status of a shop stewards' committee representing employees in the docks.

Midland Cold Storage Ltd. v. Turner
[1972] 3 All E.R. 773; [1972] I.C.R. 230
National Industrial Relations Court

The Port of London Joint Shop Stewards Committee consisted mainly of TGWU shop stewards representing dock workers. They were concerned at the loss of work for registered dock workers resulting from the activities of those, like the plaintiffs, who were involved in the loading and unloading of containers which were not designated as "dock work" for the purposes of the Dock Labour Scheme; hence it was work which could be undertaken by workers who were not dockers. The plaintiffs' cold store was blacked on the committee's instructions.

The plaintiffs ("Midland") sought injunctions against the committee. The National Industrial Relations Court held that no order could be made against the committee because it did not satisfy the statutory definition of an "organisation of workers" under the Industrial Relations Act 1971 61(1) (essentially the same as the current definition in TULRA, s.28(1)).

Sir John Donaldson P.: It follows that if Midland are to obtain an order against the committee they must satisfy us that (*a*) it is an organisation; (*b*) it consists wholly or mainly of workers; (*c*) its principal objects include the regulation of relations between workers of one or more descriptions and employers.

We have no doubt at all that the committee exists and has great influence in the London docks. We have no evidence as to its composition, other than the fact that it has a chairman and secretary, and that, as we infer from its name and our general knowledge of organisation in the docks, it is composed wholly or mainly of trade union shop stewards. It is not recognised by employers, although they are well aware of its existence and may take account of its activities. Furthermore, there is no evidence that it seeks recognition by employers as a bargaining agent for any bargaining unit or as a representative body for or of any union or unions. It is proved to be an influential pressure group. Our general knowledge of the industry tells us that its activities are to some extent co-ordinated with those of other shop stewards' committees in other docks by a national dock shop stewards' committee, but that those other committees may have different compositions and functions. If we have to be able to point to evidence to confirm what as members of an industrial court we ought to know and do know, it was provided at a late stage in the hearing by the production of a printed leaflet, purporting to be issued by the committee, referring to support from the national committee. Its most apparent activity seems to consist of recommending the taking or abandonment of industrial action in the London docks and organising any such action which may be decided on. Thereafter it does not seem to enter into negotiations with the employers but leaves this task to the established union machinery.

Against this background, we are satisfied that prima facie the committee is an organisation and that it consists wholly or mainly of workers as defined in the 1971 Act. However, we are not satisfied that there is a prima facie case for holding that its principal objects include the regulations of relations between workers of that description (namely registered dock workers) and employers. No body whose principal objects included such regulation could fail at least to seek recognition from employers and of such an attempt we have no evidence. Accordingly, we are unable to make any order against the committee as such . . . .

The evidence which has been put before us shows quite clearly that the committee has a policy of its own, namely that the scope of employment reserved for registered dock workers must be expanded to provide sufficient work for all such persons. All or most of the members are shop stewards, and thus officials, of one or other of the two unions which are concerned with dock workers, namely NASD and TGWU. The committee appears to be content to leave the regulation of relations between the dockers and employers to those unions—so long, that is, as those unions are, in its opinion, being sufficiently forceful in achieving this objective. Currently the committee is not satisfied that the unions are being sufficiently forceful. It has therefore initiated industrial action independently . . . .

Many organisations contain pressure groups formed by more active members with a common sectional interest. In framing policy and seeking to execute it the organisation has to take account of the likely reaction of such groups. It may decide that they are too disruptive to be retained within the organisation, or it may decide to modify its policy to such an extent as is necessary to appease them. But it is necessary to distinguish between, on the one hand, a pressure group whose object is to cause another organisation to try to regulate relations between employers and workers in a particular way, including bringing pressure on employers who facilitate this result, and, on the other hand, a body which itself seeks to regulate those relations.

We do not consider that the evidence which we have quoted, or any other evidence before this court, indicates a wish on the part of the committee to regulate the relations between employers and workers within the guiding principles. Rather it discloses an intention to exercise a power of veto over particular actions which TGWU might otherwise take in the course of its regulation of such relations. Accordingly, we are unable to take the next step and infer that the committee's principal objects include such regulation. It follows that we cannot be satisfied and are not satisfied that the committee is an "organisation of workers" within the meaning of the Act.

We must, however, make it clear that we have been concerned solely with the status of this particular joint committee. If the question hereafter arises in relation to some other joint committee of shop stewards, the matter will have to be fully investigated in relation to that committee. It may also be necessary to reconsider our previous acceptance of the proposition that a committee of shop stewards is necessarily a committee "wholly or mainly of workers," since it is for consideration whether they are members in their capacity as workers or in their capacity as trade union officials as defined in [the Industrial Relations Act 1971] s.167(1). It may, indeed, be that nobody can come within the statutory definition of an "organisation of workers" unless it is of a type which could reasonably be described as a trade union, whether permanent or temporary, or whether registered or unregistered.

In contrast to the *Midland Cold Storage* case, where the committee represented workers in one industry, the following case examined whether all the employees of a single enterprise constituted an "organisation of workers" under the Industrial Relations Act 1971, *ie* a "trade union".

Frost v. Clarke and Smith Manufacturing Co. Ltd.
[1973] I.R.L.R. 216
National Industrial Relations Court

The employer called upon all the employees in the enterprise to elect the members of a works committee set up by the management.

SIR HUGH GRIFFITHS P.: If they were indeed an "organisation of workers" as a result of the request to send members to the works committee, they were indeed an unusual organisation. They had no name, they had no constitution, they had no rules, they held no meetings, they kept no minutes, they had no offices, they had no property, they had no funds; indeed, they had none of the attributes of an organisation. This court finds it quite impossible to accept the argument that when an entire work force is invited to send members to a works committee by an employer, it is thereby constituted an organisation of workers. Furthermore, we are not satisfied that the principal objects of the setting up of the works committee included the regulation of relations between workers and this employer. It was, we think, properly described as a "consultative committee." We cannot hold that the employers have unwittingly created an "organisation of workers" within the meaning of [the Industrial Relations Act 1971] s.61(1) . . . .

Compare the ease with which an employment agency, the "Overseas Workers' Federation" was able to have its status as an "organisation of workers" upheld by the Court of Appeal, by the simple tactic of inserting into its constitution a form of words defining itself in terms of the statutory definition (*McCabe* v. *Edwards* [1981] I.C.R. 468 (Q.B.), (1981) New Law Journal 368). The next case illustrates how particular features of organisation and/or behaviour by the same body of workers (*eg* strikers) can determine the finding as to whether they constitute a trade union in law.

Weeks v. National Amalgamated Stevedores and Dockers' Union
[1940] 67 Lloyd's L. Rep. 282
Chancery Division

In 1923, in response to a proposal to reduce their wages, there was a strike of dockers, most of whom belonged to the Dockers' section of the TGWU. The dockers persuaded a large number of stevedores, who were mostly members of the defendant union, and lightermen, who were mostly members of the TGWU, to strike in support. The TGWU did not declare the strike official, so most of the striking dockers and lightermen joined the defendant union. The plaintiff claimed that a new union had been created comprising all the various men on strike, and that this body had then decided to amalgamate with the defendant union. However, since this amalgamation had not taken place under the then prevailing statutory requirements (*ie* the Trade Union (Amendment) Act 1876, s.12) the amalgamation was wholly ineffective and void.

FARWELL J.: When one looks at the terms of the Trade Union [Amendment] Act [1876] it is quite clear, I think, that the Act contemplates that a trade union should be some body of men with some constitution and regulations, a secretary, and other provisions of that sort so that there might be an actual entity which would form the union. I am not prepared to say . . . that under certain circumstances a strike committee or association may not be a trade union. It is enough for me to say, on the particular facts of this case and having regard to the circumstances, that I am satisfied on the evidence that this body of men who came out on strike did not in themselves constitute a trade union within the meaning of the Act.

I think it is even clearer that 6000, or approximately 6000, of the men on strike did not form a union, as is suggested in the plaintiff's pleadings. If there was a trade union at all it must have been constituted by all the persons on strike who combined together for the purpose of preventing what they thought was an injustice in the reduction of their wages; that is to say, the dockers struck for that purpose. As I gather, the stevedores and the lightermen, either in sympathy or because they were more or less compelled, came out on strike for the purpose of assisting the dockers to resist the reduction in wages; but to select 6000 or approximately 6000 of the dockers and say that they constituted a trade union seems to me to be a quite hopeless contention. In any event, I am satisfied that in this particular case the men on strike did not constitute a trade union so as to render any amalgamation necessary . . . .

. . . . As I say, I am not deciding that such a combination of men might not under other circumstances and on other evidence constitute a trade union within the meaning of the Act. It is enough for me to say that, in my judgment, the plaintiff has failed to show that there ever was a trade union such as he endeavoured to show there existed, which could amalgamate with the defendant union. Really, the question is a question of fact. I have come to the conclusion on the evidence I have heard, that no such union, as is suggested, ever existed . . . .

Cases such as this highlight the legal difficulties sometimes posed when dissident trade unionists organise to act independently of the main union, or even break off entirely to form a new organisation (*cf. ASTMS [TCO Section]* v. *Post Office* [1981] I.C.R. 278; [1980] I.R.L.R. 475 (C.A.); *British Airways Engine Overhaul Ltd* v. *Francis* [1981]

I.R.L.R. 9 (E.A.T.). Questions arise as to the legal status of trade unions generally.

(C) The Legal Status of Trade Unions

Associations of workers are in principle no different from other types of association formed for the pursuit of a common interest. The following case reviews the historical development of the legal status of trade unions.

Electrical, Electronic, Telecommunication and Plumbing Union v. Times Newspapers
[1980] 3 W.L.R. 98; [1980] 1 All E.R. 1097
Queen's Bench Division

> The plaintiff trade union, which was not a special register body for the purposes of TULRA, s.2(1), sued the defendants in libel for an article in their newspaper which, they alleged, injured its reputation. The defendants successfully pleaded that the commission of the tort depended on the existence of a legal personality and that, by virtue of TULRA, s.2(1), the union was not a body corporate and could not be treated as if it were one; therefore, as a mere unincorporated association it had no legal personality to protect.

O'CONNOR J.: Now where stands a trade union? It is not necessary for the purposes of this judgment to go into a detailed analysis of the history of trade unions in our law. It is well known that, before they were legalised, they ran foul of the law because they were unlawful combinations in the restraint of trade and suffered disabilities. But that is in the long and distant past. The Trade Union Acts since 1871 have recognised trade unions, but they were without question unincorporated associations, and as such one would have thought that they could neither sue in their own names, nor be sued, and as such could not be defamed in their proper name.

In 1901 in *Taff Vale Railway Co v Amalgamated Society of Railway Servants* [1901] A.C. 426, the House of Lords got over this difficulty, but in circumstances which were disliked by the trade union movement, by introducing what has come to be called a quasi-corporation, or a near corporation. Quite shortly, what happened was this. Looking at the registration of a trade union under the 1871 Act, and seeing the various matters dealt with in that statute, the House of Lords came to the conclusion that the trade union had a sufficient personality for that reason so that it could be sued in its own name and its funds charged in the action.

The reverse of that coin necessarily followed; if it could be sued so also could it maintain an action in its own name and, as we shall see in a moment, unions soon did so and perfectly properly. The immediate effect of the *Taff Vale* decision was to call for a change in the law to give protection to trade unions nothing whatever to do with actions of libel, but in their industrial capacity, and in 1906 Parliament passed the Trade Disputes Act in order to reverse the decision of the House of Lords in the *Taff Vale* case: that is, to reverse the decision which had enabled the plaintiffs in that case to sue the union in tort. And in 1906, in the Trade Disputes Act, Parliament passed a blanket section relieving trade unions of liability in tort.

It left quite unaffected the decision of the House of Lords that this unincorporated body, because of the effect of the statute to which it was subject, had a quasi-corporate personality . . . .

[The judge described how the Donovan Commission on Trade Unions and Employers' Associations had recommended that the position be clarified by requiring trade unions to be bodies corporate, and that effect had been given to this recommendation by the Industrial Relations Act 1971. The 1971 Act, however, had been repealed by TULRA]

. . . . Section 2 [of TULRA], the side note to which reads, "Status of trade unions," provides:

> "(1) A trade union which is not a special register body shall not be, or be treated as if it were, a body corporate . . . ."

Section 2(1) of the 1974 Act goes on, and the words have to be carefully considered:

> " . . . But—(*a*) it shall be capable of making contracts; (*b*) all property belonging to the trade union shall be vested in trustees in trust for the union; (*c*) subject to section 14 below [repealed by the Employment Act 1982, s.15(1) and Schedule 4], it shall be capable of suing or being sued in its own name, whether in proceedings relating to property or founded on contract or tort or any other cause of action whatsoever; (*d*) proceedings for any offence alleged to have been committed by it or on its behalf may be brought against it in its own name; and (*e*) any judgment, order or award made in proceedings of any description brought against the trade union on or after the commencement of this section shall be enforceable, by way of execution, diligence, punishment for contempt or otherwise, against any property held in trust for the trade union to the like extent and in the like manner as if the union were a body corporate."

If the words "or be treated as if it were" were not in s.2(1), there would be absolutely no difficulty because all those powers which are attributed and given to trade unions make it quite clear that if they are, as the section would say, not a body corporate, they had the attributes of one and they were to be treated as one, so that they could possess the necessary personalities which they could protect by [an] action of defamation: but the words are there, and the words are saying that that is exactly what is not to be done. I do not find any ambiguity in them . . . .

The fact that it can sue in tort does not mean that it can complain of the tort of libel. That is procedural. The tort of libel, as I have already demonstrated, must be founded on possession of a personality which can be libelled and s.2(1) has removed that personality from trade unions. I find nothing in the statute to show that those words are ambiguous. There are many attributes which, but for the presence of the words "or be treated as if it were" in s.2(1), would simply confirm that a trade union enjoyed a quasi-corporate personality and could bring an action in libel in its own name for the protection of its own reputation, and, as I have said, I am quite clear that apart from the law anybody would say that a trade union has a separate reputation and should be entitled to protect it; but there it is. Parliament has deprived trade unions of the necessary personality on which an action for defamation depends;. . . .

Trade unions' susceptibility to actions in tort after 1901 was combined—until the Employment Act 1982—with their virtually complete immunity in tort (TULRA, s.14), so as to protect unions from the potentially damaging legal consequences of organising industrial action. The 1982 Act's repeal of the immunity in tort revives one issue at the heart of the problem of the legal status of trade unions: their liability for industrial action. The 1982 Act holds unions liable when their members' actions have been "authorised or endorsed by a responsible person," these persons being then listed (s.15) (see below pp. 600 *et seq*.). The notions of authorisation and endorsement were explored in a similar context in the following case which vividly illustrates the problems of the legal status of trade unions and their structural complexity.

Heatons Transport (St. Helens) Ltd. v. Transport and General Workers' Union
[1973] A.C. 15
House of Lords

The jobs of dock workers were threatened by the practice of loading and unloading containers outside the areas where registered dock workers had to be employed under the National Dock Labour Scheme. Accordingly, in 1971 the respondent union adopted an official policy that the loading and unloading of containers carried by sea should be reserved for dock workers, and that this would be achieved by "blacking" lorries of firms refusing to honour this policy. The lorries of the appellants, firms of road hauliers, were accordingly blacked at Liverpool and Hull docks under the direction of an unofficial committee of shop stewards representing dock and transport workers.

The appellants complained to the then National Industrial Relations Court that the blacking of their lorries constituted an unlawful industrial practice under the Industrial Relations Act 1971, s.96, and the union was ordered to restrain the blacking. The Court of Appeal allowed the appeal on the ground that the shop stewards, as the union's agents, were acting outside the scope of their authority in blacking the lorries, so that the union were not liable for their acts. The House of Lords reversed the Court of Appeal's decision.

Lord Wilberforce: The present cases all proceed on the same basis: that is that the action complained of has been taken on behalf of the union by committees of shop stewards and that the orders made against the union have been broken by these same committees, as agents of the union . . . .

. . . . The union's contention is that the only remedy is against the shop stewards: the appellants seek to made the respondent union responsible. The essential issue is therefore one of authority: the authority of the shop stewards to take the action complained of on behalf of the union. It is necessary to emphasise that this question has to be resolved exclusively within the context of the actual disputes before the court relating to particular acts in particular localities and on the evidence before it . . . .

. . . . The original source of the shop stewards' authority is the agreement entered into by each member by joining the Transport and General Workers' Union. By that agreement each member joins with all other members in authorising specified persons or classes of persons to do particular kinds of acts on behalf of all the members, who are hereafter referred to collectively as the union. The basic terms of that agreement are to be found in the union's rule book. But trade union rule books are not drafted by parliamentary draftsmen. Courts of law must resist the temptation to construe them as if they were; for that is not how they would be understood by the members who are the parties to the agreement of which the terms, or some of them, are set out in the rule book, nor how they would be, and in fact were, understood by the experienced members of the [National Industrial Relations Court]. Furthermore, it is not to be assumed, as in the case of a commercial contract which has been reduced to writing, that all the terms of the agreement are to be found in the rule book alone: particularly as respects the discretion conferred by the members upon committees or officials of the union as to the way in which they may act on the union's behalf . . . .

What is contended is that authority to act on behalf of the union in calling for any form of industrial action by any of its members is confined to the general executive council itself or to a national or regional trade group committee or regional or district committee to whom such authority has been expressly delegated by the general executive committee. The rules, it is suggested, do not allow such authority to be delegated to shop stewards, nor has any such delegation purported to be made.

This argument based upon the necessity for delegation of authority by the general executive council commended itself to Lord Denning M.R. and to Roskill L.J. in the Court of Appeal ([1972] 3 W.L.R. 73). There are passages in their judgments where the words "the union" are used so as to mean the general executive council and senior permanent officers at its headquarters. But questions of delegation from "the top," to use the phrase adopted by Roskill L.J. do not arise if authority to take industrial action has either expressly or implicitly been conferred directly upon shop stewards from "the bottom" ie the membership of the union, whose agreement is also the ultimate source of authority of the general executive council itself. One therefore looks first at the rule book to see what kinds of action the members of the union have expressly agreed may be taken on their behalf by shop stewards.

Shop stewards are elected by the membership in a defined working place and hold office for two years. Upon ratification of their election by the appropriate district committee and regional committee they are accredited officials of the union. Their credentials may be withdrawn by the regional committee or its authorised sub-committee, but only if the shop steward is not acting in accordance with the union rules and policy.

The purpose for which shop stewards are elected is described as that of "representing membership on matters affecting their employment." This is a phrase which is both wide and vague. No doubt their main concern is intended to be the particular industrial interests of the members of the union in the work places for which they are shop stewards. This has given rise to the suggestion that they play a "dual role," in that in respect of some acts done by them they are to be treated in law as agents for the union, but in respect of others as agents only for those members of the union by whom they have been elected as shop stewards. For the latter the union is said to be not responsible in law as their principal.

This concept of duality of roles is not one which would be likely to occur to trade unionists. The rules of the Transport and General Workers' Union themselves provide that "Shop stewards shall receive the fullest support and protection from the union." Even upon the lowest basis of individual self-interest—and there is no reason to suppose that members of trade unions are actuated by this alone—it may well be thought that an improvement in the earnings or conditions of employment of any group of members will make it easier to achieve improvements for other groups and ultimately for all the members. There is thus no a priori reason why the members of the union should not agree that shop stewards should be authorised by *all* the members to take action to promote the interests of members employed in a particular work place . . . .

The basic error which underlies the judgments of the two members of the Court of Appeal from whose conclusion Buckley L.J. ultimately did not feel he should dissent lies in their acceptance of the necessity to find some express delegation of authority from the top—a necessity which the union itself consistently and publicly disclaims.

The conclusion appears clear on the evidence, and was found by the Court and substantially accepted by Buckley L.J., that before the events in question there was a general implied authority for the shop stewards to protect their men's wages and jobs by blacking. It is now therefore appropriate to see exactly what was done in Liverpool and in Hull.

At Liverpool, the initiative was taken by a body known as the Merseyside Joint Committee of Dock Workers and Road Traffic Workers (the "joint committee"). This is a joint committee of shop stewards of the two sections of the respondent union concerned with the docks and with road haulage. It was formed in 1970 for a purpose not related to containerisation. It is described as "unofficial," a term which can be accepted so long as it means no more than that it is not a committee provided for in the union's rules but it operated from Transport House, Liverpool, the union's headquarters; its existence was known to the union at the highest level and its meetings were frequently attended by union officers. It was clearly formed because the union's formal committees were inadequate to provide for co-ordination of the local interests of the dockers' and road haulage groups . . . .

. . . . As in Liverpool there is also in Hull a shop stewards' committee which is "unofficial" in the sense that it is not provided for in the rules of the union but the existence of which is recognised by the union. The committee consists not only of the 27 shop stewards who are members of the union but also of nine shop stewards who are members of another union, the National Amalgamated Stevedores and Dockers Union—NASDU—to which a minority of the dockers in the Port of Hull belong. The chairman of the shop stewards committee is a Mr Cunningham who is one of the union shop stewards . . . .

The Hull Dock shop stewards called a mass meeting of dockers for May 8, which was attended by some 2,000 of them. Mr Shenton (the TGWU's regional secretary) asked to be allowed to speak and on behalf of the general executive council called upon those present to continue normal working . . . . He then left the meeting which was subsequently addressed by some of the shop stewards. At the end those present voted unanimously in favour of continuing the blacking. After the meeting Mr Cunningham told the press that there was no split between the union and the shop stewards "just a difference of opinion in the way they went about things." He added that the shop stewards could do things on an unofficial basis which the union could not do . . . .

On April 9, the shop stewards (at Liverpool) called and addressed a meeting of about 6,000 dock workers, all members of the union. It is obvious that the shop stewards were seeking support for the policy of continuing the blacking in spite of the Court orders. They got it. Although a great deal of evidence was filed after May 3, on behalf of the union there has never been any suggestion that at this meeting or at any other time the shop stewards intimated that they were acting without any authority from the union or indeed that the union was doing other than fully supporting their policy. Moreover, Mr Lloyd, the docks district secretary for Liverpool who was a full time officer of the union, attended that meeting. He never said anything to suggest that the union disapproved of the policy being advocated by the shop stewards, let alone that in urging it, the shop stewards were exceeding the authority conferred on them by the union. Indeed, he must have known that it was his union's attitude that "the shop stewards are the union" and no doubt were so regarded by themselves and all the other members.

The effect of this evidence is summarised in the statement made by the general secretary on television already quoted: "We don't call on shop stewards to obey the union—they are the union." . . .

Finally, it was suggested that the vote of the mass meeting of dockers held at Liverpool on April 9, 1972 in favour of continuing the blacking had produced the result that thereafter the shop stewards were not acting on behalf of the union but only on behalf of the dockers who attended the meeting. That shop stewards should ascertain the wishes of the members whose interests they represent cannot affect the authority conferred upon them by the members of the union as a whole. It may be mentioned that a similar arguement was put forward with regard to the mass meeting at Hull held on May 8: it is to be answered in the same way . . . .

Summary of Opinion

The effect of this opinion may be summarised as follows:

1. In accordance with the policy of devolution followed by the Transport and General Workers' Union, and consistently with its rules and practice, shop stewards of the union have a general implied authority to act in the interests of the members they represent and in particular to defend and improve their rates of pay and working conditions. They may do so by negotiation or by industrial action at the relevant place of work. They are not authorised to do any act outside union rules or policy.

2. It was at the material time union policy to retain work in connection with containers, ie stuffing and stripping (otherwise than at manufacturers' premises) for dock workers and to prevent other workers from doing such work.

3. Shop stewards representing dock workers had implied authority to take industrial action at their place of work in furtherance of this policy. This included the blacking of haulier firms.

4. The National Industrial Relations Court was fully entitled on the evidence to conclude that the union, through its shop stewards, had been guilty of an unfair industrial practice and to issue orders restraining the continuation of this practice.

Contrast *General Aviation Services (U.K.) Ltd.* v. *TGWU* [1976] I.R.L.R. 224 (H.L.), where the plaintiffs were prevented from fulfilling contracts with various airlines at Heathrow airport by blacking organised by an unofficial committee of shop stewards largely composed of TGWU members. The House of Lords held that since the TGWU's general policy was to settle the dispute by using established negotiating machinery and to avoid industrial action, the shop stewards lacked authority to take industrial action on behalf of the union, and therefore the TGWU could not be held legally responsible. Additionally, the committee was wholly unofficial and not part of the TGWU; moreover, it had never professed itself to be acting on behalf of the union and indeed had stressed the differences between its policies and those of official TGWU committees.

These two cases show how the sometimes fragmented structures of trade unions interact with complex questions of the legal status of unions and workplace organisations to create problems in determining liability for industrial action (*cf. Thomas* v. *NUM* (*S. Wales Area*) [1986] Ch. 20).

2. TRADE UNIONS AND THE STATE

(A) Trade Unions and the Role of the State

The relation of the State to trade unions has varied from overt antagonism, prior to 1871 when unions and many of their activities were liable to prosecution, to the toleration and, at times, encouragement that unions have enjoyed during the two World Wars and under the Labour governments of the 1960s and 1970s. The 100 years following 1871 were characterised by Professor Sir Otto Kahn-Freund as an abstention of law. In their evidence to the Royal Commission on Trade Unions and Employers' Associations 1965–1968 under the chairmanship of Lord Donovan, the TUC elaborated the "abstention of law" analysis.

"*Trades Union Congress, Evidence to the Royal Commission on Trade Unions and Employers' Associations 1965–1968,*" in TRADE UNIONS (W.E.J. MacCarthy ed. 1972), p. 366 at 368–369

In setting out the case for trade unionism in the first section of this evidence, it was pointed out that the essential characteristic of free trade unions is that they are responsible to the work people themselves who comprise their membership and cannot be directed by any outside agency. No State, however benevolent, can perform the function of trade unions in enabling work people themselves to decide how their interests can best be safeguarded. It is where trade unions are not competent and recognize that they are not competent to perform a function, that they welcome the State playing a role in at least enforcing minimum standards, but in Britain this role is recognized as the second best alternative to the development by work people themselves of the organization, the competence, the representative capacity, to bargain and to achieve for themselves satisfactory terms and conditions of employment. In general, therefore, because this competence exists, the State stands aside, its attitude being one of abstention, of formal indifference.

This general attitude of abstention on the part of the State arises, be it noted, from the competence of trade unions to safeguard the interests of their members. In other words, it is where this necessary protection is lacking that the State intervenes, because free collective bargaining is absent. Virtually all the traditional activities of the Ministry of Labour [now the Department of Employment] in the field of industrial relations can be described as complementary to free collective bargaining. Wages councils, covering some 3.8 million workers, are the embodiment of this principle: they exist because satisfactory bilateral machinery cannot be established. The difficult issues which arise regarding the role of the State concern the definition of what is complementary; in other words, which function trade union should welcome the State performing and which functions if performed by the State would detract from the independence of the trade union movement. Whether seeking legislation in a particular field is the most advantageous way for trade unions to proceed is a question which cannot be answered in the abstract.

However, the considerations outlined above are relevant to every particular issue, for example, to the examination of such questions as trade union recognition, developing trade union membership, workers' rights in regard to dismissals procedure, equal pay, minimum wages and the furtherance of industrial democracy.

In an article published very shortly after the death of Kahn-Freund, Roy Lewis suggested that the abstention theory was inadequate as an explanation of British labour law as it emphasised elements of equilibrium and consensus, instead of domination and conflict in British industrial relations.

R. Lewis, *"Kahn-Freund and Labour Law: An Outline Critique"* (1979) 8 I.L.J. 202

A generation of industrial relations students has been influenced by Kahn-Freund's concept of legal abstention which he refined and brilliantly elaborated in Ginsburg, *Law and Opinion in England in the 20th Century* (1959). Abstention of the law implied a bare minimum of State intervention in the individual employment relation, which was to be regulated instead by the autonomous collective organisations. It also implied a decidedly non-interventionist character for the laws affecting the collective labour relation. Hence the absence of laws regulating trade union organisational rights and recognition, the non-contractual status of collective agreements, and the purely consensual and non-compulsory incorporation of collectively agreed terms into the individual employment contract. The same policy was promoted by the general absence of direct legal sanctions in the State's efforts to encourage industrial peace by conciliation and arbitration and to extend collectively agreed terms, and by the principle that the success of a statutory wages council was to be judged by its abolition in favour of voluntary collective bargaining. The absence of a positive legal right to strike and the legal freedom to strike in the form of negatively expressed statutory immunities from judge-made liabilities were the supreme examples of abstentionism. This seemed particularly clear in the 1950s when judicial restraint apparently brought the historic conflict between the courts and Parliament to an end. . . .

It is important to show how Kahn-Freund's legal analysis was permeated by the pluralist assumptions of equilibrium, consensus and State neutrality.

Equilibrium, the idea of a rough balance of power as between the collective forces, was postulated as a pre-condition for collective bargaining and as part (conflict was the other part) of the explanation for the historical development, lack of development and peculiar structure of British labour law. Thus, the immunities of the Trade Disputes Act 1906 were passed "to restore balance in industrial relations." Similarly, the exceptional statutory protection for individual workers (health and safety legislation in the main) was needed as a "stop-gap where disequillbrium of social forces makes its (the law's) intervention inevitable." . . .

Consensus, according to Kahn-Freund, was at the root of legal abstention and the entire voluntarist system of industrial relations in Britain. The evolution of voluntary institutions and rules reflected a distinctive ideology, adopted first by the trade unions and then by employers, the civil service and eventually even by the judges, the ideology of collective laissez-faire. He related the shared belief in the virtue of collective autonomy to the growth of a broader social consensus—"the reduction in the area of 'disputes' and the constant enlargement of the area of the 'accepted' principles of social organisation." All this met with Kahn-Freund's approval and he praised legal abstention as a reflection of the "maturity" of British industrial relations. . . .

Legal abstention was a brilliant description of the comparatively non-interventionist nature of British labour law down to the mid-sixties. It was also, more questionably, a method of explaining the law's historical development or, more typically, lack of development. Clearly, Kahn-Freund did not suggest that the parties to collective bargaining and public policy-makers sat down one day and said, "Let's have a non-interventionist labour law and a belief in collective laissez-faire." Furthermore, in relating the general absence of statutory regulation (outside the health and safety field) to the industrial strength and preference of trade unions and to the growth of collective bargaining, he recognised conflict as a dynamic factor in historical development. The question is whether his emphasis on equilibrium and consensus led him to underestimate the overriding importance of such conflict. . . .

During the nineteenth and early twentieth centuries the trade unions campaigned for a legal minimum wage and a legal limitation on maximum hours for adult males (objects only finally deleted from the T.U.C.'s constitution in 1978), but relatively little success was achieved because the balance of class forces was decisively hostile. In general, expediency rather than a belief in collective laissez-faire determined the demarcation between legislative and autonomous regulation. Factory legislation was the main example of statutory intervention and strike law was perhaps the supreme example of legal abstention. In Ginsberg, Kahn-Freund depicted the development of the former as the gradual extension of protection across industry "in ever-widening circles" on a "trial and error basis." in the interests of social equilibrium. This interpretation was later modified in [Kahn-Freund's] *Labour and the Law*, where he described the nineteenth-century development as a product of the "hazards of pressures and counter-pressures." This formulation indicated his conception of reconcilable conflict between pressure groups as opposed to class struggles waged between movements with conflicting ideologies. The history of strike law down to the First World War he depicted as a "series of dramatic conflicts between Parliament and courts," whose attitudes "reflected that of the middle class." It seemed, however, that for Kahn-Freund the importance of class conflict in the law's development permanently waned around the 1920s. But what happened in the inter-war period was that organised labour's supposed threat to the system diminished in the aftermath of the General Strike and the Depression. Hence Wedderburn's insight that the "traditional framework of British labour law really rested upon a middle class acquiescence in the current balance of industrial power." The idea of the State maintaining equilibrium between the social forces through legal abstention was simply a myth.

Richard Hyman, writing as an avowed Marxist, focuses on the notion of State "neutrality" in the abstentionist explanation of British industrial relations.

R. Hyman, INDUSTRIAL RELATIONS: A MARXIST INTRODUCTION (1975), pp. 136–137, 142–143

Even in the heyday of "voluntarism," the role of the state in industrial relations was far from neutral—and not merely because abstention from the detailed processes of collective bargaining allowed the superior power of capital to structure the terms of the relationship with trade unionism.

Through a variety of institutional arrangements, the state facilitated the routine exploitation of wage-labour by capital; and on the rare occasions when the routine was seriously disrupted, it could intervene brutally and decisively . . . .

The ostensibly neutral functions of mediation and conciliation most recently embodied in the "independent" Advisory Conciliation and Arbitration Service—in fact serve the essential purpose, for both employers and the state, of stabilising the existing mode of production. Mediation by the state, moreover, "occurs in the shadow of its known and declared propensity to invoke its powers of coercion, against one of the parties in the dispute rather than the other, if "conciliation" procedures fail. This awareness necessarily structures the trade union response.

Thus "voluntarism" has always been more apparent than real. But in recent years, the development of interventionism in general economic affairs has been accompanied by a similar process in industrial relations—and for the same reasons. The contradictions which so clearly beset contemporary capitalism limit the available options in labour relations: hence more is now required of governments than that they merely stand on the sidelines ready to repel any challenge to the rules of the political economy of capital. In previous phases of capitalist development, periods of expansion allowed a sufficient margin of profitability for employers to conduct without serious difficulty their response to the (modest) aspirations of labour; while in period of recession, the unions were ill placed to cause trouble. Yet in an era of "managed" demand, relatively full employment sustains the economic power of labour at the same time as many firms face grave problems of profitability. . . .

A more general contradiction underlies relations between trade union and the state. Put simply, recent governments have been trapped by the tension between the opposing strategies of incorporation and repression. What is at issue here is [a] "trade-off" . . . . the accommodation between trade unionism and the external power of the state. Governments have come to appreciate that if union organisation is outside the law but cannot be suppressed—and in modern times, only the brutalities of fascism have succeeded in this—its policies are likely to be militant and disruptive, perhaps involving an explicit challenge to the political regime. Conversely, if unions are assigned legitimacy—through legal protection, consultation, representation on governmental committees, "honours" for individual leaders—they are likely to form a means of integrating the working class into capitalist society, thus serving as a mechanism of social control. The state has come to *depend* on collaborative relations with trade unionism; and this dependence is particularly great when the working class is strongly organised yet is adversely affected by government economic policies.

One strategy for accommodating trade unions, particularly in connection with demands for wage restraint, has been to promote the incorporation or integration of trade unions into the operations of industry and the State. This "corporatist" strategy was analysed in the article from which the following extract is taken.

L. Panitch, *"Trade Unions and the Capitalist State"* in (1981), 125 NEW LEFT REVIEW 21

. . . the state, especially where social-democratic governments were in office, set about, partly in response to the new demands coming from the unions themselves, to integrate lower levels of the movement right down to the shop floor more effectively. This took the form of progressive legislation and state-fostered managerial practices designed to facilitate union recognition in unorganized sectors and extend union membership in organized sectors; to foster workers' participation schemes in company boards and works councils (this time under the direct aegis of the unions), to institutionalize local level bargaining and shop-steward committees; and to provide a legal framework for qualitative issues (eg, health and safety), unfair dismissals and redundancy. In one way or another this was the direction of social democratic state industrial relations practices in Sweden, West Germany and Britain in the early and mid-1970s. These reforms were progressive, but they further enmeshed the trade unions in the legal apparatus of the state and institutionalized and juridified conflict on the shop floor. Moreover, combined with the eschewing by social-democratic governments of *statutory* incomes policies, and the programmatic bow made by social-democratic parties to some form of "investment planning," these reforms constituted the new *quid pro quo* for wage restraint under resuscitated corporatist political structures . . . .

. . . in Britain, the resuscitation of corporatism *via* the Labour Government—TUC "social contract" wage-norm negotiations in 1975–76, introduced the most sustained and draconian reduction of real wages (by 8% from 1974–75 to 1976–77) in the post-war period. Strikes correspondingly fell to their lowest levels, after the intense mobilization of industrial struggle over the previous six years, for well over a decade. As in Sweden, this demobilization occurred in the context of a wage norm designed to benefit the low-paid and the tying of the reduced wage demands to decreases in taxation. But in the context of rising unemployment and falling wages in general in Britain, this at best had the effect of redistributing very marginally the burden of increased exploitation.

Each of these corporatist wage policies were negotiated in years of national economic crisis of proportions unknown in the post-war period. And corporatist political structures became the vehicle for engineering, legitimating ("in the national interest") and administering the increase in exploitation which was necessary to sustain capital in the crisis.

An alternative strategy of repression or restriction is described in the following extract.

K.W. Wedderburn and J. Clark, *"Modern Labour Law: Problems, Functions and Policies"* in LABOUR LAW AND INDUSTRIAL RELATIONS, (Wedderburn, Clark and R. Lewis eds. 1982), at pp. 197–198

By the early 1980s sustained high levels of unemployment and low levels of output have weakened the traditional economic strength of British trade unions and in many respects the political climate has turned—or was made to turn—against the sectionalism, decentralization, and unplanned nature of traditional collective bargaining, looking to the state to restore social control and order. In such a situation there is a danger that the recognition of the growing politicization of industrial relations and labour law may lead on all sides (including the trade unions) to a growing reliance on the state and the law for "solutions" to Britain's social and economic crisis. Paradoxically that danger is not decreased by the fact that the present Conservative government would vehemently—and in formal terms justly—deny that it looks to "the state" when seeking answers to the crisis. It believes in the "market." However, a necessary part of its economic and social policy (what it would describe as reducing wages to a "realistic level"; what Professor Lord Kaldor has called "smashing wage resistance") is the attack upon effective trade unionism by repressive economic and, when needed, restrictive legal force (albeit that the latter is devised in the garb of muted immunities). This onslaught moves not only labour law but an ever wider range of social relations generally nearer to the heart of the "political"arena. If the disadvantaged—whether minority urban or ethnic groups, or workers whose social wage or opportunity for employment is reduced—see little hope for the future and resort to new and possibly more desperate measures, the government that rests on market forces will not be slow to call upon the resources of the state to uphold the "rule of law". And the law must be adequate for its purposes when the moment comes. Only in this setting can we fully appreciate the current otherwise curious concern about the illegality of "political" strikes, and the significance of the Conservative labour legislation of the eighties.

The danger of an over-reliance on the state and the law at a time of social and economic crisis, itself a constant theme of Kahn-Freund's writing to the end, remains a critical problem for labour law today. In this context the experience of the Social Contract [between the TUC and the Labour Government 1974–1977] leaves a major question unanswered: can the labour movement devise an alternative strategy which recognizes the need for increased state intervention in the economy while simultaneously guaranteeing the flexibility and self-determination afforded by decentralized control of economic power, autonomous collective bargaining, and independent trade unionism?

(B) Trade Unions' Political Activities

Trade unions have historically been major contributors to the development of the modern party political system, in particular by their financial assistance to and general support of the Labour Party. As one analysis put it (J. England and B. Weekes, "*Trade unions and the State: a review of the crisis*" (1981) Industrial Relations Journal 11, at pp. 21–22):

> "The unions' power within the Labour Party can be briefly stated. Over 90% of the votes cast at Labour's policy-making annual conference come from trade union delegates. Twelve of the 27 members of the party's national executive committee are trade union representatives. The unions also have a dominant voice, through the block vote, in the election of the five women members and the Party treasurer who also sit on the executive. Thus, 18 of the 27 places are controlled by the unions. Within the Parliamentary Labour Party, anything from a third to almost a half of the members (48 per cent. in 1979) are sponsored by trade unions. Most of the Party's finances come from the unions. Even so, the unions do not dominate the Party in quite the way all this suggests, for on many issues trade union votes are split. But rarely is this the case on legislation affecting themselves."

The unions' relationship with the Labour Party was initially and temporarily put in jeopardy by the House of Lords' decision in *Amalgamated Society of Railway Servants* v *Osborne* [1910] A.C. 87. This decision was reversed by the Trade Union Act 1913; and it is that statute which, subject to the amendments introduced by the Trade Union Act 1984, Pt. III, still regulates the way in which union funds may be devoted to political purposes.

The greatest difficulty in applying the Trade Union Act 1913 lies in deciding whether or not donations are for political purposes, a question which since 1975 is adjudicated by the Certification Officer. This is an inherent difficulty (*cf.* the not dissimilar problems that have arisen in attempts to differentiate trade and political disputes for the purpose of the "golden formula", see below, p. 588). The amendments made to the 1913 Act, s.3(3) by the 1984 Act are unlikely to alter matters.

Richards v. National Union of Mineworkers
[1981] I.R.L.R. 247
Certification Officer

Mr Richards, an NUM member, complained that the union had spent money from its general fund on matters which should have been paid for out of its political fund, including money to send union officials and members and a colliery band to participate in a march and a lobby of Parliament organised by the Labour Party, and had paid for newspaper advertisements to support this march and lobby.

THE CERTIFICATION OFFICER (MR. JOHN EDWARDS): . . . Mr Daly (the union's Secretary and Treasurer) was asked in cross-examination by Mr Richards, "It is a Labour Party campaign against the Government's policy. Do you think it is a political matter?" He replied, "It is political and industrial. That is why the trade union movement was involved". Later he amended that statement and said, "It could be construed as being partly political, but our view was that the objective was mainly an industrial and economic one". Lastly he said, "Payments were made from NUM funds, from the general fund, because of this industrial objective." In my view these remarks confirm that whatever other reasons there may have been for making the payments, there was also a political reason for doing so . . . .

The third question concerns the proviso to [the NUM's] rule 47(1)(e), which has the effect of excluding from the rule payments on the holding of a political meeting if the *main purpose* of the meeting is the *furtherance of the statutory objects* [in TULRA, s.28(1)], which includes the regulation of relations between workers and masters. There is, I think, a conceptual difficulty in applying this exclusion to meetings organised by someone other than the union making the payment since the exclusion is clearly most appropriate when the meeting is one organised by the union. In my view the words "main purpose of the meeting" mean that a subjective test must be applied, with the result that it is the main purpose of the organisers of the meeting which must be determined. Obviously, however, it will usually be necessary to have regard to what the meeting was about in order to decide what purpose or purposes the organisers had in mind.

Consequently where a union makes payments on the holding of a meeting organised by another person or body it is the purpose of that other person or body in organising the meeting which must be considered in deciding whether the statutory objects' exclusion applied, and not the purpose of the union in making the payments. This is perhaps unfortunate from the union's point of view because, although it is not impossible that persons or bodies other than the union should have the statutory objects as the main purpose of their meetings, they are in the nature of things less likely to do so.

The meetings which took place on 28 November were arranged by the Labour Party as part of a campaign against the policies of the Government. They were not organised by the Trade Union Congress or by the union although the lobby was supported by those bodies. In my view this means that the strong evidence given by Mr Daly and Mr Whelan (a member of the union's National Executive Committee) as to the union's reasons for participating in the events of 28 November is not relevant to deciding the main purpose of the meetings. Similarly the evidence in the letter of 1 November from the Trades Union Congress, which placed the main emphasis on the proposed local government cuts rather than on the wider issues which were of concern to the union, is also immaterial because it indicates the reasons which the TUC had for supporting the lobby. Consequently I consider that the main purpose of the meetings was political and was not the furtherance of the statutory objects . . . .

Coleman v. Post Office Engineering Union

[1981] I.R.L.R. 427
Certification Officer

In 1980 the Canterbury branch of the defendant union had affiliated to the Canterbury District Trades Council's campaign against the then Government's public spending cuts and its general economic policies; and it had paid the £8 affiliation fee out of its general funds. The campaign published a number of leaflets and held regular public meetings, and the plaintiff, a member of the defendant's Canterbury branch, alleged that the campaign's literature and meetings were "political" within the meaning of the union's rules. Accordingly, the affiliation fee should have been paid out of the union's political fund, and the plaintiff complained to the Certification Officer of the union's failure to do so in accordance with the Trade Union Act 1913, s.3.

The Certification Officer (Mr. Alan Burridge): Were the literature and meetings political? It is difficult to define "political". The [view of the Chief Registrar of Trade Unions, the predecessor of the Certification Officer] in [*Forster* v *National Amalgamated Union of Shop Assistants, Warehousemen and Clerks* Registrar's Report 1925, Part 4 was that, in the context of the 1913 Act, "political" meant the adjectival form of "party politics" and not of "policy". Mr Reynolds submitted he was right; but Mr Coleman argued that he was not because the word in the 1913 Act was simply "political", further he said that in the *Richards* case [above p. 430] the Certification Officer had used the term "political" rather than "party political" and in his opinion the Certification Officer's view was to be preferred.

So far as the *Richards* case is concerned, it seems clear to me that the Certification Officer used "political" rather than "party political" because the meetings in question were held by the Labour Party in protest against the policies of the Government and were therefore "political" on any interpretation of the word. There was no need for the Certification Officer to go into the precise meaning of political and I do not consider that he did so; accordingly Mr Coleman is, I am afraid, mistaken in thinking that the Certification Officer was disagreeing with the approach taken by the Chief Registrar in *Forster's* case.

I agree with the Chief Registrar's distinction but he did not define closely what he meant by "party political". Unfortunately this complaint demands that I must try to do so. Mr Reynolds submitted that "political" must be interpreted having regard to the mischief which the 1913 Act was intended to deal, that mischief being expenditure in relation to Parliamentary elections. I think that is a strong submission . . . .

Should the meaning of "political" extend beyond these narrow confines? It is difficult to see where wider boundaries can be set with any conviction. For example, it seems to me to be unsatisfactory to hold that opinions which support or oppose one or more of the various matters which form Government policy or policies of other political parties are by definition "political". I do not think it would be right to conclude that people expressing a view on matters of public concern—whether politically controversial or not—are necessarily expressing a "political" view. Nor do I think the strength with which it is expressed alters the position. If a campaign expresses a number of opinions which oppose or support those of a Government or political party it may be possible to identify its political stance and some of its views may have political overtones. But I cannot accept as a general proposition that it is always "political" in the terms of the 1913 Act for people merely to distribute literature or hold meetings at which views on matters of public concern are expressed. I do not however rule out that particular cases or particular circumstances could create exceptions to this conclusion.

I cannot say with certainty that the view which I have expressed on the meaning of "political" corresponds with the view of the Chief Registrar but I think it must be close to doing so. It is a view which imposes severe limitations in its application and it may invite scepticism in the world of today; but it is in my opinion the correct view in the light of the intention and meaning of the 1913 Act.

Turning to the facts of this case, I think many people would consider that the literature distributed and the meetings held by the campaign show an identifiable political standpoint. Some but by no means all the literature shows a bias against private industry and capitalism. The leaflet quoted in paragraph 10 invites industrial action and contains criticism directed at both the present Government and the previous Labour Government from a position more likely to appeal to those on the left of British politics.

However, on the view I take that [the union's] rule 25.1(e) relates to literature and meetings held by or in support of a political party, that is not enough. The heterogeneous nature of the campaign's constituents, and particularly its sponsorship by the Canterbury Trades Council and the active support from trade unions not affiliated to the Labour Party, coupled with the variety of its targets and professed aims, exclude its activities from falling within the definition of "political" which I have attempted [above]. Accordingly, while I understand the reasons why Mr Coleman considered the campaign to be political, in my view there was no distribution of political literature or holding of political meetings within the meaning of the 1913 Act or the [union's] rule [25.1(e)] and I therefore find the complaint not justified.

In the following case, the distinction established by *Coleman* was discussed by the E.A.T.

Association of Scientific, Technical and Managerial Staffs v. Parkin
[1983] I.R.L.R. 448
Employment Appeal Tribunal

The respondent, a member of the appellant union, complained that the union was in breach of its political fund rules made pursuant to the Trade Union Act 1913, s.3 by, *inter alia*, investing money from its general fund in the development of a new headquarters building for the Labour Party. The Certification Officer upheld the complaint. The union (referred to as "the Association" in the judgment) appealed.

BROWNE-WILKINSON J.: Mr Tabachnik (for the Union) first submits, and we accept, that the political objects defined by [the Trade Union Act 1913] s.3(3) and [the Association's] rule 36(a) (which we will call the "Political Fund objects") do not comprehend all possible political objects. He submits that the Political Fund objects are to be distinguished from other political objects in two ways: first, Political Fund objects are party political objects as opposed to more general political objects (eg procuring legislation relating to vivisection . . .).

Subject to a small (but important) point of terminology, we agree with Mr Tabachnik's first point of distinction. Ever since [*Forster* v *National Amalgamated Union of Shop Assistants, Warehousemen and Clerks* Registrar's Report 1925, Pt. 4], Political Fund objects have been treated as in general covering party political (as opposed to more general political) purposes. We think there is some danger in using terminology which equates Political Fund objects with *party* politics. In our judgment the Registrar in *Forster's* case was right to construe the Act against the background of the *Osborne* decision [[1910] A.C. 87] and therefore to treat s.3 and the Political Fund objects as concerned with parliamentary representation and other representation in public elected office. Thus each of the paragraphs in sub-sections (3) (except possibly para.(e)) is directed to the election of candidates, the conduct of election campaigns and the maintenance of a candidate when elected. Therefore we agree that the broad distinction is between political activity directed towards securing representation by a candidate in Parliament (or other public body) and other political purposes. Our objection is to labelling this "party" political purposes which suggests that the support of a parliamentary or other candidate who is not a member of any party does not fall within the Political Fund purposes. In our judgment it does. The distinction is between purposes connected with representation in Parliament and other purposes. Therefore, unless and until a Political Fund has been established, a union cannot support any parliamentary candidate, whether belonging to the Labour Party or any other party or to no party at all, and, after a Political Fund has been established, must support such candidate out of the Political Fund.

3. TRADE UNIONS AND EMPLOYERS

(A) Trade Union Independence

Trade unions exist to defend the interests of their members and to represent such interests against employers. So they should clearly not be subject to employers' domination or control. The law may encourage "independence" by making it a pre-condition of entitlement to statutory rights (*cf.* Employment Protection Act 1975, s.17.: the right to information, below pp. 478 *et seq.*; s.99: the right to be consulted over redundancies, below p. 128; EPCA, ss.27–28: the right to time off work for union activities, below pp. 487 *et seq.*; EPCA, ss.23 and 58: protection against anti-union discrimination, pp. 438 *et seq.*). But insofar as trade unions need certificates of independence from a State official in order to benefit from legal rights (let alone to exist as unions, as under the Industrial Relations Act 1971), there is scope for disputes over the State's definition of "independence".

Certificates of independence are available from the Certification Officer, an independent official appointed by the Secretary of State for Employment (EPCA, ss.7–8). These certificates are granted in accordance with certain criteria which have subsequently been approved by the Employment Appeal Tribunal (*Association of HSD (Employees)* v. *Certification Officer* [1977] I.R.L.R. 261).

Certification Officer, *First Annual Report* 1976

2.16 The following paragraphs set out the principal criteria which the [Certification] Office has used in applying the statutory definition to individual cases

2.17 *History* Sometimes evidence is found that the union began with employer support and encouragement, or even as a creature of management. If that evidence relates to the recent past it is a powerful argument against the grant of a certificate. But experience indicates that over time some unions can and do evolve from a dependent to an independent state; and the decision must, of course, be based on the facts as they are at the time of the investigation and not as they were several years ago.

2.18 *Membership base* From the outset the Office has taken the view that a union whose membership is confined to the employees of one employer is, on the face of it, more vulnerable to employer interference than a broadly-based union. This is less likely to be a critical factor for a large, well-established union backed up by strong resources than for a small, weak, newly-founded organisation. In fact certificates have been issued to a number of single company unions which appear on all the available evidence to be capable of withstanding any pressure which might be brought to bear on them by the employer. Experience has confirmed that a narrow membership base may make the union's task of proving its independence more difficult but that it does not make it impossible.

2.19 *Organisation and structure* It is necessary to examine these both as they are set out in the union's rule book and as they work in practice. The main requirement is that the union should be organised in a way which enables the members to play a full part in the decision-making process and excludes any form of employer involvement or influence in the union's internal affairs. Particular attention is paid to whether employers or senior employees, especially those at or immediately below board level, are eligible to belong to the union and, if so, whether there are suitable restrictions on the part which they can play in its affairs.

2.20 *Finance* While it is exceptional to find evidence of a direct monetary subsidy from employer sources, a union with weak finances and inadequate reserves is obviously more likely to be vulnerable to employer interference than one whose financial position is strong. Particular attention is therefore paid to such questions as the main sources of the union's income, whether this matches its expenditure, the level of its subscription rate and the state of its reserves.

2.21 *Employer-provided facilities* These take the form of premises, time off and office or other services which the union receives from employer sources. In the case of single company unions the normal practice is to cost these items in order to get a rough idea of the extent of the union's reliance on them in financial terms. But it is not just a question of finance. It is necessary to look too at the administrative convenience of having facilities provided by the employer, even if they are paid for, and how easy or difficult the union would find it to cope on its own if they were withdrawn. The greater the union's reliance on such facilities the more vulnerable it must be to employer interference.

2.22 The provision of facilities is, of course, common practice among good employers, but in the context of independence its significance may vary according to circumstances. A distinction can properly be drawn between a broadly-based union, which could continue to function even if an employer withdrew facilities from one or more of its branches, and a single company union which might well find it difficult or even impossible to carry on at all if such action were taken by the firm which employs its entire membership.

2.23 *Collective bargaining record* This is almost always an important consideration. While a weak record does not indicate dependence, a strong record and the display of a robust attitude in negotiation are items on the credit side which may outweigh other factors unfavourable to the union's case. In assessing the record account must be taken of such factors as the limitations on the scope for collective bargaining imposed by incomes policy and the particular environment in which the union operates—for example, the kind of employer with whom it negotiates and the traditions and attitudes of the employees whom it represents.

2.24 This is the point at which independence and effectiveness overlap. The two concepts are not of course identical. A union is not necessarily dependent just because it cannot supply its members with the full range of services which major unions normally provide. But it is equally clear that an effective union is more likely to be independent than an ineffective one.

2.25 None of the factors listed above can be decisive by itself. It is necessary to look at the whole nature and circumstances of the union and then make a judgment about whether or not it satisfies the statutory definition. Because there is no convenient yardstick which can supply a ready-made answer there must often be a subjective element in the decisions, especially where the arguments for and against independence are finely balanced.

Association of HSD (Hatfield) Employees v. Certification Officer
[1977] I.R.L.R. 261
Employment Appeal Tribunal

The appellant association had been refused a certificate of independence by the Certification Officer under EPCA, s.8 on the grounds that although it satisfied the requirement in TULRA, s.30(1)(*a*), namely, that it was not under the domination or control of an employer, it failed to satisfy the requirement in section 30(1)(*b*), namely, that it was "not liable to interference by an employer . . . (arising out of the provision of financial or material support or by any other means whatsoever) tending towards such control''. The appellant's appeal to the E.A.T. was allowed.

KILNER BROWN J. It will be seen at once that the test is one which is strictly confined and may appear to be unduly restrictive in so far as the granting of a certificate is concerned. We recognise, as the Certification Officer has recognised, that the law does not permit an examination of the consequences of granting a certificate or whether in all the circumstances it is reasonable to grant a certificate. We do, however, unanimously support the Certification Officer in his contention that he ought to apply the definition strictly and place the burden fully upon the aspiring trade union to satisfy him or us that it can claim to be truly independent. In this context it is proper to bear in mind that no one (and that goes for both the whole body of employers and the trade union movement) wishes to see a proliferation of small bodies claiming the rights and privileges of a trade union. Still less does anyone want to see a large number of what have been termed ''splinter'' unions. On the other hand Parliament clearly recognises the right of a group of individuals to band together. What Parliament will not tolerate is the recognised and certificated existence of a band of people claiming to be an independent trade union when in reality they are unable to offer a vigorous challenge to the employers on behalf of their members whether collectively or individually.

So we turn to a detailed examination of the definition in s.30(1) of the Trade Union and Labour Relations Act. It is plain that the two sub-sections envisage a somewhat different approach, or, put another way, involve a double test. Under sub-section (a) an aspiring trade union seeking certification may fail at the first hurdle. It may be, as a question of existing fact, under the domination or control of the employer. However, even if it succeeds in surmounting that obstacle it still has to show in addition that it is not liable to interference by an employer tending towards such control. What does this mean? Whereas it may be in most cases perfectly simple to decide whether or not domination or control is there, it seems to us that liability to interference tending towards such control may be as difficult to decide as the other is simple. It involves a forward look and perhaps a degree of speculation. Certain tests and methods of appraisal with reference to the application of the definition have been followed by the Certification Officer and were approved by the Employment Appeal Tribunal in *Blue Circle Staff Association v Certification Officer* [1977] IRLR 20. They need not be repeated here. However, we are of the opinion that whereas they are valid and helpful in considering whether or not there is a domination in fact (which was the issue in the *Blue Circle* case) they may be neither helpful nor appropriate in considering whether or not there is liability to interference tending to such domination.

The courts have established that the question of trade union's freedom from an employer's domination or control is to be answered by reference to the union's vulnerability to interference; the factual question, whether such interference has actually occurred, does not need to be investigated; if the union is vulnerable, it is not independent (*Squibb United Kingdom Staff Association* v. *Certification Officer* [1979] 2 All E.R. 452 (C.A.)).

The principal question as to ''independence'' arises when ''staff associations'' apply for certification. The following extract is from a study which covered 88 organisations with a membership of about

190,000 which applied for certificates of independence between February 1, 1976 and December 31, 1978.

Supplement to the Annual Report of the Certification Officer (1979)

> . . . as commonly used "staff association" describes an organisation with two principal characteristics. First, its membership is confined to employees of a single employer (or associated employers) and these employees are almost always in non-manual or white-collar occupations. Second, it is not regarded—and often does not regard itself—as a trade union in the traditional sense and stands apart from main-stream trade unionism even if not actually hostile to it.
>
> "Staff association" is sometimes used in a wider sense to describe white-collar employee organisations in the public sector, *eg* in the Civil Service or the Police. More usually, however, the term refers to private sector employment . . . .
>
> The principal characteristic shared by all of the 88 associations is their narrow membership base. On the face of it, this is a serious obstacle to effective trade unionism. An organisation whose membership is confined to the employees of a single employer is exposed to pressures which are much less effective against a broadly based organisation; it will find it correspondingly more difficult to bargain on equal terms with that employer, particularly if the size of the undertaking places strict limits on its membership and financial resources and means that it must rely for its administration entirely on part-time officers employed by the company. Although such organisations can operate at low cost, with subscription rates far below those of competing unions, they are poorly protected against unexpected hostility from a previously benevolent employer.
>
> It is true that there are TUC unions which have all or almost all their membership in the employment of a single nationalised industry and are in no way inhibited by that fact; but these are mostly much larger bodies and have very different histories and traditions. The evidence in Chapter 2 shows that more than half of the 88 associations were actually created or inspired by management or received active encouragement from them in the early stages of their existence; this encouragement went beyond what would be expected of an employer simply prepared to respect the wishes of his staff, and is in marked contrast to traditional management attitudes to the development of white-collar unionism in many industries. Such origins may combine with the pressures already mentioned to make it even more difficult for an association to assume an effective negotiating role—some indeed never reach that stage.

(B) Freedom of Association

By virtue of ownership of the workplace and rights arising from workers' contracts of employment, the employer can curtail unions' activities on his premises. Workers' rights of free association require that employers' powers should be restricted where otherwise their exercise would prevent union activities. Legal proceedings play a relatively small part in protecting workers' freedom of association against employer interference. This is well illustrated by the paucity of decisions under the EPCA, s.77, which allows a special procedure of interim relief for complaints of dismissal for trade union reasons. Industrial action is traditionally the more usual response to challenges to union autonomy (*cf.* Chapter 13). Here, however, we focus on the statutory provisions in EPCA, ss.23 and 58, which seek to prohibit anti-union action by employers.

(i) Protection against victimisation by reason of union membership

EPCA, s.58(1)(*a*) declares unfair a dismissal by reason that the employee "was, or proposed to become, a member of an independent trade union." Section 23(1)(*a*) grants employees a right to complain about employer action short of dismissal, taken "for the purpose of preventing or deterring [them] from being or seeking to become member[s] of an independent trade union or penalising [them] for doing so." The following case reveals what some judges perceived as the policy behind this legislation and also a lamentable inability to implement that policy.

Therm-A-Stor Ltd. v. Atkins
[1983] I.R.L.R 78; [1983] I.C.R. 208
Court of Appeal

After some 60 to 65 of the employer's 70 employees joined a union, they met the union's district secretary and asked him to apply to the company for recognition, which he did on the next day. The company responded by dismissing 20 employees immediately, including Mr Crutchley. The selection was made by the chargehands, and some of those dismissed were not union members.

SIR JOHN DONALDSON M.R.: The Industrial Tribunal rejected the respondents' claims because although the reason for all four dismissals was reaction to the attempt by the union to obtain recognition, each of the four were selected for dismissal by chargehands who did not take any account of actual or proposed union membership or actual or proposed participation in union activities by those employees concerned. Accordingly the Industrial Tribunal considered that none of the four could show that the reason for his dismissal was *his* union membership or activities.

The EAT took a different view. Their reasoning is set out at the end of the judgment delivered by Mr Justice Phillips in the following terms:

> ". . . . Assume Mr Crutchley was not a member of the union. One asks oneself. 'Why was he dismissed?' The answer is that he was dismissed because the district secretary wrote the letter on 28 April, the general purport and tenor of which we have already sought to summarise. One can translate that and say that the reason for Mr Crutchley's dismissal was the involvement of the trade union; and so he would be dismissed, albeit he was not a member of the union, because of the involvement by way of reprisal for the involvement of the trade union. Well, obviously, he cannot complain in the terms of EPCA, s.58 that he was dismissed for the reason that he was, or proposed to become, a member of the union or that he had taken part or proposed to take part in the activities of an

> independent trade union: because he neither had nor did. However, if one contrasts his position with that of one of the other appellants (or, indeed, with his own position as it would be if he was a member of the trade union) surely, it can be said of him that the reason for his dismissal was that he was, or proposed to become, a member of a trade union or had taken, or proposed to take, part in the activities of a trade union? Any other conclusion, it seems to us, would put an extraordinarily narrow construction upon s.58 and render it wholly inoperative in many instances where it must have been intended to apply."

As I see it, the first question for consideration is whether the fact that the chargehands undertook the selection for dismissal means that the chargehands' reason—probably last-in, first-out—was the reason for the men's dismissal. Mr Tabachnik [counsel for the employees] submits that so to conclude is to confuse the reason for dismissal with the basis for selection. As he rightly points out they are two quite different things and are so treated in s.59 of [EPCA] in relation to redundancy. Where redundancy is the reason for the dismissal, the dismissal is not necessarily unfair. However, the method of selection for dismissal can make the dismissal unfair. For my part I think that this is right and that the intervention of the chargehands can be disregarded as being concerned solely with selection and not with the reason for dismissal.

So far so good, but the respondents still have obstacles in their way. The Industrial Tribunal did not find [that] the employers or Mr Morris [the managing director] decided to dismiss the group of twenty men because any or all of them had joined the union or proposed to do so or had taken part in union activities or proposed to do so. He decided to dismiss them by way of reaction to the union's letter seeking recognition. The reason for the dismissals was the union's plea for recognition.

Mr Tabachnik seeks to overcome this obstacle by submitting that s.58 should be construed in such a way as to recognise what he called its "collective dimension". In his submission membership of a trade union is not a solo activity—it assumes other members. Similarly it is difficult, if not impossible, to take part in the activities of a trade union unless others do so. The whole concept of union activities has an essentially plural basis. Accordingly if the respondents were members of a wider group—they were all in fact members of the TGWU—and the reason for the dismissals was the activities of that group, it follows, as he submits, that the reason for their dismissal was their union membership or activities, albeit with others.

I regard this as a valiant attempt at purposive construction of the statute, but in my judgment it goes beyond permissible limits. As I read the section it is concerned solely with the dismissal of *an* employee and provides that it shall be regarded as unfair if the reason was that *the* (ie "*that*") employee had done or proposed to do one or more specified things. The reason why each of the respondents was dismissed had nothing to do with anything which the respondent concerned has personally done or proposed to do. The section therefore has no application.

The EAT describe this as a narrow construction and said that the section, so construed, would be rendered wholly inoperative in many instances where it must have been intended to apply. If by this they meant that some protection should be given to new employees if their jobs may be put at risk merely because a trade union has applied for recognition, I would not dissent. Indeed I would go further and agree that in such circumstances the union has a justifiable grievance. It is at risk of suffering considerable damage. If an employer can act in this way with impunity, employees in other factories might well hesitate before joining a union. I also agree with the EAT that it is the duty of the courts to give effect to the intentions of Parliament. However, the concept that Parliament "must have intended" a particular result is not without its dangers. If regard is had solely to the apparent mischief and the need for a remedy, it is only too easy for a judge to persuade himself that Parliament must have intended to provide the remedy which he would himself have decreed if he had had legislative power. In fact Parliament may not have taken the same view of what is a mischief, may have decided as a matter of policy not to legislate for a legal remedy or may simply have failed to realise that the situation could ever arise. This is not to say that statutes are to be construed in blinkers or with narrow and legalistic literalness, but only that effect should be given to the intentions of Parliament as expressed in the statute, applying the normal canons of construction for resolving ambiguities or any lack of clarity.

Tempted as I am to provide the respondents with a remedy for what was an indefensible reaction to a simple request for union recognition, which could have been granted or politely refused, I cannot construe s.58 as being intended to deal with such a situation. The section is not concerned with an employer's reactions to a trade union's activities, but with his reactions to an individual employee's activities in a trade union context.

With regret, I would allow the appeal and restore the decision of the Industrial Tribunal.

Judicial confusion is also evident in the litigation over the decision of the Conservative Government to ban employees at Government Communications Headquarters in Cheltenham from trade union membership. On the one hand, the judges were prepared narrowly to interpret ILO Conventions Nos. 87 (1948), 98 (1949) and 151 (1978) guaranteeing freedom of association (see, for example, Glidewell J. in [1984] I.R.L.R. 309 (H.C.), at paras. 95–108, and Lord Lane L.C.J. in [1984] I.R.L.R. 353 (C.A.), at paras. 44–51), or simply refuse to regard them as relevant (dealt with under "minor" matters by Lord Fraser of Tullybelton in [1985] I.R.L.R. 28 (H.L.) at para. 26); *cf.* the contrary finding of the Committee on Freedom of Association of the Governing Body of the ILO dated June 1, 1984. On the other hand the House of Lords was prepared to hold as follows.

R. v. The Secretary of State and Foreign and Commonwealth Affairs, ex p. Council of Civil Service Unions

[1985] I.R.L.R. 28
House of Lords

Until January 25, 1984, the staff of the Government Communications Headquarters (GCHQ) had the right under their terms and conditions of employment to be trade union members. Six unions were represented at GCHQ, all of which were members of the Council of Civil Service Unions. On December 22, 1983, the Prime Minister, in her capacity as Minister for the Civil Service, ordered that the conditions of service be revised so as to exclude membership of any trade union, citing national security reasons. This order was implemented on January 25, 1984. The unions were not informed of the Government's decision and sought a declaration that the instruction issued varying the conditions of service was invalid.

Lord Fraser: It is clear that the employees did not have a legal right to prior consultation. The [Civil Service] Order in Council [1982] confers no such right, and article 4 [of the Order] makes no reference at all to consultation. The Civil Service handbook (*Handbook for the new civil servant*, 1973 ed. as amended 1983) which explains the normal method of consultation through the departmental Whitley Council, does not suggest that there is any legal right to consultation; indeed it is careful to recognise that, in the operational field, considerations of urgency may make prior consultation impracticable. The Civil Service Pay and Conditions of Service Code expressly states:

> "The following terms and conditions also apply to your appointment in the Civil Service. It should be understood, however, that in consequence of the constitutional position of the Crown, the Crown has the right to change its employees' conditions of service at any time, and that they hold their appointments at the pleasure of the Crown."

But even where a person claiming some benefit or privilege has no legal right to it, as a matter of private law, he may have a legitimate expectation of receiving the benefit or privilege, and, if so, the courts will protect his expectation by judicial review as a matter of public law. . . .

The test of that is whether the practice of prior consultation of the staff on significant changes in their conditions of service was so well established by 1983 that it would be unfair or inconsistent with good administration for the Government to depart from the practice in this case. Legitimate expectations such as are now under consideration will always relate to a benefit or privilege to which the claimant has no right in private law, and it may even be to one which conflicts with his private law rights. In the present case the evidence shows that, ever since GCHQ began in 1947, prior consultation has been the invariable rule when conditions of service were to be significantly altered. Accordingly in my opinion if there had been no question of national security involved, the appellants would have had a legitimate expectation that the Minister would consult them before issuing the instruction of 22.12.83. . . .

Lord Diplock: *Prima facie*, therefore, civil servants employed at GCHQ who were members of national trade unions had, at best, in December 1983, a legitimate expectation that they would continue to enjoy the benefits of such membership and of representation by those trade unions in any consultations and negotiations with representatives of the management of that government department as to changes in any term of their employment. So, but again *prima facie* only, they were entitled, as a matter of public law under the head 'procedural propriety', before administrative action was taken on a decision to withdraw that benefit, to have communicated to the national trade unions by which they had theretofore been represented the reason for such withdrawal, and for such unions to be given an opportunity to comment on it . . . .

Lord Roskill: My Lords, if no question of national security were involved I cannot doubt that the evidence and the whole history of the relationship between management and staff since 1919 shows that there was a legitimate expectation of consultation before important alterations in the conditions of service were made. No doubt in strict theory civil servants are dismissible at will and the various documents shown to your Lordships seek to preserve the strict constitutional position. But in reality the management-staff relationship is governed by an elaborate code to which it is unnecessary to refer in detail. I have little doubt that were management to seek to alter without prior consultation the terms and conditions of civil servants in a field which had no connection whatever with national security or perhaps, though the matter does not arise in this appeal, with urgent fiscal emergency, such action would in principle be amenable to judicial review.

Despite their Lordship's unanimous recognition of the GCHQ employees' legitimate expectations of union membership and consultation over proposed changes in their terms and conditions of employment, the House of Lords conceded that the Ministerial order could not be challenged in view of national security.

The *GCHQ* case and *Therm-A-Stor* v. *Atkins* (above p. 438) illustrate the low priority which the judiciary give to the collective dimension of freedom of association. However, in *Ridgway and Fairbrother* v. *National Coal Board* [1987] I.R.L.R. 80 (C.A.) refusal of a pay increase to the N.U.M. was held to be action short of dismissal taken against individual members of that union contrary to EPCA, s.23(1)(*a*) because it affected the plaintiffs both as union members and as individuals.

(ii) What are the protected "activities of an independent trade union": managerial prerogatives v. unlawful discrimination

Trade union activity often involves opposition to the employers' policies and practices. Such opposition may be inconsistent with the common law of employment which implies obedience into every contract of employment. The judges need to draw the line between "misconduct" (work-related) and "trade union activities" (non-work-related). Employers acting against the former are legitimately exercising management prerogatives. Employers acting against the latter are unlawfully discriminating against trade unionists. The policy problem is that by giving a wide interpretation to "activities of an independent trade union," the employer's control of the workplace is reduced. The dilemma facing judges and Tribunals is apparent in the following extracts. The temptation is to regard shop stewards as acting "on their own" and not on behalf of the union.

Stoke and Roberts v. Wheeler-Green Ltd.
[1979] I.R.L.R. 211
Industrial Tribunal

Miss Roberts was Mother of the Chapel at the Women's Branch of SOGAT at the employer's establishment, and Miss Stokes was the unofficial Chairman of the Chapel. There was a prolonged series of disputes and incidents between them and the management. In the last of these, Miss Roberts, with the support of Miss Stokes, refused the instruction to work a particular machine, claiming the instruction violated a rota agreement. They were both dismissed and claimed that they had been victimised because of their trade union activities. (The Code of Practice on Disciplinary Practice and Procedures (1977) para. 15(*b*) recommend that disciplinary action other than oral warnings should not be taken against part-time union officials without prior discussion of the circumstances with full-time officials of the union.)

London Industrial Tribunal (chairman: G.E. Heggs): *The applicants' case*: It is the applicants' contention that as chapel officers they were promoting the interests of their members in pursuit of their equal pay claim and grievances in relation to the distribution of work and other matters, and that because of their activities they were deliberately harrassed by Mr Connolly [the works director] and eventually their dismissal was contrived by the giving of an instruction which they would be known to refuse because they would be bound to dispute it. The applicants had been employed for seven years and they had received no written warning before the day of their dismissal and Miss Stokes had not even received a verbal warning. The dismissals were effected without prior consultation with the union as is necessary for the dismissal of chapel officers and on a day when Mr Green [the employer's managing director] was known to be away and after he had already prepared the procedure which would lead to their dismissal on the following day. The offence for which they were dismissed was a trivial offence because Miss Roberts had agreed to work the MBO [machine] and if Mrs Ellis had been assigned to work on the Brehmer [machine] nothing would have been lost and the genuine dispute as to the construction of the rota agreement could have been resolved by subsequent negotiation. Their summary dismissal that day for that reason was unjustified and should only have been carried out after prior consultation with SOGAT who would then have been able to investigate the basis of the complaint and have entered into negotiations with the respondents.

The respondents' case: It is the respondents' contention that the dismissals on 7.6.78 were the culimination of a series of events in which the applicants had shown themselves to be obstructive and unco-operative. The respondents' business entails flexibility in working machines which is assured to them by the collective agreement, it is a small business where the activities of three women acting in combination was disruptive of any form of planning and productive output and created an unhappy working atmosphere not only for the respondents but for all other employees. The applicants were acting on their own initiative without formal approval of the chapel and without the support of the union. The conduct was persisted in over a long period of time and the applicants were aware that refusal to work a machine as instructed would lead to their dismissal and by their conduct they provoked it.

What view we take upon the opposing contentions depends upon the view we take of the evidence as a whole. We have no doubt that Miss Roberts and Miss Stokes acted in what they conceived to be the interests of the women working in the factory and that some of the issues we have considered may have been seen by them in a different perspective. The work was undoubtedly hard and the constant changing of duties may often have appeared to them to be unreasonable and unnecessary. Within the limitations of the type of business which the respondents were running they appeared to us to have been satisfactory employers. They were not opposed to union activities and they had a proper working relationship with SOGAT. They were not inflexible in their attitude and they negotiated an increase in the women's wage rates to reflect the difficult working conditions. They did not refuse time off for union activities although they felt that the right was being abused, they introduced a management/chapel officers' meeting to enable grievances on any issue to be ventilated. We accept that an informal rota was introduced and maintained by the respondents for the purpose of fairly allocating duties between the women and it is our belief that the respondents endeavoured to operate it as fairly as the nature of the daily work permitted.

Were the applicants dismissed for an inadmissible reason? If it is established that the principal reason for the dismissal was that the applicants had taken part at an appropriate time in the activities of an independent Trade Union their dismissal is to be regarded as having been unfair under para. 6(4)(b) of Schedule 1 to [TULRA, now EPCA, s.58(1)(*b*)]. However, as Mr Justice Phillips pointed out in *Lyon and anor v St James Press Ltd* [1976] IRLR 215:

> "When an applicant who is alleging unfair dismissal has been engaged in trade union activities at the time of the events leading up to the dismissal and there is a connection between those activities and the conduct alleged by the employer to have justified dismissal in the terms of [EPCA, s.57(3)] the Industrial Tribunal hearing the case has a difficult task. The marks within which the decision must be made are clear: the special protection afforded by [EPCA, s.58(1)(*b*)] to trade union activities must not be allowed to operate as a cloak or an excuse for conduct which ordinarily would justify dismissal; equally, the right to take part in the affairs of a trade union must not be obstructed by too easily finding acts done for that purpose to be a justification for dismissal. The marks are easy to describe, but the channel between them is difficult to navigate."

Accordingly, following *Brennan and Ging v Ellward (Lancs) Ltd* [1976] IRLR 379 and *Dixon and Shaw v West Ella Developments Ltd* [1978] IRLR 151 we must consider which of the acts and facts relied upon in this particular case could be said to constitute activities of an independent trade union. The purpose of [EPCA, s.58(1)(*b*)] is to protect shop stewards and union members carrying on activities such as recruiting members, collecting subscriptions and convening meetings at an appropriate time and it is also apt to cover seeking advice from a union representative on the shop floor upon an industrial issue arising in the course of work and perhaps also a shop steward seeking advice on the telephone from a union official. In this instance we find that while Miss Roberts, Mrs Ellis and Miss Stokes were chapel officers and were acting in concert to promote what they considered to be the interests of their members, they were acting entirely on their own initiative without the endorsement of a chapel meeting. They did not seek to raise their grievances with management in a constitutional manner before embarking upon a course of industrial action. It is questionable whether their actions and attitude had the support of the majority of the members of the women's chapel and it is just as likely that they were representing only themselves in the action which they took and which could not be described in any sense as applying approved union practices. As was pointed out in *Chant v Aquaboats Ltd* [[1978] I.C.R. 643 (E.A.T.) [EPCA, s.58(1)(*b*)] does not read 'activities as an independent 'trade unionist' and the mere fact that one or two employees making representations happen to be trade unionists and that their spokesman happens to be a trade unionist does not make such representations a trade union activity.

In our view [EPCA, s.58(1)(*b*)] does not confer protection upon trade union members or even chapel officers who carry out unconstitutional action such as walking out without notice or refusing to carry out instructions to work in accordance with the provisions of a collective agreement incorporated as a term of their contract of employment. The action of the women in walking out on 6.6.78 was unwarranted by any standard and they were not justified in their refusal to work the machines instructed on 7.6.78 even though they may have had a genuine disagreement on construction of the rota agreement.

This was an issue which should have been resolved later by constitutional means. We accordingly find that the applicants have failed to establish that they were dismissed for taking part in the activities of an independent trade union nor was that the respondents' motive for the dismissal.

We find that the reason for the dismissal was that the applicants had over a long period adopted a concerted practice of resistance to management culminating in their walking out on 6.6.78 and refusing to work as instructed on 7.6.78 in breach of their contracts of employment. The applicants were not dismissed because of their trade union membership or because of the part they had taken in the activities of SOGAT. The applicants were accordingly dismissed for a reason related to their conduct within [EPCA, s.57(2)(*b*)].

The Marley Tile Co. Ltd v. Shaw

[1978] I.R.L.R. 238; [1978] I.C.R. 828; [1980] I.R.L.R. 25; [1980] I.C.R. 72
Employment Appeal Tribunal and Court of Appeal

Mr Shaw was nominated and approved as a shop steward by his union, the AUEW, and shortly afterwards was representing a member of his on a grievance when management informed him that they were not prepared to accept him as a shop steward. He then said he was going to call a meeting of the maintenance men he represented and also telephone the union's full-time official, Mr Garwell. Whilst telephoning the latter, one of his members met other workers who organised a meeting which resulted in a one-hour stoppage of work. This led to Mr Shaw's dismissal. An Industrial Tribunal found the dismissal unfair, and this was upheld by a majority in the Employment Appeal Tribunal, but reversed by the Court of Appeal.

Phillips J. (in the E.A.T.:) . . . . We summarise our understanding of what the Industrial Tribunal have found as follows: that Mr Shaw was dismissed for taking part in the following activities of an independent trade union, namely, taking up the grievance of the fitter, seeing and pressing for the meeting with the employers, and upon leaving that meeting calling together the maintenance men, which must have involved their leaving their work . . . [W]e have no doubt that the Industrial Tribunal were right in concluding that Mr Shaw was taking part in the activities of an independent trade union. . . .

. . . All we are concerned with is the case of a few maintenance men who were called together for what would, had things not gone wrong, have been only a short meeting, and there is no evidence that their coming together caused any disorganisation or difficulty, or that their duties were disrupted. Circumstances might well be different where what was done was with the intention of disrupting the production process. It seems to us to be all a matter of degree.

Goff L.J. (in the C.A.): The Tribunal, in paragraph 3, reviewed the situation as a whole in what they termed a broad brush approach. I read two passages taken from paragraph 13 on page 32: "Now we can see that the management was worried that Mr Shaw might be injecting a sour tone into relations at the factory. Mr Shaw had adopted a somewhat aggressive approach. There had been references by the applicant to the Communist Manifesto and [the Grunwick dispute]". Then they go on: "But as the decision in [*Lyon and Scherk v St James Press Ltd* [1976] I.R.L.R. 215] illustrates, it is not sufficient for management to be disturbed in this way if the real reason for dismissal was that the new employee was carrying on trade union activities. The very experienced lay members of this Tribunal have strongly felt that the events which took place must be considered as a whole if we are to apply what Mr Justice Bristow has recently described as our 'industrial common sense'. The events all happened quickly and flowed into each other. The applicant was quite properly carrying out trade union activities at an appropriate time when he asked, as shop steward, for a meeting with the management to discuss a grievance. The management took a step which though not unreasonable was somewhat provocative and the applicant reacted, again not unreasonably, but somewhat hastily. The men joined in and there was a one-hour stoppage. The applicant was dismissed. Looking at the matter as a whole and trying to apply the legislation with industrial common sense we would say that the applicant was dismissed for carrying on trade union activities".

In my judgment, this is too general. It does not specify the conduct of the respondent, and in particular makes no reference at all to his having called the maintenance men from their work, and I cannot regard the conclusion that the respondent was dismissed for carrying on trade union activities as a finding of fact which is binding on us. It is a conclusion purporting to be drawn from the primary facts, but on this broad brush approach the primary facts were not found.

In my judgment, the alternative approach of the Tribunal in paragraph 16 and following paragraphs in which they broke down the events was the correct one. There they divided them into three stages: 1. The raising by the respondent of the original grievance of the pay differentials with the management. As to this, they said in paragraph 16 at page 33: "The reason given by the management for dismissal does not, as we have already seen, make it clear as to whether this was a factor here". The Employment Appeal Tribunal summarised their understanding of what the Industrial Tribunal had found as follows:—and I read from page 14—" . . . that Mr Shaw was dismissed for taking part in the following activities of an independent trade union, namely, taking up the grievance of the fitter, seeing and pressing for the meeting with the employers, and upon leaving that meeting calling together the maintenance men, which must have involved their leaving their work; and that all these things were done at an 'appropriate time." With respect, however, I do not agree with the first part of that summary. It appears from my citation from paragraph 16 of the Tribunal's Decision that there was no finding that the taking up of the original grievance was the cause of the dismissal, but I do agree with the second part of that summary, which was the second phase of the Tribunal's breakdown of events. They said in paragraph 17: "The second stage was in his conduct in calling a meeting with the maintenance men and phoning Mr Garwell". I will return to this phase in a moment, but I should observe in passing that I dismiss the telephoning in working time as *de minimis*. The third is the one hour stoppage, but the Tribunal found at paragraph 10, page 34, as a fact that the respondent did not call for a stoppage. It was the shop floor men who on their own initiative joined the meeting of the maintenance men and decided on the hour's stoppage, and in paragraph 20 they concluded: " We cannot find this to be the reason for the dismissal".

There remains, as the only reason for the dismissal, the calling of the maintenance men to the canteen in working hours, and in my judgment that is the only or the principal reason and that is well supported by the evidence of Mr Aisher [the production manager] which I have read.

On the second question, was this a trade union activity, I would myself be inclined to doubt that it was because the question of the respondent's recognition as shop steward was one which fell to be determined between the company and the union, and the respondent was, as it seems to me, ventilating his own private grievance, but I will assume that it was.

Agreeing with Goff L.J., Stephenson L.J. stated: "I share his doubts whether the activity for which Mr. Shaw was dismissed was a trade union activity, but, like him, I am prepared to assume it for the purposes of this case" (para. 41).

(iii) When and where are these protected activities to be carried out?

EPCA, ss.23 and 58 impose no restriction in terms of place. On the contrary, section 23(2A)(*a*) assumes that trade union activities "extend to activities on the employer's premises". In contrast, union activities must occur at an "appropriate time". As defined in sections 23(2) and 58(2), this is either outside working hours (where the contract of employment gives the employer no control anyway), or within working hours by arrangement with, or with the consent of, the employer.

The statute does not say that this consent needs to be expressly or formally given. In what circumstances, then, will consent be implied? The policy conflicts inherent in the tension between the legal/contractual approach and the industrial relations/custom and practice approach are evident in the following extract.

The Marley Tile Co. Ltd. v. Shaw

[1978] I.R.L.R. 238; [1978] I.C.R. 828; [1980] I.R.L.R. 25; [1980] I.C.R. 72

Employment Appeal Tribunal and Court of Appeal

Facts, see p. 445 above.

Phillips J. (in the E.A.T.). Mr Irvine's submission [on behalf of the employer] is that where the employee has taken part in the activities of a trade union within his working hours it can only be at an "appropriate time" in cases where *express* arrangements have been agreed or *express* consent has been given. Such an interpretation of [EPCA, s.58(2)(*b*)] is possible, but it seems to us that this legislation must be construed against the background of industry as it is organised in practice. To interpret and apply the [sub-section] as Mr Irvine submits should be done would be tantamount to saying that there could only be an appropriate time within working hours in cases where an independent trade union had been "recognised" in the full legal sense of that word. For it is only in cases where a trade union has been so recognised that there are likely to be either express arrangements or an express consent. It is very common in practice in industry for employers to have perfectly satisfactory working relationships of an informal character with trade unions in circumstances where such unions are not, in the full sense of the word, "recognised" (*NUGSAT v Albury Bros Ltd* [1977] IRLR 173). It would be strange if in such circumstances employees had no protection against dismissal or victimisation for taking part in the activities of an independent trade union. The present case appear to be a good example of such informality or arrangement. In the course of the argument upon the hearing of the appeal, we were told that the employers recognise TGWU in respect of certain classes of workers, but have no recognition agreement with AUEW or other craft unions in respect of skilled workers. Nonetheless, occupying as they do many factories, they have a wide variety of arrangements of varying degrees of formality in different factories with the AUEW, and matters are thus satisfactorily carried on. For example, had Mr Shaw's appointment as a shop steward been eventually approved, or, if not, someone else had been appointed and approved in his place, he would have carried out within his working hours on suitable occasions the duties of a shop steward; but it is improbable that there would have been any express agreement or arrangement or consent for him to do so at particular times or places. Yet it would be very strange if in such a case there were no protection conferred by [EPCA]. Accordingly, we reject this submission.

The Industrial Tribunal deal with this matter in paragraph 16 of the decision. They say:

> "The need to interpret the definition of 'at an appropriate time ' in para 6(4A) of Schedule 1 [EPCA, s.58(1)(*b*)] in a realistic way is illustrated here. The consent of management to a shop steward raising a grievance on behalf of a member during working hours is usually accepted in industrial relations, even if the management has not specifically given permission for this. It is implied by the basic willingness of the management to work together with the union. Thus for the management to have dismissed the applicant for that conduct alone, even if the company's grievance procedure does not specifically provide for it, would be dismissing him for trade union activities at an appropriate time . . . .

We all agree with this, and accordingly agree with the conclusion of the Industrial Tribunal that Mr Shaw's doings down to and including the meeting with the employers occurred at an "appropriate time".

Our disagreement relates to the final stage, that is to say the summoning of the maintenance men away from their duties to attend a meeting with Mr Shaw, the absenting of himself to telephone Mr Garwell, and—if it be relevant—the stoppage of work. The majority—Mr Goff and I, Mr Clement-Jones dissenting—agree that the summoning of the meeting of the maintenance men and the telephoning of Mr Garwell did take place at an appropriate time, for the reasons summarised by the Industrial Tribunal in paragraph 18, namely: 'Because the type of consent referred to in paragraph 16 above, the implied consent of management arising out of the general relationship of management and union in a factory must, we would have thought, in real industrial relations terms, allow for some unusual situations where the shop steward would wish to inform his members during working hours of an unexpected development'. A different majority—Mr Clement-Jones and I, Mr Goff dissenting—disagree with the view expressed by the Industrial Tribunal in the second part of paragraph 18 of the Decision. The majority do not think that the consent of the employers can be deduced from their silence when Mr Shaw announced that he was going to call a meeting of his members and telephone Mr Garwell. The meeting ended suddenly, and on a sour note, and we think that this view of the matter is unreal . . . .

It follows that by a majority, Mr Clement-Jones dissenting on one point, we find that Mr Shaw's doings, in so far as judged relevant by the Industrial Tribunal, took place at an 'appropriate time' and that the majority would accordingly dismiss the appeal.

Mr Clement-Jones agrees that part of what Mr Shaw did was at an 'appropriate time", namely seeking to raise the grievance and meeting the management for that purpose. While, as already explained, he is in agreement with the majority in accepting the view of the Industrial Tribunal as expressed in paragraph 16 as to the correct approach to the question whether there have been "arrangements" or "consent", he does not think that it could be extended to apply to the calling together of the maintenance men and the taking over of the canteen for the purpose of the meeting, without the express consent of the employers. In his judgment, unless there is a general agreement or arrangement which covers it, the shop steward unaccredited by the management at the relevant time cannot be taken to have implied permission to call such a meeting in working hours, particularly one which ends in an hour's stoppage of the shop floor workers, even if that was not intended by the shop steward. Furthermore, Mr Clement-Jones does not agree that an arrangement for the conduct of shop steward's duties can be reasonably assumed to exist either by extension from other factories in the Marley Group, or by having regard to custom and practice at their Dewsbury plant, inasmuch as it was found by the Industrial Tribunal that neither had the AUEW hitherto nominated a shop steward nor had the TGWU done so for their membership on production in the factory.

GOFF L.J. (in the C.A.): The matter then rests on the question of consent. It is not necessary to decide whether arrangements can only be express, because this was not something done pursuant to any general arrangement. The question turns on the word "consent". In my judgment in a proper case, consent may be implied but this is not such a case . . . .
(Goff L.J. then went on, however, to reject the view that calling a meeting of members was done at an "appropriate time": (i) as per the majority in the E.A.T., consent could not be implied from silence in this case; (ii) as per the minority (Mr Clement-Jones), express or a general agreement or arrangement was needed. He went on:)

Mr Rose [counsel for Mr Shaw] submitted that the calling out of the maintenance men to discuss the unexpected situation which had arisen was incidental to the original approach to the management to discuss the fitter's differential, which the company had agreed should be in working time, by giving the respondent an appointment for that purpose and should, therefore, be treated as covered by that consent. I do not think that is right, because it was not necessary to [convene a meeting of the maintenance men] in working time and because it involved a much more significant interference with the work of the factory in which all five men were involved and not the respondent only.

Alternatively, he relied on the speech of Lord Reid in the case of *The Post Office v Crouch*, which is reported in [1971] IRLR 22 where, dealing with the precisely similar wording of s.5 of the Industrial Relations Act, 1971, his Lordship said: "But again this must be applied reasonably. It is one thing to ask an employer to incur expense or submit to substantial inconvenience. That the worker may not do. But it is a different matter to use facilities which are normally available to the employers' workers or to ask him to submit to some trifling inconvenience. Men carrying on activities of their union on their employers' premises must do so in a manner which does not cause substantial inconvenience either to their employer or to fellow workers who are not members of their trade union . . . and employers must tolerate minor infringements of their strict legal rights which do them no real harm. In my view the Industrial Tribunals are well fitted to deal with disputes about matters of that kind."

He argued that this applied to the present case and the respondent's conduct was no more than that little inconvenience which employers must accept. In my judgment, however, it was much more than that, and I think the Industrial Tribunal thought so too, when they said in paragraph 17, page 32: "Such a meeting must mean that the men are not as readily available for work as they would otherwise be, even if in this particular case these men were maintenance workers and would still be on call when in the canteen".

In my view there is no ground for inferring an implied consent to all the maintenance men being suddenly called from their place of work to a meeting, particularly one such as in the present case where the problem which had arisen did not call for a desperately urgent solution. In my judgment therefore even if the conduct for which the respondent was dismissed was taking part in trade union activities, which I have assumed, it was not at an appropriate time because it was carried out in working hours and was not in accordance with the arrangements agreed with or consent given by the company. For these reasons, I would allow this appeal, discharge the orders of the Industrial Tribunal and the Employment Appeal Tribunal and dismiss the respondent's application.

(C) THE CLOSED SHOP

One consequence of the organisation of the employees of an employer into a trade union may be the demand that all employees be or become members of that union: a trade union closed shop. From the viewpoint of trade unionists, closed shops increase the strength and solidarity of their organisation, and avoid non-union employees obtaining the benefits of collective bargaining as "free riders" on the union's back. Many employers support the closed shop as a matter of administrative and industrial relations convenience, and willingly enter into closed shop or "union membership agreements" (as they are called in legislation, *cf.* TULRA, s.30(1)). As a consequence, non-unionists may be dismissed.

The law intervenes indirectly, not by rules on the legality or otherwise of the closed shop or union membership agreements, but by rules dealing with closed shop dismissals, a sub-category of the general law of unfair dismissal. Dismissal of non-unionists is fair where there is a union membership agreement which complies with stringent conditions (*e.g.* approval by an 80 or 85 per cent. majority in secret ballot: EPCA, ss.58(3)(*c*) and 58A). These conditions present great obstacles in practice. In addition, even where these conditions can be fulfilled, dismissals will be unfair if non-unionists object to joining a union on specified grounds (*e.g.* of conscience or other deeply-held personal conviction: EPCA, s.58(4)). These practical obstacles and grounds for objection are spelled out in the Code of Practice issued by the Conservative Secretary of State for Employment which took effect on November 1, 1984.

Complaints by non-unionists when dismissed may be directed against employers, but also, unusually, against the union pressurising the employer to effect the dismissal (EPCA, s.76A). However, although extra compensation may be awarded (s.75A), re-employment of non-unionists cannot be enforced against the employer.

The policy arguments on the closed shop emerged clearly in a case considered against the background of the European Convention on Human Rights.

Young, James and Webster v. United Kingdom
[1981 I.R.L.R. 408
European Court of Human Rights

The applicants were engaged by British Rail at a time when British Rail did not require employees to be members of specified trade unions. Subsequently British Rail in 1975 concluded an agreement with the three railway unions which provided that it was a condition of employment for grades which included the applicants to be a member of one of the unions. The applicants all objected to being union members and were accordingly dismissed in 1976.

They complained to the European Commission on Human Rights that the enforcement of the legislation permitting their dismissals, when they objected on reasonable grounds to union membership, interfered with their freedoms of thought, conscience, expression and association, and that complaints under the European Convention were the sole remedies available to them. The Commission declared the complaints admissible and referred them to the European Court of Human Rights for adjudication.

THE EUROPEAN COURT ON HUMAN RIGHTS: The main issues in this case arise under Article 11 [of the European Convention on Human Rights], which reads as follows:

> "1. Everyone has the right to freedom of peaceful assembly and to freedom of association with others, including the right to form and to join trade unions for the protection of his interests.
>
> 2. No restrictions shall be placed on the exercise of these rights other than such as are prescribed by law and are necessary in a democratic society in the interests of national security or public safety, for the prevention of disorder or crime, for the protection of health or morals or for the protection of the rights and freedoms of others. This Article shall not prevent the imposition of lawful restrictions on the exercise of these rights by members of the armed forces, of the police or of the administration of the State."

A substantial part of the pleadings before the Court was devoted to the question whether Article 11 guarantees not only freedom of association, including the right to form and to join trade unions, in the positive sense, but also, by implication, a "negative right" not to be compelled to join an association or a union.

Whilst the majority of the Commission stated that it was not necessary to determine this issue, the applicants maintained that a "negative right" was clearly implied in the text . . . .

The Court does not consider it necessary to answer this question on this occasion.

The Court recalls, however, that the right to form and join trade unions is a special aspect of freedom of association (see the *National Union of Belgian Police* judgment of 27.10.75, Series A no. 19, p. 17 section 38); it adds that the notion of a freedom implies some measure of choice as to its exercise . . . .

. . . it does not follow that the negative aspect of a person's freedom of association falls completely outside the ambit of Article 11 and that each and every complusion to join a particular trade union is compatible with the intention of that provision. To construe Article 11 as permitting every kind of complusion in the field of trade union membership would strike at the very substance of the freedom it is designed to guarantee . . . .

As a consequence of the agreement concluded in 1975, the applicants were faced with the dilemma either of joining the NUR (in the case of Mr James) or TSSA or NUR (in the case of Mr Young and Mr Webster) or of losing jobs for which union membership had not been a requirement when they were first engaged and which two of them had held for several years. Each applicant regarded the membership condition introduced by that agreement as an interference with the freedom of association to which he considered that he was entitled: in addition, Mr Young and Mr Webster had objections to trade union policies and activities coupled, in the case of Mr Young, with objections to the political affiliations of the specified unions. . . . As a result of their refusal to yield to what they considered to be unjustified pressure, they received notices terminating their employment. Under the legislation in force at the time . . . their dimissal was "fair" and, hence, could not found a claim for compensation, let alone reinstatement or re-engagement.

The situation facing the applicants clearly runs counter to the concept of freedom of association in its negative sense.

Assuming that Article 11 does not guarantee the negative aspect of that freedom on the same footing as the positive aspect, complusion to join a particular trade union may not always be contrary to the Convention.

However, a threat of dismissal involving loss of livelihood is a most serious form of complusion and, in the present instance, it was directed against persons engaged by British Rail before the introduction of any obligation to join a particular trade union.

In the Court's opinion, such a form of complusion, in the circumstances of the case, strikes at the very substance of the freedom guaranteed by Article 11. For this reason alone, there has been an interference with that freedom as regards each of the three applicants.

Moreover, notwithstanding its autonomous role and particular sphere of application, Article 11 must, in the present case, also be considered in the light of Articles 9 and 10 . . . .

Mr Young and Mr Webster had objections to trade union policies and activities, coupled, in the case of Mr Young, with objections to the political affiliations of the TSSA and NUR . . . . Mr James' objections were of a different nature, but he too attached importance to freedom of choice and he had reached the conclusion that membership of NUR would be of no advantage to him . . . .

The protection of personal opinion afforded by Articles 9 and 10 in the shape of freedom of thought, conscience and religion and of freedom of expression is also one of freedom of association as guaranteed by Article 11. Accordingly, it strikes at the very substance of this Article to exert pressure, of the kind applied to the applicants, in order to compel someone to join an association contrary to his convictions.

In this further respect, the treatment complained of—in any event as regards Mr Young and Mr Webster—constituted an interference with their Article 11 rights.

JUDGE SORENSEN, joined by JUDGES VILHJALMSSON and LAGERGREN (dissenting). The so-called positive and negative freedom of association are not simply two sides of the same coin or, as the [majority judgment of the] Court puts it, two aspects of the same freedom. There is no logical link between the two.

The positive freedom of association safeguards the possibility of individuals, if they so wish, to associate with each other for the purpose of protecting common interests and pursuing common goals, whether of an economic, professional, political, cultural, recreational or other character, and the protection consists in preventing public authorities from intervening to frustrate such common action. It concerns the individual as an active participant in social activities, and it is in a sense a collective right in so far as it can only be exercised jointly by a plurality of individuals. The negative freedom of association, by contrast, aims at protecting the individual against being grouped together with other individuals with whom he does not agree or for purposes which he does not approve. It tends to protect him from being identified with convictions, endeavours or attitudes which he does not share and thus to defend the intimate sphere of his personality. In addition, it may serve the purpose of protecting the individual against misuse of power by the association and against being manipulated by its leader. However strongly such protection of the individual may sometimes be needed, it is neither in logic nor by necessary implication part of the positive freedom of association.

It follows that union security arrangements and the practice of the "closed shop" are neither prohibited nor authorised by Article 11 of the Convention. Objectionable as the treatment suffered by the applicants may be on grounds of reason and equity, the adequate solution lies not in any extensive interpretation of that Article but in safeguards against dismissal because of refusal to join a union, that is, in safeguarding the right to security of employment in such circumstances. But this right is not among those recognised by the Convention which—as stated in the Preamble—is only a first step for the collective enforcement of human rights. At present, it is therefore a matter for regulation by the national law of each State.

In 1987 a Government Green Paper (Trade Unions and Their Members (Cmnd. 95) proposed that (a) immunity should be removed from all industrial action designed to create or maintain a closed shop; and (b) EPCA, s.58(3) which allows a non-union member to be dismissed fairly on grounds of non-union membership where there is a ballot-approved closed shop should be removed.

4. RELATIONS BETWEEN TRADE UNIONS

In many workplaces and enterprises a number of unions will be recognised in respect of different sections of the workforce, and these unions must frequently co-operate if there are to be orderly industrial relations and if their members are to gain the advantages of collective bargaining. Unions also need frequently to collaborate outside specific workplaces and enterprises: hence the roles of the Trades Union Congress and local trades councils and such groupings of unions as the Confederation of Shipbuilding and Engineering Unions. On the other hand, competition between unions for membership or for employer recognition or over work allocation can result in bitter conflict. This is yet another area where the courts play little part in practice in settling differences, although such disputes not infrequently provide the background to reported cases involving trade unions.

(A) Co-operation

Official co-operation between trade unions takes place at national, local and industrial levels.

ACAS, *Industrial Relations Handbook* (1980), p.43

Any trade union with membership in England and Wales may apply for affiliation to the central co-ordinating body of the trade union movement—the Trades Union Congress (TUC), which has been in continuous existence since 1868. The TUC is an autonomous industrial body composed of affiliated trade unions paying annual fees based on memberships . . . .

The General Council

The General Council is the executive body of Congress, transacting business in the periods between each annual Congress . . . .

Neither Congress nor General Council can override the autonomy of the affiliated unions, and in most areas of collective bargaining the TUC has a peripheral role. But if TUC policy decisions are not, strictly speaking, binding, the affiliated unions have recognised a strong obligation to follow lines taken by Congress and by General Council. Certain standing orders do give the General Council, and Congress, disciplinary sanctions and responsibilities. These relate in the main to three areas of disputes: industrial disputes, inter-union disputes and disputes concerning individual union membership.

The General Council and disputes

In 1976 Congress approved a revision of the TUC's Rules 11, 12 and 13 and the regulations governing procedure in regard to disputes.

Rule 11 (Industrial Disputes) obliges affiliated organisations to keep the TUC General Secretary informed with regard to matters arising between them and their employers and/or between one organisation and another, including unauthorised and unconsitutional stoppages of work, in particular where such matters may involve directly or indirectly large bodies of workers. While it is TUC policy that neither General Council nor General Secretary will intervene while there is a prospect of settlement by the normal machinery of negotiation, advice and assistance can be offered in suitable circumstances and moral and material support appropriately organised. [The Rule now also permits the General Council or the General Secretary to use their influence to settle disputes which affect other affiliated unions.]

Rule 12 (Disputes between Affiliated Organisations) (as revised) gives the TUC considerable powers in relation to inter-union disputes—the prevention or conciliation of which has long been a major preoccupation of the TUC. The TUC first developed formal principles for handling inter-union disputes in 1924, and these were greatly extended in 1939 by the Bridlington Congress which adopted a series of recommendations designed to minimise disputes between trade unions over membership questions and to establish procedures through which the TUC would handle, and rule on, complaints by one organisation against another. Broadly designed to prevent the "poaching" of members, these Bridlington Principles play an important part in preventing the proliferation of unions in situations where more than one union is capable of representing a particular grade of worker. Their existence has substantially discouraged the formation of breakaway unions and the movement of groups of workers from one union to another.

The *Principles* were supplemented in 1969 by recommendations adopted by a Special Congress held at Croydon. Amendments to Rule 12 gave the TUC considerably greater powers is respect of official and unofficial inter-union disputes. In particular, no affiliated union was to authorise a stoppage of work in pursuance of an inter-union dispute until the matter had been considered by the TUC. As a result of Bridlington and Croydon the TUC has formal responsibilities in disputes and differences over membership, recognition, demarcation and wages and conditions of employment between member unions. Further amendments were made in 1979 [and 1985].

Rule 13 (Conduct of Affilitated Organisations) empowers the General

Council to investigate the conduct of any affiliated union on the ground that its activities may be detrimental to the interests of the trade union movement or contrary to the declared principles or declared policy of the Congress. The General Council has the (rarely invoked) ultimate sanction of suspension from membership of the Congress until the next Annual Conference.

TUC Disputes Committees

The TUC's Disputes Principles and Procedures constitute a code of good trade union practice on the handling of inter-union disputes accepted as morally binding by the affiliated organisations. Upon application by affiliated unions the General Council investigates a dispute or disagreement between such unions and, if conciliation has been unsuccessful, may require them to submit evidence to enable a Disputes Committee of the Council to adjudicate. A TUC Dispute Committee is composed of not less than three persons appointed by the General Secretary from the General Council or from experienced union officials. The Disputes Committee exercises a triple function—as a fact-finding commission, as a conciliating body and as a tribunal. When as award is made the unions in dispute are expected to abide by it and if they fail to do so there is the sanction of suspension. An account of all inter-union disputes during the year is contained in the General Council's report to Congress.

Independent Review Committee

Since 1976 a small high-level Independent Review Committee has existed to consider appeals from individual persons who have been dismissed, or given notice of dismissal, from their jobs as a result of having been expelled from, or having been refused admission to, a trade union in a situation where trade union membership is a condition of employment.

A. Marsh, *Trade Union Handbook* (1979), p. 102–103

Trades Councils exist in most major cities, towns and districts of the United Kingdom and consist of representatives of local trade union branches or lodges. Most of them meet monthly. Their function is to provide a local forum for trade union discussion; to provide a common service on industrial, civic and education matters as required, to assist in improving trade union organisation and to nominate representatives of the trade union viewpoint to committees, tribunals etc. Representatives from particular unions remain subject to the rules and policies of those unions. Councils are not regarded by the trade union movement as independent bodies competent to make local decisions which may conflict with those of national or regional trade union organisation.

ACAS, *Industrial Relations Handbook* (1980), p. 43

Despite the long-term trend towards a reduction in the number of trade unions, largely through mergers, there remain problems of "multi-unionism" in many areas. The TUC has developed machinery for handling these problems, but difficulties are also overcome to some extent by the formation of federations of trade unions, both for negotiating purposes and for the provisions of common services. In 1977 there were 43 federations, of which by far the largest was the Confederation of Shipbuilding and Engineering Unions (CSEU) coordinating the activities of 23 constituent unions in those industries.

During the 1970s the TUC also developed industrial committees which co-ordinate unions' activities, dispose of inter-union problems and formulate common policies within specific industries or groups of industries (*cf.* the Annual Reports).

Unofficial co-operation between organisations of workers at plant level takes the form of multi-union shop stewards committees, and may exist at enterprise or even industry level. These unofficial organisations can cut across trade unions' formal structure *cf. Heatons Transport (St. Helens) Ltd.* v. *TGWU* (above p. 420). (For the constitution of a shop stewards' combine committee, see (1981) 19 B.J.I.R., at 7–8).

(B) Conflict

(i) Over work

"The Isle of Grain Dispute" (1980) 18 B.J.I.R. 385 and (1981) 19 B.J.I.R. 100

A prolonged dispute involving twenty-seven laggers on the Isle of Grain, where Europe's largest oil-fired power station was under construction, came to a head when on 14 April [1980] the Central Electricity Generating Board (C.E.G.B.) announced 600 redundancies and a week later decided to cease construction work altogether at the end of June with the loss of the remaining 1,400 jobs. The dispute had begun last year after a C.E.G.B. proposal that the Thermal Insulation Contractors Association (TICA) should re-negotiate the open-ended bonus system previously agreed with the G.M.W.U. laggers in order to bring bonus payments into line with those of other skilled workers on the site. This, it was hoped, would eliminate the inter-union tensions and leapfrogging claims which the disparity had begun to generate. Estimating that the proposed £2.60 an hour bonus ceiling would cost them as much as £50 a week in wages, the laggers had refused to accept the proposal and had been suspended.

If nothing else, the decision to halt construction succeeded in re-animating a dispute which had threatened to atrophy as the direct participants left the scene. The suspended laggers had mostly taken other jobs; the contractor who employed them was no longer involved at the Isle of Grain; and the G.M.W.U., which traditionally represented laggers, had withdrawn without allowing the twenty-seven jobs to be filled. The shut-down announcement, however, stimulated two of the skilled unions, the E.E.T.P.U. and the A.U.E.W., into allowing their members to be trained by the mechanical contractors (not the insulation contractors with whom the G.M.W.U. operated a national agreement on lagging work) to fill the vacant jobs at rates of pay commensurate with those of other skilled jobs. This action reflected the seriousness with which the unions on site treated the C.E.G.B. threat, for it was generally acknowledged that lower than expected electricity demand, the high cost of fuel oil and the need to keep a tight rein on capital expenditure meant that the Board was under no great pressure to complete the new power station rapidly. Although the unions were rewarded by the C.E.G.B announcement on 16 May that construction at the Isle of Grain would continue after all, the G.M.W.U expressed "outrage" at the defiance of the Bridlington Agreement [*cf.* p. 454 above] by the E.E.T.P.U. and the A.U.E.W., urged the T.U.C. to take action to prevent the training of new laggers, and threatened to withdraw 6,000 laggers from other sites in sympathy. On 27 May in an atmosphere of considerable bitterness a 400 strong G.M.W.U. picket tried unsuccessfully to stop work at the Isle of Grain. There were thirty-seven arrests. Continued G.M.W.U. threats to escalate the dispute were accompanies by attempts by the Finance and General Purposes Committee of the T.U.C. to establish common ground upon which a resolution of the issue might be founded. These discussions continued throughout June without a great deal of progress, although, after talks involving the C.E.G.B., the G.M.W.U. decided on 19 June to postpone indefinitely a planned strike by laggers on all C.E.G.B. sites. By 9 July, however, this strike plan was revived only to be cancelled again two days later after an all night session at the T.U.C. produced fresh proposals to resolve the impasse. The Finance and General Purposes Committee called on the E.E.T.P.U. and the A.U.E.W. to withdraw their replacement laggers, believed then to number sixty, and to allow the re-employment of the twenty-seven G.M.W.U. laggers under the terms of the thermal insulation agreement which had originally caused the dispute. The concessions the G.M.W.U. were prepared to make, including an understanding that the laggers would seek to harmonise their earnings with those of other skilled workers, were not satisfactory either to the C.E.G.B. or to the two craft unions. The C.E.G.B. remained adamant that G.M.W.U. laggers could only return if they agreed to the bonus rates common to the remainder of the skilled workforce. The E.E.T.P.U. and the A.U.E.W. stood by their original contention that they would not tolerate the perpetuation of a bonus system which gave their membership second-class status and added a further complication by expressing concern about the future of the sixty newly trained laggers whom they were not prepared to see sacked. The possibility that these unions might be suspended by the T.U.C. under [its] Rule 13 for failure to comply with a T.U.C. directive was raised when the T.U.C. General Council decided to issue formal advice to the unions involved that they should accept the T.U.C.'s proffered solution.

This refusal [by the E.E.T.P.U. and A.U.E.W.] suggested that the dispute would come to a head at the T.U.C. Congress in early September with the possibility that the E.E.T.P.U. and A.U.E.W. would be suspended from the T.U.C. under Rule 3. But whilst such a public confrontation was avoided at Brighton [where the Annual TUC Conference was held in 1980], the search for a compromise based on the re-introduction of G.M.W.U. laggers on Unit 3, where insulation work was about to begin, and the continued employment of A.U.E.W./E.E.T.P.U. laggers on Unit 1, was unsuccessful. On 24 September the General Council gave the two unions until 10 October to comply with its directive or be suspended from the T.U.C. Meanwhile the ramifications of the events at the Isle of Grain became apparent as a similar dispute in Wales became increasingly prominent. Since the summer the G.M.W.U. had been accusing the A.U.E.W., E.E.T.P.U. and other unions of poaching laggers at the Texaco/Gulf oil terminal and cracking unit sites near Milford Haven. The G.M.W.U. picketing culminated in a mass demonstration on 6 October which resulted in the arrest of five of the 600 pickets. The next day G.M.W.U. delegates of the country's six thousand laggers called for a national strike. At the same time, parallel tension between the employers' groups involved was growing as T.I.C.A. became increasingly alarmed that its member firms were losing their traditional insulation work to members of the Oil and Chemical Plant Constructors Association and the Engineering Employers' Federation. As the suspension date approached, the executive of the 27,000 strong construction section of the A.U.E.W. instructed its General Secretary, Mr John Baldwin, to find a solution to the dispute by 20 October, otherwise the section would abide by the T.U.C.'s advice. However, the larger engineering section (1.2 M. members) of the A.U.E.W. together with the E.E.T.P.U. (420,000 members) confirmed their opposition to the T.U.C. proposal. The 10 October deadline passed, the suspension move being delayed until the General Council meeting on 22 October, by which time the A.U.E.W.(E) and the E.E.P.T.U. had broadly agreed to accept the T.U.C. formula, provided the fifty-seven non-G.M.W.U. laggers continued to work on the Isle of Grain "for the time being". The C.E.G.B. which was uneasy about the T.U.C. proposals, met the unions on the 27 October. This meeting decided that the G.M.W.U. would enter negotiations with T.I.C.A. firms over productivity and harmonisation of bonuses which would provide a basis for G.M.W.U. members to undertake lagging work on Unit 3. Further negotiations to arrange for G.M.W.U. laggers to complete work on Unit 1 were proposed, although the C.E.G.B. stressed that in this event there would be no work for the fifty-seven non-G.M.W.U. laggers.

(ii) Over membership

Conflicts may equally occur between unions over recruiting workers into membership; *cf.* the facts underlying such cases as *Weeks* v. *Amalgamated Stevedores' and Dockers' Union* [1940] Ll. Rep. 282 (Ch.D.), above p. 417; *Spring* v. *NASDU* [1956] 1 W.L.R. 585, below p. 637.

(iii) Over recognition

Disputes over membership may develop into disputes between two unions over claims to recognition by an employer for the purposes of collective bargaining. Indeed, the attainment of recognition is a major boost to membership, and equally the absence or loss of recognition acts as a hindrance to a union's progress, *cf.* the underlying situation in cases such as *UPW* v. *The Post Office* [1974] 1 W.L.R. 89 (H.L.); *Stratford* v. *Lindley* [1965] A.C. 269 (H.L.); *EMA* v. *ACAS* [1980] 1 All E.R. 896 (H.L.).

CHAPTER 12

COLLECTIVE BARGAINING

1. CONCEPT AND CRITIQUE

The significance of collective bargaining for contemporary labour lawyers was one of Kahn-Freund's seminal insights. Historically, however, it dates back only to the latter part of the nineteenth century; it has been suspended for lengthy periods during various national emergencies; a substantial proportion of the workforce is not affected by it; and it looks to be increasingly under threat from centralised regulation in the form of government imposed incomes policies. Thus, while its present importance justifies detailed study, other methods of regulating employment, such as unilateral employer regulation, statutory regulation, individual contract and workers' control (see above, Clegg, Chapter 11, p. 409) must always be borne in mind.

Ministry of Labour, *Industrial Relations Handbook* (1961), pp. 18–19

The term "collective bargaining" is applied to those arrangements under which wages and conditions of employment are settled by a bargain, in the form of an agreement made between employers or associations of employers and workers' organisations. In unorganised trades, the normal practice was and sometimes still is for the individual workman, when applying for a job to accept or refuse the terms offered by the employer, without communication with his fellow workmen and without any other consideration than his own position. In other words, he made with his employer an entirely individual bargain. The position is different when the employer is party to an agreement which settles the principles and conditions upon which for the time being all workmen of a particular class or grade will be engaged. When the agreement is made by a number of different employers or, as is often the case, by an employers' association acting on behalf of the whole or the greater part of the firms in a given industry within a wide area, all the workers employed by the employers concerned are secured equality of treatment, while each employer is protected against unfair competition by reason of lower wages costs in so far as his competitors are parties to the agreement. For many years collective agreements have played a most important part in the regulation of working conditions in this country. They cover a great variety of matters including not only rates of wages, but also hours of work, overtime conditions, special allowances, piece-work arrangements, holidays, allocation of work, employment of apprentices, redundancy, guaranteed week arrangements, and working conditions generally. The terms and conditions laid down in agreements are applied not only to members of trade unions but also to non-unionists. Trade agreements are also largely observed by employers who are not party to them.

This system of collective bargaining could not function smoothly without agreements between the parties regarding the procedure for dealing with questions as they arise, and much work has been done towards evolving machinery for the avoidance of strikes and lock-outs in connection with trade disputes.

The whole of the collective system rests upon the principle of mutual consent, and the value of the agreements and the machinery for settling disputes has depended upon the loyal acceptance by the constituent members on both sides of the decisions reached. This acceptance is voluntary. Loyal acceptance has in fact been the rule in all the trades concerned. Although the question has been raised from time to time of the adequacy of these methods, the view has always been taken that it was not desirable to adopt some alternative based upon principles other than that of mutual consent or to introduce any system of penalties for non-observance of agreements.

There has been occasional judicial recognition of the basic assumptions of collective bargaining, *e.g.* in *Gray Dunn & Co. Ltd.* v. *Edwards* [1980] I.R.L.R. 23 (E.A.T.), Lord McDonald said:

> "Where employers negotiate a detailed agreement with a recognised trade union they are entitled to assume that all employees who are members of the union know of and are bound by its provisions. There could be no stability in industrial relations if this were not so."

In *Nelson and Woolett* v. *The Post Office* [1978] I.R.L.R. 548 (E.A.T.) Kilner Brown J. declared:

> " . . . the whole basis of good industrial relations, particularly where it is a State industry or where the employers are represented by a national employers' federation, is that agreements arrived at between the employing authorities or the employing representation [*sic*] and the trade unions in question ought to bind everybody. It is impossible, obviously, with a democratic system under which the trade union movement believes it operates, for the individual members in the minority to have their own personal views recognised . . . it can only lead to industrial anarchy if individual branches or individual members of a trade union are entitled to opt out and to avoid the consequences of a decision democratically arrived at in an overall national connotation."

The values of stability and consensus which are highlighted as justifying collective bargaining echo values identified in Kahn-Freund's pluralist perspective, which has dominated modern British labour law (see above, Chapter 11, pp. 424 *et seq*.). The following extract criticises the pluralist perspective on collective bargaining.

R. Hyman and I. Brough, SOCIAL VALUES AND INDUSTRIAL RELATIONS (1975), pp. 162–166

. . . industrial relations pluralism is elaborated by Fox [in *Beyond Contract: Trust, Power and Work Relations*] in contradistinction to what he terms the "unitary frame of reference." This latter, Fox argues, postulates an identity of interests within the industrial enterprise and the nation as a whole; the enterprise is viewed according to a teamwork analogy, with "one source of authority and one focus of loyalty. . . . Each accepts his place and his function gladly, following the leadership of the one so appointed." Where industrial conflict occurs, those who embrace this ideology will naturally attribute it "to faults among the governed—to stupidity, or short-sightedness, or outdated class rancour, or an inability to grasp the basic principles of economics, or the activities of agitators who create mischief out of nothing." And inevitably, a commitment to the unitary frame of reference carries with it an ambivalent—if not downright hostile—attitude to trade unionism.

Against this unitary perspective, with its obvious affinities with functionalism and systems theory, Fox insists that the enterprise is "more plausibly viewed as a coalition of interests, a miniature democratic state composed of sectional groups with divergent interests. . . . " This divergence of interests provides a legitimate basis for union activity: firstly in protecting the workers' *economic* interests where these conflict with those of the employer, but secondly in defending them against the arbitrary exercise of *managerial* authority—management action "in deploying, organising and disciplining the labour force, after it has been hired." The pluralist recognises that "conflict is endemic to industrial organisation"; hence "instead of assuming disruption to be due to the impact of the more regrettable aspects of human nature upon an otherwise harmonious system, we see it instead as an outcome of group structure, group relations and group policies."

Despite the important contrasts between the two perspectives which Fox outlines, industrial relations pluralism is notable for its ambiguity. Fox's characterisation of conflict as the "outcome of group structure, group relations and group policies" fails to specify what is the nature of the group processes involved, whether the divisions within each enterprise extend across the whole political economy, and how fundamental are the resulting conflicts of interest. The possibility that the structure of ownership and control within capitalist industry may generate an *irreconcilable* conflict of interest between employers and employees is not confronted. The very adoption of the label "pluralism" would appear to imply, on the contrary, an orientation which parallels the dominant approach in recent political theory: the assumption that contemporary society, and political relations within that society, are characterised by the competition of numerous sectional groups of which none possesses a disproportionate concentration of power. Pluralism is the political equivalent of the presuppositions of utilitarian economics: just as the market is assumed to mediate neutrally between the interests of the various economic actors, so the political process is assumed to generate a "negotiated order" which accords tolerably with the interests of all. Utilitarian economics and political pluralism both admit the existence of conflicting aims and preferences on the part of the members of society: but both are predicated, explicitly or implicitly, on the existence of an underlying balance of power and interest. For in the absence of such balance, what is conceived as a negotiated order would rest in actuality on coercion or manipulation.

This same presupposition of balance is basic to industrial relations pluralism. The pluralist perspective, as Fox has expounded it, insists that "co-operation . . . needs to be engineered by structural adaptations in work organisation, work rules and work practices, and that direct negotiation with work-groups is an essential part of this process." It is an act of faith that workers' willing co-operation is forthcoming so long as managements appreciate the existence of a divergence of interest which renders legitimate the activities of workers' organisations, both within and without the workplace. This presupposition of the resolubility of conflicts of interest is, however, plausible only if it is assumed that these conflicts are less fundamental than the underlying area of common aims and interests. Fox has conceded this point in a later and more critical discussion. . . .

. . . . Thus, Fox argues, while pluralism is at first sight a theoretical perspective radically different from the unitary approach, it represents in the final analysis "no more, or no less, than enlightened managerialism." Put bluntly, pluralism assumes the existence of sufficient convergence of interest to provide a practical basis for moral integration; it endorses the notion of a common "national interest," even though this position is reached from a different route.

2. COLLECTIVE BARGAINING STRUCTURES

In the United Kingdom the organisation of collective bargaining differs widely from industry to industry, and within some industries even from enterprise to enterprise.

ACAS, *Industrial Relations Handbook* (1980), pp. 99–100

Collective bargaining is not universal throughout industry. The 1978 New Earnings Survey found that about thirty per cent of full-time employees in Great Britain were not affected directly or indirectly by any collective agreements. . . . However, collective bargaining is widespread and negotiations can take place at a number of different levels. In many industries there is machinery at national or industry level which brings together representatives of employers' associations and full-time officers of trade unions. Sometimes this machinery is a permanent ("standing") body, with its own secretariat. These bodies can go under one or other of about a dozen different titles, of which the most common are probably—national joint industrial council (NJIC), joint industrial council (JIC), and national joint committee or council (NJC). These bodies are largely based upon the model constitution drawn up by the Ministry of Labour following the report of the Whitley Committee in 1917 . . . but vary widely in their coverage of an industry, and in the nature and extent of their activities. In other industries, engineering for example, there is no separate machinery, but established arrangements for regular negotiation at national level.

In private industry, the substantive agreements at national or industry level tend to set minimum terms and conditions of employment. The items covered vary widely from industry to industry, but usually include minimum rates of pay, premia for calculating payments for overtime and shiftwork, normal hours of work, and holiday entitlements. Employers in an industry who are not "federated"—do not belong to the employers' association—are not obliged to implement these agreements, although in practice those who employ a workforce of any magnitude tend to offer terms and conditions which are no less favourable. In some industries minimum terms and conditions are determined by a wages council or other statutory machinery . . . and have statutory force. In the public services and nationalised industries where there is a single employer actual pay and conditions of employment are normally set by agreements at national level.

In industries where there is national negotiating machinery, there is sometimes accompanying machinery at regional or district level, also bringing together representatives of the employers' association and full-time officials of the trade unions. This will commonly deal with problems of applying the national agreement to the particular circumstances of an individual district, and often also operate as a stage in the procedure for resolving disputes. In some cases particular regional or district rates of pay or conditions of employment are agreed.

Bargaining at company level, covering all the establishments of a multi-plant company, or at plant or establishment level covering a single site within a company is widespread. In a large company a company-wide agreement can involve the national full-time officials of a union, while bargaining in a small company or covering an individual plant may be conducted entirely by shop stewards. Where there is no industry-wide agreement, or where an employer is not federated, negotiations at these levels may be the sole determinant of pay and other conditions of employment. In federated companies the agreements may build on the minimum rates of pay set nationally—sometimes by establishing higher actual rates, sometimes by adding a productivity scheme or other bonus arrangements—or may cover matters outside the scope of the national agreement.

Finally, at workshop level, within an individual plant, it is common for shop stewards and foremen or other management staff to bargain over detailed conditions of employment—such as the allocation of work, allowances for specific jobs, arrangements for overtime, etc. These arrangements are rarely written, but become reinforced in time through habit and custom, and are known as "custom and practice."

Two other terms are also used to identify levels at which agreements are concluded. Local level is used . . . to describe all agreements concluded below district or company level—at, for example, an individual operating unit within a nationalised industry, in a division of a company covering several plants, or at plant or establishment level. Domestic level is used to denote all agreements at or within individual companies.

In many industries in addition to negotiations there are also arrangements for consultation between managements and employees about matters of common concern which fall outside the scope of the negotiating machinery. Consultation is highly developed in the nationalised industries; in some cases the same committees are used both for negotiation and consultation. In private industry there is no industry-wide machinery; companies have their own arrangements, often a works council at each establishment and sometimes a co-ordinating committee at company level.

W. A. Brown, *"The Structure of Pay Bargaining in Britain,"* in F. T. Blackaby, THE FUTURE OF PAY BARGAINING (1980), pp. 129–137

Rather than use the imprecise notion of a bargaining "level," it is preferable in the first instance to distinguish arrangements by whether or not they involve collaboration between employers. "Multi-employer" agreements where employers act in coalition or association are thus to be distinguished from "single employer" agreements negotiated by the individual employer for his own workforce and no one else. The former strategy has been seen as offering a chance to "take wages out of competition" and present a united front to the unions, while the latter may be preferred by employers desiring greater freedom in their labour policy. . . .

Multi-employer bargaining, industry-wide at either district or national level, developed strongly in Britain in the nineteenth century and was reinforced after the First World War. A series of bodies, most often called National Joint Industrial Councils, permitted negotiations between employers' associations and groups of trade unions to determine pay and conditions of work for specific industries. For want of a better phrase, these will be referred to as "industry-wide" arrangements.

In industries where trade unionism was weak successive governments this century have sought to encourage the development of independent industry-wide bargaining arrangements through the creation of wages councils (originally called trade boards). On these the balance of votes is held by individuals held to be independent of management and of trade union representatives, and the awards made are statutorily enforceable through a Wages Inspectorate. . . .

On the continent of Europe, multi-employer industry-wide pay bargaining has remained supreme. But in Britain, with longer traditions of workplace bargaining and less commitment to employer solidarity, industry-wide agreements began to crumble with post-war full employment. Under pressure from both the labour market and their workforce, local managers became accustomed during the 1950s to augmenting industry-wide wage rates with payment-by-results bonuses, overtime and all manner of supplements. By the time the Royal Commission on Trade Unions and Employers' Associations reported in 1968 [Cmnd. 3623], the realities of wage bargaining were so remote from the formalities, particularly in much of manufacturing industry, that a fundamental change was recommended. The only way to gain control over wage drift and disputes was through formal factory agreements unhindered by commitments to industry-wide rates. In the terms of this discussion, the Commissioners proposed that much of industry should shift from half-hearted multi-employer to whole-hearted single-employer arrangements. . . . (in 1977) overall, single-employer arrangements cover around 57 per cent of the labour force, half of which is accounted for by the public sector and the remainder fairly evenly divided between the establishment and corporate bargaining. The rest of the labour force falls in roughly equal proportions between wages councils, industry-wide arrangements and no bargaining of any sort. . . . In the public sector there are strong organisational reasons for corporate arrangements covering the whole of a service; and in broad terms, the last decade has seen increased centralisation of control both within the public sector industries and between them and the government. In private manufacturing industry there has been a more fundamental change in bargaining structure since the war. Multi-employer arrangements, which in the 1930s were the principal source of pay increases for almost all manual workers, now play this role for only 27 per cent of manual workers in 36 per cent of establishments of 50 or more employees. Wages councils cover 7 per cent and industry-wide and regional agreements 20 per cent of the manual manufacturing workforce in establishments of 50 or more employees. It is negotiations with their own employer alone that principally affect the pay of 68 per cent of manual employees (in 53 per cent of establishments). For 46 per cent of employees these are at establishment level and for the remaining 21 per cent at some corporate level involving more than one establishment.

Since the above extracts privatisation of the public sector and increasing contrasts in prosperity and prices in different regions, have led to suggestions for further abandonment of industry-wide bargaining. In 1987 the Secretary of State for Education has replaced collective bargaining rights of public sector teachers with *imposed* terms and conditions of employment (*cf.* Teachers' Pay and Conditions Act 1987). Once it is appreciated that most workers' terms of employment are settled by collective bargaining, the problems for a labour law based upon the contract of employment are apparent. How does the contract of employment relate to a complex structure of collective bargaining which frequently involves negotiations at a number of different levels, which may give rise to formal written agreements or the informal rules governing workplace behaviour known as custom and practice?

(A) At What Stage in Negotiations Do Terms Become Contractually Binding?

Land and Wilson v. West Yorkshire Metropolitan County Council
[1979] I.R.L.R. 174
Employment Appeal Tribunal

In the fire service full-time firemen had frequently volunteered for "off-time" duties, and such volunteers were described as doing "wholetime/retained duties." The Fire Brigades Union, representing most firemen, adopted the policy in November 1974 that all firemen should be solely employed on a full-time basis, and that the wholetime/retained duties should be abolished. The subsequent negotiating history was as follows:

(i) in July 1975 the National Joint Council for Local Authorities' Fire Brigades, the negotiating body comprising employing authorities and union representatives, began to consider the union's policy decision;

(ii) in August 1975 the employers reserved their position and were not prepared to concede a change without further consideration;

(iii) on September 17, 1975 the NJC resolved to convene a joint working party to examine the question and make recommendations on a regional and district basis;

(iv) on September 23, 1975 a joint circular issued to all employing authorities notified employers' acceptance in principle of the phasing out of retained duties, but that the present arrangements should continue pending the outcome of negotiations. This position was confirmed on April 5, 1976;

(v) on April 8, 1976 the working party informed the West Yorkshire authority that there was no problem and no need for "retained duties";

(vi) in response to requests for guidance, the West Yorkshire authority received letters of August 26, 1976 which stated that there was no objection by the working party if they decided to implement the acceptance in principle of phasing out "retained duties."

In the West Yorkshire area, out of 1500 firemen, 126 had before October 1974 been on the retained system. Following the union decision in November 1974, most of that number ceased these duties and by August 1975 there were only 41 so employed. Some firemen, including the complainants, objected to their union's policy and in May and June of 1975 were expelled from the union. Although there was a policy decision of the union and an acceptance in principle, no clear action to implement these decisions was taken by the employing authority until October 4, 1976. On that day they wrote to the local union branch stating their agreement to abolition of retained duties. On October 14, 1976 they wrote to the 41 men asking them to accept a variation of their contracts. Seventeen refused. The change was nonetheless implemented.

Kilner Brown J.: . . . we operate under a system of freely negotiated contracts of employment. In the end it is a personal and individual relationship. Collective agreements are not by themselves of any legal significance unless and until they are translated into contractual relationship between employer and employee. This may be brought about by collective agreement which, if it is to be achieved by representative process, become binding individually upon those who are caught by the representative process. Even if the employee is outside the representative process and is not a party to the national negotiations he may individually accept the collective agreement by agreeing to a contract which is based upon such collective agreement. Authority for these propositions is to be found in *Young* v. *Canadian Northern Railway Co.* [1931] A.C. 83 (PC) and *Gascol Conversions Ltd.* v *Mercer* [1974] I.R.L.R. 155 (CA).

By extension and analogy these principles would indicate that where a variation of, or a termination of, an existing contract is to be made based upon a collective agreement such a change can only be binding upon individuals if it is accepted individually or if they were collectively represented at the time the change was agreed upon. If the applicants had still been members of the Fire Brigades Union in October 1976 none of us would have found any difficulty in this case. If they had still been members in September 1975 we might have found a way out of a difficult problem.

As our anxieties and potential division of opinion were fully exposed in the course of argument before us in court it would be appropriate to pose and adumbrate the questions which have troubled us.

Are individuals who were members of the union at the time the union took a policy decision bound thereafter by an agreement made pursuant to that policy and made when they were no longer members of the union?

Is a decision in principle which is accepted by employers' and employees' representatives binding upon both sides before it is implemented and acted upon?

Can such a decision in principle be effective and binding upon individual contracts when the Joint Council clearly indicates that the question is to be examined by a working party?

Does it make any difference to the effect of a decision in principle when the evidence reveals that the ultimate implementation was not universal, but (as in this case) not regarded by either side as a practical possibility for several employing authorities?

Can a decision in principle be effective and binding with reference to individual contracts when the Joint Council instructs employing authorities to maintain existing contracts until the Joint Council permits the employing authority to implement the decision in principle?

Does such permission relate back to the date of the acceptance of the decision in principle?

If these questions were relevant and essential to the decision of this appeal we would not shrink from coming to conclusions even if the decision exposed a division of opinion between a trade union and employer's approach to the problem with the presiding judge joining whichever side he thought were correct in law.

The E.A.T. did not attempt to answer these questions. The E.A.T.'s decision that there had been dismissals was reversed by the Court of Appeal ([1986] I.R.L.R. 87).

Tucker v. British Leyland Motor Corporation
[1978] I.R.L.R. 493
County Court

The plaintiffs, members of the TGWU employed at the defendant's Swindon plant, objected to new holiday arrangements which involved transferring certain "statutory" holidays to the period from Christmas to the New Year, so that a week's holiday could be taken. These new arrangements had been recommended in principle at national level at meetings on August 23, 1974 and October 2,

1974, and a national ballot of British Leyland employees had upheld the principle. The TGWU representatives at the Swindon plant participated in the national ballot only after a written assurance was given by Mr Hooper, the plant's industrial relations manager, to the effect that "the management accept that statutory holidays will not be transferred except by mutual agreement between themselves and all the trade unions represented within the plant." Nonetheless, in the absence of the plaintiff's union, the Swindon Works Committee (which dealt with matters of common concern at the Swindon plant) agreed to the transfer of holidays. The plaintiffs claimed that their contracts of employment were not affected by the national or plant agreements.

JUDGE JOHN MAIN Q.C.: . . . [the defendants] say that possibly the meeting of August 23, and certainly the meeting of October 2, constitute an agreement at national level with the trade unions upon the principle of a week's closure at Christmas; and that all that required local determination was the particular day or days of holiday to be transferred to enable that closure to take place. Then, say the defendants, the plaintiffs were insisting on taking holidays contrary to such agreement and not in accordance with it.

. . . I do not read document 93 [which contained an agreed statement of the agreement reached on October 2] as saying any more than that the trade unions at national level were not opposed to—and indeed recommended—the idea of a week's holiday at Christmas. . . . I do not think, however, that it was agreed at national level that individual plants were bound to accept a week's holiday at Christmas whatever their holiday traditions had been or preferences then were. There are some rough notes of what the plaintiffs were told by their national officers . . . , and what is recorded there is "Christmas/New Year is for local determination" and I do not believe that the plaintiffs told Mr Hooper anything different from that. It is also instructive to refer to document 125 dated 25.3.75, where Mr Hooper writing to Mr R. Burns stated, "The problem basically is that the trade unions within the plant do not accept that the national officers have committed them to the movement of statutory holidays without in-plant mutual agreement. The situation is greatly complicated by the fact that on the advice of [the defendants'] Corporate Industrial Relations [department], at the time that corporation-wide holiday ballot was held, I informed the TGWU that Bank Holidays could only be agreed mutually within the plant in order to obtain their participation in the ballot."

In my judgment Mr Hooper—for obvious reasons—now regrets giving the assurance that he did give and would prefer to think that he did not give it. But that assurance having been given it seems to me impossible for the defendants now to contend that there was a national agreement binding on all the unions at Swindon that there should be a week's closure at Christmas 1976. On the contrary it seems to me to be clear that there was an agreement at Swindon that statutory (as opposed to annual) holiday were to be the subject of local agreement. Such local agreement would not be obtained if it were proposed that statutory days should be moved from other parts of the year to Christmas, and Mr Hooper knew that full well.

Moreover it seems to me that it is not open to the defendants now to contend that the plaintiffs were bound to accept the holidays agreed with the works committee; the whole point about Mr Hooper's assurance was that it guaranteed that a decision as to movement of a statutory day must be agreed to by all the unions, not just a majority of them.

(B) What Local Agreements or Informal Workplace Bargaining Affect Contractual Terms?

Barratt v. National Coal Board
[1978] I.C.R. 1101
Employment Appeal Tribunal

The collective agreement governing mineworkers provided that the normal working week should be 40 hours. Clause 3 provided for the regular working of additional shifts when such additional work was necessary to ensure the safety of a pit. Under this clause it was envisaged that such arrangements might where necessary be made locally or on an area basis between the National Union of Mineworkers and the National Coal Board.

The appellant, a ventilation fan attendant, claimed that as a member of a team of men who manned the ventilation fan continuously day and night, seven days a week, he worked a 56-hour week. The question was whether this was a result of a local agreement or arrangement. The Industrial Tribunal replied in the negative.

PHILLIPS J.: There are two extremes. One extreme is an agreement of a formal nature which it is not necessary to find. In the middle is an arrangement of some kind; and it must be, to be sufficient under clause 3, an arrangement between the union and the National Coal Board. It can be quite informal and at quite a low level in the [union] hierarchy. But it is not, we would think, necessarily sufficient if all there is, is, at the other extreme, the mere private agreement or assent by one or two (or in this case, three) individual employees as a matter of personal initiative to man the ventilating system on a 24-hour basis, through the operation of a fan. It is something in between those extremes which is the minimum requirement, that is to say an arrangement of some kind, the existence of which can either be proved or disproved, made for the purpose of clause 3.

Scott v. Formica Ltd.
[1975] I.R.L.R. 104
Industrial Tribunal

The applicant was employed by the respondents as a process worker. His written particulars of employment provided that he would work shifts on request and that he could be moved "from job to job and from department to department." When redundancies had to be made, the applicant was transferred to the waste fuel boilerhouse, which involved shift work but also a cut in his basic hourly rate of pay. The Tribunal held that the applicant was entitled to refuse the transfer under his contract of employment.

NEWCASTLE TRIBUNAL (chairman A.J. BOWKER):. . . . It has been asserted on behalf of the company that some time ago, it is not quite clear when, but possibly two years or so ago, there was a verbal agreement between the company and Mr Scott's trade union under which it was agreed that if a man on transfer suffered a basic reduction in wages by one grade he had to accept this. The man however was not obliged to accept a transfer which involved a reduction of two grades or more in the basic rate of pay. It is not disputed that the transfer to the boiler house would in fact have resulted in a reduction of one grade.

The evidence of this agreement with the union is extremely sketchy. There is certainly nothing in writing before the Tribunal. Neither Mr Smith [the respondents' personnel manager] nor the union representative could say exactly when the agreement was reached nor did anyone expound its exact terms. When asked how this agreement was communicated to Mr Scott. Mr Smith said that he thought that it would be passed down the managerial chain in the usual way but he had no evidence that in fact this was done. The union representative said that they relied upon men attending branch meetings but unfortunately very few actually attended. It was said that members of the union could always read the minutes which would set out the terms of this agreement. However the minutes were not produced to us. It is said that union minutes were put up on a notice board, but no one knew quite when the minutes would have been put up and Mr Scott said that he had never heard of this agreement. In the Tribunal's view, if there is to be an important variation in a man's contract of employment resulting from an agreement between management and union, this variation must be brought to the man's attention in some way, otherwise it would not find its way into his contract of employment. An obvious way of bringing it to his attention is to issue an amended statement of the contract of employment containing the agreement. Or a slip could be placed in a man's wage packet mentioning the matter. Or the entire work force could be addressed by a union official, or by management so that the variation could be explained verbally. But nothing of this sort was done. Mr Scott said he had never heard of any such agreement and we accept his evidence. The Tribunal finds that any such agreement, since it was not brought to his attention, was not binding upon Mr Scott.

(C) What Are the Contractual Terms When There Is a Conflict Between Collective Agreements Negotiated at Different Levels?

Loman and Henderson v. Merseyside Transport Services Ltd.

(1968) 3 I.T.R. 108
Queen's Bench Division

The appellants, who were employees in the road haulage industry, became redundant and were dismissed by the respondents. The National Agreement relating to the appellant's employment specified a normal working week of 41 hours. In 1963, a "local agreement" (referred to as A.1 in the judgment below) was entered into between the employers and trade union officials which provided for a 68-hour working week. Mr Hanson, a witness, stated that the local agreement had no binding force being only a "gentlemen's agreement." The Tribunal accepted the evidence of the witness and awarded redundancy payments based on a 41-hour working week. The employees appealed.

Lord Parker L.C.J.: . . . at one time I was very surprised at Mr Hanson's evidence, and doubted whether any reasonable Tribunal could have properly accepted it, because one felt that the arrangement of A.1 must be binding. But on going into the matter further, one can see at once why a local agreement of this sort is not made contractually binding, but is adopted as a gentlemen's agreement. If locally legally binding agreements were made, departing from the National Agreement, it would undoubtedly create demands for a complete overhaul of the National Agreement. It seems to me, as Mr Hanson says, that these local arrangements are useful to iron out local labour difficulties, as under these arrangements employers, as it were, assume *ex gratia* an obligation to pay their men on the basis of a 68-hour week, whilst at the same time there is no obligation on any workman to work the 68-hour week. Accordingly both in law and in common sense it seems to me that the Tribunal were fully entitled to come to the conclusion they did, and accordingly I would dismiss this appeal.

Arguments such as that of Parker L.C.J. in *Loman* have frequently been adopted by the Courts in order to establish the primacy of national over local agreements. The judiciary have seldom heeded the fact that agreements at national (or industry) levels generally establish minima, which are then improved on by bargaining at local level (*cf.* ACAS's *Industrial Relations Handbook* (1981), p. 463 above).

(D) How Does a Change in Bargaining Arrangements Affect Contractual Terms?

Burroughs Machines Ltd. v. Timmoney
[1977] I.R.L.R. 404
Court of Session

The respondent employees were laid off without pay due to a strike by a group of the company's employees at their place of work. The company contended that they were entitled to lay off by virtue of clause 5(1)(*c*) of the Engineering National Agreement on guaranteed pay, which had been negotiated by the Engineering Employers' Federation on behalf of employers in the engineering industry. The company had been members of the Federation when the respondent employees commenced work but they had resigned from the EEF in February 1973.

The relevant term of the agreement provided for a guaranteed week for all hourly rated manual workers continuously employed by a *federated* firm for not less than 4 weeks, but provided for the guarantee to be suspended in the event of dislocation of production due to an industrial dispute in a *federated* establishment.

Lord Emslie: It is the fact that the company resigned from the Engineering Employers' Federation on 24.2.73. Before doing so the company gave a verbal assurance to union representatives that existing agreements, other than procedural agreements, would continue to apply after the resignation had taken effect. In addition, on 2.4.73 the company entered into a further agreement with the Amalgamated Union of Engineering Workers, representing the respondent's interest, which provided, inter alia, "Other than as altered by the above clauses, all other terms and conditions of employment for hourly paid workers shall remain unaltered." None of the alterations therein mentioned affected the terms and conditions relating to the guaranteed week.

There is no doubt that the act of the company in resigning from the federation had and could have had no effect whatever upon the contract of employment between the company and the respondent. Its terms and conditions were just the same after the resignation as they had been on 23.2.73. In these circumstances the Employment Appeal Tribunal first decided that the provisions of clause 5(1) of the National Agreement must be deemed to have been incorporated, word for word, in the contract of employment between the company. The Tribunal then proceeded to construe clause 5(1) and concluded: (i) that the respondent having been employed continuously by the company, when it was a "federated firm", for not less than four weeks, was entitled to guaranteed five day week employment or assured 40 hour-week earnings, and (ii) that although there was dislocation of production in the company's establishment on and after 28.8.74 within the meaning of the proviso (*c*) to clause 5(1) it was not a dislocation of production in a "federated" establishment with the result that the company was not entitled to lay off the respondent without pay.

. . . . The obvious intention of clause 5(1) of the National Agreement was that each of the members of the Employers' Federation would, by contract with each of their employees, guarantee employment for five days in each week or assured earnings throughout their service provided that certain conditions were fulfilled.

. . . . The other condition was that in certain circumstances the guarantee might be suspended. These circumstances plainly included dislocation of production in the premises where the qualified employee continued to work under his contract of employment, as the result of an industrial dispute there.

. . . . The contract of employment also included, at least during the company's membership of the federation, the right to suspend the guarantee where the cause of dislocation of production in the respondent's place of work was an industrial dispute in the establishment of any of their fellow members of the federation. We do not, however, for the purposes of this case, require to consider whether an additional right of the company could have survived their resignation from the federation, and it is sufficient for the disposal of this appeal to hold, as we do, that there was nothing in the respondent's contract of employment with the company to disable the company from suspending the respondent's entitlement to the guarantee, after their resignation from the federation, if there occurred as the result of industrial trouble in the respondent's place of work, a dislocation of production which, before the company's resignation, would have justified a suspension of that guarantee. In our opinion the Tribunal erred in thinking that clause 5(1) of the National Agreement must be deemed to have been incorporated word for word in the contract of employment of the respondent and we are content to know that we are not placed in the position of endorsing a construction of the provisions governing the guaranteed week in the respondent's contract of employment which has the thoroughly unsatisfactory, if not startling, consequences of the result reached by the Tribunal. In the result we hold that the company was not in breach of contract when they laid the respondent off without pay on 28.8.74.

Robertson and Jackson v. British Gas Corporation

[1983] I.C.R. 351 [1983] I.R.L.R. 302

Court of Appeal

The plaintiffs were employed on terms which provided, *inter alia*, that "Incentive bonus scheme conditions will apply. . . . " When their employment began there was a collectively agreed scheme which specified the bonus which was to be paid, and this was held to be imported expressly into the contract of employment, as were subsequent collectively agreed variations. In 1981, the employers gave six months' notice under the collective agreement to terminate the scheme.

KERR L.J.: It is true that collective agreements such as those in the present case create no legally enforceable obligation between the trade union and the employers. Either side can withdraw. But their terms are in this case incorporated into the individual contracts of employment, and it is only if and when those terms are varied collectively by agreement that the individual contracts of employment will also be varied. If the collective scheme is not varied by agreement, but by some unilateral abrogation or withdrawal or variation to which the other side does not agree, then it seems to be that the individual contracts of employment remain unaffected. This is another way of saying that the terms of the individual contracts are in part to be found in the agreed collective agreements as they exist from time to time, and, if these cease to exist as collective agreements, then the terms, unless expressly varied between the individual and the employer, will remain as they were by reference to the last agreed collective agreement incorporated into the individual contracts.

This was also the conclusion reached in *Gibbons* v. *Associated British Ports* [1985] I.R.L.R. 376 (Q.B.D.).

3. THE PROCESS OF COLLECTIVE BARGAINING

Out of the complexity and confusion of collective bargaining, labour lawyers try to extract rules defining the process. Allan Flanders stipulated three different functions for the procedural rules of collective bargaining:

> "First, they define the bargaining unit and the structure of relationships between the bargaining parties. Second, they determine the status and facilities to be accorded to their representatives. Third, they regulate the behaviour of the parties in the settlement of disputes; the stages to be followed and the methods to be used." (Evidence to the *Donovan Commission*, p. 572).

Lawyers fascinated with procedural rules should remain sensitive to the importance of substantive outcomes. As Richard Hyman reminds us:

> "[workers] do not admire collective bargaining simply as an elegant ritual, a procedural *pas-de-deux* as significant for its aesthetic sophistication as for its substantive outcome. They value trade unionism, more prosaically, as an effective means of pursuing interests which differ significantly from those of the employer: at the very least, as a mechanism for maintaining or improving the conditions of their working lives" . . . [there are dangers in assigning] primacy to the parties to collective bargaining and to the procedural arrangements in which they participate, and only secondary importance to the substantive outcome of their relationship. . . . The mere participation in job regulation may of course be wholly compatible with the stagnation or deterio-

ration of material conditions" ("Pluralism, Procedural Consensus and Collective Bargaining" (1978) 16 B.J.I.R. 16, at pp. 33–34).

The following extracts illustrate and assess attempts at legal intervention in the process of collective bargaining.

(A) Collective Bargaining and Recognition

In the United Kingdom, trade union recognition has generally been won through the strength of trade unions rather than by reliance on legislation. For two periods during the 1970s, there were statutory provisions whereby employers could be made to recognise unions:

(i) the Industrial Relations Act 1971, ss.44–53, repealed by TULRA, s.1; and
(ii) the Employment Protection Act 1975, ss.11–16, repealed by the Employment Act 1980, s.19(*b*).

Cases decided under the latter provisions revealed a profound judicial antipathy to statutory enforcement of union recognition (R. B. Simpson, "Judicial Control of ACAS" (1979) 8 I.L.J. 69). Such judicial resistance is still alive, as is revealed by the declaration in *Cleveland County Council* v. *Springett* [1985] I.R.L.R. 131 (E.A.T.):

> "There is, in our judgment, no place in any satisfactory system of employment law for the concept of enforced or automatic recognition thrust upon an employer by the action of a third party over which he has no control" (*per* Waite J., para. 28).

Currently, the closest legislation comes to prescribing duties to recognise are certain statutes establishing such publicly owned enterprises as the Post Office (*e.g.* the Post Office Act 1969; see *R.* v. *Post Office, ex p. ASTMS* [1981] I.C.R. 76; [1981] 1 All E.R. 139 (C.A.)) which merely impose duties to consult "appropriate" organisations. Also at this lower level of consultation, the House of Lords has held that, although there is no legal right of recognition, where a person has a legitimate expectation of such consultation by a decision-maker empowered by public law with executive powers, the courts will protect this expectation by judicial review. In *R.* v. *The Secretary of State for Foreign and Commonwealth Affairs, ex p. Council of Civil Service Unions* [1985] I.R.L.R. 28 (H.L.) (the GCHQ case), it was held (*per* Lord Roskill):

> " . . . the whole history of the relationship between management and staff [in the Civil Service] since 1919 shows that there was a legitimate expectation of consultation before important alterations in the conditions of service of civil servants were made . . . [W]ere management to seek to alter without prior consultation the terms and conditions of civil servants . . . such action would in principle be amenable to judicial review" (para. 83).

Although recognition has now to be gained mainly by autonomous action, the statutory definition of recognition (Employment

Protection Act 1975, s.126(1)) is still important. "Recognition" is a precondition to the enjoyment of certain statutory rights such as disclosure of information by employers for the purpose of collective bargaining (EPA, ss.17–21; below, pp. 478 *et seq.*); consultation over redundancies (EPA, ss.99–107, below, pp. 476 *et seq.*) or transfer of undertakings (Transfer of Undertakings Regulations S.I. 1981 No. 1794 r.10(2)); right to time off (EPCA, ss.27–28, below, pp. 487 *et seq.*), and rights to appoint safety representatives (Health and Safety at Work Act 1974, s.2(4)). Consequently, in a line of cases, the courts have had to examine whether and at what stage a trade union can be said to be "recognised for the purpose of collective bargaining" (EPA, s.126(1) and TULRA, s.29(1)).

National Union of Gold, Silver & Allied Trades v. Albury Brothers Ltd.

[1979] I.C.R. 84; [1978] I.R.L.R. 504
Court of Appeal

On May 5, 1976 eight of the company's 55 employees joined the union. Two days later the union's district secretary wrote asking the company for a meeting to discuss rates of pay, and on May 20, a meeting was held at which the wages of one employee were discussed but no agreement was reached. On May 28, four employees were dismissed on grounds of redundancy without prior consultation with the union. The union complained that the lack of consultation constituted an infringement of EPA, s.99 which requires employers to consult representatives of recognised trade unions when proposing redundancies.

Lord Denning M.R.: A recognition issue is a most important matter for industry; and therefore an employer is not to be held to have recognised a trade union unless the evidence is clear. Sometimes there is an actual agreement of recognition. Sometimes there is an implied agreement of recognition. But at all events there must be something sufficiently clear and distinct by conduct or otherwise so that one can say, "They have mutually recognised one another, the trade union and the employers, for the purposes of collective bargaining".

Then one comes to this particular case. Were those few letters and the one meeting recognition of the trade union? It is agreed by Mr Sedley [counsel for the union] that if the employer had simply banged the door and told the union representative to go off, that would not be recognition. Is it recognition when he goes along with the letter in his hand and is ready to discuss wages? It seems to me that that is not sufficient. Nor is it sufficient if he starts discussing the wages of one particular man . . . . There must be something a great deal more than that.

Cf. Joshua Wilson and Brothers Ltd. v. *USDAW* [1978] I.R.L.R. 120 (E.A.T.) where although the employer had never expressly agreed to recognise the union, there was clear and unequivocal evidence of recognition which could be inferred from:

(i) the fact that the company had allowed a union representative to put up a notice publicising a wage increase agreed by the Joint Industrial Council whose agreements the company followed;

(ii) the union representative had been consulted over changed allocation of duties;
(iii) the union representative had been permitted to collect union dues on company premises; and
(iv) management had directly consulted the union's area organiser over discipline and security.

Union of Shop, Distributive and Allied Workers v. Sketchley Ltd.
[1981] I.C.R. 644; [1981] I.R.L.R. 291
Employment Appeal Tribunal

After USDAW had recruited a number of members in the company's shops, it was granted "recognition for representation purposes" in respect of its members by an agreement of May 1978. The agreement specifically stated in clause VIII that the company did not grant "recognition to USDAW for negotiation of terms and conditions." Subsequently the company accepted the union's shop stewards and agreed that they be permitted time off but without pay because of the provisions of clause VIII.

After a meeting in January 1980 to discuss wages the company repeated that the union was not recognised to negotiate terms and conditions of employment although the union would be consulted. In February 1980 threats of strike action led to a meeting between the union and the company at which a memorandum was approved, giving the union official advance notice of any discussion of redundancies with a branch manager and staff at any branch where there were USDAW members, and providing that the union official would be available for discussions with the staff, that redundancy payments might in certain circumstances exceed the statutory minimum, and that in some cases volunteers for redundancy would be accepted. In return the union agreed to recommend its members not to take industrial action.

Subsequently the union complained that the company had failed to consult with it in advance of redundancies, as required by the Employment Protection Act 1975, ss.99–107. The only issue before the Industrial Tribunal was whether the union was "recognised" as required by section 99. The Tribunal decided that the union was not recognised.

BROWNE-WILKINSON J.: We think there are three stages to be considered:
(a) did the agreement of 8.5.78 amount to statutory recognition of the union?
(b) did the events which occurred between 8.5.78 and 29.2.80 give rise to such statutory recognition?
(c) did the events of 29.2.80 give rise to statutory recognition?

The relevant law on the matter was laid down by the Employment Appeal Tribunal in *NUGSAT v Albury Brothers Ltd* [1977] IRLR 173 at p. 175 as follows:

" . . . the following propositions have been established. First, the question of recognition is a mixed question of fact and law. Secondly, recognition requires mutuality, that is to say that the employer acknowledges the role of the union for the relevant purposes and the union assents to that acknowledgement. Thirdly, such a process requires agreement, which may be express or implied. Fourthly, if it is said to be implied, the acts relied on must be clear and unequivocal, and (usually) involve a

> course of conduct over a period of time. Fifthly, the words 'to any extent' in [EPA] s.11(2) do not refer to the strength or conviction of the recognition but to the subjects or areas to which it relates. In other words there may be partial recognition; that is, recognition in certain respects but not in others. Those decisions of the Appeal Tribunal do not refer to the question whether the agreement, express or implied, between the employer and the union must be legally enforceable in order to constitute recognition. In our judgment it need not."

That decision was upheld in the Court of Appeal: see [1978] IRLR 504 [p. 475 above].

The authorities also establish that it is a matter of substantial importance to the parties whether or not statutory recognition has occurred. It is for that reason that recognition is not lightly to be inferred from the actions of the parties. But we cannot accept that the Industrial Tribunal was right in treating the matter as a question of burden of proof where, as in the present case, there is an express written agreement. Where there is an express written agreement, there is no doubt that the parties have reached an agreement: the only area of doubt is as to what they have agreed. That question is to be answered by giving the agreement its true meaning in the context in which it was entered into.

We turn then to consider the three points mentioned above.

(a) The Agreement of 8.5.78. We agree with the Industrial Tribunal that this agreement did not afford statutory recognition to the union. We will assume in favour of the union that matters of representation in grievance procedures and the appointment of shop stewards are matters of a kind referred to in s.29(1) of [TULRA which provides part of the definition of "recognition"]. The crucial question in our view is whether Sketchley were recognising the union "for the purposes of negotiation relating to or connected with" such matters. The statutory definition requires the recognition to be for that purpose and none other. In our view, Sketchley were affording to the union limited rights to represent their members in grievance procedures, together with facilities for appointing shop stewards and collecting union dues. As the heading to the agreement states, it is an agreement to provide "recognition for representation," not recognition for negotiation purposes. This distinction is again emphasized by clause 8 of the agreement which expressly states that the agreement does not confer "recognition for negotiation of terms and conditions."

Mr Hand, for the union, submitted that the distinction between recognition for representational purposes on the one hand and recognition for negotiation purposes on the other is artificial and unworkable. We cannot agree. First, to our minds, there is a clear distinction between the role of a person who, under existing grievance procedures, is entitled to make representations on behalf of an individual on the one hand and the role of a person who is entitled to negotiate over what the procedures themselves should be, on the other hand. Secondly, those of us who have experience in industrial relations well know that the progress towards full recognition of a union by an employer is often a slow and careful one. The first stage is often to concede to the union the right to represent its own members. Thereafter matters may proceed further but normally only in carefully negotiated steps. To treat the first step (a representation agreement) as tantamount to recognition for negotiation purposes would be contrary to sound industrial relations practice. Thirdly, the dangers of so doing are great. Some employers are faced with a multiplicity of unions, each claiming to represent a section of the work force. All have representation rights for their individual members under grievance procedures, a practice which is obviously fair. However, only certain of the unions will be accorded full recognition and have negotiating rights. The employer's decision to recognise a union for negotiating purposes is carefully made, and once given, is equally carefully guarded by both sides. Quite often the recognised unions in an undertaking come together to engage in joint negotiations with the employer. What would be the cost to orderly industrial relations if every union which has obtained the right to represent its own members thereby became recognised for the purposes of s.99 and other purposes? For these reasons we do not consider that the agreement of 8.5.78 conferred statutory recognition to negotiate on the union. . . .

(b) Did the events occurring between 8.5.78 and 29.2.80 give rise to recognition? We do not think any inference of recognition can be drawn from these events. Although during this period the union is plainly trying to gain wider recognition and the employers are getting very close to negotiating terms and conditions of employment with the union, Sketchley throughout make it clear by their express words that they have no intention of recognising the union. In such circumstances, it is impossible to draw any inference of a mutual intention contrary to Sketchley's expressed intention.

(c) Did the events of 29 February give rise to statutory recognition?. . . . It will be remembered that the events of 29.2.80 took place in the face of a threat of imminent strike action. The memorandum states that the union has agreed to recommend withdrawal of such action and sets out certain redundancy procedures and rates of redundancy payment in excess of the statutory rates. It gives the union the right to prior information of a limited kind relating to redundancies. Nowhere does the agreement state expressly that the union is not being recognised for purposes of the negotiation.

In these circumstances, if the events of 29 February, culminating in the memorandum, in fact represent a bargain struck between the union on the one hand and the employers on the other, giving the union certain rights relating to redundancy in consideration of a recommendation to withdraw industrial action, in our view the Industrial Tribunal could properly draw the inference that Sketchley were indeed recognising the union for negotiating purposes. In our view, an employer who enters into an agreement with a union relating to the terms and conditions of employment of members of their union runs a severe risk that the inference will be drawn that such an employer has recognised the union as having negotiating rights in that field.

We do not feel able to decide this matter for ourselves. The memorandum itself, although in some respects it is suggesting a bargain between the union and Sketchley, in other parts suggests that the employers are merely stating their position without entering into any commitment. We must, therefore, remit the matter to the Industrial Tribunal to determine whether or not the events of 29.2.80 amounted to a bargain between Sketchley and the union and, if so, whether in all the circumstances it is right to infer a statutory recognition by Sketchley of the union.

(B) Collecting Bargaining and Disclosure of Information

The provisions in EPA which require disclosure of information to trade unions provide a clear illustration of legal intervention in the process of collective bargaining. The 1980 DE/PSI/ESRC Workplace Industrial Relations Survey found that 9 per cent. of managers in establishments with recognised unions reported receiving a request for disclosure of information under the provisions of the 1975 Act (6 per cent. of all establishments), while 20 per cent. of manual worker representatives and 14 per cent. of non-manual representatives reported making requests (W.W. Daniel and N. Millward, *Workplace Industrial Relations in Britain* (1983), p. 152). The extracts below highlight some of the problems of legal regulation of industrial relations.

H. Gospel and P. Willman, "*Disclosure of Information: the CAC Approach*" (1981) 10 I.L.J. 10

. . . . The trade unions, for their part, wanted a statutory right to more information, but from the beginning some claimed that the Employment Protection Act [1975] was too limited and hedged around with qualifications. For the most part the unions had probably not thought through what they wanted from the Act, what sort of information they required, and how they would use the information once obtained. On the employers' side, some more sophisticated managers welcomed greater disclosure as a channel of communication with employees and a means of obtaining their co-operation in the management of enterprise. Others, however, saw the statutory obligation to disclose to trade unions as an invasion of managerial prerogatives and a means whereby trade unions would enhance their bargaining power *vis-à-vis* management. Their objections were against various aspects of disclosure: the main argument was usually that based on commercial secrecy and confidentiality; they also charged that the process of information disclosure would impede effective decision-making; and they argued that the information which unions were citing was often not available or would be too costly to compile in relation to its value.

Perhaps the greatest innovation in the provisions on disclosure in EPA is that disputes are to be resolved by a tripartite, expert, but non-legally qualified Central Arbitration Committee (with an independent chairman and representative members), rather than by an Industrial Tribunal or a court. The following extracts contrast CAC procedures with traditional dispute resolution mechanisms.

(i) Procedure

H. Gospel and P. Willman, "*Disclosure of Information: the CAC Approach*" (1981) 10 I.L.J. 10, pp. 12–13

On receipt of a complaint the Committee has developed the practice of holding an informal meeting involving a Chairman (without the industrial members), both parties, and frequently an ACAS conciliator. The purpose of this meeting is to clarify the issues facing the Committee, discuss the rules applicable, and decide whether the problem can be solved by conciliation. The parties are not required to produce evidence nor to make formal statements and no minutes of the proceedings are taken. After this meeting, the trade union may withdraw the complaint if there seems no prospect of success or the employer may concede disclosure. Alternatively, if a conciliated settlement seems likely, arrangements will be made for the parties to receive ACAS conciliation. If there seems to be no prospect of agreement, the parties proceed to a full hearing. Similarly, where conciliation is unsuccessful, the parties will arrive at a full hearing after the Service [*ie* ACAS] has informed the Committee that further attempts at conciliation are unlikely to result in a settlement. The full hearing before the Chairman and industrial members is more formal. Written cases are exchanged beforehand and the proceedings themselves are minuted; occasionally, the parties are represented by counsel. The Committee then goes on to produce its written award stating whether all, part or none of the union's claim is well-founded, and indicating, under the heading of "general considerations," the logic underlying the decision.

Thus the procedure adopted has become more flexible than that implied in the [Employment Protection] Act [1975]. Whereas section 19 implies a clear division of labour between the Committee and the Service wherein the Committee makes a decision about the involvement of the Service which may subsequently involve awaiting the outcome of conciliation, then proceeding to a hearing, in practice the roles of the Service and the Committee are less clear-cut. The informal hearing can involve both the Service and the Committee Chairman in an assessment of the possibilities for conciliation. The parties thus encounter the Chairman in two different contexts: in the attempt to reach a settlement prior to the hearing and in the hearing itself.

Central Arbitration Committee, *Annual Report* (1981), para. 3.5

The aim, in accordance with [the Employment Protection Act 1975] s.19(2), is to settle these cases if at all possible by conciliation, an objective consistent with the CAC's general philosophy. To this end it is usual to hold a preliminary meeting with a CAC chairman and an ACAS conciliator so that the parties can discuss the issues and the possibility of conciliation can be assessed. Statistics show the effectiveness of this procedure: about two-thirds of all references have been withdrawn before reaching a full hearing and about two-thirds of these settled following the preliminary meeting/conciliation.

(ii) Statutory interpretation

Contrast the awards of the CAC and the decisions of the courts in their interpretation and application of statutory language in the following cases.

(a) EPA, s.17(1)(a): Material information

CAC Award No. 80/73, Ministry of Defence and Civil Service Union

The complaint followed the Conservative Government's decision to allow contractors to bid for the cleaning of government buildings rather than having the work done only by directly employed cleaners.

1. The complaint made under Section 19(1) of the [Employment Protection] Act [1975] relates to an alleged failure on the part of the Ministry of Defence to disclose to representatives of the Union information relating to (a) the number of cleaners to be employed by each contractor for cleaning services at certain of the employer's premises in Bath and (b) the number of hours to be worked by those cleaners. . . .

Main submissions on behalf of the Unions

8. The Union complained that, although on the basis of the formula contained in the Establishment Officer's Guide it could estimate the cost of

direct cleaning at each site in Bath, it could not, in the absence of information about the number of contract cleaners to be employed and the hours to be worked, calculate the cost of contract cleaning arrangements. It could not therefore validate the Ministry's claim that contract cleaning was more economical and so was impeded in collective bargaining relating to the anticipated redundancies of 68 cleaners. . . .

General considerations

18. In putting a case to the Committee a union has to establish to our satisfaction that without the information they are seeking they would be impeded to a material extent in collective bargaining, and that it would be in accordance with good industrial relations practice that such information should be disclosed. We have no doubt that on both these counts the Union's request to the Ministry of Defence is justified. We are surprised that the Ministry disagreed with the Union on this, since they maintained in their evidence that they always revealed as much information as they could to the Union and that they had nothing to hide on this issue. It is clear to us that the Union cannot negotiate effectively with the Ministry about the use of contract cleaners unless they are in a position to challenge whether the conditions which have been agreed are necessary for a change from direct labour—ie that it is more economic to put the work over to contract.

Civil Service Union v. Central Arbitration Committee
[1980] I.R.L.R. 274
Queen's Bench Division

FORBES J.: The only purpose of any collective bargaining by the union on this aspect was to show that contract labour would not be cheaper than direct labour and thus avert redundancy notices for 69 [*sic*] of their members. This involves, of course, a comparison of the costs of the two rival methods. If you wish to show that the employer is mistaken in suggesting that contract labour is cheaper than direct labour then you will seek to prove that the suggested figure for direct labour is too high or that its figure for contract labour is too low. Where both figures are estimates there is obviously room for considerable argument about the assumptions made in respect of the calculations. Where however the figure for the cost of contract labour is not an estimate but an actual tender or contract price there is no room for argument about it, unless you are going to maintain that the employer either cannot read the contract figure or is deliberately misleading you. The cost to the employer will be the contractor's price. However much you may calculate that the contractor's price ought to be "x," if it happens to be "y" the cost to the employer is "y" and not "x." So long as the union's case rests solely, as it did in this case, on the necessity of having this information so that they may show that the price ought to be "x," I cannot see how the process of collective bargaining can be impeded by the refusal to give them information to enable this calculation to be made. It is clearly an irrelevant, and therefore unnecessary, calculation and the information on which it is based is equally unnecessary for the process of collective bargaining. Now the only case made to the Committee was that they required the information to enable them to calculate the contractors' prices. On the basis of that argument I cannot see how any Tribunal properly directing itself, could come to the conclusion that the information was necessary to facilitate collective bargaining, or to put it more accurately, that the lack of such information would, to a material extent, impede the union in carrying out collective bargaining.

During the course of the argument in this case various other reasons were suggested why this information was required, in particular that it was required to enable the union to show that the contractors would be unable to do the job properly on the prices calculated on the basis of the information requested. Another possibility which occurs to me is that it might be possible to show that some of the lower tenders were suspect and that the only acceptable ones were higher than the cost of direct labour. If those had been the arguments before the Committee I can well imagine that that body might have accepted that, for that purpose, this was necessary information. But none of these matters was in fact put before the Committee.

(b) EPA, s.17(2): Recognition for collective bargaining

An even more fundamental problem to arise is the question of what constitutes collective bargaining. Employers have in recent years been seeking greater involvement of their employees through consultation with their representatives. It is acknowledged that such consultation is ineffective if the representatives have only partial information on which to formulate and present their views. Whether such discussions constitute negotiation as required by the Employment Protection Act 1975, s.17(2) is a matter for debate. No case before the Committee has yet turned upon this point. Where it has arisen as an issue, the parties have preferred to use the Committee's informal procedures to reach a domestic understanding rather than have a legal definition intruded into their relationship.

R. v. Central Arbitration Committee, ex p. BTP Tioxide Ltd.

[1982] I.R.L.R. 61; [1981] I.C.R. 843
Queen's Bench Division

BTP Tioxide recognised ASTMS by an agreement in 1974 in respect of monthly paid staff. In addition to the union gaining bargaining rights in respect of certain specified terms and conditions, ASTMS was granted "representational rights" on behalf of its members with regard to any other terms or conditions of employment and with regard to individual members' complaints under the company's grievance procedure.

In 1978 the union acquiesced in the establishment of a job evaluation scheme; maximum and minimum salary levels remained subject to collective bargaining but the placing of jobs within bands was a managerial decision based on the job evaluation scheme.

In representing a member claiming re-evaluation of his job under the scheme, ASTMS requested disclosure of certain details of the scheme from the company, in particular the "break points" between grades, job descriptions, and the points allocated to jobs. The company refused this request and ASTMS complained to the CAC under the Employment Protection Act 1975, s.19.

The company argued that ASTMS was not recognised for collective bargaining about the matters for which the disclosure was sought. The CAC, however, upheld the union's complaint on the ground that to accept the company's argument would mean that ASTMS was entitled to information in the exercise of one of its functions but not for its other function, and that such a result did not follow from a reasonable interpretation of the legislation.

The company applied to the High Court for a judicial review order to quash the CAC's decision on the ground that it had misdirected itself on a point of law.

FORBES J.: If Parliament had intended that all collective bargaining by trades unions was to attract the benefits of [E.P.A.] s.17 they could have said so. They did not. It is clear that Parliament restricted, and intended to restrict, the benefits of the compulsory disclosure of information only to such collective bargaining as is set out in s.17(2). That restriction, so far as is relevant, is to "matters . . . in respect of which the trade union is recognised." This expression itself envisages that there may be matters, which might appropriately form the subject-matter of collective bargaining but which are nevertheless matters in respect of which the trade union is not recognised. The Committee say that it is dealing with an agreement which recognises the union for two different roles—a right to negotiate and a right to represent individual members. It is the fact of recognition which, the Committee suggests, makes it contrary to the spirit of the Act to differentiate between the two roles. It is here that one must look at the definition of "recognition" [in EPA, s.126(1)]. . . .

I can see no obstacle under the Act to an agreement which recognises the union's right to collective bargaining, *ie* negotiation, about one aspect of employees' terms and conditions of employment and also recognises a right to some form of dealings with the employers, which does not answer to the description of collective bargaining, perhaps because it cannot be called negotiation, about another aspect. Indeed, it seems to me that the definition of "recognition" inevitably accepts this possibility as I have already indicated. The result of such an agreement would, of course, be that the union was entitled to information in respect of its collective bargaining role but not in respect of its other role under the recognition agreement. This seems to me to be a matter which the language of the Act plainly contemplates. But the Committee has directed itself that this result is contrary to the intention of the Act. It seems clear to me, therefore, that it misdirected itself in law, or on the intention and construction of the legislation.

(iii) The remedy: EPA, s.21(3)

The statutory enforcement procedure goes to convoluted length to avoid so far as possible a direct order that the employer must disclose the information sought by the union. If ACAS conciliation fails at the first stage of the complaint procedure, the CAC merely declares the union's rights to the information sought and states a period within which the employer *ought* to disclose it (s.19(6)). In the event of the employer's non-compliance with this declaration, the union may present a further complaint to the CAC (s.20); if the complaint is upheld, the CAC *may* award that the employer shall observe the terms and conditions specified in the claim or other appropriate terms and conditions (s.21(3); these terms and conditions then have effect as part of the contracts of employment of the employees within the claim (s.21(6)).

So the statute significantly avoids a direct intervention in the affairs of the collective parties by making an order enforceable against the employer by the union. Instead, it requires both the union, when making its complaints, and the CAC, when making an award at the final stage (s.21), to translate an essentially "collective" complaint into appropriate "individual" terms. It is scarcely surprising that a complaint of non-disclosure of information, upheld at the final stage of this procedure, may still cause the CAC difficulties in their award of a remedy, and characteristic differences between its response and that of the Courts.

(a) A contractual obligation to disclose information

CAC Award No. 79/451, Holokrome Ltd. and ASTMS, para. 17

A claim under [the Employment Protection Act 1975] s.21 may be expected to cover issues such as improved working conditions or better wages or holiday entitlement, in other words the sort of benefits the union might have been able to negotiate had they received the information awarded under s.19. In this case, however, the union limited its claim to the substance of the original complaint. We were presented with something of a problem as there can be important differences between information necessary for collective bargaining and information suitable for inclusion in an individual's contract of employment. We did not accept the argument put forward by the employer's solicitor that the Committee was not empowered to award any of the information already sought. The test is whether what is claimed is appropriate as a term or condition which can form part of an individual's contract of employment. We had no hesitation in awarding that the right to information on salary ranges and any incremental scale for the grade in which an employee falls should have effect as part of the individual's contract.

Civil Service Union v. Central Arbitration Committee
[1980] I.R.L.R. 274
Queen's Bench Division

FORBES J.: [The Employment Protection Act 1975, ss.20–21] sets out the procedure for taking a complaint, if the employer has not complied with the request, to the Central Arbitration Committee, and then there are some very curious provisions, which, despite all the ingenuity of Mr Weitzman [on behalf of the union], I have not been able to understand, relating to the method of enforcing any decision of the Central Arbitration Committee against the employer who fails to carry out what is required. Apparently, all that happens is that the finding of the Committee will then automatically be written in as one of the terms and conditions of the employment or service of the employees. How you can write in a decision that the employer should disclose some sort of information to the union in an employee's terms of service I fail to understand. As I say, Mr Weitzman has been quite unable to suggest any sensible solution to that problem. But those are the statutory provisions.

In *R.* v. *CAC, ex p. BTP Tioxide Ltd.* [1982] I.R.L.R. 61 (Q.B.D.), Forbes J. recalled his bewilderment in the above case, but declared he had since been enlightened as to the possibility of a claim which could be inserted into employees' contracts. He still did not appear able to entertain the CAC's innovatory idea of a term requiring disclosure.

(b) An award to meet the parties' future needs

Central Arbitration Committee, *Annual Report* (1980), paras. 4.6–4.7

In achieving results in cases of complexity, the Committee has found it wise always to bear in mind the possibility of associating the parties themselves with shaping the exact form of the award. The underlying thought behind this policy is that as far as possible the result of the arbitration should fit easily into the detailed structure of the parties' relationship. Although the third party—the independent arbitrators—may be able to see clearly the broad outline of an acceptable settlement, it is often advantageous to let the parties consider how best that aim can be expressed in detail.

The Committee has used this method in both equal pay and disclosure cases where the detail of the eventual settlement can be very extensive. It has involved close co-operation with ACAS conciliators who assist with the negotiations during the adjournment of the case and who are able to ensure that those negotiations and quasi-judicial decisions made by the arbitrators are kept properly separate. The aim of this added flexibility is awards so constructed that, at the level of technical detail, they meet the need in as convenient a way as possible for both sides.

R. v. CAC, ex p. BTP Tioxide Ltd.
[1982] I.R.L.R. 61; [1981] I.C.R. 843
Queen's Bench Division

FORBES J.: I should say that it seems plain to me that all the Committee was, and could be, adjudicating upon was a complaint that an employer *has failed* (the emphasis is mine) to supply information ([E.P.A.] s.19(2)). This declaration must specify, if they find the complaint well-founded, the information in respect of which they so find. I feel confident that these provisions only entitle the Committee to deal with a complaint relating to a past failure and information already refused and do not permit a declaration of what the Committee prospectively considers the employer in future cases should disclose. I feel some sympathy with the Committee on this point as a declaration made in the circumstances of this case, where the argument was a general one, might well be expected to govern all future cases of the same description, and the declaration was no doubt framed in this way to assist in avoiding future disputes about the same subject matter. Nevertheless, I consider that in this form the declaration was outside the Committee's statutory powers.

(iv) Effectiveness of legal enforcement

From the time of the introduction into force of the disclosure provisions (August 22, 1977) to the end of 1985 the CAC issued 50 awards (see CAC Annual Reports). In 24 awards the complaint was held to be not well-founded; in 22 awards the complaint was held to be well-founded or partly so (for detailed surveys, see 215 *Industrial Relations Review and Report* (January 1980) and 290 I.R.R.R. (February 1983)). As to the effectiveness of awards (215 I.R.R.R. (January 1980)):

> "Despite the fact that (an EPA) s.19 award is only declaratory, our research shows that employers have complied with the terms of the declaration in 10 out of the 12 references where the CAC has wholly or partly upheld the complaint.
>
> In order to ascertain the usefulness of the information obtained through a s.19 declaration, we contacted the union officials concerned. Our inquiries indicated that in only five out of the ten cases was the information of any practical use for bargaining purposes."

H. Gospel and P. Willman, "*Disclosure of Information: The CAC Approach*" (1981) 10 I.L.J. 10, pp. 20–21

The first conclusion to be drawn from an analysis of cases is that, because little use has been made of the provisions, their direct influence on disclosure practice appears to have been slight. But there may be a greater indirect impact. The [Employment Protection] Act [1975, ss.17–21] and the Code [of Practice on Disclosure of Information to Trade Unions for Collective Bargaining Purposes 1977 required to be issued under EPA, ss.17–18] together could operate to improve employer disclosure practice in the worst cases, by offering a statutory remedy. However, many unions do much better on a non-statutory basis, and the existence of restrictive provisions might encourage employers to be legalistic and secretive where this offered advantage: they might refuse to disclose information which had been granted in the past. Trade unions which have reasonable access to information might be reluctant to use the Act to extend their knowledge not only because they feel that their chances of success would be slight, but also because such a move might precipitate a change of employer attitudes.

Trade unionists may or may not want to collect a great deal of information about their companies, depending on their collective bargaining styles and strategies. But if they do, there are a number of ways they may collect it. They may seek to sign a formal "information agreement" with their employers, entitling the union to specified information. They may rely on information disclosed during the course of bargaining by management negotiators, accepting or rejecting such information as it suits them. They may rely on informal "grapevines" within organisations, so that union members pick up information about the company in the course of their work: in this instance, the occupational composition of the membership is important. Finally, they may rely on illicit or "stolen" information which becomes available accidentally within the organisation. In combination, these information sources may supply the union's bargaining needs. Given the expense and duration of a section 19 claim, it is likely that recourse to the Act will only occur where those other resources are inadequate.

In the nature of things, variable voluntary disclosure practices will always be more important than statutory devices. However, good disclosure practice requires more positive employer action and the development by unions of organisations and strategies which create a need for information and a determination to obtain and use it. The role of legislation is best seen as the promoter of such developments. Against this standard the present law is inadequate.

(C) Facilities and Time Off Work for Trade Union Officials

(i) Statutory provisions

Union lay officials need administrative facilities and time off work to fulfil their role in the process of collective bargaining. Until 1975 there were no statutory rights to any of these necessary supplements to collective bargaining. Even now the only matter covered to any extent is time off (EPCA, ss.27–28, and the Safety Representatives and Safety Committee Regulations 1977, reg. 4(2)), though as regards inspections of their workplace, the Safety Representatives' Regulations specify that "the employer shall provide such facilities and assistance as the safety representatives may require (including facilities for independent investigation by them and private discussion with the employees"—regs. 5(3) and 6(2)). However, even here in the event of non-co-operation by an employer, the regulations provide no legal sanction. The ACAS Code of Practice on Time Off for Trade Union Duties and Activities recommends that management should make available "facilities necessary for officials to perform their duties efficiently and to communicate effectively with members, fellow lay officials and fulltime officers," and then proceeds to make some specific suggestions as to desirable facilities which should be provided (para. 24). Once again, however, there is no directly enforceable obligation attached to these recommendations (*cf.* EPA, s.6(11)).

The statutory provisions permit union officials paid time off for "duties . . . concerned with industrial relations between (an) employer and any associated employer, and their employees; or to undergo training in aspects of industrial relations which is relevant to the carrying out of those duties" (EPCA, s.27(1)). By contrast, both officials and union members may have time off without pay in order to participate in the activities of a recognised trade union.

The principal difficulties over these provisions have been:

(1) the determination of what is *reasonable* as regards the amount of time off and the purposes for which, the occasions on which, and any conditions subject to which time off may be taken; on all these matters reference may be made to the ACAS Code of Practice on Time Off (EPCA, s.27(2) and 28(3));
(2) the demarcation between industrial relations duties (paid time off) and trade union activities (unpaid time off).

The decisions on these questions have ranged from a restrictive to a liberal view of the scope of "duties" and the amount of time off allowed. The first major case, *Sood* v. *Elliott Process Automation Ltd.* [1980] I.C.R. 1; [1979] I.R.L.R. 416 (E.A.T.) was careful to leave scope for both approaches, and is quoted at length in the leading Court of Appeal decision from which the following extract is taken. But the approach(es) in *Sood* should be contrasted with that in *Young* v. *Carr*

Fasteners Ltd. [1979] I.C.R. 844; [1979] I.R.L.R. 420 (E.A.T.), which took a liberal approach, and *Allen* v. *Thomas Scott & Son (Bakers)* [1983] I.R.L.R. 329 (C.A.) which leaned towards a more restrictive view.

Beal v. Beecham Group Ltd.
[1982] 1 W.L.R. 1005; [1982] I.R.L.R. 192; [1982] I.C.R. 460
Court of Appeal

The applicant lay union official employed by the respondent was refused paid time off to attend a meeting of the ASTMS National Advisory Committee (NAC) for the Beecham Group. Operationally, the Beecham Group was sub-divided into Products and Pharmaceuticals, each of which conducted industrial relations separately; the Beecham Group was solely concerned with pension and holiday arrangements. Within each sub-group collective bargaining was conducted with so-called Common Interest Groups (CIGs). ASTMS had agreements covering a number of CIGs which recognised the union to varying extents, ranging from full negotiating rights to representational rights only or to recognition at specified sites only. The NAC meeting was called for representatives of both sub-groups to discuss industrial relations and to plan a co-ordinated strategy for forthcoming negotiations.

The applicant complained to an Industrial Tribunal under EPCA, s.27 of the employer's refusal to grant him paid time off, and the Court of Appeal upheld the E.A.T.'s reversal of the Industrial Tribunal's rejection of the complaint.

O'Connor L.J.: Mr Field [for the employer] submitted further that the duties carried out must be consistent with the recognition afforded to the union. He recognised that for these submissions to succeed would involve over-ruling the decision of the E.A.T. in *Sood* v *GEC Elliott Process Automation Ltd* [1979] IRLR 416. That was a case which bore some similarity to this case. The same union had members employed in GEC Ltd and its subsidiary companies, of which Automation was one. The union had set up an NAC, but in addition they had set up a Products Advisory Committee, whose function was to enable representatives from various subsidiaries and sites producing similar products to meet, exchange information and experience, and supply information to the NAC. The question was whether an official attending a PAC meeting came within [EPCA] s.27(1)(*a*). . . . The Industrial Tribunal decided by a majority that attendance at the PAC was not within the section. On appeal by the employee, counsel for the employers made the same submissions as those Mr Field has made to us. The E.A.T. rejected the submissions. Slynn J., giving the judgment of the Tribunal, said. . . .

"We share the view of the whole of the Industrial Tribunal that the provision permitting time off for the purpose of enabling a trade union official to carry out his duties does not of itself mean that he is to be allowed paid time off in order to prepare himself or to make himself a better trade union representative. That in our view is covered by s.27(1)(b). We also agree with the Industrial Tribunal that the phrase 'industrial relations' is not to be narrowly construed. It is capable of covering many matters which arise in connection with the relationship of employer and employee. We do not accept Mr Pardoe's argument [on behalf of the employer] that the test of an official's duties is to be limited by the recognition. It seems to us that recognition identifies the trade union whose officials are entitled to claim time off under the section. It does not limit those duties to collective bargaining or to the precise terms of the recognition. We think that it is not the intention of Parliament that a trade union official should only have time off for the purpose of meetings with representatives of management. It seems to us that when questions involving industrial relations arise, a union official may well be entitled, as part of his duties, to take part in the planning of strategy and in discussing with other workers who are at the time negotiating with their employers, so long as the latter employers are associated with a particular trade union official's own employers. Nor do we accept the argument that a trade union official is only entitled to take time off for the purpose of negotiating where the employers have laid down the particular industrial relations structure . . . as Mr Pardoe suggests. It seems to us that the carrying out of the trade union official's duties for the purpose of the section can go wider than that. We do not accept the view of the second member of the Industrial Tribunal that the fact that these committees are set up purely by the trade unions, and for trade union functions, necessarily means that the duty of an official in connection with them prevents them from being duties concerned with industrial relations.

The intention of [EPCA, s.27] is that trade union officials should have time off to enable them to perform certain duties. We do not think that Parliament intended we should approach the section on the basis that the words should be narrowly construed. On the other hand it is clear from the words themselves that the duties must concern industrial relations between the official's employer and its employees, and an associated employer and the associated employer's employees, in a case where both employers and both sets of employees are concerned with the particular industrial relations problem. So, if two associated companies are negotiating with the trade union, or are involved in an industrial relations problem which will or may need to be negotiated, then it seems to us that the official's duties in connection with such negotiations may fall within the section.

There must however be some limit to the activities which fall within the section. In our view, the test is whether the time off is required to enable the official to carry out his duties in relation to a matter which arises in relations between employees and management. We do not consider that the mere exchange of information between the trade union officials themselves necessarily qualifies, even if those officials represent workers in a particular group of companies."

The E.A.T. held that the purpose of the PAC meeting was to exchange information and experience, and so dismissed the appeal. Like the E.A.T. I do not think it correct to limit "industrial relations" in s.27 to mean collective bargaining as defined in s.32. If that had been the intention of Parliament, s.27 would have read "concerned with collective bargaining." I agree with Slynn J. that "industrial relations" in the section are not limited by the terms of the recognition agreement and I am content to adopt the passages from *Sood* which I have quoted as correct. The recognition agreement may well be of very great importance when considering what is reasonable under s.27(2), see the case of [*Depledge* v. *Pye Telecommunications Ltd* [1981] I.C.R. 82; [1980] I.R.L.R. 31 (EAT)].

In practice matters arising in relations between employees and management are likely to be within the very wide range of collective bargaining as defined in the Act. In considering what is reasonable in all the circumstances for allowing time off with pay, s.27(2) requires that regard be had to the ACAS Code of Practice "Time off for trade union duties and activities." [The judge quoted the text of para. 13 and continued:] These provisions, which expressly are not comprehensive, show that the Code envisages that what is a union meeting may well be concerned with industrial relations. The Code uses collective bargaining in a restricted sense as it separates matters of grievance and discipline, but it shows that what may be called preparatory work and explanatory work by officials may well be in fulfilment of duties concerned with industrial relations.

Mr Field [on behalf of the employer] submitted that as the SEM CIG only had representational recognition, and as there were also invited representatives from Products and a non-accredited representative, the NAC meeting could not be a duty for the Technicians' Representatives within s.27(1)(a). Like the E.A.T., I cannot accept this submission. I am not concerned with the position of the . . representatives, but only with the respondents and if they were attending to enable them to carry out their duties concerned with industrial relations I do not think it matters who else was there. Such factors may well be relevant under s.27(2).

Finally, Mr Field submitted that as the NAC had no negotiating function with the employers—indeed no function at all with the employers—attending its meeting could not be for the purpose of enabling the official to carry out this duties concerned with industrial relations. Once it is recognised that preparatory work falls within the discharge of duties concerned with industrial relations, then one looks to see if the preparatory work had some direct relevance to an industrial relations matter, and if so, it qualifies under s.27(1)(a). As I have said, attending the NAC to exchange information would not have that direct relevance but to determine policies nationally may well be directly relevant, depending upon what the policies are. The agenda and minutes of the meeting show that some at least of the policies were concerned with industrial relations matters that were to go into the 1979 wage claim.

It follows that in my judgment when the respondents attended the NAC meeting it was for the purpose of enabling them to carry out their duties concerned with industrial relations.

The value of this guidance by the Court of Appeal is considerably diminished by decisions such as that in *Ashley* v. *Ministry of Defence* [1984] I.C.R. 298; [1984] I.R.L.R. 57 (E.A.T.). This held that whether a particular body of union representatives is sufficiently proximate to negotiations to qualify attendance to benefit from EPCA, s.27 is a question of fact with which the E.A.T. cannot interfere—even where, as in *Ashley*, the E.A.T. doubted if it would have reached the same conclusion. Similarly, in *Thomas Scott & Sons (Bakers) Ltd.* v. *Allen* [1983] I.R.L.R. 329 (C.A.), the Industrial Tribunal's decision was allowed to stand even though both the Court of Appeal and the E.A.T. expressed disagreement with it.

(ii) Collective agreements

The ACAS Code of Practice on Time Off paras. 10–12 puts great emphasis on the need for prior agreement between employers and trade unions. The following extracts from agreements illustrate the extent to which the standards prescribed both by statute and by the

Code of Practice are either improved upon or neglected by negotiators.

The National Bus Company's Agreement on Time off for trade union duties and activities, 201 *INDUSTRIAL RELATIONS REVIEW AND REPORT* (June 1979), p. 16

The appropriate trade union officials in company employ shall be granted absence with pay by arrangement for attendance at meetings with management representatives at any of the following:

(a) negotiations at national level;
(b) negotiations at company central level;
(c) negotiations at company local level;
(d) consultative meetings at national level;
(e) consultative meetings at company central level;
(f) consultative meetings at company local level.

Trade union officials in company employ attending meetings listed shall be granted absence with pay for attendance at one pre-meeting with their members directly related to each main meeting listed provided that such pre-meetings are held on the same day as the main meetings insofar as this is practicable.

Meetings with local paid union officers, or attendance at union branch or branch committee meetings, even though related to company activities shall be without pay, unless such meetings have the prior approval of management as part of the agreed negotiation and consultative procedures.

Trade union officials in company employ shall, on request, be given absence with pay for such time as is necessary in respect of the following matters:

(a) representation at company inquiries;
(b) representation at company appeals.

Unless there are special circumstances acceptable to management, it should only be necessary for one "lay" official to attend an inquiry or appeal.

Trade union officials in company employ should be allowed to meet the new employees to advise on union related matters or procedures agreed with the company wherever possible during spare or other non-working periods in the duties of the individuals concerned and where payment will be made in any event.

Both trade union officials and other union members in company employ shall be allowed absence without pay to attend union conferences and committees where these are not directly related to company activities. Absence with pay will be granted for attendance at trade union meetings convened to ratify annual wage settlements.

Leave of absence for branch members other than officials to participate in union activities must be subject to limitation in numbers consistent with maintaining the operational commitments of the unit(s) within the company concerned.

Trade union officials in company employ should not be permanently relieved of scheduled duties unless special circumstances within individual companies warrant such an arrangement. In such event the facilities should be restricted to a limited number of main centres and not provided at each individual depot.

Elsewhere, every effort should be made for at least one of the union officials to work special duties at each main depot (such as peak hour only) so as to facilitate their availability both to their own members and to local management.

If practicable, specific office accommodation furniture or fittings may be provided for trade union officials.

Such provision would normally apply only at the main depot or workshop within a company as in the case of many small depots such limited office accommodation as exists cannot reasonably be made available for union use.

Access to, but not exclusive use of, a telephone will be available to union officials for discussion of matters directly related to company activities.

Training activities

Absence with pay for trade union officials in company employ shall be for courses (approved by NBC's Manpower Department) as stated in s.27 of the Employment Protection (Consolidation) Act 1978. . . .

Absence with pay will be granted for attendance by union officials at union sponsored training activities related to the training of officials, and absence without pay in the case of other union members.

The numbers of those granted absence at any one time must be so limited as to be consistent with the maintenance of operational commitments of the unit(s) within the company concerned.

A copy of the syllabus or prospectus of any union sponsored training activities shall be supplied.

Absence with pay will also be given for in-company joint courses for company staff and union officials, or for off-the-job courses where company staff have an input into union organised courses.

The De La Rue Grosfield (Portsmouth location) and AUEW-TASS Agreement, 193 *INDUSTRIAL RELATIONS REVIEW AND REPORT* (February 1979), p. 9

(a) TASS committee members will be permitted to hold daily "surgeries" between 9.45 and 10.15 [a.m.].

(b) TASS committee members may use the company's facilities to contact full-time officials by letter or telephone. The normal courtesies shall be observed.

(c) The company will provide a facility for TASS members to meet on a monthly basis from 12.05–12.35 [p.m.] on a Friday. If it is envisaged that the meeting will continue beyond 12.35 [p.m.], TASS will inform management who will arrange for company transport to come back to pick up people delayed. Management will indicate the two Fridays [on which] it would prefer TASS not to have meetings because of workload in accounts.

(d) An annual general meeting shall be held during [the] month of December to confirm the election of the TASS committee. The company will provide a facility for this meeting and TASS will extend an invitation to management to attend and address the meeting following the completion of election business.

(e) The company will provide a facility for a joint monthly meeting of the engineering shop stewards and TASS committee members. The meeting shall be of half-hour duration during working hours.

(f) The company will not unreasonably withhold permission for TASS members to attend official trade union educational courses. Time off with pay will be provided subject to mutual agreement.

(g) Both sides recognise that despite the foregoing, special arrangements may be necessary to meet unforeseen circumstances. TASS would give at least 24 hours' notice of such a meeting and notify the reason for the meeting.

The implications of using collective agreements as a standard for what is "reasonable" time off were analysed in the following extract.

R. H. Fryer, A. J. Fairclough and T. B. Manson, "*Facilities for female shop stewards: the Employment Protection Act 1975 and collective agreements*" (1978) 16 B.J.I.R. 160, pp. 161–2

The Code [of Practice on Time Off] suggests that facilities depend, to some degree at least, on the circumstances prevailing in the place of employment, and does not lay down exact details as to how much time is to be allowed. Different circumstances are said to produce different forms of collective bargaining and a different pattern of industrial relations. Time off will therefore be expected to vary and, while [EPA] provides a right to time off, the precise amount of time off will be dependent on local circumstances. . . .

It seems likely that facility agreements and the provisions of EPA, rather than making common provision, will in fact result in unequal availability of facilities to different groups of shop stewards. In so far as local bargaining determines the level of facilities, the results of bargaining will reflect the strengths and weaknesses of union organisation. Any systematic strengths or weakness of groups of workers or occupations will therefore tend to be reproduced in the level of facilities enjoyed by those workers, and conversely, explanations for systematic variations in levels of facilities should be sought in patterns of strength and weakness.

Even where facilities agreements are negotiated, they are almost never legally enforceable as between the collective parties (see below, pp. 501–503). Even if incorporated into individual contracts of employment, the judges are reluctant to allow union representatives to enforce such contractual rights. The reasoning in the following case illustrates the policy preferences of the courts in weighing trade union rights against managerial prerogatives.

City and Hackney Health Authority v. National Union of Public Employees

[1985] I.R.L.R. 252
Court of Appeal

Mr Craig was an accredited shop steward whose contract of employment was held arguably to incorporate section IX of a collective agreement (referred to in the judgment as the "Whitley Council Agreement") whereby the employer undertook to provide facilities to enable shop stewards to exercise their functions. Following a hospital occupation, the employer suspended, and then dismissed Mr Craig, alleging misconduct. Mr Craig obtained an interlocutory injunction restraining his employer from interfering with his access to the hospital and the performance of his duties. The employer appealed.

OLIVER L.J.: . . . what I feel the very greatest difficulty about is in seeing how, assuming such incorporation [of section IX into Mr Craig's contract of employment], the privileges extended to a shop steward under section IX of the Whitley Council Agreement could possibly survive the suspension or the termination—and we are now dealing in fact, as matters have evolved since the hearing before the learned judge, with a termination—of the only agreement whereby they have their contractual force. It seems to me that this is so plainly unarguable that I would be prepared to hold on this ground alone that there was really no arguable case for saying that once his employment had been suspended—*a fortiori,* once it had been terminated as it now has, although that is still subject to a right of appeal under the conditions of service—he had a right to attend on the premises, a right which could only stem from the contract of service.

There are, however, further points which Mr Tabachnik [counsel for the employer] has taken even if that is wrong. First of all, he says this, that in effect the injunction that has been granted by the learned judge, although negatively expressed, amounts in fact to a specific performance of the provisions of section IX that the plaintiff shall give facilities for the exercise of the shop steward's function. That, he says, is something which is wrong as a matter of law because this is, although not strictly in itself a contract of service, a part of the contract of service by incorporation: indeed, it can, in conferring rights on Mr Craig, only confer such rights in law on the footing that the terms are incorporated in the contract of service. In any event, he says, and I think there is great force in this, that this is the sort of contract which must necessarily depend upon mutual confidence and is not the sort of contract in which it would be appropriate or in which the court could possibly order specific performance. In decreeing, therefore, that the plaintiff shall permit Mr Craig to come on the premises for the purposes of carrying out negotiations—and that, as I read the order, is what in fact it is doing—it is either doing something which ought not to be done (that is, specifically enforcing an agreement which is based entirely upon the mutual trust between the parties) or it is a useless injunction, because if one of the parties is not prepared to negotiate with Mr Craig (and the plaintiffs say in unequivocal terms that they have lost all confidence in him), then it serves no useful purpose. I point again to the terms of paragraph 352 of section IX of the Whitley Council Agreement where a shop steward's activities are, *inter alia,* "to make representations on such matters to the management and to co-operate with management to ensure that the agreements of the Council are observed." How one can get such co-operation when all confidence has been lost is not apparent to me, and I think there is great force in Mr Tabachnik's submission that this does in fact amount to interlocutory specific performance of a contract which, of its nature, is not specifically enforceable. . . .

On the face of it, I am bound to say that it is very difficult to imagine anything more inconvenient from the plaintiffs' point of view than having, under order, to permit on their premises for apparently as much time as he requires a dismissed employee whom they clearly distrust, who will be in constant contact with their other staff, one of the allegations made against him being that he has disrupted staff-management relations. Nor is it easy to see what useful purpose is served from Mr Craig's point of view, save this, that he has some slight financial interest in the matter of being shop steward because he gets a commission from the union of an amount we have not been told about on the introduction of new members. Apart from that, his position as shop steward, I would have thought, would be one which could serve no very useful purpose because, with the kind of feelings which are deposed by the affidavits, it does not look as if any negotiations which do take place, or might take place, if he is allowed to frequent the plaintiffs' premises, show a very fruitful prospect of success.

There are further reasons which would indicate very strongly that an injunction, in the circumstances, ought not to have been granted, which are these. It is quite clear, in my judgment, that the whole purpose of the introduction into the conditions of employment of a clause enabling the employer to suspend an employee from duty on full pay pending investigation is to enable the employer to deny the employee access to the premises while that investigation is proceeding—for obvious reasons. In cases of serious misconduct, no employer wishes to have about his premises an employee who is in constant contact with other members of his staff but in whom the employer has lost all confidence. If that liberty to the employer is to be avoided by a side-wind by the continued force given, notwithstanding the termination of the employment, to the provisions of section IX of the Whitley Council Agreement, that is undermining, as it seems to me, the disciplinary procedure which has been introduced into the contract by the terms to which I have referred.

4. CUSTOM AND PRACTICE

In section 2 we described something of the complexity of collective bargaining structures: their many levels, their varieties of personnel and degrees of formality or informality, and the legal problems which these features cause. In section 3 we examined legal interventions in the process of collective bargaining that goes on within these structures.

In this section we examine a phenomenon of industrial relations of great significance to workers which is neither captured within the structures of collective bargaining, nor adheres to the formal processes outlined above. This phenomenon is called "custom and practice," ("C & P") and the following extracts represent attempts to define and describe it.

W. Brown, *"A consideration of custom and practice"* (1972) 10 B.J.I.R. 42

. . . C & P rules [are] those transactional rules of job regulation which arise, not from any explicit and formal negotiation, but from a process whereby managerial error or omission establishes a practice that workers see as legitimate to defend. Besides being a type of job regulation rule, C & P is used as a claim and an excuse in circumstances where powerful work-forces interact with un-coordinated managements.

The importance of C & P should be emphasized. Whatever it is called, the phenomenon is evident in most of industry. In some industries it provides the basis and origin of rules of job regulation. It does not just augment formally negotiated rules; it supplants them. Even many ostensibly solid formal agreements are no more than the temporary recording of the current state of C & P rules. Once signed, these agreements may become battered by managerial deviation and worker pressure and finally dissolve into the broad flux of C & P.

If, in much of industry, C & P is king, its reign is curiously blind. Its rules do not emerge from any of the conscious bargaining processes with which industrial relations theories have concerned themselves. They do not arise from intention, deliberation or conspiracy. They are the product of management error and worker power.

H. A. Clegg, *THE SYSTEM OF INDUSTRIAL RELATIONS IN GREAT BRITAIN* (2nd ed., 1972), pp. 248–50

In industry bargaining, signed agreements are reached through recognised procedures. Even where the procedures are not embodied in an agreed document they are generally well understood and no one is in doubt about the arrangements for calling a joint meeting or for conducting its business. Members of the two sides may, of course, meet and talk outside the procedure and even come to understandings about how to handle particular issues, but the constitutional procedures and the signed agreements remain the basis of their relationship. It is very different with domestic bargaining. One of its features which helps to account for the difficulty of giving a clear account of its working and importance, and which often puzzles visitors from countries with different systems of industrial relations, is that in domestic bargaining there need be neither signed agreements nor recognised procedures.

This can easily be envisaged in a small plant with only one shop steward representing all the workers. There is no need for a procedure. He can ask to see the manager when he wants to, or the manager can send for him. Let us suppose that he convinces the manager that one group of workers is underpaid in view of the work they are doing, and the manager agrees to pay them an extra sixpence an hour. This may be done by a verbal instruction to the wages clerk, and there need be no explanation of why the payment is made; or perhaps it may be referred to as a merit rate or just a plus rate. Successive decisions of this kind can lead to a separate pay structure for the plant, quite different from the industry agreement. To settle arguments about overtime the manager may ask the steward to keep a rota of men willing to work overtime. Again there need be no record on paper except the list which the steward keeps in his pocket.

There is no clear line between bargaining of this kind and consultation. The decision is an agreement if the manager accepts that he cannot change it without the consent of the steward. The manager may be forced to do so if he finds that the men are prepared to strike or if the steward appeals to his full-time officer and through him to the industry's disputes procedure. But in any particular instance in which it has not been put to the test there may be doubt as to whether a particular managerial decision is an agreement or merely an exercise of managerial prerogatives after consultation with the steward.

Understandings of this kind are commonly called "custom and practice," but custom and practice can also arise without any conscious decision by management. Let us suppose that it is the shop steward himself who decides to keep an overtime rota, asking the foreman henceforth to follow the rota in offering overtime work. The foreman, not concerned with anything else but getting the work done, acquiesces in the arrangement, which thus becomes custom and practice, regarded as binding on the manager even though he has never heard of it. Furthermore in industrial relations as elsewhere custom can emerge without any conscious decision at all. Let us suppose the firm has its own vans to deliver its products. It so happens that the drivers stand by while their vans are loaded. No one can remember why. One day it occurs to the manager that deliveries would be speeded up if the drivers helped to load. He tells them to do so. They demur, saying that the existing arrangement is custom and practice, and if he wants to change it he must negotiate with the steward.

Domestic bargaining may be conducted in this way even in larger undertakings. A manager may deal separately with each of two or more stewards or leave his departmental managers to do so. If some common issue arises the stewards can ask to see him collectively, or he can send for all of them at once. Their joint dealings may result in nothing more than unwritten understandings. However, as the size of the undertaking increases the demands of administration are likely to bring some formality and written understandings. Where there is a number of stewards it may be convenient for one of them to call the others together from time to time and to arrange for meetings with the manager. It may also be useful to call on this senior steward or convenor to deal with issues which cannot be settled between departmental managers and their stewards. The manager may decide to keep a note of his meetings with the stewards. If he asks the senior steward to agree the note then the decisions recorded come close to written agreements.

The above descriptions of custom and practice contrast sharply with the rules which emerge from the structures and processes of collective bargaining described in previous sections. The following extract offers an analysis of the nature of the rules or norms of custom and practice.

S. Hill, *"Norms, groups and power: the sociology of workplace industrial relations"* (1974) 12 B.J.I.R. 213, 230–32

[One explanation of rules and normative regulation] presupposes an analysis of actual behaviour in specific situations, focusing attention on the relationships of workers with management and with each other. This is an interactionist perspective which lays emphasis on the nature of social relations within a social system. In this case, norms are treated as the expressions of regularities arising out of interactive behaviour rather than imposing regularity on this. Social interaction in industry may have certain characteristic features, such as the way it takes place within a system of formal authority relationships, but it can be analysed in the same terms which sociologists have developed for other forms of social relationship. Thus the regularities of industrial social relations can be understood in terms of the various bases of interaction identified elsewhere, in particular in terms of power and exchange.

Norms serve primarily to codify and formalize these interactions. There is no reason why such norms should necessarily become more than mere statements about the regularity of behaviour, because the internalization of norms as morally binding or desirable is not the necessary consequence of such interaction. Interaction can and does become habitual and can be stable overtime without either party attaching moral value to it or treating it as legitimate in terms of social values. The regularity of interaction and the growth of norms can be matters of indifference to either party, or they can be regarded as illegitimate by one side which does not, however, have the resources to change the situation. Situations where management feels itself dominated by the labour force, or vice versa . . . , are characterized by regularity of interactions and the existence of norms or rules but not by sentiments of legitimacy.

On the other hand, it is possible that interaction may develop into something which is normatively internalized, as can be seen in Brown's account [above p. 495] of custom and practice as a series of "transactional rules." This is basically an interactionist approach to workplace relations: it provides an example of a set of rules based on interaction which owes little to any prior or internalized normative regulation, but shows how the regularities can become invested with legitimacy and develop a morally binding force if continued over time. In some instances, it is possible to talk of a moral obligation to follow the rules which derives from their regular, or customary, nature. . . .

The moral force which some rules accumulate over time can make them to some extent independent of interaction, however, so that the rules themselves can be appealed to if behaviour deviates from, say, customary practices. But changes in interaction ultimately change the rules: for example, if a work group consistently breaks a rule and has the power to prevent management enforcing this, then the new action becomes the norm and the old rule ceases to operate as a standard for behaviour. The dialectical nature of this process indicates that some rules become as it were detached from interaction and exert an independent force of their own which partially constrains future actions, but that changes in the interactive base ultimately modify the norms to accord with the new reality. The structure of the workplace social system is neither inherently stable nor static, since it represents the regularities of past interactions which are modified by new ones: it is a continually evolving, adaptive process. Norms have force to the extent that they embody these previous regularities: they are taken into account, but do not necessarily determine behaviour in relationships.

Custom and practice poses numerous problems for labour law. One is the static nature of the concept of "contract" and its difficulties in accommodating a dynamic process of rule formation at the workplace. The formalities required by the law of contract (consideration, and so on) only add to the problems of fitting custom and practice into the contractual straitjacket. Some authors claim to ascertain developments by the courts to meet this problem (P. Davies and M. R. Freedland, *Labour Law: Text and Materials* (2nd ed., 1984), p. 299). It is possible, however, that even more problematic for the courts is the essentially collective nature of custom and practice, its instability and, perhaps above all, the sources of its legitimacy.

W. A. Brown, *"A consideration of custom and practice"* (1972) 10 B.J.I.R. 42, 48–9

Under the prevailing values of our industrial society . . . the underlying legitimacy of rules of job regulation stems from managerial prerogative. It may come directly from management regulation. Alternatively it may come from management's formal recognition of and negotiation with worker representatives. Either way, the legitimacy is basically managerial legitimacy.

There is another source of legitimacy present in the industrial context, one that is very different from the managerial type. This is based on custom. . . .

In the absence of other mutually acceptable criteria, then, custom can possess its own sense of legitimacy. Under what circumstances this becomes important and over-rides managerial legitimacy is a question that must await further discussion.

M. Terry, "*The inevitable growth of informality*" (1977) 15 B.J.I.R. 76, 78

Rules which differ in form, content, and authorship often apply in the same area of job control. The potential conflict thus implied is only brought to the surface when each side invokes the rule to which it adheres in a dispute situation. In these situations it then becomes possible to see that these different rules may carry different degrees of support and allegiance with the different groups involved.

Consider the common case of a dispute situation in which management base their case on a formal rule, and the shop floor base theirs on a C. & P. understanding. One example took place at one of the plants studied, and concerned a management attempt to transfer an operator between areas in a way which the men concerned considered to be in breach of custom. In cases of this sort, as happened in this particular instance, agreement may be reached which concedes the shop floor (C. & P.) claim, while emphasising that this is a "special case" and not a concession on principle. The cumulative effect of such decisions tends to be to reinforce the legitimacy of the formal provision in the minds of management and to confirm the usefulness of the custom in the minds of the stewards and the shop floor. Such situations can, and do, lead to a situation typical of many workplaces, namely that the legitimacy and authority of rules purporting to regulate the work situation are not constant across those to whom they apply and by whom they are applied. Different groups attach different importance to different rules.

To put the same point more systematically, the hypothesis can be advanced that a rule will carry the greatest authority with the group or individual who fought for, negotiated, or guarded, that rule. This implies that groups or individuals further away from the authorship or care of such rules will be more prepared than the authors or guardians to challenge such rules. Thus in the workplace C. & P. should carry greater authority for the shop floor workers than any other group, and for these workers, such rules may well carry greater authority than any other rule or set of rules, with another source or author. Further, the strength of shop-floor allegiance to C. & P. suggests that, from the shop-floor perspective, it is irrelevant whether or not the authors of such rules have any written dispensation, either from management or the union outside, to negotiate or enforce such rules.

The unwillingness of judges to integrate rules of custom and practice into contract law, and their reluctance to rely on informal practice is illustrated in the following case of refusal of management to acknowledge a custom and practice of consultation of trade union representatives.

Glitz v. Watford Electric Co. Ltd.
[1979] I.R.L.R. 89
Employment Appeal Tribunal

The appellant, who was employed on general clerical duties, worked mainly as a typist. When, after three years, she was asked to operate the duplicating machine, she was reluctant, but eventually agreed. She developed headaches, however, and when these prevented her continuing on the duplicator, she was dismissed.

ARNOLD J.: That question would be whether the agreement, which undoubtedly was forthcoming as a matter of fact, from Miss Glitz to working on the duplicator was vitiated and destroyed because of the circumstances in which it was given. Now the argument is this: that where a *fait accompli*, a decision already made by management, is presented to an employee without prior consultation, then an agreement by the employee to the proposal thus made is automatically of no effect, and that that is particularly so where no trade union assistance, or less than a desirable degree and quality of trade union assistance, is afforded to the employee in making his or her decision.

Of course there are many situations in which the necessity for consultation is required, either absolutely or within qualified terms, in order to avoid certain legal consequences. . . .

[The judge referred to the law on unfair dismissal and redundancy and continued:] But that is very far from saying that the law of contract has been changed and that somehow there has become encrusted on to the legal requirements for the valid formation of a contract between an employer and an employee, that there should be some prescribed degree of consultation before the moment of agreement, whether that involves the introduction into the negotiations of a trade union officer or not. . . .

One of the matters which arose in this context concerns the position of Mr Tomsett. Mr Tomsett in fact, according to Miss Glitz's evidence, assisted her in making up her mind. When she was describing, in the language to which we have already referred, her initial reaction to working the machine she added, after saying that she "did agree, however"—"I saw Mr Tomsett and he advised me to use it." Now at that stage no question arose between Miss Glitz and the management concerning the position of Mr Tomsett at all. But later on, when the problems stemming from the consequences to the health of Miss Glitz of using the duplicator arose, a question did arise as to whether Mr Tomsett should be regarded as representing her in her negotiation with the employers and by a transference of conception—a very natural one as it seems to us—it is said on behalf of Miss Glitz, "Well, if, at that later stage, the company was unwilling to recognise Mr Tomsett as Miss Glitz's negotiator" then no doubt the same conception prevailed earlier on so that, when he advised Miss Glitz, he had not got those advantages which he would have had if he had been the duly accredited negotiator. That is the sort of point which is put. It is very important to understand this point. Mr Tomsett was, as we understand the evidence, the duly accredited negotiator by arrangement between the union and the employers for technical staff. He was not, under any arrangement between the union and the employers, the negotiator either for clerical staff generally or for those members of his union who happened to be employed in a clerical capacity. It may be or it may not be, if it had been proposed that he should be such an accredited negotiator, that the answer would have been that he should be. That would have depended upon many factors, not least the question whether any other union was in the field. But that was the situation and it does not seem to us to be in the least surprising or shocking in those circumstances that, without there being such an accreditation, he should not formally be regarded as nevertheless being an accredited negotiator for clerical staff.

Contrast may be made with a decision of the House of Lords which recognised a continuum between collective agreements which are legally binding, collective agreements which are not legally binding, and established industrial custom and practice. It was held that an employee, who was a member of USDAW, laid off as a result of a dispute with workers in the AUEW was "directly interested" in it (and hence disqualified from unemployment benefit) because "the employers would, by reason of the factual situation at the factory, by which [the Social Security commissioner] clearly meant the established industrial custom and practice there, apply automatically the outcome of their dispute with the AUEW to other groups of workers belonging to other unions at the same factory, including the group of workers belonging to USDAW of which the claimant was one." (*Presho* v. *Department of Health and Social Security* [1984] I.R.L.R. 74 (H.L.), *per* Lord Brandon of Oakbrook, at para. 19.)

5. COLLECTIVE AGREEMENTS

(A) Legal enforceability

The legal definition of "collective agreement" in TULRA, s.30(1) gives some indication of their breadth of coverage by reference to the list of items in section 29(1). Collective agreements may contain detailed provisions on hours of work, wages, holidays, sick pay and other substantive terms, as well as procedures for grievance or dispute settlement, disciplinary rules and procedures, job evaluation criteria and procedures, substantive terms and procedures governing the introduction of new technology, redundancy terms and selection procedures, closed shop requirements and appeals procedures; they may also set up complex negotiating structures.

Collective agreements are rarely legally enforceable as between the collective parties, employers and trade unions, who negotiate them, as the following extract explains.

Green Paper on *Trade Union Immunities*, Cmnd. 8128 (January 1981)

224. It has been noted that, unlike most other countries. Great Britain has no tradition of legally enforceable agreements. They are not prohibited by law. But management and unions have chosen not to conclude agreements which are legally binding. The Donovan Commission summed up the position as follows:

> "In this country collective agreements are not legally binding contracts. This is not because the law says that they are not contracts or that the parties to them may not give them the force of contracts. . . . It is due to the intention of the parties themselves. They do not intend to make a legally binding contract, and without both parties intending to be legally bound there can be no contract in the legal sense . . . [T]his intention and policy that collective bargaining and collective agreements should remain outside the law is one of the characteristic features of our system of industrial relations. . . . It is deeply rooted in its structure." (paras. 470–471)

225. The High Court confirmed that collective agreements were not legally binding in 1969 in the case of *Ford Motor Co v Amalgamated Union of Engineering and Foundry Workers (AEF)* ([1969] 2 All E.R. 481). Mr Justice Geoffrey Lane (the present Lord Chief Justice) giving judgement said:

> "The fact that the agreements *prima facie* deal with commercial relationships is outweighed by the other considerations, by the wording of the agreements, by the nature of the agreements, and by the climate of opinion voiced and evidenced by the extra-judicial authorities. . . . Without clear and express provisions making them amenable to legal action, they remain in the realm of undertakings binding in honour."

(i) Liability of trade unions

236. In some other countries the legal enforceability of collective agreements means that trade unions themselves become liable if their officials or members break those agreements. . . .

237. . . . it is argued that trade unions are not at present equipped to supervise and monitor the multiplicity of agreements which are signed by their officials, including shop stewards. Without major changes in the structure and organisation of unions (including a substantial increase in the number of full-time officials), it is suggested that it would be unrealistic to expect them to exercise the necessary degree of control over the making of such agreements which is apparent in other countries. . . .

(iii) Attitudes of employers and trade unions

239. The third consideration lies in the attitudes of employers and unions. If both employers and trade union negotiators had accepted that it was in their interests to conclude legally binding agreements they could have done so at any time in the last 100 years. They have hardly ever done so. The 1971 [Industrial Relations] Act sought to encourage the adoption of such agreements. The experience was that management and unions were at best apathetic and at worst deeply hostile. Hostility appears to have been greater on the part of unions, reflecting their traditional suspicion of legal intervention in collective bargaining, but it is by no means clear that employers would always have welcomed the stricter obligations legal enforceability would impose on them. The informal nature of collective bargaining in Great Britain has often appeared to suit both employers and trade unions, although to different extents at different times.

240. It is argued that there needs to be some general basis of consent for the universal introduction of legally enforceable agreements into Great Britain for the system to operate effectively. The experience of other countries shows that legal enforceability works, not simply because the law provides that agreements are enforceable at law, but because it is accepted by both unions and management alike as a sensible way of regulating industrial relations which benefits employers and their employees.

In *Monterosso Shipping Co. Ltd.* v. *International Transport Workers Federation* [1982] 3 All E.R. 841; [1982] I.R.L.R. 468 (C.A.) it was held that a collective agreement, which did not state that it was intended to be legally enforceable and which was therefore under TULRA, s.18 conclusively presumed not to be legally enforceable, was not a contract at all. The essence of a contract is that it is legally enforceable. In *National Coal Board* v. *National Union of Mineworkers* [1986] I.R.L.R. 439 it was held that the effect of section 18 was to require the parties to make a statement in a collective agreement that they intend the agreement to be enforceable; in the absence of such a statement the agreement will not be legally enforceable.

(B) Incorporation of Collective Agreements into Contracts of Employment

The legal consequences of collective agreements fall mainly, therefore, on the individual employee and employer. Collective agreements are normally incorporated, expressly or by implication, into individual contracts of employment. The complex structure of collective bargaining can, as shown above (pp. 463 *et seq.*) create difficulties in establishing which collective agreement is incorporated and how this is accomplished. Here, a different problem is addressed: the suitability of the *contents* of collective agreements to be translated into individual contractual rights. Some substantive provisions of collective agreements may transfer easily into contracts of employment (*e.g.* terms on wages, hours, holidays, sick pay, etc.). But other aspects of collective agreements may present problems. The following cases illustrate the difficulties confronting Tribunals and courts seeking to apply collectively negotiated terms of employment to individual employment relationships.

(i) Job evaluation schemes

Mucci v. Imperial College of Science and Technology
[1973] I.R.L.R. 130
Industrial Tribunal

A collective agreement introduced a restructuring scheme for university technicians involving a job evaluation procedure and opportunities for appeal. The scheme was accompanied by increases in pay.

LONDON TRIBUNAL (chairman: E. G. WRINTMORE): As we understand the law, collective agreements between employers and organisations representing employees, are not necessarily incorporated into contracts between an individual employee and his employer. It does not seem that by the terms of his contract of employment the complainant in this case is bound to accept the terms of a national agreement such as this one. But it may be argued that even though not expressly bound, nevertheless by reason of his conduct he has impliedly agreed that the terms of his contract should be varied.

We find upon this evidence that Mr Mucci has accepted a rise in salary and accepted it linked with the principle of job evaluation and a restructuring of some kind. He objects that he does not fit into the National Agreement Scheme that has been subsequently devised. That may well be; it may be that he should be fitted into an academic related structure . . . and indeed it is possible that he will be; he may become a Research Officer and with this he would probably be satisfied. But in the meantime some test must be applied and some machinery must exist for assessing his duties. It is necessary that there should be some kind of job description form to see if the complainant's job can be fitted into such an academic related structure or whether it is more appropriate to the technical structure.

(ii) Disciplinary rules and procedures

Bailey v. BP Oil Kent Refinery Ltd.
[1980] I.R.L.R. 287; [1980] I.C.R. 642
Court of Appeal

Mr Bailey complained that a collectively agreed disciplinary procedure was not followed when he was dismissed. The particular clause in issue was: "Safeguard 4: The company will inform the appropriate full-time [trade union] official as soon as possible of any case in which dismissal or down-grading is contemplated."

LAWTON L.J.: The Employment Appeal Tribunal seems to have construed Safeguard 4 as a condition precedent, with which there had to be compliance before there could be a dismissal. Thus, in his judgment, Mr Justice Arnold, as he then was, said at page 13C: "We therefore come to the conclusion that there was here a failure to comply with the contractual procedure which was prescribed to be dealt with in such cases, and that, although it is quite impossible to say that had that procedure been complied with it would have led to the opposite conclusion in the event, we cannot exclude the possibility that it might have done. In those circumstances the appeal must, we think, be allowed. . . . " We are unable to accept this reasoning for two reasons: first, we do not construe Safeguard 4 as creating a condition precedent which had to be complied with before an employee could be dismissed. . . .

Safeguard 4 can only be construed as providing a condition precedent to dismissal if further words are read into it; but if it is read literally it provides no safeguard for an employee because he could be dismissed as soon as the trade union official had been informed. Doing the best we can with a badly drafted provision of the agreement, we construe it, not as creating a condition precedent but as meaning that the employers have to keep the employee's trade union official informed of what they are thinking of doing so that he can take such action as he thinks fit, including, if there is a dismissal, having the case referred to arbitration.

(iii) Disputes procedures

National Coal Board v. Galley
[1958] 1 W.L.R. 16; [1958] 1 All E.R. 91
Court of Appeal

When deputies at the defendant's colliery gave notice that they would not work on Saturdays in future, the plaintiff issued a writ claiming damages for breach of contract. The plaintiff was a member of a local trade union which was itself a member of the National Association of Colliery Overmen and Deputies and Shotfirers (NACODS), an unregistered trade union that was composed of area associations and had no individual members, and which discussed and arranged with the defendants any alterations in the terms of the deputies' employment. At issue, *inter alia*, was an agreement on "revised terms and conditions of employment of deputies" reached on July 29, 1952 and which contained the following clauses:

Clause 12. Except where prevented by sickness, accident or industrial disease to which the provisions of Part E of this schedule apply, deputies shall work such days or part days in each week as

> may reasonably be required by the management in order to promote the safety and efficient working of the pit and to comply with statutory requirements.
>
> Clause 15. If, in any case, it is alleged that the amount of time worked by any deputy or deputies is unreasonable or is not reasonably distributed between deputies in the same grade in the pit, such matter shall be settled by discussion in such manner as the Board and the Association in the division shall agree.

PEARCE L.J.: The judge thought that, since one of the objects of Nacods was to negotiate the wages and conditions of all members and the defendant was a member of the local trade union which was itself a member of Nacods, the defendant was individually bound by the Nacods agreement. But in any event, by the defendant's personal contract his wages were to be regulated by national agreements for the time being in force and the contract was to be subject to those agreements; and therefore, since the Nacods agreement was a national agreement, the defendant was bound by it. . . .

. . . as the judge said, it is clear that the [plaintiff's] personal contract of service is regulated by the Nacods agreement and the [plaintiff] by working on the terms of the Nacods agreement has entered into an agreement which contains the term now in dispute.

The [plaintiff] next contends that, even though the Nacods agreement was applicable to the [plaintiff's] employment, yet it had no contractual force, because it was too vague. It is an industrial agreement, he argues, covering a wide area, with no intention that it shall have a specific or enforceable effect.

Collieries differ, and what is reasonable in one will be unreasonable in another. The court has no yardstick to measure what are reasonable requirements. For instance, the stringency of those requirements depends on the number of deputies employed. It is a case within the principle of *May and Butcher* v *The King* [1934] 2 K.B. 17 rather than *Foley* v *Classique Coaches Ltd.* [1934] 2 K.B. 1.

But it seems to us, on a consideration of the Nacods agreement, that it was meant to have a binding effect. Realising the difficulties inherent in the situation, it provided for discussions, if it appeared to be working out unfairly for the deputies. To define with exactitude what are the duties of a servant is no easy task. The court will supply an implied condition as to reasonableness in many contracts where duties are not fully defined, as in *Hillas & Co. Ltd.* v *Arcos Ltd.* (1932) 147 L.T. 503 and *Foley* v *Classique Coaches Ltd.*

Mr Gardiner [counsel for the plaintiff] also relies on the provision in clause 15 for discussion in the event of complaints. He contends that this is typical of an industrial agreement not intended to be enforceable in the courts. We do not, however, see how in principle such a provision differs from that in *Foley* v *Classique Coaches Ltd.*, which provided for the price to be agreed between the parties. It may be that discussion is a condition precedent to action, but once discussion is repudiated or fails the matter falls to be determined by the courts. Moreover, the [plaintiff] is in this further difficulty. He is asserting that the agreement as a whole exists, while seeking to deny the enforceability of clause 12. If clause 12 is too vague to be enforceable the whole agreement is not legally binding on either side: see *Bishop & Baxter Ltd.* v *Anglo-Eastern Trading Co. Ltd.* [1944] K.B. 12; 60 T.L.R. 37.

In this contract the parties have expressly provided that reasonableness shall be the test. The fact that it is difficult to decide in a given case, should not deter the court from deciding what is a reasonable requirement by a master in the light of the surrounding circumstances. In our view, therefore, the judge was right in deciding that the term as to working was legally binding.

Compare the National Disputes Procedure in the engineering industry:

> Where any party wishes to raise a matter for resolution, there shall be discussion at domestic or national level, as appropriate. It is agreed that in the event of any difference arising which cannot immediately be disposed of, then whatever practice or agreement existed prior to the difference shall continue to operate pending a settlement or until the agreed procedure has been exhausted. In order to allow for the peaceful resolution of any matter raised by any party, there shall be no stoppage of work, either of a partial or general character, such as a strike, lock-out, go-slow, work-to-rule, overtime ban or any other restrictions, before the stages of procedure provided for in this Agreement have been exhausted.

The next extract discusses a disputes procedure in the context of an unfair dismissal claim.

Thompson v. Eaton Ltd.
[1976] I.C.R. 336; [1976] I.R.L.R. 308
Employment Appeal Tribunal

> The appellants were dismissed following their refusal to return to their normal places of work after having left their places of work to stand around so as to prevent the working of a newly installed "Montfort" machine on which management intended to start proving operations.

PHILLIPS J.: There was in force an agreement for the avoidance of disputes. One of the employees' complaints before the Industrial Tribunal was that the management had refused to put the dispute into procedure. There is no doubt that a dispute was coming into existence on March 4 [, 1975]. Whether technically the management was at fault in this respect depends in part on whether there was an existing agreement or an established practice about the proving of the Montforts within section (3) (a) of the domestic procedure agreement for the avoidance of disputes. If there was an established practice, namely, that which had been followed in September 1974, the management was entitled to go ahead and the employees should have sought consultation without the operation being brought to a standstill. If there was not an existing agreement or an established practice, then, in view of the employees' objection made clear on March 4, the management should have sought to reach an agreement or have exhausted the procedure before implementing the decision to prove the Montforts in the manner intended. But, in that event, the men were technically at fault too, because they took their action to prevent the management from proving the Montforts as intended before making any request to go into procedure. It is not possible upon the material available to the Appeal Tribunal, or to the Industrial Tribunal, to reach a wholly decisive view as to who was technically at fault. However, there seems to be no doubt that, at best, the management's approach was obtuse. We do not know enough of the background to express a detailed view, but it seems clear that after September 1974 there was no definite system agreed with the employees for the installation of the Montforts, and it was, to say the least, unwise to leave the matter until the eve of their installation before raising the question with them. On March 4 the management was aware of the employees' resistance to the course proposed. It seems likely that, had a proper discussion taken place otherwise than under the imminent intention of the management to carry out the installation of the Montforts, there would have been a happier outcome. No doubt it is for this reason that the Industrial Tribunal found that had the matter fallen to be decided in accordance with the provisions of [s.57(3) of EPCA] they would have found in favour of the employees.

Cf. Tadd v. *Eastwood and the Daily Telegraph* [1983] I.R.L.R. 320 (Q.B.D.), where it was held that although parts of a collective agreement which dealt with terms of employment were incorporated into the plaintiff's contract of employment, those parts of the agreement which set out a disputes procedure between the union and the employer were outside the ambit of the employer/employee relationship, and therefore inappropriate for incorporation into the plaintiff's contract. Nonetheless, the judge went on to hold that when the employee participated in the processing of his grievance through the disputes procedure, he thereby consented to be bound by it, a finding not appealed against in the Court of Appeal which upheld the decision ([1985] I.R.L.R. 119).

(iv) Redundancy procedures

British Leyland UK Ltd. v. McQuilken
[1978] I.R.L.R. 245
Employment Appeal Tribunal

LORD McDONALD: The respondent worked in the appellants' engineer[ing] experimental department in Glasgow. In 1976 the appellants entered into an agreement with the majority of the unions represented in their workforce (including the union to which the respondent belonged), relative to a proposed reorganisation which would involve redundancies. This provided for the discontinuation of the experimental department in Glasgow in July 1977. Clause 4 of the agreement also provided that employees affected would be interviewed by a member of the personnel department with the object of establishing a list of employees who wished to take up the option of (a) retraining or (b) redundancy. These lists were to be drawn up on or before 11.3.77. Skilled employees who did not wish to take up retraining were to be given redundancy. . . .

The terms of a collective agreement between employers and unions may or may not fall to be regarded as incorporated within the individual contract of employment of an employee. . . .

In our opinion in the present case the terms of the agreement between the appellants and the unions did not alter the respondent's individual contract of employment. That agreement was a long-term plan, dealing with policy rather than the rights of individual employees under their contracts of employment. The Tribunal seems to have considered that because the appellants did not interview the respondent prior to 11.3.77 they were in breach of their contract of employment with him. For the reasons stated we do not think they were. Moreover, if they were, we are unable to conclude that it was a significant breach going to the root of the contract entitling the respondent to terminate his employment.

(v) Productivity agreements

Joel v. Cammell Laird (Ship-Repairers) Ltd.
(1969) 4 I.T.R. 206
Industrial Tribunal

LIVERPOOL TRIBUNAL (chairman: J. CROSSLEY-VAINES): . . . it had long been the policy of Cammell Laird's Ship-repair Division to require their employees, presumably by means of appropriate terms in the contract of service, to work in the Ship-building Division (or "on new work," as the expression goes) as and when a transfer to that division was deemed necessary by the employers, and there were, of course, transfers back to ship-repairing as occasion demanded. When, however, the former employees of Grayson Rollo became employees of Cammell Laird directly, it was not thought that they could be asked to transfer to new work without the obligation being made the subject of collective (local) agreement, and the requirement of transferability or interchangeability was made a feature of a collective agreement between Cammell Laird (Ship-repairers) Limited of the one part and the member unions of the Confederation of Shipbuilding and Engineering Unions, Mersey District of the other part, dated 27th October, 1965, and declared to be with effect from 8th November, 1965. This agreement, commonly referred to in the industry as "Package Deal No. 1" represents a part of the outcome of attempts to iron out labour-management difficulties in the ship-building and repair industries, and it commences by granting substantial increases in remuneration (over £3 0s. 0d. weekly so far as the applicants were concerned) "subject to" (ie, in return for) "specific and overall conditions," including the condition round which this case revolves, contained in section II(a), *viz.*:—

> "The integration of the 'Grayson' and 'Cammell Laird' repair sections so that men and work can be freely interchanged under the repair company management. And that men can be interchanged between the repair and new work companies as the work requires. Either company to accept service with the other company as service with itself for purposes of the Contracts of Employment Act [1963, now Part I and ss.49–52 of EPCA] and Triple Benefit Plan, which Plan will be extended to the repair company as soon as this can be arranged."

Pausing here, we might say in the first place that the triple benefit plan refers to sickness and pension benefits and the like, and constituted a further inducement to acceptance by the employees; and that secondly we regard section II(a) as an unimpeachable condition, all other things being equal. We cannot agree with Mr Stannard's submission [on behalf of the employees] that it is ambiguous (and inoperative for ambiguity). Pedantically viewed it may be, as Mr Stannard suggests, ungrammatical, but in our opinion it imports into the contract of service of any employee who might properly be deemed to be affected (a qualification we shall have to consider at length) a clear and unequivocal stipulation that he must be ready to go on new work if required, and that a refusal to be transferred will amount to a breach of his contract of service.

(vi) Trade union recognition and facilities agreements

City and Hackney Health Authority v. National Union of Public Employees

[1985] I.R.L.R. 252
Court of Appeal

Mr Craig, a NUPE shop steward, was suspended, and later dismissed following a hospital occupation. He obtained an interlocutory injunction restraining the employer from interfering with his access to the hospital and the performance of his duties as a union representative. The employer appealed.

OLIVER L.J.: The plaintiff is the district health authority responsible for the administration of the hospital. It is a National Health hospital, and the plaintiff is a party to the General Whitley Councils Ancillary Staff Agreement. Paragraphs 351 to 354 of that agreement, which are contained in a section called section IX, are in the following terms so far as material:

> "351. *Recognition*
> A union steward who has been appointed in accordance with the rules of a recognised union represented on the Ancillary Staffs Council, has been duly accredited by the union and has been in the employment of the authority for at least six working days shall, upon written notification by the union to the authority of his/her appointment, be recognised as the representative of the members of that union employed as Ancillary Staff in the hospital group, hospital or other organisation, or particular section or department thereof.
> 352. *Functions*
> The functions of a union steward, within the context of this agreement, shall be to represent the union members concerned; to investigate any complaint or difficulty raised by those members; to make representations on such matters to the management and to co-operate with management to ensure that the agreements of the council are observed.
> 353. *Facilities*
> The employing authority shall give recognised union stewards facilities for exercising their functions, and stewards shall ensure the proper use of such facilities."

Paragraph 354 provides for "Other rights and duties." I do not think I need read any of those except (c) which provides:

> "Stewards shall be subject to all the provisions of the council's agreements in the same way as any other employee, but no recognised steward shall be dismissed or otherwise penalised in any way whatsoever for carrying out his functions as a steward in accordance with the provisions of this agreement."

There is also a provision in paragraph 357, which perhaps I ought to read, which relates to full-time trade union officers, and it provides:

> "Full-time union officers shall be permitted to visit the workplace in the performance of their trade union duties and for the purpose of seeing that the council's agreements are observed, provided they make prior arrangements with the employing authorities' senior representative and inform him/her of their arrival at the workplace."

At all material times up to 26 September of this year the second defendant, Mr Craig, was employed by the plaintiff at the hospital as a hospital porter. As far as the evidence goes, he was elected in September 1983 as the NUPE shop steward for the hospital for the year January to December 1984. He was accredited by the union, and he was recognised by the plaintiff. . . .

So far as the industry of counsel has been able to unearth, there is no statutory provision enabling a shop steward to go on the premises. There is a provision by a statutory instrument (S.I. 296 of 1974) which incorporates in contracts of employment certain terms and conditions . . . in paragraph 3(2) conditions of service are dealt with. That is in these terms:

> "Subject as aforesaid"—that is, subject to paragraph (3), and I need not bother about that at the moment—"where conditions of service, other than conditions with respect to remuneration, of any class of officers have been the subject of negotiations by a negotiating body and have been approved by the Secretary of State after considering the result of those negotiations, the conditions of service of any officer belonging to that class shall include the conditions so approved."

Now in fact the terms and conditions which are contained in the Whitley Council Agreement were approved, so far as is known at any rate by the Secretary of State, and that everybody is prepared to assume, and those terms and conditions are therefore incorporated in the terms and conditions of employment of Mr Craig.

Mr Tabachnik [counsel for the plaintiff health authority] has drawn attention to the table of contents which sets out the various sections of the Whitley Council Agreement, section I of which deals with grading structures and rates of pay and section II with conditions of service. He goes on to suggest that since section IX is simply getting facilities for trade unions, it does not come under the rubric "Conditions of Service" and it is not something which is incorporated. For my part, I do not find that a very convincing argument. It seems to me that there is at least an arguable case for saying that the existence and maintenance of trade union facilities at a hospital is a condition of service which can be treated as incorporated into the terms of an agreement. But Mr Tabachnik goes on to submit that, even if the whole booklet is incorporated, the only provisions which could give rise to any contractual rights are those which are clear and affect the position of an employee as an employee and not as a trade union representative. For my part, I think there may be something in that, although I do not think the contrary is totally unarguable. . . .

(After considering further arguments the judge concluded) I am bound to say that I am persuaded that it is certainly not unarguable, as Mr Tabachnik contends that section IX of the Whitley Council Agreement is in fact a condition of service which is incorporated in the contract of employment with, among other people, Mr Craig, although I express no opinion upon the ultimate outcome of that argument. It seems to me that there is an arguable case on this point.

For the outcome of this case, see above, pp. 493–495.

(C) Collective Agreements as Setting Rules and Standards for Labour Law

(i) Fair wages policy and extension of collective agreements

Fair wages policy required employers to adhere to standards of "fair" pay (see above, *Pay and Benefits*, pp. 172 *et seq.*). One standard of "fair" pay was that reflected in collective agreements. The policy of using collective agreements to set standards of fairness culminated in Schedule 11 to E.P.A. (which was repealed by the Employment Act 1980) and the Fair Wages Resolution of 1946 (which was revoked by Parliament in September 1983). The effect was that all employers, up to 1980, and government contractors, up to 1983, were liable to be summoned before an independent arbitration tribunal (most recently the Central Arbitration Committee) and charged with non-compliance with "fair" standards, *ie* terms of employment established for the trade or industry in the district where the work was carried out by machinery of negotiation or arbitration to which the parties were organisations of employers and trade unions representative respectively of substantial proportions of the employers and workers engaged in the trade or industry in the district. Collective agreements were thus indirectly enforced through this legal procedure.

(ii) Statutory rights and collective agreements

One aspect of the relation between collective agreements and law is illuminated by the number of instances where legislation provides that, if certain minimum conditions are observed, provisions in collective agreements can set standards in place of statutory provisions. The extract below analyses how collective agreements have responded to such opportunities to gain exemption from statutory provisions.

C. Bourn, *"Statutory exemptions for collective agreements"* (1979) 8 I.L.J. 85

. . . . The uneven development of collective bargaining has . . . created a difficulty where it has been desired to provide a minimum standard of rights for all workers in areas which are commonly the subject of collective bargaining. In order to avoid undermining the integrity of collective bargaining, in several instances provision has been made for the exemption of workers covered by a relevant collective agreement, where that agreement already offers a protection to the worker which is at least comparable with the benefits to be provided by the statute. Such provisions for exemption orders have been made in relation to redundancy payments, the handling of redundancy situations, unfair dismissal and guaranteed week agreements. Although these exemptions provisions were passed in order to preserve the principle of voluntarism in industrial relations, very few such exemption orders have ever been made. Two exemption orders have been made in respect of redundancy, none for handling redundancy, none in respect of unfair dismissal and eighteen in respect of guaranteed payments. The question arises as to why so little advantage has been taken of the opportunities for exemption in respect of unfair dismissal and redundancy whilst a modest number of orders have been made in respect of guaranteed payments.

Conclusions

The exemption provisions reviewed here are all directed towards the same basic purpose that of not undermining existing voluntary agreements whilst extending a basic floor of minimum rights to all employees. Contrary to the expectations of those who framed the legislation, there has been very little interest in these exemption provisions.

Several answers suggest themselves as to the reasons why these provisions have not been taken up by employers and unions. First, it was intended by those who framed the legislation to protect existing adequate voluntary agreements, but in each of the cases reviewed, with the exception of guarantee pay, there were, *at the time when the legislation was enacted,* few adequate examples of collective agreements covering these matters. Thus the incentive for the parties to a collective agreement to apply for exemption would be that a perfectly adequate set of arrangements would be confused and/or undermined by less beneficial statutory standards, but this has seldom been the case. Few good redundancy compensation agreements existed prior to 1965, few adequate dismissals procedures in terms of accessibility, independence, speed of settlement and range of remedies existed prior to 1971, especially at local level and few if any (outside the excluded cases of seamen and dockers [*cf.* EPA 1975, s.119(3) and (12]) examples existed of long pre-determined periods of consultation over redundancy before 1975. Only in the case of guaranteed payments were there any number of adequate agreements, the operation of which would be interfered with by the new statutory scheme. This was perhaps because the statutory standards for guarantee pay have been seen to be inadequate and are now in the process of being upgraded. . . .

There were thus few truly adequate private schemes in existence prior to this legislation. The legislation has, in fact, tended to encourage the formation of agreements which have supplemented the statutory standards rather as local agreements often elaborate national agreements. In fact, what the experience of exemption orders has tended to reveal is the poverty of collective bargaining in Britain rather than the adequacy of existing agreements, even though part of this effect arises from the contrast between the indicative and fluid way in which collective agreements are couched as opposed to the more rigid statutory requirements, thus making it difficult to show on paper that the relevant collective agreement offers a better standard of protection to the worker than is offered under the statute.

Contrast may be made with the references to collective agreements in various statutory provisions concerning redundancy: EPCA, s.59(*b*) and EPA, s.99(5)(*e*). Breach of non-legally binding collective agreements by employers may also be a factor in determining whether an employer has acted reasonably in a claim for unfair dismissal compensation. This was done in *Kent County Council* v. *Gilham* [1985] I.R.L.R. 18 (C.A.) where Dillon L.J. commented (para. 42):

> "It is of obvious importance, in the fields of employment law and industrial relations, that national agreements negotiated between employers and trade unions as to wages and conditions of employment should not be breached unilaterally by an employer. It could not therefore be said that no reasonable Tribunal could have regarded the Council's decision, to breach the national agreement and dismiss the dinner ladies unless they were prepared to accept a reduction of pay, as unreasonable."

But while a factor, breach of agreements does not compel a finding of unreasonableness, and while in *Gilham* it contributed to such a finding, opposite conclusions were arrived at on similar facts by two Industrial Tribunals (unreported, but cited in *Gilham*, para. 21).

(iii) Collective agreements and incomes policies

The role of collective agreements in setting standards is particularly evident when incomes policy restrains wage increases, subject to exceptions that may be collectively negotiated. It is then the case that collective agreements set the legally sanctioned standards for any wage increases. The following extract is taken from a study which examined the "productivity" exemption to the wage restraint policy of 1967–69, and the role of collective agreements at central and local levels.

W. W. Daniel and N. Millward, *"Incomes Policy and Collective Bargaining at the Workplace: A study of the productivity criterion cases"* PEP BROADSHEET 541 (May 1973), at pp. 12, 66–68

The chief effects of the inclusion of a productivity criterion exception were twofold. Where productivity agreements were already in the process of being developed and negotiated workers and trade unionists were under much stronger pressure to accept them. Whereas prior to incomes policy it had been a question of whether the increases offered by agreements were sufficiently greater than workers would normally have expected to receive in periodic wage negotiations, now acceptance of the agreement became the only means of achieving any increase at all during the nil norm period and anything but a very small increase during the subsequent period. Thus the incomes policy served as a powerful aid to management in pushing through agreements already being negotiated. Secondly, where managements were not in the process of negotiating productivity agreements, and where they were under pressure to concede wage increases through pressure from either the work force or labour market, then they began to think in terms of productivity agreements as a means of doing so. Thus, as our own findings confirm, the productivity criterion led to a rapid spread of productivity bargaining both among managements who had toyed with the idea but had not done anything concrete about it and among managements who had not previously considered such agreements at all. . . .

. . . . the principle of a national incomes policy runs counter to one of the most powerful movements in British labour relations during the past ten years, that is to say the trend towards formal plant and company bargaining. . . . Not least among the reasons were the rising expectations of industrial workers that they would have a say in the decisions that affected them, and recognition of the informal *de facto* power they exercised. In principle, however, a national incomes policy contradicts the trend towards decentralisation of collective bargaining. It suggests that earnings are settled at a level even more centralised than the industry agreement. Moreover, one of the chief fears and criticisms of incomes policy is that it is totalitarian and destroys free collective bargaining which is a touchstone of democracy. In view of this it is a nice paradox that in the agreements we looked at as part of the last incomes policy, local union officials and particularly lay officers were more heavily involved in collective bargaining over a wider range of issues than ever before. Stewards reported that the main effect of the agreements for them was that they had more influence and responsibility. This paradox highlights how there is a means of accommodating the needs for plant bargaining and greater influence on the part of workers and stewards over decisions with the need for greater control at the centre over movements in earnings. And this means conceiving of national incomes policy as a framework. The national framework agreement at company level, and indeed at industry level within nationalised industries, was a feature of the productivity bargaining phase and often very successful. The framework agreement did provide a mechanism whereby local autonomy could be accommodated within central control. Scope was provided for people at plant level still to influence events, even exercise a greater influence over events, within a regulated context . . . the implication of these different points is that a national incomes policy that seeks to represent anything more than a short-term freeze stands very much more chance of achieving its different objectives, and accommodating obstacles, if it is conceived of as a framework which not only permits, but positively encourages, company and plant agreements seeking to reform degenerated systems of payments, bring overtime under control, improve the utilisation of plant and labour, and reform labour relations institutions and procedures. Implicit in this prescription is the idea that trade unionists will be more than compensated for any apparent decline in their freedom to negotiate wage rates (though the extent to which trade unions have ever influenced the level of earnings through collective bargaining remains a matter of academic debate) by the greater scope they have to influence "control" or organisation issues as opposed to "wage" issues through an extension of joint regulation at the work place.

. . . the last incomes policy, through the productivity criterion, did give a considerable boost to reform and change at plant level in a way that increased rather than reduced worker and trade union influence.

(D) Approaches to Collective Agreements: Judges and Arbitrators

A key problem and central issue of policy is that of dealing with disputes involving collective agreements. In the following extracts we contrast judges' and arbitrators' approaches to resolving such disputes.

Central Arbitration Committee, *Annual Report (1981)*, paras. 4.2–4.8

Almost all the work of the CAC involves determining issues against the background of formal or informal collective agreements. Pay questions, equal pay, disclosure of information and a large proportion of voluntary arbitrations often depend upon an interpretation of these agreements. Committees have to be expert in penetrating to the very core of the agreement and have to appreciate the parties' attitude to provisions that they themselves have drafted and agreed.

This, at the present time, is often far from easy. It is almost impossible to find a clearly written agreement—one that is comprehensive and unambiguous. Equally, virtually all agreements are subject to the nuances of prior understandings and subsequent custom and practice. Further, deciding what the parties to a dispute originally intended, that is *before* the occurrence of the dispute itself has sharpened and even distorted their views, is an especially difficult task.

Once the particular dispute is over, the parties having reached a settlement or the arbitrator's award on the point given, it is rare for a comprehensive reassessment to be made of those formal and informal agreements which may in part have led to the misunderstanding. The reason for this is simple. Such a re-assessment would be exceptionally difficult, expensive and time-consuming but above all would almost certainly open fresh disputes. Often these would arise over matters of little practical importance since the subject-matter of a particular clause might have been included only as a contingency upon unlikely events. It would seem absurd to invite an immediate dispute when the maxim of letting sleeping dogs lie could well ensure continued peace.

At the opposite extreme, it should be pointed out that disputes often arise from over-precise wording, where unthinking applications to new circumstances give one side or the other an unexpected and plainly unfair advantage. The need is for a steady improvement of agreements within the traditional pattern—a mixture of formality, informality and custom and practice—consciously combining and balancing greater certainty and flexibility to enable agreements to be applied with fairness to new as well as previously experienced situations.

These considerations, which must be obvious to any[one] who undertake[s] industrial relations arbitration, underline the need for steady improvement in the structure and form of agreements but it is difficult to see how a real impetus can be given to this valuable and basically uncontentious aim.

It is certainly hard to envisage a rapid move to "tightly drawn" agreements of the sort that lawyers would advise. Indeed, in the complicated area of wide-ranging national agreements or complicated plant processes that type of certainty is probably not attainable, or if it is, only at the cost of great complexity and rigidity.

Arbitration

There can be no doubt that, in its various forms, the process of arbitration itself is of assistance in identifying problems inherent in collective agreements and pointing the way to improvements. Arbitration should not be thought of merely as "giving" or "refusing" a claim. It has a constructive role in improving the way in which the parties set out their understandings and agreements so that future disputes become somewhat less likely. When, in a dispute, these agreements are submitted to a specialised arbitral body which combines the skills of arbitration and background understanding of the sector of employment under review, the chances of achieving lasting solutions—without recourse to industrial action and all the damaging consequences that entails—are maximised.

To contrast the approach of arbitrators and courts to collective agreements, we have taken a case under the Equal Pay Act 1970, s.3(1) which provides:

> "Where a collective agreement . . . contains any provision applying specifically to men only or to women only, the agreement may be referred by any party to it or by the Secretary of State to the Central Arbitration Committee . . . to declare what amendments need to be made, in accordance with subsection (4) below, so as to remove that discrimination between men and women."

The following extracts reflect the attitude of the Central Arbitration

Committee and of the Divisional Court to a complaint under that section.

CAC Award No. 79/74, Hy-Mac Limited and APECCS, paras. 14–18

> Before the implementation of the Equal Pay Act 1970, the collectively agreed pay structure at Hy-Mac Ltd. specified different grades and lower rates of pay for women than for men. In order to meet the Act's requirements, it was agreed in 1974 to give the women staged increases, with a final payment to bring them up to the men's rate following completion of a job evaluation exercise in December 1975. When this failed to be completed by December 29, 1975, the implementation date of the 1970 Act, the company gave all adult women an additional £1.75 a week and introduced a revised salary structure which no longer specified different grades and rates for men and women. Subsequently a job evaluation exercise set up a new unisex structure of seven grades, CO to C6, but agreement could not be reached on the appropriate rates for each grade. The union complained under section 3(1) of the Act that the company's pay structure was still discriminatory.

We have first to determine whether the pay structure which has emerged since the job evaluation exercise is discriminatory as between men and women. Clearly the removal of the terms "male" and "female" from the earlier agreement began elimination of discrimination but we must look further and not confine our examination to the satisfactory use, or otherwise, of unisex terminology. Indeed the Union has suggested that the pay structure remains discriminatory despite the increases in pay made by the Company to adult females up to and including 29 December 1975.

We found this a difficult case and after the hearing and for several months we continued discussions with the parties to seek further information. The Company expressed the view that past practices in relation to pay on recruitment and promotion policy may have favoured men which would appear to have been the case. It can hardly be by accident or fortune that women are distributed disadvantageously throughout the pay structure.

There is no overt discrimination and we turned our attention to ascertain whether there was a failure to eradicate properly the historical concept of a woman's rate of pay. We feel that this is the case. In considering how to amend the structure the Committee have held firmly in mind first what we take to have been the broad intention of Parliament, namely to ensure that women should not be paid less than men for doing similar work, and secondly, the desirability of giving advice or making a declaration which would be realistic in industrial relations terms. The second of these considerations causes us more difficulty. Because of the close grouping of the salary bands in grades (C4–C6) we felt it necessary to adopt an approach of determining new salary bands as if it were a newly negotiated pay structure but we emphasise the difficulty of doing so, especially bearing in mind the existence of a Government pay policy. We appreciate that this may cause the Company some problems but we consider that our duty to eliminate discrimination can only be done in this way. The industrial relations considerations weigh heavily in such an approach.

Each party submitted to the Committee its own proposals for new salary bands. The Union's suggestion was to raise the rate of pay of women to the average rate of pay for men in each grade. This did not seem to us to be a sound approach as there would then be men whose rate of pay was below the men's average at the bottom of each grade. The Company's proposals were based upon market values.

Neither proposal seemed to us to be within the spirit and intention of the legislation and we have therefore determined what we think are reasonable salary bands taking into account all the evidence received. We leave for negotiation between the parties the actual salaries of individuals.

R. v. Central Arbitration Committee, ex p. Hy-Mac Ltd.
[1979] I.R.L.R. 461
Queen's Bench Division

The company applied for an order of certiorari to quash the CAC's award, on the grounds that in making this declaration the CAC had acted outside its jurisdiction.

Watkins J.: What the Central Arbitration Committee should have done in this particular case was to ask themselves these questions. Firstly, is there in existence an agreement between the employers and a collection of those employed of the kind which has been referred to us? Secondly, what are its terms and when was it made? Thirdly, does it apply specifically to men only, no matter what interpretation is put upon the meaning of the words "applies specifically" so as to give us jurisdiction to hear and determine the reference? Fourthly, if so, does it discriminate against women? Finally, if it does, what is required by way of amendments to the agreement to remove the discrimination?

What in fact the Committee did was to conduct a general policy review of job classification without going so far as to suggest what wages should be paid as a result of the adoption of their classification.

It did not attempt to confine itself within the very strict limits of s.3 of the Equal Pay Act, 1970 but embarked on this general and quite arbitrary review hoping to settle all the outstanding differences between the parties which was not what it was called upon by Parliament to do.

They may have been beguiled into this by a part of the reference letter of 14.7.77 which reads: "Discussions have taken place with the Company and the advice of the Department of Employment sought, but it has not proved possible to reach agreement on the salary range to be applied to each of the grades."

That statement of fact, if it was the fact, was preceded by this assertion: "During 1975 the Job Evaluation exercise was carried out in accordance with agreed criteria; for various reasons this was not completed until July 1976, when six basic grades were agreed upon."

This I suspect encouraged the Committee to assume the role of arbitrators and, as I indicated earlier, thereafter to pay no real attention to the strict limits of its duties as set out in s.3.

CHAPTER 13

INDUSTRIAL CONFLICT

1. INTRODUCTION: CONTEXT, PERSPECTIVES AND THEMES

Collective disputes pose the problem of what weapons are available to workers for use against the employer and conversely what weapons the employer can use against workers. The use of industrial action by workers and the implications for legal regulation were described in the following extract from a detailed study of strikes between 1966–1973.

C. T. B. Smith, R. Clifton, P. Makeham, S. W. Creigh and R. V. Burn, "*Strikes in Britain*," (1978), DEPARTMENT OF EMPLOYMENT MANPOWER PAPER No. 15, pp. 87–90

In an average year only 2 per cent of United Kingdom manufacturing plants which employ only 20 per cent of manufacturing workers experience strikes large enough to be recorded by the Department of Employment. Stoppages involving fewer than 10 workers or lasting less than one day are not recorded unless the aggregate number of days lost exceeds a hundred. Moreover, this evidence on the concentration of disputes is based on years in which the overall level of activity was high. Since most strikes do not involve the whole work force of a plant the proportion of manufacturing workers who are involved in strikes in any year is appreciably less than 20 per cent. For example even in 1972 this proportion was less than 11 per cent. If this analysis could be extended to the non-manufacturing sector there is little doubt that a similarly low proportion of work-places (establishments) would be found to be affected in most industries. (Presumably, if information were available on the incidence of very short stoppages (downers) and industrial action short of a strike, the proportion of establishments affected by *all* forms of industrial action in a year would be above 2 per cent. However, evidence . . . suggests that various forms of industrial action tend to be concentrated in much the same plants). In a hypothetical case in which an entirely new set of plants and workers were affected each year, any plant would experience strikes only in one year each half century and any workers would be involved in strikes about every tenth year. In practice the probability of a strike is much higher in a few industries and areas and markedly in some plants. This means that, for most of the economy, strikes occur even less frequently than in the hypothetical case noted above. British industry in general is certainly not widely or continually affected by industrial action; it is not "riddled" with strikes. . . .

The central point revealed by the examination of the nature of strike action is one of extreme concentration of strike activity in a few plants in certain industries and areas. . . . During the period 1971–73 a quarter of 1 per cent of all manufacturing plants employing 11 workers or more (that is only 150 plants) accounted for two-thirds of all days lost in recorded strikes. It is thus the experience of these very limited segments of the economy, combined with widespread ignorance of the experience of the vast remainder . . . that has perpetuated until now a misleading and damaging industrial relations image. . . .

In conclusion we would draw out two broad implications of the discussion of the recent United Kingdom strike record as described in this report. The first is that strikes appear to be over fundamental issues, in which economic pressures on participants are very important. This comes out in several different ways. Attention has already been drawn to the causal analyses which show that the reasons given for striking by the people actually involved are predominantly economic, the two main categories of pay and job security being very frequently cited. The predominance of pay as an issue in work stoppages was apparent when viewed historically. Equally important here is the examination of the incidence of multiple-cause strikes. . . . In 88 per cent of all industrial stoppages officially recorded over 1966–73 the participants stated one clear-cut reason for striking which was usually economic. In the remaining 12 per cent of stoppages the secondary and underlying reasons were also usually economic. These findings challenge the view in industrial sociology . . . that the issues in strikes are often so complex that classification to a single reason is of no value. . . .

The other broad implication of our results follows from the finding that strikes are in the main concentrated in a very small proportion of plants, typically the larger ones in certain industries and certain areas of the country. Although the authors of the Donovan Report [Cmnd. 3623] were well aware that strikes were highly concentrated and that in certain plants industrial action was endemic, increasing concern over the apparently large number of small unofficial strikes led to a drive towards general procedural reform and then comprehensive legislation. . . . If the extent of industrial action and of strikes in particular is the major area of concern, a general reform policy may be justifiable on the grounds that the measures involved do not adversely affect the industrial relations environment in hitherto strike-free establishments, or at least do not so badly affect the environment that such plants begin to experience strikes. However, it may also be argued that it is inappropriate to propound general remedies which must incidentally affect all plants in order to have an impact on the 2 per cent of plants which suffer strikes in an average year or—even more to the point—on the quarter of one per cent of plants which are seriously affected.

The study pointed out (p. 84) that five industries, coal-mining, ports and inland water transport, motor-vehicle manufacture, shipbuilding, and iron and steel, accounted for a disproportionate amount of stoppage activity. Between 1965 and 1976 they accounted for over a quarter of stoppages and a third of working days lost in most years, though accounting for little more than 6 per cent. of employment. The concentration of industrial stoppages was highlighted in a detailed examination of strike activity during 1971–73. Over these three years, as stated in the above extract, the average number of manufacturing plants experiencing no stoppages recorded by the Department of Employment in any year was 98 per cent. Subsequent research substantiates the earlier findings while establishing additional patterns of industrial conflict.

W.W. Daniel and Neil Millward, *Workplace Industrial Relations in Britain*: THE DE/PSI/ESRC SURVEY (1983), p. 292

Overall, our analysis confirmed, first, that the incidence of both strikes and other industrial action was strongly associated with workforce size, the preponderance of male, full time employees, the level of unionisation and with the establishment being the main locus of collective bargaining. There was little support for any strong connection between the occurrence of disputes and such matters as the presence of agreed procedures, joint consultative machinery, manufacturing technology and multi-unionism. Trade union density was the characteristic most strongly related to the proportion of the workforce involved in a stoppage. Intermittent recurrent strikes were more widespread than the national engineering stoppage in 1979 which brought them to public notice. Industrial action other than strikes was a feature of non-manual employment in particular and was particularly common among non-manual employees taking industrial action for the first time.

In view of the growing proportion of non-manual workers in the national labour force, the results suggest that the incidence of strikes is no longer an adequate measure of the level of overt industrial conflict. Indeed, broadly speaking, less than one half of the establishments affected by any type of industrial action were affected by a strike which would have come within the definition used for the official records. Our findings show that that definition provides a particularly inadequate measure of industrial conflict in local and national government and, to a lesser extent, in food and chemicals, textiles and clothing, miscellaneous manufacturing and the health and education services.

The association between all types of industrial action and systems of payment-by-results provided a second striking feature of the analysis. That association was revealed in the present survey by the way that strikes were substantially more common in workplaces where PBR operates and by earlier evidence of the extent to which disputes over rates for the job under PBR were cited as the trigger events for industrial action, at least in manufacturing.

Industrial conflict can be viewed from at least three perspectives. In the first (the unitary view of industrial relations), industrial action is regarded as harmful: self-damaging to the workers who take part in it and even more so to the enterprise and others outside it. As such it should be discouraged, if not repressed. The second perspective (pluralist) sees some degree of conflict as endemic, but again would restrict industrial action to "tolerable" limits. It attempts to seek resolution of disputes through procedural mechanisms. The third perspective (Marxist) sees conflict as fundamental and industrial action as a weapon in the hands of workers to be wielded in the course of the struggle. As such it should be encouraged and protected. The reader of this chapter should evaluate the law presented in the light of these different perspectives: is it too liberal; are alternative mechanisms preferable; does it restrain industrial action which is necessary or desirable? Once disputes erupt into open conflict, attention tends conventionally to be focussed on collective actions of the workers in the dispute. By contrast the so-called "managerial prerogatives," stemming from ownership and control of the means of production, enable employers to discipline or dismiss their employees, to re-organise their work, or to withdraw facilities from union officials or recognition from trade unions. The use of these inherent powers often suffices to resolve disputes in the employer's favour. Employers in the U.K. nowadays seldom need to resort to such classic forms of industrial warfare as lockouts, the engagement of strike-breakers or non-union labour, or concerted actions by employers' associations. This theme, the lack of congruence in the powers and weapons available to workers and employers, explains why this chapter concentrates on the weapons available to workers. Most of the weapons usually used by employers in dispute are dealt with elsewhere (see Chapters 7 and 10 on *Discipline* and *Termination*, and the section on *Changes at Work* (pp. 58 *et seq.*)). Two other themes will be evident in the chapter. First, the distinction which should be made in the case of workers' weapons between the taking of industrial action and the organising of such action. The former is done by workers; the latter by their trade unions and representatives. Industrial action by workers, whether a walk-out, working-to-rule, or picketing, is different from the acts of those organising these activities, *e.g.* writing letters or leaflets, issuing verbal instructions, making speeches, or persuading trade unionists not to walk through picket lines. The activities and legal liabilities of the different actors should be considered separately. A second theme is the need to distinguish the effect of industrial action on the employer in dispute from the effect on others, *e.g.* suppliers, customers, the public in general, and other workers. Emphasis will be laid on the differing extent to which the common law and statute seek to maintain this distinction.

2. WEAPONS USED BY WORKERS AND TRADE UNIONS

(A) The policy of the common law

(i) Strikers and breach of contract

> "A strike is . . . a temporary refusal to work in accordance with the prevailing employment contracts (or on other conditions that are not specified or implied in the contracts), combined with the firm intention, at least on the part of the great majority of the workers involved, of not terminating their contracts." (A. Flanders, *Management and Unions* (1972), p. 219)

Most strikers, and their employers, intend to continue, rather than terminate, the employment relationship after the strike. The common law has been unable to accept this reality.

Simmons v. Hoover Ltd.
[1976] 3 W.L.R. 901; [1977] 1 All E.R. 775
Employment Appeal Tribunal

PHILLIPS J.: . . . The employee, Mr Simmons, was dismissed by his employers, the respondents, by a letter dated December 27, 1974. At that time he was on strike together with his fellow employees. . . . We are satisfied that at common law an employer is entitled to dismiss summarily an employee who refuses to do any of the work which he has engaged to do: see *Laws v London Chronicle (Indicator Newspaper) Ltd.* [1959] 1 W.L.R. 698—the employee has "disregarded the essential conditions of the contract of service." Does it make any difference that the refusal occurs during, and in the course of, a strike? In *J. T. Stratford & Son Ltd. v Lindley* [1965] A.C. 269, 285, Lord Denning M.R. said: "The 'strike notice' is nothing more nor less than a notice that the men will not come to work—or, as in this case, that they will not do their work as they should—in short, that they will break their contracts. . . ."

. . . there is no doubt that it was widely believed at the time of the decisions in *Rookes v Barnard* [1964] A.C. 1129 and *J. T. Stratford & Son Ltd. v Lindley* that by taking part in a strike the employees committed a breach of contract, for which in many cases they were liable to dismissal.

One of the matters considered at length by the Donovan Commission (Royal Commission on Trade Unions and Employers' Associations 1965–68, Cmnd. 3623) was the effect of strikes on the contract of employment. In paragraph 943 of the Commission's Report there are enumerated some of the difficulties inherent in regarding the contract as suspended. In the end the conclusion was reached that it was not practicable to introduce such a conception into the law. Whether or not that be so, it was clearly the view of the Commission that at common law a contract cannot be terminated unilaterally, and that if an employee refuses to carry on working under his contract of employment his employer has the option either to ignore the breach of contract and to insist upon performance of it, or alternatively to accept such a fundamental breach as a repudiation of the contract and to treat himself as no longer bound by it: paragraph 946. In our judgment this view was in accordance with general principle and supported by authority. In short, refusal to work during a strike did not involve "self-dismissal" by the strikers, but left the parties to the contract hoping that the strike would one day be settled, and the contract be alive, unless and until the employer exercised his right to dismiss the employee.

. . . We find it impossible to think that *Morgan v Fry* [1968] 2 Q.B. 710 (C.A.) was intended to revolutionise the law on this subject. . . . It is noteworthy that Lord Denning M.R., the only member of the court unequivocally in favour of the view that the contract was suspended, although he uses the word "suspension," does not deal with any of the problems which arise when a contract is suspended in the sense that the obligations of the parties are suspended, such as those referred to in the Donovan Commission Report, for example, paragraph 943:

> "The concept is not as simple as it sounds: and before any such new law could be formulated problems of some difficulty would have to be faced and solved. They include the following: (a) To what strikes would it apply? To unofficial and unconstitutional as well as to official strikes? How would strikes be defined for this purpose? (b) Would it also apply to other industrial action such as a ban on overtime in breach of contract or to a 'go-slow'? (c) Would it apply to 'lightning strikes' or only to strikes where at least some notice was given, though less than the notice required for termination of the contract? If so, what length of notice should be required? (d) Would the new law apply to the gas, water, and electricity industries, which at present are subject to the special provisions of section 4 of the Conspiracy and Protection of Property Act 1875 [repealed by the Industrial Relations Act 1971, Sched. 9]? What also would be the position under section 5 of the same Act? (e) Would the employer still be allowed instantly to dismiss an employee for grave misconduct during the course of the strike? (Note: this is the case under French law where strikes are treated as suspending the contract of employment.) If so, what kind of acts would constitute 'grave misconduct'? (f) Would 'contracting out' of the new law be permissible, eg in collective bargains, or in individual contracts of employment? (g) Would

strikers be free to take up other employment while the contract was suspended? If so, would any obligations of secrecy in the suspended contract be suspended too? (h) If all efforts to end the strike failed, upon what event would the suspension of the contract cease and be replaced by termination?

. . . bearing in mind the many changes in the law of industrial relations which have occurred since the decision in *Morgan v Fry*, we do not feel that we are bound by that case to hold that the effect of a strike, whether preceded by a proper strike notice or not, is to prevent the employer from exercising the remedy which in our judgment he formerly enjoyed at common law to dismiss the employee for refusing to work. We accept, of course, that in most cases men are not dismissed when on strike; that they expect not to be dismissed; that the employers do not expect to dismiss them, and that both sides hope and expect one day to return to work. Sometimes, however, dismissals do take place, and in our judgment they are lawful. . . .

We do not accept that if the contract of employment was not suspended, nonetheless the employee's action in going on strike was not repudiatory of the contract. It seems to us to be plain that it was, for here there was a settled, confirmed and continued intention on the part of the employee not to do any of the work which under his contract he had engaged to do, which was the whole purpose of the contract. Judged by the usual standards, such conduct by the employee appears to us to be repudiatory of the contract of employment. We should not be taken to be saying that all strikes are necessarily repudiatory, though usually they will be. For example, it could hardly be said that a strike of employees in opposition to demands by an employer in breach of contract by him would be repudiatory. But what may be called a "real" strike in our judgment always will be.

P. Davies and M. Freedland, KAHN-FREUND'S LABOUR AND THE LAW (3rd ed., 1983), pp. 354–5

. . . Does a strike or a lockout put an end to the [workers'] contracts [of employment]? Does it suspend them? Do those taking part in a strike break their contracts so that the employer may dismiss them without notice? Or does he, by doing so, in his turn break the contract? And whether he does or not, can he be liable for unfair dismissal if he has dismissed a worker who has gone on strike or been locked out?

At this point the difference between a "right" and a mere "freedom" to strike becomes decisive. If—as in France and in Italy—the workers have a "right" to strike then they cannot, by exercising it, break their contracts. Moreover, if the contract was terminated by a strike or if the mere fact that there was a strike allowed the employer to terminate it, the right to strike would be frustrated, because the workers could exercise it only at the risk of sacrificing their jobs. Hence—and this conclusion was drawn in Italy as well as in France—the contract of employment is only suspended by the strike, and after its end the employee is entitled to re-instatement with full seniority.

(ii) Strike organisers and inducing breach of contract

Whether industrial action is premeditated or spontaneous, an individual or group of individuals will almost inevitably at some stage emerge as the source to whom the participants look for leadership. Such organisers may themselves be strikers, in which case they will frequently be shop stewards. Alternatively, they may be outsiders not employed by the employer in dispute, such as full-time union officials.

Organising industrial action may involve discussions with strikers, the convening and chairing of meetings, speech-making, the giving of written instructions, advice and financial support, organising strike ballots, leading picketing or factory occupations, or negotiating with representatives of the employer, and other groups of workers, regional or national union officials and the local police. Involvement in such activities renders the organiser vulnerable to pressure from the employer, since an obvious tactic is to seek to separate organisers from the body of strikers, and by depriving the latter of leadership, to persuade or pressurise them to return to work.

The case that determined the common law's response to strike organisers did so by establishing the tort of "inducement to breach of contract."

Lumley v. Gye
(1853) 2 E. & B. 216; 18 E.R. 749

The defendant theatre proprietor persuaded Johanna Wagner, a singer, not to honour her engagement to sing at the plaintiff's theatre. The defendant was sued for wrongfully inducing the breach of the singer's contract to appear at the plaintiff's theatre.

CROMPTON J.: . . . it must now be considered clear law that a person who wrongfully and maliciously, or, which is the same thing, with notice, interrupts the relation subsisting between master and servant by procuring the servant to depart from the master's service, or by harbouring and keeping him a servant after he has quitted it and during the time stipulated for as the period of service, whereby the master is injured, commits a wrongful act for which he is responsible at law. . . .

. . . . It does not appear to me to be a sound answer, to say that the act in such cases is the act of the party who breaks the contract. . . . Nor it is an answer, to say that there is a remedy against the contractor, and that the party relies on the contract; for . . . the action on the contract and the action against the malicious wrongdoer may be for a different matter; and the damages occasioned by such malicious injury might be calculated on a very different principle from the amount of the debt which might be the only sum recoverable on the contract. . . . The servant or contractor may be utterly unable to pay anything like the amount of the damage sustained entirely from the wrongful act of the defendant; and it would seem unjust, and contrary to the general principles of law, if such wrongdoer were not responsible for the damage caused by his wrongful and malicious act.

In a sense, the law affecting strike organisers may be perceived as merely parasitical on the law affecting strikers. If the strikers are deemed to be committing unlawful acts (*e.g.* breaches of contract), those who organise strikes may be deemed to be acting unlawfully as well. But such an approach obscures the different policy issues in the treatment of strike organisers, *e.g.* issues of freedom of speech and expression of opinion. At what point does a prohibition on strike organisers making statements or speeches, issuing instructions or giving advice infringe their freedom of speech, elsewhere regarded as a value of supreme importance. The following cases illustrate differing attitudes in the judiciary.

D. C. Thomson & Co. Ltd. v Deakin
[1952] Ch. 646; [1952] 2 All E.R. 361
Court of Appeal

When the plaintiffs, printers and publishers, dismissed a member of NATSOPA the union appealed to other unions to support them. Lorry drivers at Bowaters, the company which supplied paper to the plaintiffs, informed Bowaters, their employers, that they might not be prepared to deliver paper to the plaintiffs. Bowaters informed the plaintiffs that they would not be able to deliver paper under contract.

SIR RAYMOND EVERSHED M.R.: I appreciate that in these matters there is a difficult question of distinguishing between what might be called persuasion and what might be called advice, meaning by the latter a mere statement of, or drawing of the attention of the party addressed to, the state of facts as they were. In the case of *Camden Nominees Ltd. v Forcey* [[1940] Ch. 352], before Simonds J., it was held that the advice given was of such a nature (was of a character obviously intended to be acted upon) that it was for all practical purposes equivalent to persuasion; but, if the matter be advice merely (in the ordinary sense of the word) it seems to me that there can be no complaint about it; nor do I think that [counsel for the plaintiffs] can derive any substantial assistance by saying that Bowaters proved themselves merely chicken-hearted and that the ease with which a person may be persuaded is not a relevant consideration in determining whether the persuader was wrongful in what he was doing. That may, as a general proposition, be true; but in this case the evidence on this motion, whatever may emerge when the matter is fully investigated, falls too far short of any proof of what is required to constitute a cause of action such as would entitle the plaintiffs to an injunction. Put another way, I cannot see that the evidence establishes that there was anything done by Bowaters vis-à-vis the plaintiffs which is fairly attributable to any such pressure, persuasion or procuration on the part of any of these defendants, as would in any event cause them to be liable in tort.

Contrast with the above extract the view of Winn L.J. in the following case.

Torquay Hotel Co. Ltd. v. Cousins
[1969] 2 Ch. 106; [1969] 1 All E.R. 522
Court of Appeal

WINN L.J.: A natural and justifiable inference . . . from . . . Mr Pedley, the [TGWU] district secretary for the Exeter district . . . telephoning to the Esso depot in Plymouth on February 3, a message that there was an official dispute with the Imperial [Hotel] and any fuel supplies would be stopped, is that without regard to whether, and without investigating whether, Esso had contracted with the owners of the Imperial [Hotel] to make periodical deliveries or a specific delivery of fuel oil, Mr Pedley was thus seeking to induce them not to make such deliveries. . . .

It was one of Mr Pain's main submissions [on behalf of the defendants] that mere advice, warning or information cannot amount to tortious procurement of breach of contract. Whilst granting *arguendi causa* that a communication which went no further would, in general, not, in the absence of circumstances giving a particular significance, amount to a threat or intimidation, I am unable to understand why it may not be an inducement. In the ordinary meaning of language it would surely be said that a father who told his daughter that her fiancé had been convicted of indecent exposure, had thereby induced her, with or without justification, by truth or by slander, to break her engagement. A man who writes to his mother-in-law telling her that the central heating in his house has broken down may thereby induce her to cancel an intended visit.

Camellia Tanker Ltd. S.A. v. International Transport Workers' Federation and Nelson

[1976] I.R.L.R. 190; [1976] 2 Lloyd's Reports 546
Court of Appeal

Following a dispute between the International Transport Workers' Federation, (the ITF) and the owners of the ship named the "Camellia" concerning rates of pay, some of the crew refused to sail the tanker, the crew of dockyard tugs refused to assist in moving her and the staff at the lock gates refused to open them. The shipowners applied for an interlocutory injunction against the ITF and an official of the TGWU. (The ITF is a federation of national transport unions, including the TGWU.)

MEGAW L.J.: [Assuming these workers had thereby broken their contracts of employment] those assumptions being made, they do not avail the plaintiffs, apart altogether from any question of the effect of [TULRA], unless such assumed breaches of assumed contracts have been "induced," in the proper sense of that word in this context, by Mr Nelson [a TGWU official]. At the least, "induce" in this context involves some "pressure, persuasion or procuration" on the part of the alleged "inducer." The words "pressure, persuasion or procuration" come from the judgment of Sir Raymond Evershed, Master of the Rolls, in *D C Thomson & Co Ltd v Deakin* [1952] Chancery 646, at p. 686 [see above p. 526].

There is, in my judgment, nothing in the material at present before the Court—and it is with that alone that we can properly concern ourselves—which establishes a good arguable case, or gives the plaintiffs a real prospect of succeeding in establishing, that any breach or potential breach by tug men or by lock men of any contractual obligation owed by them to their employers was brought about by any pressure, persuasion or procuration on the part of Mr Nelson. It may, indeed, readily be accepted on the evidence that Mr Nelson desired that the tug men and the lock men should, if they were to be asked or ordered by their employers to assist in enabling "Camellia" to depart, refuse to provide their services to that end. It is, indeed, clear that Mr Nelson has passed on information, hoping and believing that that information would assist in achieving his desire. It is also clear that he has on a number of occasions asserted his belief that "Camellia" will not depart until ITF are satisfied; and that that will be so because, in part at least, of the probable action or inaction of the tug men and the lock men. It is on that basis that the plaintiffs invite the Court to draw the inference that Mr Nelson has induced breaches or threatened breaches of contracts by tug men and lock men.

But in considering whether that is an inference which it is permissible, on the material before us, to draw, one may not ignore the uncontradicted evidence of Mr Nelson himself. It would be unjust and unfair to allow an injunction to be granted against a defendant on the basis, not of direct evidence, but of an inference as to his past and future conduct, without taking into account his own categorical denial of such conduct. That dictate of fairness applies even in respect of a claim for an interlocutory injunction, particularly where, as may be the case here, the grant of an interlocutory injunction may effectively decide the action.

So one must look at what Mr Nelson says. In paragraph 40 of his affidavit, sworn on 4.2.76, he says, "I have neither instructed nor directed nor requested nor recommended industrial action on the part of the Transport & General Workers Union. I have kept the Transport & General officers in Manchester and Liverpool fully informed upon the progress of the negotiations with the owners, even though the riggers have established direct communication with the Indian crew and the dispute has from its beginning been widely reported in the local, trade and national Press and more recently on television. As an affiliate of the ITF supporting ITF Policies. I have (and have had) no doubt whatever that the Transport & General would decide to take industrial action in support of the Chinese and Indian crew. It would be their decision, not mine; and only the vessel's crew (and not me) could persuade the Transport & General to refrain from such action."

[Megaw L.J. then adopted in respect of the evidence in the instant case the penultimate sentence from Sir Raymond Evershed MR's judgment in *Thomson v Deakin* extracted at p. 526 above.]

It thus becomes a question of fact whether advice proffered, information communicated, warnings delivered, suggestions given, recommendations made or hopes expressed suffice to create liability for "inducement." For example, what is the effect of a rule in a union's rule book laying down a policy for members to follow? If the union issues an instruction in accordance with this policy, does this amount to an inducement to its members to break their contracts of employment where the instruction conflicts with those contracts? The Court of Appeal seemed to have few doubts on this score in *Associated Newspapers Group Ltd.* v. *Wade* [1979] 1 W.L.R. 697; [1979] I.R.L.R. 201 (C.A.).

(iii) A case study in common law policy: "simple" conspiracy

The two fundamental common law views: of strikes as breaches of contract and organising strikes as inducement of such breaches, persist. Their effect was, and is, to render all industrial action unlawful at common law, including that which might be perceived by others, not judges, as legitimate. It was an appreciation of industrial action as possessing some kind of legitimacy in certain cases which led the courts to the development described in the following extracts: from an initial view of industrial action as an unlawful "simple" conspiracy, to the reversal of this view. The view of a strike as a criminal conspiracy was first expressed in the following case.

R. v. Bunn
(1872) 12 Cox C.C. 316

Workers at a gas works who threatened to withdraw their labour in breach of contract after a fellow worker had been dismissed for trade union activities, were convicted of criminal conspiracy.

BRETT J. [directed the jury as follows]. . . . This is a charge of conspiracy at common law, and if you think that there was an agreement and combination between the defendants . . . to interfere with the masters by molesting them, so as to control their will; and if you think that the molestation which was so agreed upon was such as would be likely, in the minds of men of ordinary nerve, to deter them from carrying on their business according to their own will, then I say that is an illegal conspiracy, for which these defendants are liable. . . .

This judicial creation of "simple" conspiracy, namely, that an agreement or combination to pursue "illegitimate" ends was unlawful even if no unlawful act was committed, was swiftly curtailed by statute: the Conspiracy and Protection of Property Act 1875, s.3 (currently the Criminal Law Act 1977, s.1). This statutory rejection of industrial action as a criminal conspiracy did not deter the judges, who developed the notion of "simple" conspiracy as a civil wrong.

Quinn v. Leathem
[1901] A.C. 495; [1900–03] All E.R. Rep. 1
House of Lords

The plaintiff, an employer of non-unionists, and one of his best customers, were told that they would be subject to industrial action unless the non-unionists were dismissed. As a result, the plaintiff lost his customer, and he sued the defendant trade unionists.

LORD LINDLEY: What may begin as peaceable persuasion may easily become, and in trades union disputes generally does become, peremptory ordering, with threats open or covert of very unpleasant consequences to those who are not persuaded. Calling workmen out involves very serious consequences to such of them as do not obey. Black-lists are real instruments of coercion, as every man whose name is on one soon discovers to his cost. A combination not to work is one thing, and is lawful. A combination to prevent others from working by annoying them if they do is a very different thing, and is *prima facie* unlawful. Again, not to work oneself is lawful so long as one keeps off the poor-rates, but to order men not to work when they are willing to work is another thing. A threat to call men out given by a trade union official to an employer of men belonging to the union and willing to work with him is a form of coercion, intimidation, molestation, or annoyance to them and to him very difficult to resist, and, to say the least, requiring justification. None was offered in this case. . . .

Intentional damage which arises from the mere exercise of the rights of many is not, I apprehend, actionable by our law as now settled. To hold the contrary would be unduly to restrict the liberty of one set of persons in order to uphold the liberty of another set. According to our law, competition, with all its drawbacks, not only between individuals, but between associations, and between them and individuals, is permissible, provided nobody's rights are infringed. The law is the same for all persons, whatever their callings: it applies to masters as well as to men; the proviso, however, is all-important, and it also applies to both, and limits the rights of those who combine to lock-out as well as the rights of those who strike. But coercion by threats, open or disguised, not only of bodily harm but of serious annoyance and damage, is *prima facie*, at all events, a wrong inflicted on the persons coerced; and in considering whether coercion has been applied or not, numbers cannot be disregarded.

The inability of the House of Lords in 1901 to see any legitimacy in the collective action of workers was remedied by the House of Lords in 1942.

Crofter Hand Woven Harris Tweed Co. v. Veitch
[1942] A.C. 435; [1942] 1 All E.R. 142
House of Lords

Millowners on the island of Lewis who made and sold tweed cloth from locally spun yarn refused to employ 100 per cent. union labour or grant a wage increase because of competition from the appellants' mills which imported spun yarn from the mainland. The millowners and the TGWU, which had members both among the mills' workforce and in the docks serving the island, combined to counteract this competition. The union instructed dockers in the port of Lewis not to handle yarn arriving for the appellants. Such an instruction did not involve the dockers breaking their contracts of employment. The appellants sued the unions for conspiracy to injure.

LORD WRIGHT: . . . As the claim is for a tort, it is necessary to ascertain what constitutes the tort alleged. It cannot be merely that the appellants' right to freedom in conducting their trade has been interfered with. That right is not an absolute or unconditional right. It is only a particular aspect of the citizen's right to personal freedom, and like other aspects of that right is qualified by various legal limitations, either by statute or by common law. Such limitations are inevitable in organized societies where the rights of individuals may clash. In commercial affairs each trader's rights are qualified by the right of others to compete. Where the rights of labour are concerned, the rights of the employer are conditioned by the rights of the men to give or withhold their services. The right of workmen to strike is an essential element in the principle of collective bargaining. . . .

It is thus clear that employers of workmen or those who like the appellants depend in part on the services of workmen, have in the conduct of their affairs to reckon with this freedom of the men and to realize that the exercise of the men's rights may involve some limitation on their own freedom in the management of their business. Such interference with a person's business, so long as the limitations enforced by law are not contravened, involves no legal wrong against the person. In the present case the respondents are sued for imposing the "embargo," which corresponds to calling out the men on strike. The dockers were free to obey or not to obey the call to refuse to handle the appellants' goods. In refusing to handle the goods they did not commit any breach of contract with anyone; they were merely exercising their own rights. . . .

Thus for purposes of the present case we reach the position that apart from combination no wrong would have been committed. There was no coercion of the dockers. There were no threats to them. They were legally free to choose the alternative course which they preferred. . . .

English law . . . has for better or worse adopted the test of self-interest or selfishness as being capable of justifying the deliberate doing of lawful acts which inflict harm, so long as the means employed are not wrongful. The common law in England might have adopted a different criterion and one more consistent with the standpoint of a man who refuses to benefit himself at the cost of harming another. But we live in a competitive and acquisitive society, and the English common law may have felt that it was beyond its power to fix by any but the crudest distinctions the metes and bounds which divide the rightful from the wrongful use of the actor's own freedom, leaving the precise application in any particular case to the jury or judge of fact. If further principles of regulation or control are to be introduced, that is matter for the legislature. . . .

. . . The respondents had no quarrel with the yarn importers. Their sole object, the courts below have held, was to promote their union's interests by promoting the interest of the industry on which the men's wages depended. On these findings, with which I agree, it could not be said that their combination was without sufficient justification. Nor would this conclusion be vitiated even though their motives may have been mixed, so long as the real or predominant object was not wrongful. Nor is the objection tenable that the respondents' real or predominant object was to secure the employers' help to get 100 per cent membership of the union among the textile workers. Cases of mixed motives or, as I should prefer to say, of the presence of more than one object are not uncommon. If so it is for the jury or judge of fact to decide which is the predominant object, as it may be assumed the jury did in *Quinn's* case [above p. 529], when they decided on the basis that the object of the combiners was vindictive punishment, not their own practical advantage. . . .

. . . To what legitimate interests other than those mentioned the general doctrine may extend I do not here seek to define, since beyond question it extends to the present case, whether the object of the action were the prosperity of the industry or the obtaining one hundred per cent membership. But the objects or purposes for which combinations may be formed are clearly of great variety. It must be left to the future to decide on the facts of the particular case, subject to the general doctrine, whether any combination is such as to give rise to a claim for a conspiracy to injure.

Recently, the House of Lords confirmed the position of the *Crofter* case, but acknowledged the anomalous nature of "tortious combination" or conspiracy.

Lonrho Ltd. v. Shell Petroleum Co. Ltd.
[1981] 3 W.L.R. 33; [1981] 2 All E.R. 456
House of Lords

LORD DIPLOCK: Why should an act which causes economic loss to A but is not actionable at his suit if done by B alone become actionable because B did it pursuant to an agreement between B and C? An explanation given at the close of the nineteenth century by Bowen LJ in the *Mogul* case 23 QBD 598 at 616 when it was before the Court of Appeal was: "The distinction is based on sound reason, for a combination may make oppressive or dangerous that which if it proceeded only from a single person would be otherwise. . . ." But to suggest today that acts done by one street-corner grocer in concert with a second are more oppressive and dangerous to a competitor than the same acts done by a string of supermarkets under a single ownership or that a multinational conglomerate such as Lonrho or oil company such as Shell or BP does not exercise greater economic power than any combination of small businesses is to shut one's eyes to what has been happening in the business and industrial world since the turn of the century and, in particular, since the end of the 1939–45 war. The civil tort of conspiracy to injure the plaintiff's commercial interests where that is the predominant purpose of the agreement between the defendants and of the acts done in execution of it which caused damage to the plaintiff must I think be accepted by this House as too well-established to be discarded, however anomalous it may seem today. It was applied by this House eighty years ago in *Quinn v Leathem* [1901] AC 495 [above p. 529], and accepted as good law in the *Crofter* case [above p. 530] in 1942, where it was made clear that injury to the plaintiff and not the self-interest of the defendants must be the predominant purpose of the agreement in execution of which the damage-causing acts were done.

Judicial acceptance of workers' self-interest as a legitimate objective became in effect a defence of "justification" to the tort of conspiracy. Could the common law have developed similar doctrines to protect strikers from actions for breach of contract, or to protect strike organisers from actions for inducing breaches of employment contracts? For efforts in this direction, see *South Wales Miners' Federation* v. *Glamorgan Coal Co.* [1905] A.C. 239 (H.L.); *Smithies* v. *National Association of Operative Plasterers* [1909] 1 K.B. 310 (C.A.); and *Brimelow* v. *Casson* [1924] 1 Ch. 302; and for the adoption of this defence with reference to the tort of interference with business, see *Barretts & Baird (Wholesale) Ltd.* v. *IPCS* [1987] I.R.L.R. 3 (Q.B.D.) para. 69.

(iv) Industrial action and interference with business relationships

The primary objective of industrial action is to put economic pressure on the employer by disrupting his normal business activities. Given a network of business relationships, this inevitably affects others: customers, suppliers, other workers, etc. The central policy issue involves weighing the protection of workers' interests in industrial action against the interests of those involved in business relationships. The common law's values are evident from the extracts which follow.

(a) Interference with existing contracts

Strikes often prevent the employer fulfilling his existing contractual commitments to customers, suppliers and employees. To prohibit industrial action which had this effect would often amount to banning strikes altogether. Nonetheless, in the post-Second World War period, the judges declared that procuring a breach of contract by the indirect means of a strike was unlawful, as the following extracts explain.

D. C. Thomson & Co. Ltd. v. Deakin

[1952] Ch. 646; [1952] 2 All E.R. 361
Court of Appeal

For the facts, see p. 526 above.

JENKINS L.J.:. . . . The plaintiffs' case, as regards paper, is that the defendants persuaded, induced or procured employees of Bowaters (that is, drivers employed by Bowaters Sales Company Ltd., and loaders employed by Bowaters Mersey Mills Ltd.) to break their contracts of employment by refusing to drive lorries loaded with, or to load lorries with, paper destined for the plaintiffs with the object and intention of causing Bowaters to break, or making it impossible for them to fulfil, their contract for the supply of paper to the plaintiffs; and that the defendants did in fact, by the means I have stated, produce the intended result. . . .

Now, the plaintiffs' case, as I have stated it, does seem to me to involve an extension of the range of actionable interference with contractual rights beyond any actual instance of this type of wrong to be found in the decided cases. Here there is no direct invasion of the plaintiffs' rights under the contract. It was no part of their contract that these particular employees, or any particular employees, should be employed by Bowaters for the purpose of effecting deliveries of paper to them. Thus the breaches by these men of their contracts of service with Bowaters (if made out on the facts) did not in themselves involve any breach of Bowaters' contract with the plaintiffs. The breaches of the contracts of service (if made out) were, so to speak, at one remove from the breach of contract complained of. Nevertheless, I think that in principle an actionable interference with contractual relations may be committed by a third party who, with knowledge of a contract between two other persons and with the intention of causing its breach, or of preventing its performance, persuades, induces or procures the servants of one of those parties, on whose services he relies for the performance of his contract, to break their contracts of employment with him, either by leaving him without notice or by refusing to do what is necessary for the performance of his contract, provided that the breach of the contract between the two other persons intended to be brought about by the third party does in fact ensue as a necessary consequence of the third party's wrongful interference with the contracts of employment.

I take this view because I see no distinction in principle for the present purpose between persuading a man to break his contract with another, preventing him by physical restraint from performing it, making his performance of it impossible by taking away or damaging his tools or machinery, and making his performance of it impossible by depriving him, in breach of their contracts, of the services of his employees. All these are wrongful acts, and if done with knowledge of and intention to bring about a breach of a contract to which the person directly wronged is a party, and, if in fact producing that result, I fail to see why they should not all alike fall within the sphere of actionable interference with contractual relations delimited by Lords Macnaghten and Lindley in *Quinn v Leathem* [[1901] A.C. 495 (H.L.) [above, p. 529].

But, while admitting this form of actionable interference in principle, I would hold it strictly confined to cases where it is clearly shown, first, that the person charged with actionable interference knew of the existence of the contract and intended to procure its breach; secondly, that the person so charged did definitely and unequivocally persuade, induce or procure the employees concerned to break their contracts of employment with the intent I have mentioned; thirdly, that the employees so persuaded, induced or procured did in fact break their contracts of employment; and, fourthly, that breach of the contract forming the alleged subject of interference ensued as a necessary consequence of the breaches by the employees concerned of their contracts of employment.

See also *Stratford* v. *Lindley* [1965] A.C. 269 A.C. 269 (H.L.). More recently, the House of Lords again, quoting the last paragraph from Jenkins L.J.'s judgment above, asserted that "his statement of the law as to what are the essential elements in the tort of actionable interference with contractual rights by 'blacking' . . . has, for 30 years now, been regarded as authoritative," and went on to develop it further.

Merkur Island Shipping Corporation v. Laughton
[1983] 2 A.C. 570; [1983] I.C.R. 490
House of Lords

Lord Diplock: *D. C. Thomson & Co. Ltd. v Deakin* [[1952] Ch. 646 [above p. 526] was a case in which the only interference with contractual rights relied upon was procuring a *breach* by a third party of a contract between that third party and the plaintiff. That is why in the passage [quoted in the extract on p. 533 above] that I have picked out for citation Jenkins L.J. restricts himself to that form of actionable interference with contractual rights which consists of procuring an actual breach of the contract that formed the subject-matter of interference, but it is evident from the passages in his judgment which precede the passage I have cited . . . that Jenkins L.J. though using the expression "breach," was not intending to confine the tort of actionable interference with contractual rights to the procuring of such non-performance of primary obligations under a contract as would necessarily give rise to secondary obligations to make monetary compensation by way of damages. All prevention of due performance of a primary obligation under a contract was intended to be included even though no secondary obligation to make monetary compensation thereupon came into existence, because the secondary obligation was excluded by some *force majeure* clause.

If there were any doubt about this matter, it was resolved in 1969 by the judgments of the Court of Appeal in *Torquay Hotel Co. Ltd.* v *Cousins* [1969] 2 Ch. 106 [below, p. 539]. That was a case in which the contract the performance of which was interfered with was one for the delivery of fuel. It contained a *force majeure* clause excusing the seller from liability for non-delivery if delayed, hindered or prevented by (*inter alia*) labour disputes. Lord Denning M.R. stated the principle thus, at p. 138:

> "There must be *interference* in the execution of a contract. The interference is not confined to the procurement of a *breach* of contract. It extends to a case where a third person *prevents* or *hinders* one party from performing his contract, even though it be not a breach." (The emphasis is that of Lord Denning.)

Parliamentary recognition that the tort of actionable interference with contractual rights is as broad as Lord Denning M.R. stated in the passage I have just quoted is, in my view, to be found in section 13(1) of [TULRA] itself which refers to inducement not only "to break a contract," but also "to interfere with its performance," and treats them as being *pari materia*.

The House of Lords thus confirmed the new economic tort of interference with an employer's contracts by the indirect and unlawful means of inducing breach of employment contracts. This new liability for organisers of strikes was also applicable to the strikers themselves who interfered with the employer's commercial contracts by the indirect and unlawful means of breaking their contracts of employment by striking.

In the extract from *Thomson & Co. Ltd.* v. *Deakin* quoted (above, p. 533), Jenkins L.J. set out a number of preconditions for the tort. These are discussed under the following headings.

(1) Knowledge: "that the person charged with actionable interference knew of the existence of the contract and intended to procure its breach."

Emerald Construction Co. Ltd. v. Lowthian
[1966] 1 W.L.R. 691; [1966] 1 All E.R. 1013
Court of Appeal

LORD DENNING M.R.: If the officers of the trade union knowing of the contract deliberately sought to procure a breach of it, they would do wrong; see *Lumley v Gye* [(1853) 2 E. & B. 216 [above p. 525]. Even if they did not know of the actual terms of the contract, but had the means of knowledge—which they deliberately disregarded—that would be enough. Like the man who turns a blind eye. So here, if the officers deliberately sought to get this contract terminated, heedless of its terms, regardless whether it was terminated by breach or not, they would do wrong. For it is unlawful for a third person to procure a breach of contract knowingly, or recklessly, indifferent whether it is a breach or not.

Cf. Square Grip Reinforcement Ltd. v. *Macdonald* [1968] S.L.T. 68 (Inner House) where the defendants were liable for inducement to breach of contract despite their ignorance of the commercial contracts in question because they must have realised that their action in blacking the plaintiff's products would cause breach of its commercial contracts. See also *Falconer* v. *ASLEF and NUR* [1986] I.R.L.R. 331 (County Court) where the defendant unions, which had called a one-day stoppage on the railways without a ballot (as required by the Trade Union Act 1984, Pt. II) were held liable in damages for the overnight accommodation of the plaintiff, a railway passenger, who (because of the stoppage) had had to spend a night in London in order to fulfil business engagements. The defendants' plea of ignorance as to the existence of a contract between the plaintiff and British Rail was dismissed.

"In my view the plaintiff was one of a definite and identifiable group of people in contractual relationship with the British Rail Board. The fact that his actual name and description were unknown to the defendants at the time does not preclude him from beginning the action and succeeding in his claim provided he satisfies the Court in regard to other matters which must be proved.

I accept the argument advanced on behalf of the plaintiff that it is sufficient to show that the defendants knew there were existing contracts between the Board and the group or class of persons (passengers) of which the plaintiff was one."

(2) Intention: "that the person so charged did definitely and unequivocally persuade, induce or procure the employees concerned to break their contracts of employment with the intent [to procure the breach of *eg* a commercial contract]."

D. C. Thomson & Co. Ltd. v. Deakin
[1952] Ch. 646; [1952] 2 All E.R. 361
Court of Appeal

JENKINS L.J.: . . . general appeals to others to prevent a given person from obtaining goods or services . . . is a purpose capable of being lawfully carried out, and there can, therefore, be nothing unlawful in advocating it, unless unlawful means are advocated. The result of such advocacy may well be that unlawful means are adopted by some to achieve the purpose advocated, but that is not to say that a person who advocates the object without advocating the means is to be taken to have advocated recourse to unlawful means. If by reference to the form of actionable interference with contractual rights now propounded, general exhortations issued in the course of a trade dispute, such as "Stop supplies to X," "Refuse to handle X's goods," "Treat X as 'black,' " and the like, were regarded as amounting to actionable interference, because persons reached by such exhortions might respond to them by breaking their contracts of employment and thereby causing breaches of contracts between their employers and other persons, and because the person issuing such exhortations must be taken constructively to have known that the employers concerned must have contracts of some kind or other with other persons, and that his exhortations (general as they were) might lead to breaches of those contracts through breaches of contracts of employment committed by persons moved by his exhortations, then, the proposition must be accepted, that it is an actionable wrong to advocate objects which can be achieved by lawful means, because they can also be achieved by unlawful means; and to that proposition I decline to subscribe.

Intention can be distinguished from motive (hope, desire, belief) in taking action which leads to breaches of contract. The latter was held insufficient to make out the tort in *Camellia Tanker Ltd. S.A.* v. *ITF and Nelson* [1976] I.R.L.R. 190 (above, p. 527).

(3) Unlawful means: "that the employees so persuaded, induced or procured did in fact break their contracts of employment."

D. C. Thomson & Co. Ltd. v. Deakin
[1952] Ch. 646; [1952] 2 All E.R. 361
Court of Appeal

JENKINS L.J.: . . . almost every strike, if to any extent successful, must cause breaches of contracts between the employer against whom it is directed and the persons with whom he is doing business, the very object of the strike being to bring his business to a standstill or himself to terms. Again, many a strike embarked on in support of a strike in progress in some other concern must have had for its immediate object the cutting off of supplies to, or prevention of distribution of the products of, or the application of similar pressure upon, that other concern.

Yet we have been referred to no case in which the persons inciting a strike have been held liable for actionable interference with contractual relations between the strikers' employers and the persons with whom they deal; and in principle I do not think that the inciters of the strike could be held so liable in the absence of proof that they knew of the existence of a particular contract, and, with a view to bringing about its breach, counselled action by employees in itself necessarily unlawful (as, for example, breach of their contracts of employment) designed to achieve that end.

To hold otherwise would, in my view, be to admit not only an addition to the means whereby actionable interference with contractual rights may be compassed (which addition, as I have said, I am in principle prepared to accept), but also an enlargement of the character and scope of the tort itself (which I cannot agree to).

In *D. C. Thomson & Co. Ltd.* v. *Deakin* the plaintiff complained that the defendant had induced the employees of Bowaters, the paper suppliers, to break their contracts of employment, thus procuring breach of the paper supply contract between Bowaters and the plaintiffs. However, as put by Sir Raymond Evershed M.R.:

> "I need only add that there was, on the evidence, no breach of contract by any workman, since Bowaters, for reasons which I doubt not were prudent, took the line that they would not order any man either to load or to drive paper for the plaintiffs. They accepted the situation as they found it and made no attempt to contrive to get the paper to the plaintiffs by any other means."

(4) Causation: "that breach of the contract forming the alleged subject of interference ensued as a necessary consequence of the breaches by the employees concerned of their contracts of employment."

D. C. Thomson & Co. Ltd. v. Deakin
[1952] Ch. 646; [1952] 2 All E.R. 361
Court of Appeal

JENKINS L.J.: I should add that by the expression "necessary consequence" used here and elsewhere in this judgment I mean that it must be shown that, by reason of the withdrawal of the services of the employees concerned, the contract breaker was unable, as a matter of practical possibility, to perform his contract; in other words, I think the continuance of the services of the particular employees concerned must be so vital to the performance of the contract alleged to have been interfered with as to make the effect of their withdrawal comparable, for practical purposes, to a direct invasion of the contractual rights of the party aggrieved under the contract alleged to have been interfered with, as, for example (in the case of a contract for personal services), the physical restraint of the person by whom such services are to be performed. . . .

Finally, not every breach of a contract of employment with a trading or manufacturing concern by an employee engaged in services required for the performance of a contract between his employer and some other person carries with it as a necessary consequence (in the sense above indicated) the breach of the last-mentioned contract. For instance, A induces B, C's lorry driver, to refuse, in breach of his contract of employment, to carry goods which C is under contract to deliver to D, and does so with a view to causing the breach of C's contract with D. C could, if he chose, engage some other lorry driver, or arrange alternative means of transport, but does not do so. He fails to deliver the goods, telling D he is prevented from doing so by B's breach of contract. In such circumstances, there has been no direct invasion by A of C's rights under his contract with D, and, although A has committed an actionable wrong against C, designed to bring about the breach of C's contract with D, and a breach has in fact occurred, it cannot be said that the breach has in fact been caused by A's wrongful act, and therefore D cannot, in my view, establish as against A an actionable interference with his rights under his contract with C.

Contrast the reasoning of Jenkins L.J. above with the conclusion in *Falcolner* v. *ASLEF and NUR* (above p. 535) that the defendant unions were liable to the plaintiff rail passenger who had to find overnight accommodation in London due to an unlawfully called one-day stoppage on the railways.

(b) Interference with business

It is obvious that strike action will in most cases interfere with trade and business (including contracts). That is its purpose. But what if no contracts are broken or interfered with, though the strike does interfere with business generally, *eg* by precluding potential contracts being formed? In 1898 judges were asked to hold that industrial action to persuade employers not to employ non-unionists was an interference with business and *per se* unlawful (see Chapter 2 on *Access to Work*, section on a "right to work," p. 37). In *Allen* v. *Flood* (below) the trial judge and a 6:2 majority of the Court of Appeal accepted the proposition, and only by a 6:3 majority in the House of Lords was it rejected.

Allen v. Flood
[1898] A.C. 1; 67 L.J.Q.B. 119
House of Lords

LORD HERSCHELL: In *Temperton v Russell* [[1893] 1 Q.B. 715] the further step was taken by the majority of the Court, A. L. Smith L.J. reserving his opinion on the point, of asserting that it was immaterial that the act induced was not the breach of a contract, but only the not entering into a contract, provided that the motive of desiring to injure the plaintiff, or to benefit the defendant at the expense of the plaintiff, was present. It seems to have been regarded as only a small step from the one decision to the other, and it was said that there seemed to be no good reason why, if an action lay for maliciously inducing a breach of contract, it should not equally lie for maliciously inducing a person not to enter into a contract. So far from thinking it a small step from the one decision to the other, I think there is a chasm between them. The reason for a distinction between the two cases appears to me to be this: that in the one case the act procured was the violation of a legal right, for which the person doing the act which injured the plaintiff could be sued as well as the person who procured it; whilst in the other case no legal right was violated by the person who did the act from which the plaintiff suffered: he would not be liable to be sued in respect of the act done, whilst the person who induced him to do the act would be liable to an action.

I think this was an entirely new departure. A study of the case of *Lumley v Gye* [2 E. & B. 216, above, p. 525] has satisfied me that in that case the majority of the Court regarded the circumstance that what the defendant procured was a breach of contract as the essence of the cause of action.

The "*Allen* v. *Flood*" clause in the Trade Disputes Act 1906, s.3 confirmed the view of the majority in the House of Lords:

> "An act done by a person in contemplation or furtherance of a trade dispute shall not be actionable on the ground only . . . that it is an interference with the trade, business, or employment of some other person, or with the right of some other person to dispose of his capital or his labour as he wills."

This section (most recently embodied in TULRA, s.13(2)) was repealed by the Employment Act 1982, s.19(1).

The refusal of the common law to hold interference with business tortious was maintained until 1969. In that year Lord Denning M.R. crossed the chasm referred to by Lord Herschell in *Allen* v. *Flood* (above) between actions procuring breaches of contract and those falling short of this. He did this by following the path of *D. C. Thomson & Co. Ltd.* v. *Deakin* (above p. 533). As that case showed, procuring breach of contract could be accomplished directly (*Lumley* v. *Gye* above p. 525) or indirectly—using unlawful means. The House of Lords in *Allen* v. *Flood* had rejected the extension of *Lumley* v. *Gye* to include direct interference with business. Lord Denning felt able, nonetheless, to argue that *indirect* interference with business, using unlawful means, was tortious even though direct interference was lawful. He did this with apparently full awareness of its implications for the right to strike. For, as has been shown (*cf.* pp. 522 and 525 above), a strike almost invariably involves breaches of and inducement of breaches of contracts of employment—unlawful acts.

Torquay Hotel Co. Ltd. v. Cousins
[1969] 2 Ch. 106
Court of Appeal

For the facts, see p. 526 above.

Lord Denning M.R.: . . . A trade union official, who calls a strike on proper notice, may well know that it will prevent the employers from performing their contracts to deliver goods, but he is not liable in damages for calling it. *Indirect* interference is only unlawful if unlawful means are used . . . [and he referred to the distinction in *D. C. Thomson & Co. Ltd* v *Deakin* (above p. 533) between direct inducement (tortious) and indirect inducement (only tortious if unlawful means are used), and continued:] This distinction must be maintained, else we should take away the right to strike altogether.

Nearly every trade union official who calls a strike—even on due notice . . . knows that it may prevent the employers from performing their contracts. He may be taken even to intend it. Yet no one has supposed hitherto that it was unlawful; and we should not render it unlawful today. A trade union official is only in the wrong when he procures a contracting party *directly* to break his contract, or when he does it indirectly *by unlawful means*. . . .

I must say a word about unlawful means, because that brings in another principle. I have always understood that if one person deliberately interferes with the trade or business of another, and does so by unlawful means, that is, by an act which he is not at liberty to commit, then he is acting unlawfully, even though he does not procure or induce any actual breach of contract. If the means are unlawful, that is enough. . . .

This point about unlawful means is of particular importance when a place is declared "black." At common law it often involves the use of unlawful means. Take the Imperial Hotel. When it was declared "black," it meant that the drivers of the tankers would not take oil to the hotel. The drivers would thus be induced to break their contracts of employment. That would be unlawful at common law.

In *Merkur Island Corporation* v. *Laughton* [1983] I.C.R. 490 (H.L.), Lord Diplock seemed to signal unqualified acceptance of the new tort:

> "I should mention that the evidence also establishes a *prima facie* case of the common law tort, referred to in section 13(2) and (3) of [TULRA (now repealed respectively by the Employment Acts 1982, s.19(1) and 1980, s.17(8))], of interfering with the trade or business of another person by doing unlawful acts. To fall within this genus of torts the unlawful act need not involve procuring another person to break a subsisting contract or to interfere with the performance of a subsisting contract."

This is to read the "*Allen* v. *Flood* clause" (TULRA, s.13(2)) as acknowledging the tort of interference by unlawful means, instead of denying the existence of a tort of interference with business, as *Allen* v. *Flood* decided. Whether it was invented or merely revived by Lord Denning, its implications for the legality of strikes at common law are clear. Strikers, by breaking their contracts of employment, and organisers, by inducing such breaches, will indirectly interfere with the employer's business—even if he has no contracts to be interfered with—and thus be liable in tort. Moreover, in *Barretts and Bairds (Wholesale) Ltd.* v. *IPCS* [1987] I.R.L.R. 3 (Q.B.D.) it was confirmed in interlocutory proceedings that there was clearly an arguable case that a striker's breach of his employment contract constituted the necessary unlawful means for this tort.

(c) Conspiracy and intimidation: combining and threatening to interfere with business by unlawful means

Breach of contract by strikers and inducing breach by organisers are held by the common law to be unlawful means for the purposes of the torts of indirect interference with contracts or business. The questions arise: is *combining* together to do these unlawful acts a tortious conspiracy? Is *threatening* to do these unlawful acts tortious intimidation? The latter question was answered in the affirmative in the following case.

Rookes v. Barnard
[1964] A.C. 1129; [1964] 1 All E.R. 367
House of Lords

When the respondents informed the employer, BOAC (now British Airways) that there would be a strike unless Mr Rookes was dismissed, he was given due notice of dismissal. He claimed damages for the tort of "intimidation"—the respondents having threatened to break contracts of employment, causing him injury.

LORD DEVLIN: . . . It is not, of course, disputed that if the act threatened is a crime, the threat is unlawful. But otherwise is it enough to say that the act threatened is actionable as a breach of contract or must it be actionable as a tort? My Lords, I see no good ground for the latter limitation. . . . The essence of the offence is coercion. It cannot be said that every form of coercion is wrong. A dividing line must be drawn and the natural line runs between what is lawful and unlawful as against the party threatened. . . .

I find therefore nothing to differentiate a threat of a breach of contract from a threat of physical violence or any other illegal threat. The nature of the threat is immaterial. . . . All that matters to the plaintiff is that, metaphorically speaking, a club has been used. It does not matter to the plaintiff what the club is made of—whether it is a physical club or an economic club, a tortious club or an otherwise illegal club. If an intermediate party is improperly coerced, it does not matter to the plaintiff how he is coerced.

I think, therefore, that at common law there is a tort of intimidation and that on the facts of this case each of the respondents has committed it, both individually (since the jury has found that each took an overt and active part) and in combination with others.

If threatening to strike is tortious intimidation, is combining to strike a tortious conspiracy? It seems to follow logically from Lord Devlin's argument above, but he refused to commit himself:

> "I am not saying that a conspiracy to commit a breach of contract amounts to the tort of conspiracy; that point remains to be decided. I am saying that in the tort of intimidation a threat to break a contract would be a threat of an illegal act. It follows from that that a combination to intimidate by means of a threat of a breach of contract would be an unlawful conspiracy; but it does not necessarily follow that a combination to commit a breach of contract *simpliciter* would be an unlawful conspiracy."

(d) Causing loss by unlawful means

Taken together, the four torts of (1) interference with contracts or (2) business by unlawful means and (3) conspiring or (4) threatening to do an unlawful act are sometimes said to embody a principle that causing loss by unlawful means is actionable at common law. A key policy issue is how much is included in "unlawful means": breach of any statutory obligation, any criminal act, any breach of contract, any tort, contempt of court, any restrictive trade practice, and so on? The dispute in *Rookes* v. *Barnard* (above) over breach of contract as an unlawful means indicates the difficulty. As Lord Wedderburn of Charlton says: "It would make for brevity, logic and elegance if the principle could be stated that the definition of 'illegal' or 'unlawful' was the same under all four rubrics. . . . Unhappily, no such clear principle emerges from the authorities" (Clerk and Lindsell on *Torts* (15th ed., 1982), para. 809).

(v) Picketing and interference with employers' property

Picketing may involve the commission of the economic torts canvassed above: interferences with contracts and with business, as well as conspiracy and intimidation. In addition, the common law has found ways of condemning pickets for interfering with the employer's enjoyment of his property and for committing torts of nuisance, public and private, and trespass. The policy issue is to decide whether acts of picketing, which from the workers' perspective are assertions of their freedom of expression, nevertheless amount to tortious interference with—in particular—the rights of property-owners. The following early cases illustrate contrasting attitudes of the judges.

Lyons v. Wilkins
[1899] 1 Ch. 255
Court of Appeal

After failure of an attempt to persuade the plaintiffs to improve wages and alter their payment system, the union called a strike and posted pickets outside the premises of an outworker. No violence or intimidation was alleged. The Court of Appeal upheld the award of an injunction against the general secretary and other members of the union.

Sir Nathaniel Lindley M.R.: The truth is that to watch or beset a man's house with a view to compel him to do or not to do what is lawful for him not to do or to do is wrongful and without lawful authority unless some reasonable justification for it is consistent with the evidence. Such conduct seriously interferes with the ordinary comfort of human existence and ordinary enjoyment of the house beset and such conduct would support an action on the case for a nuisance at common law . . . Proof that the nuisance was "peaceably to persuade other people" would afford no defence to such an action. Persons may be peaceably persuaded provided the method employed to persuade is not a nuisance to other people.

Ward Lock & Co. Ltd. v. The Operative Printers' Assistants Society
(1906) 22 T.L.R. 327
Court of Appeal

The defendant union picketed the plaintiffs' printing works with the aim of persuading employees to join the union; it was then the intention that the new union members should give notice to terminate their employment with the plaintiffs, thereby (it was hoped) achieving a closed shop. There was no evidence of violence, obstruction or common law nuisance and the pickets were found not to have induced employees to breach their contracts of employment.

MOULTON L.J.: . . . I am therefore of opinion that in support of the plaintiffs' claim with regard to picketing, it must be shown that the defendants or one of them were guilty of a wrongful act, *ie*, that the picketing constituted an interference with the plaintiffs' action [*sic*] wrongful at common law, or, as I think it may accurately be phrased, were guilty of a common law nuisance. . . . I wish to add, that, in my opinion, there is throughout a complete absence of evidence of anything in the nature of picketing or besetting which could constitute a nuisance. . . . It appears that the discharged workmen loitered about for a day or two after leaving work—a thing which is not unlikely to happen—and that they were at times joined by others, but there is no suggestion even by the plaintiffs' witnesses that any annoyance or molestation took place.

The previous two cases were decided under section 7 of the Conspiracy and Protection of Property Act 1875, which still provides that certain acts (*e.g.* watching and besetting, or following a person in a disorderly manner) are unlawful if done "wrongfully and without legal authority." *Lyons* v. *Wilkins* concluded that the acts specified in the 1875 legislation were themselves inherently wrongful; *Ward Lock & Co. Ltd.* v. *OPAS* decided that to be criminal the acts had to be proved wrongful, *e.g.* as tortious: (*per* Moulton L.J.)

> " . . . (the section) renders nothing wrongful that was not so before. Its object is solely to visit certain selected classes of acts which were previously wrongful, ie were at least civil torts, with penal consequences. . . .

As the later case, *Ward Lock* is generally thought to prevail (see, *eg* *Thomas* v. *NUM* [1985] I.R.L.R. 136, p. 544 below), but its effect is considerably weakened by the casual manner in which various acts of picketing are found tortious. For example, following a car was held to be wrongful behaviour in *Elsey* v. *Smith* [1983] I.R.L.R. 292 (High Court of Justiciary (Scotland)): "It was of the kind calculated to harass and distress and it did harass and distress those who were followed and we have little doubt that, at the very least, its restraint by interdict [injunction] would have been justified" (*per* Lord Emslie, at p. 294, para. 4. In *The Mersey Docks & Harbour Company* v. *Verrinder* [1982] I.R.L.R. 152 (Q.B.D.), picketing aimed at "cowboy" hauliers was acknowledged to be peaceful, but the attempt to compel the employer not to use such hauliers was said to be capable of constituting a private nuisance. For a similar finding in relation to a "work-in" see *Galt* v. *Philp* [1984] I.R.L.R. 156 (High Court of Justiciary (Scotland)). Since these acts of picketing were tortious, they generally become criminal as well under the 1875 Act.

The 1875 Act contained a proviso, now enshrined in TULRA, s.15, as amended by the E.A. 1982, that watching and besetting (*ie* attendance) were not to be unlawful if done "for the purpose only of peacefully obtaining or communicating information, or peacefully persuading any person to work or abstain from working." This statutory side-wind has shaped judicial perceptions of picketing. (Elsewhere we deal with the criminal law aspects of picketing and public order, see below, pp. 584 *et seq.*). In the context of civil law, however, the legality of picketing is determined by how the courts balance the interests of pickets with those of persons affected by picketing. Previous sections have illustrated ample judicial protection of contracts and business: the interests of strike-breakers and employers are readily acknowledged in the courts as "right to strike." The collective interests of strikers, however, appear alien to the courts. They are unwilling to acknowledge that continued operation by the employer, or working by strike-breakers, results in substantial damage to strikers and thus infringes their "rights." The courts fail to recognise the strikers' interests (rights) as a balance to those of the employer or strike-breaker. This can lead to only one outcome, as the following case shows. It may be noted, however, that the strikers' interest in secondary action was given some recognition by the judge's refusal to enjoin secondary picketing as a nuisance *per se*—even though such secondary action would be unlawful.

Thomas v. National Union of Mineworkers (South Wales Area)
[1985] I.R.L.R. 136
Chancery Division

SCOTT J.: The position seems to me to be this. Some 50 to 70 striking miners attend at the colliery gates daily. Six of them are selected to stand close to the gates. The rest are placed back from the road so as to allow the vehicle conveying the working miners to pass. Abuse is hurled at the vehicle and at the men inside. Police are in attendance. This picketing or demonstrating is taking place against a background of high community tension and known anger by the pickets or demonstrators against the working miners. It is taking place not on isolated instances but on a daily regular basis. Whether there is thereby committed an infringement of the rights of the working miners I have yet to consider. Whether this picketing or demonstrating is within the rights of those taking part or is such as a trade union is entitled to organise or encourage is also for argument. But I really do not think it can be sensibly suggested that picketing or demonstrating of this sort and in the circumstances revealed by the evidence in this case would be otherwise than highly intimidating to any ordinary person. Why is it necessary for the working miners to be brought into their workplace by vehicles? Why is it necessary for police to be in attendance? Are the apprehensions of violence, intimidation or unruly conduct that prompt these precautions without foundation? On the evidence adduced in the present case I cannot think so.

I must not be taken to be doubting the sworn evidence of those lodge [*ie* branch union] officers who have deposed to their personal abhorrence of violence and to their firm lodge policy that there should be no violence on the picket lines. But where, as in this industrial dispute, feelings run high, substantial numbers of pickets are, in my view, almost bound to have an intimidatory effect on those going to work. I was struck by a remark of Mr Scrivener [counsel for the defendant union] in this connection. He invited me to imagine a large number of sullen men lining the entrance to a colliery, offering no violence, saying nothing, but simply standing and glowering. That, he said, would not be intimidating to a working miner. I disagree. It would, in my opinion, by highly intimidating. . . .

The right of the plaintiffs to relief in respect of the picketing at colliery gates raises three questions. First, there is the question whether the picketing sought to be restrained would represent the commission of a tort against a particular plaintiff or plaintiffs. As to this, I regard the phrase "unlawful picketing" as unhelpful and misleading. It is frequently used. Sometimes it is used to describe picketing in the course of which criminal offences are committed. Sometimes it is used to describe picketing which is tortious. And often it is used to describe picketing which is both tortious and criminal. This is a civil action in which the plaintiffs are asserting their private rights under the civil law. They can complain in a civil action of picketing which is tortious but not of picketing which is criminal. It is for the public prosecuting authorities or for the Attorney-General to control the commission of criminal offences in the course of picketing. It is not for these plaintiffs to do so. The question for me, therefore, is whether the picketing is tortious. The question is not whether the picketing is criminal. . . .

[The judge quoted TULRA, s.15 as amended].

The position, therefore, is that the picketing in the present case of which complaint is made will not be actionable in tort if it can be brought within this [amended] s.15. In my judgment, on any reasonable view of the defendants' own evidence, the immunity of this provision cannot be claimed for the persons who regularly assemble at the colliery gates. It may be that the six persons who are selected to stand close to the gates could bring themselves within the provision, but the many others who are present cannot do so. What is their purpose in attending? It is obviously not to obtain or communicate information. Is it peacefully to persuade the working miners to abstain from working? If that is the case what is the need for so many people, what is the need for the police, and what is the need for vehicles to bring the working miners safely into the collieries? It is fair to say that Mr Scrivener, realistically, did not invite me to deal with this application on the footing that the colliery gate picketing could claim immunity under the substituted s.15. And, of course, picketing at people's houses or places of education cannot qualify for immunity under the section.

It does not, however, follow that because picketing cannot be brought within the substituted s.15, the picketing is therefore tortious. In order to decide whether or to what extent picketing that falls outside the section is tortious, recourse must be had to the general law of tort . . . [The judge rejected alleged torts of assault, obstruction of the highway, and unlawful interference with contracts of employment. He then considered a submission as to "intimidation."] . . . I am in full agreement with [counsel for the plaintiffs'] general submissions regarding the state of affairs at the colliery gates, which, he said, represented intimidation.

The working miners are entitled to use the highway for the purpose of entering and leaving their respective places of work. In the exercise of that right they are at present having to suffer the presence and behaviour of the pickets and demonstrators. The law has long recognised that unreasonable interference with the rights of others is actionable in tort. The law of nuisance is a classic example and was classically described by Sir Nathaniel Lindley MR in *Lyons v Wilkins* [1899] 1 Ch 225 at page 267. . . . It is, however, not every act of interference with the enjoyment by an individual of his property rights that will be actionable in nuisance. The law must strike a balance between conflicting rights and interests. The point is made in Clerk & Lindsell, 15th edition, at paragraph 23.01:

"A variety of different things may amount to a nuisance in fact but whether they are actionable as the tort of nuisance will depend upon a variety of considerations and a balance of conflicting interests."

Nuisance is strictly concerned with, and may be regarded as confined to, activity which unduly interferes with the use or enjoyment of land or of easements. But there is no reason why the law should not protect on a similar basis the enjoyment of other rights. All citizens have the right to use the public highway. Suppose an individual were persistently to follow another on a public highway, making rude gestures or remarks in order to annoy or vex. If continuance of such conduct were threatened no one can doubt but that a civil court would, at the suit of the victim, restrain by an injunction the continuance of the conduct. The tort might be described as a species of private nuisance, namely unreasonable interference with the victim's rights to use the highway. But the label for the tort does not, in my view, matter.

In the present case, the working miners have the right to use the highway for the purpose of going to work. They are, in my judgment, entitled under the general law to exercise that right without unreasonable harassment by others. Unreasonable harassment of them in their exercise of that right would, in my judgement, be tortious.

A decision whether in this, or in any other similar case, the presence or conduct of pickets represents a tortious interference with the right of those who wish to go to work to do so without harassment must depend on the particular circumstances of the particular case. The balance to which I have earlier referred must be struck between the rights of those going to work and the rights of the pickets.

It was made clear in *Ward, Lock & Co Ltd v The Operative Printers' Assistants' Society* [above p. 542] that picketing was not, *per se*, a common law nuisance. The Court of Appeal was in that case considering the question from the point of view of the owner of the premises being picketed. The picketing was peaceful and *per* Vaughan Williams LJ at page 329, first column, "there was no evidence that the comfort of the plaintiffs or the ordinary enjoyment of the Botolph Printing Works was seriously interfered with by the watching and besetting." He held, in effect, that there was no common law nuisance being committed.

Similarly, in the present case, the working miners cannot complain of picketing *per se* or of demonstrations *per se*. They can only complain of picketing or demonstrations which unreasonably harass them in their entry into and egress from their place of work.

From the comments I have already made earlier in this judgment it will be apparent that I think it plain from the evidence before me that the picketing at the colliery gates is of a nature and is carried out in a manner that represents an unreasonable harassment of the working miners. A daily congregation on average of 50 to 70 men hurling abuse and in circumstances that require a police presence and require the working miners to be conveyed in vehicles do not in my view leave any real room for argument. The working miners have the right to go to work. Neither they or any other working man should be required, in order to exercise that right, to tolerate the situation I have described. Accordingly in my judgment the colliery gates picketing is tortious at the suit of the plaintiff or plaintiffs who work at the collieries in question. . . .

[The judge then held the South Wales Union vicariously responsible for the picketing. He considered whether he ought to exercise his discretion to issue an injunction.]

This is an interlocutory application and it is usual on such applications to pay particular attention to the balance of convenience until trial, and to require of a plaintiff no more than that an arguable case be shown. Mr Scrivener, however, invited me on this application not to adopt that usual approach, but to apply a more strict test to the plaintiffs' case before supporting it by the grant of interlocutory relief. He put forward two reasons why I should do so. First, he emphasised that the action was brought against the background of a bitter industrial dispute. The strike is, in South Wales, an official one. The striking miners are entitled to be on strike and entitled to picket in support of their strike. I should avoid, he said, so impeding the right to picket as might prejudice the continuance of the strike. I do not think this is a point of weight. The right to picket is, unless the case can be brought within [the amended] s.15 of [TULRA], no more than the general right which everyone has to do what he or she wants to do, if it can be done without infringing the rights of others. The striking miners have no right, whether by picketing, demonstrating or otherwise, unreasonably to harass the working miners in going to or leaving their workplace. . . . [The judge later considered the argument that secondary picketing at premises other than collieries, was bound to be tortious, and concluded that it was. As to the argument that such secondary picketing was also bound to be a nuisance (and thus criminal under section 7 of the Conspiracy and Protection of Property Act 1875), however, he disagreed.]

In my opinion, the *Ward, Lock* case provides the answer to this submission. Picketing is not a criminal "watching and besetting" under s.7 unless it is at least a tortious watching and besetting. And the Court of Appeal held in the *Ward, Lock* case that the picketing did not represent common law nuisance. Further, common law nuisance requires a balance to be struck between the respective rights and interests of the plaintiff and of the defendant. Where the balance should be struck may depend upon prevailing ideas as to the desirability of and justification for certain types of conduct. It may have been right in 1896, when *Lyons v Wilkins* was decided, to regard picketing in an industrial dispute as *per se* common law nuisance, no matter how peaceably and responsibly conducted. If so, it seems that a change had come about by 1906 when the *Ward, Lock* case was decided. But this is 1985, and prevailing ideas about strikes and picketing are nothing like what they were in 1896. If picketing in pursuance of an industrial dispute is peacefully and responsibly conducted at or near business premises I can see no reason at all why it should be regarded *per se* as a common law nuisance. Nor, in my view, does the fact that the picketing is secondary picketing invalidate this conclusion. If the picketing is secondary and involves the commission of torts, there is now, under [the amended] s.15, no immunity from tortious liability. But there is no statutory provision which makes secondary picketing *per se* a common law nuisance, and in my judgment it is not one. It follows that, in my judgment, secondary picketing will not necessarily constitute an offence under s.7 of the 1875 Act.

On the other hand, Mr Scrivener submitted that mass picketing—by which I understand to be meant picketing so as by sheer weight of numbers to block the entrance to premises or to prevent the entry thereto of vehicles or people—was not *per se* tortious or criminal. In my judgment, mass picketing is clearly both common law nuisance and an offence under s.7 of the 1875 Act.

In *News Group Newspapers Ltd.* v. *SOGAT '82* [1986] I.R.L.R. 337, paras. 111–112 Stuart-Smith J. accepted that there was force in criticisms of the new head of liability in *Thomos.* It was suggested that unreasonable interference with the rights of others should not be actionable unless those rights are recognised by the law and fall within some accepted head of tort, for which proof of damage is a necessary ingredient.

(B) Parliament and the Common Law: the Statutory Immunities

(i) The statutory immunities

Parliament's response to the policy of the common law on industrial action by workers took an unusual form. Faced with judicial condemnation of industrial action as unlawful in various ways, Parliament attempted to remove the *consequences* of such condemnation by precluding the courts from intervening. This was done by declaring certain actions by workers, held unlawful by the courts, to be *not actionable* in the courts. The workers were given an "immunity" from court action. The interplay of judicial condemnation, statutory immunity, judicial interpretation of the immunity, statutory reformulation of the immunity, etc., has produced a legal framework governing industrial action of inordinate complexity. The common law liabilities already reviewed (above pp. 522 *et seq.*) have provoked the following statutory immunities.

(a) Breach of contract

There is no immunity, except as regards common law remedies:

TULRA, s.16:

"No court shall, whether by way of—
(a) an order for specific performance or specific implement of a contract of employment, or
(b) an injunction or interdict restraining a breach or threatened breach of such a contract,
compel an employee to do any work or attend at any place for the doing of any work."

(b) Inducing breach of contract or interference with contract

TULRA, s.13(1)(*a*):

"An act done by a person in contemplation or furtherance of a trade dispute shall not be actionable in tort on the ground only—
(a) that it induces another person to break a contract or interferes or induces any other person to interfere with its performance. . . ."

(c) "Simple" conspiracy

TULRA, s.13(4):

"An agreement or combination by two or more persons to do or procure the doing of any act in contemplation or furtherance of a trade dispute shall not be actionable in tort if the act is one which, if done without any such agreement or combination, would not be actionable in tort."

(d) Interference with business (direct and indirect)

TULRA, s.13(2) (repealed by the Employment Act 1982, s.19(1)):

"For the avoidance of doubt it is hereby declared that an act done by a person in contemplation or furtherance of a trade dispute is not actionable in tort on the ground only that it is an interference with the trade, business or employment of another person, or with the right of another person to dispose of his capital or his labour as he wills."

(e) Intimidation

TULRA, s.13(1)(*b*):

"An act done by a person in contemplation or furtherance of a trade dispute shall not be actionable in tort on the ground only . . .

(b) that it consists in his threatening that a contract (whether one to which he is a party or not) will be broken or its performance interfered with, or that he will induce another person to breach a contract or to interfere with its performance.

(f) Conspiracy to do an unlawful act

TULRA, s.13(3) (repealed by the Employment Act 1980 s.17(8)):

"For the avoidance of doubt it is hereby declared that—

(a) an act which by reason of subsection (1) [*ie* interference with contracts] or (2) [*ie* interference with trade, business or employment] is itself not actionable;

(b) a breach of contract in contemplation or furtherance of a trade dispute;

shall not be regarded as the doing of an unlawful act or as the use of unlawful means for the purposes of establishing liability in tort."

As stated above (p. 541), the four torts of interference with contracts, interference with business, intimidation and conspiracy all require unlawful means to be used. TULRA, s.13(3) sought to provide immunity against these common law liabilities by declaring that the acts of strikers in breaking their contracts and strike organisers in inducing breach of or interfering with contracts were *not* to constitute unlawful means so as to provide the necessary "unlawful" ingredient for liability under any of these torts. The repeal of TULRA, s.13(3) by the Employment Act 1980 raises problems which are discussed below (p. 554).

(g) Interference with employers' property and his employees

TULRA, s.15

(1) It shall be lawful for a person in contemplation or furtherance of a trade dispute to attend—

(a) at or near his own place of work, or

(b) if he is an official of a trade union, at or near the place of work of a member of that union whom he is accompanying and whom he represents,

for the purpose only of peacefully obtaining or communicating information, or peacefully persuading any person to work or abstain from working.

It will be noted that these immunities are confined to acts "in contemplation or furtherance of a trade dispute": the "golden formula." Problems of interpreting this formula are discussed below (p. 555 *et seq.*). Also, the immunities sketched above have been withdrawn in the case of some secondary action and secondary picketing (Employment Act 1980, s.17), pressure to impose trade union membership or recognition requirements (Employment Act 1982, s.14), and where the union has not held a secret ballot which supports the action (Trade Union Act 1984, Pt. II).

The dynamic relationship between judges and Parliament will be explored under the following headings illustrating key aspects of the law regulating workers' recourse to industrial action.

(ii) Paths of common law development

The ability of the judges to create new liabilities in order to restrain workers' recourse to industrial action is evident. The response of Parliament in reversing the effect of these common law developments by providing immunities has in the past been equally apparent. The question arises whether this pattern is to continue, or whether the judges will restrain their creative urges to accord with the restrictions on the immunities laid down by Parliament in the 1980s with regard to industrial action. It is a choice between the assertion of common law autonomy and a policy of self-restraint.

Two cases can be used to illustrate these two paths of common law development. *Rookes* v. *Barnard* [1964] A.C. 1129 (H.L.) illustrates the assertion of common law autonomy. *Universe Tankships Inc. of Monrovia* v. *International Transport Workers' Federation* [1982] I.R.L.R. 200 (H.L.) illustrates a policy of restraint.

Why different choices were made in 1964 and 1982 by the House of Lords is a fascinating question. Was it the case in 1964 that, as Wedderburn put it: " . . . Middle-class opinion . . . no longer acquiesced in the 1960's in the new muscles which trade unions had, but rarely efficiently, flexed in days of full employment" ((1972) 10 B.J.I.R. 270, 275)? Was it that by 1982, with a turbulent history of controversial judicial interventions in labour law, unemployment reaching three million and a Conservative Government legislating new restrictions, the judges felt able to adopt a more restrained approach?

In 1964 the House of Lords had to decide whether workers threatening to break their contracts of employment by going on strike had committed the tort of intimidation. As we have seen (above p. 540) they decided that threatening to strike was tortious.

Rookes v. Barnard
[1964] A.C. 1129; [1964] 1 All E.R. 367
House of Lords

For the facts, see above p. 541.

LORD DEVLIN: . . . there is one argument, or at least one consideration that remains to be noticed. It is that the strike weapon is now so generally sanctioned that it cannot really be regarded as an unlawful weapon of intimidation: and so there must be something wrong with a conclusion that treats it as such. This thought plainly influenced quite strongly the judgments in the Court of Appeal. To give effect to it means either that illegal means ought not to include a breach of contract or that the statute [Trade Disputes Act 1906, the forerunner of T.U.L.R.A.] ought to be construed as wide enough to give protection. The Court of Appeal tended, I think, to apply the argument to both points indiscriminately. I see the force of this consideration. But your lordships can, in my opinion, give effect to it only if you are prepared either to hobble the common law in all classes of disputes lest its range is too wide to suit industrial disputes or to give the statute a wider scope than it was ever intended to have.

As to the former alternative, I cannot doubt that the threat of a breach of contract can be a most intimidating thing. The present case provides as good an example of the force of such a threat as could be found. A great and powerful corporation submits to it at once, for it was threatened with the infliction of incalculable loss and of grave inconvenience to the public which it serves. The threat is made by men who are flagrantly violating a pledge not to strike, at least until constitutional means of resolving the dispute have been exhausted.

It is not just a technical illegality, a case in which a few days' longer notice might have made the difference. Because of the damage that would ensue from a strike, B.O.A.C., no doubt in return for corresponding benefits, secured the pledge not to strike; and it is that pledge that is being broken. Granted that there is a tort of intimidation. I think it would be quite wrong to cripple the common law so that it cannot give relief in these circumstances. I think it would be old-fashioned and unrealistic for the law to refuse relief in such a case and to grant it where there is a shake of a fist or a threat to publish a nasty and untrue story.

I said that I thought it would be wrong to cripple the common law in such a case, but that does not mean that I am necessarily criticising the policy of the Trade Disputes Act, 1906. It is easy now to see that Parliament in 1906 might have felt that the only way of giving labour an equality of bargaining power with capital was to give it special immunities which the common law did not permit. Even now, when the scales have been redressed, it is easy to see that Parliament might think that a strike, whether reprehensible or not, ought not to be made a ground for litigation and that industrial peace should be sought by other means. It may, therefore, as a matter of policy be right that a breach of contract should not be treated as an illegal means within the limited field of industrial disputes. But can your lordships get that out of the words of the [Trade Disputes] Act [1906]? Section 3 gives immunity from action for procuring a breach of contract but not for the breach itself. In the Court of Appeal Donovan, L.J., said with great force:

> "If one may procure the breach of another's contract with impunity in a trade dispute, it is certainly odd if one cannot even threaten to break one's own."

The section could easily have read—"shall not be actionable on the ground only that it *is a breach of contract or* induces some other person" etc.; but it is not so written. It may be that, as counsel for the respondents suggests, Parliament thought it very unlikely that an employer would resort to action against workmen individually for breaches of contract and that he would get very little from it if he did: see on this point *National Coal Board v Galley* [[1958] 1 All E.R. 91]. Or it may be that Parliament did not anticipate that a threat of breach of contract would be regarded as an intimidatory weapon. Whatever the reason, the immunity is not in the statute; the section clearly exempts the procurer or inducer and equally clearly does not exempt the breaker. It is not suggested that the House can remove the oddity by reading words into the Act that are not there . . . The essence of the difficulty lies in the fact that in determining what constitutes the tort of intimidation your lordships have drawn the dividing line not between physical and economic coercion but between lawful and unlawful coercion. For the universal purposes of the common law, I am sure that that is the right, natural and logical line. For the purpose of the limited field of industrial disputes, which is controlled by statute and where much that is in principle unlawful is already tolerated, it may be that pragmatically and on grounds of policy the line should be drawn between physical and economic pressure. But that is for Parliament to decide. What the House said in *Vacher & Sons, Ltd. v London Society of Compositors*, especially per Lord MacNaghten [[1913] A.C. 107 at 148] . . . is a very clear warning, if one be needed, against the interference of the courts in matters of policy in this branch of the law.

In 1965 Parliament enacted an immunity for intimidation (see now TULRA, s.13(1)(*b*). In 1982 the House of Lords had to decide whether the use of "economic duress" by a trade union to induce an employer to part with money entitled the employer to recover the money.

Universe Tankships Inc. of Monrovia v. International Transport Workers' Federation

[1982] I.R.L.R. 200; [1982] 2 All E.R. 67

House of Lords

> In July 1978 the plaintiffs' ship, the Universe Sentinel, was prevented from sailing by being blacked by tugboat crews at the request of the defendants. The blacking was only lifted when the plaintiffs, *inter alia*, paid the defendants 80,000 U.S. dollars, including 71,720 dollars as an estimate of the shortfall in wages payable under the defendants' standard collective agreements and 6,480 dollars as a contribution to a union welfare fund. After the money was paid and the ship allowed to sail, the plaintiffs demanded repayment on the ground that the money was paid under duress.

Lord Diplock: Commercial pressure, in some degree, exists wherever one party to a commercial transaction is in a stronger bargaining position than the other party. It is not, however, in my view necessary, nor would it be appropriate in the instant appeal, to enter into the general question of the kinds of circumstances, if any, in which commercial pressure, even though it amounts to a coercion of the will of a party in the weaker bargaining position, may be treated as legitimate and, accordingly, as not giving rise to any legal right of redress. In the instant appeal the economic duress complained of was exercised in the field of industrial relations to which very special considerations apply.

My Lords, so far as is relevant to this appeal, the policy of Parliament, ever since the Trade Disputes Act 1906 was passed to overrule a decision of this House [the *Taff Vale* decision [1901] A.C. 426] has been to legitimise acts done by employees, or by trade unions acting or purporting to act on their behalf, which would otherwise be unlawful wherever such acts are done in contemplation or furtherance of a dispute which is connected with the terms and conditions of employment of any employees. I can confine myself to the kind of acts and the particular subject-matter of the trade dispute that was involved in the instant case, and I use the expression "legitimise" as meaning that the doer of the act is rendered immune from any liability to damages or any other remedy against him in a court of justice, at the suit of a person who has suffered loss or damage in consequence of the act save only a remedy for breach of contract where the act is done in breach of a direct contract between the doer of the act and the person by whom the damage is sustained.

The statutory provisions in force when the events with which this appeal is concerned took place and which point to the public policy to which effect ought to be given by your Lordships, are chiefly contained in ss.13, 14 and 29 of the Trade Union and Labour Relations Act 1974 [*ie* prior to the repeal of TULRA, s.14 and the amendment of ss.13 and 29 by the Employment Act, s.1980 and 1982]. The legislative history of these sections is referred to in the recent decision of this House in *Hadmor Productions Ltd v Hamilton* [1982] IRLR 102. In terms they are confined to bestowing immunity from liability in tort; they do not deal with immunity in any other type of action. In the case of a trade union such immunity is extended by s.14 to virtually all torts; in the case of individuals, it is extended by s.13 to defined classes of torts (which would include the blacking of the "Universe Sentinel") which are limited, not only in their nature, but also by the requirement that what would otherwise be the tortious act must be committed in contemplation or furtherance of a trade dispute as defined in s.29.

The use of economic duress to induce another person to part with property or money is not a tort *per se;* the form that the duress takes may, or may not, be tortious. The remedy to which economic duress gives rise is not an action for damages but an action for restitution of property or money exacted under such duress and the avoidance of any contract that had been induced by it; but where the particular form taken by the economic duress used is itself a tort, the restitutional remedy for money had and received by the defendant to the plaintiff's use is one which the plaintiff is entitled to pursue as an alternative remedy to an action for damages in tort.

In extending into the field of industrial relations the common law concept of economic duress and the right to a restitutionary remedy for it which is currently in process of development by judicial decisions, this House would not, in my view, be exercising the restraint that is appropriate to such a process if it were so to develop the concept that, by the simple expedient of "waiving the tort," a restitutionary remedy for money had and received is made enforceable in cases in which Parliament has, over so long a period of years, manifested its preference for a public policy that a particular kind of tortious act should be legitimised in the sense that I am using that expression.

It is only in this indirect way that the provisions of the Trade Union and Labour Relations Act 1974 are relevant to the duress point. The immunities from liability in tort provided by ss.13 and 14 are not directly applicable to the shipowners' cause of action for money had and received. Nevertheless, these sections, together with the definition of trade dispute in s.29, afford an indication, which your Lordships should respect, of where public policy requires that the line should be drawn between what kind of commercial pressure by a trade union upon an employer in the field of industrial relations ought to be treated as legitimised despite the fact that the will of the employer is thereby coerced, and what kind of commercial pressure in that field does amount to economic duress that entitles the employer victim to restitutionary remedies.

(iii) The meaning of an "immunity": is industrial action a tort (unlawful) or a risk (non-actionable)?

The immunities in TULRA, s.13(1), (2) and (4) provide that various acts are "not actionable." This is in line with a policy of protecting a "right to strike"—normal industrial action was not to lead to liability in tort. Persons affected by industrial action had to tolerate such risks to their contracts or business. However, counter to the policy of protecting industrial action, doubts were expressed by judges as to whether such "non-actionable" acts were nonetheless still unlawful. If unlawful (though non-actionable) they could still be unlawful means for the purposes of *indirect* interference with contracts or business *and* not protected by existing immunities which protected only *direct* inducements or interference. To resolve such doubts, TULRA included a new section 13(3) (above, p. 549) which declared certain acts (inducements, interference, breaches of contract) *not* unlawful means for the purposes of liability for these indirectly committed torts. The significance of section 13(3) was debated when it was proposed to repeal it in the Employment Act 1980. Opposition peers in the House of Lords alleged its repeal would revive the torts of indirect interference and cause all strikes to become unlawful (see *Parliamentary Debates*, Official Report, House of Lords, June 12, 1980, Vol. 410, cols. 672–688).

The Employment Act 1980, s.17(8) duly repealed TULRA, s.13(3). The issue debated in the House of Lords was soon afterwards brought before the courts. The House of Lords, reversing the Court of Appeal, held that section 13(3) had been otiose and that its repeal therefore did not alter the law (*Hadmor Productions Ltd.* v. *Hamilton* [1982] 2 W.L.R. 322 (H.L.)).

The real issue of policy is whether strikes which interfere with contracts and business are to bring the law down on the heads of strikers and strike organisers? Implicit is the policy choice between the interests of strikers and of those whose contracts or business is interfered with. As in the case of picketing (see p. 617 below), new approaches need to be explored. For example, the focus of attention could be shifted from the concept of "unlawful means" to the concept of "interference." The concept of "interference with contracts and business" implies a course of commercial conduct which is interfered with. This section has been concerned with the consequences of interference resulting from strikes and industrial action. But *other* interferences abound: fluctuations in interest rates, inflation, technological change, *force majeure*, etc. These are not tortious matters, but *risks* which businessmen run and against which, where appropriate, they take precautionary counter-measures (as, *eg* in *Torquay Hotel Co. Ltd.* v. *Cousins* [1969] 2 Ch. 106 (C.A.), above p. 539, where the contract between the oil supplier, Esso, and the plaintiffs contained a *force majeure* clause excepting liability for labour disputes).

Could a statutory policy be devised recognising that industrial action is not a tortious interference but a risk, and even allocate the costs of such risk? There are precedents along these lines, *eg* the rights of workers to guarantee payments in the event of lay-off are suspended if the lay-off is in consequence of a trade dispute, even if they are not involved in it (EPCA, s.13(1)). It could be statutory policy that interference with contracts and business in consequence of a trade dispute is not unlawful, at least for the strikers and strike organisers. Businessmen, as with other risks, could sort out the appropriate costs themselves, or statute could intervene in that sphere as well.

(iv) The scope of the immunities: judicial policy in interpreting the "golden formula"

Those committing the acts described in the statutory immunities are protected from legal action when they act "in contemplation or furtherance of a trade dispute"—the "golden formula." Strikers and those organising strikes are legally vulnerable unless they can bring their acts within the scope of this formula. While ostensibly a matter of textual interpretation, the judges have raised the following policy grounds in interpreting the "golden formula."

(a) The effectiveness of the industrial action

Some judges, particularly in the Court of Appeal, expressed the view that to be within the "golden formula" (*ie* to be "furthering" a dispute), the industrial action had to be *reasonably capable* of achieving the ends desired by those taking the action (*per* Lawton and Brandon L.JJ. in *MacShane* v. *Express Newspapers Ltd.* [1979] I.R.L.R. 79 (C.A.)). Other judges said that to "further" a dispute the action must have some *practical* effect in putting pressure on the other party to the dispute (Lord Denning M.R. in *MacShane*; Ackner J. in *United Biscuits (UK) Ltd.* v. *Fall* [1979] I.R.L.R. 110 (Q.B.D.)). A related view is that industrial action does not "further" a dispute where it is taken to support demands which are not susceptible of compromise by the other party, "are wholly extortionate or utterly unreasonable or quite impossible to fulfil" (Lord Denning M.R. and Templeman L.J. in *PBDS (National Carriers) Ltd.* v. *Filkins* [1979] I.R.L.R. 356 (C.A.)). Taken together, these views require the *court* to assess the effectiveness of industrial action: only that which is "objectively" effective can be said to further the dispute and thus fall within the statutory immunity. The majority of the House of Lords in *MacShane* v. *Express Newspapers Ltd.* [1980] A.C. 672 and in *Duport Steels Ltd.*v. *Sirs* [1980] I.R.L.R. 116 rejected this view.

Express Newspapers Ltd. v. MacShane
[1980] A.C. 672; [1980] 1 All E.R. 65
House of Lords

The National Union of Journalists (NUJ), of which Mr MacShane was President, called a strike against provincial newspapers. Because the local papers also got news copy from the Press Association (PA), the union called upon its members employed by the PA to come out on strike as well. About half of the PA journalists, however, remained at work, and their supplies of copy enabled the provincial newspapers to carry on despite the strike. To put pressure on the PA to stop supplying this copy, the union ordered its members employed by national newspapers to "black" PA copy—*ie* to refuse to handle copy produced by those refusing to come out on strike at the PA. The Daily Express sought an injunction restraining the defendant from inducing their employees to break their contracts of employment by refusing to handle PA copy.

Lord Diplock: My Lords, during the past two years there has been a series of judgments in the Court of Appeal given upon applications for interlocutory injunctions against trade union officials. These have the effect of imposing on the expression "an act done by a person in contemplation or furtherance of a trade dispute" for which immunity from civil actions for specified kinds of torts is conferred by s.13(1) of the Trade Union and Labour Relations Act, 1974, (as now amended), an interpretation restrictive of what, in common with the majority of your Lordships, I believe to be its plain and unambiguous meaning. The terms in which the limitations upon the ambit of the expression have been stated are not identical in the various judgments, but at the root of all of them there appears to lie an assumption that Parliament cannot really have intended to give so wide an immunity from the common law of tort as the words of ss.13 and 29 would, on the face of them, appear to grant to everyone who engages in any form of what is popularly known as industrial action.

My Lords, I do not think that this is a legitimate assumption on which to approach the construction of the Act, notwithstanding that the training and traditions of anyone whose life has been spent in the practice of the law and the administration of justice in the courts must make such an assumption instinctively attractive to him. But the manifest policy of the Act was to strengthen the role of recognised trade unions in collective bargaining, so far as possible to confine the bargaining function to them, and, as my noble and learned friend Lord Scarman recently pointed out in *The Nawala (NWL Ltd v Woods and another* [1979] 1 W.L.R. 1294, to exclude trade disputes from judicial review by the courts. Parliament, as it was constituted when the Act and the subsequent amendments to it were passed, may well have felt so confident that trade unions could be relied upon always to act "responsibly" in trade disputes that any need for legal sanctions against their failure to do so could be obviated.

This being so, it does not seem to me that it is a legitimate approach to the construction of the sections that deal with trade disputes, to assume that Parliament did *not* intend to give to trade unions and their officers a wide discretion to exercise their own judgment as to the steps which should be taken in an endeavour to help the workers' side in any trade dispute to achieve its objectives. And if their plain and ordinary meaning is given to the words "An act done by a person in contemplation or furtherance of a trade dispute," this, as it seems to me, is what s.13 does. In the light of the express reference to the "person" by whom the act is done and the association of "furtherance" with "contemplation" (which cannot refer to anything but the state of mind of the doer of the act) it is, in my view, clear that "in furtherance" too can only refer to the state of mind of the person who does the act, and means: with the purpose of helping one of the parties to a trade dispute to achieve their objectives in it.

Given the existence of a trade dispute (the test of which, though broad, is nevertheless objective, see *The Nawala*), this makes the test of whether an act was done "in furtherance of" it a purely subjective one. If the party who does the act honestly thinks at the time he does it that it may help one of the parties to the trade dispute to achieve their objectives and does it for that reason, he is protected by the section. I say "may" rather than "will" help, for it is in the nature of industrial action that success in achieving its objectives cannot be confidently predicted. Also there is nothing in the section that requires that there should be any proportionality between on the one hand the extent to which the act is likely to, or be capable of, increasing the "industrial muscle" of one side to the dispute, and on the other hand the damage caused to the victim of the act which, but for the section, would have been tortious. The doer of the act may know full well that it cannot have more than a minor effect in bringing the trade dispute to the successful outcome that he favours, but nevertheless is bound to cause disastrous loss to the victim, who may be a stranger to the dispute and with no interest in its outcome. The act is none the less entitled to immuniity under the section.

It is, I think, these consequences of applying the subjective test that, not surprisingly, have tended to stick in judicial gorges: that so great damage may be caused to innocent and disinterested third parties in order to obtain for one of the parties to a trade dispute tactical advantages which in the court's own view are highly speculative and, if obtained, could be no more than minor. This has led the Court of Appeal to seek to add some objective element to the subjective test of the *bona fide* purpose of the person who did the act.

. . . [a] test, suggested by Lord Denning in the instant case, is that the act done must have some "practical" effect in bringing pressure to bear upon the opposite side to the dispute; acts done to assist the morale of the party to the dispute whose cause is favoured are not protected. [Alternatively] there is the test favoured by Lawton and Brandon L.JJ. in the instant case: the act done must, in the view of the court, be reasonably capable of achieving the objective of the trade dispute.

My Lords, these tests though differently expressed, have the effect of enabling the court to substitute its own opinion for the *bona fide* opinion held by the trade union or its officers, as to whether action proposed to be taken or continued for the purpose of helping one side or bringing pressure to bear upon the other side to a trade dispute is likely to have the desired effect. Granted *bona fides* on the part of the trade union or its officer this is to convert the test from a purely subjective to a purely objective test and for the reasons I have given I do not think the wording of the section permits of this. The belief of the doer of the act that it will help the side he favours in the dispute must be honest; it need not be wise, nor need it take account of the damage it will cause to innocent and disinterested third parties. Upon an application for an interlocutory injunction the evidence may show positively by admission or by inference from the facts before the court that the act was not done to further an existing trade dispute but for some ulterior purpose such as revenge for previous conduct. Again, the facts in evidence before the court may be such as will justify the conclusion that no reasonable person versed in industrial relations could possibly have thought that the act was capable of helping one side in a trade dispute to achieve its objectives. But too this goes to honesty of purpose alone not to the reasonableness of the act, or its expediency. . . .

. . . The withdrawal of PA copy from the provincial newspapers would be a crucial factor in strengthening the bargaining position of the striking journalists, but in view of PA's attitude this could only be achieved by forcing it to close down or at any rate to reduce its services drastically, by withdrawing journalistic labour from it. PA was not an NUJ closed shop and for economic reasons even the NUJ members on its staff were not likely to be enthusiastic at the prospect of being called out on strike. For my part I see no reason for doubting the honesty of the belief held by Mr MacShane and Mr Dennis [another NUJ official], that the response of their members to the strike-call at PA might well be less numerous and less enduring if they knew that fellow members of their union on the national newspapers were continuing to make use of copy produced by those whom they would regard as "blacklegs" at PA.

I would allow this appeal.

LORD WILBERFORCE (dissenting): . . . My Lords, the issue which has to be resolved in the present case arises out of the very great extension of industrial action which has occurred in recent years. When trade disputes were confined to disputes between employees in an undertaking and their employers or between employees in an undertaking, it was not difficult to decide whether industrial action was in contemplation or furtherance of a trade dispute. . . .

. . . industrial action has been greatly widened. It may extend to customers or suppliers of a party to the dispute, on the basis that through them pressure upon the party is intensified. In still other cases, of which *Associated Newspapers Group Ltd v Wade* [1979] IRLR 201 is one and this is another, it may extend to customers or suppliers of such suppliers or customers. Such second stage customers or suppliers may, and probably will, have no dispute with those calling for the industrial action, and no interest in the first stage dispute though some of their workers may have sympathy with it. Moreover they may, as here, have no means of influencing that dispute or of making concessions which might bring that dispute to an end. The question therefore whether action against such innocent and powerless third parties or parties even more remote from the original trade dispute is in "furtherance" of that dispute becomes one that is difficult to answer. The answer must depend upon some test other than the possibility of pressure being exercised upon the original party, because none can be so exercised.

The answer given to this question by the appellants is that it is enough if there is a genuine belief that action against the innocent and powerless third party will further the cause of those taking the action. By to "further" they mean—and this fits the dictionary definition—to help or encourage. So what is asserted is a purely subjective test, such as might be satisfied by [the General Secretary of the NUJ,] Mr Ashton's words—"I believe that this trend (*viz* of PA journalists to join the PA strike) may be damaged or reversed if copy produced by those breaking the strike is handled by our members elsewhere."My Lords, with all deference to those of your Lordships who are of this opinion, I am unable to accept this. I recognise, of course, that the trend of recent legislation has been to widen, and to widen greatly, the extent of immunity from civil action of trade unions and officials and members of trade unions. The policy no doubt is to substitute for judicial control or review over trade disputes and their consequences, other machinery including conciliation procedures. But it would be wrong, in my opinion, to suppose that judicial review has been excluded altogether. . . .

. . . It is clear enough that "in contemplation of" are not words exclusively subjective. It cannot be enough for someone to depose, in general terms, which cannot be probed, that he had a trade dispute in mind. The words, to me, presuppose an actual or emerging trade dispute as well as the mental contemplation of it. Similarly, "in furtherance" may quite well include, as well as an intention to further, an actual furtherance (help or encouragement) or the capability of furtherance. Secondly, so to construe the phrase is not to impose upon it a limitation. There is much in the cases to the effect that "the words must be given some limitation" and to this the appellants object. The words, they say, and I agree, must be given their natural meaning and the courts must not approach them with a disposition to cut them down. But it is always open to the courts—indeed their duty—with open-ended expressions such as those involving cause, or effect, or remoteness, or in the context of this very Act, connection with, (cf *BBC v Hearn* [1977] IRLR 273), to draw a line beyond which the expression ceases to operate. This is simply the common law in action. It does not involve the judges in cutting down what Parliament has given: it does involve them in interpretation in order to ascertain how far Parliament intended to go.

The question of whether industrial action "furthers" a trade dispute is thus a *subjective* one for those taking the action. A policy test of "effectiveness" is not to be applied by the judges. As put by Lord Scarman in *MacShane* [1980] A.C. 672, 694:

> "I confess that I am relieved to find that this is the law. It would be a strange and embarrassing task for a judge to be called upon to review the tactics of a party to a trade dispute and to determine whether in the view of the court the tactic employed was likely to further, or advance, that party's side of the dispute. . . . It would need very clear statutory language to persuade me that Parliament intended to allow the courts to act as some sort of a backseat driver in trade disputes. . . ."

MacShane itself highlights the problems of the so-called "objective" test: by applying the *same* test to the facts of the case, *i.e.* whether the industrial action *was* reasonably capable of achieving its objective, Lord Wilberforce in the House of Lords, and Lawton and Brandon L.JJ. in the Court of Appeal [1979] I.R.L.R. 79 came to *opposite* conclusions. The "objective" test would replace the workers' assessment of effectiveness by that of the judge's. If legality of workers' industrial action were to depend on judicial assessment of its effectiveness, judges would be propelled into the front line of industrial relations. Not surprisingly, judges have differed in their willingness to adopt this politically exposed position. The Employment Act 1980 has placed them in that position by making the legality of secondary action depend, *inter alia*, on whether it is "likely to achieve" a specified purpose (section 17(3)(*b*) and (4)(*d*), see below pp. 561 *et seq.*).

(b) The motives for the industrial action

In some older cases (*e.g. Conway* v. *Wade* [1909] A.C. 506 (H.L.)) the view was expressed that industrial action falls outside the statutory immunity if the motive or purpose of those taking the action is not to further a trade dispute, but is an extraneous motive, *e.g.* of a political or personal nature. Some judges (again particularly in the Court of Appeal *e.g. The "Camilla M," Star Sea Transport Corporation of Monrovia* v. *Slater* [1978] I.R.L.R. 507) asserted that where the predominant purpose in a dispute was political or personal in character (even though there might be other "industrial" purposes), immunity was lost. The contrary view was upheld by the House of Lords in *NWL Ltd.* v. *Woods* [1979] 1 W.L.R. 1294, p. 578 below, on the ground that, although the ultimate objective of the defendant trade union official might well have been to pursue his union's "political" policy of blacking ships, such as the plaintiff's, sailing under flags of convenience, this did not prevent the immediate dispute between the ship-owners and the union being a dispute *connected with* the necessary subject-matter of the statutory definition of a "trade" dispute in TULRA, s.29(1).

Subsequently the requirement that the dispute had to be "connected with" the statutory subject-matter of a trade dispute has been replaced by the stricter requirement that the dispute must "relate wholly or mainly to" one or more of the statutory subjects of a trade dispute (cf. Employment Act 1982, s.18). While this removes immunity from disputes that are predominantly "political" or personal disputes (*cf. Mercury Communications Ltd.* v. *Scott-Garner* [1984] 1 All E.R. 197, p. 589 below), it does not necessarily withhold immunity from disputes where, as will frequently be the case, there is animosity between the chief protagonists but nevertheless the trade unionists are still seeking to further their cause in the dispute.

Norbrook Laboratories Ltd v. King
[1984] I.R.L.R. 200
Northern Ireland Court of Appeal

The defendant, a full-time union official, organised a strike and picketing of the plaintiff's plant. At the trial the plaintiff's counsel claimed that the trade dispute was a pretext and that the defendant was pursuing a personal vendetta against the plaintiff's managing director. At his trial, in addition to liability in nuisance and trespass (for which there is no immunity) the defendant was held liable *obiter* for inducement to breach of contract on the ground that his actions were not immune from liability because they had not been *in furtherance* of the trade dispute. The defendant appealed.

GIBSON L.J.: . . . The state of mind of the defendant is undoubtedly the critical factor in deciding whether the defendant was acting in contemplation or furtherance of a trade dispute. But the existence of hostility [towards the employer] can only be relevant if it is so extreme as to negative any genuine intention to promote or advance the dispute against the person who is the object of the hostility. I would imagine that there must be few trade disputes which reach the state of a strike where there is not some hostility on the part of the strikers or those who organise it. One must I think distinguish between the emotional attitude of the defendant towards the plaintiff and the quality of the mental resolution to take the action objected to. Once the facts pointed on the balance of probabilities towards the conclusion that the defendant did act in contemplation or furtherance of a trade dispute, any personal animus against the employer could only displace that onus if it is shown to be such that the conduct of the defendant was actuated solely by a determination to express that ill will and not to promote a resolution of the dispute. The question to be asked in such a case is, whether the defendant in taking the action he did, honestly and genuinely believed that the workers would gain some advantage in the dispute by virtue of his act. Such a belief can plainly co-exist with a malicious or malevolent disposition towards the employer. Whether the action was within the scope of immunity provided by the Order [the equivalent in Northern Ireland of TULRA, s.13] is to be judged by the intention in acting and not the motive for the act or the effect which it had.

Despite the pitfalls which lie before judges attempting to ascertain the motives of large numbers of workers taking industrial action in complex disputes, the 1980 and 1982 legislation forces them to make findings as to the principal and other motives of those taking or organising industrial action. For example, for there to be immunity, industrial action must "wholly or mainly" relate to the issues specified in TULRA, s.29(1)(*a*)–(*g*) (EA 1982, s.18), and the lawfulness of secondary action depends on the ascertainment of the "purpose or principal purpose" of the action (EA 1980, s.17(3)(*a*) and (4)(*a*), *cf.* Secondary Action, p. 595 below). Disputes with "political" elements involve particular dangers if judges disregard defendants' expressed motives as mere pretexts and decide that genuine motives are extraneous (*cf. Associated Newspapers Group Ltd.* v. *Wade* [1979] I.R.L.R. 201 (C.A.); *PBDS* v. *Filkins* [1979] IRLR 356 (C.A.); *United Biscuits (UK) Ltd.* v. *Fall* [1979] I.R.L.R. 110 (Q.B.D.); see Political Disputes p. 588 below).

(c) Remoteness of the industrial action from the trade dispute: third parties and secondary action

In a number of cases in the late 1970s certain judges asserted that industrial action directly involving third persons not party to the trade dispute was not "in furtherance" of the dispute and lost immunity (*e.g.* Lord Wilberforce, dissenting in *MacShane*, above, p. 556). Thus, most secondary action would become unlawful. The following extract is a classic instance of resistance to judicial temptations in this direction.

Duport Steels Ltd. v. Sirs
[1980] 1 W.L.R. 142; [1980] I.R.L.R. 116
House of Lords

The Iron and Steel Trades Confederation (ISTC) called out on strike their members employed by the British Steel Corporation over a pay dispute. The Union believed that BSC, a public corporation, was not offering more money because of intervention by the Government. To put pressure upon the Government, the Union decided to extend the dispute into the private steel sector and called out all their members employed by private sector steel companies. Sixteen private sector employers applied for an injunction against Bill Sirs, General Secretary of the ISTC. At first instance, the judge rejected the application. The Court of Appeal allowed an appeal and issued the injunction (Lord Denning M.R., Lawton and Ackner L.JJ.).

LORD DIPLOCK: My Lords, as recently as December 13, 1979 this House decided in *Express Newspapers Ltd v MacShane* [1980] A.C. 672 (above p. 556), that upon the true interpretation of s.13(1) of the Trade Union and Labour Relations Acts 1974 and 1976, the test whether an act was "done by a person in contemplation or furtherance of a trade dispute" and so entitled him to immunity from a part of the common law of tort, is purely subjective: *ie*, provided that the doer of the act honestly thinks at the time he does it that it may help one of the parties to a trade dispute to achieve their objectives and does it for that reason, he is protected by the section.

That conclusion as to the meaning of words that have been used by successive Parliaments since the Trade Disputes Act 1906, to describe acts for which the doer is entitled to immunity from the law of tort over an area that has been much extended by the Acts of 1974 and 1976, is (as I pointed out in the *MacShane* case) one which is intrinsically repugnant to anyone who has spent his life in the practice of the law or the administration of justice. Sharing those instincts it was a conclusion that I myself reached with considerable reluctance, for given the existence of a trade dispute it involves granting to trade unions a power, which has no other limits than their own self-restraint, to inflict by means which are contrary to the general law, untold harm to industrial enterprises unconcerned with the particular dispute, to the employees of such enterprises, to members of the public and to the nation itself, so long as those in whom the control of the trade union is vested honestly believe that to do so may assist it albeit in a minor way, in achieving its objectives in the dispute.

My Lords, at a time when more and more cases involve the application of legislation which gives effect to policies that are the subject of bitter public and Parliamentary controversy, it cannot be too strongly emphasised that the British constitution, though largely unwritten, is firmly based upon the separation of powers, Parliament makes the laws, the judiciary interpret them. When Parliament legislates to remedy what the majority of its members at the time perceive to be a defect or a lacuna in the existing law (whether it be the written law enacted by existing statutes or the unwritten common law as it has been expounded by the judges in decided cases), the role of the judiciary is confined to ascertaining from the words that Parliament has approved as expressing its intention, what that intention was, and to giving effect to it. Where the meaning of the statutory words is plain and unambiguous it is not for the judges to invent fancied ambiguities as an excuse for failing to give effect to its plain meaning because they themselves consider that the consequences of doing so would be inexpedient, or even unjust or immoral. In controversial matters such as are involved in industrial relations there is room for differences of opinion as to what is expedient, what is just and what is morally justifiable. Under our constitution it is Parliament's opinion on these matters that is paramount.

A statute passed to remedy what is perceived by Parliament to be a defect in the existing law may in actual operation turn out to have injurious consequences that Parliament did not anticipate at the time the statute was passed; if it had, it would have made some provision in the Act in order to prevent them. It is at least possible that Parliament when the Acts of 1974 and 1976 were passed did not anticipate that so widespread and crippling use as has in fact occurred would be made of sympathetic withdrawals of labour and of secondary blacking and picketing in support of sectional interests able to exercise "industrial muscle." But if this be the case it is for Parliament not for the judiciary to decide whether any changes should be made to the law as stated in the Acts, and, if so, what are the precise limits that ought to be imposed upon the immunity from liability for torts committed in the course of taking industrial action. These are matters on which there is a wide legislative choice, the exercise of which is likely to be influenced by the political complexion of the Government and the state of public opinion at the time amending legislation is under consideration.

It endangers continued public confidence in the political impartiality of the judiciary, which is essential to the continuance of the rule of law, if judges, under the guise of interpretation, provide their own preferred amendments to statutes which experience of their operation has shown to have had consequences that members of the court before whom the matter comes consider to be injurious to the public interest. The frequency with which controversial legislation is amended by Parliament itself (as witness the Act of 1974 which was amended in 1975 as well as in 1976) indicates that legislation, after it has come into operation, may fail to have the beneficial effects which Parliament expected or may produce injurious results that Parliament did not anticipate. But, except by private or hybrid Bills, Parliament does not legislate by individual cases. Public Acts of Parliament are general in their application; they govern all cases falling within categories of which the definitions are to be found in the wording of the statute. So in relation to s.13(1) of the Acts of 1974 and 1976, for a judge (who is always dealing with an individual case) to pose himself the question: "Can Parliament really have intended that the acts that were done in this particular case should have the benefit of the immunity?" is to risk straying beyond his constitutional role as interpreter of the enacted law and assuming a power to decide at his own discretion whether or not to apply the general law to a particular case. The legitimate questions for a judge in his role as interpreter of the enacted law are: "How has Parliament, by the words that it has used in the statute to express its intentions, defined the category of acts that are entitled to the immunity? Do the acts done in this particular case fall within that description?"

The first of these questions was answered by this House in the *MacShane* case in the way I have already mentioned. The principal question in this appeal is whether the Court of Appeal were right in overruling the High Court judge's finding that it was highly probable that the acts complained of in the instant case did fall within the category of acts entitled to the immunity. . . .

Lord Denning M.R. advanced an alternative reason for allowing the appeal which is not echoed in either of the other judgments. He was unwilling to accept that the majority speeches in this House in the *MacShane* case had expressed a clear opinion that the test of whether an act was done in furtherance of a trade dispute was purely subjective. This led him to conclude that this House had not rejected a test based on remoteness that he himself had adumbrated and adopted in three earlier cases. These cases, he said, had not been specifically singled out by name in the *MacShane* case as being overruled. He inferred from this that it was arguable that they still remained good authority. In the *MacShane* case this House was not concerned to decide whether the actual decisions in any of a series of previous cases in the Court of Appeal were wrong. What was considered was whether any of three different tests which had been adumbrated in those cases as applicable to determine whether an act was done by a person in contemplation or furtherance of a trade dispute, was right in law or not. Among the three tests rejected as wrong in law was the test of remoteness the authorship of which was specifically ascribed in my own speech to Lord Denning. Recognising this, counsel for the respondents has not felt able to support the judgment of the Court of Appeal on this ground either.

The House of Lords thus adopted a policy of restraint, refusing to interpret the long-standing golden formula as prohibiting the equally long-standing practice of secondary industrial action. The policies which Lord Denning and other judges attempted to implement through the common law were subsequently adopted by the Conservative Government's Employment Act 1980, which banned much secondary action (*cf.* p. 595 below). Conservative Government spokesmen openly acknowledged the debt owed by the legislation to Lord Denning's initiatives.

(d) Is there a "trade dispute?"

To know whether industrial action is "in contemplation or furtherance of a trade dispute," a definition of "trade dispute" is required. This is found in TULRA, s.29, as amended by the Employment Act 1982, s.18. The definition of "trade dispute" limits the extent to which workers can use their industrial strength lawfully, and thereby determines the boundaries of the right to strike. This can be demonstrated by looking at how the amendments to the definition by the Employment Act 1982, s.18 deprived many disputes of their previous immunity. Thus *before* the 1982 Act:

(1) trade disputes included those to which a trade union or employers' association were parties; (this is no longer the case due to the repeal of TULRA, s.29(4));
(2) a trade dispute could exist between workers and an employer *other* than their own; (this is no longer the case under the now amended TULRA, s.29(6));
(3) trade dispute included disputes between workers and workers; (they are no longer included under the amended TULRA, s.29(1));
(4) trade disputes included those relating to matters outside Great Britain, regardless of their effect in the United Kingdom; (such effect is now required by the amendment to TULRA, s.29(3));
(5) trade disputes needed only to be "connected with" the matters specified in TULRA, s. 29(1)(*a*)–(*g*); (henceforth, they need to be "wholly or mainly" related to those matters), *cf.* p. 560 above.

Since the vast majority of strikes are by workers against their employer over pay and job security, most industrial action will continue to benefit from the immunities available to "trade disputes." Further, insofar as trade disputes involve terms and conditions of employment, any demand by workers seems capable of being transformed into a trade dispute over terms of employment, as the following case indicated.

British Broadcasting Corporation v. Hearn
[1977] I.C.R. 685; [1977] I.R.L.R. 273
Court of Appeal

Mr Hearn, General Secretary of the Association of Broadcasting Staff was asked by the Action Committee Against Racialism to prevent the BBC televising the FA Cup Final to South Africa. Following this request, and in light of the ABS's anti-racialist policy, when the BBC refused to take steps to ensure that the broadcast was not transmitted, the General Secretary issued a notice to branches that the union would have to ask its members concerned in covering the Cup Final not to work on the programme. The BBC applied for an injunction. The defendant invoked the golden formula.

Lord Denning M.R.: . . . To become a trade dispute, there would have to be something of the kind which was discussed in the course of argument before us: "We would like you to consider putting a clause in the contract by which our members are not bound to take part in any broadcast which may be viewed in South Africa because we feel that is obnoxious to their views and to the views of a great multitude of people. We would like that clause to be put in, or a condition of that kind to be understood." If the BBC refused to put in such a condition, or refused to negotiate about it, that might be a trade dispute. That, I think, is rather the way in which the judge approached this case. Towards the end of his judgment he said, putting it into the mouths of members through their union: "We wish it established as a condition of employment that we shall not be required to take part in broadcasts to South Africa so long as the South African Government pursues its policy of Apartheid." If that request had been made, and not acceded to, there might be a trade dispute as to whether that should be a condition of the employment. But the matter never reached that stage at all. It never reached the stage of there being a trade dispute. There was not a trade dispute "in contemplation." It was coercive interference and nothing more. If that is the right view, it means that the trade union and its officers are not exempt from the ordinary rule of law—that men must honour their contracts, and must not unlawfully interfere with the performance of them.

In *NWL Ltd* v. *Nelson* [1979] 1 W.L.R. 1294 (H.L.) Lord Diplock seemed to accept that a trade dispute could arise in the way described by Lord Denning. But as the following case shows, it is rare for trade unionists to phrase their demands in the necessary legalistic terms. Accordingly, on these and other grounds, emanating from the amended definition of "trade dispute" in the 1982 Act, the defendant union was held not to enjoy immunity in tort.

Dimbleby and Sons Ltd. v. The National Union of Journalists
[1984] I.R.L.R. 67; affirmed [1984] I.R.L.R. 161 (H.L.)
Court of Appeal

Dimbleby and Sons Ltd. arranged to have their newspapers printed by TBF Printers Ltd., part of the TBF Ltd. group. When journalists employed by Dimbleby and Sons Ltd. learned of this, they contacted their union, the NUJ, which was in dispute with TBF Ltd.. On union advice, they refused to submit any copy to be printed by TBF Printers Ltd., and were suspended in consequence. The plaintiffs sought an injunction restraining the NUJ from inducing breaches of their employees' contracts of employment and interfering with the TBF Printers Ltd. contract. The union argued, *inter alia*, that they were immune as there was a trade dispute.

Sir John Donaldson M.R.: The defendants submit that their action in instructing the Dimbleby journalists to refuse to supply copy and other material which would be printed by TBF Printers Ltd was taken in furtherance of two different trade disputes. The first was a dispute between the plaintiffs and their journalists (a) concerning their terms and conditions of employment (s.29(1)(a) of [TULRA] as amended by s.18 of the Employment Act 1982); (b) concerning the allocation of work as between workers or groups of workers (s.29(1)(c)); and (c) concerning their suspension or dismissal (s.29(1)(b)). The second dispute was a dispute between TBF Ltd and those of the journalists whom they dismissed in 1978 and who still wish to be reinstated.

Disputes between the plaintiffs and their journalists

The learned judge held that there was no dispute between the plaintiffs and their journalists concerning their terms and conditions of service and, on the evidence at present available, this is clearly right. The journalists never suggested that they were entitled to refuse to supply the copy and other material merely because it would be printed by TBF Printers Ltd. Nor was there any suggestion that their terms and conditions of employment should be altered to make this permissible. Had there been any such suggestion, we would have had to bear in mind the dictum of Lord Cross of Chelsea in *Universe Tankships v ITF* [1982] IRLR 200, that "A trade union cannot turn a dispute which in reality has no connection with terms and conditions of employment into a dispute connected with terms and conditions of employment by insisting that the employer inserts appropriate terms into the contracts of employment into which he enters."

The learned judge also, and again rightly, held that there was no "trade dispute" between the plaintiffs and their journalists concerning the allocation of work between workers or groups of workers, because, in the light of the amended definition of "trade dispute," this can only occur when all the workers concerned are employed by the employer who is party to the dispute (in this case the plaintiffs). What was objected to was the allocation of printing work to the employees of TBF Printers Ltd.

Finally the learned judge held that there *was* a trade dispute between the plaintiffs and their journalists concerning the threat to suspend them or terminate their employment. In this I consider that the learned judge erred. Under the amended definition of "trade dispute," the dispute in order to qualify as such must "relate wholly or mainly to" one of the specified subject matters. This dispute did not relate wholly or mainly to the suspension or dismissal of the plaintiffs' journalists. It related to the decision by the plaintiffs to have the copy printed by TBF Printers Ltd.

Dispute between TBF Ltd and its dismissed journalists

This, as the learned judge held, was a trade dispute within s.29(1) since it was between an employer (TBF Ltd) and its ex-workers and it concerned the refusal of TBF Ltd to re-engage them. Although it was argued that this dispute had died of old age—it began in 1978—the evidence suggests that some of the journalists are still in receipt of dispute pay from the union and I agree with the learned judge in thinking that the dispute is still alive.

I have no doubt that the action taken by the defendants was taken in furtherance of the trade dispute between TBF Ltd and its dismissed journalists. . . .

3. WEAPONS USED BY EMPLOYERS

(A) Management Prerogatives

In the course of a collective dispute, employers may use various weapons before workers have taken industrial action, during the industrial action, or in its aftermath. Ownership of the means of production enables the employer to exert pressures of various kinds. In previous chapters we reviewed some of the weapons available to an employer in dispute with an individual worker: action short of dismissal and dismissal (see Chapters 7 and 10 on *Discipline* and *Termination*). The following cases illustrate the power of the employer to impose sanctions in the context of collective industrial conflict.

McQuade v. Scotbeef Ltd.
[1975] I.R.L.R. 332
Industrial Tribunal

Mr McQuade was the convenor of shop stewards at the employer's meat processing factory. He was one of 39 employees dismissed following frequent stoppages and disruptive action in breach of procedure agreements.

Scottish Industrial Tribunal (chairman: I. MacDonald): The Tribunal came to the conclusion that, on the overwhelming evidence, a state of indiscipline caused by lack of co-operation by a group in mainly the slaughterhouse and butchery departments, frequent disruptive industrial action and frequent breaches of procedural agreements, had persisted for a considerable period in the factory. The Tribunal considered that the applicant had been dismissed for a valid reason . . . namely his misconduct. They considered further that the respondents had acted reasonably in dismissing the applicant. The main source of trouble in the factory emanated from the slaughterhouse department and the butchery department. There were many stoppages which took place and where no notice of any stoppage was given. While the management did not claim to dismiss him because he was a convener of shop stewards, the Tribunal came to the conclusion that the applicant, in fact, made no effort to try and persuade the men to give notice of the stoppages before bringing the production line to a halt on so many occasions. The Tribunal considered that he acquiesced in these frequent stoppages. He made no attempt to stress to the men that 24 hours' notice of a stoppage was required.

Cruikshank v. Hobbs
[1977] I.C.R. 725
Employment Appeal Tribunal

Six stable lads participated in an official strike in May 1975. During the strike the number of horses at the employer's stables dropped and therefore the amount of stable work diminished. When the strike ended in July the employer, a racehorse trainer, decided to make five lads redundant, and selected five of the six lads who had been on strike. An Industrial Tribunal dismissed their application for unfair redundancy dismissal on the ground that the trainer's fear that he might have jeopardised the loyalty of the non-striking lads if he had selected any of them for redundancy was a fair basis for selection.

CUMMING-BRUCE J.: In our view a strike may be relevant to selection for redundancy in a number of ways, though its weight as a factor may be negligible. If a strike has caused or aggravated the redundancy, it may be reasonable to take account of the conduct of the strikers as causing the redundancy so that it is a factor that points to their selection rather than any of those who did not by their conduct reduce the number of jobs available. But that is not this case. Secondly, if the withdrawal of labour lasts long enough, the reintroduction into the reduced force of men who have been long absent may give rise to practical difficulties arising from technical or administrative changes which have occurred during their long absence. Thirdly, passions may be aroused during the strike, or incidents of abuse or violence between strikers and those remaining at work may have the effect that to sack men who stayed on and replace them with strikers may be expected to cause such friction between opposing groups on the shop floor that the morale and efficiency of the undertaking will be significantly impaired. In this situation it is not the strike itself, but the consequences of and incidents during the strike, which may be relevant to selection for redundancy. It is this third situation which the Tribunal appear to describe . . . and, if the evidence supports such a finding, a decision that the trainer was reasonable in giving great or paramount weight to this factor, the decision cannot be revesed on the ground that it disclosed an error of law even though we disagreed with that view.

For another example where loyalty during a strike was considered, see *Laffin and Callaghan* v. *Fashion Industries (Hartlepool) Ltd.* [1978] I.R.L.R. 448 (E.A.T.).

There is little in common law or statute to curb the use of employers' weapons in industrial conflict. Restrictions on the employer's use of his power are primarily the product of countervailing collective power by workers and their organisations, for example, the *status quo* arrangements operating in joint industrial disputes procedures.

S. D. Anderman, *"The 'status quo' issue and industrial disputes procedures: some implications for labour law"* (1974) 3 I.L.J. 131, 131–33

A status quo arrangement in a dispute procedure comes into operation when there is a dispute over a change or proposed change in existing terms and conditions of work; the arrangement deals with the status of the change or proposed change pending the resolution of the dispute or the exhaustion of procedure. The basic possibilities are fourfold:

(1) The procedure may provide that the position prior to the change is to be preserved until procedure is exhausted. This is a pure status quo clause.
(2) The procedure may stipulate that the change that has been introduced may remain in force pending the exhaustion of procedure in which case it is understood that a retrospective adjustment will be made consistent with the negotiated result. This in effect is the opposite of a status quo clause and is sometimes termed a "managerial functions" clause.
(3) The procedure may provide that the parties can agree to a temporary, *ad hoc* arrangement pending the results of negotiation; or
(4) The procedure may provide that more than one of these methods may apply depending upon the category of dispute.

Status quo arrangements have two main functions. They draw the line between action which may be taken unilaterally by either side and that which must be deferred until either jointly agreed or until procedure has been exhausted. Hugh Scanlon succinctly described this function of status quo arrangements when in 1971 he gave the following explanation for the Confederation of Shipbuilding and Engineering Union proposals for a wide status quo clause in a reformed Engineering Procedure Agreement:

> " . . . we have to get away from the conception that management make decisions and we carry them out and use a procedure to try and alter them. We want the idea to pervade throughout the industry that we discuss the problem on both sides before we make that decision, and . . . if that applies to [management] in regard to dismissal and redundancy and such like, it equally applies to [trade unions] when [they] are seeking improvement."

In that respect, status quo provisions create a line between managerial prerogatives and collective bargaining and may be viewed as an important procedural element of industrial democracy.

The relative absence of legal regulation of employers' weapons contrasts sharply with the extensive common law and statutory controls over weapons used by workers and their organisations. Here we examine the principal weapons used by employers: lockout/lay-off, dismissal/discipline, the labour injunction and, in particular, dismissal of strikers and labour injunctions against strike organisers.

The lockout/lay-off is not a frequently used weapon in the United Kingdom. Nonetheless, the contrast between the law relating to employer lockouts and that relating to workers' strikes is startling. The multitude of common law liabilities consequential on a collective withdrawal of labour are not balanced by a stringent regime applicable to employers' collective dismissals. The law not only regards the lockout as an employer's prerogative, but also intervenes to protect the employer against certain possible consequences. For example, statutory provisions prevent employees dismissed both in a lockout and a strike from complaining of unfair dismissal (EPCA, s.62; *Fisher* v. *York Trailer Co. Ltd.* [1979] I.C.R. 834 (E.A.T.)). Statutory provisions also prevent even innocent workers laid off as a consequence of a lockout, strike or other industrial action from claiming statutory guarantee payments (EPCA, s.13(3)). The law has even been interpreted as disqualifying such laid-off workers from unemployment benefit in certain circumstances (*Presho* v. *DHSS* [1984] I.R.L.R. 74 (H.L.)). Collective agreements, however, often allow for guarantee payments to workers laid off as a result of certain types of disputes, and may deny the employer the right to lay-off non-striking workers where he has work for them (see the National Engineering Agreement applied in *(1) Bond* v. *CAV Ltd.; (2) Neads* v. *CAV Ltd.* [1983] I.R.L.R. 360 (Q.B.D.)) *cf.* p. 108 above.

(B) Dismissal and Discipline

The use by the employer of weapons of dismissal and discipline against individual workers in the course of collective industrial conflict raises a number of policy issues.

(i) Individual sanctions and collective action

Is the imposition of sanctions against an individual striker an acceptable response to collective industrial action? The essence of a strike is its collective nature. If the industrial action is organised and instigated by the collectivity, a trade union, perhaps even with the opposition of some individual members, ought not the consequences of that action in the form of employer sanctions be aimed at the collectivity and not at the individual? It may be precisely the difficulties in proceeding with sanctions against the union which have led to so much emphasis on individual sanctions. These difficulties were not only practical, but in the United Kingdom also legal. Until the Employment Act 1982 unions were effectively immune from the legal consequences of strikes under TULRA, s.14. Insofar as such "collective" sanctions have become increasingly possible with the repeal of TULRA, s.14, there might be considered some balance in terms of a lessening of individual sanctions. If workers' organisations are involved in industrial action, then the consequences should perhaps fall upon the organisations, not on the workers.

To some extent, this concept of a collective approach to sanctions against strikers is recognised in EPCA, s.62. Provided the individual striker can show some discrimination between himself and other strikers with regard to dismissal or re-engagement, he can complain to an Industrial Tribunal of unfair dismissal. The principle of no discrimination or "no victimisation" encapsulated the view that industrial action is a collective and not an individual responsibility.

The principle of no discrimination has been curtailed by both statute and common law. The Employment Act 1982 amendments (section 9) decisively broke with the policy of no victimisation. Discrimination became possible in three cases:

(1) where the re-engagement takes place more than three months after the complainant's date of dismissal. So a patient employer can discriminate;
(2) where employees have been re-engaged (or are not "taking part in the action") *at the time of the complainant's date of dismissal*: and hence are not "relevant employees" within this

section (see the definition in EPCA, s.62(4)(*b*)(ii)). So by deferring dismissal of some strikers, the employer can re-engage others dismissed without fear of having the fairness of his actions judged;

(3) where the employer discriminates between establishments, by sacking strikers in one but not another. The dismissed workers cannot invoke comparison with those retained: they are no longer since 1982 "relevant" employees as defined in section 62(4)(*b*).

One major hazard facing employers tempted by option (2) may be in determining the "complainant's date of dismissal" before which other strikers may be re-engaged. If a group of workers strikes, the date of dismissal is a function of doctrines of repudiation, acceptance or waiver and affirmation (express or implied). The employer will have to show that the complainants were dismissed only after the employer had dismissed *and* re-engaged other strikers; or that those others were *never* dismissed, and the complainant only later (after the others had returned) was dismissed. In *Hindle Gears Ltd.* v. *McGinty* [1984] I.R.L.R. 477 (E.A.T.), Waite J. said (para. 2):

> " . . . the process of dismissal of a striking workforce (is) something like a game of hazard in which winner takes all, in which defeat or victory turns upon the fall of a single card, and in which the stakes increase dramatically according to the numbers involved. It is a game requiring intense concentration, each side closely watching the other. It is also, one suspects, a game in which no one does half so well as the lawyers who have become indispensable as its croupiers."

The interpretation of section 62 by the judges does not appear to support unequivocally the principle of "no victimisation." Despite lip service to this objective, the judges' interpretations display insensitivity to the realities of industrial conflict, where an employer's ability to treat strikers differently is a critical weapon. The following case illustrates this tactic which, however, failed. The E.A.T. nonetheless interpreted the three-month limitation period on claims as excluding claims based on selective re-engagement within the three months.

Highlands Fabricators Ltd. v. McLaughlin

[1984] I.R.L.R. 482
Employment Appeal Tribunal

When the entire workforce of 2,000 went on strike, the employers sent notices dismissing them all. Subsequently, letters were sent to 1,600 employees, but not the complainant, offering re-engagement. There was only a limited response to this offer. After further negotiations, the employers offered re-engagement to the remaining 400, including the complainant. Having found other employment, he rejected the offer, but claimed unfair dismissal.

LORD MCDONALD . . . The object of these provisions has been said to be to prevent victimisation by an employer of persons who took part in a strike (*Frank Jones (Tipton) Ltd v Stock* [1978] IRLR 87). It has been held that the time at which discrimination of this nature must be shown to exist is the date of the hearing before the Industrial Tribunal (*McCormick v Horsepower Ltd* [1981] IRLR 217).

S.62(2)(b) of [EPCA] has been amended by s.9(2) of the 1982 [Employment] Act and now reads as follows:

> "An Industrial Tribunal shall not determine whether the dismissal was fair or unfair unless it is shown 'that any such employee has, before the expiry of the period of three months beginning with that employee's date of dismissal, been offered re-engagement, and that the complainant has not been offered re-engagement'."

The majority of the Tribunal in the present case have held that because on 21.8.83 the appellants offered re-engagement to 1600 of their work force but not to the respondent that was an end of the matter and jurisdiction was immediately conferred upon the Tribunal by virtue of s.62(2)(b) of the 1978 Act. They were not influenced by the fact that on 16.9.83, within the three month period, re-engagement was offered to the entire striking work force, including the respondent. Neither were they influenced by the fact that, at the date of the Tribunal hearing, the respondent had been offered re-engagement.

The chairman of the Tribunal dissented. He held that all striking employees, including the respondent, had been offered re-engagement within the appropriate period, that neither of the exceptions in s.62(2) of the 1978 Act applied, and that in consequence the Tribunal did not have jurisdiction to entertain the application.

We are unanimously of the view that the dissenting chairman reached the correct conclusion. We consider that the majority placed too narrow a construction upon the wording of s.62(2). If their interpretation is correct it could lead to precisely the chaotic situations envisaged by their Lordships in the Court of Appeal in *McCormick v Horsepower Ltd.* For a variety of reasons offers of re-engagement may be made to striking employees in differing numbers and at different times. It would wreck all chance of negotiation in what is frequently a delicate and tense industrial situation if a limited offer of re-engagement were to confer immediately on employees to whom the offer was not directed a vested right to complain of unfair dismissal. Certainly if at the date of the Tribunal hearing such an employee can show that the terms of s.62(2)(a) or (b) have been complied with, the Tribunal will have jurisdiction to entertain the application. We regard the three month period introduced by the 1982 Act as something of a cooling off period, designed to achieve the very objective which was reached in the present case, *viz* settlement of a strike on terms acceptable to management and work force alike, on sensible and honourable terms. To interpret s.62(2)(b) in the manner in which the majority of the Tribunal have done would make it impossible to attain this objective and we do not consider it was the intention of Parliament that it should be construed in this way.

In another illustration, the courts were called upon to decide whether an employer who offered different terms of re-engagement to different strikers satisfied section 62(4)(*c*) so as to prevent a striker offered inferior terms claiming that the Industrial Tribunal had jurisdiction to hear his complaint of unfair dismissal. A policy of allowing inferior terms would enable the employer to single out individual strikers for less favourable terms of re-engagement and thus undermine the collective nature of the industrial action.

Williams v. National Theatre Board Ltd.
[1982] I.R.L.R. 377
Court of Appeal

LORD DENNING M.R.: In March 1979 many men at the National Theatre went on strike. This so disrupted the plays that the management dismissed all of the men who took part in the strike. As all were dismissed, none of them could claim for unfair dismissal. The management then made an offer to re-engage all those men in their own jobs, but they added a special term to the offer. It was to the effect that if they offended again they might be dismissed again. The men objected to the special term. They refused the offer of re-engagement. They remained out of work and claimed for unfair dismissal. The Industrial Tribunal turned down their claim on the ground that, under [EPCA, s.62], they had no jurisdiction to hear it. The Employment Appeal Tribunal affirmed that decision. The men appeal to this court. Now for the details. . . .

There was one woman [Miss Ellis], however, who was treated differently. She was a secretary. She sympathised with the strikers. On one day, 19 March 1979, she did not go to work, but joined the pickets and made tea for them. On the next day she stayed at home because she did not want to cross the picket line. She later changed her tactics and returned to work, but, unbeknown to the management, she helped the strikers by reporting to them from inside. The management had to dismiss her, and did dismiss her on 6 June 1979, together with all the others, else all would have a claim for unfair dismissal, see *Stock v Frank Jones (Tipton) Ltd* [1977] I.R.L.R. 278. But, believing that she had honestly returned to work, they offered her re-engagement on different terms from the others. In a letter of 23 April 1979 they said:

> "You will be re-engaged without effect on your continuity of employment and on the same terms and conditions of employment as you were under at the time of your dismissal."

She accepted the offer . . . The crucial question in this case is whether . . . 30 men were offered "re-engagement" in the job which they held before the date of dismissal.

The offer was contained in the letter of 23 April 1979 which said to each of them that:

> "You will be treated as being on second warning as described in clause 10(2) of the agreement [setting out the National Theatre's disciplinary procedure] in regard to your general conduct."

It seems to me that, by using the colloquial word "job," [in the definition of re-engagement in EPCA, s.62(4)(c)] Parliament intended it to be used with the sort of meaning which ordinary people attribute to it when they speak of a man's "job." The statutory definition is an attempt to put the colloquial meaning into Parliamentary language. If a man is offered re-engagement in the same "job" as before—that is in the same "capacity" as before—the offer is valid even though there may be some difference in the terms and conditions attached to it. He should accept it, even though there may be some strings attached to it—so long as these are reasonable in all the circumstances of the case. But not if they are unreasonable. If he were offered re-engagement on half-days only, it would not be the same "job" as before. If he were offered half-pay instead of full pay, it would not be the same "job" as before. Such offers of re-employment would be inconsistent with it being the same "job" as before. But there are some terms and conditions which may be quite consistent with it being the same "job" as before. This very case is a good illustration. It seems to me that these men were offered re-engagement in the same "capacity" as before. It was quite reasonable for the management to treat them as on second warning. It must be remembered that they had been guilty of most serious misconduct. They had been guilty of repudiatory breach of their contracts. They had inflicted heavy losses on the National Theatre. They could not fairly claim to be re-engaged on precisely the same terms as the large number of loyal employees who had stayed at work throughout the strike. It was only fair all round that these 30 men should be told: "Yes, we are ready to re-engage you in the same job in the same capacity as before, but, mark you, you must not do anything of this kind again. Otherwise you will be liable to be suspended, and may be dismissed." That condition does not, to my mind, derogate from the fact that they were offered re-engagement in the same job as before.

So also there may be some re-arrangement of hours or duties which would not derogate from the fact that they were offered re-engagement in the same job as before. It is for the Industrial Tribunal to decide whether or not the offer was re-engagement in the same "capacity" or not.

As for Miss Ellis, the men cannot complain of her re-engagement. It was for the management to decide the terms on which they would offer her re-engagement. They were not bound to treat the men the same as her or to treat her the same as them.

I find myself in agreement with the Industrial Tribunal and the Employment Appeal Tribunal. I would dismiss the appeal.

The Court of Appeal's interpretation opens the door for employers to do precisely the mischief the section was intended to prevent: to discriminate among strikers. The employer may offer less favourable terms of re-engagement to some strikers and thus deter them from returning to work. According to Lord Denning, much will depend on whether the employer steps outside the boundaries of "reasonable" terms of re-engagement. It is unsatisfactory for judges to adjudicate, in the delicate aftermath of a strike, on whether the employer was "reasonable" in his offers of re-engagement, particularly if, as did Lord Denning, they invoke the employee's breach of contract in striking as a relevant factor, without regard to the merits of the strike or the employer's conduct and responsibilities.

Once the Tribunal has jurisdiction (the striker having shown some discrimination between himself and others), the employer has to satisfy the tribunal as to the reason, and may be challenged as having acted unreasonably. The treatment of the victimised striker has to be justified, *cf.* EPCA, s.57(3). But there is little in the case law which elucidates the issues of "fair" treatment of strikers. In *Cruikshank* v. *Hobbs* little sympathy was shown for the strikers by the Industrial Tribunal, though there seemed to be some from the E.A.T. (above p. 568). A more balanced view was expressed by Phillips J. in *Laffin and Callaghan* v. *Fashion Industries (Hartlepool) Ltd.* [1978] I.R.L.R. 448

(E.A.T.), a case involving redundancies in the aftermath of a strike (para. 18):

> "A valid matter to be considered is the loyalty of those who served during the strike, but . . . by the same token to give *carte blanche* to the loyalty of those who did work is likely to cause indignation among those who out of a corresponding loyalty to their fellow workmen did not stay loyal to the management."

In theory, at least, arguments in defence of strike activity can be accomodated within the law of unfair dismissal (once the Tribunal has jurisdiction). In cases of discipline, however, the courts fall back on the traditional common law of contract (*Theedom* v. *BRB* [1976] I.R.L.R. 137 (I.T.)).

(ii) Dismissal as a sanction against strikers

In industrial practice, strike action is perceived as a temporary phenomenon. Nobody believes that workers who go on strike really want to terminate their contracts. Nor is termination the result anticipated by management. The employer normally expects the workforce to return at the end of the industrial action.

In the preceding extracts, we saw how despite this reality, under E.P.C.A., s.62 dismissal of strikers is accepted, subject to a principle of non-discrimination and sometimes even then. However, one alternative to termination adopted by many countries is suspension of the contract of employment (see Kahn-Freund, above p. 524). Naturally, the performance of the contractual obligations is altered during the strike, but the employment relationship is not broken and after the industrial action is over it resumes its normal course. The possibility of adopting a theory of suspension was canvassed in *Simmons* v. *Hoover Ltd.* (above p. 522). But that case simply confirmed the traditional common law view that strikes are breaches of contract entitling the employer to terminate the strikers' employment.

Management responses to strikes are much more flexible than common law doctrine. The following is an extract from a circular issued by the Department of Health and Social Security in late 1979 giving guidance to employers in the National Health Service on the forms of management response to different types of industrial action.

DHSS Circular, *"Forms of management response to industrial action,"* 216 INDUSTRIAL RELATIONS REVIEW AND REPORT (January 1980)

1. This Annex spells out the various forms of management response to certain forms of industrial action. This Annex, has been prepared in the light of legal opinion available to the Government, but does not purport to be a full statement of the law. Authorities should look at the terms of individual contracts before deciding what action to take and should if necessary seek specific legal advice. This should be done quickly, lest by delay or inaction [Health] Authorities are seen as acquiescing in a breach of contract by their staff. The advice given in paragraphs 2–7 is based on the premise that the conduct of the employee to whom the advice applies amounts to a substan-

tial breach of his contractual obligations, such as would have justified his dismissal at common law.

2. **Complete withdrawal of labour**
Those on strike should not be paid for the appropriate period of time and there should be no subsequent payment for the period of the strike.

3. **Lightning strikes**
Pay should be stopped for the period of the lightning strike. Where constant short-duration stoppages are so disruptive as to affect the whole work pattern, management should consider taking the action described in paragraph 6(ii) below.

4. **Bonus schemes**
There are no specific rules in NHS productivity schemes referring to industrial action. Nevertheless the codes explicitly relate the payment of bonus to performance. Where performance is affected by industrial action, local management should assess the reduction in bonus that is appropriate under the terms of the scheme and give staff notice that, failing resumption of normal working, bonus will be adjusted from the next pay period. There will usually be provision for similar action in respect of bonus schemes for ambulancemen which form part of their transferred terms and conditions of service devised by former local authorities. It will, however, be necessary to examine the details of such schemes. The "lead-in" pay agreement for ancillary staff (applicable equally to lead-in for works maintenance staff) provided for the payment to cease "in the event of staff co-operation being withdrawn or undertakings broken." This should present grounds for withdrawal of "lead-in" payments in the event of industrial action. Conditions attaching to "lead-in" payments for ambulancemen are not laid down and these should be treated on the same basis as pay.

5. **Overtime, shift allowances, units of medical time and other allowances**
In the event of an overtime ban, overtime payment should not, of course, be made. In the case of guaranteed or regular overtime, shift allowances, units of medical time and other allowances, where employees do not carry out the duties to which the allowances relate, pay should be stopped for the appropriate period and no subsequent payment made. In general, it is only in cases where the contract of employment *requires* overtime or shift working that refusal to work overtime or shifts is a breach of contract, but this point can be resolved only by examination of the contracts concerned.

6. **Restricted performance of duties**
Where staff report for duty normally but refuse to carry out their normal duties by means of working to rule, "blacking" certain areas of work, by selecting those duties they will carry out, or by deliberately restricting production, they are usually in breach of contract. An employee is not entitled to his remuneration for any pay period unless he can prove substantial performance of his contractual obligations during that pay period. Appropriate forms of management response where there has been a breach of contract will depend on local circumstances but will usually consist of one of the following courses of action:–

i. if less than the full range of duties is acceptable to management in the sense that it is willing to accept specific but limited services the staff concerned should at the outset of the action be given notice (say 24 or 48 hours in advance of the sanctions being applied) that while they refuse to undertake normal working they are in breach of contract and are not entitled to full contractual pay. Terms which would then be offered might be one of the following. Terms (a) would be for staff to be offered such proportion of normal payments as the Authority considers reasonable for the proportion of normal duties performed. Management should be careful to ensure that there has been a clear and valid direction to the employee to perform his full duties and that any payments made should not be taken as an acceptance of or acquiescence in the employee's action. It is not necessary for Authorities to devise complicated formulae for assessment purposes and a standard proportion of normal wages for groups of staff would usually be appropriate. It is sufficient that the Authority should offer a payment which they consider reasonable. The offer should be expressed to be *ex gratia* and should not be the subject of negotiation. In very exceptional circumstances, Authorities may consider that it is justifiable to continue full pay for partial working, but this should not be the normal course of action. Terms (b) would be to make clear that pay will be stopped while the industrial action continues but that management are prepared to pay (on a full-time basis) that number of staff required to maintain the level of service offered;

ii. If less than full service is not acceptable to management and the Authority can establish that the duties not being undertaken or being undertaken in an improper manner are among those which the employee has a contractual obligation to do, this could justify the sending home of the staff concerned without pay, as a serious and material breach of contract. In such a case, the appropriate staff side representatives should be informed of management's intention to send home those staff who are not prepared to perform in a proper manner their full range of duties from an operative date. A warning notice should also be issued in writing to each of the staff concerned. The exact form of notice sent will depend upon the circumstances of the case and should be the subject of legal advice. Each of the staff concerned should be asked to acknowledge receipt of the notice by signing a copy of it. Where after such notice an employee does not agree to perform in a proper manner the full range of his duties, a further letter should be issued formally suspending him from duty without pay but inviting him to indicate when he would be willing to resume the normal range of duties appropriate to his grade. Again, a receipt should be asked for. The operative date for the action should normally be the date of receipt of the second letter and there should be at least two clear working days between the issue of the first and second letters. In all cases it should be made clear that this action does not amount to termination of employment and is not being applied as a disciplinary measure within the terms of section XXXIV of the General Whitley Council Handbook.

7. **Working restricted hours**

On any day when an employee works less than his contractual hours he is in breach of contract and loses his right to be paid for that day. Management may exercise their right to withhold pay for such time as the employee was in breach of his contract or may offer an *ex gratia* payment, based upon the proportion of the day which was worked.

(C) Labour Injunctions

Labour injunctions (as they have been called in the United States) offer employers a means of restraining by court order impending industrial action involving allegedly unlawful conduct. Proceedings can be initiated very quickly by interlocutory applications, mainly decided on affidavit (*i.e.* documentary) evidence without opportunity for cross-examination. Applications used often to be made *ex parte* (*i.e.* with only the applicant employer represented); and even if the defendant to the action was in court he might have had little time in which to prepare his defence. Hence TULRA, s.17(1) was enacted to require that in a case where the defendant is likely to claim that he acted in contemplation or furtherance of a trade dispute, injunctions are not to be granted unless the court is first satisfied that all reasonable steps have been taken to allow the defendant to be heard.

In *American Cyanamid Co.* v. *Ethicon Ltd.* [1975] A.C. 396 the House of Lords reconsidered the principles on which interlocutory injunctions should be granted (a case not involving industrial conflict). These principles were that the court had to be satisfied that the application disclosed *a serious question to be tried, i.e.* was not frivolous or vexatious. Thereafter, the court should not try to resolve points of fact or law on the basis frequently of incomplete evidence and argument; these matters should be reserved to the full trial of the action. In deciding whether or not to grant an injunction pending the trial, all that the court should at that stage consider is whether the *balance of convenience* prior to the trial favoured the granting or refusal of the injunction.

However, these principles proved very disadvantageous to trade unionists. Hence the enactment of TULRA, s.17(2), the full significance of which remained uncertain until the following decision.

NWL Ltd. v. Woods
[1979] 1 W.L.R. 1294; [1979] 3 All E.R. 614
House of Lords

LORD DIPLOCK: I turn next to the effect of TULRA section 17(2) upon applications for interlocutory injunctions in cases of this kind. The nature and goals of industrial action, the virtual immunity from liability for tort conferred upon trade unions by [TULRA] section 14 [now repealed by the Employment Act 1982] and the immunity from liability for the tort of wrongfully inducing breaches of contract conferred upon all persons by [TULRA] section 13 where this is done in connection with a trade dispute, are three factors which in combination would make the balance of convenience come down heavily in favour of granting an interlocutory injunction if the usual criteria [established in *American Cyanamid Co.* v *Ethicon Ltd.* [1975] A.C. 396] were alone applied.

In the normal case of threatened industrial action against an employer, the damage that he will sustain if the action is carried out is likely to be large, difficult to assess in money and may well be irreparable. Furthermore damage is likely to be caused to customers of the employer's business who are not parties to the action, and to the public at large. On the other hand the defendant is not the trade union but an individual officer of the union who, although he is acting on its behalf, can be sued in his personal capacity only [*ie* because of TULRA, s.14 subsequently repealed by the Employment Act 1982, s.15]. In that personal capacity he will suffer virtually no damage if the injunction is granted, whereas if it is not granted and the action against him ultimately succeeds it is most improbable that damages on the scale that are likely to be awarded against him will prove to be recoverable from him. Again, to grant the injunction will maintain the status quo until the trial; and this too is a factor which in evenly balanced cases generally operates in favour of granting an interlocutory injunction. So on the face of the proceedings in an action of this kind the balance of convenience as to the grant of an interlocutory injunction would appear to be heavily weighted in favour of the employer.

To take this view, however, would be to blind oneself to the practical realities: (1) that the real dispute is not between the employer and the nominal defendant but between the employer and the trade union that is threatening industrial action; (2) that the threat of blacking or other industrial action is being used as a bargaining counter in negotiations either existing or anticipated to obtain agreement by the employer to do whatever it is the union requires of him; (3) that it is the nature of industrial action that it can be promoted effectively only so long as it is possible to strike while the iron is still hot; once postponed it is unlikely that it can be revived; (4) that, in consequence of these three characteristics, the grant or refusal of an interlocutory injunction generally disposes finally of the action: in practice actions of this type seldom if ever come to actual trial.

Sub-section (2) of section 17 which is said to be passed "for the avoidance of doubt" and does not apply to Scotland, appears to me to be intended as a reminder addressed by Parliament to English judges, that where industrial action is threatened that is prima facie tortious because it induces a breach of contract they should, in exercising their discretion whether or not to grant an interlocutory injunction, put into the balance of convenience in favour of the defendant those countervailing practical realities and, in particular, that the grant of an injunction is tantamount to giving final judgment against the defendant.

The sub-section, it is to be noted, does not expressly enjoin the judge to have regard to the likelihood of success in establishing any other defence than a statutory immunity created by the Act although there may well be other defences to alleged wrongful inducement of breach of contract, such as denial of inducement or that what was sought to be induced would not constitute a breach, or justification of the inducement on other grounds than the existence of a trade dispute. So the sub-section is selective; it applies to one only out of several possible defences and, consequently, only to those actions which, since they are connected with trade disputes, involve the practical realities which I have mentioned.

My Lords, when properly understood, there is in my view nothing in the decision of this House in *American Cyanamid Co. v Ethicon Ltd.* [1975] A.C. 396 to suggest that in considering whether or not to grant an interlocutory injunction the judge ought not to give full weight to all the practical realities of the situation to which the injunction will apply. *American Cyanamid Co. v Ethicon Ltd.*, which enjoins the judge upon an application for an interlocutory injunction to direct his attention to the balance of convenience as soon as he has satisfied himself that there is a serious question to be tried, was not dealing with a case in which the grant or refusal of an injunction at that stage would, in effect, dispose of the action finally in favour of whichever party was successful in the application, because there would be nothing left on which it was in the unsuccessful party's interest to proceed to trial. By the time the trial came on the industrial dispute, if there were one, in furtherance of which the acts sought to be restrained were threatened or done, would be likely to have been settled and it would not be in the employer's interest to exacerbate relations with his workmen by continuing the proceedings against the individual defendants none of whom would be capable financially of meeting a substantial claim for damages. Nor, if an interlocutory injunction had been granted against them, would it be worthwhile for the individual defendants to take steps to obtain a final judgment in their favour, since any damages that they could claim in respect of personal pecuniary loss caused to them by the grant of the injunction and which they could recover under the employer's undertaking on damages would be very small.

Cases of this kind are exceptional, but when they do occur they bring into the balance of convenience an important additional element. In assessing whether what is compendiously called the balance of convenience lies in granting or refusing interlocutory injunctions in actions between parties of undoubted solvency the judge is engaged in weighing the respective risks that injustice may result from his deciding one way rather than the other at a stage when the evidence is incomplete. On the one hand there is the risk that if the interlocutory injunction is refused but the plaintiff succeeds in establishing at the trial his legal right for the protection of which the injunction had been sought he may in the meantime have suffered harm and inconvenience for which an award of money can provide no adequate recompense. On the other hand there is the risk that if the interlocutory injunction is granted but the plaintiff fails at the trial, the defendant may in the meantime have suffered harm and inconvenience which is similarly irrecompensable. The nature and degree of harm and inconvenience that are likely to be sustained in these two events by the defendant and the plaintiff respectively in consequence of the grant or the refusal of the injunction are generally sufficiently disproportionate to bring down, by themselves, the balance on one side or the other; and this is what I understand to be the thrust of the decision of this House in *American Cyanamid Co. v Ethicon Ltd.* Where, however, the grant or refusal of the interlocutory injunction will have the practical effect of putting an end to the action because the harm that will have been already caused to the losing party by its grant or its refusal is complete and of a kind for which money cannot constitute any worthwhile recompense, the degree of likelihood that the plaintiff would have succeeded in establishing his right to an injunction if the action had gone to trial, is a factor to be brought into the balance by the judge in weighing the risks that injustice may result from his deciding the application one way rather than the other.

The characteristics of the type of action to which section 17 applies have already been discussed. They are unique; and, whether it was strictly necessary to do so or not, it was clearly prudent of the draftsman of the section to state expressly that in considering whether or not to grant an interlocutory injunction the court should have regard to the likelihood of the defendant's succeeding in establishing that what he did or threatened was done or threatened in contemplation or furtherance of a trade dispute.

My Lords, counsel for the respondents have invited this House to say that because it is singled out for special mention it is an "overriding" or a "paramount" factor against granting the injunction once it appears to the judge that the defence of statutory immunity is more likely to succeed than not. I do not think that your Lordships should give your approval to the use of either of these or any other adjective to define the weight to be given to this factor by the judge, particularly as the sub-section does not apply to Scotland where, as my noble and learned friend Lord Fraser of Tullybelton explains, it would be but one of several factors to be taken into consideration whose relative weight might vary with the circumstances of the case. Parliament cannot be taken to have intended that radically different criteria should be applied by English and Scots courts. The degree of likelihood of success of the special defence under section 13 beyond its being slightly more probable than not is clearly relevant; so is the degree of irrecoverable damage likely to be sustained by the employer, his customers and the general public if the injunction is refused and the defence ultimately fails. Judges would, I think, be respecting the intention of Parliament in making this change in the law in 1975, if in the normal way the injunction were refused in cases where the defendant had shown that it was more likely than not that he would succeed in his defence of statutory immunity; but this does not mean that there may not be cases where the consequences to the employer or to third parties or the public and perhaps the nation itself, may be so disastrous that the injunction ought to be refused, unless there is a high degree of probability that the defence will succeed.

My Lords, the instant case presents no problem. On the evidence before the court at each stage of these proceedings, the defendants have a virtual certainty of establishing their defence of statutory immunity. I would dismiss these appeals.

The changes in the Employment Act 1982 which render trade unions liable for industrial action led Lord Diplock to comment further on his judgment in *NWL* v. *Woods* (above p. 578), adjusting his guidelines to the new circumstances.

Dimbleby and Sons Ltd. v. The National Union of Journalists
[1984] I.R.L.R. 160; [1984] 1 All E.R. 117
House of Lords

Lord Diplock: As a result of the passing of the Employment Acts of 1980 and 1982 . . . what in 1979 were practical realities [*cf. NWL* v *Woods* above p. 578], no longer apply in 1983 to a suit against a trade union claiming damages for an injunction to restrain it from secondary action which is actionable. If the suit succeeds, the trade union will be liable not only in damages up to a substantial maximum (£125,000 in the case of the NUJ) [*cf.* the maximum damages awards, fixed by reference to total membership, which may be made against unions in respect of economic tort liability under section 16 of the 1982 Act], but also for costs without any maximum limit, and to unlimited fines or sequestration of its assets if, by breaching an injunction, it should commit contempt of court. In the paragraph of my speech in *NWL Ltd v Woods* which precedes the reference to the practical realities, I had pointed out that if the plaintiff continued the action to a successful conclusion, it was unlikely that damages on the scale that the plaintiff would have sustained would be likely to prove recoverable from the individual defendant or defendants who alone, at that time, could be made defendants to the suit. That was what lay at the root of the "reality" that I numbered (4). At so early a stage in the action as that at which an injunction is generally sought (as it was in the instant case), there is no reason for a judge to exercise his discretion on the assumption that the case will never proceed to trial and final judgment where the defendant is the trade union itself and not a mere individual office-holder in it.

For an application of the complex criteria laid down in the *NWL* case, as modified by trade unions' revived vulnerability to tort liability since the repeal of TULRA, s.14 by the Employment Act 1982, s.15, see the following dialogue.

Mercury Communications Ltd. v. Scott-Garner
[1984] I.C.R. 74; [1984] 1 All E.R. 197
Court of Appeal

For the facts, see p. 589 below.

SIR JOHN DONALDSON M.R.: . . . Proceeding by the appropriate stages, the questions and my answers are as follows:

(i) Q. Has Mercury shown that there is a serious question to be tried?
A. Yes.

(ii) Q. Has Mercury shown that it has a real prospect of succeeding in its claim for a permanent injunction at the trial?
A. Yes.

(iii) Q. If Mercury succeeded, would it be adequately compensated by damages for the loss which it suffered as the result of the union being free to continue to take industrial action pending the trial?
A. No. Mercury is in a relatively frail condition as a newcomer to the field and has very large sums invested in the project. New customers cannot be attracted whilst industrial action is threatened and the losses will vastly exceed the maximum liability which can be imposed upon the union, namely £250,000 (see section 16 of the Employment Act 1982).

(iv) Q. If the union were to succeed at the trial in establishing its defence under section 13 of [TULRA], would it be adequately compensated by an award under the cross-undertaking?
A. Yes. The union would suffer no loss since, on this hypothesis, the dispute is wholly or mainly about redundancy and there is no suggestion that a temporary cessation in the industrial action would cause or hasten any redundancy.

(v) Q. Where does the balance of convenience lie?
A. It lies in protecting Mercury pending the trial of the action.

4. COLLECTIVE DISPUTES AND THE STATE

Previously, workers' and employers' weapons have been considered mainly in terms of the common law of contract and tort, and in the context of employment law and business relationships. When the State becomes involved, this common law context is supplemented by legal rules derived from policy choices in the fields of social security, public order, the political process, public services and economic policy.

(A) Strikes and State Social Security

The following extract considers the role of the State in relation to the financial problems of strikers.

J. Gennard, *Financing Strikers* (1977), pp. 10–12

What criteria can be used by a democratic state to decide on the posture that should be taken towards strikers? Regardless of administrative pressures what political motives can be discerned to explain the posture originally taken and the changes in that policy which have taken place over this century? The issue of the stance to be taken towards strikers can be distinguished from that taken towards strikes as such. For all governments, without exception, strikes have been regarded as undesirable, to be avoided wherever possible. Of course, on some occasions this view has found expression in the treatment of strikers—access to State benefits has been restricted quite specifically to discourage striking. There have been equally obvious occasions when policies have been framed with the covert objective of discouraging strikes by discouraging strikers. There need not be anything wrong in this. However, it is by no means self-evident that a government which discourages strikes should also attempt to manipulate the provisions of the Welfare State to penalise strikers.

As soon as the merits of individual strikes are considered, the question of the fairness of the State's treatment of strikers is raised. When the question of the relative economic power of the employers and the employed is added, then the issue of fairness becomes even sharper. It is not necessary to be unduly cynical to note that few governments in any country have grasped this particular nettle of social and economic policy. The general practice in the Western world has been that the State attempts to stand aloof from consideration of merits and relative power in disputes by using the provisions of the Welfare State to penalise both sides. On the one side, the access of strikers and their families to public assistance is restricted. On the other side, the employer is prevented from using public employment exchanges [*e.g.* "Job Centres"] to recruit strike-breakers.

This balancing of penalties is, on the face of it, not only a very rough and ready way of achieving State neutrality to disputes but also begs the issues. There have been occasions when the access of strikers to public assistance has been altered with the specific objective of influencing behaviour. It has been more customary, however, for governments to leave well alone and point to the token balancing of disadvantages to each side as sufficient evidence of their aloofness.

In order to examine the rationale for governments' actions, a distinction must be drawn between *laissez-faire* and *neutrality* towards strikes. Where the State involved itself in no way with labour exchanges and public assistance, where freedom of association was allowed to both employed and employers, then *laissez-faire* might involve no more than ensuring that the peace was kept. However, there has never been a time in Britain, nor probably in any other country, where those conditions prevailed. Even if the judicial harassment of trade union activities after the emancipatory Acts of 1871 and 1875 is ignored and the last quarter of the nineteenth century is characterised as a period of *laissez-faire* in industrial relations, there were still the Poor Laws providing support for strikers' families. The mere existence of even this primitive form of public assistance meant that British governments did not even have the option of *laissez-faire*. To allow striker households full access to outdoor relief might have altered the balance of power and thus directly [have] influence[d] the outcome of disputes. To exclude striker households completely would have been to remove one of the essential props to working-class existence. Even if it could have been described as "clearing the ring" it could hardly have been described as the State not interfering. To allow striker households restricted access to outdoor relief by administrative ruling was merely the standard compromise that most governments would accept as the least controversial course of action.

Yet even if there had been no Poor Laws, and even if the other aspects of employer/employee relations had been unfettered by legislative or judicial interference, a lack of involvement by government would not have been neutral. If many workers were poorly organised, with minimal savings other than for their burials, then contests with the employer can rarely have been equal. The average length of strike was extremely long by modern standards, which must have meant that workers and their families endured extreme deprivation to achieve any improvements in working conditions. If an important function of modern government is seen to be the support of weak groups against strong, to encourage the development of countervailing power, then it can be argued that governments must justify any failure to act where the balance of power between groups is unequal. In short, a policy of State neutrality in strikes would involve active intervention to ensure that the employer and the employed could bring equal power to bear in their bargaining.

It must be a matter of personal judgement whether one would wish for a neutrality of this sort. If strikes are considered bad because they are economically wasteful, then the active encouragement of countervailing power to be brought to bear in strikes might be seen as undesirable because of the costs that might result from such a policy. The view might be taken that the disparity in power between employers and unions was so great that the only way in which it could be balanced was by providing workers with a high level of income during strikes. It might be that this could be provided by allowing full access to unemployment benefits. If it were felt that this was a misuse of the National Insurance Fund, or that the level of benefit would not be high enough to strengthen the union side, or that a more obvious gesture of public support should be made, then one might imagine an argument being made for a State Strike Fund.

When the modern State has shown itself ready to intervene in so many aspects of life, it is difficult to accept that it is being neutral when it holds itself aloof from one aspect in particular. It is equally difficult to accept that the existence of the web of State benefits does not affect labour market conditions and thus form[s] one of the inputs into collective bargaining and strikes. The State is obviously not a neutral element in strikes and to claim that it is so, simply because access to one set of benefits is restricted to non-strikers, is an obvious nonsense. . . .

Recent changes in the law illustrating a shift in State policy are described in M. Partington, "Unemployment, industrial conflict and social security" (1980) 9 I.L.J. 243.

(B) Picketing and Public Order

The problems of picketing and public order include adjustment of the conflicts of interest between the various parties affected (employers, pickets, customers, non-strikers, etc.), and the enforcement of whatever compromise emerges through the criminal law. The following two cases illustrate the workings of the criminal law in this area.

Piddington v. Bates
[1961] 1 W.L.R. 162; [1960] 3 All E.R. 660
Queen's Bench Division

The respondent, a police officer, was sent to strike-bound premises after a telephone call and found two pickets stationed at one entrance and four pickets at the rear entrance in Fowler Road, two of whom withdrew at the respondent's request. Ten to twelve pickets were in Fowler Road when the appellant approached the respondent and asked him where was the rear entrance. The respondent told him three times that in his view two pickets at each entrance was sufficient. The appellant insisted on his rights to join the pickets at the rear entrance, and gently pushed past the respondent and was gently arrested. No obstruction was caused to the highway and there was no disorder or violence created by the picketing.

LORD PARKER L.C.J.: The court has been referred to a great number of cases, both Irish and English, dealing with the position when a police constable can be said to contemplate a breach of the peace and to take action to preserve it because, of course, the question here is whether the constables in question were acting in the course of the execution of their duty when they were obstructed. I find it unnecessary to refer to those cases. It seems to me that the law is reasonably plain. First, the mere statement by a constable that he did anticipate that there might be a breach of the peace is clearly not enough. There must exist proved facts from which a constable could reasonably anticipate such a breach. Secondly, it is not enough that his contemplation is that there is a remote possibility; there must be a real possibility of a breach of the peace. Accordingly, in every case, it becomes a question of whether, on the particular facts, it can be said that there were reasonable grounds on which a constable charged with this duty reasonably anticipated that a breach of the peace might occur . . . it is said that no reasonable man could possibly anticipate a breach of the peace. It is pointed out that there was no obstruction in the street; that there was no actual intimidation; and that there were no threats or intimations of violence. It is said that there was really nothing save the fact that picketing was going on to suggest that a breach of the peace was a real possibility.

As I have said, every case must depend upon its exact facts, and the matter which influences me in this case is the matter of numbers. It is, I think, perfectly clear from the wording of the case, although it is not expressly so found, that the police knew that in these small works there were only eight people working. They found two vehicles arriving, with eighteen people milling about the street, trying to form pickets at the doors. On that ground alone, coupled with the telephone call which, I should have thought, intimated some sense of urgency and apprehension, the police were fully entitled to think as reasonable men that there was a real danger of something more than mere picketing to collect or impart information or peaceably to persuade [*ie* the sole lawful purpose of pickets *cf*. now TULRA, s.15(1)]. I think that in those circumstances the prosecutor had reasonable grounds for anticipating that a breach of the peace was a real possibility. It may be, and I think this is the real criticism, that it can be said: Well, to say that only two pickets should be allowed is purely arbitrary; why two? Why not three? Where do you draw the line? I think that a police officer charged with the duty of preserving the Queen's peace must be left to take such steps as on the evidence before him he thinks are proper. I am far from saying that there should be any rule that only two pickets should be allowed at any particular door. There one gets into an arbitrary area, but so far as this case is concerned I cannot see that there was anything wrong in the action of the prosecutor.

Moss v. McLachlan
[1985] I.R.L.R. 76
Queen's Bench Division

Four striking miners were stopped by a police cordon at a junction within one and a half miles of a colliery affected by the strike. The inspector in charge told them to turn back as he feared a breach of the peace if they continued. When they refused, they were arrested. They were convicted by magistrates of wilfully obstructing a police officer in the execution of his duty and appealed.

SKINNER J.: . . . (the appellants) contend that the police orders to turn back and their subsequent refusal to allow them to pass were unlawful. In reality, they say, the police were restricting their right to freedom of movement. Though the police have a duty to ensure that the peace is kept, they had no power to take the steps they did in this case: their only power was to admonish. In these circumstances the police were not acting in the execution of their duty and the offence accordingly was not proved.

Subject to one submission by Mr Mansfield [counsel for the appellants], to which I shall return later, the law on this subject is clear. If a constable apprehends, on reasonable grounds, that a breach of the peace may be committed, he is not only entitled but is under a duty to take reasonable steps to prevent that breach occurring. . . .

The possibility of a breach must be real to justify any preventive action. The imminence or immediacy of the threat to the peace determines what action is reasonable. If the police feared that a convoy of cars travelling towards a working coal field bearing banners and broadcasting, by sight or sound, hostility or threats towards working miners, might cause a violent episode, they would be justified in halting the convoy to enquire into its destination and purpose. If, on stopping the vehicles, the police were satisfied that there was a real possibility of the occupants causing a breach of the peace one-and-a-half miles away, a journey of less than five minutes by car, then in our judgment it would be their duty to prevent the convoy from proceeding further and they have the power to do so.

During the first 27 weeks of the miners' strike of 1984–5, the Chief Constable of Nottinghamshire stated that 164,508 "presumed pickets" had been prevented from entering his county (Civil Liberties and the Miners' Dispute: First Report of the Independent Inquiry, NCCL (1984), para. 3.40). Magistrates' attachment of restrictive bail conditions to striking miners charged with picketing offences similarly adhered to the police viewpoint (*R.* v. *The Mansfield Justices, ex p. Sharkey* [1984] I.R.L.R. 496 (Div. Ct.). Attempts to obtain recognition of the interests/rights of pickets have been rebuffed by the courts.

Hunt v. Broome

[1974] 2 W.L.R. 58; [1974] I.C.R. 84 (*sub. nom. Broome* v. *DPP*)
House of Lords

During a national building strike, Mr Broome, a trade union official, had failed to persuade a lorry driver not to drive onto a building site. When the lorry driver started to drive his lorry onto the site, Mr Broome stood in front of it blocking its path and continued his attempts to persuade the driver not to enter the site. A policeman called to the scene warned Mr Broome that he would be arrested if he did not move out of the lorry's path. He did not move and was arrested but acquitted by the justices of an offence under the Highways Act 1959, s.121 [now the Highways Act 1980, s.137].

The justices took the view that the period of nine minutes spent by Broome seeking to persuade the driver not to enter the site, interspersed, as it was, by manoeuvrings of the lorry, was not an unreasonably long time for Broome to spend in exercising his statutory right peacefully to persuade the lorry driver not to work under the predecessor to TULRA, s.15, the Industrial Relations Act 1971, s.134.

The House of Lords confirmed the decision of the Queen's Bench Division to allow the appeal by the police.

LORD SALMON: The justices seem to have construed [section 121 of the Highways Act, 1959] as conferring a right to stop anyone on the highway against his will and to compel him to listen to persuasion. If this is the true meaning of the section, it follows that it imposes a corresponding obligation upon anyone to stop and listen to persuasion whether or not he wishes to do so. It is argued that otherwise the section is meaningless and of no effect. My Lords, I can find no justification of any kind for such a construction. It involves reading words into the section which are not there and which, if they were, would seriously diminish the liberty of the subject. Everyone has the right to use the highway free from the risk of being compulsorily stopped by any private citizen and compelled to listen to what he does not want to hear. No doubt it is permissible, either by words or signs, to ask any man to stop on the highway and then to ask him to listen to what you have to say. He is free, however, to stop or go on as he pleases. If he does stop and then decides that he does not wish to listen or that he has heard enough, he cannot be compelled to stay. The Act of 1971 certainly does not expressly confer any right upon pickets to compel any man to stop upon the highway and listen to them nor does it expressly empower any pickets to stop any man from using the highway as a means of access to his place of work or to compel any man to listen to persuasion which he does not want to hear. I cannot accept that the Act confers such rights or imposes corresponding obligations by implication. Surely if such an astonishing interference with the liberty of the subject had been intended, the legislature would have made its intention plain by express and unambiguous language.

Lord Salmon's judgment was scrutinised in the following casenote, which questioned, first, the assumption that because there was no *duty* on users of the highway to listen to pickets, there was no *right* to picket; and second, the "almost absolute" nature of the right to use the highway.

G. S. Goodwin-Gill, in (1975) 91 L.Q.R. 173, 176–7

. . . the "right to use the highway" is not the sort of right which imposes duties on others. It is not a right strictly so-called in the sense of a right to proceed to the exclusion of all others. A characteristic of such a right as this is that it is subject to competition from other similar rights; it has, as it were, to be shared, and it potentially collides with other "legitimate interests."

The "right to picket," it is submitted, would be of the same family. There is no need to search for any exact, correlative obligation. The concern is not with what may be claimed in unqualified terms, but with what may justifiably be claimed when other competing interests have been taken into account. Once one has accepted the notion of a "qualified right," then the problem becomes that of determining the principles which govern or should govern the competition which will arise between them. The task is one of balancing opposing, but legitimate, interests, and to approach it within a traditional rights/duties straitjacket is to invite trouble.

It is a characteristic of qualified rights that they compete with other such rights. Thus, the right to use the highway requires to be balanced against the right of others to that use, whether for the purpose of passage to and fro, or for the purpose of access to premises adjacent to the highway. In principle, there would seem to be little reason why the right to use the highway should not on occasion be balanced against the somewhat different rights of industrial pickets. Some will argue that this would constitute too great an interference with "individual liberty," and that no man should be inconvenienced by the activities of those with whom he is not in sympathy. Indeed, it may be admitted that the present view does depend in large measure upon acceptance of the fact that, in contemporary society, there will be many groups whose legitimate interests and expectations will occasionally collide. . . .

The "right to use the highway" may thus be seen as subject not only to the reasonable exercise of similar and related rights by other members of the public, but also to the reasonable exercise of the "right to picket"—*ie* the right of participants in an industrial dispute to attend at the specified places and for the specified purposes. Delay and inconvenience may be caused to members of the public and drivers may be "obliged" to stop their vehicles; but whether or not their *right* has been infringed now becomes a question of fact to be determined in the light of what is reasonable, and with the aim of maintaining a balance between competing interests. A solution to this question cannot conveniently result from a general conclusion that pickets have no rights because no one else has any correlative duties.

In *British Airports Authority* v. *Ashton* [1983] I.R.L.R. 287 (Q.B.D.) Mann J. thought it would be "astonishing" if Parliament intended TULRA, s.15 to imply a right to attend on land against the will of the land-owner.

(C) Political Disputes

Disputes between workers and employers are usually considered as "economic" disputes and are distinguished from "political" disputes involving the State. Hostility to government policy may, however, be a factor in causing industrial action (*eg* opposition to the Heath government's employment legislation: *Sherrard* v. *AUEW* [1973] I.C.R. 421; or to the Thatcher government's policies: *Express Newspapers Ltd.* v. *Keys* [1980] I.R.L.R. 247; or to the imposition of cash limits on nationalised industries: *Duport Steels Ltd.* v. *Sirs* [1980] 1 All E.R. 529 (above p. 561); or to apartheid: *BBC* v. *Hearn* [1977] 1 W.L.R. 1004 (above p. 565)). The question of policy is whether industrial action is a legitimate weapon of workers in political disputes, or economic disputes with a political element.

British law outlaws "political" industrial action by granting immunity from liability for economic torts only where there is a "trade dispute." Prior to the Employment Act 1980, disputes with mixed economic and political content were legitimate, so long as the subject-matter of the dispute was "connected with" terms and conditions of employment etc., itemised in TULRA, s.29(1). The 1980 Act replaced the words "connected with" and inserted instead the words "wholly or mainly" related to the issues listed in TULRA, s.29(1). The problems this can give rise to are illustrated by the following case.

Mercury Communications Ltd. v. Scott-Garner
[1984] I.C.R. 74; [1984] 1 All E.R. 197
Court of Appeal

The Post Office Engineering Union, as part of a campaign against licensing competitors (liberalisation) to and privatisation of the telecommunications system in the United Kingdom, instructed its members not to effect interconnections between Mercury Communications, a new private sector company, providing public telephone services and the then publicly owned British Telecom (BT). The stated objectives of the union's campaign included the defence of the jobs and job opportunities of its members. In September 1980 the union and BT had made a formal Job Security Agreement (JSA) in the context of technological changes whereby BT undertook not to make compulsory redundancies (clause 4) but reserved the right to withdraw from this commitment in the event of manpower surplus (clause 5). The Court of Appeal reversed the trial judge's finding that there was a trade dispute.

May L.J.:. . . . The union saw the attempt to interconnect Mercury as the thin end of the wedge which could ultimately lead to the failure of their campaign against liberalisation and then privatisation. If this campaign failed, there was, it was said, a serious risk of redundancies and, amongst other things, the likelihood that B.T. would become less profitable, which would also reduce the scope for improvement in the terms and conditions of employment of its employees. In the various affidavits sworn by Mr Stanley [the union's General Secretary] and filed on the defendants' behalf in these proceedings this is repeated and emphasised—for instance in paragraph 10 of his first affidavit:

> "I therefore wish to state unequivocally and with all the emphasis at my command that the purpose and object of the industrial action complained of by the plaintiffs is to prevent the risk of job losses arising from the entry into the market of an unwelcome competitor."

Mercury's claim necessarily involves an attack on the genuineness of these contentions of Mr Stanley. Their case in brief is that the blacking of Mercury and its shareholders was part of the union's relatively long-standing campaign against Mercury and the government and the policies of liberalisation and thereafter privatisation for which they stand. Of course Mr Stanley has to base himself upon an alleged risk of redundancies, because under the relevant legislation as now enacted [*ie* TULRA, ss.13 and 29 as amended by the Employment Acts 1980 and 1982] this is the only defence that the union can have in this action, and in particular against the interlocutory injunctions now sought. . . .

Further, although I fully appreciate that we live in a time of high unemployment with fears of redundancy prevalent throughout industry, the evidence that we presently have leads me to the conclusion that to the knowledge of the union B.T. clearly anticipated being able to accommodate any job losses that might result either from competition or from technological advance, by natural wastage and retirement.

Finally, in my opinion all these matters have to be considered in the context that there is no doubt that the union is and has for some time been conducting a campaign against liberalisation and privatisation, in which the defence of its members' jobs and conditions of service has only been one of the issues. I think that from the union's own documents which are before us this has been and is in substantial degree a political and ideological campaign seeking to maintain the concept of public monopoly against private competition. I have no doubt that those who strenuously contend for the continuation of a monopoly in the postal and telecommunications fields honestly and fervently believe that this is in the best interests of the jobs and conditions of service of those working in the industry. It does not however follow that industrial action taken to further that campaign amounts to a dispute which is wholly or mainly about fears of redundancies if that monopoly is not maintained. Doing the best I can, I have come to the conclusion that it is unlikely that the defendants in this case will succeed in satisfying a court at trial that the dispute between B.T. and its employees over the blacking of Mercury and its shareholders was a trade dispute within the relevant legislation as now enacted . . . in the present case the real dispute, as I think, is not between BT and the union but between the latter and Mercury and between the union and the government. The industrial action is no doubt being used as a bargaining counter in the dispute between the union and the government . . .

Dillon L.J.: Whether the dispute between the defendants' members and B.T. and Mercury is a trade dispute has to be considered objectively. The court has to consider all the evidence and it is not concluded by the *ipse dixit* of Mr Stanley. . . .

In the present case there can be no doubt that the defendants as a union have for many months opposed with fervour the government's proposals for changes within the telecommunications industry. . . . The background to the particular dispute, and the attitude of the union which required the workers to take the industrial action and which professes to speak for the workers, must in my judgment be relevant in assessing . . . whether the dispute between the workers and B.T. and Mercury relates wholly or mainly to fear of job losses.

. . . . In this court (counsel for the union) has sought to brush [the JSA] aside because it is not a binding contract in law or on the ground that clause 5 enables B.T. to withdraw the undertaking about redundancies whenever B.T. finds the undertaking inconvenient. But that is to ignore the realities of industrial relations . . . Mr Stanley's assertions that the particular dispute and the wider dispute are all about jobs have to be set against the fact that the defendants have not, in their campaign against Mercury, liberalisation, privatisation and inter-connection, ever mentioned or invoked the Job Security Agreement. . . .

On the material before us, I would not regard the defendants' prospects of success in establishing that there is a trade dispute as overwhelming. . . . My assessment is that the defendants may succeed at the trial, but if they do it will have been a close run thing.

It follows, in my judgment, that I am entitled to exercise my own discretion as to the grant or refusal of an injunction. . . .

Sir John Donaldson M.R.: Well, which is the subject-matter—facilitating and implementing liberalisation, agreeing to interconnect, ordering interconnection or the risk to jobs? Only the latter would enable the dispute to qualify as a trade dispute. The evidence has to be looked at as a whole, but I find it impossible to conclude on the evidence at present available that the risk to jobs was a major part of what the dispute was about. I say that because I find it inconceivable that if the dispute was wholly or mainly about jobs, the union would not have approached B.T. asking for a guarantee of job security or a strengthening of the Job Security Agreement. Yet nothing of the sort appears to have happened and the union did not even think that this agreement was relevant to the present proceedings. On the other hand there is massive evidence that the union was waging a campaign against the political decisions to liberalise the industry and to privatise B.T. . . .

My conclusion on the evidence, provisional though it has to be, is reached without any doubt or hesitation. It is that it is most unlikely that the union will be able to establish that there was at any material time a trade dispute between B.T. and its employees.

(D) Collective Disputes and the "Public Interest"

The increased role of the State in society means a multitude of social and economic functions are exercised by public authorities granted powers and duties by law. Industrial action involving these authorities in their capacity as employers often results in their being unable to fulfil these statutory duties and the general public suffering in consequence. The policy question is whether industrial action is legitimate which interferes with the performance of statutory duties. In the following case, notions of conspiracy and inducement were canvassed in considering the legitimacy of such industrial action.

Meade v. London Borough of Haringey
[1979] 1 W.L.R. 637; [1979] 2 All E.R. 1016
Court of Appeal

In support of a wage claim school caretakers and ancillary staff threatened the closure of schools. Accordingly, the defendant local education authority instructed head-masters to close schools and advised parents to keep their children at home. Parents complained that the failure to make schools available for full-time education was in breach of the Education Act 1944, s.8, (which also contains procedures for complaints to the Minister (s.99)). After the schools had been closed for four weeks the plaintiff, on behalf of himself and other parents and ratepayers, sued for an order that the defendant should perform its duty under section 8 and for a mandatory injunction to put the order into effect.

Both at first instance and on appeal the injunction was refused but the claim that there had been a *prima facie* breach of statutory duty was upheld.

EVELEIGH L.J.: While it has been said that the [defendant] council were influenced by their sympathy with the union's claim, it has not been specifically alleged in the affidavits that the union and the council agreed together for the purpose of securing a rise in the employees' pay that the council would close the schools. In such a situation there could well be a conspiracy to bring about a breach of statutory duty under section 8 of the Education Act 1944. If anyone suffering damage or who might suffer damage sued the individuals concerned for the tort of conspiracy, it would not be necessary to consider the effect of section 99 of the Education Act 1944 because the cause of action would not be one for breach of statutory duty *simpliciter*. Furthermore the immunity in tort given by the Trade Union and Labour Relations Act 1974 would not apply to such a situation, for to agree with another or to induce that other to act in breach of a statutory duty does not fall within the provisions of section 13 of the Act. If a claim for damages would lie, so too would a claim for an injunction. However, the evidence necessary to present a claim on this basis would have to be strong, and I would not infer such an agreement from the affidavits before the court.

Counsel for the plaintiff says that in saying, "The schools will be closed," the union are ordering the council to close the schools and that the council's decision was simply responding to that command. This, however, is argument that the court will have to consider when the case is tried. Mr Grant [on behalf of the defendants] claims that the sentence can be read as simply a factual statement of what will be the situation when the strike starts. Again that is argument. If the union were ordering the council to act in that way, they clearly had no right to do so and it would be the duty of the council to ignore it. To withdraw their labour when the inevitable result must be that the schools will be closed is something the unions are entitled to do. On the other hand, there is a statutory duty upon the council to make the schools available, and the unions have no right to ask or demand that the council should close the schools for they would thereby be demanding that the council should commit a breach of its statutory duty. They may, in proper circumstances, induce others to break a contract in the furtherance of a trade dispute but they are not entitled with impunity to order or solicit a breach of statutory duty: see section 13 of the Trade Union and Labour Relations Act 1974 to see the extent of the immunity granted.

Cf. Barretts and Baird (Wholesale) Ltd. v. *I.P.C.S.* [1987] I.R.L.R. 3 (Q.B.D.). The one-sidedness of common law notions may tempt governments in other collective disputes, where the State may intervene to invoke the "public interest", to avoid emergencies or risks to essential services, and thereby restrict industrial action by workers. The policy issues concern the reasons for, extent to and terms on which any restrictions are proposed. These issues are explored in the following extract.

C. Crouch, "Changing perceptions of a public interest" in LABOUR LAW AND THE COMMUNITY (Lord Wedderburn of Charlton and W. T. Murphy ed., 1982), p. 107 at pp. 107–9

I shall address the question: "Will concepts of public interest in labour law within capitalist societies be merely synonymous with employer interests?"

If workers need to challenge existing powers in order to pursue their own interests (in higher wages, better working conditions, reduced redundancies, or whatever), they usually need to disrupt or at least threaten to disrupt the functioning of the operation in question. Exceptional circumstances apart, most people will prefer to see a smoothly running service than a disrupted one. Therefore the initial answer to my question is yes, the public interest in an industrial dispute is often synonymous with the employer's interest. . . .

One implication of all this is that workers who happen to be employed in vital, monopolistic sectors find that they threaten the public interest whenever they take action which is regarded far less severely when pursued by workers in less sensitive areas of the economy. One might conclude from this either that such workers must be placed under extraordinary constraints, or that, in fairness to them, the concept of the public interest should be excluded from consideration. But both are unnecessarily defeatist positions. Since at least the late 19th century there has been an assumption in public policy that exceptional forms of mediation and of pay determination should be deployed within this sector to reduce conflict to the lowest possible levels. Workers were, more or less, ensured favourable treatment, and it was assumed that they would show exceptional restraint in the use of industrial action. In some countries, particularly those within German traditions of law and administration, these reciprocal privileges and constraints were formalised and made statutory, creating the special employment position of the *Beamte* or public servant. In Britain, characteristically, the issue has been governed by voluntary understandings. For public-service unions the cost of this was a certain demobilisation of their members, but there was a *quid pro quo* in the form of greater job security and probably easier working conditions for their members than in other sectors, together with a far easier path than in many parts of the private sector for the union itself in gaining recognition and rights of consultation from the public employer. An important feature of industrial relations in the public service became the use of comparability with the market sector as the basis for establishing public-service pay, and unions found a distinctive role in manipulating the rules and conventions which thereby developed. For a long time such procedures provided a practical means of pursuing a public interest that was not equivalent to an employer's interest.

The extent to which the policy exchange between self-restraint in industrial action and alternative methods of conflict resolution has been undermined is now reflected in increasing concern over the issue of strikes in essential services (*c.f.* the Green Paper on Trade Union Immunities 1981 Cmnd. 8128 paras. 306–338).

(E) Industrial Action, Economic Policy and the Law

The law may be used to regulate industrial action in conformity with the objectives of government economic policy. Three examples follow.

(i) Industrial action and incomes policy

K. W. Wedderburn, "Industrial action, the State and the public interest" in INDUSTRIAL CONFLICT: A COMPARATIVE LEGAL SURVEY (B. Aaron and K. W. Wedderburn, eds., 1972) at pp. 378–9

. . . Statutory control of wages must involve legal limitation in the "national interest" upon the right to strike for those wages.

It was that Rubicon which the British Prices and Incomes Act crossed in 1966. The Act was repealed at the end of 1970. It gave the Government for one emergency year the power to prohibit all wage increases (though bad drafting led to successful court actions by workers who had been promised increases); and later it gave a power to the Minister to order that particular agreed increases should be postponed—so-called "standstill" orders. . . .

. . . The sanctions used were primarily the threat of criminal prosecution though none was ever brought. In civil law, apart from destroying the workers' contractual right to any increase, a standstill order was carefully excluded from giving rise to further tort liabilities. Moreover, disputes about standstill orders or the Act were expressly made "trade disputes"—a marked shift towards inclusion of political disputes within the protected area.

Any attempt by strike action or otherwise "with a view to compel, induce or influence" an employer to pay an increase contrary to a standstill order during the relevant period was a crime remediable by fines of up to £100. But workers had to have that "view"; so that when a group of lorry drivers stopped working extra hours, they claimed that that had no such object, but were merely withdrawing from their end of a bargain of which the wage increase had been "frozen" by an order. Although no one was prosecuted, the Act caused great tension between the Labour Government and the trade unions who had opposed it.

. . . The policy failed not merely because it would have been difficult to fine or imprison thousands of workers had they defied the Act.

The reason is that a law enforcing an incomes policy has to create some novel offences which upset cherished principles of democratic thought. . . . What offence are workers committing if, having given notice and observed the [agreed] procedure, they come out in support of a claim for an increase in their own pay? If we subject them to legal penalties, what liberties are safe? Then there is still the employer . . . what kind of crime is it for a man to agree to pay his employees higher wages?

It is surely for this fundamental reason that those who have, with pre-eminent logic, proposed that reforms of labour laws must now be overtly dovetailed into national Government's overall economic policy, have met with little positive response.

(ii) Unofficial strikes and "efficient" management

Report of the Royal Commission on *Trade Unions and Employers' Associations* 1965–68 (chairman: Lord Donovan), Cmnd. 3263, paras. 412–415

It is also necessary to take account of the effects on management of fear of the possibility of strikes even if they do not take place. If an employer forestalls a strike by making concessions in the face of threats which it might have been better to resist, or by refraining from introducing changes which he believes to be necessary in the interests of efficiency, then the economic consequences of his doing so may be more serious than those to which a strike would have given rise. Naturally, however, it is impossible to measure such consequences statistically.

It is in fact only when the impact on managements of unofficial strikes and other forms of unofficial action is taken into account that their gravity becomes apparent. Such action may face a manager with a sudden and acute dilemma. He may be under severe pressure from customers to produce goods or materials by a particular deadline, and in a competitive market such pressure is not easy to resist. No doubt it should be resisted if the alternative is to surrender to blackmail exerted by unofficial strikers. But it is not surprising if managers sometimes make unwise concessions which secure peace for the time being at the cost of storing up trouble for the future.

Moreover it is characteristic of unofficial action that it is unpredictable. For the most part it concerns issues which are not regulated by written collective agreements. The formal rules which are supposed to govern workplace bargaining—those contained in disputes procedures—are frequently ineffective and cannot be relied on. The informal network of rules and undertakings built up by managements and shop stewards in their day-to-day dealings with each other lack precision and stability. The upshot is that some managements lack confidence that the plans they make and the decisions they reach can be implemented rapidly and effectively or, in extreme cases, at all.

This situation is found in its most acute form in the small number of establishments where there is what might be termed an "endemic" strike situation. . . . In these establishments managers and supervisors are in a constant state of anxiety lest they do something which might inadvertently lead to a strike. There are also a growing number of establishments where occasional strikes and other forms of industrial action take place, and here managements tend to be worried lest the situation deteriorate. The economic implications are obvious and serious; the country can ill afford the crippling effect which such managerial attitudes are liable to have on the pace of innovation and technological advance in industry. . . .

(iii) Strikes and non-union labour markets

J. Clark and Lord Wedderburn of Charlton, "Modern labour law: problems, functions and policies" in LABOUR LAW AND INDUSTRIAL RELATIONS, (R. Lewis, J. Clark and Lord Wedderburn eds., 1982) pp. 162–3

How far the restriction policy could go in the eighties can be measured further by the provisions of the 1982 Employment Act concerning industrial action connected with the refusal of trade unionists to work with non-unionists. The new law removes . . . the immunities from the widest range of activity which might be used to uphold requirements that work must be performed by trade union members (either generally or of a particular union). Such "union-only" terms in commercial contracts become void. Failure to include an employer in a list for tenders or suppliers "on the ground of union membership," or to end a contract (however lawfully in other respects) or to refuse to make a contract for that reason, is unlawful and permits any person "adversely affected" to sue for damages or an injunction. In fact the "union-only" reason need be "only one of the grounds" on which action is taken. Industrial action which attempts to induce someone to take any such action is stripped of the immunities. So too is industrial action where interference with the supply of goods and services (whether or not under contract) is reasonably to be expected and where one of the reasons is that the work is being done by non-unionists.

The restriction policy is here being applied in its most explicit form, in order to free the labour market from trade union "obstruction." Although the government did acknowledge that "it has to be accepted that it is not possible to eradicate 'union-only' practices simply by changes in the law," the implications of these new legal provisions are clear. At a time of large-scale unemployment, falling union membership, and weakened union strength, it will become illegal to refuse to work alongside those who are willing, in their desperation for jobs, to be employed on an employer's unilateral conditions which undercut the rates negotiated by the union (or in construction, for example, "on the lump").

5. ISSUES OF LAW AND POLICY

Here we deal with a number of central issues of contemporary interest which cut across the structure used above to analyse the law of industrial conflict.

(A) Secondary Action

Secondary action is defined in terms of industrial action involving only an employer who "is not a party to the trade dispute" (Employment Act 1980, s.17(2)). The 1980 Act removed the immunities in TULRA, s.13(1) from *some* industrial action involving secondary employers which interferes with their commercial contracts. Not all secondary action is unlawful. It is legitimate when the criteria in the 1980 Act, s.17(3)–(5) are satisfied. In essence, these criteria look to the legal relationship between the (secondary) employer against whom the industrial action is taken and the (primary) employer in dispute. The following case illustrates this.

Marina Shipping Ltd. v. Laughton
[1982] I.C.R. 215; [1982] 1 All E.R. 481
Court of Appeal

A vessel on time charter arrived at Hull and the charterers' agents arranged for port services. However, the ship's crew members complained about conditions of service and the defendant official of the International Transport Workers' Federation (ITF) demanded that the owners of the ship pay the requisite rates and back pay. When the ship-owners declined, the ITF informed affiliated unions whose members, including lock-keepers, refused to do the work necessary to allow the ship to leave port. The owners sought an injunction.

LAWTON L.J.: The problem in this case is this. As I have already stated, had this blacking occurred before August 1, 1980, the plaintiff owners could not have come to the court asking for relief. That was so notwithstanding that, on the facts that I have recounted, they clearly had a cause of action for unlawful interference with their contract with the charterers and with such other persons with whom they had contracts for the transport of goods; and secondly, they had a cause of action, *prima facie*, for interference with their business by the use of unlawful means. The blacking through the lock-keepers kept the vessel in dock and that necessarily meant, under clause 34 of the charter-party, that time was running against them. So that head of claim was as clear as any head of claim could be. It is also reasonably clear, on the facts of this case, that the blacking of the vessel necessarily meant that she could not be going about her ordinary work as a vessel.

For the purposes of this appeal the existence of those causes of action has not been disputed. What has been pointed out and accepted by counsel on both sides has been that, before August 1, 1980, despite the fact that, *prima facie*, the owners had those two causes of action, they were not actionable against either the I.T.F. or its officials, because of the operation of section 13 of the Trade Union and Labour Relations Act 1974, as amended by the Trade Union and Labour Relations (Amendment) Act 1976. The provisions of that section, as amended, are so well known that it is unnecessary, for the purposes of this judgment, to repeat them. But as is also well known, Parliament in 1980 decided that the protection given to trade unions and their officials under section 13 was too wide and, as a consequence, an amendment was made to section 13 of the Acts of 1974 and 1976 by section 17 of the Employment Act 1980.

It is necessary for me now to refer to some of the provisions of section 17. Sub-section (1) is in these terms:

> "Nothing in section 13 of the Act of 1974 shall prevent an act from being actionable in tort on a ground specified in sub-section (1)(a) or (b) of that section in any case where—(a) the contract concerned is not a contract of employment, and (b) one of the facts relied upon for the purposes of establishing liability is that there has been secondary action which is not action satisfying the requirements of sub-sections (3), (4) or (5) below."

That provision opens the gate to proceedings. Sub-section (2) defines what is meant by "secondary action." It is in these terms:

> "For the purposes of this section there is secondary action in relation to a trade dispute when, and only when, a person—(a) induces another to break a contract of employment or interferes or induces another to interfere with its performance, or . . . "

—and then comes another paragraph which, for the purposes of this appeal, is not relevant.

On the face of it, what I.T.F., through its officials, was doing was inducing the lock-keepers to break their contracts of employment with the port authority. That was seemingly unlawful secondary action. But Parliament provided that certain kinds of secondary action should not lead to proceedings against trade unions and their officials. The relevant type of secondary action with which this case is concerned is defined in sub-section (3), which is as follows:

> "Secondary action satisfies the requirements of this sub-section if—(a) the purpose or principal purpose of the secondary action was directly to prevent or disrupt the supply during the dispute of goods or services between an employer who is a party to the dispute and the employer under the contract of employment to which the secondary action relates: and (b) the secondary action (together with any corresponding action relating to other contracts of employment with the same employer) was likely to achieve that purpose."

Sub-section (3)(b) clearly did apply to this case, because the action taken by Mr Shaw, a local official of I.T.F., succeeded in preventing the vessel from leaving Alexandra Dock. If paragraph (a) had stood by itself, for my part, I would have thought that what happened in this case came within that paragraph, because the purpose of the blacking was to deprive the vessel of the usual services provided by the port authority; the persons deprived of those services were the owners of the vessel; and the method of depriving them of the services was by inducing a breach of contract, between the lock-keepers and the port authority.

There is, however, another subsection in section 17, which is the material one for the purposes of this appeal. Sub-section (6) reads:

> "In subsections (3)(a) and (4)(a) above"—(4)(a) is irrelevant for the purposes of this appeal—"(a) references to the supply of goods or services between two persons are references to the supply of goods or services by one to the other in pursuance of a contract between them subsisting at the time of the secondary action . . . "

Under that sub-section, if there had been a contract between the port authority and the owners of the vessel, then, in my judgment, the secondary action would have been lawful within sub-section (3). On the other hand, if, at the material time, there was no such contract between the owners of the vessel and the port authority, then the secondary action would not have been lawful under the provisions of sub-section (3).

In my judgment, everything in this case turns upon this question: on whose behalf did General Freight Limited make such contract (if any) for the provision of the port authority's services? Mr Hoffmann [on behalf of ITF] has submitted that the contract was made on behalf of the owners. Mr Buckley, on behalf of the owners, has said it was not made on their behalf, it was made on behalf of the charterers.

The judge upheld the latter contention. As there was no contract between the ship-owners (the parties to the dispute), and the secondary employer subject to the industrial action (the port authority employing the lock-keepers) the action was unlawful. For similar cases see *Merkur Island Corporation* v. *Laughton* [1983] I.C.R. 490 (H.L.); *Shipping Company Uniform Inc.* v. *ITF* [1985] I.R.L.R. 71 (Q.B.D.). The legal sophistication of the commercial arrangements whereby the charterers, not the owners, made the contracts with the port authorities, defeated the claims to legitimacy of the secondary industrial action. The extent to which secondary action is thus made vulnerable to employers' legal strategies is illustrated by the following case.

Dimbleby & Sons Ltd. v. National Union of Journalists
[1984] 1 All E.R. 117; [1984] I.R.L.R. 67 (C.A.);
affirmed [1984] I.R.L.R. 160; [1984] 1 All E.R. 117 (H.L.)
Court of Appeal

For facts see above p. 565.

GRIFFITHS L.J.: . . . The union is inducing the journalists to break their employment with the plaintiffs, it is taking this action because of its trade dispute with TBF, and the plaintiffs are not a party to that dispute.

There is therefore secondary action within the meaning of [the Employment Act 1980, s.17(2)].

But not all forms of secondary action are outlawed by sub-section (1)(b); the secondary action may fall within the protection of sub-section (3), (4) or (5).

At first the union very understandably claimed that they were protected by sub-section (3) but this arose out of a misunderstanding of the way in which TBF conducted their business. T Bailey Forman Ltd do not print their newspapers on their own premises, they have them printed by an associated company. Until the plaintiffs' lawyers took the point no one regarded this as of any significance; the companies were run by the same people from the same office and with the same ethos—they did not use union labour.

But when one looks closely at sub-section (3) it can be seen to be a matter of vital importance.

In order to attract the protection of sub-section (3) the goods and services, in this case the copy, must be supplied to "an employer who is a party to the dispute." TBF Printers Ltd, to whom the goods and services are supplied, are not a party to the dispute with the NUJ; the union's dispute is with T Bailey Forman Ltd. So one arrives at the end of the journey at what seems a curious result; if T Bailey Forman Ltd had produced their papers on their own presses, the union's action would have been protected but, because the owner of the business chooses to operate through associated companies, the union is unprotected. I see no escape from this conclusion and agree with the judge that s.17 of the 1980 Act has removed the protection which the union would have enjoyed under [T.U.L.R.A., 1974 and T.U.L.R.A. (Amendment) Act 1976].

SIR JOHN DONALDSON M.R.: It may strike some people as odd that the liability of the defendants should depend upon what they may reasonably regard as almost being a matter of chance, namely, whether the directors of the TBF group decided to arrange that one subsidiary should employ journalists and another undertake printing as contrasted with deciding that one subsidiary should undertake both printing and journalism. Whether or not the defendants would be right so to regard the position, that appears without doubt to be the law.

The union's appeal to the House of Lords was dismissed ([1984] 1 All E.R. 403).

In practice, workers in dispute do seek to put pressure on persons having economic relations (whatever their legal form) with the employer in dispute as a means of exerting economic pressure. As the above cases show, however, a narrow legal definition of such economic relations (in terms of direct contracts) is inadequate to cover the varied forms these economic relations can take.

Secondary action tends to be undertaken if (1) primary action taken against the employer in dispute is ineffective or impossible whether due to workers' own collective weaknesses (*eg* difficulties of organising a geographically scattered labour force or shift-workers or part-timers) or to employers' obduracy or strength (*eg* through their ability to transfer work away from a strike-bound plant or by dismissing strikers or by obtaining injunctive relief against strike organisers); and (2) the workers are sympathetic to those in dispute (hence the term "sympathetic action" often used). This sympathy may derive from shared trade union membership, working in the same industry, similar skills, geographical proximity or simply by virtue of class solidarity.

An alternative policy to assessing legitimacy of secondary action by reference to the relations between the employer in dispute and the secondary employer, would be to use the criterion of the relationship between the workers in dispute and those taking sympathetic action. If the secondary action was undertaken by reason of industry/skill/geographical solidarity, it would be legitimate. The cases on secondary action illustrate such links (*Dimbleby and Sons Ltd.* (above pp. 565 and 598), *MacShane* (above p. 556) and *Duport Steels Ltd.* (above p. 561)—common union membership; *Marina Shipping Ltd.* (above p. 596) and other ITF cases—industry solidarity). If the contours of the law followed the lines of motivation of those involved in secondary action, recognising those motives as legitimate in at least some cases, the law would be more acceptable to workers than if its contours follow the relationships of employers, which may cut across trade union principles. The same argument can be applied to secondary picketing: see B. Bercusson, "Labour law and the public interest: a policy approach" in Lord Wedderburn and W. T. Murphy (eds.), *Labour Law and the Community* (1982), p. 179. The law on secondary action needs to be analysed not only in its technical aspects, but also in terms of its policy premises: *cf.* T. Ramm in *Industrial Conflict: A Comparative Legal Survey* (B. Aaron and K. W. Wedderburn eds., 1972) at p. 276:

> "The solutions of . . . different legal systems are based upon separate ideological and sociological approaches. It is, of course, important to know whether industrial actions are essentially considered to be class struggles in which at least all workers act or should act in solidarity, or to be part of collective bargaining and therefore principally restricted to the parties to [the collective] bargaining."

(B) Strikes and Strike Organisers: the Legal Position of Trade Unions and Workers' Representatives

(i) Trade unions' liability

The liability of trade unions for industrial action by their members raises policy questions wholly separate from those concerned with the liability of the strikers themselves. The structural problems of attributing responsibility to trade unions for the acts of their striking members are discussed in the following extract, which analyses the provisions of the Employment Act 1982.

J. Clark and Lord Wedderburn of Charlton, "Modern labour law: problems, functions and policies" in LABOUR LAW AND INDUSTRIAL RELATIONS, (R. Lewis, J. Clark and Lord Wedderburn eds. 1983), pp. 199–206

The legislation of 1982 makes trade unions as such liable in tort in the ordinary courts for the first time since 1906. The question immediately arises, liable for what and for whom? . . .

The Employment Act of 1982 and the preceding [Green Paper on Trade Union Immunities] of 1981 [Cmnd. 8128] forced vicarious liability into the centre of the labour law debates. It could not be otherwise, for it meant reviving the explosive *Taff Vale* judgment of 1901 [*cf. Taff Vale Railway Co.* v *Amalgamated Society of Rail Servants* [1901] A.C. 426] imposing liability on union funds in tort, which was, wrote Lord Asquith, so novel that it was "not surprising that public opinion was unprepared for any such decision."

It has long been a principle of English law that an employer is liable in civil law for the acts of his "employee" done within the "course of the employment," and a principal is liable for the acts of his "agent" done within the scope of his "authority." When this doctrine approached its modern form in the eighteenth century it rested upon the notion that the employer should be liable because the employee must have acted under his "command"; subsequently, it was added, his "implied command." By 1912 the master or "principal" was made similarly liable for his "agent" for acts done within the scope of the agency, even if the latter was not strictly an "employee" and had not even acted for the principal's benefit. Since then the area of the legal doctrine has expanded; but it is still rooted deeply in the concept of a "command" structure—that same "command under the guise of an agreement" which Kahn-Freund perceived behind the contract of employment.

Whatever else it is, a trade union is not based upon a "command" structure of the kind found in an employment relationship—certainly not in respect of shop stewards; and not even in relation to its full-time officers (even if they are appointed and not elected and count in law as "employees" of the union). Indeed the voice of reform, the Donovan Report [Cmnd. 3623], had warned in 1968: "Trade union leaders do exercise discipline from time to time, but they cannot be industry's policemen. They are democratic leaders in organisations in which the seat of power has almost always been close to the members." So when the 1982 Act attempts to impose upon trade unions these "common law doctrines," this policy is bound to require legislation that goes beyond the common law and which is bound to be an assault upon the integrity and the legality of their independent activities.

That much had been learnt in 1972 under the Industrial Relations Act 1971. The intellectual gymnastics of the judges in *Heatons Transport Ltd.* v *TGWU* [1973] A.C. 15 (H.L.) [above p. 420] who tried to decide whether the authority of shop stewards came "up from the bottom" or "down from the top," were essays in the absurdity of trying to apply the common law doctrine to trade unions, as they were bound by the Act to do. Indeed when Lord Wilberforce found that shop stewards "play a dual role"—sometimes acting for "the union," sometimes for their group of members—he thought such an idea so surprising that it would not be "likely to occur to trade unionists." In fact, of course, it is part of the common currency of trade union life. The House of Lords found the TGWU liable in the *Heatons* case because the shop stewards in the docks had acted with an "implied authority" (contained in the rule book, plus the customs and practices and the policies of "the union"). But four years later, [in *General Aviation Services (U.K.) Ltd.* v *TGWU* [1976] I.R.L.R. 225] by a majority, they held the union not liable for parallel industrial action launched by shop stewards at London Airport, in whom they could find no parallel "authority." The 1971 Act required a wider area of vicarious liability to be effective. Indeed Kahn-Freund, who approved of the Law Lords' analysis that authority comes "from the bottom" rather than "the top" (how could it be otherwise in this association governed by custom and practice and direct democracy as much as by rules?), nevertheless concluded: "it is the irony of the *Heatons* case that the same court which diagnosed the identity of unions and shop stewards imposed on 'the union' " (*ie* now the permanent officials of the union) the duty to enforce the court's order "by threatening to withdraw the shop stewards' credentials". . . .

In framing its proposals for legislation in 1982 the government took its cue not only from the principles applied to "common law" vicarious liability but also to those governing contempt of court. For the policy of restriction to work the union must be made to disavow industrial action wherever possible. This is the inexorable logic of the policy when it is applied to the reality of industrial life. For it is notorious that the rule books of trade unions, and even the rules plus the "practices, customs and policies" of unions, will not always make clear whether shop stewards have the "authority" (express, implied, or "ostensible") which attracts the ordinary doctrine of vicarious liability.

. . . First, under the terms of the [Employment Act 1982] the revival of the *Taff Vale* . . . doctrine makes the union generally liable in tort. But it is liable for torts arising from industrial conflict—the so-called "economic torts"—only in respect of acts authorized or endorsed by a list of "responsible persons" who are by statute declared to be the agents of the union. These include the executive committee, any person empowered by the rules to authorize acts of the kind in question, and the President and the General Secretary (whatever the "rules" have to say about their authority). It is significant that under the Act's provisions the term "rules" does not mean only the union rule book; it includes any other written provisions forming part of the "contract" between the members of the union (though it is not at all clear which documents are thereby included).

Secondly, the union is made liable for acts authorized by two other groups of "responsible persons," namely employed officials (who will usually be full-time officers of the union) and any committee to which any such officer "regularly reports." But here the liability does not arise if such persons were prevented by the "rules" from authorizing the kind of acts in question, or if the act done has been repudiated by the executive committee or the President or the General Secretary. However, such repudiation is effective only if it occurs as soon as is reasonably practicable after the act "has come to the knowledge" of the executive committee or either of those two top officers, and if the person purporting to authorize the act is informed of the repudiation without delay and in writing. Above all, the repudiation is not valid if the executive committee or either the President or the General Secretary "has behaved in a manner which is inconsistent with the purported repudiation" after it has been effected. How long after is not made clear. What is clear is that, if it takes the law seriously, a well-advised executive committee will have ready a stock of repudiation forms and will make them available to the President and the General Secretary just in case.

The logic of the 1982 scheme must lead therefore to the repudiation of union officers by their executive, President, or General Secretary. . . . On the one hand the union is responsible for acts of all persons authorized by the written documents which count as the "rules" (though it is far from clear what they are) and cannot repudiate them. So too the acts authorized by the executive committee and its two top officers create liability, whatever the "rules" may say. But those officers and that body can relieve the union of liability for acts of other full-time officials and committees to whom they answer (even if the "rules" do not prevent them from having authority) by taking the necessary steps to effect a repudiation within the carefully defined limits of that term. It is at once obvious that the pressure upon (say) a General Secretary to repudiate industrial action apparently authorized by (say) a regional officer which has been brought to his knowledge by (say) a television announcement or a newspaper reporter will be intense, especially if the claim is already being made that damage is being done to the employer or to the public which is "disastrous."

In this respect what will no doubt be claimed as a virtue of the Act . . . is on closer inspection a significant part of the policy. The union is to be liable for the industrial torts only for acts authorized by the "responsible persons," and that does not include shop stewards unless they are persons "empowered by the rules" to authorize the kind of acts in question. It may be said that the courts will not therefore have thrust upon them the difficulties inherent in interpreting the express or implied authority of stewards, as in the *Heatons* case. But there is little in the new measures to prevent a court from discovering an implied authority in the "rules" which empowers the stewards to authorize the acts in question. Indeed the "rules" are defined to include written provisions other than the rule book, a formulation which might include the cards of accreditation usually issued to stewards by their trade union. In that event a re-run of *Heatons* is a virtual certainty. The difference would seem to be that the court could not rely upon unwritten custom and practice this time to establish (or, more important, to exclude) implied authority. But if a court finds that the shop stewards do have an implied authority within these "rules" so as to make the union liable, the 1982 Act does not permit the executive committee or the two top officers to save the union by repudiating them. The repudiation provisions apply only to full-time officials and committees to which they report.

As was found in the *Heatons* litigation in 1972, concentration upon the question of legal authority tends to pull the stewards and the members at the grass roots away from the formal institutions of the union and its officers. Despite the persistent, perhaps necessary, tension which exists in Britain between shop stewards and full-time officers in trade unions suffused with direct democracy, it has been noted that this relationship has become increasingly close and the assistance of the former may often be crucial to the work of the latter. The special care which the 1982 legislation displays to encircle the full-time official with a legalistic structure of authority within the (new concept of the) "rules," bounded by a statutory procedure for repudiation of his acts, is instructive. Wedges will inevitably be driven between stewards and full-time officials, between both of them and the executive and the two top officers, and between all of them (as "responsible persons") and the membership. The "union" will increasingly appear to the members as "they" not "we." If the law works the trade union will increasingly assume the character of a policing organization.

It is not difficult to imagine the practical effect of such legal principles. The legal approach in practice would obviously be to expect liability in the union, either if shop stewards with general industrial relations functions were involved in industrial action or if a full-time officer were involved and the executive had not repudiated him, especially if the President or the General Secretary had taken any steps to endorse the action. There is nothing to exclude a finding by the courts that there has been "implied" endorsement by the executive or by such an officer. Days of legal argument might be spent (while an interim injunction stopped the strike) on whether there had been behaviour inconsistent with the repudiation before or after the repudiation itself, or whether the alleged repudiation did not contain an under-the-counter nod or wink encouraging the members to believe that it was only a legal formality.

The reality of all this is clear. Proceedings for an interlocutory labour injunction, brought at a day's notice, with the evidence all on affidavit, prepared at leisure by the plaintiff, and not subject to cross-examination—that reality makes it highly improbable that the union could establish to the satisfaction of the court in the (theoretically) interim proceedings that it had negotiated successfully the obscure paths set before it by the statutory rules on "responsible persons." Where, for example, industrial action erupts against the importation of non-unionists—the very battle against "free labour" that the trade union movement was fighting at the time of *Taff Vale* [1901] A.C. 426 (H.L.) at the turn of the century—it will hardly be easy to prove that no persons empowered by the "rules" approved it, or that every full-time local, district, or even national official who has assisted his members in what has become their illegal fight for trade unionism has been fully and properly repudiated. Meanwhile the union's legal advisers will no doubt do their duty by advising the executive committee to tell the stewards to stand aloof and to repudiate the full-time officers unequivocally, in an effort to protect the union's funds from liability for what (they will have been informed by the employer's lawyers) could amount to damages of a disastrous nature.

If the policy of restriction wishes to endorse severe financial penalties on unions by way of damages, it clearly does not wish to authorize their total destruction. An arbitrary limit has therefore been set [by the Employment

Act 1982, s.16] on the amounts that can be awarded as damages in any one set of proceedings, on a scale from £250,000 for a union of 100,000 members or more to £10,000 were there are less than 5,000 members. However, awards of damages and costs cannot be executed against "protected property" [*cf.* the Employment Act 1982, s.17] . . .

In the 1982 scheme then, the ordinary doctrine of vicarious liability has been infiltrated with other concepts, mainly because that doctrine does not easily fit trade unions. Certain agents (or "responsible persons") are appointed by the State, not by the contract in the rule book. The authority of others is to be looked at through a special concept of the "rules." But most important in practice, the need to repudiate acts of officials, the roots of which doctrine lie in the penal laws on contempt of court, is insinuated in part to determine the prior question of civil liability; and each repudiation must satisfy the statutory tests. Meanwhile the Act permits the President and the General Secretary to make the union liable by endorsing acts which lie far beyond their authority under the rules, thereby treating them, along with the executive committee, as the *alter ego* of the union and beyond the democratic control of the members whilst in office. All this is a long way from common law vicarious liability, from the maxim that "no man can become the agent of another person except by the will of that person," from the rule that the plaintiff must assume the burden of proof to establish any authority which he alleges to exist. The rules of procedure are such that in interlocutory proceedings trade union defendants pleading the trade dispute immunities have always been heavily disadvantaged. The 1982 scheme creates new disabilities. It is an attempt to build a "command" structure into the trade union, since without one the notion of vicarious liability will not work. The method by which this is done includes an admixture of quasi-criminal tests which will bring to the fore in such proceedings the issue of "repudiation" of union officials; and to that extent there is a real sense in which trade unions under this legal regime are presumed to be guilty before the litigation begins. As for the age-old problem of trade union "martyrs," the government did recognize in 1981 that "the opportunities to seek martyrdom might be reduced but would not be eliminated."

The infiltration of the law of contempt of court into the law governing liability of trade unions for their members'actions was evident in early cases on the 1982 Act's provisions.

(1) Richard Read (Transport) Ltd. v. National Union of Mineworkers (South Wales Area); (2) George M. Read Ltd. v. National Union of Mineworkers (South Wales Area)

[1985] I.R.L.R. 67
Queen's Bench Division

The plaintiffs had contracts to haul coke from the British Steel Corporation's Port Talbot depot, and their lorries were subjected to mass picketing which caused some of them to turn back to the depot. An interim injunction was granted on April 14, 1984, on prima facie evidence that the conduct of the pickets was authorised or endorsed by the president of the NUM (South Wales Area), which restrained the defendant union from instructing or encouraging its members to interfere with lorries and to withdraw any such instruction or encouragement already given. The South Wales NUM did not appear at the hearing but in a subsequent letter stated it would comply with the injunction. Picketing nonetheless continued and the plaintiffs applied to the Court with respect to the alleged contempt.

PARK J. [Having reviewed the facts which led up to the interim orders of April 17, 1984:] George M. Read's London solicitors received a letter from Mr Emlyn Williams [president of the South Wales NUM] dated 18.4.84. The letter says this:

> "In reply to your telemessage of 17 April, enclosed please find the national instruction sent down to this office, which is self-explanatory.
> It appears to us that the proceedings against the South Wales Area were misconceived. However, our members have been informed of the court decision and to the extent that it applies to the NUM (South Wales Area) we are complying with its terms."

The enclosures consisted of a copy of a letter from Mr Heathfield, the secretary of the National Union of Mineworkers, addressed to "All Regional Co-ordinators," and a copy of a document sent with that letter headed "National Guidelines." The letter to All Regional Co-ordinators contained these paragraphs:

> "The National Co-ordinating Committee of the Transport Unions and the NUM monitoring the present industrial action within the coal mining industry, has requested me to prepare and distribute National Guidelines relative to the conduct of the dispute.
> Please find enclosed copies of these guidelines for your information and I shall be pleased if you would provide copies to the other trade union offices within your region who are responsible for the conduct and co-ordination of industrial action."

The document headed "National Guidelines" contained 10 paragraphs to only three of which I need refer.

> "1. There shall be *no movement of coal or coal products* into or out of the country nor internally within the country unless by prior agreement with the NUM for specific reasons as listed below.
> 8. The National Co-ordinating Committee are further aware of the use of massive numbers of police deployed to restrict the legitimate and traditional right of workers to peaceably picket other workers. The Committee deplore the use of the Police to enforce the Tory Government's Employment Acts of 1980 and 1982. Where such action prevents the proper deployment of a trade union picket, a picket shall be deemed to exist notwithstanding the inability of trade unionists to carry out their normal function.
> 9. Any action to restrain the Trade Union activities of those involved in industrial action by resort to the courts for injunction, sequestration of union assets or damages under the provision of the 1980 and 1982 Employment Acts, shall be treated as an attack upon all of the unions. In the event of one union calling upon the others in the face of such action, all available support required shall be made available."

It is sufficient for me to say that in my judgment these documents provided strong evidence that the conduct of the pickets towards the drivers employed by the two plaintiff companies had been authorised or endorsed by all responsible persons in the defendant's union, including the president, the vice-president and secretary; and further, that any similar conduct in the future would also be authorised or endorsed unless firm steps were taken to withdraw such authority or endorsement. It seems to me that the inference to be drawn from paragraph 9 is that the union was being advised that little or no regard need be paid to court orders, and were such an order to be made, "all available support"—whatever that might mean—from other unions would be forthcoming. . . .

[The judge went on to describe alleged subsequent interference with the plaintiff's lorries involving "NUM Official Pickets":]

So it is plain from this undisputed evidence that the defendant union, by its officials, since the making of the injunction on 17 April, on numerous occasions must have instructed or encouraged the union's members to interfere with the free passage of the vehicles of both plaintiffs into and out of Port Talbot works.

By his letter of 18 April Mr Emlyn Williams had said that he and his members would comply with the terms of the injunction. There is no evidence, however, from which the inference can be drawn that Mr Williams had revoked instructions to his members to interfere with the plaintiff companies' vehicles and to intimidate their drivers.

In these circumstances, by notices of motion dated 19.7.84, both plaintiffs apply to the Court, as I said, for an order that the defendant union's officials be committed to prison for their contempt in failing to comply with the terms of the interim injunctions of 17 April. The notices of motion, together with the affidavits in support, were served on the three officials of the union and on the union on 20 and 21 July. On 24 July the plaintiffs' London solicitors received from solicitors acting for the defendant union and its officials a letter dated 23 July. That letter acknowledged the receipt by the union, and by the three officials, of the notice of motion and the accompanying documents. It contained these paragraphs:

> "We have seen a copy of the letter which the NUM (South Wales Area) wrote to you on 18 April last informing you that although they considered that the court proceedings were misconceived, their members had been informed of the terms of the court order dated 17.4.84 and informing you also that to the extent the order applied to the NUM (South Wales Area) they were complying with its terms. That has been and continues to be the position of the union and the three named officials.
>
> Our clients instruct us that your clients simply do not appreciate that so long as their vehicles travel with a large number of vehicles belonging to other companies in a single convoy, it is extremely difficult to observe the terms of the court order.
>
> We are instructed that your clients' vehicles, for many weeks past, have been travelling in convoys of anything between 50 to 130 vehicles between Port Talbot and Llanwern. There are three or four such trips a day. The convoy travels at speed, the vehicles of the various companies are bunched close together, and in these circumstances it is impossible or impractical for any person on the picket line to identify the lorries which belong to your clients and distinguish them from the remainder of the vehicles in the convoy. If your clients' vehicles were travelling in a group on their own either ahead or at the rear of the convoy and our clients were so advised of the arrangement, the position would be different as they would be clearly recognisable.
>
> We think it right to bring this to your notice as our clients do not see how it can be said that a member of the picket line can knowingly be in breach of the Injunction Order of 17.4.84 unless he knew that the specific

vehicle which would be affected by his conduct, belonged to your clients.

We are without instructions to enter an appearance, but you will no doubt disclose this letter to the Court at the hearing of your motion."

The letter thus appears to suggest that the officials have in fact ceased to instruct or encourage the pickets to interfere with the plaintiff companies' vehicles and to abuse their drivers but that, owing to the failure of the companies in some way to distinguish their vehicles from the vehicles of other hauliers, any breaches of the injunction have been unknowingly committed. It would have been interesting to know what instructions, if any, were given to pickets in relation to the plaintiffs' vehicles. On this the letter is silent. However, neither the union nor any of the officials have put before the Court any evidence to support this unacceptable explanation, even if it be true, of the events which have been happening since 17 April.

The law, so far as it is applicable to the evidence in this case, was succinctly stated by Sir John Donaldson in *Howitt Transport Ltd v Transport and General Workers' Union* [1973] IRLR 25, where he said this:

"Before leaving this matter, the members of the Court would like to say a few general words about court orders, because some of the things that have been said today have led us to suppose that there may be a possible basis for misunderstanding. First, orders of any court must be complied with strictly in accordance with their terms. It is not sufficient, by way of an answer to an allegation that a court order has not been complied with, for the person concerned to say that he 'did his best.' The only exception to that proposition is where the court order itself only orders the person concerned to 'do his best.' But if a court order requires a certain state of affairs to be achieved, the only way in which the order can be complied with is by achieving that state of affairs."

I am satisfied by the evidence so that I feel sure that, between the service of the interim injunction on the defendant union and its officials and 19 July, union officials have been guilty of numerous breaches of the injunctions resulting in serious interference with and disruption of the trade and business of both companies and in serious intimidation of their drivers. On the evidence, the officials appear to be completely indifferent to the consequences of the pickets' violent behaviour, although Mr Williams has apparently admitted to a fear that someone was going to be killed. The officials are therefore in contempt of court.

Express and Star Ltd. v. National Graphical Association (1982)

[1985] I.R.L.R. 455
Queen's Bench Division

The plaintiffs, newspaper publishers and printers, obtained an injunction restraining the defendants, their servants or agents from blacking copy emanating from the plaintiffs. Following the order, the union's General Secretary sent a circular to all branches withdrawing instructions on blacking. The plaintiffs complained about alleged breaches of the injunction. The trial judge having found as fact that certain union officials did persuade union members to break their contracts of employment by refusing to handle copy, went on to consider whether the union was vicariously responsible for the acts of various of its officials at common law.

SKINNER J.: Fundamental to . . . this . . . question is the relationship between the union and its branches. Mr Goudie [counsel for the defendants] submits that the rules of the union show them to be independent of one another. He relies upon the evidence of Professor Gennard that, historically, the branches have had an existence independent of the union and (as is confirmed by Mr Cooper) are very jealous of their independence and autonomy. He argues that the union is a federation of independent units.

The members of the branches (*ie* the members of the union) may think they are independent, but they are not. To regard the union as a federation of separate branches is, in my judgment, a wholly artificial concept, clearly contradicted by the union rules. Rule 5(6) is, in my judgment, conclusive of the matter. It reads as follows:

> "6. For the purpose of efficient administration the Association shall be divided into branches and every member of the Association shall be a member of a branch. The territorial area of each branch and the formation of new branches shall be matters for the discretion of the National Council."

The remainder of the sub-rule is irrelevant.

The NGA comprises all the branches and the branch officials are employed by the NGA. Every branch member is a member of the NGA. Every NGA member is a member of a branch. Without the branches there would be no NGA. Rule 5(6) clearly shows that the organisation of the union in monolithic and not federal.

Mr Goudie further argues that all the officials concerned—Lowe and Harris in the West Midlands and Morgan, Webb and Ellis in North Wales—were acting contrary to the orders of the union expressed through the General Secretary, Mr Dubbins, in Circular 52/85 and the subsequent correspondence and argues that they were acting on their own initiative and without authority. Can I infer, as Mr Lee [counsel for the plaintiffs] invites me to, that the circular was merely a front and an observance of the letter of the injunction only?

I am driven to the conclusion that the officials concerned were acting with the authority of the union. . . .

There were two union officials, one national and one local, paying lip service to the terms of the order but plainly breaking it. It is inconceivable that they would do that unless encouraged to do so from above. It would be totally inconsistent with the essence of trade union action and trade union strength. . . .

. . . it [is] clear to me that this was more than a nod and wink approval by the union. This was the implementation of a policy by the union to bring unlawful financial pressure on the plaintiffs in breach of the order of 1.3.85.

Skinner J. then went on to hold that the union was liable for the officials' breaches of the injunction in accordance with the provisions of the Employment Act 1982, s.15. That section repeals trade unions' immunity in tort contained in TULRA, s.14 and then provides in sub-section (2) that where proceedings in tort as brought against a union in respect of interference with contract and intimidation (as described in TULRA, s.13(1)) or conspiracy "then, for the purpose of determining in those proceedings whether the union is liable in respect of the act in question," the Act must have been authorised or endorsed by a "responsible person" (as subseqently defined). On appeal it was unanimously held that section 15 did not apply to acts in contempt of court but only to the specified torts. The only question, therefore, was whether as a matter of evidence the union by itself, its servants or agents had done the Acts which were forbidden, which the Court of Appeal had no difficulty in establishing to be the case ([1986] I.R.L.R. 222).

Notwithstanding the complex provisions of the Employment Act 1982 relating to trade unions' liability for industrial action by their members, the common law decision in *Heatons Transport Ltd.* v. *TGWU* [1973] A.C. 15 (H.L.) (above p. 220) continues to be important, since the provisions of the Employment Act 1982, s.15 only apply to proceedings in tort on a ground (*sic*) specified in TULRA, s.13(1) or conspiracy.

Thomas v. National Union of Mineworkers (South Wales Area)
[1985] I.R.L.R. 136
Chancery Division

The plaintiffs, working miners, sought injunctions to restrain the organisation of pickets at the gates of collieries at which they worked. These pickets were organised by the defendant union's local lodges (or branches) during the 1984–1985 national miners' strike, which in South Wales was an official strike.

SCOTT J.: The real question concerns the responsibilities of the lodges and through them of the South Wales Union. There is, as I have said, a real question on the evidence as to the responsibility of the lodges and their respective officers for the nature and manner of the colliery gate picketing that is taking place. But none of the lodge officers is a defendant, so unless responsibility can be imposed on the South Wales Union for what is done by the lodge officers the plaintiffs' claim in this action for injunctive relief to control the colliery gate picketing must fail.

The lodges are constituent parts of the South Wales Union. I have already referred to Rule 27 of the Rules. There are many other rules which refer to the lodges and their officers, but, otherwise than in respect of funds, contributions, accounts and other like matters, there is no rule which sets out the powers or duties of the lodges. These powers and duties are obviously and sensibly enough left to practice and custom. The Rules do, however, provide for the objects of the South Wales Union itself. The objects include under sub-paragraph (b) of paragraph 3 this:

"To advance and protect the interests of members in relation to questions of wages, hours, holidays, conditions of employment, safety, compensation and all other questions arising out of and/or in connection with the member's employment or occupation."

This object is plainly wide enough to cover the conduct of an official strike and, in my view, under the Rules the overall responsibility for the conduct of any official strike rests with the union itself. The arrangements for local picketing at collieries and elsewhere may be left to the individual lodges, but in carrying out this function the lodges are, in my judgment, acting on behalf of the South Wales Union for the purpose of enabling the union to pursue one of its own most important objects, namely the advancement of the interests of its members in connection with their employment.

Mr Scrivener [counsel for the defendants] referred me to *Heatons Transport*

(St Helens) Ltd v Transport and General Workers Union [1973] A.C. 15 on this question of the union's vicarious responsibility for its lodges. The point in that case was whether a union against which an injunction had been granted was liable for contempt of court where one of its shop stewards had acted in breach of the order. The relationship between the union and its shop stewards was examined. The House of Lords, reversing the Court of Appeal, held the union liable, not on a vicarious footing for what the shop steward had done, but rather on the ground that the union had failed to take adequate steps to try and ensure that the order was obeyed. But as to the vicarious liability point Lord Wilberforce said this at page 99:

> "In the Court of Appeal Lord Denning M.R. and Roskill L.J. in considering the scope of the shop stewards' scope of authority placed considerable reliance on the fact that the shop stewards were agents rather than servants. But we think that is not an important factor in this case.
>
> No new development is involved in the law relating to the responsibility of a master or principal for the act of a servant or agent. In each case the test to be applied is the same: was the servant or agent acting on behalf of, and within the scope of the authority conferred by, the master or principal?. . . . Usually a servant, as compared with an agent, has a wider authority because his employment is more permanent and he has a larger range of duties as he may have to exercise discretion in dealing with a series of situations as they arise. The agent in an ordinary case is engaged to perform a particular task on a particular occasion and has authority to do whatever is required for that purpose but has no general authority."

The application of the principle there expressed to the facts of the present case leads, in my judgment, to the conclusion that the South Wales Union is responsible on ordinary principles of vicarious liability for what is done by the lodges and their officers in organising colliery gate and other local picketing on behalf of and in the name of the South Wales Union.

(ii) Workers' representatives

As to workers' representatives organising industrial action, a paradox arises from the fact that activities which may give rise to common law tortious liability (inducement, threats) have also received a degree of legitimation through statutory protection of trade union members and officials. A shop steward could be legally protected from dismissal for activities leading to a strike, but liable in tort for those same activities.

Midland Plastics Ltd. v. Till
[1983] I.C.R. 118; [1983] I.R.L.R. 9
Employment Appeal Tribunal

> The works committee at the employer's factory notified management that it was the workers' intention to take industrial action as from 11 a.m. on that day if certain demands were not met. Till and three others were approached by management and asked what action they were going to take. They replied that they were going to abide by the wishes of the workforce or that they would take industrial action but without specifying what it would be. They were immediately dismissed before 11 a.m. They claimed unfair dismissal.

The employer argued that as they were engaged in industrial action, the Industrial Tribunal had no jurisdiction to hear the case under EPCA, s.62. A majority of the Tribunal rejected the employer's argument. He appealed.

BROWNE-WILKINSON J.: The Tribunal posed the question which they had to answer as being whether the threat note and the subsequent statements by the individual employees amounted, as at 9.30 to 10 that morning, to industrial action? The majority of the Tribunal found that there was no industrial action *then*. They point out that at that stage there was no walk-out, no go-slow, no work to rule, no banning of overtime, and no picketing. They then go on to accept the evidence that had been given that there was no decision as to the nature of the industrial action, if any, which was to be taken. They then express the view that the threat letter was ambiguous; it was a statement of intention in that it did not say that industrial action would necessarily occur at 11 a.m. In their view, it was no more than an indication that unless the employers acted properly and responsibly in wage negotiation, certain action might be taken in the future. They then say that in the view of the majority, the workforce were doing no more than carrying out their normal trade union duties in negotiating with management.

The chairman, on the other hand, reached a different view. He regarded the letter, taken with the statements made by the employees, as being a very clear threat of action in the immediate future which was intended to put pressure on the employers. . . .

As it seems to us, Parliament has laid down the stage at which the employer becomes entitled to dismiss without fear of unfair dismissal proceedings by reference to the time at which somebody takes part in a strike or other industrial action. Unless, as the chairman did in this case, it can be said that by threatening to take some action, you are actually taking part in that action, it seems to us that the stage defined by section 62, at which the immunity exists, had not been reached by the time these gentlemen were dismissed. We cannot accept the [minority] view of the chairman [of the Industrial Tribunal] that because the threat to take industrial action imposed pressure on the employers, such threat itself constituted the taking of industrial action. . . .

Unfortunately a substantial factor in industrial relations negotiations in this country is a display of power by one side in response to which the other side either does or does not yield to the wishes of the person displaying such power. The actual taking of industrial action is the last stage and is quite distinct from the stage at which the threat of it is being used as a negotiating weapon. Throughout the period of a strike notice what is bearing upon the employer is the risk to his business. We can see no distinction between what occurred in this case and the ordinary strike notice. In neither case has the matter matured into taking part in industrial action.

The position of the organiser who actually participates in the industrial action is ambivalent. EPA, s. 6(2) instructs ACAS to "provide practical guidance on the circumstances in which a trade union official is to be permitted to take time off under [EPCA, s. 27] in respect of duties connected with industrial action." There is some dispute as to whether the Code of Practice on Time Off, paragraphs 31–33 implements this instruction; and in any case section 27 only provides a right to claim compensation under section 30. The policy of the common law outlawing certain activities of organisers needs to be reconciled with statutory recognition of the positive role played by workers' representatives in industrial conflict.

(C) Legal Treatment of Forms of Industrial Action Other Than Strikes

The question of whether workers who participate in industrial action short of strikes ought to receive different legal treatment from strikers raises serious policy issues. Industrial relations practice does distinguish the strike which involves leaving the workplace—and results in non-payment of wages—and other industrial action, which may involve even a stoppage but does not necessarily lead to forfeiture of wages. In contrast, the law (EPCA, s.62) bars Industrial Tribunal from hearing claims for unfair dismissal arising from a "strike or other industrial action" with consequences that are apparent in the following case.

Power Packing Casemakers Ltd. v. Faust
[1983] I.C.R. 292; [1983] I.R.L.R. 112
Court of Appeal

In support of a wage claim, employees refused to work voluntary overtime and were summarily dismissed. The point at issue was whether the Industrial Tribunal lacked jurisdiction to hear a complaint of unfair dismissal.

STEPHENSON L.J.: It has not been suggested, except from the bench, that [the employees] were taking part in a strike. But were they taking part in the same kind of industrial action as a strike? For that is the question prompted by what I regard as the natural and ordinary meaning of the words in their context. There was, according to the findings of the Industrial Tribunal, a history of disputes about wages after an increase in November 1978. The employers half promised a further increase, but refused to implement the increase. "The men,"—I quote from paragraph 7 of the Industrial Tribunal's decision—"through Mr Cullinan, stated they would take industrial action." According to the Industrial Tribunal, they did. In passages from paragraphs 6 and 9 of their decision, which the Appeal Tribunal quoted, they found, first:

> " . . . that the ban on overtime which was indulged in by the workforce was in connection with wage negotiations. Undoubtedly the workforce used it as a weapon. It was industrial action but it was industrial action which did not amount to a breach of contract and was not therefore misconduct. That is the firm view of the majority of this Tribunal. . . . "

An Industrial Tribunal and the lay members of the Appeal Tribunal may be trusted to recognise industrial action when they see it, and that was how both Tribunals, as well as one appellant and one other witness, described the employees' refusal to work overtime.

Now Mr Jones submitted on the employees' behalf that they ought not to have described it so, because it was not a breach of contract. His point on construction is this: to constitute "industrial action," in the natural meaning of those words, on the part of an employee, there must be action in breach of his contract of employment. If he merely refuses to do something which he is not contractually bound to do, he cannot be taking part in industrial action. I would agree that if he refuses because he has a private commitment to visit a sick friend, or a personal preference for a football match, he is not taking industrial action. But that is not this case. If he refuses because he and others who refuse with him hope to extract an increase of wages out of his employers because their business will be disrupted if they do not grant it, that continued application of pressure is industrial action in the common sense of the words. I do not feel able to say any more about that argument of Mr Jones that that is not the natural meaning of "industrial action." And when the words come at the end of the phrase "taking part in a strike or other industrial action," [in EPCA, s.62] they seem to me to cover even more clearly a refusal used as a bargaining weapon, whether it is a breach of contract or not.

As the Appeal Tribunal said, this may be thought at first sight a somewhat startling result, a gift to employers which requires careful examination. Counsel agree that there is no authority on the question whether industrial action must involve a breach of contract, but that in all reported cases the industrial action considered has in fact involved a breach of contract. . . .

Mr Jones submits that to give these words the extended (and what, contrary to his first submission, I have held to be the natural) meaning which they bear if not confined to breaches of contract, would do injustice and defeat the purpose and object of section 62 and its predecessor in [EPA], namely, to deprive an employee of his right to complain to an Industrial Tribunal of unfair dismissal if, and only if, he has been guilty of misconduct or has broken the terms of his contract. If Mr Jones's gloss—for such, contrary to his submission, it clearly is—upon the language of the section is rejected, unscrupulous employers will be allowed, so he submits, to dismiss unfairly and unjustly those who take legitimate industrial action, without any fear of the circumstances being investigated by the statutory Tribunals, or of having to pay compensation or reinstate those unfairly dismissed employees. . . .

[Counsel for the employers] counters the potential injustice relied on by Mr Jones by submitting that the purpose and object of the section is to avoid courts of law and Tribunals being required to investigate the rights and wrongs, or to adjudicate on the merits, of trade disputes in the context of unfair dismissal applications. He referred us to what Lord Scarman said, in *N.W.L. Ltd v Woods* [1979] I.C.R. 867, 886, about the policy of TULRA, the forerunner of this part of EPCA, to exclude trade disputes from judicial review by the courts and to substitute an advisory, conciliation and arbitration process; and he pointed out that such disputes are often complex and to give the determination of them to Industrial Tribunals would defeat the legislative aim of providing cheap and speedy hearings of unfair dismissal complaints by such Tribunals. These considerations must, he submitted, have outweighed, with the legislature, the potential injustice created by the statutory ban imposed not only on determining complaints by strikers or those engaged in industrial action by section 62(1)(*b*), but imposed by section 62(1)(*a*) on determining complaints by employees locked out by employers at the date of dismissal.

I feel the force of these submissions, but no certainty as to the intention of the legislature in enacting this provision.

In threading my way from section and sub-sections to schedule and paragraphs, and from schedule back to section, I may have lost the way, or the thread, or sight of Parliament's aim and object, even if Parliament itself did not. But of this I have no doubt, that as there is no compelling reason why the words of the provision should not be given their natural and ordinary meaning, and good reason why they should not now be defined as once they were, we ought to give them that meaning and apply them, as the Appeal Tribunal did, to the undisputed facts of the case in favour of the employers. I would accordingly affirm their decision and dismiss this appeal.

The indiscriminate treatment of strikes and other industrial action which results from this controversial judicial interpretation of EPCA, s. 62 contrasts with the common law approach. The common law first of all recognises employees' freedom to act so long as such actions are not in breach of contract. Secondly, it is capable of a measured response to actions in breach of contract. The court can examine the employee's contractual breach in context, and—in the absence of gross misconduct by the employee amounting to a repudiatory breach—may allow the employer only certain (lawful) remedies, excluding dismissal, even though the non-availability at common law of specific relief in respect of employers' wrongful termination of contracts of employment and the common law rules limiting the potential damages recoverable by the employee render these restrictions on employers' freedom of action frequently insubstantial in practice. An illustration is *Laws* v. *London Chronicle (Indicator Newspapers) Ltd.* [1959] 2 All E.R. 285 (C.A.), where an employee was sacked for walking out of an interview with two others contrary to the orders of the managing director. Given the particular circumstances, this was held not to be a breach of contract amounting to a repudiation, and hence the employer's dismissal was wrongful. Parallel developments are found in the case law on unfair dismissal and the Code of Practice on Disciplinary Practice and Procedures in Employment Procedures which distinguish between various forms of employee misconduct and the sanctions and procedures deemed appropriate. It seems anomalous to lump together an all-out strike and a minor form of non-co-operation, when distinctions between various kinds of disobedience are recognised in the case law and employers' works rules. The legal response to different forms of industrial action should be structured.

(D) Positive Rights to Strike and Immunities

The contrast between continental law which provides a *right* to strike and British law which grants an *immunity* from liability raises the issue of whether this difference in legal form is significant. One document highlighted the following among a host of other problems.

Green Paper on *Trade Union Immunities,* Cmnd. 8128 (January 1981), Chap. 4, paras. 342, 345–50, 355–9, 380

Positive Rights in British Labour Law

The common law itself, which provides the guiding precepts for our whole legal system, comprises in fact a series of fundamental rights and duties which, unless abrogated by legislation or sometimes by contract, govern all relationships including those at the workplace. As has been seen, however, these fundamental rights are not sufficient to guarantee the legality of trade union activity. It is because the common law operated to make associations of workers and concerted industrial action unlawful, that a system of immunities from legal processes at common law has developed. Indeed, simply to repeal the immunities and to return to the common law could make it virtually impossible for trade unions to exist and operate lawfully at all. . . .

In short, the introduction of positive rights into the law relating to strikes and industrial action in Great Britain would be an entirely novel step. It would represent a fundamental change from the legal system based on immunities which has developed over the last hundred years. . . .

Main Characteristics of a Positive Right in Relation to Strikes

The following would appear to be the main matters to be resolved in adopting a system of positive rights.

A Right to Strike or a Right to Organise a Strike?

Most legal systems based on positive rights start with a statement of fundamental rights which forms the basis for all subsequent labour law. These basic rights are sometimes contained in the Constitution itself; sometimes they are to be found in statute. They almost all include in one form or another the right of employees to strike though, as will be seen, this right has usually been limited by subsequent legislation.

. . . . the nearest equivalent to the right to strike in Great Britain is the immunities from actions in tort under Sections 13 or 14 of the Trade Union and Labour Relations Acts 1974 and 1976 as restricted by the Employment Act[s] 1980 [and 1982]. These immunities, however, protect the *organisers* of industrial action, whether they be individuals, trade unions or employers' associations. There is no immunity for the employees who actually take the industrial action; if they do so in breach of their contracts of employment they may be sued in contract.

The exact equivalent of the current immunity in a positive rights system would not, therefore, be a right to strike, but a right to organise a strike. This is not a concept which is recognised in other countries; in most countries the right to organise a strike is held to be implicit in the right to strike itself and other protective rights such as the right to take part in trade union activities. If, therefore, there were to be a positive right in relation to industrial action in Great Britain, it is arguable that it should be a right to strike rather than a right to organise a strike.

It would also be necessary to decide whether such a right should override the law of contract and enable those who go on strike in breach of their contracts of employment to do so without fear of being sued by their employers or being dismissed. French law, for example, regards a strike as suspending the individual contract of employment. In contrast, US law states that a strike during the renegotiation of a collective agreement breaks the employment contract and allows the employer to dismiss the strikers and to take on replacement workers. . . .

Definition and Limitation of the Right to Strike

A right to strike or lock-out by itself would leave almost unlimited scope for industrial action. It would therefore be necessary to limit that right in a number of ways.

In most other countries the basic right to strike has been limited by subsequent legislation. These limitations fall into six main categories, five of which have parallels in the existing law in Great Britain. These parallels have been considered in Chapter 3. As part of a change to a positive rights system it would be necessary to determine precisely what restrictions should be placed on the right to strike in respect of:

(*a*) secondary action (Section B of Chapter 3);
(*b*) picketing (Section C);
(*c*) political strikes (Section D);
(*d*) strikes in breach of contract (Section E); and
(*e*) special groups of essential workers (Section H).

The sixth category of limitation of the basic right to strike relates to the legality of industrial action short of a strike. In most systems the right to take action short of a strike (*eg* a work to rule or "go slow") derives from the right to strike itself and is not specified separately. In some countries (such as Sweden) action short of a strike is covered by a formula such as "strike action or other similar measures." In others (*eg* France) it has been specifically declared unlawful. British law recognises no such distinctions: either the contract of employment is broken or it is not [although now see *Power Packing Casemakers v Faust*, above p. 612].

In respect of each of these restrictions it would be necessary to decide whether it should be defined so as precisely to reproduce present British law or whether any changes (*eg* those discussed in Chapter 3) should be made.

This is not an exhaustive list of the decisions and problems which would be involved in limiting a right to strike. But it illustrates the extent to which a positive right to strike would need detailed definition and limitation in legislation. It is important to note that, wherever the law was silent on a particular point, the right to strike would apply and, wherever this created uncertainty in the law, it would be for the courts to decide what the right to strike meant. . . .

It is a matter of judgment how far these benefits could be achieved. But three points seem to emerge from the examination of a positive rights system undertaken in this Chapter. First, though the language of positive rights can be more easily related to industrial reality, this does not necessarily make for a simpler legislative provision. There appears to be no escape from a detailed provision which carefully defines and constrains the application of a right to strike. Secondly, however carefully defined, there would always remain under this and under any other system some uncertainty at the margin about whether a particular action was lawful or not. Thirdly, there is no indication that a positive rights system would be any less open to judicial interpretation than a system of immunities. There would always be difficult cases for the courts to decide. Indeed, an entirely new legal framework would be likely to open up new areas of uncertainty until a corpus of judicial interpretation had developed.

For further discussion of the practical implications of enacting a positive right to strike, see Ewing (1986) 15 I.L.J. 143. The legal technicalities of the "right to strike" should not obscure the more fundamental policy question of whether workers would benefit from a simple translation of immunities into rights. Another way of putting it would be to ask whether workers *want* a right to strike. Strikes are often painful and risky exercises for workers. Other forms of effective pressure, if backed by law, might be more welcome than the enactment of a right to strike. For example, effective grievance procedures or status quo clauses. A right to strike would be infinitely more valuable if it embraced not simply the right to be absent from work without sanction, but imposed other pressures on the employer. The following extract examines some of these.

B. Bercusson, "*One hundred years of conspiracy and protection of property: time for a change*" (1977) 40 M.L.R. 268, 288–90

Outbreaks of violence on picket lines have led to proposals and legislative developments in Canadian jurisdictions which have begun tentatively to recognise the interests of strikers in closing down a plant . . . a problem arose in public employee labour relations laws when "designated" employees, who were prohibited from striking as being essential workers, had to cross the picket lines of their legally striking fellow-workers. Section 102(3)(*a*) and (*b*) of the New Brunswick Public Service Labour Relations Act 1968 attempted to resolve the problem with the following formula:

> "the employer shall not replace the striking employees or fill their positions with any other employee; and
> no employee shall picket, parade or in any manner demonstrate in or near any place of business of the employer."

As Woods [in *Labour Policy in Canada* (2nd ed. 1973), p. 317] points out: "Thus, the employee's right to picket is traded off against the employer's right to replace striking employees. The employee is guaranteed that his job will not be transferred to strike-breakers, and the employer is protected from the potential disobedience of designated employees who might otherwise refuse to report for work if picket lines were established." . . . there is here legal recognition of the function of picketing. However indirectly, the law, in the words of Lindley L.J. in *Lyons v Wilkins* [[1896] 1 Ch. 811, 822]: "confers on trade unions the power of saying to other people, 'You shall not work for those who are desirous of employing you upon such terms as you and they may eventually agree upon'." By going out on strike, workers may lawfully have the power to close a plant down.

Another step in the recognition of workers' interests in closing down a struck plant has come again from New Brunswick, though once more it is specific to a particular group of workers, this time in the construction industry . . .

The intent of the [New Brunswick Industrial Relations Act 1971] seems clear—a strike is to have the effect of closing down a construction site to the extent that none of the strikers may be replaced. No employer may enter into an agreement to replace strikers, and no union may agree to supply such employees. . . .

In addition to these two limited embodiments of the rights of workers effectively to close down a struck plant, there are two other preliminary steps in this direction. The Manitoba Labour Relations Act 1972 enacted a new section [12(1)] which allows an employee to refuse to perform work "which would directly facilitate the operation or business of another employer whose employees within Canada are lawfully on strike or locked out." In addition, section 13(1) prohibits an employer from discharging or otherwise altering the employment status of an employee "who has refused to perform all or any of the duties or responsibilities of an employee who is participating in a legal strike or lockout." The . . . Code of British Columbia . . . prohibits employers from using, or authorising or permitting the use of professional strike breakers (s.3(2)(*e*)). A professional strike breaker is defined as "a person who is not a party involved in a dispute whose primary object, in the opinion of the Board, is to prevent, interfere with, or break up a lawful strike" (s.1(1)).

One move in this direction in the United Kingdom is to be found in the regulations affecting the conduct of employment agencies (S.I. 1976, No. 715), para. 9(11) of which provides:

> "A contractor shall not supply workers to a hirer as direct replacements of employees who are in industrial dispute with that hirer to perform the same duties as those normally performed by those employees."

(E) *Justifiable Strikes*

We have seen how the law differentiates secondary action and political strikes (p. 596 and p. 588 above). The provisions on "responsible" bodies and "repudiation" in the Employment Act, 1982, s.15 attempt to regulate union liability for strikes (see pp. 600 *et seq.* above). In contrast, there is much less regulation of employers, *e.g.*, dismissal cannot be challenged when the worker is taking part in any kind of industrial action (above pp. 570 *et seq.* above). Injunctions are primarily a function of the balance of convenience, with the factors taken into account giving employers' decisive advantages in the court's decision (see p. 577 above).

Yet in practice strikes are often a function of employers' behaviour, not just workers' demands. Strikes may be defensive actions as well as offensive drives *cf. Thomson* v. *Eaton Ltd.* [1976] I.C.R. 336 (above p. 506) and *Power Packing Casemakers* v. *Faust* [1981] I.C.R. 484 (above p. 612). There seems no reason why strikes should not be differentiated so as to take account of employer conduct in their origination, except that this would bring to an end the view that it is not for the courts to assess the merits or demerits of recourse to industrial action. The following extract explored the general justification in Canada for limiting employers' right to dismiss strikers, and sought to apply it to the United Kingdom.

G. England, "*Loss of jobs in strikes: the position in England and Canada compared*" [1976] I.C.L.Q. 583, 587–9, 591, 596

From the worker's viewpoint three considerations make it unfair that he loses his job because he strikes. First, England and Canada have opted for collective bargaining as the chief institution of job regulation and a meaningful "right" to strike is essential for its existence. Of course, the different values prevalent in different societies will determine the limits of the "right" to strike, which must be defined in order to give the system its driving force. Given that a particular strike is a necessary component of the system, it is illogical and unjust to penalise the striker for participating in action that is essential to the functioning of the society in which he finds himself and from which the public derives the benefits. Secondly, the employee may be summarily dismissed for repudiatory breach when the strike is lawful *vis-à-vis* his union. The collectivity is the sum of its members. If the collectivity is acting lawfully, it is illogical and unjust that the individual may be made to act unlawfully. This would not prevent the employer from terminating the striker's employment by notice or wages in lieu, which is one reason why the boundaries of collective legality should not determine individual protection. However, it at least requires that the striker should not be penalised for his *unlawful* act in striking, when the strike is lawful on the collective plane. Thirdly, workers are subject to strong pressures to join strikes, including social ostracism, violence and expulsion from the union, with loss of their jobs in a closed shop situation. The striker has no practical freedom of choice when faced with the dilemma of losing his job through striking or being driven from it by his workmates. By itself this would justify protection in *all* strikes, but this would go too far. However, it weighs in favour of protecting the striker where his action is necessary to the functioning of the system. . . .

The principle of protecting the jobs of strikers in action essential to the functioning of the prevailing system has been recognised in all Canadian common law jurisdictions. Protection is given through statutory provisions which have a dual effect. First, there are declaratory sections conferring "employee" status on strikers and these assure them access to the enforcement sections where none might otherwise exist at common law. Section 1(2) of the Ontario Labour Relations Act 1970 typifies the common approach. It reads:

> "For the purpose of this Act, no person shall be deemed to have ceased to be an employee by reason only of his ceasing to work for his employer as the result of a . . . strike."

Secondly, there are enforcement sections making it an "unfair labour practice" for the employer to discharge employees because of their participation in lawful strikes. Thus, section 58 of the Ontario Act provides:

> "No employer . . . (a) shall refuse to employ or to continue to employ a person . . . because that person . . . was exercising any . . . rights under this Act . . . or . . . (b) shall seek by threat of dismissal . . . to compel an employee . . . to cease to exercise any . . . rights under this Act. . . . "

. . . The boundaries of collective legality are coterminous with action necessary for the functioning of the system. Canadian courts have realised that the common law is too unwieldy a tool to ensure that protection is concentrated in this area. . . .

The lawfulness of strikes at the collective level (in the U.K.) is largely governed by statutory immunities from criminal prosecution and tort action available exclusively within the formula "in contemplation or furtherance of a trade dispute." This formula should represent the ambit of legitimate action accepted by the actors in the system. By extending immunities to virtually all strikes within it, the boundaries of collective lawfulness are made to correspond with the system's ambit of legitimate action. Strikers should not stand to lose their jobs within that ambit.

The author goes on to argue that strikers' jobs should be safeguarded even in various controversial forms of strikes: strikes which are unlawful as regards the union, unofficial strikes (unauthorised by the union), unconstitutional strikes (in breach of agreed procedures), lightning strikes (without due notice), recognition strikes, strikes creating emergencies, demarcation strikes and secondary action.

The anomalous lack of protection for strikers can be illustrated by a parallel from unfair dismissal cases on refusing to accept changes at the workplace. The present position is that if the employee, as an individual, rejects such changes and walks out, he may have a claim for unfair dismissal heard by an Industrial Tribunal. However, if he walks out with *others* similarly resisting the change, this may be characterised as industrial action and the Tribunal is precluded from adjudicating on the merits of the dispute (EPCA, s.62). The argument (as in *Power Packing Casemakers Ltd.* v. *Faust* [1983] I.C.R. 292 (C.A.), above p. 612) that collective disputes are somehow qualitatively different in substance and unsuitable for Tribunal action is belied by this anomaly.

We began this chapter on industrial conflict with a comment as to how the law focussed on workers. Policy considerations dictate an equally close surveillance of employers.

(F) Ballots and Industrial Action

The Trade Union Act 1984, Pt. II now requires a secret ballot before industrial action and a response by a majority of those voting in favour of industrial action in order for a trade union to be protected by the statutory immunities of TULRA, s.13. Section 11 of the 1984 Act lays down detailed provisions as to the rights of union members balloted—not surprising when the principal justification advanced for such ballots is the desire to improve democratic decision-making in trade unions (Green Paper on *Trade Union Immunities*, Cmnd. 8128, (January 1981) para. 246). Yet the stimulus to internal democracy which secret ballots may provide raises at least two policy problems in the context of industrial conflict.

First, there is the problem of the role of employers, outsiders to the internal democratic processes of the union. The 1984 Act, by removing statutory immunity where section 11 ballots are not held, puts it in the hand of the employer (and others) to halt the industrial action. The employer's interest in stopping industrial action is likely to go beyond any desire to further union democracy, and intervention by the employer at a time of internal union dissension or industrial conflict is likely to worsen the prospects both for normal democratic processes and for resolution of the dispute. For while he is enforcing democracy in the union, he is simultaneously engaged in conflict with the union. Alternatives to employer involvement are evident in the cases where non-striking miners successfully used the courts to enforce the union's rule book requiring ballots (below, pp. 655–663).

The second problem is as to the consequences of a favourable ballot. Under the 1984 Act, such a ballot merely allows the TULRA, s.13 immunities to apply: democratic practices avoid union liability to employers and others. Yet in the context of industrial conflict, where members of the union have voted by a majority to take industrial action, the democratic principle would require that the minority adhere to the majority decision. They should be restrained from continuing to work in breach of the majority decision. And if the employer is to have a role in policing internal union democracy in cases of industrial action, he is even better equipped to ensure that a ballot in favour of industrial action is adhered to. Indeed, continuing to offer work where the union member is bound by a majority strike decision comes close to inducement to breach of the contract of membership or interference with it!

The Trade Union Act 1984, Pt. II, can be as much an employer's weapon in industrial conflict as an instrument of trade union democracy. Employers have used the Act to restrain industrial action (1) where there was no possibility of a ballot of workers (*Shipping Company Uniform Inc.* v. *International Transport Workers' Federation* [1985] I.R.L.R. 71 (Q.B.D.)): the I.T.F. is primarily a federation of trade unions so it cannot comply with the requirement of section 11 that all individual members of the union who are called upon to strike shall be entitled to vote; (2) where a majority of the trade union side of a joint negotiating committee had already voted for a strike (*Austin Rover Group Ltd.* v. *AUEW (TASS)* [1985] I.R.L.R. 162 (Q.B.D.)); and (3) where the union had already held a partial ballot which had produced an overwhelming majority in favour of industrial action (*Metropolitan Borough of Solihull* v. *NUT* [1985] I.R.L.R. 211 (Ch.D.)). On the other hand the Court of Appeal has acknowledged industrial realities to the extent of not requiring a fresh ballot where balloted industrial action is temporarily suspended to permit the resumption of negotiations and on the break-down of these negotiations the industrial action is reimposed *cf. Monsanto Plc* v. *Transport and General Workers' Union* [1986] I.R.L.R. 496.

The 1984 Act's provisions typify the way the law neglects collective issues.

CHAPTER 14

THE INTERNAL AFFAIRS OF TRADE UNIONS

In the late 1940s it was possible to assert that the courts were reluctant to intervene in the internal affairs of voluntary associations including trade unions. Most trade unionists are convinced that not only is there no trace of reluctance now, but that the trade union defendant has little chance of success. We are here concerned to contrast judicial attitudes with the practice of the unions so as to discover the extent to which rules of law take account of practice. The issues are analysed under the headings of admission to membership and discipline, trade union government, and union services and benefits.

1. MEMBERSHIP AND DISCIPLINE

(A) Admission

(i) Practice

The fact that until recently the law did not challenge the right of a trade union to admit or reject whom it chose left trade union rule makers free from legal restraint. Nonetheless, there is a remarkable similarity in trade union admission procedures. Most unions merely require employment in the relevant trade as a qualification. The only widespread ground of disqualification, that of ill-health, is presumably dictated by the function of the union as a provider of benefits to unemployed or sick members. In practice, the disqualification is rarely applied.

In the craft unions the pattern is different. As apprenticeship has become less common, it is less commonly required as a condition of full membership. Some, however, seek to secure an intention to continue at the trade by requiring experience in it. Many unions, particularly in areas where the practice is common, do not object to the admission of the self-employed. In such cases, however, it is not uncommon to find a careful line drawn to exclude those who exercise managerial authority bearing on the welfare of union members. Unions in the printing industry, however, do seek to recruit management or even require them under closed shop agreements to join the appropriate union.

Almost all unions have more than one grade of membership. Most clearly define the grades and few allow for alteration of the structure save by the normal, and usually cumbersome procedures for any amendment of the rules. Since it is normal to place admission in the hands of branches, judicial insistence on the rigidity of the contractual terms has given rise to problems for unions. There is often a tendency to adopt pragmatic solutions to individual cases.

Admission procedures are commonly elementary. Most unions require an application to be proposed and seconded, a tradition left over from their nineteenth century history and honoured mostly as a formality. On the other hand, the fact that this is not always the intended result is revealed by some rule books specifically imposing responsibility (even with penalties) on the sponsors. The admission process is normally conducted by a branch committee, or a branch meeting. It is now fairly common to require the decision of the branch to be affirmed at a higher level, at least if the decision is to reject the applicant. There is seldom a provision that the applicant should be able to appear to plead his case, but some unions provide for an appeal against rejection of applications. Occasionally, the applicant is allowed to be present in which case, in practice, he will usually be allowed to say something in support of his application.

As might be expected, the broad outline of admission procedures and qualifications laid down in union rules is habitually followed, but a considerable amount of detailed modification almost certainly takes place in procedure. This is explicable largely because most admission questions pass through the hands of a busy lay branch secretary. It would be surprising if there did not develop tendencies to short-cut routine procedures. The practice revealed in *Bonsor* v. *Musicians' Union* [1956] A.C. 104 of routine expulsions from membership of members in arrears with their payment of subscriptions for more than 26 weeks being handled by the branch secretary instead of by the branch committee, as required by the union's rules, is equally likely to appear sensible when applied to admission. Departures from rules in order to modify qualifications will not normally be handled so informally. In *Kirkham* v. *NATSOPA* [1981] I.R.L.R. 244, the large Manchester branch of a union whose branches tend to be relatively powerful within the organisation had, indeed, devised its own standing sub-categories of membership. This is likely to be a rare occurrence. Whether centrally or at district level, however, an organisation used to collective bargaining is likely to be tempted to reach the sort of compromise arrived at in *Martin* v. *Scottish TGWU* [1952] 1 All E.R. 691: the creation of "temporary members" (see p. 628 below).

Finally, the potential for conflict when a trade union admits to membership a member or former member of another union is obvious. At the annual TUC Congress in Bridlington, Yorkshire in 1939, rules were laid down for trade unions' admission procedures so as to avoid this problem. The two principal provisions of the "Bridlington Agreement" so far as membership admission is concerned are in their current wording as follows:

TUC Dispute Principles and Procedures

Preface

The following Principles constitute a code of conduct accepted as morally binding by affiliated organisations. They are not intended by such organisations or by the Trades Union Congress to be a legally enforceable contract. The Principles include the main text and the Notes and both are to be read together as having equal status and validity.

. . .

Principle 2

No one who is or has recently been a member of any affiliated union should be accepted into membership in another without enquiry of his present or former union. The present or former union shall be under an obligation to reply within 21 days of the enquiry, stating:

(a) Whether the applicant has tendered his resignation;
(b) Whether he is clear on the books;
(c) Whether he is under discipline or penalty;
(d) Whether there are any other reasons why the applicant should not be accepted.

If the present or former union objects to the transfer, and the enquiring union considers the objection to be unreasonable, the enquiring union shall not accept the applicant into membership but shall maintain the status quo with regard to membership. If the problem cannot be mutually resolved it should be referred to the TUC for adjudication

A union should not accept an applicant into membership if no reply has been received 21 days after the enquiry, but in such circumstances a union may write again to the present or former union, sending a copy of the letter to the head office of the union if the correspondence is with a branch, stating that if no reply is received within a further 14 days they intend to accept the applicant into membership. Where the union to which application is being made is dealing directly with the head office of the present or former union, a copy of this communication may be sent to the TUC.

Notes on Principle 2

(a) Where unions are in frequent contact, they should advise one another of the appropriate level at which membership enquiries should be made.

(b) No member should be allowed to escape his financial obligations by leaving one union while in arrears and by joining another.

(c) The reference to "recently" in the first sentence of Principle 2 shall normally be understood to apply to applicants who have contributed to an affiliated union during the preceding 52 weeks. Unions should however appreciate that this is intended merely as a guide and much difficulty will be avoided if enquiries are made in all cases where previous trade union membership is known.

Principle 4

A union shall not accept a member of another union where that union objects to the transfer (see Principle 2 above), or where enquiry shows that the member is:

(a) under discipline;
(b) engaged in a trade dispute;
(c) in arrears with contributions.

Notes on Principle 4

(a) It should be a general understanding that both national and local officials of trade unions should refrain from speaking or acting adversely to the interests of any other union during any period in which the members of the latter union are participating in a trade dispute. Much trouble could be avoided if unions about to participate in a trade dispute would take care to inform other unions whose members would be likely to be affected thereby. (See Congress Rule 11.)

(b) With regard to the question of arrears in (c) above, a number of affiliated unions have a rule or rules excluding members who have been in arrears for a specified period of time. However, although a union with such a rule regards an individual in such arrears as being no longer a member entitled to participate in the work of the union, it does not necessarily mean that the union regards the individual as being automatically free to join another organisation. Any union which considers that another union has unreasonably objected to a transfer on the grounds of arrears (or for any other reason) should not therefore accept an individual into membership, but should refer the matter to the TUC for adjudication.

As stated by Foster J. in *Rothwell* v. *APEX* [1976] I.C.R. 211:

> "In order that unions affiliated to the T.U.C. should be under an obligation to carry into effect the disciplinary decisions of the T.U.C. a model rule was devised which has found its way into the rules of most of the affiliated unions though not all. APEX has it in its rule book as rule 14 and it is headed 'Decisions of the T.U.C. disputes committee'. . . ."

In *Cheall* v. *APEX* [1983] I.R.L.R. 215, the House of Lords upheld APEX's expulsion of a member in accordance with this rule, where the member had been admitted into membership in violation of the Bridlington Agreement (*cf.* where there is no such express power of expulsion, *Spring* v. *NASD* [1956] 1 W.L.R. 585, below p. 637).

(ii) Legal policy

Traditionally, a trade union at law is treated as free to accept or reject applications to enter into the contract of membership (though legislation has restricted this freedom, as in the Race Relations Act 1976, s.11; Employment Act 1980, s.4). In reality, trade unions exercise an influence on the lives of working people, and to be a member, to participate in formulating and applying union policy and to benefit from union influence is vital to workers. The closed shop is only the extreme case of the importance of union membership to employment issues. The conflicting policies are, on the one hand, maintaining voluntarist associations based on contractual freedom, and on the other, recognising the social significance of membership. If an association can be regarded as in a position where its contractual freedom should be limited by overriding considerations, the temptation for judges is to invoke public policy.

Nagle v. Feilden
[1966] 2 Q.B. 633; [1966] 1 All E.R. 689
Court of Appeal

> Mrs Nagle trained racehorses. She was, however, refused a licence to do so by the Jockey Club in pursuance of its policy of never giving such a licence to a woman. In order for her horses to be allowed to run on courses controlled by the Jockey Club the licence to train was given to her "head lad." Mrs Nagle objected to this situation and sought an injunction to compel the Jockey Club to issue her with a licence. Her initial contention depended on the argument that a contract arose when she applied for a licence and it was struck out. She appealed against the decision, and the Court of Appeal in considering that interim matter was concerned simply to decide whether she had an arguable case.

LORD DENNING M.R.: Now, I quite agree that if we were here considering a social club, it would be necessary for the plaintiff to show a contract. If a man applies to join a social club and is blackballed, he has no course of action: because the members have made no contract with him. They can do as they like. They can admit or refuse him, as they please; but we are not considering a social club. We are considering an association which exercises a virtual monopoly in an important field of human activity. By refusing or withdrawing a licence, the stewards can put a man out of business. This is a great power. If it is abused, can the courts give redress? That is the question.

It was urged before us that the members of a trading or professional association were like a social club. They had, it was said, an unrestricted power to admit, or refuse to admit, any person whom they choose: and that this was established by a case in 1825 concerning the Inns of Court. In *R* v *Lincoln's Inn Benchers* (1825) 4 B&C 855, Bayley J, said: "They make their own rules as to the admission of members; and even if they act capriciously upon the subject, this court can give no remedy in such a case; because in fact there has been no violation of a right."

I venture to question this statement, notwithstanding the eminence of the judge from whom it fell. The common law of England has for centuries recognised that a man has a right to work at his trade or profession without being unjustly excluded from it. He is not to be shut out from it at the whim of those having the governance of it. If they make a rule which enables them to reject his application arbitrarily or capriciously, not reasonably, that rule is bad. It is against public policy. The courts will not give effect to it. Such was held in the seventeenth century in the celebrated *Ipswich Tailors' Case* (1614) 11 Co Rep 53, where a rule was made that no person should exercise the trade of a tailor in Ipswich unless he was admitted by them to be a sufficient workman. Lord Coke L.C.J., held that the rule was bad, because it was 'against the liberty and freedom of th subject.' If, however, the rule is reasonable, the courts will not interfere. In the eighteeenth century, the company of surgeons required as a qualification for an apprentice an understanding of the Latin tongue. The governors rejected an apprentice because on examination they found him to be totally ignorant of Latin. Lord Mansfield L.C.J. declined to interfere with their decision (see *R* v *Surgeons' Co. (Master)* (1759) 2 Burr 892).

There are not many modern cases on the subject, but they support the principle which I have stated. In *Weinberger* v *Inglis* [1919] AC 606, the rules of the Stock Exchange gave to the committee an absolute discretion to admit such persons as they "shall think proper." The House of Lords were not referred to the old cases but to the cases where directors are empowered in their discretion to refuse a transfer of shares, such as *Re Gresham Life Assurance Society, ex parte Penney* (1872) 8 Ch App 446. The House were disposed to accept this analogy and to hold that, if the committee of the Stock Exchange were to act arbitrarily or capriciously, the courts could set aside their decision—see what Lord Buckmaster, Lord Atkinson and Lord Wrenbury said. Then again in *Faramus* v *Film Artistes' Association* [1964] A.C. 925, a trade union, which kept a "closed shop," made a rule forbidding entry to any person who had been convicted of a criminal offence. Lord Pearce said:

> "Since the respondent union have a monopoly, exclusion from membership prevents a man from earning his living in this particular profession. An absolute rule that so prevents any person who may have suffered a trivial conviction many years before is in restraint of trade and unreasonable."

We cannot, of course, decide the matter today. All I say is that there is sufficient foundation for the principle for the case to go to trial. We live in days when many trading or professional associations operate "closed shops." No person can work at his trade or profession except by their permission. They can deprive him of his livelihood. When a man is wrongly rejected or ousted by one of these associations, has he no remedy? I think that he may well have, even though he can show no contract. The courts have power to grant him a declaration that his rejection and ouster was invalid and an injunction requiring the association to rectify their error. He may not be able to get damages unless he can show a contract or a tort; but he may get a declaration and injunction. . . .

All through the centuries courts have given themselves jurisdiction by means of fictions; but we are mature enough, I hope, to do away with them. The true ground of jurisdiction in all these cases is a man's right to work. I have said before, and I repeat it now, that a man's right to work at his trade or profession is just as important to him as, perhaps more important, than his rights of property. Just as the courts will intervene to protect his rights of property, so they will also intervene to protect his right to work.

In the present case Mrs Nagle does not seek admission as a member of the Jockey Club. She only applies for a trainer's licence; but this makes no difference. If she is to carry on her trade without stooping to subterfuge, she has to have a licence. When an association, who have the governance of a trade, take it on themselves to license persons to take part in it, then it is at least arguable that they are not at liberty to withdraw a man's licence—and thus put him out of business—without hearing him. Nor can they refuse a man a licence—and thus prevent him from carrying on his business—in their uncontrolled discretion. If they reject him arbitrarily or capriciously, there is ground for thinking that the courts can intervene. I know that there are statements to the contrary in some of the cases. We were referred to one by myself in *Russell v Duke of Norfolk* [1949] 1 All ER 109, at 119; but that was seventeen years ago. The right to work has become far better recognised since that time. So has the jurisdiction of the courts to control licensing authorities. When those authorities exercise a predominant power over the exercise of a trade or profession, the courts may have jurisdiction to see that this power is not abused.

The significance for trade union law of this suggestion (it was no more) is that like the Jockey Club, a trade union is a voluntary association which, unless specially protected by statute, might be treated in the same way.

This development went no further for a while, partly because in the case of trade unions, it was temporarily overtaken by the provision of a statutory right to complain of arbitrary exclusion (Industrial Relations Act 1971, s.65(2)). This provision survived in TULRA 1974, s.5(1) and was finally repealed by the Trade Union and Labour Relations (Amendment) Act 1976, s.1. Little use was made of the statutory right.

The statutory right to complain of unreasonable refusal of an application for membership of a trade union has now been revived, but only in relation to any applicant who is, or is seeking to be, in the employment of an employer with respect to which a union membership agreement (*ie* a closed shop) applies (Employment Act 1980, s.4).

The normal reluctance of the courts to intervene in admission processes by the application of legal doctrines not designed with such practices in mind may be justified. The adoption of a rigid approach to the contract of membership contrasts with the flexible and discretionary attitude usually adopted by unions towards membership.

Martin v. Scottish Transport and General Workers Union
[1952] 1 All E.R. 691
House of Lords

The plaintiff had been directed to work in the docks at Edinburgh at the beginning of the Second World War. The appropriate trade union branch was reluctant to admit such workers to membership but eventually agreed to classify them as "temporary" members. Eight or nine years later when work at the docks declined the union agreed to such "temporary" members being laid off before ordinary members. The plaintiff argued that since the rule book made no provision for temporary membership, he must be considered to have been admitted as a full member.

LORD NORMAND: Any rule governing the terms on which membership is granted must apply to all admissions until it is altered by the method prescribed by the rules themselves, and I, therefore, reject the argument put forward for the respondents that *esto* the rules in August, 1940, provided only for the admission of members without any limit on the duration of their membership, some modification of the rule so as to provide for temporary membership could be brought about by an implied ratification of admissions purporting to have been made on a temporary basis. Now, rule 15 contains this:

> "Every person upon being admitted a member of the union shall be deemed to agree to abide by the rules of the union in every respect, and be liable to forfeit membership at any time if in the opinion of the general executive council such person has failed to abide by the rules."

There is no rule providing for the admission of members on a temporary basis or for forfeiture for any reason except that prescribed by rule 15. Rule 20 provides:

> "No new rule shall be made, nor shall any rule herein contained or hereafter to be made (*sic*), or amended, or rescinded except in accordance with a resolution duly passed at the annual meeting of the general executive council."

In spite of imperfections of draftng, the sense of this rule is clear. It is common ground that rule 15 was in force in August, 1940, and that it was not thereafter altered by any resolution passed at the annual meeting of the general executive council. Therefore, the officials of the branch or of the union had no authority in August, 1940, or later, to admit the appellant to membership subject to a limitation of time, and when they purported to do so they acted in excess of their powers and their act had and has no validity. I agree with the view expressed by Lord Carmont that there was an attempt to create a class of member outside the provisions of the rules and that it necessarily fails. The conclusion that the appellant never was a member may be inconvenient to both parties, because it may be difficult to work out the equitable adjustment of rights, but that is not a consideration which can affect the decision of the present appeal. I would dismiss the appeal with costs.

Faramus v. Film Artistes Association
[1964] A.C. 925; [1964] 1 All E.R. 25
House of Lords

Faramus applied in 1950 to become a member of the respondent union. He was accepted as a member and, indeed, was later elected to its executive committee. The union, however, had a rule that "no person who has been convicted in a court of law of a criminal offence . . . shall be eligible for, or attain membership of, the Associaton." Faramus had, when 17 years old, been convicted and sentenced to three months imprisonment in Jersey for taking and driving away motor cars without their owners' consent.

LORD EVERSHED: My lords, with all respect to the opposite view adopted by the Master of the Rolls, [Lord Denning,] I cannot for my part entertain any doubt as to the meaning and effect of rule 4 (2), as could not UPJOHN, L.J. and DIPLOCK, L.J., particularly in the context in which it is found and having regard also to the heading to the rule and to the terms of the first sub-rule. I repeat the formula in the relevant sub-rule (2):

> "No person who has been convicted in a court of law of a criminal offence . . . shall be eligible for, . . . membership of the Association."

In my opinion, these words in their context can only mean, on their fair reading, that a person who has been so convicted is disqualified altogether from becoming a member. . . .

Like the majority of the Court of Appeal, I am unable to see any ground on which it could be seriously submitted that the rule could be disregarded by the court because of the vagueness of its terms or because its application in certain circumstances might not only be difficult of ascertainment but productive of embarrassment in the conduct of the respondent union's business. Nor can it, as I think, be suggested that to a rule of this kind there can be applied any principle of natural justice. The case is in no sense analogous to the case of rules applicable to someone whose contract of membership is being terminated, where it may well be that for their validity the rules must make provision to enable such a person at any rate to have a proper opportunity to put his case. In the circumstances, therefore, the only ground on which the appellant can, as I think, succeed is if he were able to establish that the terms of this rule operated as an unreasonable restraint of trade and that the rule was not saved by s.3 of the Trade Union Act, 1871 [now incorporated into TULRA, s.2(5)].

In these decisions, therefore, the courts regard substantive rules as depriving the union of power to admit.

Application of traditional principles of law has therefore either driven the courts to deny any substantial right to the rejected applicant or to consider a remedy based on public policy, regarding the social power of the association in question as placing it in a class different from that of the normal voluntary association. One recent decision offers an interesting new approach, albeit one which displays all the limitations of judicial perceptions of social reality.

McInnes v. Onslow Fane
[1978] 3 All E.R. 211
Chancery Division

> The plaintiff applied to the British Boxing Board of Control for a licence as a boxing manager. His application was rejected without a hearing or reasons. He sought a declaration that the refusal was unlawful as being unfair and contrary to natural justice.

MEGARRY V.-C.: Where the court is entitled to intervene, I think it must be considered what type of decision is in question. I do not suggest that there is any clear or exhaustive classification; but I think that at least three categories may be discerned. First, there are what may be called the forfeiture cases. In these, there is a decision which takes away some existing right or position, as where a member of an organisation is expelled or a licence is revoked. Second, at the other extreme there are what may be called the application cases. These are cases where the decision merely refuses to grant the applicant the right or position that he seeks, such as membership of the organisation, or a licence to do certain acts. Third, there is an intermediate category, which may be called the expectation cases, which differ from the application cases only in that the applicant has some legitimate expectation from what has already happened that his application will be granted. This head includes cases where an existing licence-holder applies for a renewal of his licence, or a person already elected or appointed to some position seeks confirmation from some confirming authority: see, for instance, *Weinberger v Inglis* [1919] A.C. 606; *Breen v Amalgamated Engineering Union* [1971] 2 Q.B. 175 [below p. 647]; and see *Schmidt v Secretary of State for Home Affairs* [1969] 2 Ch. 149; *R v Barnsley Metropolitan Borough Council, ex parte Hook* [1976] 1 W.L.R. 1052.

It seems plain that there is a substantial distinction between the forfeiture cases and the application cases. In the forfeiture cases, there is a threat to take something away for some reason; and in such cases, the right to an unbiased tribunal, the right to notice of the charges and the right to be heard in answer to the charges (which, in *Ridge v Baldwin* [1964] A.C. 40 at 132, Lord Hodson said were three features of natural justice which stood out) are plainly apt. In the application cases, on the other hand, nothing is being taken away, and in all normal circumstances there are no charges, and so no requirement of an opportunity of being heard in answer to the charges. Instead, there is the far wider and less defined question of the general suitability of the applicant for membership or a licence. The distinction is well-recognised, for in general it is clear that the courts will require natural justice to be observed for expulsion from a social club, but not on an application for admission to it. The intermediate category, that of the expectation cases, may at least in some respects be regarded as being more akin to the forfeiture cases than the application cases; for although in form there is no forfeiture but merely an attempt at acquisition that fails, the legitimate expectation of a renewal of the licence or confirmation of the membership is one which raises the question of what it is that has happened to make the applicant unsuitable for the membership or licence for which he was previously thought suitable . . . Counsel for the plaintiff disclaimed any contention that the Board must give reasons for their decision which would enable the plaintiff to apply to the court to set it aside. Yet if the procedure for refusing an application requires the Board to notify the plaintiff of the gist of their reasons for refusing a licence, or proposing to refuse it, I do not see why he should not found an application to the courts on those reasons; and when a refusal is made without giving the gist of the reasons, then a second application in which the gist of the reasons is required to be given may then provide a ready indication of the reasons why the first application failed, and so on. In this way the Board would be unable to refuse an application without supplying the applicant with material which would assist him in engaging the board in litigation.

In response to a question from the bench, counsel for the plaintiff said that the same procedure, with the same consequences, would apply to someone who sought to join a trade union and was rejected; and doubtless the position would be the same for any trade association or sporting body where membership or the grant of a licence was requisite for pursuing some gainful occupation or career. In all cases, a refusal would entail the two-stage procedure and the communication of the gist of the objections to the applicant, with the opportunities of resort to the courts that this would give. The way would lie open for persistent applicants and persistent litigants, with all that this entails. When I asked counsel for the plaintiff whether this procedure would not also apply to the Lord Chancellor when he refuses an application for silk, he said that it would not, since silk was not a requisite for practice at the Bar, but only an extra, as it were, authorising work at a higher level. I did not find that answer convincing; and in any case the procedure would appear to apply to anyone seeking to join an Inn of Court. Yet in a passage in *Nagle v Feilden* [1966] 1 All E.R. 689, 699 that I have already mentioned, Salmon L.J. took admission to an Inn of Court as an example of a case in which no reasons for the rejection of an applicant need be given.

However, the burdens of the procedure do not conclude the matter. If the requirement to act fairly brings these consequences in its train, then the substantial and time-consuming changes that they entail must be made. The most that can be said is that the more burdensome and far-reaching the consequences, the more carefully must be scrutinised the rule that is said to produce them. What, then, does the requirement to act fairly mean in this type of case?

As I have said, counsel accepted that the board were under a duty to reach an honest conclusion without bias and not in pursuance of any capricious policy. That, I think, is right: and if the plaintiff showed that any of these requirements had not been complied with, I think the court would intervene . . .

I find some assistance in *Breen v Amalgamated Engineering Union* [see below p. 647 below] . . .

Now of course that case is not this case. In one sense it is *a fortiori* the Board's contentions in this case; for this, of course, is a mere application case, and not a legitimate expectation case. In *Breen's* case, the plaintiff, having been elected by his fellow members, had a legitimate expectation of confirmation by the committee. If even in a legitimate expectation case there is no general right to notice of what is against the applicant, and the chance of meeting it, in a mere application case there could hardly be a greater right. On the other hand, *Breen's* case concerned not the "right to work" but a right to hold office as a shop steward. However, the loss of such an office is no triviality in the trade union world. It is something, as Lord Denning M.R. said in his dissent (on which counsel for the plaintiff relied in several respects), which "strikes deep, and not the less so because it may not strike at the pocket." Furthermore, as I have indicated, I am not at all sure how far the "right to work" can be said to include the "right" to begin a new career of the worker's choice, as distinct from continuing with an existing mode of employment. On the whole, I think that *Breen's* case provides at least a useful parallel to important factors in the case before me, and probably something more.

Looking at the case as a whole, in my judgment there is no obligation on the Board to give the plaintiff even the gist of the reasons why they refused his application, or proposed to do so. This is not a case in which there has been any suggestion of the Board considering any alleged dishonesty or morally culpable conduct of the plaintiff. A man free from any moral blemish may nevertheless be wholly unsuitable for a particular type of work. The refusal of the plaintiff's application by no means necessarily puts any slur on his character, nor does it deprive him of any statutory right. There is no mere narrow issue as to his character, but the wide and general issue whether it is right to grant this licence to this applicant. In such circumstances, in the absence of anything to suggest that the Board have been affected by dishonesty or bias or caprice, or that there is any other impropriety, I think that the Board are fully entitled to give no reasons for their decision, and to decide the application without any preliminary indication to the plaintiff of those reasons. The Board are the best judges of the desirability of granting the licence, and in the absence of any impropriety the court ought not to interfere.

There is a more general consideration. I think that the courts must be slow to allow any implied obligation to be fair to be used as a means of bringing before the courts for review honest decisions of bodies exercising jurisdiction over sporting and other activities which those bodies are far better fitted to judge than the courts. This is so even where those bodies are concerned with the means of livelihood of those who take part in those activities. The concepts of natural justice and the duty to be fair must not be allowed to discredit themselves by making unreasonable requirements and imposing undue burdens. Bodies such as the Board which promote a public interest by seeking to maintain high standards in a field of activity which otherwise might easily become degraded and corrupt ought not to be hampered in their work without good cause. Such bodies should not be tempted or coerced into granting licences that otherwise they would refuse by reason of the courts having imposed on them a procedure for refusal which facilitates litigation against them. As Lord Denning M.R. said in *Re Pergamon Press Ltd.* [1971] Ch. 388, 400 "No one likes to have an action brought against him, however unfounded." The individual must indeed be protected against impropriety; but any claim of his for anything more must be balanced against what the public interest requires.

The statutory provisions of the Employment Act 1980, s.4, allowing complaints of unreasonable exclusion, have overcome the obstacle to a substantive right of admission, and thereby confer on the courts considerable freedom in interpreting what is "reasonable" exclusion, as the following case illustrates.

Kirkham v. National Society of Operative Printers, Graphical and Media Personnel

[1981] I.R.L.R. 244 (IT); [1983] I.C.R. 241; [1983] I.R.L.R. 70
Industrial Tribunal and Employment Appeal Tribunal

In 1968 the applicant took voluntary redundancy and was given an "honourable withdrawal" from the union, discharging him from further liability to pay subscriptions to the union. In 1970 the Manchester branch of the union divided its "casual work" class of member into three categories, the third of which was to apply to anyone in the position of the applicant. Members assigned to that category were at a considerable disadvantage in seeking employment. In 1974 the applicant wished to re-enter the industry and applied to rejoin the union. Unknown to him he was assigned to the third category of casual workers. He complained to the Industrial Tribunal under the Employment Act 1980, s.4.

MANCHESTER INDUSTRIAL TRIBUNAL (chairman: H. DAY): A man has the right to be able to work and to freely compete in a particular field and an employer and employee have the right to choose each [other] in the employment field. We find that to debar a man from the regular category or the opportunity of being in the regular category, as the respondents have done, is to make it impossible for the applicant to obtain work on a regular basis, to become a member of a chapel, or to have the advantages of that work in the newsprint industry in Manchester. One of the objects of the union is stated to be "our aim is to maintain and improve the status of the members we represent in all spheres of our organisation." Mr Kirkham's aim has been to improve his status within the field of his employment, a field in which he has worked for so many years, but has been prevented from so doing by a branch resolution for which no authority or rule has been produced indicating that they have the power to make such a rule. Again, there is no evidence of any authority enabling the Manchester branch to sub-divide the casual category into the three sub-sections and/or to prevent the applicant moving into a section to enable him to work full-time.

[The E.A.T. allowed the union's appeal on other grounds but upheld the Tribunal's finding on reasonableness:]

BROWNE-WILKINSON J.: In favour of the reasonableness of the system whereby those who had accepted redundancy were placed in category 3, we would accept that in general it was reasonable for a union involved in a contracting industry to give preference in the allocation of the available jobs to those who had stayed in the industry in preference to those who had received capital payments for leaving it. But if this policy is to be adopted reasonably, it seems to two of us that the union should, in the normal case, inform its members before they leave the industry and take their severance payment that this is the policy of the union. We are all agreed that, even if the policy had been changed while an employee was out of the industry, he should be informed before he rejoins the union that he is rejoining a system that will impose a de facto disadvantage on him. The applicant left the industry without knowing that he was thereby forfeiting the chance of ever again obtaining regular employment in the industry and was readmitted to membership in 1974 apparently on the same terms as he had left but without being told that he would not be able to obtain regular employment.

In *National Graphical Association* v. *Howard* [1983] I.R.L.R. 445 the Code of Practice on the Closed Shop (para. 49) was referred to by the E.A.T. in holding that "the state of unemployment or otherwise amongst members of the union in a particular industry can be taken into account as a factor in deciding whether or not a union's refusal to admit further applicants is, or is not, reasonable" (*per* Browne-Wilkinson J., at p. 448); *cf.* also *Saunders* v. *Bakers Food and Allied Workers Union* [1986] I.R.L.R. 16.

(B) Resignation and Repudiation

A member has a common law right to resign from a trade union unless the rules provide to the contrary (*Finch* v. *Oake* [1896] 1 Ch. 409). The Industrial Relations Act 1971 for the first time prohibited rules excluding resignation. Currently, TULRA, s.7, as amended, achieves much the same effect by implying into every contract of membership a term conferring on a member, giving reasonable notice and complying with any reasonable conditions, the right to terminate his membership. The common law on this occasion reveals a greater appreciation of the actual position than does statute.

By far the most common method of resignation occurs when a member ceases to pay his dues.

Re The Sick and Funeral Society of St. John's Sunday School, Golcar,

[1973] Ch. 51; [1972] 2 All E.R. 439
Chancery Division

A society had been established in 1866 to provide sick and death benefits for the teachers and scholars of a Sunday school. In 1966 the members came to the conclusion that it had outlived its usefulness and resolved that it be wound up. In 1967 four members who had ceased to pay subscriptions in 1963 but had never been formally excluded sought to pay their arrears of dues in order to participate in the distribution of assets.

MEGARRY J.: I should be very slow to accept that a member of a society may disregard all his obligations as a member for several years, and then, when it appears that there is some advantage in resuming membership, assert that he is still a member because the correct procedure under the rules to terminate his membership has not been followed. The question, of course, is not one of expulsion, or of the society snatching at some trivial or short-lived breach of rules by a member to deny him membership; it is a question of a voluntary disregard of the obligations of membership over a continuous period of years. There must be many instances in clubs up and down the country in which this sort of thing happens. Yet if the contentions on behalf of the four members are right, either the society or the members concerned may, if it suits them, claim that the membership is still in being. Such members might find that the society is claiming many years' arrears of a substantial subscription, or the members might, as here, suddenly re-assert their membership when some advantage turns up.

I do not think that this can be right. It seems to me that the answer, or an answer, lies in the decision of the Court of Appeal in *Finch v Oake* [1896] 1 Ch. 409, which I mentioned in the course of argument. This established that a member of a society has the unilateral right, not dependent on acceptance by the society, to resign his membership at any time, even though the rules contain no provision as to resignation. In that case, the member wrote a letter saying that he desired to withdraw his name as a member of the society, and that was held to be sufficient. There can be no magic in the word "resign," nor in whether the resignation is written or oral. The essence of the matter seems to me to be whether the member has sufficiently manifested his decision to be a member no more. I cannot see why such a manifestation should not be by conduct instead of by words; the only question is whether the member's decision has been adequately conveyed to the society by words or deeds. In short, in addition to resignation by words, I think there may be resignation by conduct; and I do not see why in a proper case a sufficiency of inertia should not constitute resignation by conduct. The point seems to lack authority, and so I must resolve it on principle.

I am not suggesting that the mere failure to pay weekly subscriptions for a few weeks or quarterly subscriptions for two or three quarters would suffice per se; but three years and more is another matter. No reasonable man is likely to feel any real doubt about the intentions of a member of a society who for over three years has failed to make his weekly or quarterly payments, and has put forward not a word to suggest that this was due to some mistake, or that he has done some act showing an intention to continue a member. As I have indicated, among the many thousands of clubs and societies in the country there must be many cases of members whose membership has never been terminated in accordance with any provision in the rules, and yet who are regarded as still being members neither by themselves nor by the club or society. If their membership is said to have "lapsed," that may be another way of describing a tacit resignation. However it is described, it seems right that there should be such a doctrine, so that neither the member nor the club or society should be able to claim against the other on the basis that what has long been dead de facto still lives de jure. A moribund membership ought not to be capable of resurrection.

In the circumstances of this case, I think the four members of the society ceased by tacit resignation to be members well before the end of 1966, so that, in accordance with *Finch v Oake*, they could not thereafter withdraw their resignations; they could become members again only if they joined the society once more, and this did not occur. An alternative basis for reaching the same result is that the four members repudiated their contracts of membership by their prolonged breach of their most important duty of membership, and that the society accepted this repudiation by ceasing to treat them as members. There is nothing to suggest that any demand for their subscriptions was ever made after they ceased to pay them; the evidence points in the opposite direction. What suffices for repudiation may indeed suffice for resignation, with the difference that, unlike repudiation, resignation does not require acceptance. Accordingly, whether by resignation or repudiation, or perhaps an interesting combination of both, I hold that the four respondents in question are not entitled to claim as members. . . .

(C) Discipline and Expulsion

(i) Practice

The approach of the courts to membership issues changes radically when they consider the disciplining of members. Judicial requirements are much more demanding and the draftsmen of union rules have responded with more complete regulations. The need to do so is emphasised by the strict approach adopted by the courts to the application and construction of the contract of membership. The terms of the contract of membership of a trade union are set out in the union rule book governing the internal organisation of the union. It is reasonable to conclude that unions would be unhappy if courts of law could fill gaps with rules considered by judges to be reasonable.

The number of specific offences that might be made punishable by discipline or expulsion is considerable. Unions are well aware that it is unlikely that any draftsman would comprehend all likely causes for discipline. Accordingly, "blanket" provisions are now by far the most common type of disciplinary rule. Typically, these will permit the disciplining of any member who in the opinion of the branch or national executive committee has acted contrary to the interests of the union. Some unions do attempt to list specific offences, most often topped off by a blanket provision. Of such specific provisions, the most common are those penalising various forms of "strike-breaking" and those relating to misconduct by officers.

Rules as to disciplinary procedure owe much to legal requirements and unions' readiness to comply with these requirements. The choice of disciplinary tribunal may be influenced by the degree of internal autonomy permitted to the various levels in the structure of the union. Generally, however, disciplinary proceedings are initiated at branch level. In recent years, however, the practice of requiring confirmation of expulsion by the national executive has spread. Since the higher the tribunal is in the hierarchy, the more important it is considered, a number of rule books devote more attention to procedure at the ratification stage than to procedure at the initial hearing. Few, even now, provide anything like full guidance on the conduct of the initial hearing.

Union government is based on the assumption that the institution of disciplinary proceedings will be a rare event and that it would be inappropriate for the rule book to give the impression that enforcement of discipline was a major aspect of the union's function. It is likely, therefore, that minor defects will occur in many disciplinary cases. Lay union tribunals, inadequately guided and close to the cause of the proceedings, are inevitably prone to procedural improprieties in particular, see for example *Santer* v. *NGA* [1973] I.C.R. 60 (below p. 639).

(ii) Legal policy

The judicial approach to trade union disciplinary cases is affected by insistence on protection of the individual. The relationship of the individual to the objects of the union is sometimes asserted simplistically to accord with this policy preference. An example is the following dictum of Lord Denning in *Edwards* v. *SOGAT* [1970] 3 All E.R. 689 (C.A.):

> "A trade union exists to protect the right of each one of its members to earn his living and to take advantage of all that goes with it. If the union should assume to make a rule which destroys that right or puts it in jeopardy—or is a gratuitous and oppressive interference with it—then the union exceeds its powers. The rule is *ultra vires* and invalid."

(a) Power to discipline

(1) Implying rules. There can be no discipline without contractual provision. It is theoretically possible for that provision to be implied, but in practice the courts are unlikely to imply disciplinary powers unless no express rules exist to govern any of the relations of the members of the organisation. A good illustration of the courts' attitude is their approach to the Bridlington Agreement (above, p. 624). Their emphasis is on individual rights in a conventional contractual framework. Collective practice is not accepted as a basis for implying terms as to discipline, as the following case shows.

Spring v. National Amalgamated Stevedores and Dockers Society
[1956] 1 W.L.R. 585; [1956] 2 All E.R. 221
Chancery Division

The union had recruited members to its northern region who had previously belonged to the Transport and General Workers' Union. The latter protested that this was contrary to the prohibition contained in the Bridlington Agreement, and a TUC Disputes Committee ordered the NASD to expel the new recruits from its organisation. The recruits refused to accept such exclusion voluntarily and the NASD, therefore, expelled them notwithstanding that it possessed no rule allowing such action.

Sir Leonard Stone V.-Ch.: [The judge reviewed the facts, cited correspondence between the union and the TUC and continued:] That brings me to the points raised in paras. 14 and 15 of the defence, in regard to the implied terms, that is to say, that it was an implied term of the plaintiff's contract of membership [with] the defendant union that the union should have the right to do all things which may be necessary and proper to comply with its lawful and proper agreements; and further, that it was an implied term that members would act in conformity with the lawful and proper agreements of the defendant union, meaning thereby the Bridlington Agreement. To that line of defence several submissions were made by counsel for the plaintiff. The first was that the plaintiff in his evidence, which I entirely accept, said that it was not until "the recognition strike", that is to say, some five or six weeks after he had been accepted as a member of the defendant union, that he first heard of the Bridlington Agreement. Even in this court his ideas about its effect were quite inaccurate and imperfect. . . .
[The judge then referred to the "officious bystander" test for implying terms into a contract.]

If that test were to be applied to the facts of this case and the bystander had asked the plaintiff, at the time when the plaintiff paid his five shillings and signed the acceptance form, "Won't you put into it some reference to the Bridlington Agreement?" I think (indeed, I have no doubt) that the plaintiff would have answered, "What's that?" In my judgment, that is sufficient to dispose of this case.

Although this judgment applies a standard principle for the implication of terms, it is applied in a way that destroys any chance of it being used as a common source of implication. The learned judge poses a question framed in technical terms and interprets a hypothetical inquiry for further explanation as a negative answer. A more acceptable, if still traditional form of common law reasoning appears in the following judgment.

Radford v. National Society of Operative Printers, Graphical and Media Personnel
[1972] I.C.R. 484
Chancery Division

Mr Radford had been expelled from the union for "action taken against the union" in failing to give the union information about consultations he had had with his solicitor concerning a claim for redundancy payments.

Plowman J.: [having concluded that this was a case in which he should not exercise a discretion to defer consideration of the complaint until the domestic remedies had been exhausted, continued:] Mr Hawser [counsel for the union] then submitted a proposition of an entirely novel character in this field . . .

"Further, or in the alternative, the conduct of the [applicant] hereinbefore alleged (or specified in the further and better particulars given hereunder) was a fundamental breach of the contract between the [applicant] on the one hand and the . . . union on the other hand. By reason of the relationship between the union and its members and between its members inter se and by reason of the purposes for which the union was established and has at all material times existed (namely, for the general benefit of the members as a whole and for the furtherance of their interests) and by reason of the express terms of the contract between the union and its members and its members inter se as specified in the said rules, it was an implied term of that contract that the [applicant] would be just and faithful in his dealings with the union and his fellow members thereof and would comply with all reasonable arrangements made between the union and employers and would accept all reasonable and proper directions from the union as to his dealings with employers. The said conduct of the [applicant] was a breach of such implied term and amounted to repudiation of the said contract. At the said meeting on May 23, 1967 the union accepted the said repudiation and was entitled thereafter to treat the [applicant] as having ceased to be a member of the union."

. . . In my judgment, however, no such term can be implied. In view of the very specific enumeration in rule 20 of the circumstances in which a member can be deprived of his membership by the union there is no scope or necessity for the implication of any additional obligation, for breach of which the applicant was liable to lose his membership.

In *Bonsor* v. *Musicians' Union* [1954] Ch. 479, the courts were able to refuse to imply a term from long practice on the more acceptable but no less restrictive ground that it would contradict an express term. In *Burn* v. *National Amalgamated Labourers' Union* [1920] 2 Ch. 364, it was held that specification of a greater penalty did not confer power to impose a lesser penalty. But so strict an application of contractual rules as to implying terms may not be in the interests of the individual. In the following case, the court felt able to construe a rule specifying no other penalty than expulsion as permitting lesser penalties.

Santer v. National Graphical Association
[1973] I.C.R. 60; [1972] 14 K.I.R. 193
Queen's Bench Division

The plaintiff, having been dismissed for bad time-keeping, took employment with a company not recognised by his union. The union possessed a sub-rule so that "any member accepting work in an office not recognised by the [union] shall . . . be subject to immediate expulsion." When he appeared before his branch committee to discuss his dismissal he revealed that he was working for the unrecognised firm. He was then told that the committee intended to recommend to the executive council that he be immediately expelled from the union. He was given no hearing nor was he informed of the existence of a right of appeal. The union executive committee accepted the recommendation.

MELFORD-STEVENSON J.: It is upon the language of that sub-rule in its context in rule 37 that a great deal of argument has taken place before me, the contention on the one side being that working or accepting employment in an unrecognised office must be followed by expulsion, there being no discretion in the union. The words of the sub-rule itself, are "subject to immediate expulsion"; and the sub-rule follows a number of other sub-rules dealing with other offences, the exact nature of which I am not quite sure I understand. They include something called "smooting" and something called "farming," which can attract maximum fines of £50, as, indeed, does insulting an officer of the union, but each of those offences are offences which, I think, permit someone to continue his membership of the union, having paid any fine that may be imposed upon him. I find the fixing of those penalties for offences that can be committed during membership of the union of some assistance in construing the words "subject to immediate expulsion." The view I take of sub-rule 10 is that, although the member is subject to immediate expulsion, it is open to the committee, if they so wish, to impose a penalty which falls short of expulsion for the offence of working in an unrecognised office.

(2) Interpreting rules. Although the courts show little readiness to imply rules, they have always retained the final word in the construction of the rules of voluntary unincorporated associations, including trade unions, and whether such rules are substantive or procedural.

Lee v. Showmen's Guild of Great Britain
[1952] 2 Q.B. 329
Court of Appeal

The plaintiff and a Mr Shaw both applied for sites on the ground of the Bradford Moor Fair. The best position was allotted to Mr Lee by the local authority. Mr Shaw claimed that in accordance with a previous ruling of the guild he was entitled to the position but Mr Lee stood on his right arising from the local authority's allocation. He was fined by his professional association for "unfair competition" and expelled when he failed to pay the fine. The Court of Appeal upheld the decision of the lower court that Mr Lee's conduct could not be construed as unfair competition within the meaning of the rules.

DENNING L.J.: But the question still remains: to what extent will the courts intervene? They will, I think, always be prepared to examine the decision to see that the [voluntary association's domestic] tribunal have observed the law. This includes the correct interpretation of the rules. Let me give an illustration. If a domestic tribunal is given power by the rules to expel a member for misconduct, such as here for "unfair competition," does that mean that the tribunal is the sole judge of what constitutes unfair competition? Suppose they put an entirely wrong construction on the words "unfair competition" and find a member guilty of it when no reasonable person could so find, has not the man a remedy? I think he has, for the simple reason that he has only agreed to the committee exercising jurisdiction according to the true interpretation of the rules, and not according to a wrong interpretation. Take this very case. If the man is found guilty of unfair competition, the committee can impose a fine on him of a sum up to £250. Then, if he has not the money to pay, or, at any rate, does not pay, within one month, the man automatically ceases to be a member of the Guild: see rule 14. To be deprived of membership in this way is a very severe penalty on a man. It means that he will be excluded from all the fair grounds of the country which are controlled by the Guild or its members: see rule 11(*g*)(ii) and rule 15(*a*). This is a serious encroachment on his right to earn a livelihood, and it is, I think, not to be permitted unless justified by the contract into which he has entered. . . .

In most of the cases that come before such a domestic tribunal the task of the committee can be divided into two parts—(i) they must construe the rules; (ii) they must apply the rules to the facts. The first is a question of law which they must answer correctly if they are to keep within their jurisdiction. The second is a question of fact which is essentially a matter for them. The whole point of giving jurisdiction to a committee is so that they can determine the facts and decide what is to be done about them. The two parts of the task are, however, often inextricably mixed together. The construction of the rules is so bound up with the application of the rules to the facts that no one can tell one from the other. When that happens, the question whether the committee has acted within its jurisdiction depends, in my opinion, on whether the facts adduced before them were reasonably capable of being held to be a breach of the rules. If they were, then the proper inference is that the committee correctly construed the rules and have acted within their jurisdiction. If, however, the facts were not reasonably capable of being held to be a breach and yet the committee held them to be a breach, then the only inference is that the committee have misconstrued the rules and exceeded their jurisdiction. The proposition is sometimes stated in the form that the court can interfere if there was no evidence to support the finding of the committee, but that only means that the facts were not reasonably capable of supporting the finding.

My conclusion, therefore, is that the court has power in this case to intervene in the decision of the committee of the Showmen's Guild if no facts were adduced before them which could reasonably be considered to be "unfair competition within rule 15(*c*) which says that no member of the guilt shall indulge in unfair competition with regard to the renting, taking or letting of ground or position."

The courts, therefore, insist on the requirement that the enforcement of discipline should be authorised by the rules as construed by the courts, but without resort to implication of terms. However, just as attempts have been made in connection with admission to membership to use public policy emphasising individual rights, so a similar attempt has been made to invalidate or alter the rules of the union relating to discipline.

Edwards v. Society of Graphical and Allied Trades

[1971] Ch. 354; [1970] 3 All E.R. 689
Court of Appeal

The plaintiff was employed by an employer who accepted a union closed shop and "checked off" union dues by deductions from his employees' wages. A union official failed to take the necessary steps to see that the plaintiff's dues were so deducted from his pay so that, over a period, he fell into arrears. The plaintiff first became aware of this when told that he had ceased to be a member of the union under a rule providing for the automatic termination of temporary membership of those six weeks in arrears. It was conceded that the plaintiff had been wrongly expelled but it was relevant to the claim for damages to consider whether the union could have acted properly in expelling the plaintiff.

LORD DENNING M.R.: The union excluded him by virtue of a rule commonly called the "automatic forfeiture" rule. It is rule 18(4)(h), which provides: "Temporary Membership shall terminate automatically if the member becomes over six weeks in arrears." That rule is so positive in its language that I see no way of limiting it. Not by way of construction. Nor by way of an implied term. Why then does it not apply to this case? I think it is for this simple reason: this rule, like the other, is invalid. It is an unwarranted encroachment on a man's right to work. Just think. A man may fall into arrears without any real fault of his own. It may be due to oversight on his part, or because he is away sick, or on holiday. It may be due, as here, to the union's own fault in not forwarding the "check-off" slip. But, whatever the cause, this rule, if valid, would put it into the power of the union, as soon as a man was six weeks in arrears, either to enforce his exclusion, or to waive it, or to readmit him. It could be as arbitrary or capricious as it pleased. It could discriminate in favour of some and against others as it liked (as indeed the plaintiff thought happened to him). It could turn him out of his work without any good or sufficient cause. Such cannot be permitted. It is ultra vires. No union can stipulate for automatic exclusion of a man without giving him the opportunity of being heard, see what Lord Evershed said in the *Faramus* case [1964] A.C. 925 [above, p. 629].

SACHS L.J.:. . . . The courts have always protected a man against any unreasonable restraint on his right to work even if he has bargained that right away; and it matters not whether the bargain is with an employer or with a society (see *Pharmaceutical Society of Great Britain v Dickson* [1970] A.C. 403, and the cases there cited). A rule that in these days of closed shops entitles a trade union to withdraw the card of a capable craftsman of good character who for years has been a member, even if styled "temporary" member, for any capricious reason such as (to mix conventional and practical examples) having incurred the personal enmity, for non-union reasons, of a single fellow member, the colour of his hair, the colour of his skin, the accent of his speech, or the holding of a job desired by someone not yet a member, is plainly in restraint of trade. At common law it is equally clearly unreasonable so far as the public interest is concerned. Is it then protected by either s.3 or s.4 of the Trade Union Act 1871? It cannot be said that a rule that enabled such capricious and despotic action is proper to the 'purposes' of this or indeed of any trade union. It is thus not protected by s.3 and is moreover ultra vires. Nor can I find any protection for it in s.4. It is thus void as in restraint of trade.

Section 3 of the 1871 Act provided that the *purposes* of a trade union should not by reason that they were in restraint of trade at common law be unlawful. The provision is now included in TULRA, s.2(5) but with an extension to cover *rules* so as to deal with the penultimate sentence in the extract from Sachs L.J.'s judgment above, which was in conflict with the House of Lords' decision in the *Faramus* case (above p. 629). Section 4 of the 1871 Act was repealed by the Industrial Relations Act 1971; it provided that various union contracts, while not being unlawful, were unenforceable; these included agreements between union members and agreements for the payment by members of subscriptions or penalties to their unions. A similar effect may be achieved by applying the power to construe the rules so as to conclude that the facts reveal no offence under the rules, as in the following case, where a union member entertained reasonable doubts about their legitimacy.

Esterman v. National Association of Local Government Officers
[1974] I.C.R. 625; 118 S.J. 596
Chancery Division

The union, in pursuance of a pay claim, instructed certain branches, including that to which the plaintiff belonged, not to assist in the forthcoming local government elections. The plaintiff refused to obey this instruction and was asked to attend a disciplinary meeting to consider whether her conduct was such as to render her unfit for membership. She sought an injunction to prevent the branch taking disciplinary action.

TEMPLEMAN J.: In my judgment, when the national executive council take the serious step of interfering with the right of a member to volunteer or take work of any description outside his normal employment, the national executive council are only entitled to one hundred per cent and implicit obedience to that order if it is clear that they have been given power to issue the order and if it is clear that they are not abusing that power. If a member disobeys an order of the national executive council which does not satisfy those tests, then it seems to me that he cannot be found guilty on that account of conduct which renders him unfit to be a member of NALGO.

I should say at once that I have no doubt that the national executive council have acted in the utmost good faith, have only done what they have done in the firm belief that it is in the best interests of NALGO and that they are supported by all or a majority of the members of NALGO. It is agreed between counsel that we are to some extent in unknown territory. It may be some guidance to say that persons in the position of the national executive council must consider not only whether, by turning the rules upside down or inside out, they can spell out power to do what they want to do, but whether, in all the circumstances, it is right to demand from every member of the union immediate and unquestioned obedience to the order which they propose to give.

On this application, I have listened to very long and very learned argument on the interesting question of whether, on the true construction of the rules and also on the construction of the procedure for strike action, the national executive council had power to issue the order dated April 8, 1974 [*ie* to members not to assist in the local elections]. It is sufficient for present purposes that not only am I in some doubt now as to the answer to that question, but also that every member of NALGO who received the order could not have been clear as to whether there was power to issue that particular order. . . .

As at present advised, I emphatically reject the submission that it was the duty of every member blindly to obey the orders of the national executive council in the prevailing circumstances and that he could only disobey the order if he were prepared to take the risk of being expelled from NALGO. I also reject the submission that a member who disobeyed the particular order given by the national executive not to assist returning officers showed prima facie that he was unfit to be a member of NALGO. An Act of Parliament carries penalties for its breach, but it is a fallacy to assume that every democratically elected body is entitled to obedience to every order on pain of being found guilty of being unfit to be a member of an association. It must depend on the order and it must depend on the circumstances and, in my judgment, if implicit obedience is to be exacted, those who issue the order must make quite sure that they have power, that no reasonable man could be in doubt that they have power and that they are making a proper exercise of the power, and that no reasonable man could conscientiously say to himself that "this is an order which I have no duty to obey." In the present case, it was not so clear.

(b) Procedure

(1) Union rules. By a normal application of contractual principles the courts require the union to adhere to any disciplinary procedure laid down in the unions' rules. This is so whether the failure to adhere to that procedure produces action which is *ultra vires* the person or tribunal undertaking it (*e.g. Bonsor* v. *Musicians' Union* [1956] A.C. 104 (H.L.)), or is simply a breach of the contractual obligation to follow the specified procedure.

Santer v. National Graphical Association
[1973] I.C.R. 60; [1972] 14 K.I.R. 193
Queen's Bench Division

For the facts, see above, p. 639.

MELFORD-STEVENSON J.: Rule 38 lays down the procedure which has to be followed in the event of any contravention of the rules of the union. It says that:

> "(1) All allegations of contravention of these rules by a member shall be investigated by the committee of the branch to which for the time being the member belongs. The member concerned shall have the right at any such investigation to answer the charge, either in writing or in person, and call witnesses. The chapel officers concerned in the charge shall be present. The branch committee shall either dismiss the charge or, if they consider the charge proved, communicate their decision and the penalty recommended to the member and to the executive council. In so communicating their decision and recommendation, the branch committee shall make clear to the member that, provided he notifies the branch secretary within seven days of his desire so to do, he has the right to answer the charge before the executive council, in writing or in person, and to call witnesses. The executive council shall then investigate the charge and recommendation and, when the member has notified his desire to answer the charge and in fact attends with or without witnesses when called upon so to do, or sends to the executive council a written answer after hearing the member and his witnesses, if any, or considering any written answer, either dismiss the charge or impose the penalty recommended by the branch or any other penalty permitted by these rules as it sees fit. No penalty shall be imposed except by the executive council whose decision shall be final . . ."

Applying my mind as best I can to those two rules and in particular to rule 38, it is quite plain that rule 38 contemplates the formulation of a charge against a member when it appears that an offence against union rules has been committed. I can find no other explanation of the phrase in rule 38(1) "answer the charge," and I think that it follows that a charge having been formulated—the rule does not say "in writing" but it is, at least, desirable it should be—that the member has an opportunity to consider and prepare any defence he thinks he may have to the charge, and I cannot interpret the word "investigated" in the second line of rule 38(1) except by saying that it must contemplate an investigation by the committee in the presence of a member who has had an opportunity to prepare any answer he may wish to make to the charge formulated against him, and I am equally satisfied that in the present case the steps to which I have referred were not taken. I have no doubt that the committee did decide to recommend expulsion, but I am quite satisfied on the balance of probabilities on the evidence of the plaintiff as against the evidence of Mr Nash and Mr Donkin that not only did they not properly communicate their decision to the plaintiff, but that the committee did not make clear to him that provided he notified the branch secretary within seven days of his desire so to do, he had the right to answer the charge before the executive council in writing or in person, and to call witnesses. It follows that what, in my view, is a vital part of rule 38 was not observed. He was not told of his right to appeal and there was not the equivalent of a notice of appeal in seven days such as the rules contemplate, and there is no evidence before me to suggest (indeed, the indications are all to the contrary) that the executive council to whom the recommendation of the committee was communicated ever investigated the matter at all.

The only document which affords any indication of what happened at the executive council is a minute of June 6, 1963, which contains this bald record. First, there is a reference to Hastings, and then the statement:

> "The council accepted the recommendation of Hastings branch committee that [the plaintiff], who had taken up employment at the non-society office of Olivers at Battle, be expelled in accordance with the provisions of rule 37(10)."

The plaintiff said that he did receive a letter communicating that decision shortly afterwards on June 8,—but it is quite plain that he was not told of his right to appear before the executive council, and he did not do so and he did not call any witnesses.

The pleadings suggest that there was here a breach of the rules of natural justice. It is, I think, accepted that it is quite unnecessary for me in this case to consider the rules of natural justice in the context of the facts that are before me. It is perfectly obvious to my mind that the rules of the union were not observed, that the expulsion of the applicant from the union was a nullity, and in doing what it did the union was committing a very grave breach of contract between itself and the plaintiff. . . .

See also *Hiles* v. *Amalgamated Society of Woodworkers* [1968] Ch. 440.

(2) Natural justice. The courts have long supplemented the rules of bodies exercising judicial functions when imposing disciplinary penalties with a requirement of fair procedure usually called "natural justice." The jurisdictional basis for this requirement is uncertain, with judges invoking both public policy and common law contract doctrines.

Lawlor v. Union of Post Office Workers

[1965] Ch. 712; [1965] 1 All E.R. 353
Chancery Division

The case concerned the expulsion of a number of members by the union's executive council without any notice of the charge for which they were being disciplined or any opportunity to be heard. The union's rule 3(c) provided for an appeal against expulsion to the annual conference of the union.

UNGOED-THOMAS J.: There are authorities which suggest that the application of natural justice may be affected by such considerations as whether the decision was of a professional or trade body, or of such a social body as a club; whether the decision affects livelihood or reputation; whether the consequences are financial or social; whether the decision involves imputation of misconduct; and whether it involves an inquiry. On the one hand it has been regarded as a requirement of public policy overriding contract, and on the other hand as no more than a term, albeit implied, in a contract. Doubtless these considerations and differing views about them can be expanded. The most restricted view of the application of natural justice is that which may be based on the observations of LORD GODDARD, L.C.J., in the *Jockey Club* case, *Russell v Duke of Norfolk*, approved by TUCKER, L.J., in the Court of Appeal [1949] 1 All E.R. 109, 118. This view, advanced by the defendants in this case, is to the effect that the rules of natural justice can only be applied in a contract (i) if they are not inconsistent with what is expressed in the contract and (ii) if they are necessary to carry it out and therefore must have been intended by the parties, and not merely if the rules of natural justice make the carrying out of the contract more convenient and might have been included if the parties had thought about it. It was not controverted in the *Jockey Club* case (4), and it was accepted by the defendants before me, that if the contract contemplated an inquiry, that inquiry would, at any rate in the absence of express limitation by contract, import the rules of natural justice. Thus, on this most restricted view of the application of the rules of natural justice, the question becomes (a) are the express terms of the union rules about expulsion, which constitute the relevant contract in this case between the members, inconsistent with the rules of natural justice, and if not (b) is it necessary to the carrying out of the union rules about expulsion that the executive council should hold an inquiry, or that the persons proposed to be expelled by the executive council should be told of the charges against them and have an opportunity of being heard on those charges by that council?. . . .

All these considerations strongly indicate that the rules of natural justice apply to the making of an expulsion decision by the executive council under rule 3(e). They are considerations which are particularly appropriate to such a non-technical business document as trade union rules, but I will also make a more technical and meticulous approach. An appeal, generally at any rate, implies the contention that the decision appealed against was wrong, and a successful appeal similarly implies the conclusion that the decision was wrong. But a subjective opinion and a decision laid down as the expression or consequence of a subjective opinion cannot by its very nature be wrong, as in the words of rule 3(e), if the "opinion" is subjective in the passage:

> "Any member shall be expelled from the union who in the opinion of the executive council is not a fit and proper person for membership. . . ."

If "opinion" is subjective, it is the opinion, and that is the end of the matter. An appeal implies that the decision appealed against is of an appealable nature, and not the expression of a subjective opinion, but the expression of an opinion that can be the subject of examination on appeal and therefore arrived at judicially and objectively. So this approach also, to my mind, indicates an inquiry and the rules of natural justice.

So, in view of all these considerations, it is incredible to my mind that these union rules should not necessarily contemplate that for the executive council to consider the expulsion of a member, the member should have a statement of charges or complaints and an opportunity of being heard by the council on them. The rules of natural justice are, in my view, necessarily implied into the making of an expulsion decision by the executive council under rule 3(e), and those rules have not been observed in this case.

Alternatively, public policy is said to regard trade union disciplinary tribunals as domestic judicial tribunals subject to the normal safeguards applied by administrative law to tribunals which impose penalties.

Breen v. Amalgamated Engineering Union
[1971] 2 Q.B. 175
Court of Appeal

Lord Denning M.R.: (dissenting on the issue of whether the union had acted fairly but agreeing with the majority on the availability of such a requirement:) The judge held that it was not open to the courts to review the decision of the district committee, because it was not exercising a judicial or quasi-judicial function. It was entirely a matter for discretion whether the plaintiff was approved or not. It could be vitiated if it was made in bad faith, but not otherwise. And he declined to find bad faith. In so holding, the judge was echoing views which were current some years ago. But there have been important developments in the last 22 years which have transformed the situation. It may truly now be said that we have a developed system of administrative law. These developments have been most marked in the review of decisions of statutory bodies; but they apply also to domestic bodies. . . .

. . . So [how] should we treat this claim by trade unions. They are not above the law, but subject to it. Their rules are said to be a contract between the members and the union. So be it. If they are a contract, then it is an implied term that the discretion should be exercised fairly. But the rules are in reality more than a contract. They are a legislative code laid down by the council of the union to be obeyed by the members. This code should be subject to control by the courts just as much as a code laid down by Parliament itself. If the rules set up a domestic body and give it a discretion, it is to be implied that that body must exercise its discretion fairly. Even though its functions are not judicial or quasi-judicial, but only administrative, still it must act fairly. Should it not do so, the courts can review its decision, just as it can review the decision of a statutory body. The courts cannot grant the prerogative writs such as certiorari and mandamus against domestic bodies, but they can grant declarations and injunctions which are the modern machinery for enforcing administrative law.

Generally speaking, the requirements of natural justice in relation to trade unions have become more strict since the 1960s. Whatever concessions may be made to the facts of union organisation as regards bias (see below), none are made as regards neglect of procedure. The Industrial Tribunal principle that dismissal procedure is not unfair unless it has affected the issue (see p. 326 *et seq.* above) does not apply. The rules of natural justice or the requirements of fair procedure, whichever name is applied, essentially include a fair hearing. This requires a known charge to answer, time to prepare an answer, an adequate opportunity to present that answer and a tribunal capable of judging the quality of the answer with a mind not closed before the hearing.

(i) Notice. Union disciplinary tribunals, particularly at branch level where most disciplinary action is initiated, tend to be involved in the situations giving rise to the proceedings. They are prone to neglect strict requirements of a fair hearing because they assume that the accused has knowledge of the issues or that he has no answer to the charge. The requirement that the accused be given notice of the charge has been accepted in innumerable cases.

Annamunthodo v. Oilfield Workers' Trade Union
[1961] A.C. 945; [1961] 3 All E.R. 621
Privy Council

The appellant had been charged in writing with four specific offences each under a named union rule. None of the offences gave rise to the possibility of expulsion from the union. The initial hearing attended by the appellant was adjourned and he did not attend the remainder of the hearing. He was subsequently informed that he had been convicted of all four charges but had been expelled under a blanket rule with which he had not been charged.

LORD DENNING.: The first question is: Did rule 11(7) create a *separate and distinct offence* of "conduct prejudicial to the interests of the union"?—for in that case it ought to have been separately charged—or did rule 11(7) merely empower the general council to impose *more severe penalties* for the various *other offences* specified in the rules, provided that the conduct of which he was convicted under them was prejudicial to the interests of the union?—for in that case rule 11(7), so it was said, need not be separately charged, but only the other offences. PHILLIPS, J., in the Supreme Court and Archer and Rennie, JJ., in the Federal Supreme Court thought that rule 11(7) only empowered the general council to impose *more severe penalties*, and sought support for this view from some observations of EVE, J., in *Wolstenholme* v *Amalgamated Musicians' Union* [1920] 2 Ch. 388. But WYLIE, J., thought it created a *separate and distinct offence*, and their Lordships agreed with him. As he said (4),

> "it stands entirely on its own, authorising expulsion of a member who is proved to the satisfaction of the general council 'to have been guilty of conduct prejudicial to the interests of the union'."

In the opinion of their Lordships, it should not have been invoked for the purpose of expelling the appellant unless he was given notice of the charge under it and had a fair opportunity of meeting it. But, even if rule 11(7) only empowered *more severe penalties*, nevertheless those severe penalties could only be imposed when the conduct was prejudicial to the interests of the respondent union; and their Lordships think that, even on that view, the rule should not have been invoked without giving the appellant notice of it. Counsel for the respondent union sought to treat the specific formulation of *charges* as immaterial. The substance of the matter lay, he said, in the *facts* alleged in the letter as to the meetings which the appellant had attended and the allegations he had made. Their Lordships cannot accede to this view. If a domestic tribunal formulates specific charges, which lead only to a fine, it cannot without notice resort to other charges, which lead to far more severe penalties.

(ii) Bias. The Privy Council has warned of the inevitability of a certain amount of ill-feeling and prior knowledge of the facts under review in many disciplinary situations.

White v. Kuzych
[1951] A.C. 585
Privy Council

VISCOUNT SIMON.: Whatever the correct details may be, their Lordships are bound to conclude that there was, before and after the trial, strong and widespread resentment felt against the respondent by many in the union and that Clark, among others, formed and expressed adverse views about him. If the so-called "trial" and the general meeting which followed had to be conducted by persons previously free from all bias and prejudice, this condition was certainly not fulfilled. It would, indeed, be an error to demand from those who took part the strict impartiality of mind with which a judge should approach and decide an issue between two litigants—that "icy impartiality of a Rhadamanthus" which Bowen L.J., in *Jackson v Barry Rly Co* [1893] 1 Ch 248 thought could not be expected of the engineer-arbitrator—or to regard as disqualified from acting any member who had held and expressed the view that the "closed shop" principle was essential to the policy and purpose of the union. What those who considered the charges against the respondent and decided whether he was guilty ought to bring to their task was a will to reach an honest conclusion after hearing what was urged on either side and a resolve not to make up their minds beforehand on his personal guilt, however firmly they held their conviction as to union policy and however strongly they had shared in previous adverse criticism of the respondent's conduct.

But this tolerance does not excuse the intervention of those with particular interests over and above those inevitable in such situations.

Roebuck v. National Union of Mineworkers (Yorkshire Area) (No. 2)
[1978] I.C.R. 676
Chancery Division

The union's area president (Mr Scargill) acting on behalf of the union, had successfully sued a newspaper for libel. In the action two union members had given evidence for the newspaper. At the instigation of Mr Scargill, the area executive resolved to charge those members with conduct detrimental to the interests of the union. That executive found the charges proved and this was confirmed by the area council which had originally referred the matter to the

> executive. Mr Scargill was president of both bodies and participated in their proceedings, questioning the plaintiffs and taking part in the deliberations. He did not vote on the resolutions to suspend one of the plaintiffs from office as branch chairman and to declare the other ineligible for office in the union for two years.

TEMPLEMAN J.: Mr Roebuck and Mr O'Brien were entitled to be tried by a tribunal whose chairman did not appear to have a special reason for bias, conscious or unconscious, against them. True it is that all the members of the executive committee and the area council, in common with all members of a domestic tribunal where the interests of their own organisation are at stake, have a general inclination to defend the union and its officers against attack from any source; this fact, every trade unionist and every member of a domestic organisation knows and accepts.

But Mr Scargill had a special position, which clearly disqualified him from taking the part in the critical meetings of the executive committee and the area committee which he did take. I say that as a question of fact and not as a question of criticism. It is a fact that Mr Scargill, as plaintiff, had clearly borne the heat and burden of the libel action. It is clear from the admissions that his cross-examination had been complicated and made difficult by the actions of Mr Roebuck and Mr O'Brien. It is clear that Mr Scargill was a witness to what had happened and to what Mr Roebuck and Mr O'Brien had said and done in the course of the libel action in the High Court. Whether or not those actions of Mr Roebuck and Mr O'Brien, before and during the High Court proceedings, were detrimental to the interests of the union, it is quite plain that they must have been gall and wormwood to Mr Scargill before, during and after the trial, Mr Scargill was a plaintiff and a witness—an important witness—in the High Court proceedings. Then he reappeared as the complainant, the pleader, the prosecutor, the advocate and the chairman in the union proceedings, which followed swiftly. It is impossible to know what would have happened if Mr Scargill had recognised his impossible position and had not acted as he did. But his presence as chairman, and his conduct (admitted conduct) undoubtedly gave the impression that the dice were loaded against Mr Roebuck and Mr O'Brien. No amount of evidence can remove that impression, or establish affirmatively that the end result was unaffected by natural resentment and prejudice in the mind of Mr Scargill for prolonging his cross-examination and jeopardising the success of the action which, true enough, affected the union, but in addition vitally affected Mr Scargill, as president of the union, and as a private individual, who had been libelled. Whether he recognised the fact or not, Mr Scargill must inevitably have appeared biased against Mr Roebuck and Mr O'Brien. The appearance of bias was inevitable; the exercise of bias, conscious or unconscious, was probable. I am content to rest my judgment on the ground that it was manifestly unfair to Mr Roebuck and Mr O'Brien that Mr Scargill should have acted as chairman, and should have played the part which he admits to have played at the relevant meetings of the executive committee and the area council. . . .

In the present case, the fact that there was an overlap between the membership of the executive committee and the area council seems to me to be irrelevant. In this kind of domestic tribunal that must happen and is acceptable. But it is to be observed that the test is the likelihood of bias; in *Hannan v Bradford Corporation* [1970] 1 W.L.R. 93 Cross L.J. said, at p. 949:

> "If a reasonable person who has no knowledge of the matter beyond knowledge of the relationship which subsists between some members

> of the tribunal and one of the parties would think that there might well be bias, then there is in his opinion a real likelihood of bias. Of course, someone else with inside knowledge of the characters of the members in question, might say: 'Although things don't look very well, in fact there is no real likelihood of bias.' That, however, would be beside the point, because the question is not whether the tribunal will in fact be biased, but whether a reasonable man with no inside knowledge might well think that it might be biased."

That seems to me an answer to the plea of Mr Turner-Samuels [on behalf of the union] that the trial ought to take place so that one can find out exactly what happened at the relevant meetings; what the members of the various tribunals thought; what the plaintiffs, Mr Roebuck and Mr O'Brien thought and said; and whether in fact, despite the appearance, justice, or rough justice, was done.

As I have said already, a man before a tribunal of this kind must put up with the fact that as members of the union, and as officers, the members of the tribunal itself are rightly and properly concerned to uphold the union and its officers. But Mr Scargill was in a different position from which the likelihood of bias was plain and evident. It is not sufficient to satisfy either the court or the (and I use Mr Turner-Samuels' adjective) robust members of the trade union, that justice, or rough justice, was meted out to Mr Roebuck and Mr O'Brien. The fact is that even a guilty man is entitled to a proper tribunal and a tribunal is not properly constituted if the chairman has been personally involved and is likely to be biased, consciously or unconsciously. It is no answer to say, or prove, that Mr Scargill in fact had no influence on the result.

(iii) Appeals. There is perhaps no aspect of the law relating to discipline by trade unions where judicial thinking fails to accord with practice more than that dealing with internal appeals and resort to the courts. A large proportion of rule books contain provision for some internal review or internal appeal. Where this is provided it is common for the union to seek to restrict resort to the courts. Unions which provide for appeals wish primarily to ensure that the correct decision has been made, and they may suppose that if this is finally established, and earlier defects have been eliminated, those defects become irrelevant. In law, however, the existence of an appeal which will often produce in the eyes of the union ultimate justice will not normally cure early defects.

Leary v. National Union of Vehicle Builders

[1970] 2 All E.R. 713

Chancery Division

> The plaintiff had been a full-time area organiser of the union for 14 years. At a meeting of his branch of which he had not been given notice and which he did not attend, it was decided to exclude him from the union under a rule allowing the branch this discretion over the case of members more than six months in arrears with dues. After several other meetings, the National Executive Committee of the union, after hearing the plaintiff, endorsed this decision. His appeal was dismissed and he sought a declaration and injunction.

MEGARRY J.: Secondly, there is the question on which there appears to be no English authority, and I put it in general terms. Can a deficiency of natural justice before a trial tribunal be cured by a sufficiency of natural justice before an appellate tribunal? In the present case, the decision of the branch committee admittedly contravenes the rules of natural justice; but counsel for the union contends that this defect has been cured by the subsequent hearings by the NEC and by the appeals council. The latter admittedly complied with the rules of natural justice, and the former was at all events a perfectly proper administrative inquiry. . . .

. . . (I have) little doubt that if there is a defect of natural justice the proper course is for the body to which the jurisdiction is confided to rehear the matter de novo, rather than treat any further hearing as an appeal or, a fortiori, let the matter be consigned to some appellate tribunal or other body. No doubt if the trial body has a variable membership, so that the actual members sitting for the rehearing differ from those at the original hearing, this is all to the good. But this is not essential; nor is it essential . . . that there should be any formal annulment of the former decision before starting afresh. The sheet should be made as clean as possible; but I think that it should be the same sheet and not a different one. What is required is a venire de novo and not the process of appeal, whereby the person aggrieved may be treated as bearing the burden of displacing an adverse decision which, for lack of natural justice, ought never to have been reached. . . .

Now in the present case the hearing by the appeals council seems to me to have been in substance a complete rehearing, with the witnesses called and heard, and complete liberty of action for the plaintiff to present his case in full. Indeed, the members of the quite differently constituted branch committee might well have been put in some practical difficulty if they had been required to devote two days to disposing of the case. Nevertheless, it was not to the appeals council that the rules confided the issue of expulsion or no. It may be that the matter was properly brought before the appeals council by the combined effect of rule 2(13), rule 6(1) and the decision of the executive committee; but any such jurisdiction is merely appellate. If a man has never had a fair trial by the appropriate trial body, is it open to an appellate body to discard its appellate functions and itself give the man the fair trial that he has never had?

I very much doubt the existence of any such doctrine. Central bodies and local bodies often differ much in their views and approach; and the evidence before me certainly does not suggest that this is a union free from any such differences. Suppose the case of a member whose activities have pleased some of his fellow members in the locality but have displeased headquarters and other branches. Suppose further that in his absence, and so without hearing his explanations, a local committee is persuaded to expel him. Is it any answer to his complaint that he has not received the benefit of natural justice to say "Never mind, one of the central bodies will treat your appeal as if it were an initial trial"? Can he not say "I want to be tried properly and fairly by the only body with power under the rules to try me in the first place, namely, the local committee"? I appreciate that the appeals council is composed of members elected from each of the union's 12 divisions, and is not an emanation of the NEC or other central body; but I do not think that this affects the point.

That is not all. If one accepts the contention that a defect of natural justice in the trial body can be cured by the presence of natural justice in the appellate body, this has the result of depriving the member of his right of appeal from the expelling body. If the rules and the law combine to give the member the right to a fair trial and the right of appeal, why should he be told that he ought to be satisfied with an unjust trial and a fair appeal? Even if the appeal is treated as a hearing de novo, the member is being stripped of his right to appeal to another body from the effective decision to expel him. I cannot think that natural justice is satisfied by a process whereby an unfair trial, although not resulting in a valid expulsion, will nevertheless have the effect of depriving the member of his right of appeal when a valid decision to expel him is subsequently made. Such a deprivation would be a powerful result to be achieved by what in law is a mere nullity; and it is no mere triviality that might be justified on the ground that natural justice does not mean perfect justice. As a general rule, at all events, I hold that a failure of natural justice in the trial body cannot be cured by a sufficiency of natural justice in an appellate body.

This rule, refusing recognition to the practical role of internal union appeals procedures, is hardly surprising in the light of the general insistence of the courts upon the last word in the application of the contract of membership, and consequently upon the invalidity of any attempt to exclude the jurisdiction of the courts. This insistence has recently been tightened so that the courts take jurisdiction even where a member is himself in breach of contract in not exhausting his internal remedies.

Leigh v. National Union of Railwaymen
[1969] 3 All E.R. 1249; [1970] Ch. 326
Chancery Division

GOFF J.: Next it was submitted on behalf of the defendants that the plaintiff is not entitled to relief because he has not exhausted or indeed embarked on the domestic remedies afforded by the rules. On this point I extract from *White* v *Kuzych* [1951] A.C. 585 in the Privy Council and *Lawlor* v *Union of Post Office Workers* [1965] Ch. 712 in this court, two propositions. The first is that even where there is an express provision in the rules that the plaintiff must first exhaust his domestic remedies the court is not absolutely bound by that because its jurisdiction cannot be ousted, but the plaintiff will have to show cause why it should interfere with the contractual position. This is consonant with the rule in the case of a submission to arbitration where the court always has a discretion whether to stay an action but cause must be shown why it should not. The second is largely the converse of the first, namely that in the absence of such a provision the court can readily, or at all events more readily, grant relief without prior recourse to the domestic remedies but may require the plaintiff to resort first to those remedies. Thus UNGOED-THOMAS, J., in *Lawlor*'s case, said at pp. 733, 734):

> "Trade union rules clearly cannot oust the jurisdiction of the courts. Contracts, including a contract constituted by trade union rules, may provide that recourse to domestic tribunals shall be exhausted before there is recourse to the courts, and the courts may recognise and give effect to that contract; but that does not oust its jurisdiction. So in this case, the court has jurisdiction, and here there is no contractual provision requiring domestic remedies to be exhausted before resort to the courts. Should that jurisdiction be exercised now, or should it be withheld, in the circumstances, pending appeal to annual conference? This case involves the construction of the rules of the trade union, and it is for

> the courts, and not a domestic body, to decide questions of construction, as matters of law. It involves questions of natural justice, which again are matters for the courts to decide."

Counsel for the plaintiff concedes that he cannot, on the evidence on this motion, show cause why an express provision, if there be one, requiring that domestic remedies should be first utilised should be disregarded, and the defendants submit that the rules, and in particular rule 3(6) and rule 9(4), have that effect. I must therefore first determine whether this is so, and I am not prepared to accept that submission. The rules purport to exclude the jurisdiction of the court altogether and to that extent are void on the authority of *Lee* v *Showmen's Guild of Great Britain* [1952] 2 Q.B. 329, but that is no reason for construing them as requiring recourse to the domestic tribunal first. The two things are inconsistent.

Then ought I, notwithstanding the absence of such a provision to refuse relief because the domestic remedies have not been adopted? In my judgment, on the facts of ths case, I ought not. It is true that *Lawlor's* case was one of expulsion and infringement of the rules of natural justice and is therefore much stronger than the present. On the other hand, this is at least one of refusing the opportunity of election to an office of honour and profit and it is one turning on construction, which, as UNGOED-THOMAS, J., observed in the passage I have quoted, is peculiarly appropriate for the court.

2. TRADE UNION GOVERNMENT

One of the problems in discussing democracy within trade unions lies in the fact that the union branch is the member's local link with the national government of the union, but in many industries has little part to play in industrial relations at the place of work. Whether the national leadership is responsive to the pressures of factions or the rank-and-file, ensuring democracy within the union's rules of government is less relevant to the individual member than his influence on his workplace shop stewards. To the extent that rule books concentrate on formal union government, to the detriment of workplace organisation, the courts, operating within the compass of the rule book, can do little to draw together the different strands. In reality, the government of trade unions, like the government of the United Kingdom, is regulated by a constitution only part of which consists of written documents. To treat the rule book as the key to understanding trade union government could lead to ill-advised interventions in union internal affairs. The resolution of individual and collective interests in trade union government poses particular problems for judges in the context of industrial conflict, where the common law has proved very hostile to collective industrial action. This was evident in the litigation arising out of the miners' strike of 1984–85. The following extracts illustrate the grounds on which the courts intervene in trade union government (*cf.* trade union services, *Oddy* v. *TSSA* [1973] I.C.R. 524 (N.I.R.C.), below, pp. 691). We look at a number of problem areas: union policy-making and executive action, conflicts between unions' decision-making organs, elections, the position of union officials, and workplace organisation.

I turn to the rules of the Derbyshire Union. Rule 68 is headed "General Strike and mode of voting" and reads:

> "When any question of a general strike or lock-out is before the branches in accordance with rule 41 of the National Rules the voting shall be taken by ballot and shall be conducted as follows: the Area general secretary shall forward to each branch a sufficient number of voting papers on which members must record their votes at such time and place as may be determined upon by the branch committee. The branch secretary shall send the voting papers together with a summary of votes for and against to the Area General Secretary on the completion of the ballot. There must be 55% of the members who vote in favour of a strike before rule 41 of the National Union's Rules is invoked."

On the constitution of the Derbyshire Union it is sufficient for me to say that subject to the authority of the NEC the general management of the affairs of the Derbyshire Union is vested in a council called the Area Council which consists of the area president and vice-president, and representatives appointed by the branches. Subject to the authority vested in the NEC and in the Area Council, the general business of the Derbyshire Union is supervised and dealt with by the Area Executive Committee, which consists principally of the area president and vice-president and representatives of panels of branches. . . .

[The judge then described the NEC's resolution, the Derbyshire ballot and the Area Council's actions.]

I consider first the claim that the strike is unlawful. First, I must reiterate my regret that neither the Derbyshire Union nor the NUM, has seen fit to present to the court any evidence or submissions in support of the lawfulness of its conduct. Their decision not to defend the proceedings is the more regrettable, and surprising, in view of the seriousness of the allegations made against them. However, in my view a deliberate choice by the defendants not to defend a claim ought not to be allowed to prejudice the position of the plaintiffs. On the material before me, in my judgment it is plain as a pikestaff that so far as the Derbyshire area is concerned, which is the only area with which this action is directly concerned, the strike call by the Derbyshire Union and by the NUM was in breach of the rules of the Derbyshire Union and of the NUM and, hence, invalid. No national ballot has been held, so the strike call cannot stand as a lawful call for a national strike under NUM rule 43. The result of the only ballot held in the Derbyshire area was a very slim majority against a strike, so the strike cannot stand as a lawful strike of the Derbyshire area (*ie* of the Derbyshire Union) under NUM rule 41 and Derbyshire Union rule 68. That is the beginning and end of the matter, so far as the Derbyshire area is concerned.

Paragraph 2 of the defence of the first three defendants . . . alleges the existence of a custom and practice of the Derbyshire Union for many years, and therefore by implication a rule, that strikes of some or all of the members of the Derbyshire Union may occur without a prior ballot. On this it suffices to say that apart from any other considerations no evidence of such a custom or practice was called. . . .

I should add that the primary way in which Mr Lyell [counsel for the plaintiffs] put forward this part of the plaintiffs' case was that the strike called is a national strike and not a call for a strike by one or more areas, and that since no national ballot has been held with the necessary majority in favour, the strike is unlawful. He submitted that what the NUM has sought to do is to exercise a discretion under rule 41 to achieve a purpose (*ie* a national strike) which can only be achieved properly under rule 43. It seems to me that the provisions in the NUM rules regarding a national strike cannot be circumvented by the NUM merely avoiding use of the words "national strike." If it calls upon all its members to stop work that is a call for a national strike. Again, if it calls upon all its members not to cross picket lines and takes steps to organise or encourage the setting up of picket lines throughout the country, that equally would be a call for a national strike within NUM rule 43. The evidence before me includes evidence to the following effect. On 8 March the NEC passed its resolution approving as official strike action in opposition to pit closures which any area might choose to call; on 19 April the NUM special delegate conference resolved that the future development of picketing should be co-ordinated by the national office, and called on all areas to strike; since then the national office has directed or co-ordinated the strike activities, picketing (including picketing of power stations and coal imports at ports) and the preparation and circulation of black lists of haulage firms crossing "official picket lines"; pickets have been deployed from one area into areas such as Nottingham where the area has resolved not to take strike action; the NUM has threatened to discipline local officers who encourage miners to cross "official picket lines"; and there was evidence that in Nottingham (an area not on strike) Mr Scargill [the NUM's national president] described the strike as "official" following the conference decision of 19 April.

Again, refraining from formally "declaring" a national strike, and from instructing or directing members to strike (confining the action to a "call") does not in my view take the strike action outside the ambit of rule 43 when, as here, picket lines are set up as "official." The NUM relies heavily on the long-standing trade union tradition of not crossing picket lines. A national call to strike by the NUM conference, coupled with the organisation of "official" picket lines on a national basis and with threats to officers who encourage miners to cross such picket lines, seems to me in practice to place a miner deciding whether or not to work in a position not substantially different from that existing where there is a formal declaration of a national strike or an instruction to strike. A national call coupled with threats and the need to cross a so-called "official" picket line to get to work in my judgment is entering upon a national strike.

Accordingly, although the strike action in the Derbyshire Area purports to be area action, Mr Lyell's submission that the strike in which the Derbyshire Union is participating is not a stoppage of work of one or more areas within rule 41 but is national action falling to be justified if at all under rule 43 is, in my judgment, well-founded so far as concerns Derbyshire (which is the only area with which this action is directly concerned).

From the conclusion that the strike call is in breach of the Unions' rules so far as the Derbyshire Area is concerned, it follows that the Unions may not properly issue instructions or directions to the membership to strike or not to work or not to cross picket lines in that area. Any strike action taken, or any picket lines mounted, in that area can at best be "unofficial," and the plaintiffs are entitled without thereby breaching any rule or obligation they owe to the Union, not to strike, and to disregard the call to strike and to cross such picket lines.

From this decision it also follows, it seems to me, that the failure of the plaintiffs to heed the calls of the Derbyshire Union or the NUM to strike and not to cross picket lines cannot properly be the subject-matter of any disciplinary measures or proceedings. The same must apply to other members of the Derbyshire Union. Accordingly the purported indefinite suspension of the plaintiffs on 22 May was void and of no effect. For good measure that suspension was also void on other grounds: the plaintiffs were given no prior notice of the complaints against them or of the action proposed to be taken, and were given no opportunity of presenting their case, and an indefinite suspension was not one of the penalties for misconduct prescribed in rule 36 (the relevant Derbyshire Union rule). . . .

I come now to the relief sought. The making of declarations is discretionary. Is this an appropriate case for declarations? The plaintiffs' case—and in fairness to them it should be said—is that they are loyal NUM members, ready to abide by decisions of their Union, reached constitutionally. Their complaints in this action are not based on mere technicalities, lawyers' quibbles on nice points of interpretation of obscure rules. The rules are the constitutions of the Unions. They exist for the benefit and protection of all the members. The rules regarding strikes are explicit, but for a period of over six months now the officers of the NUM and the Derbyshire Union have chosen to disregard the constitutions under which they hold office, and to ride roughshod over their members by taking action which could be taken lawfully only with the support of a majority vote on a ballot. When challenged to justify their actions, both Unions declined to do so. Meanwhile members of the Derbyshire Union who wish to do no more than exercise their right to work are vilified, harassed, disciplined by their Union, and sought to be intimidated by violent mass picketing and in other ways, and they and their families in the communities where they live are abused or ostracised and threatened with physical violence. In my view this is a proper case for the court to exercise its discretion and grant declarations on the invalidity of the strike call in the Derbyshire Area, on the plaintiffs' entitlement in law to disregard picket lines, and on their entitlement in law not to be disciplined by their trade unions for disregarding picket lines and continuing to work.

Accordingly, although I will hear counsel on the precise wording, I propose to make declarations and grant permanent injunctions. . . .

[The judge issued declarations and injunctions to this effect.]

Taylor and Foulstone v. (1) National Union of Mineworkers (Yorkshire Area), (2) National Union of Mineworkers

[1984] I.R.L.R. 445
Chancery Division

The plaintiffs, non-striking miners and members of the NUM (Yorkshire Area) sought injunctions and mandatory orders relating to the strike called by the NUM, and sought to restrain the use of new disciplinary rules.

NICHOLLS J.: I turn to the Yorkshire Union rules . . . Rule 53, under the heading "Strikes and Lock-outs" provides:

> "No Branch or portion of a Branch shall be allowed to strike or leave off work, unless such course is sanctioned by 55% of the members composing the Branch and the provisions of National Rule 41 have been observed. The decision of the Branch shall be ascertained by a Ballot Vote (which Ballot Vote must be first sanctioned by the Area Executive Committee or Area Council) on a question as to whether the course suggested should be adopted; but in no case shall such vote be legal unless three-fourths of the members composing such Branch record their Votes by Ballot, and 55% of the members of the Branch be in favour of the course suggested. The result of such Ballot shall be immediately sent to the Area General Secretary, who shall lay the facts before the next Area Council Meeting. If the Ballot is favourable, and the dispute not settled,

> the Area Council shall have power to say when notices to cease work shall be tendered. When any Branch is on strike or locked-out, a Vote by Ballot of the whole of the Branches of the Union may be taken for the purpose of deciding whether there shall be a general strike of all the members of the Union with a view to compelling a settlement of such dispute."

—and omitting the immaterial words:

> "(b) On the question of a general strike the Ballot shall be one of all the members of the Union [that is, of the Yorkshire Union] and shall not be legal unless three-fourths of the members vote, and 55% of those voting are in favour of such strike."

And (c) under the heading "National Union—Disputes, etc.":

> "In the event of a dispute arising in the Yorkshire Area or applying to the workers in any Branch likely or possible to lead to a stoppage of work the questions must be immediately reported to the National Executive Committee which shall deal with the matter forthwith, and in no case shall a cessation of work take place by the workers without the previous sanction of the National Executive Committee, or of a Committee (whether consisting of members of the National Executive Committee or of other persons) to whom the National Executive Committee may have delegated the power of giving such sanction, either generally or in a particular case and no funds of the National Union shall be applied in strike pay or other trades dispute benefit for the benefit of workers who shall have ceased work without the previous sanction of the National Executive Committee."

I now turn to the events giving rise to this motion. I must start as far back as January 1981. Early in that month it became known that the National Coal Board was considering the closure of some 25 collieries, and there were fears that one of these might be Orgreave colliery in the Yorkshire area. In January 1981 the Yorkshire Union balloted its members on the question: "Are you in favour of giving the NUM (Yorkshire Area) authority to take various forms of industrial action (including strike action, if necessary) to stop the closure of any pit, unless on the grounds of exhaustion?" 85.6% of the votes cast were "Yes" votes. Within days the NCB [the National Coal Board, now British Coal, the employers] announced its intention to close Orgreave colliery and the Area Council immediately called a strike which lasted some two weeks, until the Board withdrew its closure plans. Some months later, in June, the Area Council again resolved to take industrial action, failing agreement by the Board to agree to develop the workable coal reserves found to exist at Orgreave, but within a few days this dispute with the Board was satisfactorily resolved.

There then followed over the period from January 1982 to March 1983 three national ballots, all concerning strike action. The first was held in January 1982 concerning a wages dispute with the National Coal Board. On that occasion 55% of the NUM members voting were against giving the NEC authority to call a national strike if necessary. On an Area basis, 66.5% of the members of the Yorkshire Union voted in favour of giving the NEC such authority. On 28–29.10.82 a second national ballot was held, on a question which related both to pit closure and wages. The question put was:

> "Are you in favour of the Special Conference recommendation that the NEC be given authority to take industrial action if necessary to prevent the closure or partial closure of any pit, plant or unit other than on

grounds of exhaustion and at the same time bring about a satisfactory settlement of our wages claim?''

On a national basis 61% of the votes cast were against; on an Area basis, 56% of the Yorkshire Area votes were in favour. The third and most recent national ballot on strike action was held on 3.3.83. This time the question related solely to pit closures and was in these terms:

> ''Are you in favour of the NEC's unanimous recommendation that the NEC be given authority to take industrial action to prevent the closure or partial closure of any pit, plant or unit, other than on the grounds of exhaustion, including those currently threatened in South Wales?''

On a national basis 61% of the votes cast were against strike action; in the Yorkshire Area, 54% were in favour of strike action.

Pausing there, that ballot result would not suffice for the calling either of a national strike by the NUM or of an Area strike by the Yorkshire Union. . . . on 1 March [1984] the area director of the NCB announced the proposed closure of Cortonwood Colliery. On 5 March the Yorkshire Area Council met and resolved that ''in conformity with the 1981 Yorkshire Area individual ballot vote of 85.6% to call on all branches and members to strike'' as from Friday 8 March'' to stop the action of the NCB to butcher our pits and jobs,'' and called upon the NEC in accordance with NUM rule 41 to declare the action official, and on all areas to join in taking industrial action. A resolution to allow special meetings for branches to discuss the matter with a view to reporting back before the Area Council decided on strike action was defeated.

On 8 March the NEC met and declared that in accordance with NUM rule 41 the proposed strike action in Yorkshire and Scotland and in any other area which took similar action be official. Thus the NEC gave a nationwide, blanket sanction to all areas, in advance (save as to Scotland and Yorkshire) of any requests made, to take official action in those areas. . . .

Finally I come to the relief concerned with the claim that the strike in the Yorkshire Area is invalid. On this the plaintiffs first seek, in short, injunctions restraining the defendant Unions from instructing or seeking to persuade the plaintiffs or other members of the Yorkshire Union to strike or not to cross picket lines by describing the strike or picket lines as official or by threatening disciplinary action. That the strike is not lawful national action is self-evident; rule 43 has not been complied with. But can the strike be justified as lawful Area action under Yorkshire Union rule 53 and NUM rule 41? The plaintiffs submit in effect that although sought to be dressed up as area by area action, what the Yorkshire Union and the NUM have entered upon is, and is alone, national action. Hence it cannot be justified in Yorkshire under rule 41. Moreover, even considered on an area by area basis as the NUM would seek to do, the strike in the Yorkshire Area did not comply with rule 53: an Area ballot was needed, and none was held, the 1981 ballot being too remote in time and there having been too much change in the branch membership of the Area since then for that ballot to be capable of justifying a call to strike action two and a half years later.

This is not the trial of the action. Suffice it for me to say that in my view on the evidence that I have referred to above the plaintiffs have a highly arguable case on these points in support of a claim that the strike is in breach of the rules and constitution of the two Unions and as such is unlawful.

Since what is at issue is the right of the plaintiffs to go to work and earn their living, I have no hesitation in concluding that this is a proper case in which to grant injunctive relief as sought pending the trial. The plaintiffs have been kept from working now for many months. They have constant police protection and their houses are surrounded by police officers. Conversely if, despite the injunction, the Unions wish to continue to describe the strike as official in the Yorkshire Area then, as was pointed out by Mr Burton for the plaintiffs, they have a remedy in their own hands: ballot their members. The Unions can then let the majority votes determine their policy, as the NUM president said when successfully proposing a reduction in the majority required on a ballot in April of this year.

But on this part of the case the plaintiffs go further and ask for a mandatory order that the NUM do now conduct a national ballot. For me to grant such an order I would have to find in the rules of the NUM, expressly or impliedly, a positive legal obligation on the NUM to hold such a ballot, of which obligation it was currently in breach. The only relevant rule is rule 43. The relevant part of the rule is expressed in negative terms. It limits the circumstances in which if national action is proposed by the NUM a national strike may be entered upon. The limit, the prerequisite of a valid national strike, is a ballot vote taken in pursuance of a resolution of Conference and (as recently amended) a simple majority of those voting on the ballot being in favour of such a strike. In short, a national strike shall not be declared unless the national ballot condition is satisfied. Thus if, in contravention of that rule, the NUM declares (or "enters upon") a national strike without the national ballot condition being satisfied, the NUM is acting beyond its powers and unlawfully, and it can be restrained from so doing. What for my part I at present do not see (and I choose my words bearing in mind that this is not the trial of the action and it is not for me on this motion to seek to decide the point) is how, if the NUM does act *ultra vires* and unlawfully, by calling for a national strike without a national ballot being held pursuant to an appropriate resolution of a NUM Conference, there then arises a positive obligation on the NUM to conduct such a ballot regardless of whether Conference has resolved that there be a ballot or not. The NUM's acts will not be lawful unless and until it does duly hold a national ballot which shows a majority in favour of the strike. But, as at present advised, I am unable to spell out of rule 43 by implication any such positive obligation entitling a member to compel the NUM to hold a ballot. The member's right under the rules is confined to being able to insist that a national strike cannot lawfully be held without a national ballot; but he has no greater right than that in respect of a national ballot. The point is, I accept, arguable, but following the approach to the grant of a mandatory injunction which I have stated above, I do not think I should on this interlocutory application make a mandatory order for the NUM to hold a national ballot.

I should mention one last matter. Very properly, Mr Burton for the plaintiffs drew to my attention the following passage of the judgment of the Lord Chief Justice (then Lane L.J.) in *Stephen v Post Office* [1977] 1 W.L.R. 1172 at 1180E:

> "Finally, and most seriously as I see it, the ground on which I would primarily base my decision would be this; that it can only be in very rare circumstances, and in the most extreme circumstances, that this court should interfere by way of mandatory injunction in the delicate mechanism of industrial disputes and industrial negotiations. It is likely if mandatory injunctions are imposed in these circumstances that more damage might be done than good and the results are both unforeseeable and may be grave."

That case concerned an application by a company for a mandatory order against the Post Office for the delivery up of mail addressed to the company which, by reason of industrial action, the Post Office was unable to deliver.

The mandatory order could only have been given effect to by the striking workers returning to work and [ceasing their unlawful discrimination] against one user of the Post Office service. I am in no doubt that when saying what I have quoted above the Lord Chief Justice did not have in mind a case such as the present one where members of a trade union are invoking the court's assistance to prevent that union from acting in contravention of its rules to the prejudice of its members and their right to work. In such a case the context may often be an industrial dispute; clearly this is a matter to be taken into account when deciding whether to grant relief, but it is a type of case very different from that with which the Lord Chief Justice was concerned in *Stephen v Post Office*. I can see nothing in the passage which I have read precluding me from granting the relief I have already indicated in this case. As Mr Burton put it for the plaintiffs, if the court will not protect the members in the present dispute, the rules of the union might as well not be there.

In contrast to the previous two cases, the issues were considered in the following case, where the difficulties of applying the common law rule in *Foss* v. *Harbottle* to trade unions were recognised, if not at the stage of principle, at least at the stage of remedy.

Taylor v. National Union of Mineworkers (Derbyshire Area) (No. 3)
[1985] I.R.L.R. 99
Chancery Division

The plaintiffs, non-striking miners and members of the NUM (Derbyshire Area) sought injunctions restraining the union and its officers from applying its funds in support of the strike, and damages against individual officers. (For further facts, see page 655 above.)

VINELOTT J.: [After referring to the judgment of Nicholls J. in *Taylor* v *NUM (Derbyshire Area)* [1984] I.R.L.R. 440 (above p. 655)]:

The first question is whether the plaintiffs are in a position to maintain an action against the individual defendants in effect on behalf of the Derbyshire Union whose members have not been consulted on the question whether proceedings should be brought against the individual defendants. A great wealth of authority has been cited on this issue. The position, in my view, is not open to serious doubt. I need only refer to two cases, both cases concerning the National Union of Seamen, *Cotter v National Union of Seamen* [1929] 2 Ch 58 and *Edwards v Halliwell* [1950] 2 All E.R. 1064.

In *Cotter*'s case the plaintiffs, members of the union, commenced proceedings to restrain the union and its officers from making an interest-free loan of £10,000 to the Miners' Non-Political Movement and for a declaration that a special general meeting had been invalidly convened and that a resolution of that meeting to make the loan was accordingly invalid. It was held by Romer J. and the Court of Appeal that it was within the power of the union to make the £10,000 loan, that an irregularity in calling the meeting and in passing the resolution could be cured by a confirmatory resolution passed at a meeting properly convened, and that in those circumstances the plaintiffs as a minority of the union were not entitled to sue on behalf of the union. Thus the court applied to the union the principle known to company lawyers as the rule of *Foss v Harbottle* after the case of that name in 2 Hare 461.

I do not propose to cite extensively from the judgments in *Cotter's* case. The point is made shortly in two passages in the judgment of Romer J., which was affirmed by the Court of Appeal. At p. 71 he said:

> "The principle, as I understand it, [that is, the principle in *Foss v Harbottle*] does not depend upon the existence of a corporation. The reasoning of it surely applies to any legal entity which is capable of suing in its own name and which is composed of individuals bound together by rules which give the majority of them the power to bind the minority."

At that time trade union law was still governed by the principles laid down in the Trade Union Act 1871. S.8 of that Act provided for the property of a union to be vested in trustees for "the use and benefit of the trade union and the members thereof." It had been held in the well-known case of *Taff Vale Railway Company v Amalgamated Society of Railway Servants* [1901] A.C. 426 that the effect of the Act was that a union could be sued in its own name and that the effect of s.8 was that the property so held for the benefit of the union and its members was the property of the union which was the beneficial owner of it.

The principle so laid down was, of course, an essential step in the reasoning of Romer J. and the Court of Appeal. The trade union was treated as analogous to a company for the purposes of the rule in *Foss v Harbottle* because as regards its property it was to be treated as a separate legal entity governed by the code constituted by its rules and could be sued and be made liable to the extent of its property in its name. The argument of the unsuccessful plaintiff in *Cotter's* case was that the concluding words of the passage in s.8 which I have cited preserved the members' beneficial interest in the funds of that union. So, it was said, as in the case of any other unincorporated society such as a club any member could restrain an application of the funds of the union made otherwise in compliance with the rules of the union. That argument was rejected by both Romer J. and the Court of Appeal.

In *Edwards v Halliwell* the plaintiff, a member of the same union, claimed that a resolution increasing the contributions of employed members was invalid. Under the rules such a resolution required a two-thirds majority obtained at a ballot vote. The purported resolution was passed without a ballot. The Court of Appeal held that the rule in *Foss v Harbottle* did not apply to bar the plaintiff's right to sue. The failure to hold a ballot was not a mere irregularity. Any member was entitled to refuse to pay an increased subscription unless made payable by a valid resolution. In a classic exposition of the rule in *Foss v Harbottle*, which is often cited but which I shall cite again, Jenkins L.J. said:

> "The rule in *Foss v Harbottle*, as I understand it, comes to no more than this. First the proper plaintiff in an action in respect of a wrong alleged to be done to a company or an association of persons is *prima facie* the company or the association of persons itself. Secondly, where the alleged wrong is a transaction which might be made binding on the company or association and on all its members by a simple majority of the members, no individual member of the company is allowed to maintain an action in respect of that matter for the simple reason that, if a mere majority of the members of the company or association is in favour of what has been done, then *cadit quaestio*. No wrong has been done to the company or association and there is nothing in respect of which anyone can sue. If, on the other hand, a simple majority of members of the company or association is against what has been done, then there is no valid reason why the company or association itself should not sue. In my judgment, it

is implicit in the rule that the matter relied on as constituting the cause of action should be a cause of action properly belonging to the general body of corporators or members of the company or association as opposed to a cause of action which some individual member can assert in his own right.

The cases falling within the general ambit of the rule are subject to certain exceptions. It has been noted in the course of argument that in those cases where the act complained of is wholly *ultra vires* the company or association the rule has no application because there is no question of the transaction being confirmed by any majority. It has been further pointed out that where what has been done amounts to what is generally called in these cases a fraud on the minority and the wrongdoers are themselves in control of the company, the rule is relaxed in favour of the aggrieved minority who are allowed to bring what is known as a minority shareholders' action on behalf of themselves and all others. The reason for this is that, if they were denied that right, their grievance would never reach the court because the wrongdoers themselves, being in control, would not allow the company to sue. Those exceptions are not directly in point in this case, but they show, especially the last one, that the rule is not an inflexible one and it will be relaxed where necessary in the interests of justice."

I have read that passage in full, because Jenkins L.J. makes it clear that the protection afforded by the rule in *Foss v Harbottle* to a company and a trade union does not extend to cases where the plaintiff seeks to prevent or remedy an application of the funds of the body which is outside the powers conferred by its constitution. The reason is that such an application cannot be ratified by a mere majority of the members or indeed by any majority, however large. Any member is entitled to insist that the funds of the body be used exclusively in furtherance of its objects, those objects to be inferred from its constitution. . . .

[There followed a discussion of the House of Lords decision in *Howden* v *Yorkshire Miners' Association* [1905] A.C. 256, decided under the Trade Union Act 1871.]

The trade union legislation has undergone many changes since 1871. It was provided by the Industrial Relations Act 1971, s.74, that a trade union which was registered under the Act if it was not then a body corporate should thereby become a body corporate. A union which did not register remained a mere unincorporated association. The law was further altered by the Trade Union and Labour Relations Act 1974. S.2 of that Act provides as follows:

"(1) A trade union which is not a special register body shall not be, or be treated as if it were, a body corporate, but:. . . . "

That section remains in force subject to a minor modification. As I see it the effect of that section is to restore the law as it was under the 1871 Act, in particular as interpreted by the Court of Appeal in *Cotter*'s case. . . .

The principles which emerge are, I think, clear. *Foss v Harbottle* applies to a union but does not bar the right of an individual to maintain an action joining the union and its officers as defendants and claiming that a particular application by the officers was *ultra vires* and an injunction to restrain further application of the funds of the union for the same purposes and requiring the officers to make good the loss to the union. Being *ultra vires* the misapplication cannot be ratified by any majority of the members.

The central issue in this case is whether the payments, amounting to over

£1.7 million, were misapplications of the funds of the union within the exception to the rule in *Foss v Harbottle*. . . .

. . . Were the applications of the funds of the union in question misapplications beyond the powers of the union?. . . .

[The judge then quoted from various rules of the Derbyshire Union, including Rule 3:

"The objects of the Union shall be. . . .

(b) To provide in accordance with these rules a weekly allowance for the support of the members and their families when the member is out of work, on strike, locked out or victimised. . . ."

and Rule 66:

"(a) Members on strike by the authority of the National Executive Committee, or locked out, shall be paid, in addition to the amount provided under the rules of the National Union (and then there are set out the amounts).

(b) The amounts made by resolution of Council be reduced in accordance with the number of men involved, and the duration of the stoppage."]

It is clear in the light of Nicholls J.'s judgment [in *Taylor* v *NUM* (*Derbyshire Area*) (*No. 1*) above p. 655] that strike pay cannot be paid under that rule, because the members are not on strike properly called with the authority of the NEC.

The correct approach to construction of the rules of a union is set out in an often-cited passage in a speech of Lord Wilberforce in *Heaton's Transport (St Helens) Ltd v Transport and General Workers Union* [1973] A.C. 15 at p. 101, where he said:

> "The basic terms of that agreement [that is, the agreement entered into by a member joining a union] are to be found in the union's rule book. But trade union rule books are not drafted by parliamentary draftsmen. Courts of law must resist the temptation to construe them as if they were, for that is not how they would be understood by the members who are the parties to the agreement of which the terms or some of them, are set out in the rule book, nor how they would be, and in fact were, understood by the experienced members of the court. Furthermore, it is not to be assumed, as in the case of a commercial contract which has been reduced into writing, that all the terms of the agreement are to be found in the rule book alone, particularly as respects the discretion conferred by the members upon committees or officials of the union as to the way in which they may act on the union's behalf. What the members understand as to the characteristics of the agreement into which they enter by joining a union is well stated in the section of the TUC Handbook on the Industrial Relations Act [1971] which gives advice on the content and operation of the union's rules. Paragraph 99 reads as follows:
>
> 'Trade union government does not however rely solely on what is written down in the rule book. It also depends upon custom and practice, by procedures which have developed over the years and which, although well understood by those who operate them, are not formally set out in the rules. Custom and practice may operate either by modifying a union's rules as they operate in practice, or by compensating for the absence of formal rules. Furthermore the procedures which custom and practice lay down very often vary from workplace to workplace within the same industry, and even within different branches in the same union.' "

That passage was cited and approved by Lord Diplock in *Porter v National Union of Journalists* [1980] I.R.L.R. 404. Mr Potts [counsel for the plaintiffs] relied on a passage in the speech of Lord Dilhorne in that case. He said at p. 410:

> "In construing these rules I adhere to what I said in *British Actors' Equity Association v Goring* [1978] I.C.R. 791, namely that different canons of construction to those applied to any written document are not to be applied to the rules of a union. I regard it as our task to construe them so as to give them a reasonable interpretation which accords with what in our opinion must have been intended. The more imprecise the language the greater may be the difficulty in deciding what was intended. I agree with my noble and learned friend Lord Wilberforce that the rules must not be construed as though drafted by parliamentary draftsmen and that custom and practice may operate to moderate a union's rules as they operate in practice (see *Heaton's Transport v Transport and General Workers Union*). But custom and practice, while it may moderate the operation of a rule, cannot in my opinion entitle a union to act in conflict with it."

It is quite clear that Lord Dilhorne did not intend to express a different opinion as to the correct approach to the construction of union rules. He in terms agrees with the speech of Lord Wilberforce in *Heaton*'s case. The point made by Lord Dilhorne, I think, is that while the principles of construction to be applied to the union rule book are the same as those applied to any other contract, the factual context into which the rules must be set is far wider than is normally the case. In particular the rules govern a continuing body with a fluctuating membership. Custom and practice at a particular moment must be borne in mind in construing the rules and seeing what is to be implied in them. But if the rules are clear, custom and practice cannot be given effect if they conflict with the rules.

[The judge then returned to the *Howden* case and an even earlier case, in *Re Durham Miners' Association, Watson* v *Cann* 17 T.L.R. 39:]

The case for the plaintiffs is simply this. It is said that under rule 3 the union has power to provide in accordance with the rules an allowance for the support of members and families of members when on strike. That provision is made by rule 66. That rule in conjunction with the other rules lays down the procedure to be followed before payments can be made to men on strike. It is clear from the judgment of Nicholls J. [in *Taylor* v *NUM* (*Derbyshire Area*) (*No. 1*) that the men are not on strike within the rule. As in the *Howden* and *Durham Miners Association* cases the rules are inconsistent with and preclude the assistance of men who are on strike, but which is not authorised by the rules but indeed has been called in breach of the rules.

The case for the defendants is that there is, as admittedly there is, an industrial dispute between the Durham Union, the National Union, and the NCB and that under the general object in (b) of the national rules [which provide broad powers "to advance and protect the interests of members . . . arising out of and/or in connection with members' employment or occupation"] the executive committee and the Area Council, subject in each case to the overriding authority of the [National Executive Committee], has power to do anthing they or the NEC consider expedient in furtherance of that dispute. It is said that it has long been the practice to support miners on unofficial strike in this way. The fact that the union may be liable for acts done by shop stewards in calling an unofficial strike and for the conduct of the strikers was recognised by the House of Lords in *Heaton*'s case. It is said that it would be anomalous that the union should be liable for acts of such persons but not able to use its funds to support an unofficial strike. Mr Scrivener [counsel for the union] submitted that the only practical effect of rule 66 is that under that rule in the case of an official strike members have an entitlement to strike pay. In the case of an unofficial strike they have no entitlement but the union has a discretion to make payments in support of pickets and in relief of hardship of those who have refused to work.

That last submission, to my mind, rings somewhat hollow in the light of the fact which emerged in the course of argument that in 1972, when there was an official strike, the officers of the Derbyshire Union were instructed by the NEC of the National Union not to pay strike pay in order to conserve the funds of the union. The officers of the Derbyshire Union, I understand, complied with that instruction.

I find myself unable to accept that Mr Scrivener has established that there is in this case even a fairly arguable case that the payments in question were within the powers of the union or that they might be found to be within the powers of the union if the matter were to go for hearing and if the question were to be decided in the light of the past practices of the union. As Lord Wilberforce pointed out in the *Heaton* case:

> "All members [that is, of a union], whether they take part in a strike or not, have an interest in preserving its funds. The rules provide that dispute benefit should only be payable if the strike or lock-out has been approved or recognised by the general executive council or, in the case of a strike involving the whole of the members of the union, by a delegate conference. There is no express provision confining to the general executive council or a delegate conference the power to call strikes which involve only a part of the membership. On the contrary, the rules appear to contemplate that strikes may be called by other committees or officials of the union, but that, if this is done, dispute benefit is not payable out of the union funds without the sanction of the general executive council. One sense in which a strike may be said to be 'unofficial' is that it has not been recognised by the general executive council as entitling the members who take part to receive dispute benefit."

There, of course, Lord Wilberforce was not concerned with the right of a member to strike pay, but the earlier observation that all members have an interest in preserving the funds and ensuring that benefit is only payable if the rules so provide is of general application.

It seems to me that if the rules of a union provide expressly for allowances to be made to members on what I will for convenience call an "official strike"—that is, one called in accordance with the procedures prescribed by the rules—it is impossible to imply consistently with that a power for officers to make a precisely similar allowance to members on "unofficial strike"—that is, one called or followed in breach of the rules of the union. Every member of the union, as he has an interest in preserving the funds of the union, is, it seems to me, entitled to prevent the funds of the union being used in that way. That was quite clearly the approach of the Court of Appeal and the House of Lords in *Howden*'s case, and although there is no doubt that today a more liberal approach to the construction of the rules of a union is appropriate, that principle seems to me equally applicable. . . .

I find myself therefore driven to the conclusion, uncomfortable though it is, that once it is accepted that the payments in question were made, as they admittedly were made, to pickets and otherwise in furtherance of the strike or for the relief of miners on unofficial strike from hardship caused by the stoppage of work and wages, the conclusions that follow inevitably are first that the payments were beyond the powers of the union; secondly that the two officers, the second and third defendants, who made or sanctioned the payments, are liable to reimburse the union; thirdly that the plaintiffs are entitled to maintain this action; and fourthly that the misapplication of the union's funds cannot now be ratified by any majority of the members, however large. Should I, therefore, make the order which is sought?

I have come to the conclusion that I should not. My reasons are shortly as follows. Although the misapplication of the funds of a corporate body (I include for this purpose funds belonging to a union) cannot be ratified by any majority of the members, however large, it is open to a majority of the members, if they think it is right in the interests of the corporate body to do so, to resolve that no action should be taken to remedy the wrong done to the corporate body and such a resolution, if made in good faith and for the benefit of the corporate body, will bind the minority. The majority of the members of a trading company, for instance, might properly take the view that the publicity, costs and the inevitable loss, let us say, of the services of a managing director, who would be the defendant, would outweigh any benefit to the company—although, of course, a contractual release of the right of action, as compared with the decision simply not to institute proceedings, would require to be supported by some consideration.

In the instant case there is an impressive body of evidence filed on behalf of the defendants which is designed to establish that the overwhelming majority of members approves the expenditure in question. It must, I think, follow that they would most probably not [*sic*] oppose proceedings for [its] recovery. At a meeting of a special area council on 19 October it was resolved there that:

> "The Area Council reaffirms its decision of 19.3.84 and endorses the actions taken by the Derbyshire NUM full-time officials both before and after the commencement of the aforesaid legal proceedings and ratifies and approves all items of expenditure incurred by them in relation to the strike, notwithstanding the terms of the order made against them by the Derbyshire NUM and its full-time officials dated 28.9.84."

Affidavits have been filed by the branch secretaries of every one of the union's 13 branches to say that at branch meetings the members have passed similar resolutions. . . . the circumstances of this case seem to me wholly unprecedented. When the ballot was held on the question whether the members should go on strike, the resolution in favour was defeated, albeit by a very small margin. Nonetheless, when the National Union and the Derbyshire Union called on their members to go on strike, the call, although in contradiction and indeed in flagrant breach of the rules of the Derbyshire Union, was obeyed by 85% of the members. Even now, as I understand it, over 60% are on strike. I cannot speculate as to the reasons why members, having voted against a strike, should obey instructions to go on strike and in particular whether the conduct is to be explained by loyalty to the leaders of the National Union or the Derbyshire Union or to the picketing and violence that has ensued.

It is not in dispute that the payments in question were made in the honest belief that the Derbyshire Union had power to make them. There is no question, as I see it, of payments having been made in conscious breach of the rules, far less that they have been made for the personal private benefit of the defendants. I do not feel that in these wholly exceptional circumstances it would be safe to rule out entirely the possibility that a majority of members may in the future be able, properly and lawfully, to take the view that it would not be in the interests of the union that the individual defendants should be made personally liable. . . .

It follows from what I have said that the plaintiffs are entitled to an injunction to restrain further misapplications of the union's funds. . . .

Mr Scrivener submitted that the evidence showed that the majority supported the continuance of the payments in question and that it would be wrong for the wishes of the majority to be thwarted by an injunction in this way. My answer to that submission is that it is open to the officials of the Derbyshire Union or to a sufficient number of the members of the union to call for a further ballot on the question of whether a strike should or should not now be called. If there is a majority in favour of a strike, the funds of the union can be applied in furtherance of the strike to the extent that the rules supported or supplemented by reasonably implied powers so permit. If the majority continues to be opposed to the strike, then they cannot, as the rules now stand, require or sanction the use of the union's funds in pursuance of a strike called otherwise than in accordance with the ballot.

For a critical comment on the relationship of *ultra vires* and the rule in *Foss* v. *Harbottle* to the voluntary association characteristic of trade unions, see Lord Wedderburn in (1985) 14 I.L.J. 127. Vinelott J.'s interpretation of the rules to exclude from the union the power to make payments to striking miners relied on the incorporation of rule 66 of the Derbyshire Union, which purports to deal with strike pay, into rule 3, which purports to deal with the objects of the union. The combination was said to *restrict* the powers of the union. Contrast the following case, where a similar exercise produced the opposite result.

Bourne v. Colodense Ltd.
[1985] I.R.L.R. 339
Court of Appeal

Mr Bourne authorised his union to claim damages from his employers for an industrial injury. His action was dismissed with costs of £50,000, which the union refused to pay. The employers issued a summons asking for a receiver to take proceedings in Mr Bourne's name against the union to claim an indemnity in respect of these costs. Apart from whether any undertaking to indemnify had been given, expressly or impliedly, the question arose as to whether the union had the power to grant such an indemnity.

LAWTON L.J.: Much turns on the rules. They seem to have been put together in a haphazard way. They are far from clear and difficult to construe. I have reminded myself, first, that I must try to construe them as they would be understood by the members (see *Heatons Transport v TGWU* [1972] I.R.L.R. 25 per Lord Wilberforce [above p. 240]), and, secondly, that I must not assume that all terms of the agreement between the members and the Union are to be found in the rule book, particularly as respects the discretion conferred by the members on committees or officials of the Union as to the way in which they may act on the members' behalf, see *Heatons Transport*.

The objects of the Union are set out in Rule 2. The general effect is for the Union to try and look after the interests of the members at work, in sickness, in old age, and in adversity. One circumstance of adversity is when a member requires legal advice. This is specifically dealt with in rule 2(g). The material part is in these terms:

"Legal advice also to be made available to members' wives up to three months after death of a member for the purpose of clearing up members' affairs and assistance to members instituting legal proceedings in connection with matters pertaining to their employment or securing compensation to them for injury by accidents."

In my judgment, members would construe this rule as meaning that the Union would stand by them if they had to institute legal proceedings to secure compensation for injury by accident—and standing by them would not mean deserting them when faced with an order for the payment of costs. Sub-rules (k) and (l) are as follows:

"(k) To provide such other benefits as the membership from time to time determine by ballot and generally to do all things which a trade union may lawfully do.
(l) To take any steps considered necessary in the opinion of the executive council to achieve any of the preceding objects . . . "

Unions can lawfully indemnify their members against all risks arising out of litigation. Sub-rule (l) gives the Executive Council a wide discretion to do what, in its opinion, is necessary to achieve any of the specific objects in rule 2. This would include indemnifying against all litigation risks a member who was being put forward, as the plaintiff was, in a test case for the benefit of a number of other members. The rule which Mr Sedley [counsel for the Union] has submitted prevents the Union from discharging the plaintiff's liability for costs is rule 33. It is headed "Benefits" and defines what benefits members are entitled to receive, such as unemployment, incapacity and funeral benefits. Section (E) of the rule deals with legal benefits. Paragraphs 1 and 2 specify the procedure to be followed when making application for benefit. Paragraph 2 continues as follows:

"All such applications shall be placed before the Executive Council who shall consider the same and decide whether or not assistance shall be granted. In the event of the application being granted the Executive Council shall give directions as to the nature and extent of the assistance to be given to the member and shall impose such conditions upon the member as in its discretion it considers advisable provided that at the termination of legal proceedings in connection with any of the matters referred to in Rule 2 a member may apply for assistance or further assistance if as a consequence of such proceedings the member is under any liability for costs or damages. . . . "

The Executive Council has the obligation, as is shown by the use of the word "shall," to give directions as to the nature and extent of the assistance to be given to a member. No limit is put upon the extent of the assistance; and, if the Executive Council considers litigation is necessary for securing the payment for compensation for injuries to a member, or a number of members, it can take all the steps which it considers necessary. Since many members, probably most in this Union, are likely to be buying their houses on mortgage, a necessary step to safeguard their interests would be to protect them from the risk of costs being awarded against them. If this paragraph stopped after the words "it considers advisable" there could be no doubt that the rules give the Executive Council power to give a member a full indemnity against an order for costs. The question is whether the following words, starting "provided that," limit the powers of the Executive Council. They deal with situations in addition to those in which an application for legal assistance has been granted under the first part of the paragraph. This is shown by the use of the word "assistance" as well as the words "further assistance." They also deal with the case in which the Executive Council have only granted limited assistance, as they are empowered to do under the first part of sub-rule (2). Sub-rule (3) gives a specific power to refuse further assistance if the member shall have been adjudged in any proceedings to have been guilty of specified kinds of misconduct. In my judgment, the latter part of sub-rule (2) and sub-rule (3) do not in any way restrict the power of the Executive Council to give assistance to any extent they consider to be necessary for achieving any of the objects of the Union—and one of them is securing compensation to their members for injury by accidents. It follows that the full indemnity which I am sure the Executive Council gave the plaintiff was not ultra vires the Union.

Again, in the next case, the judge took a liberal view of the union's capacity to be liable for picketing, in contrast to the restrictive view as to the union's capacity to pay benefits to striking members in *Taylor* v. *National Union of Mineworkers* (*Derbyshire Area*) (*No. 3*) (above p. 663).

Thomas v. National Union of Mineworkers (South Wales Area)
[1985] I.R.L.R. 136
Chancery Division

The plaintiffs, non-striking miners and members of the NUM (South Wales Area), sought injunctions to restrain the Union or its officers organising picketing at the gates of collieries at which they were working.

SCOTT J.: It is clear from the defendants' evidence, and not disputed by the plaintiffs, that the organising of picketing at each of the collieries in the South Wales area is the responsibility of the lodge of that colliery. Rule 27 of the South Wales Union's Rules provides that "lodges shall be formed for every colliery at which there are 50 or more men employed . . . " and goes on to provide for the constitution of lodges. The rules do not expressly impose on the lodges the duty to organise local picketing, but it is clearly the policy and practice of the South Wales Union that its lodges should do so. There was no evidence before me to suggest that colliery gate picketing had been or was being organised by the Area Executive, or *a fortiori*, by the National Executive. It was and is treated as a local responsibility. . . .

I now come to the question whether the defendants, or any of them, can be held responsible in law for the colliery gates picketing. . . .

. . . under s.2 of the Trade Union and Labour Relations Act 1974, a trade union is a hybrid; corporate for certain specified purposes but not for others. . . . [see p. 418 above].

[The judge thereupon granted an injunction to restrain the union organising tortious picketing.]

I will now turn to the second part of the plaintiffs' case. The plaintiffs seek to restrain the South Wales Union by itself or by its lodges from organising any picketing whether within or outside the South Wales Area, that is "unlawful." The cause of action asserted for this purpose is that it is *ultra vires* the Rules of the South Wales Union to organise picketing that is "unlawful." It is sought by this means to control picketing, first, at colliery gates of all South Wales pits, whether or not they are pits at which individual plaintiffs work, and secondly, at other industrial premises.

Locus standi

Before I come to consider the substance of the plaintiffs' case there is a *locus standi* point raised by Mr Scrivener [counsel for the Union] with which I must deal.

He submitted, and it is not disputed, that the rule in *Foss v Harbottle* applies to trade unions. He pointed out, correctly, that the plaintiffs are suing in their own right, and are not suing in a representative or derivative capacity. He then submitted, as I understand it, that a claim for injunctive relief to restrain *ultra vires* acts by the South Wales Union ought to have been brought as a derivative action and to have been justified under one of the exceptions to the rule in *Foss v Harbottle*. I do not think there is anything in this point. The plaintiffs are not in this action seeking, from any defendant, the restitution of money belonging to the South Wales Union or the payment of damages for a wrong done to the South Wales Union. They are seeking to restrain the South Wales Union from engaging in an *ultra vires* activity in breach of the Rules. The Rules represent the contract between the members of the union *inter se* and between the individual members and the union, and there is no bar, in my view, to a member suing on his own behalf to restrain *ultra vires* activity. I do not think *Foss v Harbottle* has anything to do with this case.

The Rules

The plaintiffs' proposition is that unlawful picketing is *ultra vires* the union. Mr Blom-Cooper [counsel for the plaintiffs] made it clear that he was using the word "unlawful" to cover not only criminal but also tortious conduct.

I start with the Rules themselves and refer once again to sub-paragraph (b) of para. 3 which I have already read. That sub-paragraph plainly empowers the union, if it thinks fit, to take industrial action, and to arrange for picketing in support of its industrial action. I repeat that this strike is, it is accepted for the purposes of this application, an official strike.

Mr Blom-Cooper submitted that sub-paragraph (b), and indeed the Rules generally, must be read subject to an implied limitation restricting the authority of the union to that which was lawful. In my view that is too general a proposition to be satisfactory.

First, I would agree that it must be *ultra vires* for a union, or indeed any company, deliberately to embark on a series of criminal acts. No objects clause could lawfully expressly authorise that to be done, and no implication to that effect would ever be read into an objects clause.

Secondly, it would not, in my view, necessarily be *ultra vires* for a union or a company to embark on a series of acts which carried the risk that criminal offences might be committed in the course thereof. If the acts were possible to be done lawfully there is no reason why they should not be authorised under an objects clause.

A fortiori, it would not be necessarily *ultra vires* for a union or a company to embark on a series of acts which carried the risk that torts might be committed. Indeed, I am sure that in the ordinary conduct of business a large number of companies take this sort of risk open-eyed and frequently. In the present case the union is entitled under its rules to engage in picketing. It would be *ultra vires* for the union to embark on a form of picketing that would be bound to involve criminal acts. It would not, in my view, be *ultra vires* for the union to embark on a form of picketing which was capable of involving criminal acts but not bound to do so. As to whether it would be *ultra vires* for the union to embark on a form of picketing which was bound to involve tortious acts I am not clear. The answer might depend upon the nature of the tort since, in the final analysis, it would, I think, be considerations of public policy on which the answer would depend. In addition, whenever a union or a company becomes exposed to tortious or criminal liability, questiions may arise as to whether officers of the union or the company have been in breach of their duties of management in causing or permitting this to have happened.

I must now apply these general principles to the particular picketing to which exception is taken in this case.

Colliery gate picketing

I have concluded on the evidence I have seen that the nature and manner of the picketing at the five collieries in question is tortious. I would be prepared to accept that the nature and manner of the picketing also represent offences under s.7 of the 1875 [Conspiracy and Protection of Property] Act. But I have no evidence of the picketing at the other South Wales collieries. I have not been asked by Mr Blom-Cooper to infer that that picketing is similar to the picketing of which I have had evidence, although that might not have been a difficult inference to draw in the case of collieries where people have returned to work.

It may be the case that colliery gate picketing at all these collieries is of a character that makes it inevitable that criminal acts will be thereby committed. If that is so, this picketing is, in my view, *ultra vires* the South Wales Union. . . .

[The judge nonetheless declined to grant an injunction to control picketing at other South Wales collieries, on various grounds of practicality, evidence and that:

> "(iv) It is obviously possible for colliery gate picketing to be carried out without involving any tortious, let alone criminal acts."

The judge went on to hold that secondary picketing was probably bound to be tortious, and mass picketing was both tortious and criminal. He concluded:]

In my judgment, therefore, there is nothing necessarily *ultra vires* in the South Wales Union organising secondary picketing. On the other hand, it would, in my judgment, be *ultra vires* for the union to organise mass secondary picketing. It would thereby be deliberately setting out to do something that would be bound to be criminal. . . .

As I have said it must be almost certain that all the secondary picketing has exposed the South Wales Union to liability in tort for, at least, interference with contract. But I am not prepared to hold that the picketing is, on that ground, *ultra vires* the union.

If there had been evidence that the South Wales Union had been persistently organising mass secondary picketing, with the inference that it would, unless restrained, continue to do so, I would have thought it right to grant an injunction to restrain the continuance of what would, in my view, have been clear *ultra vires* conduct. But, in the absence of any such evidence, I am not prepared to grant an interlocutory injunction to restrain secondary picketing.

Given the extensive range of civil liabilities, and the restricted and uncertain scope of the statutory immunities in respect of torts committed in the course of industrial action, a doctrine which held industrial action which was likely or bound to be tortious or criminal to be *ultra vires* the union (as a breach of its rules) would be an explosive common law development of restraints on union policy-making and executive action in the sphere of industrial conflict. It would allow for restraining litigation along procedural lines quite separate from those heretofore developed for traditional labour injunctions sought by employers (see Chapter 13 Industrial Conflict). It is not even clear what the role of the statutory immunities would be in relation to such litigation. An insight is gained by the attempt in *Thomas* v. *NUM (South Wales Area)* (see above) to enjoin the NUM (and one of its organs, the National Co-ordinating Committee), from inducing or encouraging *ultra vires* secondary picketing. Scott J. thought this was protected by TULRA, s.13(1), (para. 185). He accepted that the acts alleged did not fall within the Employment Act 1980, s.17, so as to remove the section 13 immunity, and similarly, that section 16(2) of the 1980 Act did not remove the section 13 immunity in this case (para. 189). So while the South Wales Union could be enjoined for acting *ultra vires* (in breach of its rules and hence of the contracts of membership), an inducement to do so was protected by TULRA, s.13!

Judicial control of union policy and action in the context of industrial conflict may, following the miners' strike, have shifted to the contract of membership. The miners' litigation was extremely valuable in demonstrating the extent to which members can use the rule book to restrain the union from a policy of supporting industrial action. That this result need not inevitably ensue is, however, apparent from the next two extracts.

Drake v. Morgan
[1978] I.C.R. 56
Queen's Bench Division

> Rule 10(p) of the National Union of Journalists' rulebook empowered the National Executive Committee to authorise expenditure of union funds to assist members in such legal matters as it deemed necessary to protect the interests of the union and in the payment of legal charges, costs and damages. The NEC passed a resolution that the union would indemnify its members in respect of fines imposed for picketing offences. The plaintiff, a member of the union, sought an injunction restraining the use of funds in this way.

FORBES J.: The first argument of Mr Melville Williams [for the defendant] is that the resolution comes within the first sentence of rule 10(p), because (if I may abridge his argument) the N.E.C. is the sovereign authority and rule 10(1) gives them power to determine what is or what is not a purpose of the union. It is quite clear from the rules that the N.E.C. is intended to be the sovereign authority between annual delegate meetings and it is so described in rule 21(c): "Nothing in this rule shall derogate from the N.E.C.'s sovereign authority between A.D.M.s." But as I read the first part of rule 10(1) the N.E.C. is only empowered to act on behalf of the union in accordance with the rules themselves. The committee is thus circumscribed by those rules. Indeed, in my view, the first sentence of rule 10(p) makes a deliberate distinction between the expenditure of money for union purposes, which must be purposes specified in the rules, and the expenditure for those purposes set out in (i) and (ii) over which the N.E.C. are to have an absolute discretion.

I cannot find that the payment of fines for members is a purpose specified in the rules, so that the first sentence of rule 10(p) does not, in my view, cover these resolutions. . . .

Both counsel accept that rule 10(p)(ii) cannot cover these resolutions: it refers in terms and only to legal charges, costs and damages and cannot, therefore, cover the payment of fines. But Mr Melville Williams says that rule 10(p)(i) does cover the situation. The payment of a fine for a member must, he says, be assistance in a legal matter or proceeding and as long as the N.E.C., in its absolute discretion, deems it necessary to pay such a fine to protect the interests of the union, such a decision falls squarely within this sub-rule.

Mr Still [counsel for the plaintiff] will not accept this. First he says you must read (i) and (ii) together and thus read (i) as a general provision which is particularised in (ii). I do not think this rule can be so read. It is clear that (i) and (ii) are intended to be two separate matters on which money can be expended by the N.E.C. in its absolute discretion. They are both concerned with legal matters and proceedings: (ii) specifically deals with legal charges, costs and damages; (i) is much wider and must be assumed to be dealing with matters other than those detailed in (ii). I can see no reason for excluding the payment of fines from the ambit of rule 10(p)(i) subject to one matter to which I shall have to return.

Mr Still's other point is that it cannot be in the interests of the union that its members should be encouraged to break the law by having their fines paid, or that justices imposing penalties should increase them in the knowledge that the union was paying, or even impose penalties other than financial in order to hit the offender rather than the union. There is much force in this argument, but the rules, it seems to me, do not provide for intervention by the courts on this ground. A judge cannot substitute his judgment for that of the N.E.C., because the rules provide that it is the N.E.C. who shall have absolute discretion and be the sole judge of what is necessary to protect the interests of the union. It may be that if the N.E.C. decided to do that which no reasonable committee could possibly think was in the interests of the union the courts might interfere, but that is very far from being this case.

Hopkins v. National Union of Seamen
[1985] I.R.L.R. 157
Chancery Division

The Executive Council of the National Union of Seamen approved payments out of the Union's general fund to the National Union of Mineworkers. The plaintiff, a member of the NUS, contended that the executive council was acting beyond its powers under the union's rules.

Scott J.: The plaintiff contends that it is *ultra vires* the executive council to devote Union funds to assisting the National Union of Mineworkers.

The power of the executive council to utilise the general fund of the Union in pursuit of the objects of the Union is to be found in sub-rule 32 of rule 6. For convenience I will read this sub-rule again.

> "The executive council shall have power to authorise . . . expenditure of the general fund for all or any of the objects of the union. . . . "

The plaintiff, therefore, has to say that the payment of £5000 and £10,000 to the National Union of Mineworkers were not made in pursuance of any of the objects of the Union and that any future payments to that Union would not be in pursuance of those objects.

Mr Slater, [the NUS General Secretary], in his affidavit, has set out the reasons why, in his view (and no doubt in the view of the executive council as a whole), the application of the funds of the National Union of Seamen in assisting the National Union of Mineworkers was and would be within the objects of the National Union of Seamen. He has identified three particular purposes. I have referred to these already and I will briefly mention them again.

First, he says that the payments were made to protect the interests of the many members of his Union whose employment would be adversely affected by the closure of pits. He referred to the seamen working on ships carrying coal around the coasts of this country.

Secondly, he says that the payments were made in order to promote the trade union principle of solidarity. Co-operation and mutual support between trade unions are, he says, fundamental principles of the trade union movement.

Thirdly, he makes the point that payments providing assistance to his own members whose employment has been dislocated by the miners' dispute are within the objects of his Union. As to the last point, no one has argued to the contrary and it is obviously correct.

Mr Morland [counsel for the plaintiff] accepted that payment by the Union from Union funds to assist another Union engaged in an official industrial dispute could be within the powers of the executive council. Mr Morland drew the distinction, however, between official disputes and unofficial disputes. He contended that a payment to assist the National Union of Mineworkers in its conduct of what he referred to as "an illegal strike" or as "an unlawful strike" could not be a payment made in pursuit of any of the objects of the National Union of Seamen.

The use of the adjectives "illegal" and "unlawful" in that proposition means (and I think means no more than) that the strike of the National Union of Mineworkers is, as has been held by Nicholls J. [in *Taylor* v *NUM* (*Derbyshire Area*), (*No. 1*) above p. 655], a strike called otherwise than in accordance with the rule book of that union.

There are a number of other features of the strike regarding the use of pickets and regarding incidents which have taken place on the picket line which might well justify the description of "unlawful"; but that is not, I think, part of Mr Morland's submission. His submission does not depend on such special circumstances as those. His submission depends simply upon the proposition that the industrial action taken by the National Union of Mineworkers is not industrial action which has been authorised in accordance with the rules of the National Union of Mineworkers and, accordingly, is not an official strike.

I do not think that the distinction between an official and an unofficial strike provides a proper yardstick for deciding whether or not payments made out of National Union of Seamen's funds are in pursuance of the objects of the National Union of Seamen.

In the view of the executive of the National Union of Mineworkers, their strike is, as I understand from press reports, official. According to the judgment of Nicholls J., and in the view of others, their strike is unofficial. But if the strike is in the pursuit of objectives which will further the objects of the National Union of Seamen, then it seems to me to be capable of support out of the funds of the National Union of Seamen consistently with the Rules of that Union irrespective of whether it is official or unofficial.

[The judge refused to grant an injunction restraining the transfer of funds to the NUM.]

(B) Conflicts between Unions' Decision-Making Organs

Hopkins v. *National Union of Seamen* (above p. 676) raised the issue of a conflict not only between members and their trade union, but also that between different organs within the union's internal structure. The court held that the union's executive council had acted *ultra vires* in raising a weekly levy, a power conferred by the rules only on the biennial general meeting or a special delegate meeting. In the following two cases, similar conflicts between organs within the union were at issue: in *Goring*, the general meeting against the membership as a whole; in *Gormley*, the National Executive Committee against the delegate conference. In these cases, the problem is judicial competence in deciding between the democratic alternatives of ballots and meetings, an issue which can, at the risk of over-compression, be expressed as, *passive voting* versus *active participation*.

British Actors Equity Association v. Goring
[1978] I.C.R. 791
House of Lords

A dispute had arisen within the union as to the construction of the union rules dealing with alteration of the rules. The union itself brought proceedings against two members representing the conflicting points of view to determine the issue. The Court of Appeal held that an alteration could only be effected at a general meeting, but that any such alteration was subject to the result of any subsequent referendum of the membership. The House of Lords reversed this decision in part. The two rules in question read:

34. "REFERENDUM. (1) The council has powers to conduct a vote of the entire association on any question or resolution whenever the council deem it necessary. (2) Any member or members declaring their disapproval of any resolution passed at an annual general meeting or a special general meeting can, upon presentation to the council of a petition signed by 100 members in full benefit, demand that a vote of the entire association be taken on the resolution. (3) The result of a referendum of the membership taken in accordance with this rule shall be binding upon the council. Non-voters shall not count either for or against."
43. "ALTERATION OF RULES. Alterations to the rules shall be made at an annual general meeting properly convened, or at a special general meeting, at which in either case a quorum is present. 21 days' clear notice shall be given by circulation to the entire membership of the proposed alterations. Any proposed alteration not having been passed by the council must bear at least 40 signatures of members in full benefit before it can be considered at a general meeting. A grand total shall be made of the votes cast for and against by all present and entitled to vote at a general meeting. It shall require at least two-thirds majority of the grand total to carry a motion for the alteration of rules."

LORD DILHORNE: While it cannot be said that the rules are a fine example of legal drafting, I do not think that, because they are the rules of a union, different canons of construction should be applied to them than are applied to any written documents. Our task is to construe them so as to give them a reasonable interpretation which accords with what in our opinion must have been intended.

The respondents place great weight on the opening words of rule 43. "Alterations to the rules shall be made at" a general meeting. They say that these words mean that an alteration shall only and can only be made at such a meeting. . . . [The judge then considered a number of ambiguities and problems in relating the two rules. He continued:]

As I have said, one would expect the rules to enable a vote of the entire membership to be taken on a matter of vital importance. In my view rule 34(2) does this. If it did not, it would mean that an important rule could be altered and a new rule made by a minority of the members—for surely a hall could only accommodate a minority—contrary to the wishes of the council and of the majority of the members.

I think it implicit from rule 34(2) that a member or members who disapprove of a resolution must demand a referendum within a reasonable time, and, while it appears that an alteration of a rule made in accordance with rule 43 takes place when the motion to alter it is carried, the effect of reading rule 34(2) with rule 43 is that the alteration comes into force but without prejudice to the right to appeal to the entire membership. They can veto what has been done at a general meeting.

I now turn to the more difficult question: can there by a referendum when an alteration of a rule is desired and has been put to a general meeting but does not get the support of at least two-thirds of those who vote? If there can then be a referendum and there is a majority in favour of the change, will the result of the referendum change the rule?

It is clear that in those circumstances there can be no referendum at the instance of a member or members but can there be one at the instance of the council?

Rule 34(1) is very wide in its terms. They could hardly be wider. One does not know what were the reasons which led to it being added to rule 34(2) in 1948 but one reason may have been that it was then realised that for the entire association merely to have power to veto a change of the rules was not enough and that there should be power in the association to bring about a change when it had been considered at a general meeting and had not received the support of at least two-thirds of those voting.

The council can take the vote of the entire association on any question. It clearly can ask the members to vote on whether a particular change to the rules is desirable but it does not follow that if a majority thinks it is, that will operate to change the rule. That the respondents say can only be done at a general meeting.

Rule 34(1) gives the council power to refer not only any question but also any resolution. They can, should they consider it desirable, submit to the entire association any resolution including a resolution to alter a rule which was passed or not passed at a general meeting while the right given to a member or members by rule 34(2) is only in relation to a resolution which has been passed.

If the council, the governing body of the union with 63 members, thinks it desirable in the interests of the members to submit to the vote of the entire association a resolution which has been passed or not passed at a general meeting, it would, I think, be extraordinary if the decision of the association had no operative effect. As I have said, in my view a resolution which has been passed at a general meeting can be annulled by the vote of the entire association if action is taken by a member or members under rule 34(2). It would indeed be odd if a vote of the association on a resolution which has been passed, taken as a result of action by the council under rule 34(1), did not have the same effect.

If the vote of the entire association on a resolution passed in accordance with rule 43 and referred by the council can annul the resolution, as in my opinion it can, I fail to see any valid reason why a resolution not passed at a general meeting should not if supported by a majority on a referendum be regarded as passed and as having operative effect. That must, I think, have been intended. It cannot surely have been intended that a resolution to alter a rule which has been considered at a general meeting but which has not been supported by at least two-thirds of those voting at the meeting should, if referred by the council to the entire association and voted for by a majority of those voting on the referendum, have no effect and that it should still be necessary for the council to obtain a two-thirds majority at a general meeting for the rule to be altered.

I think that the rules show that it was intended that any change of rules should be initiated at a general meeting. That is where rule changes will ordinarily be considered and made. In my opinion rule 34 gives a right of appeal to the entire association to a member or members who disapprove of a rule or of an alteration to a rule passed at such a meeting and to the council both in relation to a resolution which has been passed and one that has not been.

I do not think that it was intended by the rules that the council should be able to by-pass rule 43 and to bring about an alteration to a rule by submitting a question to the entire association. Rule 43 in my opinion requires a rule change to be considered in the first place at a general meeting. If it is passed, a member or members are given a right of appeal by rule 34, and that rule gives the council a right of appeal whether or not it has been passed.

National Union of Mineworkers v. Gormley

The Times, October 20, 1977
Court of Appeal

The National Executive Committee of the NUM proposed a ballot of the membership on an incentive scheme with the National Coal Board which they recommended. The Kent area, a constituent body of the union, asked for an injunction to restrain the holding of the ballot, claiming that such schemes were contrary to resolutions passed at previous national delegate conferences.

Lord Denning M.R.: Unions were a kind of thing on their own; and the real authority managing the NUM in between conferences was the NEC. Its powers to call a ballot were in no way limited. If it desired to obtain the opinion of all the workers on particular problems it was entitled to hold a ballot. Indeed it was proper and desirable that it should hold a ballot; when every worker would be affected in his terms of employment by the scheme it seemed as plain as could be that the NEC was fully entitled to take that course to ascertain the opinions of members on a most important agreement.

The conference consisted of some 200 delegates who might not speak with the true voice of all members. They were, so to speak, independent and voted according to their own particular views. The conference should not be held to be the sole governing body of the union. The real power under the rules on day to day affairs and management was fixed in the NEC. Its proposal for a ballot was certainly valid . . .

. . . The ballot was a sensible and reasonable proposal by the NEC to take the views by the democratic method of a secret ballot of all the workers affected. It was a far more satisfactory and democratic method than leaving it to the delegates of a conference who might not be truly representative in their individual capacities of views of the various men they represented.

His Lordship would dismiss the application.

The subsequent membership ballot did in fact reject the NEC's recommendation. When the NEC persisted in authorising incentive schemes, another application was made for an injunction to stop them. Yet the judge (Watkins J.) refused it, once again upholding the NEC, relying on Lord Denning's judgment above (see *The Times*, December 20, 1977).

(C) Elections and the Rule Book

Although there is a rough similarity in the provisions of union rule books relating to admission to membership and discipline, there is no similarity in election rules. This divergence is understandable and, indeed, necessary in the light of the differing structures of trade unions. Unions differ very much in the autonomy they are prepared to allow to branches and districts. Some trade unions, and notably the National Union of Mineworkers, are technically a federation of area unions and in them the equivalent of district organisation is relatively important. For others, sometimes because of the fact that they operate in small units, the district official is a representative of the central organisation and the branch is insignificant. The hierarchy of authority is usually much the same, but the methods of electing and controlling the heirarchy may differ considerably. The Trade Union Act 1984, Part I, imposes a degree of uniformity by requiring secret ballots in elections for certain positions.

In dealing with complaints of electoral irregularity, the courts adhere closely to the contractual approach which we have seen is the normal basis for their jurisdiction in other matters relating to the internal organisation of the union (see *Leigh* v. *National Union of Railwaymen* [1970] Ch. 326 (Ch.D.); *Breen* v. *Amalgamated Engineering Union* [1971] 2 Q.B. 175 (C.A.). But the bland application of a contractual approach can produce surprising results, as in the following case.

Losinska v. Civil and Public Services Association
[1976] I.C.R. 473
Court of Appeal

The plaintiff was the national president of the defendant union, and a candidate for re-election. She contributed an article to "Readers' Digest" headed "The Marxist Battle of Britain" in which she made allegations about the extent and purpose of the influence of the militant Left within the union. The national executive committee of the union passed a resolution deploring this action as irresponsible and an improper use of the office of president. It ordered that this resolution should be published in the union's journal. Following the issue of a writ for an injunction to restrain the publication of this resolution, the NEC rescinded the earlier resolution and passed another deploring the views expressed in the article. Brightman J. granted the plaintiff an interlocutory injunction restraining the publication of either resolution. Subsequently, Fox J. granted the plaintiff an interlocutory injunction restraining the union from circulating any agenda for its annual delegate conference which contained any motion to censure the plaintiff.

LORD DENNING M.R.: The solution of this case must depend on the rules of the union. I would agree with what Mr Dehn [on behalf of the union] has said so forcibly. Unless there is something in the rules which would prohibit it, there is no doubt whatever that this trade union and its members can reply to the article which Mrs Losinska wrote with just the same force as that with which she herself wrote it. If there is nothing in the rules to prevent it, they too can condemn her as she condemned them. This is the elementary principle of free speech which means not only freedom to express those views of which we approve, but also those views which we wholeheartedly detest. So, unless there is something in the rules to stop it, the union can certainly go ahead with their motion, their resolutions, their censures and the like, subject only to the limitations imposed by the law of libel.

Now what about the rules? They form, as we know, the contract between the members, under which they associate together. We have to see what the rule says, particularly about discipline. . . .

It is quite plain to me that it is a very carefully framed procedure, which sets up a hierarchy of original hearings and appeals: initiation by the NEC; hearing by the inquiry tribunal; sentence by the NEC; appeal to the whole conference. In that disciplinary procedure the NEC itself plays a key role. It seems to me that it is essential that, playing this key role, it should be above suspicion in the sense that it must not take it upon itself to condemn the party before the necessary disciplinary procedures are gone through. It must not condemn him before it hears (as it may have to hear) an appeal by him as to sentence or the like; and equally it must not prejudice the matter in the eyes of the annual conference, to whom the eventual appeal lies. Indeed, the annual conference must keep itself impartial and independent just as must the NEC. It must not pre-judge the case by condemning the party in advance of the hearing of the proper disciplinary measures. That is the very ground on which Brightman J. held that the original motion was erroneous and ought to be stopped. On reading the first resolution of March 3, Brightman J. said that in it the NEC had expressed the opinion that the president had been guilty of improper use of her office; of perpetrating a public demonstration of gross irresponsibility. It described her conduct as doing widespread injury to the union. That was plainly an assertion of conduct which was detrimental to the interests of the union. On the face of it, it shows that the NEC was condemning a president for conduct detrimental to the interests of the union, when that was a matter which had yet to be considered by the inquiry tribunal if that were thought proper.

Trade unions usually adopt a surprisingly restrictive attitude to electioneering. Factions exist in most sizeable unions and these factions often become associated with one or other of the recognised shades of political opinion. Trade unions may attempt, not without success, however, to exclude a political overtone from electioneering and, to this end, either forbid or curtail the publication of election addresses and other forms of canvassing (see *Boyce* v. *Amalgamated*

Society of Woodworkers The Times December 13, 1961). These restrictions, normally clearly stated in the rules, are perforce accepted by the courts.

The conduct of ballotting is, not unexpectedly, even more closely controlled by the rules. But here the courts have been prepared to adopt a more flexible approach, based on other electoral experience.

Brown v. Amalgamated Union of Engineering Workers
[1976] I.C.R. 147
Chancery Division

The plaintiff was declared elected to the office of union divisional organiser and gave up his existing employment to take the job. Complaints were received concerning the conduct of the election in which, by mistake, one branch had not received any ballot papers and other ballot papers were delivered late. A fresh ballot was held before the hearing of the plaintiff's appeal against the decision to hold it and as a result another candidate was declared elected. Five months after this person had assumed office, the plaintiff's appeal was successful and he assumed office three months later. A year after its first decision, the appeal body purported to rescind it and confirmed the decision to rescind it six months later. The plaintiff sought a declaration that these two decisions were *ultra vires* and void and an injunction restraining the union from acting on them.

WALTON J.: In my judgment, the power of the executive council to order a fresh ballot, which is a power I think conferred upon them by rule 2(7), that is to say, is part of their general power of control of the election, comes to an end when the election itself comes to an end. And the election itself comes to an end when the result is declared. Down to that time, the election still continues, and fresh ballots may be ordered if the circumstances so justify. After that time, the election is over, and neither the power in rule 2(7) which has ended with the ending of the election, nor the power in rule 15(18) which, if it permitted the elected candidate to be deprived of office, would be contrary to rule 2(4), which provides that the candidate who receives a larger number of votes than the remainder combined is to be declared elected, apply.

I think that this conclusion—although I can see that it may conceivably lead to difficulties where irregularities come to the notice of the executive council long after the declaration of the result—is in accordance with common sense. There is no obligation on the executive council to declare the result within any particular time; in the present case, for very good reasons indeed, they took their time about it. They had, by the time of the declaration of the result, been fully appraised of the fact that there had been malfunctionings of the electoral machine, but they still went ahead and declared the result, because at that stage they thought that while there had been some mistakes and imperfections in the ballot, there was not enough to require or to justify the ordering of any new ballot. Thereafter, so it appears to me, unless some factors emerge which demonstrate that the whole election was a nullity—for example, that the candidate declared elected was not duly qualified, or that a sizeable slice of the votes had been cast by persons, not members of the union (or even members thereof who had no right to cast them at all) then there appears to me to be no rule under which the candidate declared elected can be deprived of his office. The rules do not provide for anything in the nature of an election petition. . . .

I do not of course shut my eyes to the fact that this may mean that a corrupt candidate . . . may, as a result of the declaration of the poll be no longer liable to be called to account. Be that so; I think that this is a situation which is far preferable to leaving minor irregularities hanging over his head for an indefinite period. It is of the essence of any fair system for invalidating elections that any objection should be presented within fairly narrow time limits: compare section 109 of the Representation of the People Act 1949 in relation to a Parliamentary election.

Hughes v. Transport and General Workers' Union
[1985] I.R.L.R. 382
Chancery Division

Mr Hughes, a TGWU member, asked for a ruling that every member of the union was entitled to access to union records to obtain information about the result of a union election for General Secretary at all branches of the union at which ballots took place, and not merely the result at his own branch.

VINELOTT J.: The position in my judgment is that the property of the union is vested in trustees who are bound to deal with it in accordance with the proper directions of the governing body of the union and of persons authorised by them. No individual can claim the right of access to the books and records otherwise than in accordance with the directions of the general executive council or its delegates save to the extent that that right is conferred by or by necessary implication from the rules governing the union.

Mr Goldblatt [counsel for the plaintiff] submitted that such a right is inherent or necessarily implicit in the relationship between the members and the governing body of a union which is established and governed by democratic principles. He relied in particular upon sub-rule (2) paragraph (d) of rule 1 which provides that "every member not being an honorary member shall, subject to the following rules, have an equal voice in all the concerns thereof and in the administration of all the property thereof. An honorary member shall not be entitled to claiming." I do not think that that sub-rule can be relied on in establishing any right to or access to information. As Mr Tabachnik [counsel for the union] expressed it the rule embodies the principle of non-discrimination; a member's rights are to be found elsewhere in the rules but the rules must be construed in the light of the general principle that the members are to be treated equally. . . .

I can find nothing in the rules which can be construed as conferring or confirming the existence of a right as extensive as the right claimed by the plaintiff, nor is it in my judgment necessary to import any such right to ensure that the rights of members as members of a democratic body are protected. The right of a member to participate in a ballot is established by rule 13 and every member is entitled to know the result of the local ballot at his branch or at the regional or sub-regional office where he himself cast his vote. He must be taken to have confided to his elected representatives the task of collating the results at regional and national level.

(D) The Position of Union Officials

The fact that a union official, elected or appointed, may also be an employee has caused problems largely bearing upon remedies. The courts see no objection to ordering a union to treat a wrongly expelled member as a full member and their attitude to restoration to office is governed by the same principle. They may, however, hesitate to order a union to accept an employed official whom the union genuinely believes to be unsuitable, using concepts drawn from the common law of employment.

Leary v. National Union of Vehicle Builders
[1970] 2 All E.R. 713.

For the facts, see above, page 651.

MEGARRY J.: The case most closely in point is an unreported decision of Buckley J., *Shanks v Plumbing Trades Union* (unreported, November 15, 1967) a motion in which the only issue was removal from the office of district secretary of a union. Having reached the conclusion that the plaintiff had made out a prima facie case that he was likely to succeed in the action, Buckley J. said:

> "It has been submitted on behalf of the Union that this is a case in which the Court ought not to grant the relief sought because that will be tantamount to specific performance of a contract of employment. It seems to me that very different considerations apply when one is dealing with an elected officer when somebody other than those who elected him is seeking to remove [him] from office, than apply in the ordinary case of employer and employee. In the circumstances, I propose to grant the plaintiff the injunction he seeks until judgment in the action."

In that case, the plaintiff had been removed from office on a charge that he had failed in his duty of giving full information during an inquiry about the number of certain ballot papers that had been issued. On the basis of the plaintiff having established a prima facie case of being not guilty on the charge, the court restored him to office despite the lack of confidence that the union might feel in him; a prima facie case is not, of course, one that has been finally established.

On the other hand, Citrine [*Trade Union Law* (3rd ed. 1967) pp. 295–6] distinguishes between on the one hand the governing bodies and officers of a union who are responsible only to the membership that elected them, and not to any superior body in the union, and on the other hand officers who are employed under a contract of service. If wrongly excluded from office, the former can, in a proper case, obtain an injunction restoring them to office, whereas the latter will be left to their remedy in damages. Consider also *Taylor v National Union of Seamen* [1967] 1 W.L.R. 532. Some of the cases cited in support of this distinction were cited to me, but unfortunately a number of them were only somewhat brief newspaper reports. Nevertheless, until I was referred to *Shanks v Plumbing Trades Union* (15 November 1967 unreported), I think that I should have accepted the distinction made in Citrine. The question is what it is right to do in view of that decision.

I accept what Buckley J. said about very different considerations applying to elected officers as contrasted with those employed under the ordinary relationship of employer and employee. It does not, however, appear from the judgment whether the cases relied on by Citrine were put before Buckley J., *eg Tanner v National Union of Seamen* (1928) *The Times* 30 November, and *Lewis v National Union of General and Municipal Workers* (1948) *The Times* 31 July. Even if I assume that the case before me is one in which I have the power to grant the injunction sought, I feel much hesitation about whether it would be right to do so. . . .

. . . Indeed, this must be implicit in many cases in which there is any question of what in effect is akin to the specific performance of a contract of service. For myself, I should be very slow to make any such order on motion, although in a clear and compelling case there is no doubt jurisdiction to do so. I do not think that this is a case of that sort. A union must of necessity depend in large measure on the loyalty and reliability of its officers in what is plainly often a difficult and controversial field of human activity.

(E) Workplace Organisation and the Rule Book

The position of the shop steward was summarised by W. E. J. McCarthy in the following extract.

W. E. J. McCarthy, *THE ROLE OF SHOP STEWARDS IN BRITISH INDUSTRIAL RELATIONS*, Research Paper No. 1 for the Royal Commission on Trade Unions and Employers' Associations (1967)

Union Rules

7. Union rule books are not always an accurate reflection of the workplace situation as it affects shop stewards. Some make no specific reference to workshop representation in any form, although this may well exist. Thus B. C. Roberts, after an analysis of 134 rule books, concluded that six made provision for the election of "Shop representatives and collectors"; and a further 48 provided for collectors "whose function, according to the rules, is limited to the collection of contributions and the checking of membership cards." In other words, in a sample of some 20 per cent. of British unions, which probably included most large organisations, only a third made any reference to shop stewards in our generic sense. On the other hand almost all the bigger unions who are known to have workplace representatives of one sort or another make some reference to them in their rules. What is perhaps more significant is that these references are sometimes ambiguous, and usually fail to cover certain important matters. These include:—

The Method of Appointing and Dismissing Stewards

8. Most stewards are elected by a "show of hands" in the workplace. But many rule books do not specifically prescribe for this, and often simply state baldly that they "shall be appointed." Others say nothing about how the election is to be conducted, or how often it is to take place. Most rule books specify the body under whose "jurisdiction" shop stewards operate, but it is sometimes unclear who has the power to deprive them of their credentials and for what reason.

The Representative Functions of Shop Stewards at the Workplace

9. Generally rules are more specific and comprehensive concerning the responsibilities of stewards in recruiting and retaining members than they are about representing them before employers. Some confine themselves to the negative injunction that employees should not be interviewed without a witness. Others do not mention representation at all.

The Relationship Between Workplace "Democracy" and the Formal Organs of Union Authority

10. It has been said that most stewards emerge as a result of some "democratic" process in the workplace, and it is understandably widely believed that they remain, in some sense, "accountable" to those who have elected

them. Moreover, if they are to undertake negotiations on behalf of any considerable group of members they must normally arrange to meet them collectively, in order to sound out their views and report back on progress made. Even where grievances and claims are raised on behalf of a single member it may be necessary to approach others for guidance and support. The most common way of achieving all these objectives is by means of short, informal, shop floor meetings, at which resolutions can be tabled and decisions made. These may take place either in the firm's time, or during a convenient break. If this is impossible, or not considered necessary in a particular instance, stewards may consult their members individually, in the most effective manner open to them.

Yet few rule books mention the shop floor meeting at all, and, outside printing, most of them do not try to prescribe for the processes of workplace "democracy" and consultation. Since as individuals both stewards and their constituents are subject to the various levels of union authority set out in the rules, it is always maintained by union executives, with justification, that no shop floor meeting, or other system of collecting opinion, can authorise policies which are at variance with union policy as laid down by the formal bodies established under the rules. Nevertheless this is usually implied, rather than specifically stated, and in practice little attempt is made to prescribe and regulate the processes of mandation and consultation in the workplace by union rule.

• • •

The 1980 DE/PSI/ESRC survey of *Workplace Industrial Relations in Britain* (1983) did not reveal much deviation from this pattern (see Chapter 4).

The critical position of workplace representatives makes them likely targets of attack either by constituents or more senior officials. In *Shotton* v. *AUEW* (unreported, October 20, 1976), Oliver J. ordered the union to recognise as effective the plaintiff's election as a shop steward. The district committee of the union had required from the plaintiff an undertaking that he would carry out its instructions regardless of whether they were in accordance with union rules after he had refused to take part in an unofficial strike contrary to the instructions of the same district committee. In the absence of that undertaking, the committee had refused to confirm the plaintiff's election.

The position of the shop steward was most clearly and fully presented to the courts in the following case.

Heatons Transport (St. Helens) Ltd. v. Transport and General Workers' Union
[1972] I.C.R. 308
Court of Appeal

For the facts, see Chapter 12 on Organisations of Workers, p. 420.

LORD DENNING M.R.: On the one hand, a "shop steward" is the representative of his work group, that is, his fellow-workers in a particular place of work, such as a factory, depot or wharf or a section of it. He is one of them. He works alongside them. He is employed by the same employer as they are. He is their leader. He speaks for them. If any of them has a grievance with the management, he takes it up. He negotiates on their behalf with the employers on any point specially connected with that particular shop, such as, who is to do this piece of work or that, whether they should work overtime and so forth. He is often appointed by the workers unopposed, but, in case of difference, they hold an election to decide who it shall be. If there are other "shops" with similar problems, he may join with other shop stewards in a "shop stewards' committee" so as to present a united front in their negotiations. In all this, he is essentially the representative of his own work group. The work group is, as the Royal Commission [on Trade Unions and Employers' Associations 1965–1968 Cmnd. 3623] said, at p. 27, para. 104:

> " . . . the basis of the shop steward's power. He could not of his own volition impose a limit on output or a ban on non-unionists. This can only be done by decision of the group of workers which he represents."

On the other hand, a "shop steward" is also a representative of a trade union. He is accredited to the union. He collects the men's contributions to the union or sees that they are collected. He sees that new men join the union. He keeps his fellow-workers informed of the policy of the union and of the decisions of branches. If the union decides to take action of one kind or another, he would be responsible for carrying it out in his shop. But he is not paid by the union. He is not an "officer" of the union. He is only an "official." He is paid by his employers and is the servant of his employers: but they allow him to spend part of his time—and sometimes the whole of it—on his shop steward duties. They may allow him an office and the use of a telephone. This is because he is so valuable a person in the whole set-up. I would quote the words again of the Royal Commission, at p. 29, para. 110:

> "the shop-floor decisions which generally precede unofficial strikes are often taken against the advice of shop stewards. Thus shop stewards are rarely agitators pushing workers towards unconstitutional action. In some instances they may be the mere mouthpieces of their work groups. But quite commonly they are supporters of order exercising a restraining influence on their members in conditions which promote disorder."

So the shop steward has a dual role. He is at one and the same time the representative of his own work group: and also the representative of the trade union. Suppose now that he, by himself or in conjunction with other stop stewards, calls on his fellow-workers to take industrial action. Does it mean that he is acting with the authority of the union? I think not—or not necessarily. He may be acting on behalf of his own work group and under pressure by them—without any authority from the union at all. If he is to have authority from the union so as to make the union responsible for unlawful action by him, it must be found in the rules or the [union's] handbook or in the course of dealing. I have studied all these with the greatest care. I find that a shop steward, by himself or in conjunction with others, has authority to negotiate terms with his employers; but this, as I see it, does not include taking industrial action. Industrial action is not to be regarded as ancillary to or incidental to the negotiations. I find no authority in a shop steward—or in a shop stewards' committee—to take industrial action on his or their own initiative. The matter must first be put before one of the official committees of the union before it can be made responsible. It must at least be approved by the district committee of the union. That is the lowest body to which the rules permit industrial action to be delegated: see rules 3(9) and 6(15) and (16). It is no good getting the approval of an officer of the union. It must be by an official committee of the union.

Take Hull as an example. There is a shop stewards' committee. It has 38 members. They are elected through machinery set up by the Hull Dock Labour Board, which is nothing to do with the unions. There are two rival unions in Hull. The dock workers elect these members to represent them, irrespective of their trade union. There is nothing to show at the elections to which union any candidate belongs. Even on the committee they do not speak or vote by unions. Research shows that, out of the 38 shop stewards on the committee, some 26 belong to the Transport and General Workers Union, and 12 to the "blue" union, N.A.S.D.U. Some of them may belong to both. If the committee decide on a course of action, it is impossible to say that it is taken on behalf of one union or the other or both. No one knows how the voting went. In addition, on June 2, 1971, the matter was distinctly raised at a meeting of a joint port committee in Hull which consisted, as I have said, of representatives of employers, work-people and the Hull Dock Labour Board. The upshot was recorded in the minutes in these words:

> "Whilst there was no objection on the part of the T. & G. to the shop stewards forming a committee from amongst themselves, the committee would have no statutory power [under the Dock Labour Board legislation] so far as the T. & G. was concerned, and any policy changes or negotiations which the shop stewards' committee might think necessary *must still be processed through the medium of the Hull Docks District Committee* (of the union) . . . authority would have to be given by that body" [the regional committee.]

There is no corresponding minute for Liverpool. But the same rules and handbook apply there: and I see no reason to doubt that the shop stewards' committee there have no more authority to bind the union than the shop stewards' committee at Hull.

As I read the evidence in both Liverpool and Hull, the permanent officers of the union were well aware of what was going on; but they were powerless to prevent it. They did not turn a blind eye to it. They did not approve it by a nod or a wink. Some of them, indeed, did what they could to get the shop stewards to call off the "blacking": but it was no good. The shop stewards were not acting in this regard as representatives of the union. They were acting as representatives of their own work group[s]. But in each case their action was endorsed overwhelmingly by the mass meetings of the dock workers. I do not think the "blacking" was within the express or implied authority of the union: nor was it ratified by the union.

For the House of Lords' reversal of the Court of Appeal's judgment, see Chapter 11 Organisations of Workers, p. 420.

The next extract provides an example of judicial policy on the important question of how unions select shop stewards.

Breen v. Amalgamated Engineering Union
[1971] 2 Q.B. 175
Court of Appeal

LORD DENNING M.R.: The plaintiff was elected by his fellow workers at the Fawley oil refinery as their shop steward for the coming year. It was, however, subject to approval by the district committee; rule 13(21) states that:

> "Shop stewards elected by members are subject to approval by the District Committee and shall not function until such approval is given."

On 9th December 1965 the district committee met. In previous years they had approved his election. This year they rejected him. There was little discussion at the meeting, says the judge, but general agreement that the plaintiff was not a person who, in view of his history, could be approved by the committee as a shop steward. On 18th December 1965, the plaintiff wrote a letter to Mr Townsend [the secretary of the district committee] protesting at the committee's decision:

> " . . . I wish to protest most strongly at their decision to disqualify me . . . and would ask them to reconsider this decision. No reason has been given to me for this action. . . . "

On 30th December 1965 the district committee met again. There was again little discussion. They affirmed their previous decision and told Mr Townsend to write to the plaintiff and tell him the reason. On 31st December 1965 Mr Townsend wrote to the plaintiff. It is the most important letter in the case:. . . .

[The letter contained false reasons. Lord Denning went on to hold that the courts could review the committee's decision if the complaint was that the rules of natural justice had been violated (see above p. 647).]

So here we have the plaintiff. He was elected by his fellow workers to be their shop steward. He was their chosen representative. He was the man whom they wished to have to put forward their views to the management and to negotiate for them. He was the one whom they wished to tell the union about their needs. As such he was a key figure. . . .

Seeing that he had been elected to this office by a democratic process, he had, I think, a legitimate expectation that he would be approved by the district committee, unless there were good reasons against him. If they had something against him, they ought to [have told] him and to [have given] him a chance of answering it before turning him down. It seems to me intolerable that they should be able to veto his appointment in their unfettered discretion. This district committee sit in Southampton some miles away from Fawley. None of the members, so far as I know, worked in the oil refinery. Who are they to say nay to him and his fellow workers without good reason and without hearing what he has to say? To be fair to them, the district committee did not claim that they could act without good reasons. They said that they had good reasons. They were set out by their secretary with their authority in the letter of 31st December 1965. And, when examined, the very first reason it gave was a bad reason. It was that the plaintiff had misappropriated union funds seven years ago, whereas in truth he had done nothing of the sort and had been acquitted of the charge. So long as that letter stands as the vehicle of their reasons, their disapproval must be utterly invalid; for, on the face of it, they were actuated by a highly prejudicial consideration which was entirely erroneous and which they ought not to have taken into account at all. Call it prejudice, bias, or what you will. It is enough to vitiate the discretion of any body, statutory, domestic, or other. To make it worse, they did not give him a chance of answering it or correcting it. They condemned him unheard.

3. SERVICES AND BENEFITS

Despite the predominance in the case law of issues of membership, discipline, the closed shop and trade union government, it is likely that foremost in the minds of union members is the union's bargaining function in maintaining and improving terms and conditions at work. Similarly, representation of individual grievances must figure prominently, although the need for such a service is likely to be considerably more intermittent. Together, the bargaining and grievance representation functions of the union form a class of membership services of first importance. Another, less significant class of benefits are financial, *e.g.* the now nominal rights to sickness and dispute benefit. Somewhere between these two distinct classes of benefits in order of significance lies the group of individual services a union may offer its members of which the single most important example is probably legal aid and advice, first established in relation to industrial injury claims, and recently extended on the establishment of Industrial Tribunals. Without it, most employees would not otherwise receive legal representation, though in practice a great deal of such representation before Industrial Tribunals is conducted by full-time district officials of trade unions. In the following sections we look at each of these classes of benefits from the point of view of legal entitlement and legal control of the quality of the service provided.

(A) Collective Bargaining and Grievance Representation

Despite the significance of the union's bargaining function, the courts are reluctant to concede to the member a right to representation.

Oddy v. Transport Salaried Staffs Association
[1973] I.C.R. 524
National Industrial Relations Court

The employee's applications for a number of more senior positions with British Rail, his employer, were rejected on the ground that he lacked the detailed knowledge required. His union branch passed a resolution rejecting this as a ground of unsuitability and requesting the union's general secretary to make representations to the employer. When the employee sought independent legal advice the general secretary refused to discuss the matter with the employers. The plaintiff asked the court to construe a right to such representation from a provision in the union rules declaring it to be an objective of the union "to improve pay and conditions and protect the interests of its members."

Sir Hugh Griffiths: [referring to provisions in the now repealed Industrial Relations Act 1971] The rule of TSSA upon which the employee relies is that which describes the objects of the organisation. It is entitled "Objects" and these are set out in paragraphs lettered (a) to (n), covering the wide ranging scope of activities which are the proper province of unions. As one would expect, it includes among its objects rule 5(b) which reads: "(b) To improve the conditions and protect the interests of its members."

The employee's complaint was that the general secretary, in ignoring the resolution of the branch, was failing to protect both the collective interests of members of the union (because they have an interest in seeing that branch resolutions are acted upon) and his own particular interests with British Railways. However, this is not a complaint against the union as such but against a particular officer of the union, for which the remedy would be first to raise the matter with the executive committee and, if dissatisfied with their decision, to appeal under rule 47 to the next delegate conference. The [industrial] tribunal pointed this out in their reasons, but they rested their decision upon broader grounds with which we will deal shortly.

Since the hearing before the tribunal the employee has pursued his complaint against the general secretary to appeal before the delegate conference. His appeal has been unsuccessful, but it is not a matter with which we are concerned in this case.

The tribunal held that no remedy lay under section 107 of the Act of 1971 for the alleged breach of the objects rule. They said:

> "[TSSA] say that this is not a 'rule' as contemplated in section 107(3)(*b*). Although it comes under the heading of rules in the rule book, they say that rule 5(b) does not give any individual rights, but is merely part of a rule which states the main objects of the organisation, what may be done with its funds, and the rest of its powers, in the same way as many other organisations, such as limited companies and members' clubs, have objects clauses.
>
> We certainly think that the objects in the rule amount to a definition of the powers of the organisation which are to protect the interests of the members collectively and it is not contemplating giving a right to a particular individual. What may be in the interests of one member may be against the interests of another member. If we were to accept the [employee's] contention, it seems that it would open the door very widely to the intervention by tribunals into the affairs of unions. We can only intervene where we are given jurisdiction to do so. If the [employee] is correct, then his principle would mean that the tribunal would have to investigate, for example, every complaint of slackness or delay in dealing with everyday correspondence as not protecting the interests of the members and this, we feel, was not the intention of Parliament when enacting these provisions. On this specific matter of promotion, where one person is selected out of a number of applicants it seems that any unsuccessful applicant might claim that it was the duty of the union to protect his interests and press his case as opposed to the member who had been successful and who then might himself allege a breach of rules.
>
> If we take the interpretation which we think is correct, namely that the object of rule 5(b) is to improve the conditions and protect the interests of the members as a class, then the [employee's] case does not involve any breach of such a rule, even though we accept all his contentions of fact. This is a matter which in our opinion should be dealt with within the internal organisation of TSSA and does not afford the [employee] any remedy under section 107."

We agree with the reasoning of the tribunal. Section 107 is dealing with individual rights and is concerned with breaches of those rules that regulate the rights of members in their relationship with the organisation to which they belong. By way of example in the context of this case, rule 47 provides:

> "(a) Any matter not provided for in these rules shall be dealt with as the executive committee may determine, but any member, officer, or branch aggrieved thereby shall have the right to appeal to the next delegate conference."

If the employee had been refused a hearing by the delegate conference, he would have had grounds for complaint under section 107(3)(*b*), but as already recorded this was not so. But rule 5(b) is not such a rule. It does no more than state one of the overall aims of TSSA. It does not purport to confer any right upon an individual member of the union and is not a "rule" within the meaning of section 107(3)(*b*). This appeal must, therefore, be dismissed.

A failure to negotiate or a lack of impartiality in negotiation based on grounds of race or sex might fall under the Race Relations Act 1976, s.11(3) or the Sex Discrimination Act 1975, s.12(3). But the following case simply highlights the general absence of any enforceable right to adequate or efficient representation.

Furniture, Timber and Allied Trades Union v. Modgill
[1980] I.R.L.R. 142
Employment Appeal Tribunal

Sixteen African Asian workers complained under the Race Relations Act 1976 that their union had not permitted them to have their own shop steward and had failed to give them support in their efforts to achieve better wages and a more satisfactory wage structure, that the shop steward had failed to provide adequate support to those wishing to be transferred, that the union had discriminated against them by not supporting their desire to work a 40-hour week and that there had been a lack of communication by the union.

SLYNN J.: On the matters where they have come out in favour of the applicants, the Tribunal clearly have been satisfied that the union did not give sufficient support to, or have sufficient understanding about, the applicants' desire for a shop steward of their own. But what is significant here is that they do not say that any other section of the company's works had been treated more favourably than these applicants. On the contrary, there was evidence given, and it emerges from the decision of the Tribunal itself, that one of the reasons why it was felt that there should not be a shop steward in this particular section was that, if that were done, a number of other small sections in the factory would also require that they too should have their separate shop steward. As we see it, there is really nothing in the evidence to indicate that there had been here a less favourable treatment of this particular group of workers than any other group of workers. The fact that the applicants felt themselves aggrieved, the fact that no shop steward was provided, and the fact that it might have been a great deal better if a shop steward had been provided, does not, it seems to us, go far enough. We do not for one moment dissent from the view expressed by the Tribunal that the union had not fully appreciated and taken care of the problems of these men in this paint shop. But the Tribunal did not ask themselves whether what had happened amounted to less favourable treatment than the treatment afforded to other people. We do not consider that it is necessary for us to send the case back for them to answer that question. It seems to us that there was simply no evidence before them on which they could possibly have concluded that there had been less favourable treatment. Certainly there was nothing to indicate that such acts as had been complained of were in any sense attributable to racial discrimination.

Then the other matter which exercised the Tribunal, and upon which they concluded in favour of the applicants, was on the basis that there had been inadequate communication. Again, this may show to some extent, in the view of that Tribunal, a breakdown in the functions of some of the trade union officials. It may (as the Tribunal thought) or it may not amount to a lack of efficiency in some respects; the machinery may not have been adequate or worked properly. In regard to the complaints about transfers, segregation, wage negotiations and industrial action there clearly was a lack of understanding and a sense of grievance on the part of the applicants. But there is no question asked here by the Tribunal as to whether that amounted to less favourable treatment than was afforded to other members of the union in the factory. Again we have considered whether the failure to answer that question means that we ought to send the case back, but we are all satisfied that here there was no evidence upon which the Tribunal could possibly conclude that the applicants, even if treated inefficiently, had been treated less favourably than other members of the union in other sections of the factory.

The general attitude of local union officials to grievance procedures is that it is their right to represent the union member concerned and to decide how best to do this. Tribunals appear not to take exception to this practice.

Gray Dunn and Co. Ltd. v. Edwards
[1980] I.R.L.R. 23
Employment Appeal Tribunal

The employee was summarily dismissed for being under the influence of alcohol at work. Before dismissal he was interviewed in the presence of his shop stewards, but management refused to interview certain witnesses as to his fitness to work. He appealed to the assistant general manager who also declined to hear the witnesses and confirmed the dismissal. The employee was not present at the appeal, which was conducted by shop stewards.

LORD McDONALD: The Tribunal appear to have considered that because the respondent was not present at every stage of the inquiry, but represented by his trade union officials there was some denial of natural justice in the investigation of his offence. We cannot accept this. The concept of natural justice does not include the automatic right to be present throughout a disciplinary hearing provided the interests of the employee are safeguarded by his duly accredited representatives (*Pirelli General Cable Works Ltd v Murray* [1979] IRLR 190). If the presence of the respondent was considered necessary by these representatives they could have insisted upon it. There may well have been reasons why they deemed it was not in his best interests to be there. Accordingly the only reasonable inference from the evidence is, in our opinion, (a) that the respondent did have an opportunity to defend himself and state his position and (b) that if this was done at any stage on his behalf by his trade union representatives and in his absence, there was no denial of natural justice.

Ultimately, if the standard of trade union representation proves unacceptable, the member may resign. The existence of a closed shop, however, may result in dismissal. In *Home Delivery Services Ltd.* v. *Shackcloth* [1984] I.R.L.R. 470 (E.A.T.), the employee complained that the union had let him down in a whole series of respects, set out in a "List of Grievances" containing 11 items ranging from a lack of consultation by the union with the membership before accepting a major change in working conditions, to a failure to see that the members' workplace was treated on a par with others with respect to holidays. He resigned from the union and was dismissed. The E.A.T. held the dismissal unfair under EPCA, s.58(4): an objection to union membership on grounds of a deeply-held personal conviction "that (the union)) had failed to look after his interests: for to have your interests looked after is why you join and pay your subscription" (*per* Bristow J., para. 25, p. 473). *Cf.* an opposite conclusion on the facts in *McGhee* v. *Midland British Road Services Ltd.* [1985] I.R.L.R. 198 (E.A.T.), confirmed by the Court of Appeal (see 303 Industrial Relations Legal Information Bulletin 13).

(B) Contractual Financial Benefits

The provident benefits which were a major incentive for workers to join the early trade unions have now diminished into insignificance. Strike benefit, however, can still impose a considerable drain on a union's funds (though now less important to individual members). Entitlement under the rule book is normally only for officially sanctioned disputes. But most industrial action is initiated at the workplace either by shop stewards or by unofficial shop floor groups whose action the shop stewards may or may not subsequently confirm.

The Report of the Royal Commission on *Trade Unions and Employers' Associations* 1965–1968, Cmnd. 3623, paragraphs 402–405

In many trade unions there is no rule under which members are expressly forbidden to go on strike without prior authorisation. What the official attitude of the union should be to a strike begun without prior authorisation is a question which has to be considered only if the strike lasts long enough to make intervention by full-time officials necessary or if there is a question of paying dispute benefit (*ie* strike pay). The majority of unofficial strikes are however over too quickly for either eventuality to arise. . . . In some unions, such as the Amalgamated Engineering Union, the General and Municipal Workers' Union and, until recently, the Electrical Trades Union, dispute benefit is paid only if a stoppage lasts three days or more.

Nevertheless when an unofficial strike does last long enough for the strikers to apply for strike benefit, the trade union's attitude towards the strike has to be made clear retrospectively, since the authorisation of dispute benefit appears in all unions which pay such benefit to be a matter for decision by the executive. Most of them permit the executive to decide to pay benefit in respect of strikes which did not have prior authorisation by the union. We examined the position in the fourteen largest unions in the country, organising between them some $6\frac{1}{4}$ million workers. We found that in 1965 the payment of dispute benefit was authorised in respect of nearly 200 strikes which did not have prior approval; and that the corresponding figure for 1966 probably exceeded 150. Virtually all these cases were confined to five out of the fourteen unions.

It is important to consider why unions authorise benefit in these circumstances. In the case of one union, the Electrical Trades Union, the rules make it clear that members are entitled to strike first and to seek to have the strike made official afterwards. In many other cases the union executive concerned took the decision to pay strike benefit because the strike involved other unions with more members involved; so that its own members had little choice but to join in, or alternatively were laid off in circumstances which disqualified them from receiving unemployment benefit. In yet other cases action without prior authorisation was regarded as justified because of "provocation" by the employer, or because the union's vital interests were thought to be involved, for example by the dismissal of a shop steward, or by the actions of a breakaway union. Finally unions occasionally regard the retrospective payment of benefit as justified in a case where a claim at workplace level has initially been refused more or less out of hand by an employer, and then conceded as soon as the strike takes place.

It may be concluded therefore that in the majority of unofficial strikes the unions do not officially declare an attitude; and that in a substantial proportion of the remainder they are prepared to pay dispute benefit after the event.

It will be recalled how differently the courts approached the payment of strike benefit during the miners' strike of 1984–85 (as in *Taylor* v. *NUM (Derbyshire Area) (No. 3)* (above p. 663)). Their attitude can be contrasted with the readiness of the Court of Appeal in the following case to *imply* a right to financial assistance with legal proceedings.

Bourne v. Colodense Ltd.
[1985] I.R.L.R. 339
Court of Appeal

Mr Bourne authorised his union to take legal action on his behalf, which they did. When his claim failed, the question arose as to whether the union was liable to indemnify Mr Bourne against the legal costs of the action given against him.

LAWTON L.J.: I feel impelled to accept that no one on behalf of the Union told the plaintiff in express terms that the Union would give him an indemnity against any costs which he might be ordered to pay. The question is whether, having regard to all the surrounding circumstances, there must have been an understanding, amounting in law to a contract, that the Union would discharge any liability for costs which the plaintiff might incur. Without the complication caused by the Union's rules upon which the plaintiff relies, I have no hesitation at all in adjudging that, when the plaintiff agreed to accept the legal assistance offered by the Union, it was on the understanding of both parties that the Union would keep the plaintiff free from personal liability if his claim was dismissed. It is inconceivable, in my opinion, that a sick, elderly, married man who had lost his job through ill health would have become involved in this litigation without being assured by someone on behalf of the Union that they would stand behind him in all circumstances.

DILLON L.J.: There are cogent grounds for arguing that such an indemnity is to be implied on the officious bystander test [*cf. Shirlaw* v *Southern Foundries (1926) Ltd.* [1939] 2 K.B. 206, 227 *per* MacKinnon L.J.], into any agreement by the Union to give assistance to the respondent in connection with these proceedings. . . .

(C) Advice and Assistance

A third major class of services available to trade union members consists of the provision of advice and assistance, particularly in connection with legal disputes. The range of services available is described in the following extract.

G. Latta and R. Lewis, "TRADE UNION LEGAL SERVICES" (1974) 12 B.J.I.R. 56, pp. 56, 66–67

Most unions are empowered by their rule books to provide legal assistance to their members in connection with employment problems. In practice the bulk of this legal workload normally results from industrial accidents. The union role in relation to accidents embraces advice and representation in members' social insurance claims, and the handling of common law claims for damages.

Apart from accidents, unions provide a number of other legal services to members. These are often related to specific types of membership. Thus the Musicians' Union and Equity deal with a number of cases of breach of contract, while teachers' unions handle cases involving their members' tenure in their jobs, and alleged assaults on pupils. Unions also provide a service in representing members before the Industrial Tribunals, usually in redundancy and unfair dismissal issues. . . .

Some unions deal with specialized employment problems outside the problems of accidents and dismissals. Unions in the entertainment industry place considerable emphasis on collecting debts owed to members, and in dealing with copyright questions. Advice on contracts, or cases involving their breach, are also common for some other white-collar unions. The National Union of Agricultural and Allied Workers are concerned with cases involving the eviction of members from "tied cottages," while a number of unions support claims before the Criminal Injuries Compensation Board, if the member has been attacked in the course of his employment, *eg*. the Union of Post Office Workers.

Several unions provide legal defence for members who are criminally prosecuted for matters arising out of their employment. The provision of defence in Road Traffic Act prosecutions is particularly important for unions whose members' jobs depend on their driving licences. Thus the Transport and General Workers' Union and the United Road Transport Union are especially involved in this. Most unions with members who might be involved in such cases, about twenty-five in all, provide this service. A rather smaller number also provide defence for members who are charged with other criminal offences arising out of their employment, *eg* theft at work, although most unions are careful to ensure that such a service is discretionary.

Eleven of the forty-nine unions [studied] provide a scheme whereby the member is entitled to a free interview, or a free letter of advice from a solicitor on any matter at all. The issues which arise most frequently concern hire-purchase, divorce[,] and trouble with landlords and neighbours, and are similar to the kind of issues a Citizens' Advice Bureau would handle. Discussions with union legal officers suggest that members are often unaware of their legal rights, or are seeking reassurance, and there is little tendency to rush off and see a solicitor unless a genuine problem has arisen. The union's role here is especially valuable in view of the cost of legal advice and the general mistrust of lawyers.

Among other problems affecting workers availing themselves of trade union advice services is that of the standard of service they are entitled to expect. The duty of care applicable to trade union officials was dealt with in the following case.

Cross v. British Iron, Steel and Kindred Trades Association
[1968] W.L.R. 494
Court of Appeal

The rules of the union required it to give legal assistance to its members, *inter alia*, on the happening of any event which would reasonably appear to entitle the member to claim damages at common law. The plaintiff sustained an accident at work and reported it to his branch secretary, who prepared a report which was put before a competent solicitor of the union. That solicitor advised, in effect, that the plaintiff had no case. Two years later, the plaintiff raised the matter again with the branch secretary, but no further action was taken. After expiration of the three years limitation period for personal injuries, the plaintiff requested the union to look into the matter and subsequently alleged negligence against the union in relation to the claim.

SALMON L.J.: I incline to the view that on the true construction of [the union's] rule 36(1), the defendant union perform their duty in the circumstances there postulated if they make available to their members the legal services of solicitors or barristers whom on reasonable grounds they believe to be reasonably competent, skilful and of good reputation. As at present advised, I do not think that the defendant union warrant that the solicitor or barrister concerned shall perform his duties carefully or skilfully, still less that the legal advice given is right.

When an event happens which would reasonably appear to entitle the member, amongst other things, to claim damages at common law and, therefore, to receive legal assistance under rule 36(1), there is no doubt that the branch secretary has to obtain from the member, and the member is obliged to supply, if he can, the full particulars of the event. Those particulars are then sent by the branch secretary to the central office to be forwarded to the defendant union's solicitor. In this case that is exactly what occurred. I am not prepared to decide whether in any special circumstances there might be an obligation on the defendant union's officers to look for further information. In the present case the branch secretary, Mr Morley, certainly did look for further information and he got it from a Mr Moxon, who was operating the machine which expelled the piece of steel which crushed the plaintiff's finger. He sent forward that information given to him by Mr Moxon, together with the particulars supplied by the plaintiff, to the defendant union's solicitor, Mr Walker. Mr Walker said in evidence that he had ample information in those documents to enable him to come to a conclusion.

The conclusion at which he arrived is expressed in the letter which LORD DENNING, M.R., has read dated May 9, 1958. As I read that letter, and as I have no doubt the defendant union's officials read that letter, it meant (whatever Mr Walker said he intended it to mean) that there was no prospect of a claim succeeding and there was no necessity to make further enquiries. On receipt of that letter, Mr Morley communicated its contents to the plaintiff, who at that stage appeared to accept them. The case, as I understand it, against the defendant union is that Mr Morley was negligent because he did not make any further enquiries. The judge has found that Mr Walker, in advising as he did, did not fall short of the standard of care demanded of a solicitor. That finding is perhaps not very important if the defendant union do not, as I think they do not, warrant that their solicitor will in fact use reasonable skill and care. In any event, there is no cross-notice in respect of that finding.

The letter from the solicitor is, however, of the greatest importance. I think it would be quite wrong to find that the officers of a union were negligent because they accepted the advice of their solicitor whom they had every reason to believe was competent and careful. They cannot be expected to be any wiser than he was.

Despite this refusal to apply to unions the full effect of the principle that the duty of care cannot be delegated, trade unions have taken on in recent years a range of new legal services which potentially impose upon them considerable and complex duties. The possibility of liability for negligence is clearly demonstrable (see *Papparis* v. *Charles Fulton and Co. Ltd.* [1981] I.R.L.R. 104).

The problem of defining precisely the extent of the advisory function of trade union officials is rendered complex by their bargaining/representational functions—which are carried on simultaneously. The following cases illustrate how different policies towards dispute resolution can shape the judge's concept of trade union officials' advisory duties.

Owen v. Crown House Engineering Ltd.
[1973] I.C.R. 511
National Industrial Relations Court

The union raised with the employer the possibility of claims for unfair dismissal by two former employees dismissed for redundancy. The employer requested time for the board of directors to consider an offer of better redundancy terms. The union accordingly did not pursue the claim until informed that no improved offer would be made. By then the claim was out of time under what is now EPCA 1978, s.67(2) and could not be entertained unless it was not "practicable" to have presented it within the limitation period.

Sir Hugh Griffiths: Within the context of industrial relations where emphasis is rightly placed upon the vital importance of attempting to settle all differences by amicable negotiation, it is unrealistic to exclude the likely consequence of a course of action in considering whether or not it is practicable. At the end of the meeting on August 16, Mr Mott [the union official negotiating on behalf of the employees] was left with the impression that a better offer would be forthcoming. Mr Muir [one of the employer's directors] said as much in evidence. What would have been the practical effect if Mr Mott had ignored Mr Muir's request to hold his hand but had pressed on with the application for unfair dismissal? The answer must be that it would almost certainly have killed any hope of a fruitful outcome to the negotiations. . . .

In the view of this court, the Tribunal placed too much weight upon the physical possibility of presenting the application and paid insufficient attention to the almost certain ruin of the negotiations attendant upon such action. The particular circumstance so important in this case is that the presentation of the application was delayed at the specific request of the employers. This is a circumstance which the court is entitled to and should take into account in considering whether or not it was practicable to make the application. In the face of such a request we have no doubt that it was not "practicable" to make the application within the meaning of the proviso. This is not to say that in all cases where parties are negotiating an employee is relieved of observing the time limit. This is a special case and founded upon the action of the employers which caused the employees to hold their hand.

Times Newspapers Ltd. v. O'Regan
[1977] I.R.L.R. 101
Employment Appeal Tribunal

Cumming-Bruce J.: First, Mrs O'Regan knew, as she said, that she could claim for unfair dismissal; she knew that in June. Further she knew that the claim must be made within three months [under what is now EPCA 1978, s.67(2)]. Where she got that from we know not. She said: "I thought the three months ran from the time the negotiations were exhausted," and from a letter that she wrote to the Tribunal it appeared that she got that impression as a result of advice which she obtained from the assistant branch secretary of the union when she asked him what would happen if she wanted to take her case to an Industrial Tribunal. From that moment she proceeded on the basis that as long as the negotiations were continuing, and until the negotiations had reached a final termination, the time would not begin to run against her.

We accept the findings of the Industrial Tribunal that the negotiations, in her genuine belief, were protracted over two periods, the first being the period when the union were trying to negotiate, first, re-engagement, without success, and then a money payment, with some success; and then, as she strongly believed, the negotiations were continuing between the union and the employers with the object of obtaining for her a written reference from *The Times*. So, it was only when she was satisfied that the negotiations to obtain a reference had failed, which was in October, that she thought that the three months time began to run against her. The Industrial Tribunal took the view on those facts that her belief was not unreasonable, and that she was not unreasonable in holding out or refraining from bringing a claim until October when she realised that she was not going to get a reference. So the Industrial Tribunal held that it was not reasonably practicable for her to have brought the application within three months of 12 June, and they extended the period.

We are all clearly of the view that therein the Industrial Tribunal has gone wrong in law. . . .

She knew that she had a right to claim to an Industrial Tribunal; she knew that in June. Also in June she knew that there was a time limit—a time limit of three months. When she mentioned those facts to the assistant branch secretary of the union, he advised her—if that is the right way to describe what he said that gave her the impression upon which she later relied—that the time would run from the determination of the negotiations. It is clear that at that time both the union secretary and Mrs O'Regan thought it was so likely that the negotiations would be brought to a successful termination, that it was unlikely that she would ever have to implement the contingent intention of bringing a claim before an Industrial Tribunal on the ground of unfair dismissal. So she knew of the right; she knew of a time limit; but she had a mistaken belief about the date from which the time ran—a belief that was either implanted or fortified by mistaken advice from her union adviser. Unfortunately she did nothing about it until the three months time period had long expired, because she did not intend or expect to have to do anything until she knew that the negotiations had failed, if they did.

. . . We have no doubt at all that, on these facts, a person who seeks redress for unfair dismissal, who knows that there is a right to seek a remedy from an Industrial Tribunal, and knows that there is a time limit, and knows the length of that time limit, is under a duty to make such inquiries, either herself, or through a union or other adviser, so as to confirm the impression that she or the union adviser may initially have about the date from which the time runs. And if, without giving any warning to the employers that an application to an Industrial Tribunal is in contemplation if all else fails, they then allow the time to run out without making further inquiries in order to confirm the date from which the time runs, that is a situation in which it has been reasonably practicable for the applicant to present the claim to the Industrial Tribunal in time, and the failure to do so must be regarded as a matter of law as being due to a set of circumstances in which the applicant cannot show a specific and acceptable explanation for not acting within the four weeks.

We are satisfied that as, in the first place, it appears that Mrs O'Regan herself knew that there was a time limit and the time limit was of three months, she was under a duty herself to check, for example, by finding out from a [job centre], or such other means as may have been open to her, from what date the time limit ran; and if she got it wrong because she relied upon her first impression and upon bad advice given by the union agent whom she asked about it, in either case, for the purposes of determining whether it was reasonably practicable, or not, it must be regarded as her fault, or the fault of her advisers, that the claim was not presented within the time limit. Here, there was no just cause or excuse for not presenting the complaint within three months as to make it right as a matter of law for the Industrial Tribunal to hold, however sympathetic they may have been with her position, that it was not reasonably practicable for her to present her claim in time.

INDEX